THE CAMBRIDGE HISTORY OF

THE AMERICAN NOVEL

This ambitious literary history traces the American novel from its emergence in the late eighteenth century to its diverse incarnations in the multi-ethnic, multi-media culture of the present. Original essays by internationally renowned scholars present fresh readings of American classics and break new ground to show the role of popular genres – such as science fiction and mystery novels – in the creation of the US literary tradition. In an exciting departure from its predecessors, the essays in this book talk to each other. Their dialogue highlights surprising connections within and across eras. As a collective, interwoven chronicle of America's dominant literary genre, *The Cambridge History of the American Novel* will change the way we think about the history – and the future – of American literature.

LEONARD CASSUTO, Professor of English at Fordham University, New York, is the author of *Hard-Boiled Sentimentality: The Secret History of American Crime Stories* (2009), which was nominated for the Edgar and Macavity Awards. Other books include *The Inhuman Race: The Racial Grotesque in American Literature and Culture* (1997) and three edited volumes. Cassuto is also an award-winning journalist, writing about subjects ranging from sports to the scientific search for room-temperature semiconductors.

CLARE VIRGINIA EBY, Professor of English at the University of Connecticut, is the author of *Dreiser and Veblen, Saboteurs of the Status Quo* (1998) and editor of the Norton Critical Edition of *The Jungle* (2003), the Dreiser Edition of *The Genius* (2008), and (with Leonard Cassuto) *The Cambridge Companion to Theodore Dreiser* (2004). She is completing *Until Choice Do Us Part: The Theory and Practice of Marriage in the Progressive Era.*

BENJAMIN REISS is Professor of English at Emory University, Atlanta, Georgia. He is the author of *The Showman and the Slave: Race, Death and Memory in Barnum's America* (2001) and *Theaters of Madness: Insane Asylums and Nineteenth-Century American Culture* (2008). He is at work on a book about sleeping in the modern world.

THE CAMBRIDGE HISTORY OF THE AMERICAN NOVEL

★

General Editor

LEONARD CASSUTO

Associate Editors

CLARE VIRGINIA EBY

and

BENJAMIN REISS

CAMBRIDGE UNIVERSITY PRESS

CAMBRIDGE UNIVERSITY PRESS
Cambridge, New York, Melbourne, Madrid, Cape Town,
Singapore, São Paulo, Delhi, Tokyo, Mexico City

Cambridge University Press
The Edinburgh Building, Cambridge CB2 8RU, UK

Published in the United States of America by Cambridge University Press, New York

www.cambridge.org
Information on this title: www.cambridge.org/9780521899079

First published 2011

Printed in the United Kingdom at the University Press, Cambridge

A catalogue record for this publication is available from the British Library

Library of Congress Cataloguing in Publication data
The Cambridge history of the American novel / Leonard Cassuto, general
editor ; Clare Virginia Eby, associate editor ; Benjamin Reiss, associate editor.
p. cm.
ISBN 978-0-521-89907-9 (hardback)
1. American fiction – History and criticism. I. Cassuto,
Leonard, 1960– II. Title.
PS371.C36 2011
813′.009–dc22
2010030376

ISBN 978-0-521-89907-9 Hardback

Contents

PART TWO
REALISM, PROTEST, ACCOMMODATION

Illustrations

Tables

Contributors

LEONARD CASSUTO, Professor of English at Fordham University, New York, is the author of *Hard-Boiled Sentimentality: The Secret History of American Crime Stories* (2009), which was nominated for the Edgar and Macavity Awards. Other books include *The Inhuman Race: The Racial Grotesque in American Literature and Culture* (1997) and four edited volumes. Cassuto is also an award-winning journalist, writing about subjects ranging from sports to the scientific search for room-temperature semiconductors. www.lcassuto.com.

CLARE VIRGINIA EBY, Professor of English at the University of Connecticut, is the author of *Dreiser and Veblen, Saboteurs of the Status Quo* (1998), and editor of the Norton Critical Edition of *The Jungle* (2003), the Dreiser Edition of *The Genius* (2008), and (with Leonard Cassuto) *The Cambridge Companion to Theodore Dreiser* (2004). She is completing *Until Choice Do Us Part: The Theory and Practice of Marriage in the Progressive Era*.

BENJAMIN REISS is Professor of English at Emory University, Atlanta, Georgia. He is the author of *The Showman and the Slave: Race, Death and Memory in Barnum's America* (2001; rpt. 2010) and *Theaters of Madness: Insane Asylums and Nineteenth-Century American Culture* (2008). He is at work on a cultural and intellectual history of sleep.

JONATHAN ARAC is Andrew W. Mellon Professor of English and founding Director of the Humanities Center at the University of Pittsburgh. He also serves on the *boundary 2* editorial collective, and he chairs the Advisory Committee for the Successful Societies Program of the Canadian Institute for Advanced Research. His next book is *Impure Worlds: The Institution of Literature in the Age of the Novel.*

VALERIE BABB is Professor of English and African American Studies at the University of Georgia and editor of the *Langston Hughes Review*. Among her published works are *Whiteness Visible: The Meaning of Whiteness in American Literature* (1998) *and Culture* and *Ernest Gaines* (1991). While a Professor at Georgetown University, Babb was the creator of the video documentary *Black Georgetown Remembered*, which evolved into the book, *Black Georgetown Remembered: A History of Its Black Community from the Founding of the "Town of George" in 1751 to the Present Day* (1991), now in its second printing.

JAN BAETENS is Professor of Cultural Studies at the University of Leuven (Belgium). He has published widely, although most often in French, on word and image studies, mainly in the field of so-called minor genres such as the photonovel, the graphic novel, and novelization. With Ari Blatt, he coedited a special issue of *Yale French Studies* (114 [2008], "Writing and the Image Today"). He is also the author of nearly fifteen books of poetry.

HESTER BLUM is Associate Professor of English at Pennsylvania State University, where she directs the Center for American Literary Studies. She is the author of *The View from the Masthead: Maritime Imagination and Antebellum American Sea Narratives* (2008) and the editor of William Ray's Barbary captivity narrative *Horrors of Slavery* (1808; 2008).

CARRIE TIRADO BRAMEN is an Associate Professor of English at the University at Buffalo (SUNY) and Executive Director of the University of Buffalo Humanities Institute. She is the author of *The Uses of Variety: Modern Americanism and the Quest for National Distinctiveness* (2000), which won Harvard University Press's Thomas J. Wilson Prize for best first book. She is currently working on a book entitled *American Niceness*.

LAWRENCE BUELL is Powell M. Cabot Professor of American Literature at Harvard University, and author of numerous books, including *Literary Transcendentalism* (1973), *New England Literary Culture* (1986), *Emerson* (2003), and three ecocritical books. He is a former Guggenheim and NEH Fellow and a member of the American Academy of Arts and Sciences. He is presently at work on a cultural and critical history of the dream of the Great American Novel.

DONNA CAMPBELL is Associate Professor of English at Washington State University. She is the author of *Resisting Regionalism: Gender and Naturalism in American Fiction, 1885–1915* (1997). Recent publications include work on the American artist and writer Gertrude Christian Fosdick (2008) and "*At Fault*: A Reappraisal of Kate Chopin's Other Novel" in *The Cambridge Companion to Kate Chopin* (2008). Her current project is a book on American women writers of naturalism.

RUSS CASTRONOVO is Jean Wall Bennett Professor of English and American Studies at the University of Wisconsin-Madison. His books include *Fathering the Nation: American Genealogies of Slavery and Freedom* (1996), *Necro Citizenship: Death, Eroticism, and the Public Sphere in the Nineteenth-Century United States* (2001), and *Beautiful Democracy: Aesthetics and Anarchy in a Global Era* (2007).

ROBERT CHODAT is the author of *Worldly Acts and Sentient Things: The Persistence of Agency from Stein to DeLillo* (2008), as well as essays on Richard Powers, Philip Roth, Lorrie Moore, and other postwar authors. He is currently working on a book about the American philosophical novel and a book about the "two cultures" debate in postwar American culture. He teaches at Boston University.

ROBERT COOVER is a worker in this book's field. More than a share-cropper, less than a proprietor. *The Origin of the Brunists, The Universal Baseball Association, J. Henry Waugh, Prop., Pricksongs & Descants, A Theological Position, The Public Burning, A Political Fable, Spanking the Maid, Gerald's Party, A Night at the Movies, Whatever Happened to Gloomy Gus of the Chicago Bears?, Pinocchio in Venice, John's Wife, Briar Rose, Ghost Town, The Grand Hotels (of Joseph Cornell), The Adventures of Lucky Pierre, Stepmother, A Child Again, Noir*. Also teaches experimental and electronic (including immersive 3D) writing at Brown University.

GREGG CRANE is Associate Professor of English at the University of Michigan and the author of *Race, Citizenship, and Law in American Literature* (2002) and *The Cambridge Introduction to the Nineteenth-Century American Novel* (2007).

KIRK CURNUTT is Professor and Chair of English at Troy University Montgomery in Montgomery, Alabama. He is the author of eleven books of fiction and criticism, including the novels *Breathing Out the Ghost* (2008) and *Dixie Noir* (2009) and such scholarly works as *The Cambridge Introduction to F. Scott Fitzgerald* (2007). Among his other works are *Coffee with Hemingway* (2007), an entry in Duncan Baird's series of imaginary conversations with great historical figures, and the short-story collection *Baby, Let's Make a Baby* (2003).

JUDE DAVIES is Professor of American Literature and Culture at the University of Winchester and editor of *Theodore Dreiser's Political Writings* (forthcoming). His previous books include *Diana, A Cultural History: Gender, Race, Nation and the People's Princess* (2000), and as joint author, *Gender, Ethnicity, and Sexuality in Contemporary American Film* (1998).

ANNA MAE DUANE is an Assistant Professor of English at the University of Connecticut, and is the Director of UConn's American Studies program. She is the author of *Suffering Childhood in Early America: Colonial Violence and the Making of the Child-Victim* (2010).

MICHAEL A. ELLIOTT is Winship Distinguished Research Professor of English and American Studies at Emory University Georgia. He is the author of *The Culture Concept: Writing and Difference in the Age of Realism* (2002) and *Custerology: The Enduring Legacy of the Indian Wars and George Armstrong Custer* (2007). He is also, with Claudia Stokes, the co-editor of *American Literary Studies: A Methodological Reader* (2003).

JOHN ERNEST, the Eberly Family Distinguished Professor of American Literature at West Virginia University, is the author of *Resistance and Reformation in Nineteenth-Century African-American Literature* (1995), *Liberation Historiography: African American Writers and the Challenge of History, 1794–1861* (2004), and *Chaotic Justice: Rethinking African American Literary History* (2009), as well as several editions of texts by nineteenth-century African American writers.

ROBERT FAGGEN is the Barton Evans and H. Andrea Neves Professor of Literature at Claremont McKenna College, California, and Director of the Gould Center for Humanistic Studies. He is currently completing a biography of Ken Kesey. Faggen is also the author of *Robert Frost and the Challenge of Darwin* (1997) and the editor of *The Notebooks of Robert Frost* (2006), *The Cambridge Companion to Robert Frost* (2001), and *Striving Towards Being: The Letters of Thomas Merton and Czeslaw Milosz* (1997).

MARIA FARLAND has taught at Johns Hopkins, Wesleyan, and Columbia Universities, and is currently Associate Professor of English and American Studies at Fordham University in the Bronx. She has published numerous essays on American literature that focus on feminism, gender, and science, in venues like *American Literature*, *American Literary History*, *English Literary History*, and *American Quarterly*.

JENNIFER L. FLEISSNER teaches English at Indiana University, Bloomington. She is the author of *Women, Compulsion, Modernity: The Moment of American Naturalism* (2004) as well as essays in *Critical Inquiry*, *ELH*, *American Literary History*, *American Literature*, *Novel*, *differences*, and other journals. Among her current projects is *Eating and Time: American Literature and the Embodied Everyday*, which focuses on appetite and individuation in late nineteenth-century fiction.

WINFRIED FLUCK is Professor and Chair of American Culture at the John F. Kennedy Institute for North American Studies of Freie Universität Berlin. He studied at Freie Universität Berlin, Harvard University, and the University of California, Berkeley, and has taught at the Universität Konstanz, the Universidad Autonoma Barcelona, and Princeton University. His books include *Ästhetische Theorie und literaturwissenschaftliche Methode* (1975); *Populäre Kultur* (1979); *Theorien amerikanischer Literatur* (1987); *Inszenierte Wirklichkeit. Der amerikanische Realismus 1865–1900* (1992); *Das kulturelle Imaginäre: Eine Funktionsgeschichte des amerikanischen Romans* (1997); *Romance with America: Essays on Culture, Literature, and American Studies* (2009), and *German-American Literature: New Directions in German-American Studies* (2002), co-edited with Werner Sollors. He is a founding member and director of the Graduate School of North American Studies at Freie Universität Berlin and co-director of the "Futures of American Studies" Institute at Dartmouth College, New Hampshire.

ELIZABETH FREEMAN is Associate Professor of English at the University of California, Davis and the author of *The Wedding Complex: Forms of Belonging in Modern American Culture* (2002). She specializes in nineteenth-century American literature, LGBTQ Studies, and Cultural Studies. Her current book, *Time Binds: Queer Temporalities, Queer Histories*, is forthcoming.

PAUL GILES was Professor of American Literature at the University of Oxford from 2002 to 2009; from 2010, he will be Challis Chair of English at the University of Sydney. Among his books are *The Global Remapping of American Literature* (forthcoming), *Atlantic Republic: The American Tradition in English Literature* (2006), and *Virtual Americas: Transnational Fictions and the Transatlantic Imaginary* (2002).

NANCY GLAZENER, Associate Professor of English at the University of Pittsburgh, is the author of *Reading for Realism: The History of a US Literary Institution, 1850–1910* (1997). She is currently at work on two book projects: a history of US literary culture in the nineteenth century and a study of forms of moral personhood in US novels.

JENNIFER RAE GREESON is Assistant Professor of English at the University of Virginia. She is currently completing a book entitled *Our South: Geographic Fantasy and the Rise of National Literature* (2010).

SANDRA M. GUSTAFSON is the author of *Eloquence Is Power: Oratory and Performance in Early America* (2000) and the editor of *Early American Literature*. Among her works are an essay collection co-edited with Caroline F. Sloat on *Cultural Narratives: Textuality and Performance in the United States before 1900* (2010) and a forthcoming monograph, *Imagining Deliberative Democracy: Politics and Letters in the Early American Republic*. She teaches in the English Department at the University of Notre Dame, Indiana.

URSULA K. HEISE is Professor of English and Director of the Program in Modern Thought and Literature at Stanford University. She specializes in ecocriticism and theories of modernization, postmodernization, and globalization. She is the author of *Chronoschisms: Time, Narrative, and Postmodernism* (1997) and *Sense of Place and Sense of Planet: The Environmental Imagination of the Global* (2008). Her most recent project is a book on species extinction and modern culture.

MICHAEL HILL is Assistant Professor at the University of Iowa. Along with his wife, Lena Hill, he has co-written *Ralph Ellison's "Invisible Man": A Reference Guide* (2008). Currently, he is working on *The Ethics of Swagger*, a book about prize-winning African American novels between 1977 and 1993.

ANDREW HOBEREK is Associate Professor of English at the University of Missouri-Columbia and the author of *The Twilight of the Middle Class: Post-World War II American Fiction and White-Collar Work* (2005). He is currently pursuing projects on post-1960 US fiction and the poetics of foreign policy and on contemporary fiction writers' fascination with popular genres.

BARBARA HOCHMAN is Associate Professor of American Literature at Ben-Gurion University of the Negev, Israel. She is the author of *The Art of Frank Norris: Storyteller* (1988), *Getting at the Author: Reimagining Books and Reading in the Age of American Realism* (2001), and diverse essays on nineteenth- and twentieth-century American fiction. Her current project, "Uncle Tom's Cabin and the Reading Revolution," explores radical differences in what Stowe's novel meant – to commentators, editors, illustrators, and the "common" reader – before and after the Civil War.

AMY HUNGERFORD is Professor of English and American Studies at Yale University. She is the author of *The Holocaust of Texts: Genocide, Literature and Personification* (2003) and *Postmodern Belief: American Literature and Religion since 1960* (2010). Current projects include *The Cambridge Introduction to the American Novel since 1945*. Her survey course on the American novel since 1945 is available in full (video, audio, and searchable transcripts) online through Open Yale Courses (oyc.yale.edu).

GREGORY S. JACKSON is Associate Professor of English at Rutgers University, New Jersey. He is the author of *The Word and Its Witness: The Spiritualization of American Realism* (2009).

CATHERINE JURCA teaches American literature and film at the California Institute of Technology. She is the author of *White Diaspora: The Suburb and the Twentieth-Century American Novel* (2001).

Lovalerie King is Associate Professor of English, Affiliate Faculty in Women's Studies and African and African American Studies, and Director of the Africana Research Center at Pennsylvania State University. She is the author of *Race, Theft, and Ethics: Property Matters in African American Literature* (2007), and The *Cambridge Introduction to Zora Neale Hurston* (2008), and the editor of three other volumes.

Susan Koshy is Associate Professor of English and Asian American studies at the University of Illinois, Urbana-Champaign. She is the author of *Sexual Naturalization: Asian Americans and Miscegenation* (2004), selected as a *Choice* Outstanding Academic Title, and co-editor of *Transnational South Asians: The Making of a Neo-Diaspora* (2008). She is working on a book on race, globalization, and postmodernity.

Andrew Lawson is Senior Lecturer in English at Leeds Metropolitan University. He is the author of *Walt Whitman and the Class Struggle* (2006), and is currently completing a book to be called *Downwardly Mobile: The Changing Fortunes of American Literary Realism.*

Rodrigo Lazo is Associate Professor of English at the University of California, Irvine, where he teaches courses in hemispheric American studies, Latino literature, and US literature and culture.

Stephanie Le Menager is Associate Professor of English at the University of California, Santa Barbara. She has published *Manifest and Other Destinies: Territorial Fictions of the Nineteenth-Century United States*, which won the 2005 Thomas J. Lyon award for Best Book in Western American Literary Studies, and articles in *ALH*, *ELH*, and *American Literature.*

Jonathan Levin is Dean of the College of Liberal Arts and Professor of English at Drew University, New Jersey. He previously taught at Columbia University and Fordham University (where he chaired the English Department), and served as Dean of the Humanities at Purchase College, State University of New York. His book, *The Poetics of Transition: Emerson, Pragmatism, and American Literary Modernism*, was named a Choice "Outstanding Title" in 1999. His other work includes edited volumes by H. D. Thoreau, Gertrude Stein, and Walt Whitman.

Robert S. Levine is Professor of English and Distinguished Scholar-Teacher at the University of Maryland. He is the author of *Conspiracy and Romance* (1989), *Martin Delany, Frederick Douglass, and the Politics of Representative Identity* (1997), and *Dislocating Race and Nation* (2008), and the editor of a number of volumes, including *Martin R. Delany: A Documentary Reader* (2003), *The Norton Anthology of American Literature, 1820–1865* (2007), and (with Caroline Levander) *Hemispheric American Studies* (2008).

Tom Lutz is the author of *American Nervousness, 1903: An Anecdotal History* (1991), *Crying: The Natural and Cultural History of Tears* (1999), *Cosmopolitan Vistas: American Regionalism and Literary Value* (2004), and *Doing Nothing: A History of Loafers, Loungers, Slackers, and Bums in America* (2006). He teaches at the University of California, Riverside.

SEAN McCANN is Professor of English at Wesleyan University, Connecticut. He is the author of *Gumshoe America: Hard-Boiled Crime Fiction and the Rise and Fall of New Deal Liberalism* (2000) and *A Pinnacle of Feeling: American Literature and Presidential Government* (2008).

BARBARA McCASKILL is Associate Professor of English at the University of Georgia. With Caroline Gebhard, she published *Post-Bellum, Pre-Harlem: African American Literature and Culture, 1877–1919* (2006). She has written extensively on race and slavery, including a forthcoming book entitled *A Thousand Miles for Freedom: William and Ellen Craft in Transatlantic Literature and Culture*. As co-director of The Civil Rights Digital Library (www.civilrightslibrary.org), she conducts collaborative research on the Civil Rights Movement.

MARK McGURL is Professor of English at the University of California, Los Angeles. He is the author of *The Novel Art: Elevations of American Fiction after Henry James* (2001) and, more recently, *The Program Era: Postwar Fiction and the Rise of Creative Writing* (2009).

WALTER BENN MICHAELS is Professor of English at the University of Illinois at Chicago. He writes on literary theory (*The Shape of the Signifier*, 2006) and on American literature (*The Gold Standard and the Logic of Naturalism*, 1987 and *Our America*, 1995). His most recent book is *The Trouble with Diversity* (2006).

JULIA MICKENBERG is Associate Professor of American Studies at the University of Texas at Austin. She is the author of *Learning from the Left: Children's Literature, the Cold War, and Radical Politics in the United States* (2006) and co-editor (with Philip Nel) of *Tales for Little Rebels: A Collection of Radical Children's Literature* (2008).

DAVID T. MITCHELL AND SHARON L. SNYDER are the authors, most recently, of *Cultural Locations of Disability* (2006). David is on the faculty in the College of Education at Temple University and Sharon is the founder of Brace Yourselves Productions. In 1995 they began a foray into collective work on representational issues of disability with their production of the feature-length documentary *Vital Signs: Crip Culture Talks Back*. They also edit a book series, Corporealities: Discourses of Disability, for the University of Michigan Press.

GRETCHEN MURPHY is the author of *Hemispheric Imaginings: The Monroe Doctrine and Narratives of US Empire* (2005) and *Shadowing the White Man's Burden: US Empire and the Problem of the Color Line* (2010). She teaches English at the University of Texas at Austin.

PETER NICHOLLS is Professor of English at New York University. His publications include *Ezra Pound: Politics, Economics and Writing* (1984), *Modernisms: A Literary Guide* (1995), *George Oppen and the Fate of Modernism* (2007), and many articles and essays on literature and theory. He has co-edited with Giovanni Cianci *Ruskin and Modernism* (2001) and with Laura Marcus *The Cambridge History of Twentieth-Century English Literature* (2004).

ELIZABETH NOLAN lectures in the Department of English at Manchester Metropolitan University. She has contributed an essay on Kate Chopin to *The Cambridge Companion to Kate Chopin* (2008). She co-edited *The Awakening: A Sourcebook* (2004), *Lives of Victorian Literary Figures IV: Edith Wharton* (2006), and *Edith Wharton's "The House of Mirth"* (2007).

TIM PRCHAL is the co-editor of *Visions and Divisions: American Immigration Literature, 1870–1930* (2008) and author of articles appearing in *MELUS*, *Studies in American Fiction*, *American Literary Realism*, and *Leviathan*. He focuses on comparative ethnic literature and, specifically, American immigration literature from the late nineteenth and early twentieth centuries. He is currently a Visiting Assistant Professor at Oklahoma State University.

PAMELA REGIS is Professor of English at McDaniel College in Westminster, Maryland. In *Describing Early America* (1992) she investigated the nature writing of William Bartram, Thomas Jefferson, and J. Hector St. John de Crèvecoeur. In *A Natural History of the Romance Novel* (2003) she defined this form of literature and traced its history.

ROBERT F. REID-PHARR, Professor of English and American Studies at the Graduate Center of the City University of New York, is one of the nation's leading scholars of both early African American literature and the emerging field of race and sexuality studies. His latest book is *Once You Go Black: Choice, Desire, and the Black American Intellectual* (2007).

BRUCE ROBBINS is Old Dominion Foundation Professor in the Humanities at Columbia University. His most recent book is *Upward Mobility and the Common Good* (2007). He is also the author of *Feeling Global: Internationalism in Distress* (1999), *The Servant's Hand: English Fiction from Below* (1986), and *Secular Vocations: Intellectuals, Professionalism, Culture* (1993).

JOHN CARLOS ROWE is USC Associates' Professor of the Humanities and Chair of the Department of American Studies and Ethnicity at the University of Southern California. His most recent books are *Literary Culture and U.S. Imperialism: From the Revolution to World War II* (2000), *The New American Studies* (2002), and *Blackwell's Companion to American Studies* (2009).

RAMÓN SALDÍVAR is the Hoagland Family Professor of Humanities and Sciences in English and Comparative Literature at Stanford University. He is author of *Figural Language in the Novel: The Flowers of Speech from Cervantes to Joyce* (1984), *Chicano Narrative: The Dialectics of Difference* (1990), and *The Borderlands of Culture: Américo Paredes and the Transnational Imaginary*, which was awarded the 2007 MLA Prize for best book in the area of US Latina/Latino and Chicana/Chicano Literary and Cultural Studies.

DAVID SCHMID is an Associate Professor in the Department of English at the University at Buffalo (SUNY). He has published on a variety of subjects, including celebrity, film adaptation, and crime fiction, and he is the author of *Natural Born Celebrities: Serial Killers in American Culture*.

DeNel Rehberg Sedo is based at Mount Saint Vincent University in Halifax, Nova Scotia, Canada, and works in the sociology of literature. Her scholarly interests include the social contexts of reading, women's reading practices and learning communities, feminist epistemology and ontology. Along with Danielle Fuller from the University of Birmingham (UK), she is conducting an investigation of contemporary reading cultures in Canada, the UK, and the USA.

Milette Shamir is a Senior Lecturer at Tel Aviv University, where she is Chair of the Department of English and American Studies. She is the author of *Inexpressible Privacy: The Interior Life of Antebellum American Literature* (2006) and the co-editor of *Boys Don't Cry? Rethinking Narratives of Masculinity and Emotion in the US* (2002).

Shelley Streeby is Associate Professor of Literature at the University of California, San Diego. She is the author of *American Sensations: Class, Empire, and the Production of Popular Culture* (2002) and co-editor of *Empire and the Literature of Sensation: An Anthology of Nineteenth-Century Popular Fiction* (2007). She serves on the editorial board of *American Quarterly*.

Timothy Sweet is Professor of English at West Virginia University. His publications include *Traces of War: Poetry, Photography, and the Crisis of the Union* (1990), *American Georgics: Economy and Environment in Early American Literature* (2002), and articles on early, antebellum, and Native American literature.

Sean Kicummah Teuton is Associate Professor of English and American Indian Studies at the University of Wisconsin. He is the author of *Red Land, Red Power: Grounding Knowledge in the American Indian Novel* (2008).

Cecelia Tichi is the William R. Kenan Jr. Professor of English at Vanderbilt University, Tennessee. She is the author of six scholarly books as well as the editor of several others, including *Exposés and Excess: Muckraking in America 1900/2000* (2003). She has also published three novels.

Candace Waid is the author of *Edith Wharton's Letters from the Underworld: Fictions of Women and Writing* (1991) and the editor of numerous editions of Wharton's work, including the Norton Critical Edition of *The Age of Innocence* (2003). Her essays on Faulkner have appeared in *Faulkner and the Artist* (ed. Donald Kartiganer, 1996) and *The Faulkner Journal* (2007). Waid teaches courses on Faulkner and Southern literature in the Department of English at the University of California, Santa Barbara.

Alan M. Wald is the H. Chandler Davis Collegiate Professor of English Literature and American Culture at the University of Michigan. The concluding volume of his trilogy on the US literary Left, *American Night: The Literary Left in the Era of the Cold War*, is forthcoming.

Priscilla Wald teaches at Duke University, North Carolina and is the author of *Constituting Americans: Cultural Anxiety and Narrative Form* (1995) and *Contagious: Cultures,*

Carriers, and the Outbreak Narrative (2008). She is editor of *American Literature*, is on the editorial boards of *ESQ* and *Literature and Medicine*, co-edits a book series, *America and the Long 19th Century*, and chairs the Faculty Board of Duke University Press.

BRYAN WATERMAN is a member of the Department of English at New York University and the author of *Republic of Intellect: The Friendly Club of New York City and the Making of American Literature* (2007). His writing on early American literature and culture has appeared in *Early American Literature, American Literary History, The William and Mary Quarterly*, and elsewhere.

CINDY WEINSTEIN is Professor of English at the California Institute of Technology. She has edited or co-edited several volumes and is the author of *Family, Kinship and Sympathy in Nineteenth-Century American Literature* (2004) and *The Literature of Labor and the Labors of Literature: Allegory in Nineteenth-Century American Fiction* (1995).

JAMES L. W. WEST III is Edwin Erle Sparks Professor of English at Penn State University. He is a biographer, book historian, and scholarly editor. He is the author of *American Authors and the Literary Marketplace* (1988), *William Styron: A Life* (1998), and *The Perfect Hour: The Romance of F. Scott Fitzgerald and Ginevra King* (2005). West is the general editor of the Cambridge Fitzgerald Edition; his edition of *Trimalchio: An Early Version of The Great Gatsby* appeared in 2000.

ELIZABETH YOUNG is Professor of English and Gender Studies at Mount Holyoke College, Massachusetts. She is the author of *Black Frankenstein: The Making of an American Metaphor* (2008), and *Disarming the Nation: Women's Writing and the American Civil War* (1999); and co-author, with Anthony Lee, of *On Alexander Gardner's "Photographic Sketch Book" of the Civil War* (2007).

MARY SARACINO ZBORAY is Visiting Scholar in Communication at the University of Pittsburgh and co-author of *A Handbook for the Study of Book History in the United States* (2000), *Literary Dollars and Social Sense: A People's History of the Mass Market Book* (2005), and *Everyday Ideas: Socioliterary Experience among Antebellum New Englanders* (2006), which won the annual book prize of the Association for Education in Journalism and Mass Communication's History Division, and the International Reading Association's E. Jennifer Monaghan Award for best book in the history of literacy.

RONALD J. ZBORAY is Professor of Communication, Cultural Studies, and Women's Studies at the University of Pittsburgh, author of *A Fictive People: Antebellum Economic Development and the American Reading Public* (1993), and co-author of *A Handbook for the Study of Book History in the United States* (2000), *Literary Dollars and Social Sense: A People's History of the Mass Market Book* (2005), and *Everyday Ideas: Socioliterary Experience among Antebellum New Englanders* (2006).

DAVID A. ZIMMERMAN is Associate Professor of English at the University of Wisconsin–Madison. He is the author of *Panic! Markets, Crises, and Crowds in American Fiction* (2006). His essays have appeared in *American Literature, ESQ, Arizona Quarterly*, and *Dreiser Studies*.

Acknowledgments

It takes a village to raise a book like this. In a volume that is explicitly dedicated to the idea of collaboration, it's a pleasure to recognize some of the many who have helped us assemble this omnibus.

First of all, we thank the contributors to this book, who have cheerfully and generously complied with a set of compositional and editorial requirements that so often veered sharply away from standard operating procedure. Their willingness to talk to each other in print has created a different – and richer – literary history. For special assistance of various kinds beyond their fine essays, we put our hands together for Jonathan Arac, Gregg Crane, Michael Elliott, John Ernest, Maria Farland, Paul Giles, Andrew Hoberek, Barbara Hochman, Amy Hungerford, Robert S. Levine, Cecelia Tichi, James L. W. West III, and Elizabeth Young.

Others who have aided us on the long road to completion include Rachel Adams, Chris Castiglia, Martha Cutter, Frances Smith Foster, Teresa Goddu, Ezra Greenspan, Glenn Hendler, June Howard, Lawrence Jackson, James Kim, Elizabeth Long, Jerome McGann, W. J. T. Mitchell, and Christopher Wilson. We also thank the anonymous referees whose comments on the original book proposal helped so much in the planning stages. (One of those referees, Gregg Crane, was kind enough to sign his referee's report on the proposal for this project before going on to contribute to it.)

Among those at Cambridge University Press, we're grateful to Chloe Howell, Thomas O'Reilly, and Maartje Scheltens. We especially thank Ray Ryan for his good counsel and unflagging confidence in this book, and for the alacrity with which he has always supplied both. The innovations showcased in this history would have been impossible without Ray's support. He's been a terrific partner in this venture.

One of the most important of those innovations has been the notorious *Cambridge History of the American Novel* (*CHAN*) wiki, the intramural website that so centrally affected the reading and writing of this book. For designing the wiki we thank Shawn McCauley of Emory University.

A heartfelt thank you to our superb research assistants, Meredith Benjamin and especially Paul Thifault, without whom we would all be many steps closer to the grave. And thanks to Fordham University for funding them both.

Finally, we thank our families, who let us do this, and whom we do it for.

Leonard Cassuto
Clare Virginia Eby
Benjamin Reiss

Note on the text

Secondary sources (i.e., criticism and contextual scholarship) are fully referenced in the endnotes that follow each chapter, but the novels – because they often exist in multiple editions – are not sourced.

General introduction

LEONARD CASSUTO

Hundreds of thousands of novels have been published since the first novel was written by a North American in the early days of the republic. Between 1789 and 1800, about thirty novels written by Americans were published in the United States, at a time when "American" meant something very different, and much less separate, from what it means now. During that period about 350 other titles were published,[1] creating a distinctly transatlantic (and very British) literary landscape.[a] As late as 1875, the number of novels both written and published in the United States had never exceeded 175 per year. Not until the 1880s, in a booming economy – now featuring what has been termed "the industrial book"– did new American fiction titles exceed 1,000 per year.[2] The numbers have been climbing exponentially ever since, flagging only slightly during economic downturns. The total had doubled again by the 1950s, and again by the 1980s. It had doubled yet again by the 1990s, and once more in the 2000s.[3] At this writing, near the end of the first decade of the twenty-first century, a book of fiction is being published in the United States every hour, on average (and that figure excludes vanity press and self-publishing ventures).[4] That's more than 10,000 works of fiction – mostly novels – each year. Not only do rumors of the death of the novel appear greatly exaggerated, but these numbers alone (and the swiftly shifting landscape they portend) suggest that we need to consider the history of the novel anew.

Any history of the American novel must pick a path through the multitudes of books, and provide a rationale for that path. Like all literary histories, *The Cambridge History of the American Novel* is a document of its time. It reproduces the categories of its time and the debates of its time even as it produces new

a Various characteristics of this early transatlanticism are addressed in many chapters in the first part of this volume, including those by Paul Giles, Bryan Waterman, Anna Mae Duane, and Ronald Zboray and Mary Saracino Zboray. In Part Two, Nancy Glazener considers the transatlanticism of American print culture during the postbellum period.

ones alongside. But unlike most of its notable predecessors, it calls attention to its own internal conflicts and especially to the contingency – historical and otherwise – of its methodology and approach, and of the categories that it creates. It is with that contingency in mind that this book has been organized.

To begin with, this history synthesizes the divisions between the author-centered literary history of yesterday and the context-centered efforts of recent years.

The older American literary histories (that is, the ones before the mid-1980s) practice different versions of the Great Man Theory, arguing that literary history is the story of illustrious writers seeking timeless truths, allowing their books to rise above quotidian surroundings. Context, where it does appear in these older books, is often straight biography, and historical apparatus centers on grouping writers into movements which are then aligned with a thesis-driven, millennialist narrative of American literary exceptionalism and national progress.[5]

Richard Chase's widely scoped and still influential *The American Novel and Its Tradition* (1957) is a case in point. Chase sought the "originality and 'Americanness'" of the American novel in the ways that it "incorporate[es] an element of romance."[6] Monumental summative works by Alfred Kazin, Charles Feidelson, R. W. B. Lewis, Richard Poirier, and others present similarly thesis-driven surveys of large chunks of American literary history, almost always concentrating on the longer fiction by the famous men whose precincts scholars, critics, and readers have since widened.

These ambitious weavers of American literary historical fabric frequently reviewed each other's works, mostly generously. Their less guarded moments of mutual critique offer a window onto their own views of their vaulting literary historical projects. Consider Lewis's 1954 review of Charles Feidelson's *Symbolism and American Literature* (1953), written while Lewis was presumably finishing his own such reappraisal, *The American Adam*, which appeared the next year. In *Adam* Lewis would hold up his method ("intellectual history") as a way to expose "the dominant ideas of a period, or of a nation."[7] But in his reading of Feidelson, Lewis places himself at an ironic distance from such monumental critical tasks, and proposes instead that the practice of critics and historians reflects the preoccupations of their own times.

Is American literature not, asks Lewis in his review, overly "susceptible to the big idea?"[8] That question serves to unify the brief critical historiography that I've been unfurling here. From D. H. Lawrence forward, histories of the American novel (and of American literature more generally) long centered on the "big idea." Big ideas – displayed, for example, in a raft of older books with the phrase "American Mind" in their titles – have charisma, but they reveal pitfalls. Most notable of these is tendentiousness. Or as Lewis puts it: does the big idea "not sometimes skirt those rare exceptions" that don't fit its frame?[9] Books built around big ideas rarely squint, but there is much more focus today on those "rare exceptions," which turn out not to be so rare after all. The expanding literary canon, a salutary and ongoing development, demands that we squint.

The most expansive literary histories of our era have sought to uproot and overturn the old vision of the big idea. These more recent works have nearly all been multi-authored collections, as the big idea gives way to a diversity of ideas – and to diversity itself. In the era of the expanding canon, it may be that no one person can fully represent the diversity of the American literary tradition, even within one genre. Bernard W. Bell's important survey of the African American novel succeeds by limiting its scope in order to cover a lot of chronological ground, but most of the ambitious and influential works of American literary history during the past generation have been wide rather than long. The contributors to this volume have benefited, for example, from the work of Cathy N. Davidson's new historicist reading of the early American novel (which also makes use of methods from book history), and from Jane Tompkins's fusion of literary criticism with some of the methods of cultural studies, and Amy Kaplan's innovative use of postcolonial and transnational scholarship.[10] These major new visions have brought new ways of reading old books and focused our attention on new ones; they encompass approaches and methodologies that have emerged in recent decades to offer different models of inquiry – but without much historical sweep. The histories that cross periods these days (that is, diachronic works) have been books with many authors.

Literary history has also confronted new ways of doing history itself. Intertwined with parallel trends in historical study (which has lately focused on the travails of ordinary people rather than famous ones), the current emphasis in literary study is strongly bottom-up rather than top-down, stressing the idea that literature is of its time, and that writers do not (and indeed cannot) transcend their contexts. Newly invigorated by historical scholarship, multiculturalism, and cultural studies, literary study has become not only more historical but also more generally interdisciplinary in its approach during the past twenty-five years, developments which are reflected, for example, in the monumental *Cambridge History of American Literature*.[11]

Accordingly, the 1991 *Columbia History of the American Novel*, the last major effort along the lines of the present volume, is divided up into chapters whose titles mention no author by name, and whose literary-historical approach entwines the novelists into a many-branched narrative that is fully context-driven. This fine book initiates some of the projects that continue in *The Cambridge History of the American Novel*, such as the study of the novel in the book market, and the sustained analysis of minority literatures in the context of a larger literary whole. The result of the "thematic" approach of the Columbia history is a rich depiction of backdrop – the setting against which American novels have been written – that de-emphasizes individual writers.[12]

But writers may also have influence that can allow them to affect the course of literary history beyond their own times. (For example, a chapter in this volume argues for the influence of Herman Melville on the Beat writers of the 1950s; another traces Ernest Hemingway's influences on post-World War II Jewish novelists.) We can learn a lot from the context that produces a novel, but as critics of earlier generations remind us, there is also much to learn from the mind of the author who wrote the book.

The Cambridge History of the American Novel accordingly aims at a Howellsian "middle way" that synthesizes the shifts in method and emphasis of this generation, but without tossing out the idea that writers can influence history as well be influenced by it. It's appropriate that Howells has emerged as a figure of signal importance in this history who is discussed across a number of chapters. "The Dean" proves significant not so much for his own novels (which receive their due here) as for his central role – coupled with his awareness of that role – in promoting realism as the most truthful, most democratic way to tell a story.[b] Howells knew that his novels, reviews, editorial pronouncements, and support of younger authors were both shaping and reflecting a new turn in American literary history, even if he didn't know what that history would look like later on. In this literary history we have highlighted the ground that we've covered even as we seek future trailheads.

The dialogic method

How *The Cambridge History of the American Novel* works is inseparable from the thick braid of interwoven stories that it tells. So let me turn briefly to the structure and inner workings of the volume.

b For discussions of this aspect of Howellsian realism in this volume, see the essays by Michael Elliott ("Realism and radicalism: the school of Howells," chapter 17), and Carrie Tirado Bramen ("James, pragmatism, and the realist ideal," chapter 18).

One might say that *The Cambridge History of the American Novel* is founded upon a series of productive collapses. I don't mean the kind of collapse where something (or someone) falls apart, of course. Rather, a productive collapse mixes things together, creating new juxtapositions of the familiar and unfamiliar, new similarities and contrasts, and an expanded overall scope.

This book is founded on the idea that a narrative history by many hands must necessarily be a collaborative history. Moreover, such collaboration should, for the sake of unity, be as explicit as possible.

Accordingly, the most important collapse that structures this volume is the breaking down of the boundaries that ordinarily separate the contributors to an edited volume. So many such volumes convey the effect of the contributors laboring in a row of hermetically sealed glass booths, unable to talk to each other until after the task is done. (There have been cases in my own experience of writing for scholarly collections when I haven't even learned who else was in the table of contents until I saw the finished book.) The process of writing and editing *The Cambridge History of the American Novel* combines the immediacy of a conference proceeding – in which the contributors actually converse with one another – with the rigor of a carefully planned and structured literary history. The overall goal has been to foster collaboration at every stage to create a multivoiced yet integrated literary history.

We've drawn on twenty-first-century technology to promote dialogue, combined with the old-fashioned notion that the writers of a collective history should read each other's work as they write their own. To promote that goal, we posted contributors' work – starting with abstracts and continuing through successive drafts – on a wiki, a shared private website that enabled contributors to access each other's work in progress. Throughout the composition process, the editors have noted who might benefit from reading whom, and have relayed this information to the contributors, who have also read freely on the wiki on their own.

Having read the work of their colleagues, chapter authors have engaged each other *within their chapters* in order to create literary conversations within and across time – just as American novels do. Readers of *The Cambridge History of the American Novel* will find tangible results of that dialogue in the form of many intramural references within. The footnotes in the text are exclusively devoted to reproducing such dialogue, with traditional bibliography reserved for the endnotes. But the main results of this collaborative approach go beyond intramural references. They guide and structure the story that's being told by linking the chapters through various pathways threading among them. The effect, as one of the contributors to this book noted at a

2009 conference, invokes hypertext: numerous links that draw chapters together, and with them the book as a whole.

The strong dialogical emphasis in this book generates horizontal and vertical continuity (that is, unity within and across time). It also generates productive disagreement. For example, *The Cambridge History of the American Novel* represents the current identity categories that drive today's study of the American novel, especially in its more recent incarnations. But the volume also contains a critique of those categories that describes them as "neoliberal" and criticizes them for attending to racial and ethnic identity rather than economic inequality.[c] These dissenting views explicitly clash in ways that allow the reader to witness the ongoing process of creating literary history.

The Cambridge History of the American Novel thus intertwines multiple texts and contexts to create a web of interlocking conversations and overlapping conflicts rather than a master narrative or even a giant diorama (an image which also connotes orderly representation).[13] This book surveys the field differently. The tradition of the American novel is tangled, and the goal of this book is to represent that tangle and follow many strands within it, not to unravel it in search of any separate strand.

This goal entails more than bringing groups of books together (though this history surely does that). The chapters in the volume speak to each other in a way that encourages the migration of themes, ideas, and authors across boundaries. As an example, consider race and the American novel, a subject treated on its own in scores of scholarly books. The editors have sought to keep matters of race (and African American novels) from being relegated (we might say "segregated") to chapters that separately trace the African American tradition. Eric J. Sundquist has written of "the necessity of living with the paradox that 'American' literature is both a single tradition of many parts and a series of winding, sometimes parallel traditions that have perforce been built in good part from their inherent conflicts."[14] The *Cambridge History of the American Novel* enfolds such conflicts so as to show the complex interrelationships among them. Sundquist's important 1993 book, even as it guides efforts to reconceive literary history along these lines, nevertheless scrutinizes race separately from other issues. One of the advantages of assembling a history of this scope lies in the opportunity to complicate race and turn it outwards in a way that extends Sundquist's paradigm and embodies his larger purpose.

c See Walter Benn Michaels, "Model minorities and the minority model – the neoliberal novel" (chapter 61).

All of this interchange is possible because the authors have read and referenced each other in ways that follow themes from chapter to chapter, and place them in different contexts. At seventy-one chapters, *The Cambridge History of the American Novel* has more than twice as many chapters as its most recent predecessor. The large number is designed to generate a multiplicity of literary-historical perspectives that weave together (and sometimes bump into each other) in complicated ways. That means, for example, that Charlotte Perkins Gilman's utopian *Herland* (1915) is read in one chapter as an outgrowth of the sentimental tradition, and in another chapter as a forerunner of the queer gender-bending that proliferated in the twentieth century, in a third as a meditation on American imperial adventures, and in a fourth as a protest novel. From the discussion of protest the reader may follow the theme of propaganda (in protest novels) into a discussion of the influence of mass media on the literary representation of protest, and from there into the proletarian tradition of the 1930s, and so on – with all of these linked via footnoted references. As with hypertext, one may follow the links of one's choice to create one's own literary historical narrative.[d] Such internal dialogue within this history corresponds to the property that Mikhail Bakhtin says is "the fundamental constitutive element of all novelistic style."[15] The form of this history thus dovetails with that of its subject.

It may be that future literary histories will be found on the internet, where actual electronic hypertextual references will allow readers to bounce from entry to entry. That approach will have its strengths and weaknesses (and some of these are assessed in forward-looking analyses by Ursula Heise and Robert Coover in this book). But today, right now, *The Cambridge History of the American Novel* represents an innovation: a narrative history by more than seventy tellers working together in virtual space.

Invention versus discovery

What kind of collective story is being told by these more than seventy tellers? The sheer number of American novels, and the accompanying reality that no one can read them all, together raise the question of whether historians – literary and otherwise – create the story or uncover it. Exactly what do literary historians make up (or construct) in a case like this and what do they discover?

d Chapters referenced here include "The woman's novel beyond sentimentalism" (34); "Reimagining genders and sexualities" (57); "Imperialism, Orientalism, and empire" (32); and "Novels of civic protest" (23), as well as "The novel, mass culture, mass media" (41) and "Steinbeck and the proletarian novel" (40).

And how much "there" is already there? The post-Civil War movement toward realism in American fiction, for example, is a heavily documented literary historical event. Likewise, the fame and influence of, say, Nathaniel Hawthorne in his own time is a fact that literary historians ignore at their peril, though they will naturally interpret that fact differently. We may expect legitimate literary histories to consider such matters. On the other hand, what is the significance of introducing a category like *manhood* into American literary history?

The focus on "invention" of the story in *The Cambridge History of the American Novel* is twofold. First, we've sought to invent new categories that reshape old histories. Accordingly, this book is the first-ever history of the American novel to devote a chapter to the "worlding" of the American novel (a category which encompasses, among other topics, the development of the American novel after the attacks of September 11, 2001), to name one example. And following developments in the new field of masculinity studies, *The Cambridge History of the American Novel* identifies and follows the relation between changing meanings of American manhood and changes in the American novel.[e]

But another aspect of invention centers on devising histories for new things that simply didn't exist at the time of earlier histories. This volume sets aside space for analysis of televised book clubs and other twentieth- and twenty-first-century reading communities. These communities descend from earlier reading groups whose development is also chronicled here, but are also distinct from them because they have evolved in different media. Consider also the example of graphic novels, an ambitious recent outgrowth from comic books that now cross-pollinates with literary fiction, the memoir, and the movies. *The Cambridge History of the American Novel* is the first history of the American novel to bring graphic novels into the larger narrative of the novel as a genre – and in tracing the separate history of the graphic novel, old *Krazy Kat* cartoons come into view as precursors, and these then become part of the diverse root system of the American novel.

One may justly question the way that this history singles out the United States. The most tempting response is pragmatic: people already study American literature and American novels, so those categories already exist, and there is practical value to extending discussions that have already been joined. In the preface to one of the earliest scholarly histories of American

e This thread begins with "Manhood in the early American novel" (chapter 11) and extends through many later chapters in the volume.

fiction, Arthur Hobson Quinn tasks himself with showing the development of the nation's fiction as "an artistic form" that will "show its relation to American life."[16] Leslie Fiedler, in one of the first expansive histories of the American novel alone, defended his theme ("Love and Death") as the necessary method to serve his exceptionalistic purpose ("to make clear the divergence of our own novelistic tradition from the continental ones").[17] Assumptions stack atop each other like cordwood in the introductions to these books, and Quinn's and Fiedler's reasoning can easily be made to look self-referential despite the continuing value of their books.

The structure of this history acknowledges the contingency of ideas about nation even as its organization argues for the value of tracing national literary traditions and the shared literary self-consciousness that they provide. In other words, if the novelists wrote with an idea of America in mind, there's value in tracing the tradition they created that coheres about that idea. Even so, from its consideration of the transatlanticism of the early American literary scene to its focus on the complex literary interchanges surrounding the borders of the United States, *The Cambridge History of the American Novel* also contributes to what has recently been termed the "hemispheric turn" in American studies.[f]

But why separate the story of the American novel from the rest of American literature? To answer this question, let's go back to what happens when we consider the graphic novel as a kind of novel. By making a case for the significance of the graphic novel, Jan Baetens shows that we must perforce consider – and consider in a new and different way – the significance of the wordless woodcuts of the 1920s that are, along with cartoons, another important source for the graphic novel. The enormous flexibility and absorptive qualities of the novel (called "hybridity" in the current critical lexicon) make the case for studying its history. Or as one of the genre's eminent practitioners, Emile Zola, puts it, the novel is an "eminently seductive form" that "has monopolized all space, absorbed all genres . . . It is what one wishes it to be."[18] In short, the novel is a cultural prism with enormous power to focus and refract its surroundings, bringing history and culture into view from simultaneous and differing perspectives.

Analysis of new "invented" categories like graphic novels and the culture of readers and reviewers on Amazon.com may be distinguished from efforts to interpret literary phenomena that we agree are significant (e.g., what was realism all about?– a "discovery" question). This history presents the two together. The volume continues the discussions that explore traditional

f Chapters with a central hemispheric component include those by Gretchen Murphy, Rodrigo Lazo, and Ramón Saldívar (chapters 33, 65, and 62 respectively).

literary historical categories, but also invents new kinds of literary history and new approaches to it. Readers may question to what extent we are driven by new critical categories, and to what extent by new facts on the ground – and they may decide for themselves.

Collapsing high and low, periods and isms

The Cambridge History of the American Novel pays more attention to genre fiction than previous histories of American literature, and it accords them the importance they deserve in the shaping of literary fiction and the history of the American novel generally. If all literary histories ask, "What is 'literature'?" then this volume argues that the study of popular genres alongside more self-consciously literary productions will help us to answer that question.

The rise of genre fiction is a story that begins early. Eclipsed genres like the sea novel helped to shape books that we read today as literature, as Hester Blum demonstrates in her chapter in this volume. And later genres such as the crime novel or science fiction, which flowered in the twentieth century, have cross-pollinated with so-called literary fiction and inspired novelists from Hemingway to Marge Piercy. We have also seen notable entries from within a genre take their places on the high cultural podium.

The critical study of genre fiction begins somewhat later, as it took awhile for scholars to acknowledge the importance of formula-driven fiction as art, or as a source of literary influence and cultural insight. This history devotes chapters to "strong genres"– so called because they register with particular clarity the collectively held beliefs, hopes, and anxieties of the context in which they are produced. David S. Reynolds, one of the first to implicate genre writing with the development of canonical literature, writes of the way that early American genre writing reflected "profound fears and fantasies" during a period of rapid change.[19]

We've placed chapters on genres at the point in the chronology where they peaked in visibility, readership, and influence: in other words, at the point in time where they matter most to the larger history by affecting developments outside of themselves. The Western, a form which thrived in the dime novels that proliferated after the Civil War and into the twentieth, has always informed conceptions of the frontier, a connection demonstrated in numerous chapters herein,[g] but most critics agree that its long heyday has now passed, so

g See, most notably, Stephanie Le Menager's "Imagining the Frontier" (chapter 31), and Shelley Streeby's "Dime novels and the rise of mass market genres" (chapter 35).

these chapters mainly appear earlier in this book. John G. Cawelti, one of the pioneers in the serious study of the Western and of US popular culture generally, suggests that contemporary readers are no longer comfortable with the way that Westerns handle the clash of cultures on the frontier, with two main results: first, the mass popularity of the genre has fallen off; and second, today's Westerns tend to be self-reflexive high art.[20] Many contemporary genres, meanwhile, gained in popularity during the mid twentieth century, when the popularity of the paperback (a phenomenon which is the subject of a separate chapter in this volume[h]) affected the reading habits of US residents and also soldiers fighting abroad.

This intersection between the story and the form in which it's packaged points to the way that *The Cambridge History of the American Novel* collapses the traditional barrier between literary and book history. Book historians (who focus on books as material and commercial artifacts and reading as consumption) and literary historians (who focus on the words between the covers) have been leading parallel existences for some time. Book historians have their own methodologies, generate their own findings, and write their own histories – which amount to an interesting, complementary reversal of today's literary criticism, where context is so important to interpretation. In the case of book history, what is often treated as context by the critic becomes central, and particular books, or even groups of books, become only one type of evidence for making claims about the work of books as a whole. *The Cambridge History of the American Novel* brings these two perspectives together; in a series of chapters appearing throughout and cross-referenced in the dialogues that structure the volume, this book traces the history of American novels as objects that are made, sold, and read – together with the history of what's inside them.[i]

Along with genres, *The Cambridge History of the American Novel* tracks themes, ideological preoccupations, and conventions that persist through the centuries of American novels. While some of the chapters in the book are timebound (such as those devoted to individual authors), others (such as "Supernatural novels") range across centuries. As with genre-based chapters, we have sought to place "time-traveling chapters" at points in the chronology that coincide with the emerging importance of their preoccupations.

h See James L. W. West III, "Twentieth-century publishing and the rise of the paperback," chapter 47.

i See in particular the chapters by Mary Saracino Zboray and Ronald J. Zboray, Nancy Glazener, Barbara Hochman, James L. W. West III, DeNel Rehberg Sedo, and Robert Coover (chapters 4, 20, 36, 47, 70, and 71 respectively).

Accordingly, the chapter on science fiction is positioned at mid-twentieth century (the time of the genre's "Golden Age"), while "Novels of civic protest" appears in the section focusing on the age of realism, even though the story that the chapter tells ranges both forward and back from the era that cultural historian Alan Trachtenberg has termed "the age of incorporation."[21]

The self-conscious juxtaposition of time-limited chapters with time-traversing ones again calls deliberate attention to the act of assembling a narrative history. Different chapters in this history explore – and sometimes challenge – the logic underlying the periodization through which most of us learn literary history. In US literary history, the boundaries of the foundational periods (romanticism, realism, modernism, etc.) are mainly linked to the dates of wars.[j] Conventional period markers thus carry an ideological weight that is rarely acknowledged. Some of the contributors to this book work within conventional period boundaries, while others critique them. As the development of the novel itself shows, there are not only many ways to tell stories, but also many ways to combine them. The structure of this volume accordingly accepts and traces the "isms" (romanticism, realism, etc.) that once dominated literary history – because their influence is evident in the way that most scholars have learned the subject.

This conjunction of the synchronic and the diachronic highlights the larger mission and method of *The Cambridge History of the American Novel*. Through the contrast of chapters with vastly different temporal scopes and conceptual frames – many of them implicitly linking global and local perspectives – this book takes wide views. But by putting sweeping and detailed views together, the book also acknowledges the inevitable narrowing of dimension (whether length or width) that accompanies each one. By juxtaposing the wide and the narrow, the traditional and the contemporary, and the settled and the speculative, this history – through its content and structure together – presents the big idea along with critique and corollary. It also frames the impulse (so common among critics of American literature as to be almost ingrained) to seek it. There are many paths through *The Cambridge History of the American Novel*, just as the volume traces many histories within its larger history. And that is exactly the point.

j John Carlos Rowe explores the connection between war and literary history in "US novels and US wars" (chapter 49), as does Elizabeth Freeman in "Reimagining genders and sexualities" (chapter 57); Freeman also considers gender bias in periodization. Clare Eby explores this issue further in her introduction to Part Three of this volume.

Notes

1. Lyle H. Wright, *American Fiction 1774–1850: A Contribution Toward a Bibliography* (1948; 2nd rev. edn., San Marino, CA: The Huntington Library, 1969), 363; Herbert Ross Brown, *The Sentimental Novel in America, 1789–1860* (Durham, NC: Duke University Press, 1940), 15.
2. Lyle H. Wright, *American Fiction, 1851–1875: A Contribution Toward a Bibliography* (San Marino, CA: The Huntington Library, 1965); in totaling Wright's titles by year from 1851 to 1875, see Perry Willett, ed., *Wright American Fiction, 1851–1875*. Indiana University Digital Library Program, www.letrs.indiana.edu/web/w/wright2.
3. For figures from 1991 to 2007, see "Book Title Output and Average Prices," from *The Bowker Annual Library and Book Trade Almanac*, volumes XXXIX to LI, ed. Catherine Barr, Gary Ink, Dave Bogart, Andrew Grabois, Catherine Barr, and Constance Harbison (New Providence, NJ: R. R. Bowker, 1994–2008); for R. R. Bowker figures from 1880 to 1990, see William S. Lofquist, "A Statistical Perspective on U.S. Book Publishing," in *International Book Publishing: An Encyclopedia*, ed. Philip G. Altbach and Edith S. Hoshino (New York: Garland Publishing, 1995), 344–346.
4. Laura Miller, "How Many Books Are Too Many?" *New York Times* (July 18, 2004).
5. In the *Literary History of the United States* produced by Robert E. Spiller and others, for example, Henry Seidel Canby describes the writing of the period named by F. O. Matthiessen the "American Renaissance" as expressing "the climax of a long growth from colonial beginnings to self-conscious and organized nation"; "Address to the Reader" (1948), *The Literary History of the United States*, ed. Robert Spiller *et al.* (3rd rev. edn., New York: Macmillan, 1963), xxiii.
6. Richard Chase, *The American Novel and Its Tradition* (Garden City, NY: Doubleday Anchor Books, 1957), vii–viii.
7. R. W. B. Lewis, *The American Adam: Innocence, Tragedy, and Tradition in the Nineteenth Century* (Chicago: University of Chicago Press, 1955), 2.
8. R. W. B. Lewis, "Literature and Things," review of *Symbolism and American Literature*, by Charles Feidelson, Jr., *The Hudson Review* 7 (1954): 311.
9. *Ibid.*, 312.
10. Bernard W. Bell, *The Afro-American Novel and its Tradition* (Amherst: University of Massachusetts Press, 1987); Cathy N. Davidson, *Revolution and the Word: The Rise of the Novel in America* (1986; rev. edn. New York: Oxford University Press, 2004); Jane Tompkins, *Sensational Designs: The Cultural Work of American Fiction, 1790–1860* (Oxford: Oxford University Press, 1985); Amy Kaplan, *The Anarchy of Empire in the Making of U.S. Culture* (Cambridge, MA: Harvard University Press, 2002).
11. Sacvan Bercovitch, ed., *The Cambridge History of American Literature*, 8 vols. (Cambridge: Cambridge University Press, 1994–2006).

12. Emory Elliott, "Introduction," in *The Columbia History of the American Novel*, ed. Emory *et al.* (New York: Columbia University Press, 1991), xv.
13. For example, Robert E. Spiller and his editorial cohort sought "a single and unified story" in their landmark literary history of the USA from an earlier time (Spiller, "The Second Edition" [preface, 1953], *The Literary History of the United States*, ix).
14. Eric J. Sundquist, *To Wake the Nations: Race in the Making of American Literature* (Cambridge, MA: Harvard University Press, 1993), 18.
15. M. M. Bakhtin, "From the Prehistory of Novelistic Discourse," in *The Dialogic Imagination: Four Essays by M. M. Bakhtin*, University of Texas Press Slavic Series, No. 1, ed. Michael Holquist, trans. Caryl Emerson and Michael Holquist (Austin: University of Texas Press, 1981; rpt. 2004), 46.
16. Arthur Hobson Quinn, *American Fiction. An Historical and Critical Survey* (New York: Appleton-Century Crofts, Inc., 1936), vii.
17. Leslie A. Fiedler, *Love and Death in the American Novel* (New York: Criterion Books, 1960; rev. edn., New York: Stein and Day, 1966), 11.
18. Frederick Brown, *Zola: A Life* (Baltimore: Johns Hopkins University Press, 1995; rpt. 1996), 411.
19. David S. Reynolds, *Beneath the American Renaissance: The Subversive Imagination in the Age of Emerson and Melville* (New York: Alfred A. Knopf, 1988), 82. It's worth noting that Reynolds saw these genres as exerting pressure from "beneath" the more prestigious canonical literature, with their importance lying in the way that they serve as subversive sources for the canonical works. Thanks to Carlo Rotella and Sean McCann for inventing and clarifying the concept of "strong genres."
20. John G. Cawelti, *The Six-Gun Mystique Sequel* (Bowling Green, OH: Bowling Green State University Popular Press, 1999), 99–126.
21. Alan Trachtenberg, *The Incorporation of America: Culture and Society in the Gilded Age* (New York: Hill and Wang, 1982).

PART ONE

*

INVENTING THE AMERICAN NOVEL

Introduction: inventing the American novel

BENJAMIN REISS

Sandra Gustafson's chapter in this section begins with the image of a map of North America in 1715 that shows the familiar British colonies abutting territories identified as French, Spanish, Iroquois, Apachee, Kikapou, Illinese, Esquimaux, Mozeemleck, and even Danish – picturing "a mixture of the familiar, the less familiar, the unknown, and the fantastic." The map is a fitting backdrop not only for the novels of James Fenimore Cooper, the main subject of her chapter, but also for other fictional works that attempted to bring order to the chaotic and often violent conditions of life in the New World.

The map can also remind us that while literary historians – and a great many novelists themselves – have long seen the development of the novel as tied up with the history of nations, both nations and novels have origins far more complex than any simple linear narrative or national map can convey. And so while the hunt for the origins of the American novel has tended to stress indigenous forms, themes, settings, and other patterns that reinforce exceptionalist models of US literary history, we do best, as Paul Giles suggests in the opening chapter of this book, to map the American novel onto a broader swath of the globe. Specifically, Giles argues, "cultural traffic across the Atlantic in both directions" shaped a number of literary conventions, themes, and formats out of which later critics and writers would try to find patterns suggestive of a national tradition. And an accurate temporal mapping, Gregory S. Jackson shows, reveals that ideas stretching over millennia provided ballast for depictions of the novelty of American life – in the hundreds of overtly religious novels that were some of the most widely read of the time (as they continue to be today), as well as in many of the acknowledged masterpieces like *Moby-Dick* (1851) that incorporate the world's religious traditions into their epic structures.

Accordingly, the chapters in this section stress the circulation of ideas – as well as of persons and goods (including books) – across terrain that stretches well beyond national geography or temporality. Some of the ideas and stories moving across the Atlantic traveled in a well-appointed passenger's cabin, like the elite Enlightenment philosophical and scientific ideas that Bryan Waterman shows were dramatized in Charles Brockden Brown's novels or the heady romantic metaphysics that animated Hawthorne's writing, in Jonathan Arac's account. Others rode below, swabbing the decks or cleaning out the hold, as in the sailor's tales that in Hester Blum's analysis animated so much of Melville's writing. And Winfried Fluck shows that even the early impulse to define a national culture through historical romance drew on European theories of historical progress, including those disseminated in fictional form by a Scottish nationalist, Sir Walter Scott.

Cooper was the first American novelist to be read widely abroad, but for any book to find its audience, as Ronald Zboray and Mary Saracino Zboray remind us, networks of production and distribution must be established. Their chapter inaugurates a strand of inquiry in this volume that examines the novel as a material artifact, brought into being by publishers and authors working within and even helping to expand the economic markets of their time.[a] The ability to turn market pressures to one's advantage was a prized cultural trait through the mid-nineteenth century. Not surprisingly, this trait was featured in many early American narratives of self-making, which, as Milette Shamir argues, pitted a typically masculine drive toward social mobility and economic independence against "traditional social bonds." The result was a "crisis" that was productive for many nineteenth-century literary artists, from Walt Whitman and Melville to Martin Delany and Frederick Douglass – who embraced self-made manhood as the antithesis of slavery. But the emphasis in early American novels on novelty, movement, and self-making, Shamir shows, made the genre seem a "moral hazard" within certain elite, tradition-bound corners of the culture.

Novels were thus not simply a kind of cargo that circulated through the Atlantic world and penetrated American interiors, but also tools for representing new ways of life in the spaces and places their authors encountered (or imagined encountering). Timothy Sweet's chapter shows that while many popular novels were curiously placeless, others (including works by Brown,

[a] Other contributors who explore the American novel within the context of book history include Barbara Hochman (chapter 36), Nancy Glazener (chapter 20), James L. W. West III (chapter 47), DeNel Rehberg Sedo (chapter 70), and Robert Coover (chapter 71).

Cooper, and Caroline Kirkland) prioritized setting, affording it nearly the centrality of character. Like painters of the period, these novelists turned to natural scenes to found an American aesthetic, one that rendered the taming of the wilderness as a measure of civilization and national progress. Indeed, the drama of historical romances often turned on genteel white men bringing order to wild frontier spaces, giving these works– as Fluck shows – a generally conservative tilt. Popular historical romances written by women such as Lydia Maria Child and Catharine Maria Sedgwick complicate these gendered dynamics, however, by casting protagonists as "strong, independent-minded and outspoken heroines who depart from an ideal of female deference."

Cargo of the human kind animated stories not of circulation but of confinement. Robert S. Levine makes clear the extreme constraints on African American novelists, even those who had never been enslaved. They had virtually no access to major US publishing houses and had to turn to abolitionist or black-run publishers – sometimes located abroad – just to find ways to circulate their manuscripts. And once their manuscripts found readers, they faced intense skepticism and even open hostility from white readers. Their work nonetheless added to and drew liberally from the broad flow of transatlantic ideas and narratives: their influences included the Brontë sisters, Charles Dickens, and Adam Smith. And, of course, Harriet Beecher Stowe, whose *Uncle Tom's Cabin* (1852) probably had more influence (both as model and provocation) on the African American novel than any other single text. John Ernest shows that Stowe did not present any new elements in the arguments against slavery or about white/black relations more broadly; it was instead her comprehensive, and combustible, mixture of existing elements that afforded her novel such a prominent place in the politics (and literary culture) of the day. Her work helped both to create and reinforce stereotypes that African American writers would react against for at least the next century; *Uncle Tom* thus represented a kind of literary confinement they must escape and a challenge that would spur them to circulate new ideas and images.

Stowe's work also helped circulate topics that were difficult for women to address in the public realm. According to Cindy Weinstein, in Stowe's novels and those of other popular sentimental writers like E. D. E. N. Southworth, one finds a tension between rigid generic conventions (which to some extent mirror social expectations for women) and the authors' challenging of those conventions from within. Thus "Southworth's plots work to establish for women a degree of agency and freedom within an institutional framework that legally allows neither," just as her plots test the limits of sentimental conventions. The almost equally popular seduction novels of a previous generation that so influenced the sentimental writers were never quite as bold as works by Stowe or Fanny Fern in protesting oppressive social conditions. However, they too focused "on the fraught role of women in the new republic," as Anna Mae Duane argues. By almost ritualistically recurring to scenes of female entrapment, these early novels revolved around agonizing questions of "whether one could ever fully possess his or her own body," a key concern animating debates in political philosophy across the Atlantic world.

The idea of self-dispossession is just as prominent, but in a more abstract – indeed, otherworldly – vein in supernatural fiction. As Elizabeth Young shows, the idea of losing oneself (anathema to the Lockean notion of self-possession that undergirds the American political system) recurs in our most compelling fictions of slavery, from *Uncle Tom's Cabin* to Toni Morrison's *Beloved* (1987). Even in its less openly political uses, the supernatural attaches itself to depictions of "people dispossessed of their rights," in works ranging from Edgar Allan Poe's *The Narrative of Arthur Gordon Pym* (1837) to Stephen King's *The Shining* (1977). Other novelistic forms first developed in the early national period that have persisted over the centuries are the historical novel, which Fluck shows evolved from a justification of the social order into a vehicle for dispossessed groups to claim their past; and the romance, that variant of the novel especially associated with Hawthorne. As Arac argues, Hawthorne decisively turned the novel inward – from grand dramas of national emergence toward a philosophical focus on what Emerson called "the growth of the individual" – and in the process claimed an exalted position for the novel, a high status that had once belonged to poetry. And yet it is worth noting that his works often turn on visions of haunting that Young shows have long been a staple of popular culture. Herman Melville also incorporated lofty philosophical ideas into his work, but as Blum argues, he did this in part to toy with reader's expectations based on the popular formulas from which he drew so heavily. Genre thus provides a kind of productive constraint for Melville, one that allows him to portray himself as throwing off the yoke of established literary and popular convention, even as he tells tales of seekers throwing off their shackles and following the wondrous circulatory currents of the oceans.

Freedom, mobility, and circulation were sometimes portrayed as ambiguous or even dangerous ideals. Beginning with the snares set for young women that represent the seductions of false liberty in the novels of Susanna Rowson and Hannah Foster (in Duane's account) and the dangers of embracing a secular worldview untethered from traditions of piety and deference in the novels of Charles Brockden Brown (according to Waterman), American writers through the mid nineteenth century approached their country's declared ideals with equal measures of exhilaration and wariness. Nowhere is this wariness more evident than in novels by southern writers, as John Ernest and Jennifer Rae Greeson reveal. To northern writers, Greeson shows, the South often functioned as a pre-modern space, characterized by stasis and stubborn resistance to development. But southern novelists increasingly characterized the North as promoting a dangerously unregulated "conflict between labor and capital" (in the words of leading pro-slavery politician John C. Calhoun); in stark contrast, plantation fiction pictured the southern slave system as a model of (to use twenty-first-century terminology) sustainability. One might want to dismiss southern antebellum writers' critique of northern unfettered capitalism because it was deployed in defense of a system now generally viewed to be abhorrent. Yet to look ahead, much of the writing surveyed in Part Two chronicles not only the extraordinary damage done by the slave system they defended, but also by the free-market capitalist system they feared.

I

Transatlantic currents and the invention of the American novel

PAUL GILES

Like all histories, the history of the novel has always been written retrospectively, producing in the celebrated work of Ian Watt and Cathy N. Davidson powerful alignments of theories of fiction with the emergence of national narratives. In Watt's case, this involved the valorization of a masculine, middle-class individualism that, in *The Rise of the Novel*, he took to typify the realistic idiom of the English novel in the eighteenth century. Writing some thirty years later, Davidson identified in the early American novel a predominantly female discourse of sentimentalism, whose "distinctive voice" she understood as combating the "demoralizing derision of Anglo-European arbiters of value and good taste," and as a counternarrative that constituted a resource for "those not included in the established power structures of the early Republic."[1] Both Watt and Davidson sought to inscribe generic and national types, but it is equally important to acknowledge the inherent instability of both these typological categories throughout the eighteenth century, with formal and generic mutations of the novel being akin to the amorphous, fluctuating nature of national formations. The Derridaean maxim that the "law of genre" is inherently self-contradictory since it establishes norms only for the purpose of violating them thus has a particular historical resonance in the case of the novel, since, as Homer Obed Brown notes, the novel as an "institution" did not begin to be consolidated or canonized until the early nineteenth century.[2] In the eighteenth century, by contrast, it was a much more inchoate form of expression, encompassing letters, journalism, and other kinds of imaginative or descriptive writing; indeed, Lennard Davis observes that within the "news/novel discourse" of the time, fact and fiction were seen as a continuum, with the novel being "presented as an ambiguous form – a factual fiction which denied its fictionality and produced in its readers a characteristic uncertainty or ambivalence as to whether they were reading something true or false."[3]

Daniel Defoe is perhaps the best known of these eighteenth-century writers who deliberately mixed fact and fiction – in *The Storm* (1704), for example, he combines real letters from correspondents all over Britain about the tempest of 1703 with supplementary "letters" written by himself under a variety of pseudonyms. Such hybrid forms are, of course, far from unknown in our own day – witness the "new journalism" of Tom Wolfe and others – but the prevalence of such a style necessarily complicates any attempt to pin down a discrete origin for the American novel as a mode of prose fiction.[a] Hector St. John de Crèvecoeur's *Letters from an American Farmer* (1782), for example, is not normally thought of as a novel, but its epistolary structure mirrors that of much eighteenth-century fiction, while its examination of how public affairs affect the private domain of the book's narrator, the fictitious farmer "James," ensures that Crèvecoeur's text inclines as much toward the condition of novel as documentary reportage.[4]

Concomitant with such generic instability is the difficulty of attributing national labels to such works as Aphra Behn's *Oroonoko* (1688). William C. Spengemann has claimed that *Oroonoko* is the "earliest American novel" on the grounds that it is "a literary work written in English about America by someone who claims to have lived there."[5] In truth, Behn's reported trip to the Caribbean in 1663 and 1664 was of limited duration; but *Oroonoko*, which sets its scene "in a Colony in America, called *Surinam*, in the West-Indies," does directly address issues of slavery and monarchical authority in the British overseas territories, issues toward which the author herself, as a Tory and a Catholic living in the reign of King Charles II, maintained an ambiguous stance. The plot of *Oroonoko* turns upon ways in which the eponymous hero, a "Royal Slave," rebels against the island's colonial rulers to highlight "the Miseries, and Ignominies of Slavery," but the narrative is more concerned with emphasizing the exemplary human characteristics of the slave leader than with interrogating the system of slavery as such. The spoofing of local authority figures in *Oroonoko* does not extend to any stringent critique of the parameters of royal power.

What is apparent from Behn's example, however, is the extent to which America in the seventeenth and eighteenth centuries entered into British colonial consciousness. Nancy Armstrong and Leonard Tennenhouse, who have dismissed the whole question of the "cultural origins" of any novelistic tradition as "slightly ridiculous," have pointed out how it was Indian captivity

a David Schmid explores this hybridity in "The nonfiction novel," chapter 59 in this volume. For a focus on the New Journalism, see 997.

narratives such as that published in 1682 by Mary Rowlandson that helped to shape the trajectory of the eighteenth-century English novel, with Samuel Richardson's *Pamela* and *Clarissa* sharing a hermeneutics of captivity and redemption with their New England predecessor. Just as Rowlandson's *Sovereignty and Goodness of God* was very popular in England, so *Pamela* and *Clarissa* were widely reprinted in colonial America, often in abridged editions that highlighted the seduction plots more than the extended ruminations upon their fate preferred by Richardson's characters.[6]

The extent of the cultural traffic across the Atlantic in both directions during the eighteenth century is also exemplified by the case of Charlotte Lennox, who was nominated by Gustavus Howard Maynadier in 1940 as his candidate for the title of "first American novelist," though later research has shown that Lennox was born in Gibraltar rather than New York, as Maynadier thought (although she did live in the province of New York between 1739 and 1742).[7] Lennox's first novel, *The Life of Harriot Stuart, Written by Herself* (1750), is clearly based on her own experiences of what its heroine calls the "unsettled condition" of transatlantic displacement, recounting the heroine's adventures in London before her departure for America, and then her "wild and romantic" escapades with Indians and lovers in the New World before her eventual return to England. Lennox's last novel, *Euphemia* (1790), returns to this transatlantic scene in a more sophisticated manner, incorporating familiar scenes of captivity melodrama – Euphemia's son Edward is carried off by Native Americans at the age of three, only to reappear as a "handsome Huron" at the end of the novel – but also contemplating in a more reflective way the quandaries of exile. Euphemia's father initially repairs to America to salvage his fortunes, but in the last volume Mrs. Mountfort wonders to herself whether or not it would be wise to return home after the death of her husband: "I left England in the bloom of youth and beauty," she says, "how can I bear the thoughts of returning thither, thus altered, that none of my former friends would know me." The kind of dilemma that characters face in the novels of Henry James a hundred years later is also embodied in *Euphemia*: a fully realized, complex world where questions of family, career, and even pension rotate in complicated ways upon a transatlantic axis. As Amanda Gilroy and W. M. Verhoeven have remarked, the form of the epistolary novel favored by Lennox and other eighteenth-century novelists, predicated upon the idea of correspondents distant in space, allowed authors to exploit a transnational framework to good effect.[8]

Lennox's most famous novel in her own lifetime was *The Female Quixote* (1752), another exercise in genre-crossing, which chronicles the tendency of its heroine, Arabella, to misinterpret her life by refracting it through the lens of "romantic Forms." The novel's comic aspects lie primarily in its mock-epic deflation of Arabella's pretensions, her tendency "to magnify the most inconsiderable Trifles into Things of the greatest Importance"; yet the book also embodies a significant reflexive element, since it foregrounds the question of how and why events can or should be interpreted in a certain manner. This is also the theme of *Female Quixotism*, published in 1801 by American novelist Tabitha Gilman Tenney, who similarly satirizes the "strangely extravagant" tendency of her heroine, Dorcas Sheldon, to misread the world according to the hyperbolic figures of fiction rather than the more solid evidence of empirical fact. *Female Quixotism* is, however, a more conservative novel than its predecessor: whereas Lennox draws the reader into Arabella's comic flights of fancy, Tenney, the wife of a prominent Federalist politician, sternly aligns the threat to her heroine's serenity with the forces that were threatening to disturb the social hierarchies of the new American republic. Thus, Dorcas receives a proposal from a South Carolinian who had gone to France and "had there thoroughly imbibed all the demoralizing, and atheistical principles of that corrupt people." As with *The Female Quixote*, though, there is a self-conscious disquisition in *Female Quixotism* on the status of fiction: Richardson, Tobias Smollett, and various other writers are mentioned by name, while the Cervantes prototype ensures that *Female Quixotism* (like *The Female Quixote*) can be regarded as, in Cynthia J. Miecznikowski's phrase, "a satiric parody of the eighteenth-century romance that is also a parody of a parody, *Don Quixote*."[9]

In the second half of the eighteenth century, then, the Atlantic becomes a contested discursive space where novelists and other writers take up different, often deliberately antagonistic, positions on the meaning of the Quixote legend and other iconic aspects of Western culture. Just as political philosophers such as Edmund Burke and Tom Paine clashed over the meaning of democracy and revolution, so Hugh Henry Brackenridge's *Modern Chivalry* – published sequentially between 1792 and 1805, with additional materials appearing in 1815 and 1819 – mediates debates about contemporary manners and politics in America. The sprawling nature of Brackenridge's narrative reflects the continual revisions in the author's own views on the state of Pennsylvania running through Brackenridge's multi-volume work, whose final episode appeared twenty-seven years after its first installment. In this sense, as Jared Gardner notes, the structure of eighteenth-century American fiction was specifically designed to accommodate "contradictory positions," not on account of any "insufficiency of the nascent literary culture," nor any psychological "instability of the individual author," but because discursive cross-currents were what the early American novel was all about. Again, the epistolary form was ideally suited to such a "complex weave of contradictory voices," and, as Gardner says, Hannah Foster in *The Coquette* (1797) positions herself as "editor/curator" of the letters she reproduces rather than as their mere fabricator, thereby allowing within her work a hypothetical space for voices beyond the author's own.[10]

The early American novel's formal situation, as a rhetorical site for the mediation of contrasting positions, correlates to its late eighteenth-century fixation on the dynamics underpinning the War of Independence. The war was a motif to which American novelists kept returning long after the last shot had been fired, partly because (as Ernest Hemingway later realized) the scenario of war itself always offers aesthetic enticements and opportunities, partly because of patriotic pride at the revolutionary outcome, but also partly because the trauma of insurrection created a general sense of discomfort in the American body politic that took many years to work through.[b] One of the most popular novels of the 1790s in the new United States was *The History of Constantius and Pulchera, or Constancy Rewarded*, first published anonymously in 1794, which went through many editions. Patriotically subtitled "An American Novel," *Constantius and Pulchera* describes how the romance between its central protagonists was forestalled by the intervention of "Monsieur le Monte, only son and heir to a rich nobleman in France," who turns the head of Pulchera's father and forces her to flee from such "cruel parental authority." Despite cross-dressing in "a neat suit of red regimentals" in an effort to avoid detection, Pulcehra, in her guise as Lieutenant Valorus, is "captured by a forcible British cruiser" and detained in Canada. True love eventually works itself out, of course, but it is significant that the authenticity of this romantic sentiment is correlated with, and verified by, the ritual of transatlantic crossings – "we will cross the Atlantic, we will revisit the land of freedom" – and also by a fictional use of the Revolutionary War as an analogy to this quest for self-fulfillment.

Cross-dressing is also integral to Herman Mann's novel *The Female Review* (1797), which is similarly set during the Revolutionary War and which follows the fortunes of Deborah Sampson, who absconds from the marriage arranged by her mother in their small New England village and runs away to serve as a man in the American army. *The Female Review* is narrated in the first person,

b On ways in which American writing relates theoretically to the experience of war, see John Carlos Rowe's essay in this volume, "US novels and US wars," chapter 49.

and the novel's detailed attention to the history and geography of the war – replete with dates, and with close-up descriptions of military personnel such as Washington, Cornwallis, and Lafayette – offers a hybrid blend of fact and fiction; indeed, the novel attempts to authenticate its narrative in the final pages by quoting from a 1784 New York newspaper about the case of a female soldier who passed by the name of "Robert Shurtlieef." What is most noticeable about the character of Deborah Sampson, however, is how she implicitly conflates gender reversal with national rebellion: "All nature seemed in one combustible convulsion," she remarks, and it is not difficult here to infer parallels between America's violent disruption of Britain's naturalized social hierarchies and the heroine's determination to "swerve from my sex's sphere." The overall effect of this historical novel, published nearly a generation after American independence had actually been won, is not only to mythologize these "events [as] the most singular and important we have ever known," but also to acknowledge the widespread feelings of disturbance and anxiety that went along with such heroic insubordination.

One of the side effects of the war's outcome was to divide the eighteenth-century novel, and indeed Anglo-American culture generally, into two discrete national traditions. This, however, created intense difficulties for the large body of American Loyalists: historians today estimate that while about two-thirds of those living in the American colonies supported the struggle for independence, fully one-third did not. After 1783, this Loyalist minority tended to keep quiet, feeling that ritualistic invocations in the new United States of the heroic nature of this revolutionary enterprise naturally tended to exclude them. Nevertheless, as Sarah J. Purcell observes, the fact that a novel such as Samuel Jackson Pratt's *Emma Corbett* (1780) was consumed so avidly in America, even though it was published by a British author at the height of the conflict, reflects "the ubiquity of these rifts" in the American colonies around the struggle for secession.[11] Drawing upon the metaphor of the Anglo-American family as one organic nation, a trope that informed much conservative thinking at this time, *Emma Corbett* mournfully chronicles a family torn apart by the war. The title character's father sympathizes with the American cause, but the story ends up badly for him, as he loses not only his property interests in America but also most of his family to death on the battlefield. Lamenting "that civil fury which hath separated the same interests of the same people," Corbett foresees that the wounds of this conflict will lead to "deep-mouthed gashes in the heart of Britain." On one level, *Emma Corbett* can be read as a British colonial novel – Sir Robert Raymond, one of the candidates for the hand of Emma, has recently returned from an administrative tour of duty in India – but its central character is strongly critical of British policy toward America. Just as many American post-revolutionary novelists portrayed Britain as an unnaturally cruel parent, so Pratt's novel organizes its discourses of family sentiment around representations of civil war as a transgression against the laws of nature: "Nature herself lies bleeding on thy shore," laments Corbett, "and there the inhuman mother has plunged the dagger (with her own barbarous hand) into the bowels of her child!"

In light of this focus upon war, Davidson's model of late eighteenth-century American fiction as impelled by a progressive, feminist sentiment needs to be qualified by a recognition of how, as Terence Martin observed back in 1957, the early American novel usually fell "into one of two categories, the historical and the sentimental." Although the "virtue in distress" formula of the "American sentimental novel" was very popular, historical fiction – often focused on the revolutionary battlefield and, by extension, the fate of the nation – was equally recognizable.[12] One writer of this era who straddled both categories was Isaac Mitchell, who published a series of novels reconfiguring gothic forms of melodrama within a carefully delineated American social setting. *Albert and Eliza* (1802) takes place in colonial New York, in the early settlement of North America, and it represents the ocean as a stimulus to both romance and intrigue. The heroine comes from a family that had emigrated from England to New York with a splendid fortune, and when Albert is called away to Europe on a business trip she fears he might get distracted by "some trans-atlantic beauty" – although his failure to return home promptly is actually brought about by the misfortune of having been taken prisoner by an Algerine corsair on the Atlantic, carried to Algiers, and sold into slavery. *Melville and Phalez* (1803), another novel first published in serial form, similarly spans wide geopolitical space – various scenes are set in Turkey, Russia, Switzerland, and other countries – and it considers ways in which mercantile values pose an implicit threat to the stability of the American republic in this early national period. Set amidst a world of trade, gambling, and speculation, *Melville and Phalez* contemplates the viability of autonomous domestic virtue in a multipolar world.

Mitchell's most enduring work of fiction, however, was *Alonzo and Melissa*, another novel set during the Revolutionary War that was first published in serial form in 1804. The work was then revised by the author and published in book form as *The Asylum* in 1811, and it remained popular in the United States throughout the nineteenth century. Mitchell's novel shadows modern American landscapes, in which the natural world and its seasons are lovingly evoked, with the specter of gothic intrigue, represented here as a perverse force from the Old World whose malign influence threatens the protagonists' happiness. Again, trade and travel are integral to the story, and when Alonzo sets sail from America to Europe, his native shore appears to him "like a semicircular border of dark green velvet on the edge of a convex mirror." It would appear from this evocative image as though the Atlantic Ocean itself were the prime mover behind the fortunes of these characters, with its scene of traversal a correlative to their perennial fear of finding themselves, both spatially and metaphorically, at "cross purposes": at the end of the novel, the narrator reports with a sigh of relief how "No *cross purposes* stood ready to intervene their happiness." The real *deus ex machina* who engineers this happy ending is none other than Benjamin Franklin, described here as "the great dispenser of all mercies," who encounters Alonzo in Paris and, on the strength of his old acquaintance with Alonzo's merchant father, ensures safe passage back to America for the hero.

In a note appended to the serialized version of *Alonzo and Melissa*, which was published in the Poughkeepsie weekly newspaper *Political Barometer* from June 5 through October 30, 1804, Mitchell says he would have liked to place more emphasis on "the most important events of the American war," but that such narrative detail would have been too time-consuming for his newspaper readers. Mitchell amply remedies these deficiencies in *The Asylum*, putting in many more elaborate descriptions of naval battles and other aspects of warfare. He also includes in *The Asylum* what he calls a "Preface: Comprising a Short Dissertation on Novel," an extended essay which bears comparison with Nathaniel Hawthorne's famous preface to *The House of the Seven Gables* forty years later in the way it seeks to map out parameters and possibilities for the American novel.[c] Mitchell attempts here to boost the status of the novel and redeem it from the charge of immorality, a charge made frequently by American Christian ministers, by claiming that such fiction should aspire to represent an idealized world in which "the scenery should be natural, the sentiment pure." He thus distinguishes the novel from the old generic model of romance, whose features of "licentiousness and impurity," as well as its reliance on "enchantments" rather than verisimilitude, led to a disproportionate emphasis on the "power of darkness." In this way, Mitchell radically reinterprets Western literary history to position its most exalted models as generic prototypes for the American novel:

c On the preface to *The House of the Seven Gables*, see Jonathan Arac, "Hawthorne and the aesthetics of American romance," chapter 8, 136–137.

> The most sublime specimens of fine writing, the most splendid productions of *belleslettres* genius, of either ancient or modern date, have been presented to us in the form of Novel. The Iliad of Homer, the Aenead of Virgil, Ossian's Fingal, Milton's Paradise, Dwight's Conquest, Barlow's Columbiad, and several other similar performances, are, in fact, epic novels, possessing the polished and superior advantages of loftv and majestic numbers.

Just as American patriots at the turn of the nineteenth century regarded the new United States as a culmination of older civilizations, as westward the course of empire took its way, so Mitchell here somewhat bizarrely appropriates the Bible and *Paradise Lost* as precursors to his novelistic idiom. While admitting that the American novel still retains "irregularities" that derive from "the copious mixture of alloy" in its generic inheritance, Mitchell nevertheless seeks to justify this form by comparing it to biblical parables in its capacity to impart "the most solemn and important truths."

In this sense, the language of *The Asylum* – which the author claims to be "of the middle class, neither soaring to that sublimity which dazzles the understanding by its perpetual glitter, nor sinking to dull and trite inelegance" – is of a piece with his desire to evoke a world of "connexion and regularity" rather than "disorder and interruption." Such a sense of order is, in turn, aligned with a specifically patriotic impulse: "The production is entirely American," says Mitchell of *The Asylum*, and the poetic excerpts "from the geniuses of our own country." It is true, of course, that various contradictions between gothic irregularity and pastoral sublimity are played out within the novel's narrative, and it is also true, as Joseph Fichtelberg has observed, that as a novelist committed to serial publication Mitchell was necessarily implicated within the chaotic world of international trade and commerce against which, through its final inward gesture of romantic retreat, *The Asylum* ultimately turns its face.[13] His novel can thus be read as an allegory of the emergence of American exceptionalism, of attempts at the beginning of the nineteenth century to carve out a discrete cultural and political space for the new nation that might set it apart from the rest of the world. Just as the lovers withdraw into "the native charms of their retired village," so the United States in this Jeffersonian era began to contemplate the virtues of blocking itself off from ancestral corruptions by an "ocean of fire."[14]

For all of its avowed patriotic zeal, then, *The Asylum* is implicitly haunted by various Atlantic cross-currents. In general terms, this idiom of conscious reduplication, predicated upon a pattern of intertextual dialogue or other structural double binds, is common throughout early American fiction. William Hill Brown's *The Power of Sympathy* (1789), once conventionally credited as the first American novel, cites Jonathan Swift, Laurence Sterne, and, most significantly, Goethe's *The Sorrows of Young Werther*, a copy of which is found on the bedside table of the repentant seducer, Harrington, after he has killed himself. Goethe's novel originally appeared in Germany in 1774, with a first American edition published in translation in Philadelphia in 1784 and five more American editions appearing over the next eighteen years. Because of its theme of adulterous love, Goethe's novel was generally deemed immoral in Christian America, but Brown's novel might be said to represent a domestication of Goethe, in the way its seducer-turned-sentimentalist advances, under *Young Werther*'s tutelage, to his ultimate demise.[15] There is also an elaborately reflexive aspect to Brown's novel, exemplified by Mrs. Holmes's frequent critical remarks on literature: she talks, for example, of how ridicule is "evidently a transatlantick idea, and must have been imbibed from the source of some *English* Novel or Magazine." Brown's novel uses this play of intertextuality to interrogate the status of sentimentalism, or what its title classifies oxymoronically as "the *power* of *sympathy*." The inner world of emotional affect is here redescribed in relation to worldly force, and such a discourse of paradoxical transposition is commensurate with the character of Harrington himself, who is described as "a strange medley of contradiction – the moralist and the amoroso." Such contradictions are also integral to the emotional impulse of this kind of sentimental novel which, as Mr. Worthy observes, mixes "pain" and "pleasure" in equal measure.

The early American novel thus developed within an intellectual framework of sensibility, the grounding of knowledge in experiential perception rather than *a priori* concepts; yet, as Julie Ellison has observed, sensibility in the late eighteenth century was "a transaction, not a character type," a form of exchange intimately linked to the circulation of commodities, and, by extension, to slavery.[16] Bernard Bailyn has observed that the Atlantic was the first ocean ever to be located at the heart of an economy, while Stephen Shapiro argues that the American novel in its early years was shaped more by the bartering of both tangible and intangible assets – not only slaves, but also sensibility and sentiment – across international borders, rather than by any incipient form of nationalism.[17] The popularity in America of the works of Laurence Sterne – author of *A Sentimental Journey* (1768), who was Thomas Jefferson's favorite novelist – and of Jean-Jacques Rousseau testifies to the popularity in the new United States of radical Enlightenment ideas around sentimentalism, the intertwining of moral belief with human emotion.[18] It is useful to remember that Charles Brockden Brown, sometimes misconstrued in purely nationalistic terms as an isolated primitive writing about the "trackless forest," was in fact part of a transatlantic intellectual movement that sought systematically to critique the epistemological and ethical implications of traditional social hierarchy.[19] Also part of this movement were William Godwin – whose work Brown much admired, and who admired Brown's novels in return – Mary Wollstonecraft, and Wollstonecraft's lover Gilbert Imlay, whose novel *The Emigrants*, concerning the prospects for dissenters intending to migrate from Britain to America, appeared in 1793. Indeed, according to Pamela Clemit the radical group of writers in early nineteenth-century Britain centered around the Shelleys was "swift to claim [Brown] as one of their own," as a writer with a distinctive political imagination rather than merely the oddball figure he often seemed within the United States, and indeed Mary Shelley read *Wieland* just before starting work on *Frankenstein* in 1816.[20] From this perspective, the patterns of displacement, comparison, and exchange that are self-evident in Olaudah Equiano's *Interesting Narrative* of 1789 might be said to epitomize American fiction in the late eighteenth century more generally. Just as Equiano's persona charts his (factual or fictional) movements from Africa and Europe to America, from slavery to freedom, so early American novelists negotiate the transference of cerebral commodities such as emotional sensibility and political dissent across a wide geopolitical spectrum.[21]

The constitutional doubleness of the early American novel, involving a condition of alienation as well as domesticity, is exemplified again by Peter Markoe's *The Algerine Spy in Pennsylvania*, which first appeared in 1787. Although Markoe's novel was published in Philadelphia and preceded *The Power of Sympathy* by two years, it is normally disqualified from the perhaps invidious title of "first American novel" on the grounds that its author was born at St. Croix, in the Caribbean, and educated at Oxford University, even though after a career as a lawyer in London he took his oath to the State of Pennsylvania in 1784 and remained there until his death in 1792. *The Algerine Spy in Pennsylvania* filters observations on the new United States through the eyes of "a native of Algiers," Mehemet, who has moved to Pennsylvania to report back on the condition of "the political Aetna of the world." The novel's prefatory note claims that "the work is but a translation," a rendering in English of letters written in Arabic and other languages, and this reinforces our sense of Markoe's novel situating itself amidst a global network of power. Algiers itself declared war on the United States in July 1785, encouraged to do so by the British who, having lost the War of Independence, wanted at least to drive American commerce out of the Mediterranean, and, as Markoe's novel implies, images of the Muslim world as an inveterate enemy of the American people were ubiquitous in the early years of the republic.

The Algerine Spy in Pennsylvania is, on one level, a typically American patriotic narrative, since by the end of the novel Mehemet becomes so convinced of the virtues of his adopted country that he decides never to return to Algiers. Mehemet particularly contrasts state tyranny in his African homeland with the prospect of freedom of speech in America: "Were an Algerine supposed to have imagined only in a dream what a Pennsylvanian speaks, prints, publishes, maintains and glories in," he says, "he would suffer the severest tortures." Yet the doubleness that runs through Markoe's spy narrative ensures that American "pillars of freedom" are always refracted through an idiom of estrangement, whereby the new United States is creatively reimagined from a position of alterity: American Christians, for example, are always referred to by Mehemet as "the Nazarenes." This kind of transatlantic defamiliarization also informs Royall Tyler's novel *The Algerine Captive* (1797), which similarly plays American and Algerine, Christian and Muslim, off against each other. Tyler's novel, which features a former New England schoolmaster taken captive by the Algerines and forced to spend seven years away from home, foregrounds questions of historical and geographical perspective as it draws explicit parallels between the state tyranny in Algiers and the system of slavery in the southern United States, thereby facilitating what Timothy Marr has aptly described as "a critical transnational consciousness from the comparative perspective of Algerine space."[22]

The novels of both Markoe and Tyler are more explicitly philosophical in their orientation than Susanna Rowson's play *Slaves in Algiers; or, A Struggle for Freedom* (1794), which straightforwardly pits Islamic bondage against the political freedoms enjoyed by America. Nevertheless, *Slaves in Algiers* exemplifies how Rowson's work is also informed crucially by transnational currents. Rowson's bestselling novel, *Charlotte Temple*, was actually written in England and first published there in 1791 as *Charlotte: A Tale of Truth*, before being repackaged with great success for the American market.[d] With its popular theme of virtue in distress, however, *Charlotte Temple* is much less ambitious in scope than *Reuben and Rachel* (1798), Rowson's three-volume epic about the foundation of the United States, which starts off in the days of Christopher Columbus and then traces the course of a family's history over

d On ways in which *Charlotte Temple* touched a popular nerve, see Anna Mae Duane, "Susanna Rowson, Hannah Webster Foster and the seduction novel in the early USA," chapter 2, 38–40.

some 300 years, through religious struggles in England, the Reformation, and emigration to Pennsylvania in the eighteenth century. By charting how the Dudley family criss-crosses the Atlantic over several generations in search of economic wealth and freedom of conscience, Rowson's novel invokes such displacement as both a precursor to and an emblem of the US national narrative: Reuben and Rachel willingly renounce their English titles at the end, saying they are "distinctions nothing worth" compared to the joy of having sons who are "true-born Americans," with the prospect of "blessings" for their "posterity." In this sense, *Reuben and Rachel* sets out deliberately to rewrite the history of the new nation, projecting its roots back in time to lend the unstable new republic a distinguished mythological antecedence.

The eighteenth-century American novel, then, developed across a transatlantic axis and was shaped by European prototypes as much as by US political pressures. It was a radically unstable form, mixing fiction, philosophy, and epistolary conventions, and this kind of formal hybridity coalesced with a historical era in which geographic boundaries were being reconceptualized and the limits of empire and nation radically redrawn. Noah Webster asserted in 1783 that "America must be as independent in literature as she is in politics," but this was clearly a proleptic statement rather than a description of the state of national letters at the end of the Revolutionary War. The attempts in the next generation to enunciate a specifically American cultural tradition, as in the work of Mitchell and Rowson, often involved a conscious appropriation and reconfiguration of the past. This kind of historical metafiction, centered upon the idea of the Atlantic as a contested discursive space, continued into the nineteenth century, as we see in Washington Irving's *Sketch Book* (1819), which broods nostalgically over the cultural legacy of Europe and its memorializing relevance within the US national domain. In this sense, even though the term metafiction has more frequently been associated with postmodernist fiction, it is not difficult to see how American fiction has always incorporated a metafictional dimension, one that has sought to interrogate the parameters of its own discursive domain.[e] From the start, the affiliation of the American novel with a notion of US cultural identity was a fractious and ambiguous enterprise, one expounded vigorously by patriotic proselytizers but circumscribed by the amorphous quality of literary genre and by the always permeable boundaries of the nation itself.

e On "metafiction" in the second half of the twentieth century, see Ursula Heise, chapter 58, 966–974 and Winfried Fluck, chapter 7, 132.

Notes

1. Ian Watt, *The Rise of the Novel: Studies in Defoe, Richardson and Fielding* (London: Chatto and Windus, 1957); Cathy N. Davidson, *Revolution and the Word: The Rise of the Novel in America*, 2nd edn. (New York: Oxford University Press, 2004), 3, 150. The first edition of Davidson's book was published in 1986.
2. Jacques Derrida, "La Loi du Genre/The Law of Genre," *Glyph: Textual Studies* 7 (Spring 1980): 176–232; Homer Obed Brown, *Institutions of the English Novel: From Defoe to Scott* (Philadelphia: University of Pennsylvania Press, 1997), xviii–xix.
3. Lennard J. Davis, *Factual Fictions: The Origins of the English Novel* (New York: Columbia University Press, 1983), 77, 36.
4. Elizabeth Heckendorn Cook, *Epistolary Bodies: Gender and Genre in the Eighteenth-Century Republic of Letters* (Stanford, CA: Stanford University Press, 1996), 7.
5. William C. Spengemann, *A Mirror for Americanists: Reflections on the Idea of American Literature* (Hanover, NH: University Press of New England, 1989), 45.
6. Nancy Armstrong and Leonard Tennenhouse, *The Imaginary Puritan: Literature, Intellectual Labor, and the Origins of Personal Life* (Berkeley: University of California Press, 1992), 198; Leonard Tennenhouse, "The Americanization of *Clarissa*," *Yale Journal of Criticism* 11.1 (Spring 1998): 177–196. On Richardson's influence in America, see also Jay Fliegelman, *Prodigals and Pilgrims: The American Revolution against Patriarchal Authority, 1750–1800* (Cambridge: Cambridge University Press, 1982), 83–89.
7. Gustavus Howard Maynadier, *The First American Novelist?* (Cambridge, MA: Harvard University Press, 1940).
8. Amanda Gilroy and W. M. Verhoeven, eds., *Epistolary Histories: Letters, Fiction, Culture* (Charlottesville: University Press of Virginia, 2000), 9.
9. Cynthia J. Miecznikowski, "The Patriotic Mode and the Patriarchal Imperative: Reading the Female Reader(s) in Tabitha Tenney's *Female Quixotism*," *Early American Literature* 25.1 (1990): 42.
10. Jared Gardner, "The Literary Museum and the Unsettling of the Early American Novel," *ELH* 67.3 (Fall 2000): 745, 755.
11. Sarah J. Purcell, *Sealed with Blood: War, Sacrifice, and Memory in Revolutionary America* (Philadelphia: University of Pennsylvania Press, 2002), 69.
12. Terence Martin, "Social Institutions in the Early American Novel," *American Quarterly* 9.1 (Spring 1957): 73–74.
13. Joseph Fichtelberg, *Critical Fictions: Sentiment and the American Market, 1780–1870* (Athens: University of Georgia Press, 2003), 17.
14. Thomas Jefferson, letter to Elbridge Gerry, May 13, 1797, in *Writings* (New York: Library of America, 1984), 1044.
15. Maxine Grefe, *"Apollo in the Wilderness": An Analysis of Critical Reception of Goethe in America, 1806–1840* (New York: Garland, 1988), 165.
16. Julie Ellison, *Cato's Tears and the Making of Anglo-American Emotion* (Chicago: University of Chicago Press, 1999), 98.

17. Bernard Bailyn, "The Idea of Atlantic History," *Itinerario* 20.1 (1996): 30; Stephen Shapiro, *The Culture and Commerce of the Early American Novel: Reading the Atlantic World-System* (University Park: Pennsylvania State University Press, 2008), 13, 40.
18. Andrew Burstein and Catherine Mowbray, "Jefferson and Sterne," *Early American Literature* 29.1 (1994): 19–34.
19. Spengemann, *Mirror for Americanists*, 138. On the transatlantic intellectual context of Brown's writing, see Bryan Waterman, "Charles Brockden Brown and the novels of the early republic," chapter 3.
20. Pamela Clemit, *The Godwinian Novel: The Rational Fictions of Godwin, Brockden Brown, Mary Shelley* (Oxford: Clarendon Press, 1993), 106.
21. For the suggestion that "the accounts of Africa and the Middle Passage in *The Interesting Narrative* were constructed" and that Equiano "probably invented an African identity," see Vincent Carretta, *Equiano The African: Biography of a Self-Made Man* (Athens: University of Georgia Press, 2005), xix–xv.
22. Timothy Marr, *The Cultural Roots of American Islamicism* (New York: Cambridge University Press, 2006), 55.

2

Susanna Rowson, Hannah Webster Foster, and the seduction novel in the early US

ANNA MAE DUANE

For much of its history, the seduction novel was absent from the origin tale literary historians have spun about American literature. While Susanna Rowson's *Charlotte Temple* (1794) and Hannah Webster Foster's *The Coquette* (1797) included both the love and the death that critics like Leslie Fiedler insisted were the building blocks of the American literary tradition, these novels had the details all wrong.[1] Following a European template, these texts told a story of dependence, deceit, and downfall – hardly the stuff of national origin myths. But as Cathy Davidson and others have demonstrated, these were precisely the stories that resonated among early Americans. Seduction was everywhere in early America – not only in novels, but in magazines, newspaper accounts, and in the privileged realms of privately circulating letters and manuscripts. According to Mildred Doyle, seduction outstripped all other topics in the periodical literature of the period.[2] The two novels I shall discuss in this chapter certainly tapped into the era's general fascination with the subject. Matthew Carey, *Charlotte Temple*'s American publisher, estimated that the book had sold well over 50,000 copies by 1812.[3] Foster's *The Coquette* went through at least ten editions between 1797 and 1866.

Once these novels were rediscovered in the twentieth century as part of a widespread recovery effort by feminist scholars, two major critical narratives emerged about them. The first focused on the seduced woman as a symbol for a young and vulnerable nation. As Jan Lewis writes, the seduction novel heroine's "attempt to navigate between the eighteenth-century Scylla of overweening power and its Charybdis of seductive liberty was the nation's plot as well."[4] Julia Stern, Carroll Smith-Rosenberg, and others have illustrated how seduction functioned as a structuring metaphor for American nation-building. These political readings echo John Adams's eighteenth-century analysis of the seduction heroine's plight when he warned that "democracy is Lovelace, and the people are Clarissa."[5]

Another, often overlapping, critical narrative about these texts focuses specifically on gender and the proto-feminist subtext that emerges when we read these novels against the grain. As Charlotte and Eliza, the respective protagonists of *Charlotte Temple* and *The Coquette*, defy the expectations of their parents and guardians to take up with unsuitable men, critics such as Gillian Brown argue that they are pushing the boundaries of agency and consent for women.[6] Cathy Davidson argues that *The Coquette*'s emphasis on Eliza's ability to choose emphasizes how constrained women's choices were in the eighteenth century, while Marion Rust contends that *Charlotte Temple* articulates "a unique set of concerns for the self-aware female reader." Charlotte's histrionics, and her fate, Rust argues, awakened the eighteenth-century woman reader to "her own dissatisfaction with the limited arena in which her powers of choice and selection were seen to operate."[7]

Both critical foci – nation-building, and the fraught role of women in the new republic – testify to a transatlantic conversation about the relationship between personhood and property, and how emotion mediates between the two. While literary historians have placed *The Coquette* and *Charlotte Temple* in a tradition that begins with Samuel Richardson's seduction novels and moves forward to the nineteenth-century sentimental novel, this chapter places these texts in a broader literary constellation. While these novels undoubtedly played a key role within an evolving sentimental genre, I suggest that they also belong within a diverse transatlantic tradition bound together by a common focus on whether one could ever fully possess his or her own body.

Self-possession, as articulated by Enlightenment thinkers, was a key element in emergent ideas about American citizenship and its underlying ethos of possessive individualism. John Locke is perhaps the most influential of thinkers on the subject. "Every man has a 'property' in his own person," Locke wrote in the *Second Treatise of Government* (1690). "This nobody has a right to but himself."[8] The idea that one could "own" one's own body supported the argument that individuals were capable of the self-government necessary for democracy. As C. Leiren Mower has argued, the "very act of imagining a proprietary interest in one's body reinforces a vital link between liberal political theories of government and the self-controlled citizen who performs these political theories."[9] In early America, however, the embrace of self-ownership was tentative and contradictory – while theorists adopted the notion of self-possession as a corollary to natural rights, they also had to account for rather glaring exceptions. The bodies of enslaved blacks and women for instance, were clearly the property of someone else. As Cindy Weinstein discusses in this volume, questions of consent and self-possession would continue to occupy a prominent role in much of the American fiction that would follow Rowson's and Foster's work.[a]

In the midst of a generation in which the relationship between personhood and property was a topic of concern for the founding fathers as well as the fare of cheap periodicals, *Charlotte Temple* and *The Coquette* speak to a nightmare haunting a nation founded on rational self-determination – a scenario in which the body's claims overrule the mind's wishes. This nightmare was articulated in Indian captivity narratives, slave narratives, and in a rash of contemporary works about Americans taken captive in Algiers. As Paul Giles argues in this volume,[b] the themes of captivity and redemption – or lack of it – circulated through much British and American fiction in the late eighteenth century. In these cases, an outside force – the captor – steals the captive's liberty, and at least for a short while, that captive's very sense of self. In *Charlotte Temple* and *The Coquette* the calculus plays out differently: rather than an outside force capturing the protagonists' bodies, it is the body itself that undoes the women's selfhood.

Alongside this anxious literary conversation about the horrors that accompany the loss of self-control, Great Awakening sermons and preachers extolled the bliss of kenosis – of surrendering one's body to the divine force. It is within this context that *Charlotte Temple* and *The Coquette* gloss the frightening specter of self-immolation with the sheen of religious redemption. Ultimately, I suggest, extended focus on pregnancy in *The Coquette* and *Charlotte Temple* articulates an ongoing debate between the Enlightenment belief in the individual's ultimate control over the body, and the traditional religious belief that God was the ultimate proprietor of all bodies. To trace how this debate unfolds in these two popular novels, I begin with an analysis of how the rhetorical interplay between slavery and seduction functioned in questions about print, personhood, and the power of sympathy to elucidate the stakes of *Charlotte Temple* and *The Coquette*. More precisely, I demonstrate how these novels move between the poles of self-abdication (found in slavery, seduction, and in a different way, religious submission) and self-ownership. I then place

a See Cindy Weinstein's essay on "Sentimentalism" in this volume (chapter 12), esp. 213.

b See Paul Giles, "Transatlantic currents and the invention of the American novel," chapter 1 in this volume, 23–24.

these novels in the context of Great Awakening preaching to reveal the fraught counternarrative these tales of ruined women offered to the national story of autonomous individualism.

It is no coincidence that the first American seduction novel (William Hill Brown's *The Power of Sympathy*) and the first major autobiographical account of slavery (*The Interesting Narrative of the Life of Olaudah Equiano*) both emerged to a receptive public in 1789, in the midst of tumultuous battles for liberty that raged on both sides of the Atlantic. Both the seduction tale and the slavery narrative, after all, feature protagonists who were trying to determine how to lay claim to their own bodies in the midst of a system which rendered those bodies the property of another. *Charlotte Temple* and *The Coquette* were published when both the USA and England were experiencing the first wave of anti-slavery fervor, and the first concrete moves toward manumission in New England states. New York, the site of Charlotte Temple's demise, passed its first gradual manumission law in 1799. These legal meditations on slavery found echoes in literary representation. *Charlotte Temple* and *The Coquette* emerged at a moment when seduction and slavery were mutually reinforcing discourses in much of Anglo-American print culture. As Bryce Traister has argued, both the rake and the fallen woman were depicted as enslaved by forces beyond their control.[10]

The Power of Sympathy opens with the rake Harrington's letter hailing "the gentle God of Love" who "rivetest the chains of thy slaves." Benjamin Rush and Jeremy Belknap, two prominent commentators on post-revolutionary life, had a correspondence that moved rather easily from enthusiasm for abolition to hand-wringing over the fate of the seduced Elizabeth Whitman (the real-life inspiration for *The Coquette*, and for a lengthy footnote in *The Power of Sympathy*).[11] Susanna Rowson, a writer obviously concerned with the politics of seduction, also penned *The Slaves of Algiers* (1794), a play in which racialized female sexuality became central to negotiating the poles of captivity and liberty.[12] The critical and rhetorical intersections between seduction and slavery invest the *Coquette*'s and *Charlotte Temple*'s harrowing and ultimately deadly pregnancies with resonances of the horror of captivity – women who first feel that they can control (if not fully "own") their own bodies eventually succumb to a powerful physical process that overrides their wills and ultimately takes their lives.

Charlotte Temple's and *The Coquette*'s evocation of virtual enslavement and erasure deviate from the plot of English seduction novels written earlier in the century. The amatory fiction created by Eliza Haywood, Aphra Behn, and

Delarivier Manley, otherwise known as the "triumvirate of wit," were able to depict women as sexual agents capable of thinking and writing their way through a host of seductive pleasures. To take just one example, Aphra Behn's 1684 *Love-Letters between a Nobleman and his Sister* features a heroine who is the object of a libertine's desire. She succumbs but still wins for herself, as Ros Ballaster writes, "the life of a classless adventuress."[13] Indeed, far from being enslaved by their passions and punished for their transgressions, the heroines of early amatory novels are rewarded for their skills at duplicity and manipulation. The sexually adventurous woman was not featured solely in the work of women writers, either. Daniel Defoe's eponymous heroines Roxana (1724) and Moll Flanders (1722) were transgressive women who, after their seductions managed to prosper, if only for a while. Notably, although these women were not free from the encumbrances of pregnancy, motherhood did not prevent them from making their way in the world.

The success of Samuel Richardson's models from 1740 and 1747–1748, in which Pamela's meek virtue wins her a husband and Clarissa's sentiment-laden decline and death wins her love and approval (albeit posthumously), heralds a shift in the politics of seduction toward a model in which submission becomes a strategy for those excluded from contractual relations.[14] There is an important continuity, however, between the savvy seductresses of Behn's and Haywood's amatory fiction and the virtuous innocence of Pamela and Clarissa. In both these early female-authored novels, and in Richardson's later works, the heroine wields some control over her fate through her skill with the pen. In Pamela's case, it is actually the discovery of her letters that leads to her eventual triumph and virtuous marriage. Although Clarissa's avid letter-writing does not save her from ruin, her talents as a writer do allow her to control the dispensation of both her body and her story beyond even her own death. For these heroines, the ability to skillfully manipulate language provides a means of escaping the fate that often accompanied the vulnerable female body.

As they used their pens to articulate a form of personhood that transcended sexual mores, the protagonists of early seduction novels subscribed to a transatlantic belief in print's transformative power. Michael Warner has argued that the early American public sphere of letters provided an abstract realm in which one might imaginatively leave behind the needs of particular bodies to participate in a linguistic community that fostered national belonging.[15] The 1780s and 1790s saw African Americans, women, and other marginalized Americans enter into print culture to escape the encumbering narratives attached to their bodies and claim the sort of independent personhood that would qualify them for a meaningful place in the new nation. As one might expect, for both African Americans and women, entry into the public sphere was a highly contested affair. The stories they sought to tell were challenged, and, at times, co-opted by powerful white male writers. Similarly, stories of seduced women that inspired both *Charlotte* and *The Coquette* were the subject of embellishment and debate by powerful men in several public forums. Certainly, the authors of these two novels were not exempt from the difficulties facing women who sought to enter the public sphere of letters. Susanna Rowson, saddled with a chronically under-employed husband, helped to support her family with her prodigious output. She wrote ten novels, several plays, and several volumes of poetry. Her work often met with the harsh words of male critics. Hannah Foster, who enjoyed a somewhat less volatile financial environment as she wrote and raised her six children, was nonetheless aware of the social dangers facing a woman who took on controversial topics. She wrote political pieces for various newspapers, and *The Boarding School* (1798), a work about female education in the USA. Notably, however, Foster's name did not appear on her most famous work, *The Coquette*, until 1866.

For an American public anxious about the dangers of powerful rhetoric on self-governance, the seduction story's twin footing in fact and fiction was an irresistible draw. Tales of seduction in the early republic's print culture moved adroitly between real life, fiction, and the gossip networks that mediated between the two. The case of the seduced and suicidal Fanny Apthorp (1788), the inspiration for Brown's *The Power of Sympathy*, made the local newspapers, and received intent notice from luminaries such as John Adams and James Bowdoin. *Charlotte Temple* – first billed as a "Tale of Truth" – was the subject of widespread speculation and commentary from critics and readers alike. As I shall discuss in depth later in this chapter, readers were intent on rendering Charlotte a historical figure, even when history itself offered little corroborating evidence.[16] The story of Elizabeth Whitman – a girl of good family who died of puerperal fever after giving birth to an illegitimate child in a Danvers, Massachusetts tavern, and became the inspiration for *The Coquette*, was a topic of public fascination and debate. At least some of the discussants of Whitman's demise directly attributed her downfall to her over-identification with novels. Worries about women's engagement with the public sphere as both readers and writers emerged in a host of contemporary sources. *The Power of Sympathy* features a long digression (which references Whitman) on what women could safely read. Both Charlotte Lennox's *The Female Quixote* (1752) and Tabitha Tenney's *Female*

Quixotism (1801) satirize the role of romance novels in the formation of female character.

In the midst of an increasingly anxious conversation about what women read and wrote, two bestselling novels of republican America feature women who grow increasingly wordless as their stories grow increasingly complex. Unlike many of the besieged women before them, the heroines of *Charlotte Temple* and *The Coquette* are not able to benefit from the power of the pen. In this respect they fit the epistolary template established by Brown's *The Power of Sympathy*, in which the masculine voice of Harrington dominates the narrative and the action.[17] The letters that comprise *The Coquette*'s narrative gradually eclipse Eliza's voice, and the narrative itself serves to discredit her choices thoroughly. Most notably, the epitaph that marks her gravestone is a narrative constructed entirely by friends who conclude her story for her "in the very mode of its telling."[18] Charlotte is even further removed from the telling of her own life's story. *Charlotte Temple* abandons the epistolary mode altogether in favor of a pedantic narrator who repeatedly breaks into the telling of her tale to instruct readers in the proper way to read Charlotte's story.[19] Moreover, as Marion Rust argues, Charlotte's fate is in fact largely sealed because of her inability to get her letters read.[20]

This muting of the heroine's voice, I suggest, is part of both novels' investigation of an increasingly touted ethos of self-abdication as a strategy for the powerless. American revolutionaries may have loved *Clarissa*'s depiction of a battle between the tyrant father and oppressed child, but that child's success only comes through the sympathy she manages to evoke as she succumbs to the fate she cannot escape. The notion that the feelings evoked by the powerless could somehow subvert a legally instituted hierarchy was a popular response to the paradox that both women and the enslaved posed for a nation whose founding documents proclaimed the equality of all. In 1776, Abigail Adams implored her husband to "remember the ladies" as he worked on documents of liberty, in the hopes that women could be granted the same claims to self-ownership being bestowed on elite white men.[21] Adams's rejoinder echoed a common refrain – that the legally powerless actually exerted formidable emotional leverage over the powerful. "Depend upon it," he responds, "we know better than to repeal our masculine systems," but "We are obliged to go fair and softly, and, in practice, you know we are the subjects. We have only the name of masters."[22] Even Jean-Jacques Rousseau, a passionate Enlightenment spokesman on matters of equality, nonetheless argued for women to deploy the strength of weakness: Woman's "strength is in her charms," he argues in *Emile* (1762), "by their means she should compel him to discover his strength and to use it."[23] As Rust argues, the post-revolutionary resolution offered to women contained a paradox: "to attain a status that allowed one material comfort, the respect of one's peers, and a measure of public influence, one needed to perform a 'deliberate evocation of powerlessness.'"[24]

"A deliberate evocation of powerlessness" fairly describes the plotlines of both *Charlotte Temple* and *The Coquette*. Although many critics have read these novels as warnings about the dangerous power of sympathy, in fact they chronicle the *failure* of sympathy to protect those who were written out of the social contract. Their respective heroines seek to win their seducers' hearts – at first through charm and beauty, later by tears and pleas. Both women fail miserably. Notably, their pregnancies, which could conceivably create bonds of sympathy between lovers, as well as between mother and infant, isolate and invalidate the women. Their pregnancies render them vulnerable and pathetic. Yet instead of their weakness eliciting the beneficence of more powerful individuals, the vulnerability created by pregnancy cuts them off from those who might help them.

In these two novels, in which the vulnerabilities of the female body end fatally, the women begin their tales by exhibiting control over the signals their bodies send. Eliza is particularly adept at manipulating her body language so that she might convincingly embody different personas. Her pleasant yet demure demeanor charms the rather stodgy Reverend Boyer. To the hedonist Sanford, however, Eliza emerges as "the very soul of pleasure." Charlotte Temple is far more naïve than Eliza, yet she is not so innocent that she cannot create a cover story for a misbehaving body. After an anxious night tossing and turning over plans to elope with Montraville, her body betrays – to paraphrase Madame Du Pont – an apparent "languor." Charlotte is savvy enough to create a narrative that overrules her body's symptoms. In the process, she disrupts the sentimental formula in which one's face perfectly reflects one's feelings.

Before their pregnancies, the heroines *of The Coquette* and *Charlotte Temple* are able to function under the logic of self-possession, in which the mind can control the body as one might manage a valuable piece of property. Yet their bodies soon exert a force all their own. Notably, while neither woman is physically held captive (as Clarissa is for much of Richardson's novel) their bodies in general, and pregnancy in particular, emerge as a force that overwhelms the women's will and their personality – the very fears associated with captivity in the eighteenth century. As they lose control of their bodies, Charlotte's and Eliza's investment in individual goals and pleasures gives way to the religious language of self-immolation. Rather than simply revealing a woman's sin, these pregnancies act as a force outside the woman's will, literally reforming her from the inside out. In these novels, the fetus both disciplines and transforms the woman who can no longer hide beneath a deceptive exterior. Both Charlotte and Eliza grow physically weaker and more emotionally transparent as their pregnancies progress.

The self-abdication catalogued in the description of these heroines' pregnancies resonates with the voices of the Great Awakening, which glorified a form of physical surrender in stark contrast to the republican investment in self-possession. For Great Awakening ministers, the object was to surrender control of one's body in order to allow for the touch of grace. George Whitefield is the most famous of these ministers, and for good reason. Like the rakes that were populating the pages of periodicals and novels, he was a smooth talker with a flair for performance. One reason why Whitefield's rhetoric was so successful was that he grounded his words with an emphasis on bodily suffering. Whitefield's sermons often focused on the physical pain that he felt was inextricable from the transmission of grace. In one sermon, Whitefield argues that conversion comes with the realization that "I am conceived and born in Sin . . . I am full of Wounds and Bruises and putrefying Sores."[25]

As Bryan Waterman discusses in this volume, novelists of the late eighteenth century often placed their protagonists in the contentious space between Lockean rationality and the mysteries of the spiritual realm explored by Whitefield. For instance, Charles Brockden Brown's *Wieland* (1798) features a heroine who deploys Lockean rationality in the face of seductive mysteries and ominous portents. While the supernatural is eventually discredited, the novel's endorsement of Enlightenment reason seems rather thin, as logic does little to prevent the wholly irrational tragedy that ultimately occurs.[c] In the early American seduction novel, pregnancy provides a space for the authors to play out Lockean ideals of self-possession against the evangelical model of self-surrender. In the Bible, pregnancy was a particularly popular example of God's ultimate ownership of the human body. The origin story of Christ himself tells of God's miraculous hand in Mary's virginal conception. The pain of childbirth was also of great significance in Protestant dogma, as it verified God's sustained punishment of original sin. The anguish of labor was God's penalty for Eve's attempts to hide her desires

c Bryan Waterman, "Charles Brockden Brown and the novels of the early republic," chapter 3 in this volume, 53.

and actions from the divine, and thus emerges as God's way of correcting a woman's will by asserting his ownership of her body.

In George Whitefield's calculus, resistance to conversion, followed by the physical pain of descending grace, was testimony of God's direct intervention upon sinners. Their suffering bodies are manifestations of the hand of God, and are proof positive of the folly of the notion of self-possession. As pregnancy progresses, regardless of a woman's feelings about it, so does conversion work against one's "free will."[26] The willful Eliza is certainly purged of her "unruly affections" by her pregnancy. She leaves for her final trial echoing the words of Christ as he finished his: leaving her mother's house, Eliza declares "it is finished."

After dismantling the heroine's ability to use performance and language to manipulate the meanings assigned to her body, disciplinary pregnancy illustrates the failure of the vulnerable female body to elicit the sort of sympathy that could protect it. Eliza moves to try to bring Sanford to his own spiritual epiphany, but she falls notably short of Whitefield's efficacy. Whatever sympathy she manages to evoke in Sanford has little effect on her own fate. Charlotte's failure to generate sympathy through her weakness drives the very plot of the novel. Almost from her first arrival in America, the weakened and pitiful Charlotte fails to tug sufficiently on the heart strings of her lover, her neighbor, or her teacher. None of them is moved to protect the vulnerable girl. "I am a villain," her seducer tells himself, but that moment of self-awareness does not prevent him from eventually abandoning Charlotte to a lonely death. Both Charlotte Temple and Eliza Wharton succumb to their deaths holding on to the inarticulate assurances of the spirit. Notably, we don't get to hear Eliza herself speak as she meets her end, and must instead make do with accounts passed on to her friends about "the state of her mind, in her last hours." Although Charlotte's words are confused at the time of her death, her silent body speaks volumes: as she moves closer to death her haggard face becomes "serenely composed." As she passes, she lights up with a "beam of joy." The deceptive language they were able to deploy at the beginning of their stories has been replaced by their silent but transformed bodies. The women ultimately succumb to a wordless embrace of the unutterable divine.

Read against the philosophy of the Great Awakening, both Charlotte and Eliza have been saved from the folly of self-possession by bodies that first displayed their sin, and then redeemed them from it. But, for Charlotte and Eliza such painful physical conversions offer none of the power that Whitefield gleaned from the experience. For women self-surrender may be the sole path to redemption, but it is also a sure road to self-destruction. Motherhood, rather than a path that allows women to influence future members of the republic, forecloses any opportunity for their voices to be heard at all.[27] Both *Charlotte Temple* and *The Coquette* end with their heroines ultimately silenced by forces beyond their control, forces that overrule any pretensions the heroines had to owning their bodies.

Yet if the novels themselves chronicle – even as they lament – the progressive silencing of their heroines, the public response to these bestselling seduction novels provides a space for "speaking" with these women long after their official stories had ended. As the epistolary form in these novels, and in early America, declined in favor of a more controlled narrative voice, both *Charlotte Temple* and *The Coquette* inspired a remarkable group of readers who reimagined and retold the stories of heroines in both print and through performance. *The Coquette* helped to foster a diverse and long-lasting display of devotion as readers mourned at Elizabeth Whitman's real-life grave, appropriating an authoritative print narrative and remaking it through their own physical pilgrimages.[28] The 1848 *History of the Town of Danvers* describes "Eliza Wharton's" grave as a "Mecca for all who love the Romantic." Visitors to Elizabeth Whitman's grave exchanged tangible tokens at the gravesite, seeking to elicit and create meaning from the silenced woman whose story had been so often told by others. The Danvers historian describes a "footstone demolished," and a headstone partially carried away, "piecemeal, by acquisitive pilgrims."[29]

Charlotte Temple's grave offers an even more remarkable story – since there was no historical evidence that a real Charlotte Temple ever existed. Nonetheless, Charlotte's alleged resting place became the stuff of real-life legend. As late as 1905, *The New York Times* asserted that "the grave of Charlotte Temple is the second point of interest of any of the many relics of old days in old Trinity Churchyard" as readers sought to pay (the fictional) Charlotte the respect she was so thoroughly denied in the story.[30] As Cathy Davidson writes, "[R]eaders flocked to her grave like pilgrims searching for the One True Cross,"[31] leaving emblems of their own lives such as flowers, letters, and even locks of hair. Generations after the novel's initial publication, powerful personages took it upon themselves to rewrite Charlotte's story in a way that extended her the sympathy she had been famously denied. In 1835 Philip Hone, former Mayor of New York and Warden of Trinity Church, was confronted with an urban plan that would disrupt the actual graveyard in which Charlotte was fictionally interred. As the *Times* correspondent tells us, Hone was decisive about the fate of her body and his own role as protector of it: "'No,' he said, she was treated like – when she was alive, and I'll be blanked if her grave shall be violated now that she is dead."[32]

Hone's protective gesture toward a literary character is perhaps the quintessential sentimental response. The readerly tears elicited by Charlotte and Eliza – and the urge to sanctify their socially suspect deaths through acts of communal mourning – anticipate some of the most powerful themes of the sentimental genre that would dominate the nineteenth-century marketplace. As Cindy Weinstein points out in this volume, sentimental novels often picked up where *Charlotte Temple* and *The Coquette* leave off – by lamenting the lack of desirable choice for the *feme covert*.[d] Arguably the nineteenth-century sentimental novel offers a bleaker account of women's roles as wives and mothers than Foster's and Rowson's novels – where the heroines never achieve either status. Rowson's sequel to *Charlotte Temple, Lucy Temple (*1828) implies that the only happy ending for a young woman is one that avoids marriage and family altogether. Rowson allows Charlotte's illegitimate child to grow up, but not to marry – and certainly not to reproduce. For Lucy, the solution is a form of secular nunhood – she opens a school, remaining unattached and celibate for life. For many antebellum sentimental novels, the sad fate of the choiceless, property-less woman manifests in the helpless deaths of young girls. Wildly popular novels including *Uncle Tom's Cabin* (1852) on the American side of the Atlantic and Charles Dickens's *The Old Curiosity Shop* (1841) on the British, mourn the sad fate of a young girl who dies because her pure heart renders her too tender to survive in a harsh world (and, arguably, the harsh marriage that the world would demand). Charlotte and Eliza – and the outpouring of feeling their "deaths" elicited – presage these other unfortunate daughters who would rivet an antebellum reading public consumed with sympathy for fragile and unprotected characters, even as contemporary legal structures remained indifferent toward the nation's most vulnerable inhabitants.

Notes

1. The 1794 publication date refers to *Charlotte Temple*'s first American edition. The novel was first published in England in 1791. Leslie Fiedler, *Love and Death in the American Novel* (1960; rpt. Champaign, IL and London: Dalkey Archive Press, 2003). Although *Charlotte Temple* is mentioned in passing during Fiedler's analysis, he spends little time on its contribution to the American literary tradition and rather brushes it off with the observation that rakes like Montraville functioned as "the masturbatory fantasy figure of bourgeois ladies," 69.

d See Cindy Weinstein, "Sentimentalism," chapter 12 in this volume, 213–215.

2. Mildred Doyle, *Sentimentalism in American Periodicals, 1740–1800* (New York: New York University Press, 1944).
3. Cathy Davidson, "The Life and Times of Charlotte Temple: The Biography of a Book," in *Reading in America: Literature and Social History*, ed. Davidson (Baltimore: Johns Hopkins University Press, 1989), 159.
4. Jan Lewis, "The Republican Wife: Virtue and Seduction in the Early Republic," *William and Mary Quarterly* 44.4 (1987): 693.
5. John Adams, letter to William Cunningham, March 15, 1804, in *Correspondence between the Hon. John Adams and the Late William Cunningham, Esq.* (Boston, 1823).
6. Gillian Brown, *The Consent of the Governed: The Lockean Legacy in Early American Culture* (Cambridge, MA: Harvard University Press, 2001).
7. Cathy Davidson, *The Revolution and the Word: The Rise of the Novel in America*, 2nd rev. edn. (New York: Oxford University Press, 2004); Marion Rust, *Prodigal Daughters: Susanna Rowson's Early American Women* (Chapel Hill: University of North Carolina Press, 2008), 51.
8. John Locke, *The Second Treatise of Government*, ed. C. B. Macphereson (Indianapolis: Hackett Publishing, 1980), chapter 5, section 27.
9. C. Leiren Mower, "Bodies in Labor: Sole Proprietorship and the Labor of Conduct in *The Coquette*," *American Literature* 74.2 (2002): 326.
10. Bryce Traister, "Libertinism and Authorship in America's Early Republic," *American Literature* 72.1 (2000): 8.
11. Jeremy Belknap to Benjamin Rush, August 16, 1788, *Rush Letterbooks*, vol. XXX (Library Company of Philadelphia / Historical Society of Pennsylvania), quoted in Carla Mulford, "Introduction," in William Hill Brown and Hannah Webster Foster, *The Power of Sympathy* (New York: Penguin, 1996), ix.
12. Rust, *Prodigal Daughters*, 201.
13. Ros Ballaster, *Seductive Forms: Women's Amatory Fiction from 1684 to 1740* (Oxford: Clarendon Press, 1992), 1.
14. *Ibid.*, 21.
15. Michael Warner, *The Letters of the Republic: Publication and the Public Sphere in Eighteenth-Century America* (Cambridge, MA: Harvard University Press, 1990). Elizabeth Dillon's *The Gender of Freedom* (Stanford, CA: Stanford University Press, 2004) provides a fascinating critique of Warner's argument, with an alternative history of women's role in mediating the private / public divide.
16. For more on the grave of Charlotte Temple, see Davidson, "Life and Times."
17. For more on the masculine narrative in *The Power of Sympathy*, see Davidson, *Revolution and the Word*, 185–186, and Bryce Traister, "Libertinism and Authorship."
18. Davidson, *Revolution and the Word*, 228.
19. For more on the narrators of both *The Coquette* and *Charlotte Temple* see Julia Stern, *The Plight of Feeling: Sympathy and Dissent in the Early American Novel* (Chicago: University of Chicago Press, 1997).
20. Rust, *Prodigal Daughters*, 61.

21. Abigail Adams to John Adams, March 31, 1776. www.masshist.org/digitaladams/aea/letter/.
22. John Adams to Abigail Adams, April 14, 1776. www.masshist.org/digitaladams/aea/letter/.
23. Jean-Jacques Rousseau, *Emile* (North Clarendon, VT: Orion Press, 1993), 385.
24. Rust, *Prodigal Daughters*, 7. The internal quotation is from Catherine Allgor, *Parlor Politics: In Which the Ladies of Washington Help Build a City and a Government* (Charlottesville: University of Virginia Press, 2000), 33.
25. George Whitefield, *The Marks of the New Birth* (Philadelphia: Andrew and William Bradford, 1742), 19.
26. George Whitefield, "A Penitent Heart is the Best New Year's Present," Sermon 32. www.reformed.org/documents/index.html?mainframe=/documents/Whitefield/WITF_032.html.
27. The concept of republican motherhood was introduced by Linda Kerber, "The Republican Mother: Women and the Enlightenment – An American Perspective," *American Quarterly* 28.2 (1976): 187–205. Jan Lewis (cited above) and Margaret A. Nash are among some of the critics who have complicated the term. Margaret A. Nash, "Rethinking the Republican Mother: Benjamin Rush and the Young Ladies' Academy of Philadelphia," *Journal of the Early Republic* 17.2 (Summer 1997): 171–191.
28. For a compelling and comprehensive analysis of the literary and performative responses to Eliza Whitman's death, see Bryan Waterman, "Elizabeth Whitman's Disappearance and Her 'Disappointment'," *WMQ* 66.2 (2009): 325–364.
29. J. W. Hanson, *The History of the Town of Danvers, from its Early Settlement to the Year 1848* (published by the author: Danvers, 1848), 211.
30. M. A. T., "Charlotte Temple in Fiction and in Fact," *The New York Times* (July 9, 1905): 11.
31. Davidson, "Life and Times," 159.
32. M.A.T., "Charlotte Temple in Fiction and in Fact," 11.

3

Charles Brockden Brown and the novels of the early republic

BRYAN WATERMAN

Shortly after the close of the American Revolution – at first in magazines, beginning with Jeremy Belknap's nationalist allegory *The Foresters*, serialized in Philadelphia's *Columbian Magazine* in 1787, and soon following in book form, beginning with William Hill Brown's *The Power of Sympathy* in 1789 – American writers and printers unleashed a surge of native fiction that often but not always self-identified as "novels."[1] Although this surge gained momentum through the turn of the century, domestic productions in the novel still did not come close to rivaling the numbers and popularity of foreign imports and reprints available from booksellers and circulating libraries. As Paul Giles indicates in this volume, accounts of the American novel – whether nationalist accounts or accounts of developing nationalism – that fail to consider the totality of writing consumed by early American readers inevitably fail to comprehend the character of these first American fictions.[a]

The tendency toward reading the "national" over other contexts has been particularly true of critics of Charles Brockden Brown (1771–1810), a Philadelphia native born to Quaker parents on the eve of the war. Brown's six novels – published between 1798 and 1801 – have most often been treated by literary historians as indices of American character, political conflict, and nascent nationalism.[2] Such approaches often take writers rather than readers as key subjects, making Brown one among a handful of writers who advocated – successfully or not – for some distinctively American traits in the new nation's literary productions; they also take for granted Brown's status as representative of an incipient "American novel" tradition and, at times, of the

a See Paul Giles, "Transatlantic currents and the invention of the American novel," chapter 1.

new nation's public sphere or literary culture as a whole. Although these studies have validated Brown's self-conception as a careful observer of social and political environments, they have largely failed to acknowledge that Brown's work took shape not simply in relation to the new political and cultural terrains of the American republic but in the context of a late Enlightenment intellectual project that was transnational by definition. Brown's transnational philosophical orientation marks his fiction as unique among early United States writing in several ways; if his writing is not representative of early US letters at large, it nevertheless opens up key insights into the possibilities for literary writing in the new American republic.[b] The depth of his philosophical probing accounts (along with a nationalist impulse toward canon-making) for his status as the United States' first canonical novelist.

With his major novels behind him, in the spring of 1800 Brown described his early books as "doleful" and possibly unappealing to average American readers due to their fixation on "the prodigious and singular": religious fanaticism, spontaneous combustion, axe murders, ventriloquism, somnambulism, cosmopolitan conspiracy, Indian uprising, and yellow fever epidemics.[3] Responses from Brown's circle to his work suggest that his readers would have recognized behind these sensational elements a specific set of broad moral-philosophical concerns – engagements with philosophies of history, matter, and mind, and their social implications, from Newton and Locke to Hartley and Hume – as his key motivation for writing. For example, the Columbia law professor and Federalist jurist James Kent, an associate of Brown's, expressed some objections to *Wieland* when it was published in the fall of 1798, based both on its dark tone and on its indebtedness to the moral-philosophical outlook of the British radical William Godwin, whose reputation was just beginning to suffer amid a transatlantic anti-Jacobin backlash to the French Revolution. Responding to Kent's criticism, Brown's roommate and Kent's protégé, a young New York City lawyer named William Johnson, defended Brown in terms that help explain both Brown's agenda for his fiction and some readers' reluctance to embrace it. According to Johnson, Brown planned to *avoid*, in future publications, "the development, or discussion of

b Brown's engagement with the radical philosophy of William Godwin, Mary Wollstonecraft, and their circle, as well as a longer and more diverse Englightenment tradition, belies the notion that American literature before Emerson was bereft of ideas, a thesis put forward by Philip Rahv among others. See Robert Chodat, "Philosophy and the American novel," chapter 39 in this volume, esp. 653–654.

any principles, which will shock even your prejudices, on certain subjects . . . The major propositions of Mr. G[odwin] and Mr. B[rown] are hypothetical, and the inferences are correctly made; – yet they afford not a rule of conduct for the beings who now walk the earth. – But enough."[4] Johnson's explanation highlights the degree to which Brown imagined a moral-philosophical program for his fiction, an ideal set of principles that may have united with his fiction's "doleful tone" in falling afoul of some readers. This approach to literary writing began with his early enculturation in Enlightenment ideals of encyclopedic knowledge and unreserved communication.

Brown's Enlightenment origins are apparent in the literary culture from which he emerged, which one historian has referred to as an "associational world."[5] When Brown described his early novels as highlighting "the prodigious and singular" he aligned them with a particular strain of eighteenth-century empiricism that aimed to discount supernatural understandings of "prodigies" – natural phenomena that were seemingly monstrous or aberrant – by incorporating them into the systematizing (and secularizing) schemes of modern science.[6] In this way, Brown's ventriloquists, sleepwalkers, and even his rational women (prodigious considering educational inequalities) are, to some degree, analogous to the five-legged animals that populate scientific correspondence in the era. They may, that is, be exceptional, but they must be accommodated by philosophical system and understood without recourse to superstition or the supernatural. Carwin, the anti-hero of Brown's *Wieland* and *Memoirs of Carwin the Biloquist*, uses this formulation to explain the phenomenon of the echo, which precipitated his ventriloquism: it would, he notes, have been "formerly regarded as prodigious." In *Wieland*'s preface, Brown notes that some of the novel's "incidents" – Carwin's abilities in particular – "approach as nearly to the nature of miracles as can be done by that which is not miraculous." Nevertheless, such apparent miracles will be shown to have natural explanations. Although several critics have argued that Brown's fiction (like the gothic novel tradition on which it obviously draws) aims to expose Enlightenment limits, the intellectual context for his fiction finds him ultimately placing confidence in the ability, through rigorous observation and reflection, to arrive at clearer understandings of unusual phenomena and moral systems than previously existed.[7] Such impulses stand for larger movements toward the secularization of social authority.

Although Brown's writing bears obvious influence of works by key eighteenth-century writers including Richardson, Rousseau, and Schiller, his most significant influence was the philosophical and fictional writing published in the 1790s in London by William Godwin and his circle, a group that included Mary Wollstonecraft, Mary Hays, Thomas Holcroft, and sympathetic writers elsewhere such as Robert Bage. These writers, dubbed from their age to ours as "British Jacobins," saw fiction as an ideal vehicle for disseminating their brand of radical rationalism. Indeed, despite Brown's calls for fiction suited to the "condition" of the new United States, his philosophical aesthetic squares almost perfectly with the Godwinian agenda for prose fiction. This program was outlined by Mary Hays in the September 1797 issue of the London *Monthly Magazine*, a publication Brown and his circle read closely.[8] Hays's description anticipates Brown's writing, particularly her suggestions that fiction should serve philosophy and truth; that it could do so by stimulating thought and conversation; that the novelist's language should be direct rather than overly artful; and that fiction should illustrate mistakes rather than ideal examples. Hays's emphasis on the experience of reading also anticipates Brown's fiction, which locates its action as much in the thought processes of its characters as in plot development and which models thought as the bedrock of morality.

Beginning with the fictional dialogue *Alcuin* (1798), his first publication in book form, Brown aimed to intervene in a range of intellectual debates at the turn of the century, from discussions of women's education and rights, to religion's place in public life, to the nature and treatment of yellow fever, which plagued the eastern US seaboard at the turn of the century. Though Brown's novels ultimately take sides in such debates, his narrative method allows characters to represent various, sometimes opposing, positions or opinions; the narratives sometimes allow for the resolution of disputes or, at times, illustrate the effects that flow from a particular set of actions or beliefs. In addition to promoting distinct philosophical or scientific positions, Brown's fiction also aimed to produce what Frank Shuffelton has described as a juridical public: "Brown's democratic lessons," he argues, "emerge not out of the content, the 'moral' of his fiction" so much as from "the act of reading itself and the continuous judgments it simultaneously necessitates and problematizes."[9]

Content, however, contributes just as much as the establishment of formal processes of judgment to Brown's civic intellectual agenda. To engage with questions of gender and intellectual culture, *Alcuin* explicitly takes its form – the philosophical dialogue, and conversation more generally – as its principal topic. It also stems directly from his interest in mental improvement, which he, like Mary Wollstonecraft, whom he admired, believed was uneven among men and women for cultural, not natural, reasons.[10] In essence, the characters pit Godwin's critiques against Wollstonecraft's; both score points, the *salonnière* widow Mrs. Carter on the need for coeducation in order to make mixed-sex conversation meaningful, and Alcuin, a New York schoolmaster, on the need to rethink society to its foundations. In the end, her arguments (which were curtailed considerably in the Philadelphia *Weekly Magazine*'s serialization) would seem most likely to encourage reform, not least because Alcuin's more radical utopian imagining of a society without gender was censored twice: first within the dialogue itself, when he hesitates to report on sexual relations among the utopians, and again when Brown and his friends, in an uncanny parallel, kept the dialogue's continuation from press.

Alcuin lays important groundwork for the novels Brown would shortly produce not simply in its obvious concern with philosophical inquiry but also because its form anticipates the dialogic nature of Brown's fiction. Like *Alcuin*, Brown's novels put abstract philosophical propositions to the test, sometimes by pitting them against one another, but more often by attaching ideas to characters who represent the contingency of real-world motivations, mistakes, and misunderstandings, as Hays had advocated. In addition to testing one principle against another, Brown often weighs one narrator's account of events against the next, forcing characters and readers to scrutinize other characters' actions for signs of motive, and motives for underlying philosophical justification.

This formal preoccupation with dialogue and the weighing of evidence is dramatized memorably in Brown's first published novel, *Wieland, or the Transformation, An American Tale*, which he completed in New York in the summer of 1798 and sent to press less than a year after *Alcuin* had seen print there. Although *Wieland* also deals with questions of gender and education – particularly in its emphasis on the equal education offered to the brother and sister who form half of the novel's core characters – the book pays more attention to matters of religion and epistemology in general. The novel's narrator, Clara Wieland, begins with the history of her parents, who moved from England to the Pennsylvania frontier as missionaries to the Indians following her father's conversion to a form of millenarian Protestantism. His religious enthusiasm ends in what appears to be death by spontaneous combustion while he is engaged in prayer; his wife dies shortly after. Clara and her brother Theodore are then educated by an aunt in "most branches of useful knowledge," but the bulk of the novel's action takes place after the two have fully inherited the riverside estate, which they occupy with their childhood friends, Catharine and Henry Pleyel. Theodore marries Catharine; Clara seems destined for Henry until a series of disembodied voices (eventually attributed to an itinerant ventriloquist named Carwin) throws their society into disarray, climaxing in Theodore Wieland's brutal murder of his young family at what he takes to be God's command.

The voices – and the murders – generate a crisis of sensory evidence and experience, topics the characters discuss obsessively. Clara's observations take on the tenor of an eighteenth-century treatise on intellectual faculties. Her principal mode of encountering the world is diagnostic: "All his actions and practical sentiments," she writes of her brother, "are linked with long and abstruse deductions from the system of divine government and the laws of our intellectual constitution. He is, in some respects, an enthusiast, but is fortified in his belief by innumerable arguments and subtilties [*sic*]." We are, in other words, what (and how) we think; Clara's process of making sense of Theodore's reaction models the reader's attempt to make sense of the book's events as well.

As *Wieland*'s characters judge the evidence of their senses, the book simultaneously asks the reader to judge the characters' judgments. Almost immediately, Clara is seduced by the possibility that "there are conscious beings, beside ourselves, in existence, whose modes of activity and information surpass our own," an idea the novel works strenuously to undermine. When Theodore is arraigned for his crimes, his self-defense foregrounds the question of accountability and religious first principles: if he believes he has acted according to divine will, is he responsible for his actions? The novel pits this line of self-defense against the suggestion that disembodied voices offer insufficient evidence about their origins, and that to act on such limited sensory evidence might even indicate insanity. Clara's early worries about Theodore's "dangerous symptoms" seem to be confirmed in the novel's late inclusion of a footnote citing Erasmus Darwin's *Zoonomia*, a medical work taken by contemporaries to be aligned with Godwinian moral philosophy. The footnote annotates an explanation of Theodore's actions by his uncle, a physician: "Unquestionably [Theodore's] illusions were maniacal. They are all reducible to one class, and are not more difficult of explication and cure than most affections of our frame." The statement (and the note) does more than simply pit a scientific explanation against a religious one; it diagnoses the religious explanation itself as a form of madness.

Though *Wieland* seems, at first glance, simply to suggest the limits of sensory experience, it also suggests that the characters' fault lies in insufficient corroboration of this evidence.[11] Brown seems most concerned with prejudices that affect how we evaluate and act on sensory evidence. If one believes in divine intervention, for example, one is apt to be duped by pretension to divine authority. (By invoking the notion of "inner voice," Brown seems to render a particularly harsh indictment of his family's Quaker faith.) In the end, some ambiguity remains concerning Carwin's agency – the ventriloquist refuses to admit he threw the final voice that sent Theodore on the murder spree – and we are also left to question Clara's status as a frenzied narrator still traumatized by the events she narrates. Though the Darwin note (and others like it) suggest the book favors secular, scientific explanations for the events it recounts, it nevertheless puts the audience in the role of judge and jury; we are left to "moralize on this tale" and to weigh the various explanations for its terrifying content.

Immediately following *Wieland*'s publication in September 1798, New York suffered a yellow fever epidemic that left Brown infected and his friend Elihu Smith dead, a loss that haunts each of Brown's remaining novels. Returning to the city later that fall, Brown threw himself into multiple writing projects, including what would become his second published novel, *Ormond, or the Secret Witness*, published in January 1799. *Ormond* furthers Brown's effort to promote debate among readers through the use of another unreliable narrator – this one embodying the suspect position of Christian moralist rather than traumatized observer. *Ormond* supplants *Wieland*'s framework of multiple testimonies, though, with a relatively simpler one in which a series of seduction plots doubles as an occasion to compare and contrast modes of female education, which quickly emerges as the novel's chief concern.

Ormond's heroine, Constantia Dudley, is educated by her father in science and history rather than feminine graces; in the novel's opening chapters she proves her mettle by preserving her family and neighbors in the midst of Philadelphia's 1793 yellow fever epidemic. Her fortitude and intellect make her, to borrow Brown's term, somewhat prodigious. Constantia is for a time taken with the title character's own engaging conversation and imagines that he may be the friend and intellectual equal she seeks, but Ormond turns out, in time, to be a villain who only feigns interest in her favorite topics in order to seduce her. After dispensing with rivals for her affection – including her father – Ormond seeks to sequester Constantia in a country manor, where he plans to rape her. She escapes this fate in the end by killing her attacker instead. In allowing its heroine to murder the would-be rapist, *Ormond* critiques the tradition of the seduction novel – Richardson's *Clarissa* (1748) in particular – by undermining its dependence on a gender essentialism that would suggest women were incapable of violent self-defense and consign them instead to wasting away following sexual assault.[12] In the end, the novel suggests that "the education of Constantia Dudley" – her Wollstonecraftian worldview and her arguments for women's moral and intellectual independence – have, indeed, won the day.

Brown's next two books – the first volume of *Arthur Mervyn, or Memoirs of the Year 1793* and *Edgar Huntly, or Memoirs of a Sleep-Walker* (both published in 1799) also bring epistemological issues to the fore, paying particular attention to the place of medical and scientific authority in the new century and the new nation. *Edgar Huntly*, a long excerpt of which appeared in Brown's own New York-based *Monthly Magazine and American Review* in April 1799, builds on Brown's preoccupation with erratic narrators and problems surrounding accurate judgment by making its narrator (the title character) unaware of his own actions through much of the novel. Sentences in *Edgar Huntly* are often phrased as questions; Huntly pieces things together in this novel, narrating his inferences and endless decision-making processes as he goes, at much the same pace as his readers consume his account. Take, for example, Huntly's minute description of a box he hopes to open:

> I surveyed it with the utmost attention. All its parts appeared equally solid and smooth. It could not be doubted that one of its sides served the purpose of a lid, and was possible to be raised. Mere strength could not be applied to raise it, because there was no projecture which might be firmly held by the hand, and by which force could be exerted. Some spring, therefore, secretly existed which might forever elude the senses, but on which the hand, by being moved over it, in all directions, might accidentally light.

It is as if we are so closely aligned with the narrator that we have to live his every thought; by letting us into his mind in such detail, he allows us to understand why he places too much confidence in his rationalism, and why his somnambulism threatens to undermine it. Huntly's box serves Brown as an apt figure for the human mind, whose springs and motives remain hidden to all but the most diligent observers.

Huntly narrates the bulk of the novel as a single letter to his fiancée, Mary Waldegrave, the sister of his recently deceased friend. He begins with an account of finding a half-naked man digging furiously beneath a stately elm – the very spot where Waldegrave was murdered. Convinced that this man is Waldegrave's killer, Huntly later follows him through wilderness forests and caves and eventually confronts him.[c] The man, Clithero Edny, who has been

c For a reading of the novel that focuses on Brown's aesthetic engagement with the American landscape, see Timothy Sweet, "American land, American landscape, American novels," chapter 5 in this volume, esp. 89–90.

sleepwalking through these rambles, eventually lays out a tale in which he confesses not to Waldegrave's murder, but to the murder of Mrs. Lorimer, his benefactress in Ireland. Clithero's confused tale of impulsive attacks and mistaken consequences mirrors Huntly's own chaotic account of his wilderness adventures, which include his killing of a number of Indians in the process of rescuing a kidnapped girl; he becomes indistinguishable from them in appearance and fierceness and even exchanges fire with a white rescue party. Later he learns that he had himself gone missing nights earlier during a bout of somnambulism. Huntly's and Clithero's stories continue to shadow one another when the sleepwalking Irishman arrives, wounded by Indians. Huntly attempts to clear Clithero's name, but the novel concludes abruptly with news that Clithero, descended into madness, has drowned en route to an insane asylum – news we may, as readers, have reason to doubt, given that Huntly himself (and, indeed, Mrs. Lorimer's brother Wiatte) earlier survived such an apparent drowning.

Brown's enduring concern with psychological experience is served well by somnambulism, "one of the most common and most wonderful diseases or affections of the human frame," as he writes in the preface. The phenomenon, which he (like Erasmus Darwin and the American physician Benjamin Rush) treats as a disease or a form of insanity, raises questions about motivation, agency, and accountability. The novel's invocation of key moments in the history of settler/native contact also reveals preoccupations with national experience, reminding us that Brown also aims, according to the novel's preface, "to exhibit a series of adventures, growing out of the condition of our country." Perhaps the "condition of our country," critics have suggested, is one of sleepwalking, of forgetting the violence of whites' land appropriation schemes in particular.[13] Considering somnambulism as a medical crisis with moral implications allows us also to see ways in which Brown gestures toward questions of national morality and accountability.[d] In this way Edgar Huntly offers a fictional counterpart to medical theories on either side of the Atlantic from thinkers like Darwin and Rush; in doing so, as Justine Murison has argued, "Brown articulates how the analogy between mind and nation poses national identity as always vulnerable to disease, even at its most quotidian moments."[14] Brown has attempted, quite literally, to diagnose the public mind.

d These concerns are especially pertinent, as John Carlos Rowe demonstrates in chapter 49, "US novels and US wars," in the context of the American Revolution (see esp. 814–815).

The key issue of medical (and intellectual) authority in the new nation is even more apparent from first to last in *Arthur Mervyn*. The novel opens with Dr. Stevens's discovery of Mervyn, fever-stricken, on his doorstep. The doctor takes him in and listens to his story of relocating from the country into the city, including his varied misadventures leading up to contracting the fever. On Mervyn's arrival in Philadelphia, a wealthy merchant named Thomas Welbeck had given him a home and offered him a job as a confidential secretary. Arthur quickly became unwittingly wrapped up in Welbeck's schemes and made an unwise promise not to reveal his background to any of Welbeck's acquaintances. Several episodes ensue in which Mervyn's integrity is compromised because he will not break the promise to Welbeck, and the novel's first part (published in May 1799) ends as Mervyn attempts to return to the country but collapses, fever-stricken, before he can leave town.

If *Edgar Huntly* (which was published between the two volumes of *Arthur Mervyn*) conducts an extended interrogation about how well we know ourselves, volume two of *Arthur Mervyn* asks how well we can ever know others, their motivations, or their intentions. This second part of the novel (published in the summer of 1800) emphasizes the significance of conveying accurate information, especially in a crisis like an epidemic. Mervyn attaches the need for good information to his newfound desire to become a doctor. The relationships Brown had fostered between literary writing and the medical and scientific professions becomes explicit in Mervyn's story and the novel's form as the title character comes, in the conclusion, into full control of the narrative. In so doing, *Arthur Mervyn* relies on slightly different narratological devices than Brown had previously used. Much of the novel is narrated by Dr. Stevens, but especially in the second part, Mervyn's virtue is tested as he competes with a parade of witnesses recounting multiple versions of his story. Once he takes the reins as narrator, Mervyn is fully aware of his own motivations (though perhaps he's the only one fully aware of them) whereas Clara Wieland and Edgar Huntly are, to some degree, unknown to themselves; for this reason many of Brown's modern readers have assumed that Mervyn manipulates the truth in self-serving ways.[15] Mervyn's self-narration, however, emphasizes his benevolence and his eagerness to rectify Welbeck's crimes. What appears to be duplicity on Mervyn's part may simply be hard lessons on the way to Godwinian sincerity and benevolence.[16] It is, after all, in the second part of *Arthur Mervyn* that we find this sentiment: "Good intentions, unaided by knowledge, will, perhaps prove more injury than benefit, and therefore, knowledge must be gained ... [M]eanwhile we must not be unactive [*sic*] because we are ignorant. Our good purposes must hurry to performance, whether our knowledge be greater or less." The first half of the quotation could be taken as the moral to *Edgar Huntly*'s cautionary tale or to *Arthur Mervyn*'s first part alike. The second half of the quote seems to suggest that Mervyn's imperfections are excused by his industry, as long as he is consciously engaged in the search for greater knowledge. The novel's confident ending – if one agrees to read it without irony – both redeems the uncertainty that haunts *Edgar Huntly* (character and novel alike) and offers a bridge to the domestic moral dilemmas that make up the content of Brown's final two novels.

Clara Howard and *Jane Talbot*, both published in 1801, mark, along with the conclusion to *Arthur Mervyn*, a decided shift in tone – the shift Brown described to his brother as moving from a gothic mode to the courtship romance. As this shift also marked an adoption of epistolary forms, Brown's critics, from the earliest forward, have often written off the two final novels as evidence of Brown's (lamentable) conversion from Godwinian radicalism to anti-Jacobin conservatism. Yet both novels – though undoubtedly trying to reach readers who were turned off by Brown's earlier focus on the frightful and freakish – have more at stake than a simple narrative of political and aesthetic conservatism would allow. *Clara Howard* reworks some of the love-triangle dynamics from the earlier novels to create an ethical dilemma faced by a young man who loves one woman but has promised himself to another. As in *Arthur Mervyn*, the question of promises is of utmost importance in one's engagement with the world, and the novel leaves open the issue of whether promises are wise or should be binding, even when they conflict with what is just. (Godwin had argued the negative.)

Brown's last novel, *Jane Talbot*, also returns to Godwin's *Political Justice*, this time dealing not only with its ideas but with its reputation. The central couple is classic Brown: Jane Talbot is a married older woman whose husband will pass away during the course of the story, while Henry Colden faces a triangular dilemma somewhat like the one in *Clara Howard*. But here the moral monitoring comes not from the lovers but from Jane's surrogate mother, Mrs. Fielder, who strenuously objects when the time comes for Henry and Jane (who is now widowed) to marry. Her objection, again reminiscent of the testimony provided by Arthur Mervyn's antagonists, is that Henry has been a Godwinian, an infidel, and, in her mind, a potential libertine. The novel never fully proves wrong her account of Henry's beliefs, and in the end Henry undergoes a conversion to Christianity that puts his sentiments in harmony with Jane's. Brown's supposed turn from Godwin would seem to be complete if this characterization of Godwinian doctrines weren't coming from the novel's voice of false delicacy and rigid conservatism, the source of Jane and Henry's misery. Indeed, throughout the novel Jane repeatedly affirms that Henry's skepticism helps her refine her own faith. In the end, the epistolary form turns out to hold quite a subversive potential, keeping alive Brown's tendency to frame his reading audience as jury, since we know less about Henry's actual beliefs than about others' views of him and his own self-interested epistolary performance.

It is tempting to read Brown's final novel as a brief for those who had abandoned Christianity in the revolutionary fervor of the 1790s but now believed it might have a place in the new republic. But *Jane Talbot* may just as easily have been part of a public performance designed by Brown to protect his career and his character from the same kinds of accusations Henry Colden faces. In May of 1800, only months before he began writing *Clara Howard* and *Jane Talbot* – and well into the transatlantic anti-Jacobin backlash against Godwin and Wollstonecraft – Brown told his friend Margaret Bayard that he still believed Godwin's to be "the most perfect" philosophical system he had encountered. It may be that Henry's concession at the novel's end was intended in part as a signal of Brown's own conversion, perhaps a prerequisite for his courting a minister's daughter. Nevertheless, Brown's reputation was already fixed as a radical: almost a year after *Jane Talbot* was published, for instance, Thomas Boylston Adams was still inclined to describe Brown, in a letter to his brother John Quincy Adams, as "a small, sly Deist, a disguised, but determined Jacobin."[17]

This question of Brown's politics has haunted criticism of his novels for nearly two centuries, with influential readings mounting on all sides of the debates. If readers come to Brown expecting partisan statements they will find little to nothing explicitly addressing contemporary American politics; they will, however, find engagement with the broader, transatlantic cultural politics that gave rise to the Godwinian moral philosophy Brown so admired. Contemporary evidence exists that at least some readers (James Kent, William Johnson, the Adamses) comprehended the novels' political and philosophical character and associated them with Jacobinism. The British *Antijacobin Review*'s response to *Ormond*, which had been reprinted in London, drew the same conclusions, excoriating the novel and calling its author a "mad-headed metaphysician."[18] Certainly Brown's novels, early or late, are not as politically transparent as such American anti-Jacobin fiction as Sarah Wood's *Julia or the Illuminated Baron* (1800), which like *Ormond* and the serialized *Carwin the Biloquist* responds to the turn-of-the-century fear of foreign conspirators infiltrating American institutions – including marriage. Nor are they as transparently nationalistic as the historical-mythmaking fiction of the generation just behind Brown's: James Kirke Paulding, Washington Irving, John Pendleton Kennedy,[e] and James Fenimore Cooper.[19]

In the social experience of Brown and his friends, reading and discussing fiction was one of many methods for achieving the Godwinian ideal of "unreserved communication," or the "intercourse of mind with mind."[20] This ability to transcend the local political contexts in which the novels were received by focusing on broader philosophical debates has helped Brown's novels endure with generations of critics – not only those psychoanalytic and historicist critics who find them to be careful archives of mental or historical processes but also those who appreciate his influence on later American writers like Poe, Hawthorne, and Fuller. Brown's early and persistent canonization owes as much, perhaps, to his immediate associations – especially to the same friendships that fostered his intellectual development – as they do to popularity then or now or to those he influenced.[21] In the case of the Reverend Samuel Miller, Brown's associate in the intellectual circle known as the Friendly Club, the bonds of association trumped Brown's evident disregard for religion. Miller made an exception in his routine condemnation of novels to praise Brown for "a vigorous imagination, a creative fancy, strong powers of description, and great command, and, in general, great felicity of language." Brown's early high standing among a politically and religiously diverse set of intellectual associates bears witness to efforts made during his lifetime and shortly following his death to canonize him as the first American novelist "deserving respectful notice," to use his friend Miller's phrase.[22] When, as an old man in the 1840s, Brown's early acquaintance James Kent was asked to recommend a reading list for young readers in a mercantile library, he included Brown's novels ("American productions of great energy, but of grave character") and William Dunlap's biography of Brown, as well as Godwin's *Caleb Williams*.[23] Perhaps the aging federalist jurist was finally convinced by the Godwinian argument that stimulus to thinking and debate – the clash of mind on mind – would outweigh any reservations about the dangerous character of their contents.

e On the role of these and other historical novelists in the production of American nationalism, see Winfried Fluck, "The nineteenth-century historical novel," chapter 7 in this volume, esp. 118–123.

Notes

1. On Belknap and other writers of early American magazine fiction, see Patricia Okker, *Social Stories: The Magazine Novel in Nineteenth-Century America* (Charlotesville: University of Virginia Press, 2003), ch. 2.
2. Compare the pride of place given Brown, vis-à-vis an "American" novel tradition, in key studies from the last quarter-century such as Cathy Davidson, *Revolution and the Word: The Rise of the Novel in America* (New York: Oxford University Press, 1986; 2nd rev. edn., 2004); Michael Warner, *The Letters of the Republic: Publication and the Public Sphere in Eighteenth-Century America* (Cambridge, MA: Harvard University Press, 1990); Christopher Looby, *Voicing America: Language, Literary Form, and the Origins of the United States* (Chicago: University of Chicago Press, 1996); Jay Fliegelman, *Declaring Independence: Jefferson, Natural Language, and the Culture of Performance* (Stanford, CA: Stanford University Press, 1993). For a contrary view and critique of the canon-making politics that long enshrined Brown as the "father" of the American novel, see Jane Tompkins, "Susanna Rowson: The Father of the American Novel," in *The (Other) American Traditions: Nineteenth-Century Women Writers*, ed. Joyce Warren (New Brunswick, NH: Rutgers University Press, 1993), 29–38. Tompkins herself had devoted multiple chapters to Brown in her influential *Sensational Designs: The Cultural Work of American Fiction, 1790–1860* (New York: Oxford University Press, 1986).
3. Charles Brockden Brown to James Brown, April 1800, in William Dunlap, *The Life of Charles Brockden Brown* (Philadelphia: James Parke, 1815), II:100.
4. William Johnson to James Kent, December 8, 1798 [copy], James Kent Papers, vol. II, Library of Congress. Johnson, along with Brown's friend Elihu Hubbard Smith, had been directly involved in plotting a "suitable catastrophe" for the novel. See Smith, *The Diary of Elihu Hubbard Smith, 1771–1798*, ed. James Cronin (Philadelphia: American Philosophical Society, 1973), 458 (July 29, 1798).
5. Peter Clark, *British Clubs and Societies, 1580–1800: The Origins of an Associational World* (New York: Oxford University Press, 2002).
6. William E. Burns, *An Age of Wonders: Prodigies, Politics, and Providence in England, 1657–1727* (New York: Manchester University Press, 2002), esp. "Conclusion: from Reverence to Ridicule," 185–187.
7. As such his novels function as many eighteenth-century novels do, in John Bender's terms, to "validate Enlightenment canons of knowledge." John Bender, "Enlightenment Fiction and the Scientific Hypothesis," *Representations* 61 (1998): 6–28. Markman Ellis, *The History of Gothic Fiction* (Edinburgh: Edinburgh University Press, 2000), 123–140, emphasizes Brown's use of gothic forms for rational ends. For an argument that sees Brown testing the limits of Enlightenment, see William L. Hedges's two important essays, "Benjamin Rush, Charles Brockden Brown, and the American Plague Year," *Early American Literature* 7.3 (Winter 1973): 295–311 and "Charles Brockden Brown and the Culture of Contradictions," *Early American Literature* 9 (1974): 107–142.

8. M. H. [Mary Hays], "On Novel Writing," *Monthly Magazine* (London) 4 (September 1797): 180–181. In both this essay and in the preface to Hays's 1796 novel *Memoirs of Emma Courtney*, which Brown and his friends read appreciatively, Hays cited Godwin's *Caleb Williams* as the chief example of the kind of fiction she described.
9. Frank Shuffelton, "Juries of the Common Reader: Crime and Judgment in the Novels of Charles Brockden Brown," in *Revising Charles Brockden Brown: Culture, Politics, and Sexuality in the Early Republic*, ed. Philip Barnard, Mark Kamrath, and Stephen Shapiro (Knoxville: University of Tennessee Press, 2004), 88–114, quote on 91.
10. For a more detailed study of how Brown and his contemporaries understood and evaluated Wollstonecraft's arguments, see Bryan Waterman, *Republic of Intellect: The Friendly Club of New York City and the Making of American Literature* (Baltimore: Johns Hopkins University Press, 2007), chapter 3.
11. For a contrary view that sees Brown as mounting an attack on sensory perception, see Roland Hagenbüchle, "American Literature and the Nineteenth-Century Crisis in Epistemology: The Example of Charles Brockden Brown," *Early American Literature* 23 (1988): 121–151.
12. Brown would make this critique more explicitly in one of his magazines. See "Objections to Richardson's *Clarissa*," *Monthly Magazine, and American Review* (November 1800): 321–323.
13. See especially Peter Kafer, *Charles Brockden Brown's Revolution and the Birth of American Gothic* (Philadelphia: University of Pennsylvania Press), chapter 6.
14. Justine Murison, "The Tyranny of Sleep: Somnambulism, Moral Citizenship, and Charles Brockden Brown's Edgar Huntly," *Early American Literature* 44.2 (Spring 2009): 243–270.
15. See especially Michael Davitt Bell, *The Development of American Romance: The Sacrifice of Relation* (Chicago: University of Chicago Press, 1980), 56–59.
16. See Dorothy Hale, "The Profits of Altruism: *Caleb Williams* and *Arthur Mervyn*," *Eighteenth-Century Studies* 22.1 (Fall 1988): 47–69.
17. Philip Barnard, "Culture and Authority in Brown's Historical Sketches," in *Revising Charles Brockden Brown*, 330n11. The exchange between the Adamses comes in response to Brown's repudiation of the arguments in a conservative take on the French Revolution that John Quincy Adams had translated.
18. *Antijacobin Review* 6 (August 1800): 451.
19. Philip Barnard, "Retold Legends: Washington Irving, James Kirke Paulding, and John Pendleton Kennedy," in *A Companion to American Fiction, 1780–1865*, ed. Shirley Samuels (Malden, MA: Blackwell Publishing, 2004).
20. William Godwin, *Enquiry Concerning Political Justice, and Its Influence on Morals and Happiness* (Philadelphia: Bioren and Madan, 1796), 239, 238. A reprint of the second London edition.
21. Cathy Davidson has noted that copies of Brown's novels in association libraries such as the American Antiquarian Society (most of which date precisely to the era of Brown's publishing) appear to have been little read, which suggests an

expressed purpose of purchasing them for high-minded collections; copies of more popular books were acquired later, deemed only retrospectively to have historical significance, and often bear evidence of prior ownership. See *Revolution and the Word*, 338.

22. Samuel Miller, *A Brief Retrospect of the Eighteenth Century* (New York: T. & J. Swords, 1803), II:171.
23. James Kent, *Outline of a Course of English Reading, based on That Prepared for the Mercantile Library Association of the City of New-York* (New York: Putnam, 1853), 46, 107; for his recommendation of Godwin, which was not included in the 1853 published version, see William Kent, *Memoirs and Letters of James Kent* (Boston: Little and Brown, 1898), 256.

4

The novel in the antebellum book market

RONALD J. ZBORAY AND MARY SARACINO ZBORAY

The market for antebellum American novels has yet to be materially considered within its broader socio-cultural field.[1] Their production, distribution, and consumption have been too often distorted by scholarly focus on the canon, non-canonical influences upon it, and, in rare cases, a few bestsellers or obscure imprints that shed light on social issues, then and now. Overlooked are entrepreneurs like Boston's Frederick Gleason, who produced more first-edition American-authored titles than anyone, even Harper and Brothers. Gleason specialized in short pamphlets between 60 and 120 pages, while Harper and Brothers issued mostly hardcovers, the format of canonical works.[2] The well-remembered Harpers' road led to "serious literature," and the forgotten Gleason paved the way to cheap popular literature. The two roads were mere exploratory paths within the publishing landscape compared with longstanding highways filled with standard works, religious propaganda, schoolbooks, business ephemera, partisan newspapers, and reference material. Still, these pathfinders of American novel publishing set the direction for future longer-length American fictional ventures in print and other media.

This discussion follows novels through their production, distribution, and consumption. Beginning in the 1820s, entrepreneurial publishers nurturing their own house lists gambled to an unprecedented degree on American-authored novels, as they issued nearly five times as many titles as in the previous decade. Prior to that, such novels as Susanna Rowson's *Charlotte Temple* (1794) or Charles Brockden Brown's *Wieland* (1798) represented highly unusual speculations by their locally oriented publishers, who not surprisingly paid their authors very little, if anything at all. By contrast, in the antebellum years, while most fiction authors continued to write for scant "literary dollars" for periodicals, a few became *littérateurs*, renowned enough nationwide to make a living from books. James Fenimore Cooper, having secured lasting fame first in Europe, led the way.[3] By the 1830s, the home-grown celebrity novelist had arrived, thanks to publisher-impresarios with stereotype plates as their major capital investments and puffery as their main marketing method. Having publicized their authors, publishers used mid-century transportation developments, such as railways, canals, and steamboat lines, to get books out to consumers. Selling books to a national market in addition to local ones proved pivotal to novel consumption, although nonfiction and European novel reprints outnumbered American-authored volumes. Still, that consumers bought American novels at all encouraged native production. That they read them suggests these novels' role in constructing a national identity.

Production

Between the two financial panic years of 1837 and 1857, publishers produced at least 2,305 new American-authored fiction titles in book form, the vast majority being novels (Table 1).[4] The boom in fiction publishing was fueled by factory production, electrotyping, steam-powered presses, and a national distribution system enabled by the transportation revolution.[5] The outpouring continued until the panic of 1857 sent many houses into ruin and the ensuing Civil War disrupted national book distribution patterns.[6] During the antebellum high tide, New York, Boston, and Philadelphia accounted for 84 percent of new fiction titles.[7] Although New York published the most titles overall, it dominated only during the decade after 1847. Before that, Boston had become the national fiction-publishing capital. Its 1845 record-high number of fiction titles was not even approached by New York until 1853. Over the two decades, Philadelphia saw less than half of Boston's production, and just under a third of New York's (Cincinnati was a distant fourth). That these cities' fiction output seldom moved in synch suggests that the national market had yet to replace local sales, but the corresponding large print runs and widespread advertising indicate that both near and distant audiences were targeted. Beyond the three main northeastern cities and Cincinnati, ninety different secondary centers published the remaining titles. Production in these publishing outposts took off in 1844, partly because of the "city-mysteries" fad stirred by translations of Eugène Sue's *Les Mystères de Paris* (1842–1843) that at once helped launch a paperback revolution and stimulated a taste for lurid exposés in local settings.[a] By the Civil War no fewer than sixty-four "mysteries" novels

a At first glance, the cutting-edge entrepreneurialism of the most advanced fiction-publishing firms would seem very similar to that described in James L. W. West's "Twentieth-century publishing and the rise of the paperback" (chapter 47 in this volume). However, the later firms operated within a very different business landscape dominated

Table I *New American fiction titles, 1837–1857.*

YEAR	New York	Boston	Philadelphia	Cincinnati	Other	TOTAL
1837	6	16	7	0	8	37
1838	17	16	9	2	5	49
1839	20	9	8	0	11	48
1840	9	10	7	0	3	29
1841	22	13	7	0	9	51
1842	15	11	6	0	4	36
1843	35	20	26	0	4	85
1844	31	45	20	1	18	115
1845	43	87	18	0	23	171
1846	53	73	17	1	14	158
1847	48	48	13	3	16	128
1848	42	66	16	8	22	154
1849	41	27	17	3	18	106
n.d.* 1840s	3	3	0	0	0	6
1850	46	36	27	6	12	127
1851	38	22	30	8	14	112
1852	52	26	34	7	21	140
1853	80	34	26	10	23	173
1854	55	29	21	6	26	137
1855	72	23	25	12	10	142
1856	76	28	18	6	15	143
1857	58	25	13	1	12	109
n.d.* 1850s	45	1	1	1	1	49
TOTAL	907	668	366	75	289	2305

Source: Lyle Wright, *American Fiction*, vols. I and II.*n.d.=no date on title page.

appeared, most as paperbacks issued out of secondary municipalities.[8] Of course, such minor cities saw other types of novels published, too. Baltimore, with forty-one titles, published at least twice as many as Auburn (NY), Providence, St. Louis, Richmond, Lowell, and Buffalo. Scattered southern secondary cities issued slightly more titles than their counterparts elsewhere, whereas in the middle states, publishing concentrated in upstate New York with its access to western markets. So, competition from the three key cities did not entirely eliminate fiction publishing elsewhere.

by a much more highly rationalized corporate model. For a discussion of mysteries of the city, see Sean McCann's essay, "The novel of crime, mystery, and suspense," chapter 48 in this volume.

Table 2 *Top American fiction publishers, 1837–1857. Parenthetical numbers reflect the number of titles each firm published.*

1. F. Gleason (Boston, 180)
2. Williams Brothers (Boston, 130)
3. Harper and Brothers (New York, 85)
4. Carey and Hart (Philadelphia, 62)
5. J. C. Derby (New York, 60)
6. D. Appleton (New York, 57)
7. Lippincott, Grambo & Co. (Philadelphia, 52)
8. Burgess, Stringer & Co. (New York, 48)
9. Charles Scribner (New York, 46)
10. T. B. Peterson & Brothers (Philadelphia, 45)
11. G. P. Putnam (New York, 41)
12. Samuel French (New York, 37)
13. DeWitt & Davenport (New York, 36)
14. H. Long & Brother (New York, 34)
15. Lea and Blanchard (Philadelphia, 31)
16. Redfield (New York, 30)
17. Phillips, Sampson & Co. (Boston, 26)
18. William H. Graham (New York, 25)
19. John P. Jewett and Co. (Boston, 23)
20. Stringer & Townsend (New York, 19)
21. Garrett & Co. (New York, 19)

Most fiction publishers played the game for only a year or two. For the few who continued on, novels were minor entries in their larger lists. Beginning in the mid-1840s, a very few firms, however, began to specialize in fiction. As a result, fiction publishing became concentrated in the top twenty-one firms (Table 2). Representing but 3.5 percent of all fiction publishers, they produced 47 percent of all titles. Boston's ascendancy was owed to the nation's two most prolific firms operating there: Frederick Gleason and the Williams Brothers, which together published nearly a tenth of all titles. Unlike New York's Harper and Brothers, in existence since 1817 and ranked third with mostly hardcover titles, Gleason and the Williamses specialized in American pamphlet fiction and operated only for about a decade. Despite their importance to the American novel's history, these two firms are shrouded in mystery. Appearing out of nowhere in the 1840s, they found rapid but fleeting success. The German-born Gleason published his initial novel in 1842, Joseph Holt Ingraham's town-and-country temperance tale, *Edward Austin*. The story became typical Gleason fare, with a high death rate of its main characters due to suicide, dueling, or grief. Gleason went on to found a story paper, *The*

Flag of Our Union (1846) and the nation's earliest illustrated newspaper, *Gleason's Pictorial Drawing Room Companion* (1851). His papers carried serialized novels subsequently repackaged as pamphlets produced in his Publishing Hall, the nation's first fiction factory that integrated under one roof all facets of book production. Paper, print, ink, and novel manuscripts came in one door, while paperbound, finished books came out another.[9]

Even less has been recovered about Nova-Scotia-born George H., Henry L., and Edward P. Williams, known collectively as the Williams Brothers. Like Gleason they published story papers, such as their *Uncle Sam*, which yielded their novelettes.[10] On that paper's fifth anniversary in 1845, the proprietors confessed, "We began our editorial career five years ago, poor, [and] unknown," before they boasted, "We have published more original matter, we believe, than any other paper in the nation."[11] They issued their first novel and six others in 1843, all by Joseph Holt Ingraham. Both Gleason and the Williams Brothers quickly faded in the early 1850s. The victim of an 1853 newspaper war with P. T. Barnum, whose recently purchased *Illustrated News* competed at a ruinous price with the *Companion*, Gleason, who had been earning $50,000 a year, sold his backlog of novel copyrights to Samuel French in New York, and his newspapers to his editor. After a few modest publishing ventures, the destruction of his office by fire in 1871, and his ensuing bankruptcy six years later, Gleason died penniless in 1896 in a Boston home for "Indigent Business Men." The Williams Brothers relocated to publish the daily New York *Morning Star* in February 1848, before vanishing without trace by 1855.[12]

The houses of Gleason and the Williams Brothers foreshadowed later production. They established the American novel as a marketable literary property, promoted for being original, not a European reprint. They developed the author-stable system and factory techniques to produce vast numbers of titles quickly in great volume. They proved the "paperbackability" of the American novel, and found new distribution outlets for it in periodical depots. With their low-priced (12.5–25 cents) rousing adventure tales, they set the stage for later dime novels.[b] They also pioneered book-and-periodical

b For further detail on some of the players in the pre-dime-novel era of cheap publishing, see Shelley Streeby's "Dime novels and the rise of mass market genres" (chapter 35 in this volume); in light of what she writes, the movement from the earlier period to the later was largely from experimentation and unpredictability of content apparently intended as scattershot to hit different types of readers, toward fairly predictable genre-fication aimed at specific demographics within a highly segmented market. Nancy Glazener, in her treatment of the bestseller of the 1890s, *Trilby*, shows how the serialization-to-book synergy, adopted by genteel houses; a Harper brother described his firm's intent for its magazine as merely "a tender to our business."[13]

The book-publishing part of Harpers' business involved little American fiction among its thousands of European reprints and standard works. Although it was the nation's premier hardcover publisher, its differences from the top Boston publishers should not be overdrawn, however. It did its share of cheap publishing, even translating Eugène Sue's *Mysteries of Paris* in 1843. The prolific Ingraham worked with all three houses. His *Lafitte* and *Captain Kyd* – published by Harpers in 1836 and 1839, respectively – differ little from his tales for Gleason or the Williamses; the latter brought out his sequel to *Lafitte*, entitled *Theodore* (1844). Still, Harpers did produce hardcovers bespeaking a transatlantic gentility that was only enhanced when in 1850 it launched America's first successful general-interest monthly, *Harper's*, which by the end of the fifties paid its marquee authors at the very respectable rate of five dollars a page.[14] Amid the house's generally lackluster American fiction list could be found Herman Melville's early novels and the ill-fated *Narrative of Arthur Gordon Pym of Nantucket* (1838) by Edgar Allan Poe, which was poorly received by critics and public alike, for its obvious shortcomings as a faux Arctic expedition account. The firm did pay novelists who sold well, while reducing royalties for those who did not. For example, Melville's Harper contracts show his plummeting estimation as a novelist: from "one half of the net profits" for *Moby-Dick* (1851), to "twenty cents per copy" for *Pierre* (1852) – one weak-selling book followed by a total commercial failure.[15]

The rest of the top twenty-one can be mapped within a spectrum from the Boston cheap publishers to Harpers (Table 2). Toward the Harper end were several names associated with today's well-remembered authors: New York's Appleton, Scribner, and Putnam, who published, respectively, poet Fitz-Greene Halleck, essayist Nathaniel Parker Willis, and novelist Susan Warner, whose Christian domestic tear-jerker, *Wide, Wide World*, found wide readership in 1851. Philadelphia had Carey and Hart, Lea and Blanchard (two related firms who issued William Gilmore Simms's Southern historical romances), and Lippincott, Grambo, who published some of Timothy Shay Arthur's longer moral tales, like *Ten Nights in a Bar-Room* (1854). Thriving in the 1850s afterglow of Boston's cheap publishers were Phillips, Sampson (who brought out Jacob Abbot's "Rollo" series of children's books), and John P. Jewett; the latter sold over 310,000 copies of Harriet

practices continued on in the Harpers' magazine ("The novel in postbellum print culture," chapter 20, 339–341). Glazener also analyzes the practice of branding, which we raise presently.

Beecher Stowe's *Uncle Tom's Cabin* (1852).[16] The sole Gleason–Williams-style firm in Philadelphia was T. B. Peterson, who, with forty-five titles, specialized in cheap originals and reprints, a potpourri of rousing sea tales, bloody western adventures, and genteel Southern romances. The final nine obscure New York publishers fall between the spectrum's middle and Gleason–Williams end: Burgess and Stringer (Cooper's later publisher), DeWitt and Davenport (who issued George Foster's urban exposés), Samuel French (publisher of plays and pamphlet adventures, like those of Sylvanus Cobb), Garrett (Ned Buntline's swashbucklers), William H. Graham (Westerns and Indian tales), Long and Brother (sea yarns, and Fanny Fern's essays), Redfield (later works by Simms and posthumous writings of Poe), and Stringer and Townsend (sportsman Frank Forrester). J. C. Derby, with sixty titles, ranging from feminist author Elizabeth Oakes Smith's reformist *The Newsboy* (1854) to Benjamin Penhallow Shillaber's humorous *Life and Sayings of Mrs. Partington* (1854), differed from these in that he forged strong co-publishing arrangements with brothers in Cincinnati and Buffalo, and with Phillips, Sampson in Boston. The very number of New York firms in the top echelon heralds that city's rise as the national fiction capital. Conspicuous by its absence from that echelon is Boston's Ticknor and Fields, Nathaniel Hawthorne's publisher, who, though focused on belles-lettres, became famous for poetry and reprints, and for its signature blue and gold binding, an early form of product branding. The house published scarcely over a dozen novels before 1857.

The antebellum American novel improbably thrived without international copyright laws, meaning that publishers could widen profit margins by stealing books from abroad rather than paying authors at home. In light of this, Edgar Allan Poe exaggerated perhaps only a little when he remarked in 1842 that "without an international copyright law, American authors may as well cut their throats." American publishers could reprint at will – with no royalties to authors or fees to original publishers – any novel not registered for US copyright, which was established under 1790 Federal legislation protecting owners for fourteen years, renewable for a second term.[17] Moreover, the "pirated" foreign novel had advance publicity through mostly European reviews. American reprinters could simply rely upon European *littérateurs'* established reputations, which is one reason why Harpers' or Peterson's lists brim with foreign works.[18] No pirate, however, could count on being the sole reprinter. Rather than compete with pirates head-on, some publishers, like Gleason or the Williamses, followed a strategy that depended on federal copyright protection: motivate American authors to write prolifically by all but guaranteeing publication and by paying them, albeit at a low enough rate to stimulate output. The threat of copyright litigation in cases of infringement discouraged domestic piracies. The resulting flood of novels could then be marketed as original and American, not retread and "foreign." Meanwhile, the authors collected cash.[19]

Some novelists who took the cheap publishers' bait became the most prolific among the 873 writers of fiction in book form between 1837 and 1857. Nine percent of all titles were written by just two novelists, Ingraham with 99 and Timothy Shay Arthur with 106. Ingraham was a Maine migrant to Mississippi, where he began writing his adventure tales in 1835, before becoming a college teacher, girls' boarding school proprietor, and eventually an Episcopalian minister renowned for his bestselling 1855 biblical novel *Prince of the House of David*. Arthur was a Baltimorean who adopted Philadelphia as his home around 1840 after gaining fame with temperance stories. He became the sentimental chronicler of the moral dilemmas of the nation's upwardly mobile urban petty bourgeoisie. He has been called a proto-realist for the occasionally critical stances he took against unethical business practices in novels such as *Debtor and Creditor* (1847) and *Nothing But Money* (1861), as well as in his long-running *Arthur's Home Magazine* (1852–1898). The dimensions of his and Ingraham's massive output were somewhat diminished by the fact that their books were short paperbacks that averaged in print 174 and 93 pages, respectively. However, these pamphlets, with their characteristically small typefaces, narrow margins, larger pages, and reduced interlineal spacing could contain as many words as conventionally longer hardcover novels. Indeed, fifteen of the most prolific early American authors wrote in similar pamphlet formats, and most were Boston-based, due to greater opportunities afforded by the cheap fiction publishers there. Overall, only about a third of novices published a second novel. Among the top twenty, only two appear in conventional literary histories: James Fenimore Cooper and William Gilmore Simms. The sole Westerner was Emerson Bennett, mostly published in Cincinnati. Just two of the 261 women who wrote novels fall in the top twenty: Caroline Lee Hentz and E. D. E. N. Southworth. Only in Boston in the mid-1850s did the number of titles by women exceed that by men. Otherwise, despite Hawthorne's 1855 complaint that "America is now given over to a d[amne]d mob of scribbling women," the typical antebellum novel was written by a man and the typical novelist was a man.[20] Still, men *and* women proved that American novelists could live by their pens.[21]

Professional novel-writing emerged alongside amateur and social authorship (for circulation among known acquaintances).[22] Beyond the drive for literary dollars from market-conscious entrepreneurial publishing were several intersecting "authorial economies" (to use Leon Jackson's phrase) advanced by the ample opportunities periodical publishers provided for getting into print, albeit by offering low contributor fees – or none at all. In this light, the legions who published one or two obscure novels might count as market failures, but only by one standard. If Harriet Wilson's *Our Nig* (1859) brought her a few needed dollars, while demonstrating that an African American woman could write a novel and help some white "children understand the injustices blacks suffered throughout the United States," not just in Southern bondage, can that be called a failure? Navigating these authorship systems challenged novelists, few of whom had fully adopted market ethics, and many of whom felt tension between writing for money and for other ends, especially interpersonal "social sense," grounded in traditional local moral economies of helping, guiding, and educating.[23] Suspended between these moral economies and the market, the antebellum American novel, through its successes and proliferation, passed an important threshold: it was here to stay.

Distribution

A novel manuscript may be prepared and submitted by authors, accepted and edited by publishers, printed and bound by jobbers, and be readied for warehouse shipping, but scholars often ignore what intervenes between this and the book getting into consumers' hands: distribution.[24] Absent consideration of this, a supply-side fallacy ensues: if publishers build it, consumers will come – increased production creates corresponding demand. This obscures the immense marketing hurdles publishers faced. They had to sell small batches of different products to a consumer base of millions stretched across a continent. How could a thousand or so copies, a common small print run, find their purchasers among these masses? Fiction publishers labored under an even greater burden: in a largely utilitarian nation long suspicious of anything in print short of the truth, they had to proffer "impractical" goods of imagination. Publishers of American fiction had the bar set higher: the popularity of European novels had long made their American counterparts mere novelties.[25]

The solutions that evolved were tentative, multifarious, and, ultimately, complex in order to avoid risky reliance on a single strategy. Antebellum novel distribution was like a game with fixed pieces played upon a checkerboard where new squares constantly appeared. The game pieces included subscription sellers, canvassing agents, trade sale auctioneers, booksellers and other storekeepers, periodical depot dealers, newsboys, advertisers, newspaper and magazine editors, book reviewers, lecturers, librarians, schoolteachers, panorama exhibitors (oral performers providing scripted narration and selling tie-in print material), and shipping agents of varying stripes. The game board expanded constantly because of innovations in intermodal transportation, as new rail lines opened that connected with coastal shipping packets, canal barges, or riverboats, which in turn interfaced with stagecoach express services. As books were subject to several transshipments involving different transport modes and shippers, they often were lost or damaged.[26] With loss inevitable, limiting it became a goal.

All American commercial publishers shared in this game, but those who issued original novels particularly relied upon aggressive advertising. A *Yankee Blade* ad for Maria Susanna Cummins's *The Lamplighter* (1854) exemplifies the making of an American bestseller. It boasted of the book's rapid success, "65,000 Published in 5 Months," before underscoring this popularity claim: "The Charming Story of Uncle True and Little Gerty which has already delighted Hundreds of Thousands of Readers and is destined to be read universally, not only in English, but in the various dialects of Europe, and is now being translated into the French language at Paris, and the German at Berlin."

The translations, useless to English-speaking Americans unable to buy these piracies, attested to the book's universal importance. John P. Jewett, *Lamplighter*' s publisher, tried to turn piracies to his advantage, capitalizing and centering the line, "Seven Rival Editions." "The sale of this Great American Romance" – Jewett's "Great-American-Novel" claim is centered and highlighted – "has been greater than those of any other book its size, in the same space of time, from the pen of an UNKNOWN Author."[27] With such gestures toward nationalist symbolic consumption trumping descriptions of the book's qualities, antebellum American novel publishers showed that they had learned to tell their own "fables of abundance"[28] foreshadowing turn-of-the-century advertising.[c]

What Jewett and other fiction publishers hoped to achieve through such marketing bears spelling out. The main line of distribution went to booksellers and other retailers. Advertising aimed to get prospective purchasers to ask their retailers to order the books, but also tried to persuade

c See Glazener's discussion of fiction's place in national-advertising-driven ten-center magazines of the 1890s in chapter 20 of this volume (esp. 339–341), and West's treatment of twentieth-century book clubs and other mass-marketing ventures in chapter 47 (esp. 787–792).

booksellers to place orders ahead of the demand the ad publicized. This is why pre-publicity for *The Lamplighter* explicitly discussed distribution channels: "A great curiosity has already been excited, a large demand will be created, and *early* orders from the principal houses in the trade are solicited, to govern the size of the first edition," proclaimed a notice in the February 1854 *Home Journal*. Once the retailer ordered the books, they would be shipped at a quarter to one-third discount off the published price, in this case one dollar, with payment due in a few months.[29] The retailer sold the book at price and took profit out of the difference from the discounted cost. Retailers did their own advertising by displaying the book or promotional materials in plate glass windows fronting stores, to attract street traffic. Once inside a bookstore, shoppers encountered a visual cornucopia. When Phillips, Sampson moved their Boston store in February 1855 (until well after the Civil War most publishers also maintained a retail business), the *True Flag* described the new retail space below wholesale offices: "The ladies will be pleased to hear that . . . superb editions of our favorite poets lie side by side with the last new novel, and farther on, solid works of history are interspersed with costly and elegant annuals."[30] A less specialized country outlet like Cushing's Bookstore in tiny Great Barrington, Massachusetts was "the place to find most anything a person can want in the line of books, stationery, Perfumery of all kinds, Fancy Articles, Brushes, Fancy Soaps, Hair Oils, Combs, Penknives, Silver Pencils, Purse Trimmings, Cheap Novels and Pictures of all kinds." Such was the novel's place in the emerging world of goods.[31]

Store purchase was not the only way books got into consumers' hands. Cheap novels could be "publicly hawked about the streets" of cities "by mere lads," or throughout the countryside by pedlars.[32] Some firms hired agents. One promised "A Chance for the Million / $50 to $150 Per Month / can be easily made selling the Popular Books Published by Miller, Orton, & Mulligan." The firm's ad explained that "The great Masses of the People who want them and will have them are not within reach of the local bookstores."[33] Publishers not only saw opportunity in balancing the competitive cities with the under-served countryside, but also in converting the conveyances between them into venues in which books, especially pamphlet fiction, were sold. "Especially to those traveling on railroads or in steamboats, they are capitally adapted, being so cheap they can afford to leave them by the way after reading," Gleason's *Flag of Our Union* wrote of the firm's "Fresh Nouvelletes."[34] Some urban periodical depots operated near transportation centers, allowing travelers to purchase reading before boarding.[35] One observer blamed newspapermen's "puffery" – fulsome praise of unread books posing as reviews occasionally lubricated with publishers' bribes – for "a dozen novels now circulating on the rail-road cars . . . which have no more merit in them than a saw-dust pudding has of nutrition."[36] By mid-century, the distribution of American novels had become effective, indeed.

Consumption

"The community must and will have books, even as they must have food," *Norton's Literary Gazette* announced in 1854.[37] If reading had become a necessity of life, did that include American novels?[38] Excoriating "yellow-visaged pamphlets of the . . . [George] Lippard school" as "murderous weapons to kill time," the *Yankee Blade* in 1849 would seem to believe it did not: "What a quantity of sickly novel-reading for the million is daily poured into our cities." But was not the *Blade*, as a story paper, guilty of what it condemned? Gleason's *Flag of Our Union* had charged "weekly papers . . . decrying . . . Novels and Romances" with "toadyism," when "their very columns are filled with the very same class and style of articles." The Gleason sheet offered a positive defense, similar to others of the period, suggesting that hardened attitudes against novels – that reading them resulted in time-wastage, mental deterioration, moral turpitude, ill-health, criminality, insanity, even abortion – were softening. Far from being "immoral," "romances" like those under Gleason's banner "inculcate a high order of morality . . . by contrast[ing] the hideousness of vice and the loveliness of virtue." (One of his 1852 ads listed eight such romances among thirty-seven novelettes, including Ned Buntline's *Red Revenger; or, the Pirate King of the Floridas*, George Canning Hill's *Esmeralda: or, The Italian Peasant Girl*, Fred Hunter's *The Heiress of Toulon*, F. Clifton Barrington's *Conrado de Beltran; or, The Buccaneer of the Gulf*, and John Hovey Robinson's *The Child of the Sierra*.) Romances were then defined by imaginative excess defying the "real" world supposedly represented in novels, with a tinge of exoticism and a love story at the center. But, according to the *Flag* editorial, these Gleason works uniquely publicize "noble qualities of generosity, magnanimity, courage, [and] self-sacrifice." The editorial then summoned civic virtue by asserting that Czar Nicholas charged double import duties on novels to discourage their use: "He fears novels because they teach the people to hate tyrants and tyranny, and to love freedom and heroes." In 1853, after *Uncle Tom's Cabin* had vindicated this fusion of morality, virtue, and civic purpose between novel covers, the *Flag* reminded readers that such literature must be presented to cloak "instruction in such a garb to make it pleasant and agreeable." To weigh the quality of this blend of entertainment and moral utility, realist criticism emerged by the mid-1850s: "A true picture of life is neither all dishpans, nor all gaslight and gay dresses," the *True Flag* editorialized in its 1856 survey of recent fiction "too often untrue to nature."[39] Indeed, criticism of novels' verisimilitude[d] – the previous century's anti-fiction diatribes took aim at their frivolity and failure to portray truth – had become a mainstay for both book reviewers and common readers.[40] In light of the novel's mid-century triumph, critics largely replaced efforts to eradicate it thoroughly with advice on separating the wheat from the chaff to guide fiction-hungry public taste.

The fiction mania grabbing hold of the nation seemed pandemic by mid-century. "Americans . . . [are] a novel reading people," British traveler James Dixon declared as early as 1849. He found cheap novels vended "At every public place, the terminal of the railroad, landing-places of the steamboat, and often on board as well," where he spotted, to his horror, a mother so absorbed in one that she left care of her toddler to her husband. He determined that "this pernicious habit is eating into the American mind."[41] The consumers were being consumed. As a minister, Dixon may have been less sanguine than other contemporary critics about novel reading, but his observations raise a question of evidence. Given the prior decades of discourse that argued that novels wasted time, dissipated attention, enthroned error, introduced vice, sentimentalized reality, overexcited the phlegm, heightened the passions, or seduced the virginal,[e] had reading cheap novels become a guilty if small pleasure deemed little worthy of note by diarists and letter writers?[42]

Seen another way, *someone* had to have read the enormous number of American novels. One Gleason pamphlet, *Fanny Campbell* (1845), by Maturin Murray Ballou, for example, sold 80,000 copies nationwide within months, far exceeding the initial 65,000 claimed by *The Lamplighter*'s publisher. The cover illustration even shows up on sailors' scrimshaw.[43] A comprehensive survey of 931 New England readers' records, however, found no references to Ballou's pamphlet about a woman cross-dressing as a pirate.[44] By contrast, *The*

d In light of the essays by Michael Elliott ("Realism and radicalism: the school of Howells") and Lawrence Buell ("Theories of the American novel in the age of realism"), chapters 17 and 19 in this volume, verisimilitude should be considered but one rather technical component within a larger agenda of what might be called instrumental realism – that is, a writerly practice meant to deploy claims of "the real" in a way that did not jettison moral or social "truths," but, indeed, could be said to prove and prop them up.

e For a discussion in this volume of the continuing difficulties involved in disentangling discourses about the novel-reading habit from evidence of reading behavior, see Barbara Hochman's "Readers and reading groups" (chapter 36).

Lamplighter, deemed a more moral book, received twenty-four citations, some showing it was not exempt from criticism. "It[']s exciting to the extreme, but of no utility," complained a drygoods shopkeeper who "read [it] till late" before measuring it by the realist yardstick: "its characters are very fine, but purely imaginary, existing only in the mind of the writer."[45]

The quotation also warns against taking too seriously the constant railing against female fiction readers, for both sexes read novels, and, with oral group reading at least as common as individual silent reading, they often read them together: "Commenced reading the Lamplighter to my husband," a newlywed recorded of one characteristic instance. Indeed, that aforementioned survey of New Englanders revealed no difference between men's and women's reading patterns in terms of genre.[46] The depiction of the antebellum novel reader – like that of the novel writer, discussed above – as characteristically female was little more than an artifact of anti-novel (and anti-woman) discourse: a misogynistic bugaboo.

The prevalence of groups reading aloud suggests that in estimating numbers of readers exposed to a book, one must multiply copies sold by an unknown factor of listeners. The book acquired still more readers, as it was passed from hand to hand, borrowed, or cut apart for scrapbooks. Some books were rented, at rates ranging from six to twelve and a half cents per volume, from the commercial circulating libraries that increasingly specialized in novels at mid-century as the newly founded free public libraries mostly eschewed fiction. Other books were charged from membership-based "social libraries" more friendly to fiction in the Harper's style than that of Gleason. There were, too, abundant book clubs and reading groups. Some of the latter, such as the Ladies' Sewing and Reading Society founded in Pittsfield, Massachusetts, in 1840, and lasting for thirty-eight years, had a benevolent cast that combined several activities, like collecting donations for missionary work, with reading. (Such "ladies'" associations frequently had male members or guests). In these groups, a single book could change hands several times, or be read aloud to dozens at a single sitting, thus vastly widening the circle of readers. And many published books had prior lives as serialized novels reaching large audiences via story weeklies that themselves circulated well beyond the point of sale. Thus consumption, if defined as purchase, becomes but a gateway into much subsequent reading not directly registering as aggregate sales.[47] Such reading helped build authors' reputations and could influence sales of their future work or even of the book's genre, so it was not without market impact.[f]

This is one more reason to consider cheap publishing within the same cultural field as genteel publishing. Pamphlet novels' extensive circulations provide primary evidence that many readers were exposed to a multiplicity of narrative strategies employing recognizable American character types in local settings. Ingraham's novels alone feature a Dickensian cast of main protagonists, including the young artisan, artist, genius, chief of the "Abenaquies," and "gentleman born in a cellar." Among his other male title characters may be found the "American lounger," "hackney coachman," printer's apprentice, "little news vender," "raftsman of the Susquehanna," and so on. Among women, there is the "maiden of the inn," "pretty haymaker," "beautiful cigar vender," "bonnet-girl," "milliner's apprentice," "forger's daughter," "strawberry girl," and "the heroine of the Kennebec."[48] Occasionally speaking in local dialect, these heroes and heroines encounter American landscapes and cityscapes peppered with corresponding villains.

Exposed to this jumbled reiteration of American characters, settings, voices, and themes, some fledgling writers, like Louisa May Alcott, learned their craft from cheap fiction and incorporated its lessons in their later practice. Alcott's 1863 novelette, "Pauline's Passion and Punishment," for example, concludes with a murder scene involving the scorned protagonist seeking to use a wealthy man she subsequently married, Manuel Larouche, to take revenge on her quondam lover, Gilbert Redmond. The stylistic similarities to the story weeklies' purple prose are obvious in the denouement set on a precipice overlooking the sea: "Then the wild beast that lurks in every strong man's blood leaped up in Gilbert Redmond's, as, with a single gesture of his sinewy right arm he swept Manuel to the verge of the narrow ledge, saw him hang poised there one awful instant, struggling to save the living weight that weighed him down, heard a heavy plunge into the black pool below, and felt that thrill of horrible delight which comes to murderers alone."[49] The scene bears the genetic traces of blood-and-thunder cheap fiction that Alcott evidently read in her youth.

Other readers not inclined to the pen like Alcott glimpsed in the American novel other ways of life in their nation. For example, ensconced on a Virginia

f This social aspect to readership differs from contemporary forms of it treated by DeNel Rehbergh Sedo in chapter 70 of this volume ("Twentieth- and twenty-first-century literary communities") primarily by virtue of its position within new media's matrix of power relations hidden beneath – if sometimes challenged by – personal communication technologies.

plantation far from the radicalism of Fourierist communalism, Margaret Junkin Preston reported in an 1850 letter her experience of reading Hawthorne's new book, *The Blithedale Romance*, to a group of "young ladies." Amidst the "veiled lady" exhibition chapter about Priscilla, the impecunious seamstress, under a mesmerist thrall, Preston employed a related trope, when the household had to scrounge up "an old-fashioned wrought-tissue veil" for a domestic slave "to be married to a servant from a neighboring plantation." In the ensuing chaos, Preston concluded, "I was content to give up the weakly, gentle Priscilla, and the queenly Zenobia [the novel's Margaret Fuller character] for the nut-brown maid 'Rhinie.'" The interregional gaze took place from the other end of the telescope, too. When a Philadelphia matron in California received *Uncle Tom's Cabin* via a San Francisco bookstore, she found it revealed Southern conditions of which she was unaware. "I read it all and enjoyed it," she wrote in November 1852, "Only sometimes I got quite mad at the d – s of slave-holders, and of course I had to do some crying and no little laughing." As much as American-authored novels could provide glimpses of different ways of life across the Mason-Dixon Line, they could enculturate sojourners in any region. Philadelphian Charlotte Forten, having left her native African American community behind to attend school in Salem, Massachusetts, eagerly adapted herself to a less racially oppressive climate, while reading in 1854 a steady diet of books with local settings, like John Townsend Trowbridge's send-up of the Boston cheap publishing scene, *Martin Merrivale, his 'X' Mark* (1854), Elizabeth Stuart Phelps's stories of Yankee ministers' wives, *Sunny Side* (1851) and *A Peep at Number Five* (1852), and Hawthorne's hometown melodrama, *House of the Seven Gables* (1851). That she received many of these texts from her grammar school teacher suggests the important role they played in social relations built upon a foundation of a budding consciousness of nationhood.[50] Overall, these experiences with varied fictive regional representations helped Americans deprovincialize their reading taste and refine their national imaginary.

Simply put, the American novel was not born in the antebellum years, but it matured during that period. Through the efforts of a generation of publishers, distributors, and consumers, the American novel went from novelty to ubiquity. An 1853 *Flag of Our Union* editorial thus exaggerated little when it proclaimed, based on the growing domestic success and international renown of the nation's novelists, "American literature is now of age, fit to speak for itself."[51]

Notes

A 1983 Albert Boni Short-Term Fellowship in Publishing History and a 1993 American Antiquarian Society-National Endowment for the Humanities Long-Term Fellowship provided funding for Ronald J. Zboray's research on this chapter. The two tables are based on information taken from Lyle Wright, *American Fiction, 1774–1850* [and *1851–1875*]: *A Contribution toward a Bibliography* (San Marino, CA: Huntington Library, 1969, 1956).

1. For example, Scott E. Casper, Jeffrey D. Groves, Stephen W. Nissenbaum, and Michael Winship, eds., *A History of the Book in America*, vol. III, *The Industrial Book, 1840–1880* (Chapel Hill: University of North Carolina Press, 2007), contains no chapter on novel publishing, no index entry for "novel," and only six indexed page references to "fiction."
2. Short formats did not necessarily feature lower word counts due to cheap publications' smaller type, narrower margins, larger pages, and reduced interline spacing.
3. Lyle Wright, "A Statistical Survey of American Fiction, 1774–1850," *Huntington Library Quarterly* 2 (1938–1939): 309–318; Ronald J. Zboray and Mary Saracino Zboray, *Literary Dollars and Social Sense: A People's History of the Mass Market Book* (New York: Routledge, 2005); Willard Thorpe, "Cooper Beyond America," *New York History* 35 (October 1954): 522–539.
4. The following discussion is based on Ronald J. Zboray and Mary Saracino Zboray, "American Fiction Publishing, 1837–1857," a paper delivered at the Annual Convention of the Society for the History of Authorship, Reading, and Publishing, July 15, 1994, Library of Congress, Washington, DC, on deposit at the American Antiquarian Society, Worcester, MA. That paper reports the results of an analysis of bibliographical information given in Lyle Wright's two volumes of *American Fiction*. Cf. Wright's "A Statistical Survey."
5. Ronald J. Zboray, *A Fictive People: Antebellum Economic Development and the American Reading Public* (New York: Oxford University Press, 1993), 3–68.
6. *American Publishers' Circular and Literary Gazette* 3 (October 31, 1857): 502, and 7 (July 20, 1861): 229.
7. Cf. William Charvat, *Literary Publishing in American, 1790–1850* (1959; Amherst: University of Massachusetts Press, 1993), 17–37.
8. Ronald J. Zboray and Mary Saracino Zboray, "The Mysteries of New England: Eugène Sue's American 'Imitators,' 1844," *Nineteenth-Century Contexts* 22.3 (September 2000): 457–492; Mary Noel, *Villains Galore: The Heyday of the Popular Story Weekly* (New York: Macmillan, 1954), 21–22.
9. He was born in Hamburg, according to his June 3, 1848 passport application, *U.S. Passport Applications, 1795–1925*, via Ancesty.com; George Waldo Browne, "Pioneers of 'Popular Literature: New Hampshire Authors among Them," *Granite State Monthly* 3.2 (February 1907): 49–56; *Gleason's Pictorial Drawing Room Companion* 2 (April 3, 1852): 221.

10. *US 1850 Census Manuscript Population Schedules*, via Ancestry.com, roll: M432_336, p. 12, image 236.
11. *Uncle Sam* 6 (September 20, 1845): 2; Noel, *Villains Galore*, 18–24, 27–29.
12. "A Word to the Public," *Flag of Our Union* 8 (July 23, 1853): [3]; Charles E. L. Wingate, "Boston Letter," *The Critic* 23 (May 25, 1895): 388; Browne, "Pioneers," 51–52; *Boston Daily Advertiser* (November 11, 1872, June 4, 1877); *Massachusetts Vital Records, 1851–1910*, via NewEnglandAncestors.org; Margaret Becket, "Williams Brothers ..." in *American Literary Publishing Houses, 1638–1899*, ed. Peter Dzwonkoski, 2 vols. (Detroit: Gale, 1986), II:493–494; Noel, *Villains Galore*, 28.
13. Fletcher Harper, quoted in Henry Mills Alden, "Fifty Years of Harper's Magazine," *Harper's New Monthly Magazine* 100 (May 1900): 948.
14. Jennifer Phegley, "Literary Piracy, Nationalism, and Women Readers in *Harper's New Monthly Magazine*, 1850–1855," *American Periodicals* 14 (2004): 88n28.
15. Herman Melville and Harper & Brothers, "*Moby-Dick*, or the Whale," (September 12, 1851), and "Pierre" (February 20, 1852), Contract Books, Harper & Brothers Papers, Rare Books and Manuscripts Library, Columbia University. See William Charvat, "Melville's Income," in *The Profession of Authorship, 1800–1870*, ed. Matthew Bruccoli (Columbus: Ohio State University Press, 1968), 190–200.
16. Not only was Warner's book not representative of the corpus of the period's sentimental novels (as Cindy Weinstein points out in "Sentimentalism," chapter 12 in this volume, 211–212), such novels rarely appeared under the Putnam imprint. Harrison T. Meserole, "The 'Famous Boston *Post* List': Mid-Nineteenth-Century American Bestsellers," *Papers of the Bibliographical Society of America* 52 (1958): 93–110.
17. Edgar Allan Poe to Frederick W. Thomas, August 27, 1842, in *The Letters of Edgar Allan Poe*, ed. John Ward Ostrom, 2 vols. (Cambridge, MA: Harvard University Press, 1948), I:210. For some qualifications of this generalization, see Meredith McGill, "Copyright," in Casper *et al.*, *History of the Book*, 158–178.
18. Indeed, the cover of Meredith McGill's *American Literature and the Culture of Reprinting, 1843–1853* (Philadelphia: University of Pennsylvania Press, 2003), shows Charles Dickens before a projection of Peterson's enormous list of his works. Elsewhere in this volume, Nancy Glazener discusses how lack of international copyright would remain a problem until passage of the Chace Act in 1891. (See Glazener, "The novel in postbellum print culture," chapter 20, 343.)
19. Zboray and Zboray, *Literary Dollars*, 78–81, 213–214.
20. Warren G. French, "Timothy Shay Arthur: Pioneer Business Novelist," *American Quarterly* 10 (1958): 55–65. James D. Wallace, "Hawthorne and the Scribbling Women Reconsidered," *American Literature* 62 (1990): 201–222, quotation on 204. For other uses of Hawthorne's comment, see the chapters in this volume by Cindy Weinstein ("Sentimentalism," chapter 12) and Jonathan Arac ("Hawthorne and the aesthetics of American romance," chapter 8).
21. Mary Kelley, *Private Woman, Public Stage: Literary Domesticity in Nineteenth-Century America* (New York: Oxford University Press, 1984).

22. Margaret J. Ezell, *Social Authorship and the Advent of Print* (Baltimore: Johns Hopkins University Press, 1999).
23. Zboray and Zboray, *Literary Dollars*; Leon Jackson, *The Business of Letters: Authorial Economies in Antebellum America* (Stanford, CA: Stanford University Press, 2008); Eric Gardner, " 'This Attempt of Their Sister': Harriet Wilson's Our Nig from Printer to Readers," *New England Quarterly* 66 (1993): 226–246.
24. But see Zboray, A *Fictive People*, 1–87, and Zboray and Zboray, *Literary Dollars*, 125–168. Distribution studies usually do not focus on fiction: e.g., Michael Hackenberg, ed., *Getting the Books Out: Papers of the Chicago Conference on the Book in 19th-Century America* (Washington, DC: Library of Congress, 1987); see also Casper *et al.*, *History of the Book*, 117–157.
25. Robert B. Winans, "The Growth of a Novel-Reading Public in Eighteenth-Century America," *Early American Literature* 9 (1975): 267–275.
26. Zboray, *A Fictive People*, 55–68.
27. "The Lamplighter," advertisement, *Yankee Blade* 14 (September 16, 1854). Cummins as the author figured in her later *Mabel Vaughan* (1857) advertisements; see *American Publishers' Circular and Literary Gazette* 3 (August 29, 1857): 39. English advertisements for *Uncle Tom's Cabin* had employed the phrase, "Great American Novel," according to Lawrence Buell, "The Unkillable Dream of the Great American Novel: *Moby-Dick* as a Test Case," *American Literary History* 20.1 (2008): 135. *The Lamplighter* ad used the term to appeal to an American audience in a story paper featuring nationalistic fiction, and it thus prefigures, in essential ways, John De Forest's fuller development of the concept in 1868, which Buell explores in chapter 19 of this volume, 333–334.
28. T. J. Jackson Lears, *Fables of Abundance: A Cultural History of Advertising In America* (New York: Basic Books, 1994).
29. "A Thrilling Book," advertisement, *Christian Review* 19 (April 1854): 320; Michael Winship, "Distribution and the Trade," in Casper and *et al.*, *History of the Book*, 123–125.
30. *True Flag* 4 (February 3, 1855): [3].
31. "Cushing's Bookstore," *Berkshire Courier* (July 2, 1846): [3]; Ronald J. Zboray and Mary Saracino Zboray, "Books, Reading, and the World of Goods in Antebellum New England," *American Quarterly* 48 (1996): 587–622.
32. "Licentious Books and Prints," *Uncle Sam* 3 (January 1, 1844); H. Long and Brother, advertisement in Thurlow Weed, *Autobiography* (Boston: Houghton Mifflin, 1884).
33. *Star Spangled Banner* 8 (April 8, 1854): [3].
34. *Flag of Our Union* 48 (November 7, 1848): [3]; Zboray, *A Fictive People*, 74.
35. Ronald J. Zboray and Mary Saracino Zboray, "The Boston Book Trades, 1789–1850: A Statistical and Geographical Analysis," in *Entrepreneurs: The Boston Business Community, 1700–1850*, ed. Conrad Edick Wright and Katheryn P. Viens (Boston: Massachusetts Historical Society, 1997), 258.
36. "American Literature and Reprints," *Putnam's Monthly Magazine* 7 (February 1856): 213; Charvat, "Melville's Income," 168–189.

37. N.M., "Correspondence," *Norton's Literary Gazette* 1 (May 11, 1854): 219.
38. William J. Gilmore-Lehne, *Reading Becomes a Necessity of Life: Material and Cultural Life in Rural New England, 1780–1835* (Knoxville: University of Tennessee Press, 1989).
39. "The Light Literature of the Day," *Yankee Blade* 6 (September 26, 1849): 2; "Novels and Romances," *Flag of Our Union* (August 25, 1849): [3]; "New Publications," *Gleason's Pictorial Drawing Room Companion* (November 13, 1852): 309; "Winter Evenings," *Flag of Our Union* 8 (January 29, 1853): [3]; "Fiction and Life," *True Flag* 5 (August 23, 1856): [3]. Examples of anti-novel discourse include: "K," "Novel Reading," *Literary Messenger* 2 (June 1841): 3–4; "Penseur," "Novel Reading," *Christian Parlor Magazine* (June 1845): 45; "Novels and Insanity," *Zion's Herald and Wesleyan Journal* 18 (30 June 1847): 102; John Moore, "Novel-Reading," *Christian Advocate and Journal* 27 (February 19, 1852): 29; "Letters from New York," *Yankee Blade* 7 (November 27, 1847): [3]. Jonathan Arac captures the rhetorical elasticity of the romance–novel distinction through the lens of Nathaniel Hawthorne's writings ("Hawthorne and the aesthetics of American romance, chapter 8 in this volume).
40. Nina Baym, *Novels, Readers, and Reviews: Responses to Fiction in Antebellum America* (Ithaca, NY: Cornell University Press, 1984), 152–72; Ronald J. Zboray and Mary Saracino Zboray, *Everyday Ideas: Socioliterary Experience among Antebellum New Englanders* (Knoxville: University of Tennessee Press, 2006), 263–264.
41. "Book Manias," *True Flag* 6 (April 18, 1857): [3]; James Dixon, *Personal Narrative of a Tour through the United States and Canada* (New York: Lane and Scott, 1849), 39.
42. G. Harrison Orians, "Censure of Fiction in American Romances and Magazines," *PMLA* 52 (March 1937): 195–214. Zboray and Zboray, *Everyday Ideas*, 301n15, 171–172.
43. Peter Benson, "Gleason's Publishing Hall," in *Publishers for Mass Entertainment in Nineteenth-Century America*, ed. Madeleine B. Stern (Boston: G. K. Hall, 1980), 139; Susan S. Williams, "'Promoting an Extensive Sale': The Production and Reception of *The Lamplighter*," *New England Quarterly* 69 (June 1996), 185; Zboray and Zboray, "Books, Reading," 621n87.
44. Zboray and Zboray, *Everyday Ideas*.
45. George Foster Allen, May 24, 1854, Diary, vol. II, George Foster Allen Papers and Diaries, 1850–1871, Phillips Library, Peabody Essex Museum, Salem, MA.
46. "Ellen," "Novel Readers," *Boston Cultivator* 12 (April 6, 1850): 109; Zboray and Zboray, *Everyday Ideas*, 132–144; Frances Jocelyn Peck, April 17, 1854, Diary, Jocelyn Family Papers, Connecticut Historical Society, Hartford, CT.
47. Zboray and Zboray, "Part II. Dissemination," *Everyday Ideas*, 71–147; David Kaser, *A Book for a Sixpence: The Circulating Library in America* (Pittsburgh: Beta Phi Mu, 1980), 62–85; *Young Ladies' Sewing and Reading Society* (Pittsfield, MA), Records, 1840–1878, Schlesinger Library, Radcliffe Institute, Harvard University; Caroline J. Lawes, *Women and Reform in a New England Community, 1815–1860* (Lexington: University Press of Kentucky, 2000), 63–64; Patricia Okker, *Social*

Stories: The Magazine Novel in Nineteenth-Century America (Charlottesville: University Press of Virginia, 2003).

48. Bibliographical information on the titles mentioned can be found in Wright, *American Fiction*, 1:172–85.
49. Madeleine B. Stern, "Introduction," in *Freaks of Genius: Unknown Thrillers of Louisa May Alcott*, ed. Daniel Shealy, with Madeleine B. Stern and Joel Myerson (Westport, CT: Greenwood Press, 1991), 1–5; "Pauline's Passion and Punishment," *Frank Leslie's Illustrated Newspaper* (January 10, 1863): 249.
50. Elizabeth Preston Allan, ed., *The Life and Letters of Margaret Junkin Preston* (Boston: Houghton, Mifflin, 1903), 50–54; Anna Lee Marston, ed., *Records of a California Family; Journals and Letters of Lewis C. Gunn and Elizabeth Le Breton Gunn* (San Diego: n.p., 1928), 185; Brenda Stevenson, ed., *The Journals of Charlotte Forten Grimké* (New York: Oxford University Press, 1988), 68, 71, 75–76, 79, 89, 95; on Forten's relationship to New England, see Zboray and Zboray, *Literary Dollars*, 43–57.
51. "American Books in England," *Flag of Our Union* 8 (January 22, 1853): [3].

5

American land, American landscape, American novels

TIMOTHY SWEET

While "nature" has figured prominently in the aesthetic production of American identity, approaches to the natural environment have varied by medium and genre. Painters facing the problem of subject matter in the supposed thinness of American culture turned to nature to develop a national aesthetic during the antebellum era. Thomas Cole's sometimes nostalgic celebrations of wilderness as a special site of divine presence were reinterpreted in nationalist terms by the next generation of painters, who became known as the Hudson River school. These painters depicted optimistic narratives of the transformation of wilderness into cultivated space, while developing a visual culture in which a certain landscape form became identified as the national landscape. Their synecdochic nationalism presented nature's newness as symbolic of America's newness, the wilderness as ready to receive culture's imprint.[1] Ironically, in transforming the wilderness, cultivation obliterated nature's newness and with it, the American promise of exceptionalism.[2] Moreover, for all the Hudson River school's claims to aesthetic nationalism, their paintings originated in observations of a particular region's landscapes. This tension between aesthetic nationalism and local representation took a more complex form in the antebellum novel, where cultural narratives with claims to national scope, such as the pastoral retreat or the progress of civilization through stages of economic development, were inflected through or conflicted with local narratives and landscape forms.

In discussions of the prospects for a national literature, theorists of the novel were divided on the question of the thinness of American culture and its implications for setting as the ground of a distinct tradition.[a] James

a As Lawrence Buell observes in chapter 19, "Theories of the American novel," literary theory was seldom addressed as a topic in itself before the 1880s; see 322–323. Rather, theorizing was undertaken sporadically in reviews and author's prefaces.

Fenimore Cooper was among those who lamented American cultural thinness, observing in *Notions of the Americans* (1828) that a great "obstacle against which American literature has to contend, is in the poverty of materials." In contrast to Europe, America offered "no annals for the historian; no follies ... for the satirist; no manners for the dramatist." Nathaniel Hawthorne, whose early fiction mined the American historical archive, turned finally to Italy for a "congenial" setting for "romance," explaining in his preface to *The Marble Faun* (1860) that American settings provided "no shadow, no antiquity, no mystery, no picturesque and gloomy wrong, nor anything but commonplace prosperity, in broad and simple daylight." Charles Brockden Brown had argued on the contrary, in his preface to *Edgar Huntly* (1799), that a unique novelistic aesthetic, replete with shadow and mystery, could be founded on peculiarly American materials such as "incidents of Indian hostility, and the perils of the Western wilderness." Such materials, claimed William Gilmore Simms in his preface to the second edition of *The Yemassee* (1853), comprised "the natural romance of our country." Simms observed that Cooper was the first to have "opened the eyes" of Americans to these literary "resources," through a characteristic plot which fixes on "one man, and flings him upon the wilderness."[3]

In practice, novelists developed more complex and varied engagements with American land and landscape than even such divided theorizing implied. Two significant issues emerged during the antebellum era, one concerning the novel's generic commitment to setting and another concerning the possibility of imagining a "national" landscape. First, in an era that saw the flowering of loco-descriptive poetry and prose, the novel was not the pre-eminent landscape genre, for a novel could get by with only minimal response to the sheer materiality of non-human nature. Nevertheless, through its primary generic commitment to the socio-economic world of character and plot, together with its generic history of absorbing a disparate range of discourses, the novel could provide an important means to observe and even to shape the reciprocal interaction of human culture and natural environment.[4] Second, for the novel, there was no national landscape parallel to that developed in visual culture through the institutionalization of the Hudson River school aesthetic, even if some of the more visually conscious novelists evoked painterly landscape modes so as to claim participation in this national visual culture. Rather, individual novels engaged, to greater or lesser degrees, with particular local landscapes, much like the diverse productions of genre painting and regional landscape traditions that flourished in antebellum America.[5] Regional identifications were defined through loose chronotopical affiliations, including frontier adventure novels, novels of agricultural transformation, domestic pastorals (in eastern and western variants), plantation novels (both anti- and pro-slavery), and fictionalized accounts of travel to exotic landscapes beyond North America.[6] Thus the novel's commitment to material setting, activated through its primary commitment to the social world, could connect a local setting with national concerns.

The first American novel to engage substantially with landscape was Charles Brockden Brown's frontier adventure, *Edgar Huntly* (1799). Especially interested in the workings of the mind, Brown developed a critique of perception, cognition, and moral judgment by transporting the European picturesque aesthetic to wild and pastoral American landscapes.[b] A key feature of the picturesque aesthetic was the capacity to judge a physical landscape as if it were a painting, appreciating signs of a benevolent deity in the complex harmony of nature or a beneficent social organization in the order of a rural scene.[7] Experimenting with such ideas concerning the moral correlation of landscape, Brown sends his protagonist Huntly into a "mazy" wilderness, near a fully settled agricultural district, where he encounters Lenape Indians bent on revenge for the expropriation of their lands.[8] Brown here undercuts assumptions of Huntly's cognitive mastery of the landscape and associated capacity for moral judgment. He often makes it unclear whether landscape forms are being internalized through Huntly's perception or his mental states are being externalized through projection. In either case, Huntly's judgments often turn out to be erroneous, as when he learns that he and a close friend have shot at each other across a ravine, each mistaking the other for an Indian. As Huntly journeys from the wilderness back to the settlement, further incidents of violence and debauchery question the conventional association of rural landscape with happiness and virtue.

The most popular and influential frontier adventure novels were Cooper's Leatherstocking series: *The Pioneers* (1823), *The Last of the Mohicans* (1826), *The Prairie* (1827), *The Pathfinder* (1840), and *The Deerslayer* (1841).[c] Although these

b On Brown's concern with judgment and psychological experience, see Bryan Waterman, chapter 3, "Charles Brockden Brown and the novels of the early republic," 55–61. On the importation of European paradigms, see Paul Giles, chapter 1, "Transatlantic currents and the invention of the American novel," 31–34, and Waterman, chapter 3, 53–54.

c The frontier adventure became the most popular American form of the historical novel. As Winfried Fluck argues in chapter 7, "The nineteenth-century historical novel," *Pioneers* was crucial in the Americanization of historical fiction; see 127–129. On the Leatherstocking novels' ideology of frontier violence, see Stephanie LeMenager, chapter 31, "Imagining the frontier," 518–520.

came to be understood, in retrospect, as presenting a national narrative, they originated in a distinctly local narrative of agricultural transformation.[9] In *The Pioneers*, a historical novel set in 1793–1794 and based on the founding of Cooperstown, Cooper introduced the character of Natty Bumppo, a hunter who is displaced westward by agricultural settlement. With the exception of *The Prairie*, which (implausibly) finds Natty working as a fur trapper on the Platte River, the Leatherstocking novels are set in upstate New York and northwestern New England, a terrain Cooper knew well and could deploy to thematic advantage. In none of the subsequent Leatherstocking novels, however, did Cooper return significantly to *The Pioneers'* motivating theme of the agricultural transformation of wilderness (though he did return to it in other novels, such as the Littlepage trilogy). In *The Pioneers*, Natty decries the clearings and "betterments" that drive away the game, depriving him of his livelihood as a market hunter. His description of a landscape scene in the Catskill Mountains, which displays "the ordering of God's Providence" untouched by the "hand of man," anticipates Thomas Cole's adaptation of picturesque aesthetic theory to the upstate New York landscape, identifying a setting that Cole would in fact paint several times, as for example in *Falls of the Kaaterskill* (1826). In a trans-media doublecross, Cole subsequently devoted several canvases to scenes from *Last of the Mohicans*. In these, the first painterly illustrations of an American novel, mountain and forest scenery overwhelms the human action such that the landscape appears as the primary subject.

In Cooper's aesthetic progression through the Leatherstocking series, the English modernist D. H. Lawrence observed "a decrescendo of reality, and a crescendo of beauty."[10] Cooper's landscape aesthetic changed partly as the result of travels in Europe. His later novels value either settled agricultural landscapes or pure natural spaces within the wilderness, such as Lake Glimmerglass of *Deerslayer* or the forest clearings of *Pathfinder*, but they show increasing uneasiness in transitional landscapes. Distaste for the "disfigured" landscapes of the early stages of agricultural transformation is evident, for example, in *Satanstoe* (1845), the first novel of the Littlepage trilogy centering on the Anti-Rent Wars in New York State, and is elaborated in the second, *The Chainbearer* (1845), where Cooper asserts that "lovers of the picturesque" would find "little satisfaction" in the scenery of "a new country," the first settlers "having done so much to mar the beauties of nature, without having yet had time to supply the deficiencies by those of art." Cooper associates such liminal landscapes with unsettling political potential. They require both aesthetic and political-economic consolidation, as General Littlepage remarks in *Chainbearer*: "Nothing contributes so much to the civilization of a country as to dot it with a gentry." In *The Pioneers*, Judge Temple had checked the first-wave settlers' egalitarian impulses. Backwoods squatting in *Chainbearer* and anti-rent agitation in *Redskins* (1846), the third of the Littlepage trilogy, appear as dangerous instances of the lower classes' infringement on the property rights of the owning class. In *Redskins*, property in large holdings is said to be "associated with all the higher feelings of humanity." Cooper's later novels thus consolidate an ideology of the picturesque in which visual possession and aesthetic appreciation of the prospect view is correlated with rightful legal-economic possession of the land.[11]

Framed as the pre-history of agricultural transformation, the frontier setting implied, even when it did not explicitly address, questions of landscape aesthetics. Robert Montgomery Bird's *Nick of the Woods* (1837), for example, opens proleptically with a quick sketch of the "flood" of emigration to Kentucky in the 1790s – including a critique of John Filson's Edenic rendering of the landscape in his narrative of Daniel Boone's exploits, *The Discovery, Settlement, and Present State of Kentucke* (1784)– before settling into its account of Indian warfare in the 1780s. Bird, an accomplished amateur watercolorist whose landscapes harmoniously integrate culture with nature, occasionally punctuates *Nick* with jarring prolepses, as when Nathan "plunged with his companion into a maze of brake and forest; neither of them then dreaming that upon the very spot where they toiled through the tangled labyrinths, a few years should behold the magic spectacle of a fair city, the Queen of the West" (i.e., Cincinnati).[12] Such oscillation between wild and cultivated landscapes had large cultural resonance, famously treated visually in Cole's *The Oxbow* (1836). Here the composition strictly divides rugged hillside terrain from the neat farms of the Connecticut River valley below, providing no narrative of the transition between wild and cultivated states. Like the later Cooper and Cole, Bird avoids messy, transitional landscapes; unlike them, he evokes little nostalgia for the wilderness.

Novels of agrarian transformation focused on the liminal settings that Cooper and Cole found disconcerting, drawing out two larger cultural narratives that often remained only implicit in the wilderness adventure: the pastoral retreat and the progress of civilization through stages. The pastoral retreat imagined the restorative power of a "middle landscape" between unfriendly wilderness and stifling urban or European environments.[13] Even in its specifically American form, the pastoral mode carried assumptions of class hierarchy from its English antecedents. These assumptions interacted with the history of settlement on the ground, as understood according to a

1 Asher B. Durand's *Progress (The Advance of Civilization)* (1853).

second narrative, stadialist cultural theory. Developed by French and Scottish Enlightenment philosophers, stadialist (stage-wise) theory described the progress of civilization through distinct socio-economic stages, from a savage state through herding and farming to a culmination in metropolitan commercial culture – although some, such as Thomas Jefferson, thought that metropolitan commercial culture represented regression rather than progress.[14] Stadialist theory could be grafted onto classical republican pessimism (such as Jefferson's) concerning the inevitability of corruption, as for example in Cole's allegorical series of landscape paintings, *The Course of Empire* (1834–1836).[15] When applied to westering American settlement, stadialism translated temporal progress into spatial form. This spatialization of history is evident, for example, in Asher Durand's reworking of the compositional form of Cole's *Oxbow* in an expansive painting entitled *Progress (The Advance of Civilization)* (1853). Here, intermediary stages of culture – from log cabin in the foreground to steamboats and city shining in the distance – supply and extend the narrative of landscape transformation that is elided in the two halves of Cole's canvas.[16]

Pastoralism and stadialism both addressed issues of race and class and the disposition of labor confronting expansionist nationalism, especially as manifested in the agricultural transformation of wilderness.[d] The presence of indigenous Americans of course frustrated expansionist nationalism. In the frontier setting, the stadialist idea of cultural progress implied the narrative of the vanishing Indian, a recurrent theme in Cooper's Leatherstocking series and other wilderness adventures (and discussed in more detail in this volume by Sandra Gustafson).[e] The idea of the vanishing Indian subsumed local, tribal specificity within an overarching national narrative, so that Cooper's account of English and French settlers' relations with Lenape and Iroquois in *Last of the Mohicans*, for example, could be taken to represent white America's relation to all indigenous peoples – although perhaps even Cooper himself wondered about this synecdoche, since in *The Prairie* he replayed *Mohicans'* dynamic of settler culture's interaction with two mutually hostile peoples (this time, Sioux and Pawnee). The narrative of the vanishing Indian persisted, as a dichotomous choice of "civilization or extinction," even in writers with a primarily northeastern cultural orientation such as Catharine Sedgwick, Lydia Maria Child, Nathaniel Hawthorne, and Herman Melville, and even when material evidence went against the analogy, as in the case of the removal of the Cherokees and other "civilized" indigenous nations from their home lands in the southeastern United States.[17]

In terms of class – that is, the organization of labor within the white settler culture – stadialism had interacted with another Enlightenment cultural theory, environmental determinism, to map regional and class differences as early as J. Hector St. John de Crèvecoeur's *Letters from an American Farmer* (1782).[18] Where stadialism identified the commercial culture of the middle-Atlantic seaboard as the height of civilization, an early pastoral novel such as Gilbert Imlay's *The Emigrants* (1793) countered by imagining an agricultural utopia in the trans-Appalachian west, whose hierarchical social structure and grid-like ordering of the land are alike evident in the elevated prospect of Captain Arl–ton's landscape aesthetic. Subsequent novels of agricultural transformation would interweave the assumptions of class hierarchy inherited from pastoral's European antecedents, as evident in *The Emigrants*, with Crèvecoeur's and Cooper's uneasiness regarding first-wave settlers.

d Stadialism and pastoralism can thus be understood, in terms of Le Menager's analysis of frontier discourse, as narrative strategies by which Americans evaded the hard facts of the frontier; see chapter 31, 515–516.

e Gustafson argues in "Cooper and the idea of the Indian" that although Cooper failed to imagine a successful resolution to the conflict between Euro-American imperial expansion and traditional Native American life, he nevertheless explored numerous options for race relations; see chapter 6, 109–115.

The organization of the rural class structure is a primary theme of Caroline Kirkland's important novel of agricultural transformation, *A New Home – Who'll Follow?* (1839), set during the Michigan land boom of the 1830s. Kirkland negotiates class tensions through humor, finding amusement in the first-wave settlers' egalitarian practices such as their indiscriminate borrowing. Beneath the humor, the stadialist narrative of cultural progress reassures Kirkland's middle-class readers. The most "vicious and degraded" of the first-wave settlers are displaced by well-off farmers or speculators who take over and improve on the landscape transformations wrought by the first settlers, employing tenants or landless laborers to work the land.

Confirming Kirkland's narrative of cultural progress and the sorting out of the rural class structure, women novelists developed a domestic-pastoral tradition, sending characters out to already transformed western landscapes, as for example E. D. E. N. Southworth's *India: The Pearl of Pearl River* (1856) or Maria Cummins's *Mabel Vaughan* (1857).[19] The point-of-view and stylistic register of such novels is identified with the genteel northeast, the source of economic and cultural capital, while other landscapes and settler cultures provide explicit counterpoints in the identification of regional particularities. A deeper understanding of the cultural history embedded in landscape is evident in Alice Cary's *Clovernook* sketches (two volumes, 1852 and 1853), the first western fiction written by a native Westerner. The narrative perspective, that of a woman recollecting girlhood experiences, deliberately disavows omniscience to concentrate on the framing of particular incidents and views. Presented as a set of sketches, these close observations nonetheless interweave several narrative lines to form a novelistic account of the transformation of the Cincinnati environs from the earliest permanent white settlement (whose traces are evident in a few log cabins that still dot the region's landscape) through capital-intensive, market-oriented agriculture (with its accompanying refinements in architecture and consumer goods) to urbanization. Throughout *Clovernook*, the increasing differentiation of landscape correlates to an increasingly differentiated class structure. As Cary observes, "the lines which divide rusticity from the affluent life in country places, or the experience of the middle classes in towns, are very sharply defined," and even among the "rustics" exist numerous fine divisions. While Cary addresses the same cultural narrative as does Kirkland – the "improvement" of both landscape and manners driven by the input of eastern capital and the extraction of western resources – her capacity for empathy with a range of class positions provides a greater critical understanding of the interaction of human culture and landscape form. Moreover, Cary's attention to landscape transformation anticipates deeper engagements with environmental history in later rural novels such as Willa Cather's *O Pioneers!* (1913) and *My Ántonia* (1918) and William Faulkner's *Go Down, Moses* (1942), and even in the ecofiction of the 1960s and following (which is discussed by Jonathan Levin later in this volume).[f]

In the South, where the class structure was defined by slavery, the shaping of the landscape through a long history of slave labor was variably evident in artistic productions.[20] During the early antebellum era, landscape paintings commissioned by wealthy planters to display their estates usually excluded any depiction of slaves, but as sectionalist tensions increased in the 1850s, apologists presented pleasant rural scenes depicting slavery as a benevolent institution. Harriet Beecher Stowe's abolitionist novel *Uncle Tom's Cabin* (1852) takes this pro-slavery landscape as its point of departure. On the Shelby farm in Kentucky, slavery appears in relatively benign form, amenable to treatment by a genre painter such as Eastman Johnson, who painted scenes from *Uncle Tom's Cabin* before turning to his most famous work, *Old Kentucky Home (Negro Life at the South)* (1859).[21] The landscapes in *Uncle Tom's Cabin* become more ominous as the narrative moves southward, following a conventional picturesque correlation of landscape form and moral quality. Tom is carried on a "middle passage" up the Red River, through "dreary pine barrens" and "long cypress swamps, the doleful trees rising out of the slimy, spongy ground, hung with long wreaths of funeral black moss," to Simon Legree's plantation, one of "the dark places of the earth."

A swamp such as the one surrounding Legree's plantation is a prevalent and distinctive topographical feature of the plantation novel. Imagined as the other of the manor house, the swamp tested the bounds of the conventional picturesque aesthetic, bearing variable historical resonances and moral-political connotations.[22] In William Gilmore Simms's writings on the Revolutionary War in South Carolina (which include eight novels and an 1844 biography of Southern Revolutionary War commander Francis Marion), the swamp setting is associated with liberty, but ambivalently so. Providing places of refuge for guerrilla brigades commanded by the "Swamp Fox" Marion and other partisans, swamps are also the haunts of ruffians, such as "Hell-Fire Dick" in *The Forayers* (1855) or the squatter Bostwick in *Woodcraft* (1852). As a pro-slavery apologist during the increasing sectionalism of the 1850s, Simms comments further on the association of wilderness with liberty by twisting the prominent

f As Levin details, ecofiction emerged in the context of the new environmental awareness of the 1960s and 1970s ("Contemporary ecofiction," chapter 68).

cultural image of the fugitive slave in the swamp: Captain Porgy hides his slaves in a swamp to prevent them from being confiscated for debt repayment.[g] Taking up this setting in *Dred* (1856), Stowe developed the picturesque correlation of landscape form and moral quality she had begun to explore in *Uncle Tom's Cabin*.[h] Son of frustrated slave rebel Denmark Vesey, the title character had escaped to the Great Dismal Swamp at age fourteen and has lived there ever since, becoming the leader of a maroon community.[23] The swamp imagery interweaves two lines of landscape tradition, one in which raw nature invites cultivation, and another in which pure nature connotes liberty.

Novels set in the long-settled landscapes of the northeast drew variously on the narrative of pastoral retreat, while engaging with the picturesque's moral correlation of culture and nature. An important development in this regard was aesthetic tourism, as for example the Hudson River to Niagara route, which became popular with the fashionable elite and their middle-class emulators after the completion of the Erie Canal in 1825.[24] Aesthetic conventions were disseminated via travel books, often illustrated with landscape scenes, such as Nathaniel Parker Willis's *American Scenery* (1840). Especially in sentimental novels, touristic episodes often addressed the moral dimension of the picturesque aesthetic, using a character's sensitivity to landscape beauty to indicate a capacity for qualities such as piety, sympathy, taste, and refinement.[i] In Maria Cummins's *The Lamplighter* (1854), for example, a mountaintop view near Saratoga Springs marks a key stage in the heroine's growth: reflecting on her unhappy childhood, Gerty responds to luminist imagery as a sign of divine presence and, moreover, enacts sympathy in teaching this response to others: "the light shines brightly above the clouds."

Rebecca Harding Davis's depiction of an industrial landscape in *Life in the Iron-Mills* (magazine publication, 1861) added new intensity to the conventional pastoral contrast between country and city. Anticipating explorations of environmental determinism by naturalist writers such as

g As Jennifer Greeson observes in "Imagining the South," chapter 14 in this volume, Simms's sectionalism played out in surprising ways in his Revolutionary War novels, which concentrate not on triumphalist narratives but rather on British tyranny and threats to patriots; see 245–246.

h In writing *Dred*, Stowe may have been responding as much or more to African American criticisms of *Uncle Tom's Cabin* as to "anti-Tom" plantation novels; see John Ernest, "Stowe, race, and the antebellum American novel," chapter 15, 264 in this volume.

i On the sentimental novel's focus on women's emotional lives, see Cindy Weinstein, "Sentimentalism," chapter 12.

Stephen Crane, Frank Norris, or Jack London,[j] Davis opens on a view of the iron mills of Wheeling, Virginia, with a description that registers the constraints on workers' lives: "the sky sank down before dawn, muddy, flat, immovable." Illuminated by the glowing furnaces at night, the same scene appears "picturesque" to middle-class travelers who view it with an "artist's eye," but "looks like t' Devil's place" to the workers. Characterizing the protagonist Hugh, a Welsh iron puddler, as a natural artistic genius whose development is blocked by class barriers, Davis further thematizes the moral correlations of visual aesthetics. Although Hugh's attempt to realize his freedom ends tragically, a companion does escape to a rural setting, a Quaker farm "overlook[ing] broad, wooded slopes and clover-crimsoned meadows," above which appears a luminist cloudscape "where, in the flickering, nebulous crimson, God has set the promise of the Dawn."

In *Pierre* (1852), Herman Melville developed critical responses to the conventions of the pastoral retreat, the picturesque aesthetic, and the trope of landscape as moral correlative. The opening paragraph's promise of a "green and golden world" of rural "repose" dissipates as Melville restores the historical associations often obliterated by the visual presentism of pastoral and picturesque. Revisiting the setting of Cooper's Littlepage trilogy, the manorial holdings of upstate New York, Melville traces an aristocratic family's unbroken land tenure from the bloody Indian wars of the colonial era to the impoverished tenantry and anti-rent strikes of the 1840s, while revealing a genealogy in which the hero Pierre is drawn to a pretended marriage with a woman whom he believes to be his illegitimate half-sister. Pierre's embrace of this flawed genealogy compels him to reverse the pastoral retreat's conventional trajectory in a flight to the labyrinthine urban wilderness of New York City. As in the ambiguous correlation of landscape forms with mental states in Brown's *Edgar Huntly*, Pierre experiences the urban labyrinth as both environment and moral compass.[25] Disconnected from landed income, he struggles unsuccessfully to make a living as a writer. Reflecting on his titanic struggle, he returns in memory to a prominent landscape feature of his ancestral holdings: a prototypically picturesque scene of flower-dotted fields surrounding the "beautiful, but not entirely inaccessible-looking purple precipice" of the Mount of the Titans becomes, on closer view, a weed-choked waste

j See Donna Campbell's account of "classic naturalism" in "The rise of naturalism," chapter 30, 502–506.

fronting a forbidding summit ravaged by rock slides: "Stark desolation; ruin, merciless and ceaseless; chills and gloom, – all here lived a hidden life, curtained by that cunning purpleness, which, from the piazza of the manor house, so beautifully invested the mountain." Delineating a contrast between distant and close views so as to play with the picturesque's capacity for moral correlation (as investigated, for example, by Brown, Stowe, Cummins, or Davis) and the convention of the prospect view as inviting possession (as developed, for example, by Cooper), Melville thus critiques the Hudson River school aesthetic on its home ground.

Novelistic accounts of travel following Euro-American imperial encroachment beyond North America extended pastoral tropes to exotic landscapes.[k] Edgar Allan Poe's *Narrative of Arthur Gordon Pym* (1838), for example, drawing on the travel-hoax *Symzonia* (1820) as well as factual accounts of voyages by Captain James Cook and others, depicted a highly organized natural world inhabited by a savage human culture. In the South Sea environment of Poe's imagination, the color palette becomes increasingly monochromatic as latitude approaches the pole. Contrasting with Poe's black and white allegory are Melville's ambiguous accounts of south Pacific islands in *Typee* (1846) and *Omoo* (1847), drawn from first-hand experience as a sailor on whaling ships that used the islands as supply bases.[l] Melville anatomizes Polynesian cultures whose food seems to emerge spontaneously from the landscape without labor, but who also have a history of cannibalism. As colonial production alters the inhabitants' relation to the landscape, native abundance turns to want, suggesting a narrative of the vanishing indigene parallel to that of the vanishing Indian of North America.

In order for painters or novelists to present any landscape as raw wilderness awaiting cultivation, they had to remove the indigenous inhabitants, imaginatively if not literally – enacting, as in Cooper's *Last of the Mohicans*, a proleptic nostalgia for the vanishing Indian. In some cases, another pattern of removal might follow, erasing traces of labor in the presentation of a settled agrarian landscape, a suburb, a city, or even an industrial complex, as the natural state of the landscape. In the novel's narrative structure, however, lay the capacity to understand any landscape as an embodiment of human history.

k On the American novel's imperial engagements, see Russ Castronovo, "Imperialism, Orientalism, and empire," chapter 32 in this volume, especially 539–542.

l On the genealogy of the American maritime novel, including sources in nonfiction narrative, see Hester Blum, "Melville and the novel of the sea," chapter 9, 151–155.

Notes

1. On the celebration of divinity in wilderness, see Barbara Novak, *Nature and Culture: American Landscape and Painting, 1825–1875* (New York: Oxford University Press, 1980). On the development of synecdochic nationalism, see Angela Miller, *The Empire of the Eye: Landscape Representation and American Cultural Politics, 1825–1875* (Ithaca, NY: Cornell University Press, 1993).
2. See Perry Miller, "The Romantic Dilemma in American Nationalism and the Concept of Nature," in *Nature's Nation* (Cambridge, MA: Harvard University Press, 1967), 197–207.
3. Quotations from George Perkins, ed., *The Theory of the American Novel* (New York: Holt, Rinehart, and Winston, 1970), 17, 64, 7, 41; Richard Ruland, ed., *The Native Muse: Theories of American Literature from Bradford to Whitman* (New York: Dutton, 1976), 333, 336.
4. On the novel's absorptive tendencies, see M. M. Bakhtin, "Discourse in the Novel," in *The Dialogic Imagination*, trans. Caryl Emerson and Michael Holquist (Austin: University of Texas Press, 1981), 259–422. On the interaction of culture and natural environment in literature, see Raymond Williams, *The Country and the City* (New York: Oxford University Press, 1975); Timothy Sweet, *American Georgics: Economy and Environment in Early American Literature* (Philadelphia: University of Pennsylvania Press, 2002).
5. For a regionalist approach to American genre painting, see Elizabeth Johns, *American Genre Painting: The Politics of Everyday Life* (New Haven: Yale University Press, 1991). In the present volume, Tom Lutz contends that a regionalist sensibility has been perhaps the central form of American literary representation (chapter 26, "Cather and the regional imagination").
6. This sense of the term "chronotope" (literally, time–space) is a geographically oriented adaptation of Bakhtin's sense of the term; see "Forms of Time and of the Chronotope in the Novel," in *The Dialogic Imagination*, 84–258. Here "chronotope" captures the sense of a typical configuration of landscape at a particular historical moment.
7. On Brown's landscape aesthetics, see Dennis Berthold, "Charles Brockden Brown, *Edgar Huntly*, and the Origins of the American Picturesque," *William and Mary Quarterly* 41 (1984): 62–84.
8. The Lenape had been dispossessed of enormous tracts of land by the fraudulent "Walking Purchase" of 1737 and the Easton Conference treaty of 1758. On Brown's allusions to the history of Lenape dispossession, see Sydney J. Krause, "Penn's Elm and *Edgar Huntly*: Dark 'Instruction to the Heart,'" *American Literature* 66 (1994): 463–484. John Carlos Rowe's chapter in the present volume locates *Huntly* within the racialized context of American wars for empire (chapter 49, "US novels and US wars," 814–815).
9. On Cooper and national narrative, see Jonathan Arac, *The Emergence of American Literary Narrative, 1820–1860* (Cambridge, MA: Harvard University Press, 2005), 5–16.

10. D. H. Lawrence, *Studies in Classic American Literature* (1923; New York: Viking, 1964), 50.
11. On the development of this ideology, see Albert Boime, *The Magisterial Gaze: Manifest Destiny and American Landscape Painting, c. 1830–1865* (Washington, DC: Smithsonian Institution Press, 1991).
12. Reproductions of Bird's watercolors are on view at www.library.upenn.edu/exhibits/rbm/bird/.
13. On the "middle landscape" ideal, see Leo Marx, *The Machine in the Garden: Technology and the Pastoral Ideal in America* (New York: Oxford University Press, 1964), 34–144.
14. Jefferson expressed this view, for example, in a famous paean to agrarian culture in Query XIX of *Notes on the State of Virginia* (1785). On stadialism, see Henry Nash Smith, *Virgin Land: The American West as Symbol and Myth* (Cambridge, MA: Harvard University Press, 1950), 211–224; George Dekker, *The American Historical Romance* (Cambridge: Cambridge University Press, 1987), 84–96.
15. On republican political theory, see J. G. A. Pocock, *The Machiavellian Moment: Political Thought and the Atlantic Republican Tradition* (Princeton: Princeton University Press, 1975).
16. On the painterly narration of agrarian transformation by the generation following Cole, see Miller, *Empire of the Eye*, 137–165.
17. On the "vanishing Indian" narrative, see Roy Harvey Pearce, *The Savages of America: A Study of the Indian and the Idea of Civilization* (Baltimore: Johns Hopkins University Press, 1965). On the "civilization or extinction" dichotomy in Sedgwick, Melville, Hawthorne, and others, see Lucy Maddox, *Removals: Nineteenth-Century American Literature and the Politics of Indian Affairs* (New York: Oxford University Press, 1991).
18. On the environmental determinism debate, see Antonello Gerbi, *The Dispute of the New World: The History of a Polemic, 1750–1900*, trans. Jeremy Moyle (Pittsburgh: University of Pittsburgh Press, 1973). The antebellum novel's engagement with issues of class continues to receive scant critical attention; see, however, Amy Schrager Lang, *The Syntax of Class: Writing Inequality in Nineteenth-Century America* (Princeton: Princeton University Press, 2003).
19. On westering, domestic-pastoral novels, see Annette Kolodny, *The Land Before Her: Fantasy and Experience of the American Frontiers, 1630–1860* (Chapel Hill: University of North Carolina Press, 1984), 159–226.
20. Lewis Simpson identifies the accommodation of slavery to the pastoral ideal as the defining problem of Southern literature in *The Dispossessed Garden: Pastoral and History in Southern Literature* (Athens: University of Georgia Press, 1975). On Southern landscape painting, see John Michael Vlach, *The Planter's Prospect: Privilege and Slavery in Plantation Paintings* (Chapel Hill: University of North Carolina Press, 2002); Angela D. Mack and Stephen G. Hoffius, eds., *Landscape of Slavery: The Plantation in American Art* (Columbia: University of South Carolina Press, 2008).

21. On Johnson's paintings of slave life, see Johns, *American Genre Painting*, 127–35; Mack and Hoffius, *Landscape of Slavery*, 105–09.
22. On the swamp's aesthetic values and cultural associations, see David C. Miller, *Dark Eden: The Swamp in Nineteenth-Century American Culture* (Cambridge: Cambridge University Press, 1989); Anthony Wilson, *Shadow and Shelter: The Swamp in Southern Culture* (Jackson: University of Mississippi Press, 2006), 3–61; M. Allewaert, "Swamp Sublime: Ecologies of Resistance in the American Plantation Zone," *PMLA* 123 (2008): 340–357.
23. Maroons (from the French *marron*, fugitive) were runaway slaves who lived independently in marginal areas such as mountains or jungles. Among Stowe's sources on the maroon community of the Great Dismal Swamp was W. C. Nell's *Colored Patriots of the American Revolution* (1855); see Robert S. Levine, Introduction, in Harriet Beecher Stowe, *Dred* (Chapel Hill: University of North Carolina Press, 2000), xxi.
24. On landscape aesthetics and the growth of tourism, see John F. Sears, *Sacred Places: American Tourist Attractions in the Nineteenth Century* (New York: Oxford University Press, 1989).
25. On *Pierre* in the context of antebellum landscape aesthetics, see Samuel Otter, *Melville's Anatomies* (Berkeley: University of California Press, 1999), 172–207. On the labyrinth form in *Pierre*, see Wyn Kelley, *Melville's City: Literary and Urban Form in Nineteenth-Century New York* (Cambridge: Cambridge University Press, 1996), 145–161.

6
Cooper and the idea of the Indian

SANDRA M. GUSTAFSON

A map of North America first published in 1715 shows a continent where European settlements intermingle with indigenous powers.[1] Running down the eastern seaboard, and bounded by the Sea of the British Empire (that is, the Atlantic Ocean), are the colonies of New England, New York, Virginia, and the Carolinas. Iroquois country is west of New York. Further west, large territories bear the names of New France and Louisiana, while to the west and south lay New Mexico, New Spain, and "Apaches de Navaio." A region identified as New Britain or Eskimaux lies to the north. Interspersed with the larger colonial and native powers are some smaller territories and less familiar place names. New Denmark and New Ultra appear at the upper edge of the map on Buttons Bay, just north of New North Wales and northeast of "The Bogs Morasses & Lakes of the Assinopovals." The "Kikapous" and other tribes of the northern plains appear west of the Great Lakes. "Ilinese" country separates New France from Louisiana, while New Scotland divides New Foundland from New England. The region of northern California claimed by Francis Drake in 1578 is identified as New Albion, while California itself appears as a large island separated from the mainland by the Gulf of California and the Red Sea. East of the Gulf of California, and immediately north of Apaches de Navaio, is "Great Teguia." Still further north and merging into "Parts Unknown" is "Mozeemleck Country," based on a description from the Baron Lahontan, and said to include "many villages." This is an image of North America as a mixture of the familiar, the less familiar, the unknown, and the fantastic. It is a cosmopolitan terrain that calls for new forms of knowledge and representation.

In his eleven Indian-themed novels James Fenimore Cooper created a fictional analogue to the cosmopolitan world portrayed in Herman Moll's map. As Cooper considered the moral challenges that his characters face in confronting their world, he developed an approach that shares important emphases with the philosopher Kwame Anthony Appiah's ethic of rooted cosmopolitanism. Appiah suggests that the ethical requirements of modernity are best met by promoting an ideal that combines a sense of place and tradition derived from one's own background (rootedness) with a commitment to engage people from other societies in mutually respectful dialogue (cosmopolitan conversation).[2] Cooper's rootedness displayed itself in two ways: in his devotion to Cooperstown and the upstate New York region where he grew up; and in his well-known American nationalism, which rested on his belief that the modern republic was the best available political form, embodied in the United States Constitution and in the native societies of North America. His cosmopolitanism was initially fostered by his childhood experiences in a region peppered with Iroquois towns, villages of Christian Indians who were refugees from New England, and hamlets such as Cooperstown where migrants of different religions and national backgrounds commingled. It was further nurtured by his early years as a sailor, developing additional dimensions when, after establishing himself as a writer, he lived and traveled extensively in Europe from 1826 to 1833. Already in his early fiction Cooper had manifested a comparative approach and an interest in cultural difference, and these aspects of his work were further stimulated by his European travels.[3]

The world of Cooper's Indian novels is one where difference is the norm and strategies for managing difference are a persistent central concern. Cooper explores the elaborate struggles for power and efforts at coexistence pursued by indigenous communities and European settler communities, and he offers a variety of approaches to the elaborate reality depicted on Moll's map, including warfare and conquest, intermarriage, friendship, conversation and deliberation, habit and tradition, and religious conversion. He portrays conflicts between European settlers and indigenous Americans that parallel relationships between members of competing European colonial powers, between representatives of rival native powers, and between Native Americans and African Americans. The novels set before the Revolution show a world like Moll's map, overwritten with dense affiliations and rivalries between indigenous Americans, ethnic Europeans, and creole Americans. Cooper's novels with post-Revolutionary settings reveal a nation that is the heir of this cosmopolitan world.

No single Cooper novel captures the full range of his representations of Indians or reveals all the dimensions of his cosmopolitan worldview, for his project was neither simple nor static. Cooper typically explored basic social conflicts using his fictions as laboratories to test out different approaches and try out a range of perspectives. He wrote problem novels, often returning to an issue over the course of several works to regard it from another angle or develop it more fully. *The Oak Openings* (1848) is no more Cooper's definitive word on the Indian because it is his last Indian novel than *The Pioneers* (1823) is definitive because it was his first such novel or *The Last of the Mohicans* (1826) is definitive because it was his most popular work.

Cooper has frequently been treated as a proponent of a view that Roy Harvey Pearce influentially described as "savagism," that is, a belief that indigenous American life was destined to be overwhelmed and replaced by white civilization. Pearce found in Cooper a foundational rendering of this belief system. According to Pearce, Cooper drew upon views of native society that were widely held by white Americans, who defined the savage "in terms of the ideas and needs of civilized life." Later Pearce writes that "all Cooper's Indian stories are civilized fictions in which the Indian is imaged as a measure of the noncivilized and is made to die as both Chingachgook and Leatherstocking have died."[4] Pearce's first claim here is only partly true, and his second claim is simply inaccurate. Many of Cooper's Indian characters survive past the end of his novels, sometimes even getting the last word, as Old Peter does in Cooper's final Indian tale, *The Oak Openings*. Despite its inaccuracies and partial readings, this approach to Cooper's Indian novels informs a longstanding tradition of Cooper criticism that includes such influential works as D. H. Lawrence's *Studies in Classic American Literature* (1923), Leslie A. Fiedler's *Love and Death in the American Novel* (1960), and Richard Slotkin's *Regeneration through Violence* (1973). In *Empire and Slavery in American Literature, 1820–1865* (2006), Eric J. Sundquist offers a historicized version of this approach, arguing that Cooper fictionalized a view that was embodied in a wide variety of forms and disciplines, including the ethnography of Henry Rowe Schoolcraft; the histories of Thomas McKenney; and the poetry of Henry Wadsworth Longfellow. The approach that predominates in these works understands "American Indians as a people who belonged to a passing phase of human development, destined to die out if they remained unable to accept acculturation into the new nation."[5] Readings like these treat Cooper's Indian novels as an ideological justification for Jacksonian America's most pernicious tendencies: racial purity and Indian Removal.[a]

Such ideological readings do some justice to Indian-themed novels that predate Cooper, such as Charles Brockden Brown's *Edgar Huntly* (1799), where the Indian characters exist more symbolically than actually; or John Neal's

a The pervasiveness of this approach is clear from the examples of it in this volume, including the treatments of Cooper in essays by Winfried Fluck (chapter 7), Stephanie Le Menager (chapter 31), and Russ Castronovo (chapter 32).

Logan (1822), which portrays an exceptionally complicated interracial animosity that ends with the deaths of all the major characters.[6] This approach does not work so well with Cooper, at whose feet the whole history of literary savagism has sometimes been placed. Cooper certainly believed that Native American life as it had developed prior to European conquest and settlement was coming to an end, and his Indian novels examine the ethical dilemmas posed by this prospect. He sometimes describes the probable outcome as the triumph of white civilization over red savagism. A passage such as this one, from Cooper's 1832 Paris introduction to *The Prairie* (1827), seems to support Pearce's and Sundquist's contentions about Cooper's fiction: "The Great Prairies appear to be the final gathering place of the red men. The remnants of the Mohicans, and the Delawares, of the Creeks, Choctaws, and Cherokees, are destined to fulfill their time on these vast plains. The entire number of the Indians, within the Union, is differently computed, at between one and five hundred thousand souls." Here Cooper is in part engaging in an end-time scenario for the indigenous peoples of the United States, but his language does not foreclose other possibilities. The passage immediately follows his description of the Great Prairies as a "comparative desert" presenting "a barrier to the progress of the American people westward." Moreover his travels in Europe, where he wrote this introduction, heightened his skepticism regarding linear progressive histories and alerted him to the idea that ethnic minorities and nomadic peoples could survive and even flourish in the presence of dominant settler cultures.[7]

The chronology of Cooper's fictions offers important insights into his method. Of the eleven novels that Cooper wrote with prominent Indian characters and Indian-related themes, five were set in the thirty-five-year period of imperial warfare that began around 1740 and ended with the American Revolution. These novels depict a world of elaborate and shifting alliances and rivalries. They include three of the Leatherstocking Tales: *The Last of the Mohicans* (1826) is set in 1757; *The Pathfinder; or, The Inland Sea* (1840) takes place in the late 1750s; and the events of *The Deerslayer; or, The First War-Path* (1841) occur from 1740 to 1745. The main events of *Satanstoe; or, The Littlepage Manuscripts: A Tale of the Colony* (1845), the first novel in Cooper's anti-rent trilogy that examines political conflicts over property rights, occur soon after the massacre at Fort William Henry depicted in *The Last of the Mohicans*, during the imperial conflict on the New York frontier. And *Wyandotté: or, The Hutted Knoll* (1843) portrays the consequences for a New York settlement of the Revolutionary events of 1775 and 1776. Five further novels explore the post-Revolutionary years up through 1848, when Cooper published his last Indian novel, *The Oak Openings; or, The Bee-Hunter* (1848), set on the Michigan frontier. *The Pioneers; or, The Sources of the Susquehanna* (1823), which introduced Natty Bumppo as a relict of an earlier era and launched the Leatherstocking series, is set in the 1790s, while Natty's death in *The Prairie: A Tale* (1827) takes place on the plains as the United States underwent its first dramatic period of expansion following the Louisiana Purchase. The novels set in the post-Revolutionary period also include *The Chainbearer; or The Littlepage Manuscripts* (1845), which occurs during the years following independence; and *The Redskins; or, Indian and Injin: Being the Conclusion of the Littlepage Manuscripts* (1846), which takes place in the early 1840s. Three of these novels are set on the plains and the remaining seven occur predominantly in New York.

Cooper wrote just one Indian tale of the seventeenth century, *The Wept of Wish-ton-Wish* (1829), which is set in western Connecticut before and during King Philip's War. The place of this novel in Cooper's *oeuvre* helps clarify his distinctive approach to the treatment of his Indian characters. In it, Cooper confronts the contested legacy of Puritanism to American race relations and establishes the deep background for the rivalries and conflicts of the Leatherstocking Tales. *The Wept of Wish-ton-Wish* portrays the early history of the Mohican nation's relations with the English colonists and establishes the background to Natty's close relationship with Chingachgook. *Wept* also explores an event (King Philip's War) and develops a theme (marriage between whites and Indians) that were central to literary writings about Native Americans during the years when Indian Removal was debated, the Indian Removal Act passed (1830), and the Cherokees and other eastern tribes forcibly moved west (1831–9). In the 1820s and 1830s, novelists including Lydia Maria Child and Catharine Maria Sedgwick, playwrights such as John Augustus Stone, poets like James Wallis Eastburn, and orators including Edward Everett and William Apess focused on this period in colonial history as a formative era that continued to shape race relations in the early American republic.

Were the Puritans the source of a high-minded progressive society, as Daniel Webster claimed in 1820? Or did they produce a Manichean worldview that demonized others, as William Apess asserted in 1836?[8] Cooper took a point of view closer to Apess's on this subject. The Yankees in his novels most often are characterized by such unattractive traits as greed, self-righteousness, or impracticality. He expressed his own form of sectional nationalism drawn from the rich history of New York State, which he presented as more respectful of varied traditions and more cosmopolitan than the New England ideal with its emphasis on purity and iconoclasm. The place of New England in Cooper's Indian novels emerges with the greatest clarity in *Wept*, which responds to the works of Child and Sedgwick. During the 1820s these two Massachusetts-based authors wrote novels examining the entwined issues of religious and racial tolerance in seventeenth-century New England by focusing on intermarriage, a controversial topic that played a prominent role in debates about the future of native America. Child's *Hobomok: A Tale of Early Times* (1824) is set in Naumkeak (later Salem) during the first years of settlement, where her heroine Mary Conant marries the warrior Hobomok in a desperate effort to escape from her virulently Puritan father. When Mary's Anglican lover Charles Brown unexpectedly returns, Hobomok relinquishes her and their son and fades into the western wilderness. The marriage of Hobomok and Mary does nothing, finally, to reduce interracial conflict. Rather, it provides a mechanism to reconcile English Protestants to one another. Hobomok's son eventually drops his Indian name and is absorbed into English society.

In *Hope Leslie; or, Early Times in Massachusetts* (1827), Sedgwick picks up temporally and thematically where *Hobomok* left off, with much of the action taking place in 1643. As is the case with Roger Conant and Corbitant in *Hobomok*, both the Puritan leader John Winthrop and the Pequot chief Mononotto elevate religious principle over humanity, and their unshakable ideological commitments help to produce a devastating cycle of attacks and counterattacks. Interracial marriage is equally unsatisfying as an alternative to conflict as in *Hobomok*, however. Neither the childless union of Hope Leslie's sister Faith with her husband Oneco nor the love between Magawisca and Everell presents a successful means to reconcile warring communities. The novel closes with the consolidation of the Puritan settlement amid reports that war has broken out between the tribes of Miantunnomoh and Uncas. So long as there is conflict between native communities, the Puritans conclude, their own communities are safe.

If we treat Child's and Sedgwick's novels as two installments in the history of Indian–white relations in Puritan New England, Cooper's *The Wept of Wish-ton-Wish* provides the third segment in this chronicle. He picks up the story where Sedgwick left it: with the aftermath of the war between Miantunnomoh and Uncas. The ongoing conflict is shaped by the religious dogmatism of the Puritan minister Meek Wolfe, who demonizes rather than reconcile the warring parties, and the more humane character of patriarch Mark Heathcote, whose experience of suffering tempers his demanding religious views. Cooper also offers a textured portrait of Miantunnomoh's son

Conanchet, who is educated by Puritans but retains his allegiances to his own people, even as he marries Heathcote's granddaughter, with whom he has a son.

Against the backdrop of King Philip's War, Conanchet is unjustly executed by Uncas (an ancestor of the character who appears in *The Last of the Mohicans*) upon the orders of Meek Wolfe, with Cooper laying the blame upon both men. His wife dies of grief, but the novel remains oddly silent about the fate of their son. Cooper does stress the significance of another lineage: the novel ends with a postscript that describes the Reverend Meek Lamb as a descendant of the Reverend Meek Wolfe, the change in name effected by "time and intermarriage," which have also affected "doctrinal interpretations of duty." New England Puritans have mellowed, Cooper suggests. This pre-history to *The Last of the Mohicans* gives roots to the alliance between Natty, Chingachgook, and Uncas and recasts the later Uncas's death as a cosmic retribution for the sins of his fathers.

Moreover the unaccounted-for offspring of Conanchet and Ruth Heathcote offers a tantalizing if undeveloped alternative to the racial politics of *The Last of the Mohicans*. When Uncas and the mixed-race Cora Munro die in the concluding chase scene of that novel, the surviving couple Alice Munro, Cora's all-Scottish half-sister, and Duncan Heyward, a creole American of pure British ancestry, seem poised to provide an all-white lineage for the United States. Read as it falls chronologically between *Hobomok* and *Hope Leslie*, *Last of the Mohicans* forms part of an all-white ideological fabric.[9] Yet this narrative of white hegemony is complicated in the very next Leatherstocking Tale. Set in 1805 in the heart of the newly acquired Louisiana Purchase, *The Prairie* features Captain Duncan Uncas Middleton, the grandson of Duncan and Alice, who has recently married the Spanish American Inez Augustin, only to lose her to the slave stealer Abiram White on the day of their wedding. Yet Inez finally reunites with her husband and they return east, where with the help of his father-in-law Middleton pursues a political career at the national level.[10] This tale of ethnic intermarriage offers a precedent for the union of Canonchet and Narra-Mattah.

The Prairie marks the end of the first phase of Cooper's Leatherstocking series, and *The Wept* was his last Indian novel for eleven years. During Cooper's hiatus from Indian fictions, two major writers produced novels on the theme. In 1835 William Gilmore Simms published *The Yemassee: A Romance of Carolina*, which resembles Cooper's New York novels in its time-period (early eighteenth century) and its main theme (struggles for possession of colonial South Carolina by the English, the Spanish, and the Yemassee). Like

Cooper, Simms registers the painful facts of colonization and Indian displacement and represents some of his Indian characters as tragically heroic.[b] Robert Montgomery Bird takes a strikingly different approach in *Nick of the Woods* (1837), which explores the psychology of Indian hating, a subject for which Cooper had little taste. While Simms extended Cooper's method, Bird picked up the uglier strain of Indian fiction represented by Neal's *Logan*.

When he returned to Natty Bumppo in the 1840s in *The Pathfinder* and *The Deerslayer*, Cooper returned as well to the terrain of upstate New York and engaged the question of interracial relations in a more philosophical vein. These novels move backward in time from *The Last of the Mohicans*, seeking the roots of the values and beliefs that animate Natty's choices in the first three novels. Marriage again factors largely in the plots. In *The Pathfinder* we see Natty in love and find out why he was rejected by the woman he would have married, and in *The Deerslayer* we see him reject a proposal from a woman who would have married him. In both cases the recipe for successful romance hinges on forms of likeness and difference that include but go beyond racial identity to encompass traits such as age, attractiveness, and virtue. In *The Pathfinder* Natty is drawn to the fresh and lovely Mabel Dunham, though he recognizes that their differences in age and education make them an ill-assorted couple. Natty repeatedly insists that "like loves like," as Mabel is drawn to Jasper Western, who more nearly matches her age, good looks, and background. In *The Deerslayer*, the youthful Natty turns down two marriage proposals in quick succession, again treating likeness as a principle guiding him in the choice of a marriage partner. His radical application of the principle results in his failure to reproduce.

Natty relaxes his stringent criteria for similitude when he forms friendships and other non-blood ties, such as adoptive relationships. D. H. Lawrence and Leslie Fiedler have famously commented on the pseudo-marriage between Natty and Chingachgook that anticipates the relationships between Ishmael and Queequeg, Huck and Jim, or the Lone Ranger and Tonto, arguing that through these relationships white creoles claim a mythic bond with nature and suppress or expiate their guilt for appropriating a continent and exploiting its inhabitants. Lawrence famously describes the tie between Natty and Chingachgook as "the nucleus of a new relationship" based upon "the stark, loveless, wordless unison of two men who have come to the bottom of

b Elsewhere in this volume, Jennifer Rae Greeson (in chapter 14, "Imagining the South," 245–246) and Winfried Fluck (in chapter 7, "The nineteenth-century historical novel," 130–131) consider the specifically Southern quality of Simms's novelistic worldview.

themselves" and out of that unison found "a new society" based on violence. Recently critics have identified more pacific possibilities in this relationship. Ivy Schweitzer considers Cooper's treatment of the friendship between Natty and Chingachgook as a model affiliation with implications for civic life. Building on Schweitzer's work, Dana Nelson has claimed that through his depiction of this friendship Cooper explored "alternative civic possibilities for white America" and suggests that in this portrait of "passionate interracial feeling" Cooper modeled a relationship that "served as the basis for some of the most radical ideals and actions of black and white male abolitionists in the 1840s and 1850s."[11]

These interracial friendships develop through cosmopolitan conversations, which Cooper presents as an idealized form of deliberation.[12] Rather than "wordless," the interactions between Chingachgook and Natty frequently involve extended discussion. These deliberations may involve practical matters, such as deciding on a course of action. Occasionally they take a more philosophical direction, as in the early scene in *The Last of the Mohicans* where the reader first encounters the pair on the bank of a stream debating the relative brutality of the European conquest of Indian tribes compared to the conquest of tribes by one another. Natty insists that there is a moral equivalence between these types of imperial domination, but Chingachgook disagrees emphatically and at length. Natty listens carefully to Chingachgook's arguments, and in the end he is persuaded to his friend's point of view. This scene contrasts with the preceding scene, where Duncan Heyward wrongly suppresses Alice Munro's misgivings about Magua and leads them into danger. It also provides the paradigm for later scenes in the novel where variously configured groups discuss their course of action. In several of these scenes Natty gives Heyward explicit advice about how to participate more effectively in group decision-making. His most important lessons include the need to listen and respect his Indian companions and avoid the arbitrary exercise of authority. These lessons are central to the larger context of the novel, which is framed by Cooper's introductory reflections on the "Babel" of languages on the New York frontier and which includes a diplomatic exchange conducted in English and French that ultimately leads to the massacre at Fort William Henry.

The participants in these cosmopolitan conversations do not shy away from sensitive topics. Cooper's novels are filled with scenes where Indian characters reproach their white companions for settler depredations upon native lands. In *The Pathfinder*, the Tuscarora Dew-of-June speaks harshly to Mabel, saying: "Yengeese too greedy – take away all hunting grounds – chase Six Nation from morning to night; wicked king – wicked people. Pale Face very bad." They are frequently supported in the novels by both the white characters and the narrator. Here, Cooper writes, Mabel "felt the justice of the rebuke . . . too much to attempt an answer." When Whittal Ring and Ruth Heathcote reunite with their families after many years with the Narragansetts late in *The Wept of Wish-ton-Wish*, Cooper conveys the extent of their acculturation by having them express anger at the whites for taking away native lands. In these scenes Cooper suggests both the justice of their complaints and the ideological function that such critiques played in consolidating native opposition and promoting conflict.

Cooper developed an even more complex ethnic palette in his second cluster of Indian novels, which begins in 1843 with *Wyandotté*, includes the *Littlepage Manuscripts*, and concludes with *The Oak Openings*. The Leatherstocking Tales and associated works divide the scene between Indians and whites; each category is further split internally, with Iroquois and Delaware Indians in opposition and French and English imperial forces similarly opposed. In *Wyandotté* Cooper introduces ethnic English speakers, including Irish and Dutch New Yorkers whose heavy dialects mark competing white identities. At other times a strong dialect links a white character to a nonwhite character, or suggests a connection between two nonwhite characters. In his persona as Saucy Nick, the Tuscarora warrior Wyandotté is drawn together with the Irishman Michael O'Hearn through a shared love of liquor and a propensity for inflicting head wounds with unusual weapons (tomahawks and shillelaghs). *The Littlepage Manuscripts* similarly highlights the ethnic variety of New York, and for the first time Cooper juxtaposes Indian characters with prominent African American characters. The New York frontier is portrayed less as the scene of imperial conflict in these novels and more as the site of nation formation, imagined as a process of negotiating and ameliorating differences through habit, shared experience, and the formation of tradition. Deliberation retains a prominent place in these novels, but it is often complicated by demagoguery and the divisiveness it engenders, conflicts which for Cooper often have a New England source.

In *Wyandotté* Cooper returned to a plot device that he had developed in *The Last of the Mohicans*, making physical punishment the catalyst for long-lasting interracial animosities. The major themes and plot devices in that novel – flogging, authentic and inauthentic Indian identity, and property – are developed at greater length in the *Littlepage Manuscripts*. *Satanstoe*, the first in the series, repeats the beating scenes of *The Last of the Mohicans* and *Wyandotté*, but with some crucial differences: Corny Littlepage's slave Jaap beats Muss, a

Huron prisoner. Cooper writes that Jaap "had a sort of natural antipathy to all Indians" and that "the Indians repaid" the feeling "by contempt indifferently concealed." Attitudes toward power and punishment are at the root of these differences. Susquesus explains that, though typically stoic and reserved, Indians are exceptionally sensitive to insult when it comes to a beating. By contrast Jaap combines emotional expressiveness with a tolerance of physical discipline borne of his condition. Moreover, Jaap understands human property to be defined by its susceptibility to whipping: "Muss was *my* prisoner, and what *good* he do me, if he let go widout punishment," he asks. For Jaap the satisfactions of possession hinge on the possibility of inflicting harm.

This conversation brings to life the racialist trope of black and red "natures" as they manifest different understandings of domination and liberty. Antebellum race theorists claimed that blacks were well suited by nature and habit to subordination and servitude. Indian men, on the other hand, were thought to be overly devoted to personal freedom and thus incapable of accepting even the most benign forms of hierarchy. In *Satanstoe* Cooper suggests that these positions are not static natural facts or essential identities. Instead they are attitudes that arise from slavery and colonization, and they lead to conflicts that often reinforce and perpetuate antagonisms between groups rather than ameliorate them. But as Cooper goes on to show in *The Chainbearer*, the second novel in the Littlepage trilogy, group differences can also be gradually eroded through familiarity and the building of a common history.

A desire to protect the environment and a rejection of individualist values unite the landlords and Indians in *The Redskins; or, Indian and Injin*, Cooper's final Littlepage novel. Here the anti-rent Injins are misled and manipulated by demagogues into a false assertion of rights; the real Indians pose a sharp contrast as they pay their respects to Susquesus, a "living tradition" whose reputation as a "just Indian" is widely known on the Prairie. In this novel the prejudices between groups that are a central topic of Cooper's fiction are replaced by a moral grid, in which "the good red-men and good pale-faces do what is right; the bad, what is wrong." Susquesus declines the invitation to return to the Prairie, stating that "half of my heart is white; though the other half is red." He bears both "the traditions of my fathers" and "the wisdom of the stranger," and finds himself increasingly drawn to Christianity. Cooper leaves the question of Susquesus's ultimate spiritual disposition unresolved in *The Redskins* and defers a full treatment of Christian conversion until *The Oak Openings*.

Set on the Michigan frontier in 1812, *The Oak Openings* takes up the subject of Christian missions in a manner unprecedented among Cooper's works. The action centers on Parson Amen, an idiosyncratic but well-meaning missionary, and Scalping Peter, who views Amen as part of a colonizing force that he has long resisted. Peter contributes to the events that lead to Amen's execution and witnesses his prayer for his executioners. The consequences of this scene are not fully realized until the final chapter, set in 1848, when the narrator meets Peter and learns that for years he has been preaching the Gospel, and particularly the principle of forgiving those who harm us. Cooper concludes the novel with a description of the convert "wishing naught but blessings on all colors alike" and ends with Peter's speech rejecting Indian traditions as falsehoods and exhorting all to forgiveness, as he had seen Parson Amen do. When a man "got de force of de Holy Spirit, de heart of stone is changed to de heart of woman, and we all be ready to bless our enemy and die." In his final Indian novel Cooper thus turns to Christianity as a universal system of belief that transcends cultural differences and provides a means of reconciling warring parties, a position espoused by some native rights activists including Apess.

The rich legacy of Cooper's Indian fiction includes dime novels and westerns, as well as a less familiar cosmopolitan tradition of fiction concerned to represent cultural encounters.[c] These encounters take a variety of forms. In 1829, while Cooper was living in Europe and enjoying great literary acclaim in France, Honoré de Balzac published *The Chouans*, the first novel in what became his epic series *The Human Comedy*. Balzac drew explicitly on Cooper in his treatment of the conflict between the French republican army and the royalists of Brittany. He portrayed the Catholic, Celtic Bretons as a premodern people and compared them repeatedly to Mohicans. A later Cooper fan, Joseph Conrad, produced one of the most important and controversial treatments of cultural encounter in *Heart of Darkness* (1899), where he exposed the psychological sources of white racism and colonialism. Postcolonial fiction reflects Cooper's influence either directly or indirectly through Conrad. Building on these precedents, novels such as Chinua Achebe's *Things Fall Apart* (1958), N. Scott Momaday's *House Made of Dawn* (1968), and Toni Morrison's *A Mercy* (2008) present the experiences of colonized people with an insight that Cooper never achieved and attend more fully than he to the

c These legacies are traced further in the chapters by Shelley Streeby ("Dime novels and the rise of mass market genres") and Stephanie Le Menager ("Imagining the frontier"), chapters 35 and 31 in this volume.

dynamics of power in cosmopolitan conversations. In doing so, they help fill in the features of the world that he began to map in his Indian novels.[d]

Notes

1. Herman Moll, "To the right honourable John Lord Summers . . . this map of North America . . . is most humbly dedicated" (London, 1715). The map was published in several editions as late as the middle of the eighteenth century.
2. "To engage in dialogue with others around the world about the questions great and small that we must solve together, about the many projects in which we can learn from each other, is already to live as fellow citizens of the world." Kwame Anthony Appiah, "Rooted Cosmopolitanism," in *The Ethics of Identity* (Princeton: Princeton University, 2005), chapter 4, 271. See also Kwame Anthony Appiah, *Cosmopolitanism: Ethics in a World of Strangers* (London: Allen Lane, 2006).
3. Wayne Franklin, *James Fenimore Cooper: The Early Years* (New Haven: Yale University Press, 2007). Franklin's biography of Cooper is the first comprehensive treatment of his life.
4. Roy Harvey Pearce, *Savagism and Civilization: A Study of the Indian and the American Mind* (1953; rpt. and rev. edn., Berkeley: University of California Press, 1988), 202, 209.
5. Eric J. Sundquist, *Empire and Slavery in American Literature, 1820–1865* (Jackson: University Press of Mississippi, 2006), 70. Jonathan Arac offers a more nuanced version of this argument in *The Emergence of American Literary Narrative 1820–1860* (Cambridge, MA: Harvard University Press, 2005), 5–16. Both Sundquist's and Arac's books first appeared in *The Cambridge History of American Literature*, vol. II, ed. Sacvan Bercovitch (Cambridge: Cambridge University Press, 1995).
6. In *Love and Death in the American Novel*, rev. edn. (New York: Stein and Day, 1966), 157–161, Leslie A. Fiedler influentially treated *Edgar Huntly* as a psychodrama. Jared Gardner challenged this reading, focusing instead on Brown's treatment of race and nationalism, in *Master Plots: Race and the Founding of an American Literature, 1787–1845* (Baltimore: Johns Hopkins University Press, 2000), chapter 3. For discussions of *Logan* see Teresa Goddu, *Gothic America: Narrative, History, and Nation* (New York: Columbia University Press, 1997), chapter 3; and Dana D. Nelson, *National Manhood: Capitalist Citizenship and the Imagined Fraternity of White Men* (Durham, NC: Duke University Press, 1998), esp 90–94.
7. In *Gleanings in Europe: France* (1837; Albany: SUNY Press, 1983) Cooper commented on the presence of "gypsies," or Romani, in England (43).

d In "The worlding of the American novel," chapter 66 in this volume, Bruce Robbins writes that "there is no doubt that, as the regions of the world that are obscurely tugging on each other's everyday life have increased, the demand has grown for better maps, more complex and reliable global positioning systems" (1098). Cooper's Indian novels create a paradigm for one type of fictional "worlding."

8. In his 1820 address at Plymouth, Daniel Webster deemphasized the oppressive features of Puritan settlement, referring to the native inhabitants as "barbarians" and describing their displacement as the progress of civilization. Responding to this version of New England history, Pequot orator and writer William Apess delivered a "Eulogy on King Philip" in Boston in 1836, where he emphasized that the Puritan tradition contained a strain of bigotry that shaped white attitudes toward people of color. Against Webster and his associates, Apess contended that Puritanism was the source of contemporary prejudice, not its antidote. I discuss this history in Sandra M. Gustafson, *Imagining Deliberative Democracy in the Early American Republic* (Chicago: University of Chicago Press, 2011).
9. Richard Slotkin develops this approach to Cooper's novel in his introduction to *Last of the Mohicans* (Penguin: Harmondsworth, 1986). Using a conflict-of-civilizations model, Slotkin considers Cooper's place in American culture in *Regeneration through Violence: The Mythology of the American Frontier, 1600–1860* (Middletown, CT: Wesleyan University Press, 1973), and *The Fatal Environment: The Myth of the Frontier in the Age of Industrialization, 1800–1890* (Middletown, CT: Wesleyan University Press, 1985).
10. Sandra M. Gustafson, "Natty in the 1820s: Creole Subjects and Democratic Aesthetics in the Early Leatherstocking Tales," in *Creole Subjects in the Colonial Americas: Empires, Texts, Identities*, ed. Ralph Bauer and José Antonio Mazzotti (Chapel Hill: University of North Carolina Press for the Omohundro Institute of Early American History and Culture, 2009), 465–490.
11. D. H. Lawrence, *Studies in Classic American Literature* (New York: Thomas Seltzer, 1923), 78; Fiedler, *Love and Death in the American Novel*; Ivy Schweitzer, *Perfecting Friendship: Politics and Affiliation in Early American Literature* (Chapel Hill: University of North Carolina Press, 2006); Dana D. Nelson, "Cooper's Leatherstocking Conversations: Identity, Friendship, and Democracy in the New Nation," in *A Historical Guide to James Fenimore Cooper*, ed. Leland S. Person (New York: Oxford University Press, 2007), 123–143; quotations at 136 and 142. The other essays in the *Historical Guide* contribute further to the revision of the Lawrence–Pearce–Fieldler–Slotkin approach to Cooper.
12. In chapter 7 of *Imagining Deliberative Democracy in the Early American Republic*, I develop a reading of *Mohicans* as "the great American deliberative novel."

7

The nineteenth-century historical novel

WINFRIED FLUCK

In the history of the novel, the historical novel was a breakthrough genre. Until its arrival in the early nineteenth century, political and cultural elites had dismissed the novel as immature and childish, as "mere fiction." Educators warned that readers would form dangerous illusions about reality by reading novels. The popular success of sentimental novels contributed to a perception of the novel as a primarily female genre. Literary activities by gentry-elites were limited to "respectable" literary forms such as the heroic verse epic, historical writing, the stage tragedy, the essay, or satirical prose forms in which the "Quixotism" of naïve novel readers could be exposed to ridicule. These authors were not yet professional writers but gentleman-amateurs who often did not sign their work by name in order to avoid the suspicion of writing for fame. The historical novel eventually changed all that: by shifting its subject to the serious matter of history, the novel gained cultural respectability and successfully countered charges of frivolous irrelevancy; by depicting a cross-section of classes, social groups, and regional characters, the novel redefined itself as a medium of national representation; by skillfully mixing historical references, sketches of local customs and manners, scenes of adventure, family sagas, as well as love stories in which national and personal fate coincided, the historical novel generated a new reading public that comprised both sexes more evenly and broke down the gender division in readership; finally, by focusing on grand topics such as revolutionary wars or key conflicts in a nation's history, the novel could be elevated to the rank of a modern epic that depicted the formation of a nation and captured the soul of its people.

The epic dimension made it possible to introduce heroic deeds and exciting action characteristic of the romance of adventure; the terms "historical novel" and "historical romance" were therefore used almost interchangeably at the time (and will be here). Novel and romance effectively complement each other in the historical novel: the novel can provide an air of reality, while the romance can take advantage of the license of fiction to create an imaginary space for, as one reviewer summarized recurrent motifs of the historical romance, "wars, Indians, wild beasts, witches, trials, hangings, mobs, pirates, regicides, all conspiring against the reader's peace in every page."[1]

The historical novel's combination of a realism of representation and themes of adventure taken from the romance gave the novel a popularity never seen before. As the critic George Dekker put it: "For more than a century and a half, the biggest bestsellers, the favorite fictions of succeeding generations of American readers, have been historical romances. No other genre has even come close to the consistent popularity enjoyed by historical romances from *The Spy* in 1821 down to *Gone with the Wind* (1936) and *Roots* (1976) in recent times."[2] The category has consistently transcended taste levels; its appeal remains undiminished today. This chapter will focus on the period between 1820 and the Civil War when the genre established a new form and function of the novel and had its greatest impact on the development of American literature.

The rise of the historical novel can be traced to the international success of the English writer Walter Scott, whose publication of *Waverley; or, 'Tis Sixty Years Since* in 1814 changed the public perception of the role of fiction, and made the historical novel, as Georg Lukács has shown in his magisterial study *The Historical Novel*, the major literary form in the first half of the nineteenth century, including in America.[3] Scott inspired writers like Washington Irving – who was very much interested in historical subject matter, although he did not write historical novels himself – and James Fenimore Cooper, who praised Scott for having raised the novel to the dignity of the epic.[4] Until 1820 no American author had been able to sustain himself financially by his writing. Irving's *The Sketch Book* (1819), which contained a number of historical sketches, and Cooper's historical novels *The Spy: A Tale of the Neutral Ground* (1821), a story about the war for American independence, and *The Pioneers. A Descriptive Tale* (1823), his first Leatherstocking novel, helped to transform literary authorship into a profession. The improvement of printing technologies and transportation, as well as cheaper rates for sending books by mail, facilitated the emergence of a national literary market driven by the growing acceptance and popularity of the novel.[a] Between the 1820s and mid-century, the number of American novels multiplied by ten and so did their average print run.

a Ronald and Mary Saracino Zboray provide the larger picture in chapter 4 in this volume, "The novel in the antebellum book market."

Women notably profited from this development, since there were no legal or academic barriers to keep them out of the profession. Together with Cooper, successful female authors like Catharine Maria Sedgwick, one of the major writers of early American literature, and Lydia Maria Child, a versatile writer and tireless reformer, were pioneers in adapting the genre of the historical novel to American themes and conditions. The new market for novels also attracted writers who set aside careers in other fields (such as medicine or the law) in order to pursue a literary career, and who eventually moved on to other literary genres or occupations. John Neal, a lawyer and journalist with the image of an erratic genius, strongly propagated the use of native materials and wrote six novels between 1817 and 1828, of which his story of the Salem witchcraft trials, *Rachel Dyer: A North American Story* (1828), has remained the best known. James Kirke Paulding, who started his literary career as editor of the journal *Salmagundi*, became a popular historical novelist who represented Swedish life in Delaware in *Koningsmarke, the Long Finne: A Story of the New World* (1823) and Dutch life in New York in *The Dutchman's Fireside* (1831). His novels *Westward Ho!* (1832) and *The Puritan and His Daughter* (1849) deal with religious fanaticism, while *The Old Continental; or, The Price of Liberty* (1846) uses the Revolutionary War to discuss questions of false suspicions and divided loyalties. James McHenry was a poet, writer, and physician who provided two early contributions to a growing body of historical novels, *The Spectre of the Forest* (1823), a novel about the witchcraft trials, and *The Wilderness; or Braddock's Times. A Tale of the West* (1823). Timothy Flint, best known for his *Biographical Memoir of Daniel Boone, the First Settler of Kentucky* (1833), was a schoolmaster but also a missionary, who found time to write five novels in the period between 1826 and 1830, among them *Frances Berrian, or The Mexican Patriot* (1826), *George Mason, the Young Backwoodsman; or, "Don't Give Up the Ship"* (1829) and *The Shoshonee Valley; a Romance* (1830). Daniel Pierce Thompson practiced law and engaged in politics before he wrote *The Green Mountain Boys* (1839), a Robin Hood story in Vermont and one of the most popular of the historical novels of the period. Robert Montgomery Bird pursued careers as a dramatist, a novelist, and a physician at various times of his life, and tried his hand at several historical novels, among them the Revolutionary War story *The Hawks of Hawk Hollow, a Tradition of Pennsylvania* (1835), and *The Adventures of Robin Day* (1839). In between, he came up with one of the most powerful frontier novels of the period, *Nick of the Woods, or The Jibbenainosay; a Tale of Kentucky* (1837), still known for its unrelenting Indian-hating violence. An author who made the transition from historical to psychological romance is Nathaniel Hawthorne, who returned again and again to historical topics in his tales and in his "Puritan" novels *The Scarlet Letter* (1850) and *The House of the Seven Gables* (1851).[b]

After a slow beginning, the historical novel also became an attractive literary forum for Southerners. John Pendleton Kennedy, originally a lawyer, wrote three novels, of which *Horse-Shoe Robinson* (1835), a novel about the Revolutionary period, was the most successful. (Kennedy's *Swallow Barn* [1832, 1851] is probably his novel best remembered today, and was an early example of plantation fiction.)[c] Nathaniel Beverley Tucker idealized the planter aristocracy in *George Balcombe* (1836). Similarly, William Alexander Caruthers wrote three historical novels in which the superior civilization of the South was celebrated, among them *The Cavaliers of Virginia, or, The Recluse of Jamestown* (1835). William Gilmore Simms must be considered the major Southern novelist of the time; his frontier novel *The Yemassee: A Romance of Carolina* (1835) about the colonial wars over the possession of South Carolina is still in print today.

Many of these authors were writers with an expansive literary output that included poetry, drama, stories, pamphlets, historical writing, biography, travel writing, religious tracts, and regional novels of manners. Cooper wrote thirty-two novels and almost fifty books during his thirty years as a professional author, Sedgwick ten novels and didactic works and over 100 tales and sketches; Simms wrote eighty-two books during his literary career, thirty-four of which were works of fiction. Such a large output was possible because modernist criteria of strict formal control and a search for the "right word" were not yet in place. In order to meet contractual obligations and pressing deadlines, authors wrote at a rapid pace, revised rarely, and often did not know themselves how their plots would turn out in the end. (In a review of Cooper's *The Spy*, the reviewer expressed his hope that Cooper would write his next book "before he prints it."[5]) Authorial digressions, standardized plot patterns, proliferating subplots, and coincidences that strained credibility were used to stretch a manuscript to the required length. Lively and exciting scenes were more important than their successful aesthetic integration into an overall pattern. These conditions of literary production can help to put into perspective some features of historical novels that were later criticized as shortcomings. The historical novel was part of a cultural moment in which a convincing

b In his essay on "Hawthorne and the aesthetics of American romance" (chapter 8), Jonathan Arac describes the way in which the romance takes on oppositional meanings in the process. See especially 136–137.

c For the plantation novel's depiction of slavery see John Ernest, "Stowe, race, and the antebellum American novel," chapter 15 in this volume, esp. 255–257.

realistic representation of history and of national circumstances (realistic in the sense of providing a credible illusion) was considered an important cultural achievement on its own; and matters of formal unity or linguistic experimentation were not yet an issue.

The rise of the historical novel has to be seen in the larger context of the increased importance of historical consciousness in the nineteenth century, when past events were no longer understood merely as illustrations of moral laws. Instead, their meaning was now derived from their place in a historical process which could only be understood by the study of history itself. However, in order to make meaningful connections between isolated events that would otherwise remain fragmented and meaningless, authors needed a philosophical assumption about the larger pattern at work in historical development. A historical novel is thus not merely "a fiction set in the past" which the writer cannot have experienced himself, as traditional definitions have it. Identifiable historical times, identifiable localities, and, for some critics, historical figures are indispensable elements of the genre. What makes them part of a historical novel is a story in which history functions as a transformative force and is interpreted on the basis of a historical law. Although historical novelists liked to stress the importance of their works by claiming historical truthfulness, the historical novel is clearly more than a historical record, if only because historical facts have no meaning in themselves without a narrative pattern by which they can be linked and "emplotted."

Scott had provided such a pattern. In drawing on theories of the Scottish Enlightenment, a philosophy that conceived of history in terms of a sequence of stages from savagery, barbarism, and a pastoral, agricultural state to modern commercial society, the central drama Scott saw at work in history was the conflict between different stages of social development.[6] His novels draw their drama from the confrontation of cultures that belong to different stages, such as the Scottish Highland clans and modern English commercial society in *Waverley*, or the Saxons and Normans in *Ivanhoe* (1819). This confrontation, often a conflict over contested territory, is staged from the perspective of an eighteenth-century theory of the civilizing process which insists on the superiority of modern civilization over the savagery of tribal societies but, at the same time, also regards modern times as a threat to communal values and republican principles. Modernity corrupts and undermines traditional virtues. The goal is thus not simply to praise modern civilization. On the contrary, historical novels often contain significant social criticism and pleas for social reform in order to exert influence on the development of a nation that is still in the making. Many leading American writers of historical novels may be labeled critical conservatives who used the novel to link national identity with republican virtues that seemed to be threatened by a selfish materialism.

Scott's lasting achievement was to demonstrate the usefulness of fiction for the purpose of national self-definition. In the United States, as in many European countries, he inspired a search for a national literature that could be seen as expression of a nation's identity and its true values.[7] The fact that the United States had not, in the view of most of its literati, yet produced a literature which could demonstrate its historical importance, had become a source of embarrassment in the early republic. In the self-perception of the political and cultural elite, the American republic had reached a new stage of historical development by realizing the ideals of the Enlightenment. But it had not yet developed a literature of its own that could provide distinction, so that the new nation might "take a place, by its authors, among the lights of the world."[8] In response, a strong literary nationalism developed after the war of 1812. Elites affiliated with magazines like the influential *North American Review* played a leading role in challenging American writers to create a national literature worthy of the glory of the new nation. Without cultural independence, they argued, the promise of American democracy was not yet fully realized. "We boast of our political institutions," said poet and critic William Ellery Channing, but "receive our chief teachings, books, impressions, from the school of monarchy."[9]

In order to do its work of national self-definition successfully, the historical novel had to be accepted as a truthful representation of history and of national conditions. Historical novels thus aim at a reality-effect produced by claims of accuracy in historical reference and verisimilitude in the description of customs and locales. In the preface to *The Deerslayer, or The First War-Path* (1841), Cooper insists that, "the lake, mountains, valley and forests, are all believed to be sufficiently exact, while the river, rock and shoal are faithful transcripts from nature." In order to strengthen an impression of objective representation, historical novels are almost always told by an omniscient narrator who is able to link the fates of individualized but "typical" characters to the national conditions which shape their existence. Their stories can thus gain metaphoric significance and become emblematic of the nation as a whole. For depicting this whole, historical novels draw on representational modes of the novel of manners and the regional sketch to present a wide variety of character types, a multitude of local peculiarities, and a range of social and cultural diversity, often including remarkable, not yet sufficiently examined multicultural and multi-linguistic dimensions. However, the historical novel always presents this multitude with the goal of integration in order to demonstrate that everything, the general and the particular, the national and the personal, is significantly linked. The nation is seen as an organic body, often compared to the family, where all parts or members have their place and function – which also means that existing social hierarchies can be presented as seemingly "natural" and political disagreements can be reconceptualized as family quarrels.

In deploring the lack of a national literature in the United States, critics often pointed out that the young nation could not yet draw on a long and rich history comparable to European countries. Under these circumstances, what could be suitable topics for American historical novels? Again, it was Scott who showed the way out. His two recurring topics were the turmoil of political revolutions and the historical conflict between different stages of civilization. The popularity of these narrative patterns led American authors to look for similar motifs in their own history. In the debates about a national culture, three stages of American history were identified as especially influential for the formation of an American identity: the Puritan beginnings, the violent conflicts on the frontier, and the American Revolution. Around 1830, a fourth topic became prominent, the myth of a chivalrous South contrasted with a materialistic North. Famously, in *Life on the Mississippi* (1883) Mark Twain laid the blame for the Civil War on the impact that Scott's historical novels had on the romantic self-image of the American South.

In choosing one of these topics, historical novels joined an active dialogue about national self-definition. What were the origins of the American nation, its special virtues, as well as its remaining shortcomings? Who were the true founding fathers of the American nation? John Winthrop and the Puritans? Daniel Boone and the pioneer settlers? Or George Washington and the revolutionaries? The Revolutionary Wars (including the War of 1812) had the greatest patriotic potential, but they could not yet provide the new nation with a long and venerable history. Puritanism offered that possibility, but only at a price, for although the Puritan founders' firmness of character was generally praised, their stern authoritarianism and religious dogmatism posed a problem for a nation defining itself as the land of liberty. Eventually, the frontier experience proved to be the most popular choice, because it provided new and suggestive material for the adaptation of Scott's culture conflict formula to American conditions.

At first blush, the American struggle for independence seemed the most promising topic for a home-grown American historical novel. After all, it had been the American Revolution that had created the new nation. The topic offered lots of dramatic potential: death-defying rebels, exciting battle scenes, captures, escapes, divided families, mistaken identities, espionage, false suspicions, trials, and lovers torn apart by divided loyalties. Three of Cooper's first five novels are set during the Revolution. By 1850 over one hundred novels about the Revolutionary Wars had appeared, including Cooper's first serious novelistic effort, *The Spy*, and his *Lionel Lincoln; or, the Leaguer of Boston* (1825), as well as sea novels filled with swift and violent action, *The Pilot* (1824), and *The Red Rover* (1828).[d] With *Wyandotte* (1843) Cooper returned to the Revolutionary period. Child's novel *The Rebels; or Boston Before the Revolution* (1825), Sedgwick's *Redwood* (1824), and *The Linwoods; or, "Sixty Years Since" in America* (1835) introduced strong, independent-minded and outspoken heroines who depart from an ideal of female deference and find ways to play an active part in support of the nation. Again national and individual fates are intertwined. National independence holds a promise of personal liberation, but in the end, the individual pursuit of happiness has to serve the task of developing the new nation. In novels like *Redwood, The Linwoods*, or the Civil War novel *Miss Ravenel's Conversion from Secession to Loyalty* (1867) by John William De Forest, the best historical novel written in the age of realism, the conflicting sides are finally reunited in marital union, so that the nation can be symbolically reintegrated and personal independence finds its limits in the ideological trope of the national family. As Michael Davitt Bell has put it, "marriage is always the final symbol of the new civilization."[10]

For historical novelists, turning to Puritanism seemed to hold the promise of finding a heroic origin for the American nation.[11] The topic became a staple of historiography and the historical novel during the antebellum period. Starting with the serial publication of the anonymous *Salem Witchcraft* in 1820, McHenry's *The Spectre of the Forest,* and Harriet V. Cheney's *A Peep at the Pilgrims in Sixteen Hundred Thirty-Six: A Tale of Olden Times* (1824), continuing with Child's *Hobomok; a Tale of the Times* (1824) published originally anonymously, Sedgwick's *Hope Leslie; or, Early Times in the Massachusetts* (1827), Neal's *Rachel Dyer*, as well as Cooper's response to Sedgwick, *The Wept of Wish-ton-Wish* (1829), and going on to such novels as Eliza Buckminster Lee's *Naomi; or Boston, Two Hundred Years Ago* (1848), Henry William Herbert's *The Fair Puritan, an Historical Romance of the Days of Witchcraft* (1844–1845), and Hawthorne's *The Scarlet Letter*, around thirty "Puritan" novels were published in the first half of the nineteenth century.

d On Cooper's influence on the genre of the sea novel, see Hester Blum, "Melville and the novel of the sea," chapter 9 in this volume, 154.

However, in most of them, Puritanism is treated ambivalently. On the one hand, the story of bold, undaunted founding fathers in a "howling wilderness" confirmed the idea of an American exceptionalism driven by moral determination. For many, the Puritans were national heroes "founding the liberties of America on the Plymouth rock."[12] On the other hand, the religious dogmatism of the Puritan founding fathers and their "spirit of fanaticism"[13] seemed to bequeath a dark legacy of intolerance. Puritanism was thus useful not only in its evocation of the beginnings of American society but even more so for a liberal reconceptualization of American society, often inspired by Unitarianism's critique of a stern orthodox Calvinism symbolized by the Salem witchcraft trials. In this sense, historical novels on Puritanism are also novels about the present as much as the past; they use Puritanism to determine what traditions and values should prevail in the nation. In this debate, they often champion the rights of individual dissenters against the claims of traditional authority in order to affirm the idea of liberty.

In some cases, these liberal sympathies were extended to the treatment of cultural encounters with Native Americans and the possibility of a peaceful coexistence. Two novels, long neglected but now rediscovered and newly appreciated as major examples of the American historical novel, are especially noteworthy in this respect. Both Child's novel *Hobomok* and Sedgwick's *Hope Leslie* are set in the early colonial period and revise accounts of Puritan encounters with Indians as a Manichean struggle between devilish savages and godly Puritan founders. In *Hobomok*, Child jokingly places her narrator not even "within sight of the proud summit which has been gained either by Sir Walter Scott, or Mr. Cooper." But then, under this cover, she undertakes the daring task of revising conventional views of the Wampanoag chief King Philip and presents him as an example of racial tolerance in contrast to Puritan intolerance. For the liberal Unitarian Sedgwick, who had already criticized religious dogmatism in her regional novel of manners *A New England Tale* (1822), rewriting Puritan history also opens up the possibility of challenging patriarchal authority. Sedgwick's rebellious heroine begins to reject the claims of paternal guardian figures and to question their authority, even in the case of John Winthrop, the exemplary Puritan. In *Hope Leslie*, which Carolyn Karcher has called the most multivocal and technically innovative of nineteenth-century frontier romances,[14] it is not traditional authority but the heroine's willingness to listen to her own inner nature that turns out to be her best guide. An authority based on religious orthodoxy is replaced by an inner moral sense inspired by nature which no longer needs tradition for guidance. This development is dramatized with a good measure of irony when John Winthrop recommends the unloved William Hubbard as a possible husband and the heroine rejects him: "Thus our heroine, by her peculiar taste, lost at least the golden opportunity of illustrating herself by a union with the future historian of New England."

At a closer look, then, historical novels are not merely and not even primarily novels about historical events but about the question of who should have authority in the new nation and what rights the individual should have in that new social order. They provide a medium of national self-definition but also one of an individual empowerment in which claims for recognition are asserted against the constraints of tradition and then rechanneled as a force of national regeneration. However, where recent readings have tried to emphasize the progressive race and gender politics of these novels, they also had to acknowledge its limits. Although Sedgwick and Child present "rebellious daughters,"[15] who have the courage to defy patriarchal authority, these new heroines remain legally and socially subordinated and without political rights in the end. Similarly, Hawthorne's Hester Prynne, who starts out as a defiant nonconforming individual in *The Scarlet Letter*, accepts the necessity of traditional social arrangements in the end and accepts her place in that order willingly.

Once one realizes that historical novels are not merely stories about the past but also about claims of the individual against established authority – so that the struggle for national independence also promises individual empowerment – it is not hard to understand why the frontier novel became the most popular American version of the genre and helped to give it a characteristic American turn. Frontier novels began to proliferate in the early 1820s, starting with *Hobomok*, *Hope Leslie*, and *The Pioneers*, Eliza Lanesford Cushing's *Saratoga* (1824), McHenry's *The Wilderness, or Braddock's Times*, and then continuing with Cooper's Leatherstocking series, his *The Wept of Wish-ton-Wish*, Simms's border romance *The Yemassee*, and Bird's *Nick of the Woods* among many others. The topic was ideally suited to transfer the theory of social stages from the complex class societies of Europe to a socially less stratified American settler society. The border warfare with Indians could be reconceptualized as an epic struggle between an ancient and a modern stage of civilizatory development in which Native Americans could be assigned the role of Scott's Highland clans. By drawing analogies with the mythic world of antiquity, and especially with Homer's epics, it became possible to give American civilization a heroic pre-history and thereby to make Indians a part (however involuntarily) of American national history: ironically enough, the "savage warrior who was not less beautiful and bold in his figurative diction than in his attitude of death"[16] could thus become a model of republican virtue. The imaginary construct of the Noble Savage effectively linked two seemingly contradictory motifs: by associating the Indian with a "savage" state of history, his defeat and removal could be justified as an inevitable fate, while, on the other hand, this safely removed Indian could be idealized as a heroic warrior, embodying virtues that seem to have been lost in modern civilization.[e]

Cooper's adaptation of the culture conflict formula to depict the defeat and eventual expulsion of Indians as historically inevitable marks the American historical novel's modification of Scott's narrative pattern: in the frontier novel, the culture conflict formula does not end in reconciliation or integration but remains forever arrested in violent conflict and struggles of survival. A few novelists attempted to overcome this split, yet all of them failed. *Hobomok*, although initially violating the taboo against interracial marriage, then suggests a policy of "assimilating the Indians into white culture through education" and through a gradual erasure of Indian identity.[17] *Hope Leslie* contains the only lasting Indian–white marriage in the nineteenth-century novel, but the marriage occurs offstage and remains apparently childless. The novel thus "seems to arrive at an impasse, having tested and found wanting three modes of accommodation between Indians and whites: peaceful coexistence, interracial marriage, and friendship."[18] In his *The Last of the Mohicans. A Narrative of 1757* (1826), Cooper wards off miscegenation by the death of the interracial couple Uncas and Cora. In *The Wept of Wish-ton-Wish*, the marriage between the noble Indian chief Conanchet and Ruth Heathcote fails because of Puritan intolerance. In all of these novels, the prospect of a peaceful coexistence of cultures is eventually rejected. Ultimately, this narrative disjunction could be taken to justify the official antebellum policies of Indian removal.[f] The best possible compromise was to create "white Indians" like Cooper's Leatherstocking figure who "acquires the traits Anglo-Americans most admire in the Indian, yet remains racially 'pure'."[19]

For an understanding of the gradual Americanization of the historical novel, Cooper's first Leatherstocking novel *The Pioneers* is crucial. Clearly, what Cooper initially had in mind was not yet a "Leatherstocking novel" in the adventure mode. The beginning of the novel, in which the twenty-four hours of Christmas Eve in a frontier town are described in fifteen long-drawn

e For an account of how Native writers have responded to this pervasive narrative, see Sean Kicummah Teuton,"The Native American Tradition," chapter 67 in this volume, esp. 1108–1110.

f For a different view in this volume see Sandra Gustafson, "Cooper and the idea of the Indian" (chapter 6), esp. 105–106.

chapters, focuses on the portrayal of an earlier period and, thus, on a nation still in the making. Cooper identifies three problems that put the legitimacy of the new nation into question. To start with, the extent of democratization seems excessive and has to be reined in. Ecological recklessness (illustrated by wanton pigeon shooting and bass fishing), lawlessness (illustrated by hunting without legal permission), and narrow commercial self-interest pose threats to the pastoral peace of the new nation.[g] In response, the project of the novel is the symbolic containment of these potentially anarchic and destructive forces. In order to achieve this, Cooper wants to strengthen the authority of the landed gentry, the bearer of civilized standards. For this, it becomes necessary to counter the suspicion that the gentry's social status and wealth, based on the possession of land, results from the dispossession of Indians, because in that case the moral authority of the new nation would be severely tainted. However, what first looks like historical guilt is merely a fantasy of the young hero Edward, who can imagine history only along the lines of European moral corruption. As it turns out, the new order does not need to suppress its past. Although it may still be uncivilized and somewhat rude in places, it is nevertheless not morally tainted, and Cooper leaves no doubt that the lack of civilized manners will be corrected by the next generation. The novel can therefore end with a restitution of the social order on new grounds, symbolized by the marital union of two representatives of initially hostile factions. At the same time, the characters symbolizing an earlier, barbaric stage, who are outside the possibility of ever being "civilized," are expelled from the exemplary new order which the novel has created. This narrative pattern – the eventual reintegration of mildly deviant and eccentric characters into a symbolic order and the elimination of all those who refuse to be integrated – is the basic configuration of nation-formation in the historical novel.

In Cooper's representative frontier town of Templeton (based on Cooperstown, New York, which was founded by his father), the characters who would later become heroes of the Leatherstocking series remain on the margin, even though their status and importance increases during the novel. Chingachgook, in later Leatherstocking novels the exemplary noble Indian, is introduced pathetically as the drunken Indian John, and Natty Bumppo, the Leatherstocking figure, is at the beginning hardly more than an eccentric outsider, named after his crudely eclectic leggings. As an odd loner, he is only

g For a related reading of *The Pioneers* elsewhere in this volume, see Timothy Sweet, "American land, American landscapes, American novels," chapter 5, 91–92.

one figure in a gallery of quaint regional types that provide the historical novel with local color. However, in the course of the novel he begins to grow in stature because of his moral intuition, his code of honor, and his extraordinary shooting skills by which he saves the life of the daughter of the village patriarch Judge Temple. The importance of Natty and the elements of adventure increase together in the novel, whereas the role of history decreases. This becomes even more obvious in the second Leatherstocking novel, *The Last of the Mohicans*, the best known and most popular of the series, which, by changing Natty into a heroic warrior, transforms the "descriptive tale" of *The Pioneers* into a fast-paced adventure tale of flight and pursuit, with history now functioning mainly as a source of dramatic energy for a romance of adventure.

In the 1830s, Cooper's writing moved beyond the adventure formula toward social commentary on republican principles and the state of American democracy. In three historical novels set in Europe, *The Bravo* (1831), *The Heidenmauer; or, The Benedictines* (1832), and *The Headsman of Berne* (1833), Cooper cautioned Americans that republics are always in danger of deteriorating into dictatorship. His attacks on commercialism and the unprincipled character of democracy increased and gained in intensity. Dispossession of a new kind became a topic; while a novel like *The Pioneers* seeks to justify the dispossession of the Indians by the landed gentry, the gentry itself now feels threatened by dispossession. Cooper's work, which started out in proud support of American independence, ended in growing discontent with an America in which the tyranny of English kings had been replaced, in his view, by the tyranny of a majority that interfered with individual rights. Many of his later works, including *Home as Found* (1838), and the so-called "Littlepage Trilogy" – *Satanstoe* (1845), *The Chainbearer* (1845), and *The Redskins* (1846), in which he contrasts the integrity of the landed gentry with modern greed and opportunism – contain strong criticisms of American democracy. Eventually, Cooper retreated to an idea of self-reliant, "principled" individuality that finds its apotheosis in the later Leatherstocking versions of *The Pathfinder* (1840) and *The Deerslayer*.

In their sequence, Cooper's first two Leatherstocking novels illustrate conflicting tendencies in the politics of the historical novel. On the one hand, historical novels justify existing social hierarchies by describing them as the "progressive" result of historical development; on the other hand, the popularity of the historical novel derives from elements of violent struggle and heroic adventure that undermine established social hierarchies. Those characters who are best equipped to succeed in the struggle for survival gain the greatest authority, while the traditional father figure is decisively weakened. In the later Leatherstocking novels, genteel heroes disappear altogether and only the "lowly" Natty remains, a character, as Cooper himself put it, "that possessed little of civilization but its highest principles."[20] He stands for the possibility of a natural nobility in individuals from the lower ranks. Natty may lack the education and manners of the gentry, but he has something they do not have, namely an inner moral sense developed in communion with nature, which is the source of his moral superiority. However, as the saga unfolds Natty can remain faithful to himself and his inner nature only outside of society. Cooper thus creates the figure of a self-reliant individual, resulting in the paradox of a conservative writer who, in trying to define a new nation, ended up creating one of the most powerful visions of unconnected radical individualism. This ironic logic has consequences. If class distinction can no longer have the same importance, another source of distinction must take its place: race replaces class and class differences dissolve in racial warfare. Social conflicts are displaced by conflicts with outside others, thereby creating a legacy that would dominate later versions of the frontier novel like the Western.[h] The Leatherstocking series may therefore be considered a major contribution to the creation of the American myth of regeneration through violence.[21]

William Gilmore Simms, who admired Cooper and became the principal man of letters in the antebellum South, introduced the topic of the South into the historical novel. In doing so, he showed that its narrative patterns could easily travel and be appropriated for different purposes. Like other Southern writers of the time such as George Tucker in *The Valley of Shenandoah; or, Memories of the Graysons*(1824), Nathaniel Beverley Tucker in *The Partisan Leader* (1836), and Caruthers in his *Cavaliers of Virginia*, Simms tells stories about the formation of an ideal civilization that is threatened from within, but even more so from forces outside, including a materialistic-minded North. Consequently, Simms's "ideal civilization" is no longer that of the American nation as a whole but rather of the American South, and his historical novels aim at giving the South a separate identity. In a seven-volume series about the

h In chapter 31 in this volume,"Imagining the frontier," Stephanie LeMenager traces the ways in which "exceptionalist thinking" has shaped the frontier tradition in American literature, esp. 516–518. Fittingly, Russ Castronono characterizes the American novel in the first half of the nineteenth century as "an imperial romance" in chapter 32 ("Imperialism, Orientalism, and empire"), 537. As Shelley Streeby shows in her chapter on "Dime novels and the rise of mass market genres" (chapter 35),the historical romance of adventure, including the frontier novel, has shaped some of the most important genres of US-American mass culture.

American Revolutionary War in the lower South (*The Partisan* [1835]; *Mellichampe* [1836]; *The Kinsmen* [1841], later re-titled *The Scout*; *Katharine Walton* [1851]; *The Sword and The Distaff* [1852], revised as *Woodcraft* [1854]; *The Forayers* [1855]; and *Eutaw* [1856]) as well as a series of border romances (*Guy Rivers* [1834], *Richard Hurdes* [1838]; *Border Beagles Beauchampe* [1842]; *Helen Halsey* [1845]; and *Charlemont* [1856]), Simms traces the rise of the South through colonial times and the subsequent confrontation of Southern civilization with a series of historical challenges. Most of these novels are forgotten today, but his frontier novel *The Yemassee* has become a classic of early Southern literature. Like other Southern writers, Simms conceptualized his ideal Southern order as a hierarchy, in which everybody occupies the place he or she deserves. This arrangement includes the justification of slavery as God-given and "natural." Simms was a fervent, unrepentant defender of white supremacy and spent a good deal of his life apologizing for the antebellum South and its policies. The South was declared a model for the American nation and the fictional reconstruction of its history became its heroic, "epic" legitimation.[i]

After the Civil War, the historical novel lost its dominant status in highbrow culture but lived on as a popular form. A new generation of writers, inspired by Hawthorne to pay more attention to the psychology of characters than to the melodrama, dismissed the historical novel as old-fashioned. Already in 1846, in a review of a book of review articles by Simms, Hawthorne notes: "The themes suggested by him . . . would produce nothing but historical novels, cast in the same worn out mould that has been in use these thirty years, and which it is time to break up and fling away."[22] The charge was revived in Mark Twain's 1895 essay "Fenimore Cooper's Literary Offenses," in which he made fun of what he considered Cooper's stilted language, his wooden characters, and the implausibility of his plots. In Twain's *The Adventures of Tom Sawyer* (1876), historical novels are characterized as the stuff of overheated boyish fantasies. When William Dean Howells, the broker of realism, dismissed historical novels as "pernicious fiction," he was already referring to a new type of popular historical romances at the turn of the century in which history becomes the backdrop for quaint costume dramas and imperial fantasies.[23] In the twentieth century, the genre retained its strong role in the literature of Southern self-apology, starting with revisionist

i In "Imagining the South" (chapter 14 in this volume), Jennifer Rae Greeson redefines "the Southern novel" and puts it in the wider context of a national and worldwide setting, tracing its development from the early Republic to the end of the nineteenth century.

histories of the Ku Klux Klan such as *The Clansman* (1905) by Thomas Dixon, continuing in *Gone with the Wind*, and reaching a tragic interpretation in Faulkner's modernist novels with their growing uncertainty about the meaning of a past filtered through consciousness and memory. Radical writers rediscovered the genre for revisionist narratives of the thirties and the hysterical anti-communism of the fifties, as in E. L. Doctorow's *The Book of Daniel* (1971) and Robert Coover's *The Public Burning* (1977). However, in showing how history can be revised by a change of narratives, these writers also paved the way for the postmodern critique of grand master-narratives that falsely claim to provide authoritative versions of history. In a paradoxical move, historiographic metafiction[24] attempts to reopen access to history by creating an awareness of the traps of narrativization, for example in Thomas Pynchon's postmodern novels *V.* (1963) and *Gravity's Rainbow* (1974), where we can never be sure whether we are confronted with history or paranoia. The awareness that history needs a narrative to gain meaning but that narratives introduce their own structural and linguistic order has made the historical novel a central genre again for postmodern metafiction and its project of demonstrating that such seemingly self-authorizing references as "reality" or history are hopelessly entangled in language.[j]

However, postmodern metafiction is by no means the concluding chapter of the story of the historical novel. The historical novel revives wherever a need is felt to show how the past shapes the present. In Toni Morrison's novels about slavery, above all *Beloved* (1987), or in Charles Johnson's *Middle Passage* (1990), historical events are the points of departure for traumatic experiences that determine present-day identities.[k] Consequently, the representation of history can no longer take place in a straightforward chronological manner, but is interwoven with memories, fantasies, and everyday impressions. The historical novel, created in the search for a national identity, has thus moved on to the histories of marginalized groups and diasporic experiences. As a durable literary form with, by now, a venerable history of its own, it remains a vital part of an ongoing conversation about a reality that cannot be understood without going back to history.

j In "Postmodern novels" (chapter 58 in this volume), Ursula Heise discusses historiographic metafiction in the larger context of postmodern metafiction and its development through several stages. See especially 972–973.

k For more on Morrison's and Johnson's novels, see Michael Hill, "Toni Morrison and the post-civil rights African American novel," chapter 64, 1176–1177. See also the important role of the historical novel in borderland fiction, as described by Ramón Saldívar in chapter 62, "The American borderlands novel."

Notes

1. W. H. Gardiner, *"The Wilderness* and *The Spectre of the Forest,"* in *Americans on Fiction, 1776–1900. Vol. I*, ed. Peter Rawlings (London: Pickering & Chatto, 2002), 97.
2. George Dekker, *The American Historical Romance* (Cambridge: Cambridge University Press, 1987), 1. For a classical survey, see also Ernest Leisy, *The American Historical Novel* (Norman: University of Oklahoma Press, 1950).
3. Georg Lukács, *The Historical Novel*, trans. Hannah and Stanley Mitchell (Boston: Beacon Press, 1963).
4. See Cooper's review of Lockhart's *Memoirs of Sir Walter Scott*, rpt., in *American Romanticism: A Shape for Fiction*, ed. Stanley Bank (New York: Capricorn Books, 1969), 126.
5. W. H. Gardiner, "James Fenimore Cooper's *The Spy*," in Rawlings, *Americans on Fiction*, 74.
6. For a succinct description of this concept of history see George Dekker's chapter "Historical Romance and the Stadialist Model of Progress," in *The American Historical Romance*, 73–98.
7. In that sense, the American historical novel was part of a transatlantic culture of letters. But it is one thing to emphasize transnational dimensions and quite another to focus on the use that has been made of them.
8. William Ellery Channing, "Remarks on National Literature," in *The American Literary Revolution 1783–1837*, ed. Robert E. Spiller (New York: Doubleday, 1967), 343.
9. *Ibid.*, 352.
10. Michael Davitt Bell, *Hawthorne and the Historical Romance of New England* (Princeton: Princeton University Press, 1971), 183.
11. *Ibid.*; Philip Gould, *Covenant and Republic. Historical Romance and the Politics of Puritanism* (New York: Cambridge University Press, 1996); Michael J. Colarcurcio, *Doctrine and Difference. Essays in the Literature of New England* (New York: Routledge, 1997); and Lawrence Buell, *New England Literary Culture: From Revolution through Renaissance* (Cambridge: Cambridge University Press, 1986), 193–213.
12. Gardiner, "James Fenimore Cooper's *The Spy*," 62.
13. *Ibid.*
14. Carolyn L. Karcher, "Introduction," in Catharine Maria Sedgwick, *Hope Leslie or Early Times in the Massachusetts* (New York: Penguin, 1998), xxxiii.
15. See Michael Davitt Bell's chapter on "Fathers and Daughters" in his *Hawthorne and the Historical Romance of New England*, chapter 4.
16. Gardiner, "James Fenimore Cooper's *The Spy*," 62.
17. Lucy Maddox, *Removals. Nineteenth-Century American Literature and the Politics of Indian Affairs* (New York: Oxford University Press, 1991), 102.
18. Karcher, "Introduction," in Sedgwick, *Hope Leslie*, xxviii.
19. *Ibid.*, xxxi.

20. Arvid Shulenberger, *Cooper's Theory of Fiction. His Prefaces and Their Relation to His Novels* (Lawrence: University of Kansas Press, 1955), 80.
21. Cf. Richard Slotkin, *Regeneration Through Violence: The Mythology of the American Frontier, 1600–1860* (Middletown, CT: Wesleyan University Press, 1973).
22. Randall Stewart, "Hawthorne's Contributions to *The Salem Advertiser*," *American Literature* 5 (1934): 331.
23. Cf. Amy Kaplan, "Romancing the Empire. The Embodiment of American Masculinity in the Popular Historical Novel of the 1890s," *American Literary History* 2 (1990): 659–690.
24. An excellent discussion of historiographic metafiction is provided by Linda Hutcheon, *A Poetics of Postmodernism. History, Theory, Fiction* (London: Routledge, 1988).

8

Hawthorne and the aesthetics of American romance

JONATHAN ARAC

Nathaniel Hawthorne called his long narratives "romances" to claim their difference from the novels of his day. He appealed to a familiar and conventional distinction in order to launch a radical innovation. Romance in European culture, after its medieval dominance, had been killed by Cervantes in *Don Quixote* (1605) and its revival, in quite different form, two centuries later gave a name to the Romantics. In Britain, Walter Scott's historical romance in prose, beginning with *Waverley* (1814), offered a new freedom of action-packed storytelling, while the romanticism of William Wordsworth and Samuel Taylor Coleridge in the poems of *Lyrical Ballads* (1798) opened a path into the human mind. Hawthorne adopted the term used for the externally oriented works of Scott and his American counterpart James Fenimore Cooper, but he sought inwardness, the "truth of the human heart."[1]

Romance gave Hawthorne resources to establish an independent imaginative space, to gain for his works freedom from compromising involvement with his personal political commitments as a Democratic party loyalist or with larger, national controversies over slavery. It defined the space of fictionality from which American literary narrative arose.[2] Romance was the term by which American prose narrative first began to take over cultural authority from poetry, on the way to a new definition of literature.[3]

In the early twenty-first century, what American bookstores sell on the "Literature" shelves is serious fiction, that is, the kind that highbrow culture validates. This is the mode Hawthorne invented for the United States, in his extended works from *The Scarlet Letter* (1850) through *The House of the Seven Gables* (1851), *The Blithedale Romance* (1852), and *The Marble Faun* (1860). In the prefaces he wrote to his long fictional works, Hawthorne highlighted the term "romance," and through his usage the term became important again in mid-twentieth-century claims for a tradition of fiction treated as specifically

American, adumbrated in a line of critics from Lionel Trilling and Richard Chase to Harry Levin and Leslie Fiedler.[4]

Herman Melville dedicated *Moby-Dick* to Hawthorne, and it has often been discussed as the consummate American romance, but Melville did not make the point Hawthorne did of attempting to define his works' genre, except for *Mardi* (1848). In a letter to his British publisher, John Murray, Melville characterizes what he's doing in *Mardi* as "*real* romance," that is something "original," marked by "freedom & invention." He distinguishes this from the "true narrative" of his previous works, *Typee* and *Omoo*, which incredulous reviewers had taken as fiction, accusing him of "being a romancer in disguise."[5] Melville uses "romance" in two different ways – at times to value something as poetic, at times to condemn something as false – and Hawthorne did similarly in the prefaces he wrote a few years later.

Hawthorne's term "romance" takes its meaning both affirmatively and oppositionally. Oppositionally, romance contrasts to everyday life. In the preface to *The Marble Faun*, Hawthorne explains that he chose Italy "as the site of his Romance," because it offered "a poetic or fairy precinct, whose actualities would not be so terribly insisted upon as they are, and must needs be, in America." He gave much the same explanation in the preface to *The Blithedale Romance*: his concern with a "socialist community" similar to Brook Farm (where he had a decade earlier involved himself) was "merely to establish a theatre, a little removed from the highway of ordinary travel," in order to avoid "exposing" his work to "too close a comparison with the actual events of real lives." These self-formulated accounts sound a defensive note that is a major feature of Hawthorne's prefaces. More important than any consistent theory of fiction within them may be Hawthorne's attempt to escape the hostility of those in his native Salem who resented the critiques of named or recognizable local personalities in *The Scarlet Letter* and *The House of the Seven Gables*.[6] Even in these earlier works, Hawthorne tried to mark his distance from the local. In the "Custom-House" sketch introducing *The Scarlet Letter*, he defined "neutral territory" as the proper ground for the "romance-writer." In "appropriating" for *The House of the Seven Gables* a "lot of land which had no visible owner," Hawthorne sought a space secure from "inflexible" and "dangerous" criticism, insisting that his romance had "a great deal more to do with the clouds overhead" than with "the actual soil" of his home county.

A second oppositional sense of "romance" does not separate art from life, but distinguishes one form of writing from another. Romance as a kind of fiction contrasts to novel. Hawthorne begins his preface to *The House of the*

Seven Gables, subtitled "A Romance": "When a writer calls his work a Romance, it need hardly be observed that he wishes to claim a certain latitude, both as to its fashion and material, which he would not have felt himself entitled to assume had he professed to be writing a Novel." The novel seeks "a very minute fidelity . . . to the probable and ordinary course of man's experience," but the choice of "circumstances" for the romance is much more greatly "of the writer's own choosing or creation." Hawthorne was adapting a distinction with some currency in the eighteenth century and more recent support from Walter Scott, even if it was not always uniformly observed.

When used as if it had self-evident meaning, "romance" is not much different from "fiction." This usage derives from debates over the "Romantic" in German literary theory around 1800, where the mixture of modes and the breakdown of "classical" genres helped to define the modern, "Romantic" product of verbal art. The novel (*Roman* in German, *roman* in French) was the name given to this genre to end genre. The novel was the prose epic of the modern world. The emphasis on romance and the rise of the literary in mid-nineteenth-century America also connect in other ways to the romanticism of earlier generations. In both Germany and Britain, the basis for what is now understood as "literature" was laid through the sharp sense of an absent public sphere. Deprived of an acceptable world of political exchange and no longer in a position to enjoy the aristocratic patronage of an earlier age, the Romantic writers had to develop their work in relation to market concerns. The relation they chose was opposition.

In the United States, as in England, what we now know as literature emerged in relation to the market. The moment at which "literature" took shape was also the moment the "bestseller" arose. 1850, the year that *The Scarlet Letter* was published, was also the year that Susan Warner's *The Wide, Wide World* set sales records that two years later were topped by Harriet Beecher Stowe's *Uncle Tom's Cabin* (1852) but by few other books of the nineteenth century.[a] The very moment Hawthorne reached a substantial public coincided with his dismay over what he called, in a letter to his publisher, the "d–d mob of scribbling women," who reached a much larger public.[7] Having a potential readership greater than that in any European nation because of its high literacy rates, the United States, by 1850, had become available as a national market because of both the improved transportation

a Within this volume, see Cindy Weinstein's warning against too easily taking these two works as representative of the sentimental genre, "Sentimentalism," chapter 12, 209–212.

that railroads permitted and the new steps in the technical organization of publishing and bookselling that made this audience actual.[b]

Hawthorne's *Scarlet Letter* began to establish the basis for the cultural leadership that was exercised through the *Atlantic Monthly* (founded 1857) and that made Boston for several generations a publishing center of greater cultural weight than New York. Through differentiation and stratification of audiences, by 1851 Hawthorne could make a living through publishing his kind of fiction (a degree of success that escaped Herman Melville), while publishers could do well financially with the work of more popular authors like Warner.

By 1850, the United States was at once more intensely national and more intensely sectional than it had been when Hawthorne had begun his career writing sketches and tales, around 1830. The expansion to the Pacific, the Mexican War, and the whole apparatus of manifest destiny, sealed by the astonishing growth of overland railroad connections, brought the nation to a new level of power. Yet the tensions that developed over the future of slavery tremendously enhanced both solidarity within sections and antagonism between sections. Political questions of the utmost consequence were shunted away from the forums of debate on the grounds that they threatened the sacred Union. Politics was displaced most dramatically by the Compromise of 1850, which made slavery solely a matter for states and thus a topic unfit for national debates. In the characters of separate individuals, matters banned from public politics could be resolved silently and privately. Ralph Waldo Emerson wrote in "Politics" (1844) that the "antidote" to the "abuse of formal Government" is "the influence of private character, the growth of the Individual."[8] This curative role provided the opportunity Hawthorne seized.

"Individualism," Alexis de Tocqueville had argued in *Democracy in America*, was a new word for a new thing; it was not merely selfishness, which is a passion, but a "reflective and peaceable sentiment that disposes each citizen to isolate himself from the mass of those like him." Selfishness corrupts all virtue, said Tocqueville, but individualism, at least at first, "dries up only the source of public virtues."[9] The solitary powers of the literary writer, the romancer, were very much individual.

In this situation, "literature" could fill a new function. It offered an internalized psychology, and it took place in a "neutral territory" that was neither here nor there, neither national nor local, with regard to the intensely debated

b For far richer insight into antebellum book distribution, see Ronald J. Zboray and Mary Saracino Zboray, "The novel in the antebellum book market," chapter 4, 75–78.

political issues of the day. It proposed eternal questions of "the human heart," rather than discussing more immediate and controversial issues.

Hawthorne's romances emphasize the private as the reality that public life either mocks or conceals. In the "Custom-House" preface to *The Scarlet Letter*, the documents about Hester Prynne left by Surveyor Pue are available for Hawthorne's imaginative use because they were "not official, but of a private nature."[10] This emphasis on the private joins Hawthorne to a practice of writing that we usually think of him as opposing. Only the popular female writers of the time are commonly known as sentimental novelists, but Hawthorne's fiction is also committed to sentiment, as were works by other men of his time.[11] The homely hearth replaced the great natural landscapes of James Fenimore Cooper as the locus of a natural moral virtue on which the preservation of America depended.[c] This focus on homely virtue was the tendency of Hawthorne's fiction, just as it was that of the women writers he criticized.

Hawthorne's "neutral territory" for the romance writer's imagination had a strange relation to the imaginative spaces of the West that around 1850 in the minds of ideologists were being peopled with slaves or free farmers. Purist logic held, as Lincoln would later suggest, that the nation must be either all slave or all free. The corollary was usually unspoken, except by Garrisonian abolitionists and, increasingly, by Southern "fire-eaters," namely, that if Americans remained divided by slavery there would no longer be a Union. The moderate position, favored by Hawthorne, tried to reconcile the claims of slavery (or freedom) and union.

Such reconciliation of opposites was the specific task of the imagination, as Coleridge had defined it in the *Biographia Literaria*, and the imaginary resolution of these real problems was one of the means by which romance in Hawthorne's hands helped to negotiate the moment of political crisis in the middle of the nineteenth century. But Hawthorne could only perform this resolution in literature by distancing himself from actual politics. In "The Custom-House," Hawthorne had been dejected, he explained, because "imagination" was incompatible with receiving "public gold." Thus he established his authority by a radical and thoroughgoing redefinition of literature in which successful imaginative activity creates a literary world that stands free from the world of everyday life as an independent whole. This is one crucial meaning of Hawthorne's practice of romance.

c For a more nuanced characterization of Cooper in this vein, see Timothy Sweet, "American land, American landscape, American novels," chapter 5, 91–92.

This interiority where imagination works and growth develops, where character is known and formed, is the privileged space of the literary, both in authors and in their characters. Shakespeare's Hamlet has "that within which passes show." Yet this creative originality was not supposed to diverge utterly from common life. Hawthorne, in the preface to *The House of the Seven Gables*, had emphasized that the romancer – even while freed from ordinary probabilities – remained bound to observe "the truth of the human heart."

Interdependence between everyday life and romance marks the relation of "The Custom-House" to "The Scarlet Letter," that is, of the introductory sketch of modern life to the long tale of the seventeenth century with which it shares a book. Because the phrase "the scarlet letter" names both the whole book and one of its parts, "The Custom-House" occupies a space that in its absence would not be recognized as vacant. It adds something that was not required and so complicates the tale that follows.

The authorial figure of "The Custom-House" resembles in several ways the characters of "The Scarlet Letter." Both Hester in the tale's opening and the character of Hawthorne in the sketch suffer disapproval from an imagined crowd of Puritan authorities. Both Dimmesdale in the tale and Hawthorne in the sketch are split by a passionate inner life wholly at odds with their "official" public positions. Both Chillingworth in the tale and Hawthorne in the sketch display prowess as critical analysts of character. These and other resemblances integrate "The Custom-House" thematically with "The Scarlet Letter." Such resemblances, however, also undermine the self-sufficiency of "The Scarlet Letter," making the tale an allegory of the writer's situation in 1850.

Harried dejection is a recurrent mood of "The Custom-House," emphatic near its end. It leads Hawthorne to welcome his "execution" in the change of political administrations that costs him his patronage job. It is as if, he explains, a man planning suicide had "the good hap to be murdered." From this mood issues forth "The Scarlet Letter," only to end where it began, in the mood of the questions the heartsick women of Massachusetts ask Hester: "why they were so wretched and what the remedy." For the man alone in 1850 as for the women alone in the seventeenth century, no action will bring happiness. With luck one will be decapitated, or else, as Hester envisions, "the angel and apostle of the coming revelation" will appear. The only remedy is patient trust in the future. "The Scarlet Letter" does, however, propose a specific source for the misery: Hester's past action, which both found her a child and lost her its father. Action lies only in the past, feeling in the present, and hope in the future.

This structure in *The Scarlet Letter* resonates with the politics of sentiment that Daniel Webster and others proposed as the means to negotiate the threat of disunion over the issue of slavery. Politics is internalized and personalized, and issues are removed from consideration in the public world in which Hawthorne wrote, just as they are in the private world that he wrote about. Hawthorne's campaign biography of his friend Franklin Pierce (1852) emphasizes character over issues just as his romances do. Hawthorne's critique of the emptiness of life under the eagle of "Uncle Sam" in the custom-house is accurate. "Official" politics were cut off from anything that might seem real. The paralytic calm of the 1850s fed Hawthorne's greatest commitment to writing.

The crisis of action also structures *The House of the Seven Gables*. In that romance redemption comes from replacing all human action, which is guilt-ridden, with the beneficent process of nature, which has been domesticated, in keeping with the book's intense household focus. The dreadful pattern of stasis in the house and repetition in the crimes of its inhabitants is undone by the natural development of the housekeeper Phoebe, as she matures from girl to woman.

The House of the Seven Gables, flouting Aristotle, enacts a plot to erase and undo all action. Just as Holgrave is about to repeat his ancestor's mesmeric possession of a Pyncheon woman, he holds back, which makes possible his union with Phoebe through the natural course of love. The apparent murder of Jaffrey proves to be death by natural causes, and likewise the earlier death for which Clifford had been imprisoned. In both cases "a terrible event has, indeed, happened ... but not through any agency." Even Jaffrey, we learn, had not actively committed any crime in allowing Clifford to be convicted. The long-standing class conflict between owners and workers, Pyncheons and Maules, is mediated through modest marriage. The daughter of the Pyncheons, Phoebe, is herself a housewife rather than a lady waited on by servants; the son of the Maules, Holgrave, is both a radical and an entrepreneur.

Action is intolerable then; character takes its place. This is the romantic internalization that moved Shakespeare off the stage and into the book.[12] No longer the traditional Aristotelian one who acts, nor, as in many great novels, one who speaks, a character becomes simply one who is known. Following the technique he developed in writing his tales, Hawthorne, in his longer works, maintains an extremely high proportion of narration to dialogue, while at the same time abandoning most of the materials – that is, the actions – of traditional narration. His fiction technically anticipates that of Gustave Flaubert and Henry James in its emphasis on its characters, as narrated.

Hawthorne's narrative inquisition takes part in a great dual movement of the nineteenth century: scholars in the social sciences produced vast new amounts of knowledge about individuals, while officers and bosses exercised vast new powers over individuals. When the discourse is not social science but literature, its special concern is to represent as personalized what actually depended on impersonality. In *The Scarlet Letter* the reader does not penetrate the "interior" of Dimmesdale's "heart" until Chillingworth has led the way there. The relation between the two men more closely anticipates psychoanalysis than it corresponds to any actual medical practice in either the 1850s or the 1640s, and it allows Hawthorne to achieve a powerfully ambivalent fantasy of being perfectly known: the dream of therapeutic intimacy and the nightmare of analytic violation.[d]

In *The Scarlet Letter* the turn from action to character means that the terms of contradiction emerge in Hawthorne's analysis of what prevents a character from acting – as when Hester tempts Dimmesdale in the forest. Hester's "intellect and heart had their home . . . in desert places, where they roamed as freely as the wild Indian." In contrast, Dimmesdale "had never gone through an experience calculated to lead him beyond the scope of generally received laws," although "in a single instance" he had transgressed one. Hawthorne elaborates, "But this had been a sin of passion, not of principle, nor even purpose." Dimmesdale, "at the head of the social system . . . was only the more trammeled by its regulations, its principles, and even its prejudices." Therefore, "the framework of his order inevitably hemmed him in."

Instead of plot, the interrelations of principle and passion give meaning to the characters of *The Scarlet Letter*. Dimmesdale himself is defined by passion without principle; opposed to him is the "iron framework" of Puritanism, principle without passion. Lacking both passion and principle is Chillingworth: he "violated, in cold blood, the sanctity of a human heart." Violation negates principle, and cold blood negates passion. At times, however, the text marks Chillingworth with "dark passion," making him a double of Dimmesdale (for they are the two men with claims on Hester). Finally, the combination of passion and principle defines the ideal Hester. Readers may construct this figure but then must confront Hawthorne's failure to actualize her in his text, for in most of the book Hester buries her passion and is dominated by ascetic principle, making her as cold and hard as the Puritan establishment's iron framework.

d See Milette Shamir's "Manhood in the early American novel" (chapter 11, esp. 204) for a richer contextualization of the dynamic between the two men.

The organization of (in)action in romance works through a structure of conflicting values related to the political impasse of the 1850s. The famous ambiguity of Hester's scarlet letter may also be related to the fundamental problems in the 1850s over the meanings of such documents of American life as the Declaration of Independence and the Constitution.[13] The turn to the courts to adjudicate constitutional issues made these documents no less subject to interpretation than was Hester's letter. The letter enters into a career of indeterminacy that allows it to combine the celebratory communal hopes of "A" for "angel" in the sky after Winthrop's death and the anguished solitary pain of Dimmesdale's "A" in his flesh. The identification of Pearl with the letter further emphasizes that its meaning must be understood through experience, growth, and development.

This double vision preempted action, and in refusing to open itself to the new issues of the day, the system, shared by Andrew Jackson and Daniel Webster, became a dead letter, even as Hawthorne made it the basis for a new cultural form in the shimmering life of the scarlet "A."[14]

Hawthorne knew that his chosen romance form was fragile and unreliable. Echoing a figure that Coleridge had used in the *Biographia Literaria* to characterize the effect he and Wordsworth had sought in *Lyrical Ballads*, Hawthorne defined the special "medium" of the romance writer as "moonlight, in a familiar room." This domesticates the external nature in Coleridge's "moonlight or sunset diffused over a known and familiar landscape."[15] Even if Hawthorne's primary tool is the uncanny atmospheric effect – the ordinary made strange by moonshine – nonetheless, he makes high claims for his art. In *The House of the Seven Gables*, the task of romance is defined as "the attempt to connect a bygone time with the very present that is flitting away from us." The persistence of the past and the evanescence of the present teach a lesson that Hawthorne offers while shying away from any too emphatic a "moral" claim. Too obtrusive a moral, like an "iron rod" or a "pin through a butterfly," causes a story to "stiffen in an ungainly and unnatural attitude." Thus between the mobile, evanescent present of the novel and the totally static moral, the romance mediates.

These metaphors for his accomplishments and his concerns help to explain some of the major tensions in Hawthorne's long fictions. He focuses on temporal processes: Hester's long penance in *The Scarlet Letter*; the working out over centuries of Maule's curse in *The House of the Seven Gables*; the consequences of bringing together old Moodie's previously separated daughters in *The Blithedale Romance*; the emergence of modern consciousness and conscience in Donatello in *The Marble Faun*. Yet his technique is also strongly oriented to optical presentation, whether of hovering atmospheric, picturesque effects or of allegorical fixities. Hawthorne's temporal concerns emphasize persistence with development. Their effect is not change (although *The Transformation* was the title of the English edition of *The Marble Faun*); rather, it is the unfolding of an essence, in accord with the laws of the human heart. Hawthorne tends to place the decisive moment of origination offstage, away from the main narrative, which itself presents an aftermath. He prefers to stage a "theater," in which things may be contemplated, rather than a drama, in which people do things.

The key figure in Hawthorne's long narratives, in keeping with his theatricality, is the "sensitive spectator."[e] At times this role is embodied in one of the fictional characters, but more frequently the role names an achievement that the author is implicitly claiming for himself and challenging the reader to match. The sensitive spectator is another of the bridging devices by which Hawthorne's romances function. In Hawthorne's romances, he maintains a relationship he had first developed in his magazine sketch-writing. The author maintains a distance from the narrated characters and establishes closeness to the reader. In the long fiction the social level of the scene rises somewhat, and the tightly focused vision of the sketch is generalized by its extension over a full-length narrative.

The Scarlet Letter invokes the sensitive spectator both early and late in the book to guide readers' responses to Hester. Within a page of Hester's first appearance in the tale, the narrator describes her and her effect on the assembled viewers as she emerges from prison with her baby and her letter. The sensitive spectator responds to the absent and contrary features of a face or context, feeling the pain in bravery and the triumph in humility that together make Hester a reconciliation of opposites, embodying the power Coleridge had attributed to the imagination in *Biographia Literaria*.

In *The House of the Seven Gables* a similar complexity is established through imagining the sensitive spectator in relation to the House itself. After the long easterly storm during which Jaffrey Pyncheon dies in the House, the weather finally dawns bright and beautiful. Hawthorne first conjures "any passerby," who might wrongly surmise from the "external appearance" that the history of the House must be "decorous and happy." Even a "person of imaginative temperament," who would give a second look and become "conscious of something deeper than he saw" might still imagine that the House bore an

e On realist spectatorship in the later nineteenth century, see Lawrence Buell, "Theories of the American novel in the age of realism," chapter 19, 327–330.

ancestral "blessing," rather than the curse around which the book revolves. One feature in particular would "take root in the imaginative observer's memory" – the great "tuft of flowers" called "Alice's Posies." The power of imaginative observation perceives the beauty of Alice's Posies and recognizes, even in the history of crime, the utopian potential that motivates the book's end.

The narrative structure of *The Blithedale Romance* highlights the complexities of spectatorship. Departing from his usual technique, Hawthorne experiments with a first-person narrator. The speaker and setting are unusually close to Hawthorne's own life, for "Blithedale" is transparently a version of Brook Farm, and Miles Coverdale, the narrator, is a literary artist. Coverdale himself is the primary sensitive spectator in *The Blithedale Romance*, and he offers contradictory descriptions of his role. At one point Coverdale criticizes himself for "making my prey of other people's individualities," which would make him hardly any different from the more assertively egotistic Hollingsworth. But only a few pages earlier, Coverdale observed that he would have done something only "had I been as hard-hearted as I sometimes thought." His spectatorship compromises his relation to the community at Blithedale. He often retreats to his "observatory," a hidden nook up in a tree. Its isolation and secrecy, he thinks, "symbolized my individuality." Yet his spectatorship also implicates him in the affairs of the others.

Coverdale gives an intricate summary of his position. He reflects that Zenobia should have been able to appreciate:

> that quality of the intellect and the heart which impelled me (often against my own will, and to the detriment of my own comfort) to live in other lives, and to endeavor – by generous sympathies, by delicate intuitions, by taking note of things too slight for record, and by bringing my human spirit into manifold accordance with the companions whom God assigned me – to learn the secret which was hidden even from themselves.

In its union of mind and heart, its scrupulous attentiveness, and its quest for the unrevealed, even the unconscious, this self-image presents an ideal of what Hawthorne's narrative and his readers might seek. Yet in *The Blithedale Romance*, this ideal is compromised by its location in a flawed character. Even in this passage, Coverdale's case is obviously exaggerated by the force of defensiveness and desire alike.

The sensitive spectator was never a simple matter, even in Hawthorne's earlier romances. In *The Scarlet Letter* Chillingworth is the character who most fully penetrates the secrets of others through intimate knowledge, fueled by intuition as much as by science. Still, Chillingworth, however wronged and suffering, is the villain. The covert and malicious, yet institutionally legitimated, surveillance that he carries out on Dimmesdale is echoed more coarsely in *The House of Seven Gables*, where Jaffrey Pyncheon searches into "the secrets of your interior" to threaten Clifford with incarceration for lunacy. Although Holgrave descends from the Maules and is implicated in the history of the House, he presents himself only as a "privileged and meet spectator," whose task is to "look on" and "to analyze." Phoebe, however, is distressed that he speaks "as if this old house were a theatre," because "the play costs the performers too much, and the audience is too cold-hearted."

The power to harm by distance, the uncaring irresponsibility that refuses to act on knowledge, may be distinguished from another dangerous power, what, in *The House of Seven Gables*, Hawthorne calls the power of the "sadly gifted eye" of a "seer." Faced with the "tall and stately edifice" of character presented to the outside world by a hypocrite like Jaffrey, this seer's power of vision causes the "whole structure" to melt "into thin air," until all that remains is the evidence of the original, hidden crime: "the hidden nook, the bolted closet ... or the deadly hole under the pavement, and the decaying corpse within." Here Hawthorne echoes the commonplaces of another variety of romance that he refunctioned in his work, the gothic.

Hawthorne's fiction does not challenge the political order, yet there are respects in which it stands against its age. The power of his hesitant stylistic effects to undo the reality of what they describe, as the seer unsees the reality of the edifice, provoked one reviewer to complain, "We want the result, and not the process ... We want *things*."[16] Because a book is a marketable commodity, and therefore itself a thing, are readers entitled to demand that it also contain things? Hawthorne resisted this demand. Even while operating within the market system and the whole machinery of business that made half his life seem to him like no life at all, Hawthorne tried to find a space for freedom in his romances. By highlighting a process of creation that had not yet solidified into things, Hawthorne tried to distinguish imagination from commodity.

In *The Marble Faun* these issues are most elaborately turned over, for with three artists among the four main characters, the question of vision and its relation to life is crucial. Fully equal in sensitivity to the artists is the Italian naïf Donatello, whose roots in the countryside link him to both cultural antiquity and natural vitality. He loves Miriam and he hates her persecutor, the mysterious Capuchin; when the Capuchin menaces her, Donatello hurls him off the Tarpeian Rock. He explains, "I did what your eyes bade me do, when I asked them with mine." This dialogue of the eyes proves the true love between the couple, yet it is proved in a surge of hatred and its criminal response. The sensitive spectator, when not an artist but a person of no reflective consciousness, may prove a dangerous agent. The look is not only deadly but also contagious, when it is seen with responsive sympathy.

There is a further force at play in this sequence, still another coercive spectator. Hawthorne's "Postscript" explaining the police plot was added to the second English printing of the book, after reviewers had complained about the lack of resolution in the original ending. The romance enacts a compromise. Hawthorne may give the appearance of being "free and self-controlled" as an artist, but his conceptions are under surveillance by a powerful readership whose demands he must meet. Hawthorne's revision attributes to politics (the secret police) responsibility for what is actually a matter of economics (his audience), but elsewhere in the book he does focus attention on the economic conditions of artistic production.

The image of artistic wholeness does not wholly cover the division of labor on which it depends as a business. The establishment of literary narrative in Hawthorne's romance made possible the dream of an autonomous world of art and pleasure, which proved however to depend on economic and political conditions that produced misery at the personal, local, and national levels. Hawthorne's romances powerfully proclaim the separation of art from life, even as they show that such separation is impossible. In becoming established as a relatively autonomous practice and institution, literature was at once more powerful than it feared and more responsible than it wished.

After the Civil War, Hawthorne's first major critic and inheritor, Henry James, no longer found use in the term "romance" in his biocritical study *Hawthorne* (1879) for the "English Men of Letters" series.[17] "Realism" was the buzzword in the time of James and Howells, as Michael Elliott demonstrates elsewhere in this volume.[f] Yet in the preface James wrote for the New York Edition reprint of his early novel *The American* (1877), he offered a formulation later emphasized by Lionel Trilling and others in discussions crucial for the mid-twentieth century. While "the real" encompasses "the things we cannot possibly *not* know, sooner or later, in one way or another," by contrast romance includes "the things that, with all the facilities in the world we never *can* directly know." These things "can reach us only through the beautiful circuit and subterfuge of our thought and our desire." He elaborates

f Michael A. Elliott, "Realism and radicalism: the school of Howells," chapter 17, esp. 289–291.

this line of thinking into a figure of the "balloon" of romance as floating freely aloft, no longer tied to earth.[18]

At about the same time as James's prefaces, in the wake of works by Robert Louis Stevenson and Rudyard Kipling, an American renewal of romance in quite a different vein from James's occurred, in works by Winston Churchill, Thomas Dixon, and others. This new movement returned to the conventions of Scott and Cooper rather than to the complexities of Hawthorne, which had been appropriated into Jamesian realism. In the next generation, around the Great War, T. S. Eliot undergirded his collapsed epic poem *The Waste Land* (1922) with topoi from the medieval Grail romance. In "Mr. Bennett and Mrs. Brown" (1924) the British modernist feminist Virginia Woolf put a case that could readily be rephrased in Hawthorne's terms: against the externally descriptive so-called realism of Arnold Bennett, she sought a realer real in the truth to the human heart and mind of an ordinary woman, "Mrs. Brown." Building from international modernism, William Faulkner brought back the narrative apparatus of historical romance, achieving an unparalleled combination of violent action and mysterious interiority. Yet the year that Faulkner's *Absalom, Absalom!* appeared (1936), Margaret Mitchell won the Pulitzer Prize for her exteriorized historical romance *Gone with the Wind*. The two strains of fiction Hawthorne had already observed and lamented continued.

A century after Hawthorne, not in the run-up to a terrible war but rather in its aftermath, romance returned as a major critical operator, both in the nationalist/exceptionalist historical criticism of Richard Chase and others, and also in the systematizing theory of the Canadian Northrop Frye (*Anatomy of Criticism*, 1957).[19] Chase defined the American novel *as* romance, in its violent, abrupt, and melodramatic differences from the English social novel canonized by F. R. Leavis in *The Great Tradition* (1948). Frye made romance the star player in his taxonomy, functioning both as the plot form that stands between comedy and tragedy and also as the narrative mode positioned between myth and realistic mimesis. In the last thirty years, Americanist political criticism and deconstructive theory alike have purged romance, rejecting its seductions and compromises, as I have to some degree done in this chapter. Yet the most admired American novel of this period is Toni Morrison's *Beloved* (1987) a soul-sear[ch]ing ghost story that combines historical and gothic romance with deep interiorization.[g] The film that defined

g Elsewhere in this volume Elizabeth Young joins *Beloved* to *The House of the Seven Gables* through the figure of the haunted house in "Supernatural novels," chapter 13, 225, 232.

a new age was *Star Wars* (1977), a space romance. In bookstores, it is far easier to find romance – labeled crime, horror, Harlequin, western, gothic, science fiction – than to find the inheritors of Hawthorne, called literature.

Notes

1. For a good overview of current Hawthorne scholarship, see Richard H. Millington, ed., *The Cambridge Companion to Nathaniel Hawthorne* (Cambridge: Cambridge University Press, 2004).
2. For the full-length elaboration of this argument, see Jonathan Arac, *The Emergence of American Literary Narrative, 1820–1860* (Cambridge, MA: Harvard University Press, 2005), originally written for *The Cambridge History of American Literature*, ed. Sacvan Bercovitch, vol. II (New York: Cambridge University Press, 1995).
3. For the development of the term "literature" to refer to a special body of writing, see Raymond Williams, *Keywords: A Vocabulary of Culture and Society* (New York: Oxford University Press, 1976), 150–154.
4. For Trilling, see especially several essays in *The Liberal Imagination: Essays on Literature and Society* (New York: Viking Press, 1950); for his student and colleague Richard Chase, see *The American Novel and Its Tradition* (Garden City, NY: Doubleday, 1957); Harry Levin, *The Power of Blackness: Hawthorne, Poe, Melville* (New York: Knopf, 1958); Leslie Fiedler, *Love and Death in the American Novel* (New York: Criterion Books, 1960).
5. Letter of March 25, 1848, in Herman Melville, *Correspondence*, ed. Lynn Horth, volume XIV of *The Writings of Herman Melville* (Evanston, IL and Chicago: Northwestern University Press and Newberry Library, 1993), 106–107. For further discussion in this volume of this letter and of *Mardi* as romance, see Hester Blum, "Melville and the novel of the sea," chapter 9, 156–157.
6. These local details may be pursued in the major biographies by James Mellow (*Nathaniel Hawthorne and His Times* [Boston: Houghton Mifflin, 1980]), Arlin Turner (*Nathaniel Hawthorne: A Biography* [New York and Oxford: Oxford University Press, 1980]), and Brenda Wineapple (*Hawthorne: A Life* [New York: Knopf, 2003]).
7. Hawthorne, letter of January 19, 1855, in *The Letters, 1853–1856*, ed. Thomas Woodson *et al.*, *Centenary Edition of the Works of Nathaniel Hawthorne*, vol. XVII (Columbus: Ohio State University Press, 1988), 304.
8. Ralph Waldo Emerson, "Politics," in *Essays: Second Series* (1844), in *Emerson: Essays and Lectures*, ed. Joel Porte (New York: Literary Classics of the United States, 1983), 567.
9. Alexis de Tocqueville, *Democracy in America*, trans. Harvey C. Mansfield and Delba Winthrop (1835, 1840; Chicago: University of Chicago Press, 2000), 482–483.
10. On the relationship between psyche and politics in the case of Surveyor Pue, see Donald E. Pease, "Hawthorne in the Custom-House: The Metapolitics, Postpolitics, and Politics of *The Scarlet Letter*," *boundary 2* 32 (2005): 53–70, which reviews, criticizes, and advances from earlier work by Jonathan Arac, Sacvan Bercovitch, and Lauren Berlant.

11. See Mary Chapman and Glenn Hendler, eds., *Sentimental Men: Masculinity and the Politics of Affect in American Culture* (Berkeley: University of California Press, 1999)
12. See Jonathan Arac, "The Media of Sublimity: Johnson and Lamb on *King Lear*" (1987), in *Impure Worlds: The Institution of Literature in the Age of the Novel* (New York: Fordham University Press, 2010).
13. For a fuller development of this argument, see Jonathan Arac, "The Politics of *The Scarlet Letter*," in *Ideology and Classic American Literature*, ed. Sacvan Bercovitch and Myra Jehlen (Cambridge: Cambridge University Press, 1986), 247–266.
14. The richest exploration of Hester's letter comes in Sacvan Bercovitch, *The Office of "The Scarlet Letter"* (Baltimore and London: Johns Hopkins University Press, 1991).
15. Samuel Taylor Coleridge, *Biographia Literaria*, in *The Complete Works of Samuel Taylor Coleridge*, vol. III (New York: Harper & Brothers, 1868), 364.
16. See the invaluable compendium edited by J. Donald Crowley, *Hawthorne: The Critical Heritage* (London: Routledge, 1970), 311–312.
17. On Hawthorne's impact on the next generation of writers, see Richard Brodhead, *The School of Hawthorne* (New York: Oxford University Press, 1986).
18. Henry James, preface to *The American* (1907), in Leon Edel, ed., *Henry James: Literary Criticism: European Writers and The Prefaces* (New York: Literary Classics of the United States, 1984), 1062–1065.
19. By far the most substantial scholarly treatment from this period has had very little influence because of its belated publication, but it is still essential for anyone who would advance on this topic. The great Americanist Perry Miller delivered a lecture series in 1956 that was only published posthumously in 1967. See "The Romance and the Novel" in Miller, *Nature's Nation* (Cambridge, MA: Harvard University Press, 1967), 241–278. See also, more recently, Winfried Fluck, "'The American Romance' and the Changing Functions of the Imaginary," *New Literary History* 27 (1996): 415–457.

9

Melville and the novel of the sea

HESTER BLUM

By the time Herman Melville began work on his third novel, *Mardi* (1849), he had already enjoyed popular and critical success with his first two sea narratives, *Typee* (1846) and *Omoo* (1847). The earlier Polynesian writing had reflected to some degree his experiences as a sailor and beachcomber in the South Pacific, where Melville had spent time after deserting a whaleship. In fact, *Typee* and *Omoo* were presented to the reading public as narratives of experience, rather than novels; yet they were held to be fantastic by many reviewers, many of whom shared the judgment of one early commentator: "We cannot escape a slight suspicion . . . that there is an indefinite amount of romance mingled with the reality of his narrative."[1] The seemingly opposed generic categories of "romance" and "narrative" used to identify his first two works are explicitly taken up by Melville in the brief note that opens *Mardi*. Here, Melville refers to the reception of the earlier sea narratives in terms of such formal distinctions: "Not long ago, having published two narratives of voyages in the Pacific, which, in many quarters, were received with incredulity," he begins, "the thought occurred to me, of indeed writing a romance of Polynesian adventure, and publishing it as such." His goal in doing so, he writes somewhat wryly, is "to see whether, the fiction might not, possibly, be received for a verity; in some degree the reverse of my previous experience." Aiming for "the reverse" of his previous experience, Melville would achieve it in ironic and unanticipated fashion: whereas *Typee* and *Omoo* were well-received bestsellers, *Mardi* mystified reviewers and frustrated readers. Yet in the preface Melville proposes to anticipate such misreading, and "this thought," he concludes, "was the germ of others, which have resulted in Mardi." What Melville sees as the misapprehension of the expectation of his novels is presented as generative rather than disheartening.

To think of *Mardi* as the result of willfully playful or genre-bending energies is itself, in turn, a productive way to consider Melville's relationship to maritime writing and, more broadly, to the nineteenth-century novel. The generic terms Melville uses to characterize his published work in *Mardi*'s preface would be familiar to his contemporary readers: *Typee* and *Omoo* are identified as "narratives," and thus factual accounts, and *Mardi* itself is designed as a "romance," the form of the American novel made popular by writers such as Cooper and Hawthorne.[a] The intermingling of fact and fiction characteristic of Melville's three Polynesian novels was also a hallmark of the early American novel.[b] In the mid-1840s literary world in which Melville's first works were published, the forms of the narrative and the romance were both adapted in the service of maritime writing.

This chapter takes up Melville's interest in the generic forms and presumptions of sea writing and of popular novels more generally. It refers in some degree to all of his sea writing, including *Typee* (1846), *Omoo* (1847), *Mardi*, *Redburn* (1849), and *White-Jacket* (1850); special attention is paid to *Moby-Dick* (1851), even as this chapter provides a genealogy for Melville's sea novels whose trajectory does not presume a logical or inevitable end in that brilliantly experimental work. There is a structural distinctiveness in the genre of sea writing, one that Melville perceives, theorizes, and redeploys in the service of a reorientation of the form of the novel. What is distinct about sea writing is in part the novelty of the experience it represents: the facts of nautical life conveyed by sea literature would be new, if not inaccessible, to land-based readers. More to the point, nautical facts – in all their minute and obscure detail – are fundamental to the genre of sea writing. No matter the individual forms maritime writing takes, the specificity of the details of nautical verisimilitude is central to the structure of the works. In sea literature, in other words, fact and fancy (or truth and imagination) are not just formal categories, but instead are the source of productive tensions that animate the genre.

While water has always provided a medium for metaphorical reflection, Melville's writing shares with maritime literature a fastidious interest in the material facts of labor at sea. The experience or knowledge of the conditions of maritime labor becomes the hallmark of the sea novel in its technical language and descriptions of nautical practices.[2] An imaginative or fictive response to the sea, in turn, only succeeds through a recognition of the material conditions of nautical labor in its collaborative nature. This quality for the most part has gone unrecognized by a reading public whose interest in nautical writing's scenes of novelty and adventure preclude the possibility

a Jonathan Arac describes the genealogy of the romance in "Hawthorne and the aesthetics of American romance," chapter 8, 135–136.

b For examples and analysis of such "factual fictions," see Paul Giles, "Transatlantic currents and the invention of the American novel," chapter 1, 22–23.

of a novelty of form. Melville's recognition of what is innovative in the genre of sea writing, more broadly, has a social as well as categorical dimension, which can be used to take up issues such as sentiment, sexuality, race, empire, and class – and the chapter therefore considers also the implications of Melville's frustration of generic expectations in the form of his domestic novel *Pierre* (1852) and riparian novel *The Confidence-Man* (1857).

Melville was a diagnostic reader of sea writing and of its place in literary culture, and his own sea fictions can be read within the context of the two generations of maritime writing that preceded his work, such as James Fenimore Cooper's eleven popular sea novels.[c] Other forms of maritime writing predate the sea novel. A variety of genres provided aesthetic conceptions of the ocean as well as literary expression for nautical experience, such as first-person narratives of working sailors, and the ephemeral ballads, chanteys, pamphlet novels, seaman-directed religious tracts, and pirate tales that also circulated in the antebellum literary public sphere. Colonial encounters with the Americas were necessarily sea voyages, and narratives of such nautical passages presented the sea as space for providential deliverance (or punishment), or for economic opportunity.[3] Sensational accounts of such events as storms, shipwrecks, or North African captivity were popular from the sixteenth to the nineteenth centuries. In the federal era writers such as Philip Freneau (in his many nautical-themed poems), Susanna Rowson (in her play *Slaves in Algiers* [1794]), and Royall Tyler (in his novel *The Algerine Captive* [1797]) used the sea as a stage for nationalist projects, while the eighteenth-century Black Atlantic was a feature of the writings of Olaudah Equiano, Venture Smith, and John Jea, whose narratives described their authors' fraught circulation throughout the Atlantic world.[4]

The origin of the novel of the sea can be seen as coincident with the origin of the novel: Daniel Defoe's *Robinson Crusoe* (1719) has been considered (most influentially by Ian Watt) the first novel in English. It shares with nonfictional maritime writing a close attention to the minutiae of nautical practice, and like some early maritime writing, *Crusoe* represents the sea as a sphere of providential deliverance or punishment. More directly, the genealogy of the American sea novel can be traced to the mid-eighteenth-century picaresque novels of Tobias Smollett, whose grotesque rendering of sailors was also reinforced in popular cartoons, ballads, and plays. Walter Scott's novel *The*

c Although rarely read today, Cooper's sea novels – and his several naval histories – were in many ways as popular and as well received as his Leatherstocking tales (which are discussed by Sandra Gustafson in "Cooper and the idea of the Indian," chapter 6).

Pirate (1821) marks a turning point in the fictional portrayal of sailors, as the travails of the titular buccaneer Captain Cleveland take the form of historical romance, a genre James Fenimore Cooper adapted for the first American sea novels.[5]

Cooper's sea fiction was written as a response to Scott's novel, which Cooper found insufficiently expert in nautical matters, as he recorded in a late-career revised preface to his first sea novel, *The Pilot* (1823). His maritime romances served as a model for many mid- to late-century cheap fictions – enjoyed by sailors – by popular writers such as Joseph Holt Ingraham and Ned Buntline (nautical pen name of Edward C. Z. Judson).[d] The "nautical romances" of the late 1820s and 1830s generally credited Cooper as an influence, but not in the manner he might have intended, as working seamen found Cooper's picture of maritime labor to be as inaccurate as Cooper had found Scott's.[6] Sailor memoirists of the antebellum period (including those who had served in the largely maritime War of 1812) sought a corrective to the romantic and inexpert portrayal of life and work at sea provided by Cooper, who had served briefly in the Navy but could not claim substantial maritime experience. The narrative that best fit this expectation – and one that would become the best-known and most important sailor narrative of the period, and a huge influence on Melville – was *Two Years before the Mast* (1840) by Richard Henry Dana, Jr., a Harvard student who went to sea "before the mast," or as a common working seaman, to cure eye problems presumed to be caused by too much reading. Dana's attention to the sea as a place for labor, as well as a place for contemplation, set off a wave of imitations, and became characteristic of the narratives written by American sailors of the mid-nineteenth century.[7] Just as Cooper tried to improve on the nautical authenticity provided by Scott's writing, and in turn was revised by subsequent sailor writing, Dana's narrative itself spurred an increased interest in the supposed facts of life at sea, rather than the romance of it. A shared sense of what was "productive" about the truth of maritime life would be a point of "affectionate sympathy" between Dana and Melville, who called Dana his "sea-brother" in their correspondence and thanked him for suggesting that he write up "the 'whaling voyage.' "[8]

The admixture of fact and fancy in Melville's novels was crafted from a variety of material, including many first-person sailor narratives; Melville

d Buntline was also a hugely prolific writer of city mysteries, Westerns, and other dime novels, as Shelley Streeby details in "Dime novels and the rise of mass market genres," chapter 35, 589–591.

borrowed widely from books about the sea in his fictions.[9] Scholars, most visibly David S. Reynolds, have generally concluded that Melville adapted and revised his source material to create works elevated from and more "literary" than their origins.[10] But such a judgment neglects the composite and collaborative nature of sea writing, which is analogous to sea labor in its collective practices. If Melville relied heavily on other works about the sea, he did so in accordance with the conventions of maritime writing. The "Extracts" that open *Moby-Dick*, for example, are designed to advertise and place such influences at hand. The recurrent tension between factual narrative and romance in Melville's fiction constitutes a substantiation of the special structural properties of sea writing: labor and contemplation are simultaneous and collective, both in maritime writing and in maritime work. His critical attention to the genre is notable, even though the form of the sea narrative has received little scrutiny, whether in Melville's day or in ours. And yet viewing Melville's work within its most salient generic context brings into focus Melville's compulsion to test the elasticity of the genre. What happens, Melville's novels seem to ask, when the expectations and codes of a literary genre are stretched to their furthest point? In what follows, this chapter discusses Melville's novels in an effort to explore the structural radicalism he identifies in sea writing and deploys, and tests, in his own works.

Polynesia, and three voyages thither

Typee describes a sojourn on the South Pacific island of Nukuheva in the Marquesas that begins when the narrator, known as "Tommo," jumps ship along with his friend, Toby. They seek a respite in the Typee valley from oppressive life aboard a long-voyaging ship, hoping that their hosts are not cannibals, as they fear. Tommo soon settles into an Edenic existence with the Typee, companionably lounging and recreating with the lovely Fayaway and the attentive Kory-Kory (Toby having mysteriously disappeared). More an ethnography than a nautical narrative, *Typee* resembles the South Sea romances described by Jonathan Lamb in *Preserving the Self in the South Seas* (2001) in its emphasis not on the superiority of the social and political structures of the white travelers, but on the feelings of disruption, confusion, and displacement they experience.[11]

The novel tests the limits of respectability in various ways, particularly in its critique of Christianizing impulses and Western senses of sexual and bodily propriety, and in its representation of Kory-Kory's onanistic fire-making session. Tommo's role as narrator presents similar challenges – and not just because we never learn his true name, nor even come to the name "Tommo" itself until later in the book. In the first chapter, the narrator cites several then-well-known sea narratives by David Porter, Charles S. Stewart, and William Ellis (whose works would continue to provide Melville with source material in his future novels), but then claims that he "never happened to meet with" Porter's naval memoir before. This impish and manifestly untrue statement is just the first of what will become in Melville's novels a serial and unreliable disavowal of narrative control, method, or genealogy, even as his works adhere to templates provided by sea literature. Just as Tommo fears facial tattooing but is willing to offer his arm – which would be concealed by Western shirts – to a Typee tattoo artist, Melville's novels themselves offer one face to the world and tease the reader with the "hieroglyphics" that undergird their formal structure.

In *Omoo*, the follow-up to *Typee*, this narrative coyness continues, as the name "Tommo" is discarded and the narrator is called variously Typee or Paul, or perhaps more generally Omoo, a Polynesian word that means "rover." (The progression of narrative aliases finds its apotheosis in *Moby-Dick*, in which the narrator famously invites the reader: "Call me Ishmael.") *Omoo* takes up where *Typee* leaves off, and critics celebrated its easy, engaging, sailor style, seeing its author as the "American Rabelais."[12] Melville himself described the narrative as presenting "the 'man about town' sort of life, led, at the present day, by roving sailors in the Pacific – a kind of thing, which I have never seen described anywhere."[13]

The popular and critical reception of Melville's first two novels did not always recognize the terms of his engagement with the formal aspects of nautical literature. During the composition of *Mardi*, Melville began to articulate the problems and frustrations with literary form and the literary marketplace that would become recurrent themes of his later novels, his correspondence, and the critical response to his work. In a letter to John Murray, his London publisher, Melville describes how a "change in [his] determinations" would produce a different sort of sea novel than *Typee* or *Omoo*:

> To be blunt: the work I shall next publish will in downright earnest [be] a "Romance of Polynesian Adventure" – But why this? The truth is, Sir, that the reiterated imputation of being a romancer in disguise has at last pricked me into a resolution to show those who may take any interest in the matter, that a *real* romance of mine is no Typee or Omoo, & is made of different stuff altogether.[14]

In this pronouncement Melville paradoxically embraces the formal label with which he has been tagged, and simultaneously disavows it. He maintains that he must disrupt expectations, and *Mardi* makes good on this promise. The book does indeed, as Melville wrote to Murray, "open like a true narrative,"[15] as the narrator, later called Taji, finds himself jumping ship (like Tommo and *Omoo*'s narrator before him) with an older sailor, Jarl. They fall in with a Polynesian ship that has survived a mutiny, and upon encountering a mysterious white maiden named Yillah, Taji pursues her futilely across the Mardi archipelago.

At this point *Mardi* departs from the conventions of South Sea romances, and away from those of sea fiction more generally. Accompanied by his loquacious Mardian companions King Media, Babbalanja (a philosopher), Mohi (a historian), and Yoomy (a poet), Taji and his companions spend the remainder of the novel engaged in satirical and philosophical speculation and debate. In this sense *Mardi* has been seen as a precursor to the metaphysical reflections in *Moby-Dick* and in *Pierre*. Formally, the novel is as open-ended as its plot, although the rewards of Melville's fictional toils were few: *Mardi* proved to be a critical disappointment for being too wild – exceeding Melville's prediction that it would be "wild enough" – in its formal innovations and its turn toward metaphysics. In its double reversal of "verity" and success, *Mardi* is not unlike Edgar Allan Poe's sea novel of the previous decade, *The Narrative of Arthur Gordon Pym* (1837), which itself had had a mixed reception on the grounds of its presumed lack of veracity and formal coherence.[16] A description in *Mardi* of the famed Mardian poet Lombardo's work as unplanned and chartless, even incomplete, would become a common theme in Melville's descriptions of his own narrative method in his future fictional output, most familiarly in *Moby-Dick* ("For small erections may be finished by their first architects; grand ones, true ones, ever leave the copestone to posterity. God keep me from ever completing anything. This whole book is but a draught – nay, but the draught of a draught"). Yet before *Moby-Dick*, Melville produced two further sea adventures, novels that restored to some degree the critical and popular good name bruised by *Mardi*.

Writing the other way

Melville himself notoriously dismissed *Redburn* and *White-Jacket* as "*jobs*,"[17] akin to chopping wood. Yet the novels present attitudes toward the construction of literary monuments that are similar – if not quite identical – to that seen in *Moby-Dick*. When the irredeemably naïve Wellingborough Redburn finds that the guidebook to Liverpool that his dead father had left him is out of date and thus worthless, he reflects, "For the cope-stone of to-day is the corner-stone of to-morrow; and as St. Peter's church was built in great part of the ruins of old Rome, so in all our erections, however imposing, we but form quarries and supply ignoble materials for the grander domes of posterity." In this passage, as in the similar one above, Melville describes the process of literary composition as necessarily fragmented and indefinite. The architectural metaphors in *Redburn* and *Moby-Dick* (and also in *Pierre*[18]) suggest, however, that the "grand" or "true" work will achieve some kind of completion or perfection in an unattainable future. Yet for young Redburn, who has embarked on a transatlantic merchant voyage in the face of his family's financial distress, there is little hope that his father's expired guidebook will be future material, however "ignoble," for any monument. The guidebook is one of many unreliable texts in circulation in the novel – and many of the rest are maritime materials.

Redburn's shipmates, whom he had presumed to be pious men, in fact read the kind of coarse materials popular with seamen, such as *The Newgate Calendar* (an infamous annual crime report), *The Pirate's Own Book* (an anthology of pirate tales) and mystical "Dream Books" of sham navigation. Redburn himself brings along Adam Smith's *Wealth of Nations* on his cruise, yet he soon finds that it serves better as a pillow than as nautical reading matter. Melville's invocation of maritime sources in *Typee* and his earlier works is redoubled in *Redburn*, but with a difference: rather than demonstrating a legible genealogy of influence, the texts Melville cites in *Redburn* and in many of his later novels do not necessarily hasten the completion of any given project, whether intellectual or literary.[19] In this sense the novel can be seen as a *Bildungsroman* in reverse, in which the protagonist gains no knowledge and ends up owing money by the novel's end.

Redburn toys with the expectations of the maritime initiation narrative in another way: Wellingborough Redburn is presented with several sexual signs, cues, and invitations from his shipmates, but fails to process their import. For this reason, he is unlike the sailors of Melville's other novels, or those in maritime writing more generally, whose own expressions of queer sexuality or homosocial love (however encoded) are recognized and recognizable by fellow sailors and by many readers.[20] For Redburn these expressions are all opaque, whether the actions of his "perfectly formed" friend Harry Bolton, whom he first encounters "standing in the doorways" of seaport boarding houses; the nature of Aladdin's Palace, the homosexual brothel to which Harry takes him in London (and which Redburn's wildest imagination can only suspect is a gambling den); or his response to the power of the splendid organ of the beautiful Italian boy Carlo. Melville had earlier faced some censorship in *Typee* for crossing lines of propriety in his representations of religion and the sexuality of the island women, but his repeated invocations of queer sexuality were never censored. Indeed, they become progressively more explicit in and central to his works, as Melville continued to push the bounds of the sea novel. Push, but not puncture, for other sailors' narratives documented, in their own oblique way, the "situational homosexuality" (to use the term more recently applied to sailors, soldiers, prisoners, and athletes) common to shipboard life.

Melville had promised his publisher that *Redburn* would be all "cakes & ale," "no metaphysics,"[21] and indeed, it is arguably his funniest work. Yet its humor depends in part upon the reader's recognition of the novel's deviation from what would be the standard formula of sea narratives and other narratives of experience: the acquisition and deployment of knowledge. While many sailor tales are light and comic, the source of the comedy in *Redburn* is its first-person narrator's own ineptitude, rather than the high spirit of life at sea. Even in *White-Jacket*, in which the narrator is a more skilled seaman than the beggarly Redburn, the jacket that gives the narrator his moniker is a joke: a composite, ill-fitting, and utterly unseaworthy garment pieced together by circumstance. *White-Jacket* was written and published quickly, just as *Redburn* had been, and draws again from Melville's own nautical experience, this time his return to the USA aboard an American man-of-war; the novel primarily focuses on the ill-treatment and arbitrary violence suffered by sailors at the hands of naval officers. In the novel's dramatic close, White-Jacket survives a fall from the main topgallant yardarm, a plunge precipitated by the jacket. Only upon cutting himself free from the garment (which is then mistaken for a white shark and harpooned by his mates) does the narrator save himself. The jacket answers to all purposes save the one it is supposed to – keeping its wearer warm and dry. In its multiply-stuffed pockets, sprawling and incomplete tailoring, voluminous matter, and dedication to utility – however inadequately realized – the jacket's best metaphorical role may be as a stand-in for the form of the sea narrative.

Moby-Dick, Melville's next novel, shares the jacket's formal motley. It models a variety of narrative forms, and references to books or other texts proliferate. The Usher inaugurates the novel with his grammar books; the Sub-Sub Librarian presents the fruits of his textual research in the Extracts; and once Ishmael's voice commandeers the narrative, the endlessly multiplying bibliography that makes up the "grand programme" of *Moby-Dick* is increasingly detailed for the reader. Whales are classified as books, with their skin, foreheads, and various bodily parts potentially legible; other texts to be read in the novel include the doubloon, the coffin-lifebuoy, Ahab, the whale's forehead, and Ishmael's and Queequeg's tattoos. This narrative urge to catalogue has been frequently noted in criticism on *Moby-Dick*, although its practice has been general throughout Melville's fiction. In this sense, we might think of the novel as a commonplace book for seamen's experience, a demonstration of the collectivity of their labor and of their literary engagement.

Constant attrition

While "Call me Ishmael" is routinely cited as the opening line of *Moby-Dick*, the novel in fact opens with the line: "The pale Usher – threadbare in coat, heart, body, and brain; I see him now." The opening sections "Etymology" (which traces the genealogy of the word "whale") and "Extracts" (which cites various reference to whales in literary history) serve as composite introductions to *Moby-Dick*. Their mixed form forecasts the heterogeneity of the novel itself, as readers are faced with the task of reconciling the action-driven revenge plot with Melville's mazy dissertations on the science and literature of whaling. But as "Etymology" and "Extracts" suggest, a balanced accounting of these different registers is neither an easy nor, perhaps, a desired task. The etymologies provided by the consumptive Usher for the word "whale" themselves are inconsistent, which suggests that the book's interest in taxonomy has no fixed end, no necessary unity, accrete as it will. The quotations about whales that follow in the Extracts, likewise furnished by a fictional character (a "Sub-Sub Librarian"), are themselves "random" and "higgledy-piggledy." They forecast the contingent nature of the encyclopedism of the novel to follow. More to the point, the Extracts call attention to the existence of a body of maritime knowledge that circulates in literature as well as in labor. If the Etymology and the Extracts are an archive of information about whaling, drawn from philology, taxonomy, natural history, and literature, then Melville's sea novels themselves can be seen as commonplace books of seamen's experiential knowledge.

Throughout *Moby-Dick* Melville aligns the science of whaling with the practice of reading and writing books. A prime example of this comes in the chapter "Cetology," which finds Ishmael cataloguing whales in terms of book formats, identifying the largest whales as folios and the smallest as duodecimos. His categorization system is designed, in part, to preserve himself from the sea's "unshored, harborless immensities"; but as Ishmael acknowledges, he is essaying "the classification of the constituents of a chaos." As such, taxonomies of this sort must always be in "draught" form, like the narrative itself ("a draught of a draught") – for as Ishmael reiterates in various ways throughout the novel, "any human thing supposed to be complete, must for that very reason infallibly be faulty." By reason of the fact that they are in draft form, the classification systems at play in *Moby-Dick* invite a reader's participatory labor in the reading process; "I am the architect, not the builder," Ishmael reminds the reader. Assimilation of the terms and disparate elements of the novel incorporates the reader into the *work* of the broader genre of the sea narrative – the manual labor that operates the ship, as well as the intellectual labor exemplified by the sailor's engagement with the materiality of texts.

"Cetology" is one of many chapters that dramatize the work of interpreting texts. In "The Doubloon," the second mate Stubb – the *Pequod*'s resident materialist – theorizes the seamen's varied approaches to the task of interpretation. Ahab had nailed a doubloon to the mast, promised as a reward for the first sailor to spot Moby Dick. As the crew members pause to contemplate the coin, Stubb records how the men approach the text and images on the Ecuadoran gold coin variously; each provides "another rendering" of the "one text" that is the doubloon. Each reading, too, is an experiential one, speaking to the individual crew member's ideology or prejudice. Ahab sees himself exemplified in the coin's tower, volcano, and cock, for example, while pious Starbuck sees God's divinity; Queequeg marks traces of the doubloon's symbols on his own tattooed flesh; and Stubb's own reading is astrological. This act of simultaneous reading prompts Stubb's apostrophe: "Book! you lie there; the fact is, you books must know your places. You'll do to give us the bare words and facts, but we come in to supply the thoughts." In putting books in their places, Stubb makes clear that the works he cites are themselves reference books of the mathematic, navigational, astrological, or meteorological symbols relied upon by seamen. Yet the active work of thinking must be done by the reader. Playfulness is not disallowed in this equation: as Pip's contribution to the readings of the doubloon reminds us, if the doubloon is the ship's navel, and all are "on fire to unscrew it," the consequence of such an act, colloquially, is that one's bottom will fall off (and out). Even in the face of such potential bottomlessness, as *Moby-Dick* insists, taxonomies or classifications must be dynamic and participatory. This formulation is derived by Melville from his reading of sailor narratives, whose commonplaces provide the "bare words and facts" of *Moby-Dick*.

One of the most memorable passages in the novel comes in "The Quarter-Deck," in which Ahab reveals to the crew that the true mission of their voyages in not a general whale hunt, but their captain's inexorable search for the legendary white whale that had taken his leg. Among the crew there is one principal objector, the upright first mate Starbuck, who thinks that taking "vengeance on a dumb brute" is absurd, even blasphemous. In response, Ahab famously rationalizes his pursuit:

> All visible objects, man, are but as pasteboard masks. But in each event – in the living act, the undoubted deed – there, some unknown but still reasoning thing puts forth the mouldings of its features from behind the unreasoning mask . . . That inscrutable thing is chiefly what I hate; and be the white whale agent, or be the white whale principal, I will wreak that hate upon him.

Ahab has little curiosity about the unfathomable force that governs action in the world; the "unknown but still reasoning thing" that determines causality is for him only something to hate and destroy. The question of whether *Moby-Dick*'s seeming malice toward Ahab originated with the whale, or with some broader, unseen force on whose behalf the whale acted, in other words, is not relevant to him.

Ahab's relative indifference to questions of causality stands in marked contrast to a comparable passage in *Pierre* (1852), in which Pierre Glendinning decides that a fateful letter he has received from a woman claiming to be his half-sister must be truthful. Like Ahab, Pierre perceives a distance between the visible surface of things and their unaccountable depths; but unlike Ahab, Pierre wishes not to strike blindly through the concealing mask, but to see and know its wearer. As he comes to his determination to believe Isabel Banford's story of her paternity, Pierre declares,

> I will lift my hand in fury, for am I not struck? . . . Thou Black Knight, that with visor down, thus confrontest me, and mockest at me; lo! I strike through thy helm, and will see thy face, be it Gorgon! . . . From all idols, I tear all veils; henceforth I will see the hidden things; and live right out in my own hidden life!

Generic distinctions can help explain the difference between Ahab's drive to obliterate causality without perceiving it, and Pierre's desire to commit violence in order to expose causality: if sea narratives are above all interested in the mutually sustaining work of labor and contemplation, then Ahab's failure in *Moby-Dick* might be seen to lie not in his misplaced attribution of agency to the whale, but in his failure to do his job. In other words, Ahab's reasoning is distorted when he abandons the whaling mission, as the epistemology of sea writing depends upon the experience of maritime labor.

A wholly separate epistemology governs *Pierre*, which takes the form of a domestic novel of sentiment and sensation.[e] The work failed commercially and critically, in part because of its scandalous representations of incest. Much of the scholarly debate on *Pierre* has focused on whether Melville was trying sincerely to write a sentimental novel and not succeeding, or whether he intended the work more bitterly as an attack on the popular form.[22] But while set far from the sea, this novel, too, finds Melville exploring what is possible within the given terms and expectations of a genre. In the majority of sentimental novels, the heroine eventually marries a young man who has been in her life as a brother figure, or a cousin, or a father figure. If we think of Melville as working consciously within the genre of the sentimental novel, then the relationships between Pierre and Isabel (and Pierre and his mother, and Pierre and his cousin Glen) follow this logic to its final point: the resultant relationships must be incestuous.

Critics and readers found *Moby-Dick* and *Pierre* to be, in a sense, confidence games, engaging a reader's expectations about what form each of the novels should take. Yet we might see Melville not so much violating the reader's expectations as retraining the reader to see the elasticity of possibility within a given genre – or the logical extrapolation of what the form might dictate. What Melville seems to have most chafed at in terms of his market reputation was the idea that his novels failed out of poor planning or inconsistency. He would return to this theme in *The Confidence-Man*. The work consists of a sequence of exchanges (both dialogic and financial) between passengers on a Mississippi steamboat and a confidence man who assumes a variety of forms. In a chapter whose title advertises its circular logic – "Worth the Consideration of Those to whom it May Prove Worth Considering" – Melville reflects on fiction's requirements for characters, including the idea that "while to all fiction is allowed some play of invention, yet, fiction based on fact should never be contradictory to it; and is it not a fact, that, in real life, a consistent character is a *rara avis*?" *The Confidence-Man* is marked throughout by this very unwillingness to mediate between the contradictory demands for fiction to be consistent and yet truthful. The paradox in many ways revisits the question of whether fiction exemplifies fact or fancy that had marked Melville's early writing career; it remained unsolvable for him.

e Cindy Weinstein discusses novels of sentiment more generally, and *Pierre* in particular, in chapter 12, "Sentimentalism"; see esp. 214.

After *The Confidence-Man* Melville would publish no further novels in his lifetime.[f] Often quoted is one of his letters to Nathaniel Hawthorne, written as he was completing *Moby-Dick*, in which he makes the aching confession that "What I feel most moved to write, that is banned, – it will not pay. Yet, altogether, write the *other* way I cannot. So the product is a final hash, and all my books are botches." Yet immediately preceding these sentences is a less familiar but arguably more evocative fear about the process of writing: "I shall at last be worn out and perish, like an old nutmeg-grater, grated to pieces by the constant attrition of the wood, that is, the nutmeg."[23] Melville does not characterize himself here as the nutmeg, the thing that is ground down – which would be the assumption in such a metaphor. Instead, he is the nutmeg-grater: the engine of production. Rather than the substance shredded by the critics, Melville is the shaper shredded by the effort of his craft. The figure of the nutmeg recurs within the text of *Moby-Dick*, too. In "The Chase – Second Day," Stubb's and Flask's boats are destroyed by the whale, and the broken bits of the cedar wreckage resemble "the grated nutmeg in a swiftly stirred bowl of punch." The startling image, in its evocation of sociable cheer, is an odd flourish to a scene of devastation. But like the grater invoked by Melville in his letter to Hawthorne, this nutmeg serves as a reminder of the presence of the shaping hand that resists being ground down by convention and critical expectation. The figure stands in for Melville's career as a novelist: he inhabits a form that ultimately cannot maintain its constitutional integrity in the face of its work as the fashioning agent for the matter contained within.

Notes

1. *Harbinger, Devoted to Social and Political Progress* 2.17 (April 4, 1846): 263.
2. For more on the structure of maritime labor, see C. L. R. James, *Mariners, Renegades, and Castaways: The Story of Herman Melville and the World We Live In* (New York: Schocken Books, 1985); Cesare Casarino, *Modernity at Sea: Melville, Marx, Conrad in Crisis* (Minneapolis: University of Minnesota Press, 2002); and Marcus Rediker, *Between the Devil and the Deep Blue Sea: Merchant Seamen, Pirates, and the Anglo-American Maritime World, 1700–1750* (Cambridge: Cambridge University Press, 1987).
3. The overview of sea writing in this section has been aided by Thomas Philbrick, *James Fenimore Cooper and the Development of American Sea Fiction* (Cambridge, MA: Harvard University Press, 1961); Haskell Springer, *America and the Sea: A Literary History* (Athens: University of Georgia Press, 1995); Bert Bender, *Sea-Brothers*

f For a discussion of the posthumously published *Billy Budd*, see Gregg Crane, "Law and the American novel," chapter 46 in this volume, 768.

(Philadelphia: University of Pennsylvania Press, 1988); Robert Foulke, *The Sea Voyage Narrative* (London: Routledge, 1997); and John Peck, *Maritime Fiction* (New York: St. Martin's, 2000).

4. On the subject of such narratives, see David Kazanjian, *The Colonizing Trick* (Minneapolis: University Minnesota Press, 2003); Jeffrey Bolster, *Black Jacks* (Cambridge, MA: Harvard University Press, 1997); and the anthology *Pioneers of the Black Atlantic*, ed. Henry Louis Gates, Jr. and William L. Andrews (Washington, DC: Civitas, 1998).
5. On the development of sea writing in America, see my *The View from the Masthead* (Chapel Hill: University of North Carolina Press, 2008); Philbrick, *James Fenimore Cooper and the Development of American Sea Fiction*; and Springer, *America and the Sea*.
6. Sailor author Nathaniel Ames spoke for many when he condemned the "ridiculous language" used by Cooper in rendering sailor speech, finding Cooper's "sea dialogues" to be "disgusting and absurd, from being stuffed with sea phrases." Nathaniel Ames, *A Mariner's Sketches* (Providence, RI: Cory Marshall and Hammond, 1830), 238–239.
7. See my *The View from the Masthead*.
8. Melville to Richard Henry Dana, October 6, 1849, in *Correspondence*, ed. Harrison Hayford, Hershel Parker, and G. Thomas Tanselle (Evanston, IL: Northwestern-Newberry, 1993), 141; Melville to Richard Henry Dana, May 1, 1850, *ibid.*, 162.
9. A few of his most frequently used sources include William Ellis, *Polynesian Researches* (New York: J. & J. Harper, 1833); J. Ross Browne, *Etchings of a Whaling Cruise* (New York: Harper & Brothers, 1846); David Porter, *A Voyage in the South Seas, in the Years 1812, 1813, and 1814 with Particular Details of the Gallipagos and Washington Islands* (London: Phillips & Co., 1823); Anon., *Life in a Man-of-War, or Scenes in "Old Ironsides" during her cruise in the Pacific* (Philadelphia: Lydia R. Bailey, 1841); and C. S. Stewart, *Private Journal of a Voyage to the Pacific Ocean, and residence at the Sandwich Islands, in the years 1822, 1823, 1824, and 1825* (New York: John P. Haven, 1828).
10. David S. Reynolds, *Beneath the American Renaissance: The Subversive Imagination in the Age of Emerson and Melville* (Cambridge, MA: Harvard University Press, 1988).
11. Jonathan Lamb, *Preserving the Self in the South Seas, 1680–1840* (Chicago: University of Chicago Press, 2001). Other compelling readings of the novel, such as those by Samuel Otter in *Melville's Anatomies* (Berkeley: University of California Press, 1999) and by Geoffrey Sanborn in *The Sign of the Cannibal* (Durham, NC: Duke University Press, 1998), stress *Typee*'s exploration of race, ideology, and the body.
12. Philarète Chasles, "The Actual and Fantastic Voyages of Herman Melville," *Literary World* [New York], 131 (August 4, 1849): 89.
13. Melville to John Murray, January 29, 1847, *Correspondence*, 78.
14. Melville to John Murray, March 25, 1848, *Correspondence*, 106.

15. *Ibid.*
16. Melville's preface to *Mardi* echoes Poe's to *Pym* in many ways, as the character "Pym" worries in his narrative's introduction about "the probability . . . that the public at large would regard what I should put forth as merely an impudent and ingenious fiction." Presenting it to the public as fiction, "Pym" finds, has the opposite effect: "the public were still not at all disposed to receive it as fable." Elizabeth Young, on the other hand, reads *Pym* as pure fable – specifically, a fiction of race – in "Supernatural novels," chapter 13 in this volume, 223–225.
17. Melville to Lemuel Shaw, October 6, 1849, *Correspondence*, 138.
18. Pierre, on contemplating his ancestral legacy:

    > For in the ruddiness, and flushfulness, and vaingloriousness of his youthful soul, he fondly hoped to have a monopoly of glory in capping the fame-column, whose tall shaft had been erected by his noble sires. In all this, how unadmonished was our Pierre by that foreboding and prophetic lesson taught, not less by Palmyra's quarries, than by Palmyra's ruins. Among those ruins is a crumbing, uncompleted shaft, and some leagues off, ages ago left in the quarry, is the crumbling corresponding capital, also incomplete.

19. See Michael Rogin, *Subversive Genealogy: The Politics and Art of Herman Melville* (New York: Knopf, 1983).
20. See Robert K. Martin, *Hero, Captain, and Stranger* (Chapel Hill: University of North Carolina Press, 1986); James Creech, *Closet Writing/Gay Reading* (Chicago: University of Chicago Press, 1994); and Eve Kosofsky Sedgwick, *Epistemology of the Closet* (Berkeley: University of California Press, 1990).
21. Melville to Richard Bentley, June 5, 1849, *Correspondence*, 132.
22. See in particular Cindy Weinstein, *Family, Kinship, and Sympathy in Nineteenth-Century American Literature* (Cambridge: Cambridge University Press, 2006), and Richard H. Brodhead, *Hawthorne, Melville, and the Novel* (Chicago: University of Chicago Press, 1973).
23. Melville to Nathaniel Hawthorne, [June 1 ?], 1951, *Correspondence*, 191. On Melville's tortured relationship to the act of writing, see Elizabeth Renker's *Strike Through the Mask: Herman Melville and the Scene of Writing* (Baltimore: Johns Hopkins University Press, 1996).

10

Religion and the nineteenth-century American novel

GREGORY S. JACKSON

In 1874, a decade after the death of his father-in-law, Nathaniel Hawthorne, George Parsons Lathrop, assistant editor of the *Atlantic Quarterly*, observed in his essay "The Novel and Its Future" that "Christ's thought, however slow to manifest itself firmly in the details of our social, political, and religious organization, has assuredly taken root in the novel."[1] In light of the perceived deficiencies of social institutions in enacting Christian principles, Lathrop's observation bespeaks the value of a particular narrative tradition. What did he perceive the novel to be doing that social, political, and religious organizations had failed to do? What did he mean by "Christ's thought"? He was not, of course, alluding to theology or doctrine. He was suggesting something about the capacity of narrative to instill proper moral feeling or Christian sentiment, or as Harriet Beecher Stowe had similarly put it in *Uncle Tom's Cabin* (1852), the capacity to bring the readers' sympathies "in harmony with the sympathies of Christ," to "*feel* right." He was also suggesting something about the capacity of narrative to represent reality as Christians understood it. Unlike secular, more materialist understandings that made the object world an end in itself, American Protestants in the Augustinian tradition understood the world, like the novel, as another form of representation that largely obscured, while occasionally disclosing, the invisible reality beyond the material. Lathrop's observation suggests the novel's capacity as a literary form to address deficiencies in the sermon, catechism, religious tract, and other extra-biblical genres. Once the staple of Protestants' in-home devotional practice, these genres were becoming less relevant in an increasingly modern, mechanized world.

Although the novel failed to gain the traction in the American colonies that it had in eighteenth-century England, its influence on religious pedagogy is perceptible after the mid-century New England and mid-Atlantic revivals. In the aftermath of these protracted evangelical awakenings, Baptist,

Congregational, Presbyterian, and Methodist ministers and exhorters began incorporating narrative strategies in their sermons that relied on visually oriented rhetoric, snippets of realism – discursive details meant to evoke readers' own sense experience in real time – that eroded the sermon's largely conceptual frame.[2] In this transformation, the religious tract, crafted by elder ministers for a generation then in seminary, gradually shifted from theodicy – justifying the ways of God to man with elaborate, scripturally based theological scaffolding – to narrative-driven tracts aimed at wider audiences. Broadly speaking, the generic distinctions and discursive strategies that would comprise the American religious novel began to emerge in the eighteenth century through narrative developments that constitute what we might think of as the novelization of the sermon. The disparity between religious tracts and the sermon, on the one hand, and Jacob Abbott's representative early nineteenth-century story tracts and heuristic juvenilia, on the other, mark the sermon's path toward the religious novel and its highly specialized form that I have identified as the "homiletic novel."[3] In place of the minister's authoritative voice in the sermon emerged the disembodied narrator, whose moral opprobrium was a judgment predicated not on ministerial condemnation but on the reader's informed moral autonomy. Most famously, like Abbott and others innovating on the sermon form, Mason Locke Weems crafted vividly evocative tales filled with the hellish wages of sin. In his influential "Looking Glass" series (1812–1822), "Parson" Weems revealed with the sensationalism of the hellfire sermon and the narrative development of fiction the chilling consequences of sin, from the gateway vices of drinking, gambling, adultery, and dueling, to the darkest deeds of rape and murder. By the late antebellum period, as the novel finally superseded the sermon as the most popular print genre in the United States, religious educators began novelizing homiletic pedagogy, creating new modes of discursive realism that showcased sumptuously graphic and visually evocative narratives intended to simulate reality for the young in order to exercise their volition while feeding their appetites for newly popular literary forms.[a]

Compounding ministers' dissatisfaction with traditional pedagogical forms was the pervasive eighteenth-century epistemological shift predicated on the growing ascendancy of empiricism, rationalism, and inductive reasoning. If, in accordance with the doctrine of the fall, traditional Christian epistemology circumscribed the limits of human knowledge, the new scientific mode, fueled

a For an account of the novel's emergence and print ascendancy in the United States, see Barbara Hochman's "Readers and reading groups," chapter 36 in this volume.

by an optimism born of Enlightenment humanism, diminished the theological proscription, lifting the bar on knowledge previously deemed beyond human ken. Following Bacon and Locke, empiricism emphasized experience as the catalyst for knowledge formation, and in so doing, overturned for many Protestants the Pauline dictum at the core of Christian epistemology for millennia that instructed the faithful to "walk by faith and not by sight" (2 Cor. 5:7). The epistemic break divided even the religious – less by sectarian affiliation than by educational and evangelical commitment – into those who downplayed the authority of Enlightenment rationalism and those who incorporated it into their theology, fostering what became, as E. Brooks Holifield has demonstrated, a widespread, though contested, intersectarian adherence to "evidential Christianity."[4]

By the late eighteenth century, experience had come to occupy so important a place in Protestant theories of moral and spiritual maturation that it led to an arsenal of exercises and homiletic instruments meant to provide the young with controlled exposure to sin, with abstract perils and their eternal consequences manifested in discursively detailed scenes. Ministers shaped homiletic pedagogy as a defense against a perceived decline in moral vigilance and the worldliness it presaged. Seeking to shape children's conception of the temporal world, eighteenth-century revival sermons increasingly relied on homiletic realism's "aesthetics of immediacy": visual language, the personalization of religious narrative, and the evocation of intense emotions, especially fear – all of which worked to foster readers' identification with protagonists struggling for moral control and spiritual transcendence.[5] Facing the encroachment of secular culture (particularly the allure of popular entertainment) nineteenth-century ministers adapted the Christian message and traditional pedagogy to new, popular narrative forms. The novel's form – with its focus on ordinary individuals, iteration in diachronic time, dramatization of cause and effect through character development and reflexively unfolding plots, and narrative length that mandated serialized reading – heightened its epistemological verisimilitude, allowing readers to imagine the novel's action as a simultaneous reality unfolding in real time. Put another way, through its adaptation of sermon realism, the novel encouraged readers to bridge the difference between reality and representation by helping them cast their lives – their own spiritual development – within the frame of narrative time.

So profound was America's colonial religious legacy that it is difficult to imagine a nineteenth-century novel that does not address religion, systems of belief, or personal or institutional faith. There is, nonetheless, a difference between novels that invoke spiritual themes or recount religious histories and novels specifically aimed at religious audiences. For one thing, the homiletic novel's roots in the sermon preserved a range of reading practices among a broader, class-diversified population than literary history fully accounts for. The novels taught in college courses today, like the content of literary histories, account for a fraction of novel production, elevating particular aesthetic values and literary movements at the expense of a representative cultural history. The bestselling nineteenth-century novels were not written by Cooper, Melville, Hawthorne, James, Dreiser, or Crane. With the exception of Stowe's *Uncle Tom's Cabin* and Alcott's *Little Women* (1868), they emerged from the pens of authors who have been, relatively speaking, critically neglected, and included such works as Susan Warner's *Wide, Wide World* (1850); T. S. Arthur's *Ten Nights in a Barroom* (1854); Maria Susanna Cummins's *The Lamplighter* (1854); Horatio Alger's *Ragged Dick* (1868); Elizabeth Stuart Phelps's *The Gates Ajar* (1868); Edward P. Roe's *Barriers Burned Away* (1872); Lew Wallace's *Ben-Hur* (1880); Charles Sheldon's *In His Steps; Or, What Would Jesus Do?* (1896); and Mary Johnston's *To Have and to Hold* (1900).[b]

In its focus on specific paradigms of literary formalism, culturally elite aesthetic values, and critical methodologies little relevant to the religious novel's purpose of moral instruction and spiritual inculcation and its function as a devotional template, contemporary criticism has skewed literary history, projecting a modern-day aesthetic and secular hegemony onto a past in which belief systems, religious literature, genre, and generic function, to varying degrees, operated differently among class-integrated communities. This neglect continues into the present day, as the bestselling religious novels of the twentieth century, such as Harold Bell Wright's *The Shepherd of the Hills* (1907) and Francena Arnold's *Not My Will* (1940) and contemporary works such as the stunningly popular "Left Behind" series (1995–2003) remain largely unexamined by literary critics. In the last thirty years, the literary canon has expanded to include clusters of novels once aimed at popular audiences, yet these para-canonical works tend to constellate around the social categories of race, gender, and class. Screened through these categories, novels are either stripped of their religious affinities or do not compete with academia's secular humanism.

b For an account of antebellum bestsellers within the broader book market, see Ronald Zboray and Mary Saracino Zboray, "The novel in the antebellum book market," chapter 4 in this volume.

Much of the criticism of religious novels is predicated on aesthetic values alien to these novels' homiletic strategies, discursive exercises that, at times, make these novels seem more akin to devotional texts than to the novel. As Josiah Gilbert Holland writes in the preface to his novel *The Bay-Path* (1857),

> Religious fiction . . . persistently traduced by those who do not comprehend its true mission, has . . . the highest sanctions of Christianity. The Author of the Christian system spake in parables in the illustration of important practical truths. In fact . . . the great principle in human nature which called Him into the world, is identical with that on which the claims and power of legitimate fiction rests. He came to embody abstract truth in human relations, and the naked, incomprehensible idea of God, in the human form.

Employing a range of discursive strategies, homiletic novels – like Christ, Holland insists – incarnate not just abstract spiritual truths but divine incomprehensible realities. Examining them is thus key to a reassessment of American religious cultures and literary history, and the faith-based practices of ordinary communities across a broad spectrum of classes, ethnic backgrounds, and doctrinal affiliation.[6]

The homiletic novel

The homiletic novel highlights how evangelicals have long understood participatory pedagogies as vital to developing moral agency. It illustrates the major themes of Protestant education: the eighteenth-century shift in epistemology that emphasized personal experience for salvific transformation and spiritual growth; the emergence of narrative forms and discursive modes intended to intensify readerly identification aimed at simulating personal experience; and the gradual shift from the sermon's conceptual frame to a lifelike realism generated by the novel's emphasis on connections between text and life. In religious novels, those connections include the parallel tracks between character and readerly development and between the novel's temporal sequencing and modernity's emphasis on diachronic progression. Additionally, the novel's cause-and-effect-driven resolution parallels the causal relation between moral and spiritual development, a connection such novels use to strengthen the reciprocity between self-transformation and eternal salvation. By reading the books in this way, religious readers could render their own lives as texts, allegorical in the way in which Augustine encouraged the faithful to see this life as a simulation of (and thus preparation for) the world beyond. Homiletic authors understood that experience was managed, at least in part, by the individual's agency and commitment to the temporal as an allegory of the eternal.

As a powerful heuristic, the homiletic novel, like the sermon before it, was meant to circumscribe the Protestant principle of personal interpretation, to contain the possibility of meaning. Because Protestantism was predicated on *sola scriptura* – the Bible alone – it privileged both readers' interpretive authority and private judgment ("liberty of conscience," in Reformation theology). Unlike modern habits of readerly consumption in which individuals read narratives for plot, propelled by temporal and developmental progressions, homiletic reading demanded a different epistemology, what David Hall, drawing on the work of Rolf Engelsing, calls an "intensive" rather than "extensive" reading practice.[7] "Intensive" articulates a level of exegesis associated with sacred texts, in which a given book – the Bible, primers, catechisms, spiritual allegories – might be incorporated into momentous life-cycle activities, such as births, conversions, baptisms, marriages, spiritual changes, and deaths, while also transforming the novel's temporal and developmental progression into allegory, the spiritual journey inwardly shadowing one's literal path through time. "Extensive" reading, on the other hand, denotes reading practices fostered by the print revolution, in which readers browse broadly for informational content or plot, a more passive reading mode associated primarily with information gathering.[8]

This bifurcation of reading modes complicates the study of homiletic novels. Novels written in one register often made the transition into the hermeneutic register of another, highlighting the difficulty of using literary genre or content as an index of whether any given reading practice is – to use Raymond Williams's formulation – "emergent," "dominant," or "residual."[9] If, for instance, the young today read Alcott's genteel classic *Little Women* as a secular novel about how a family of sisters coped with the deprivations of wartime New England (a dominant twentieth-century interpretation), they do so against the novel's explicit frame within an older Christian heuristic tradition. Today, the novel's repeated reference to Bunyan's *The Pilgrim's Progress* is little more than an allusion to an all but forgotten text. Yet Alcott's original audience intimately knew Bunyan's proto-novelistic allegory; it is likely that *The Pilgrim's Progress* was the most widely read book after the Bible in eighteenth- and nineteenth-century America.[c] Alcott's contemporary

c For a discussion of the proto-novelistic sources that helped give shape to early American novels, see Paul Giles, "Transatlantic currents and the invention of the American novel," chapter 1 in this volume.

readers would have understood the March sisters' use of Bunyan's allegory as a homiletic template for conquering their moral enemies in order to become *types* of Christian (the name of Bunyan's everyman protagonist).

As the sisters personalize *The Pilgrim's Progress* by inserting themselves into its narrative structure, personifying their own moral failings after Bunyan's allegorical antagonists, so Alcott implicitly invites young readers to engage the moral action of *Little Women*, to become participants in a narrativized struggle against anger, selfishness, greed, and fear. By illustrating how the sisters read Bunyan, *Little Women* negotiates the difference between the universality of allegory *and* the specificity of the novel's formal realism, most significantly the individual localized in history. While the characters reflect the uniqueness of individuals, they are, like Bunyan's Christian, also universal (or at least national) types in their facilitation of readerly identification. "There are," Alcott's narrator announces, "many Beths in the world, shy and quiet ... and living for others." And by extrapolation, many Megs, Jos, and Amys.[d]

For Alcott's readers, the personal register encourages the inexperienced to tailor their identification to their own moral faults. Just as each sister identifies with an aspect of Bunyan's Christian, so Alcott's allegory invites readers to choose the appropriate Christian model from characters within the novel. The universal register of the everyman template then encourages them to transcend the personal, and to see their individual lives within the pilgrimage-plot of Christian allegory. Only through such identification can readers, in effect, textualize themselves, becoming, as the March sisters do, "heroines" in their own personal progress. Such a residually intensive reading mode thrives today among those trained in the heuristic tradition from which hosts of novels emerged. The universal register of the everyman template encourages them to transcend the personal, and to see their individual lives within the pilgrimage-plot of Christian allegory. In contemporary works such as William Young's *The Shack* (2007) and Mel Odom's *Apocalypse* series (2003–2008), as well as in their bestselling twentieth-century precursors like Wright's *The Shepherd of the Hills*, Barton's *The Man that Nobody Knows* (1925), Arnold's *Not My Will*, and Roger Elwood's 1980s novels with celestial narrators, we can see the continuation of this kind of identificatory homiletic realism.

Homiletic literature's continuing capacity to co-opt new forms should thus caution against assuming, as critics have, that Christian allegory, with its explicit reading epistemology, has given way to a modern, implicit

d For an alternative reading of *Little Women*, see Julia Mickenberg's "Children's novels" chapter 52 in this collection, 863–864.

epistemology exemplified in the rise of the secular novel.[10] In fact, many nineteenth-century novels we think of as more secular still engage sustained spiritual themes or derive their structure from spiritual allegory, even when religion seems less central or apparent in the plot.[e] Novels such as Catharine Maria Sedgwick's *A New-England Tale* (1822), Melville's *Moby-Dick* (1851), Hawthorne's *The House of the Seven Gables* (1851), Elizabeth Stoddard's *The Morgesons* (1862), Josiah Gilbert Holland's *Sevenoaks* (1875), and Harold Frederic's *The Damnation of Theron Ware* (1896) invoke religious themes, biblical motifs, and Protestant typology – traditionally, the link between Christ and Old Testament personages whose lives imperfectly prefigured his – but they are not, strictly speaking, "religious" novels. *Moby-Dick*, for example, by turns meditates on the presence and absence of an authoritarian God, yet concerns itself less with spiritual salvation than with the redemption of honor and dignity, with a pre-Christian need for vengeance or *wergild* as a reclamation of status, or in its denial, the Job-like recourse to decry God as an antagonist for harassing humanity for sport. Ahab's obsession with the white whale is a Faustian struggle as much indebted to classical epic and drama – to Homeric, Virgilian, and Senecan themes of heroic hubris, hype, and misconstrued destiny – as it is to the Book of Job and Dantean, Spenserian, and Miltonic allegories of humanity's struggle with a bifurcated nature. Among earthly creation, humanity alone has the capacity to rise or fall on the ontological scale, to slip from its place just beneath the angelic orders to the depths of the bestially transmogrified.

Many novels after the Civil War exhibit modern cultural shifts even as they draw on shared schema of not only Protestant theology but also reading practices. In Oliver Wendell Holmes, Sr.'s *Elsie Venner: a Romance of Destiny* (1861) and Edward Bellamy's *Looking Backward* (1890), for instance, science and technology trump traditional belief, while simultaneously incorporating key elements of it.[f] *Elsie Venner* inscribes evolutionary determinism over the tracks of Calvinist predestination to peddle a scientized belief we might think of as Calvinist eugenics. *Looking Backward*, like Howells's *A Traveler from Altruria* (1894) and its sequel, *Through the Eye of the Needle* (1907), offers the optimism of technology as a corrective to the Gilded Age extremes of religious fervor,

e Amy Hungerford's essay in this volume, "Religion and the twentieth-century American novel" (chapter 44), focuses ostensibly on secular novels' appropriation of religious forms and concerns, from the turn of the twentieth century to the present.

f Holmes's blend of science, psychology, and the spiritual in *Elsie Venner* prefigures the connection between Freud, faith, and science fiction, a point Elizabeth Young takes up in "Supernatural novels," chapter 13 in this volume.

tolerance for impoverished suffering, and market greed, projecting onto a utopian future (without Howells's irony) the rational élan not of biological but social evolution, not of laissez-faire industrialism, but the leveling capacity of social institutions, among them state-regulated religion.[g] Other novels draw on the conventions of the historical romance, and, in so doing, interweave biblical typology and regional hagiography, Old Testament genealogy and national history. With their focus on the nation's past, works such as Nathaniel Hawthorne's *The Scarlet Letter* (1850) and *The House of the Seven Gables*, Harriet Beecher Stowe's *Oldtown Folks* (1869) and *The Minister's Wooing* (1859), John W. De Forest's *Witching Times* (1856), Lydia Maria Child's *Hobomok* (1824), Nathan Henry Chamberlain's *The Autobiography of a New England Farmhouse* (1865), Edward P. Roe's *Without a Home* (1881), and Catharine Maria Sedgwick's *A New-England Tale* (1822) recount, revise, and critique the nation's religious history, incorporating spiritual scenes and unfolding plots about faith, belief, or a redemption socially, institutionally, or theologically denied.

Like Melville's *Moby-Dick*, many other novels rely on the structure of allegory, and could take for granted readers' skills in Christian hermeneutic practices. These novels underscore the continuing influence of religious reading practices that homiletic novels help us discern. A hermeneutic that had once parsed scripture into four levels of allegory (literal, allegorical, anagogical, and tropological), survived in nineteenth-century Christian reading practices, despite the novel's supposed hegemony of formal realism and sequential progression. Trained in biblical exegesis, contemporary readers with a range of denominational affiliations came to texts armed with the capacity to understand the thematic and structural overlay of typology and allegory – the thematic recurrence between Old and New Testaments, or between prophecy and its fulfillment – and, as with Warner's use of Bunyan's allegory in *Wide, Wide World*, by the superimposition of a new literary genre across older heuristic conventions. With a high tolerance for anachronism, nineteenth-century Protestant readers possessed the analogical imagination not only to make typological connections between Adam, David, Daniel, or Samson as Christ types *and* Christ, but also to divine through the palimpsest of New World history the sacred patterns of Old Testament typology, discerning a national teleology that could become manifest as a special providence.

g In "Science fiction," chapter 50 in this volume, Priscilla Wald explores how the vogue for science fiction in the postbellum era fostered cultural movements of utopianism, spawning, in fact, utopian communities and galvanizing social idealism into national political movements. See especially 835.

Read from this perspective, Hawthorne's tragic romances focus on events occasioned by individuals' inability to assess providential signs or, more cosmically sinister, the outcome of communities torn by the possibility of multiple interpretations. At the climactic end of *The Scarlet Letter*, for example, the town's failure to achieve a unified interpretation of what the comet portends – "A" for angel, the scarlet letter, adulterer, and so on – seems playful only when we forget the damage that their inability to interpret celestial signs has already caused, or the devastating consequences of a sign's plural meaning for a society whose system of justice depended on linguistic precision, the moral certainty of an authoritative meaning. In Hawthorne's work, as to an extent Melville's, allegory's resistance to traditional hermeneutic practices – its resistance to a consistent scriptural rendering – does not merely pull characters into the maelstrom of meanings and the ambiguity of conflicting signs, but also spins centrifugally outward into historical specificity and material reference, constituting a supra-realism. Yet destabilized by the juxtaposition of material detail and transcendent meaning, even historical particularity and material specificity finally slide back into allegory. It is this teetering between realism and allegory that produces the "unreality" that the literary critic Amy Kaplan identifies as the aesthetic concern occupying literary realism in works such as Stephen Crane's *The Red Badge of Courage* (1895), Jack London's *The People of the Abyss* (1903), and Frank Norris's, *McTeague* (1899).[11] From this perspective, even in works epitomizing American literary realism the relationship between formal realism and homiletic reading discloses the extent to which this modernist aesthetic still had its moorings in allegory.

Young adults and homiletic reading practices

Because religious instruction sought to inculcate moral habits early, the first American novels for young adults were religious, yet less inspirational than admonishing in their refrain against imprudence, moral laxity, and the habituating nature of vice. Sarah Savage's *The Factory Girl* (1814) and *Filial Affection; or, the Clergyman's Granddaughter* (1820), like Weems's "Looking Glass" tales, featured the harsh realities of early national life, warning children of their birthright in sin and preparing them for life-long vigilance against pride, anger, lying, and libidinous impulses. Unlike the celebration of religious austerity in Savage's and Catharine Sedgwick's works, later novels increasingly trace the declining arc of Calvinism, when innate depravity linked tragedy to hereditary sin or retributive justice. Savage's novels depict protagonists exemplary in their humility and narrative asides praise them for their self-accusation and shame for seemingly unavoidable events. They prescribe a strict diet of self-denial and recreational austerity, illustrating the degree to which, particularly in rural America, the belief in children's natural depravity forestalled modern childhood as a time bracketed from the moral, physical, and economic pressures of adulthood.

This paradigm gradually changed with Protestant theology over the course of the nineteenth century. As political sentiment shifted early in the century away from class-privileged hierarchies associated with Federalism, a theology predicated on pre-existing covenants and God's arbitrary sovereignty was becoming incompatible with the linchpin of commerce and contract, the individual's free and informed consent. By mid-century, the logic of imputation theology, in which one person is bound over to the law for the crime of another – Adam's descendants for his deeds – seemed irrational in an age that championed inalienable rights and advocated voluntary contractual forms of political obligation.[12] In particular, the decline in the belief in original sin meant that the young did not have an inchoate sense of depravity that might otherwise protect them from being surprised by sin. As theology accompanied changes in institutional attitudes toward children and childrearing in the home, particularly in the decades before and after the Civil War, it cultivated Sunday school curricula that spilled over into secular education. We can see these paradigms at work in novels that exemplified spiritual duty through child development in ordinary activities, such as Jacob Abbott's *Rollo at Work* (1835), *Rollo at Play* (1835) *Rollo's Experiments*(1839), and *Rollo's Travels* (1855), and in novels by familiar authors such as Alcott, Maria Susanna Cummins, Elizabeth Stuart Phelps, E. D. E. N. Southworth, and Warner. But in the nineteenth-century novels published by scores of forgotten writers, young readers found protagonists with whom they sympathized through an *a priori* structure of identification that modernized the *imitatio Christi* by channeling it through exemplary protagonists who struggled daily for moral self-mastery.[13]

Under the pseudonym of Sophie May, Rebecca Sophia Clarke began a series of stories in 1861 that introduced the nation's young to the "Little Prudy Parlin" characters, and to a range of gentler childrearing practices. Extending a modernized child psychology in her "Maidenhead" series, Clarke wrote her next series for older girls, who, at an age perceived more vulnerable for girls than boys, required sterner medicine. These novels portray not the cycles of sin and expiation that had earlier characterized the narrative realism of Hannah Webster Foster's *The Coquette* (1797) and Susanna Rowson's *Charlotte Temple* (1794) but scenes in which caution vigilantly exercised averts moral and spiritual calamity, consequences occasionally forecast in direct-address narrative interruptions outside the narrative frame. Similarly, Isabella Macdonald Alden and Mrs. C. M. Livingston co-authored novels about children encountering the temptations of a modern age. Beginning with Bible histories, they went on to pen more than sixty novels under the pseudonym "Pansy" (1873–1896) including, *Esther Ried: Asleep and Awake* (1870); *Four Girls at Chautauqua* (1876); *Ruth Erskine's Cross* (1879); *A New Graft on the Family Tree* (1880); *Mrs. Harry Harper's Awakening* (1880); *An Endless Chain* (1887); and *Making Fate* (1895).

Late antebellum and early postbellum novels for the young were inspirational, if formulaic, but seldom engaged doctrine, theological disputes, or scriptural exegesis. Drawing on Christian concepts keyed less to doctrine than to the popular theological trends suffusing postbellum culture – such as atonement theology's emphases on sacrifice and suffering, labor and poverty, and on millennial prosperity – these novels transcended denominational affiliation to achieve the Sunday School Association's purpose of providing a broad evangelical education.

Advertisements for these novels assured parents that "their heroes bring us face to face with every phase of home life, and present graphic and inspiring pictures of the actual struggles through which victorious souls must go."[14] In just two years, beginning in 1870, Susan Warner wrote her series "A Story of Small Beginnings" for older adolescents, which included *What She Could* (1871); *Opportunities* (1871); *The House in Town* (1872); and *Trading* (1872). If these works demonstrate how literature gendered Christian education by cautioning young girls about the need for vigilant reflection to avert irreparable moral damage, they are inversely mirrored by novels like Elizabeth Oakes Smith's *The Newsboy* (1854) and later, by Horatio Alger's "second-chance" novels for boys, beginning with *Ragged Dick* (1868), that extolled honesty, charity, and chastity, and in contrast to girls' fiction, peddled "luck and pluck" as a means of social advancement. The gradual secularization of religious values associated first with boys' novels is especially clear in *Ragged Dick*'s aptly titled sequel *Fame and Fortune; or, the Progress of Richard Hunter* (1868).

This largely unexamined body of material regularly drew on homiletic pedagogies emerging from sweeping changes during the century in views about epistemology and children's moral aptitude, registered in literary form's perceived capacity to instantiate spiritual growth. In *The Young Christian* (1832), Jacob Abbott reminded educators of the necessity of vivid, picturesque language to transport young listeners into the narrative frame: "Words that have been often repeated gradually lose their power to awaken vivid ideas in the mind."[15] He contrasts a father's "cold reading" of a Bible passage to a vivifying homiletic rendering:

> Suppose that this same father could, by some magic power, show to his children the real scene which these verses describe. Suppose he could go back through the eighteen hundred years since these events occurred, and taking his family to some elevation . . . from which they might overlook the country of Galilee, *actually show* them *all that this chapter describes*.[16]

By reading in a way that he referred to as "experiential," Abbott assured teachers that children could experience what they read, not as passive consumers but as engaged participants.

Homiletic novelists set about experimenting with discursive strategies that would produce new forms of realism, an aesthetics of immediacy that would generate firsthand experience through scenes so vivid that they transported readers inside the narrative frame. In *Ben-Hur*, for example, Wallace illustrates and explains the function of such narrative immediacy. Instructing young Judah in Hebrew history, his mother asks him to imaginatively envision all she describes. With confirmation that he hears the very music with which she sets the scene, she responds:

> You can use your fancy, and stand with me, as if by the wayside, while the chosen of Israel pass us at the head of the procession. Now they come – patriarchs first. I almost hear the bells of their camels and the lowing of their herds. Who is he who walks alone between the companies? An old man, yet his eye is not dim . . . In such a light as I could, I have set our great men before you – patriarchs, legislators, warriors, singers, prophets.

Just as *Little Women* proffers templates for moral development by depicting how the Marsh sisters study *The Pilgrim's Progress* daily and apply its lessons to their lives, so *Ben-Hur* indicates the mode of its own reading by illustrating the proper mental orientation ("use your fancy, and stand with me, as if by the wayside") to homiletic realism. These novels thus model one way that heuristics trained readers to insert themselves within novelistic representations, and, conversely, to furnish traditional allegories with vivid, temporally specific realism.

The Catholic novel and historical Christianity

The private space of reading and the novel's capacity to foster ideological commitment through characters with whom readers identified helped neutralize the dogmatic nature of verbal debate and the narrowly focused doctrinal and denominational partisanship associated with sermons and religious tracts. Fictional narrative dramatized theological difference in the idiom of ordinary life, disengaging it from the locutionary pace of orality and the dialectical structure of verbal argument, while articulating it with a realism that passed for readers' everyday experiences. Religious educators initially viewed the novel's serialized unfolding with concern. They worried that its capacity to pace thought and defer judgment over time could disarm young Christians, whose moral resistance would be worn away by the novel's structure of identification, narrative repetition, fictional escapism, and emotional appeal.[h] The Catholic literary critic Orestes Brownson, formerly part of Concord's transcendentalist coterie and later editor of the influential *Brownson's Quarterly Review*, for instance, excoriated the novel in an 1846 review. Not only did he repudiate it generally, but he took aim at the Catholic novel for its Protestant derivation: although such novels "have a Catholic costume and inculcate some Catholic doctrines, they have too many affinities with the spirit of Protestant novels and romances, and feed a sickly sentimentalism rather than nourish a robust piety."[17]

Yet religious authors also came to see how these same features might transform the novel into a powerful, self-regulating instrument for morally fortifying the masses. If the religious novel could enlist readers into desired political or intellectual positions by fostering ideological identification through narrative content, it could equally undermine partisanship or heal the fracture caused by overheated interdenominational debates that plagued the sermon form. In response to the novel's enormous popularity and proselytizing success among Protestants, Brownson, its detractor a decade before, did an about-face: such "literature is a power, and it is a power which we should possess ourselves. Let every man, every woman, old or young, that can write a passable book, write it." Attesting to the novel's relevance as an instrument of religious education apart from any concern for aesthetics, Brownson suggested that "even trash is better than nothing."[18]

No category of novel better illustrated educators' faith in the genre's capacity to defuse ideological and inter-faith hostility than the Catholic novel. Through rational explanation, it sought to neutralize anti-Catholic sentiment among middle-class readers in a century that saw the rise of the anti-Catholic Know-Nothing Party in the 1850s and the American Protective Association in the 1880s. The Catholic novel also confronted a backlog of stereotypes and libels that circulated in perennially published novelized

h For a useful history of the novel's cultural acceptance, see Hochman, chapter 36.

pamphlets, such as Rebecca Reed's *Six Months in a Convent* (1835) and Maria Monk's *Awful Disclosures* (1836), and in lurid tales spun after the fashion of George Lippard's *Quaker City; or, the Monks of Monk-Hall* (1844). Against this anti-Catholic propaganda – popularized in narratives of fugitive nuns, lascivious monks, and cloister intrigue – Catholic novelists presented the case for Catholicism over Protestantism in measured tones, often incorporating scenes in which Catholic and Protestant characters undertake a scriptural study together.

In many novels, Catholics walk Protestants through the rudiments of their theology and liturgy. The scores of novels written by Anna H. Dorsey, for example, center on Catholic children who must win the approval of a Protestant family. In *Conscience; or the Trials of May Brooke* (1856), the orphan May converts her stern uncle to Catholicism when he learns on his deathbed of her secret works of charity. While an important resource for increasing the faith and piety of the laity, novels by Charles James Cannon, Mary Hughs, William B. MacCabe, George H. Miles, Charles Constantine Pise, John T. Roddan, George Sand, and W. P. Strickland employed a range of strategies for engaging Protestant readers. Cannon's *Father Felix* (1845) dramatizes scenes in which Catholics respond to Protestant persecution, yet avoid the feeling-focused emotionalism of Protestant fiction that appealed to interdenominational evangelical audiences. The dialogue between the Protestant protagonist Adrian and his Catholic tutor Father Felix is an elaborate setup for explaining Catholicism to converts. Playing to the Protestant emphasis on biblical authority – a view in its extreme known as "bible-onlyism" – Catholic authors keyed these passages to scripture, rarely referencing outside authority, including the more Protestant-tolerated Patristic authors, Augustine, Jerome, and Aquinas. A rare exception, Hughs's *Julia Ormond; or, the New Settlement* (1846), depicts the conversion of an Andover Seminary graduate by a young Catholic woman on the Mississippi frontier. In the novel, Julia dispassionately explains to her Protestant auditor why the church fathers are as well informed as biblical authors, whose stories, she points out, were not canonized as the New Testament until the fourth century by the very authorities Protestants would disqualify. Taking advantage of Protestant interest in biblical historicism – the "higher criticism" emerging out of German universities that viewed the Bible as a historical document – postbellum Catholic novels more forcefully defended the use of extrabiblical authority at a time when Protestants began dividing over the question of the Bible's infallibility and living-word theology.

As with Cannon and Hughs, Pearl Craigie, under the pseudonym John Oliver Hobbes, and Frances Christine Tiernan, under the pseudonym

Christian Reid, wrote scores of novels illustrating how lived piety, charity, and logical argument assist Catholic protagonists in converting Protestants through rational rather than reactionary scriptural examinations. When these novels entered a dialogue with Protestant faith groups, they did so primarily with more formal or high-church denominations, "Old School" Congregationalists and Presbyterians, Episcopalians, and Anglicans. Catholic novels often lampooned the religious practices of their chief detractors, revivalist denominations, especially Baptists, Methodists, and Campbellites, while reserving their derision for Mormons, Millerites, and Methodist exhorters riding frontier "circuits."

In American Protestantism and Catholicism generally, the past and the present merged in symbolic scenes of rebirth. Protestant authors frequently turned to the nation's colonial or regional origins: Lydia Maria Child in *Hobomok* and Nathaniel Hawthorne in *The Scarlet Letter* and *The House of the Seven Gables* to colonial Massachusetts; Mary Johnston in *To Have and to Hold* to colonial Virginia; John Fox Jr.'s *Little Shepherd of Kingdom Come* (1903) and Harold Bell Wright's *The Shepherd of the Hills* to frontier Kentucky and Arkansas; and Thomas Dixon Jr.'s *The Clansman* (1905) and *The Leopard's Spots* (1902) to the New South, where, after Reconstruction, white supremacy passed for Anglo-Saxon hagiography to give it the burnish of a biblical and biological pedigree. Millenarian novelists downplayed nationalist rhetoric to claim their authority not from region or nation but from the invisible Kingdom whose earthly dispensation did not transcend nationalism altogether since, if these novels did not always locate the Second Coming in America's not-so-distant future – as with the "Left Behind" series of today – they augured America's place as a privileged site in the end-times events prophesied in the Book of Revelation. All of these works tied themselves to themes of renewal by linking themselves to the cyclical patterns of biblical typology, in which prophecy is enacted in histories foreshadowed and repeated through time. Pauline Hopkins's *Of One Blood* (1903) returns its protagonist to Africa, from which, as the novel's scriptural title suggests (Acts 17:26), an ancient and recycling stream of biblical history issued.

Such narrative strategies hardly escaped the notice of Catholic novelists. They often set their works in the Middle Ages, in plots that revealed the church's ancient authority before New World colonization. Scenes of holy ritual lent credence to Catholicism in a language that fed Americans' absorption with the past, with an antiquity that justified the nation's sense of exceptionalism and themes of manifest destiny. While Anna Dorsey set novels in colonial America, for instance, she also set them in ancient Ireland and

England. *Mona the Vestal* (1869) dramatizes the transition between the Ireland's fourth and fifth-century Druid religion and the church under the missions of Pope Celestine I; *The House at Glenarra* (1887) extends that story through history, making Irish immigration part of New World eschatology (a redemptive theme still detectable in contemporary narratives such as Frank McCourt's *Angela's Ashes* [1996]) and initiating a market in the next century for medieval Christian allegories in the stamp of C. S. Lewis's *The Chronicles of Narnia* (1950–1956) and J. R. R. Tolkien's Middle-Earth trilogy, *Lord of the Rings* (1937–1949).

Primitive Christianity and the homiletic novel

Following the Civil War, novels about ancient Christianity fostered the development and spread of Christian primitivism, a popular theology emerging from Bible-onlyism and stripped-down Christian movements spearheaded early in the century. The shift in evangelical theology toward religious primitivism, in turn, boosted sales of religious novels that elevated the spiritual status of poverty and suffering and peddled themes of spiritual pilgrimage and martyrdom. The degree to which readers emphasized the literal dimensions of the pilgrimage theme as a template for their own spiritual development depended to an extent on race and class. African American and impoverished white men and women, whose fugitive status, dispossession, or itinerancy led them on protracted migrations, would read as literal the hardships offered by a template still defined in America by Bunyan's allegorical progress. Eighteenth- and early nineteenth-century spiritual autobiographers like David Brainerd, John Wesley, Charles Finney, and Zilpha Elaw emphasized the correlation between biblical metaphors and their impoverished followings, individuals living from hand to mouth on the nation's margins.

Yet after mid-century, with the Industrial Revolution's reach into rural life, the increasingly visible disparity between the poor and wealthy and between agrarian labor and urban industry fostered markets for novels that recast poverty in the virtuous mold of first-century Christians. Such a narrative construct not only revalued the lives of the working classes – whose value had been driven down by urban economies newly supported by immigrant labor and machines – but also revivified parables and homiletic allegories as structures for imagining their lives in a way that transformed physical hardship and mental suffering into the biblical idiom of laborer, soldier, servant, beggar, and redeemed thief. By privileging suffering, these narratives fueled interest in the historical details of the first martyrs, outcasts of the empire and the fodder of Roman blood sports. Fictional accounts of first-century Rome such as E. L. Carey's *The Martyr* (*c.*1820) and Henry Hart Milman's *The Martyr of Antioch* (1822), both of which enjoyed wide circulation in the United States, multiplied after mid-century, inspiring a lasting tradition of fiction set in the apostolic age. In the introduction to *Carey's Library of Choice Literature*, James Carey describes the first disciples in a way that captured the religious status enjoyed by the rural poor, day laborers, indigent farmers, and free and enslaved African American men and women: those "bred in the camp and the field, encompassed with hardships and dangers, would be little encumbered with learning or philosophy, therefore more open to conviction."[19]

In the wake of higher criticism, ministers like Joseph Holt Ingraham turned to writing historical novels that described Bible scenes with the imaginative detail and temporal immediacy that Abbott advocated for Christian fiction.[20] If Catholic novels drew on medieval traditions to depict a time when the church alone illuminated the Western world's fall into darkness, validating the church's claim of unbroken authority, Protestant novels turned back still further to Christianity's apostolic origins. By depicting Christianity's simple beginnings, they portrayed Catholic liturgy as a corruption of later ages. No novel evoked a more detailed, historical account of Christianity's tumultuous birth than Wallace's *Ben-Hur*. With greater historical sophistication than Cummins's *El Fureides* (1860) – also set in the ancient Middle East – Wallace's novel, like Cummins's before it, fed a passion among evangelicals for realistic literary tapestries of early Christian survival. In evocative detail, *Ben-Hur* gives flesh to plausible, if extra-biblical, events from the Nativity to the Crucifixion. Readers meet Judah Ben-Hur first as a Jewish prince straining against Roman oppression, only to follow him through a crucible of suffering, as galley slave and bereaved brother and son, until consumed with vengeance, he learns how his mother and sister contracted leprosy under a false imprisonment. While the novel depicts Christ obliquely, as a mysterious figure whose path intersects *Ben-Hur*'s, the book's subtitle, *A Tale of the Christ*, reminds readers how Judah's and Jesus' stories, like their own, are one and the same through the imitative mechanism of Christian typology. By emulating Christ, Christians learn to walk *in his steps* – literally, *imitatio Christi* – or, in a radical imitation theology advocated by W. T. Stead in *If Christ Came to Chicago* (1894), they are enjoined to "Be a Christ!"

The Social Gospel

Fiction about first-century Christianity collaborated in the popularity of atonement theology and the nineteenth-century Trinitarian debates that focused on

Christ's ontological status, whether the incarnation rendered him God, man, or "god-man." After the Civil War, identification with Christ not as awe-inspiring Messiah but – as Elizabeth Phelps depicted him in *The Gates Ajar* – in the gentle, suffering Jesus, generated an ethos of "Christian stewardship" (the Social Gospel credo Charles M. Sheldon popularized as the subtitle of *His Brother's Keeper* [1895]) that emerged in the 1880s as the Social Gospel. Out of abolitionism, women's suffrage, and temperance emerged a host of religiously rooted postbellum agendas to address poverty, labor, immigration reform, and urban renewal. Social reform proliferated as the decline in predestinarianism invigorated the idea of human volition, championing individuals' capacity to alter the social world in anticipation of a pan-continental salvation army.

For a broad spectrum of Protestants, the focus on Jesus as "son of man" rather than "Son of God" made his carnal struggle against sin, sorrow, doubt, and even erotic desire into a triumph of spirit over flesh to which humanity could aspire. (This thematic history peaked with Martin Scorsese's film *The Last Temptation of Christ* [1988].) The radical end of religious humanism – the belief in humanity to approximate Christ – modernized this revivified *imitatio Christi*, producing an absorption with Christ's poverty that granted respectability to poorer classes, and in turn whetted the evangelical appetite for novels that portrayed the rich arming themselves for duty as God's earthly stewards. Sheldon epitomized the *fin-de-siècle* mood in scores of novels depicting well-heeled protagonists sacrificing wealth, family, and dreams to assist the urban poor.

Because such a structure of identification required greater knowledge of Christ's life than the Synoptic Gospels recorded, homiletic novels dramatized the immensity of Christ's suffering for humanity in realistic detail, rendering him as homeless in Judea, in rags in a Chicago street, and, in Bruce Barton's *The Man Nobody Knows* (1925), in business attire on Wall Street. Like Barton's novel, Albion Tourgée's *Murvale Eastman* (1890), Sheldon's *In His Steps* and *The Crucifixion of Philip Strong* (1894), W. E. B. Du Bois's short stories "Jesus Christ in Georgia" (1911) and "Jesus Christ in Texas" from *Dark Water* (1920), and Rebecca Harding Davis's *Life in the Iron-Mills* (1861), countless narratives spun hypotheticals about Christ's incognito visits to Gilded Age cities as a charwoman, laborer, and in Du Bois's fiction, as a black man lynched by white Christians who failed to recognize their Savior beneath an "olive" complexion. Shamed by their complacency toward the "undeserving poor," Social Gospel Christians increasingly measured their worth by the ability to see in the suffering, disabled, and dying the visage of their Lord.

Through such an identificatory structure, the homiletic novel became a powerful agent of reform. The genre's emphasis on how moral choices alter plot and, thus, individuals'– both characters' and readers'– impact in and outside historical time is a crucial yet critically overlooked mechanism for how homiletic practices instrumentalized narrative in the service of Christians' moral maturation. This emphasis also marks the intersection between more secular realism and the homiletic novel. Yet, as a homogeneous category, the "Social Gospel novel," a rubric taken from Charles Hopkins's 1940 study, obviates the disparate ends novels in this period served, obscuring theological nuances and the unique reading practices that differentiated religiously themed novels from the more devotional works that shaped the way the religious experienced the world.[21] The label fails to distinguish between novels that, like Howells's *Annie Kilburn* (1889) and Jesse Jones's *The Christian Commonwealth* (1900), embraced culturally suffused Christian values as part of American life, and those that, like Henry Wood's *Edward Burton* (1890) and Bradley Gilman's *Ronald Carnaquay: A Commercial Clergyman* (1903), offered blueprints for individual and social reform. Additionally, it fails to distinguish either of these from novels like Washington Gladden's *The Christian League of Connecticut* (1883), Edward Everett Hale's *How They Lived in Hampton* (1888), and Howells's *Altruria* sequel, *Through the Eye of the Needle* (1907), that endorsed social reform in varying degrees of millennial utopianism. As a catchall, the "Social Gospel novel" homogenizes the movement's broad appeal between the sectarian extremes of formal and popular Christianity and between evangelicalism and ethical secularism. Where secular realism focused on individuals' ethical behavior in a world defined by social and physical forces, the homiletic novel emphasized identification with the sordid and suffering masses in an effort to highlight the relationship between representation and material reality and between the temporal and the spiritual. While both secular and homiletic realism grounded themselves in the novel's psychological and formal realism, for the homiletic novel such realism – the very materiality of reference – was the beginning rather than the end of signification. It was the fulcrum by which religious readers lifted themselves above the facts and figures of material existence into what they deemed *the* authentic reality beyond.

Among the novels emerging during the Social Gospel era, these differences were subtle but real. Tourgée's *Murvale Eastman*, like Davis's earlier *Life in the Iron-Mills*, promoted Christian ethics in the service of labor reform, whereas

Wright's *That Printer of Udell's* (1903) promoted temperance as one means among many to social salvation. Howells's *The Rise of Silas Lapham* (1885) posits the individual's moral struggle as the building block from which social reform is incrementally constructed, while Sheldon's and Wright's novels make collective organization key to reformation as the trigger for social salvation. Whereas Howells's novels promote reform in this world as a moral end in itself (a point Michael Elliott parses in greater detail in this volume), Sheldon's and Wright's promote it as a means to communal transcendence into the next.[i] By accounting for these divergent end-games, we can better isolate and define the generic distinctions that comprise the novel's ideological and aesthetic breadth and the range of its spiritual inflection and political and devotional instrumentalism.

A key formal feature that distinguishes homiletic novels from their secular counterparts is their refusal of narrative closure. Far from an aesthetic weakness, narrative disruption was an invitation to complete the text, a participatory mechanism intended to simulate the moral challenges Christians might confront. The homiletic novel's realism belonged to a tradition of "inoculation theology" that had emerged with the hellfire sermon and continues today in alternative media forms that, like the homiletic novel, attempt to simulate plausible realities intended "virtually" to engage readers in hypothetical moral dilemmas in an effort to exercise judgment and volition. Such a reading practice is an example of the particular habits of imagination that allowed the religious to see their lives unfold through Bunyan's transformative allegory or, more recently, to accept the characterological impersonation demanded by "Left Behind: Eternal Forces"– in which players enact the role of Christ's soldiers in a post-Rapture landscape – or in modern-day hell houses, where the young tour graphic vignettes of human suffering to experience the eternal consequences of vice and sin. Readers came prepared for the homiletic novel's abruptly ending plots and open-ended resolutions meant to simulate the personal experience of the conversion process and the inevitability of spiritual backsliding. In Christian tradition going back to the early church, the faithful were encouraged to piece their experiences into a unified pattern after the fact, a personal teleology construed from temporally disjointed events. Narrative breaks simulated emotional disruption, stalled conversions, spiritual stagnation, and the doubt that besought salvific assurance. Such disruption

i For a study of Howells that complicates the conventional popular and critical assessment of his canon as a purveyor of Social Gospel ideology, see Michael Elliott's "Realism and radicalism: the school of Howells," chapter 17 in this volume.

could be properly accounted for only through imaginative exercises that pieced seemingly discrete experiences into a unified expression of one's spiritual progress. By filling in narrative gaps or completing storylines, modern readers emplot the homiletic novel, exercising moral judgment and, in so doing, learn strategies for devising a spiritual narratology for their own lives. In the same way that colonial Protestants had earlier used typology to structure their journals into spiritual autobiographies – sweeping narratives revealing particular providences – later religious readers drew on the homiletic novel's frame as a heuristic device for revealing spiritual development and organizing personal experience into meaningful patterns that manifested the purpose-driven life.

Through the connection between interactive narrative and the muscularization of readerly agency, the homiletic novel wore away at the twin *fin-de-siècle* legacies of Christian and scientific determinism and promoted a host of reform movements. While critically overlooked, it was as much to this broad focus on men *and* women's volitional capacity as to the narrow emphasis on masculinity that "muscular Christianity" came to characterize religious reform in the early twentieth century, an ethos fostered through readers' engagement with homiletic novels. In Sheldon's *In His Steps*, characters struggle with the moral complexities of the modern world, and interracial congregations took up the novel as an exercise through which they collectively engaged moral hypotheticals, unifying community values and fortifying individual faith. Novels such as Tourgée's *Murvale Eastman*, Katherine Pearson Woods's *Metzerott, Shoemaker* (1889), Hjalmar Boyesen's *The Social Strugglers* (1893), and Sheldon's *His Brother's Keeper* (1896) provided blueprints for reform that were implemented in real life. Spiritual challenges encountered first in narrative became blueprints for community reform, much as when *In His Steps* inspired Sheldon's white congregation to integrate with a neighboring black church, and to organize kindergartens and vocational classes for adults, a development that later became the basis for another homiletic novel, *The Redemption of Freetown* (1899).

Nineteenth-century religious novelists counted on readers' ability to personalize the novel's plot structure by overlaying its heuristic frame across the text of their own experience. In so doing, they intended their readers to draw connections between literary representation and daily life to reveal how, like fiction, experiences were themselves merely representations of the eternal reality behind the temporal. As the novel's plot unraveled in empty, homogeneous time – incrementally revealing God's unfolding plot – it did not so much undermine readers' commitment to their part in the providential design as strengthen their perception of the protagonist's (and thus their own) agency in shaping or emplotting that destiny. While more secular novels laid out their fictive landscapes in a linear path commensurate with secular readers' perception of time, homiletic novels fostered identification with allegory, a typological script whose action unfolds simultaneously inside and outside historical time. To "read" narratives in this way is to understand oneself as a historically located subject with transhistorical agency. It was to this end above all that nineteenth-century homiletic novels provided a counter-balance to life in an increasingly modernizing nation by encouraging readers to reconnect their lives with ancient sacred stories and templates. They did so by drawing both on the most modern of literary forms, the novel, and the older genres of sermon, parable, and homily.

Notes

1. George Parsons Lathrop, "The Novel and Its Future," *Atlantic Monthly* (September 1874): 313–334: 313.
2. Unless denoted as postbellum or late nineteenth-century "literary realism," I use "realism" throughout this chapter in a broader critical sense, referring to a discursive mode of literary representation emerging in the eighteenth- and nineteenth-century United States that complemented the emergence of empirical method, particularly the Lockean emphasis on sensory experience.
3. For a full discussion of the category of the "homiletic novel," see Gregory S. Jackson, *The Word and Its Witness: The Spiritualization of American Realism* (Chicago: University of Chicago Press, 2009), 157–214.
4. Brooks E. Holifield, *Theology in America: Christian Thought from the Age of the Puritans to the Civil War* (New Haven: Yale University Press, 2003), 127–217.
5. For a larger discussion of the sermon's "aesthetics of immediacy," see Jackson, *The Word and Its Witness*, 31–35; 189–214.
6. Gregory S. Jackson, " 'What Would Jesus Do?' Practical Christianity, Social Gospel Realism, and the Homiletic Novel," *PMLA* 121 (May 2006): 277–310.
7. David D. Hall, "The Uses of Literacy in New England, 1600–1850," in *Printing and Society in Early America*, ed. William L. Joyce *et al.* (Worcester, MA: Oak Knoll, 1983), 1–47.
8. For the prominence of this bifurcated reading practice in American literary history, see Cathy N. Davidson, *Revolution and the Word: The Rise of the Novel in America* (New York: Oxford University Press, 1986); and Paul David Nord, *Faith in Reading: Religious Publishing and the Birth of Mass Media in America* (New York: Oxford University Press, 2004). For a historical perspective on the American practice of reading, see David D. Hall, *Ways of Writing: The Practice of Text-Making in Seventeenth-Century New England* (Philadelphia: University of Pennsylvania Press, 2008).

9. Raymond Williams's formula for the simultaneous temporal stratification of culture into distinct epochs marked by "emergent," "dominant," and "residual" cultural strains, provides a useful model for conceiving how individuals or communities can coexist in different times. These concepts are most fully developed in his *Marxism and Literature* (Oxford: Oxford University Press, 1977).
10. Michael McKeon and Leopold Damrosch, Jr. have both demonstrated the significant extent to which Bunyan's *The Pilgrim's Progress* is an originating source of the English novel: McKeon, *The Origins of the English Novel, 1600–1740* (Baltimore: Johns Hopkins University Press, 1987); Damrosch, *God's Plot and Man's Stories: Studies in Fictional Imagination from Milton to Fielding* (Chicago: University of Chicago Press, 1985).
11. See Amy Kaplan, *The Social Construction of American Realism* (Chicago: University of Chicago Press, 1988), 4–11.
12. Taking this logic to its natural conclusion, anti-Catholic and anti-Mormon novels depicted scenes in which young women were coerced into taking vows, often collapsing at the moment of consent, the trigger of lawful contract. Maria Ward's *The Mormon Wife* (1873; originally *Female Life Among the Mormons*), Metta Victoria Fuller's (pseudonym, Metta Victor) *Mormon Wives* (1856), A. G. Paddock's *The Fate of Madame La Tour: A Tale of Great Salt Lake* (1881), Mary W. Hudson's *Esther the Gentile* (1888), and Alfreda Bell's *Boadicea the Mormon Wife* (1855) depict such scenes, figuring the contest for citizens' informed consent and the motivation for their political obligation. See Nancy Bentley, "Marriage as Treason: Polygamy, Nation, and the Novel," in *The Futures of American Studies*, ed. Donald Pease and Robyn Wiegman (Durham, NC: Duke University Press, 2003), 341–370; and Gregory S. Jackson, "'A Dowry of Suffering': Consent, Contract, and Political Coverture in John W. De Forest's Reconstruction Romance," *American Literary History* 15.2 (Summer 2003): 277–310.
13. Novels exemplifying appropriate Christian conduct included Thomas Bailey Aldrich, *Prudence Palfrey* (1874); Mary Baskin, *Released* (1878); and many others.
14. Citation comes from the flyleaf of Pansy books published in the 1860s. In the same pattern, Martha Finley wrote nearly thirty volumes recounting the adventures of her heroine Elsie Dinsmore in the decades following the American Civil War.
15. Jacob Abbott, *The Young Christian; or, A Familiar Illustration of the Principles of Christian Duty* (New York: American Tract Society, 1832), 229–230.
16. *Ibid.*, 230.
17. Orestes Brownson, *Brownson's Quarterly Review* (July 1846): 402–403.
18. Orestes Brownson, *Brownson's Quarterly Review* (April 1856): 271–272.
19. James Carey, *Carey's Library of Choice Literature* (Philadelphia: E. L. Carey and A. Hart, 1936): 18–30: 19.

20. *The Prince of the House of David* (1855), Ingraham's most enduring novel, depicted scenes that focused not only on historical events but also on the everyday smells, sounds, and sights of the Mediterranean world.
21. Charles Howard Hopkins, *The Rise of the Social Gospel in American Protestantism* (New Haven: Yale University Press, 1940). For a fresh take on the racial dimensions of the Social Gospel, see Ralph E. Luker, *The Social Gospel in Black and White: American Racial Reform, 1885–1912* (Chapel Hill: University of North Caroline Press, 1991).

11

Manhood and the early American novel

MILETTE SHAMIR

In the decades between the American Revolution and the Civil War, both the concept of manhood and the genre of the novel underwent important transformations. With changes in the economy, the political system, and family structure, the relatively secure patriarchal paradigms of colonial manhood were becoming noticeably threadbare. A new fiction of masculinity – spreading forth from the nascent white middle class in the urban northeast – gradually revised all major relations by which manhood is defined. The new paradigm of "self-made manhood" changed how men saw themselves in relation to their fathers (and thus their understanding of paternal authority), to women (and the emergent ideal of domestic womanhood), and to their peers (and, more broadly, the homosocial public sphere). These changes, pitting a new concept of manly self-regard against traditional social bonds, resulted in tensions and ambiguities sometimes described by historians of antebellum manhood in terms of a "crisis."[1]

During the same decades, the novel arose from the status of a morally questionable genre at the end of the eighteenth century to that of the most popular literary form by the middle of the nineteenth. Early critics of the novel found in the genre, ironically, both the danger of solipsism and the threat of risky social affiliations. The novel was criticized for luring its readers into a privatist, isolated existence, *and* for fostering in them alternative identifications and imaginary bonds that threatened to erode existing structures of power.[2] The "triumph of the novel" did not end such concerns. While, by the 1850s, the legitimacy of the novel as such was seldom questioned, its relative linguistic freedom, open form, and mounting diversification kept debates over its moral hazards alive.[a] Antebellum reviewers continued to express concern

a Barbara Hochman points out elsewhere in this volume that "Until well into the twentieth century fiction-reading was an extremely popular but still contested social practice" ("Readers and reading groups," chapter 36, 600).

over some novelistic themes, styles, and subgenres that were seen to inculcate self-centered individualism or to promote compromising social connections.[3]

To discuss "manhood and the early American novel," then, is to align two shifting and unstable domains. We can neither simply examine the novelistic representations of a fixed definition of antebellum manhood, nor analyze a paradigmatic novel within which ideas of manhood can be found and assembled. But it is precisely the diversity and flexibility of the novel as a genre that makes it a fertile terrain for understanding the transforming concept of manhood during the first half of the nineteenth century. The conflicting ways in which the novel was described – as encouraging privatism and promoting sociability – reflected the major tension in self-made manhood between a fantasy of unfettered autonomy and a need to depend upon others. After describing the rise of the self-made man with his constitutive ambivalences, this chapter will focus on how the novel offered a useful vehicle for writers working through the prescriptions and limits of this fraught ideal of manhood.

Fathers and sons

Our modern understanding of masculinity owes its shape largely to Sigmund Freud. After centuries in which masculinity was hidden under the mantle of invisibility and universality, in which it assumed the privilege of the self-evident and natural, it was Freud who first offered a sustained analysis of the concept. Freud told a powerful story about the formative moments of masculine identity in the oedipal complex, the son's feelings of rivalry and identification with his father. He attributed the resolution of that story to the terror of castration, which causes the frightened boy to intensify his identification with his father, give up his desire for the mother, and find consolation in the future promise of adult male power, internalizing in the process the father's authority in the form of the super-ego. Freud, however, never regarded masculinity as simply "achieved" at the oedipal resolution. He regarded normative masculinity as harboring the elements of its own undoing, its promise of phallic power forever haunted by alternative desires and identifications, by illusions of power as well as by feelings of guilt, subservience and inadequacy. The son's conflict with the father, for Freud, is never quite over.[4]

But as post-Freudian scholarship has shown, the idea that manhood is shaped through a father–son dynamics of desire, rivalry, and separation appeared in America only around the time of the Revolution.[5] During much of the colonial era, a boy became a man not during a delimited period of childhood, but in the course of a gradual, lengthy process of assuming private and public responsibilities; not by proclaiming his individuality and autonomy, but by patient obedience and deference to authority. True manhood was achieved when a man became a mature, moderate, authoritative head of a household, capable of taking care of his dependants, a father whose unshaken position in the home mirrored the ideal of patriarchy within the polity. A man proved his virility by "demonstrat[ing] his worth in the domestic context of service to his family and community."[6] The most important relationships were indeed those he held with his father and later on with his sons, but these relations were patterned on continuity rather than conflict. As late as in 1782, Hector St. John de Crèvecoeur imagined his American Farmer as saying: "why should not I find myself happy ... where my father was before? ... he left me a good farm, and his experience."[7] Based on land ownership, clearly defined masculine roles, and intergenerational continuity, colonial manhood was influenced but little by the tumultuous father–son relation upon which Freud would later come to focus.

But by the time Crèvecoeur published *Letters from an American Farmer*, this colonial model of manhood was already in rapid decline, particularly in the northeast. In *Prodigals and Pilgrims* (1982), Jay Fliegelman attributes this change to a crucial transformation within the family as, in the second half of the eighteenth century, a more affectionate and egalitarian ideal of parenting replaced authoritarian patriarchy.[8] Rather than demand deference, fathers were now encouraged to prepare their sons, through love and nurturing, for complete independence and self sufficiency.

No eighteenth-century text captures this transformation better than *The Autobiography of Benjamin Franklin* (1771), which opens with young Franklin's unyielding replacement of paternal discipline with self-discipline. Optimistic and self-assured in tone, Franklin's *Autobiography* seldom dwells on some of the more troubled aspects of this new model, which provided what Fliegelman calls the "quintessential motif" for the Revolutionary revolt against the Father-king. [9] Early American novels, however, often did. While the widespread suspicion about the novel was partially due to its common thematization of filial disobedience, early novels did not simply celebrate the figure of the independent son, but often turned to the feelings of anxiety and guilt that accompanied his revolt and to the problematic status of manly power achieved through *defiance* of paternal authority. The plot of William Hill Brown's *The Power of Sympathy* (1789), for example, tells of the tragic fate of a rebellious son who discovers that ties to the father can never be severed, as the woman he defies his father by loving turns out to be this father's illegitimate daughter. Royall Tyler's *The Algerine Captive* (1797) follows the tracks of a prodigal New England son who, rather than independence, finds bondage and submission in his travels away from home. With greater psychological depth, Charles Brockden Brown's *Wieland* (1798) imagines the lethal consequences of filial autonomy. Its eponymous hero loses his father at an early age and grows up free of the kind of paternal pressures experienced by the young Franklin. But as Wieland himself matures to the position of husband and father, he begins to hear, or imagine hearing, the voice of God demanding he sacrifice his family. He promptly slays his wife and children. *Wieland* thus psychologizes the experience of manhood in post-Revolutionary America,[b] where an absent father is reincarnated as an abstract voice, where filial independence transforms into pathological submission, and where the line between paternal love and paternal violence appears dangerously thin.[10] It is with novels such as *Wieland*, we might say, that Freud's oedipal son was born on American soil.

Self-made manhood

It is only during the next generation, however, that Revolutionary notions of filial independence coalesced into a full-fledged ideology of masculinity. Self-made manhood – the term itself was coined by Henry Clay, who lauded in 1832 "the enterprising and self-made men, who have whatever wealth they possess by patient and diligent labor"[11] – was advanced during the Jacksonian era by a number of prominent myths. There was, to begin with, the near-mythic status of President Andrew Jackson himself, who came to be regarded as the epitome of independent, self-generated manhood. No less significant was the growing popularity of frontier fiction. Carroll Smith-Rosenberg has shown that tall-tales such as those in the Davy Crockett almanacs helped promulgate the progressive ideal of the free-floating, autonomous male who defies paternal control and embraces the violence of the wilderness.[12] This ideal received fuller treatment in frontier novels, which constructed American manhood in contrast to both European paternalism and Native American tribalism; James Fenimore Cooper's *The Last of the Mohicans* (1826), William

b For an extended discussion in this volume of *Wieland* and of Brown's understanding of gender, see Bryan Waterman's "Charles Brockden Brown and the novels of the early republic," chapter 3, 54–57.

Gilmore Simms's *The Yemassee* (1835), and Robert Montgomery Bird's *Nick of the Woods* (1837) are among the most famous examples.

These Jacksonian-era myths of self-made manhood reflected a number of historical changes: expanding democracy, the market revolution that liberated men from traditional occupations, westward expansion that lessened the land-based hold of fathers over their sons, and, perhaps above all, the birth of a self-conscious middle class in the fast-urbanizing northeast, a class that defined itself through new norms of "true" manhood and womanhood. "Mobile, competitive, aggressive in business," writes Michael Kimmel, "the Self-Made Man was also temperamentally restless, chronically insecure, and desperate to achieve a solid grounding for masculine identity."[13] It is this precarious nature of the new middle-class ideal of manhood that worried antebellum observers; for shunning external authority, driven by self-interest, and anchored in an increasingly fickle economy, what was to ensure the moral behavior of self-made men? The answer devised by educators and reformers was a growing emphasis on self-discipline and self-restraint. To achieve true manhood, men were instructed to erect firm boundaries around the self and avoid any violation of these boundaries, whether in promiscuous sexual behavior, excessive emotional outpouring, or immoderate consumption. By the middle of the nineteenth century, Herman Melville's *Moby-Dick* (1851) would celebrate the "rare virtue of thick walls" and call upon the male reader to "admire and model [him]self" after the thick-skinned, impenetrable whale.

By the time Melville published his masterpiece, the middle-class ideal of manhood had become a veritable "cult," promoted in dozens of behavior guides, biographies of representative men, political speeches, and works of fiction.[14] We should not forget that meanings of manhood varied widely between merchants and laborers, slaves and masters, farmers and urbanites, Southern gentlemen and Northern reformers. But these different styles and practices were all influenced to some degree by the prescriptions of middle-class manhood, which circulated nationally in such successful books as John Frost's *Self Made Men in America* (1848) and Charles Seymour's *Self Made Men* (1858). Groups of men excluded from the privileges of the white, northern middle class, and often severely critical of this class, nevertheless claimed manhood by appropriating the terms of self-making. The nascent working class, for example, borrowed the language of individualism and self-possession even if it spoke this language with a markedly different accent. The post-bellum dime novels of Frederick Whittaker and John E. Barrett, for instance, sought to reconcile in their heroes the bourgeois norms of manly self-advancement with proletariat ideals of class solidarity.[15] Similarly, African

American writers often used the tropes of self-made manhood in order to argue for the manliness of those deprived of it by the paternalistic, effeminizing rhetoric of slavery. Martin Delany in *Blake* (1859) and Frederick Douglass in "The Heroic Slave" (1853) attributed to their heroes – in both cases leaders of slave rebellions – the revolutionary son's love of liberty, and the self-made man's calculated rationality and self-restrained aggression.

Manhood and the domestic woman

"The Heroic Slave" expresses the dominant fiction of manhood in another respect as well. Douglass underlined his protagonist Madison Washington's virility by emphasizing his devotion to his wife and his determination to liberate her (as did Delany in regard to Blake); but he preceded Washington's final emergence as a free, autonomous man with this wife's sudden death. This kind of ambivalence toward women – where the wife is presented as both evidence for and hindrance to true manhood – has often been described as one of the defining features of masculine identity. Second-wave feminist scholars (such as Nancy Chodorow, Dorothy Dinnerstein, and Jessica Benjamin), revising Freud's account of oedipal masculinity, have pointed out that the emphasis on the father–son conflict pushed out of view the active role that women play in masculine formation. Manhood is defined in opposition to womanhood, they claimed, and it simultaneously depends on the presence *and* the repudiation of femininity. In their account, the dread a male subject feels toward the pre-oedipal, all-powerful mother who threatens to "lure" him back into a state of dependence, far supersedes the father's threat of castration. It leads to the hyper-idealization of women as the "lost Eden" as well as to the need to belittle and dominate women.[16]

This feminist account is useful for understanding the shape mainstream American manhood took during the antebellum period, when the role of mothers in male socialization increased dramatically. As much as antebellum culture demanded that men control themselves, it insisted that the mechanisms of self-discipline had to be instilled early on by proper mothering; the more closely manhood became identified with the interest-driven, fluctuating marketplace, the larger the role that was assigned to domestic women to counter the chaotic, selfish nature of the economic sphere. The internalized voice of the mother replaced that of the colonial father in ensuring that young men would preserve their moral character even as they ventured out of the home in quest of their fortunes. After the young man married, his wife, with her gentle suasion, was to take over this supervising role. Paradoxically, self-made men were made by women.

By the middle of the nineteenth century, the popular genre of the sentimental novel adopted the influence of mothers over their sons as one of its central themes.[c] Harriet Beecher Stowe's *Uncle Tom's Cabin* (1852), for example, tirelessly traces back both the evil deeds of the slaveholders and the virtue of the abolitionists to their relation with their mothers; thus, Stowe attributes the sadism of fiendish slaveholder Simon Legree to his early repudiation of his mother, while she portrays the "liberator" George Shelby as a prosthetic male extension of his mother's sound moral principles.

But the very changes that permitted women to play such a crucial role in shaping manhood also prescribed that men grow up to define themselves *against* domestic womanhood. If during the colonial era manhood was constructed largely along a generational axis, now the middle class began to conceptualize manhood primarily through gender opposition, through the disavowal of the dependencies, intimate bonds, and self-sacrifices associated with domestic womanhood. In other words, the conflict identified by feminist theorists between an early reliance on the mother and a later imperative to negate her became pivotal only with the solidification of the gendered binaries that characterized the bourgeois worldview. This conflict, typically hidden in the sentimental novel, found violent expression in other genres. Gothic fiction, such as Edgar Allan Poe's horror stories or George Lippard's popular *Quaker City* (1844), responded to the sentimental "empire of the mother" [17] by imagining repeated scenes of the violent mastering and even rape of virtuous women.[d] The internalized maternal voice – constantly reminding self-made men of their lingering desires and dependencies, and exposing the limits of their self-possession and self-control – was projected in the gothic scenario onto the figure of the submissive, middle-class maiden who could then be violently subdued in fantasy.[18]

c For an extended consideration of the sentimental novel, see Cindy Weinstein's essay in this volume (chapter 12). Weinstein points out that the dichotomous form that the critical debate over sentimentalism has taken tends to obscure important themes of the genre ("Sentimentalism," 209–212). Certainly the sentimental novel's concern with autonomous, self-made manhood – especially as contrasted with the relative lack of autonomy of the heroine (213–214) is one such theme.

d This fantasy of the violent restoration of masculine power is one example of what Elizabeth Young describes in this volume as a main feature of the supernatural novel, "to preserve or restore traditional hierarchies of power" ("Supernatural novels," chapter 13, 222).

In the romances of Hawthorne (which straddled the line between the sentimental and the gothic) the self-made man's ambivalence toward domestic womanhood finds expression in the split representation of women. As T. Walter Herbert points out, Hawthorne's several avatars of self-made manhood – Dimmesdale of *The Scarlet Letter* (1850), Holgrave of *The House of the Seven Gables* (1851), and Hollingsworth of *The Blithedale Romance* (1852) – required the magical touch of domestic womanhood in order to fully transform into true men. But alongside sentimental female creations such as Phoebe, Priscilla, or the reformed Hester Prynne, Hawthorne enlisted antithetical figures of female power and sexual allure – the early Hester or Zenobia – outward projections of the masculine dread of unregulated desire or undissolved dependencies.[19] Indeed, this shuttling between repudiated and idealized womanhood arguably defined the very shape of the male literary canon. As critics such as Nina Baym and Annette Kolodny have claimed, this canon can be read as an extended "melodrama of beset manhood," in which the male hero (and writer) flees from the threat of coercion and dependence evoked by the mother or wife, only to project his pre-oedipal fantasies onto a natural landscape imagined as the edenic "lost" mother or as a subdued virgin.[20]

Between self-made men

Against this increasingly complex generational and gendered dynamics, antebellum fiction often depicted fraternal bonds as relatively simple and natural. As historians of manhood have pointed out, during the nineteenth century a newly forged boy culture (so well captured in the novels of Mark Twain and Horatio Alger after the Civil War) offered a space of liberation from both paternal pressure and feminine socialization. This boy culture performed the dual task of symbolizing democratic, egalitarian fraternity, and helping prepare the boy for the actualities of his future life in the competitive male workplace. The centrality of adult homosocial bonds – particularly interracial bonds – to the antebellum novel has been long recognized by critics, beginning with Leslie Fiedler's *Love and Death in the American Novel* (1960).[21] But, as more recent critics such as David Leverenz, Christopher Newfield, Dana Nelson, and David Anthony have shown, these homosocial bonds were no less complex and fraught than familial ties, no less troubled by the binary pull between self-possession and autonomy on the one hand, and desire and submission on the other. The Whitmanesque ideal of fraternal intimacy as the bedrock of American democracy, that is, clashed with the middle class's increasingly compulsive demands for matrimony and procreative heterosexuality. Even more profoundly, it clashed with the realities of a modern marketplace in which homosocial relations were structured on mutual suspicion, cut-throat competition, and strict hierarchies. In an economy based on credit and debt, and punctuated by periodic panics, idealized fraternal bonds were often reimagined as relations of domination and violation of boundaries.[22]

These re-interpretations of fraternal bonds in early American culture draw upon the insights offered by queer theory. Over the past two decades, queer theorists have critiqued Freudian thinking for its normalizing tendencies and feminist theory for adhering to a strict masculine–feminine binary. Judith Butler (to cite a particularly influential example) argued that both the boy's rivalry/identification with his father and his repudiation of the mother depended on a yet earlier formative moment: the foreclosure of homosexual attachment and its internalization in the ego as an unrealizable but ungrievable desire. This, for Butler, is the "melancholy" aspect of normative masculinity.[23]

Queer theory's argument about the melancholy of heterosexual men applies with special force to antebellum manhood, a form of masculinity that both celebrated intimate ties between a democratic band of brothers *and* regarded these ties as dangerous to the norms of self-possession and sexual propriety. In the antebellum novel, the spaces and practices of male association are often presented as powerfully attractive – as exciting masculine zones of escape and fulfillment – but also as deeply repelling, harboring the dangers of humiliation, submission, and even implied sodomy.[e] In the urban writing of Edgar Allan Poe and George G. Foster, the strange man encountered in the city and its crowds is at once a magnetizing object of fascination and a source of uncanny threat. Theodore Winthrop's *Cecil Dreeme* (1861) fully captured this duality by involving its hero in two homosocial relations: one a spiritual and platonic friendship with a delicate soulmate (who is conveniently revealed to be a woman in disguise by the end of the novel), and the other a dangerous, sensual relation with a sporting man of fashion, who combines the threats of economic and sexual exploitation.[24] Against a very different backdrop, Richard Henry Dana's *Two Years before the Mast* (1840) and Herman Melville's sea novels at once idealized the close relations of sailors on

e Elizabeth Freeman writes in this volume that "even the most canonical history of the American novel is already a queer one, if by queer we mean imaginatively and stylistically committed to a multiplicity of alternative gendered and sexualized subject-positions." See "Reimagining genders and sexualities," chapter 57, 942.

the ship and presented them as potentially tainted and risky; such books often described, alongside fraternal egalitarianism, scenes of exploitation, violation, and brutal tyranny between men.

Emphasizing self-possession and self-control, then, the dominant ideology of manhood in pre-Civil War America was structured upon a number of relations of intimacy, need, and indebtedness, both in the private and public spheres. Prescribing detachment and self-sufficiency, it could not silence voices that expressed the need for connection, the lure of desire, or the fear of loneliness. Perhaps the best articulation of the melancholy of self-made manhood belongs to Hawthorne. "You know how I sprang out of mystery, akin to none," the hero of his posthumously-published *Etherege* (1860–1861?) divulges,

> how all through my boyhood I was alone; how I grew up without a root, yet continually longing for one – longing to be connected with somebody – and never feeling myself so . . . I have tried to keep down this yearning, to stifle it, annihilate it, with making a position for myself, with being my own past, but I cannot overcome this natural horror of being a creature floating in the air, attached to nothing.[25]

Writing manhood

Much of the self-made man's negotiation between striving to be "attached to nothing" and "longing to be connected to someone" took place in the novel, the middle class's most important form of literary representation. Since the novel was itself a relatively recent phenomenon, still seeking full cultural authority and often experimenting with genres, themes, and forms, it served as a testing ground on which the ideas and emotions surrounding self-made manhood could be laid out and explored.

One way to account for the usefulness of the novel in this respect is to consider the genre's inherent pull between individualism and sociability. As novels were typically read in private, they were regarded as promoting the enclosure of the self from the world; but to the extent that they were often shared by family members or close friends and produced imaginary communities across traditional social boundaries, novels were also understood as a social and socializing medium. Authors, on the one hand, were increasingly worshiped as isolated geniuses, writing in the privacy of their homes about truths that transcended the contingencies of the social world and the marketplace. But on the other hand, authors became increasingly dependent upon that very marketplace and upon a consumer-minded readership that often demanded of them to expose their most private souls in public. Novels could be understood as the most individualistic of literary forms (as Ian Watt famously described them), centering on the sole protagonist and his process of self-making and pursuit of happiness; but they could also be seen as the most social genre of writing (as Mikhail Bakhtin no less famously defined them), blending together a host of characters, social identities, and voices that produce meaning only through their multiple interactions.[26]

Mindful of these dualities, antebellum novelists used several literary techniques to express complex attitudes toward self-made manhood. One technique was the construction of a particular kind of hero, labeled the "American Adam" in R. W. B. Lewis's classic study, and helpfully redescribed as the "man beyond desire" in David Greven's more recent one.[27] This type of hero embodies the pure principle of inviolate manhood; socially disembedded and isolated, and emotionally, sexually, and psychically unavailable either to women or to men, he is depicted as intensely desirable but also without desires of his own. Cooper's Natty Bumppo – fatherless and childless, an avowed bachelor and avoider of white company – is a perfect example of this type, as are Melville's enigmatic clerk Bartleby and the immaculate Billy Budd in their eponymous narratives. Surprisingly, perhaps, one of the most interesting avatars of this "man beyond desire" was created by a woman writer. Julia Ward Howe. *The Hermaphrodite* (*c.*1846–1847) – a never-completed novel by a writer better known for "The Battle Hymn of the Republic" – tells the story of Laurence, who was born with the sex organs of both genders. Socialized and self-identified as male, Laurence grows up to inflame the passion of women and to be fervidly sought after by men. His physical condition, however, means that he returns the love of neither gender, and it is precisely this condition of purity that turns him into the consummate poet. Freed from the pull of desire, disowned by his parents, and radically alone, the hermaphrodite comes to stand for perfect self-contained manhood. (To a woman writer, the idea that masculine autonomy, privilege, and creativity are best achieved without a male body was no doubt attractive.)

But, as D. H. Lawrence was among the first to notice, the inviolate hero of antebellum fiction often turned out to be a sad figure, lonely to the point of dehumanization, a "republican machine" indeed. By way of compensation, novelists sometimes projected the emotional and sexual ties repudiated by this hero upon a secondary character, particularly a character of a different race.

Paul Gilmore has argued that the more deeply steeped in the modern marketplace self-made manhood had become, the more it relied upon the fantasy of primitive, nonwhite masculinity in its search for an authentic self that lies outside bourgeois norms of self-restraint and discipline.[28] The Native American or African American sidekick could serve as a repository for those emotions, desires, and intimate ties disavowed by the white hero; through his friendship, that hero could experience human connection by proxy, without endangering his boundaries. This is an aspect of the interracial male couple that Fiedler had overlooked: the fact that the nonwhite partner is typically depicted in antebellum fiction as embedded within a collection of intimacies and affiliations beyond his relationship with the hero. Natty's friend Chingachgook is anything but solitary: not only is his relationship with his son Uncas in *The Last of the Mohicans* a projection of the self-made man's feelings of guilt toward or longing for the deposed father, but his romance with the Indian maiden Hist-oh!-Hist in *The Deerslayer* (1841) also balances Natty's disparagement of heterosexual love. Throughout the *Leatherstocking Tales*, the Mohican chief stands for fraternal loyalty and respect, ideals that were fast becoming problematic in competitive, market-oriented America. Chingachgook, along with such other phantasmatic racial creations as Melville's Queequeg (in *Moby-Dick*) and Twain's Jim (in *Huckleberry Finn*), project precisely those desires and identifications that negatively defined the inviolate hero.[29]

The conventional plot of the novel as it developed in Europe followed the path of the hero from a state of isolation and detachment to a denouement of social integration. In such prototypical travel novels and *Bildungsromans* as Johann Wolfgang von Goethe's *Wilhelm Meister*(1795), Daniel Defoe's *Robinson Crusoe*(1719), or Charles Dickens's *David Copperfield* (1850), the position of privileged manhood was reached with the hero's final incorporation in or return to society, further confirmed by marriage and fatherhood. But in the context of the relatively stronger emphasis on individualism and self-reliance in the American dialects of manhood, this denouement often appeared problematic – a sacrifice of masculinity rather than its fulfillment. More than their European counterparts, that is, American novelists were mindful of the contradiction inherent in a plot that celebrates integration into a society initially depicted as limiting, oppressive, and cruel to the male individual.

Thus, some of the most prominent antebellum novelists rewrote conventional plots to convey skepticism over the value of social integration. In Hawthorne's romances, for example, the framing plot mimics European convention, but the middle section dwells upon themes of perverted social ties with such dark intensity as to radically undermine at the end of the novel the desirability of social integration. The happy ending of *The House of the Seven Gables*, when the self-made Holgrave marries the angelic Phoebe and gains both house and status, can barely dispel the horrors of intersubjective violation and psychological domination explored in the middle chapters. Nor can Hester's re-integration in the Boston community at the end of *The Scarlet Letter* counter the force of the earlier chapters devoted to the sadomasochistic relations of Dimmesdale and Chillingworth. Dimmesdale's inability to combine public, self-made success with private desire, and his ironic, posthumous "marriage" to his tormentor physician, all but empty out the positive meanings of Hester's return.[30]

Another alternative plot devised by antebellum writers was that of the open ending. As Joseph Boone has argued, the absence of the return to society at the end of such novels as Poe's *The Narrative of Arthur Gordon Pym* (1838), Melville's *Moby-Dick*, and Twain's *The Adventures of Huckleberry Finn* (1884), bespeaks the author's refusal to re-subjugate his hero to the conventions and deprivations of social life. In an ending left open, the hero is allowed to escape both the tyrannies of marriage and domesticity and the alienation and hierarchies of the capitalist workplace. For critics Boone and Robert Martin, Melville's *Moby-Dick* evolves around the homoerotic interracial bond aboard the ship, a bond that symbolizes a truly egalitarian, loving alternative to the misogyny, racism, and homophobia of modern American manhood represented by Captain Ahab; Melville's refusal to end his novel with an account of Ishmael's return expresses his pessimism over the possibility of sustaining this alternative on American shores.[31]

The negotiation between autonomy and sociability entered also into the choice of narrational voice. One example is the frequent deployment of a narrator who is a bachelor. As Bryce Traister and Katherine Snyder have shown, beginning in the 1820s with the writing of Washington Irving, the bachelor-narrator was favored as a vehicle for exploring the contradictory aspects of emerging self-made manhood. By the 1850s, novels such as Ik Marvel's *Reveries of a Bachelor* (1852) and Hawthorne's *The Blithedale Romance* privileged the point of view of the bachelor because of his liminal status: the bachelor was depicted as outside domesticity yet defined by it, isolated yet sentimental and "soft," treading the fine line between homosocialibity and homosexuality. Through the bachelor-narrator, novelists could vacillate between "proximity and distance ... specular vicariousness and spectacular self display," and thus bring to the forefront the tensions at the core of self-made manhood.[32]

Finally, antebellum novelists investigated the norms of self-made manhood through the voice of the implied author. In a period during which female novelists gained success by using the techniques of sentimental expression, emotional identification, and confessional self-exposure, thus capitalizing on illusions of intimacy with the reader, male authors defined their voices *as* men by opposing themselves to what Hawthorne notoriously called "the damned mob of scribbling women." Many male writers did write sentimental prose – Ik Marvel, for example, as well as writers of temperance fiction such as T. S. Arthur and others.[33] But several male writers tried self-consciously to define their masculine voice by using emotional self-restraint and by avoiding public exposure. Hawthorne, forever conscious of the feminizing demands of the marketplace, engaged in the prefaces to his romances in a complicated game with the reader, deploying a confessional/autobiographical mode of writing while insisting that his true self remains "veiled." Melville, too, developed a complex and increasingly vituperative relation with his readership, expressing, as early as in his introductory remarks to *Mardi* (1849), sarcasm over his reader's hunger for biographical "truth." And Poe brought the art of enticing and baffling the reader to perfection, his several famous literary hoaxes constituting a game of hide-and-seek with his audience. In all three cases, an insistence on authorial privacy served to define the masculine writer in distinction to his sentimental, feminine competitors (whose desire was often, by contrast, to break the walls of privacy that domesticity imposed upon them).

Students of gender in American culture have long argued that the expansion of female readership in the first half of the nineteenth century, the novel's site of production in the home, the rise of the woman celebrity author, and the popular success of domestic fiction, all meant that the novel underwent "feminization" in the antebellum USA. Important feminist interventions in the history of the novel, such as Nancy Armstrong's in *Desire and Domestic Fiction* (1990), have made the case that one cannot separate the rise of the novel from "the production of the new female ideal" in the late eighteenth century, and have rewritten the novel's genealogy accordingly to highlight women authors, characters, and subgenres.[34] But to overemphasize the feminization of the antebellum novel is to risk overlooking how useful this literary genre had been for male writers such as Cooper, Hawthorne, and Melville, in their insistent, rigorous, and sometimes pained explorations of their own melancholic, self-made manhood.

Notes

1. On the tendency of scholars to regard American manhood *as* and *in* crisis, see Bryce Traister, "Academic Viagra: The Rise of American Masculinity Studies," *American Quarterly* 52.2 (2000): 274–304.
2. On the privatism associated with the early novel, see Patricia Meyer Spacks, "The Privacy of the Novel," *Novel: A Forum on Fiction*, 31.3 (1998): 304–316; on the early novel's promotion of subversive social affiliations see Cathy N. Davidson, *Revolution and the Word: The Rise of the Novel in America* (Oxford: Oxford University Press, 1986).
3. Nina Baym, *Novels, Readers, and Reviewers: Responses to Fiction in Antebellum America* (Ithaca: Cornell University Press, 1984).
4. See, for example, Sigmund Freud, "The Ego and the Super-Ego (Ego-Ideal)," in *The Ego and the Id*, ed. James Strachey (New York: Norton, 1962), 22–35.
5. John Demos was among the first to show that the Freudian model begins to apply in America only in the nineteenth century; see his "Oedipus in America: Historical Perspectives on the Reception of Psychoanalysis in the United States" (1978), rpt. in *Inventing the Psychological: Toward a Cultural History of Emotional Life*, ed. Joel Pfister and Nancy Schnog (New Haven: Yale University Press, 1997), 63–78.
6. Anne S. Lombard, *Making Manhood: Growing Up Male in Colonial New England* (Cambridge, MA: Harvard University Press, 2003), 10.
7. J. Hector St. John de Crèvecoeur, *Letters from an American Farmer*, ed. Susan Manning (Oxford: Oxford University Press, 1998), 25.
8. Jay Fliegelman, *Prodigals and Pilgrims: The American Revolution against Patriarchal Authority, 1750–1800* (Cambridge: Cambridge University Press, 1982), 1.
9. *Ibid.*, 3.
10. On the latter, see Elizabeth Barnes, "Loving with a Vengeance: *Wieland*, Familicide and the Crisis of Masculinity in the Early Nation," in *Boys Don't Cry? Rethinking Narratives of Masculinity and Emotion in the US*, ed. Milette Shamir and Jennifer Travis (New York: Columbia University Press, 2002), 44–63.
11. Quoted in Michael S. Kimmel, *Manhood in America: A Cultural History* (New York: Free Press, 1995), 26.
12. Carroll Smith-Rosenberg, "Davy Crockett as Trickster: Pornography, Liminality, and Symbolic Inversion in Victorian America," in *Disorderly Conduct: Visions of Gender in Victorian America* (New York: A. A. Knopf, 1985), 90–108.
13. Kimmel, *Manhood in America*, 17.
14. *Ibid.*, 26.
15. Michael Denning, *Mechanic Accents: Dime Novels and Working-Class Culture in America* (London: Verso, 1987), 167–84. See also Gregory L. Kaster, "Labour's True Man: Organised Workingmen and the Language of Manliness in the USA, 1827–1877," *Gender & History* 13.1 (2001): 24–64.
16. See, for example, Nancy J. Chodorow, "Being and Doing: A Cross-Cultural Examination of the Socialization of Males and Females," in *Feminism and Psychoanalytic Theory* (New Haven: Yale University Press, 1991), 23–44.

17. The term is Mary P. Ryan's, in *The Empire of the Mother* (New York: Haworth Press, 1982).
18. T. Walter Herbert, "Pornographic Manhood and the Scarlet Letter," *Studies in American Fiction* 29.1 (2001): 113–120.
19. T. Walter Herbert, *Dearest Beloved: The Hawthornes and the Making of the Middle-Class Family* (Berkeley: University of California Press, 1993).
20. Nina Baym, "Melodramas of Beset Manhood: How Theories of American Fiction Excluded Women," in *The New Feminist Criticism: Essays on Women, Literature, and Theory*, ed. Elaine Showalter (New York: Pantheon, 1985), 63–80; Annette Kolodny, *The Lay of the Land: Metaphor as Experience and History in American Life and Letters* (Chapel Hill: University of North Carolina Press, 1975).
21. Leslie Fiedler, *Love and Death in the American Novel* (New York: Criterion Books, 1960). On American boyhood culture see Anthony E. Rotundo, *American Manhood: Transformations in Masculinity from the Revolution to the Modern Era* (New York: Basic Books, 1994), 31–55.
22. David Leverenz, *Manhood and the American Renaissance* (Ithaca: Cornell University Press, 1990); Christopher Newfield, *The Emerson Effect: Individualism and Submission in America* (Chicago: University of Chicago Press, 1996); Dana Nelson, *National Manhood: Capitalist Citizenship and the Imagined Fraternity of White Men* (Durham, NC: Duke University Press, 1998); David Anthony, "The Helen Jewett Panic: Tabloids, Men, and the Sensational Public Sphere in Antebellum New York," *American Literature* 69.3 (1997): 487–514; and David Anthony, "Banking on Emotion: Financial Panic and the Logic of Male Submission in the Jacksonian Gothic," *American Literature* 76.4 (2004): 719–747.
23. Judith Butler, "Melancholy Gender/Refused Identification," in *Constructing Masculinity*, ed. Maurice Berger, Brian Wallis, Simon Watson, and Carrie Mae Weems (New York: Routledge, 1995), 27.
24. Michael Millner, "The Fear Passing the Love of Women: Sodomy and Male Sentimental Citizenship in the Antebellum City," *Arizona Quarterly* 58.2 (2002): 19–52.
25. The title *Etheridge* for the unfinished manuscript from which the quotation is taken was given by the *Centenary Edition of the Works of Nathaniel Hawthorne*, vol. XII: *The American Claimant Manuscripts*, ed. Edward H. Davidson, Claude M. Simpson, and L. Neal Smith (Columbus: Ohio State University Press, 1977).
26. Ian Watt, *The Rise of the Novel: Studies in Defoe, Richardson, and Fielding* (Berkeley: University of California Press, 1957); Mikhail Bakhtin, *The Dialogic Imagination* (Austin: University of Texas Press, 1981).
27. R. W. B. Lewis, *The American Adam: Innocence, Tragedy and Tradition in the Nineteenth Century* (Chicago: University of Chicago Press, 1955); David Greven, *Men Beyond Desire: Manhood, Sex, and Violation in American Literature* (New York: Palgrave Macmillan, 2005).
28. D. H. Lawrence, *Studies in Classic American Literature* (London: Penguin Classics, 1991); Paul Gilmore, *The Genuine Article: Race, Mass Culture, and American Literary Manhood* (Durham, NC: Duke University Press, 2001).

29. On the development of such racial surrogacy in the preceding decades, see Carroll Smith-Rosenberg, "Surrogate Americans: Masculinity, Masquerade, and the Formation of a National Identity," *PMLA* 119.5 (2005): 1325–1335.
30. On the relationship between manhood and Hawthorne's alternative plot structure see Scott S. Derrick, "'A Curious Subject of Observation and Inquiry': Homoeroticism, the Body, and Authorship in Hawthorne's *The Scarlet Letter*," *Novel: A Forum on Fiction* 28.3 (1995): 308–326; see also Christopher Castiglia, "The Marvelous Queer Interiors of *The House of the Seven Gables*," in *The Cambridge Companion to Nathaniel Hawthorne*, ed. Richard H. Millington (Cambridge: Cambridge University Press, 2004), 186–206. On Hester's "disappearance" from her own romance see Leverenz, *Manhood and the American Renaissance*, chapter 9.
31. Joseph Allen Boone, *Tradition Counter Tradition: Love and the Form of Fiction* (University of Chicago Press, 1987); Robert K. Martin, *Hero, Captain, and Stranger: Male Friendship, Social Critique, and Literary Form in the Sea Novels of Herman Melville* (Chapel Hill: University of North Carolina Press, 1986). For a critique of the idealization of interracial fraternity in American Studies, see Robyn Wiegman, "Fiedler and Sons," in *Race and the Subject of Masculinities*, ed. Harry Stecopoulos and Michael Uebel (Durham, NC: Duke University Press, 1997), 45–68.
32. Bryce Traister, "The Wandering Bachelor: Irving, Masculinity, and Authorship," *American Literature* 74.1 (2002): 111–137; Katherine Snyder, *Bachelors, Manhood, and the Novel, 1850–1925* (Cambridge: Cambridge University Press, 1999), quotation at 15.
33. See Glenn Hendler, *Public Sentiments: Structures of Feeling in Nineteenth-Century American Literature* (Chapel Hill: University of North Carolina Press, 2001).
34. Nancy Armstrong, *Desire and Domestic Fiction: A Political History of the Novel* (Oxford: Oxford University Press, 1990), 8.

12

Sentimentalism

CINDY WEINSTEIN

In an 1867 *New York Ledger* article, Fanny Fern observed: "at this day it is difficult to find [a woman] who does not write, or has not written, or who has not, at least, a strong desire to do so."[1] A quick glance at the names of authors, especially the bestselling ones in the years leading up to and following the Civil War, proves her point: Susan Warner, Maria Cummins, E. D. E. N. Southworth, Mary Jane Holmes, Caroline Lee Hentz, Elizabeth Stuart Phelps, and, of course, Harriet Beecher Stowe. Their output was remarkable. Southworth, for example, wrote more than sixty novels, Holmes almost forty, and even the less prolific ones were nonetheless quite productive. The entire body of sentimental novels numbers in the many hundreds.

This enormous archive has, for all intents and purposes, been distilled for reasons both pragmatic and problematic into a representative twosome, with Stowe's *Uncle Tom's Cabin* (1852) and Warner's *The Wide, Wide World* (1851) standing in for the genre known as the sentimental novel. Despite the distinctive aspects of individual novels (features upon which I shall elaborate in this chapter), whether at the level of plot, ideology, or aesthetics, the category of sentimentalism and its general features have nevertheless been extremely useful to literary critics. These features include a focus on day-to-day activities in the domestic sphere, a concentration on relationships, and a profound interest in the emotional lives of women. With the publication of F. O. Matthiessen's *American Renaissance* (1941), which ushered in the academic study of nineteenth-century American literature, sentimentalism stood as the dividing line between high and popular literature, between male and female writers, between serious and maudlin representations of American life in literature. Matthiessen's critical legacy has dictated that sentimental fiction, by virtue of its putative antithesis to the canonical works of the American Renaissance, has minimal art, as it were, and little to express other than the allegedly mundane matters of romance and reproduction. This could not be less true. Not only are these novels worth reading for their aesthetic contributions, but what they are trying to express is also deeply important: yes, many of these novels are emotional, maudlin, self-absorbed, and bourgeois, but they are also judicious, pragmatic, critical, and engaged.

One might say that in the last three decades or so, sentimentalism has been recovered and cast as art and expression in the age of Stowe and Warner. First, they wrote the most popular novels of the nineteenth century. *The Scarlet Letter* (1850) and *Moby-Dick* (1851) did not come close to the sales figures of Stowe and Warner (or Cummins or Holmes), and as a result Hawthorne famously denounced "that damned mob of scribbling women," while Melville in *Pierre* (1852) complained about "that countless tribe of common novels."[2] To the chagrin of Hawthorne and Melville, women were authoring the nation's first home-grown fictional bestsellers, and because nineteenth-century readers read them in numbers previously unheard of, literary critics quite rightly believe that these novels' popularity tells us many things about the culture (and its readers) in which these books by women flourished. Second, taken together, *Uncle Tom's Cabin* and *The Wide, Wide World* capture many dimensions of the antebellum period: its religious concerns (Uncle Tom's self-sacrifice and Ellen Montgomery's submission to God's will), economics (Colonel Shelby's sales of slaves and Aunt Fortune's Protestant work ethic), gender roles (Eliza's crossing the Ohio and John Humphrey's constant scrutinizing of Ellen's behavior), and regional sensibilities (St. Clare's opulent New Orleans quarters in contrast to the plain style of Warner's New England homes). Third, these texts indicate much about the reading tastes of the antebellum audience, as well as the elaborate system of distribution and advertisement that, according to Ronald and Mary Saracino Zboray's chapter in this volume, was being developed during this period. Long novels with many characters presented no obstacle to these readers, who also had a high tolerance for tearful scenes and outrageous coincidences and a low tolerance for plots that did not end in marriage and characters that did not get their just deserts.

But as illustrative of their historical moment as Stowe and Warner are, there are serious limitations in casting them as representative. First, just as Matthiessen's emphasis on Hawthorne, Melville, Emerson, and Thoreau not only led to a critical occlusion of women's fiction, but also to fiction written in regions other than New England, so the focus on Stowe and Warner – both of whom lived most of their lives in the New England/upstate New York area – renders invisible Southern writers such as Hentz (who, though born in Massachusetts, spent her adult life in Alabama and North Carolina), Georgia natives Maria McIntosh and Augusta Jane Evans, and Southworth, who was born in Washington, DC, to name just a few of the women writers who lived south of New York City. This regional bias leads to a second problem with seeing Stowe and Warner as representative. The concentration on Stowe's *Uncle Tom's Cabin* gives us only one perspective on the most important issue of the time – slavery. To be sure, Stowe's worst slaveowners hailed from the North, which reflects her effort to denounce the institution rather than the region. But Southern writers of fiction had their own ideas about how they wanted to represent slavery, both in response to *Uncle Tom's Cabin* and as an attempt to create new storylines that implicitly endorsed slavery. What slaves and slavery look like in pro-slavery texts cannot be adequately appreciated or understood if Stowe stands in for all positions on the topic.

Nor should *The Wide, Wide World* be taken as the final word about sentimental novels in their alleged dismissal of antebellum politics. One might be tempted to assert, based on the 1850 edition of Warner's novel, that sentimental fictions had nothing to say about race and slavery – the most significant issues confronting the nation. The fact is, and we do not know why, two extremely suggestive scenes about race were deleted from Warner's 1849 manuscript. In fact, many sentimental novels *do* engage the twinned issues of race and slavery, but at a more subterranean level, in a manner quite different from Stowe's explicit confrontation. The case of Warner, along with the following examples, further demonstrate the point made in John Ernest's chapter in this volume that "race was in many ways fundamental to the creation of a distinctively American tradition in fiction."[a] Thus, in Maria Cummins's *Mabel Vaughan* (1857), we seem to have the conventional story of a proud woman brought to abjection through poverty and bad judgment, on her part and her father's, only to find out that her father's speculations in Kansas have run up against the problems of Bleeding Kansas. Nor is slavery irrelevant to the romantic aspect of the plot, for Mabel's love interest is not only a prince charming, but also an ardent abolitionist.

I raise the question of Stowe and Warner's representativeness in order to register some of the elements that have been missing from our understanding of sentimentalism. One is that the presence of slavery has not been adequately examined, *pace Uncle Tom's Cabin*. Another is the conventional wisdom about the genre's ideological commitment to the heteronormative, middle-class status quo. Ever since Ann Douglas labeled sentimentalism as "rancid" because of its excessive and self-gratifying emotionalism, and Jane Tompkins responded with a reading of Stowe and Warner that placed them

a John Ernest, "Stowe, race and the antebellum American novel," chapter 15, 254.

at the center of a subversive female world of love and ritual, to invoke Carroll Smith-Rosenberg's influential account of distinctive female bonding practices in the nineteenth century, analyses of the genre have by and large been stuck in an either/or paradigm.[3] That is, either the novels written by women are cast as ahistorical, fatally conservative, and self-centered, or they are celebrated for plots and characters critical of dominant ideology in the ways available to a woman in the antebellum period. Unfortunately, this dichotomy leaves very little room for novels to do what they do best, which is to take a straightforward situation and reveal its complexities in ways that challenge readers to rethink their assumptions.

Indeed, one of the most complex issues taken up by sentimental fiction is the marriage relation, because sentimentalism demands that its novels conclude in marriage. Yet virtually all of the novels are acutely aware of just how vulnerable a woman is when she marries. Her marriage makes her liable to physical and mental abuse (Lydia Maria Child's *The Romance of the Republic* [1867] takes up the former; Hentz's *Ernest Linwood* [1856] represents the latter), and legally speaking, she becomes a *feme covert*, literally a hidden woman whose husband takes her property, her name, her very self. Novel after novel represents marriage as both a mistake and a joyous fulfillment of a woman's destiny. Bad marriages abound. Mary Jane Holmes's *Ethelyn's Mistake* (1869) makes the point clearer than most, but one can easily point to Mary Leon in *Ruth Hall* (1854), whose husband abandons her, takes their child, and drives Mary to the insane asylum, or Metta Victoria Fuller's (who also wrote widely under the pseudonym of Metta Victor) temperance novel, *The Senator's Son* (1853), in which a husband's alcoholism destroys his marriage and his family. Although many sentimental writers represent the chasm between an ideal of marriage and its reality, Southworth does it more relentlessly (and voluminously) than just about anyone else. Marriage is often a trap for Southworth's women, and her plots are frequently dedicated to releasing them (often, I should add, from a bad marriage into a happy one). For many women's rights advocates of the period, and I would include Southworth here, a woman's position vis-à-vis her husband was not unlike that of a slave. If the heroine's *Bildungsroman* represents a journey toward self-possession, which culminates in the decision to marry the man of her choice, what then happens to that story of self-possession when she becomes legally possessed by another? When she becomes, analogically speaking, like a slave?

I cry

One of the first things she does is cry. But characters in sentimental novels cry for all sorts of reasons: they have lost a child or a parent, seen a loved one fall from spiritual grace, endured cruel treatment, had a letter intercepted, missed out on a job opportunity, been forced to wear ugly clothes, chosen the wrong man to marry. An exemplary illustration of a crying woman can be seen in this passage from *The Senator's Son*, where the protagonist's mother has just witnessed the death of a friend's child: "The want – the wrong – the wo – came over her soul like a rushing cloud, and, sinking beside the bed, she sobbed aloud. Her weeping was contagious. It melted the icy grief of the mourner down to the level of natural expression; she threw herself upon the couch with cries and tears." There is indeed a contagion of weeping, but the targeted weeper is, of course, the reader. To get the reader to cry is to engage her in an act of sympathy, which is the ideal affect in sentimental fiction. With tears, the logic goes, comes relief for the sufferer. In this scene from *The Senator's Son*, the suffering mother can only cry once the viewer of her suffering has cried. Here is a classic sentimental tableau: the witness, clearly a stand-in for the reader, displays her sympathy, which then allows the truly aggrieved mother – the one who has lost her child – to mourn.

Although some sentimental novels by women place suffering men at the center of their plots (for instance, *The Senator's Son*, Hentz's *Marcus Warland* [1854], and Southworth's *Ishmael, or in the Depths* [1863]), by and large, women are the primary sufferers and weepers. Like their eighteenth-century predecessors, fictional women in nineteenth-century novels have been seduced, abandoned, and even when they have gotten married, have by definition become *femes covert* whose legal identities are subsumed within their husbands'. These women disappear, or as one character in Hentz's *Ernest Linwood* cogently puts it, a wife "loses her own identity in his." Sentimental fiction replaces the anxieties about autonomy and self-separation, which are constitutive of classic American Renaissance novels by men, with tremendous obstacles toward autonomy. As Milette Shamir explains in her chapter in this volume, middle-class manhood in this period is conceptualized "primarily through gender opposition, through the disavowal of the dependencies, intimate bonds, and self-sacrifices associated with domestic womanhood."[b] What this means for domestic womanhood, then, is that there is, legally speaking, no longer any self from which to separate because that self has

b Milette Shamir, "Manhood in the early American novel," chapter 11, 198.

been incorporated by the husband at the moment of the wedding vow. And if that wedding vow is broken (or even fraudulent), what is left for that woman without a self, and without the property she may have brought to the marriage, to do? Or what if the wedding vow is made and conditions intervene to make it deeply problematic?

This quandary, it should be noted, is quite similar to the one in which two of American literature's most canonical heroines find themselves – Hester Prynne and Isabel Banford of Melville's *Pierre* (1852). This correspondence powerfully illustrates how Matthiessen's dividing line between sentimental and canonical texts does not hold.[4] Hester is left without a husband in sight (she believes Chillingworth has died while she has been in New England), and yet the marriage vow holds her in its vise-like grip. Without evidence to the contrary, she remains married to someone who may or may not exist. Pearl's story, moreover, is the search for her last name, a plotline of *The Scarlet Letter* that neatly overlaps with the sentimental novels *Lena Rivers* (1856) and *The Lamplighter* (1854). The case of *Pierre* takes up the question of the wedding vow, and to what extent the vow made in private has the authority of the vow made in public. Legal historian Hendrik Hartog has uncovered an extra-legal landscape of "multiple marital regimes" in which persons simply declared their marriage and it was so or couples were geographically separated and, without the permission of the court, remarried.[5] Thus, Pierre's "secret marriage" to Isabel is just as good (or bad) as the real thing. Despite Melville's protests to the contrary, *Pierre* could be read as just as good (or bad) as "countless" sentimental novels, such as two of Southworth's, *Ishmael, or in the Depths* and *The Fatal Marriage* (1863), with that very same plot device. Indeed, because Southworth devotes her entire career both to situating her female protagonists within the limitations of being *femes covert* and finding a way within or beyond those limitations, let us turn to some of the texts comprising her remarkable *oeuvre*.

I do, or *The Fatal Marriage*

The problem of marriage is the driving force behind virtually all of Southworth's plots, and it is almost in spite of those plots that her novels conventionally conclude with happy marriages. But Southworth takes a long time getting there, partly because she introduces so many characters whose intersecting lives and relationships must be disentangled before a marriage can occur and partly because there are so many awful scenarios, so many negative possibilities that must be represented before they can be cleared away – exorcised, as it were – in order for the union to take place. I do not mean to gainsay the very real economic motives driving Southworth to write long and numerous books (she was the sole supporter of two children and had been abandoned by her husband), but I do think that her frenzied compositional pace and voluminous output are usefully viewed in terms of her vexed relation to a literary tradition that demanded an ending – marriage – about which she was deeply suspicious. Moreover, it is hard to believe, with titles such as *Family Doom, The Fatal Marriage, The Maiden Widow,* and *The Missing Bride*, that marriage is the relation to which women ought to aspire and the one in which women will be emotionally and economically cared for. By examining Southworth's rendering of the act of making a vow – who says it, who means it, where it is said – we can begin to understand her attempts to carve out a space where women are not simply the victims of their "I do's," but subjects with an active role in shaping the meanings of those vows.

Southworth goes so far as to suggest that even a marriage that follows all of the legal formalities is not necessarily binding if one of the parties is an unwilling participant in the ceremony. Thus, in the case of *The Fatal Marriage*, much of the novel revolves around the question of exactly what it means when a fifteen-year-old boy and a twelve-year-old girl are forced to marry. As the protagonist Orville Deville falls in love with another woman, he wonders about the legality of what the narrator refers to as his "baby-marriage" with Adelaide Lorne: "Is it binding? Should it be binding? Should a betrothal solemnized at the instance of their guardians between a boy and girl who were then for the first time and never afterwards met again, be binding upon either party?" Deville decides that these ties are not binding. He marries Lionne Deforêt and in the eyes of the law commits bigamy because the "baby-marriage," "though only nominal, being the *prior*, is consequently the *legal* one." The meaning of a marriage, in Southworth's analysis, is not fixed but rather subject to the context in which it takes place. If the wedding is forced, if the couple is too young, if the wife is unsure, if the husband is lying – all of these contexts play into Southworth's sense of the legitimacy of a marriage. Thus, the words "I do" are necessary but not sufficient to make a marriage binding. One might think of this slippage as potentially liberating for all concerned, because if marriages can be mistakenly or unintentionally entered into, presumably they can also be dissolved.

But it is much more difficult for women than men to make the case that, on the grounds of a compelling context, a marriage should be discounted. Deville, for example, initially justifies his second marriage to Lionne by declaring his first to Adelaide null and void because "we could neither have known each other or understood the purport of what we mutually promised." Yet when he begins to like Adelaide and covet her utter devotion to him, he invokes that same marriage whose validity he had denied just a few pages before as absolutely binding upon her. Lionne's only (lousy) option is to make her first marriage to Deville (but his second, at least in certain of his moods) binding, and if she cannot do so on the grounds of affection, she will try to do so by invoking the authority of the law. Thus, despite her belief that she is the wife of Deville's "true marriage," she carries at all times the marriage certificate in order to document legally her status.

There is no good resolution here for the two protagonists. Lionne, heartbroken but deeply vengeful (and a mother, thanks to Deville), loses her mind and devotes her every waking moment to destroying him. Deville's "secret" second, bigamous marriage is ultimately revealed at a public trial, and he commits suicide the moment the guilty verdict is read. Perhaps the most fascinating and unexpected aspect of the novel's conclusion is Adelaide's reward. In the final paragraph, we are told that "in due time, [Adelaide's] hand was sought by the Duke of Donaldben, a gentleman in every way worthy to make her forget the sorrows of her youth, and with whom she lived a long life of nearly perfect married love and happiness." As much a victim of Deville's ethical lapses as Lionne, Adelaide at one point actually tries to give Deville back to Lionne; in other words, when she discovers his secret marriage, she acknowledges the second wife's rights and recognizes that, in fact, the "baby-marriage" was an unfair manipulation of two children who did not know any better. Such a stand is astonishing, especially since Adelaide has been trained from very early on to obey, to please, and to submit. She does, however, attempt to run away and vanish into the Maryland countryside, but she is unsuccessful and is brought back to Deville in order that the novel can continue questioning the validity of both marriages.

I call attention to Adelaide's fate at the very end of the novel because it is so bizarre and truncated. That fate also supports the notion of Southworth's conflicted relation to sentimentalism. Adelaide gets over the death of the man who was the *raison d'être* of her life in record time, and quickly experiences "renewed health and peace." We are informed that she was "not destined to wear her days out in mourning over the past," which is a kind way of saying good riddance to the man in her life who wreaked such havoc. And then, she marries again. It all happens so quickly and so seemingly unnecessarily, until one remembers that marriage is the only acceptable conclusion for sentimental novels. For all intents and purposes, the novel ends with the rapid-fire deaths of Deville, Lionne, and Deville's mother (one of the guardians who forced the marriage), which means that Adelaide is now free to do anything but the one thing that the novel has shown us will lead to unhappiness. That, of course, is marry. But Southworth must give her audience a marriage. It is, perhaps, odd to argue that in a novel full of unbelievable twists in the plot (and I have only outlined a few), one can point to a moment that stands out for its inauthenticity. That moment is Adelaide's second marriage, which gets two sentences in a long novel, and the terse description speaks volumes about the arbitrariness of the convention that a sentimental novel must end in marriage. Southworth wants to reward Adelaide for her good works and kindness toward Lionne (after all, Adelaide is the only main character not to die), but the only way she can do so is by granting her character perfect happiness in marriage, a condition that the novelist has shown to be virtually impossible. Southworth is in a bind. While sentimentalism places certain demands on her plot, her plot has demonstrated the profound limitations of those very requirements. Thus, Adelaide is given a moment in the story where she defies the role of *feme covert*, only to be put back into that position – as a reward – at the novel's utterly inauthentic end.

"What did you mean?"

Southworth rarely receives so close a reading. That kind of critical attention is usually reserved for canonical texts. Despite this longstanding tendency, women's fictions of the postbellum period – by Elizabeth Stuart Phelps and Elizabeth Stoddard, for example – are increasingly studied for their linguistic complexity and sophistication, in much the same way as Elizabeth Nolan's essay in this volume (chapter 34) focuses on the linguistic experimentalism of Kate Chopin and Willa Cather. Language, however, is also very much on the minds of Southworth's characters, as the quotation from *The Maiden Widow* (1870) with which this section begins, implies. Southworth's characters exist in a chronic state of misunderstanding, which on the most obvious level functions to propel the plot. But I would submit that rather than characters not recognizing each other or letters getting lost in the post (typical ways that conflict is produced and plot generated), the misunderstandings in this novel are quite clearly linguistic, and organized around the very particular issue of marriage and how men and women talk about it before they actually marry.

As with *The Fatal Marriage*, but on a considerably larger scale (more characters, more plot complications, an additional volume), in *The Family Doom* (1869) proposals, pledges, promises, vows are constantly made, except that no one seems to know exactly what they mean. With a title like *The Family Doom*, one might imagine that a fatal marriage is somewhere in the offing. It is not, though, because it has already happened in the story of the widows of Henniker House. Granted, marriage happened four times, but the point of the novel is to prevent it from happening again. And Southworth manages to avert a fifth generation of marital disaster by giving her protagonist, not a future without marriage, but rather a way to make sure she enters into the right one. Within the framework of perpetually ambiguous speech acts that characterizes *The Family Doom*, Southworth's novel allows women a chance to renege on their pledges, and everyone is happier for it.

The Family Doom and its sequel, *The Maiden Widow*, tell the story of several generations of women who have married and lost their husbands because of an ancient Native American curse, which has exerted its fatal grip over multiple generations. It can only be broken "When the maid shall be widowed / Before she is wed." Although the novel ends in multiple marriages, virtually all of the female characters are faced with the choice of embarking upon a marriage, which they have at one point or another vowed to enter into, that will obliterate their self-respect, or breaking that vow and marrying the person who will allow them, within the limits of coverture, a degree of self-possession. This may not seem like much of a choice, but in the world of the novel, the difference between the first, wrong marriage and the second, right one matters immensely. Thus, minor and major characters, mostly women but sometimes men, constantly make pledges from which they are allowed to extricate themselves. A "half promise" to marry and even a "whol[e] promise" are undone in order that true love will prevail. Characters say, "I'm bound to you forever," but they are not. Even Berenice Brooke, who "has bound herself to the solemn vow never to marry Vane Vandeleur," is allowed to unbind that vow and marry him. Although circumscribed by marriage and the demands of sentimental convention, Southworth's plots work to establish for women a degree of agency and freedom within an institutional framework that legally allows neither.

I would, however, call attention to the fact that three characters do remain unmarried, and these are the widows of Henniker House, where "Woman's Right's [*sic*] and Petticoat Government reigns." Indeed, early on in the novel, Captain Storms, one of the novel's many main characters, hypothesizes the following reason for why they do not marry: "It is said that a woman is neer free until she is a widow. In her girlhood she is under her parents; in her wifehood she belongs to her husband; but in her widowhood she belongs to herself." Unlike Adelaide of *A Fatal Marriage*, once these women have been released from coverture, Southworth does not force them to become hidden again. They have, as it were, served their time, and Southworth must have believed her readers satisfied with the five marriages that conclude the novel.

Southworth had "a strong desire" to write, to return to Fanny Fern's claim. So did Warner, Hentz, Stowe, and the many other women who deployed the sentimental format in order to do the very unsentimental business of feeding and clothing their children, paying the rent, and watching the male head of the household, if he were present, bungle their financial future. Fern was in charge of her own writing career, and after one happy marriage that sadly ended in her husband's death from typhoid fever and another unhappy one that she left (that husband later divorced her on the grounds of desertion), Fern eventually wrote her autobiographical novel *Ruth Hall* (1854), which ends with Fern a widow who quite clearly, in the words of Southworth, "belongs to herself." Like Fern, many writers of sentimental novels had personal stories to tell about the importance of sympathy, the difficulties of marriage, and the fact of unfulfilled expectations. True, they had to tell their stories in such a way that their novels would sell, which means an adherence to certain generic requirements. True, their stories feature outlandish coincidences (more so than finding one white whale in the middle of the Pacific Ocean?). And true, their characters act in ways that are not always identifiably realistic (less so than Isabel strumming her guitar while Pierre hungrily watches?). That said, art and expression in the age of antebellum women's fiction is complicated and diverse, both constituted by the limiting experiences of women at the time and invigorated by a commitment to represent as fully as possible those limitations and to move beyond them.

Notes

1. Fanny Fern, "The Women of 1867," in *Ruth Hall and Other Writings*, ed. Joyce W. Warren (New Brunswick, NJ: Rutgers University Press, 1986), 342.
2. Letter, October 12, 1854, Nathaniel Hawthorne to William Ticknor, quoted in Frank L. Mott, *Golden Multitudes: The Story of Best Sellers in the United States* (New York: Macmillan, 1947), 122.
3. Ann Douglas, *The Feminization of American Culture* (New York: Avon Books, 1977), p. 307. Much literary criticism on sentimentalism is a response to Douglas and to Jane Tompkins's *Sensational Designs: The Cultural Work of American Fiction* (New York: Oxford University Press, 1986), who makes the powerful case that sentimental fiction "represents a monumental effort to reorganize culture from the woman's point of view . . . [and] is remarkable for its intellectual complexity, ambition, and resourcefulness" (124). Also see, Gillian Brown, *Domestic Individualism: Imagining Self in Nineteenth-Century America* (Berkeley: University

of California Press, 1990); Philip Fisher, *Hard Facts: Setting and Form in the American Novel* (New York: Oxford University Press, 1985); Shirley Samuels, ed., *The Culture of Sentiment: Race, Gender, and Sentimentality in Nineteenth-Century America* (Oxford: Oxford University Press, 1992); and Lora Romero, *Home Fronts: Domesticity and its Critics in the Antebellum United States* (Durham, NC: Duke University Press, 1997).

4. See Romero, *Home Fronts*, and Mary Chapman and Glenn Hendler, eds., *Sentimental Men: Masculinity and the Politics of Affect in American Culture* (Berkeley: University of California Press, 1999).
5. Hendrik Hartog, *Man and Wife in America: A History* (Cambridge, MA: Harvard University Press, 2000), 248. Also see Michael Grossberg, *Governing the Hearth: Law and the Family in Nineteenth-Century America* (Chapel Hill: University of North Carolina Press, 1985), and Nancy Cott, *Public Vows: A History of Marriage and the Nation* (Cambridge, MA: Harvard University Press, 2000).

13

Supernatural novels

ELIZABETH YOUNG

The history of the "supernatural novel" is occluded – even occulted – by problems of definition. The first problem is with the term "novel." The writer at the center of any discussion of the supernatural, Edgar Allan Poe, notoriously favored the short work, because "[T]here is a distinct limit, as regards length, to all works of literary art – the limit of a single sitting."[1] Many of the most famous nineteenth-century supernatural works are short stories, or at longest novellas; in the twentieth century, supernatural novels are plentiful, but they often become most visible when they are adapted into horror films. A greater problem is "supernatural," which colloquially signals ghosts, haunting, devils, and the spirit-world. If these are its defining features, how is the American supernatural to be distinguished from "American gothic," which is a more established critical category?[2] Both the gothic and the supernatural are anti-realist zones of haunting and strangeness, but the supernatural also crosses over into a world of spirits, as the gothic need not; conversely, the gothic always invokes fear, while the supernatural may offer friendly ghosts. Most supernatural texts are gothic, but not all, and vice versa, or as one critic puts it, "The supernatural is permitted but not essential to the Gothic."[3] The supernatural is not only difficult to separate spatially from other genres; it is also often only a temporary zone within individual works, entered and then abandoned as other explanations for mysteries arise. In Charles Brockden Brown's *Wieland* (1798), for example, the narrator considers "notions of supernatural agency" as the source for the mysterious voices she hears, only to have their human source revealed.[a] From its first appearances in the American novel, the supernatural is often asserted only to be denied, or asserted through the very process of denial.

a For discussions elsewhere in this volume of the supernatural elements of *Wieland*, see also Anna Mae Duane, "Susanna Rowson, Hannah Webster Foster, and the seduction novel in the early USA," chapter 2, 45–46, and Bryan Waterman, "Charles Brockden Brown and the novels of the early republic," chapter 3, 55–57.

In this chapter, rather than trying to stabilize the supernatural novel, I highlight its instabilities. I argue for the significance of "dispossession," in several senses, to American supernatural writing. "Possession," by ghosts, the devil, and the spirit world, is one of the major plots of the supernatural, and supernatural fiction features possessed people, places, and things. With possession comes the possibility of dispossession: the major threat of the supernatural is, accordingly, the loss of one's regular self, settings, and objects. The item most easily lost in supernatural fiction, however, is the mind. The supernatural turns on the absence of mind as much as the presence of ghosts, and it registers the problem of remaining self-possessed.

I also mean "dispossession" in a political sense, whereby supernatural traits in fiction signal people dispossessed of rights.[b] Most prominently, the supernatural has provided an evocative vocabulary for fictional discussions of slavery and its aftermath. From the antebellum period onward, American writers have used supernatural fiction to denaturalize the power hierarchies, coercive embodiments, and repeated repressions that characterize enslavement. This impulse extends to other forms of political dispossession: supernatural writing by women, for example, often denaturalizes gender hierarchies. Yet the supernatural has also been used to express desires to preserve or restore traditional hierarchies of power. Such works are less denaturalizing but similarly concerned with dispossession, albeit from the other direction; they worry about imminent or past losses of power. A mode for representing something lost, the supernatural is also a privileged mode for getting something back – for repossessing politics, history, and, especially, one's self.

I present these arguments chronologically in three sections, starting with Poe and touching on Harriet Beecher Stowe, Hannah Crafts, and Nathaniel Hawthorne; interpreting fiction from Reconstruction through the first decades of the twentieth century by S. Weir Mitchell, Elizabeth Stuart Phelps, Charlotte Perkins Gilman, Henry James, and H. P. Lovecraft; and concluding with later twentieth-century fiction by Shirley Jackson, Stephen King, Toni Morrison, Joyce Carol Oates, and Anne Rice. Intertwining "high" and "low" cultural registers, I focus throughout on categories of identity, particularly race, gender, and sexuality; since critical discussions of the supernatural often focus on single categories of identity, the goal is to initiate an analysis that brings together multiple themes using the larger framework of

b For a complementary approach to the politics of possession, see Duane, chapter 2, especially 38–40.

"dispossession." My analysis also moves from literary to visual modes. This movement occurs not only because numerous twentieth-century supernatural novels have become films, or even because earlier media such as painting and photography have influenced supernatural literature, but also because the literary supernatural often turns on representations of visuality. Insistently pressured from without and within by new ways of seeing, the supernatural novel has long been possessed by visions.

Of the numerous candidates for founder of supernatural fiction in America, Edgar Allan Poe is the most important, both because he wrote a novel with supernatural inflections, *The Narrative of Arthur Gordon Pym* (1838), and because he so meticulously explored the idea of the supernatural throughout his fiction. Poe's short stories of the 1830s and 1840s abound in strange phenomena and in the reasons his characters advance for them, including madness ("The Tell-Tale Heart [1843]), opium ("Ligeia" [1838]), and electricity ("The Fall of the House of Usher" [1839]). In this spectrum of explanations, the supernatural serves as the outer limit, to which the narrator is most reluctant to advance, since it concedes all to the irrational.

In *The Narrative of Arthur Gordon Pym*, the supernatural horizon stretches across water to the ends of the earth.[c] *Pym* includes numerous elements marked as supernatural, such as strange landscapes, ghost-like ships, and moments of haunting. When Pym and his fellow sailor Dirk Peters descend a cliff, for example, "[T]here came a spinning of the brain; a shrill-sounding and phantom voice screamed within my ears; a dusky, fiendish, and filmy figure stood immediately beneath me; and, sighing, I sunk down with a bursting heart, and plunged within its arms." Since these arms turn out to belong to Peters, the "phantom voice" and "filmy figure" are dispossessed of their supernatural elements. But similar elements recur without such dispossession, as at novel's end, when Pym nears the South Pole: "[T]here arose in our pathway a shrouded human figure, very far larger in its proportions than any dweller among men. And the hue of the skin of the figure was of the perfect whiteness of the snow." With the appearance of this large, white, shrouded figure, the novel ends with what seems to be the quintessential character of supernatural fiction: the ghost.

c For discussions of *Pym*, see Hester Blum, "Melville and the novel of the sea," chapter 9, 157; Russ Castronovo, "Imperialism, Orientalism, and empire," chapter 32, 539; John Ernest, "Stowe, race, and the antebellum American novel," chapter 15, 256–257; Jennifer Rae Greeson, "Imagining the South," chapter 14, 246; and Timothy Sweet, "American land, American landscape, American novels," chapter 5, 99.

Although generations of criticism overlooked it, it is now difficult *not* to interpret the whiteness at the end of *Pym* racially. Poe depicts the "savages" of *Pym* in racial terms, "their complexion a jet black, with thick and long woolly hair." When he learns that their "apparent kindness of disposition was only the result of a deeply-laid plan for our destruction," the threat is that of slave rebellion. In an era of massive anxiety about slave revolt – including that of Edgar Allan Poe's fellow Virginian Nat Turner – the gothic fear is that the faithful "Sambo" conceals the rebellious "Nat."[4] The haunted final landscape at the end of *Pym* focuses these anxieties on whiteness as well as blackness. Toni Morrison has argued that Poe's concluding "figurations of impenetrable whiteness" offer a "strong suggestion of paralysis and incoherence; of impasse and non sequitur."[5] Poe's novel suggests the particular capacity of the supernatural to represent white paralysis and impasse. Notably, while Poe describes black revolt in gothic terms – the "savages" were "among the most barbarous, subtle, and bloodthirsty wretches that ever contaminated the face of the globe" – he does not represent this revolt supernaturally, in the way that he does his conclusion. The turn from fears of black revolt to anxieties about white authority seems, in literary terms, to parallel the slide from gothic demon to supernatural specter. At the end of the novel, this slide is complete: the specter appearing to the white protagonist is white, while the violence that figure might inflict is white-on-white. As the supernatural comes into novelistic focus in America in the 1830s, then, its quintessential figure, the ghost, highlights white fears of dispossession.

Two decades later, with the crisis over slavery threatening to fracture the nation, supernatural fiction often featured fantasies of black repossession as well as anxieties of white dispossession. Three examples suggest the importance of the racialized supernatural in the novels of this period. In *Uncle Tom's Cabin* (1852), sentimental tears are the primary affective goal,[d] but at a key point, Stowe also foregrounds supernatural fears. Late in the novel, Cassy watches Simon Legree as he reads "stories of bloody murders, ghostly legends, and supernatural visitations." He asks her, "You don't believe in ghosts, do you, Cass?" This passage inaugurates a reversal of power between the enslaved Cassy and the slaveowner Legree. Establishing a safe hiding-place in Legree's attic by convincing him that it is haunted, she manipulates the supernatural. In a world in which African Americans are literally possessed by others, Cassy uses the supernatural as a means of self-repossession.

d For a more detailed analysis of sentimentalism, see Cindy Weinstein, "Sentimentalism," (chapter 12).

Cassy's project also involves a gender reversal. Women are central to the supernatural, both embodying its terms – they often appear as witches, ghosts, demons, or mediums – and strategically manipulating its stories. African American women are prominent in this manipulation, as suggested not only by Cassy but also by numerous African American women characters in Hannah Crafts's *The Bondwoman's Narrative*. This novel of the 1850s – its date of composition is not known[e] – is suffused with supernatural subplots, including the story of Rose, a slave whose master, Sir Clifford, orders her to kill her beloved dog and then hangs them both from a tree. Dying, she declares, "I will hang here till I die as a curse to this house, and I will come here after I am dead to prove its bane . . . I will brood over this tree, and weigh down its branches . . . Such was the legend of the Linden as we had heard it told." Crafts here offers the material basis for a ghost, in the violence inflicted on Rose. At the same time, this passage emphasizes the *story* of a ghost – "the legend of the Linden" – rather than the ghost itself. Like Simon Legree reading "ghostly legends," the narrator of *The Bondwoman's Narrative* invokes the meta-effect of a supernatural story. The "we" of this passage suggests the multiple roles of African Americans as authors and auditors of the supernatural, and of the intermediate zone between invented narrative and factual aftermath occupied by supernatural accounts of slavery.[6]

The haunted estate of Sir Clifford resembles that of a third novel of the 1850s, Nathaniel Hawthorne's *The House of the Seven Gables* (1851). In a novel that turns on questions of literal possession – who has title to the seven-gabled house – the losing party, Matthew Maule, takes compensatory spiritual possession. In a novel that features paintings and photographs, supernatural possession is inseparable from visual representation: "Turn our eyes to what point we may," declares the character known as the "Daguerreotypist" of a significant portrait, "a Dead Man's white, immitigable face encounters them, and freezes our very heart!" And in a novel that names an "Indian deed" as the origin of much Pyncheon property – "a map of the Pyncheon territory [is] grotesquely illuminated with pictures of Indians and wild beasts" – the legacy of the "white, immitigable face" carries a racial charge as well. Hawthorne's version of the supernatural brings the icy whiteness of the South Pole of *Pym* home to the foundational racial struggles of New England.[7]

Producing 600,000 dead bodies in less than five years, the Civil War provided new ground for representing the supernatural. Civil War fiction

e On the uncertainties surrounding this work, see Robert S. Levine, "The early African American novel," chapter 16, 278–280.

by male authors like Ambrose Bierce and S. Weir Mitchell often focused on the injured male body, dispossessed of its usual authority; in Mitchell's "The Case of George Dedlow" (1866), for example, wartime amputation produces the ghost of the phantom limb. Conversely, women's supernatural fiction in the 1860s often depicted women in possession of unusual power. Elizabeth Stuart Phelps's bestselling novel *The Gates Ajar* (1868) defangs the supernatural of its gothic force, as Mary Cabot, mourning the death of her soldier-brother, learns to imagine the afterlife as a gentle, domestic space. In a feminized heaven, women are prominent, and the novel's ghosts are friendly ones: "How pleasant it will be to see . . . faces I never saw in this world!" imagines Mary's aunt.

Supernatural fiction in the late nineteenth century is riven with tensions over gender and sexuality, particularly in the many short stories by women writers which feminist critics have made more visible in the literary history of the period.[8] These tensions saturate Charlotte Perkins Gilman's "The Yellow Wallpaper" (1892), the most famous of these recovered texts, and Henry James's *The Turn of the Screw* (1898). Both works feature female protagonists who insist, in unreliable first-person voice, upon the presence of mysterious characters, and who are seen as psychologically unstable by others; both works, moreover, register the rise of psychoanalysis as a field. Gilman's story drew on her experience with S. Weir Mitchell's "rest cure," which reflected Mitchell's own shift from the "phantom limbs" of male veterans to the study of female hysteria – the defining disease of early psychoanalysis. James knew of the experiments of Charcot, which influenced Freud, and critics have also suggested resemblances between *The Turn of the Screw* and specific Freudian case studies.[9] Both Gilman and James wrote in a world where the interiors of supernatural fiction and female psyche were being reshaped by psychoanalysis.

In both stories, the supernatural opposes the psychoanalytic: either Gilman's woman in the wallpaper, and James's Quint and Jessel, are psychic projections of the narrator, or they are supernatural apparitions. Both authors introduce this dichotomy with a preemptive disavowal of ghosts. Gilman's female narrator declares, "I would say [it is] a haunted house, and reach the height of romantic felicity – but that would be asking too much of fate."[f] James uses the word "ghost" once, at the start, when the male narrator who introduces the governess's story responds to hearing another account of the

f For other analyses of Gilman, see Elizabeth Nolan, "The woman's novel beyond sentimentalism," chapter 34, 580–582 and Castronovo, chapter 32, 546–548.

supernatural: "I quite agree – in regard to Griffin's ghost, or whatever it was – that its appearing first to the little boy ... adds a particular touch." This passage establishes the story's opaque relation to the ghost story, which it both possesses and dispossesses; "supernatural" and "ghost-story" both appear in quotation marks in James's later Prefaces, and here "whatever" offers unspoken but similarly ironizing scare quotes. "Whatever" is also a synecdoche for the ambiguities of the larger narrative, in which questions of sexual transgression – of "whatever" kinds – go unresolved.

Elsewhere in turn-of-the-century literature, the mark of the supernatural was transformed in overtly racialized ways. Some African American writers, for example, drew from potentially supernatural elements of African culture, as in Charles Chesnutt's stories of "conjuring" in *The Conjure Woman* (1899).[g] Others mobilized ideas about the occult toward radical, anti-racist ends, in such works as Pauline Hopkins's *Of One Blood* (1902–1903) and W. E. B. Du Bois's *Darkwater* (1920).[10] The most overtly supernatural fiction of the early twentieth century, however, was also the most overtly racist. H. P. Lovecraft created imaginary worlds with ancient histories, occult practices, and untranslatable languages; for example, his well-known story"The Call of Cthulhu" (1928) centers on the words, "Ph'nglui mglw'nafh Cthulhu R'lyeh wgah'nagl fhtagn." That his unglossed phrase is chanted by "diabolist Esquimaux" and "Louisiana swamp priests" suggests Lovecraft's interest in the supernaturally demonic and the socially foreign, qualities he insistently links to racial others.[11] In an era when the supernatural was transformed by new understandings of psyche and politics, Lovecraft's fiction offers a protest, untranslatable and uncanny, against modernity.

In the late twentieth century, the supernatural proliferated anew in American fiction, often in novels by authors who are themselves extraordinarily prolific. Joyce Carol Oates, for example, has repeatedly revivified the supernatural in many of her novels. *Bellefleur* (1980), a complex historical novel, is filled with "Haunted Things," as one chapter is titled, including the "ghosts, demons [and] spirits" of its upstate New York landscape, the "haunted closets and baths and mirrors and drawers" of its titular castle, and the "haunted things in human form" who populate its plots. That the supernatural suffuses this novel is not, for Oates, a rejection of more realist modes but an enhancement of them: as she wrote in a later Preface to *Bellefleur*, "The imaginative construction of a 'Gothic' novel involves the systematic

g For discussion of conjuring elements in African American writing, see Barbara McCaskill, "The African American novel after Reconstruction," chapter 29, 490–491.

transposition of realistic psychological and emotional experiences into 'Gothic' elements. We all experience mirrors that distort." The supernatural, along with the gothic and the grotesque, is one of Oates's most frequent distorting mirrors, used in stylized ways to refract psychological interiors. Across Oates's *oeuvre*, the supernatural retains a productive power to illuminate texts, histories and persons as "haunted things in human form."[12]

If Oates's fiction introduces the circulatory vitality of the supernatural in contemporary fiction, three very different "haunted house" novels – by Shirley Jackson, Stephen King, and Toni Morrison – show the supernatural's continuing exploration of dispossession and its changing entanglement with visual representation. Shirley Jackson's *The Haunting of Hill House* (1959) presents a house possessed by spirits – "Hill House, not sane, stood by itself against its hills, holding darkness within it," and a group of people who become possessed by that house. The emphasis is on a woman, Eleanor, who refuses to leave the house, a refusal which she understands as her own possession of it – "Hill House belongs to *me*" – and which culminates in her suicide, an act she registers as a loss of self-possession: "In the unending, crashing second before the car hurled into the tree she thought clearly, *Why* am I doing this?" Written just before the emergence of modern feminism, the novel offers a female protagonist whose susceptibility to supernatural possession suggests her own distorted rage at her powerlessness. Eleanor comes to Hill House after many miserable years as caretaker to her now-dead mother. Eleanor's relation to the house is symbolically that of daughter, while the house acts as a possessive mother, or as another character describes it, "A mother house . . . a housemother, a headmistress, a housemistress." The intensity of mother/daughter dynamics in the novel offers a psychoanalytic foundation for its depiction of the supernatural, while also supplying a metaphor for Jackson's own place in the history of the genre. *The Haunting of Hill House* is heir to a tradition of feminist supernaturalism, particularly Gilman's "The Yellow Wallpaper," but unlike that story – in which the narrator experiences the women in the wallpaper as her allies – Jackson's novel showcases an intense ambivalence about relations between women. If Hill House symbolizes not only a mother but a matrilineal literary heritage for the American supernatural, that heritage is a version of the monstrous-feminine.[13]

The house also ambivalently incorporates a different kind of relationship between women: lesbianism. Eleanor's roommate at Hill House is the glamorous Theodora, who immediately becomes a source of fascination, identification, and desire for her. Theodora is her guide to adventure: "[Theodora] called back 'Follow, follow,' and ran down the path . . . [Eleanor] caught at her hand and held her back and then, laughing, they fell together against the bank." Here, the haunted estate is less a symbolic mother than an eroticized female body, an embodiment reinforced by its architectural shape, "concentric circles of rooms," harboring a den "entirely furnished in rose-colored satin." The house's embodiment of same-sex desire intertwines, however, with homophobic panic. During another haunting, Eleanor tightly clutches Theodora's hand, but then finds, to her horror, that she was on the other side of the room: "[W]hose hand was I holding?" Eleanor's panic is apparently resolved by her abjection of Theodora as "beastly and soiled and dirty." But her suicidal embrace of the house at novel's end also suggests a more fundamental "hand-holding" with the homoerotic. Jackson disavowed lesbian interpretations of her fiction, but eroticism between women remains a ghost haunting *The Haunting of Hill House*.[h] Lesbian possibilities gain even greater visibility in Robert Wise's 1963 film adaptation of the novel. *The Haunting* elliptically connects the supernatural with the homoerotic, while linking the diegetic gazes of women onscreen to those of the film's female – and possibly lesbian – spectators.[14]

Other supernatural novel/film pairings in the 1960s and 1970s focused similarly on the haunting of female bodies, but located the agent of haunting differently. *Rosemary's Baby*, first a novel by Ira Levin (1967) and then a film directed by Roman Polanski (1968), brought the supernatural into a New York apartment building and, within this interior, inside the pregnant body of a young wife, Rosemary. *The Exorcist*, first a novel by William Peter Blatty (1971) and then a film directed by William Friedkin (1973), located its horror in a Georgetown mansion and, within this domestic space, inside the body of a twelve-year-old girl, Regan. These novels and films seem to react against the rise of contemporary feminism, suggesting that the truest haunted houses are the violent interiors of women, from womb to throat to psyche.[15] Male demons are the agents of haunting: Satan rapes Rosemary, while the satanic Pazuzu occupies Regan. Possessed by men, women are dispossessed of any authority they might have of their own, although *Rosemary's Baby* may also be seen as a critique rather than simply an enactment of misogyny.[i]

At the intersection of the supernatural novel and the modern horror film, Stephen King has written hundreds of novels and stories, many of which have

h On the intimacy between ghost stories and queer sexual possibilities, see Elizabeth Freeman, "Reimagining genders and sexualities," chapter 57, 948–949.

i For a related discussion, see Catherine Jurca on *The Stepford Wives*, "The American novel and the rise of the suburbs," chapter 53, 885.

been adapted into well-known films. His writing suggests the possibilities for appreciating the supernatural in contemporary life. In the contrast between the otherwordly implications of haunting and the everydayness of its expression, these representations often have an absurdist edge, as in *Christine* (1983; film dir. John Carpenter, 1983), which focuses on supernaturally possessed cars. King also celebrates the marginalized; he began his career writing about poor New Englanders already dispossessed by class and other hierarchies. In *Carrie* (1974) – King's first novel, and an alternative to *The Exorcist* as an account of a demonically possessed young woman – "telekinesis" is Carrie's revenge on the popular teenagers who pelt her with tampons when she first menstruates. In King's canny version of supernaturalism in New England, the high school girls' locker room is another haunted house, and supernatural possession is the revenge of the abject female body against its social dispossession.

The Shining (1977) is King's most important supernatural novel, both for its manipulation of the genre and for the sophistication of the 1980 film adaptation by Stanley Kubrick. *The Shining* moves the supernatural to a resort hotel in Colorado in winter, a setting at once vast and claustrophobic; the body of the hotel is filled with pressurized spaces – boiler rooms, kitchens, bathrooms, guest rooms – while its mind is possessed by the murderous spirits of its past inhabitants. However, for the novel's protagonists – Jack and Wendy Torrance and their son Danny – the Overlook Hotel does not so much introduce the supernatural as elicit its presence within them. The son, Danny, possesses the gift of "shining," but the novel's true breeding ground for the supernatural is the father, a perilously recovered alcoholic, failed teacher, and blocked writer who is so full of rage that he once broke Danny's arm. Increasingly possessed by the spirit of a previous hotel caretaker, Jack is drawn toward murder, but his masculinity is already in a condition of emergency from the start. Perceived threats against it include effeminacy and homosexuality: the novel opens with Jack's fury at his job interviewer, who moves "with the prissy speed that seems to be the exclusive domain of all small plump men."[16] If Eleanor's suicide at the end of *Hill House* crystallizes the self-negation of the daughter's role, then Jack's fatal descent at the end of *The Shining* suggests that adult masculinity is self-consuming. The father who fears that he will become dispossessed of masculine authority – or who suspects that he has always been so – cannot survive, while the son, who lives, may keep on shining.

The visuality of the supernatural – "shining," "Overlook" – is signaled throughout the novel in its transformation of words into hieroglyphic marks. The tradition of the hieroglyph is central to American supernatural writing from Poe onward. *Pym* includes five illustrations that Poe presents as Pym's drawings of mysteriously shaped caves. Although these shapes resemble "alphabetical characters," they do not resolve themselves into letters, but remain opaque forms that must be looked at as visual spectacles. In Gilman's story, the "dead paper" on which the narrator writes words is inseparable from the designs on the wallpaper, "great slanting waves of optic horror" that constitute another form of non-verbal hieroglyph. In Jackson's novel, the characters are terrified by the sight of the phrase "HELP ELEANOR COME HOME" mysteriously appearing on a wall in letters "almost too large to read": distorted by size, the supernatural registers here as the literal writing on the wall. King's version of such hieroglyphic writing centers on the marks that Danny sees without understanding: "redrum." The mystery of "redrum" is solved when he sees in the mirror that it spells "murder" backwards. Both a noun and a verb, a summary of past crimes and an imperative to commit future ones, "murder" is the hieroglyph "redrum" made legible. Kubrick estranges the word orally and visually. The film offers "redrum" repeated in voiceover, in strained, grainy, urgent tones, while Danny takes a lipstick from the bedside of his sleeping mother and writes the word in lipstick on the bedroom door; Wendy, waking, hugs Danny, then reads the word in the mirror as "murder." This sequence unites "redrum" and "murder," son and mother, writer and reader, as well as literary and cinematic versions of the supernatural.

In both novel and film, this circuit cannot be separated from the other character with the ability to "shine." Dick Hallorann, the hotel's African American cook, is a "tall black man with a modest afro that was beginning to powder white." Racism is a named horror in the novel – when Jack is demonically possessed, he wants to kill the "dirty, interfering nigger" – but racial hierarchy is its foundation. Safely removed to Florida for the winter, Hallorann "had come to terms with his blackness – happy terms . . . Was he going to chance the end of that – the end of *him* – for three white people he didn't even know?" In both versions of the story, the answer is clearly yes: the kindly, self-sacrificing, black man saves the young white boy. Hallorann dies in the film and lives in the novel, but in both cases he serves as Jim to Danny's Huck.[17] At the same time, the story pushes race elsewhere, onto the white *mise-en-scène* of the Overlook in winter. The overwhelming, and overwhelmingly negative, whiteness of the snow – frozen, muffling, terrifying – implies an impasse in racial whiteness as well. As Toni Morrison notes of whiteness in Poe's *Pym*, the suggestion is of "paralysis and incoherence." King's black characters are saviors while Poe's are "savages," but *The Shining* similarly intertwines blackness with whiteness. The "powder white" of Hallorann's hair spreads to the white powder of snow, and this story of supernatural possession overlooks a vista of dispossessed whiteness.

As in earlier eras, supernatural fiction of the late twentieth century opened many other racially marked vistas. African American revisions of the supernatural include Gloria Naylor's *Mama Day* (1988), which locates an African American "conjure woman" with supernatural powers, also a version of Prospero, on an island off the Carolinas, and Jewelle Gomez's *The Gilda Stories: A Novel* (1991), which centers on a black lesbian vampire, in a series of episodes that begin in slavery in Louisiana and end in a future New England. It is Toni Morrison's *Beloved* (1987), however, which most fully enters into the tradition of supernatural fiction, reversing its dominant racial gaze. Perhaps the most canonical American novel of the late twentieth century,[j] *Beloved* also engages in close conversation with noncanonical fiction, as a brief comparison with *The Shining* suggests. Both are haunted house novels that attribute supernatural abilities to African American characters. In *The Shining*, Hallorann has the gift of "shining," and so does Beloved, in a sexualized version of the concept: "Beloved was shining and Paul D didn't like it." Even the repetitive syllables of "redrum" echo faintly in Morrison's use of "red heart," when Paul D has sex with Beloved: "[W]hen he reached the inside part he was saying, 'Red heart. Red heart ... Red heart. Red heart. Red heart.' " The point here is not so much whether Morrison was influenced by King, but rather that both writers revise a common vocabulary of supernatural writing, from the haunted house to the hieroglyphic word.

Morrison's revisions reinflect the tropes of American supernatural fiction toward African American experience. The foundational haunted house of *Beloved* is the slave ship, and its founding ghost population is the "Sixty Million and more" people of African descent killed by slavery to whom the novel is dedicated. *Beloved*'s most horrific version of supernatural hieroglyphs involves literacy itself: to those who cannot read, marks on paper – like the writings of the racist Schoolteacher – are enigmatic visual spectacles that enforce enslavement. Sethe's struggle with a "haint in [her] house" is at once a crisis of supernatural possession, political dispossession, and psychological self-possession: in the wake of slavery, "Freeing yourself was one thing; claiming ownership of that freed self was another." These struggles show the

j For fuller discussion of *Beloved*, see Michael Hill, "Toni Morrison, Gender, and the post-civil rights African American novel," chapter 64, 1077–1078.

inseparability of the novel's supernatural and political projects, or as Morrison has characterized this relationship: "The fully realized presence of the haunting [in *Beloved*] is both a major incumbent of the narrative and sleight of hand. One of its purposes is to keep the reader preoccupied with the nature of the incredible spirit world while being supplied a controlled diet of the incredible political world."[18]

"Spirit" and "political" worlds have combined in radically different ways in more recent American supernatural fiction. Since 1995, more than fifty million copies have been sold of the multi-volume *Left Behind* series of Christian fiction, co-written by Rev. Tim LaHaye, an evangelical Christian minister, and Jerry B. Jenkins, a former journalist.[19] These novels are marketed not as supernatural fiction but as Christian thrillers, with a conservative political agenda; they depict the aftermath of the Rapture, when the faithful are suddenly spirited to Heaven, as a period when those left behind must become true Christians and unite to fight the Antichrist. But the supernatural is directly coupled with religion in this series, from the outset of its inaugural volume.[k] After the Rapture, those left behind struggle to understand what just happened, as a character explains: "I mean, it has to be something supernatural or otherworldly, but–." The ambiguities of "but–" are resolved after characters turn to Christianity, which subsumes the supernatural. When the novel's most skeptical character finds faith, for example, he understands afresh an earlier episode, during which he had witnessed the mysterious destruction of planes preparing to bomb Israel: "[He] had to acknowledge that something otherworldly – yes, supernatural, something directly from God almighty – had been thrust upon those dusty hills in the form of a fire in the sky." "[O]therworldly, supernatural, and God almighty" are appositively and positively aligned, in an all-consuming religious framework that pushes the supernatural backward to Revelation, outward to the Holy Land, and upward to the "fire in the sky" adventures of the end of days.

Secular supernaturalism remains: for example, the interest in vampire novels, sparked by Anne Rice's *Interview with the Vampire* (1976), remains unabated, thriving in new niches of the publishing world, such as Stephenie Meyer's successful "Twilight" series of vampire novels aimed at teenage girls. But it is telling that even Anne Rice has now shifted from vampires to Jesus, in the novels *Christ the Lord: Out of Egypt* (2005) and *Christ the Lord: The Road to*

k For discussion of *Left Behind* in the context of American religious writing, see Amy Hungerford, "Religion and the twentieth-century American novel," chapter 44, 745–746.

Cana (2008). After returning to the Catholic church, she has set aside her previous career – which includes erotic novels along with the queer narratives of her vampire fiction – for the consecration of her writing to God. At the same time, she notes the continuity between these themes: "After all, is Christ Our Lord not the ultimate supernatural hero, the ultimate outsider, the ultimate immortal of them all?"[20] It is not only that contemporary American novels both renounce and extend the terms of the supernatural; as the case of Anne Rice segueing seamlessly from the undead vampire to the resurrected Jesus suggests, renunciation is another form of extension. The flourishing of the Christian publishing industry in recent decades suggests the strength of this tilt. In the twenty-first century, the raptures and resurrections of Christian fiction may be one of the few places in American culture in which novels of any kind – let alone supernatural novels – are not left behind.

Notes

1. Edgar Allan Poe, "The Philosophy of Composition," in Poe, *Poetry, Tales, and Selected Sketches* (New York: Library of America, 1996), 1375.
2. For a classic interpretation of the "American gothic," see Leslie A. Fiedler, *Love and Death in the American Novel* (New York: Criterion Books, 1960); for an important reassessment, see Teresa A. Goddu, *Gothic America: Narrative, History, and Nation* (New York: Columbia University Press, 1997).
3. Charles L. Crow, "Introduction," in *American Gothic: An Anthology, 1787–1916*, ed. Crow (Malden, MA: Blackwell, 1999), 1.
4. On the relation between these figures, see Leonard Cassuto, *The Inhuman Race: The Racial Grotesque in American Literature and Culture* (New York: Columbia University Press, 1997), 160–167.
5. Toni Morrison, *Playing in the Dark: Whiteness and the Literary Imagination* (New York: Vintage, 1993), 32–33.
6. For discussion of this passage, see Priscilla Wald, "Hannah Crafts," in *In Search of Hannah Crafts: Critical Essays on "The Bondwoman's Narrative,"* ed. Henry Louis Gates, Jr. and Hollis Robbins (New York: Basic, 2004), 213–230.
7. On whiteness in the novel, see David Anthony, "Class, Culture and the Trouble with White Skin in Hawthorne's *The House of the Seven Gables*," in *The House of the Seven Gables*, ed. Robert S. Levine (New York: W. W. Norton, 2006), 439–459. On Crafts and Hawthorne, see Robert S. Levine, "Trappe(d): Race and Genealogical Haunting in *The Bondwoman's Narrative*," in *In Search of Hannah Crafts*, 276–294.
8. See, for example, Jessica Amanda Salmonson, ed., *What Did Miss Darrington See? An Anthology of Feminist Supernatural Fiction* (New York: Feminist Press, 1989); Lynette Carpenter and Wendy K. Kolmar, eds., *Haunting the House of Fiction: Feminist Perspectives on Ghost Stories by American Women* (Knoxville: University of Tennessee Press, 1991); and Jeffrey Andrew Weinstock, *Scare*

Tactics: Supernatural Fiction by American Women (New York: Fordham University Press, 2008).

9. On Charcot, see Leon Edel, Introduction to *The Ghostly Tales of Henry James* (New Brunswick, NJ: Rutgers University Press, 1948), xii–xiv; on Freud, see Paula Marantz Cohen, "Freud's *Dora* and James's *The Turn of the Screw*: Two Treatments of the Female 'Case,'" *Criticism* 28: 1 (Winter 1986): 73–87.
10. On the supernatural, see James W. Coleman, *Faithful Vision: Treatments of the Sacred, Spiritual, and Supernatural in Twentieth-Century African American Fiction* (Baton Rouge: Louisiana State University Press, 2006); on the occult, see Susan Gillman, *Blood Talk: American Race Melodrama and the Culture of the Occult* (Chicago: University of Chicago Press, 2003).
11. On Lovecraft's racial politics, see S. T. Joshi, *A Dreamer and a Visionary: H. P. Lovecraft in His Time* (Liverpool: Liverpool University Press, 2001) and Annalee Newitz, *Pretend We're Dead: Capitalist Monsters in American Pop Culture* (Durham, NC: Duke University Press, 2006), 91–100.
12. Joyce Carol Oates, Preface to *Bellefleur*, reprinted in Oates, *(Woman) Writer: Occasions and Opportunities* (New York: Dutton, 1988), 370. For Oates's own assessment of American gothic traditions, see her Introduction to *American Gothic Tales*, ed. Oates (New York: Plume, 1996).
13. On mother–daughter imagery in the novel, see Bernice M. Murphy, ed., *Shirley Jackson: Essays on the Literary Legacy* (Jefferson, NC: McFarland, 2005). On the "monstrous-feminine," see Barbara Creed, *The Monstrous-Feminine: Film, Feminism, Psychoanalysis* (London: Routledge, 1993).
14. On the film, see Patricia White, *Uninvited: Classical Hollywood Cinema and Lesbian Representability* (Bloomington: Indiana University Press, 1999), 61–93.
15. On gender in these films, see Creed, *Monstrous-Feminine*; and Lucy Fischer, "Birth Traumas: Parturition and Horror in *Rosemary's Baby,*" and Vivian Sobchack, "Bringing it All Back Home: Family Economy and Generic Exchange," both in *The Dread of Difference: Gender and the Horror Film*, ed. Barry Keith Grant (Austin: University of Texas Press, 1996), 412–431, 143–163.
16. See Steven Bruhm, "Picture This: Stephen King's Queer Gothic," in *A Companion to the Gothic*, ed. David A. Punter (Oxford: Blackwell, 2000), 269–280.
17. Samantha Figliola, "Reading King Darkly: Issues of Race in Stephen King's Novels," in *Into Darkness Peering: Race and Color in the Fantastic*, ed. Elisabeth Anne Leonard (Westport, CT: Greenwood Press, 1997), 146–147.
18. Toni Morrison, "Unspeakable Things Unspoken: The Afro-American Presence in American Literature," in *Within the Circle: An Anthology of African American Literary Criticism from the Harlem Renaissance to the Present*, ed. Angelyn Mitchell (Durham, NC: Duke University Press, 1994), 396.
19. This sales figure is from Amy Johnson Frykholm, *Rapture Culture: Left Behind in Evangelical America* (New York: Oxford University Press, 2004), 3.
20. Anne Rice, "Author's Note," *Christ the Lord* (New York: Knopf, 2005), 321.

14

Imagining the South

JENNIFER RAE GREESON

"The South" as addressed in this chapter is a place of the imagination; and it is from the start a cardinal point for the broader imaginative geography of the US novel. The following pages track this South from the novels of the early republic, through the Civil War and to the rise of the more programmatic regionalist writing addressed in the second section of this volume by Tom Lutz, Barbara McCaskill, and Robert Reid-Pharr.[a] Past studies of the South in the US novel have tended to create a sequestered subgenre – "the Southern novel" – which entails certain presuppositions about the regional (and, tacitly, racial) identity of the author of a book, as well as his or her predominant setting, worldview, and technical preoccupations.[1] With the comparatively late development in the southern states of commercial book publishing and broad audiences for fiction, "the Southern novel" defined in this way makes a laggardly entry into US literary history; John Pendleton Kennedy's otherwise largely forgettable *Swallow Barn, or a Sojourn in the Old Dominion* (1832) usually is identified as the point of origin for this alternate, sub-national, tradition.[2] Focusing a study on the regional identity of authors, though, masks the pervasiveness of the South in the broader history of the US novel. Never an isolatable term, the South is always relational, if complexly so: oppositional in its definition, delineated only against an implied "North" (or, more accurately, "nation"), the South is nonetheless intrinsic to the United States.[3]

When we take this wider view, we see that the South functions as a domestic or internal other for the US novel, lying simultaneously outside and inside the national imagination. As such, it becomes foremost a site of

a See Tom Lutz, "Cather and the regional imagination" (chapter 26); Barbara McCaskill, "The African American novel after Reconstruction" (chapter 29); Robert Reid-Pharr, "The postbellum race novel" (chapter 28).

connection between the United States and what lies outside the nation[b] – a connection to the larger world, to Western history, to a guilty colonial past and an imperial future both desired and feared.[4] In four chronological sections, this chapter sketches the changing incarnations of the South across the first century of the US novel, with particular attention to its evolving functions in delineating national space and time. Spatially, the South in the US novel marks both the limit of the nationalizing early republic, and, increasingly, the continental and hemispheric horizon toward which US imperial desire projects. Martin Delany's locution for his white Southern characters in *Blake, or the Huts of America* (1858–1862) – "the South Americans" – operates at just this intersection of internal regional variation and external imperial design. Temporally, the South in the US novel serves as a conduit to the past, a backward glance against which to gauge national independence, modernization, and development; as an *Atlantic Monthly* writer put it after the Civil War, local color fiction of "the Southern mountains" was valuable for delivering to US readers accounts of "our contemporary ancestors."[5] As novelists posit the South as premodern and undeveloped, though, it comes to serve a forward-looking temporal function as well, emerging as a domestic site upon which the racialist, civilizing power of US expansion and empire abroad may be rehearsed and projected.[c]

Novels of the early republic

Locating the South in the novels of the early republic is challenging, for it at first seems totally absent. Not only were no novels produced out of the southern states in these years, but also no novel was set primarily in, or plotted primarily around, a Southern locale or character. Yet looking beyond this primary lack, we may perceive that the South is in fact everywhere in the margins of the novels of the early republic, as a key point of reference that organizes the understanding of the place of the new nation in the world. The South continually intrudes on the main, centrally located action of these novels via incursion (of Southern characters, letters, inheritances, disease)

b Seeing the domestic South as crucial to the "worlding" of US literature also bears upon the debate in this volume between Lutz, chapter 26, 441, and Bruce Robbins ("The worlding of the American novel," chapter 66) on the "cosmopolitanism" or geographically restricted imagination of the postbellum novel.

c In a related move within this volume, Russ Castronovo connects the foreign contexts and exoticism of the US imperial novel to the setting of "the Southern slave plantation" ("Imperialism, Orientalism, and empire," chapter 32, 538).

and excursion (trips taken "to the southward" by protagonists), and the shape of these Southern intrusions varies among the major categories of the early novel: picaresque, gothic, and sentimental.[6]

We would expect to find the South somewhere in the early picaresque novel, since that subgenre itself implies nationalist geography. By following a protagonist through a range of disparate localities – either the varying internal regions that make up the new United States, or foreign territories in the Old or New Worlds – the picaresque novel proposes on the one hand the internal coherence of the new nation, and on the other hand its external distinctiveness, the difference between the United States and the rest of the world.[d] The role of the South as a connecting term in this project comes into particular focus in the novel usually considered the finest example of the subgenre, Royall Tyler's *The Algerine Captive* (1797).[e] Tyler's plot raises interconnected foreign and domestic challenges to republican ideology. By taking for his subject the Algerian captivity crisis in which Barbary pirates captured US merchant ships, enslaved their crews, and held them for ransom, Tyler probes the greatest affront to US sovereignty of the 1790s, which he also uses as a painful reminder of the hypocritical constitution of the United States as a slaveholding society. To hold his picaresque hero, the New Englander Updike Underhill, plausibly innocent of the threats to republican integrity inherent in the plot, Tyler inserts a sojourn in the South between Updike's account of his early life in New England and his travel to the northern coast of Africa aboard a slave-trading ship. In the combination of intra- and international geography Tyler formulates, the South serves as a sort of buffer; Updike must pass through "one of the states, southward of Philadelphia," in order to enter into the Atlantic world of empire, enslavement, and anti-republican power extremes.

To maintain this effect, Tyler insists upon a radical disjuncture between the culture, social organization, and even language of the US national center and that of the South. *The Algerine Captive* contains perhaps the first extended use of Southern dialect in a US novel, in the form of an epistolary challenge to a duel addressed to Updike early in the novel by a Harvard student "born at Carolina." "Dear Sir," the letter begins, "Them there very extraordinary pare

d Timothy Sweet considers the connection of local settings to national concerns in antebellum novels ("American land, American landscape, American novels," chapter 5).

e Elsewhere in this volume Paul Giles treats Tyler's novel in the context of other works generated in response to the Algerian captivity crisis ("Transatlantic currents and the invention of the American novel," chapter 1, 33).

of varses you did yourself the onner to address to a young lada of my partecling acquaintance calls loudly for explination. I shall be happy to do myself the onner of wasting a few charges of powder with you on the morro morning." Countering the civilized literary production of the young national protagonist with a barbarity of both behavior and spelling, the would-be Southern duelist establishes that US citizens and US Southerners speak different, and hierarchically posed, languages – making them, in the purely linguistic world of the novel, essentially different peoples.

While the gothic novels of the early republic often seem closely derived from British precedents, the South plays a key role in the American geography within which Charles Brockden Brown set his six novels published between 1798 and 1801. Brockden Brown's South, which always lies below the Mason-Dixon line but often expands into the Caribbean, consistently serves as a repository for a complex of inherited traits and ideological residue from the recent colonial past of the new United States. The uncanny Southern presences in his novels evoke the persistence of racial slavery in the republic and the specter of race war as a logical continuation of the American Revolution; the bad economic foundation of the republic in the plantation production of staple commodities; and the presumably degenerative tropical climate of the Western hemisphere, as well as the racial heterogeneity of its population. Even though Brockden Brown set each of his six published novels primarily in the middle states – Pennsylvania and New York – the South proves crucial to his formulation of a gothic mode specific to the early republic, providing the source for haunting and horrifying irruptions of New World coloniality into a tenuously independent national center.

The symbolic weight of the South in Brockden Brown's gothic comes into particular focus in his two novels organized around stolen inheritances and yellow fever epidemics, *Arthur Mervyn; or, Memoir of the Year 1793* (1799–1800) and *Ormond; or The Secret Witness* (1800). Inheritance is itself an uncanny term in a new republic focused on breaking ties with hereditary monarchy, and Brown recognizes the problematic stature of inheritance when he sources the fortunes at stake in these novels to a variety of southern locations – Baltimore, Charleston, Jamaica, Tobago – that blur the boundaries between domestic (national) and foreign (colonial) plantation production. Yellow fever on its own conjures immediate association with the South, as a disease of tropical America; setting his novels in Philadelphia during fever epidemics thus provides Brown another apt figure in which a Southern intrusion on the US center becomes a metaphor for the imperfect decolonization of the new republic.

The most popular subgenre of the early US novel, the sentimental novel, long has been seen by literary historians as creating allegories for the political situation of the early republic.[f] The early sentimental novels organized around seduction plots appear to fictionalize the perceived vulnerability of the United States to threats internal and external: in the plight of the accosted maiden one might see the innocent reader in the new nation;[g] and in the machinations of the depraved seducer appear the wiles of the anti-republican conspirator, the demagogue, the imperial tyrant.[7] It is therefore striking to note that over the course of the 1790s, the geographical affiliation of the anti-republican seducer in US sentimental novels shifts from British redcoat to Southern planter – from past exogenous oppressor to present enemy within. The first US seduction novels – such as *Amelia, or the Faithless Briton* (1787) and Susanna Rowson's *Charlotte Temple* (1791) – seem to reprise the contest for American independence. Set during the Revolutionary War, these novels subject the virtue of an innocent proto-American lass to the assaults of a domineering British swain. As the decade progresses, though, novelists dispense with the British identity of the seducer, and instead render intranational tales of struggle between republican virtue and internal despotism in which seducers almost always are aligned in some way, even if fleetingly, with the South. In the serial *Story of Margaretta* (1798), for instance, the virtue of Judith Sargent Murray's heroine is assailed by a Southern planter ominously named Sinisterus Courtland; in *Jane Talbot* (1801), Brockden Brown's most conventional epistolary seduction novel, the Philadelphian Jane is addressed by the vaguely Godwinian, fiery, and ironically named Henry Colden, who writes his letters from Baltimore. By 1801, Tabitha Tenney's rollicking picaresque/seduction hybrid, *Female Quixotism: Exhibited in the Romantic Adventures and Extravagant Opinions of Dorcasina Sheldon*, seems to comment on this trend of characterization; Tenney's romance-deluded heroine misapprehends her only honorable suitor, a Virginian, to be a diabolical seducer precisely because of his Southern origin.

In the sentimental novel of the era most acclaimed by current critics, Hannah Webster Foster's *The Coquette* (1797), the seducer Sanford's initially conflicted and potentially honorable intentions toward heroine Eliza Wharton

f Cindy Weinstein examines related allegorical dimensions of the sentimental novel, particularly in its focus on the marriage plot, in the antebellum decades ("Sentimentalism," chapter 12 in this volume).

g Anna Mae Duane (chapter 2) elaborates upon "how seduction functioned as a structuring metaphor for American nation-building," in her treatment of both *Charlotte Temple* and *The Coquette* ("Susanna Rowson, Hannah Webster Foster, and the seduction novel in the early USA," quotation at 38).

are transmuted irrevocably for the worse by a "tour to the southward," where he is himself seduced by the trappings of aristocracy. Making a mercenary marriage to a planter's daughter, Sanford returns to Hartford a confirmed villain, converted to anti-republican Southern "opulence" and bent on "possessing" Eliza out of wedlock. Herein lies a deeper worry of Foster's seduction novel: how fragile, ultimately, are republican "virtue" and metropolitan "learning" in the new nation, built as they are upon the rather dull and tedious ground of self-restraint and self-cultivation? How susceptible are readers of the early republic to being led astray by the (figuratively Southern) "palms" still acceded to imperial opulence and dominion?

Novels of the "Age of Jackson"

In the decades between the War of 1812 and the clearly defined sectional conflict that arose in the 1830s, US literature became a more commercially viable, novel-centered, and programmatically nationalist enterprise. At the same time, the primary US nationalist concern of demonstrating independence from Britain began to be supplanted by expansionist ambitions for continental dominance known as "Manifest Destiny." The interrelation of these two trends – and the role of the South at their nexus – is nicely exemplified by the literary career of James Kirke Paulding. One of the first US authors to make a life-long profession of authorship, Paulding initially came to public attention not as a novelist, but as a periodical essayist, with *Salmagundi* (1807–1808), which he co-wrote with another early American professional writer, Washington Irving. It was not until the commencement of the War of 1812 that Paulding published his first long prose work, *The Diverting History of John Bull and Brother Jonathan* (1812), a political allegory in which he personified Britain and the United States as father and son. He followed this popular work with more recognizably proto-novelistic travelogues on the same theme, *A Sketch of Old England, by a New England Man* (1822), and *John Bull in America; or the New Munchausen* (1824). In these texts Paulding explored the contrast between the two warring countries by creating a consistent narrator representative of one nation, and then rendering his picaresque adventures in the territory of the other. After the close of the war, Paulding turned this nationalistic and proto-novelistic formula away from the transatlantic contrast, and instead toward the defining intranational contrast of US literature, with *Letters from the South, by a Northern Man* (1817).

Having finally abandoned the defining United States/England contrast for its domestic North/South counterpart, and having moved entirely into the novel genre, Paulding finally produced the book for which he is best remembered today, *Westward Ho!* (1832). Here Paulding develops an influential narrative schema for mapping US expansion, in which readers first travel South in order to venture West: the novel begins in Virginia, with the aptly named Cuthbert Dangerfield, a well-defined type of the enervated, bankrupt Southern planter. The main action of the novel follows an emigrating Dangerfield to Kentucky, where he plants the utopian colony of Dangerfieldville – ideally transmuting the "dangerous fields" of the Southern plantation, in other words, into a more civilized town, an emblem of stadial progress, in the West.[h] Paulding's circum-location of westward expansion through the South represents not only his attempt to "salvage the impecunious and failure-bent Cavalier," as William R. Taylor has put it, but also his routing of the new external empire of the western territories through the old internal US empire of Southern plantation slavery.[8]

The features that characterized Paulding's work at the end of his career – his allegiance to the novel form, his commercial success, his focus westward for primary setting and plot, and his nationalist intent of creating a historical tradition in literature on the model of Walter Scott – all immediately bring to mind James Fenimore Cooper's career trajectory.[i] As it does for Paulding, the South plays an inescapable role for Cooper in negotiating these nationalist, generic, and geographic aims. His first influential novel, *The Spy: A Tale of the Neutral Ground* (1821), revisits the Revolutionary contest between Britain and the nascent United States, but on top of the past transatlantic contest, Cooper maps the domestic North–South opposition of his present day, which had just been brought into sharper political focus with the Missouri Compromise of 1820. The "neutral ground" of Cooper's subtitle – western New York State, a favorite setting of his – may be read as a middle ground both in the past contest between imperial metropolis and provincial colonies, and in the rising conflict between domestic North and South. In his Revolutionary-era New York woods, Cooper revises the iconic nationalist figure George Washington, presenting him as part of a company of Virginia dragoons and as a more southern than purely national figure. An unexpected nationalist counter-hero emerges in the person of the New England pedlar Harvey Birch, the "spy" of the title, whose modern facility in disguise, trade, and fluid self-transformation enables him to outwit both Southern and British gentlemen.

h On stadial theory and its use in novels of the era, see Sweet, chapter 5 in this volume, esp. 92–94.

i Elsewhere in this volume, Winfried Fluck charts the emergence of the historical novel in the United States, the importance of the model of Scott, and the purchase of Cooper ("The nineteenth-century historical novel," chapter 7, 118–121).

In other words, it is only against the imperfectly independent Southern gentleman-slaveholder that US novelists of the 1820s were able to elevate the decidedly unromantic Yankee – trader at the dawn of industrialism, emigrant at the frontier of expansion, and all-around avatar of the modern era – to the stature of heroic protagonist in the national saga.[9] The trend is evident not only in historical novels, but also in the most important domestic novel of the decade, Sarah Josepha Hale's *Northwood: A Tale of New England* (1827). Hale's plot centers on Sidney Romilly, an uprightly reared child of Massachusetts who as an adolescent is immersed in the glittering world of the Southern plantation. Nearly losing his moral bearings in South Carolina, Romilly must be reintroduced to his native section in order to achieve full maturity. Once he has renounced his aristocratic ways and consolidated his intranational geographic identity by marrying a Yankee lass, Hale sends him South again at the end of the novel to take over the plantation he has now inherited. In so doing, she inaugurates Romilly as an early agent of the emigrating, expanding "universal Yankee nation" whose civilizing mission begins not in the Western territories, but at home, in the unregenerate South.

The charged weight of the South in this transitional era of US literary history is epitomized by another Cooper novel, *The Last of the Mohicans* (1826). Cooper's Leatherstocking "tales" set on the colonial Anglo-American frontier consciously operate in service of archetypes and myths that stretch the imaginative fund of the new nation back into a primeval past.[j] In this particular novel, Cooper offers the reader what amounts to two interrelated sets of Ur-parents for the United States. Race is a major factor in Cooper's pairing of the half-sisters Cora and Alice Munro with the Mohican prince Uncas and the Anglo-American colonial officer Duncan Heyward, respectively, since Cora is the daughter of a mixed-race mother from the West Indies, while Alice is of "pure" Scottish descent.[k] But geographical origin is equally important in the pairings, as Cooper reveals in the telling exchange between Munro and Heyward, when the latter asks for Alice's hand, and unwittingly enrages her father for not expressing interest in Cora, the elder daughter. Munro is outraged by what he believes to be Heyward's racial prejudice, which he attributes to the fact that Heyward was "born at the South." Heyward denies the charge as "unworthy of [his] reason," but secretly admits to himself that the accusation is indeed just, and his bias "as deeply rooted as if it had been

j Fluck examines the nationalist work of antebellum historical novels, chapter 7, 122–126.
k Sandra Gustafson complicates this "narrative of white hegemony" with the context of Cooper's subsequent career as a novelist ("Cooper and the idea of the Indian," chapter 6, quotation at 109).

ingrafted in his nature." Here we see an intimate geographic connection between Cora and Heyward: they are both primally Southern characters who embody the racial bifurcation of plantation society. Cooper asserts what amounts to a "natural," if "embarrassing," white supremacy for the United States that is "ingrafted" in the nation by its South.[1]

As he consolidates the Ur-parentage of the United States by marrying his light couple, Southerner Heyward and Scotswoman Alice, Cooper annihilates his dark couple, Southerner Cora and Indian Uncas. Cooper's archetypal double-romance thus insinuates that national ascendancy is born out of and predicated on the destruction of internal others. He reinvigorates the South present in novels of the early republic, finding in it not only a past over which to weep, but also a model of racialist, civilizationist nationalism perfectly calibrated for his own expansionist era.

Novels of sectionalism

The 1830s saw a fundamental alteration in the relationship of the South to the rest of the United States. Immediate abolitionism emerged in New England at the start of the decade with William Lloyd Garrison's founding of *The Liberator*; at the same time, sectionalist politics reached a new pitch in Congress with the Nullification Crisis, when South Carolina claimed that the state could overrule Federal law. What we recognize today as a binary North/South opposition increasingly became an organizing principle in US politics, achieving a new centrality after the Compromise of 1850 (which included the Fugitive Slave Law), and culminating in the Civil War. As we would expect, a new cultural formation came into being in US letters along with this political shift: we see for the first time novelists who self-identify as "Southern," and who feel themselves to be at variance with the centers of US literary production in Boston and New York City; and we see as well across these decades a consolidating "Northern" identity, in which New England metamorphoses from a strange and distinct region into an integral part of all that is *not* "the South."[10] Self-proclaimed, self-consciously "Southern" and "Northern" writers began to do battle over which of their antithetical sections should be seen as the true seat of the republic, and the novel quickly proved the most influential genre of the antebellum era.

1 Castronovo proposes that Cooper's regionalized and historicized plot "gentrifies imperialism" by "relegating frontier warfare to a thing of the past," while also registering "the risk of miscegenation that the nation invites with its expansive military policies" (chapter 32, 538–539).

Charlestonian William Gilmore Simms is unquestionably the most significant "Southern" novelist in this era, both because he published a prodigious, and generally well received, number of novels between the early 1830s and his death in 1870, and because he prominently involved himself in the sectionalist critical wars of these decades. Simms's novelistic methods and concerns are not much distinguishable from Cooper's, or, perhaps more to the point, from Scott's: Simms seeks to create a deep, archetypal story and a mythological and symbolic fund for US nationalism. "The original literature of a Nation," he wrote in 1839, "is no less important to its interests, than its valour and its virtue." The great difference between Cooper and Simms comes in the form of geography: Simms insists upon a Southern locus for the nationalist tales he spins, with his sectionalism not antagonistic to, but rather inextricable from his nationalism; he boasted in 1851 that thanks to his Revolutionary War novels, "South Carolina is regarded as a very storehouse for romance. She has furnished more materials for the use of art and fiction, than half the states in the Union."[11]

Given his nationalist mission, the plots of Simms's series of Revolutionary War novels – usually considered his best – are surprising today. Instead of creating triumphal tales that take into account the ultimate victory of the colonial rebellion, Simms chooses as his subject the period in 1780–1781 when the South Carolina armies had surrendered to the British and were in disarray, and Charleston was an occupied city. The business of the war is thus carried on offstage in his novels, only as guerrilla warfare from the surrounding swamps, and Simms instead delineates a home front under tyrannical occupation, with patriots unjustly executed, their daughters threatened, and their homes confiscated and destroyed. In his introduction to the first novel of the series, *The Partisan* (1835), Simms explains that as a US romancer, he will serve the cause of nationalism by "dwel[ling] earnestly upon our disasters," belligerently refusing to celebrate even the primary victory that established the nation in the first place. For instance, *Katharine Walton* (1851) revolves around the unjust imprisonment of patriot colonel Richard Walton and a variety of schemes to effect his freedom, but the novel ends with the failure of all patriot plots and Walton's martyrdom by execution.

It is difficult to read Simms's particular approach to the Revolutionary War without thinking of the coming Civil War, and indeed, his personal, nonfictional accounts of the later war are almost indistinguishable from the formulas he created for his historical romances in the antebellum decades. Recalling Twain's 1883 admonishment that "Sir Walter [Scott] had so large a hand in making Southern character, as it existed before the war, that he is in great measure responsible for the war," we see that any such trajectory of cultural causality would have to be followed directly through Simms, whose novels remind us of the often infinitesimal distance between narratives of nationalist history and nationalist romance.[12]

The novel was not the preferred form of Edgar Allan Poe, the most important self-identifying "Southern" writer of the antebellum decades, but Poe's single foray into the genre, *The Narrative of Arthur Gordon Pym* (1838), replaces Simms's lengthy and moody dwellings in a mythological past with a taut, formally complex, and narratively wild jaunt into the present and future of US empire. Poe's novel insistently maps the domestic sectional conflict onto the seemingly limitless global appetite of nascent US imperialism, in the form of the journey of an emigrating New Englander –"Arthur Gordon Pym of Nantucket" – into a sublimely infinite realm for his global domination – to the South and "STILL FARTHER SOUTH."

From Poe's Southern perspective, the imagination of nineteenth-century imperialism originates in the white-over-black binary of racialized slavery, and his quasi-science-fiction novel of exploration unfolds a radical white/black polarity between antagonistically posed civilized explorers and savage others.[13] In the much-interpreted archetypal ending of the main plot of *Pym*, Poe on the one hand seems to assert an apocalyptic ascendance of absolute whiteness, in the form of the "shrouded human figure, very far larger in its proportions than any dweller among men" with skin "of the perfect whiteness of the snow," whose appearance abruptly cuts off Pym's narration.[m] But on the other hand, in the final "Note" with which Poe ends the novel, an unidentified authoritative narrator dismisses the accounts of both "Mr. Pym" and his "editor," "Mr. Poe," to reveal that the ultimate meaning of the novel is to be found in a literal subtext: in buried writing Pym discovered, but misrecognized as nonliterate, in chasms below the earth during his Southern explorations. These writings, the authoritative narrator explains, are in Arabic, Egyptian, and Ethiopian languages – a revelation stemming equally from Poe's fascination with theories of the African origins of knowledge, and from his Southern insight that strains from Africa underwrite both US culture and the US novel.

Both Simms's less distinguished but copious novels and Poe's masterful single work in the genre eclipse in significance the plantation-nostalgia

m Both Elizabeth Young ("Supernatural novels," chapter 13, 223) and John Ernest ("Stowe, race and the antebellum American novel," chapter 15, 256–257) treat this scene as the ultimate end of the novel.

novels of Southern writers such as John Pendleton Kennedy, Nathaniel Beverley Tucker, John Esten Cooke, and Caroline Lee Hentz. The novels of these Southern partisans usually are seen by literary historians as symptomatic responses to the rapid modernization of US society in the antebellum decades, providing backward glances to an idealized agrarian basis for the republic in the South, and concomitantly an implicit or explicit critique of the rise of industrial capitalism in the North.[14] But the cultural work of these plantation novels must also be understood in tandem with the political conceptualization of a Southern pro-slavery argument in the antebellum decades: when South Carolina Senator John C. Calhoun in 1837 declared Southern slavery "a positive good," he did so only by comparison to nascent Northern industrial capitalism – under which economic system, he claimed, the inherent "conflict between labor and capital" could not be regulated as it was with the racialized, ostensibly paternalist system of production in the South.[15]

The most influential innovation in imagination of the South in the antebellum era thus comes in the form of Harriet Beecher Stowe's *Uncle Tom's Cabin, or Life Among the Lowly* (1852), which boldly discards the binary between Southern slave capitalism and Northern industrial capitalism upon which the plantation-nostalgia novels depend. Instead, Stowe makes the South emblematic of the most fearful dimensions of the transforming Northern economy, drawing her allegorical "picture" of a Southern "slave establishment"– Simon Legree's plantation – to look like nothing more than a New England factory town.[16]

Stowe is by no means alone in this revelatory conflation of the cotton plantation with the textile mill; for instance, Hollis Robbins has pointed out that the recently rediscovered antebellum anti-slavery novel *The Bondwoman's Narrative* (c.1853–1861?) borrows directly and copiously from *Bleak House*, transporting Dickens's descriptions of London's urban masses directly to accounts of slave life on rural Southern plantations.[17] These remarkably modern, transformed novelistic imaginings of the South eviscerate the critique of industrial modernity put forth by the plantation-nostalgia novelists. And more, Stowe and the novelists who follow her render an intimate connection between metropolitan development and the peripheral expansion and exploitation that underwrite it. As they re-envision the South on the eve of the Civil War, US novelists narrativize the very symbiosis between industry and empire that Edward Said has bemoaned as lacking in British novels of the same era.[18]

Novels of the Civil War and beyond

With the coming of the Civil War, US novelists took a step back from Stowe's ultra-modern, dystopic imagination of the South, and instead returned overwhelmingly to romance plots organized around the progress (or thwarting of progress) of a couple toward marriage. This trend continued through the postbellum period examined in the next section of this volume. As Robert Reid-Pharr astutely points out, many of the most prominent and popular of these postbellum romances set in the South appear "embarrassing" and "juvenile" in their racialist preoccupations[n] – which may explain why many of these novels have received more sustained interest from historians – ranging from C. Vann Woodward to Nina Silber to David Blight – than from literary critics.[19] Historians have held up these romance novels as symptomatic of the extreme divisions of their time, quite literally routing questions of national union through questions of marriage. The desire for union presumably sublimated in these plots sometimes skews toward transcending the rift between the races that persists beyond the abolition of slavery. For instance, both Julia C. Collins's unfinished, serialized novel *The Curse of Caste* (1863), and Lydia Maria Child's *Romance of the Republic* (1867) revolve around interracial unions engineered by pairing phenotypically white women of mixed race with white men. While this interracial romance plot did not disappear entirely in the decades after the war – as Barbara McCaskill notes, Charles Chesnutt returns to it in a tragic register in *The House Behind the Cedars* (1900)[o] – postbellum romance novelists tended more consistently to focus instead on transcending the rift between sections. The focus on cross-sectional pairings, though, usually served to heighten the rift between the races, a point made clear in Frances E. W. Harper's *Iola Leroy* (1891), which is a plain rewriting of Collins's and Child's earlier interracial romances. Harper's phenotypically white Southern protagonist deliberately rejects her ardent white Northern suitor for a black Northern spouse, in order to maintain allegiance, above all, to her "African blood."

More often, and more disturbingly, cross-sectional romance plots swing toward consolidating a white racial identity as the basis for a reconstituted national family. Cross-sectional romances between white protagonists are organizing principles of even such realist treatments of the South such as John W. De Forest's war novel – whose title says it all – *Miss Ravenel's*

n Reid-Pharr, chapter 28 470.
o McCaskill, chapter 29 486–487.

Conversion from Secession to Loyalty (1867), and Albion W. Tourgée's novel of Reconstruction, *A Fool's Errand* (1879). Similarly, George Washington Cable's *The Grandissimes* (1880), often considered the most important "local color" novel of the era, is framed by a cross-sectional romance. Later in this volume (chapter 28) Reid-Pharr examines the peak, or indeed nadir, of this overarching trajectory of sectional reconciliation, achieved at the price of hardening racial division, in turn-of-the-century romance novels of the South under Reconstruction.

Walter Benn Michaels and others have seen these cross-sectional romances at the start of the twentieth century – whether the racialist work of a novelist such as Thomas Nelson Page (*Red Rock*, 1898), or the blatant white supremacy of a novelist such as Thomas Dixon (*The Clansman*, 1905) as inflected with a geopolitical awareness that far exceeds the North/South sectional crisis of the past.[20] Instead, these novels revisit the domestic, yet other, territory of the South to explore the increasingly global geographical imaginary of nascent US empire overseas, in the Caribbean and the Pacific. Across the first century of the history of the US novel, the South had blurred the line between self and other, identity and difference. Now, at the dawn of the "American Century," it emerged as an essential register for figuring the questions of union, equality, consent, dominance, and submission articulated by the writers of national romance plots. It is intriguing, in the end, to think about the extent to which the US novel has been able to register the contrasts between colony and nation, between republic and empire, between center and periphery – precisely because of the internal–other, outside-and-inside South of our imaginations.

Notes

1. The identity-based definition of "Southern literature" was codified most influentially in the last generation by Louis B. Rubin *et al.*, eds., *The History of Southern Literature* (Baton Rouge: Louisiana State University Press, 1985).
2. For instance William R. Taylor, *Cavalier and Yankee: The Old South and American National Character* (1961; reissue edn., New York: Oxford University Press, 1993), 178–188.
3. The classic study that takes into account literature of the South not written by southern writers is Jay B. Hubbell, *The South in American Literature, 1607–1900* (Durham, NC: Duke University Press, 1954).
4. This is the argument of Jennifer Greeson, *Our South: Geographic Fantasy and the Rise of National Literature* (Cambridge, MA: Harvard University Press, 2010).
5. William Goodell Frost, "Our Contemporary Ancestors in the Southern Mountains," *Atlantic Monthly* 83.497 (1899): 311–320.

6. Here I follow Cathy N. Davidson's categories of the early US novel in *Revolution and the Word: The Rise of the Novel in America* (New York: Oxford University Press, 1986).
7. Jay Fliegelman, *Prodigals and Pilgrims: The American Revolution against Patriarchal Authority, 1750–1800* (Cambridge: Cambridge University Press, 1982); Ruth Block, "The Gendered Meanings of Virtue in Revolutionary America," *Signs* 13.1 (Autumn 1987): 37–59; Elizabeth Barnes, *States of Sympathy: Seduction and Democracy in the American Novel* (New York: Columbia University Press, 1997).
8. Taylor, *Cavalier and Yankee*, 246.
9. This is Taylor's central argument.
10. Fred Hobson's *Tell about the South: The Southern Rage to Explain* (Baton Rouge: Louisiana State University Press, 1983) provides a wonderful account of the rise of a Southern self-consciousness in literature of this period as an intrinsically defensive enterprise, produced in response to extant cultural characterizations and uses of "the South." Useful work on the relationship of the sectionalist "North" in antebellum US culture to the nation as a whole includes Peter J. Parish's posthumous collection of essays, *The North and the Nation in the Era of the Civil War* (New York: Fordham University Press, 2003), and Susan-Mary Grant's *North over South: Northern Nationalism and American Identity in the Antebellum Era* (Lawrence: Kansas University Press, 2000).
11. Simms to George Frederick Holmes, August 15, 1842, in *Letters of William Gilmore Simms*, ed. Mary C. Simms Oliphant *et al.*, 5 vols. (Columbia: University of South Carolina Press, 1952–1956), I:319.
12. Mark Twain, *Life on the Mississippi* (Boston: James R. Osgood and Co., 1883).
13. Here Poe continues the overmapping of westward expansion and Southern plantation seen in Cooper. For more on the civilized/savage binary in US culture, see Roy Harvey Pearce's classic study, *Savagism and Civilization: A Study of the Indian and the American Mind* (Baltimore: Johns Hopkins University Press, 1953).
14. Lewis P. Simpson, *The Dispossessed Garden: Pastoral and History in Southern Literature* (Baton Rouge: Louisiana State University Press, 1975). Timothy Sweet also examines this contrast in the late, somewhat de-sectionalized instance of Davis's *Life in the Iron-Mills* ("American land, American landscape, American novels," chapter 5 in this volume, 97–98).
15. For the connections between pro-slavery ideology and modern critique of industrial capitalism see Richard Hofstadter on Calhoun as the "Marx of the Master Class" in *The American Political Tradition and the Men Who Made It* (New York: Knopf, 1948), and Louis Hartz, *The Liberal Tradition in America: An Interpretation of American Political Thought since the Revolution* (New Haven: Yale University Press, 1955).
16. Stephen Nissenbaum tracks the journey into industrialization in *Uncle Tom's Cabin* in "New England as Region and Nation," in *All over the Map: Rethinking American Regions* (Baltimore: Johns Hopkins University Press, 1996).
17. Hollis Robbins, "Blackening *Bleak House*," in *In Search of Hannah Crafts: Critical Essays on the Bondwoman's Narrative*, ed. Henry Louis Gates (New York: Basic Civitas, 2004).

18. Edward Said, *Culture and Imperialism* (New York: Knopf, 1993).
19. C. Vann Woodward, "A Southern Critique for the Gilded Age," in *The Burden of Southern History*, 3rd edn. (Baton Rouge: Louisiana State University Press, 1993); Nina Silber, *The Romance of Reunion* (Chapel Hill: University of North Carolina Press, 1993); David Blight, *Race and Reunion* (Cambridge, MA: Harvard University Press, 2005).
20. Walter Benn Michaels, *Our America: Nativism, Modernism, Pluralism* (Durham, NC: Duke University Press, 1993). See also Harilaos Stecopoulos, *Reconstructing the World: Southern Fictions and U.S. Imperialisms, 1898–1976* (Ithaca, NY: Cornell University Press, 2008).

15

Stowe, race, and the antebellum American novel

JOHN ERNEST

In her 1892 novel *Iola Leroy*, the African American writer and activist Frances E. W. Harper has one of her characters, Dr. Latimer, encourage another, Iola Leroy, to write "a book to inspire men and women with a deeper sense of justice and humanity." When Iola doubts both her ability and the receptiveness of readers to a black woman's writings, Dr. Latimer responds, "Miss Leroy, out of the race must come its own thinkers and writers. Authors belonging to the white race have written good racial books, for which I am deeply grateful, but it seems to be almost impossible for a white man to put himself completely in our place. No man can feel the iron which enters another man's soul." Prominent among those white writers who wrote influential "racial books" was Harriet Beecher Stowe, whose 1852 novel *Uncle Tom's Cabin* Harper admired deeply. In writing *Iola Leroy*, a novel that leads to a call for black novelists, Harper was participating in a tradition with deep roots in the period before the Civil War when writing about race increasingly meant writing about black Americans, and when literature about race was complexly intertwined with competing notions of social order, justice, and humanity. At stake in this tradition are not only thorny questions about novelistic authority and authorial authenticity but also fundamental questions about how race might be represented in literature. These questions, too, are deeply rooted in the antebellum period, and the effects of this earlier period of literature influenced greatly what Robert Reid-Pharr characterizes in this volume as the "shockingly discordant cacophony of form, theme, content and style" that one encounters in post-Civil War novels that deal explicitly with race.[a]

That *Uncle Tom's Cabin* brought such questions to the forefront of American politics and literature is evident from the immediate, varied, and often vitriolic

a Robert Reid-Pharr, "The post-bellum race novel," chapter 28, 470.

responses to Stowe's novel. Pro-slavery commentators "called it libelous and Stowe a liar," finding "dirty insinuations in the novel" and "the hoof of the beast" beneath Stowe's skirts.[1] Black and white abolitionists alike both celebrated the novel's powerful anti-slavery stance and worried about the perceived limitations of its sentimental appeal[b] as well as the dubious value of Stowe's politics. Both in spite of and because of such responses, readers turned to Stowe's novel as if their lives depended on it. The novel appeared first in serial form, in the pages of the *National Era*, from 1851 to 1852, and when it was published in book form in 1852 "more than three thousand copies sold the first day, fourteen power presses ran day and night to keep up with demand, and within a year there were 120 editions and 300,000 copies sold."[2] The book was soon translated into numerous languages, and Stowe's novel was firmly established not only as an unprecedented bestseller but also as a deeply influential commentary on slavery and a lasting example of the power of the novel to highlight issues of social justice. But as is perhaps suggested when Harper devotes her novel to a black woman who is advised to write a novel, the most lasting, complex, and devastating influence of *Uncle Tom's Cabin* has to do with its representation of race.

It must be noted, though, that in crafting an anti-slavery novel, Stowe was far less interested in race than in the dynamics of gender, the ways in which women might influence the moral course of the nation, though Stowe's approach to women's power betrayed the influence of her own regional, class, and racial position.[3] The novel's title itself, focusing on Uncle Tom's *cabin* rather than on Uncle Tom himself, indicates what many readers have considered Stowe's singular accomplishment in this novel, her success in locating anti-slavery political and sectional debates in the seemingly universal domestic spaces – the cabin, the kitchen, the parlor, the home – associated with women and especially with maternal love and authority.[4] In a central scene in the novel, a fugitive mother and son, Eliza and Harry, seek shelter and protection from their pursuers at the home of Senator and Mrs. Bird. The Senator and his wife have just had a disagreement about slavery, with the senator arguing for the "great public interests" that have led him to be a prominent legislative force for the protection of the system of slavery, and with Mrs. Bird arguing for Christian benevolence, what her husband characterizes as "private feeling." Although the Senator has only recently, in

b As Cindy Weinstein observes in this volume, the sentimental novel tradition has continued to be dismissed by some critics who see it as too far removed from the field of pragmatic political action, especially slavery. See "Sentimentalism," chapter 12, 209–211.

Washington, "scouted all sentimental weakness of those who would put the welfare of a few miserable fugitives before great state interests," his wife soon has reason to tell him that she knows him better than he knows himself, as his encounter with Eliza changes his mind and quickly moves him to help her in her escape. Such domestic encounters – the influence of wives over husbands, and the force of otherwise abstract political debates when they are given form and voice in the home – are central to Stowe's strategy throughout *Uncle Tom's Cabin*. But even those domestic revelations are framed by the dynamics of race, for Eliza's entrance into this home is facilitated by the Birds' "colored domestic, old Aunt Dinah" and by "old Cudjoe, the black man-of-all-work." More fully realized black characters are similarly viewed in the contexts provided by white domestic spaces, and even Uncle Tom's cabin itself seems an unlikely combination of slave quarters and a middle-class white home.

But while her domestic strategies made *Uncle Tom's Cabin* especially influential in the development of "racial books," Stowe was hardly the first to write a novel about race, and African American characters only gradually came to play prominent roles in American novels. Indeed, race was in many ways fundamental to the creation of a distinctively American tradition in fiction. In addressing the increasingly complex realities of race in the young nation, novelists both reflected and contributed to the development of an increasingly conscious and deliberate white supremacist ideology that was explicit by the 1850s and that would dominate social, economic, and political discourse by the century's end. The Constitution had equated Native Americans with foreign nations, and thus the "otherness" of Native Americans was significant in novels that explored the shifting geographical interests and boundaries of the white national order – in such novels, for example, as Lydia Maria Child's *Hobomok* (1824), Catharine Maria Sedgwick's *Hope Leslie* (1827), and James Fenimore Cooper's highly successful Leatherstocking novels.[c] Other racialized categories, like Irish and black, were more intimately connected with economic markets, developing class structures, and corresponding concepts of labor, and their presence in American fiction worked to either expose or obscure the increasing centrality of race in US social and political thought.[5] H. H. Brackenridge's *Modern Chivalry* (1792–1797), for example, deals largely

c On the portrayal of Native Americans by white American authors, see Sandra Gufstafson, "Cooper and the idea of the Indian," chapter 6, esp. 103–106;. For commentary on the ways in which later Native American authors negotiated with the "arduous psychological demands from readers moored to a colonial imagination," see Sean Kicummah Teuton, "The Native American Tradition," chapter 67, 1110.

with an Irish servant, Teague O'Regan, whose ability to attract the respect of the people he encounters reveals the folly of the American populace and thus the weaknesses of the democratic ideal. Other fictional treatments of the challenges facing the young nation included Michel-Guillaume Jean De Crèvecoeur's fictional sketches *Letters from an American Farmer* (1792) and Royall Tyler's *The Algerine Captive* (1797), both of which address African Americans as a racial presence almost incidentally in extended meditations on the ethical dilemmas posed by the system of slavery.[d] By the 1820s, though, African Americans became a more prominent presence in fiction by white writers, inaugurated by the publication of James Fenimore Cooper's *The Spy* (1821), which features a black servant, Caesar, whom one contemporary reviewer called "a character which we have never before seen truly depicted."[6]

The emergence of African Americans in American novels was tied to the development of the issue of slavery as the centerpiece, by mid-century, of political debates over race. French observer Alexis de Tocqueville famously explored the relations between the "three races" (white, red, and black) inhabiting the United States in *Democracy in America*, the first American edition of which was published in 1838. In white American historian George Bancroft's *History of the United States* (1834–1874) this exploration becomes a fundamental narrative and ideological principle, with the protection of Caucasian, Anglo-Saxon, or white interests at its core. When the institution of slavery entered a significant new phase in the 1830s – the result of the rising significance of cotton in the southern economy and a shift toward a more insistent anti-slavery movement – the situation of enslaved African Americans in the South, Irish laborers and domestics in the North, and displaced Native Americans across the continent took on increasing significance. "Many Americans now actively defended slavery," Tremaine McDowell notes, "where once they had merely excused it,"[7] and with the increasingly heated debates over slavery came other social and political shifts. Over time, the Irish "became white," as the title of one study of this period has it, and African Americans became the most conspicuous racial presence in American politics, and subsequently in American fiction.[8]

Both the social order fundamental to the system of slavery and the philosophical questions raised by that order helped to promote the development of

d This incidental treatment of race is reflective of the cultural and philosophical affiliations of early white American novelists. See, for example, Bryan Waterman, "Charles Brockden Brown and the novels of the early republic," chapter 3, 51–52.

novels devoted to depicting plantation life in the South.[e] In his exploration of the struggle by white Southerners to define the South, John Grammer notes that "as it became clear in the 1830s that slavery was a permanent feature rather than a temporary blemish on the southern landscape, Southerners were increasingly compelled to contemplate the conflict between their intellectual legacy and their present social order."[9] In many ways, this tradition begins with a novel that echoes *The Algerine Captive* and *Letters from an American Farmer* in treating slavery as a moral problem, albeit one that resisted any quick or straightforward, simple solution: George Tucker's *The Valley of the Shenandoah* (1824). Tucker's novel includes philosophical meditations on the moral and political "evil" of slavery along with sympathetic representations of the condition of the enslaved, including a slave auction, but this is still a novel that envisions a system of slavery that would last for hundreds of years. Similarly, John Pendleton Kennedy's *Swallow Barn; or, A Sojourn in the Old Dominion* (1832) depicts practices sanctioned by the system of slavery as morally wrong, but Kennedy argues against the termination of slavery more strongly than did Tucker, instead finding his solution to this moral problem through a reorganization of laws and policies governing the system.

As political tensions between the North and the South developed, the representation of race, both black and white, became an increasingly pronounced presence in novels that addressed ideals of society, economy, and governance. Nathaniel Beverley Tucker broke with the troubled meditations on slavery in the work of George Tucker and Kennedy, and broke as well with his father's anti-slavery leanings, in novels that insisted on the South as a distinct region led by men of a superior race. Convinced that northern politicians were "bloated vampyres sucking at the heart's blood" of the South, Tucker wrote *The Partisan Leader* (1836) in part to undermine Northerner Martin Van Buren's candidacy for the presidency. The novel depicts events in the then-future of 1849, and tells the tale of how Southerners feel themselves left with little choice but to secede from the Union. In another novel by Tucker published that same year, *George Balcombe*, the eponymous hero reflects at one point, "Is it not a higher honour to be sprung from a race of men without fear and without reproach – the ancient cavaliers of Virginia?" Similarly, Edgar Allan Poe, an admirer of Tucker, published in 1838 his *Narrative of Arthur Gordon Pym*, a novel of exploration

e On the development of southern novels, and on the gradual conceptualization of the South as both region and ideology, see Jennifer Rae Greeson, "Imagining the South," chapter 14, esp. 236–237, 241–247.

and adventure, influenced by the racial "science" of the time and including grotesque characterizations of nonwhite bodies, that leads readers ultimately to an encounter with "pure whiteness." "In *Pym*," as Jared Gardner has argued persuasively, "the landscape of American writing is shown to be fundamentally bound up with the landscape of racial difference, even as the latter threatens to consume the nation in an apocalyptic race war."[10]

Of course, such white supremacist novels were not limited to the productions of Southern writers, for white Northerners also explored the subject of race in an effort to delineate the boundaries of the white national polity. Many early Northern novels about Native Americans, which ranged in perspective from sympathy to unapologetic racism, involved the image of the Indian vanishing into a disappearing wilderness, or included reflections, both negative and positive, on the effects of intermarriage between white and native people. But while the presence of Native Americans raised questions about what James Madison termed "the red on our borders," more troubling to white writers in the antebellum era was what Madison called "the black race within our bosom."[11] Among the strangest of the meditations on this bosomy threat was Robert Montgomery Bird's 1836 novel *Sheppard Lee*, in which the main character inhabits and thereby reinvigorates various dead bodies. At one point Lee inhabits the body of a Quaker, and is horrified to discover that he is not only thus associated with abolitionism (for Quakers had a reputation, which some of them earned, for anti-slavery work) but also that he is to be persecuted for these views in the South – until, that is, he manages to inhabit the body of an enslaved black man and finds happiness in slavery. But even beyond such dramatic representations, northern American novelists often assumed that both their readers and the nation itself were essentially white, as Herman Melville does when in his tale of the American Revolution, *Israel Potter*, readers are presented with the story of a nation described by the narrator as "sharing the same blood with England."

What is most significant, and most "racial," about *Uncle Tom's Cabin*, then, is not that it involves a wide range of black characters, but rather that it so comprehensively presents a complex and explosive meeting of a wide and politicized field of racial types associated with debates over the system of slavery. Stowe's novel cannot be viewed, then, simply as a Northern response to Southern horrors, nor as a wholly original exposé of the abuses committed under the authority of the system of slavery, for various anti-slavery authors had recorded such abuses in great detail in other works, and at least a few anti-slavery novels had been published. To a great extent, what distinguishes this novel is that Stowe addresses struggles over slavery by way of characters who represented the various racial types that had come to inhabit the American social and literary landscape: stereotypical blacks, white Southerners troubled by slavery, white Southerners who aggressively defend both slavery and the South, white Northerners who assume the moral superiority of the North, anti-slavery Quakers, and submissive, loyal, and pious slaves. Troubling these categories and driving both the novel's plot and its moral trajectory are various characters who do not quite fit into their assigned or assumed racial categories – a white Southerner who is described as a "non-sequitur," light-complexioned African Americans who give voice to national ideals, and a US Senator whose views on slavery are transformed by his encounter with the realities of slavery in the faces and the story of a mother and her son seeking refuge in his home.

Stowe's black characters, though, constitute the most prominent and conspicuous racial group in the novel, and while they are diverse, Stowe regularly gathers them into a single category. Although none can claim African birth, *Uncle Tom's Cabin* frequently ties its black characters to a condescending vision of Africa, and it is full of unselfconscious commentary on the supposedly essential nature of those of African origins. Readers are told that Africans are "naturally patient, timid and unenterprising"; that cooking is "an indigenous talent of the African race"; and that "the invariable 'Yes, Mas'r,' " has been "for ages the watchword of poor Africa." Racial contrasts abound, as when the narrator pauses to explain a moment in the plot, as she does frequently. "The negro, it must be remembered," the narrator offers at one point, "is an exotic of the most gorgeous and superb countries of the world, and he has, deep in his heart, a passion for all that is splendid, rich, and fanciful; a passion which, rudely indulged by an untrained taste, draws on them the ridicule of the colder and more correct white race." This story of the fortunes of a particular group of enslaved African Americans involves as well various reflections on the destiny of Africa. In this emphatically Christian novel, Africans are presented as naturally religious people who have discovered (through enslavement) the news of "a compassionate Redeemer and a heavenly home." "The principle of reliance and unquestioning faith," the narrator adds, "is more a native element in this race than any other," grounded in the "gentleness" of Africans, "their lowly docility of heart, their aptitude to repose on a superior mind and rest on a higher power, their childlike simplicity of affection, and facility of forgiveness." What this has to do with successful escapes from slavery, hopeless lives left in enslavement, and even the murder of Uncle Tom becomes clear only by way of Stowe's deeply racialized theological vision. While awaiting the great day of that vision, readers are left with what George M. Fredrickson has called the "romantic racialism" central to Stowe's novel – that is, the idealization of Africans (including all those of African heritage) as more spiritual, more emotional, and more submissive than Anglo-Saxons.[12]

While Stowe did not create these racial categories and stereotypes, the enormous success of her novel helped to popularize them, establishing certain stereotypes as virtual icons in American culture and around the world. Almost immediately following the publication of *Uncle Tom's Cabin*, an unprecedented popular culture began to develop devoted to characters drawn from the novel. Before Stowe's novel, images of blacks in the United States and abroad had been circulated in pamphlets, broadsides, jewelry, and other tokens in service of the British and American anti-slavery movements. Often these images involved generalized and even faceless black bodies or silhouettes. Other images – caricatures of black bodies and gross parodies of contrived gestures and attitudes – were similarly popularized on the stage, both in dramatic productions and especially in blackface minstrel shows. Blackface minstrelsy, known in the nineteenth century as Ethiopian minstrelsy or Negro minstrelsy, was a popular form of entertainment involving white performers who would play burlesque versions of invented black "types," the most famous of which was Jim Crow.

While the pages of *Uncle Tom's Cabin* are often devoted to attempts to delineate a more complex, humane, and even more fully human black character, many of these characters are of mixed race with light complexions, while the darker African Americans in the novel often call to mind established stereotypes, including those promoted in minstrelsy. These traces were highlighted as staged versions of Stowe's *Uncle Tom's Cabin* began to appear, shows that often carried more than a trace of minstrel entertainment.[13] Even beyond the minstrel stage, though, the presence of *Uncle Tom's Cabin* was everywhere apparent. Characters were referenced frequently, often torn from their original contexts, in newspapers and books, and virtually every prominent African American male soon found himself compared with Uncle Tom; the novel's events were dramatized in various illustrations, printed on dishes, wallpaper, and jewelry; and the novel's fame was used to sell a variety of products (for example, "Uncle Tom's pure unadulterated coffee") and was made the subject of jigsaw puzzles, board games, and card games.[14]

For Stowe, of course, the point of the novel was not to promote characterizations of African Americans, real or imagined; ultimately, the black racial presence in *Uncle Tom's Cabin* serves the needs of a broader philosophical or theological project, Stowe's response to slavery that she claimed was inspired by God. And that broader project becomes the vehicle by which various black racial types are arranged in the white social landscape. It is significant, as many African American readers noted at the time, that Stowe seems uncertain about what to do with her African American characters as she approaches the end of the novel. One can only note, after all, that the main black characters in the novel either leave the country for Africa, are murdered in the South, are left to the care of white guardians, or are simply left behind, unaccounted for, as the novel works toward its concluding appeal that quite clearly targets white readers.

What is most racial about *Uncle Tom's Cabin*, when viewed within the white supremacist culture that both inspired and produced it, is the way in which reckless stereotypes and shallow assumptions are given authority under the cover of a reform or protest novel. Indeed, this was James Baldwin's complaint in his forceful critique of the novel, and of the tradition it inspired, in his 1949 essay "Everybody's Protest Novel." Such stereotypes and assumptions were encouraged as well by the many novelists who responded to *Uncle Tom's Cabin* – sometimes to add to Stowe's voice of protest, and sometimes to counter Stowe's portrayal of the slavery and white Southerners.

While some anti-slavery novels had been published prior to *Uncle Tom's Cabin*, the great majority of such novels were published in the 1850s.[15] Stowe's novel, in short, variously inspired or provoked what amounts to a virtual subgenre of the American novel: fictional condemnations, defenses, and explorations of slavery. And with novels about slavery came dramatic renditions of race, representations of both whiteness and blackness, representing both regional and national concerns. Indeed, as Sarah Meer observes, "In 1852 both Northern and Southern periodicals called for writers to answer Stowe in novel form: George Frederick Holmes argued in the *Southern Literary Messenger* for 'a native and domestic literature' to provide the most telling responses to *Uncle Tom*, while the *Pennsylvanian* asked 'friends of the Union' to 'array fiction against fiction.' "[16] Such appeals were hardly necessary, though, for the response to *Uncle Tom's Cabin* was both swift and voluminous. W. L. G. Smith's *Life at the South; or, Uncle Tom's Cabin as It Is* was published in the same year as Stowe's novel. Other novels were less direct in announcing their response to Stowe's novel, though still clear in positioning themselves in the field that Stowe had popularized, and they were regularly considered with *Uncle Tom's Cabin* in reviews and commentaries. Anti-*Uncle Tom* novels explored slavery from the perspective of various cabins – Mary H. Eastman's *Aunt Phillis's Cabin* (1852) or John W. Page's *Uncle Robin's Cabin in Virginia and Tom Without One in Boston* (1853) – and other plantation sites, as in T. B. Thorpe's *The Master's House* (1854). Some, in effect, followed the trail of Stowe's closing gesture to attempts to colonize Liberia (established for this purpose) with former slaves, as in Sarah Josepha Hale's *Liberia* (1853). Others emphasized regional relations and tensions, as in Caroline Lee Hentz's *The Planter's Northern Bride* (1854) or Caroline E. Rush's *North and South, or, Slavery and Its Contrasts* (1852), and some picked up on Stowe's emphasis, in her subtitle, of "life among the lowly," as did Maria Jane McIntosh in *The Lofty and the Lowly; or, Good in All and None All-good* (1853).

Whether pro-slavery or anti-slavery, the representation of black life and identity in these novels leaves much to be desired, and the popularity and influence of such representations posed both possibilities and problems for African American writers. On the one hand, Stowe had helped to establish fiction as a powerful forum for promoting the anti-slavery cause, and many African American writers were enthusiastic in their appreciation of Stowe's achievements. Indeed, they drew from the fame, and sometimes from the storylines, of Stowe and other writers to create their own fictional treatments of slavery and its aftermaths. It is perhaps significant that novels by African American writers emerged only after the publication of *Uncle Tom's Cabin*, and that African American writers felt compelled to comment on Stowe's novel and sometimes to respond to it directly in their work, both before and after the Civil War. One can trace the influence of Stowe's novel in such important works as William Wells Brown's *Clotel; or, The President's Daughter* (1853), Frederick Douglass's novella *The Heroic Slave* (1853), and in the work of such postbellum novelists as Frances E. W. Harper and Charles W. Chesnutt. While I disagree with Robert Levine's suggestion in this volume that Stowe could be termed "an African American writer of sorts," I agree that Stowe's influence on African American writing was significant.[f]

Writers also discovered in Stowe's novel significant challenges in representing the realities and complexities of African American life. As the Christian submission of Uncle Tom became ever more obsequious in the plays that followed *Uncle Tom's Cabin*, as loyal slaves and servants increasingly populated the pages of American novels, as earthy and wise fieldhands and cooks served their social superiors with dialect-heavy wisdom in countless publications, and as violently sexual bucks and warmly embracing mammies emerged in the pages of white supremacist fiction to take their places respectively as threats to civilization and honorary members of white families, African American writers faced a literary world that both reflected and promoted the stereotypes upon which the racist culture seemed to depend. For black writers, telling

f Robert S. Levine, "The early African American novel," chapter 16, 270.

stories true to life became a matter not just of representing the complex challenges, the multiple inspirations, and the communal joys of African American experience but also, and more pressingly, a matter of responding to, revising, and otherwise resisting the dominance of various "Negro types" in American fiction. They did so against the odds. It is hardly surprising that the most direct African American response to *Uncle Tom's Cabin* in novel form, Martin R. Delany's *Blake* – like Stowe's novel, first published serially – did not appear in book form until the 1970s. Access to mass-market publishing and distribution remained firmly under white control until well into the twentieth century, making it difficult for African American writers to challenge images of race created by white writers.

On such uneven playing fields, then, the battle over the representation of race and its role in US history has been fought throughout American literary history, and one can trace Stowe's influence, both direct and indirect, in most of those battles. As Baldwin recognized, *Uncle Tom's Cabin* has remained a pivotal example of the ways in which novelistic explorations of social justice have often worked to highlight, obscure, complicate, and otherwise shape the concept and social experience of race in and beyond the antebellum American novel. Stowe's handling of the black racial presence in *Uncle Tom's Cabin* reminds one of Toni Morrison's observation that white American novelists often represent black characters not in the interests of a faithful representation but rather in the interests of white fears, desires, or investments in racial identity. "The subject of the dream is the dreamer," Morrison observes, and "the manipulation of the Africanist narrative (that is, the story of a black person, the experience of being bound and/or rejected)" thus becomes "a means of meditation – both safe and risky – on one's own humanity."[17] By such means, white novelists used the narrative of black experience, Morrison suggests, "for discourse on ethics, social and universal codes of behavior, and assertions about and definitions of civilization and reason," and ultimately for "the construction of a history and a context for whites by positing history-lessness and context-lessness for blacks."[18] Morrison reminds us, in other words, to think about both the occasion and the audience for such representations, for many texts "about" race clearly were not "written *for* black people – no more than *Uncle Tom's Cabin* was written for Uncle Tom to read or be persuaded by."[19]

As Morrison's comments might lead one to expect, some of the most popular and influential novels in American literary history, as well as numerous other novels that have since been recognized as important landmarks in American or African American literary history, have focused on racial divisions in exploring varying concepts of history, social order, and justice. Many of these novels are devoted to the racial oppression of African Americans, as is the case with Albion Tourgée's *A Fool's Errand* (1879) and *Bricks Without Straw* (1880), Harper's *Iola Leroy* (1892), and Chesnutt's *The Marrow of Tradition* (1901). Some novels have been devoted, in turn, to presenting African Americans as threats to social order and even civilization, as is the case with Thomas Dixon's white supremacist trilogy *The Leopard's Spots* (1902), *The Clansman* (1905), and *The Traitor* (1907). Some have tried to approach the protest novel tradition[g] associated with Stowe from an African American perspective, such as Richard Wright, whose first book was a short story collection suggestively named *Uncle Tom's Children* (1938), and who was criticized by Baldwin for replicating Stowe's errors in *Native Son* (1940). Still others have represented race in attempts either to glorify the white southern past – like Margaret Mitchell, whose *Gone with the Wind* (1936) continues to define the pre-Civil War South for many readers[h] – or to draw readers into challenging re-interpretations of the past, as in Ishmael Reed's *Flight to Canada* (1976), Morrison's *Beloved* (1987), and Charles Johnson's *Middle Passage* (1990). The many visions of the histories of slavery and its aftermath that one encounters in the pages of American fiction are, in short, not only dramatically different but ideologically incompatible, and those incompatibilities speak volumes about the history of race in the United States.

Stowe herself struggled with those fundamental tensions in American culture as she attempted to extend and refine the epochal commentary on slavery that she began in the novel that both reflected and redefined the American political landscape. In *Uncle Tom's Cabin*, Stowe devoted herself to a novel not about race but about slavery, but her moral and political concerns became the means by which stereotypes and other one-dimensional representations of African Americans were ushered in to new prominence in American fiction. In her defense of the novel, and in her interactions with readers from various positions on the political spectrum, Stowe found herself entering more deeply into the chaotic terrain of American racial history. To her credit, she was attentive to African American criticism of her novel, both

g For an overview of the protest novel tradition, see Cecelia Tichi, "Novels of civic protest," chapter 23, esp. 397–398, 404.

h *Gone with the Wind* represents an influential later development of the plantation novel genre. See Candace Waid's discussion in "Faulkner and the Southern novel," chapter 45, 753.

friendly and sharp, and Robert S. Levine has argued that "these encounters and exchanges had a major impact on the racial politics" on Stowe's other major novel about slavery, *Dred* (1856). This problematic later novel, Levine argues, "with its heroic portrayal of a prophetic black conspirator seeking to bring about the slaves' deliverance, can be regarded as an African American-inspired revision of *Uncle Tom's Cabin*."[20] Other readers, while noting Stowe's attempt to attend to criticisms of *Uncle Tom's Cabin*, have found in *Dred* less an inspired revision than a novelistic manifestation of the contradictions, tensions, and seemingly irreconcilable ideological priorities of a nation divided by region and race. *Dred*, such readers conclude, gestures toward many possibilities, slave rebellion among them, but Stowe seems incapable of imagining how any of those possibilities might be realized

It remains revealing that the great majority of scholars and other readers still talk about race in the American novel almost exclusively when they are addressing texts that feature prominent characters who are not white. In the antebellum period, increasingly sharp political exchanges over slavery promoted the creation of black fictional characters whose primary purpose was to variously promote and define the contours of white political and moral identity, and even those white writers most willing to envision a more complex approach to race – Herman Melville, most prominently – struggled mightily with the force of this central American dynamic. Hester Blum's emphasis in this volume on the fluid nature of Melville's use of the sea narrative, allowing for metaphysical and cultural as well as geographical explorations, identifies an important aspect of Melville's struggles with "issues such as sentiment, sexuality, race, empire, and class," struggles that often produced mixed results.[i] Although the considerable ambiguities of Melville's most direct commentary on slavery, the novella "Benito Cereno" (1855), resist any settled accounting of the text's commentary on either slavery or race, there is still reason to accept Maggie Sale's judgment that the text "normalizes white supremacy."[21] Lesser writers, or those more deeply invested in the priorities of white supremacy, worked toward similar ends by cruder means. Identifying those crude representations is only a small part of the story of the racial presence in and of the American novel. The larger story has to do with why such representations seemed either necessary, persuasive, or compelling, and what to make of the largely unexamined whiteness behind the racial curtain.

i Hester Blum, "Melville and the novel of the sea," chapter 9, 153.

Notes

1. Elizabeth Ammons, "Introduction," in *Harriet Beecher Stowe's "Uncle Tom's Cabin": A Casebook*, ed. Elizabeth Ammons (Oxford: Oxford University Press, 2007), 3.
2. *Ibid.*, 8.
3. For white Southern responses to Stowe's presentation of domesticity as an anti-slavery forum, see Anne Goodwyn Jones and Susan V. Donaldson, eds., *Haunted Bodies: Gender and Southern Texts* (Charlottesville: University Press of Virginia, 1997); and Joy Jordan-Lake, *Whitewashing "Uncle Tom's Cabin": Nineteenth-Century Women Novelists Respond to Stowe* (Nashville, TN: Vanderbilt University Press, 2005). For particularly compelling commentaries on the cultural and ideological terms of Stowe's domestic approach, see Gillian Brown, *Domestic Individualism: Imagining Self in Nineteenth-Century America* (Berkeley: University of California Press, 1990); and Marianne Noble, *The Masochistic Pleasures of Sentimental Literature* (Princeton: Princeton University Press, 2000).
4. For historical, international background on the use of domestic fiction for the purposes of anti-slavery commentary and persuasion, see Carolyn Vellenga Berman, *Creole Crossings: Domestic Fiction and the Reform of Colonial Slavery* (Ithaca, NY and London: Cornell University Press, 2006).
5. On race and the early labor movement, see David R. Roediger, *The Wages of Whiteness: Race and the Making of the American Working Class* (London: Verso, 1991).
6. W. H. Gardner, *North American Review* 15 (October 1822): 265.
7. Tremaine McDowell, "The Negro in the Southern Novel Prior to 1850," in *Images of the Negro in American Literature*, ed. Seymour L. Gross and John Edward Hardy (Chicago and London: University of Chicago Press, 1966), 56.
8. Noel Ignatiev, *How the Irish Became White* (New York and London: Routledge, 1995).
9. John M. Grammer, *Pastoral and Politics in the Old South* (Baton Rouge: Louisiana State University Press, 1996), p. 12.
10. Jared Gardner, *Master Plots: Race and the Founding of an American Literature, 1787–1845* (Baltimore and London: Johns Hopkins University Press, 1998), 159.
11. Quoted *ibid.*, 1.
12. On the concept of romantic racialism and *Uncle Tom's Cabin*, see George M. Fredrickson, *The Black Image in the White Mind: The Debate on Afro-American Character and Destiny, 1817–1914* (New York: Harper, 1971), 97–129.
13. On this, see Eric Lott, *Love & Theft: Blackface Minstrelsy and the American Working Class* (New York: Oxford University Press, 1993), 44, 46, 211.
14. See Marcus Wood, *Blind Memory: Visual Representations of Slavery in England and America, 1780–1865* (New York: Routledge, 2000), 146–147. To view reproductions of many of these materials, see www.iath.virginia.edu/utc.
15. For an overview of anti-slavery novels, see Donald Edward Liedel, "The Antislavery Novel, 1836–1861" (PhD diss., University of Michigan, 1961). Liedel

has calculated that "the number of antislavery novels written in America between 1836 and 1861 is approximately five dozen." Of these, "less than a dozen were published before 1850; over fifty in the decade after 1850" (2).

16. Sarah Meer, *Uncle Tom Mania: Slavery, Ministrelsy, and Transatlantic Culture in the 1850s* (Athens: University of Georgia Press, 2005), 75.
17. Toni Morrison, *Playing in the Dark: Whiteness in the Literary Imagination* (New York: Vintage, 1992), 16, 53.
18. *Ibid.*, 53.
19. *Ibid.*, 16–17.
20. Robert S. Levine, *Martin Delany, Frederick Douglass, and the Politics of Representative Identity* (Chapel Hill: University of North Carolina Press, 1997), 146.
21. Maggie Montesinos Sale, *The Slumbering Volcano: American Slave Ship Revolts and the Production of Rebellious Masculinity* (Durham, NC: Duke University Press, 1997), 166.

16

The early African American novel

ROBERT S. LEVINE

For a long while, or at least up to the early 1980s, the history of the early African American novel could be told in fairly straightforward fashion. The first published novel by an African American writer, critics agreed, was William Wells Brown's *Clotel; or, The President's Daughter* (1853), which was followed by Frank J. Webb's *The Garies and Their Friends* (1857) and Martin R. Delany's serialized *Blake; or, The Huts of America: A Tale of the Mississippi Valley, the Southern United States, and Cuba* (1859, 1861–1862). Some critics also included Linda Brent's *Incidents in the Life of a Slave Girl* (1861) in their histories of the early African American novel. Rounding out that familiar group were the three revisions and reconceptualizations of *Clotel* that Brown published during the 1860s: the serialized *Miralda; or, The Beautiful Quadroon. A Romance of American Slavery, Founded on Fact* (1860–1861), *Clotelle: A Tale of the Southern States* (1864), and *Clotelle; or, The Colored Heroine* (1867). Then there was supposedly a gap in African American novelistic writing, a "nadir" of sorts, until the publication of Frances Harper's *Iola Leroy; or, Shadows Uplifted* (1892), which to some extent was inspired by Brown's portrayal of the "colored heroine" in his 1867 *Clotelle.*

A resurgence of interest in African American writing during the 1960s and 1970s inspired new scholarship that gradually revised and corrected this familiar narrative. In 1983, Henry Louis Gates, Jr., announced his "discovery" of the first novel by an African American woman, Harriet E. Wilson's *Our Nig; or, Sketches from the Life of a Free Black*, which was published in 1859; and in 1987 Jean Fagan Yellin provided compelling evidence that Brent's *Incidents in the Life of a Slave Girl* was actually an autobiographical narrative authored by the former slave Harriet Jacobs. There was more to come. In 1996, Frances Smith Foster published an edition of three virtually unknown novels by Frances Harper which had been serialized in the *Christian Recorder* – *Minnie's Sacrifice* (1869), *Sowing and Reaping* (1876–1877), and *Trial and Triumph* (1888–1889) – and ten years later, in 2006, William L. Andrews and Mitch Kachun proclaimed the "discovery" of yet another serialized novel in the *Christian Recorder*, Julia C. Collins's *The Curse of Caste; or, The Slave Bride* (1865), which they trumpeted as the first novel published by an African American woman. Andrews and Kachun could make such a claim because in 2005 P. Gabrielle Foreman and Reginald H. Pitts presented evidence in a new edition of *Our Nig* that Wilson's seemingly fictional narrative was based in large part on her experiences, and that the work itself was more autobiographical than fictional. In making their claim for *The Curse of Caste* as the first novel published by an African American woman, however, Andrews and Kachun had to emphasize the "published" aspect of this "first," because in 2002 Gates brought out Hannah Crafts's *The Bondwoman's Narrative* (*c*.1855), which he discovered in manuscript and asserted was in all likelihood the first novel *written* by an African American woman. As for the first novel written by an African American man, there is some debate about the generic status of Frederick Douglass's *The Heroic Slave*, a story or short novel about black revolt at sea that Douglass published in his newspaper (and also in a fundraising volume) around the time that *Clotel* was published in 1853. A fictional work about the 1841 slave revolt on the *Creole*, the story or novella, with its emphasis on a white man's sympathetic embrace of the black Madison Washington's violent resistance to slavery, may well have been written in 1852, at a time when Douglass was extolling Harriet Beecher Stowe's *Uncle Tom's Cabin* (1852) for helping to make whites more sympathetic to the sufferings of enslaved blacks.[1]

As this brief overview is meant to suggest, the history of the early African American novel is not fixed or stable. Because African American writers did not have ready access to US publishing houses, they had to self-publish or find sympathetic publishers in Great Britain or in abolitionist newspapers and black journals. Additional novels may yet be discovered in manuscript or in obscure newspapers and journals, in which case the literary history of the early African American novel may have to be revised yet again, with ongoing debate about which novel or novels deserve the label of "first" (along with concomitant debate about the value of assigning such a label).

There are other key problems in mapping out a literary history of the early African American novel. Literary history typically focuses on questions of influence and tradition, but it remains unclear whether these early black novelists read one another. Brown's *Clotel* and Webb's *Garies* were both published in England and not widely reviewed. Wilson's *Our Nig* was self-published in a limited printing, and serialized fiction was generally available to just a small number of subscribers. Harper clearly read Brown's 1867 *Clotelle* but not necessarily the formally very different 1853 *Clotel*. Most nineteenth-century African American novelists knew Stowe's *Uncle Tom's Cabin*, which had a profound influence on all of the works discussed in this chapter.[a] That these novelists engaged Stowe, some as admirers and some as debunkers, suggests a sense of tradition, as does the fact that early African American novelists all sought to use their fiction to attack slavery and racism. Stowe remains key here, for central to these writers' techniques of attack were appropriations and sometimes archly ironic revisions of Stowe's use of the sentimental and gothic, which she herself had appropriated from a wide range of writers in an effort to make her readers apprehend the inhumanity and horror of slavery. In this respect, the early African American novel was profoundly intertextual and political, indebted not only to Stowe but also to the British philosopher Adam Smith, whose *The Theory of Moral Sentiments* (1759) had an enormous impact on literary sentimentalism in the eighteenth and nineteenth centuries, and to such sentimental and gothic novelists as Horace Walpole, Charles Dickens, Nathaniel Hawthorne, the Brontë sisters, and a number of other political, philosophical, and literary writers whom one might not immediately think of in relation to an African American literary tradition.[b]

In addition to questions of tradition, genre must also be addressed as an interpretive problem in any history of the early African American novel, for uncertainties remain as to whether those works regularly identified as novels are truly novels. In his editions of *The Bondwoman's Narrative* and *Our Nig*, Gates includes the word "novel" in his title pages, even though the authors themselves never use that word. Given the uncertain authorship of *The Bondwoman's Narrative*, it is impossible to say whether the work was intended as an autobiography or novel – or what it was intended for at all. The same could even be said for *The Curse of Caste*, for we know very little about Julia Collins's personal history. But of course many novels draw on autobiographical sources. There are certainly autobiographical elements in *Clotel*, *Garies*, and other African American works fully accepted as novels, and it is important

a See John Ernest's "Stowe, race, and the antebellum American novel," chapter 15 in this volume, for a comprehensive, and somewhat critical, assessment of Stowe's racial representations. Ernest also limns a fuller pre-*Uncle Tom's Cabin* history of racial representation in the US novel. For a discussion of Stowe's influence on African American novelists, see 261–264.

b In her wide-ranging chapter on "Sentimentalism," chapter 12, in this volume, Cindy Weinstein makes clear that *Uncle Tom's Cabin* was just one of a number of sentimental novels that addressed the politics of slavery. That said, she does not specifically discuss African American writers, who, I'm suggesting, had an important impact on the development of sentimentalism in the US novel.

to note that the slave narrative itself as a genre owes a considerable debt to the history of the novel, starting with Defoe's *Robinson Crusoe* (1719). Frederick Douglass's second autobiographical narrative, *My Bondage and My Freedom* (1855), shows the influence of his reading of Dickens's *David Copperfield* (1850) and *Bleak House* (1852–1853) in the way he addresses questions of personal identity and economics through a more fleshed-out representation of his orphanhood,[2] and Jacobs's often novelistic *Incidents* draws on the conventions of the seduction novel pioneered by Samuel Richardson in the eighteenth century.[c] Because of the close connection between the slave narrative tradition and anti-slavery fiction, it would be fair to say that generic blurring and hybridity (mixings of personal narrative, essayistic documentation, and fictional invention) are more pronounced in early African American novels than in novels written by Britons and other Americans of that time.

There are other problems in conceptualizing a history of the early African American novel that should be noted, and these involve questions of race and nation. Must an African American novel be written by a black person? The historian Sterling Stuckey has argued that Melville's *Moby-Dick* (1851) and *Benito Cereno* (1855) reveal such a profound grasp of African culture and history that we should regard Melville as one of the great "African American" artists of the century.[3] Along these same lines, one could be tempted to term Stowe an African American writer of sorts because of her significant influence on African American literary traditions. Gates has made the case for *The Bondwoman's Narrative* as an African American novel in ways that *Uncle Tom's Cabin* is not, based on his belief that Hannah Crafts is the pen name of a black writer, possibly the escaped slave Jane Johnson. But what if the novel were written by a white woman abolitionist or, as two British critics have suggested, a white male British abolitionist? Does the novel suddenly become "white"?[4] One of the large themes of *Clotel*, *Bondwoman's*, and other early African American novels is that racial identity is always uncertain, impure, and a sort of fiction. If so, some flexibility concerning the racial identity of authors may be in order.

The very term "African American novel" also raises questions about identity, specifically the question of the meaning of the "American" in "African American." Brown wrote about blacks emigrating to England and Haiti; Delany advocated emigration to the southern Americas and Africa (and

c Anna Mae Duane offers illuminating insights into the close connections between the seduction novel and notions of self-possession central to anti-slavery novels in her chapter in this volume; see "Susanna Rowson, Hannah Webster Foster, and the seduction novel in the early US," chapter 2, 38–40.

his diasporic vision informs *Blake*); and Webb, like the character George Winston in *Garies*, moved to the southern Americas in the late 1850s. The Supreme Court's 1857 Dred Scott decision, which affirmed that blacks never were and never could become citizens of the United States, additionally complicated the question of what it meant to be a mid-nineteenth-century African American writer. Unlike white novelists of the 1850s, blacks had an uneasy relation to the nation and often wrote with a diasporic or racial consciousness that challenged fixed notions of "America."

In short, during the period ranging from 1853 through Reconstruction (and beyond), the African American novel was extraordinarily fluid and unstable, wrestling with generic hybridity and racial and national uncertainties. With respect to the practices and traditions of the early African American novel, to paraphrase Emily Dickinson, we might say that it is in the instabilities where the meanings are.

Instabilities are central to Brown's *Clotel*, generally regarded as the first African American novel. Published in London in 1853, the novel appeared at a time when Brown, an escaped slave, was still legally a slave within the borders of the United States. (His British admirers would purchase him from slavery in 1854.) Brown was inspired to write a novel when he noted the extraordinary impact of *Uncle Tom's Cabin* on readers in the United States and Great Britain. Like Brown and other black abolitionists, Stowe was outraged by the Fugitive Slave Act (part of the Compromise of 1850), which compelled US citizens, North and South, to return runaway slaves to their supposed masters, and in *Uncle Tom's Cabin* she attempted to make her white readers feel for the slave by emphasizing the pain and suffering that attends the separation of families. Brown underscored Stowe's message, but with a more subversive interest in the interracial family. "Marriage," Brown writes in the opening chapter of *Clotel*, "is, indeed, the first and most important institution of human existence – the foundation of all civilisation and culture – the root of church and state"; and in the novel he focuses on the destruction done to blacks and whites, and ultimately to US "civilization," by Southern white racists' unwillingness to legally sanction any "marriage" involving blacks. Even more subversively, he raises questions about the differences between "white" and "black" in light of the nation's history of interracial relations.

Drawing on the secret history of Thomas Jefferson and his black slave paramour Sally Hemings (named Currer in the novel), Brown presents as a given that this metaphorical father of the nation was also the father of slaves, implicitly suggesting the close connections among all of Jefferson's "children." At the novel's center are Jefferson's two "black" but white-to-the-eye daughters, Althesa and Clotel, who come to unhappy ends in the manner of the "tragic mulatta" of much anti-slavery fiction.[5] Typically, authors deployed the figure of the tragic mulatta in an effort to gain the sympathies of white readers for "black" characters and to raise questions about the nature of race itself. Like many such characters, Clotel is caught between two cultures and at home in neither. Purchased by a white man who seems to love her, Clotel is eventually sold by her beloved "husband" after he legally marries a white woman. In the most dramatic and politically powerful scene in the novel, Clotel, who had been in search of her daughter, attempts to flee from a group of fugitive-slave catchers after escaping from a slave prison in the District of Columbia. Realizing that she is about to be caught, she decides that "death is freedom" and leaps from the Long Bridge into the Potomac River. This "appalling tragedy" occurs "within plain sight of the President's house and the capital of the Union." Brown underscores the contradictions of that tragedy: "Thus died Clotel, the daughter of Thomas Jefferson, a president of the United States; a man distinguished as the author of the Declaration of American Independence, and one of the first statesmen of that country." Eventually, Clotel's light-complected daughter, Mary, escapes from slavery to Europe, and thus escapes the fate typically befalling the mulatta in US slave culture.

This brief summary may make it sound as if Brown were engaged in conventional storytelling, following the plight of Clotel and her daughters in the way that Stowe follows the plight of Eliza and her son in *Uncle Tom's Cabin*. But the book is less about plot than about the cultural discourses of slavery. From beginning to end, Brown constructs his narrative from a variety of texts that he appropriates from US slave culture and then recontextualizes in his novel, including portions of a short story by Lydia Maria Child, "The Quadroons" (1842), which he uses to tell Clotel's early history as a kept slave woman and mother; an 1815 speech by Andrew Jackson praising the black soldiers at the battle of New Orleans, which he puts into the mouth of the novel's admirable anti-slavery Southern white woman, Georgiana; excerpts from slave narratives; bits of pro-slavery speeches and sermons; accounts from abolitionist books and journals; contemporary writings about Jefferson and his slave mistress; and many other works, including some that championed scientific racism. At times *Clotel* can seem less a novel than a compilation of texts, a sort of bricolage or pastiche that works with metafictional techniques in the manner of the experimental novels of Ishmael Reed in the twentieth century. (Reed acknowledged the important influence of Brown on his own writings by making him one of the characters of his bicentennial novel *Flight to Canada* [1976].) Brown's ironic method points to the limits of Stowe's and Child's sentimental strategies and acknowledges the difficulty, if not impossibility, of representing the full horror of slavery. But perhaps his largest accomplishment in the novel is his searing portrayal of the US nation as nothing short of an ideological madhouse – a place where humans turn other humans into property and attempt to legitimate such practices through religion and "science." Brown wanted his novel to mobilize white abolitionists against slavery, but the complexity of his ironies and the disruptive instabilities of his pastiche-like narrative make *Clotel* less a call to action than a call to thought.[6]

Frank J. Webb's considerably more conventional *The Garies and Their Friends*, which was published in England four years after *Clotel*, begins somewhat like *Clotel*, with a "marriage" between a slaveowner, the Georgian Clarence Garie, and a slave woman, Emily, whom he purchased for two thousand dollars. But *The Garies* takes a very different turn from *Clotel* when Emily convinces her husband/owner to move to Philadelphia, where the marriage could be legally sanctioned and their two children protected from falling back into slavery. Through much of the twentieth century, critics attacked Webb's novel for what they regarded as its melodrama and sentimentalism.[7] But the recuperation of *Uncle Tom's Cabin* and other bestselling novels of the 1850s has helped critics to recognize that Webb's sentimentalism and melodrama are crucial to the novel's powerful social realism and anti-racist politics. Influenced by Dickens as well as Stowe, who wrote an admiring preface, Webb exposes the workings of racism in antebellum Philadelphia, invoking the long history of African Americans' efforts to achieve economic success and equal rights in a city that remained hostile to their efforts and was the site of recurrent anti-black riots. When the Garies come North, they face discrimination from clerics, landlords, and other whites who attempt to maintain clear property lines between the races. But the Garies also encounter hardworking blacks in the Ellises, who own their own home and business, and in the capitalist Mr. Walters, a millionaire of "jet-black complexion" who at times can seem selfishly focused on mere moneymaking but is ultimately analogized to the Haitian revolutionary Toussaint L'Ouverture in his willingness to fight for blacks' rights.

At the melodramatic heart of *The Garies* are the efforts of the white racist lawyer George Stevens to force the Ellises and other blacks to flee from an area of Philadelphia that he wants to purchase at a low price and then sell for considerable profit. This crucial plot element shows Webb's acute awareness of connections between race and real estate, a subject that would remain of critical importance to later African American novelists such as Charles Chesnutt, Richard Wright, and Toni Morrison. In the novel's most harrowing scene, Stevens directs Irish immigrants and other working-class whites to stage a riot against blacks, who resist with the help of Walters but still end up losing most of their property. The elder Ellis, who works with his hands, is permanently crippled and brain-damaged when rampaging whites pursue him to the top of a building and chop off his fingers as he hangs from the roof. Taking advantage of the chaos of the riot, Stevens kills Mr. Garie, to whom he secretly knows he is related, and Emily Garie dies of shock while giving birth to a stillborn child. Stevens thus inherits a fortune that would have gone to Garie's mixed-race children.

But the novel doesn't stop with these multiple tragedies. Webb follows the fates of the characters over the next fifteen years, depicting blacks' unflagging determination to rise in Philadelphia. Ellis's son Charlie fights against various forms of racism, and with the help of sympathetic whites eventually finds a job. The light-complected Clarence Garie, however, is raised as white and chooses to continue to pass (with the disastrous results befitting a "tragic mulatto"), while his light-complected sister, Emily, aligns herself with the African American community, declaring in the novel's most destabilizing remarks on race: "You walk on the side of the oppressor – I, thank God, am with the oppressed." What Webb appears to be saying through Emily's bold formulation is that race is just as much a matter of politics as of biology. Consistent with her views, the light-complected Emily chooses to marry the dark Charlie Ellis. Yet even as the narrator hails the ability of Emily, Charlie, and others to find some happiness within racist Philadelphia, Webb is hardly naïve about the problems that continue to plague the black community. Within the larger context of the novel, the half-mad elder Ellis looms as the group's most prescient realist. "There they come! there they come!" he shouts again and again from within his visions. Amidst the wedding's festive plenty, he sees just another raging white mob.[8]

There are no celebrating African Americans or raging white mobs in Harriet Wilson's *Our Nig*, which charts the struggles of a solitary black, Frado, as she grows from girlhood as an indentured servant in New Hampshire to womanhood in Massachusetts as a single mother with an ailing child. The book's full subtitle is "Sketches from the Life of a Free Black, In a Two-Story White House, North. Showing that Slavery's Shadows Fall even There." Like Webb (and Frederick Douglass and Harriet Jacobs), Wilson depicts the antebellum North as deeply implicated in slavery and racism. But there are fascinating twists to *Our Nig* that we don't see in *Garies* or in

Douglass's and Jacobs's autobiographies. For instance, the most abusive of Frado's "owners" (under the terms of the implied indenture agreement) are not the male but rather the female members of the Bellmont household. Mrs. Bellmont herself is called a "she-devil," and she and her older daughter regularly torture Frado, who just as regularly fights back through her comic resourcefulness (such as when she refuses to eat from Mrs. Bellmont's dirty plate until it is licked clean by a dog). Stowe in *Uncle Tom's Cabin* assumes the existence of a cross-racial sisterhood based on black and white women's shared experience of motherhood and the oppressions of patriarchy, but in *Our Nig* it is the white men – the uxorious Mr. Bellmont and his sons – who most exhibit a "womanly" sympathy.

Wilson troubles race as she troubles gender, for whereas Stowe and other anti-slavery writers generally present the mixed-race slave as the product of a forced union between a white man and a black woman, in *Our Nig* Frado's mother, Mag Smith, is white and her husband is "a kind-hearted African" who takes pity on her after she has been disgraced by a seducer. Following the death of her husband, Mag moves in with another black man and eventually abandons the six-year-old Frado at the home of the Bellmonts. Frado's anger at her mother suffuses the entire work, and in the final chapters, when she's desperately attempting to care for the son she had with a black con-artist, she presents herself as attempting to do for her child what her mother had failed to do for her.

In this regard, yet another remarkable aspect of *Our Nig* is its blending of autobiography and novel. The opening chapter titles, for instance, are cast in the first person – "Mag Smith, My Mother," "My Father's Death," "A New Home for Me"– before reverting to the third person ("A Friend for Nig," and so on). But those opening chapter titles signal what critics have recently learned: that much of *Our Nig* is based on Wilson's life, and that she herself had an ailing child whom she was trying to support by selling her self-published book and other merchandise. At the end of her autobiographical novel, Wilson describes Frado/Wilson's situation in Massachusetts, which was known as a center of abolitionist reform: "Watched by kidnappers, maltreated by professed abolitionists, who didn't want slaves at the South, nor niggers in their own houses, North. Faugh!" Testimonial letters in the book's appendix reveal that Wilson wasn't entirely on her own; but her son did die shortly after the book's publication, and the evidence suggests that Wilson took up spiritualism in a grief-stricken effort to speak with the dead.[9]

In 1859, the same year that Wilson published *Our Nig*, Martin Delany serialized Part One of *Blake; or, The Huts of America* in the July–December issues of the *Anglo-African Magazine*, and two years later he began a serialization of the complete novel in the *Weekly Anglo-African*, which ran from November 1861 to late April or May 1862. (Several April and May issues are missing, so *Blake* is a novel without an ending.) Delany was a leading black nationalist figure of the time who initially worked with Frederick Douglass as co-editor of the *North Star*, and then broke with him over the matter of black emigration shortly after the passage of the Fugitive Slave Act in 1850. Unlike Douglass, Delany loathed *Uncle Tom's Cabin*, which he regarded as racist, and urged blacks to consider emigrating to the southern Americas or Africa. Delany's interests in black emigration and diaspora inform *Blake*, which provides an uncommonly broad view of the problem of slavery in the Americas by focusing on the efforts of the eponymous hero to plan a coordinated black revolution in the United States and Cuba.[10]

The novel is divided between the United States and Cuba, nations which Delany describes as intimately linked through the history of slavery in the Americas. In Part 1, Blake flees from the slave plantation in Mississippi after his wife, Maggie, has been sold away, and then returns to plan a revolt among the slaves of the plantation. Or so it initially seems. But Blake has a larger conspiratorial vision of fomenting a black rebellion across the slave South. He travels from plantation to plantation, state to state, and even to Indian territories in Arkansas, to lay the groundwork for a slave rebellion that would occur at an agreed-upon moment when Blake is certain that blacks are prepared to fend for themselves. He then journeys to Cuba as a "servant" to a white captain, with the hope that he can find his wife. There, as described in Part 2, he continues to encourage what he now envisions as a hemispheric black rebellion against white enslavers in the United States and Cuba. In the context of the 1850s, a time when the US government contemplated taking possession of Cuba, Blake's plot poses a challenge to the Cuban and US slave powers, and to US imperialism and expansionism as well. Delany further enlarges the frame by having Blake sail to Africa to gain additional recruits for what can now be viewed as a Pan-African uprising. The African scenes at a notorious West African slave market invoke the global history of the slave trade; the return voyage to Cuba invokes the horrors of the middle passage. Once back in Cuba, Blake declares that he is for "war upon whites," and the novel moves steadily toward the moment when the uprising is set to erupt. The closing words of the extant novel come from one of Blake's black associates in Cuba: "Woe be unto those devils of whites, I say!" In the missing concluding chapters, Delany may have represented a bloody war between the races. Or perhaps he found a way to suggest the possibility of nonviolent reforms. Because the truncated conclusion keeps alive various possibilities, the resultant nonending may well be the most powerful ending of all.

However we imagine the conclusion, Delany's black nationalist pride is absolutely central to *Blake*. Black to the eye, Blake is known as the "intelligent slave" who wants to bring about "the redemption of the race." In this regard it is worth noting that Brown, who ended the 1853 *Clotel* with the suggestion that Clotel's daughter (and Jefferson's granddaughter) Mary and her husband were content to pass for white in England, decided to rethink that ending in order to convey his own racial pride. In Brown's three revisions and reconceptualizations of the novel published during the 1860s, Mary's light-complected husband George Green, now named Jerome, becomes black to the eye, and in the 1864 and 1867 versions Green returns to the United States to fight in the Civil War. Suggestive of Brown's pessimistic assessment of race relations immediately after the Civil War, however, Jerome in the 1867 *Clotelle* is needlessly killed when a white racist Union officer orders him to retrieve the body of a dead white officer. His grief-stricken wife, now named Clotelle, subsequently emerges as an "Angel of Mercy" as she devotes herself to improving the condition of the freed people in the United States.[11]

Brown's vision of the key role of African American women in black uplift profoundly influenced Frances Harper, whose three serialized novels of the 1860s–1880s appeared in the *Christian Recorder*, the national newspaper of the African Methodist Episcopal Church. In *Minnie's Sacrifice* (1869), the title character, a white-to-the-eye young woman, learns from the shocking appearance of a black woman claiming to be her mother that her genealogical history had been hidden from her by her adoptive Quaker parents. Expelled from her Northern school for being "black," she returns to the South to open a school for the freed people, choosing to devote her life "to the up-building of the future race" at a moment that she calls "the negro woman's hour." Minnie makes her declaration at the same "hour" that the Ku Klux Klan has begun to "spread terror and death." In a scene that will remain ambiguous until missing issues of the *Christian Recorder* are recovered, she is killed, perhaps lynched, in all likelihood by the Klan. In the closing chapter, the narrator states, in the spirit of *The Garies*, that the "lesson of Minnie's sacrifice is this, that it is braver to suffer with one's own branch of the human race." But as Harper's novel shows so dramatically, given the genealogical entanglement of white and black in American history, race can sometimes be nearly impossible to determine. In Harper's subsequent serialized novel, *Sowing and Reaping*, which focuses on temperance reform, Harper, as in her temperance short story "The Two Offers" (1859), creates racially ambiguous characters who are impossible to identify with any one "branch of the human race." Here, the emphasis is on the need for morality and self-control in the human race more generally. Racial pride returns to the forefront in *Trial and Triumph*, serialized in the late 1880s, with the figure of the strong-willed black reformer Annette Harcourt, a character who looks forward to Harper's portrayal of Iola Leroy in 1892.[d]

Several years before the appearance of *Minnie's Sacrifice*, and perhaps helping to inspire it, Julia C. Collins serialized *The Curse of Caste; or, The Slave Bride* in issues of the 1865 *Christian Recorder* running from February through September. Little is known about Collins beyond the fact that she resided in Williamsport, Pennsylvania, while writing the novel and died before completing it. (There are also four missing chapters in issues of the 1865 *Christian Recorder* that have not yet been recovered.) Set in Louisiana and Connecticut, *Caste*, like *Minnie's Sacrifice*, centers on a white-to-the-eye young woman, Claire Neville, who is descended from a white man and a slave woman he marries against his father's wishes, an act for which his father shoots him. Claire's mother dies in childbirth and her wounded father believes his child stillborn, and exiles himself to France. Years later, in the present of the novel, Claire (who believes herself white) is hired as a governess by her dastardly grandfather in New Orleans. The novel builds to the moment when Tracy returns to New Orleans to confront his father and cast his eyes on the woman, "a *quadroon* and once a *slave*," who some say closely resembles him. But the novel stops before the ailing Collins could complete it. In an editorially audacious move, Andrews and Kachun, in their modern edition of the novel, supply two possible endings, which they call "The Happy Ending" and "The Tragic Ending," imagining racial and familial reconciliation, on the one hand, and vengeful murder, on the other. It says much about the difficulties of recuperating a coherent tradition of the early African American novel that the work now touted by some critics as the first published novel by an African American woman lacks four chapters and an ending, and was authored by someone about whom we know next to nothing.[12]

In the spirit of underscoring the instabilities of the "tradition" or history of the early African American novel, it would be useful to conclude with *The Bondwoman's Narrative*, which was written sometime in the 1850s or early 1860s by someone who used the pen name of Hannah Crafts. Until it was

d On Harper's revisionary strategies, see Barbara McCaskill, "The African American novel after Reconstruction," chapter 29 in this volume, 485–487.

published as a "novel" by Henry Louis Gates, Jr., in 2002, *Bondwoman's* existed in manuscript with no clear indication that it was a novel at all. That said, there is much about the work that is novelistic, as indicated by the author's allusions to Brontë's *Jane Eyre* (1847), Dickens's *Bleak House*, and Hawthorne's *The Scarlet Letter* (1850) and *The House of the Seven Gables* (1851). *Bondwoman's* is a first-person narrative in which the light-complected "Hannah" chronicles her life as a house-slave and servant as she moves from a plantation in Virginia to Washington, DC, and then to a plantation in North Carolina. Everywhere Hannah goes, she encounters gothic histories of racial entanglement in which white women are revealed as "black" and white men as fathers of numerous white-to-the-eye "black" children. The resourceful Hannah finally escapes from slavery, finding her way to a vibrant African American community in New Jersey where she is reunited with her mother and some of her friends who had also managed to escape from slavery.[13]

With its depiction of the evils of slavery and racism, *Bondwoman's* resembles a number of African American novels of the period. That said, the happiness and great promise of the novel's concluding scene in New Jersey, compared to the provisional happiness of *The Garies* and the bleakness of *Our Nig*, raise questions about whether the author knew much or anything about the difficulties facing Northern free black communities. Moreover, the recurrent gothic turns of the narrative make it seem more fictional than autobiographical, to the point that one might wonder if the novel weren't written by a Northerner more familiar with the conventions of anti-slavery fiction than with the experience of slavery itself.

Would it make a difference if the author of *Bondwoman's* were white? Arguably, the novel itself suggests that identifying Crafts's race ought not to make such a difference, insofar as one of the oddly disconcerting aspects of the text is the way that it can trap those readers who insist on working with essentialized racial categories in order to establish "authentic" identities. It does so through the figure of the elderly lawyer Trappe, who spends his time "hunting, delving, and digging into family secrets," specifically the secrets of racial genealogies. Through the characterization of Trappe, "Crafts" suggests the invidious implications of identifying race as the single most important aspect of an individual or culture, especially given that the novel again and again points to the contingencies of racial difference. Trappe is eventually killed by Southern white fugitive-slave hunters because, as they have come to realize, "No blood-hound was ever keener in scenting out the African taint than that old man." Proclaiming that Trappe would sell his own mother into slavery, the white men implicitly convey their concerns that Trappe could sell out their own mothers (and themselves as well). When they shoot him in the head, they are doing their small part to preserve the racial fictions upon which their culture is based.

To some extent, arguments that insist on Crafts's blackness are doing their own part to preserve the racial fictions upon which traditional understandings of the history of the early African American novel have been based. Whether authored by a man or woman, black or white, *Bondwoman's* is one of the great African American novels (or narratives) of the period, in part because it raises questions about racial identity and genre so compellingly, in part because it so powerfully conveys the sufferings of the enslaved through its sentimental and gothic strategies, and in part because it aligns itself with the aspirations of the black community and (most particularly) with the aspirations of the oppressed. The very instabilities of the novel thus help to suggest some of the key themes and motifs that can help to bring coherence to our understanding of the history of the early African American novel, pressing us to beware the traps, or Trappes, of our own contemporary moment, in which race all too often becomes an overdetermined and defining category at the expense of the political, social, and literary.[e]

Notes

1. This paragraph draws on the introductions and textual materials in the following editions: Harriet E. Wilson, *Our Nig; or, Sketches from the Life of a Free Black*, ed. Henry Louis Gates, Jr. (New York: Vintage Books, 1983); Harriet A. Jacobs, *Incidents in the Life of a Slave Girl, Written by Herself*, ed. Jean Fagan Yellin (Cambridge, MA: Harvard University Press, 1987); *Minnie's Sacrifice, Sowing and Reaping, Trial and Triumph: Three Rediscovered Novels by Frances E. W. Harper*, ed. Frances Smith Foster (Boston: Beacon Press, 1994); Julia C. Collins, *The Curse of Caste; or, The Slave Bride*, ed. William L. Andrews and Mitch Kachun (New York: Oxford University Press, 2006); Harriet E. Wilson, *Our Nig; or, Sketches from the Life of a Free Black*, ed. P. Gabrielle Foreman and Reginald H. Pitts (New York: Penguin Books, 2005); and Hannah Crafts, *The Bondwoman's Narrative: A Novel* (New York: Warner Books, 2002). On *The Heroic Slave*, see Maggie Montesinos Sale, *The Slumbering Volcano: American Slave Ship Revolts and the Production of Rebellious Masculinity* (Durham, NC: Duke University Press, 1997); and Robert S. Levine, *Martin Delany, Frederick Douglass, and the Politics of Representative Identity* (Chapel Hill: University of North Carolina Press, 1997), 83–89. For a good overview of the early African American novel, see Dickson D. Bruce Jr., *The*

e See Walter Benn Michaels's "Model minorities and the minority model – the neoliberal novel," chapter 61 in this volume, for a provocative discussion of the problematics of racial identity politics.

Origins of African American Literature (Charlottesville: University Press of Virginia, 2001), chapters 6–7.

2. Douglass serialized *Bleak House* in the April 15, 1852 through December 16, 1853 issues of *Frederick Douglass' Paper*. On Douglass and Dickens, see Elizabeth McHenry, *Forgotten Readers: Recovering the Lost History of African American Literary Societies* (Durham, NC: Duke University Press, 2002), 124–126.
3. Sterling Stuckey, *African Culture and Melville's Art: The Creative Process in Benito Cereno and Moby-Dick* (New York: Oxford University Press, 2008).
4. On the problem of racial identity in Crafts, see Celeste-Marie Bernier and Judie Newman, "*The Bondwoman's Narrative*: Text, Paratext, Intertext and Hypertext," *Journal of American Studies* 39 (2001): 147–165.
5. The figure of the tragic mulatto is at the center of Richard Hildreth's *The White Slave: or Memoirs of Archy Moore* (1836), arguably the first anti-slavery novel published in the United States. For discussions of the tragic mulatto and mulatta, see Nancy Bentley, "White Slaves: The Mulatto Hero in Antebellum Fiction," *American Literature* 65 (1993): 501–522; and Giulia M. Fabi, *Passing and the Rise of the African American Novel* (Urbana: University of Illinois Press, 2001).
6. On Brown's use of his sources, see the Bedford Cultural Edition of *Clotel; or The President's Daughter*, ed. Robert S. Levine (Boston and New York: Bedford/St. Martin's, 2000). Also useful are *William Wells Brown: A Reader*, ed. Ezra Greenspan (Athens: University of Georgia Press, 2008); *The Works of William Wells Brown: Using His "Strong, Manly Voice,"* ed. Paul Garrett and Hollis Robbins (New York: Oxford University Press, 2006); John Ernest, *Resistance and Reformation in Nineteenth-Century African-American Literature* (Jackson: University of Mississippi Press, 1995), 20–54; and Ann duCille, *The Coupling Convention: Sex, Text, and Tradition in Black Women's Fiction* (New York: Oxford University Press, 1993), 17–29.
7. See, for example, Vernon Loggins, *The Negro Author: His Development in America to 1900* (1931; Port Washington, NY: Kennikat Press, 1964), 251; and Blyden Jackson, *A History of Afro-American Literature, Volume I: The Long Beginning, 1746–1895* (Baton Rouge: Louisiana State University Press, 1989), 344. For an excellent edition of Webb's extant writings, see *Frank J. Webb: Fiction, Essays, Poetry*, ed. Werner Sollors (New Milford, CT, and London: The Toby Press, 2004). Sollors provides an overview of the criticism along with new biographical information.
8. For an excellent recent discussion of the novel, see Samuel Otter, "Frank Webb's Still Life: Rethinking Literature and Politics through *The Garies and Their Friends*," *American Literary History* 20 (2008): 710–730.
9. On key critical and biographical issues in *Our Nig*, see JerriAnne Boggis, Eve Allegra Raimon, and Barbara A. White, eds., *Harriet Wilson's New England: Race, Writing, and Region* (Durham, NH: University of New Hampshire Press, 2007).
10. On *Blake*, see Ifeoma C. K. Nwankwo, "The Promises and Perils of U.S. African American Hemispherism: Latin America in Martin Delany's *Blake* and Gayl Jones's *Mosquito*," in *Hemispheric American Studies*, ed. Caroline F. Levander and

Robert S. Levine (New Brunswick, NJ: Rutgers University Press, 2008), 187–205; and Jeffory A. Clymer, "Martin Delany's *Blake* and the Transnational Politics of Property," *American Literary History* 15 (2003): 709–731.

11. On Brown's *Clotelle* and the Civil War, see Jennifer C. James, *A Freedom Bought with Blood: African American War Literature from the Civil War to World War II* (Chapel Hill: University of North Carolina Press, 2007), 34–53.

12. In a special issue devoted to *The Curse of Caste*, critics take up questions of African American literary history and other issues raised by Andrews and Kachun's edition of Collins's novel; see *African American Review* 40 (Winter 2006).

13. For a wide-ranging collection of essays on Crafts, see *In Search of Hannah Crafts: Critical Essays on The Bondwoman's Narrative*, ed. Henry Louis Gates, Jr. and Hollis Robbins (New York: Basic Books, 2004).

PART TWO

*

REALISM, PROTEST, ACCOMMODATION

Introduction: realism, protest, accommodation

CLARE VIRGINIA EBY

In William Dean Howells's exemplary realist novel *A Hazard of New Fortunes* (1890), German-American socialist Berthold Lindau sounds a voice of pure protest, underscoring how more complacent (if well-intentioned) liberal characters accommodate rather than contest the ascendant capitalist masters. Choosing to live in poverty, missing a hand from his Civil War service, and speaking in heavily accented English, Lindau embodies the fracturing of late nineteenth-century America into multiple populations based on class, ethnicity, politics, and region of origin. *Hazard* suggests Howells's ambivalence as to whether such differences could ever be overcome and fear that socio-economic power would increasingly be concentrated in fewer and fewer hands. Yet Lindau also personifies Howells's hope that realism might provide, as Michael Elliott notes in the opening chapter in this section, a "salutary engine for change."[a] For all of these reasons, Lindau provides an effective introduction to the issues informing this section.

As both Lawrence Buell and Barbara Hochman document in their chapters, the American novel gained unprecedented prestige during the late nineteenth and early twentieth centuries. If the novel had serious work to do, then certainly protest was an important part of that work. Cecelia Tichi delineates a tradition of "civic protest" and asks that we make a place for the role of propaganda in literary studies, while Tim Prchal proposes we read immigrant novels for "what they hope to reform or, indeed, what they argue *against*." Elizabeth Nolan emphasizes the feminist protests of Kate Chopin and Charlotte Perkins Gilman, while Jennifer Fleissner traces Edith Wharton's "multifaceted critique of American modernity," including her ambivalence toward the New Woman heroines championed by some of her contemporaries. Donna Campbell argues that naturalism differs from reform fiction in

[a] See Michael Elliott's chapter in this volume, "Realism and radicalism: the school of Howells" (chapter 17), 298–299, for an extended discussion of *Hazard* and Lindau.

declining to represent solutions, while Robert Reid-Pharr's analysis of Thomas Dixon shows that protest can also serve reactionary ends.

The terms "realism," "protest," and "accommodation" may patrol, but they cannot enforce, firm boundaries around literary modes. Novels that start out in protest often drift toward accommodation, as Andrew Lawson demonstrates in his reading of the iconic *Adventures of Huckleberry Finn* (1884) and *The Adventures of Tom Sawyer* (1876), and Tichi shows in her analysis of *The Jungle* (1906). David Zimmerman argues that novels aiming to expose capitalism assume "the frame of the capitalist imagination" and so accommodate what they protest against. Moreover, the boundary that champions of realism such as Howells might wish to stake around their preferred literary mode proves highly permeable. Realism is continually stalked by the very literary forms it sought to replace – sentimentalism (see Zimmerman, Nolan) and, particularly, romance, as seen in Gretchen Murphy's discussion of historical and "border romances" and Russ Castronovo's consideration of what he terms the "imperial romance." In tracing the development of the African American novelistic tradition after the Civil War, Barbara McCaskill shows how Pauline Hopkins and others create hybrid forms by fusing realism with oral and vernacular forms such as blues, spirituals, and sermons. And as Campbell remarks of realism's second cousin, naturalism is so multiform it might best be understood as "naturalisms."

Howells's Lindau identifies another important issue when he asks, "What iss Amerigan?" As the question "what is an American novel?" unites the chapters in Part One, Lindau's question threads through those in this section. One aspect of the question involves what sort of community remains possible, an inquiry lying at the heart of Carrie Bramen's chapter on William and Henry James as well as Elliott's on Howells. Who is included in and who excluded from American communities? The question of whether the nation lives up to its own principles is addressed here by Prchal, Reid-Pharr, and McCaskill, while Castronovo and Murphy take issue with the nation's central myth about itself: the premise of American exceptionalism. Stephanie LeMenager demonstrates how exceptionalism allows Euro-American novelists to dodge "recalcitrant facts" – a deeply ironic move given the dedication of most realists to faithful transcription of reality.[b]

To Lindau's *What* is an American, we might also add, *Where* is America? As Buell explains, novelists disagreed over whether "the 'Americanness' of US

[b] See Leonard Cassuto's introduction to this volume for discussion of how ideas of national exceptionalism have influenced American literary history (esp. 2–3).

literature resided in the 'part' – specificity of region, race, subculture – or in some broader national perspective." The relationship of part to whole, local to global, lies at the center of Tom Lutz's discussion of Willa Cather and regionalism. Other chapters track attempts to capture the relationship between an imagined national whole and its parts, variously defined in terms of gender (Shelley Streeby, Fleissner, Nolan), race or ethnicity (Prchal, McCaskill, Reid-Pharr, Castronovo, Le Menager, Hochman), class (Nancy Glazener, Jude Davies, Streeby, Lawson, Zimmerman, Elliott), and region (McCaskill, LeMenager, Lutz).

New configurations of national identity emerge in the late nineteenth century. Various forms of "New Americans" – to borrow the title phrase of Prchal's examination of immigrant literature – vie for the position of exemplary American. Theodore Dreiser's Carrie Meeber, a consumer with "no interiority" (Zimmerman), becomes, in Davies's reading, "*the* paradigmatic American identity of the twentieth century." Focusing on the open West rather than the crowded East, LeMenager explains how "writers of the frontier tend to derive character, or even the category of the human, from landscape" and illustrates the exemplary nature of Owen Wister's cowboy, in spite (or perhaps because) of the figure's anachronism and the novelist's "complete denial of Native American history." For many novelists the paradigmatic American becomes the figure that Charles W. Chesnutt termed "the future American": the mulatto or mulatta.[1] Elliott, Castronovo, LeMenager, Murphy, McCaskill, and Reid-Pharr examine tales of race passing and other "melodramas of miscegenation" (as Murphy puts it). While Richard Wright would insist in 1957 that "the Negro is America's metaphor," the biracial individual captured the imagination of many novelists seeking to understand America during the period straddling the late nineteenth through early twentieth centuries.[2]

As the physical bodies of these "future Americans" attest to their hybrid ancestries, they also serve as a reminder that, in the age of realism, American identity is articulated on a global stage. From Glazener's examination of the "international circulation of manuscripts and publications" to Murphy's study of the hemispheric novel's "constructions of an interconnected New World identity"; from Elliot's analysis of Howells's cosmopolitan aesthetic through Castronovo's look at how the East becomes "a screen for understanding as well as obscuring race relations at home"; from Bramen's look at James's inversion of "the Ur-journey of Anglo-American nationhood" to Lutz's discussion of regionalism's "cosmopolitan commitments," the chapters in this section show that America derives meaning in reference to other nations.

Placing the American novel on the world stage invariably entails acknowledging the global reach of one of the nation's major exports, capitalism. Concerns with the transformed economy – which was increasingly based on consumption and increasingly pervasive – mark another throughline for this group of chapters. Glazener traces what she calls "branding" in publishing, the process by which consumers come to expect, and seek out, particular narrative forms, a phenomenon that Streeby also takes up in her discussion of dime novels. Along with what Buell terms "increasing marketplace differentiation" in publishing comes the multiplication of readers, which Hochman, who reminds us that the term "bestseller" emerged in 1892, explores in her analysis of multiple reading groups. The marketplace and consumer culture become the explicit subject of novelists examined by Davies, Fleissner, and Zimmerman, among others. Endlessly fascinating in its creative destructiveness, capitalism spawns realism, romance, protest, and accommodation, in messy but often compelling combinations.

Notes

1. Charles W. Chesnutt, "The Future American" (1900). The three-part essay is reprinted in Charles W. Chesnutt, *Essays and Speeches*, ed. Joseph R. McElrath, Jr., Robert C. Leitz, III, and Jesse S. Crisler (Stanford, CA: Stanford University Press, 1999), 121–135.
2. Richard Wright, "The Literature of the Negro in the United States," in *White Man, Listen!* (Garden City, NY: Anchor Books, 1964), 72.

17

Realism and radicalism: the school of Howells

MICHAEL A. ELLIOTT

> Perhaps no higher compliment can be paid to Mr. Howells than to state that those who undertake to write about Realism in America will inevitably find themselves dealing with it as though it were his private property, instead of with the doctrines and assertions of a system.
>
> William Roscoe Thayer, "The New Story-Tellers and the Doom of Realism" (1894)

Appearing in *Forum*, William Roscoe Thayer's critical essay on the rise and, to his mind, imminent fall of American literary realism neatly presages the scholarly tradition that would follow in his wake. From Thayer's time forward, literary critics have frequently treated "Realism in America" as though it were the "private property" of William Dean Howells, the novelist, editor, and critic who shaped the field of American letters from his positions at *The Atlantic Monthly*, *Harper's Monthly*, and *Harper's Weekly* during the final three decades of the nineteenth century. "And yet," Thayer continues, "for a dozen years a horde of Realists, great and small, have been filling the magazines with their products and turning out an average of two novels a day."[1] From Thayer's vantage point, American literary realism seemed less like a private enterprise and more like a joint-stock company.

In their treatment of literary realism in the late nineteenth-century United States, Thayer's contemporaries and his critical heirs have validated Thayer's predication by neglecting the "horde of Realists" in favor of the figure of Howells. As much as has been written about Henry James, Mark Twain, Sarah Orne Jewett, or Stephen Crane – all of whom Howells considered realists – literary historians rarely address those figures as advocates for realism itself. Unlike these other major writers of the period, Howells left in his essays and reviews an archive of rough thinking that focuses, relentlessly, on the place of realist literature in the United States with a breadth and depth that has no equal among his contemporaries. At the same time, the unruliness of this critical corpus has meant that twentieth- and twenty-first-century readers have had difficulty finding the "doctrines and assertions of a system" that Thayer describes. Howells's columns are more ephemeral and less critically consistent than the theoretical essays of his friend Henry James, and those inconsistencies – the half-finished thinking combined with journalistic prose – have offered fodder for readers both sympathetic and not. As Lawrence Buell notes in this volume, even a term as basic as "realism" itself sometimes seems to elude precise definition in Howells's writing – and what he *did* write was contested vigorously by the critics who succeeded him.[a]

Howells sought nothing less than to make literary reading central to the creation of a more just and durable American social order, one held together by bonds across divisions of class and culture, and one that offered an increasing – though not immediate – sense of social equality. At a time of political ferment, in other words, Howells believed that literature could offer a more modest, more carefully managed, and perhaps even more salutary engine for change than the violence of mass strikes, demonstrations, and revolutions. Yet Howells's stated ambitions for the role of literary fiction in American society can call attention to the shortcomings of his own novels. Simply put, Howells the critic makes promises and poses questions that Howells the novelist cannot always fulfill or adequately answer.

Yet Howells never regarded his literary labors as solitary. Calling realism "the only literary movement of our time that has any vitality," he believed that its promise could be met only through the efforts of what Thayer called a "horde" of fellow writers.[2] At the height of his influence, Howells combined the offices of editor and critic: attempting to shape the taste of the American reading public, identifying the literary talent that he sought to cultivate, and trying to give a name, realism, to those things that he admired. In the process, he promoted the fiction of many of the writers whom we still read (James, Twain, Jewett, Crane, for starters) as well as many that we do not (Edward Eggleston, Joseph Kirkland, Henry Harland, to name a few). Howells became the canon-maker of his time, holding unmatched influence until the second decade of the twentieth century. Because of his tireless advocacy on behalf of American realism – particularly vis-à-vis English fiction, which he believed to be in a state of decline – Howells is too often considered solely as a literary nationalist. "We have something worse than a literary past: we have a second-hand literary past, the literary past of a rich relation," he wrote in one of his "Editor's Study" columns for *Harper's Monthly*. But Howells was not a literary

a Lawrence Buell, "Theories of the American novel in the age of realism," chapter 19, 324 isolationist. For him, literary realism offered American writers the chance to establish their place on the global stage by broadening the scope of their literary relations. Earlier in the same "Editor's Study" column, Howells mentions more than a dozen writers whom he read seriously from France, Spain, Italy, England, and especially Russia.[3]

In spite of his own status as a literary tastemaker bringing both foreign and domestic writers before the American reading public, Howells stressed that the principles of literary realism were not commandments that he was handing down from his perch atop the literary establishment. He insisted that the United States did not have a "literary center," and crucial to his belief in the democratic nature of literary realism was a sense of it as emanating from the careful observation of the variety of contemporary lives, meaning that it would take on a variety of literary forms as well as a variety of subjects.[4] While Howells's own novels largely centered on middle-class manners, his criticism also placed dialect fiction, short stories, poetry, and even some drama under the banner of realism. All that was required was that the work meet Howells's nebulous question: "We must ask ourselves before we ask anything else, Is it true?"[5]

Howells saw his pursuit of the truth in literature as embattled. Indeed, as Claudia Stokes has recently observed, "The late century was riven by wide disagreement about the ethical and aesthetic merits of realism."[6] In her essay on sentimentalism in this volume, Cindy Weinstein describes how antebellum writers such as Hawthorne and Melville derided the female-authored best-sellers as aesthetically inferior and emotionally cheap.[b] Howells became the critical heir to this tradition of hierarchy. He sought to associate the realm of literary realism with a masculine professionalism and lambasted sentimental novels for their emotional excess and melodrama. Even though one might locate the roots of realism in the careful description of anti-slavery and regional writers like Stowe, Howells believed that the sentimental romance had a corrupting effect on its female readers, who were too likely to mistake fiction for the world in which they lived. He was equally skeptical of male-authored sensational fiction and the aesthetic decadence that he found emanating from England. Critics such as Thayer derided Howells and his fellow realists for turning literature into the scientific description of minor people and events, for failing to tell stories that were either entertaining or morally instructive. Yet Howells believed that the cornerstone of literary writing should be detailed, careful, distanced observation that could knit together a

b Cindy Weinstein, "Sentimentalism," chapter 12, 209–210.

society increasingly fractured by social class and ethnicity – even if a single work of literature could only depict a small corner of that society. For Howells, the very "narrowness" of American realism – its ability "to acquaint us intimately with half a dozen people, or the conditions of a neighborhood or class" – could be its strength. "Democracy in literature," he writes, "wishes to know and to tell the truth, confident that consolation and delight are there; it does not care to paint the marvelous and impossible for the vulgar many, or to sentimentalize and falsify the actual for the vulgar few. Men are more alike than unlike one another: let us make them know one another better, that they may be all humbled and strengthened with a sense of their fraternity."[7]

Amy Kaplan argues that a central anxiety that motivates Howells's version of realism is the question of what kind of literary truth would promote social unity.[8] Or to use Howells's terms, how could fiction allow men (and presumably women) to "know one another better" in a way that could strengthen their sense of solidarity, rather than emphasize their differences? Howells seemed deeply aware that the turbulent economy of his time, the industrialization and organization of labor, and the increasing populations of urban immigrants all threatened to shred the social fabric of the nation. In 1890, Howells commented in a *Harper's Monthly* column that the American novelist possessed "an inherent, if not instinctive perception of equality,"[9] but his usual optimism about the office and effect of fictional representation is undermined by a private letter that he wrote less than two years previously to James in which he admits that "I'm not in a very good humor with 'America' myself . . . After fifty years of optimistic cant with 'civilization' and its ability to come out all right in the end, I now abhor it, and feel that it is coming out all wrong . . ."[10]

We might locate Howells's novels somewhere between these two passages, the sanguine critic cheerfully promoting equality and the shaken citizen dreading that it will never come. Both of these statements occur in the aftermath of Howells's most controversial moment in public life, his petition for clemency on behalf of the so-called Haymarket anarchists, eight men accused of planning a bombing during a Chicago rally in 1886 – a position that earned him widespread scorn from the American press. These statements also occur at the conclusion of a remarkable decade of fiction that included those novels that constitute his full turn to literary realism – *A Modern Instance* (1882) and *The Rise of Silas Lapham* (1885) – and that ended with his writing the most ambitious social novel of his career, *A Hazard of New Fortunes* (1890). It is possible to find in these novels both Howells's optimism about his own ability to register "an inherent, if not instinctive perception of equality," yet also discern the frustrated citizen unable "to trust pen and ink with all the audacity of [his] social ideas."[11] Throughout this period, Howells sought to steer a course for American fiction that would be grounded in careful observation of society, and therefore reflect the very real faultlines of American society, but would somehow produce a sense of cohesion tangible enough to hold the country together.

Amanda Claybaugh places Howells's brand of realism, therefore, in the lineage of the Anglo-American "novel of purpose." Like George Eliot, Howells distances his work from the didactic, sentimental tradition in which writing serves as an arm of social movements, and instead makes a claim for the power of the realist novel "by redefining the purposefulness of realism as a kind of substitute for reform."[12] The key term here is "reform" rather than "revolution," as Howells showed in his review of James's *The Princess Casamassima* (1886) when he omitted any mention of the novel's revolutionary plot.

"Reform" was not a term that Howells himself used frequently, but it appeared everywhere in the late nineteenth century, particularly during the decades when he waged his critical campaign on behalf of literary realism. One observer in 1890 called the term "the popular war-cry of our age" and noted that "the very atmosphere of America" had become "redolent with reforms of every kind. We have tariff reformers and temperance reformers, divorce reformers, social reformers and suffrage reformers, religious reformers, political reformers, ballot reformers, labor reformers, reformers of every imaginable tribe and species . . ."[13] As the proliferation of groups suggests, the notion of social improvement through carefully managed change was so widespread that it could become the object of ridicule. As Albion Tourgée, a judge, radical Republican, and sometime novelist whose work Howells admired, put it in 1881, " 'reform' is a cloak which may cover a multitude of sins." Tourgée noted that the name of reformer "is particularly flattering to the self-regard of one who assumes it, as well as irritating to the consciousness of equality on the part of the one who opposes or doubts."[14] As the tone of these comments suggest, American intellectuals of the late nineteenth century frequently supplemented their activism with a measure of skepticism, an ambivalence that Howells sometimes seems to share.

Howells's own novels from the 1880s often revolve around the question of how much members of different social classes can be held together with any sense of "real equality." Even when Howells's novels avoid taking on the most difficult divisions of class and race that threatened the fabric of US society, his fiction still seems unable to imagine how "real equality" could occur. *The Rise of Silas Lapham* (1885) remains a standard-bearer for American literary realism because its plot allows a character to articulate Howells's belief in the dangers of sentimentalism of the kind that he believed prevalent in popular fiction. When one of the characters considers abandoning the object of her affections because of her sister's love for the same man, the novel supplies a Howellsian mouthpiece, the Reverend Sewell, to advise against heroic self-sacrifice in a favor of a more moderate approach. Equally significant, Sewell blames fiction for instilling in young ladies notions of romance and tragedy that poorly prepare them for the actual difficulties of life. "The novelists might be the greatest possible help to us if they painted life as it is," he states, "and human feelings in their proportion and relation, but for the most part they have been and are altogether noxious."

But there is more to *Silas Lapham* than a cautionary tale about the dangers of emotional excess. As David Zimmerman states in this volume, *Silas Lapham* is a business novel that attempts to narrate the moral complexities of life in a complex, interdependent world of economic unpredictability.[c] As a novel of manners, the book revolves around the conflict between two families: the Laphams, *arrivistes* profiting from their rural paint farm, and the Coreys, blue-blooded Bostonians who have fallen upon hard economic times. While money influences the relationship between the Laphams and the Coreys at every level, it is not a discrepancy of wealth that divides them. Rather it is their social standing, customs, and manners. The Coreys have wine at their table and paintings on their walls; the Laphams drink ice water and place statuettes allegorizing "Faith and Prayer" in their drawing-room window. The experiment of the novel rests on the question of whether the financial rise that the title character has enjoyed might allow his family to ascend to the level of high culture represented by the Coreys, a possibility engendered by the eventual engagement of Tom Corey to Penelope Lapham.

"It's a curious thing, this thing called civilization," says Bromfield Corey, Tom's father. "We think it is an affair of epochs and nations. It's really an affair of individuals." Yet the individuals in question have dispersed by the end of the novel in a way that reveals the substantial differences among them. The Coreys remain in Boston, but Silas Lapham's business failure sends him and his wife back to rural Vermont, where Lapham becomes again "rather shabby and slovenly." The newly wed Tom and Penelope remove even farther, to Mexico, where, as Tom's sister remarks, "there's a chance that she will form

c David A. Zimmerman, "Novels of American business, industry, and consumerism," chapter 24, 415–416.

herself on the Spanish manner, if she stays there long enough, and that when she comes back she will have the charm of not olives, perhaps, but *tortillas*, whatever they are: something strange and foreign, even if it's borrowed." Given Howells's own internationalism, we might find a note of hopefulness in the possibility that Penelope Lapham could be received as an exotic import, but it is not likely that her parents would be able to recognize that optimism from their Vermont home. Social reconciliation, in other words, may require both time and travel that extends beyond what the elder Laphams have at their disposal.

In the resolution of *Silas Lapham*, Howells finds the middle path that characterizes his fiction – an even-handedness that avoids both the full-bore pessimism of tragedy and the triumphant resolutions of comedy. In the end, social harmony remains neither impossible nor fully realized: Howells's novels do not efface social differences, but rather show characters struggling to manage them. "Realism thus participates in constructing a society which appears more interdependent and interconnected than ever before," Kaplan writes, "while the connections between people appear more invisible and elusive."[15] In the case of *The Rise of Silas Lapham*, it is equally significant that the events that both throw characters together and then separate them seem beyond their individual control. Speaking of his business failure, the title character describes the chain of events as a row of bricks tumbling like dominoes: "It wa'n't in the nature of things that they could be stopped until the last brick went." This kind of flat fatalism offers little opportunity for locating responsibility, for finding a villain, or for any other kind of easy moralizing. Small actions have unintended consequences, and the forces that threaten to fracture society are too large to be met with anything more than a measured response.

This narrative pattern – in which a novel throws together characters from diverse social classes only to separate them by its conclusion – recurs throughout the major novels that Howells wrote in the five years after *The Rise of Silas Lapham*.[16] What changes is that Howells gradually raises the stakes from one novel to the next, so that the efforts to bridge social differences become more deliberate on the part of the characters, and the consequences of their failures grow in significance. *The Minister's Charge, or The Apprenticeship of Lemuel Barker* (1886) reprises the character of the Reverend Sewell, who takes on an even greater role than in *Silas Lapham*. Here, Sewell sets into motion the action of the novel when he falsely flatters the poetry of a young man, Lemuel Barker, living in the rural town where the Sewells are summer boarders. The minister instantly regrets his insincere encouragement of Barker's literary talent, and preaches a sermon on the necessity of practicing a difficult but "affectionate" honesty – a teaching that falls squarely within Howells's realist tenets. As far as Barker is concerned, though, the damage is already done: he soon comes to Boston in the hope of publishing his poetry, only to be told by Sewell of its true worthlessness. A series of misadventures leaves Barker penniless on the Boston Common, and then he slowly begins his own "rise": through the network of social institutions (the police station, a charity workhouse), to a servant's position, to the occupation of clerk at a middle-class hotel, and finally to the home of the Coreys, where an aging Bromfield Corey employs him to read novels aloud in the evening.

The novel reads like a parable about the networks of social obligation that comprise modern urban life. The upward mobility of Lemuel Barker affords Howells the chance to chart the social divisions of the city, as well as to give readers glimpses of the institutional spaces emblematic of them. As a result, the novel performs a journalistic function by documenting the hidden spaces of urban life for its readers. Equally important, the novel seems to be acutely aware of its appropriation of the journalistic role, to the extent that the process of professional observation by newspaper reporters and others stands as one of the novel's main subjects. In other words, one of the means of holding together the disparate populations of the city is writing itself.

The consequences of including journalists and other professional observers in *The Minister's Charge* – as in other novels by Howells – does more than to offer a foil for realist fiction. It also puts into question the ability of writing to produce a sense of tangible connection among the constituent parts of society. This latter function is particularly significant, since the newspaper articles in the novel serve to notify Sewell of Barker's situation and play a key role in continuing the connection between them. However, the extent of Sewell's obligation to Barker, and how exactly he should act on that obligation, recurs as a question in the book. By recognizing Sewell as a stand-in for a realist critic (who failed, momentarily, to discharge his critical duty when he praised Barker's verse), we can see that the novel wants to make us aware that realist fiction strains to maintain a sense of connection among its far-flung subjects.[17] At various times, the city threatens to swallow Barker up, to take him completely out of the orbit of Sewell, yet he repeatedly returns – sometimes because he seeks Sewell, sometimes the reverse.

The novel uses the term "complicity" to describe the relationship of Sewell to Barker, and the minister preaches a widely circulated sermon on the topic near the novel's conclusion. Yet it is difficult to know exactly how tightly the characters of *The Minister's Charge* have been bound to one another. Sewell repeatedly acknowledges an obligation to Lemuel Barker, but he often does so reluctantly, only when Barker seeks him out in the remove of his home. The novel introduces us to a variety of social spaces, including the boarding house of two working-class women, but the only common thread that connects them is Barker's improbable career. Via Barker, the reader of the novel travels through the social classes of Boston, but the more ordinary citizens of the novel have no means of meeting one another. In the end, a streetcar accident finally forces Barker to leave Boston and return to his rural home, where he plans to support his working-class fiancée (whom he no longer loves) by teaching school. We are told that this marriage does not come off, and that Barker is then able to marry the object of his true love, an art student. Despite Barker's apparent success in crossing class lines, the narrator gives us this information in a final sentence of the novel that refuses to explain how such a turn of events might actually occur, leaving that story "for some future inquiry." The novel's conclusion reads as though Howells himself recognized that this romantic success does injury to his own realist principles.

The question of cross-class sympathy – how it can be cultivated and what form it should take – becomes even sharper in *Annie Kilburn* (1888). There, the title character returns to her family's Massachusetts home with philanthropic motives after the death of her father, a Congressman. However, the moral center of the book, the minister Julius Peck, recognizes that Kilburn's plan (a social union, lyceum, and so forth) for wage laborers will be recognized as condescension because it does not proceed from a true recognition of equality. The money of the elite, Peck tells Kilburn, has a limited capacity to effect reform: "Because sympathy – common feeling – the sense of fraternity – can spring only from like experiences, like hopes, like fears." Howells described the novel in a letter to Hamlin Garland as being "from first to last a cry for *justice*, not *alms*," and Peck's sermon, in fact, is one of the more impassioned pieces of writing to appear under Howells's name.[18]

In *Annie Kilburn*, Peck chooses to put into practice the doctrine of complicity that Sewell preaches in *The Minister's Charge*: he elects to leave the ministry in order to work among laborers in a mill town, either as a schoolteacher or in the mills himself, so that he can find "a social way that will bring me into immediate relations with the people," even though the novel cuts Peck's social experiment off with a fatal train accident. (The accident also serves the plot by allowing Kilburn to adopt Peck's daughter.) Kilburn, for her part, ends up creating the social union, but only by giving the money raised from a benefit theater performance to leaders of the working class so that they can build it themselves. There is little evidence, though, that the union becomes a point of serious exchange among the classes – that it actually produces "social union." At the novel's conclusion, it constitutes neither "a brilliant success" nor a "failure." Howells wrote the novel at the time that the Haymarket affair was unfolding, and the injustice suffered by the accused, as well as the public censure that he received for speaking on their behalf, not only reinforced the moral quickening that he was experiencing from reading Leo Tolstoy, but also shook his fundamental optimism. The kind of equanimity that he voices in *Annie Kilburn* seems to be all the success for which he can allow himself to hope. "[I]f you read it to the end," Howells wrote to Edward Everett Hale about the novel, "you'll see that I solve nothing, except what was solved eighteen centuries ago. The most that I can do is perhaps to set a few people thinking; for as yet I haven't got to *doing* anything myself."[19]

What Howells did do next was to write his most ambitious novel, and the one in which he takes on the economic and political divisions of American urban life most directly. *A Hazard of New Fortunes* (1890) shifts the urban setting from Boston to New York, just as Howells himself had once moved to take up the *Harper's* editorship. It is a sprawling novel, larger in its size and range than anything Howells had previously written. The central figure is Basil March, a recurring character in Howells's fiction whose career bears a striking resemblance to Howells's own. March comes to New York with his wife, Isabel, to edit a new, fortnightly publication, *Every Other Week*. He mixes with an improbably diverse set of neighborhoods and social types. David Shi contends that March's perspective evolves "from the aesthetic to the ethical,"[20] but it might be more accurate to say that his ruminations on the city provide Howells the opportunity to meditate on the difficulty of disentangling these two attitudes. It is hard to discern where March's spectatorial pleasure in the visible variety of social difference ends and his "sense of complicity" begins. Howells draws further attention to the conjunction of the aesthetic and the ethical in the literary marketplace by having March compose sketches of New York life – presumably similar to paragraphs in *A Hazard of New Fortunes* – for the fictional *Every Other Week*. The magazine's founder, March tells the publisher, "believes that there's no subject so fascinating to the general average of people throughout the country as life in New York City." The publisher, the son of an oil baron who is bankrolling the magazine, responds with what sounds like Howellsian doctrine: "If you can make the comfortable people understand how the uncomfortable people live, it will be a very good thing, Mr. March. Sometimes it seems to me that the only trouble is that we don't know one another well enough; and that the first thing is to do this."

But there are people in *A Hazard of New Fortunes* who seek to do more – as well as some who seek to do a good deal less. Berthold Lindau is a German-born socialist who lost his hand in the Civil War and works as a translator for the magazine. His opposite is the publisher's father, Jacob Dryfoos, a millionaire who believes in self-reliance and refuses to countenance any kind of labor organization. The strength of the novel is not in the characterization of either of these figures or their ideas, but in Howells's portrayal, through March, of a liberal sensibility that tries to hold them together in a productive dialogue. As Kaplan argues, *A Hazard of New Fortunes* unfolds as a contest between the centripetal and centrifugal forces of literary realism, trying on the one hand to "make men know one another better" in a way that holds them together, and at the same time showing how that same knowledge of each other threatens to drive them apart.[21] "What iss Amerigan?" retorts Lindau at his most dangerous. "Dere *iss* no Ameriga any more!" The novel concludes with a series of events that dramatize the fragmentation at the heart of Lindau's rhetoric. In the midst of a streetcar strike, the tycoon's son, Conrad Dryfoos, is killed as he tries to protect Lindau from being beaten by a police officer; Lindau dies from his wounds soon after. These deaths, though, do little to moderate the position of the elder Dryfoos, who ends up selling *Every Other Week* to March and a partner. The magazine therefore continues, but with a reduction in both its staff and its aspirations. The literary center does not hold.

A Hazard of New Fortunes was Howells's most dramatic fictional statement about the divisions that threatened American society, but the most pronounced effect of the novel is its demonstration of literary realism's inability to meet the challenges of ameliorating those divisions. Howells would continue to write fiction for another two decades – his last novel would be published in 1916 – but he gradually became less aggressive in his attempts to document the social realities of American life. Soon after *Hazard*, he would publish his novel most directly concerned about race, *An Imperative Duty* (1892), a book that attempts to rewrite the "tragic mulatta" romance that had been a staple of American race fictions throughout the nineteenth century.[d] W. E. B. Du Bois would later praise the novel for facing "our national foolishness and shuffling and evasion" by avoiding the hysteria with which most Americans respond to histories of miscegenation, but Howells does little to depict the world of African Americans in Boston, where the book is set.[22] The central character in the novel, a young woman who has recently learned

d For a discussion of this plot elsewhere in this volume, see Robert S. Levine, "The early African American novel," chapter 16, 272.

of an African American grandmother, can barely tolerate the physical presence of the black men and women that she meets in a church; the male protagonist then talks her out of seeking her African American relations in favor of marrying him and leaving the United States for Rome. This aversion to facing the difficult truths of American racism suggests something of how both the characters of *An Imperative Duty* and its author are more prepared to confront ideas about race, racism, and racial equality in the abstract than to document their operation in the lived experiences of African Americans.[23] A similar retreat governs the version of the utopian novel that Howells penned in the 1890s, *A Traveler from Altruria* (1894), which takes place in a rural, New England resort, where the visitor from the utopia of Altruria can inquire about the absurdities of American life in cool comfort. Whatever the merits of *Imperative Duty* or *Altruria*, they do not seem to share in the same mimetic project of Howells's major fiction from the 1880s, in which the novels constitute their own form of thinking about the project of social representation.

As a critic, however, Howells did continue to champion works that shared the representational aspirations of novels like *The Minister's Charge* and *Hazard*. Even though, as Nancy Glazener notes in this volume, the "very capaciousness of realism made it unwieldy for branding," it also flourished, particularly in the form of regionalism and urban writing, a variety of regionalism.[e] Writing about the New York fiction of Stephen Crane and Abraham Cahan, for instance, Howells states that

> both of these writers persuade us that they have told the truth, and that such as conditions have made the people they deal with, we see their people. If we have any quarrel with the result we cannot blame the authors, who have done their duty as artists and for a moment have drawn aside the thick veil of ignorance which parts the comfortable few from the uncomfortable many in this city.[24]

The implication here is clear: by drawing "aside the thick veil of ignorance," Crane and Cahan are creating the possibility that the "conditions" under which their immigrant subjects live might be ameliorated by the influence of the "comfortable few." Indeed, the most optimistic notes of Howells's criticism in the years surrounding the publication of *Hazard* rely on the notion that the aggregate of American literature could achieve more than any single novel could. For Howells, literary realism was an aesthetic with a wide embrace; his list of exemplary authors in this column includes everyone from Whitman, Twain, and James to Mary Noailles Murfree, whose fiction

e Nancy Glazener, "The novel in postbellum print culture," chapter 20, 347.

about Appalachian life Howells admired, and James Whitcomb Riley, whose dialect poetry made him known as "The Hoosier Poet."

In the decade that followed, Howells also became the advocate of two African American writers, Paul Laurence Dunbar and Charles Chesnutt, though his critical comments about them prove deeply instructive about the limits of his own vision for literary realism in the United States.[f] In the case of Dunbar, Howells urged that he develop his dialect poetry but forgo his interest in more conventional verse.[25] In the case of Chesnutt, Howells praised the short fiction of *The Conjure Woman* (1899) and *The Wife of His Youth* (1899) but found too much anger in Chesnutt's portrayal of the Wilmington race riot in *The Marrow of Tradition* (1901).[26] Howells's comments on the novel bear careful reading because of what they reveal about the limitations of the literary realism that he championed:

> [Chesnutt] stands up for his own people with a courage which has more justice than mercy in it. The book is, in fact, bitter, bitter. There is no reason in history why it should not be so, if wrong is to be repaid with hate, and yet it would be better if it was not so bitter. I am not saying that he is so inartistic as to play the advocate; whatever his minor foibles may be, he is an artist whom his stepbrother Americans may well be proud of; but while he recognizes pretty well all the facts in the case, he is too clearly of a judgment that is made up. One cannot blame him for that; what would one be one's self?[27]

Howells chastises and sympathizes with Chesnutt in nearly the same breath. Howells names Chesnutt's anger at the violence suffered by African Americans in Wilmington as placing him outside the boundaries of the professional observation that constituted the realist project; yet Howells also understands Chesnutt's bitterness as an inevitable result of his blackness. It is no accident that Howells refers to Chesnutt as a "stepbrother" to American artists – a term of kinship that Howells seems to intend as an approbation. For Howells seeks to signal his sympathy for Chesnutt's political sentiment, but only if he can simultaneously distance himself and the realist project from the emotion, confrontation, and possible violence that could surely result from the racial politics that Chesnutt's novel depicts. As Nancy Bentley puts it, "To reveal oneself as bitter is to reveal oneself as black, and to be a black author is to be racially excluded from the detached objectivity that is Howells's pre-requisite for Realist analysis."[28]

f For fuller discussions of the fiction of Dunbar and Chesnutt, see essays in this volume by Barbara McCaskill (chapter 29, "The African American novel after Reconstruction"), and Robert Reid-Pharr (chapter 28, "The postbellum race novel").

Reading this review within the arc of Howells's career, we might add more: *The Marrow of Tradition* has the wide social ambit that Howells attempted to provide in the novels he published a decade before Chesnutt's. But Chesnutt allowed himself to go where Howells would not: into the acts of violence themselves and the minds that perpetrated them, into a direct plea for a more just social order. *The Marrow of Tradition* does not contain anything like the abstract social thinking of the realist mouthpieces of Howells's novels – the ministers Sewell and Peck, or even the editor March. Instead, Chesnutt's novel is embedded in the direct experience of what happens when men and women forget that they are "more like than unlike," when they stop being interested in coming to "know one another better." If Howells found Chesnutt's novel too "bitter" to swallow, it might be because he had refused the same medicine for so many years before.

Notes

1. William Roscoe Thayer, "The New Story-Tellers and the Doom of Realism" (1894), rpt. in Donald Pizer, ed., *Documents of American Realism and Naturalism* (Carbondale, IL: Southern Illinois University Press, 1998), 164.
2. William Dean Howells, *Selected Literary Criticism*, 3 vols., ed. Ulrich Halfmann, Donald Pizer, and Ronald Gottesman, vols. XIII, XXI, XXX of *A Selected Edition of William Dean Howells* (Bloomington: Indiana Univerisity Press, 1993), I:337.
3. *Ibid.*, II:82
4. *Ibid.*, II:290.
5. *Ibid.*, II:45
6. Claudia Stokes, *Writers in Retrospect: The Rise of American Literary History, 1875–1910* (Chapel Hill: University of North Carolina Press, 2006), 27–28.
7. Howells, *Selected Literary Criticism*, II:62, 63
8. See, generally, Amy Kaplan's chapter "The Mass-Mediated Realism of William Dean Howells," in *The Social Construction of American Realism* (Chicago: University of Chicago Press, 1998), 15–43.
9. Howells, *Selected Literary Criticism*, II:141.
10. Howells to Henry James, October 10, 1888, in William Dean Howells, *Selected Letters, Volume 3: 1882–1891*, ed. Robert C. Leitz III *et al.*, vol. XIX of *A Selected Edition of William Dean Howells* (Boston: Twayne, 1980), 231.
11. *Ibid.*
12. Amanda Claybaugh, *The Novel of Purpose: Literature and Social Reform in the Anglo-American World* (Ithaca: Cornell University Press, 2007), 121.
13. George H. Hubbard, "How and Where to Begin Reform," *The New Englander and Yale Review* 52 (February 1890): 107.
14. Albion W. Tourgée, "Reform Versus Reformation," *North American Review* 132 (April 1881): 306.

15. Kaplan, *The Social Construction of American Realism*, 43.
16. I should mention that my analysis of Howells's fiction from 1885 to 1890 omits two novels, *Indian Summer* (1886) and *April Hopes* (1887), which have little to say about social matters.
17. Stokes points out that Sewell's inability to communicate his true judgment of Barker's poetry is an example of failed literary professionalism (*Writers in Retrospect*, 122).
18. Howells to Garland, November 6, 1888, in Howells, *Selected Letters, Volume 3*, 234.
19. Howells to Hale, August 30, 1888, in Howells, *Selected Letters, Volume 3*, 228–229.
20. David E. Shi, *Facing Facts: Realism in American Thought and Culture, 1850–1920* (New York: Oxford University Press, 1995), 198.
21. Kaplan, *The Social Construction of American Realism*, 44–64.
22. W. E. B. Du Bois, "Howells and Black Folk" (1913), in *Writings*, ed. Nathan Huggins (New York: Library of America, 1986), 1147. For a more detailed consideration of *An Imperative Duty* and the writing of Du Bois, see Henry B. Wonham: *Criticism and the Color Line: Desegregating American Literary Studies* (New Brunswick, NJ: Rutgers University Press, 1996), 126–139.
23. However, Howells's attempt to address race and racism seem no less "undercooked" than the other "Postbellum race novels" written by white authors during this period, as discussed by Robert Reid-Pharr, chapter 28 in this volume, 470.
24. Howells, *Selected Literary Criticism*, II:278.
25. I discuss Howells's treatment of Dunbar's poetry in *The Culture Concept: Writing and Difference in the Age of Realism* (Minneapolis: University of Minnesota Press, 2002), 69–72. For a more recent discussion of the relationship between Howells and Dunbar, see Gene Andrew Jarrett, *Deans and Truants: Race and Realism in African American Literature* (Philadelphia: University of Pennsylvania Press, 2006), esp. 29–51.
26. The reviews in question are "Mr. Charles W. Chesnutt's Stories," *Atlantic Monthly* 85 (May 1900): 699–701; and Howells, "A Psychological Counter-Current in Recent Fiction," *North American Review* 173 (December 1901): 872–888.
27. Howells, "A Psychological Counter-Current in Recent Fiction," 882.
28. Nancy Bentley, "Literary Forms and Mass Culture, 1870–1920," in Sacvan Bercovitch, gen. ed., *The Cambridge History of American Literature, Volume 3, Prose Writing, 1860–1920* (New York: Cambridge University Press: 2005), 208.

18

James, pragmatism, and the realist ideal

CARRIE TIRADO BRAMEN

Albert Einstein once said that the most important question facing humanity is whether the universe is a friendly place. For William and Henry James, the universe is decidedly unfriendly, especially in terms of satisfying the dreams and desires that individuals imaginatively create but are unable to realize. This gulf between desire and actuality constitutes the defining tension of both Jamesian pragmatism and Jamesian realism, a tension that is best described by William James in *Pragmatism* (1907): "Is all 'yes, yes' in the universe? Doesn't the fact of 'no' stand at the very core of life?"[1] At their most fundamental level, pragmatism and realism are ways to explore the psychological, social and philosophical consequences of a world that says "no."

In 1896, Henry James wrote to his friend A. C. Benson, "I have the imagination of disaster and see life as indeed ferocious and sinister."[2] This baleful perspective when translated into James's fictional world has a tragic and at times a comic dimension, leading to a situation in which the protagonists are robbed of precisely what they desire, namely a profound intimacy with another.[3] Whether it is Christopher Newman's romantic rebuff in *The American* (1877), or Isabel Archer's miserable marriage in *The Portrait of a Lady* (1881), or Milly Theale's terminal illness in *The Wings of the Dove* (1902), James repeatedly constructs a fictional world that withholds intimacy from its major characters. When William Dean Howells chides James for not ending *The American* with the marriage of Christopher Newman and his French fiancée Claire de Cintré, James admits that such an ending would have been "prettier," but Newman and de Cintré, he insists, represent an "impossible couple." "We are each the product of circumstances," James explains to Howells in 1877, "and there are tall stone walls which fatally divide us."[4] This image of "tall stone walls" creating insurmountable obstacles to human intimacy lies at the heart of Jamesian realism, an aesthetic that emerges from an understanding of the world as fundamentally hostile, constituted by limits and constraints of all kinds, beginning with those established by our own mortality. Jamesian realism explores the trickle-down effect of this world that says "no" from external obstacles such as "tall stone walls" to the internalization of these walls in the darkest reaches of the human psyche.

Pragmatism provides a way to grapple with the flux and uncertainty of the modern world not by escaping it but by engaging it through a strategy of adaptability. "Everything here is plastic," William James writes in "What Pragmatism Means" (1907), and this idea of plasticity is central to his worldview where "new truth marries old opinion to new facts as ever to show a minimum of jolt, a maximum of continuity."[5] Jamesian pragmatism provides a crisis management guide to modernity, where the metaphor of marriage inscribes change within structures of continuity that avoid Henry Adams's nightmare of entropic chaos. In contrast to Adams, who believes that there is no foundational order, only "a chaos of anarchic and purposeless forces," Jamesian pragmatism is oddly optimistic, a therapeutic response to an insecure world that insists on the compatibility of flux and continuity.[6] The world, in other words, may be comprised of swarming atoms and a mass of maggots, but James also insists that most people are "sympathetic."[7] Pragmatism, in combining the grotesque with hope, provides a way to maneuver within an unpredictable world through strategies of accommodation and flexibility.

Whereas William James, the Harvard-trained physician and internationally renowned psychologist, wants to grapple with an unfriendly universe not so much to banish fear but to cope with it, the novelist Henry James wants to sustain "the ache of fear" in all of its emotional intensity. "Where emotion is," James once exclaimed, "there am I!"[8] The vehicle for exploring this emotional intensity is the novel, a genre that possesses the flexibility to capture the multiplicity of experience, while at the same time providing narrative parameters that give shape to the "myriad forms" of reality. As Henry James writes in "The Art of Fiction" (1884), "[e]xperience is never limited, and it is never complete," yet "art," by contrast, is "essentially selection," a process of exclusion whereby experience is given meaning and significance. The novel, for Henry, emerges from a dialectic of plasticity and limits, where the form is sufficiently flexible and dynamic to embrace innovation, while at the same time insisting on a principle of aesthetic exclusion: that a work of art requires that the author knows when to say "no." To borrow an adage from his brother William, "the art of being wise is the art of knowing what to overlook."[9]

Whether it is Henry's understanding of the novel or William's theory of the mind, both brothers emphasize the importance of saying "no" in an uncertain world that can so easily overwhelm the individual. Both underscore the vulnerability of the human subject and the tenuous basis of one's sense of well-being. This recognition of the fragility of the self derived in part from their father's faith in the therapeutic effect of social connection. According to F. O Matthiessen, Henry James, Sr. repeatedly told his children: "we need never fear not to be good enough if we were only social enough."[10] For him, "the origin of spiritual evil" is derived from "a rigidly personal or finite consciousness" that perverts creative energy into "purely selfish or unsocial issues." The only way to realize our spiritual potential is through "self-effacement," which he describes as "a spontaneous death to ourselves."[11] Redemption in the form of social solidarity can only be realized by renouncing the self, or what he calls a "moral suicide, or inward death to the self in all its forms."[12] Society, then, has a deeply spiritual resonance as the manifestation of the divine on earth.

Henry James the younger did not share his father's enthusiasm for social salvation. In a 1915 letter to his friend Hugh Walpole, he wrote: "I have 'seen' very few people – and I see as few as possible. I can't stand them, and all their promiscuous prattle."[13] Although these words can be dismissed as the misanthropic sentiments of an aging curmudgeon, they are also indicative of an important paradox in Jamesian realism, namely that his main characters long for human connection – even for that social-spiritual ecstasy that Henry James Sr. envisioned – but they rarely, if ever, find it. And if they do, it quickly ends.

This epistolary glimpse into the seventy-two-year-old novelist actually resounds in one of his earliest characters, the invalid bachelor Clement Searle in "A Passionate Pilgrim" (1871). This novella, which William Dean Howells considered one of his favorites and described as the first of James's "international novels," offers an early instance of how a deep suspicion of sociability is combined with an intense longing for companionship.[14] First serialized in *The Atlantic Monthly* in 1871, then published as part of a collection of short stories in 1875, the same year that *Roderick Hudson* appeared, this novella represents the earliest fiction that James included in *The New York Edition* (1907–1909). In the 1908 Preface to this narrative, James, in a rare gesture of personal confession, admits that the story still "indescribably touches" him, because it represents a "documentary of myself."

By combining cheerfulness with melancholia, "A Passionate Pilgrim" provides an early example of how the notion of an unfriendly universe enters James's work as a way to question his father's philosophical belief in the redemptive value of social fellowship: does sociality have the power to save us? The novella represents a transitional moment in the movement of thought across generations and within James's own *oeuvre*, in that James embraces a residual belief in the therapeutic effects of sociality – suggesting that one can find meaningful connections with others – while also showing that insurmountable obstacles cut short such connections. The perspective that develops in this narrative offers an implicit critique of his father's social optimism and instead paints a less hopeful picture of the irrepressibility of self-interest. The self cannot be banished from Henry's worldview, and neither can desire.

"A Passionate Pilgrim" depicts the son's rebellion against his father's philosophical idealism through a transatlantic allegory, in which the son leaves the land of his father to return to the ancestral home of his great-grandfathers. The novella inverts the Ur-journey of Anglo-American nationhood – the Pilgrims arriving in the New World. England, the site of Puritan alienation and expulsion, is now a spiritual homeland. The pilgrim, the forty-three-year-old Searle, is a melancholic and terminally ill Anglophilic bachelor who arrives in England not to begin a new life, but to die in a land in which he wishes he had been born.[15] Searle is the first of Henry's invalid bachelors, a predecessor to Ralph Touchett in *The Portrait of a Lady* (1881), both passionate figures of unconsummated desire.[16]

Searle decides to go to England to make a claim on his distant family's estate, Lockley Park, because of an unjust settlement a century earlier. John Simmons, Searle's Jewish American attorney and old school friend, is not optimistic and he advises his friend to return to New York: "But I know Englishmen, and I know you. You're not one of them, Searle, not you. You'll go under here, sir." When Searle rejects his friend's advice and flatly refuses to return to New York, Simmons asks: "What is the matter? Are you afraid?" – a question that will surface again, as I will show presently, in *The Ambassadors* (1903), "The Beast in the Jungle"(1903), and *The Golden Bowl* (1904). Searle responds by quoting, in part, Gratiano from Shakespeare's *The Merchant of Venice*: "Yes, I'm afraid! 'I thank thee, Jew, for teaching me that word!'" Fear is here associated with Jewishness *and* Americanness; but where the Jew represents a figure who is fearful (and with whom Searle identifies), America suggests a place that inspires fear. Searle is afraid of returning to the USA with its compulsive work ethic, and its concomitant model of manliness based on productivity, since this fusion of virility and Americanism has indirectly depleted the weakening aesthete to the extent that he wants to die in England.[17]

By moving to England, Searle fulfills his death-wish: he literally wants to be incorporated in English soil, interred in an "English churchyard" underneath an "English yew" in the land of his great-grandfathers, so that he can die an authentic death where he can claim indigenous status as an English gentleman. This postcolonial return to the ancestral home, where settler whiteness can once again become authentic Englishness, has a sexual subtext as well: this move from the USA to England is also about finding a queer home within the pastoral life of the Old World.[a] This story of return migration inverts a national narrative of the American fatherland to celebrate another type of inversion, the pleasures of homosocial bonding in the traditional setting of Britain. Where Searle is "afraid" of living in the USA, he finds comfort in England, primarily in the form of an American traveler, the anonymous narrator, who is also an Anglophilic bachelor. The two men instantly befriend each other at Hampton Court, and they walk arm and arm through the corridors and gardens of the palace. Where Simmons, the Jewish American, warns that English sociality is cold and unfeeling, Searle discovers the opposite: an amiable world of fellowship, which is marked in "the noble friendliness of the scenery." Male companionship provides moments of shared pleasure, a sense of that social utopia imagined by James the Elder, not by forgetting the self, but by becoming fully conscious of the self, a consciousness that can only be realized by connecting to another.

In embracing the self rather than banishing it, Henry James revises his father's social vision by insisting on the inseparability of self-consciousness and social consciousness. The two are, for the son, inextricably linked. But this critique of the father goes beyond the self; Henry James also emphasizes the transient and illusory nature of social harmony. The notion of a friendly universe, even in England, is ultimately a delusion that culminates in Oxford, whose atmosphere creates "the sweet illusion that all is well in this weary world, all perfect and rounded . . . England's safe!" As the illusion of safety dissipates, so Searle's body grows "daily thinner." Yet even in his weakened state, at the point of dying, Searle's final words underscore a lasting theme in James's work, introducing an element that serves as the final nail in the coffin of his father's social utopia: "Here I lie, worn down to a mere throbbing fever-point; I breathe and nothing more, and yet I *desire*! My desire lives." Searle is speaking specifically here of his desire to marry Miss Searle, his quiet and repressed English cousin and inhabitant of Lockley Place, to whom he proposes after a single afternoon. Although Searle's sudden passion for his cousin seems rather unconvincing, James emphasizes the protagonist's dying words –"I *desire*" – because they create a dynamic and restless energy that characterizes social encounters in James's fictional world. To imagine the social world as sacred, James the Elder

a Elizabeth Freeman's "Reimagining genders and sexualities," chapter 57 in this volume, also cites the prominence of queer identities in the novels of Henry James (942). However, as *The Bostonians* (1886) demonstrates, Henry James could be extremely reluctant to imagine an intimate relationship among women.

must kill the self, which is to say he must kill desire. Henry Jr., however, puts desire back into the social equation, creating a far more indeterminate world, one that can never be redemptive because it cannot remain sufficiently stable.

Perhaps one reason why Howells was so fond of "A Passionate Pilgrim" is that it shows James at his most optimistic about social fellowship. Companionship does not cure Searle but, according to his doctor, it prolonged his life by a month, which for James is the closest a reader gets to a feel-good ending. Howells, who was raised a Swedenborgian and considered it his "inherited faith," believed in the therapeutic potential of the social, a theme he underscores in his review of Henry James, Sr.'s *The Secret of Swedenborg* (1869).[18] Howells's summary of this book could also describe his own outlook: "the regeneration which is to take place will be a social, not a personal effect; not so far as a man obeys God, but as far as he loves his fellow, is he saved."[19] Howells, more than Henry James Jr., believes in the divine potential of social "solidarity," a term that Michael Elliott also uses in relation to Howells elsewhere in this volume,[b] and his realism communicates this faith, despite his melancholic depictions of middlebrow America with its petty jealousies, mundane preoccupations, and crass materialism.

This temperamental difference between Howells and Henry James can be seen in their respective forms of realism. Whereas Jamesian realism explores sociality through its impact on the psyche and its hidden desires, Howells focuses on the Victorian social world as a way to escape from the mysteries of the mind. Where Henry James analyzes the "true monsters" (to use William James's phrase) of the subconscious, Howells flees from them. Howellsian realism is more outwardly directed, committed to the democratization of American letters as a way to validate the lowly and the common as worthy of aesthetic representation. The realist author has an ethical obligation to render the ordinary interesting, thus making it a source of serious aesthetic engagement and elevating the status of the novel by making it socially relevant. "He adores the real," writes Henry James of his lifelong friend in 1886, "the natural, the colloquial, the moderate, the optimistic, the domestic, and the democratic; looking askance at exceptions and perversities and superiorities, at surprising and incongruous phenomena in general."[20] Where Jamesian realism explores the tensions between types and individuals, between asymmetrical relations and the desire for reciprocity, and the queer and incongruous amidst the ordinary, Howellsian realism, however strained and unconvincing at times,

b Michael Elliott, "Realism and radicalism: the school of Howells," chapter 17, 292.

still tenaciously holds onto a therapeutic vision of social solidarity, based on typicality, ordinariness, and the common.

For both Henry and William James, there is simply no alternative to the social world. As William wrote to a friend in 1868, "[e]verything we know and are is through men. We have no revelation but through men . . . however mean a man may be, man is the best we know."[21] At its most fundamental level, Henry's fiction can be understood as the aesthetic rendering of these fraternal words. His novels are ineluctably social, and this is the quality T. S. Eliot appreciated most about James, in that the focus of attention is always on "a situation, a relation, an atmosphere, to which the characters pay tribute," and that "the real hero, in any of James's stories, is a social entity of which men and women are constituents."[22] Both William and Henry elaborate upon their father's deeply social worldview by conceptualizing sociality as an intricate and potentially boundless web of relations and influences; but for the sons, this web is no longer idealized as a source of divine revelation. For them, social relations can be disappointing, painful, and lonely.

For Henry James, the question of boundary-making constitutes the "perpetual predicament" of the writer, a question that is perhaps best illustrated by Madame Merle in *The Portrait of a Lady*: "What shall we call our 'self'? Where does it begin? Where does it end?" Madame Merle's anxiety about the pliability and amorphousness of the self is actually symptomatic, for James, of novelistic as well as typological concerns. More specifically, Madame Merle's personal angst reflects a distinctly American dilemma. "Americans, rightly or wrongly," writes James in *The Portrait of a Lady*, "are commended for the ease with which they adapt themselves to foreign conditions." Americans, in other words, are too accommodating, too pliant, traits that make them ideal pragmatists. William's *Pragmatism* appeared one year before the New York edition of *The Portrait of a Lady* (1908), but where William advocates plasticity and flexibility as a therapeutic cure for an insecure and unsafe world, Henry explores how the cure can create its own pathology. Isabel Archer, who possesses "an unquenchable desire to please," loses a sense of her own self. Gradually, Isabel's mind becomes muddled and unclear: "there was a confusion of regrets, a complication of fears." Like Clement Searle, who arrives in England already familiar with its culture through books, Isabel Archer arrives at Gardencourt likening her encounter with Lord Warburton to a scene from a romantic novel. But where Searle dies soon after seeing the illusion of "safe England" dissipate, Isabel must grapple with the aftermath of this post-romantic vision, or what her American friend Henrietta Stackpole calls "grim reality."

What happens to the innocent American who arrives in Europe expecting to be "as happy as possible" but instead discovers suffering? When Isabel arrives in Britain fresh from her father's library in upstate New York, she expects the world to be a friendly place, a world where suffering is optional: "The young lady seemed to have a great deal of confidence, both in herself and in others." In contrast to Maggie Verver in *The Golden Bowl* (1904), whose confidence increases as she grapples with "grim reality," Isabel's confidence diminishes and she is overcome with fear – fear of her husband Gilbert Osmond, fear of herself. As Peter Jones has remarked in "Pragmatism and *The Portrait of a Lady,*" there are more than fifty references to fear, dread, and terror in the last third of the book. Fear is a "criterion of dawning awareness," as Jones points out, but an awareness that ultimately incapacitates James's heroine.[23] Isabel is a failed pragmatist: she may be accommodating but she is too tender-hearted to deal with violence, evil, and cruelty. She is unable to relinquish her pristine ideals or to acknowledge fully the capacity for evil among those she has trusted. She may be a good reader of books, but she is unable to read others effectively, and as a result she cannot cope with the consequences of her own errors. Although she is quite skilled in declining suitors, she is ultimately unable to say "no" in an ontological sense, and so cannot protect the boundaries of her own personhood.

Perhaps William James had Isabel Archer in mind when he warned against novel-reading. In *The Principles of Psychology* (1890), he casts these dangers in particularly dramatic language: "The habit of excessive novel-reading and theatre-going will produce true monsters" by creating a person who indulges in feelings at the cost of action. (For more on the moral and psychic hazards seen in novel-reading at this time, see the chapters by Glazener and Hochman in this volume.[c]) He criticizes "the nerveless sentimentalist and dreamer, who spends his life in a weltering sea of sensibility and emotion, but who never does a manly concrete deed."[24] But William's critique of the novel is specifically directed toward men and it betrays his fears about the insecurity of manliness, where reflection and idleness, the supposed antitheses of manly deeds, are highly gendered terms suggesting sexual deviance.[25]

William James's worst nightmare about the feminizing effect of novels is borne out in his brother's first acknowledged novel, which centers around an unconventional male friendship between a sculptor, Roderick Hudson, and

c Nancy Glazener, "The Novel in postbellum print culture" (chapter 20); Barbara Hochman, "Readers and reading groups" (chapter 36).

his patron, Rowland Mallet, and their intimate time together in Italy spent in idle contemplation. *Roderick Hudson* (1875) explores idleness, precisely that which William James shuns, and in doing so, the novel – far more than philosophical pragmatism – explores the gothic interiors of the mind, its conscious and unconscious dimensions, with a certain fearlessness at what it may find: the internal demons or "true monsters" that come to the surface of the novelistic canvas during the open-endedness of idle reflection. Rowland Mallet, an independently wealthy art patron, admires a Hellenistic sculpture of a naked man in his cousin's parlor in Northampton, Massachusetts. When he meets the artist, the handsome and youthful Roderick Hudson, he insists that the two of them depart for Rome for an extended period of time so that Roderick can cultivate his genius in the proper artistic milieu. Rowland takes Roderick from the narrow puritanical confines of New England to the "effete civilisation" of Europe, where the "burden and the obloquy of idleness are less heavy."

Emblematic of the geographic migration from puritan New England to profligate Rome, *Roderick Hudson* initiates a key theme in Henry James's work, namely the desire to overcome fear and to experience the freedom of letting go. In prefiguring the advice that Lambert Strether will give Little Bilham in *The Ambassadors*, Rowland says to Mary Garland, Roderick's distant cousin and long-suffering fiancée who has just arrived in Rome: "Trust yourself, let yourself go . . . I don't believe it's in you to be *really* afraid of anything." Alongside this embrace of fearlessness, however, is a counter-pull toward safety. The novel recognizes the loss that accompanies risk, such as the loss of security. Mrs. Hudson pleads, for instance, with her son to marry Mary Garland and return to Northampton where they "shall all be safe and quiet and happy." Roderick rejects the safety of home and at the end of the novel, while climbing in the Swiss Alps during an "Alpine Tempest," he disappears. Worried about the fate of his beloved friend, Rowland desperately tries to convince himself that Roderick has found a "safe chalet" to protect himself until the storm ends. But Roderick instead falls to his death, either intentionally or accidentally, and his body is discovered the following day near a "great rugged wall." Rowland's desire to imagine that Roderick finds safety in a chalet is a fantasy, itself a somnambulistic evasion of reality, one that ignores the cruelty of the world, to which Rowland awakens after Roderick dies. With this romantic figure (beautifully) dead, Rowland's "personal world" now looks "void and blank and sinister as a theatre bankrupt and closed."

Roderick Hudson illustrates a quintessential Jamesian theme, namely the asymmetry of intimacy, which is to say its incommensurability and impossibility.[26] Desire is rarely reciprocal in Henry James's fictional world, and intimacy is too often thwarted. One of James's early reviewers, Thomas Powell, perceptively comments on this trend in his 1875 review of *Roderick Hudson:* " None of his books end in a conventional way, probably because he is not a conventional writer, and those who look for 'and they lived together happily ever after' at the end of the last chapter of any of his novelettes will be disappointed."[27]

Marriage, for James, is not synonymous with intimacy but an obstacle to it. The reason that happy coupledom doesn't exist in James's fictional universe is best summarized by Christina Light when she observes that the "world's idea of possible relations, either for man or woman, is so poor – there would be so many nice free ones." In juxtaposing "is" with the conditional "would," Christina Light contrasts the actual with the possible: through an accumulation of habits, customs, and fears, we have conceived of intimacy in such narrow terms that we foreclose the possibility of truly creative, unconventional unions. James critiques social conventions not by imagining alternatives but rather by depicting the thwarted, and indeed tragic lives, produced out of the desire for connection.

This desire for connection continues to be played out spatially in James's novels through the *mise-en-scène* of Europe, which changes from the amiable landscapes of England to the sublime and dangerous terrain of Europe, whether in the form of the Alps or the inscrutability of Paris. In contrast to Clement Searle, for whom England is always already familiar, Lambert Strether, like Roderick before him, has a far more disorienting experience of Europe. *The Ambassadors* (1903), which was James's favorite of his novels, focuses on the encounters of Strether, who is sent to Europe as a familial ambassador to retrieve Chadwick Newsome, the wayward son of his imperious fiancée, Mrs. Newsome, from the feminine seductions of Paris. From Woollett, Massachusetts, Strether arrives in Europe to find Chadwick greatly improved, with a cosmopolitan sensibility that is epitomized in his "new face" and a charismatic presence of "massive young manhood." An ambassador who is distracted from his mission, Strether finds Paris all-consuming and experiences a late awakening, where "everything is different. Nothing is manageable, nothing final – nothing, above all, for poor Strether, natural."[28]

This disorientating response to Europe is at once liberating and terrifying, throwing into relief Strether's own sexual disorientation, as an anomalous figure deviating from normative heterosexual masculinity. As Eric Haralson has pointed out, critics throughout the twentieth century have noted the character's ambiguous sexuality, with Leslie Fiedler, for instance, describing Strether as "the most maidenly" of James's protagonists; others have observed that he possesses a "typical thinness of feeling wherever passion is concerned" and is "incapable . . . of carnality" and exhibits "a lack of male reciprocation" to female desire.[29] "So compromised is Strether's masculinity by his sexual (non) performance," argues Haralson, "that even the body of James's text suffers by association, drawing censure as an 'emasculated leisure-class novel.' "[30]

Perhaps as an implicit way to resolve the sexual ambiguity of James's protagonist, R. P. Blackmur insists on reading Strether as a "pilgrim" rather than an ambassador. Blackmur inscribes Strether within a Christian narrative of renunciation, which strongly echoes Henry James the Elder's spiritual vision, where the body is exchanged for the spirit who transcends desire: "We follow rather the Christian pattern of re-birth, the fresh start, the change of life or heart – arising from the pity and terror of human conditions met and seen – with the end not in death but in the living analogue of death, sacrifice, and renunciation."[31] Sacrifice – including the sacrifice of his supposed love interest Maria Gostrey – represents the condition of possibility for consciousness and conscience.

But what if we were to read Strether as a pilgrim, not in terms of Christian transcendence, but as a "passionate pilgrim" in the tradition of James's own Clement Searle, whose final words are "I *desire*"? What happens to the pilgrim's explicit expression of desire in *The Ambassadors*? The answer lies in the question that appears in both works, specifically: "Are you afraid?" In "A Passionate Pilgrim," the question is uttered in the context of a possible return to the USA, when Searle admits that the journey to New York would certainly kill him. Staying in England is a way not to escape death, but to allay his fear of death, finding comfort in the image of being buried underneath an English yew.

When that same question –"Are you afraid?"– appears in *The Ambassadors*, it is asked first by Chad, who is inquiring into Strether's fear of women. Strether admits that he is afraid of Madame de Vionnet (who Strether later discovers is Chad's lover) because of her seductive powers. Chad reassures Strether that "she won't do anything worse to you than make you like her," which is precisely what Strether fears. He also confesses to being afraid of Chad's mother Mrs. Newsome, his future wife, "perhaps even more." The question appears a second time in the final exchange between Strether and Chad, a conversation that is at once affectionate and sexually charged. Now, Strether is the one asking Chad if he is afraid. "Afraid?" asks Chad. "Of doing wrong, I mean away from my eye," laughs Strether, who adds: "I *am*, certainly, prodigious."

Clement Searle's declaration of "I desire" gives way to a more nuanced coupling of desire and fear in *The Ambassadors*: Strether wants to let himself go, or as he tells Chad's friend Little Bilham – "Live all you can; it's a mistake not to" – but is unable to do so. "*Will* you give yourself up?" Maria Gostrey asks. "I never can," says Strether, but he adds that he "unspeakably" wants to. Strether is unable to practice what he preaches: and this disjuncture between word and deed is precisely what leads him to characterize his life as a failure in terms of "relations," meaning that he has been unable to find intimacy, a sense of reciprocated desire with another.

A chain of asymmetrical desires defines this novel as much as *Roderick Hudson*: Maria Gostrey desires Strether, who may desire Chad, who desires (and finds requited love with) Madame de Vionnet. But unlike Roderick Hudson, who romantically falls to his death in the midst of a storm, Strether returns to the USA, enacting Mrs. Hudson's advice to her own son to marry and settle in New England where all shall be "safe and quiet and happy." Where *Roderick Hudson* and "A Passionate Pilgrim" explore the desiring subject within an impersonal fictional world that ultimately witnesses the premature death of the protagonist, *The Ambassadors* turns inward to depict how the "great rugged wall" becomes internalized within the psyche of the American pilgrim. Now the pilgrim returns home, not as a sacred figure of sacrifice and renunciation, but as a self-conscious subject, awakened to his own desires and yet overcome by his inhibitions. *The Ambassadors* represents in microcosm the *sine qua non* of Jamesian realism, namely an aesthetic based on fear.

In James's fiction, danger befalls those who are not fully self-aware and socially conscious, those who live delusional and solipsistic lives or what James describes in "The Beast in the Jungle" (1903) as "hallucination" in the midst of a social world of possibility and limits. In *The Golden Bowl*, published one year after "The Beast in the Jungle," Prince Amerigo's greatest fear is to be wrong "*without* knowing it" and he asks his confidante Mrs. Assingham to force him to see what he may not like, then "I shall know. And of that I shall never be afraid." But when Mrs. Assingham asks him if he's afraid about his impending marriage to the American Maggie Verver, the daughter of the millionaire and museum collector Adam Verver, he admits that he is "terribly afraid. I've now but to wait to see the monster come." Marriage is the monster in Prince Amerigo's closet and Mrs. Assingham admits that "it's a fearful thing at the best," but "don't run away from it." James's last completed novel takes what Blackmur calls "the harsh terror of love" and confronts it. *The Golden Bowl* is Henry's most pragmatic novel, where there is no innocent way out.[32]

In contrast to William James's grotesque image of life as "a mass of maggots in their carrion bed,"[33] Henry's novel depicts horror in the midst of affection, in the gilded halls of European luxury, when Maggie Verver awakens to her reality and finds that her close friend Charlotte Stant, who has married her widowed father Adam, was Prince Amerigo's lover before their marriage, and is now his mistress. But unlike Milly Theale, who dies after realizing she has been betrayed, Maggie Verver becomes more alive. At the start of the novel, Maggie is the embodiment of the innocent American girl, or what Leslie Fiedler calls the "Good Good Girl", and we are told, "she wasn't born to know evil. She must never know it." Maggie, too, wants to protect herself from the suffering and wounds of love: "I don't *want* to know!"[34] Yet the price of this innocence is a self-image based on fear. In contrast to Charlotte Stant, who is "not afraid – not of anything," Maggie confesses that "I live in terror . . . I am a small creeping thing." During the course of the novel, however, Charlotte becomes increasingly fearful as she is unable to decipher the actions of those closest to her, while Maggie finds strength in awakening to the nuanced world of deception and betrayal. Her goal, as she confides to Mrs. Assingham, is "not to be afraid." Maggie's response to this betrayal, to "innocence outraged," is not rejection or flight but acceptance. She simply cannot give her husband up.

Like her acceptance of the flawed golden bowl with its crystalline crack, Maggie has to forsake a youthful idealism for a pragmatic clarity that sees her marriage as an imperfect intimacy. But for her marriage to continue, she has to remove Charlotte Stant from Europe and banish her to American City, which also means that she must forsake her father – that he too must return to American City with his wife. Maggie's marriage depends on sacrificing her beloved father. Paternal loss enables marital continuity.

To bring about this arrangement, Maggie implements a plan that exemplifies the methodological flexibility of Jamesian pragmatism, a plan that coerces through affection. In "What Pragmatism Means" (1907), William James describes pragmatism as an amiable woman who knows when to say no: "you see already how democratic she is. Her manners are as various and flexible, her resources as rich and endless, and her conclusions as friendly as those of mother nature." Pragmatism assumes the character of the Nice American Girl, and both represent the "happy harmonizer" and "reconciler" who is, according to William, "completely genial."[35] "Amiability," writes Henry in *The Golden Bowl,* " is an aid to success." Maggie, who is described at the start as "very nice," uses this trait to persuade her husband to stop his affair and return to her, but she never confronts him directly; she never expresses rage, but instead asks for nothing. When Prince Amerigo realizes how she is maneuvering to resolve this marital crisis his response is "joy": "her kindness, gentleness, grace, her charming presence and easy humanity and familiarity had inspired him." Like the Jewish shopkeeper who was "intensely coercive" through his muteness, Maggie manipulates through "mute communication." "I am not extraordinary," confesses Maggie, "but I *am*, for everyone, quiet."[36]

Maggie Verver is a rarity among James's characters: she experiences terror and comes out the other side, thus achieving her goal: "Not to be afraid *not* to speak." When Prince Amerigo realizes that her amiability is not just a banal expression of American innocence, but comes from a far deeper knowledge of suffering and imperfection, he falls more profoundly in love with her. The final scene, when the two embrace but avoid each other's eyes, is interpreted by some as inhumane and cruel, where marriage represents a form of entrapment, but this final scene – which is also James's final scene as a novelist – is the closest we come to a happy ending.[37] Intimacy is possible in the last instance, but a flawed intimacy founded on loss, hurt, and a silent understanding.

James's novels create, as Blackmur argued in 1951, "a whole territory of human relations hitherto untouched or unarticulated. I do not say not experienced, only unarticulated."[38] Far from William James's characterization of novel-reading as sentimental escapism, Henry James's novels, and realism more generally, grapple with that which we have been afraid to discuss. Where William's pragmatism begins with the premise that we are afraid and offers a coping strategy of melioration, Henry's realism interrogates fear and casts doubt on the adequacy of such strategies. "Are you afraid?" is ultimately a question that James asks of his discomfited readers.

Notes

1. William James, "Pragmatism and Religion," in *Pragmatism* (1907), in *Writings, 1902–1910*, ed. Bruce Kuklick (New York: The Library of America, 1987), 616–617.
2. *Letters to A. C. Benson and Auguste Monod*, ed. E. F. Benson (London: Elkins Mathews & Marrot, 1930), 35.
3. For more on the comic aspects of Henry James, see Richard Poirier, *The Comic Sense of Henry James: A Study of the Early Novels* (New York: Oxford University

Press, 1960); Adrian Poole, "Nanda's Smile: Teaching James and a Sense of Humor," *Henry James Review* 25.1 (Winter 2004): 4–18.

4. *Henry James Letters*, ed. Leon Edel, 4 vols. (Cambridge, MA: Harvard University Press, 1974), II:205. See also Michael Anesko, *Letters, Fictions, Lives: Henry James and William Dean Howells* (New York: Oxford University Press, 1997).
5. William James, "What Pragmatism Means," in *Pragmatism*, in *Writings, 1902–1910*, 513.
6. Henry Adams, *The Education of Henry Adams: An Autobiography* (Cambridge, MA: Massachusetts Historical Society, 1918), 289.
7. Though depicting his pluralistic universe in rather bleak terms, William James insists that the "majority of men are sympathetic." He continues: "Not to demand intimate relations with the universe, and not to wish them satisfactory, should be accounted signs of something wrong." *A Pluralistic Universe*, in *Writings, 1902–1910*, 644–645. For a discussion of sympathy and intimacy in William and Henry James, see Kristin Boudreau, "Henry James's Inward Aches," *The Henry James Review* 20.1 (1999): 69–80.
8. R. P. Blackmur, "Henry James," in *The Literary History of the United States*, 3rd edn., ed. Robert Spiller *et al.* (New York: Macmillan, 1963), 1039. The phrase, "the ache of fear," comes from Henry James's Preface to *Roderick Hudson*, in *Literary Criticism*, 2 vols., ed. Leon Edel (New York: The Library of America, 1984), II:1040.
9. Henry James, "The Art of Fiction" (1884). Rpt. in Hazard Adams, ed., *Critical Theory since Plato* (New York: Harcourt Brace Jovanovich, 1971), 665, 668; William James, *The Principles of Psychology*, 2 vols. (New York: Henry Holt & Co., 1890), II:369. The full quotation is: "The art of reading (after a certain stage of one's education) is the art of skipping, so the art of being wise is the art of knowing what to overlook."
10. F. O. Matthiessen, *Henry James: The Major Phase* (1944; New York: Oxford University Press, 1963), 140. See the most recent biography of the James family, Paul Fisher, *The House of Wits: An Intimate Portrait of the James Family* (New York: Henry Holt & Co., 2008).
11. Henry James, Sr., *Society: The Redeemed Form of Man* (Boston: Houghton, Osgood & Co., 1879), 98–99.
12. Henry James, Sr., *The Literary Remains of the Late Henry James*, ed. William James (Boston: James Osgood & Co., 1885), 216.
13. Henry James, *The Letters of Henry James*, ed. Percy Lubbock, 2 vols. (New York: Charles Scribner's Sons, 1920), II:501–502.
14. William Dean Howells, "Henry James, Jr.," *The Century* 25 (November 1882): 27.
15. Clement Searle possesses the traits that Eric Haralson has described as a proto-gay type, which James would continue to develop as a distinct figure three years later in *Roderick Hudson*. Eric Haralson, *Henry James and Queer Modernity* (Cambridge: Cambridge University Press, 2003), 27–53.
16. Katherine Snyder argues that the bachelor as a character type is a highly eroticized figure who complicates the cultural boundaries of bourgeois

domesticity and normative manhood. See her *Bachelors, Manhood, and the Novel, 1850–1925* (Cambridge: Cambridge University Press, 1999).

17. Martha Banta discusses James's critique of the narrow parameters of gender in the USA, especially in terms of American masculinity, which was "mainly associated with the making of money." See Banta, "Men, Women, and the American Way," in *The Cambridge Companion to Henry James*, ed. Jonathan Freedman (Cambridge: Cambridge University Press, 1998), 23.
18. William Dean Howells refers to Swedenborgianism as his "inherited faith" in *Literary Friends and Acquaintance: A Personal Retrospect of American Authorship* (New York: Harper and Brothers, 1900), 228. In this same volume, Howells offers a vivid portrait of Henry James, Sr., describing him as "incommensurably more Swedenborgian" than himself, since James the Elder "lived and thought and felt Swedenborg with an entirety and intensity far beyond the mere assent of other men" (266). For a discussion of Howells's Swedenborgianism, see Walter Meserve, "Truth, Morality, and Swedenborg in Howells' Theory of Realism," *The New England Quarterly* 27.2 (June 1954): 252–257.
19. William Dean Howells, Review of Henry James Sr., *The Secret of Swedenborg, The Atlantic Monthly* 24 (1869): 763.
20. Henry James, "William Dean Howells," *Harpers Weekly* (June 19, 1886); rpt. in *Literary Criticism*, 1:503.
21. From a letter to Thomas Ward (1868). Quoted in William James, *The Philosophy of William James: Drawn from His Own Words*, ed. Horace Kallen (New York: Modern Library, 1925), 249.
22. T. S. Eliot, "On Henry James" (1918), in *The Question of Henry James: A Collection of Critical Essays*, ed. F. W. Dupee (New York: A. Wingate, 1947), 110. Lionel Trilling also valued this quality in James since the novel as a form "is a perpetual quest for reality, the field of its research being always the social world, the material of its analysis being always manners as the indication of the direction of the soul." *The Liberal Imagination* (New York: Viking Press, 1950), 212.
23. Peter Jones, "Pragmatism and *The Portrait of a Lady,*" *Philosophy and Literature* 5.1 (Spring 1981): 58.
24. William James, *The Principles of Psychology*, vol. I (New York: Henry Holt & Co., 1890), 125. See also Nancy Bentley's discussion of this passage in "Literary Forms and Mass Culture, 1870–1920," in *The Cambridge History of American Literature*, vol. III: *Prose Writing, 1860–1920*, ed, Sacvan Bercovitch (Cambridge: Cambridge University Press, 2005), 263.
25. On idleness and effeminacy in Henry James, see Hugh Stevens, *Henry James and Sexuality* (Cambridge: Cambridge University Press, 1998); Eric Haralson, *Henry James and Queer Modernity* (Cambridge: Cambridge University Press, 2003); Ross Posnock, *The Trial of Curiosity: Henry James, William James and the Challenge of Modernity* (New York: Oxford University Press, 1991). For a discussion of Victorian anxieties of virility and effeminacy from a psychoanalytic perspective, see Christopher Lane, *The Burdens of Intimacy: Psychoanalysis and Victorian Masculinity* (Chicago: University of Chicago Press, 1999). According to Alan

Sinfield, the effeminate dandy in the late nineteenth century connoted a heterosexual philanderer, and was not exclusively or primarily associated with gay men. See Alan Sinfield, *The Wilde Century: Effeminacy, Oscar Wilde and the Queer Moment* (New York: Columbia University Press, 1994). For an analysis in this volume of masculinity in relation to the rise of the American novel, see Milette Shamir's "Manhood and the early American novel" (chapter 11).

26. For a discussion of Victorian asymmetry in the portrayal of same-sex desire, see Lane, *The Burdens of Intimacy*.
27. Quoted in Kevin Hayes, *Henry James: The Contemporary Reviews* (Cambridge: Cambridge University Press, 1996), 9.
28. Henry James, *The Complete Notebooks*, ed. Leon Edel and Lyall H. Powers (New York: Oxford University Press, 1987), 561. Quoted in Posnock, *The Trial of Curiosity*, 222.
29. Quoted in Eric Haralson, "Lambert Strether's Excellent Adventure," in Freedman, *Cambridge Companion to Henry James*, 171.
30. Haralson, *Henry James and Queer Modernity*, 108.
31. R. P. Blackmur, "The Loose and Baggy Monsters of Henry James: Notes on the Underlying Classic Form in the Novel," in *The Lion and the Honeycomb: Essays in Solicitude and Critique* (New York: Harcourt, Brace & World, 1955), 276.
32. R. P. Blackmur, "Introduction," *The Golden Bowl* by Henry James (New York: Grove 1952). Rpt. in R. P. Blackmur, *Studies in Henry James*, ed. Veronica Makowsky (New York: New Directions, 1983), 158.
33. William James, "The Dilemma of Determinism" (1884), in *The Will to Believe and Other Essays* (New York: Dover, 1956), 177.
34. Martha Nussbaum focuses on the nature of Maggie Verver's moral aspiration. Maggie wants to be "as good as possible," to quote Nussbaum, by "never breaking a rule, never hurting." Nussbaum, "Flawed Crystals: James's *The Golden Bowl* and Literature as Moral Philosophy," *New Literary History* 15.1 (Autumn 1983): 25–50. For Leslie Fiedler's use of the "Good Good Girl," see *Love and Death in the American Novel* (New York: Criterion Books, 1960), esp. Part II: "Achievement and Frustration."
35. William James explicitly refers to pragmatism as a "she": "Pragmatism says no, and I fully agree with her." See "What Pragmatism Means," 521–22. Given the strong symbiosis between William's pragmatism (as an amiable woman) and Henry's Maggie Verver, William reacted quite hostilely to *The Golden Bowl*. In a letter to his brother, William wrote: "Why don't you just to please Brother, sit down and write a new book, with no twilight or mustiness in the plot, with great vigor and decisiveness in the action, no fencing in the dialogue, or psychological commentaries, and absolute straightness of style." *The Correspondence of William James*, vol. VIII (1895–June 1899), ed. John McDermott *et al.* (Charlottesville: University of Virginia Press, 1997), 463.
36. For an interpretation of Jewishness in *The Golden Bowl*, see Jonathan Freedman, *The Temple of Culture: Assimilation and Anti-Semitism in Literary Anglo-America* (New York: Oxford University Press, 2002). See also Liesl Olson, "'Under the

Lids of Jerusalem': The Guised Role of Jewishness in Henry James's *The Golden Bowl*," *Modern Fiction Studies* 49.4 (Winter 2003): 660–686.

37. Where Blackmur in his second introduction to *The Golden Bowl* (1963) considers the novel to be cruel, Gore Vidal in his introduction to the Penguin edition describes James's last completed novel as possessing a "spaciousness" and "even joy." Blackmur's 1963 introduction is reprinted in *Studies in Henry James*, 221–230. Gore Vidal, "Introduction," *The Golden Bowl* (New York: Penguin, 1987), 11. See also Quentin Anderson, "Why R. P. Blackmur Found James's *Golden Bowl* Inhumane," *ELH* 68 (2001): 725–743.
38. Blackmur, "The Loose and Baggy Monsters of Henry James," 281.

19

Theories of the American novel in the age of realism

LAWRENCE BUELL

The novel gained unprecedented prestige in the age of realism. The chief ground of opposition to the upstart form had largely been contained by mid-century – moralistic alarm at its alleged powers of seduction.[1] But only after 1865 did the dream of "the great American novel" displace the dream of a national epic. Fiction, declared William Dean Howells at century's end, had become "the chief intellectual stimulus of our time, whether we like the fact or not." "To-day is the day of the novel," Frank Norris agreed.[2] Posterity has confirmed the verdict. No span of US literary history before or since has been defined so predominantly in terms of its prose fiction.

Fiction *theory* lagged behind practice. In 1884, Henry James could call "The Art of Fiction" an almost untouched topic. "Only a short time ago," in the days of Dickens and Thackeray, the English novel "had no air of having a theory, a conviction, a consciousness of itself behind it," as if "a novel is a novel, as a pudding is a pudding," and "our only business with it could be to swallow it."[3] The situation soon improved considerably. Important American writers published such notable critical books as Howells's *Criticism and Fiction* (1891), Hamlin Garland's *Crumbling Idols* (1894), and Edith Wharton's *The Art of Fiction* (1925). James raised the genre of the authorial preface to a plane of unequaled sophistication. Close reading reached its first maturity between James's *Hawthorne* (1879) and William Crary Brownell's *American Prose Masters* (1909). The first histories of American literature date from the postbellum period, the first critical handbooks from the early twentieth century. But relative to the novelists' achievements, criticism remained impressionistic. "Literary" scholarship by academics was more historical-philological than belletristic; American literature was deemed the province of undergraduate and secondary teachers, not serious researchers.[4] No book-length work of theory or criticism principally about American fiction before D. H. Lawrence's

Studies in Classic American Literature (1923) is widely read anymore except as "background."

For the most part, this was a Linnaean period, an era of diagnostic taxonomy: of ABC-level articulation of fictional elements – plot, character, theme; of endless parsing of a handful of controverted rubrics (realism, romance, regionalism, naturalism, etc.). As Mark McGurl wryly remarks of one symptomatic case, despite the "tedious imprecision" and "unwieldy semantic accretions" surrounding both terms, few pundits failed "to weigh in on the great, awful Realism–Romance Debate."[5] (See Jonathan Arac's chapter in this volume for Hawthorne's influential insistence on this distinction.[a]) Further muddying the critical waters was the tendency to invoke such categories as fixed entities but define them variously.

Yet turn-of-the-twentieth-century US fiction criticism can hardly be dismissed. For one thing, this messy impressionism formed the substructure for critical debates that persist to this day. Four especially deserve mention. One was the question of the primary distinctive mimetic register of US fiction. In particular, was it to be "realism" or "romance"? As we shall see, 1865–1920 was a heyday for realist claims, but they were neither wholly consistent nor universally accepted. Another issue was the extent to which the "Americanness" of US literature resided in the "part"– specificity of region, race, subculture – or in some broader national perspective. For turn-of-the-twentieth-century US critics, "American" effectively meant Euro-american, but regionalism was much more often held up as the preferred pathway to a distinctively American literature than it is today. Third, critics debated, as they still do today, the validity of conceiving US fiction apart from a wider transnational field. However, the discussion during these years centered exclusively on the issue of US literature's distinction from its Anglo-American antecedents and evinced a lingering postcolonial anxiety about persistent cultural dependence on British models and British critical opinion. The thought of US literature as having been significantly shaped by black Atlantic, transpacific, and/or hemispheric influences was scarcely conceivable. A fourth question was the responsibility of fiction and criticism to "art" versus social practice, a discussion that critics of the period carried on in what seems today a naïve and amateurish idiom that masks the similarities of the underlying divisions and allegiances. That all these issues were discussed before 1920 in emphatic but desultory fashion partly reflected a combination of salience and inherent difficulty that ensured their continuance on the

a Jonathan Arac, "Hawthorne and the aesthetics of American romance," chapter 8.

critical agenda long after "American literature" became an academic specialization.

In the process, the vocabulary of fiction criticism during 1865–1920 became more sophisticated even in spite of itself. Take "realism." Howells often sounded certain that he knew what "realism" was: "nothing more and nothing less than the truthful treatment of material," i.e., probable fictive characters and events rendered fully and precisely in their social interactions. Yet he also granted that "I do not expect a novel to be wholly true"; however we hide it, "the joint is always there, and on one side of it are real ground and real grass, and on the other are the painted images of ground and grass." And when it came to specifying what "truth" itself was, other than material objects, Howells confessed that he meant "truth to human experience," which "is so manifold and so recondite, that no scheme can be too remote, too airy for the test."[6] This in effect if not intent opened up the possibility of more subjectivist-experimental accounts of realism like Sherwood Anderson's "A Writer's Conception of Realism" (1939).

Anderson here insists that whatever "reality" is (he claims not to know), "the life of the imagination will always remain separated from" it. Far from being the "exact picture of Ohio village life" sometimes supposed, *Winesburg, Ohio* (1919) "was written in a crowded tenement district of Chicago," with "the hint for almost every character" taken "from my fellow lodgers." Indeed, "all of the so-called great realists were not realists at all and never intended being." Now set this anecdote of *Winesburg*'s genesis next to Upton Sinclair's of how personal privation catalyzed his journalistic investigation of the Chicago stockyards into *The Jungle* (1906): "Externally, the story had to do with a family of stockyard workers, but internally it was the story of my own family. Did I wish to know how the poor suffered in wintertime in Chicago? I had only to recall [our] previous wintertime in the cabin . . ."[7] Sinclair stresses the fit between external and internal landscapes, Anderson the mismatch; but both ground fiction in *some* actuality (for Sinclair, two actualities) with due recognition of the non-identity between the represented world and the inner authorial world. Such back-of-the-envelope pronouncements show an incipient awareness of the complications embedded in "realism" that later critics have labored to unpack.[8]

By the same token, it was during these years that the production, consumption, and social function of prose fiction began to be seen as deserving, indeed demanding, methodical analysis. Howells proposed that critics should "classify and analyze the fruits of the human mind very much as the naturalist classifies the objects of his study, rather than to praise or blame them."[9]

Objective professionalism, here likened to botanical science, was needed to offset the irresponsibilities of old-style sententiousness. Mark Twain was spoofing this turn toward "scientific" criticism when he lambasted James Fenimore Cooper for violating eighteen of the nineteen "rules" of romantic fiction.[10] Gertrude Stein tapped into a mentality already long in place in tracing her interest in character typology and variant to the psychological research she had done under William James at the turn of the century. The most famous, and most sweeping, of the period's art-as-science manifestos, Emile Zola's "Le Roman Expérimental" (1880), envisaged the model novelistic project in grandly reductionist terms: "to show the working of the intellectual and sensory manifestations such as physiology will explain them to us, under the influences of heredity and the surrounding circumstances," with "man living in the social milieu which he himself has produced . . ."[11]

Even more basic to these calls for greater rigor than their occasional appeals to science was the insistence on novel-writing as *discipline*: not only against whimsy but also against didacticism. For James, "questions of art" were questions "of execution; questions of morality are quite another affair." Even Frank Norris's vehement defense of "the novel with a 'purpose'" ("take from [fiction] the power and opportunity to prove that injustice, crime, and inequality do exist, and what is left?") went so far in distinguishing art from advocacy as to insist that "the page-to-page progress of the narrative" must have been "more absorbing" for Stowe as she composed *Uncle Tom's Cabin* "than all the Negroes that were ever whipped or sold"; otherwise, "that great purpose-novel never would have succeeded." (See Cecelia Tichi's chapter in this volume for intensive discussion of the relation of art and advocacy during this period.[b]) Norris's downpeddling both of Stowe's *agon* of composition and his own commitment to art as social practice is a telling barometer of the ongoing displacement of the prespecialized models of the writer as genius, prophet, public citizen, and amateur enthusiast favored by all the major antebellum writers but Poe.[12] Stowe herself lent partial support for the new professionalism in a series of how-to magazine essays giving tips to aspiring young women writers about the craft.

The view of fiction as craft was understood quite variously, however. For "serious" novelists, it meant a quest for what James called the "perfect work."[13] It made sense that the modernist aesthetic of difficulty evolved during these years, and with it the avant-gardist conception of "the few who make writing," as Stein put it.[14] It made sense that this was the era when an increasing number

b Cecelia Tichi, "Novels of civic protest," chapter 23.

of women writers of fiction as well as men started to think of themselves as devotees of craft, "writing for immortality"[15] – writers such as Sarah Orne Jewett, Willa Cather, Edith Wharton, Mary Austin – as Elizabeth Nolan's chapter in this volume explains in detail.[c] (And that Charles Chesnutt took African American fiction to an unprecedented pitch of stylistic refinement.) But craft-consciousness could just as easily be put to use in the burgeoning mass market. Already by the 1850s the largest book market in the Anglophone world, the United States in the late nineteenth century became the world leader in "machine-made fiction," as novelist-critic Robert Herrick mordantly observed.[16] James deplored the correlation between "the high prosperity of fiction" with "the vulgarisation of literature in general,"[17] but others could contend, as one dime novelist did, for the superior discipline required by formula fiction, whose readers "want every word in it made to help out the story."[18] (See Shelley Streeby's chapter in this volume for more on the relation between the "industrialization" of the dime novel and issues of craft.[d]) From a high canonical standpoint, the evolution of fiction during this period is the story of the modernist "art novel" as practiced by James, Conrad, and others emerging from middlebrow philistinism. Viewed in the most comprehensive terms, however, the main storyline between 1865 and 1920 is increasing marketplace differentiation, as the number of writers, readers, and publishing venues proliferated; as the players and to some extent also the publishers became more dispersed nationwide beyond their initially northeastern base; and as the realist aesthetic fashionable from the start of the period and predominant to the end started to fission in the later nineteenth century.

Realism and (some of) its discontents

Realism was well suited to be the option of choice for writers with a newly intensified sense of novel-writing as discipline who also sought a wide readership, "an aesthetic with a wide embrace," as Michael A. Elliott remarks of Howells elsewhere in this volume.[e] It was hardly the only game in town, as other chapters in this section make clear, e.g. Nancy Glazener's analysis of the phenomenal success of Du Maurier's topical psychological-gothic thriller *Trilby* (1895).[f] In addition, historical romance, frontier melodrama, and utopian fantasy, for instance, continued to thrive even more vigorously than before

c Elizabeth Nolan, "The woman's novel beyond sentimentalism," chapter 34.
d Shelley Streeby, "Dime novels and the rise of mass market genres," chapter 35.
e Michael A. Elliott, "Realism and radicalism: the school of Howells," chapter 17, 300.
f Nancy Glazener, "The novel in postbellum print culture," chapter 20, esp. 337–345.

the Civil War. Yet even these were inflected by realist practices, as with the period's biggest-selling novel, Lew Wallace's *Ben-Hur* (1880), a biblical-historical romance into which was packed an astonishing amount of minute narrative description based on the author's historical research; and the period's bestselling utopian fantasy, Edward Bellamy's *Looking Backward* (1888), a dream vision of the wonders of the year 2000 fleshed out in the form of a profuse documentary panorama, as future everyday realities.

Although realism's ground rules and social/philosophical underpinnings were not fully articulated until well after the modernist revolution, the novels themselves show a quite sophisticated working sense of its main premises. Realism and its principal offshoots, regionalism and naturalism, operate via "surveillance" of a social scene "subjected to a disciplinary spectatorial gaze."[19] Typically they use undramatized narration to create an illusion of transparency that seems to show rather than tell, even as character deployment is unobtrusively managed with care, e.g. by free indirect discourse. Take this glimpse, from Howells's *A Modern Instance* (1881), of the unfortunate heroine through the venal protagonist's eyes: "There were many things about his relations with Marcia Gaylord which were calculated to give Bartley satisfaction. She was, without question, the prettiest girl in the place, and she had more style than any other girl began to have. He liked to go into a room with Marcia Gaylord; it was some pleasure." The toned-down flatness enables, as florid rhetoric would not, subtle digs at Bartley's vulgarity. "The prettiest girl in the place"; "she had more style than any other girl"; "it was some pleasure" – these light ironic touches tip one off as to his coarseness of feeling and perception, as does the singsongy repetition of "Marcia Gaylord" and the metaphor of "calculation." Narrative realism functions as regulated surveillance (often, as here, of acts of surveillance), using its discursive seismograph to record tiny deviations from propriety. This obviously isn't going to be everybody's cup of tea. You have to get over your initial reaction against the generic boy-sees-girl bit as hopelessly insipid to notice how the narrative voice quietly slices Bartley to bits. Small wonder Sinclair Lewis, a realist of more emphatic bent, sneered that Howells "had the code of a pious old maid whose greatest delight was to have tea at the vicarage."[20] But Lewis himself didn't so much break from Howells's genteel spectatorialism as disrupt it from within, as when the fastidious heroine of *Main Street* (1920) is regaled by an amateur local vocalist in a Gopher Prairie parlor scene:

> Carol was shuddering with the vicarious shame which sensitive people feel when they listen to an "elocutionist" being humorous, or to a precocious child

> publicly doing badly what no child should do at all ... She tried to look admiring, for the benefit of Miss Sherwin, that trusting admirer of all that was or conceivably could be the good, the true, and the beautiful.

Compared to Howells, Lewis lays his satire on thick, but he too nuances his portrait in his own way, by playing hinterland middlebrow crudity off against Eastern finickiness. And he maintains the same ethnographic frame. This is the narrative-realist default practice throughout our period – and beyond. The ductility and variegation it admits help explain both realism's remarkable durability and its capacity, as we shall see below, for abetting the heresies of naturalism and modernism.

On the one hand, the spectatorial presider might subjectify by delegating the work of observation to center(s) of consciousness, as in Lewis, or in Edith Wharton's *House of Mirth* (1905), when the embattled heroine wakes up in her cousin's downscale bedroom:

> In the cold slant of light reflected from the back wall of a neighbouring building, she saw her evening dress and opera cloak lying in a tawdry heap on a chair. Finery laid off is as unappetizing as the remains of a feast, and it occurred to Lily, that, at home, her maid's vigilance had always spared her the sight of such incongruities.

Though Lily remains caught within the spectator's subtly denigrating gaze, more than in Lewis the passage acts as conduit for her chagrin, so that even the narrator's aphorism ("Finery laid off," etc.) seconds her distaste. Suppress the commentator further, and you enable the late Jamesean rhetoric, as in the following passage from *The Ambassadors* (1903):

> What he saw was exactly the right thing – a boat advancing around the bend and containing a man who held the paddles and a lady, at the stern, with a pink parasol. It was suddenly as if these figures, or something like them, had been wanted in the picture, had been wanted more or less all day, and had now drifted into sight, with the slow current, on purpose to fill up the measure. They came slowly, floating down, evidently directed to the landing-place near their spectator and presenting themselves to him not less clearly as the two persons for whom his hostess was already preparing a meal.

Here the protagonist Lambert Strether perceives the slow advance of a couple that turns out (several serpentine sentences later) to be Chad Newsome and Madame de Vionnet, an arrival that does indeed complete the "picture" – to everyone's consternation. The metaphor refers to an old-fashioned French landscape painting that's long haunted Strether and has drawn him hither in futile retreat from his patroness's solemn charge to retrieve her son from the clutches of his French mistress. This chance meeting will confirm what Strether has doggedly refused to believe: their relation *is* sexual. Like our previous passages, this is another frame-up. Indeed Strether is framed twice over, by the narratorial gaze and by the picture metaphor. Yet the device of making descriptive narration behave like impressionist painting (recognizable figures slowly congealing out of phrasal bits), is made possible by foregrounding the experience of spectatorship, making the scene focus itself through Strether's complex process of anticipation, visual alertness, and receptivity. Narrative overview begins to dissolve into something like a rendition of the motions of the mind at ground level.

Delegation of voice was no less important for realism than delegation of consciousness. One of realism's hallmarks, as in regional or "local color" fiction – place-based writing whose basic premise was to render symptomatic scenes of off-the-beaten-track districts and subcultures – was attempted scripting of the actual speech. Here Howells and James diverged. Dialogue interested James less as his style evolved. He advised Howells to use it more sparingly. Howells, by contrast, claimed he could fathom James's increasingly convoluted style best by reading through the conversational parts, then eking out what the rest might mean. He liked to mime or echo slangy, regional, and ethnic speech, like Bartley's twang. This was partly what drew him to Mark Twain, next to James his closest friend among leading contemporary novelists – a fact that says as much about realism's range as about Howells's receptivity. His relish for the perceived lifelikeness of nonstandard language led him to promote much more enthusiastically than others among the all-WASP critical establishment such writers as Paul Laurence Dunbar, Charles Chesnutt, and Abraham Cahan.

Of these, Chesnutt was the most consummate practitioner of spectatorial realism modulated by dialogue. The opening chapter of *The House Behind the Cedars* (1900), for instance, ends in a subtle counterpoint of looking versus not-looking, where the narrative overvoice describes the interruption of a "gentleman"'s covert scrutiny of a mysterious house at sensing he's been spotted by a black workman in a house across the street. "I jes' wonder who dat man is, an' w'at he's doin' on dis street," says this youth. His father-boss, still another surveillant, admonishes him to get back to work: "You spen's enti'ely too much er yo' time stretchin' yo' neck atter other people." Whereupon "the younger man resumed his work, but still found time to throw a slanting glance out of the window" as "the gentleman, he perceived," also ventures a last look before separating. This trivial bit of small-town vigilance conjoins two aspiring young men with consuming but discrepant interest in the mulatta heroine: her passing-as-white brother returned under an alias at risk to his safety, and her local admirer-from-a-distance. The clashing language registers, together with the furtive reciprocity with which they eye each other, foreshadow the firm-seeming but factitious social divide between them. As with realism's delegation of consciousness, dialect is kept within managed bounds. But linguistic delegation is as crucial to Chesnutt's social representation, here and elsewhere, as the delegation of interiority for psychological nuance is in later James.

Still another mutation of standard realism is destabilization of the convention of character coherence itself, as in Stephen Crane's *The Red Badge of Courage* (1895):

> To the youth the fighters resembled animals tossed for a death struggle into a dark pit. There was a sensation that he and his fellows, at bay, were pushing back, always pushing fierce onslaughts of creatures who were slippery . . .
>
> When, as in a dream, it occurred to the youth that his rifle was an impotent stick, he lost sense of everything but his hate, his desire to smash into pulp the glittering smile of victory which he could feel upon the faces of his enemies.
>
> The blue smoke-swallowed line curdled and writhed like a snake stepped upon. It swung its ends to and fro in an agony of fear and rage.

Amid the fog of war, individuality gets forced into type ("the youth"), deliberate choice into instinct ("he lost . . . everything but his hate"), and human into animal. In this telegraphic sequence, conscious perception degenerates into sensation and the soldiers' rage gets collectively bestialized into the panicky snake. But "sequence" is not the right term for the oscillation effect here and elsewhere – the jumpy reiterative perspectival shifts – although the narrative spectator device itself remains constant. In its emphasis on unleashed emotion and extreme action, its portrayal of character reduced to compulsion, its blurring of borderlines between human and animal, its fusion of individual with collective, *Red Badge* crosses the porous border between "realism" and "naturalism," even while maintaining a cerebral, aestheticized, distance from the spectacle of emotional chaos more akin to traditional realism, and not pursuing to the limit the hallmark naturalist storyline of the fall into oblivion and/or degeneracy *à la* Norris's *McTeague* (1899), Dreiser's Hurstwood in *Sister Carrie* (1900), or Crane's own *Maggie, A Girl of the Streets* (1890).

The passages we've surveyed should have demonstrated the logic of conceiving realist narration in the first instance as a strategy for maintaining top-down aesthetic – and with it ideological – control by giving transparency and orderliness to potentially refractory materials. Such control often included considerable self-censorship. Well might one doubt, with Peter Brooks, whether there ever was such a thing as Anglophone narrative "realism" if only given its evasion of sex relative to the French – and suspect American so-called realism of still greater timidity.[21] Howells freely granted that "between the editor of a reputable English or American magazine and the families which receive it there is a tacit agreement that he will print nothing which a father may not read to his daughter, or safely leave her to read herself."[22] James's writing, too, patently perpetuated the "immense omission" that as critic he ascribed to Anglophone fiction's chronic "mistrust of any but the most guarded treatment of the great relation between men and women."[23] Yet partly by dint of this same hypersensitivity to taboo, realism renewed itself by edging toward "forbidden" terrain, especially as it verged into naturalism, with its greater emphasis on physical and emotional turbulence, concentration on underclasses, interrogation of conventional morality and the myth of the free-standing individual. Indeed *A Modern Instance*, cited above as a work of quintessential realism, helped initiate this process, as the first major American novel to tackle the subject of divorce head on.

So too did realism extend itself "horizontally" as well as "vertically," toward mimesis of "the actual speech of the people," in keeping with the view that "dialect is the life of a language."[24] This conviction, of highest priority to advocates for proper representation of neglected non-mainstream subcultures, enabled a more calibrated representation of class, race, and region and consequent issues of cultural division, as we begin to see in Chesnutt. Yet linguistic differentiation could also produce encryption effects analogous to late Jamesean opacity, when much of the narrative work was delegated to non-mainstream voices, as in the greatest late nineteenth-century regional novels, George Washington Cable's *The Grandissimes* (1880) and Mark Twain's *Huckleberry Finn* (1884). But the *ne plus ultra* of linguistic encryption is the upcountry Vermont local colorist Rowland Robinson in *Sam Lovell's Boy* (1901): "Bah gosh, den Ah leek you for show you de Canada mans he an't rembler so much every day as de Yankee mans know all hees laf-tam!" Here a French Canadian man retaliates against the boy-protagonist Sammy's irritated ethnic putdown after hearing his juvenile success at fox-shooting derided. Antoine retorts, roughly, that a "Canada" man grasps as much in a day as a Yankee in a lifetime. Like most regional fiction, *Sam Lovell's Boy* is narrated in third-person standard English. Usually, and understandably, critics read such nested dialect as genteel condescension toward the low-life figures it thereby other-izes.[25] Carried beyond a certain degree of idiosyncrasy, though, dialect also cuts in a quite different direction, disorienting the reader-outsider and sometimes the characters themselves. Sammy understands Antoine's *words*, even as the reader struggles; but he's thrown into equal confusion by Antoine's strange pugnacious gesticulations (whereupon Sammy grabs a rock in self-defense); and even after things calm down he never figures out, much less do we, whether he overreacted. So the text drives home how semiotic opacity (body-language as well as words) spells trouble for cross-ethnic understanding.

Of all of the ways of turning realism against itself by pressing it to the limit, the most striking is to perturb the spectatorial narrative voice itself by warping it away from its customary role as lucid, stay-on-task rational analyst. Crane's semi-redundant telegraphic jumpiness and James's ponderous hesitancies inch toward that. But no American writer did so more purposefully to the end of modernizing narrative practice than Gertrude Stein. *Three Lives* (1909) and *The Making of Americans* (1908–1911, 1925), she wrote, aimed to elaborate "the complexities of using everything and of a continuous present and of beginning again and again and again."[26] Stein deconstructs realist objectivism through deadpan tonelessness (pushing neutralist narrative rhetoric to extremes), by exposing character individuation as permutation of type, and especially by reflexive contortions of standard managerial rhetoric, driving home the inherent redundancy of narrative exposition as such – tendencies that Peter Nicholls explores at more length elsewhere in this volume.[g] For Stein, the motor that drives it all is the inexhaustible attempt to comprehend "all kinds of men and women" (as she puts it in *The Making of Americans*), given minute idiosyncrasies, unstable lifelines, changing social relations, etc. Her repeated resetting of the narrative clock satirically liberates the "eternal present" occluded by the linear momentum of conventional realist plots.

Whether one sees it as an audaciously innovative "cubist" experiment in multiplication of minute gradients of perspective or as a dreary self-indulgent slog, *The Making of Americans* stands as the ultimate extension and undoing of panoramic realism before Dos Passos's *U.S.A.* (1930–1938). Indeed it's the most exhaustive satirical anatomy ever of an American (middle-class) family saga, particularly in its cornucopia of semi-interchangeable characters and its scripting of the thinness of social texture and historical amnesia (another motive for the restart device). Small wonder that (some) later American novelists, notably Anderson and Hemingway, tried their own versions of Stein's rhetorically monotoned, obsessively recursive prose. And small wonder Mary Austin, with no thought of Stein in mind, issued a synchronous prescription for

g Peter Nicholls, "Stein, Hemingway, and American modernisms" (chapter 37).

"The American Form of the Novel." "The democratic novelist," Austin declared, "must be inside his novel rather than outside in the Victorian fashion of Thackeray," striving "not so much for judgment as for revelation, quick, nervous appreciations of place, relationship and solidarity."[27] Taken together, the pronouncements and practices of this quite discrepant pair – the iconoclastic modernist and the dyed-in-the-wool regionalist – point to a prevailing conception of "American" fiction *circa* 1920 as tied at least tenuously to realist aesthetics but hardly the same as the conventional article.

American novel theory Americanized?

To self-identify as an American writer, as did even the expatriates James and Stein, was not in itself to see "the American novel" as formally distinct. American writers knew perfectly well that realism, naturalism, even regionalism were European imports. James was far more interested in Anglo-European fiction than American, and Howells almost as much so, despite being much more immersed in the American literary scene. The same held for most of those whose primary genre was literary history, like Barrett Wendell, or literary criticism, like Brownell.

Yet postcolonial anxiety about the need to define a distinctive national literary voice continued to run strong. In fiction theory, the key instance was the dream of "the great American novel," first sketchily defined by novelist John De Forest in 1868, although we find anticipations of the idea as early as the 1850s, as Ronald and Mary Zboray show in an earlier chapter in this volume.[h] The phrase became a critical mantra that, despite soon degenerating into a media cliché, persisted throughout the period. Howells often reverted to it; Norris, Dreiser, and Wharton all weighed in with critical essays that took the idea seriously. To a large extent the dream of the great American novel, or chimera, presupposed a realist aesthetic. De Forest's prescription was effectively a realist manifesto: the great American novel was to provide a recognizable portrait of the nation in all its geographic and social diversity. Indeed, he surely wrote with his own just-published novel in mind, *Miss Ravenel's Conversion from Secession to Loyalty* (1867), regularly cited as a realist breakthrough, which in fact deploys one of the favored structural templates for great American novel contenders: a plot that negotiates a sectional and/or racial divide via amatory or familial-dynastic tangles.[28]

h Ronald Zboray and Mary Zboray, "The novel in the antebellum book market," chapter 4, 76.

By ruling Hawthorne out as a provincial romancer, and holding up Stowe's *Uncle Tom's Cabin* (1852) as the nearest approximation, De Forest reopened two big critical agendas broached during the antebellum years: whether American cultural distinctiveness was imaginable except at a regional level, and whether "romance" might be the more appropriate vehicle for expressing American distinctiveness than the (realist) "novel." Both issues remained a subject of lively – and snarled – polemic. Norris, for example, argued yes on both counts, whereas British novelist Arnold Bennett, viewing Norris as a serious great American novel contender, read Norris's *The Octopus* (1901) as national rather than sectional and as "romantic-sociological" rather than "purely romantic."[29] But most discussions of how the novel might be properly Americanized attached themselves less to matters of form than to matters of content or ideology.

Position statements were often delivered as remedies for existing deficiency. Robert Herrick, for instance, found the American novel sexually inhibited, religiously effete (he prescribed a strong dose of Christian socialism), neglectful of the emerging "epic" of woman's "struggle for life and accomplishment," and culpable for failing to create a memorable embodiment of the "great epic figure" of recent times, the ruthless capitalist.[30] In retrospect, this Menckenesque excoriation seems oddly diffident: too self-critical to perceive what was underway. Such as Dreiser's *The Financier*, published that same year (1912). Or the imminent Melville revival. Or the string of American Nobel laureates in literature (all for fiction) starting in 1930. True, in 1920 "the American novel" was still working out its identity. No consensus had been reached as to what it should be. No serious critic was prepared to claim that the USA was anything like the international player in fiction that it was in economics or politics. Yet many more American novelists now imagined themselves as a part of a burgeoning cohort of significant practitioners than in 1865, when Hawthorne seemed the one unassailably canonical American novelist. A quarter-century later it had become second nature, both at home and abroad, to think of US fiction as having reached distinction by the early twentieth century if not well before.

Notes

For valuable research assistance, grateful thanks to Kimberly August and Margaret Doherty.

1. Nina Baym, "The Triumph of the Novel," in *Novels, Readers, and Reviewers: Responses to Fiction in Antebellum America* (Ithaca, NY: Cornell University Press, 1984), 26–43. Also see Barbara Hochman, "Readers and reading groups," chapter 36 in this volume.

2. William Dean Howells, "Novel-Writing and Novel Reading," in *Selected Literary Criticism, Volume III: 1898–1920*, ed. Ronald Gottesman *et al.* (Bloomington: Indiana University Press, 1993), 227; Frank Norris, "The Responsibilities of the Novelist," in *The Literary Criticism of Frank Norris*, ed. Donald Pizer (Austin: University of Texas Press, 1964), 95.
3. Henry James, "The Art of the Novel," in *Literary Criticism: Essays on Literature, American Writers, English Writers* (New York: Library of America, 1984), 44.
4. Elizabeth Renker, *The Origins of American Literature Studies* (Cambridge: Cambridge University Press, 2007).
5. Mark McGurl, *The Novel Art: Elevations of American Fiction after Henry James* (Princeton: Princeton University Press, 2001), 43.
6. William Dean Howells, *Criticism and Fiction*, ed. Clara Marburg Kirk and Rudolf Kirk (New York: New York University Press, 1959), 38; "Novel-Writing and Novel-Reading," 216, 222, 217.
7. Sherwood Anderson, "A Writer's Conception of Realism," in *The Theory of the American Novel*, ed. George Perkins (New York: Holt, 1970), 299; Upton Sinclair, *Autobiography* (New York: Harcourt, 1962), 127.
8. Contemporary US realism theory was catalyzed by Eric Sundquist, ed., *American Realism: New Essays* (Baltimore: Johns Hopkins University Press, 1981). On the subject of mimetic register, see especially Michael Davit Bell, *The Problem of American Realism* (Chicago: University of Chicago Press, 1993).
9. Howells, *Criticism and Fiction*, 20.
10. Mark Twain, "Fenimore Cooper's Literary Offenses," in *Collected Tales, Sketches, Speeches, & Essays, 1891–1910* (New York: Library of America, 1992), 180–192.
11. Emile Zola, "'The Experimental Novel," slightly modifying George J. Becker's translation in *Documents of Modern Literary Realism*, ed. Becker (Princeton: Princeton University Press, 1963), 174. On turn-of-the-twentieth-century American fiction's employment of social science-driven paradigms, see Nancy Bentley, *The Ethnography of Manners: Hawthorne, James, and Wharton* (Cambridge: Cambridge University Press, 1995), and Susan Mizruchi, *The Science of Sacrifice* (Princeton: Princeton University Press, 1998).
12. James, "The Art of the Novel," 62; Norris, "The Novel with a 'Purpose,'" *Literary Criticism of Frank Norris*, 93, 92.
13. James, "Art of the Novel," 63.
14. Gertrude Stein, "Composition as Explanation," in *Writings 1903–1932* (New York: Library of America, 1998), 523.
15. Anne E. Boyd, *Writing for Immortality: Women and the Emergence of High Literary Culture in America* (Baltimore: Johns Hopkins University Press, 2004).
16. Robert Herrick, "The American Novel," *Yale Review* 3, n.s. (April 1914): 424.
17. Henry James, "The Future of the Novel," in *Literary Criticism* (New York: Library of America, 1984),103.
18. Frederick Whitaker, "Dime Novels: A Defence [*sic*] by a Writer of Them," *New York-Tribune* (March 12, 1884).

19. Christophe Den Tandt, "American Literary Naturalism," in *American Fiction, 1865–1914*, ed. Robert Paul Lamb and G. R. Thompson (Malden, MA: Blackwell, 2005), 105, is a helpful, concise account drawing upon the Foucaultian analysis introduced into nineteenth-century American fiction scholarship by Mark Seltzer, *Henry James and the Art of Power* (Ithaca, NY: Cornell University Press, 1984).
20. Sinclair Lewis, Nobel Prize Address (1930), in Perkins, *Theory of the American Novel*, 307.
21. Peter Brooks, *Realist Vision* (New Haven: Yale University Press, 2005), 96; and Brooks, *Henry James Goes to Paris* (Princeton: Princeton University Press, 2007).
22. Howells, *Criticism and Fiction*, 75.
23. James, "The Future of the Novel," 107.
24. Hamlin Garland, *Crumbling Idols*, ed. Jane Johnson (Cambridge, MA: Harvard University Press, 1960), 62.
25. See especially Gavin Jones, *Strange Talk: The Politics of Dialect Literature in Gilded Age America* (Berkeley: University of California Press, 1999).
26. Stein, "Composition as Explanation," 525.
27. Mary Austin, "The American Form of the Novel" (1922), in *Selected Essays*, ed. Reuben J. Ellis (Carbondale: Southern Illinois University Press, 1996), 87.
28. Lawrence Buell, "The Unkillable Dream of the Great American Novel: *Moby-Dick* as Test Case," *American Literary History* 20.1 (2008): 132–155.
29. Norris, "The Great American Novelist," in *Literary Criticism of Frank Norris*, 122–124; Arnold Bennett, "The Future of the American Novel," *North American Review* 195 (January 1912): 83.
30. Herrick, "The American Novel," 425–435.

20

The novel in postbellum print culture

NANCY GLAZENER

America's runaway bestseller in 1895 was George Du Maurier's *Trilby* (1894), a novel that surged into prominence and soon receded, leaving behind mainly the epithet "Svengali" and a style of felt hat. Set in mid-century Paris, *Trilby* nostalgically depicts a bohemian community of artists and their devotion to Trilby O'Ferrall, a tomboyish artist's model who becomes a famous singer under Svengali's hypnotic tutelage. Americans' fascination with *Trilby* took many forms, and media coverage of the fascination became another manifestation of it. There were Trilby shoes and Trilby sausages, a Trilby ice cream concoction, Trilby clubs and Trilby parties (sometimes featuring Trilby tableaux). A dramatic version of *Trilby* was a hit; satirical parodies sent up the novel and the play; and because the novel used music in many pivotal scenes, concerts featured the songs in *Trilby* and new songs inspired by it. Even scandals were folded into *Trilby*'s popularity. The commemorative volume *Trilbyana* (1895), which reprinted reviews and articles about *Trilby*'s popularity, also documented James McNeill Whistler's charge that the novel libeled him, a controversy about whether Trilby's sexual involvements made the novel unsuitable for public libraries, and allegations that Du Maurier had plagiarized an earlier novel.[1]

Given the extraordinary public response to *Trilby*, its reception has been interpreted as a watershed in book marketing or even a sign of the consolidation of that slippery phenomenon, mass culture.[2] Although "mass-marketed" has become a handy term to indicate publications available to large and diverse readerships, especially non-elite readerships, "mass culture" has a special history as a term designating the effects of large-scale industrial production and distribution on cultural commodities and consumers.[3] The more scholars learn about the intricate and surprising possibilities of reception,[a] especially in cheeky fan cultures, the less plausible it is to assume that

a In this volume, Barbara Hochman's "Readers and reading groups," chapter 36, and DeNel Rehberg Sedo's "Twentieth- and twenty-first-century literary communities," audiences consume the products of mass culture passively and unthinkingly, as some early analysts proposed.[4] However, the task that initially led scholars to identify mass culture remains important: the work of understanding how increasingly industrial, standardized, rationalized forms of production and distribution affect people's relationships with commodified cultural products. This question can be taken up in a number of ways. Indeed, versions of this question are at stake in many contributions to this volume.[b]

Literature has often been cast as an alternative or antidote to mass culture, insofar as works of literature are credited with distinctiveness and lasting value.[c] However, the case of *Trilby* instructively refutes this distinction. In its heyday, *Trilby* was not only a popular sensation and but also, for most reviewers, a literary novel. "No one who wishes to keep abreast of the best fiction will neglect 'Trilby,' " insisted an 1894 review in *The Chautauquan*, a publication committed to serious culture and self-improvement.[5] The designation of a current novel as literary does not compel the admiration of readers (including academic readers, who play a special role in prolonging or shortening the careers of novels). However, it has long been possible to market novels on the basis of their literary value, even though marketing might seem to be at odds with literariness. By examining the culture of print commodities in which these marks of value operate, we can learn more about how the publishing industry has mediated readers' encounters with novels and novelists' access to readers.

From this perspective, American literary history is the history of an important domain of print culture whose boundaries are patrolled especially intensely and have often been disputed. The boundary-patrolling around the category of literature shapes novels inside and outside of it in important ways. Moreover, this boundary-patrolling is volatile: there are usually competing ideas

chapter 70, properly emphasize the fact that readers read in unpredictable ways, crossing and complicating the demographic categories envisioned by publishers, librarians, and print culture scholars.

b Essays in this volume which take up this question especially directly include Mary and Ronald Zboray's "The novel in the antebellum book market," chapter 4, 67, which discusses the early development of two "roads" leading to "serious literature" and "cheap popular literature" (as well as the wider range of publishing ventures); discussions by Stephanie LeMenager (chapter 31), Sean McCann (chapter 48), Pamela Regis (chapter 51), and Shelley Streeby (chapter 35) of the various negotiations, creative and otherwise, accomplished in mass-marketed genres; James West's discussion of the paperback as a mass-market form (chapter 47); Julia Mickenberg's account of processes by which children's literature was differentiated from mass-marketed genres aimed at young people (chapter 52); and Mark McGurl's presentation of twentieth-century novels' relationship to the emerging mass media (chapter 41).

c Jonathan Arac's "Hawthorne and the aesthetics of American romance"(chapter 8, 137–140) addresses some of the most important terms of literary value circulating around nineteenth-century fiction.

about what literature is and who has literary authority, and the competing ideas keep changing. Focusing on novels, this chapter will examine one of the most interesting transformations in American print culture: the coherence of a centralized national literary establishment during the decades after the Civil War, an establishment challenged by the emergence of several new sources of literary authority around the turn of the century. In spite of this turn-of-the-century reconfiguration, however, many publishing practices that were shaped by the special conditions of postbellum book publishing continued to affect literary culture into the twentieth century and even operate today.

Marketing literary fiction

Trilby was by no means the first novel to inspire clever merchandising as well as less commercial forms of homage in the USA. An American reviewer had diagnosed "Jane Eyre fever" as early as 1848, and only a few years later, Harriet Beecher Stowe's *Uncle Tom's Cabin* (1852) spun off successful dramatic versions, parodies, and collectibles.[6] However, *Trilby*'s publicity coincided with two important innovations that would wreak significant changes in print culture by the early twentieth century. One was the national tracking of bestsellers: *The Bookman* magazine began to compile comprehensive bestseller lists in 1894, motivating publishers to gear their operations to produce bestsellers. *Trilby* was one of the earliest novels publicized as a bestseller. The other was the emergence of a set of ten-cent magazines (*McClure's*, *Ladies' Home Journal*, and others) that undersold established periodicals of literary standing (such as *The Atlantic Monthly* and *Harper's Monthly*) to achieve unprecedented circulation figures.[7]

The most important mark of the literary aspirations held for *Trilby* is that it was serialized in *Harper's Monthly* – *not* one of the new high-circulation magazines – as a prelude to being published in book form by Harper & Brothers. Beginning before the Civil War and continuing for several decades afterward, it was a common publication pattern for a publisher to serialize a novel in its house magazine, issue it as a book, and then review it in the same house magazine.[d] Harper was one of a number of firms that laid claim to publishing literature, and these firms' house magazines usually reviewed each other's publications.[8] Dime novels and works of fiction published in story papers were usually not reviewed in these magazines, nor were books sold by

d About the origins of this practice before the Civil War and its place within an array of modes of publication, see Zboray and Zboray, (chapter 4, 71–72).

subscription or produced by religious presses.[9] Although any book that was reviewed could be panned, just getting noticed in these magazines meant that literary value was on the table.

Trilby's literariness was compounded by its association with Henry James, who had for two decades been established as a highly literary author. *Trilby* lore made much of the fact that James, a friend of Du Maurier's, had encouraged him to write novels and endorsed the premise of *Trilby* in particular. Indeed, a copy of the novel autographed by both Du Maurier and James was auctioned at a New York City fundraiser for the Kindergarten Association in 1895; J. Henry Harper's wife was prominent in that organization, completing the links between *Trilby*, its publisher, and an upper class that endorsed cultural goods such as literature.[10] Yet another sign of *Trilby*'s literary pedigree was the good reception of Du Maurier's previous novel, *Peter Ibbetson* (1891).[11] *Peter Ibbetson* even appeared as the literary standard at the top of a "reading ladder" constructed by library school students in 1902.[12] The ladders were designed to help librarians lead readers to better and better books that resembled novels they already liked (in this case, novels with supernatural elements), thereby promoting literary tastes.[13]

Neither the Harper & Brothers colophon, the sponsorship of Henry James, nor the authorship of Du Maurier could guarantee that critics would like *Trilby*. Nevertheless, these factors meant that the novel would receive literary attention, which doubled as a particular form of commercial exposure. *Trilby* was marked for anyone who bought, borrowed, or gift-wrapped it as a novel supporting the cultural enterprise known as literature. On the same grounds, it was also likely to be ordered by libraries (and it was, in spite of the controversy about its heroine's sexual history). Since literary attention, then as now, was characterized by discretionary judgment, novels marketed as literary could not be guaranteed to satisfy a given reader's or reviewer's sense of literary value. In the twentieth century, readers, reviewers, and academics came to find *Trilby* less satisfyingly literary, but at the time of its initial circulation, *Trilby* was a promising contender for literary approval.[14] Having an opinion about *Trilby* – even thinking it was overrated – was a way of participating in literary culture in 1895.

Trilby was marked as literary except in one respect: it included 120 illustrations by the author, a famous cartoonist for *Punch*. At the time, the number and character of illustrations in a commercial book connoted its status in complex ways. For example, an expensive *édition de luxe* might reprint a classic text innovatively bound, strikingly typeset, and swaddled in illustrations, turning the text into a collector's piece or an heirloom without jeopardizing its literary status.[15] On the other hand, subscription books peddled by traveling booksellers were ridiculed in literary culture for playing up their illustrations, as if more illustrations (or more expensive ones) made for a better book.[16] The standard practice of trade publishers such as Harper was to issue a current, serious literary novel either with no illustrations or with a frontispiece and three or four full-page illustrations, often of high quality. (Even an artist as famous as Winslow Homer produced some book illustrations.[17]) A similar practice governed the illustration of novels serialized in literary magazines. Edith Wharton and Henry James both disliked this format, perhaps because the illustrations tended to be keyed to pivotal moments in the novels, turning passages from the text into portentous captions. James's innovative choice to illustrate the New York Edition with photographs of locations mentioned in his novels achieved a subtler relationship between image and text.[18] Mark Twain, who supervised publication of his own works when he headed his own subscription publishing company, tried out another form of interplay by publishing *The Tragedy of Pudd'nhead Wilson* (1894) and other works with running marginal illustrations. (Figure 2 shows a page of *Pudd'nhead Wilson* featuring Twain as iconic author.) Perhaps because of Du Maurier's fame as an artist, and perhaps because *Trilby* participated in a *fin-de-siècle* trend of reclaiming the pleasures of childhood reading for adults, its copious illustrations did not appear to lessen its literary standing.[19]

The nation-state and the literary novel

As the case of *Trilby* suggests, the study of print culture makes trouble for familiar categories of literary history such as "the American novel." Because literary studies has been organized mainly according to national literary traditions, the transnational circulation of texts has only lately come into scholarly focus.[20] *Trilby*, an American bestseller whose primary publisher was based in the USA, was not an American novel, at least by the conventions of national literary traditions: it was written in England by a British citizen. However, its American success is only one instance of the many ongoing cultural interchanges between Britain and the USA that made nineteenth-century USA literary culture effectively Anglo-American.[e] American and British literary magazines kept tabs on each

e Paul Giles's "Transatlantic currents and the invention of the American novel," chapter 1 in this volume, recounts some of the important seventeenth- and eighteenth-century dimensions of novels that registered exchanges between North America and Europe, especially Great Britain. In keeping with this perspective, Bryan Waterman's "Charles Brockden Brown and the novels of the early republic" (chapter 3) emphasizes the importance of understanding Brown's career in an international context.

A WHISPER TO THE READER.

THERE is no character, howsoever good and fine, but it can be destroyed by ridicule, howsoever poor and witless. Observe the ass, for instance: his character is about perfect, he is the choicest spirit among all the humbler animals, yet see what ridicule has brought him to. Instead of feeling complimented when we are called an ass, we are left in doubt.—*Pudd'nhead Wilson's Calendar.*

A PERSON who is ignorant of legal matters is always liable to make mistakes when he tries to photograph a court scene with his pen; and so I was not willing to let the law chapters in this book go to press without first subjecting them to rigid and exhausting revision and correction by a trained barrister—if that is what they are called. These chapters are right, now, in every detail, for they were rewritten under the immediate eye of William Hicks, who studied law part of a while in southwest Missouri thirty-five years ago and then came over here to Florence for his health and is still helping for exercise and board in Macaroni Vermicelli's horse-feed shed which is up the back alley as you turn around the corner out of the Piazza del Duomo just beyond the house where that stone that Dante used to sit on six hundred years ago is let into the wall

15

2 Mark Twain, *The Tragedy of Pudd'nhead Wilson and the Comedy of those Extraordinary Twins* (Hartford, CT: American Publishing Company, 1894), 15.

other and reviewed new publications in both countries. Many British novels sold well in the USA, but the fact that *Trilby* was published after 1891, when the USA passed the Chace Act protecting international copyrights, made it easy for Harper & Brothers to protect its edition of the novel from the unauthorized reprinting that had been known as "piracy" even when it was legal.[21] The new bestseller lists were also made possible by this legislation, since pirating had made it hard to get a comprehensive count of any foreign novel's US sales.[22]

Amid this international circulation of manuscripts and publications, though, national conditions, ideologies, and laws shaped print culture in important ways. There is no way of knowing whether the US Congress deliberately fended off international copyright legislation until westward settlement had dissolved the frontier, but the political and economic project of developing national markets of readers was certainly advanced by the decades of convenient piracy.[23] The rupture of the Civil War, whose violence was often figured as birth-pangs of a new nation, made it important to produce a renovated national literary culture. Moreover, even before the Civil War, the US–Mexican War of 1848 and the doctrine of Manifest Destiny had laid the groundwork for an imperial dimension to the nation's identity.[f] A nation aspiring to the global influence of an empire needed to combine distinctive national virtues with cosmopolitan awareness of the other global players. In light of literature's role in the collective imagination, therefore, it made sense that inexpensive reprints of foreign (especially Anglophone) novels remained legal during the decades of rapid westward settlement. Like low postal rates for newspapers and legislation providing for public libraries, the availability of cheap reprinting fostered literacy and the habit of reading: equipment for citizenship and for print consumerism.[24]

Literary publishers mainly supported international copyright, but it is important to recognize that their advocacy was influenced by their market position as an informal cartel.[25] One mark of their mutual interest is the fact that in the period before the Chace Act was passed, literary publishers such as Harper – or rather, the men who headed these firms – made a gentleman's agreement to honor each other's informal contracts with British authors.[26] The practice was a boon to British authors and Anglo-American cultural relations, but it also reflected high-end publishers' tendency to present their work as a form of benevolent patronage

f In this volume, contributions by Russ Castronovo (chapter 32), Gretchen Murphy (chapter 33), Robert Reid-Pharr (chapter 28), and Shelley Streeby (chapter 25) also chart ways in which US fiction was affected by the nation's imperial incursions, ambitions, and self-understanding.

benefiting authors. Indeed, after the Civil War, these publishers wrapped their business in a worldly literary nationalism that could trend toward the promotion of US authors (as in the case of Ticknor & Fields and its successors, Fields & Osgood and Houghton, Mifflin & Co.) or the authorized presentation of the finest British literature to American readers (as in the case of Harper & Brothers). The gentleman-publishers similarly refrained from trying to lure authors away from each other, and some of them bitterly resented authors who began to insert literary agents into these friendly patronage relations.[27]

Literary publishers also worked in concert to distinguish trade publishing from subscription publishing, even though many trade firms, named for their reliance on third-party retailers, also had subscription departments.[28] By the mid-nineteenth century, firms that distributed their books mainly by sending traveling agents directly to customers were known as subscription publishers.[29] Since subscription publishers and mail order publishers (who included publishers of dime novel series and story papers) could reach readers in areas that could not support retail bookshops, these sectors of the publishing industry often made first contact with new readerships or readers in new locations.[30] This advantage may have fueled the vehemence with which literary commentators attacked the kinds of print texts that were distributed primarily or conspicuously by mail or direct sales. Story papers, dime novels, and subscription books were usually dismissed in literary culture as inferior and potentially contaminating,[31] in spite of Mark Twain's enthusiastic foray into subscription publishing with *The Innocents Abroad* (1869). These blanket dismissals invoked literary standards, but they targeted the sectors of the publishing industry most threatening to trade publishers.

Because most publishers used the US postal service to mail books or magazines to at least some distribution points or customers, postal regulations enabled another sort of national influence on literary culture: censorship. Modeled on Civil War anti-pornography legislation, the Comstock Act of 1873 (and related state laws) made it illegal to distribute printed materials deemed obscene – including information about birth control and abortion – through the US postal system. Under the Comstock laws, for example, there were successful prosecutions of booksellers and publishers who sold Zola's *La Terre* (1887) and Tolstoy's *Kreutzer Sonata* (1889), and Shelley Streeby describes in this volume Comstock's special animus toward dime novels. Even an unsuccessful prosecution, as in the case of James Branch Cabell's *Jurgen* (1919), or a threat of prosecution, as in the case of Dreiser's *The "Genius"* (1915), could discourage booksellers and make publishers wary.[32] The

Comstock laws also had trickle-down effects, since editors and publishers sometimes consulted Comstock's office about manuscripts before publication or simply internalized Comstock's standards of policing. When Harper & Brothers asked Du Maurier to cut certain sections of *Trilby* in the version serialized in *Harper's* (twenty-seven "passages referring to artist's models sitting in the nude, matters of Christian belief, [and] references to Jews and mistresses," as one scholar summarized them), the firm Americanized the novel in a way incalculably influenced by Anthony Comstock and his Society for the Suppression of Vice.[33]

Branding literary fiction

As the literary marking of *Trilby* and the collaboration among gentleman-publishers demonstrate, what we now know as branding – the creation of a recognizable market identity that entices consumers to buy a commodity and shapes their expectations of it – thrived in postbellum literary culture. The most obviously branded books were published in labeled series with uniform bindings and cover formats, such as George Munro's Seaside Library.[34] Each member of a series effectively advertised the others, so series provided one solution to the book trade's need to advertise disparate wares efficiently. The imprint of the Seaside Library did not carry literary weight, but its inclusion of literary novels such as George Eliot's *Middlemarch* (1871) marked the porousness of literary boundaries.[35] (Transatlantic piracy operated in both directions: Henry James was startled to spot a cheap edition of *The American* (1877) in an English railway book-stall just a few months after his novel was published in the US.[36]) There were also more upscale series. Advertising for Henry Holt & Co.'s Leisure Hour Series, begun in the 1870s, kept its literary potential in play even as it perpetuated a vision of novel-reading as casual, relaxed, and integrated into daily routines and holidays.

A publisher's list was yet another form of branding that had consequences for novels. When T. B. Peterson & Bros. of Philadelphia called itself the "Cheapest book house in the World," it appealed to thrift or savvy spending but made no attempt to present its offerings as anything other than consumer goods.[37] At the other end of the spectrum of branding, the mid-century firm Ticknor & Fields's blue and gold bindings of small, pocket-sized books made the very color combination of blue and gold signify a certain kind of high-culture literary claim, with the result that it was widely imitated.[38] Mark

Twain was even advised against binding *The Adventures of Huckleberry Finn* (1884) in blue because the color had been overused.[39]

Theodore Dreiser's *Sister Carrie* (1901) was a particularly notable casualty of the branding of publishers' lists. Frank Norris, a novelist working as a reader for Doubleday, Page & Co., was enthusiastic about the manuscript, and the firm's junior partner, Walter Hines Page, talked with Dreiser about publishing the novel. However, the senior partner, Frank Doubleday, strongly disapproved of the book, perhaps on the grounds that Carrie's sexual transgressions were never punished. The firm received legal advice that Page's oral contract with Dreiser was legally binding, so it published a small edition and refused to publicize the novel. Doubleday was "heard to say that . . . the book was bound to succeed sooner or later, and preferred that the stigma of its success should not rest upon his house."[40] Clearly, the character of a publisher's list could be a valuable asset.

The following year, Doubleday, Page & Co. published Thomas Dixon's *The Leopard's Spots: A Romance of the White Man's Burden, 1865–1900* (1902), with fanfare. The novel inaugurated Dixon's theme – developed in a trilogy whose second novel, *The Clansman* (1905), inspired D. W. Griffith's film *The Birth of a Nation* (1915) – that the terrorism of the Ku Klux Klan was justified by the evils of Reconstruction and "negro rule."[g] In retrospect it seems bitterly ironic that Dreiser's sexual frankness offended Doubleday while Dixon's white supremacy did not, during a period when violent attacks on African Americans were epidemic. Dixon's imperial nationalism was in tune with the dominant political culture of the day, as manifested in recent American bids to conquer or control Cuba, Guam, Puerto Rico, the Philippines, and Hawaii. However, even a reviewer who reviled *The Leopard's Spots* for spreading the "poison virus of imperialism" understood that the book made sense on its publisher's list. The reviewer grouped it with two other Doubleday novels, Allen French's *The Colonials* (1901), set in Revolutionary-era Boston, and Ellen Glasgow's *The Battleground* (1902), set in the Civil War, and noted the firm's recent prominence as a publisher of American historical romances.[41]

In this way, the branding of particular genres could contribute to the branding of publishers. Realism, the best-known genre of late nineteenth-century fiction, was promoted by establishment consensus because it held in

g In this volume, Robert F. Reid-Pharr's "The postbellum race novel" emphasizes the instructiveness of *The Leopard's Spots* for understanding the politics of race and empire at the turn of the twentieth century (chapter 28, 472–475).

solution potentially incompatible literary values: civic-political, aesthetic, and moral-emotional justifications for novels.[h] The very capaciousness of realism made it unwieldy for branding, but one of its varieties, regionalism, was a very serviceable literary brand. Regionalist writings – known at the time as works of "local color" – could often be identified by their titles or subtitles: witness George W. Cable's *The Grandissimes: A Story of Creole Life* (1880), Mary Noailles Murfree's *In the Tennessee Mountains* (1884), Mary Wilkins Freeman's *A New England Nun and Other Stories* (1891), Sarah Orne Jewett's *The Country of the Pointed Firs* (1896), Gertrude Atherton's *The Californian* (1898), and Booth Tarkington's *A Gentleman from Indiana* (1899). Authors of local color fiction responded especially astutely to the post-Civil War desire for cultural renovation. In place of the sectional opposition between North and South, they offered a peaceable array of regions whose distinctive histories and ways of life could be sampled without controversy.[i] The quasi-ethnographic mission of local color fiction aligned it with realism's emphasis on the empirical observation of culture, especially across the kinds of differences believed to make sympathy challenging and urgent. The promotion of local color fiction enabled northeastern-based publishers of books and magazines to demonstrate their national range and significance at a time when they were trying to develop national markets. Because local color fiction lent itself to short stories, the trend meant that publishers could groom writers from various regions on the low-overhead basis of short magazine fiction before issuing a novel or collection of short stories.

There is reason to believe that the genre of local color writing was initially a product of marketing (including reviewing) rather than authorial invention, although authors and readers made it their own. Its onset might be dated to

h In "Realism and radicalism: the school of Howells" (chapter 17), in his discussion of William Dean Howells's canon-setting advocacy of realist fiction, Michael Elliott also emphasizes how hard it is to pin down realism. Both Arac (chapter 8) and Lawrence Buell (chapter 19) emphasize the extent to which the distinction between realism and romance nevertheless organized many discussions of literary value in general and characteristically American literary developments in particular.

i Tom Lutz's "Cather and the regional imagination" (chapter 26) emphasizes the serious political and intellectual stakes of many regionalist works, a valuation process which I see as operating somewhat against the grain of the official promotion of regionalism in late nineteenth-century US literary culture. Enthusiasm in literary culture for the cross-sectional romances of the postbellum era discussed elsewhere in this volume by Jennifer Rae Greeson (chapter 14) and Reid-Pharr (chapter 28) might be examples of the same pacifying tendency. Elizabeth Nolan, in "The woman's novel beyond sentimentalism" (chapter 34), argues persuasively that many women writers in the early twentieth century took care to distance themselves from what they considered the constraining traditions of regionalism and sentimentalism.

1869, when Stowe's *Old Town Folks* was praised in a review for its "local color" and "pure American atmosphere." Also in 1869, Stowe's publisher, James Osgood, made contact with Bret Harte, the California writer who had recently published "The Luck of Roaring Camp" in the *Overland Monthly*. When Osgood issued a volume of Harte's short stories about California frontier life in 1870, a reviewer praised its "local color."[42]

The 1869 completion of the transcontinental railroad, emblem of the infrastructure for national distribution, symbolically linked Stowe in Connecticut and Harte in California under the sign of local color, opening a new possibility for breaking into literary fiction.[j] Under the auspices of local color, as Richard Brodhead has emphasized, a range of new authors founded careers, especially authors who had reason to think of themselves as literary outsiders.[43] The African American writers Paul Laurence Dunbar and Charles Chesnutt entered literary culture as local color writers on the basis of poems and stories that featured dialect speakers and settings in the antebellum South or the postbellum Black Belt. Local color may have had an impact on literary insiders as well. Henry James's development of the international novel, launched by *The American* (1877), makes sense in this context as a way of transposing local color fiction's characteristic encounter between an outsider (either a character or the implied reader) and a region to encounters between Americans and Europe or Europeans and the United States.

The edges of literature

Even though novels continued to be promoted and praised by being likened to the landmark *Uncle Tom's Cabin*, the powerful political and religious appeal of that novel was not really compatible with the restrained, officially secular version of literature that was being worked out in the decades after the Civil War.[k] The reviewer who stamped *Old Town Folks* as local color hinted delicately at this point, noting, " Generally as a work of art it is altogether of a higher type [than *Uncle Tom's Cabin*] . . . The striking realism of [Stowe's]

j Moreover, once regionalism or local color fiction was recognized as a genre, literary historians could trace ancestries for the representational strategies used in these novels. In this volume, Lutz's "Cather and the regional imagination" (chapter 26) traces a regionalist sensibility that began well before "local color" began to circulate as a generic label. Timothy Sweet's "American land, American landscape, American novels" (chapter 5) also addresses a number of regionalist works as instances of landscape writing and explorations of rural class relations.

k On the initial and continuing influence of *Uncle Tom's Cabin*, see John Ernest's "Stowe, race, and the antebellum American novel," chapter 15, 259–264.

pictures is unimpeachable."[44] Novels that made people want to become part of movements – such as Edward Bellamy's *Looking Backward: 2000–1887* (1888), which inspired clubs dedicated to Bellamy's futuristic utopian vision, or Charles M. Sheldon's *In His Steps: What Would Jesus Do?* (1897), one of several novels influential in the Social Gospel movement – were not valued highly in literary culture.[l] If these novels were even reviewed in literary periodicals, they tended to be deprecated or treated gingerly (as when *Appleton's* review of the Rev. E. P. Roe's religious novel *Barriers Burned Away* (1872) observed, "The work is well calculated to please the religious reader").[45]

Succeeding on literary terms could even undercut a novel's political potential. This was the case with Helen Hunt Jackson's *Ramona* (1884), which the author had planned as a reform novel supporting her nonfiction indictment of the government's treatment of Native Americans, *A Century of Dishonor* (1881). "If I could write a story that would do for the Indian a thousandth part of what *Uncle Tom's Cabin* did for the Negro, I would be thankful the rest of my life," Jackson vowed before starting *Ramona*.[46] Contrary to her hopes, *Ramona* was overwhelmingly and lovingly received as a local color work about the history of Southern California, thereby demonstrating the potential for genres to outwit authors. Moreover, illustrators of the novel tended to depict Ramona as Spanish,[m] even though her mother was Native American, so that Ramona's story was assimilated to the romantic Spanish heritage of ranchos rather than the US history of injustice toward Native Americans.[47]

Ramona's reception, together with the constraints experienced by African American literary successes such as Chesnutt and Dunbar,[n] suggests why

l Elsewhere in this volume, Cecelia Tichi's "Novels of civic protest" (chapter 23) advocates rethinking this traditional literary hostility to political commitments understood as "propaganda," while Alan Wald's "Steinbeck and the proletarian novel" (chapter 40) details a related twentieth-century controversy over the literary value of proletarian fiction.

m For a related discussion of the cultural work of *Ramona*, see Gretchen Murphy's essay in this volume, "The hemispheric novel in the post-revolutionary era," chapter 33, 564–566.

n Scholarship about both Chesnutt and Dunbar recounts constraints on their literary careers, due partly to white readers' and editors' presuppositions about minority writers, and partly to the white-dominated literary establishment's squeamishness about works of literature – at least by African Americans – that used violence to criticize white racial oppression. In this volume, see especially Elliott's discussion of Howells's double-edged support for these writers (chapter 17, 301–302), Hochman's account of Chesnutt's difficulty in publishing *The House Behind the Cedars* (1900) (chapter 36, 605), and Barbara McCaskill's account of both writers' efforts to counter racist presuppositions (chapter 29, 488–490, 495–496).

some novelists with serious political and religious commitments might have been skeptical of the literary establishment. An active Christian press, mainly organized by specific denominations and their Sunday-School movements; an emerging Jewish press, including publications in English and Hebrew; publications serving specific immigrant populations; and a range of presses with political commitments, such as the Populist-Progressive Arena Publishing Company – all of these published some fiction, novels that could envision spiritual and social renovation without observing the political or aesthetic constraints at work in literary culture.[48] No wonder that Harriet Beecher Stowe effectively managed a double life in print, addressing specifically Christian readerships in certain publication venues but taking care not to alienate them when she published in the more secular (though Protestant-inflected) literary magazines.[49]

In spite of the controversy generated by the canon wars of the late twentieth century, most of the novelists that came to be rediscovered had been highly respected in literary culture during their lifetimes – a fact that can tell us a great deal about the circumstances that conditioned their aspirations. Charles Chesnutt, Kate Chopin, Paul Laurence Dunbar, Mary Wilkins Freeman, Charlotte Perkins Gilman, Sarah Orne Jewett, Elizabeth Stuart Phelps, and Albion Tourgée were all authors whose works were marked as literary, for example. An instructive exception is Sutton E. Griggs, who is now well known but who was definitely not a literary insider during his lifetime. Griggs operated his own press in Memphis, Tennessee, and sold his novels directly to readers, most of them African American.[50] Although his novels share many features in common with literary novels from the same era, the most important contexts for his work were remote from the literary establishment of his day: the black Baptist Church and the political force field generated by the relationship between black nationalism and African American visions of interracial cooperation.

As Griggs's example suggests, the importance of subscription publishing and religious publishing for African American readers in rural areas has only begun to be understood, especially given the astounding increases in African American literacy between 1880 and 1910.[51] Griggs, who owned more than 2,000 books at the time of his death, was part of a generation of black ministers moving to a greater reliance on print culture and literacy.[52] There is no evidence that Griggs even tried to place manuscripts in the highly literary venues where Chesnutt and Dunbar published, and it seems unlikely that he would have succeeded.[53] His first novel, *Imperium in Imperio* (1899), whose publication he financed, depicted a secret African American conspiracy to launch an independent nation based in Texas; among his writings, this work has received the most attention from academic critics.[54] His subsequent self-published novels moved away from revolutionary possibilities to social criticism, but they indicted white violence and political corruption more directly and unapologetically than was common before the Harlem Renaissance.

Griggs conducted his career as a novelist outside of literary culture, even though he didn't lack writerly confidence. His career nevertheless maintained dialogue with literary culture, evinced by the National Baptist Convention's vote to support a novel by Griggs that would offer a "suitable answer" to Dixon's *The Leopard's Spots* (1905).[55] As it happens, Dixon had been a Baptist minister before making a career as a writer, and the title of *The Leopard's Spots* references Jeremiah 13:23, "Can the Ethiopian change his color, or the Leopard his spots?"[56] Griggs's answering novel, *The Hindered Hand*, countered by referencing Psalms 68:31, "Princes shall come out of Egypt; Ethiopia shall soon stretch forth her hands unto God," a passage crucial to the black Christian tradition of Ethiopianism that provided support for black nationalism.[57] In a domain of print culture invisible to the literary establishment, *The Hindered Hand* reframed Dixon's novel as part of an argument among Christians.

The reconfiguration of literature in the early twentieth century

The ten-cent monthly magazines that invaded the turf of *Harper's* and the *Atlantic* initially relied on the literary judgments of the establishment whose monopoly they challenged. For example, the *Ladies' Home Journal*, which reached a circulation of one million in 1903, combined articles about domestic management with fiction by writers who were already stamped as literary. William Dean Howells's *The Coast of Bohemia* was *LHJ*'s eyecatching serial in 1892–1893.[58] Whereas many of the older magazines owed their existence to their implicit function of advertising books, the high fees that the new magazines paid to authors were made possible by high revenues generated by ads for national brands of household commodities.[59] Lavishly illustrated, with a new emphasis on cover and layout design, these magazines' success in recruiting and promoting literary authors was one symptom of a shake-up in literary publishing, a transformation that James West's contribution to this volume examines in relation to long-term trends within the publishing industry.[60]

Although these new high-circulation magazines nurtured some important fiction-writers – such as Willa Cather, a protégée of *McClure's* proprietor S. S. McClure – and supported many more, these magazines were not designed to mark their contents as literary in the decisive way that their predecessors had done. Rather, the new magazines helped to circulate the work of authors whose literary stature was established elsewhere: by the old literary monthlies that survived; by new magazines with bold cultural and political platforms; by upstart book publishing firms that crafted new literary platforms; and by university-based intellectuals, now that universities were developing increasingly close ties with public literary culture.[61] Innovative publishing firms such as Boni and Liveright, Random House, and Alfred A. Knopf carved out literary reputations by publishing modernists (including poets, of course) and edgier, grimmer realist authors such as Dreiser and Sherwood Anderson.[62] These publishers' literary standing was established in part by reviews of their books in both the older and the newer literary magazines (including *The Yale Review*, for which Edith Wharton recruited writers).[63]

In the diversified literary culture of the new century, writers with literary aspirations could do business in multiple literary currencies. Sherwood Anderson, for instance, published his first short story in the venerable *Harper's* in 1914 soon after he published manifesto essays in the opening issues of the gutsy, flamboyantly anti-establishment magazine *The Little Review*, whose publisher would be prosecuted in 1920 for serializing chapters from James Joyce's *Ulysses* (published in Paris in 1922).[64] (*The Little Review* was one of a number of periodicals nicknamed "little magazines" because they valued innovation and commitment more than large circulations.) Anderson also published early chapters from *Winesburg, Ohio* (1919) in the radical journal *The Masses* around the time he was trying to place his novel *Windy McPherson's Son* (1916) with either of two long-established firms, Henry Holt and Company or Macmillan.[65]

Moreover, novelists now changed book publishers more casually, as James West details elsewhere in this volume, and usually made their own arrangements for serialization or excerpted publication. In this respect, authors gained more control in branding their bodies of work (including selling the rights for translations and stage and film adaptations) than they had had before 1900 or so, with the result that they were likely to be more aware of managing their authorship as a brand. As Jonathan Auerbach has described, Jack London deliberately managed his authorial brand in relation to a particular narrative context – the Yukon, initially – and conceived of his name as a trademark, very much as Mark Twain had done.[66] By the early twentieth century, there was no longer a cartel to discourage authors or their agents from negotiating the best possible financial deal for each novel. Indeed, the expanded field of literary publication multiplied the possible print environments in which readers might encounter a literary novel and, therefore, the varieties of branding and recontextualization that might affect an author's works.

It is remarkable, for example, that Edith Wharton's Pulitzer Prize-winning novel, *The Age of Innocence* (1920), was first presented to American readers as a serial in the house magazine of a dressmaking pattern company. Wharton's novels were published in book form by long-established firms such as Appleton and Macmillan, but around 1916 she began to serialize her novels on the most profitable terms she could arrange. The *Pictorial Review*, which had a circulation of 2 million at the end of World War I, was one of the six bestselling women's magazines of the era and paid Wharton well. However, in its pages, *The Age of Innocence* was bordered by advertisements for nationally branded household products – including Rexall laxatives and Heinz Oven-Baked Beans – as well as columns with expert advice about parenting and Dolly Dingle paper dolls to cut out.[67] In this respect, the serialization of *The Age of Innocence* was tailored to women readers in the professional-managerial class that coalesced in the early twentieth century (as Richard Ohmann has charted), a class that channeled the Progressive movement's faith in secular expertise and scientific management into consumer culture and homemaking.[68]

Any serialized novel is encountered by readers within the general context of a magazine's brand as well as within the contexts of its layout on the page and its juxtaposition with other contents of the issue. These contexts can reinforce, undermine, or reinterpret features of the novel in significant ways. In the case of the serialization of *The Age of Innocence*, the aspirations and emotional dramas of the novel's contrasting main female characters are amplified and inflected by the surrounding text. The *Pictorial Review* was perhaps the most feminist of the high-circulation women's magazines, explicitly supporting women's suffrage and emphasizing women's successes in various fields of work.[69] Its commitment to women's political independence and careers shored up Wharton's depiction of Ellen Olenska, Newland Archer's free-spirited cosmopolitan love interest, but the dressmaking magazine's baseline domesticity resonated with the character of May Archer, Newland's wife.[o] An

o Jennifer Fleissner explores ways in which active consumerism integrated into the greater autonomy of the New Woman in "Wharton, marriage, and the New Woman," chapter 27 in this volume.

inset plot summary asking "Was Ellen Olenska justified in seeking a divorce?" was indirectly answered in the same issue by an article lobbying for more liberal, nationally consistent divorce laws.[70] However, the layout of *The Age of Innocence* in the *Pictorial Review* also brought some powerfully domestic illustrations and poems into the novel's orbit, echoing May's possessive wifely stance in the novel. Figure 3 shows the placement of Sara Teasdale's poem "The Strong House" within the layout of the novel, so that the poem appears to fill in May's emotional experience – not presented directly in the novel – by voicing a woman's uneasy concern that someone is trying to invade the "strong house" of her love.[71]

The print culture world in which *The Age of Innocence* was serialized was different from the one in which Edith Wharton had first formed her literary ambitions. She had begun her career as a novelist publishing in the old-fashioned way, serializing *The House of Mirth* (1905) in *Scribner's Monthly* before Charles Scribner & Sons published it as a book. That *The Age of Innocence* helped sell household products in the *Pictorial Review* in 1920 tarnished Wharton's reputation not at all. Indeed, her literary reputation was so solid that when the Pulitzer Prize committee proposed giving the prize to Sinclair Lewis's *Main Street* (1920), the Columbia University trustees awarded the prize instead to *The Age of Innocence*, objecting that Lewis's novel did not uphold American values.[72] Although the trustees' reading of *The Age of Innocence* might not be ours – and might not have been shared by Lewis, who went on to dedicate *Babbitt* (1922) to Wharton – Wharton's characters may have been integrated into the national project of post-World-War domestic consumerism by the *Pictorial Review* in a way that Lewis's dissatisfied Carol Kennicott had not been.

Rather than upholding a distinction between literature and mass culture, then, the study of print culture reveals that every work of fiction issued by the publishing industry is shaped by the organization of that industry, including its market stratification and characteristic forms of competition. Publication is at once a physical process by which print materials are manufactured in specific forms and an economic process by which these materials are given significance as commodities. In both aspects, publication involves novels in networks of cultural meaning that negotiate forms of value, especially relationships to literary value. For all these reasons, it makes sense to understand publication as constitutive of a published novel, rather than treating publication as something separate or extraneous that happens to some novels and not others. What would Edith Wharton have written if she had not been aiming at publication? What would Edith Wharton have written if her own novel-reading had not

22 *Pictorial Review for September, 1920*

THE STRONG HOUSE

By SARA TEASDALE

OUR love is like a strong house
Well roofed against the wind and rain—
Who passes darkly in the sun
Again and again?

THE doors are fast, the lamps are lit,
We sit together talking low—
Who is it in the ghostly dusk
Goes to and fro?

SURELY ours is a strong house,
I will not trouble any more—
Who is it stealing at midnight
To try the locked door?

Drawings by Kerr Eby

3 Sara Teasdale's "The Strong House" inset in an installment of *The Age of Innocence*, *The Pictorial Review*, September 1920, 22.

consisted mainly of novels selected for publication, novels that she encountered in particular forms determined by the state of the publishing industry? To the extent that these questions are unanswerable, hypothetical to the point of being absurd, we can see how crucial the study of print culture is to the study of novelists' aspirations. Equally importantly, the study of print culture sheds light on what novels can mean and do for readers as well as what they have already meant and done.[73]

Notes

1. J. B. and J. L. Gilder, eds., *Trilbyana: The Rise and Progress of a Popular Novel* (New York: The Critic Co., 1895).
2. L. Edward Purcell identified the success of *Trilby* as a factor contributing to publishers' reorientation around the production of bestsellers in "Trilby and Trilby-Mania, the Beginning of the Bestseller System," *Journal of Popular Culture* 11 (1977): 62–76; Emily Jenkins located the reception of *Trilby* as an important early moment in mass culture in "*Trilby*: Fads, Photographers, and 'Over-Perfect Feet,'" *Book History* 1 (1998): 221–267. Jenkins relies heavily on Richard Ohmann's persuasive, nuanced discussion of mass culture, which emphasizes the "homogenization" of cultural products but not the "passivity" or "uniformity" of audiences. Richard Ohmann, *Selling Culture: Magazines, Markets, and Class at the Turn of the Century* (New York: Verso, 1996), 14.
3. Many studies have explored ways in which literary or high cultural forms and mass or low cultural forms were interdependent or similar during this period. One especially comprehensive discussion is Nancy Bentley's "Literary Forms and Mass Culture, 1870–1920," in Sacvan Bercovitch, ed., *Prose Writing 1860–1920*, vol. III of *The Cambridge History of American Literature* (New York: Cambridge University Press, 2005), 63–284.
4. The foundational critique of mass culture as standardized and manipulative can be found in "The Culture Industry: Enlightenment as Mass Deception," a chapter in Max Horkheimer and Theodor W. Adorno, *Dialectic of Enlightenment*, trans. John Cumming (New York: Continuum, 1986), 120–167. Originally published as *Dialektik der Aufklärung* (New York: Social Studies Association, 1944).
5. "Talk about Books," *The Chautauquan* (November 1894): 253.
6. The phrase "Jane Eyre fever" was coined in a review article, "Jane Eyre, An Autobiography," *North American Review* (October 1848): 354; it inspired recent analysis in Cree LeFavour, "'*Jane Eyre* Fever': Deciphering the Astonishing Popular Success of Charlotte Brontë in Antebellum America," *Book History* 7 (2004): 113–141.
7. *Trilby* was in second place as an American bestseller of 1895 behind Ian Maclaren's *Beside the Bonnie Brier Bush* (1894); however, neither Maclaren's novel nor the other bestsellers for 1895 surpassed the publicity around *Trilby*. Alice Payne

Hackett and James Henry Burke, eds., *80 Years of Best Sellers, 1895–1975* (New York: R. R. Bowker, 1977), 59.

8. About the magazines' collaborative construction of an understanding of literature, see Nancy Glazener, *Reading for Realism: The History of a U.S. Literary Institution, 1850–1910* (Durham, NC: Duke University Press, 1997), 20–50.
9. Subscription publishers and religious publishers overlapped significantly. Indeed, the antebellum book pedlars who were agents of religious publishers were known as *colporteurs*, and their practices – along with those of some antebellum agents of trade publishers – provided a model for the lively subscription publishing business that emerged after the Civil War. Ronald J. Zboray and Mary Saracino Zboray, *Literary Dollars and Social Sense: A People's History of the Mass Market Book* (New York: Routledge, 2005), 129–139, 187–190; David Paul Nord, *Faith in Reading: Religious Publishing and the Birth of Mass Media in America* (New York: Oxford University Press, 2004), 110–111.
10. *Trilbyana*, 11–12, 20; Purcell, "Trilby and Trilby-Mania," 71.
11. Sample favorable reviews are "Recent American and English Fiction," *Atlantic Monthly* (May 1892): 694–707, and "Peter Ibbetson," *The Literary World* (January 2, 1892): 3.
12. Esther Jane Carrier, *Fiction in Public Libraries 1900–1950* (Littleton, CO: Libraries Unlimited, 1985), 202.
13. About the civic mission of librarians, see Barbara Hochman's essay in this volume (chapter 36, 603–608). Three important sources analyzing the intellectual and civic roles of librarians (as well as libraries' crucial role in circulating and valuing books) are Dee Garrison, *Apostles of Culture: The Public Librarian and American Society, 1876–1920* (New York: Free Press, 1979); Thomas Augst and Wayne Wiegand, eds., *Libraries as Agencies of Culture* (Madison: University of Wisconsin Press, 2002); and Thomas Augst and Kenneth Carpenter, eds., *Institutions of Reading: The Social Life of Libraries in the United States* (Amherst: University of Massachusetts Press, 2007). An instructive study of the way a particular library functioned in the postbellum decades is Christine Pawley, *Reading on the Middle Border: The Culture of Print in Late-Nineteenth-Century Osage, Iowa* (Amherst: University of Massachusetts Press, 2001).
14. For the sake of simplicity, this chapter will use "literary" to refer to the literary aspirations established by a book's marketing as well as to the canonicity accorded to works taught and studied within the academy long after their initial publication.
15. A good guide to American book illustration, including *éditions de luxe* by private presses that influenced trade publishing, is Gerald W. R. Ward, ed., *The American Illustrated Book in the Nineteenth Century* (Winterthur, DE: Wintherthur Museum; distributed by the University Press of Virginia, 1987), especially Susan Otis Thompson's essay "The Arts and Crafts Book in America," 171–200.
16. See for example "On the Inspiration of the Moment," *Scribner's Monthly* (November 1880): 167.

17. David Tatham, "Winslow Homer," in *American Book and Magazine Illustrators to 1920*, ed. Steven E. Smith, Catherine A. Hastedt, and Donald H. Dyal, vol. CLXXXVIII of *The Dictionary of Literary Biography* (Detroit: Gale Research Company, 1998), 153–165.
18. On Wharton's dislike of illustrations, see John Tebbel, *The Expansion of an Industry 1865–1919*, vol. III of *A History of Book Publishing in the United States* (New York: R. R. Bowker, 1975), 666; about James's response to book illustration practices and the photographs in the New York Edition, see Ralph Bogardus, *Pictures and Texts: Henry James, A. L. Coburn, and New Ways of Seeing in Literary Culture* (Ann Arbor: UMI Research Press, 1984), 51–74.
19. On the wave of enthusiasm for novels that simulated or appropriated the reading pleasures of childhood, see Glazener, *Reading for Realism*, 147–188.
20. Novels circulated internationally and took on transnational significance in ways too diverse to summarize, but an illuminating example from recent scholarship is the publication of several of Edith Wharton's novels in Macmillan's Colonial Library, marketed to India, Canada, and other parts of the empire; Shafquat Towheed, ed., *The Correspondence of Edith Wharton and Macmillan, 1901–1930* (Houndmills, Basingstoke, Hampshire: Palgrave Macmillan, 2007), 15–16, 22.
21. On antebellum pirate reprinting, see Ronald and Mary Saracino Zboray, "The novel in the antebellum book market" (chapter 4). For more on the Chace Act and its relation to American book publishing, see Michael Winship, "The Transatlantic Book Trade and Anglo-American Literary Culture in the Nineteenth Century," in *Reciprocal Influences: Literary Production, Distribution, and Consumption in America*, ed. Steven Fink and Susan S. Williams (Columbus: Ohio State University Press, 1999), 98–122; and Meredith L. McGill, "Copyright," in *The Industrial Book, 1840–1880*, ed. Scott E. Casper, Jeffrey D. Groves, Stephen W. Nissenbaum, and Michael Winship, vol. III of *A History of the Book in America* (Chapel Hill: University of North Carolina Press, 2007), 158–177.
22. Hackett and Burke, *80 Years of Best Sellers*, 59.
23. Historian Frederick Jackson Turner first analyzed the closing of the frontier in a famous paper delivered in 1893, relying on the conclusion drawn by the Superintendent of the Census for 1890. Frederick Jackson Turner, *The Frontier in American History* (Huntington, NY: Robert E. Krieger Publishing Company, 1976), 1. The continuing settlement of the country meant that the postbellum decades provided the opportunity for even the most successful antebellum publishers to continue reaching more remote populations. On publishers' forays into bigger geographical markets before the Civil War and the crucial problem of distribution, see Zboray and Zboray (chapter 4); and Meredith L. McGill, *American Literature and the Culture of Reprinting, 1834–1853* (Philadelphia: University of Pennsylvania Press, 2003), 270.
24. On the impact of postal rates for story papers that included novels, see Tebbel, *The Expansion of an Industry*, 38–40.
25. About publishers who did and did not support international copyright at various junctures, *ibid.*, 637–640.

26. On this practice, see Jeffrey D. Groves, "Courtesy of the Trade," in Casper and Groves, *Industrial Book*, 139–147. Correspondence among Henry Holt, Henry Harper, Daniel Heath, and other publishers negotiating informal proprietary rights to particular authors and works can be found in Ellen D. Gilbert, ed., *The House of Holt, 1866–1946: A Documentary Volume*, vol. CCLXXXIV of *The Dictionary of Literary Biography* (Detroit: Gale Research Company, 2003), 39–43.
27. Henry Holt, "The Commercialization of Literature," *The Atlantic Monthly* (November 1905): 580. An important exposé of the financial practices of publishers who followed the patronage model was Gail Hamilton's *A Battle of the Books* (1870). The significance of Hamilton's critique for women authors in particular is examined by Susan S. Williams in *Reclaiming Authorship: Literary Women in America, 1850–1900* (Philadelphia: University of Pennsylvania Press, 2006), 124–150. James West discusses the important role agents would play in helping novels navigate the twentieth-century marketplace of literary publishing and related media in "Twentieth-century publishing and the rise of the paperback" (chapter 47, 784–785).
28. On trade publishers' reliance on traveling subscription agents, see Madeleine B. Stern, "Dissemination of Popular Books in the Midwest and Far West during the Nineteenth Century," in *Getting the Books Out: Papers of the Chicago Conference on the Book in 19th-Century America*, ed. Michael Hackenberg (Washington, DC: Library of Congress, 1987), 76–97; and Sarah Wadsworth, *In the Company of Books: Literature and its "Classes" in Nineteenth-Century America* (Amherst: University of Massachusetts Press, 2006), 74. Tebbel also discusses trade publishers' use of direct sales in the early twentieth century, *The Expansion of an Industry*, 16–18.
29. The practice which gave subscription publishing its name, that of enlisting subscribers in advance to offset the costs of publication, became less common in the nineteenth century, although sometimes subscription sales began in advance of printing. Marjorie Stafford, "Subscription Book Publishing in the United States, 1865–1930" (MA thesis, University of Illinois at Urbana, 1943), 1, 30. Stafford's thesis remains one of the most comprehensive studies of subscription publishing.
30. About subscription agents making contact with remote readers, see Hackenberg, "The Subscription Publishing Network," in *Getting the Books Out*, 45–75; and Lisa Lindell, "Bringing Books to a 'Book-Hungry Land': Print Culture on the Dakota Prairie," *Book History* 7 (2004): 215–238. An invaluable compilation of documents used by subscription canvassers is Keith Arbour, *Canvassing Books, Sample Books, and Subscription Publishers' Ephemera 1833–1951 in the Collection of Michael Zinman* (New York: Ardsley, 1996).
31. "[A]n author of established reputation, who resorts to the subscription plan for the sake of making more money, descends to a constituency of a lower grade and inevitably loses caste," according to one commentator. "Subscription Books," *The Literary World* (August 1, 1874): 40. On Twain's career in subscription

publishing, see Bruce Michelson, *Printer's Devil: Mark Twain and the American Publishing Revolution* (Berkeley: University of California Press, 2006).

32. Edgar MacDonald, *James Branch Cabell and Richmond-in-Virginia* (Jackson: University Press of Mississippi, 1993), 206–207, 244–245; Richard Lingeman, *Theodore Dreiser: An American Journey* (New York: John Wiley & Sons, 1993), 127–140.
33. Louis N. Feipel, "The American Issues of 'Trilby,' " *Colophon* 2 (1937): 541. There is no direct evidence that *Harper*'s cuts responded to the Comstock Act, but a satirical poem in which Comstock threatened Trilby demonstrates Americans' continuing awareness of Comstock's power. C. S. A., "Anthony, Censor," *Liberty* (June 16, 1894): 1. On the secondary effects of Comstock laws, see Tebbel, *The Expansion of an Industry*, 611–622.
34. The granddaddy of cheap libraries was Routledge's Railway Library in England, founded in 1848; its offerings were visually uniform (known as "yellowbacks," as James West, chapter 47, 789–790, discusses) and portable (one volume, compared to the three-decker then common in England). John Feather, *A History of British Publishing*, 2nd edn. (London: Routledge, 2006), 106–111. In the USA, the earliest series of this sort issued by a book publisher appears to have been the Lakeside Library begun by Donnelley, Loyd & Co. in 1875. Wadsworth, *In the Company of Books*, 112; Tebbel, *The Expansion of an Industry*, 298.
35. Wadsworth, *In the Company of Books*, 121. Wadsworth identifies series such as the Seaside Library with branding on 133.
36. Leon Edel, *Henry James: A Life* (New York: Harper & Row, 1985), 214.
37. Tebbel, *The Expansion of an Industry*, 488. Zboray and Zboray discuss the Peterson firm elsewhere in this volume (chapter 4, 73).
38. Wadsworth's chapter 6, "A Blue and Gold Mystique," discusses the influence of Ticknor & Fields's most famous binding (*In the Company of Books*, 161–183). See also Jeffrey D. Groves, "Judging Literary Books by Their Covers: House Styles, Ticknor and Fields, and Literary Promotion" in *Reading Books: Essays on the Material Text and Literature in America*, ed. Michelle Moylan and Lane Stiles (Amherst: University of Massachusetts Press, 1996), 75–100.
39. *Huckleberry Finn* ended up being available to subscribers in either green or blue bindings. Michelson, *Printer's Devil*, 84, 123–124.
40. Accounts of the Doubleday / Page response to *Sister Carrie* conform exactly to *The Bookman*'s report of a publisher's remarks about an unnamed book, so I have attributed the quotation reported in *The Bookman* to Doubleday. The *Bookman* columnist cagily recounted the suppression of the unnamed book across the page from his notice that *Sister Carrie* was about to be reissued by another press. "Chronicle and Comment," *The Bookman* (March–April 1902): 11. About the firm's grudging publication of the novel, see Richard Lingeman, *Theodore Dreiser: An American Journey* (New York: John Wiley & Sons, 1993), 159–169. For discussions of the innovative sexual politics of *Sister Carrie* in this volume, see Jude Davies, "Dreiser and the city," chapter 22, 386–389, and

Jennifer Fleissner, "Wharton, marriage, and the New Woman," chapter 27, 452–453.

41. "Three Epochs of American History Mirrored in Fiction," *The Arena* (August 1902): 218, 215.
42. "Oldtown Folks," *Every Saturday* (October 9, 1869): 200, 197; "Editorial Notes," *Putnam's Magazine* (June 1870): 722.
43. Richard H. Brodhead, *Cultures of Letters: Scenes of Reading and Writing in Nineteenth-Century America* (Chicago: University of Chicago Press, 1993), 116–118.
44. "Oldtown Folks," 197.
45. "Literary Notes," *Appleton's Journal* (January 11, 1873): 90.
46. Helen Hunt Jackson to Thomas Bailey Aldrich (May 4, 1883), in *The Indian Reform Letters of Helen Hunt Jackson*, ed. Valerie Sherer Mathes (Norman: University of Oklahoma Press, 1998), 258.
47. As Gretchen Murphy explains ("The hemispheric novel in the post-revolutionary era," chapter 33, 565), *Ramona* was repoliticized – and Ramona affirmed as a *mestiza* – when the novel was translated in 1887 by José Martí as a text important for Cuban independence and indigenous nationalisms within the Americas. This important connection was raised by Susan Gillman in "Otra Vez Caliban / Encore Caliban: Adaptation, Translation, Americas Studies," *American Literary History* 20.1–2 (2008): 187–188. For *Ramona*'s role in the production of a popular version of California history, see Dydia DeLyser, *Ramona Memories: Tourism and the Shaping of Southern California* (Minneapolis: University of Minnesota Press, 2005); on the depiction of Ramona in illustrations, see Michelle Moylan, "Materiality as Performance: The Forming of Helen Hunt Jackson's *Ramona*," in Moylan and Stiles, *Reading Books*, 233–247.
48. About religious publishing, Paul C. Gutjahr, "Diversification in American Religious Publishing," in Casper and Groves, *Industrial Book*, 194–202; and Tebbel, *The Expansion of an Industry*, 540–559. About immigrant presses, see Wadsworth, *In the Company of Books*, 198–199.
49. In spite of strict patrolling by reviewers in religious periodicals, Stowe was loyal to this readership and seems to have managed her appearance in secular publications with care. Joan D. Hedrick, *Harriet Beecher Stowe: A Life* (New York: Oxford University Press, 1994), 334.
50. W. E. B. Du Bois believed that Griggs had a larger African American readership than any other writer of the time. Wilson Jeremiah Moses, *The Wings of Ethiopia: Studies in African-American Life and Letters* (Ames: Iowa State University Press, 1990), 224; Finnie D. Coleman, *Sutton E. Griggs and the Struggle against White Supremacy* (Knoxville: University of Tennessee Press, 2007), 23.
51. On the gains in literacy and other resources that made rural African Americans likely customers for subscription books, see Michael Benjamin, "Print Culture, Agency, and Africanity: The Origins and Meaning of Murray's 'Historical and Biographical Encyclopedia of the Colored Race Throughout the World'" (PhD dissertation, Drew University, NJ, 2007), 175–205. Elizabeth McHenry emphasizes gains in African American literacy betweens 1880 and 1930 in a study of

literary societies and reading rooms that promoted both literacy and active citizenship on the part of African Americans. Elizabeth McHenry, *Forgotten Readers: Recovering the Lost History of African American Literary Societies* (Durham, NC: Duke University Press, 2002), 4. Frances Smith Foster discusses African Americans' involvement in denominational Christian publishing in "African Americans, Literature, and the Nineteenth-Century Afro-Protestant Press," in Fink and Williams, *Reciprocal Influences*, 24–35.

52. On Griggs's book collection, see Roy Kay, "Sutton E. Griggs," in *African-American Authors, 1745–1945: A Bio-Bibliographical Critical Sourcebook*, ed. Emmanuel S. Nelson (Westport, CT: Greenwood Press, 2000), 189. On Griggs's link to a generation of ministers promoting literacy and print culture, see Evelyn Brooks Higginbotham, *Righteous Discontent: The Women's Movement in the Black Baptist Church, 1880–1920* (Cambridge, MA: Harvard University Press, 1993), 43–44.
53. Griggs was interested in getting his novels reviewed and recognized nationally, however: he sent some of his novels to influential African American intellectuals and to a number of publications for review. Griggs mentions several newspapers that reviewed his books, and *The Hindered Hand* was reviewed in *Alexander's Magazine*, a short-lived African American magazine (Moses, *The Wings of Ethiopia*, 212, 236). It is not known where Griggs sent all the review copies of his novels, but *Frank Leslie's Popular Monthly*, a general New York magazine, received *Imperium in Imperio*. "New Books Received," *Frank Leslie's Popular Monthly* (August 1899): 448. Sutton E. Griggs, *The Story of My Struggles* (Memphis, TN: The National Public Welfare League), 8–13.
54. *Imperium in Imperio* was published by the Editor Publishing Company of Cincinnati, whose advertisements in literary magazines suggest that it was a vanity press (see *The Literary World* [July 9, 1898]: 224, and *The Dial* [August 1, 1899]: 82). Griggs's *The Story of My Struggles* also implies that the selling and marketing of *Imperium* was left to Griggs alone (8–9).
55. Griggs notes that "The promised support of the National Baptist Convention never came," but it isn't clear whether the convention had made a financial commitment or merely endorsed the book. Griggs, *Story of My Struggles*, 12–13.
56. Raymond A. Cook, *Thomas Dixon* (New York: Twayne Publishers, 1974), 65.
57. Moses, *The Wings of Ethiopia*, 231.
58. Frank Luther Mott, *A History of American Magazines*, 5 vols. (Cambridge, MA: Harvard University Press, 1957), IV:538–545.
59. On the development of national brands and national advertising, see Ohmann, *Selling Culture*, 82.
60. Brad Evans's work, which pays ample attention to publication design, suggests that established magazines and book publishers were also undergoing aesthetic renovation around the time the new high-circulation magazines were being launched. Brad Evans, *Before Cultures: The Ethnographic Imagination in American Literature, 1865–1920* (Chicago: University of Chicago Press, 2005), 82–151.

61. Although American literature was not securely established as an academic discipline until the 1920s or 1930s, by the late nineteenth century the academic credentials and positions of university-based intellectuals added to the authority with which they wrote in public literary culture. About the slow and contested institutionalization of American literary studies, see Gerald Graff, *Professing Literature: An Institutional History* (Chicago: University of Chicago Press, 1987); Elizabeth Renker, *The Origins of American Literature Studies: An Institutional History* (Cambridge: Cambridge University Press, 2007); David R. Shumway, *Creating American Civilization: A Genealogy of American Literature as an Academic Discipline* (Minneapolis: University of Minnesota Press, 1994); and Gerald Graff and Michael Warner, eds., *The Origins of Literary Studies in America: A Documentary Anthology* (New York: Routledge, 1989).
62. One reason why there was room for new literary publishers is that a number of older literary publishers encountered financial problems in the early twentieth century; the new firms that thrived tried out new business practices, such as the regular preparation of royalty statements, and were open to experimentation. Some of the new firms were also headed by Jews moving into publishing outside the WASP-dominated postbellum establishment. Kim Becnel, *The Rise of Corporate Publishing and Its Effects on Authorship in Early Twentieth-Century America* (New York: Routledge, 2008), 9–11, 55–58.
63. On Wharton's connection to *The Yale Review*, see Frank Luther Mott, *A History of American Magazines*, vol. v (Cambridge, MA: Harvard University Press, 1968), 336. Wharton first published in *The Yale Review* in 1919, and she received an honorary D.Litt from Yale in 1923. Edgar F. Harden, *An Edith Wharton Chronology* (New York: Palgrave Macmillan, 2005), 61; Hermione Lee, *Edith Wharton* (London: Chatto & Windus, 2007), 598–599.
64. Walter B. Rideout, *Sherwood Anderson: A Writer in America*, 2 vols. (Madison: University of Wisconsin Press, 2006), 1:174, 181. Mott, *History of American Magazines*, 174.
65. "Windy McPherson's Son" was rejected by Henry Holt in 1913 and submitted to Macmillan some time before 1915; the British-based firm John Lane finally published it. Anderson had been friends with an associate editor of *The Masses* since 1913 and published two Winesburg stories there in early 1916. Rideout, *Sherwood Anderson*, 212–214.
66. Jonathan Auerbach, *Male Call: Becoming Jack London* (Durham, NC: Duke University Press, 1996), 18–20, 26–28, 228–229.
67. *The Age of Innocence* was serialized in the *Pictorial Review* in the issues of July–August 1920, September 1920, October 1920, and November 1920. About the magazine's circulation, see Kathleen Endres, "*Pictorial Review*," in *Women's Magazines in the United States: Consumer Magazines*, ed. Kathleen L. Endres and Therese L. Lueck (Westwood, CT: Greenwood Press, 1995), 276. Edie Thornton discusses the serialization of Wharton's *The Mother's Recompense* (1925) in the *Pictorial Review* in her essay "Selling Edith Wharton: Illustration, Advertising, and *Pictorial Review*, 1924–1925," *Arizona Quarterly* 57.3 (Fall 2001): 29–59. An

excellent discussion of a division of ideological labor between advertisements and other features of a magazine is Martha Banta's "Periodicals Back (Advertisers) to Front (Editors): Whose National Values Market Best?" in Fink and Williams, *Reciprocal Influences*, 173–198.

68. Ohmann, *Selling Culture*, 119–221.
69. Endres, "*Pictorial Review*," 276–277.
70. The inset box appears in *Pictorial Review* (October 1920): 24. In the same issue, see Helen Ring Robinson, "Taking 'The Cure' at Reno: Why Can't We Have a Uniform Divorce Law?" 17.
71. Sara Teasdale, "The Strong House," *Pictorial Review* (September 1920): 22. The illustrations accompanying the poem link the ungendered speaker to the woman depicted.
72. Richard Lingeman, *Sinclair Lewis: Rebel from Main Street* (New York: Random House, 2002), 183–184.
73. I am grateful to Finnie D. Coleman and Alisha R. Knight for insights into Sutton E. Griggs's career; to William C. Daw of the University of Pittsburgh Library System for assistance with illustrations; and to Marah Gubar for guidance about the history of juvenile fiction for girls.

21

Twain, class, and the Gilded Age

ANDREW LAWSON

In 1865, with the South defeated and the peculiar institution of slavery finally eradicated, American capitalism had what Vernon Parrington called "its first clear view of the Promised Land."[1] Liquid capital which had accumulated in Philadelphia and New York banks during the war could now be released into railroads, stockyards, refineries, and mills. Suddenly, there were vast new fortunes to be made from livestock, timber, steel, petroleum, and wheat, as well as unparalleled opportunities for corruption. America may have been a "vast, uniform middle-class land," in which every citizen was putatively "dedicated to capitalism," but government subsidies, tariffs, and land-grants were carefully steered toward the corporate elite, in what Parrington dubbed "the great barbecue."[2] Most notoriously, the Philadelphia banker, Jay Cooke, obtained 50 million acres of western lands for his Northern Pacific Railroad and established a separate company, the Credit Mobilier, to channel subsidies directly into the pockets of company directors, while the railroad's coffers were opened to provide Republicans with sweeteners in the form of campaign money and railroad stock. Ordinary Americans had believed in an open society, one that was competitive and fluid, in which entrepreneurial energy and ingenuity would be rewarded. Now it appeared that "amoral wealth-seekers" were blocking access to the "social escalator."[3] An onlooker at this spectacle was Samuel Langhorne Clemens, who, as Mark Twain, became both a sharp critic of capitalist excess and the virtual spokesman for a confused and contradictory middle class, buffeted and transformed by the period he named the Gilded Age.[4]

Twain was a child of the frontier lower middle class. His father, John Marshall Clemens, was of an old Virginian family which had suffered financial losses. The father's indigence meant that the son had to go out into the world to shift for himself. As his career developed, Sam Clemens made the primal clash between the genteel and the uncouth central to the comedic self-constitution of a "new, westward-moving middle class."[5] Cultural historians have settled on a broad definition of the middle class as "those families who, while lacking great wealth or long-established social prominence, gained comfortable livings from nonmanual occupations."[6] In the post-Civil War period, a growing professional cadre of lawyers, physicians, dentists, pharmacists, and engineers was joined by a newly expanded corps of business managers and corporate employees – accountants, advertisers, wholesalers, insurance agents, traveling salesmen – along with increasing numbers of public-service personnel, all of them sporting the crisp, detachable collars that saved on laundry bills and gave the white collar workforce its name. Finding itself uncomfortably positioned between the capitalist class of financiers, speculators, and railroad barons, and an increasingly immiserated industrial workforce, the salaried middle class retreated en masse to the streetcar suburbs, where it evolved its own "normative ideal of culture": polite, refined, relentlessly uplifting. In parlors replete with patterned wallpaper, miniature plaster sculptures, and chromolithographic prints, the new middle class sought to defuse class conflict in an atmosphere of "evasive banality."[7] But what these histories have overlooked is that the post-Civil War middle class, as it expanded, was itself transformed by its new surroundings.[8] Here, in an unformed society, where Victorian propriety and genteel cultural standards had less prescriptive force, a different cultural tone was set by a more relaxed middle class, one that was still polite, but more at ease with itself, still anxious about status and in want of information, but needing to be entertained. The young Sam Clemens witnessed the emergence of the new middle class on the frontier at first hand.

In 1861, Clemens journeyed to the Nevada Territory, where his brother, Orion, had landed a government post. Clemens took a job as a reporter for the *Territorial Enterprise* in Virginia City. The Washoe area, booming after the discovery of the Comstock Lode of silver ore, was a visibly stratified society where cock fights competed with lyceum lectures and fine wine sat alongside tarantula juice.[9] Here, the Northeast's normative ideal of culture was opposed and travestied at every turn.

In a series of burlesques and extravagant hoaxes published in the *Enterprise*, Clemens perfected what became the Mark Twain voice: ably described by Ron Powers as "iconoclastic, exuberantly outsized, funny, instinctively populist, and intensely observant."[10] Whether providing hyperbolic descriptions of extravagant ball gowns, or telling the story of the body of a petrified man found in the desert, Twain gave the impression of speaking directly into the ear of his listener, displaying evidence of a finely honed native wit. Contained in Twain's sly whimsy was an "implicit invitation to throw off adult decorum," as well as a capacity for moral indignation.[11] That mix was what made Mark Twain so beguiling and irresistible to the new middle class of clerks, shopkeepers, and small professionals who found themselves caught between elite pretension and frontier roguery. This readership welcomed the racy frontier tales of Bret Harte, editor of the *Californian*, who won national fame with his stories "The Luck of Roaring Camp" (1868) and "The Outcasts of Poker Flat" (1868), and went on to write the bestselling novel *Gabriel Conroy* (1876). Harte's gallery of gamblers, prostitutes, and miners, with their heavily inflected dialogue and uncouth manners, helped to create the vogue for "local color," and marked an important literary advance by daring to suggest that apparently vulgar figures on the margins of polite society could also act morally, with "hearts of gold." If the "hustler energy" of the Gilded Age was "retool[ing] factories, new stores, and proliferating railroads," then writers like Harte and Twain were engaged in the process of retooling polite literature to meet the demands of a "new-blooming audacity of the Self, a Self set loose from old pietistic constraints."[12]

Many of the key authors of nineteenth-century fiction began their careers as travel writers: William Dean Howells's first success was *Venetian Life* (1866), while Henry James produced a volume of *Transatlantic Sketches* (1875). Twain's first book was the story of his journey to the Holy Land on an excursion sponsored by Henry Ward Beecher's Plymouth Church, *The Innocents Abroad* (1869). Knowing that his readers were people who wanted to be "amused into respectability rather than sermonized into refinement," Twain built "the first great popular mass reading audience for an individual writer in the nineteenth century."[13] In its first year, *The Innocents Abroad* sold over 70,000 copies and remained Twain's bestselling book during his lifetime.

Twain's early travel writing prompted him to call for fiction to "cease to lie about life," to "portray men and women as they are," and to "speak the dialect, the language, that most Americans know – the language of unaffected people everywhere."[14] But while the travel writing of Howells and James is cultivated and high-toned, Twain's capacity for independent vision is matched by a consciousness of his difference from the old middle class, satirized as irremediably stuffy, inhibited, and genteel. If Southwestern humor thrives on the friction between the genteel and the plebeian, Twain explores a similar zone of tension within the middle class. In *The Innocents Abroad*, he mocks "solemnity, decorum, dinner, dominoes, prayers, slander" on behalf of the middle classes' newly arrived frontier cousins, eager both to learn the rules of Eastern highbrow culture and to bend them, infusing them with the more unruly, vital energies of the West.

Twain's second book, *Roughing It* (1872), revisits the flush times of the Nevada silver mines. Twain's flexible skill in yarn-spinning indicates the extent to which his new middle-class readership was making itself up: improvising, dreaming, fabricating a future and an identity in the new cultural space the West opened up. This space is as yet uncharted, an indeterminacy which the tacked-on "moral" of the book implies: "If you are of any account, stay at home and make your way by faithful diligence; but if you are 'no account,' go away from home, and then you will *have* to work, whether you want to or not." Dry and matter of fact, ironic and self-aware: this is virtually a manifesto for the frontier middle class, who are of "no account" in the sense that they are under-capitalized venturers on new territory. *The Innocents Abroad* and *Roughing It* are not merely travelogues but guide books for this venture, pedagogic aids in the anxious and uncertain process of class-formation. The next stage of Twain's career saw him moving both geographically and culturally, as he left the new frontier middle class behind and joined the professional middle class of the Northeast.

One of Twain's fellow passengers on the trip to the Holy Land was the seventeen-year-old Charles Jervis Langdon. Twain married Langdon's sister Olivia in 1870, while Langdon Senior set him up as the proprietor of the Buffalo *Express* newspaper, as well as gifting the couple a $40,000 house. Twain's process of entry into the Northeastern middle class was completed when, in 1875, he built a spacious and well-appointed house in the Nook Farm suburb of Hartford, Connecticut. Over the course of three months in 1873, Twain and his Connecticut neighbor, Charles Dudley Warner, took turns in writing alternate sections of a novel, reading passages aloud for the amusement of their wives.

Twain begins *The Gilded Age* (1873) with thinly disguised autobiography. Ultimately, the novel is less a straightforward satire of grossly speculative parvenus on behalf of a moral middle class than a kind of fantasy compromise with the new cultural and economic order. Philip Sterling, the New Englander-turned-frontier surveyor repents of his speculative habits, and settles down to a "regular profession" studying law. The woman he left behind, Ruth Bolton, constructs a proto-feminist rebellion against her Quaker parents and embarks on a medical career before she realizes that she has pushed her "theories of a certain equality of power" too far. They become an affianced couple on the basis of a mutual recognition of insufficiency and limitation, rather than the dream of limitless wealth and instant abundance. But Philip persists with the mining enterprise he has acquired even after his capital is exhausted. Laying off his men, he sets the charges and wields the pick-axe himself, in a last-ditch display of manly exertion. Philip combines good solid work with feverish speculation, and at last finds the coal seam which has eluded him. While he nurses Ruth, "worn down with work [,]" back to health, Mr. Bolton brings the wealth of the mine to market. The New England gentleman (as represented by Charles Dudley Warner) has been invigorated by the frontier (as represented by Mark Twain), and fastidious Eastern capital replenished by sharp practice. The novel's cultural work is thus to present a testament to the capacity for the self-renewal of the middle class: as the Chinese epigraph has it, "[b]y combined strength, a mountain becomes gems: by united hearts, mud turns to gold."

At first blush, Twain's next novel, *The Adventures of Tom Sawyer* (1876), constitutes an exercise in unalloyed nostalgia for the lost world of boyhood innocence, simplicity, and wonder. When Tom sheds the restraints of "modern civilization" to join his friends Joe Harper and Huckleberry Finn on Jackson's Island, Twain's prose acquires the quickened pulse, the heightened sense of license, of the Nook Farmer on vacation, "bound[ing] away barelegged, with fluttering shirt" to feast "in a wild free way in the virgin forest." On one of their picnics, Huck improvises a pipe from a corn cob, and smokes "in the full bloom of luxurious contentment"; in the "cool dim grey of the morning" the boys awake to "a delicious sense of repose and peace," before swimming naked in the river, "chasing after and tumbling after each other in the shallow limpid water of the white sand-bar." Huckleberry Finn, "the juvenile pariah of the parish," represents the unconfined, sensual world of what Freud called oceanic feeling, "dreamy, reposeful, and inviting." Invented by Mark Twain, the professional writer of Nook Farm, he acts as tour guide to the "Delectable Land" of free white boyhood, as seen from the shore of the "harassed," the "hampered," the "respectable." Huck occupies an alternative economy of primitive wealth in which one desire is swapped for another. When he first appears, he carries a dead cat, bought for "a blue tick and a bladder." Before long, Tom has traded his loosened tooth for one of Huck's ticks; on Jackson Island, Tom hides "certain school-boy treasures of inestimable value" in his hat, "among them a lump of chalk, an india rubber ball, three fish-hooks, and one of that kind of marbles known as a 'sure 'nough crystal.' " Huck has no need of, and is in fact allergic to, what he calls "cussed smothery houses."

But throughout the novel Twain blends nostalgia with accommodation to more commercial imperatives. Tom has shown himself to be thoroughly entrepreneurial in outlook by persuading his friends to whitewash Aunt Polly's fence and pay him for the privilege, insouciantly coordinating their efforts like one of the new breed of business executives described by Alfred Chandler, who subject the anarchy of market forces to rational scrutiny and control.[15] Like a parody of a Gilded Age robber baron, Tom gives himself "a nice, good, idle time" and ends up "rolling in wealth." He then uses the profits to buy up the Sunday school tokens his friends have earned for memorizing Bible passages, substituting sharp dealing for "industry and application." The passage, with its uneasy blend of satire and celebration, indicates the extent to which Twain could be critical of the get-rich-quick mentality and still equate success with business acumen.[16] The business of Twain's novel is to make Tom's enterprise pay off in cash terms, while purifying it of narrow, mercenary motives, instilling the quest for profit with the spirit of boyhood adventure by setting both protagonists off on a treasure-hunt. Huck is Tom's ideal business partner, always on the look-out for an "enterprise offer[ing] entertainment and requir[ing] no capital." But Twain carefully marks the differences between them. While Huck says he will use the treasure to "have a pie and a glass of soda every day," Tom says he will "buy a new drum," a "red necktie, and a bull-pup, and get married." Tom aims to settle down, while Huck cannot imagine doing so.

Twain launched his career by playfully smoothing over what Jackson Lears calls "the enduring tension between coercion and release at the heart of market culture," but his move to Hartford seems to have sharpened the friction between decorum and licence in his own mind.[17] The treasure-hunt, while it lasts, defuses the problem through sheer wish-fulfillment. Not only do Tom and Huck discover Injun Joe hiding his $600 in looted silver in the haunted house, they also witness him finding thousands of dollars in gold in a buried chest. If the Gilded Age has made real fantasies of unimaginable wealth achieved by robbery and speculation, then that wealth can be made to cross the border between the legitimate and the criminal. This is not, any longer, the schoolboy treasure of the primitive economy, but the filthy lucre of the adult world and the capitalist market. When Tom traces the treasure-box to the cave, Twain is wincingly exact about the value of Tom's share: $12,000, invested at 6 percent, producing an income of $1.25 per week. Tom's accounting gives vent to the anxiety involved in holding one's own in Nook Farm, of maintaining position among a "moderate-income circle of professional people."[18] These tensions resurface in yet more oblique form in the novel's sequel, *The Adventures of Huckleberry Finn* (1884).

Generations of readers have responded positively to the moral education undergone by Twain's protagonist. In joining the escaped slave, Jim, on a raft journey down the Mississippi, Huck learns to shed at least some of his culture's racist values, attitudes, and perceptions, and see Jim not as an ignorant and recalcitrant child, but as a grown man, a human being possessed of dignity and feeling. Jim's quest for freedom becomes part of Huck's attempt to escape the shackles of "civilized" society. But while Ernest Hemingway famously declared that "[a]ll modern American literature" came from *Huckleberry Finn*, he also advised readers of the novel to avoid the final chapters, which were, in his opinion, "just cheating."[19] In those chapters, Tom Sawyer abruptly arrives on the scene and tells Huck he will help steal him from his new owners, the Phelpses, who keep Jim locked up in a cabin. Jim's escape is delayed interminably by Tom's insistence on inventing "difficulties and dangers" for the sake of "honor," following the conventions of historical romances like Alexandre Dumas's *The Man in the Iron Mask* (1848). Tom proposes sawing Jim's leg off to free him from his chains, making him keep a journal despite his illiteracy, forcing him to keep a pet rattlesnake despite his fear of snakes, and watering a plant with his own tears. But when Tom is injured in the escape attempt, Jim loyally sacrifices his own freedom for the sake of "Mars Tom." Finally, Tom reveals that Miss Watson has freed Jim in her will, and gives him $40 "for being prisoner for us so patient."

Ralph Ellison corrected Hemingway by arguing for the "structural, symbolic, and moral necessity" of the novel's ending as a stark demonstration of how, in Twain's own time, the Negro had been "pushed into the underground of the American conscience."[20] A growing number of critics have followed Ellison in reading Tom's "Evasion" as a disguised protest against the racial violence, intimidation and discrimination unleashed against African Americans in the post-Reconstruction South, once the Northern army of occupation had been withdrawn by President Hayes in 1877.[21] There is, certainly, no shortage of contemporary parallels to support the idea of Twain's "protest." After 1877, the plantation elite resumed control of the South's black population. Negro convicts were leased to private corporations plowing Northern capital into new railroads and mining operations. Under the convict-lease system, black men were routinely beaten, starved, and housed in filthy conditions.[22] The South passed Jim Crow laws which discriminated against Negroes, and black voters were effectively disenfranchised by systematic violence and intimidation. Jim is, in Shelley Fisher Fishkin's decoding of the allegory, "[i]ncarcerated in a tiny shack" by "an authority figure who claims to have his best interests at heart," denied "information that he needs," and "forced to perform a series of pointless and exhausting tasks."[23] Twain's ending appears to perform the function of political allegory.

The problem with this interpretation is that Jim, as Twain makes clear, is actually well treated by his Southern owners. When Tom and Huck dig into his cabin, they find him "hearty and healthy." Jim tells them that Uncle Silas comes in to pray with him, and that Aunt Sally checks to make sure he is "comfortable" and has "plenty to eat." Jim's torments are caused, not by the Phelpses, but by an interfering outsider, Tom Sawyer, who poses first as "William Thompson," "a stranger from Hicksville, Ohio." When Tom declares that his baroque attempts to free Jim are "the best fun he ever had in his life, and the most intellectural [*sic*]" it's possible to read the allegory in precisely the opposite direction to that of Fishkin and the critical consensus: as a critique, not of the post-Reconstruction South, but of Reconstruction itself as the unrealistic, self-serving, and doomed project of deluded Northerners who, as Huck says of Tom, had "gone and took all that trouble and bother to set a free nigger free." Twain's allegory might, in this reading, come to the conclusions of Albion W. Tourgée's *A Fool's Errand* (1879): that Northern radicals "tried to superimpose the civilization, the idea of the North, upon the South at a moment's warning," with Tom as the representative of that quixotic effort.[a]

There exists a third possibility: that Huck's complacency and his impotent spectatorship is actually Twain's own satirical self-reflection as a member of the Northern middle class who, "irritated by the long bother of Reconstruction," forsook freedmen in favor of business deals with Southern "redeemers."[24] When, in January of 1875, Ulysses S. Grant reluctantly sent federal troops in response to the mass murder of blacks by a white mob in Warren County, Mississippi, the beleaguered President is said to have remarked that the "whole public are tired out with these annual autumnal outbreaks at the South."[25] In the election of 1876, the Republican candidate, Rutherford Hayes, made it clear he would seek accommodation with the "Solid South," urged on by opinion-makers such as E. L. Godkin, editor of *The Nation*, who advised his readers to "have nothing more to do" with the Negro.[26] When Aunt Sally cries that "they've got [Jim] back, safe and sound," we can hear the voice of disillusioned Northern liberals, washing their hands of the Negro they had sworn to protect.

Perhaps the greatest obstacle to reading the ending as straightforward "protest" is Twain's emphasis on Jim's passivity, along with the strangely detached and affectless recording of his torment, and the lingering

a Here, Twain might be seen as making the gestures toward sectional reconciliation discussed by Jennifer Greeson in "Imagining the South," chapter 14, 248–249.

stereotyping of his speech.[b] It comes as a shock to read the excerpt from the novel published in *The Century* for January 1885, alongside George Washington Cable's "The Freedman's Case in Equity" in the same issue. Cable writes against the Supreme Court's overturning of the Civil Rights Act, and the South's assumption of "broad powers of police over any and every person of color."[27] While his tone is restrained, Cable leaves his readers in no doubt about his moral repugnance at the spectacle of six million people subjected to "the hot branding iron of ignominious distinctions" and a section turned over to "lynch law."[28] As Stephen Railton has established, *Huckleberry Finn* comes close to minstrelsy, with Huck acting as Jim's polite interlocutor:

"What did you speculate in, Jim?"
"Well, fust I tackled stock."
"What kind of stock?"
"Why, live stock. Cattle you know. I put ten dollars in a cow. But I ain' gwyne to resk no mo' money in stock. De cow up 'n died on my han's."[29]

Black dialect in Twain's usage is farcical, but not as straightforwardly racist as the dialect that appears in the novels of his contemporaries Joel Chandler Harris and Thomas Nelson Page. The satire cuts both ways. Twain disbursed over $100,000 in a single year, 1881, including $46,000 in speculative investments in new mechanical inventions of the kind that, with the Paige typesetter, would eventually bankrupt him.[30] But, while Jim's tale of throwing good money after bad indicts the speculative frenzy of the Gilded Age, it hardly offers an image of the freedman's capacity for citizenship. In all of Jim's suffering at Tom's hands there is dignity, forbearance, and endurance, but no articulation of his case "in equity." Twain's insistence on Jim's abjection seems to echo the disillusioned Northern view, articulated by Tourgée, that no enslaved race has ever "leap[t] at once" from "absolute chattelism" to "complete self-rule."

The problem with irony is its indirection. Twain, like Huck, "cannot speak openly about his purposes" and, since he seeks refuge in "metaphor," those purposes remain fundamentally opaque.[31] We do know, however, that when Hayes accepted the nomination in 1876, Twain publicly announced his support for his candidacy at a Republican rally in Hartford.[32] It was around this time that Twain began to write about conscience. The narrator of "The Facts Concerning the Recent Carnival of Crime in Connecticut" (1876) wants to be

b For a discussion of contrasting representations of African American agency and resistance, see Barbara McCaskill's essay in this volume, "The African American novel after Reconstruction," chapter 29, 485–488.

"calmly, peacefully, contentedly indifferent," but is tormented by his conscience, which appears to him in the form of a "shriveled, shabby dwarf" and reminds him of his acts of meanness and lack of charity.[33] In a like manner, Huck decides that a conscience is both uncontrollable and burdensome: "[i]t takes up more room than all the rest of a person's insides, and yet ain't no good, nohow." If there is satire of the Northern middle class in the ending of *Huckleberry Finn*, it may be that Twain is queasily aware of sharing in their apostasy: that a confused admixture of protest and accommodation, rationalization and guilt, is driving the allegory and producing its tensions and contradictions, as well as Huck's tone of "irritable fatigue."[34]

"Other places do seem so cramped and smothery, but a raft don't," Huck tells us: "[y]ou feel mighty free and easy and comfortable on a raft." As James Cox points out, "[c]omfort and satisfaction are the value terms in *Huckleberry Finn*."[35] Twain sought comfort and middle-class prosperity in the charmed circle of Nook Farm, but maintaining that comfort meant doing deals, not least with the Solid South. When Twain returned to the South in April, 1882, he reported, in *Life on the Mississippi* (1883), that he was impressed by "changes uniformly evidencing progress, energy, prosperity," and by the "wholesome and practical nineteenth-century smell of cotton factories and locomotives." The rhetoric resembles that of the cardinal Gilded Age booster, Andrew Carnegie, who declared, in *Triumphant Democracy* (1886), that "the old nations of the earth creep on at a snail's pace" while "the Republic thunders past with the rush of the express."[36] Twain knew in his heart that the Northern capital he craved was accumulating on the basis of white supremacy. As the republic thundered on, he just couldn't help feeling guilty about it.

The novels of Twain's friend William Dean Howells, notably *The Rise of Silas Lapham* (1885) and *A Hazard of New Fortunes* (1889), deal with contemporary issues of unemployment, strikes, and the widening division between classes in the cities. Silas Lapham is purported to be a real-life figure from a newspaper column, "Solid Men of Boston": a manufacturer suddenly made wealthy by the discovery of a paint-mine on his Vermont farm, who must now navigate the commercial and moral hazards of life in respectable, middle-class society. Even Henry James, normally associated with the novel of manners, was moved to address contemporary issues in a novel with an anarchist plot, *The Princess Casamassima* (1886). Twain, however, continued to show a preference for indirection, for burlesque, satire, and allegory, following *Huckleberry Finn* with a medieval fantasy, *A Connecticut Yankee in King Arthur's Court* (1889). He was not, however, alone in this preference: in late nineteenth-century America the Middle Ages were in vogue. Many middle-class Americans, "[i]mpatient with the stodginess of bourgeois virtue," were drawn to an imaginary medievalism of chivalry, spontaneity, exuberance, and animal spirits. Magazine stories conjured a world of "jolly friars, winning jongleurs, [and] passionate lords and ladies," popular writers retold the stories of Lancelot and Guenevere, Paolo and Francesca, and Tristan and Isolde, while historians like Henry Charles Lea and Charles Eliot Norton produced scholarly studies of medieval culture.[37]

At first blush *A Connecticut Yankee* seems to participate in the escapist mood of the time. Hank Morgan, the superintendent of an arms factory in Hartford, Connecticut, is knocked unconscious in a fight with a worker and wakes to find himself in sixth-century Camelot. King Arthur's court presents Morgan with "a gay display of moving and intermingling colors," and the Arthurians appear to gambol in childlike innocence. With his description of a royal banquet, in which the "gilded minority" of lords and ladies gorge themselves on dishes brought to them by liveried servants, Twain throws in some mild satire of extravagant Gilded Age feasts at Delmonico's, in which "the pompous and the powerful donned laurel crowns and dined amid faux antiquities."[38] For Howells, increasingly attracted to the Christian socialism of Tolstoy, the message of the novel was clear: "we see that the noble of Arthur's day" is "one in essence" with the present-day "capitalist" who "grows rich on the labor of his underpaid wagemen."[39]

Twain's politics, however, are nothing like as straightforward as this. Morgan lectures the Arthurian workmen on their artificially high wages, arguing that their system of protection only produces higher prices. Throughout the novel, Twain's sympathies appear to lie less with organized labor than with the enterprising individual. Morgan establishes a patent office and uses Yankee know-how to create factories producing soap, sewing machines, newspapers, melodeons, and barbed wire, as well as a clandestine system of schools that will turn the "groping and grubbing automata" of feudalism into sturdy, self-reliant "*men*." But when Morgan's dream of a republic is frustrated by feudal habits of deference to authority, he is transformed from Yankee republican to dictatorial "Boss." Arthur and Lancelot go to war over Guenevere, and Morgan seizes the opportunity to construct a fortress of electrified fences and hidden dynamite, in an attempt to overthrow the feudal order. In a nightmarish triumph for modern technology, Morgan's electrical currents, high explosives, and Gatling guns allow him to kill 35,000 knights at the touch of a button. The central contradiction of the novel is that Morgan, whose narrative voice directs the satire of monarchy and aristocracy, is also the agent of techno-capitalist tyranny and mass slaughter. Twain appears to begin by putting his faith in American capitalism, only to send that faith up in smoke.

Twain's faith in progress had been shaken by the continued failure of the Paige typesetting machine, and his financial problems developed against a background of industrial unrest and violence. When the Baltimore and Ohio Railroad cut wages in 1877, Maryland troops killed ten striking workers in Baltimore. Federal troops turned Gatling guns on rioters in Pittsburgh, killing twenty-five people, while street battles between Chicago police and workers left between forty and fifty dead. On May 4, 1886, in Haymarket Square, Chicago, an anarchist bomb killed eight policemen. Labor leaders were rounded up, and, with no evidence to support the charges against them, four were executed, a judicial murder which sparked an outraged protest from Howells.[40] But to many Americans fearful that socialist revolution was imminent, "medieval brutality" was more attractive than due process.[41] A writer in *The Atlantic Monthly*, appalled by "the increasing frequency" of acts of "atrocious and wilful crime," called for the return of the "reeking scaffold" and urged the necessity of retributive justice.[42]

Placed in its historical context, Twain's novel appears less a far-fetched flight of the comic imagination than a grimly realistic fable for the times. When Morgan turns the Gatling gun on the Arthurian knights it's possible to detect another potently ambivalent mix of feelings in Twain: dismay at the remnants of feudal hierarchy which remain stubbornly embedded in a modern democracy like the United States, frustration at the shortcomings of modern technology, and a misanthropic rage at the "groping and grubbing automata" produced by the industrial system.

Perhaps what Twain's writing demonstrates most clearly are the fears and frustrations of a new middle class which found itself caught in the struggle between a class of predatory capitalists like Jay Cooke and a class of immiserated wage-earners, forced to exist on ninety cents a day. Twain helped that class to loosen up: to laugh at Victorian pomposity and stuffiness, to feel the zest and novelty of its American identity. But other Gilded Age realities could not be laughed away as easily: wealth and power concentrated in the hands of the few, the vaunting of technical rationality alongside an irrational business cycle which produced regular panics and depressions; a stubbornly persistent racism; eye-watering levels of inequality. Vivid, contradictory, and inconsistent, Twain's works form a series of enduringly resonant reports from American capitalism's Promised Land.

Notes

1. Vernon Louis Parrington, *Main Currents in American Thought: An Interpretation of American Literature from the Beginnings to 1920*, 3 vols. (New York: Harcourt, Brace & Company, 1930), III: 3, 8.
2. *Ibid.*, 26.
3. Robert E. Weir, "Mark Twain and Social Class," in *A Historical Guide to Mark Twain*, ed. Shelley Fisher Fishkin (New York: Oxford University Press, 2002), 199. On Gilded Age financiers and financial scandals, see Steve Fraser, *Every Man a Speculator: A History of Wall Street in American Life* (New York: HarperPerennial, 2006), 106–151.
4. For recent assessments of the Gilded Age, see Rebecca Edwards, *New Spirits: Americans in the Gilded Age 1865–1905* (New York: Oxford University Press, 2006); Scott Sandage, "The Gilded Age," in *A Companion to American Cultural History*, ed. Karen Halttunen (Malden, MA: Blackwell, 2008).
5. Ron Powers, *Mark Twain: A Life* (London: Pocket Books, 2007), 70.
6. Stuart M. Blumin, "Social Implications of US Economic Development," in *The Cambridge Economic History of the United States, Vol. 2: The Long Nineteenth Century*, ed. Stanley L. Engerman and Robert E. Gallman (Cambridge: Cambridge University Press, 2000), 849.
7. Alan Trachtenberg, *The Incorporation of America: Culture and Society in the Gilded Age* (New York: Hill & Wang, 2007), 144; Jackson Lears, *No Place of Grace: Antimodernism and the Transformation of American Culture, 1880–1920* (New York: Pantheon Books, 1981), 7.
8. See Brian Roberts, *American Alchemy: The California Gold Rush and Middle-Class Culture* (Chapel Hill: University of North Carolina Press, 2000).
9. Powers, *Mark Twain*, 111. See also Gunther Peck, "Manly Gambles: The Politics of Risk on the Comstock Lode, 1860–1880," *Journal of Social History* 26 (1993): 701–723.
10. Powers, *Mark Twain*, 113.
11. *Ibid.*, 130–131.
12. *Ibid.*, 175, 167.
13. Burton J. Bledstein, "Introduction: Storytellers to the Middle Class," in *Middling Sorts: Explorations in the History of the American Middle Class*, ed. Burton J. Bledstein and Robert D. Johnston (New York: Routledge, 2001), 13.
14. William Dean Howells, "The Truthfulness of Mark Twain's Fiction" (1887), in *Selected Literary Criticism, Vol. 2*, ed. Ulrich Halfmann *et al.* (Bloomington: Indiana University Press, 1993), 49–50.
15. See Alfred D. Chandler, *The Visible Hand: The Managerial Revolution in American Business* (Cambridge, MA: Harvard University Press, 1977).
16. For a discussion of this contradiction, see Gregg Camfield, "A Republican Artisan in the Court of King Capital," in Fishkin, *Historical Guide to Mark Twain*, 95–126.
17. Jackson Lears, "Reconsidering Abundance: A Plea for Ambiguity," in *Getting and Spending: European and American Consumer Societies in the Twentieth Century*, ed. Susan Strasser *et al.* (Cambridge: Cambridge University Press, 1998), 463.

18. Kenneth R. Andrews, *Nook Farm: Mark Twain's Hartford Circle* (Cambridge, MA: Harvard University Press, 1950), 102.
19. Quoted in Arnold Rampersad, "*The Adventures of Huckleberry Finn* and Afro-American Literature," in *Satire or Evasion? Black Perspectives on "Huckleberry Finn,"* ed. James S. Leonard, Thomas A. Tenney, and Thadious M. Davis (Durham, NC: Duke University Press, 1992), 216.
20. Ralph Ellison, quoted in Shelley Fisher Fishkin, *Lighting Out for the Territory: Reflections on Mark Twain and American Culture* (New York: Oxford University Press, 1996), 197–198.
21. See, for example, Neil Schmitz, "Twain, *Huckleberry Finn*, and the Reconstruction," *American Studies* 12 (1971): 59–67; Charles H. Nilon, "The Ending of *Huckleberry Finn*: 'Freeing the Free Negro,'" in Leonard, *Satire or Evasion*, 62–76; Fishkin, *Lighting Out for the Territory*, 194–203.
22. See C. Vann Woodward, *Origins of the New South 1877–1913* (Baton Rouge: Louisiana State University Press, 1971), 213–214.
23. Fishkin, *Lighting Out for the Territory*, 198.
24. George Carrington, Jr., quoted in Harold Beaver, *Huckleberry Finn* (London: Allen & Unwin, 1987), 43.
25. See Nell Irvin Painter, *Standing at Armageddon: The United States, 1877–1919* (New York: W. W. Norton & Company, 1989), 7. See also George C. Rable, *But There Was No Peace: The Role of Violence in the Politics of Reconstruction* (Athens: University of Georgia Press, 1984), 145–150.
26. See Woodward, *Origins of the New South*, 214.
27. George Washington Cable, "The Freedman's Case in Equity," *The Century: A Popular Quarterly* 29.3 (1885): 411.
28. *Ibid.*, 414, 417.
29. See "Blackface Minstrelsy," Mark Twain in His Times, Electronic Text Center, University of Virginia. http://etext.virginia.edu/railton/huckfinn/minstrl.html June 11, 2008.
30. Walter Blair, *Mark Twain and Huck Finn* (Berkeley: University of California Press, 1960), 263.
31. Nilon, "Ending of *Huckleberry Finn*," 66.
32. Excerpts from Twain's speech appear in Henry Nash Smith and William M. Gibson, eds., *Mark Twain–Howells Letters, Vol. 2* (Cambridge, MA: Harvard University Press, 1960), 864–865.
33. Mark Twain, "The Facts Concerning the Recent Carnival of Crime in Connecticut," *The Atlantic Monthly* 27.124 (1876): 641.
34. Forrest G. Robinson, *In Bad Faith: The Dynamics of Deception in Mark Twain's America* (Cambridge, MA: Harvard University Press, 1986), 216.
35. James Cox, *Mark Twain: The Fate of Humor* (Princeton: Princeton University Press, 1966), 178.
36. Quoted in Lears, *No Place of Grace*, 8.
37. *Ibid.*, 163.
38. Weir, "Mark Twain and Social Class," 200.

39. William Dean Howells, "Editor's Study," *Harper's New Monthly Magazine* 80.476 (1890): 320.
40. See Painter, *Standing at Armageddon*, 15–18, 47–50.
41. Lears, *No Place of Grace*, 110.
42. E. P. Evans, "Medieval and Modern Punishment," *The Atlantic Monthly* 54.323 (1884): 308, 302.

22

Dreiser and the city

JUDE DAVIES

"New York!" he said. "That's not a place, it's a dream."

Ralph Ellison, *Invisible Man* (1952)

The city is never simply a place. In a 1925 essay Chicago School sociologist Robert E. Park asserts that the city is "something more than a congeries of individual men and of social conveniences – streets, buildings, electric lights, tramways, and telephones." For Park, the city is "something more, also, than a mere constellation of institutions and administrative devices – courts, hospitals, schools, police, and civil functionaries of various sorts." Rather, he argues influentially, the city is "a state of mind, a body of customs and traditions, and of the organized attitudes and sentiments that inhere in these customs and are transmitted with this tradition."[1] It is exactly this sense of the city lived and imagined by individuals in relation to the material, economic, social, and cultural cityscape that animates many of the best-known novelists of the thirty years preceding Park's essay, from the work of Henry James and Edith Wharton, to Rebecca Harding Davis's pioneering *Life In the Iron-Mills* (1861) and realists and naturalists like William Dean Howells, Stephen Crane, Frank Norris, Theodore Dreiser, and Upton Sinclair.

The American city novel[2] depicts the blurring of the boundaries between the self and the city, and between self and society, as creating the conditions for an independence that elicits both desire and fear. Theodore Dreiser's *Sister Carrie* (1900) is a typical example. At one level, it affirms Chicago and New York as the privileged sites for the "American dream" of self-reinvention and social mobility. In its protagonist Carrie Meeber, Dreiser extends the scope of success narratives to include a protagonist who is not only female, but who also breaks contemporary conventions of sexual morality by living with first one and then a second man outside marriage, and who ends the novel as a successful actress, indifferent to the attentions of wealthy male admirers. Presenting what David A. Zimmerman elsewhere in this volume calls "the first non-censorious drama of consumer subjectivity,"[a] *Sister Carrie* affirms a, possibly *the*, paradigmatic American identity of the twentieth century. Yet Dreiser also associates the city with class conflict, poverty, despair, and downward mobility, plotting the rise of Carrie Meeber alongside the fall of her lover George Hurstwood. The closing chapters of the novel condense urban society into two extremes, contrasting Carrie's wealthy lifestyle with the condition of New York's homeless, among whom Hurstwood becomes numbered. As Carrie enjoys her "comfortable chambers" at the prestigious Waldorf Hotel overlooking Fifth Avenue, Hurstwood commits suicide in a Bowery flophouse. Moreover Dreiser interrogates the promise of happiness held out by the dream of success, portraying Carrie as perpetually dissatisfied, the victim as well as the beneficiary of an urban society based upon performance, spectacle, and consumption. Celebrating and questioning the urban dream of self-fulfillment, *Sister Carrie* also occupies a historically pivotal position, looking back toward the success myths of Horatio Alger, and anticipating some of the modernist tropes found in writers such as Richard Wright and Henry Miller.[b] Ranging across this trajectory, this chapter suggests how the American city novel tradition affirms the possibilities, and marks the historical limits, of urban modernity and the democratic individualism associated with it.

Sister Carrie was written into an existing tradition of urban social mobility fiction that is primarily associated with Horatio Alger, author of more than one hundred novels for young people published between 1864 and 1899.[c] Widespread views of the city as corrupting required effort in the latter part of the nineteenth century and the early twentieth century to reimagine the city as the privileged site of democratic individualism, and Alger expends that effort. The inspirational message of Alger's dime novels is that, in the face of the contingencies of urban life and capitalist economics, character determines narrative. Steeped in the Protestant ethic of hard work and investment in the self, Alger's narratives portray male protagonists, typically in the city,

a David A. Zimmerman, "Novels of American business, industry, and consumerism," chapter 24, 424.

b The thematically and historically pivotal nature of *Sister Carrie* and Dreiser's business novels *The Financier* and *The Titan* is elaborated elsewhere in this volume by David A. Zimmerman, who shows how Dreiser's characteristic ambivalence has been interpreted according to a variety of political positions. See Zimmerman, chapter 24, 421–424.

c On Alger's position in the tradition of the business novel, see Zimmerman, chapter 24, 420; on Alger as children's novelist see Julia Mickenberg's essay in this volume, "Children's novels," chapter 52, 864.

moving from rags to respectability by a mixture of "luck and pluck" and aided by the patronage of an already successful older male. Persistently mythologized throughout the twentieth century, and pervasively misrepresented as "rags to riches" tales of manly self-reliance, Alger's novels have only since the 1970s been regarded as employing complex strategies to negotiate the uncertainties of urban life. Serialized in boys' magazines such as *Student and Schoolmate*, Alger's fictions present the city as a site of potential confusion exploited by the unscrupulous, but ultimately knowable given the right guide.

Alger's bestselling and paradigmatic work, *Ragged Dick, or, Street Life in New York among Boot Blacks* (serial 1867, book publication 1868) presents itself as a geographical and practical guide to New York as much as an ethical handbook for self-advancement. Alger describes the most striking buildings on Broadway, distinguishes among the respectable and criminal businesses carried out on different streets, gives the approximate number of volumes in the Mercantile Library on Eighth Street (a footnote added to the book registered the library's growth since its serial publication), and directs readers to the statue of Washington in Union Park and to the largest and cheapest stores in New York. More important even than these forms of "useful knowledge" is Alger's description of a series of urban hazards and demonstration of how to avoid them. During the course of the book, its readers are introduced to various urban perils: a rip-off shop selling "everything for a dollar" and a series of confidence tricks involving dud checks, the "drop-game," and offers of worthless company stock in the Erie Railroad, whose over-capitalization and collapse had been a recent national scandal. In addition the novel's protagonist Dick Hunter overcomes false accusations of theft and passing counterfeit money, and the theft of his newly acquired bankbook.

Alger thereby presents urban experience and capitalist economics as fields of semiotic and moral uncertainty, which are countered by Dick's local knowledge, street smarts, and innate honesty. Yet there is a contradiction here. A keen spectator of popular amusements such as those promoted by P. T. Barnum, a spirited player of roles and master of witty repartee, and a "young gentleman on the way to fame and fortune," Dick is involved in the very kinds of simulation and speculation against which Alger's explicit project is ranged.[3] Alger's fictions acknowledge the destabilizing effects of capitalist speculation, social mobility, and the emphasis on performance associated with urban modernity, but Alger ultimately endows his heroes with a core moral character that can be read behind the surface appearances presented to any observer. Very early in *Ragged Dick*, Alger introduces his protagonist from the perspective of a pedestrian observing the street-boy for the first time. Dick is "somehow attractive" despite his "dirt and rags" and it "was easy to see that if he had been clean and well dressed he would have been decidedly good-looking." In comparison to other street-boys, "Dick had a frank, straight-forward manner that made him a favorite." This inherently moral nature remains central to Dick's character through the adventures of *Ragged Dick*, which involve multiple changes of home, clothes, and name – from Ragged Dick to Dick Hunter, the name signed on his first bankbook, to "Richard Hunter, Esq," adopted on the final page of the novel. "Esq." sets the seal on Dick's upward narrative of social mobility, which has been predicated throughout on spontaneous bonds of trust and recognition between males generated in the public space of the street.

The implied homoerotics of the "attractiveness" which made Dick "a favorite" invites contextualization with respect to Alger's own homosexuality and pedophilia (accusations of which led to Alger's resignation as a minister, indirectly precipitating his career as a novelist), and also to the clandestine sexual interactions facilitated by the anonymity of urban life. Alger might thus be read as opening a door upon a repressed history of (in this case cross-class) homosexual encounters.[d] Still, it is Alger's sublimation of the homoerotic gaze into the homosocial that has placed him in the mainstream of twentieth-century US culture, enabling his narratives to be reinvented for the era of corporate capitalism as myths of cross-class male patronage.[4] Alger's avuncular narrator figure, and the successful adult males who become Dick's patrons, gaze upon the bootblack not only with admiration but also with recognition; and what they recognize is a younger version of themselves in everything but class position: white, male, and Anglo-American. This sense of racial, ethnic, and gendered sameness authenticates the narrative of upward mobility.

Alger's double-dealing no doubt generates the ire evident in satires and attacks by Stephen Crane, James Thurber, Nathanael West, Ralph Ellison, and Henry Miller, some of which will be discussed later. But if Alger assuages fears of usurpation, his work also gets to a more universal anxiety that would also be exacerbated in the later nineteenth and twentieth centuries: a fear of independence itself. The combination of investment in and fear of the city's potential to destabilize the self typifies the American city novel. That this duality is a central and essential part of urban experience is suggested by the sociologist Georg Simmel in the 1903 essay "The Metropolis and Mental Life." Observing that "it is by no means necessary that the freedom of man be

d See Elizabeth Freeman's essay in this volume, "Reimagining genders and sexualities," chapter 57, for work representing queerness directly.

reflected in his emotional life as comfort," Simmel argues that in the metropolis the boundaries between self and society are blurred, in ways that promise autonomy and self-transformation, but also threaten dispersal and alienation. For Simmel, the metropolitan concentration of human activity in buildings, institutions, and community life offers "such an overwhelming fullness of crystallized and impersonalized spirit that the personality, so to speak, cannot maintain itself under its impact."[5] What most makes the city a desirable place, its embodiment of human spirit, also creates a threat of expropriation, confronting humans with a more powerful version of their own essence, but in objectified form. Such desires, hopes, and anxieties about independence are articulated in urban fiction from a variety of subject positions, and in somewhat different historical circumstances. From the 1890s onward writers increasingly contested the two key elements of Alger's depiction of the city: his assertion of a simple moral core to identity in the face of the destabilization associated with urban modernity, and his gendered and ethnic particularity.

Mixed with this development was the elaboration of specific characteristics of different cities into emblematic significance – crudely, Boston meant old wealth, Chicago stood for industrial capitalism, and New York became a synecdoche for an ethnically diverse nation, the"one city that belongs to the whole country," in the words of a character in William Dean Howells's *A Hazard of New Fortunes* (1890). Howells played a major role in the realist turn in fiction toward the end of the nineteenth century.[e] Having established a considerable literary reputation as the social historian of Boston's middle classes in the 1870s and 1880s, Howells moved to New York in 1889. His New York novels are often taken as signaling a shift in the American literary center of gravity, one that began to acknowledge the class and ethnic diversity of American society (Howells himself became a socialist), and made a small but significant step toward the eventual recognition of the centrality of ethnic difference to American literature.

Howells's New York is overtly shaped by the rapid changes in the USA attendant upon mass immigration, industrialization, and the rise of finance capitalism. It has become the "cosmopolis" where difference (especially among races, classes, and genders) is made manifest as spectacle, and in so doing the city becomes emblematic of American national identity.[6] Howells

e On the important role of Howells, see especially Michael A. Elliott's essay in this volume, "Realism and radicalism: the school of Howells" (chapter 17). Howells's commitment to social solidarity is compared with Henry James's pessimistic individualism in Carrie Tirado Bramen's essay in this volume, "James, pragmatism, and the realist ideal," chapter 18, 309–310.

depicts the spectatorship and consumerism by which individuals came to know the city and its people. In *A Hazard of New Fortunes*, after moving to New York Basil and Isabel March take their "chief pleasure" in its "quality of foreignness." They enjoy olives and other foods from an Italian grocery, and after experimenting with Spanish restaurants, favor "the table d'hôte of a French lady, who had taken a Spanish husband in a second marriage, and had a Cuban Negro for her cook, with a cross-eyed Alsatian for waiter, and a slim young South-American for cashier." Wryly suggesting the economic asymmetry of such interactions, Howells goes on to describe the quintessential urban experience as the product of mechanized urban transport systems. The Marches travel a good deal on the Elevated roads, which, Basil remarks, "gave you such glimpses of material aspects in the city as some violent invasion of others' lives might afford in human nature." If Alger figures an exclusive kind of social cohesion by gazes exchanged between Anglo-American males, Howells foregrounds a change in the visual relationships between people, one which he portrays as being conditioned by the spatial arrangements of urban modernity exemplified by the rapid transport system. The egalitarian exchange of looks, and the frankness and autonomy so implied, is replaced by a one-sided gaze equated with "some violent invasion of others' lives."[f]

Naturalist city novels at the turn of the century such as Stephen Crane's *Maggie: A Girl of the Streets* (1893), Frank Norris's *McTeague: A Story of San Francisco* (1899), and Upton Sinclair's *The Jungle* (1906) go still further than Howells in exploring the dangerous independence of urban life, expanding the social range of the novel to focus in detail on working-class and underclass subjects. A key element in Sinclair's propagandist narrative is the gradual dehumanization of Lithuanian immigrants initially depicted in the full vitality of a colorful, musical folk culture.[g] Crane's *Maggie* epitomizes naturalism's concern with environmental determinism; its subtitle indicating a liberation from an abusive home, but also a stigmatized social position, a form of labor, and ultimately a death sentence. At the same time, Crane is half in love with the sheer spectacle of the public spaces of the Bowery and the Lower East Side, as the novella abounds in scenes set in bars, at theater and vaudeville performances, in the streets, and in verbs of looking, seeing, appearance, and observation. This ambivalence suggests wider shifts in the views of public and private space, such that the home no longer figures as an authenticating refuge

f For a more detailed discussion of Howells's depiction of New York in *A Hazard of New Fortunes* see Elliott, chapter 17, 298–299.

g On Sinclair's activist definition of the novel see Cecelia Tichi's essay in this volume, "Novels of civic protest," chapter 23, 394–397.

for the self.[7] Due to the neglect, cruelty, alcoholism, and misguided religiosity of her parents, Maggie never really has a "home" in the first place, at least not one that provides a nurturing familial domestic environment. But Crane ironizes middle-class notions of domesticity as well as Maggie's underclass situation. Her attempts to create a home in the slum such as by the "purchase of flowered cretonne for a lambrequin" poignantly echo the middle-class respectability to which she aspires. Yet she is undone by the combination of her home environment, dominated by her monstrous mother,[h] and her middle-class aspirations, especially her romantic view of abusive lover Pete, whom she imagines in the role of provider with herself as homemaker. When Maggie tries to return home after Pete has abandoned her, her mother's response is to turn the domestic into public space, repeatedly demanding that family members "Lookut her" and deliberately staging the humiliation of her daughter in front of an audience of neighbors watching through an open door.

Norris's *McTeague* also dramatizes the failure of "home" to preserve itself as the recuperative, humanizing counterpart of the public urban spectacle. The novel's ill-matched central couple, Trina and McTeague, have little in common except the desire to share a domestic space. "Nothing could have been more delicious" than their ability "to close the sliding door to shut themselves off from the whole world" during their courtship, when they lunch together in a private hotel room. Subsequently, the setting up of a marital home in a suite of rooms, albeit constantly under threat by the invading odors and noise of the city, provides a brief romantic interlude in which the couple's qualities are balanced, McTeague's tendency to drink and Trina's miserliness kept in check. In a novel preoccupied with the relations between humans and objects, the McTeague home has the temporary ability to humanize commodities, epitomized by the couple's Nottingham lace curtains, melodeon, and wedding photograph, which are then sold as auction lots when the home is broken up. Though Norris mocks the aspirations to middle-class status associated with the goods consumed by Trina and McTeague – as Crane does with Maggie – he elicits sympathy for their doomed attempts to establish a home, all the more poignant for its fragility and brevity.

Dreiser's *Sister Carrie* opens with yet another home-leaving, immediately framed by the narrator with respect to the patriarchal dualism of female virtue and the fallen woman. "When a girl leaves her home at eighteen," the narrator

h For further discussion of this character, see Donna Campbell's essay in this volume, "The rise of naturalism," chapter 30, 504.

assures readers, "she does one of two things. Either she falls into saving hands and becomes better, or she rapidly assumes the cosmopolitan standard of virtue and becomes worse. Of an intermediate balance, under the circumstances, there is no possibility." The rest of the novel travesties these remarks and the ideologies they invoke. Homeliness, it appears, carries no weight for the novel's principal characters Carrie Meeber and her lovers Drouet and Hurstwood. Drouet enjoys the freedom conferred by the mobility of his profession as a "drummer" or traveling salesman, while Dreiser apotheosizes "[a] lovely home atmosphere" as "one of the flowers of the world" only to emphasize the utter lack of such delicate, nourishing and "mystic chords" in Hurstwood's marital residence. For both Carrie and Hurstwood home is something to escape, at best a place from which to observe the human spectacle of the city that promises a better life. After a little mental wavering at the opening, Carrie gives her familial home in a midwestern small town scarcely another thought, while her sister's apartment in Chicago holds only one attraction: the doorway from which she can watch the street. After living in a succession of rented apartments, at novel's end Carrie is living in a hotel, able to watch the street from her suite of rooms.

At key moments in the novel Carrie is fascinated by the spectacle presented by fellow urbanites in the public spaces of the city. She is repeatedly made conscious of her own "inferiority," but then energized to emulate and eventually supplant others. What Carrie first experiences as lack, when she imagines others as happy by virtue of their appearance, is also what will give her the resources to perform successfully on and offstage. Her face becomes, as her friend Robert Ames tells her late in the novel, "a thing the world likes to see, because it's a natural expression of its longing." Carrie is able to harness that energy as part of her own performances as an actress and as a woman.

This ability to remake oneself out of experiences of lack also resonates with Walter Benjamin's sense of urban experience as a series of shocks which enable productive self-transformation.[8] A loosely Benjaminian reading of *Sister Carrie* could trace how Carrie's personal and social existence is continually remade out of the sense of mingled desire and lack excited in her by the urban scene, whether the clothes that call out to her from the department store display, promising to transform her, or the middle-class parade on Broadway. But Dreiser seems more pessimistic, limiting a sense of the social utility of Carrie's performances to brief asides from the narrator, and some hopeful urgings by Robert Ames in the novel's concluding chapters. As a result, *Sister Carrie* might be better categorized according to Franco Moretti's argument that instead of proliferating public space, the city proliferates modes of individual privatization.[9] The keynote of the urban for him is not shock, but mediation. As Amy Kaplan has pointed out, while a labor strike crashes into the consciousness of Howells's characters in *A Hazard of New Fortunes*, in *Sister Carrie* "the conflict" (even though Hurstwood as a strikebreaker is the target of missiles) "is more contained and less threatening – as though roped off in a separate sphere."[10] Analogously, Carrie manages to rope off spaces temporarily, conjuring homeliness in rented rooms, restaurants, hotels, and even onstage.[11] Dreiser's later novels describe a variety of homemaking activities, including the unconventional establishment set up by Jennie Gerhardt in Chicago's Hyde Park to house herself, her father, her lover Lester Kane, and Vesta, her out-of-wedlock child by another man (*Jennie Gerhardt*, 1911); and the Chicago mansion in which Frank Cowperwood assembles the artistic spoils of his commercial power in *The Titan* (1914). In each of these, Dreiser shows as commonplace the permeability of distinctions between public and domestic space, distinctions whose breakdown is presented as entailing disastrous consequences in novels like *Maggie* and *McTeague*.

American critics of succeeding generations have theorized the blurring of borders among individual, social life, and the outside world in ways that also inform the city novel. After the character-driven urban narratives of Alger and the association of the urban with national ethnic diversity by Howells, *Sister Carrie* offers a more explicit account of what I have been calling, after Simmel and James Donald, the dangerous independence of individuals in the conditions of urban modernity. If *Sister Carrie* depicts a painful but productive making and unmaking of the self, comparable dialectical patterns can be found in a range of twentieth-century city novels employing a variety of thematics. These include immigration and other narratives concerned with what Tim Prchal calls the "complications of assimilation"[i] such as Mary Antin's autobiographical *The Promised Land* (1912), Abraham Cahan's *The Rise of David Levinsky* (1917), and Anzia Yezierska's *The Bread Givers* (1925). Similarly, the fiction of James T. Farrell, especially the *Studs Lonigan* trilogy (1932–1935), plays out its narratives of human striving against a tightly geographically defined ethnic neighborhood, in this case Chicago's South Side, which constrains at least as much as it enables. Novels of racial exclusion such as Richard Wright's *Native Son* (1940), Ann Petry's

i See Tim Prchal's essay in this volume, "New Americans and the immigrant novel," chapter 25, 432.

The Street (1946), and Ralph Ellison's *Invisible Man*, all discussed elsewhere in this volume, more explicitly contest the Alger paradigm by demonstrating the interpenetration of environment and "character," the social barriers and boundaries ignored by the Alger myth, or in the case of Paul Laurence Dunbar's *The Sport of the Gods* (1902) by presenting an Alger- (or Carrie-) style success story as a corruption of black female identity. Especially for women and writers of color, the relationship between self and urban space is often not nearly as synergistic as it is depicted in *Sister Carrie*. At its most extreme, as in Petry's *The Street*, urban space is a direct effect of racial power, constraining the self and ultimately denying it any autonomy. In Petry's novel the streets of Harlem *are* "the North's lynch mobs."

While Petry explicitly reacts against what she sees as the specious individualism of Benjamin Franklin's *Autobiography*, Ellison writes back directly to Alger. In *Invisible Man*, the unnamed protagonist travels from a Southern "negro college" to Harlem, following the uncertain "dream" delineated in this chapter's epigraph. The invisible man rejects the narrative of corrosive assimilation embodied by the college authorities, describing them as enacting "the black rite of Horatio Alger." He also rejects the black nationalism he finds proclaimed in parts of Harlem, and affiliates himself instead with the "Brotherhood," a communist-type organization that he sees as "the one place in the country where we were free and given the greatest encouragement to use our abilities." The invisible man's hope is to mediate between the largely white Brotherhood and the black "community" referred to simply as "Harlem." This promise is betrayed when it becomes apparent that the Brotherhood has deliberately fomented a race riot in order to provoke official retaliation. Instead of joining the black uprising, the Brotherhood is simply staging it so as to discredit the political status quo. In thereby manipulating the struggle of black people for its own political ends, the Brotherhood reasserts the racial hierarchy of the assimilationists. The invisible man reflects on their shared invocation of the Alger myth: "that lie that success was a rising *upwards*. What a crummy lie they kept us dominated us by." Temporarily energized (and also made fearful) by the mobilization of the black community on the streets during the riot, the invisible man eventually embraces the condition of invisibility and the duplicitous, multiple selfhoods it determines, retreating to the "hole" on the borders of Harlem from which the story is narrated.

Alger figures as the antithesis of other modernist writers such as Amiri Baraka ("The Death of Horatio Alger," 1967), Nathanael West, especially in the Alger parody *A Cool Million* (1934), and Henry Miller, whose New York novel *Tropic of Capricorn* (1938) also looks back in some respects to *Sister Carrie*, especially in its evocation of street life, including an eroticized vision of a woman on Broadway. Miller represented the birth of his own writing in retaliation to a superior's suggestion that he write a Horatio Alger-style book. Recounted in *Tropic of Capricorn*, this anecdote leads to one of Miller's trademark rushes of textuality:

> I saw the Horatio Alger hero, the dream of a sick American, mounting higher and higher, first messenger, then operator, then manager, then chief, then superintendent, then vice-president, then president, then trust magnate, then beer baron, then Lord of all the Americas, the money god, the god of gods, the clay of clay, nullity on high, zero with ninety-seven thousand decimals fore and aft.

What Miller finds outrageous is not only what he takes to be Alger's giving a moral dimension to the making of money, but also his imposition of order on the radically destabilizing city. Miller's embrace of multiplicity and his insistence on uncertainty and chaos at the center of existence – both of which determine his resistance to conventional novelistic forms – are given voice as a series of autobiographical urban narratives and reflections.

"One can feel his way about, take bearings, observe passing phenomena; one can even feel at home," Miller half reflects, half commands, in *Tropic of Capricorn*. "But there is no taking root." There is a clear link here with Carrie Meeber's continual desiring, performing, and homemaking, but Miller's modernist stream-of-consciousness otherwise seems a long distance from Carrie's, and the attendant linkage between city novels and urban sociology noted at the opening of this chapter. The links between urban sociology and urban fiction (and politics, as Cecelia Tichi's contribution to this volume makes clear) were at their strongest in the early twentieth century, epitomized by Robert E. Park and the Chicago School. Long before writing the essay on "The City" with which this chapter began, Park had himself produced a novel, which remains unpublished. Like Crane, Norris, and Dreiser, Park was a journalist in the 1890s, and he used "reportorial realism" as a model for sociological discourse, famously advising his students to "get your pants dirty in real research."[12] The Chicago School notion that the detailed study of one city may yield wider insights into the metropolitan condition also resonates with the novelists. It is hardly surprising then that in "The City" Park acknowledged a debt to "writers of fiction" for "our more intimate knowledge of urban life[,]" even as he called for the "more searching and disinterested study" that sociology could provide.[13]

Notes

1. Robert E. Park, "The City: Suggestions for the Investigation of Human Behavior in the Urban Environment," in Robert E. Park and Ernest W. Burgess, *The City: Suggestions for Investigation of Human Behavior in the Urban Environment* (Chicago: University of Chicago Press, 1925), 1–46; 1.
2. Blanche Housman Gelfant's pioneering *The American City Novel* (Norman: University of Oklahoma Press, 1954) defines the field in terms of the depiction of "urban life as an organic whole."
3. Hildegard Hoeller demonstrates how in the *Ragged Dick* series Alger squares this circle by portraying Dick as a particular kind of "freak," a figure through which the destabilizing effects of finance capitalism and social mobility can be symbolically contained by being brought within the structure of performer/audience. Hildegard Hoeller, "Freaks and the American Dream: Horatio Alger, P. T. Barnum, and the Art of Humbug," *Studies in American Fiction* 34.2 (Autumn 2006): 189–214.
4. See Michael Moon, "'The Gentle Boy from the Dangerous Classes': Pederasty, Domesticity and Capitalism in Horatio Alger," *Representations* 19 (Summer 1987): 87–110. The concept of the homosocial is elaborated by Eve Kosofsky Sedgwick in *Between Men: English Literature and Male Homosocial Desire* (New York: Columbia University Press, 1985). While the term is often used to describe the "queering" of overt heterosexuality due to patriarchy's relegation of women to inferior status, in Alger the converse is also true – homosexual desire is sublimated into a homosocial bond between males, which serves to reinforce patriarchal assumptions that the only relations that matter are those between men, while the destabilizing effects of the city are projected onto females.
5. Georg Simmel, "The Metropolis and Mental Life" ["Die Grosstädte und das Geistesleben"] in *Simmel on Culture*, ed. David Frisby and Mike Featherstone (London: Sage, 1997), 174–185, 181, 184. An influential and accessible development of Simmel's ideas is James Donald, *Imagining the Modern City* (London: The Athlone Press, 1999).
6. See Thomas Peyser, *Utopia and Cosmopolis: Globalization in the Era of American Literary Realism* (Durham, NC: Duke University Press, 1998).
7. Hana Wirth-Nesher describes the shift from the earlier notion of the "home" as private refuge to modern orientations of public and private in *City Codes: Reading the Modern Urban Novel* (Cambridge: Cambridge University Press, 1996), 18–19.
8. See Walter Benjamin, *Charles Baudelaire: A Lyric Poet in the Era of High Capitalism*, trans. Harry Zohn (London: New Left Books, 1973), and Walter Benjamin, *The Arcades Project*, trans. Howard Eiland and Kevin McLaughlin (Cambridge, MA: The Belknap Press of Harvard University Press, 1999).

9. Franco Moretti, "Homo Palpitans: Balzac's Novels and Urban Personality," in *Signs Taken for Wonders: Essays in the Sociology of Literary Forms*, trans. Susan Fischer, David Forgacs, and David Miller, rev. edn. (London and New York: Verso, 1988), 109–129.
10. Amy Kaplan, *The Social Construction of American Realism* (Chicago: University of Chicago Press, 1988), 155. Mediation is also key to Kaplan's overall view of *Sister Carrie* as "imagining and managing the contradictions of a burgeoning consumer society" (143).
11. In *City Codes* Wirth-Nesher develops more fully a Moretti-inspired reading of *Sister Carrie*.
12. See Eugene Rochberg-Halton, "Life, Literature and Sociology in Turn-of-the-Century Chicago," in *Consuming Visions: Accumulation and the Display of Goods in America, 1880–1920*, ed. Simon J. Bronner (New York: Winterthur, 1989), 311–338, for an account of the interweaving of sociology and literature, using Park, Sinclair, and Dreiser as principal examples. Rochberg-Halton points to the intersection of literary and sociological discourse in "reportorial realism" (315).
13. Park, "The City," 3.

23

Novels of civic protest

CECELIA TICHI

In the mid-1920s, a pugnacious Upton Sinclair published *Mammonart*, an overview of Western literature that included a sweeping manifesto on art. Unabashedly Sinclair proclaimed in italics that *"all art is propaganda . . . universally and inescapably propaganda."* The author of the bestselling fictional exposé of wage slavery and industrial meat contamination, *The Jungle* (1906), Sinclair had also published *King Coal* (1917) and was gathering materials for yet another novel of social reform, *Oil!* (1927). In these and other novels (and nonfiction), Sinclair critiqued capitalism as culpable for workplace danger, food contamination and adulteration, starvation wages, lethal violence, racism, environmental spoliation, child labor, sexual abuse, business criminality, and political corruption. He validated his manifesto in terms of personal experience, claiming the *bona fides* of a working artist whose convictions were shaped by "a stream of other men's work" and by a quarter-century of "experiment and blunder" in his own literary production.[1] Intellect and hard-earned craft, Sinclair indicated, qualified him to make a definitive statement on art, which is to say, on propaganda.

In addition, speaking for himself, Sinclair arguably gave voice to a literary tradition that included Harriet Beecher Stowe's *Uncle Tom's Cabin* (1852), Rebecca Harding Davis's *Life in the Iron-Mills* (1861), and Charlotte Perkins Gilman's *Herland* (1915). Sinclair's statement, furthermore, anticipated the strategies of John Steinbeck's *The Grapes of Wrath* (1939), Richard Wright's *Native Son* (1940), Norman Mailer's *The Armies of the Night* (1968), Edward Abbey's *The Monkey Wrench Gang* (1975), John Grisham's *The Appeal* (2008), and numerous other novels that have exposed moral and social injustice in a bid to reshape public opinion and thus to hasten positive social change in the United States of America and beyond. Whether urging the abolition of chattel slavery, industrial peonage, economic oppression, misogynistic patriarchy, child labor, militarism, racism, judicial corruption, or an end to environmental damage, these and other American novels from the nineteenth century onward have operated, like Sinclair's, as exposés and manifestos for social change. They have worked, that is, both to protest against conditions deemed harmful to society and to initiate and advance more equitable social arrangements. The issues that are exposed by narrators, fictional characters, and plotlines in this canon are thus meant to serve the public interest and so these texts are rightly termed novels of civic protest. In this regard, they are allied with nonfiction and fictional narratives known as muckraking.

Not that other novelists in the USA (and abroad) had avoided remediative social criticism. Exposure of social failings and foibles was a mainstay of the realist and naturalist tradition, visible in the writing of such figures as William Dean Howells, Kate Chopin, and Theodore Dreiser, just as it was a staple of the American novel from the eighteenth and early nineteenth centuries, when Charles Brockden Brown, Susanna Rowson, William Wells Brown, and James Fenimore Cooper, among others, asserted the utility of fiction for lessons in history, in virtue, and in moral philosophy. Nineteenth-century women's sentimental novels by such figures as E. D. E. N. Southworth and Susan Warner, moreover, were replete with lamentation on poverty and orphanage.

Sinclair's US predecessors and contemporaries, however, had largely fallen short in the central mission of the novel as he understood it. They had failed, that is, to exploit their propagandistic opportunity for social amelioration. By his activist test – that *"the true purpose of art is to alter reality"* – most writers and critics had gone in dangerously errant directions, in Sinclair's view.[2] His denunciation of literary misconceptions and deceptions can help clarify his conception of the workings of the novel of civic protest. "Art for art's sake," Sinclair said, was the sop of social degenerates, while doctrinaire traditionalists thwarted narrative innovation in the guise of fealty to established "classics." The art that drew critics' praise for its entertainment value instead warranted censure for its wasteful trivializing dilettantism, while a self-styled aesthetic cognoscenti of pseudo-elites excluded their fellow human beings from access to art. Those who relegated art to realms outside of and beyond morality were intellectual perverts, wrote Sinclair, while still others who denied the linkage of art with propaganda were, he wrote, the most egregious of liars.

The long-range importance of propaganda to the novel of civic protest exceeds the historical moment of Sinclair's pronouncement, but utilizing the term is difficult because it bears the burden of pejorative usage over time. "Propaganda" entered common parlance after 1918, and Sinclair's emphasis on its possibilities for advocacy risks lexical enmeshment in "a much more sinister popular connotation."[3] The close of World War I, as two recent historians of communications observe, brought a sobering assessment of "the apparent power that propaganda had exhibited as the conflict raged over almost all the entire planet."[4] The term has since become allied especially with repressive and genocidal regimes, and notable literary critics have advanced and reinforced these associations, from Kenneth Burke's 1941 analysis of the rhetoric of Adolf Hitler and the Nazi bureaucracy to Raymond Williams's glossary of keywords that names "war propaganda machines."[5]

The hostility of literary critics to propaganda, however, must be overcome to enable recognition of the particular historical moment in which Sinclair spoke and, moreover, the far wider time frame in which the US novel of civic protest has operated. The core meaning of the term as Sinclair invokes it grows out of the nineteenth-century social theory of a mediated society. Not that propaganda was identified solely with the rise of theories of "mass society" in the nineteenth century, for historians trace its origins to classical antiquity, while a chronicler of propaganda in America has found a continuum of far-reaching antecedents. These include promotional literature of the 1600s, the politicized newspapers of the late 1700s, the pamphlets of Thomas Paine, and such facilitating technologies as the hydraulic printing press (1785) and the electric telegraph (1839).[6]

A writer of Sinclair's generation knew the exponentially more formidable power of syndicated newspapers, motion pictures,[a] expositions, mass market magazines, photoengraving, radio, etc., to serve the interests of the government, of corporations, religious groups, political parties, and social movements.[7] Ever since the post-Civil War Gilded Age, every US writer has been positioned to grasp the power of advertising, branding, and public relations whose cardinal founding figures, Ivy Lee and Edward Bernays, demonstrated the ability of individual effort to shape public opinion for specific purposes. In 1906–1908, for instance, Lee helped the International Harvester Corporation avert an anti-trust battle by planting news stories emphasizing the benefits of corporate largeness.[8] By 1919, Bernays, a former wartime government propagandist, was defining himself as "public relations counsel," and his later book, *Propaganda* (1928), would argue that the public willingly avoids "confusion" by "consent[ing] to have its choice narrowed to ideas and objects brought to its attention through propaganda."[9]

Assumptions about the role of propaganda in mass society gained a particular American slant that gave rise to Sinclair's position and broadly characterizes the novel of civic protest. Late nineteenth-century European theorists,

a For a broad discussion of the power of mass media to affect fiction (and vice versa), see Mark McGurl's "The novel, mass culture, mass media," chapter 41 in this volume, especially his discussion of the adaptation of Steinbeck's *The Grapes of Wrath* for the screen (693–696).

notably Gabriel Tarde and Gustave Le Bon, anguished over the rise of the "masses." They focused on crowds' criminal and deranged behavior and warned about class divisiveness and political alienation. Le Bon's influential *The Crowd* (*La Psychologie des foules*, 1895), however, also commended the heroism and sacrifice of crowds in helping to create modern civilization. He emphasized crowd control by elites as the key to social stability and material progress. The American response, not surprisingly, sharply differed once the crowd was conceived as the body of citizenry. Public opinion in America was treated as an avenue of "enlightened discussion" to "be judged by an educated citizenry."[10]

The novel of civic protest relies on what Jacques Ellul calls "the fundamental psycho-sociological bases on which a whole society rests, the [ideas] . . . shared by all individuals in a society," including those of different classes and political affiliations. The core appeal of these novels to the common sense of their imagined readership can be explained by Ellul's warning that "a propaganda pitting itself against this fundamental and accepted structure would have no chance of success." What Ellul calls "fundamental currents of society" can be identified in all the novels considered here, but *The Jungle* will serve to illustrate the point.[11] Though Sinclair was a vegetarian and advocate of collective socialist-utopian cooperatives, his landmark novel does not endorse these lifestyle commitments. On the contrary, it actively or tacitly supports prevailing widespread social arrangements. *The Jungle* deplores dishonesty and cruelty in the industrial plants that victimize his sympathetic characters, for instance, but it does not challenge the legitimacy of industrial production as a foundation of the modern world. It condemns the callous slaughter of livestock but presumes the appropriateness of industrial agriculture to provide meat as a mainstay of the modern diet. Embracing the principle of private property, it enshrines the ownership of a house as an American ideal. (Sinclair's ardent pro-temperance stance is strongly reinforced in the novel, but temperance was a mainstream social movement when *The Jungle* was published.)

Another presumption of the novel – of its efficacy as an agent of social change – testifies to its utility as propaganda. Nearly 100,000 copies of *The Jungle* were in print by the end of 1906, and social pressures exerted by public response to the novel helped to pass the 1906 Pure Food and Drug Act, which mandated the federal inspection of food, beverages, and drugs that were shipped across state lines.[12] No longer were food producers free to sell tubercular meat or to ship hams embalmed with coal tar dyes – at least, not with impunity. The meat packers of course had their own organs of propaganda, for their products were sold via seductive advertising copytext, while the *Chicago Tribune* served their interests by denouncing Sinclair as a "distempered ... pseudo social reformer."[13]

Sinclair's novel, however, proved to be a more powerful instrument of propaganda than theirs. Sinclair's now-legendary lament that *The Jungle* failed to inspire labor rights legislation (that it hit the American stomach instead of its heart) ignores the fact of the novel's efficacy in shaping public opinion, policy, and law. In functional propagandistic terms, Sinclair's novel of civic protest worked even though it didn't accomplish its intended goal. In sum, the art of the American novel was to be a force for positive, activist social change.

In this regard, the mid nineteenth-century novels of Stowe and Davis are precursors. One scholar of communications typifies those who have found *Uncle Tom's Cabin* to be a "powerful propaganda novel" by citing its first-year sales figures of 300,000 copies and its efficacy in "contributing significantly to the abolitionist movement."[14] The first, serialized edition of *The Jungle* claimed descent in exactly these terms, and Sinclair called Stowe "a great-hearted woman [who] set forth the sufferings of the black chattel-slave, *and aroused a continent to arms*" (italics mine). Her success strengthened his determination "to write the *Uncle Tom's Cabin* of the labor movement."[15]

Davis's *Life in the Iron-Mills* also can be understood in this way. In Davis's novel (as in *The Jungle*), plantation chattel slavery is reframed as industrial slavery, and the need for abolition is once again the urgent message. Set in a river-valley industrial city, *Life in the Iron-Mills* features a sickly, poor immigrant Welsh iron worker, Hugh Wolfe, and his female cousin, Deborah, a textile mill operative. Just as Stowe presented Uncle Tom's material life in middle-class terms that were certain to engage readers' sympathies (the cabin or "cottage" that Tom shares with his spouse Chloe being replete with the signifiers of white middle-class domestic life from flower garden to carpet), so Davis strategically endows Hugh with appreciable native talent as a self-taught sculptor, a man of art. He, like cousin Deb, is desperate to escape the grinding poverty of the mill and gain a share of education and spiritual fulfillment amid surroundings of aesthetic beauty.

Davis, like Stowe, challenges her middle-class readers to recognize their complicity with abhorrent social arrangements and, upon that recognition, to take remedial action. Just as *Uncle Tom's Cabin* exposes readers to horrific cruelties on the deep South plantation overseen by "Mas'r" Simon Legree, so *Life in the Iron-Mills* goads its audience with descriptions of the industrial-era iron mill as a Dantean inferno. In addition, the novel prods readers to corrective action via a scene in which the mill is visited by a group who represent Davis's readers. A physician, a journalist, a manager, a minister, and a well-to-do gentleman all see the conditions in the mill firsthand and learn its human cost when encountering Hugh and seeing the powerful sculpture he has fashioned from ash waste matter. The sculpted figure of a spiritually starved and desperate woman expresses Hugh's (and by extension Deb's, and legions of other industrial workers') deep hunger for a decent life, as the visitors recognize. They represent society's elites, the owners, managers, and professionals who have the opportunity to help emancipate the man who is enslaved by the modern industrial order.

Yet they fail to take action. Absolving themselves of responsibility, they become the looking glass to which Davis summons her readership, before whom she lays bare the industrial peonage that furnishes the material comfort of the readers' lives, from their kitchen stoves to their doorstep boot scrapers, in order to prompt affluent Americans to take reformist action. The "great hope" expressed by the narrator is that the readers, once energized by the novel and fortified by the teachings of Christianity, will commute the collective industrial death sentence. "I have a great hope," proclaims the narrator, "and I bring it to you to be tested."

The rhetoric of *Life in the Iron-Mills* and the other novels of civic protest is overtly extreme for reasons that will warrant explanation presently. Davis's text, for instance, forswears the conventionally cozy "dear reader" of the nineteenth-century sentimental novel (and its eighteenth-century precedent) for a direct address that borders on hostile confrontation. Narrative decorum gives way to urgency of purpose because readers must be addressed at a high rhetorical decibel level. "A cloudy day," the narrator announces at the outset, immediately accusing the reader of willful ignorance in not grasping what such "nightmare fog" means "in a town of iron-works." Heretofore the reader(s) – i.e. "You" – have enjoyed several escape routes from the nightmare and may yet evade your responsibilities by dismissing the story of Hugh Wolfe and the industrial workers as a merely "tiresome" account of "dull" lives that are "vainly lived and lost." If so, however, you fail as a human being because you ignore the most profoundly dire, abhorrent economic and social facts. Your redemption, the narrator implies, can only begin with full engagement, and you are collared by the narrator's direct order: "Stop a moment." The narrator continues:

> This is what I want you to do. I want you to hide your disgust, take no heed to your clean clothes, and come right down with me, – here, into the thickest of

> the fog and mud and foul effluvia. I want you to hear this story. There is a secret down here, in this nightmare fog, that has lain dumb for centuries: I want to make it a real thing to you.

The narrator's mandate and the marching orders leave the reader no moral or ethical escape. The world of the "nightmare fog" must become the reader's provenance and responsibility.

Novels of civic protest speak in tones of extreme urgency and, in addition, typically "make it a real thing" in powerful one-dimensional images that recall the propagandist Edward Bernays's objective of sparing the public "confusion" by narrowing the range of ideas and objects that are brought to public attention. The quintessential power of maternity is projected in the image of Stowe's Eliza crossing the ice floes of the Ohio River to escape to freedom with baby Harry cradled in her arms (an incident which Stowe averred as a "well-known fact"). Congruently, Gilman's *Herland* bids to represent essential womanhood (*her* story against *his* tory). Or consider Steinbeck's "Okies," the four-generational Joad family in their jalopy crossing the country toward California in the depths of the 1930s Depression. They are a salt-of-the-earth template of American family solidarity and courage, and Tom Joad a figure of ideal male Americana (a hard worker, a faithful son, a fighter for justice and fairness).

Mailer's self-fashioned protagonist in *The Armies of the Night* is a kindred spirit of Tom Joad and thus a clear-cut paradigm of American manhood. Mailer casts himself as a typical American G.I. with the "veins and roots of the local history of every state and county in America." Abbey's Monkey Wrench Gang becomes a uni-dimensional protagonist grouping in which the group identity supervenes and governs. By the late twentieth- and early twenty-first centuries, the novelist John Grisham had long been excoriated for his one-dimensional characters. Such critique, however, misses an important linkage of the popular novelist with his categorically literary confrères, namely, that his Mississippi small-town lawyer characters in *The Appeal*, Wes and Mary Grace Payton, represent middle-class family values and grass roots citizenship in action. They are not individuated but typical by design. All the foregoing fictional figures from Sinclair through Grisham devolve from – and perpetuate – cultural stereotypes whose meanings are manifest with utter clarity.

Novels of civic protest thus reveal certain shared traits despite their particularities of diction and syntax, their congeries of disparate characters, their rhetorical moves and different settings and time periods. All exhibit a disciplined curtailment of interpretations, reflecting Ellul's emphasis on coercion over consent. "Propaganda," he writes, "tends to make the individual live in a separate world; he must not ... be allowed a moment of meditation or reflection in which to see himself vis-à-vis the propagandist, as happens when the propaganda is not continuous. At that moment the individual emerges from the grip of propaganda."[16] The grip of the novel of civic protest is applicable in these terms. Novels of civic protest, put simply, seek not to be susceptible to wide-ranging inquiry in search of nuance, subtlety, ambivalence, ambiguity, and so on. Their grip on the reader must be maintained through other techniques, often through highly dramatic plot design that is a staple of genre fiction (e.g., detective or mystery fiction).

The worlds in which these novels operate, in fact, can be considered Manichean. They are as clearly divided as light and darkness. The Mason-Dixon line (together with the Canadian border) separates the unalterably opposed worlds of *Uncle Tom's Cabin*, as does the color "line" in Wright's *Native Son*, which divides the racially white Chicago world of material plenty from the black world of hand-to-mouth struggles of the poor living in dilapidated rental housing and shopping for groceries sold at predatory pricing. The concluding scenes of Davis's text are limned in a pastoral idyll that is worlds away from the infernal iron mills as readers glimpse a house (Deb's new home) "whose windows overlook broad, wooded slopes and clover-trimmed meadows ... where the air is warmest, the air freshest." Some of these Manichean polarities are temporal, as in *Herland*, where Gilman looks back upon Western civilization as an unrelenting history of male-dominated brutal and destructive warfare, conquest, enslavement, and genocide. In contrast, Herland is a female realm whose origins include "farms and gardens ... in full production" and "industries ... in careful order," its modern status quo a sisterhood that is governed by "the power of mother-love," which is defined as the "maternal instinct ... raised to its highest power."[b]

The Monkey Wrench Gang also shows a historical split when Abbey contrasts the pristine American old West with that of its recent human imprint.[c] Readers experience a river journey that hearkens to the primal (perhaps

b Elsewhere in this volume, Russ Castronovo describes *Herland* as an "amalgam of utopia and colonialism" ("Imperialism, Orientalism, and empire," chapter 32, 547). Elizabeth Nolan, on the other hand, reads *Herland* as a story in which the "conventions of the traditional family home are overturned" ("The woman's novel beyond sentimentalism," chapter 34, 581). The novel's reform premise draws its energy from both of these contexts.

c Jonathan Levin calls this the "wilderness ethos"; in *The Monkey Wrench Gang*, this worldview is stoked by radical individualism that motivates the main characters' planned violent protest. (see "Contemporary ecofiction," chapter 68, 1123).

ahistoric) past: "river, the canyon, the desert world was always changing, from moment to moment, from miracle to miracle, within the firm reality of mother earth." One character recalls "the golden river flowing to the sea," canyons with names like Hidden Passage and Twilight, and "strange great amphitheaters called Music Temple and Cathedral in the Desert." All of these, however, "now lie beneath the dead water of the reservoir," behind which stands a dam with its "thickets of power cables," its "steel towers" and ironically irreligious "mass of cement" serving the cities of the West (e.g., Phoenix, Las Vegas), their names interlarded with Sodom and Gomorrah. Environmentally speaking, Steinbeck's Joads never rhapsodize about the Dust Bowl-era "dry earth" of their lost tenant farm as they depart for their own Californian Gomorrah, but readers understand that their decades-long hardscrabble lives had a certain sufficiency and a rich family history before the dust bowl sent them into exile. Their past, we understand, is now "spoiled" and certain to "cry to them in the coming days" of their diaspora. In Grisham's *The Appeal*, the past indeed cries out in the face of the current spoilage of the community of small-town lawyers, friends and neighbors who lived in peace and health (if not economic affluence) before the Krane Chemical company poisoned their water with cancer-causing chemicals and precipitated a lawsuit that was to politicize – that is, to infect – the state judicial system at its highest levels.

The "Armies of the Night" in Mailer's novel, once again in Manichean terms, fight in, and over, two mutually exclusive Americas. Marching with writers Robert Lowell and Dwight Macdonald to protest the Vietnam war, Mailer feels "a sharp searing love for his country," the America of the labor movement that "jack[ed] the country up from the Depression" and recently birthed the Civil Rights Movement. This is an America of virility and athleticism. Its nemesis is an America whose political and corporate authority has lobotomized the country and filled the earth and sky with a "barrage of helicopters, TV cars, monitors, loudspeakers," and above all, with a military draft that conscripts young men into a criminal war in southeast Asia. Mailer denounces "the progressive contamination of all American life in the abscess of Vietnam." He understands the moment as an historic schism, a "wrinkle in time": "He felt as if he stepped through some crossing in the reaches of space between this moment, the French Revolution, and the Civil War, as if the ghosts of the Union Dead accompanied them now to the Bastille . . . the true and high church of the military-industrial complex, the Pentagon."

Another phrase that most aptly and usefully designates novels of civic protest is one that is commonly applied to stage versions of *Uncle Tom's*

Cabin: melodrama. This term, too, has borne the brunt of longstanding critical scorn, but melodrama warrants attention here. Just as propaganda establishes the motives of persuasion in the novels of civic protest, so the theory of melodrama opens the epistemological means of their operation. Later nineteenth-century popular dramas such as Adolphe D'Ennery and Eugene Cormon's 1875 *The Two Orphans* and the stage version of E. D. E. N. Southworth's *The Hidden Hand* (based on her 1859 novel) exemplify how melodrama affects its audience. One scholar summarizes their familiar characteristics of stagecraft and script, including thrilling incidents and blatant spectacle, along with an "open display of violence and catastrophe" and "exaggerated expression of emotion."[17]

The novel, too, has come in for close, congruent examination as melodrama in Peter Brooks's *The Melodramatic Imagination* (1976), where Brooks affirms the relation of fiction to the art form that is most closely linked to his key term. For Brooks, a "fundamental characteristic of the melodramatic mode" is "the desire to express all," for "nothing is spared because nothing is left unsaid; the characters ... utter the unspeakable, give voice to their deepest feelings."[18] The concepts in play, moreover, are expressed in hyperbolic "absolute purity and polarization," which is to say with hyperbolic emphasis.[19] Melodramatic rhetoric, Brooks writes, "tends toward the inflated and the sententious. Its typical figures are hyperbole, antithesis, and oxymoron: those figures, precisely, that evidence a refusal of nuance and the insistence on dealing in pure, integral concepts."[20] Further, "the conflict of good and evil ... must hence be led to confrontation, articulation, acting out."[21] Having recognized these characteristics in the foregoing survey of American novels of civic protest, we can also appreciate Brooks's core hypothesis as central to them:

> Melodramatic rhetoric, and the whole expressive enterprise of the genre, represents a victory over repression. We could conceive this repression as simultaneously social, psychological, historical, and conventional ... The melodramatic utterance breaks through everything that constitutes the "reality principle," all its censorships, accommodations, tonings-down. Desire cries aloud its language in identification with full states of being.[22]

Melodrama, in this sense, turns the world inside out. To "make it a real thing," in Rebecca Harding Davis's term, requires violation of the "reality principle." Melodrama refuses to dissemble or defer or delay. It blurts and blares – though ever congruent, in Ellul's term, with "the fundamental currents of the society it seeks to influence." Managing that paradox is crucial to what Sinclair called its "technical competence" and its "vitality and importance."[23]

Social amelioration and civic advancement pose a positivist test for these novels. To what extent have the societal ills that they expose been remedied and given way to a more equitable state? Operating as melodrama under an overarching rubric of propaganda, how have these novels fared? From racism to militarism, sexism, environmental damage, and so on, can the American novel of civic protest attain its own internally stated goals – or is it, with few exceptions, more properly considered to be the novel of civic aspiration? (The venture of Sinclair into a gubernatorial race in California in 1933–1934 and Mailer into a New York City mayoral contest in 1969 imply their recognition of the limits of the novel to spur social change in the short term.)

The novelists themselves seem to recognize these limitations: vast sectors of the public beyond their pages are represented in their work as impervious to activism. The propagandist news media in *Native Son* stirs the public into a frenzy to lynch Bigger Thomas and seals his doom by stereotyping the youth as a black male monster driven to rape and homicide. In *The Armies of the Night*, the same news media has persuaded the American public ("Middle America," in Richard Nixon's propagandist catchphrase) that warfare in Vietnam protects the USA against the evils of atheistic communism. *Herland* allows only three representative American men to enter the all-female society but thereby reveals the daunting task of reeducating an entire patriarchal America. Further, the "eco-raiders" in *The Monkey Wrench Gang* stage their acts of rebellion in a country that is eager to consume the products of industrial agriculture, environmentally rapacious suburban housing, and hydroelectric power that ruins rivers and wildlife.

These novels speak *for* and *of* their major characters, but cannot speak *to* or *with* them. In 1915, the year of the publication of *Herland*, Gilman's women lacked the right to vote in national elections (as did the abolitionist-minded New Englander, Ophelia, in *Uncle Tom's Cabin*). Otherwise, major characters who are victimized by the existing social arrangements are emphatically too hobbled to take the initiative necessary for urgently needed reform. Literacy and articulate speech, the stock-in-trade of the novel, are denied to Sinclair's Lithuanian immigrant manual workers, to Davis's foundryman, to Wright's Bigger Thomas. The Joads are at most semi-literate and, like Bigger and the immigrants, cannot speak standard English. Preoccupied with the daily struggle to survive, neither the Joads, nor Sinclair's Jurgis Rudkis, nor Davis's Hugh Wolfe has the free time to mount and lead a progressive initiative. Unable to read the books in which they themselves appear, neither can they buy them.

The actually imprisoned Bigger might stand for the novels' own de facto social imprisonment.[d]

A corollary question becomes: to what extent has the audience (or audiences) of these novels been mobilized into action? What is the mechanism for the changes on which the novels insist? Ellul's theory is once again helpful, for he differentiates between the propaganda of agitation and that of integration. Agitation, he finds, opposes the existing order and seeks revolutionary change. The novels themselves serve this function, persuading readers that the status quo is intolerable. In this regard, the texts are as thoroughly detailed as they are tonally outraged, and readers are drawn into this outrage and simultaneously into the specifics of the social wrongs. The readers, in effect, are thus enlisted as proselytizers for the texts' causes, from living wages to healthful working conditions, good childcare, education, cessation of race-based oppression and imperial war, an impartial judiciary free of corporate-funded election campaign manipulation, and so on. These are the terms that must then prompt what Ellul calls "integration propaganda," which "aims at stabilizing the social body, at unifying and reinforcing it." Those most receptive to integrative propaganda, says Ellul, are "the more comfortable, cultivated, and informed," including "intellectuals."[24] Literate, educated, and affluent, they are the readers of these novels. Although Ellul pits the propagandist agitators against the integraters, civic protest novels present these two readers' functions sequentially. First, they – or we – are stirred into agitation for positive change and must not relent until its goals are attained. As agents of change, we thereafter become instruments of a social stability that is justified by the new social order called for in the novels. Prospects for the future, however, are guarded in these novels. Wright's reliance on the individually willed identity of existentialist experience shows his doubt that the "millions" of American Bigger Thomases, both black and white, can bring about the necessary social change to correct psycho- and sociopathologies of race and class. Sinclair's frustration in concluding *The Jungle* to his (and his readers') satisfaction also belies his apparent certitude that an era of industrial

d Valerie Babb's reading of *Native Son* in this volume provides an interesting corollary to this point, as she opposes Wright and Zora Neale Hurston on the subject of how best to represent African American experience. Hurston's ethnographic, folkloric approach contrasts with Wright's portrayal of what Babb calls the "entrapment of predestined black failure" by "a racial past that mires black progress" ("Wright, Hurston, and the direction of the African American novel," chapter 42, 709). Such a desperate and hopeless representation is, paradoxically, key to advancing Wright's reform agenda.

capitalism, fueled by greed and oppression, can be superceded by a socialist workers' movement.[25]

Gilman relied much more on nonfiction tracts to advance feminist principles, even as social theorists began to cast serious doubt on the likelihood of positivist outcomes of propaganda. From the twentieth-century era of formalism through literary theory and cultural studies, critics have largely avoided measuring the leverage of novels in securing social changes. Historian Jill Lepore, however, outlines a viable approach for doing so. Tracing the late nineteenth-century divorce of belles-lettres from the writing of history, she reminds us that historical writing allied with science to promote the core value of factual accuracy, while literary production (case in point: the novel) was thereafter valued for imaginative storytelling of people's lives.[26] The exposure of this schism implies a way to reframe the novel of civic protest in relation to the findings sought by the historian. Rather than accord the novels a "separate sphere" status and evaluate their relation to social dynamism in that vacuum, the literary critic of the novel of civic protest might regard the text as one – not *the*, but *one* – agent of the change(s) advocated.

Grisham's *The Appeal* provides one recent case study of the novel of civic protest that literary critics can best understand in the wider socio-cultural context indicated by Lepore. As an aggressively marketed novel by a prolific brand-name author of bestselling fiction, *The Appeal* is positioned to influence public opinion in its story of the catastrophic consequences of the private funding of judicial election campaigns, which are increasing throughout the United States in the early twenty-first century. Aligned with the other novels of civic protest, *The Appeal* is an instrument of propaganda providing public education via entertainment. Grisham's "Author's Note" makes explicit the take-away message of the novel: "As long as private money is allowed in judicial elections we will see competing interests fight for seats on the bench."

As a novel of civic protest, *The Appeal* is optimally viewed within a larger realm of public discourse. The parameters can be suggested here in brief. The commercial publication of the reference book, *John Grisham: A Critical Companion*, indicates the stature of the author's two decades of legal thriller fictions that have shaped an audience alerted to recurrent themes of uses and abuses of law.[27] A typical book-review blog, in addition, blurbs *The Appeal* as "a story that will leave readers unable to think about the US electoral process or judicial system in quite the same way ever again."[28] From the highest levels of the judiciary have come similar disquieting expressions, one from former US Supreme Court Justice Sandra Day O'Connor, who publicly stated in 2008, "We put cash in the courtrooms, and it's just wrong." O'Connor's remarks, in turn, were quoted in a *New York Times* op-ed essay of April 2008 with the headline: "The Selling of the Judiciary: Campaign Cash in the Courtroom." In melodramatic rhetoric, the journalist warned of the threats to impartial justice in "a grubby new era of multimillion-dollar campaigns for important state judgeships ... slugfests largely underwritten by well-heeled interest groups – including insurance companies, tobacco firms, the building and healthcare industries, unions and trial lawyers – that have seized upon judicial contests as a promising avenue for influence-peddling."[29] A follow-up *Times* front-page article appeared the next month in the Sunday edition, "Rendering Justice, With One Eye on Re-election."[30] Thus like other novels of civic protest, the potential civic efficacy of *The Appeal* is best assessed in its synergistic relation to wide-ranging, myriad public statements and texts in print and online. One can anticipate possible debates conducted in online blogs, postings, magazine and newspaper articles, symposia, TV segments, investigative commission reports, congressional testimony, and so on.

Whether the special-interest financing of judicial campaigns is curbed or outlawed in years to come cannot be known. But if the trend is reversed, at least one novel will be a part of the necessary "*changes of feeling, belief, and action*" that Sinclair sees as arts ultimate purpose.[31] The record from the past seems relevant here. Suffrage, workplace safety, civil rights, and anti-child labor legislation – these were not in place when the novels advocating them were published. But public officials, clergy, investigative journalists, academics, academically trained professionals, and activist citizens (organized, for instance, in women's clubs nationwide) – all exerted pressures for social change through coalitional arrangements. Gradually their efforts succeeded in public education and legislation. Novels of civic protest have been a significant part of this campaign literature.

Notes

1. Upton Sinclair, *Mammonart: An Essay in Economic Interpretation* (1925; Westport, CT: Hyperion, 1975), 9, 8. Sinclair's title asserted the enmeshment of art production and material wealth, and he defined the artist as "one who represents life imaginatively by any device, whether picture or statue or poem or song or symphony or opera or drama or novel" (8).
2. *Ibid.*, 9.

3. See Richard Alan Nelson, *A Chronology and Glossary of Propaganda in the United States* (Westport, CT: Greenwood, 1996), ix. For dating of the common usage of the term, see Garth S. Jowett and Victoria O'Donnell, *Propaganda and Persuasion*, 4th edn. (Thousand Oaks, CA: Sage, 2006), 100. Jowett and O'Donnell remark that "the term [propaganda] is often used as a catch-all for suspicious rhetoric" (3).
4. Jowett and O'Donnell, *Propaganda and Persuasion*, 206. Sinclair remarks on this point. See Sinclair, *Mammonart*, 10a [*sic*].
5. See Kenneth Burke, "The Rhetoric of Hitler's 'Battle,'" in *Readings in Propaganda and Persuasion: New and Classic Essays*, ed. Garth S. Jowett and Victoria O'Donnell (Thousand Oaks, CA: Sage, 2006), 149–168. See also Raymond Williams, *Keywords: A Vocabulary of Culture and Society*, rev. edn. (New York: Oxford University Press, 1983), 73.
6. The history of propaganda from classical antiquity is recounted in Jowett and O'Donnell, *Propaganda and Persuasion*, 49–92. US antecedents are chronicled in Nelson, *Chronology and Glossery*, 1–21.
7. See Nelson, *Chronology and Glossary*, 22–50.
8. On Ivy Lee and the International Harvester campaign, *ibid.*, 30–31.
9. Edward Bernays, *Propaganda* (New York: Horace Liveright, 1928), 11.
10. See Gabriel Tarde, *On Communication and Social Influence*, ed. Terry N. Clark (Chicago: University of Chicago Press, 1969), and Gustave Le Bon, *The Crowd* (1895; New Brunswick and London: Transaction, 1995). "The American response," quoted in Jowett and O'Donnell, *Propaganda and Persuasion*, 100.
11. Jacques Ellul, "The Characteristics of Propaganda" (1965), rpt. in Jowett and O'Donnell, *Readings in Propaganda and Persuasion*, 1–49.
12. For an account of the politics of the Act, see Anthony Arthur, *Radical Innocent: Upton Sinclair* (New York: Random House, 2006), 72–82. See also Robert Crunden, *Ministers of Reform* (New York: Basic Books, 1982).
13. See Arthur, *Radical Innocent*, 68–69. In *The Jungle*, Sinclair thinly disguises the products of August Swift and Phillip Armour as "Brown's Imperial Hams and Bacon" and "Durham's Pure Leaf Lard".
14. Nelson, *Chronology and Glossary*, 15. For more on the reception of *Uncle Tom's Cabin*, see John Ernest's essay in this volume, "Stowe, race and the antebellum American novel" (chapter 15).
15. Quoted in Arthur, *Radical Innocent*, 43.
16. Ellul, "The Characteristics of Propaganda," 11.
17. See Jeffrey Mason, *Melodrama and the Myth of America* (Bloomington: Indiana University Press, 1993), 17.
18. Peter Brooks, *The Melodramatic Imagination: Balzac, Henry James, Melodrama and the Mode of Excess* (1976; repr. New Haven: Yale University Press, 1995), 4.
19. *Ibid.*, 24–25.
20. *Ibid.*, 40–41.
21. *Ibid.*, 159.
22. *Ibid.*, 41.

23. Ellul, "The Characteristics of Propaganda," 21; Sinclair, *Mammonart*, 10.
24. Ellul, "The Characteristics of Propaganda," 37.
25. Sinclair wrote numerous endings for *The Jungle*, and the serialized version contains a different one from the published novel. See, for example, *The Lost First Edition of Upton Sinclair's "The Jungle,"* ed. Gene DeGruson (Memphis: St. Luke's Press, 1988).
26. Jill Lepore, "Just the Facts, Ma'am: Fake Memoirs, Factual Fictions, and the History of History," *The New Yorker* (March 24, 2008): 79–83. Lepore's discussion does not include biography or memoir, nor does she address narrative techniques employed by historians.
27. See Mary Beth Pringle, *John Grisham: A Critical Companion* (Westport, CT: Greenwood, 1997).
28. See http://writerscrunch.blogspot.com/2008/01/novels-of-month-january-2008.html
29. Dorothy Samuels, "The Selling of the Judiciary: Campaign Cash in the Courtroom," *New York Times* (April 15, 2008): A22.
30. Adam Liptak, "Rendering Justice, With One Eye on Re-election," *New York Times* (May 25, 2008): 1, 13. Liptak writes,

    > Last month, Wisconsin voters did something that is routine in the United States but virtually unheard of in the rest of the world: They elected a judge. The vote came after a bitter $5 million campaign in which a small-town trial judge with thin credentials ran a television advertisement falsely suggesting that the only black justice on the state supreme Court had helped free a black rapist. The challenger unseated the justice with 51 percent of the vote, and will join the court in August.

31. Sinclair, *Mammonart*, 10.

24

Novels of American business, industry, and consumerism

DAVID A. ZIMMERMAN

Between 1865 and 1917, American writers produced hundreds of novels focusing on business, labor relations, financial speculation, economic crises, consumerism, and other economic phenomena. A handful of these novels, including William Dean Howells's *The Rise of Silas Lapham* (1885) and Theodore Dreiser's *Sister Carrie* (1900), have secured a high place in today's literary canon. A number of others, such as Edward Bellamy's *Looking Backward* (1888) and Frank Norris's *The Pit* (1903), were national bestsellers. A few, including John Hay's *The Bread-winners* (1883) and Upton Sinclair's *The Jungle* (1906), gained brief but explosive notoriety. Many others are deservedly obscure.[1] Although they are often lumped together as "economic novels," most of them fall within recognizable subgenres: the economic reform novel (which encompasses labor jeremiads, Populist polemics, and utopian lectures), the success tale (which includes rags-to-riches stories, Wall Street romances, and novels about financial titans), and consumer fiction, the sentimental and narrative formulas for which evolved over the latter half of the nineteenth century.

These novels aim to attach familiar meanings, emotional significance, and, for literary naturalists at the turn of the century, philosophical and aesthetic import to the vertiginous economic changes transforming American culture and rendering it, in the eyes of older observers, unrecognizable. Written to alarm, disarm, entertain, regenerate, as well as mobilize readers, they offer storylines, images, and characters through which American economic modernity – the industrial, corporate, and financial forces reshaping cities, rural landscapes, social relations, and identities – could be comprehended and, at least imaginatively, controlled. Although they focus on challenges posed by new kinds of economic activity to regional, domestic, and personal life – to class, gender, and generational relations; to inherited definitions of success and status; and to older notions of agency and responsibility – these narratives are consistently framed as national dramas. They adapt the narrative grammar of familiar, often obsolescent, economic regimes (such as mercantilism, labor republicanism, entrepreneurialism, contract liberalism) to make sense of dizzying national developments and to give sentimental force to their rendering of the nation's character as it changed from a primarily rural, agricultural society to an urban, industrial one dominated by massive corporations.

Different structures of feeling animate these novels. Reform novels, constituting the largest part of this fiction, mourn the passing of small producers, regional markets, and the forms of identity and democratic belonging they anchored. These novels traverse the phases of grief: populist novelists, for example, typically express rage, helplessness, and nostalgia, while progressive authors labor to accommodate themselves to the new corporate dispensation. In contrast, success novels, which gained their widest audience during the economy's dazzling rise from crisis at the end of the 1890s, are actuated by optimism. These books spotlight the national benefits of corporate gigantism and the material progress, social stability, and cultural advance it promised. A final group of novels, harder to categorize by theme or ideological aim, is energized by awe. Written at the turn of the century when hundreds of colossal corporations were blooming into being, these works register in their plotlines and their form the overwhelming scale and speed of capitalist creation and destruction. They convey the terror as well as the excitement that business novelists such as Theodore Dreiser privately confessed to feeling when they confronted the sublime market forces remaking urban and rural economic life.

All of these novels identify American capitalism with profound, often sensational, change. Much of this fiction appears to arraign capitalism by appealing to some idea, place, or time seemingly impervious to flux – chivalric love, moral character, gender identity, aesthetic harmony, Christian service, country life, and so on. Many novels, especially before 1890, appear to condemn capitalism by emphasizing the contrast between "business" sentiments and more culturally sanctified ones, or by tracing how "business" infects realms supposedly sealed from market imperatives and values – realms such as the home, heart, and halls of government. However, it is important to keep in mind that all of this fiction speaks about American capitalism from within the frame of the capitalist imagination. With the possible exception of socialist utopias, which offer a perspective from a speculative vantage point outside of capitalist time and geography, no economic fiction indicts, supports, or even studies "capitalism" as such. Instead, these novels, even the shrillest anti-banker melodramas, typically dramatize conflicts between less and more modern trajectories *within* capitalism's development, between residual and emergent forms of market organization, economic morality, and profit-seeking. These historical tensions typically take shape in the novels as contests between representative figures (e.g. the old, timorous banker vs. the young, fearless financier) and spaces (e.g. the family farm vs. the wheat exchange). Capitalism, this fiction reminds us, produces not only goods but also the narratives that reveal and refract its internal conflicts and contradictions.

Economic reform fiction

The economic reform novel extends from factory exposés and speculation panoramas of the 1870s to Wall Street dramas and socialist prophecies at the turn of the century. Unlike antebellum financial melodramas, these novels are not cautionary tales warning against the personal and domestic ruin following from speculative recklessness and other failures of self-possession in the marketplace. Instead, they deploy stories involving laborers, financiers, corporate builders, journalists, and other economic victims, villains, and witnesses to highlight national sins and failures accompanying the sweeping transformation of the economy after the Civil War: in the 1870s, the political and moral corruption fueled by the national mania for speculation; in the 1880s, industrial labor conflict and the social rupture it portended; in the 1890s, economic crisis and the apparent demise of small-producer democracy; and after 1900, the entrenchment of industrial trusts and the apotheosis of the Wall Street titan.

Novels focusing on the misery and militancy of a burgeoning industrial underclass in the decades after the Civil War punctured the moral confidence of Republicans and supporters of northern business enterprise who saw Appomattox as "a sacred turning point in the saga of inexorable progress."[2] For these politicians and businessmen, the westward spread of railroads across the newly united nation, funded by federal and state government in coordination with northeastern finance capitalists, would create a truly national market and usher in a golden age of industrial growth and prosperity, spreading economic democracy in its wake. As the editor of *The Nation* predicted in 1865, "the great strife between the few and the many, between privilege and equality, between law and power" would soon end.[3]

Labor novelists documented the failure of this sanguine vision. Fiction about factory life, much of it focusing on female millworkers in Lowell, Massachusetts, had been popular since the 1840s. It wasn't until the 1860s and 1870s, however, with the national proliferation of large mechanized factories and the wage system, that American novelists, beginning with Rebecca Harding Davis and Elizabeth Stuart Phelps, gave sustained attention to the social and moral problems posed by the entrenchment of a permanent industrial working class. These early industrial jeremiads centered on the deafness of factory managers, investors, and other beneficiaries of the new industrial order to the moral and spiritual claims of impoverished factory workers. Davis's novella *Life in the Iron-Mills* (1861), a proto-naturalist artist tale set within the brutalizing realm of the factory, established a template for this fiction.[a] Phelps's *The Silent Partner* (1871), adapting narrative formulas established by antebellum women's sentimental novels and British industrial fiction, also exposed for bourgeois readers the widening gulf between laboring and leisure classes.[b] Mingling grim realism and dreamy lyricism, *The Silent Partner* reimagines the True Woman as a labor sympathizer and grounds this labor evangelism in an assertive feminism: in order to exercise her Christian duty to the laboring poor in the mill in which she has inherited a stake, the protagonist must first break the gender norms limiting her social experience and authority to the home. More radically, she can exercise her moral influence only by abjuring marriage and intervening in the masculine world of labor management.

Phelps's confidence in the power of compassionate communication to salve class suffering and worker outrage became increasingly untenable after the national railroad strike of 1877 and the explosion of an anarchist bomb in Chicago's Haymarket Square in 1886. Observing the escalating warfare between industrial labor and capital, writers flooded the market with reform polemics and apocalyptic prophecies about "The Coming Climax" and "The Impending Crisis." As faith in a natural harmony of interests between bosses and workers gave way to fears about the irreconcilable antagonism between capital and labor, conservative novelists found commercial success by marginalizing labor's menace. Evoking the urban upheavals of 1877, for example, future Secretary of State John Hay's *The Bread-winners* (published anonymously in 1883) was so disparaging of worker grievances – it presents labor

a For a discussion of *Life in the Iron-Mills* as a protest novel, see Cecelia Tichi, "Novels of social protest," chapter 23, 397–399.

b On this earlier sentimental tradition, see Cindy Weinstein, "Sentimentalism," chapter 12.

reformers as parasites on honest workers, "apostles of plunder" driven by class envy and sexual jealousy – that it provoked several protest novels in response.

Dozens of utopian novels in the last decades of the century also confronted the impasse between labor and capital by envisioning the ethical and economic benefits to the nation after this impasse has been peacefully resolved. These works, many capitalizing on the blockbuster success of Edward Bellamy's Christian socialist utopia, *Looking Backward*, detail futures that, if not doing away with capital altogether, put an end to the competitive economic conditions that caused mass wage cuts, worker violence, and national discord. This fiction offered middle-class Americans safe passage to the future, tempering the most explosive features of industrial capitalism, but also defanging radical socialism's threat by foreclosing the need for revolutionary upheaval. Mark Twain's *A Connecticut Yankee in King Arthur's Court* (1889) (about a Hartford machinist and weapons manufacturer who awakens in medieval England, tries to modernize the political and social system, and ends up engineering a holocaust) is sometimes read as a satire of utopian fiction and its optimism. Some readers, building on Henry Nash Smith's landmark discussion in *Mark Twain's Fable of Progress* (1964), view the novel as an allegory of American industrial modernity, an interpretation that invites as many questions as it answers: is the Yankee a figure for enlightened industrial progress, as portions of the text suggest, for example, or for demoralizing tendencies within capitalist development, as the horrifying climax might indicate?[4]

Economic reform novels centered not only on industrial labor and production but also on what Henry James called the "special and occult" realm of business and finance.[5] In the 1870s, business novels, most famously Twain and Charles Dudley Warner's *The Gilded Age* (1873) and Josiah Holland's *Sevenoaks* (1875), focus on the moral vertigo and political corruption fueled by the national mania for land and stock speculation after the Civil War, a mania inflamed by the railroad boom and climaxing in a series of sensational financial scandals that rocked Wall Street and Washington between 1868 and 1872. Panoramically tracing the connection between the speculative mania and the nation's moral decline, *The Gilded Age* weds two genres popular after the war, the western land speculation novel (David Locke's *A Paper City* [1878], for example), and the lobbyist novel (such as John W. De Forest's *Honest John Vane* [1875]). Moving from fruitless land speculations on the western frontier to corrupt profit-seeking in Wall Street and Washington, *The Gilded Age* portrays speculation as a national pastime, a craze both energizing and corrupting the country. Only in America, the novel wryly observes, can a speculator earn respect by reporting, "I wasn't worth a cent two years ago, and now I owe two millions of dollars." *The Gilded Age* documents the dislocations caused by speculation, fueled by reckless confidence and easy credit.[c]

Where *The Gilded Age* centers on the visionary delusions of small speculators, Josiah Holland's *Sevenoaks*, a "fixture on every middle-class reading table" alongside Bunyan and the Bible in the late 1870s, emphasizes the moral depravity of a rogue capitalist.[6] Written by the founding editor of *Scribner's*, the novel centers on an industrialist who gets rich off a stolen patent, starves his factory workers, uses his ill-gotten wealth to manipulate stocks on Wall Street, and exploits a ruinous oil stock mania in his hometown in Pennsylvania. Drawing on Dickens and Milton (and welcomed by one reviewer as "a masculine bass" balancing the "soprano and treble" of popular New England women's fiction[7]), it introduced a number of character types, including a prototypical "robber baron" figure and his female proxy, a profligate fascinatrix, that would become standard in later reform melodramas.

Exposing the moral and political laxness encouraged by the nation's financial lawlessness, *The Gilded Age* and *Sevenoaks* urge moral rather than economic reform. Indebted to their antebellum precedents, they focus their criticism on the domestic and political dangers of unchecked individual desire and ambition unloosed by the emerging political economy, not on forms of social injury or inequality intrinsic to capital development. Over the next three decades, reform fiction would offer more sweeping and politically charged indictments of modern capitalists and capitalism.

The populist or anti-monopolist novel dominated this protest trajectory in the 1880s and 1890s. Dramatizing the cutthroat practices of monopolies and the concentration of wealth and economic power in the hands of railroad barons and Wall Street speculators, this protest fiction gained traction with Henry Keenan's *The Money-Makers* (1884), the most notorious of the responses to Hay's *The Bread-winners*, and T. S. Denison's *An Iron Crown* (1885), an early muckraking epic. These sprawling novels aim to awaken readers to the emergence of a capitalist oligarchy ruthlessly bent on amassing wealth and social power. Insisting on sovereign labor as the enduring foundation of economic value and democratic citizenship, they dramatize how corporate rapacity triggers worker violence and social chaos. In crisis tones that became a signature of subsequent reform fiction, they prophesy that Americans, unless they mobilize politically, will soon find their

c For further discussion of *The Gilded Age* and *A Connecticut Yankee in King Arthur's Court*, see Andrew Lawson, "Twain, class, and the Gilded Age," chapter 21, 368–369, 374–376.

economic and political freedoms stifled by "the great momentum of corporate influence."

Like the fiction produced by workingmen's parties and other enemies of large capital in the decades after the Civil War, these protest novels remind us that the development of modern American capitalism was fiercely contested, especially along lines of region, class, and race, as in Thomas Dixon's 1902 bestseller *The Leopard's Spots* (where Simon Legree, the ruthless slaveholder from *Uncle Tom's Cabin*, returns as a Wall Street operator).[d] Novelists often saw themselves as active participants in the political and imaginative construction of the emerging political economy. They galvanized public opinion, pressured policymakers, and aroused the popular press. Reform novelists shaped, and occasionally incited, explosive public debates over the moral premises and social meanings of unrestrained markets, economic centralization, and, above all, the cultural and political identity of the nation.

Although protest fiction forms only a small, late part of his work, William Dean Howells offers the most sustained examination by a major American writer in the 1880s and 1890s of the ways business values and social relations under industrial capitalism penetrate the nation's cultural and moral life. In seven novels published between 1885 and 1894, Howells anatomized, with increasing despair, how industrial capitalism, by dividing rich from poor and subjecting individuals to the mercilessness of what he once called "this economic chance-world," retarded the recognition of commonality necessary for national cohesion and mutualist ethics.

The Rise of Silas Lapham is Howells's first work to focus squarely on business themes. It showcases his emerging ideas about realism in its refusal to reduce the businessman to flat caricature and its equally novel treatment of the complexities of moral action in a contingent, socially interdependent universe, exemplified by the stock market. It narrates the halting but ultimately successful rapprochement between two social classes, one represented by Lapham, a Vermont roughneck who made his fortune manufacturing paint, and the other represented by Brahmin Bostonians, the Coreys, whose son's interest in business and in Lapham's daughter brings the two sets of parents into embarrassed contact. Studying how one can deal in paint without being stained by the taint of business, the novel is framed around familiar oppositions between commercial and cultural values, parvenu crassness and Old World refinement, masculine productivity and feminine leisure. Like many

d For a discussion of Dixon's novel and the role race plays in its apprehension of American modernity, see Robert Reid-Pharr, "The postbellum race novel," chapter 28, 472–478.

business novelists, Howells entrusts the younger generation with reconciling these oppositions, ultimately finding common ground between them in the entrepreneurial aptitude and romantic fitness of the Corey son; he also finds common ground between them in the market success of one specialty brand of Lapham's paint, a high-quality type that embodies a felicitous middle ground between the mass commodity on which Lapham built his fortune and the refined art gracing the Coreys' home, and that "held its own against bad times and ruinous competition." The fate of Lapham's Persis Brand (its name suggesting persistence and continuity) offers hope that competitive capitalism can provide a secure, if circumscribed, place for moral integrity, productive work, and aesthetic distinction.

Howells's subsequent fiction, inspired by his reading of Tolstoy, Bellamy, and Spencer and culminating in two utopian novels written during the economic crisis of the 1890s, reflects his increasing doubt about the capacity of capitalism – and American democracy under capitalism – to accommodate social difference and nurture the civic benefits of individuals' "useful and wholesome labors." Awakening, like many middle-class contemporaries, to the intensifying conflict between industrial capital and labor, and outraged by the unjust treatment meted out to the Haymarket anarchists in 1887, Howells abandoned his complacent conviction that American novelists should "concern themselves with the more smiling aspects of life, which are the more American," and his fiction began to confront more directly the social and ethical costs of economic uncertainty, predatory competition, and class inequality.[8] *A Hazard of New Fortunes* (1890), culminating in labor violence, a climax more jarring and inconclusive than in any other work by Howells, marks the limits of his realism's capacity to dramatize, let alone normalize, the common character and conditions required for national cohesion and Christian brotherhood.[e]

Many novelists struggled as Howells did to map an older moral vision onto a rapidly changing economic landscape. They understood the nation, battered by economic crisis, labor strikes, and social disorder, to be at a crossroads, its economic, political, and cultural future up for grabs. One of the most widely read alarms of this sort came from Ignatius Donnelly, a three-term Populist congressman from Minnesota, whose novel *Caesar's Column* (1890), a lurid counter-vision to Bellamy's *Looking Backward*, follows a war between the capitalist

e For further discussion of *The Rise of Silas Lapham* and Howells's commitment in his major fiction and criticism to bridge class and other divisions threatening American society, see Michael Elliott, "Realism and radicalism: the school of Howells," chapter 17; and for discussion of *A Hazard of New Fortunes*, *ibid.*, 298–300; and Jude Davies, "Dreiser and the city," chapter 22, 384–385.

gold conspiracy and the oppressed poor to its nightmarish finale, set in 1988. Socialist novelists, most famously Upton Sinclair and Jack London, also delineated the disastrous endgame toward which industrial expansion and banker hegemony seemed to be projecting the nation. Viewing economic developments as expressions of strict teleological laws, these "scientific" socialists viewed corporate centralization as the logical culmination of capitalist evolution, an advanced mode of economic organization that must be commandeered by working people, not dismantled or neutralized, as Populists had urged. The most sensational and formally inventive of their apocalyptic prophecies is London's *The Iron Heel* (1907), which takes the form of a private manuscript found and glossed by scholars around the year 2600, after centuries of revolutionary insurgency have finally overthrown capitalism, but penned in 1932 by the wife of an American socialist leader, one of London's prototypical Anglo-blond supermen. Drawing on Donnelly's sensational conclusion, it ends with a traumatized depiction of the capitalist military casting its overwhelming might against Chicago's working class, massacring hundreds of thousands of laborers and mercenaries, and riding over streets mountained with corpses. The narrative breaks off mid-sentence, highlighting the disillusioning distance, political and imaginative, between the abortive revolution witnessed by the narrator and the post-capitalist utopia of the putative editors.

This preoccupation with the relation between national destiny and the narrative shape of American capital development is also evident in economic novels that focus on the historical past. Predictably, novelists outraged by corporate gigantism used their storylines to link corporate and financial modernity with various forms of social trauma, generational conflict, gender confusion, racial trespass, and moral or psychological fracture (see, for example, William "Coin" Harvey's *A Tale of Two Nations* [1894]). But pro-corporate novelists, too, used historical plots to dramatize threats to the nation's future. Writers such as Emerson Hough (whose 1902 bestseller *The Mississippi Bubble* imagines the New World exploits of the eighteenth-century financial pioneer John Law) and Frederic Isham (whose 1904 romance *Black Friday* sensationally pairs treacherous Wall Street gold speculators in 1869 and feminist anarchists in Paris in 1871) used their historical narratives to allegorize how the corporate juggernaut at the turn of the century, guided by enlightened and patriotic capitalist visionaries, would end economic crises, labor radicalism, anarchic business competition, and the cultural disintegration that threatened to deflect the nation from its progressive economic course. Rather than viewing the past as a refuge from modern capitalism's creative destruction, these novels enshrine corporate and financial modernity as the culmination of tradition, the heroic legacy of American capitalism's pioneers and founding fathers.

Of all the economic transformations between 1865 and 1917, the most disorienting, and the most important for the history of American economic fiction, was the industrial trust boom at the turn of the century. Thrown into crisis by the depression of the 1890s, American capitalism underwent a dizzyingly rapid reconstruction. In the space of a decade, a new corporate regime featuring large industrial trusts displaced an older competitive system in which railroads and manufacturing firms engaged in ruinous competition and wasteful investment. Wall Street, financing this wave of mergers, assumed its central place in the national and world economy, and investment bankers, many associated with J. P. Morgan, took direction of hundreds of corporations, insurance companies, and banks. American economic reform fiction came of age during these years. Between 1900 and 1910, these novels became popular for the first time with urban, middle-class audiences, buoyed by the public's fascination with Wall Street and its controlling figures, by growing debate in the popular and academic press about whether to regulate or dismantle the new trusts, and, most important, by a surge of mainstream journalistic interest in municipal and corporate crimes.

Most of the bestselling reform novelists of the muckraking era, including Upton Sinclair and David Graham Phillips, were also journalists (or in Thomas Lawson's case, corporate whistleblowers). They viewed their fiction, like their magazine exposés, as a way to educate an unseeing citizenry and arouse the public's democratic outrage and activism. Their novels typically follow an unsuspecting worker or investor into the iconic spaces of capitalist mystery (the stock exchange, the corporate boardroom, the factory floor, the residences of the leisure class), where they witness the systematic exploitation of abject innocents and come to discern the sublime reach of monopoly and its machinery of oppression. Sinclair's explosive bestseller *The Jungle*, sensationally detailing the exploitation, waste, and corruption of Chicago's Packingtown and climaxing in the protagonist's conversion to socialism, is the most famous of these fictional exposés.[f]

f Tichi discusses *The Jungle* in chapter 23, 396–397. The melodramatism that, for Tichi, gave American protest fiction its moral force during this period also helped incite the backlash against the literature of exposure after the publication of Sinclair's novel. Critics, most notably Theodore Roosevelt, condemned the rhetorical recklessness of Sinclair, Phillips, and Lawson, denouncing their "indiscriminate assault upon men in business." Some critics feared that corporate muckraking, appealing to public unrest and indignation at a time when violent labor strikes rocked the nation, would tip the nation toward socialism. At the center of the cultural firestorm over economic protest literature's galvanizing

All of these reform novels personalize capitalism, even those, like Sinclair's, that are meant to illuminate structural dynamics beyond the control of any single individual. They harness sentiment and melodrama to show how not only factory workers but also – for the first time in fiction – middle-class shareholders and bank depositors, are trapped within suffocating causal webs that force them to participate in the economic system that victimizes them. They emphasize how the risk of commercial dependence and moral complicity saturates the entire system.

The success tale

As the gloom of economic depression lifted in the late 1890s, there emerged alongside these reform melodramas a wave of business novels studying and sympathizing with capitalist titans. Frank Norris, Jack London, and Theodore Dreiser, along with commercially popular writers such as Edwin Lefèvre (a Wall Street insider who advised Norris on *The Pit*), produced novels exalting speculative visionaries and corporate empire builders and identifying them with the powerful, even sublime, commercial forces transforming the United States. Many of these novelists were literary nationalists who saw the muscular and mysterious world of heroic business action as a new, masculine, and quintessentially American subject for literary exploration.[9] Some, like Norris and Dreiser, updating Emerson and Whitman, represented captains of finance and industry as heroic artist figures – creators, organizers, and diviners of formal order beneath the surface flux of commercial life, virtuoso manipulators of symbolic realms (e.g., debt arbitrage, commodity futures) whose blend of mental labor and worldly consequence illuminated the capacities and limits of the novelist's own art. Other fiction writers, including Lefèvre and the prolific business novelists Henry K. Webster and Samuel Merwin (co-authors of Ayn Rand's favorite novel, the 1901 bestseller *Calumet K*), spurned the populists' savage caricatures and, adopting the imagery used during the trust boom by pro-corporate spokesmen, portrayed the capitalist titan as a trustee of American civilization and progress.

Before the trust boom, the businessman in American fiction had served to confirm the equation, conventionalized in Horatio Alger's bestselling "rags-to-respectability" stories in the 1870s and 1880s, between moral character and

potential was Lawson, who threatened to use his power as the nation's most conspicuous stock promoter and financial writer to create a massive Wall Street panic and throw the nation's financial system into disarray.

success.[10] In *Ragged Dick* (1868), *Strive and Succeed* (1871), and scores of other didactic boys' tales, Alger, an ex-minister expelled from the clergy for pedophilia, dramatized how good fortune inevitably awaited honest, enterprising, and quick-witted boy strivers. In the moral universe of Alger and other early business novelists, greedy and grasping business villains fail to restrain the selfish passions awakened by the marketplace, and they are punished for it; meanwhile, the noble impulses of plucky urchins and patrician capitalists are rewarded.[g] In contrast, fiction about business titans, written just as financiers and industrial barons were displacing self-made entrepreneurs as exemplars of capitalist success, was emphatically uninterested in the fate of the moral personality in the business world. Drawing explicitly on Darwin, Spencer, and Nietzsche, novels like Jack London's *Burning Daylight* (1910) (which compares the worlds of masculine, heroic endeavor in the Yukon wilderness and capitalist gamesmanship in the United States) portray the business universe as a jungle where male economic animals, acting out their natural instincts to compete, gamble, and dominate, battle each other. In this amoral arena, subject to nature's ruthless testing and triage, only supermen endowed with extraordinary personal "force" and shrewdness thrive.

This fiction marks the literary apotheosis of the businessman. In these narratives, natural law gives metaphysical warrant to the titan's overweening ambition and ruthlessness, to his creation of vast market empires and monopolies, and to the failure of the mass of other men. Most titan novels aim to convey the limits of this vision: *Burning Daylight* dramatizes how capitalism ultimately corrodes the superman's natural capacities; Robert Herrick's *Memoirs of An American Citizen* (1905) and Abraham Cahan's *The Rise of David Levinsky* (1917), the first modern immigrant business novel, reveal how the internalization of American capitalist subjectivity fails to assuage deeper, unacknowledged forms of erotic and ethnic longing; and Harold Frederic's *The Market-Place* (1898) shows how the titan, hard-wired to practice power, can find cultural gratification only outside of business, in political philanthropy.

Turn of the century novelists fixed their attention on financial and corporate barons and the complicated sovereignty they exercised in and over vast market systems. While they emphasized the extraordinary personal force of market visionaries, literary naturalists like Norris, Dreiser, and London crafted their narratives to show how these men were also instruments, mediums of abstract, totalizing forces – the evolution of capital, the expansion of American

g On Alger's fiction and its legacy, see Davies, chapter 22, 381–384, 388–390; and Julia Mickenberg, "Children's novels," chapter 52, 864.

commercial empire, the workings of macroeconomic laws – acting out through them. Indeed, treating economic forces as natural agencies, the naturalists figure economic processes as discrete, often sublime, subjects –"the market," "capitalism," "the economy"– that subsume, even dwarf, human agents.

Norris's *The Octopus* (1901), the first novel in his unfinished epic trilogy about the global economics of wheat (*The Pit* is the second), offers perhaps the most striking instance of this reification and reduction. Continually evoking and undermining anti-monopolist idioms and imagery, the novel ends with the protagonist, Presley, an aspiring writer, embracing progressive evolutionism and coming to see that individuals count for nothing when compared to the transcendent natural laws propelling the inexorable expansion of corporate power and directing the production and distribution of wheat. Every economic outcome in this turgid, sprawling novel is finally sanctified by Nature: the snuffing of small, disorganized businessmen-farmers by the colossal railroad monopoly, the live burial of a railroad agent inside the hold of a ship filling with corporation wheat, and the climactic extension of American commercial markets across the Pacific – an enactment, we are meant to see, of Nature's law that supply (that is, surplus American wheat) follows demand (here, starving Asians, whose consumption of American wheat is meant to signify Anglo-Saxon racial and commercial supremacy). In the end, Presley abandons his earlier romanticization of human political agency and welcomes the idea that "the Wheat," seemingly of its own volition, "indifferent to the human swarm," carried by the triumphant corporation, follows a divinely appointed destiny westward. And more: a beneficent proxy of divine Nature, "the Market" turns out to be the ideal aesthetic object Presley has spent the novel searching for. Embracing the globe, the circulation of the American commodity comprises a transcendent, unified "whole," all the more "perfect" because niggling human agents have been evacuated from it.[11]

Dreiser's *The Financier* (1912, revised 1927), the most famous titan novel, is justifiably celebrated for both culminating and deconstructing the liberal trajectory in American business fiction. It is the first novel (followed by *The Titan* [1914] and *The Stoic* [1947]) in Dreiser's massive "trilogy of desire" about Frank Cowperwood, a pioneering traction magnate based on Charles Tyson Yerkes. *The Financier* presents its protagonist as a financial superman, indifferent to conventional morality and civic responsibility and compelled by his own "chemic" nature to seek profit and power. However, Dreiser delineates an inescapably intersubjective conception of individuality, one that comprehends the superman only in relation to the social, economic, and historical arenas in which he gains his power and acts out his desire. What sets Dreiser apart from earlier business fiction writers, except perhaps Norris, is that he refuses to be alarmed or scandalized by this dissolution of personal sovereignty. Indeed, this dissolution motivates Dreiser's literary innovation, the creation of a new kind of novelistic genre, what we might call, to borrow a phrase from television, the "nature special." Immersing his novel in the details of Cowperwood's accounting schemes, Dreiser shows that conventional narratives can never adequately depict the irreducible chanciness of the natural world, the relentlessness of human plotting and counterplotting, and the dense web of interdependencies that form the basis of individuals' identity and power.

Consumer fiction

For recent generations of literary critics, the naturalist novels of Norris and Dreiser, formally innovative, stylistically eccentric, and thematically fertile, represent the literary high-water mark of American business fiction. But naturalism also occupies a privileged place in the literary historiography of economic novels because of its apparent artlessness – its fidelity to, and in more recent accounts, identification with market culture. Beginning with Vernon Parrington in the late 1920s, generations of literary historians viewed naturalism, with its ostensibly sociological emphasis on environment and its documentary interest in the "facts" of society, as the first American literature squarely to confront the agents and effects of industrial and business growth.[12] The idea that naturalist fiction, written during the nation's corporate makeover, turned "of necessity" to economic themes – class conflict, commodities, consumerism, gambling, gold, greed – was revamped by New Historicist critics in the 1980s, especially by Walter Benn Michaels in *The Gold Standard and the Logic of Naturalism* (1987), a book that for two decades energized critical discussion of turn-of-the-century economic fiction.[13]

What provoked so much sustained and strident response to Michaels's book was his argument, inspired by theorist Michel Foucault, that novels written at the turn of the century could not be critical of corporate and consumer capitalism, since whatever feelings or attitudes the authors (or their characters) expressed in relation to it were themselves produced and conditioned by it. The exemplary case, for Michaels, is Dreiser's *Sister Carrie* (1900). Recommended for publication by Frank Norris and released over the objections of its publisher,[14] the novel follows a young woman's unceasing, desire-driven gravitation toward increasingly reified sites of modern urban capitalism: from her country home to the urban sweatshop to the department store to the commercial stage and finally to a city billboard, where, as a celebrity actress whose advertised image provokes the emulative longing of other city newcomers, her identity merges with that of modern consumerism itself. The novel offers the first sustained delineation in US fiction of the ways the emergent mass consumer-oriented economy saturates the everyday experience and emotions of city inhabitants, and, by tempering the feelings of alienation it produces, safeguards capitalism from its own contradictions. The novel emphasizes the ubiquitous looking and display that fuel class emulation and consumer longing, and it shows how Carrie's character is fashioned and fulfilled within this specular realm. Unlike earlier tales of consuming, desiring, and imitative women, the novel refuses to moralize against Carrie's rise (or the sexual "fall" that advances it). Instead, it studies Carrie (and by extension the woman consumer) as an emblem and instrument of the transformed American economy.[h]

Michaels insists in *The Gold Standard* that we stop "worrying about whether Dreiser liked or disliked capitalism – not only because capitalism provides the objects of fear and desire but because it provides the subjects as well."[15] In other words, because "the market" forms the discursive system that constitutes subjects as well as their productions, naturalist literature, rather than reflecting on or even representing capitalist culture, merely exemplifies it. For Michaels, all naturalist fiction, in this sense, is market fiction, whether or not it explicitly thematizes economic concerns.

Sister Carrie represents a major turn in the history of novels of American business, industry, and consumerism. Earlier economic fiction had focused on consumption, typically deriding the conspicuous spending habits of parvenu capitalists, female social climbers, and the idle rich. (On rare occasions, as in Bellamy's *Looking Backward*, economic novels envisioned the emancipatory promise of new modes of consumption.) *Sister Carrie*, presenting the first non-censorious drama of modern consumer subjectivity, offers American fiction's earliest and fullest recognition of the nation's transformation into a mass consumer-oriented society, one that had shifted in the forty years since the Civil War from valorizing productive labor and self-denial to endorsing consumer indulgence and the corporate agencies, such as mass advertising and department stores, encouraging it. Historians have described this shift as a

h For further discussion of *Sister Carrie*, see Donna Campbell, "The rise of naturalism," chapter 30, 500–501, 506; Jude Davies, chapter 22, 380–381, 386–389; and Jennifer Fleissner, "Wharton, marriage, and the New Woman," chapter 27, 452, 457–458.

passage from a culture of scarcity to one of abundance, from a political economy based on economic sovereignty to one based on corporate subjection, from a moral economy idealizing entrepreneurial individualism to one promoting bureaucratic belonging. Leftist historians, viewing the hegemony of corporate capital and consumerism as politically and spiritually disabling, have represented this passage as a tragedy, a tale of lost social possibility; in contrast, revisionist historians, insisting that the corporate reconstruction made new forms of democratic subjectivity available, have represented this passage as an "unfinished comedy."[16]

Literary historians are also cultural storytellers, and whether we see this historical shift, at least as represented in American novels, as a decline or advance – whether we tell our literary historical narrative as a comedy or tragedy – depends on the ending we construct for it. We might, for example, close our survey with a popular novel like George Barr McCutcheon's *Brewster's Millions*, a bestseller in 1903, which cheerily makes peace with modern consumerism by dramatizing how it serves, rather than subverts, the older economic morality. Or we might end with a canonized critique like Sinclair Lewis's *Babbitt* (1922), which savagely satirizes how bourgeois business culture and standardized mass consumption in Fordist America suffocate individual freedom and democratic openness – how the system that produces the corporate booster then threatens to swallow him. Or we might close with perhaps the most celebrated American novel about business and consumerism, Fitzgerald's *The Great Gatsby* (1925), which highlights both the sordid failure and the transcendent promise of the commodity world, a promise famously linked with the throbbing desire of Dutch sailors hoping to establish themselves commercially on American shores.

Notes

1. Surveys and full-length studies of this fiction include Lisle Abbott Rose's not always reliable "A Bibliographic Survey of Economic and Political Writings, 1865–1900," *American Literature* (January 1944): 381–410; Walter Fuller Taylor, *The Economic Novel in America* (New York: Octagon, 1964); Wayne W. Westbrook, *Wall Street in the American Novel* (New York: New York University Press, 1980); Michael Spindler, *American Literature and Social Change* (Bloomington: Indiana University Press, 1983); George L. Henderson, *California and the Fictions of Capital* (New York: Oxford University Press, 1999); Laura Hapke, *Labor's Text: The Worker in American Fiction* (New Brunswick, NJ: Rutgers University Press, 2001); and David A. Zimmerman, *Panic! Markets, Crises, and Crowds in American Fiction* (Chapel Hill: University of North Carolina Press, 2006).

2. Nancy Cohen, *The Reconstruction of American Liberalism, 1865–1914* (Chapel Hill and London: University of North Carolina Press, 2002), 25.
3. Quoted in *ibid.*
4. Henry Nash Smith, *Mark Twain's Fable of Progress: Political and Economic Ideas in "A Connecticut Yankee"* (New Brunswick, NJ: Rutgers University Press, 1964).
5. Henry James, "The Question of the Opportunities" (1898), in *Literary Opinion in America*, ed. Morton Dauwen Zabel, 3rd edn., 2 vols. (New York: Harper, 1967), 1:54.
6. Westbrook, *Wall Street in the American Novel*, 39.
7. R. F. Littledale, book review (untitled), *Academy* (November 27, 1875): 549.
8. William Dean Howells, *Criticism and Fiction and Other Essays* (New York: New York University Press, 1959), 62.
9. See, for example, James, "The Question of the Opportunities," 51–55; and Frank Norris, "The True Reward of the Novelist" (1901), in *Novels and Essays* (New York: Library of America, 1986), 1147–1151.
10. Carl Bode, Introduction to *Ragged Dick and Struggling Upward*, by Horatio Alger, Jr. (New York: Penguin, 1985), ix.
11. W. E. B. Du Bois, possibly inspired by *The Octopus*, also spiritualized a natural commodity, cotton, in his own American economic epic, *The Quest of the Silver Fleece* (1911).
12. Vernon Louis Parrington, *Main Currents in American Thought* (New York: Harcourt, Brace, 1930), 3:173–188.
13. Other important studies focusing on the naturalism/capitalism relation include June Howard, *Form and History in American Literary Naturalism* (Chapel Hill: University of North Carolina Press, 1985); Rachel Bowlby, *Just Looking: Consumer Culture in Dreiser, Gissing, and Zola* (New York: Methuen, 1985); Mark Seltzer, *Bodies and Machines* (New York: Routledge, 1992); Christophe Den Tandt, *The Urban Sublime in American Literary Naturalism* (Urbana: University of Illinois Press, 1998); and Mohamed Zayani, *Reading the Symptom: Frank Norris, Theodore Dreiser, and the Dynamics of Capitalism* (New York: Peter Lang, 1999).
14. Two considerably different versions of the novel exist. One is the shortened and censored version published by Doubleday in 1900; the other is the Pennsylvania Edition of the restored, original text, released in 1981.
15. Walter Benn Michaels, *The Gold Standard and the Logic of Naturalism* (Berkeley and Los Angeles: University of California Press, 1987), 20.
16. James Livingston, *Pragmatism and the Political Economy of Cultural Revolution, 1890–1940* (Chapel Hill: University of North Carolina Press, 1997), xx.

25

New Americans and the immigrant novel

TIM PRCHAL

Concern about immigration to the USA is nothing new. Even before the Revolution, in 1751, Benjamin Franklin stated his qualms regarding newcomers, including those "who will shortly be so numerous as to Germanize us instead of our Anglifying them, and will never adopt our Language or Customs any more than they can acquire our Complexion." Franklin goes on to explain that "the Number of purely white people in the World" is dwarfed by the "black or tawny" of Africa and Asia, and even most Europeans "are generally of what we call a swarthy Complexion." Only the Saxon Germans and the English should be allowed into the colonies, Franklin says, so that the "lovely White and Red" of the region can shine up to the heavens. Less color conscious, Thomas Jefferson worried more about the challenges faced by immigrants who leave strict monarchies for a nation governed by "the freest principles of the English constitution, with others derived from natural right and natural reason." Immigrants attempting this shift, Jefferson says, "will bring with them the principles of the governments they leave, imbibed in their early youth; or, if able to throw them off, it will be in exchange for an unbounded licentiousness." These polar positions will be passed on to their children and, via the democratic process, lead to legislation being determined by "a heterogeneous, incoherent, distracted mass."[1] Both Franklin and Jefferson reveal a position often taken in subsequent immigration discourse: national security is founded on commonality, whether that commonality is a matter of complexion or of cultural conformity.

But this position often conflicts with an equally persistent, more open-armed stance regarding immigration. George Washington voiced this view in 1783 when he said, "The bosom of America is open to receive not only the Opulent and respectable Stranger, but the oppressed and persecuted of all Nations and Religions; whom we shall wellcome to a participation of all our rights and previleges [sic] . . ." Exactly one century later, Emma Lazarus's famous poem "The New Colossus" (1883) reaffirmed Washington's sentiment by portraying the "Mother of Exiles" bidding a "world-wide welcome" to the tired, the poor, and the "huddled masses yearning to breathe free." This is what Charlotte Perkins Gilman probably had in mind when, in 1915, she described the founding fathers as having "opened wide their gates to 'the poor and oppressed of all nations,' supposing that the accommodations were not bounded and that the immigration was." Immigration had changed by the early twentieth century, and Gilman declares, "Whatever our forefathers thought about their country, it is now our country – not theirs." Gilman's own position lies closer to Franklin's and Jefferson's in that she concludes by calling for the gate to be closed against "a stream of non-assimilable stuff as shall dilute and drown out the current of our life, and leave this country to be occupied by groups of different stock and traditions, drawing apart, preserving their own nationality, and making our great land merely another Europe."[2]

Developments in immigration during the late nineteenth and early twentieth centuries only intensified such debate. New streams of immigration were considered by many to be dangerous to the American melting pot. Though they made up only .002 percent of the nation's population in 1880,[3] immigrants from China were blocked with the Chinese Exclusion Act of 1882. By 1917, the restriction extended to almost all Asian populations despite the fact that Asian immigration was statistically minor compared to a growing flood from Europe. While newcomers from the western nations of Europe made up 87 percent of total immigrants in 1882, those from southern and eastern nations had grown to 78.9 percent in 1905. Reformist John Commons contended that eastern Europe was " so remote in the main attributes of Western civilization" that the shift "should challenge the attention of every citizen."[4] With incoming immigration numbers now in the millions, a literacy requirement was instituted in 1917 to favor the northern and western European groups, but it proved ineffective. A strict quota system introduced in the early 1920s much more successfully curtailed immigration overall, especially from southern and eastern Europe.

Amid soaring immigration figures, nativist rhetoric, and legislative action, immigrant novels presented a wide range of views on subjects such as opportunity and exploitation, assimilation and cultural preservation, and aspirations and disillusionment. Many of these works are didactic, clearly designed to promote a particular socio-political stance in the tradition of, say, Lydia Maria Child's *Hobomok* (1824) or Harriet Beecher Stowe's *Uncle Tom's Cabin* (1852). This is not to say that novels addressing immigration are necessarily romantic or sentimental, though some certainly are. As Michael A. Elliott explains in his chapter in this volume, immigration was just one part of the turbulence of the late nineteenth century, and several authors turned to realism to prompt reform and to bring stability to American life.[a] Much of this reform was aimed at securing social cohesion, a goal that could align with restricting immigration. However, many novelists sought to illustrate the common humanity that their immigrant characters share with native-born Americans – their struggles, dreams, and faults – thereby promoting a sense of equality.

A useful way of reading immigrant novels from the late nineteenth and early twentieth centuries, then, is to approach them in terms of what they hope to reform or, indeed, what they argue *against*. Read this way, the novels can be seen as protest novels of the sort discussed in this volume's chapter by Cecelia Tichi. Indeed, Tichi shows how Upton Sinclair's *The Jungle* (1906) is designed not to simply represent reality, but "to protest *against* conditions deemed harmful to society."[b] Read in terms of what reforms immigration novels aim to effect, they can be grouped into subcategories that illustrate the surprisingly diverse ways that literature participated in immigration discourse. Furthermore, since this discourse was hardly limited to immigrants themselves – or even to native-born authors sympathetic to immigrants – this approach expands upon the typical notion of what constitutes an "immigration novel," becoming more inclusive and integrative in regard to authors.

One of the earliest of these subcategories includes works that relate the tragedy of an immigrant unable to adjust to life in the new land. These novels prompt reform of the American values and/or institutions against which such newcomers struggle. The immigrant tragedy has roots that go back to an important work not generally thought of as immigrant literature at all, namely, Rebecca Harding Davis's *Life in the Iron-Mills* (1861).[5] More often seen as early proletariatian fiction, Davis's novel established a working-class protagonist, the son of a Welsh immigrant, who succumbs to harsh working conditions. Sinclair's *The Jungle* and Michael Gold's *Jews Without Money* (1930) are prime examples of the same plot, written with an eye toward illustrating how socialism could alleviate the suffering of immigrants. Pietro di Donato's *Christ in Concrete* (1939) also tells the story of the son of an immigrant. Despite his Italian bricklayer father's dream of erecting a better life for his family, the main character ultimately fails to achieve economic stability and suffers a sort of spiritual death in the process.

a Michael Elliott, "Realism and radicalism: the school of Howells," chapter 17.
b Cecelia Tichi, "Novels of civic protest," chapter 23, 394 (emphasis added).

Henryk Sienkiewicz's *Za chlebem* (1880) typifies the immigrant tragedy. Though originally written in Polish and published in Poland, it was based on the author's firsthand experiences in the USA and features a protagonist who is lured to the USA by the promise of financial opportunity, greater freedom, and self-improvement. However, this protagonist suffers terrible disillusionment after arriving, following a downward path from slum life and starvation to eviction and street life. The novel was widely read by Polish immigrants and Polish-Americans in the late nineteenth century, and in 1897, an English translation titled *After Bread: A Story of Polish Emigrant Life to America*, extended the novel's reach to a much wider American audience. In this respect, the novel is like Ole Edvart Rølvaag's *Giants in the Earth*, the chronicle of Scandinavian immigrants on the northern plains, which was first written in Norwegian and published in Norway before the still-popular English translation was released in 1927. *After Bread* predates two other very important immigrant tragedies, Sinclair's *The Jungle* and Alirio Díaz Guerra's *Lucas Guevara* (1914). The latter work has been cited as the first Hispanic novel of immigration,[6] written in Spanish but first published in the US. (See Gretchen Murphy's essay in this volume, chapter 33, for the historical context of this "hemispheric novel.") The diversity exemplified by Sienkiewicz, Sinclair, and Díaz Guerra – a Pole, a native-born American, and a Columbian – reveals the reach and flexibility of the immigrant tragedy. *After Bread* may be read as a counter-romance in that Sienkiewicz melodramatically warns his fellow Poles against tales that glorify America as a promised land. Díaz Guerra and Sinclair similarly comment less on the immigrants themselves and more on the flawed social environment that engulfs them. The title character of *Lucas Guevara* drowns himself in the end, a telling metaphor of an immigrant succumbing to the chaos and obstacles of life in a foreign city. Jurgis Rudkis of *The Jungle* fares somewhat better, but as an editor for *Scribner's* pointed out, Jurgis "dwindles into insignificance as the story is unfolded." [7] While this shift might be seen as an artistic weakness, it allows the author to redirect readers toward the larger social issues that prevent immigrants from succeeding.

A few novelists saw immigration itself as the larger social issue deserving censure. Instead of tragedies portraying immigrants as suffering individuals, these works portray immigrants as dangerous masses. Whether or not such works fit into the category of the immigrant novel is debatable. Perhaps immigration novel would be more fitting, but in any case, a look at novels hostile toward immigrants reveals the general climate in which novelists interested in capturing the experience of individual newcomers operated.

Expanding the territory to consider the immigration novel also reveals much about how novelists participated in this pivotal era of immigration discourse. For instance, William F. Wu explains that a "fear of massive Chinese immigration created its own particular type of fiction" in the late nineteenth century. With the emergence of these xenophobic works, "the term *Yellow Peril* came into its own, as the United States is shown to be seriously threatened, clearly doomed, or destroyed in all of them." [8]

Prominent among these "Yellow Peril" works, Pierton W. Dooner's *Last Days of the Republic* (1880) illustrates how even a highly speculative novel could accommodate anti-immigration rhetoric. Dooner's work is probably the first American entry into a swell of "future war" stories that had first risen in Europe. Other entries include H. G. Wells's *The War of the Worlds* (1898), which innovatively makes the invading army extraterrestrial, and Jack London's "An Unparalleled Invasion" (1910), which depicts Chinese invaders of the United States. As in London's story, Dooner portrays the Chinese – and, specifically, the sheer numbers of them – as the antagonists. With the conceit of looking at future events in retrospect, Dooner describes how unchecked immigration lets the "coolie" workforce saturate the western states, replace African Americans in the South, and infiltrate New England and the Midwest – all part of a grand Chinese conspiracy to erase "every term and vestige of distinction as to color and race . . . from the naturalization laws of the United States," thereby making Asians eligible for citizenship and voting. Dooner's novel surely tapped into and may have exacerbated the xenophobia that led to the Chinese Exclusion Act.

The threatening-mob imagery used to arouse fears of the Chinese was easily adapted to southern and eastern European immigrants. Katharine Metcalf Roof's *The Stranger at the Hearth* (1916), for instance, is a Whartonesque work of realism involving the upper echelon of New York City. It is among this society that Nina Varesca grew up before completing her education in Europe. Back in the United States several years later, having married an Italian count, she is repeatedly confronted by crowds of a new kind of immigrant described as primitive – with "vague" eyes, "parted lips," and groping hands – and as typical of those who had sailed in steerage during Nina's trip home. Discussions in Roof's novel about the dangers of admitting such immigrants parallel ideas expressed in influential nonfiction books of the early twentieth century such as Madison Grant's *The Passing of a Great Race* (1916). In the novel, the subject is raised by Daniel Griscom, a "man of justice" who declares that "barbarian invaders" have loosed a "destructive, disintegrative force . . . that threatens to destroy the most precious heritage of our race – the Anglo Saxon ideas inculcated in a great democracy."

Against this hostile backdrop developed what might be called the "immigrant adjustment novel," a subcategory that differs from both the anti-immigration and immigrant tragedy traditions. The immigrant adjustment novel features characters who manage to take root in America, thereby affirming the ideal of the land of opportunity. At the same time, the dangers, struggles, and sacrifices of taking root often remain key features of these novels, which range from Henry Roth's seminal *Call It Sleep* (1934) to more recent works such as Gish Jen's *Typical American* (1991). Jen might be included on a list of prominent ethnic (as opposed to strictly immigrant) authors whose works either fit, extend, or complicate this category, especially as they shift the focus from the adjustment of immigrants to that of the generation(s) following them. James Farrell does so with his Studs Lonigan series, which narrates the life of an Irish-American character in three novels, starting with *Young Lonigan* (1932). John Fante similarly explores the struggles of Italian-American Arturo Bandini in four novels that begin with *Wait Until Spring, Bandini* (1938). Mario Puzo's *The Fortunate Pilgrim* (1965) is an interesting entry in that it harkens back to the great wave of early twentieth-century immigration from Italy.

In fact, with late nineteenth- and early twentieth-century immigrant adjustment novels as a backdrop, readers can better understand the permutations of ethnic and racial relations exhibited in later novels. Such literature and the new concerns it has generated are discussed in this volume by Susan Koshy, who traces Asian American novels through three historic phases, and Walter Benn Michaels, who explores how Asian American authors have addressed the "model minority" stereotype. Rodrigo Lazo and Ramón Saldívar review works that challenge the notion of sharp national boundaries in their chapters on hemispheric American novels and American borderlands novels.[c]

To place these earlier novels of immigrant adjustment within their own historical contexts, though, it is useful to examine how such adjustment had been understood and categorized by their authors' contemporaries. In 1920, Isaac B. Berkson described the three reigning "theories of ethnic adjustment" as the "Americanization," the "Melting Pot," and the "Federation of Nationalities" schemes.[9] The first, also known as "Anglo-conformity," casts the USA as a country steeped in its British roots and, indeed, very much an Anglo-Saxon nation. According to the Americanization template, immigrants relinquish all incompatible traits and adopt those traits deemed to be in

c Chapters 63, 61, 65, and 62, respectively.

keeping with this dominant culture. The second theory portrayed immigrants as contributing their distinctive traits to the national melting pot rather than abandoning them. Here, the USA becomes a mix of nationalities (though the period's discourse typically limited these to European). The third scheme has evolved into what is now called cultural pluralism. It counters the goal of homogeneity found in the other two theories by contending that cultural heterogeneity better befits a democratic society that values self-realization. This theory also maintains that the preservation of diversity enhances the quality of life for all.[10]

Among the many early novels championing the Americanization theory, Anzia Yezierska's *Bread Givers* (1925) stands out as a work still often read today. This work follows a structural pattern that, according to David Fine, organizes many of the period's novels endorsing some form of immigrant assimilation. The pattern opens with an "initial *embrace* of everything American, coupled with the rejection of the father, who symbolizes the Old World." It moves to a "*recoil* from the harsh actualities of America" and ends with the protagonist finding the means to settle into American life.[11] The first component is especially relevant to *Bread Givers* in that Yezierska employs the motif of rejecting the Old-World father to advocate female independence. In other words, assimilation – at least, in the sense of immigrants relinquishing Old-World values and customs – is the first step in imagining the USA as a land of freedom, especially for women.[12]

Sara Smolinsky, the narrator and protagonist of *Bread Givers*, suffers under the hand of her gruff, orthodox father. An argument over two cents triggers Sara's rebellion: "For seventeen years I had stood his preaching and his bullying . . . Should I let him crush me as he crushed [my mother and sisters]? No. This is America, where children are people." She defies the Torah by striking out on her own, claiming, "In America, women don't need men to boss them." Despite loneliness, sexism, and other obstacles, she finally succeeds at becoming a teacher. Following the pattern outlined by Fine, Sara first recoils from the harsh realities of American life, then she finds a way to adjust to American life by embracing its freedoms. Certainly, those freedoms were qualified by gender (and Yezierska at no time suggests that Sara achieves gender equality). *Bread Givers* ends more hopefully than happily, and its ambiguous conclusion reveals that Americanization does not resolve all of an immigrant's problems of adjustment.

Exploring the complications of assimilation, Yezierska followed the precedent of Abraham Cahan's *The Rise of David Levinsky* (1917), certainly among the most important novels that highlight this theme. Though its title character "rises" in terms of material wealth via assimilation, David also "falls" by forsaking his devotion to religion and education. In addition – and perhaps as a result– he fails to secure the emotional connections that would make him content. In a sense, this novel straddles the categories of immigrant adjustment and the immigrant tragedy in that David's losses allow Cahan to portray American culture as overly materialistic. However, the novel is at least as much a character study as a social commentary. Cahan carefully grounds David's trajectory in his boyhood experiences in Russia, where poverty, anti-Semitism, and the vengeful feelings they incite all drive David to prove his worth once he arrives in America's capitalist system. While some popular Jewish novelists had endorsed Americanization, such as Elias Tobenkin in *Witte Arrives* (1916), Cahan emphasized the double-edge of assimilation.

Edward A. Steiner's *The Mediator* (1907), a novel that attempts to advocate a melting-pot view of immigrant adjustment, exposes a problem inherent in imagining the fusion of disparate groups. Its protagonist, Samuel Cohen, is born a Russian Jew, but the strict religious teachings imposed by his father stifle him. He gradually converts to Christianity, even becoming a Catholic cleric. However, as in *Bread Givers* and *Call It Sleep*, breaking entirely from his father is difficult for Samuel, and he finds himself torn between both communities. He reclaims his Jewish identity yet clings to Christian beliefs. The trouble arises when Steiner devises a plan to convince Jews to accept Christ as the messiah – yet doing so without necessarily having them sacrifice their allegiance to Judaism. Through the character of Samuel, Steiner advocates what has come to be called Messianic Judaism, whose controversial nature probably needs no explanation.[13] Novels envisioning such unifying plans can seem out-of-touch or simply odd today– and perhaps that's why they have lost (or, perhaps, had never found) much resonance with readers.

Cultural pluralism, on the other hand, is an ideal still embraced today, often under the banner of "multiculturalism." In an era when many Americans value preserving ethnic distinctions over working toward cultural homogenization, Willa Cather's *My Ántonia* (1918) survives as one of the most popular pieces of immigrant fiction written in the early twentieth century. Several critics have explored how the novel illustrates Cather's support of cultural pluralism, especially in its conclusion. [14] Yet few have considered how *My Ántonia* positions her endorsement of pluralism against the melting-pot and the Americanization modes. As Linda Joyce Brown says, "Rejection of the melting pot metaphor of assimilation is central to cultural pluralism."[15] Pluralism just as strongly rejects Anglo-conformity, as does Cather by revealing the materialistic strain of America's capitalist culture. Readers first see this indictment in the character of Peter Krajiek, countryman of and interpreter for the Shimerdas, who arrived in Nebraska from Bohemia. Krajiek is alleged to have taken financial advantage of the Shimerdas, presumably because his earlier arrival has made him more assimilated. The corrupting influence of American capitalism then becomes even more apparent in Larry Donovan, whose Irish surname suggests an earlier wave of immigrants widely recognized for their success in assimilating. Donovan, we learn, first loses his job as a railroad conductor "for knocking down fares," and the last Ántonia hears about him is that he might have gone to Mexico to "get rich there, collecting half-fares off the natives and robbing the company." In addition, Cather denigrates the melting pot through Ántonia's unfortunate relationship with Donovan. The melting-pot theory, Berkson notes, holds that "new strains of blood are mingled with the old stock through intermarriage."[16] The imagined dangers of such intermarriage, specifically interbreeding, panicked the likes of Gilman, Roof, and Grant. That same panic bolstered the eugenics movement, which had far-reaching impact during the late nineteenth century and well into the twentieth.[d] Interestingly, *My Ántonia* casts an ominous shadow on such marriages by rejuvenating a time-worn stock character of literature: the rake who seduces the heroine. Of course, the ruination of Ántonia brought about by Donovan's sexual (and financial) misuse of her proves to be temporary. In this regard, Cather revises eighteenth-century seduction novels such as Samuel Richardson's *Clarissa* (1747–1748) and the first American novel, William Hill Brown's *The Power of Sympathy* (1789), which Anna Mae Duane considers in her contribution to this volume.[e]

Only after Cather has explored the pitfalls of the Americanization and the melting-pot modes of adjustment does she segue to valorizing cultural pluralism. To be sure, Ántonia's first daughter, Anna, is the product of the melting pot. However, she is easily absorbed into the Cuzak family, a close-knit, energetic group that preserves its Bohemian roots through its food, language, and music. Cather illustrates that, even though assimilation and blending are a part of immigrant experience, cultural preservation ultimately creates vital American families. The complexity of Cather's work, then, lies in its combining the three modes of adjustment. According to Cather's vision, America is not exclusively Anglo-Saxon, though the pressures to conform to this cultural strain are formidable. It is not an efficient melting pot, though some cross-cultural blending

d See in this volume Donna Campbell, "The rise of naturalism" (chapter 30), and David Mitchell and Sharon Snyder, "Disability and the American novel" (chapter 60).

e Anna Mae Duane, "Susanna Rowson, Hannah Webster Foster, and the seduction novel," chapter 2, 40–42.

certainly happens. Even cultural pluralism, while preferable to the other two, cannot exist on its own.

The narrative of immigrant adjustment seems to have maintained a special attraction for authors and readers while the immigrant tragedy and anti-immigration plots have waned (though perhaps not vanished altogether). Perhaps this can be attributed to the modernist emphasis on exploring individual, psychological experience, as in Roth's *Call It Sleep*, as well as its rejection of explicit socio-political reform agendas. Regardless, all three strains of the immigration novel can be better understood in juxtaposition to one another and to their relationships to immigration discourse of the late nineteenth and early twentieth centuries. These were, after all, the formative decades of immigration literature. It was a time when immigrant and native-born authors, writing in English and other languages, mirrored and fractured each other's ideas of how to define an American – and how to become one.

Notes

1. Benjamin Franklin, "Observations Concerning the Increase of Mankind, Peopling of Countries," in *The Autobiography and Other Writings by Benjamin Franklin* (New York: Bantam, 1982), 226. Thomas Jefferson, *Notes on the State of Virginia* (New York: Penguin, 1999), 91.
2. George Washington, *The Writings of George Washington from the Original Manuscript Sources*, ed. John C. Fitzpatrick, vol. XXVII (Washington, DC: US Government Printing Office, 1938), 254; Emma Lazarus, "The New Colossus," in *The Poems of Emma Lazarus*, 2 vols. (Boston: Houghton Mifflin, 1889), 1:202–203. Charlotte Perkins Gilman, "Let Sleeping Forefathers Lie," *Forerunner* (October 1915): 261–262. Washington significantly qualifies those he welcomes when he adds the phrase "if by decency and propriety of conduct they appear to merit the enjoyment" of American rights and privileges.
3. Ronald Takaki, *Strangers from a Different Shore: A History of Asian Americans*, rev. edn. (Boston: Little, Brown, 1998), 110.
4. John R. Commons, *Races and Immigrants in America* (New York: Macmillan, 1915), 69–71.
5. One might trace the roots of the immigrant tragedy to a work published much earlier than Davis's novel. Susanna Rowson's *Charlotte Temple* (1794) fits this category rather well in that its tragic title character is an immigrant from England.
6. Nicolás Kanellos and Imara Liz Hernández, Introduction, *Lucas Guevara*, by Alirio Díaz Guerra (Houston: Arte Público, 2003), vii.
7. "The Point of View," *Scribner's* (November 6, 1907): 635.
8. William F. Wu, *The Yellow Peril: Chinese Americans in American Fiction, 1850–1940* (Hamden, CT: Archon, 1982), 30.

9. Isaac B. Berkson, *Theories of Americanization: A Critical Study with Special Reference to the Jewish Group* (New York: Teachers' College, Columbia University, 1920), 55–93. David M. Fine also discusses these three views in the second chapter of his foundational work on late nineteenth- and early twentieth-century immigration literature, *The City, The Immigrant and American Fiction, 1880–1920* (Neuchen, NJ: Scarecrow Press, 1977). For more recent discussion, see the separate introductions to the sections titled "The Assimilation Debate," "The Melting Pot Debate," and "The Cultural Pluralism Debate" in Tim Prchal and Tony Trigilio, eds., *Visions and Divisons: American Immigration Literature, 1870–1930* (New Brunswick, NJ: Rutgers University Press, 2008).
10. Walter Benn Michaels's *Our America: Nativism, Modernism, and Pluralism* (Durham, NC: Duke University Press, 1997) remains one of the most influential works of literary criticism examining the rise of pluralism in the Progressive Era. Michaels situates pluralism within a wave of "nativist modernism," a term he uses to describe modernist authors' efforts to embed American identity in race.
11. Fine, *The City, The Immigrant, and American Fiction*, pp. 105–106. Italics in original.
12. Drude Krog Janson's *A Saloonkeeper's Daughter* (1887) is an earlier example of a novel that combines immigrant and feminist themes. Originally written in Norwegian and published in Minneapolis, Janson's novel is now available in English. (Trans. Gerald Thorson [Baltimore: Johns Hopkins University Press, 2002].)
13. The organization now known as Messianic Jewish Alliance of America was founded eight years after the novel appeared. Originally, it was called the Hebrew Christian Alliance of America.
14. See Ann Moseley, "A New World Symphony: Cultural Pluralism in *The Song of the Lark* and *My Ántonia*," *Willa Cather Pioneer Memorial Newletter* 39.1 (1995): 1, 7–12; Guy Reynolds, *Willa Cather in Context: Progress, Race, Empire* (New York: St. Martin's, 1996); Katrina Irving, *Immigrant Mothers: Narratives of Race and Maternity, 1890–1925* (Urbana: University of Illinois Press, 2000); and Linda Joyce Brown, *The Literature of Immigration and Racial Formation: Becoming White, Becoming Other, Becoming American in the Late Progressive Era* (New York: Routledge, 2004).
15. Brown, *The Literature of Immigration*, 90.
16. Berkson, *Theories of Americanization*, 76.

26

Cather and the regional imagination

TOM LUTZ

Isn't it interesting that, despite having been trained for decades in the impossibility of the encyclopedia, we should continue to attempt encyclopedic projects like this *Cambridge History*? We can't summate, we must summate. No matter how many times, or in how many ways, we admonish each other to eschew the metanarrative and adhere strictly to *petits récits*, we are drawn, again and again, to the big picture. No matter how often we insist on the particularities of persons, perspectives, and populations, we are drawn to the generalized, the generic, the survey, the overview.

This predicament and proclivity is something we have in common with the regionalists, that group of writers and critics who from the 1880s through the 1930s maintained an ongoing conversation about the relation of part to whole, of center to periphery, about the interdependence – conceptually, politically, materially – of the local and the global. I say the 1880s to the 1930s, but I may as well say from the beginnings of American literature to the present, because the regionalist sensibility has always been and continues to be a central, perhaps even *the* central form of American literary representation.

To make such a sweeping claim begs the question of what we mean by "regionalist," but this chapter will avoid any real adjudication of the definitional debates that have informed the scholarship in this subfield for decades.[1] Are regions cultural constructs or natural formations? I'll just say both – that is, Appalachia is a cultural construct with mountains; Maine is a cultural construct with a coastline and fishermen. Are they monocultural or multicultural? Always multicultural, and yet we do recognize something distinct about regional cultures when compared to each other – Appalachia and California are different – and thus some identifying generalizations are necessary, generalizations that will sound somewhat monocultural. Do regions have distinct borders or do they overlap? They overlap, but Maine is not Mississippi, and therefore there must be a zone somewhere that we can adduce as separating them. Are regions bounded by the nation or are they transnational? Some are one and some the other.[2] Are regions constructed by power? Yes. By powerlessness? Yes. Do the authors associated with various regions adequately represent those regions? Of course not, but at the same time who does so better? Do regionalist texts promote a false sense of the social reality of their regions? Often, and often a more accurate representation of social reality than existed otherwise. Do these texts patronize or belittle their local characters? Often. Do they patronize or belittle their interloping outsiders, the urban sophisticates contrasted to the locals? Often. Are these texts written by women from women's perspectives about women's lives? Often (e.g., Mary Wilkins Freeman, Sarah Orne Jewett, Willa Cather), and they are also often written by men from men's perspectives about men's lives (Hamlin Garland, Bret Harte, Frank Norris), by women about men's lives (Cather, Alice Dunbar, Mary Noailles Murfree) and men about women's lives (Garland, Sinclair Lewis, Paul Laurence Dunbar). Does the term "regionalism" refer simply to a story's setting or to a novelist's sustained examination of a regional ethos and its relation to larger polities? Are regionalist texts reactionary or progressive? On the side of the powerful or the powerless? Constitutive of or resistant to the nation? Homogenizing or heterogenizing? Open to difference or hostile to it? For all these questions, the answer is: sometimes one, sometimes the other. The debates about local color and regionalist literature that have been central to literary studies for the last several decades, in other words, while they have opened up our reading of these texts, have not, finally, settled any of the fundamental issues.

In more narrow, literary, critical-evaluative terms, "regionalist" can be used pro or contra, to celebrate or to marginalize, to announce a text's value or lack thereof. For some critics and reviewers, to call something regionalist was to label it as minor. For others, the regionalist is someone who takes a firm stand against a national or international enemy – be it standardization, embourgeoisement, industrialism, modernization, or some synecdoche for these, like Washington, New York, Europe, businessmen, or bankers – in the name of the real people threatened by these forces. Hamlin Garland claimed so in *Crumbling Idols* (1894), for instance, and it was central to the project of the Agrarian manifesto *I'll Take My Stand* (1930). Depending on which option one chooses, then, regionalists can appear as racist or inclusive, isolationist or the opposite, feminist or sexist, populist or elitist, and thus have they appeared, on one side or another of these dichotomies, in the majority of literary histories written over the last hundred-plus years.

I have been arguing for some years that Cather and the other important literary regionalists fit none (or perhaps all) of these reductive images. They took for granted that the relation of their fictional locales to larger polities was of enormous significance, and some of their work was designed to explore that very relation. They also used their locales to stage numerous other debates – about the status of women, class, aesthetics, or political action, for example – that necessarily went far beyond local issues. Certainly some writers might be properly caricatured for presenting hopelessly distorted, romantic, condescending, marginalizing portraits of provincial types, but these writers – Zona Gale comes to mind – are not remembered very well by literary history. Gale is mentioned in one sentence in the *Columbia Literary History of the United States*, shows up in one list in the *Columbia History of the American Novel*, and in one list (of her agent's clients) in James West's chapter in this volume. People mistook her for a literary writer briefly precisely because she peppered her sentimental tales of quaint Wisconsin buffoons with discussions of the telephone and other such modern innovations, and thus seemed to be involved in the kind of broad, cosmopolitan, inclusive examination of social life which the literary writers regularly produced.[3] But she wasn't, and she quickly fell out of any canon on which she may have had tentative claims.

Gale's novels and stories do, though, fit the mold provided by critics like Amy Kaplan, who argues that local color stories afford a kind of narrative "management" of social anxiety, and they also fit Richard Brodhead's description of regionalist texts as the literary equivalent of the middle-class vacation, since Gale writes (to use an ahistorical metaphor) a kind of theme-park localism, one in which the picket fences are always nicely painted white or picturesquely dilapidated, and the character dialogue is always cutely misspelled.[4] Theories of regionalism like those of Brodhead and Kaplan, however, are considerably less convincing when applied to a writer of the literary stature of Cather or Mark Twain or William Faulkner, or even, I would argue, writers in the middle of the literary canon, like Mary Wilkins Freeman, Sarah Orne Jewett, Charles Chesnutt, Kate Chopin, Paul Laurence Dunbar, Hamlin Garland, or Frank Norris. What kind of management of social anxiety does *Huckleberry Finn* (1884) afford, or *McTeague* (1899), or Freeman's "Old Woman Magoun" (1905)? If one wanted to worry less about race or class or gender or sexuality, if one wanted to manage one's anxieties in the 1880s or 1890s or 1910s, one would be better off not reading these fictions. And who in their right mind would choose, as a vacation, *Ethan Frome* (1911) or *The Sound and the Fury* (1929)?

Gale and Faulkner are both regionalists in that they both represent the particularities of an identifiable locale as their stage, they both assume specifically local mores and folkways are significant frames for their characters' understanding of the world and each other, and they both take for granted that elsewhere people and their doings are understood somewhat dissimilarly. The difference between Gale and Faulkner is not the relative level of respect they afford their characters, as Marjorie Pryse and Judith Fetterly have suggested should be the test for a difference between literary regionalism and subliterary "local color."[5] Gale may be patronizing, but Faulkner hardly exercises respect: his characters tend to range from seriously misguided to venal to despicable. Gale's cultural commitments side more or less in one direction – toward a supposedly common decency that transcends local standards for more national ones, toward a reinforcement of the superior understanding of urban elites (the characters that match the self-image of the readers finding solace in her books), and away from the more difficult realities facing the residents of the region about which she writes. Gale thus is a much better than Faulkner as a cultural bureaucrat, managing social anxiety and maintaining social divisions, much better as a foot-soldier in the nation-building project some critics have concluded is the cultural work of the genre. Her writing smoothes away and trivializes cultural difference and dissension while writers like Faulkner do the opposite: they dramatize precisely those fractures Gale would efface and insist on the salience of the conflicts she would minimize. Faulkner and the other regionalists in the current canon might seem, on the one hand, to suggest the value of metropolitan standards, since they show how local mores and chauvinism can corrupt decency and justice, but they also show the corruption inherent in metropolitan values. They represent the limits of provincial, popular understanding, but also the limits of urban elite conceptions. They address the most pressing issues facing the populations they describe, without overt or explicit judgment or prejudice.

William Dean Howells, who as an editor and critic championed most of the regionalist authors we still read, was one of the first to fully articulate this particular literary ethos, although it is evident already in Harriet Beecher Stowe and Herman Melville. Howells's various defenses of realism are well known, his advocacy for a literature open to the full range of human experience free of moral or cultural bias. Literary writers were "to classify and analyze the fruits of the human mind very much as the naturalist classifies the objects of his study," he wrote in *Criticism and Fiction* (1891), "rather than to praise or blame them."[6] Writing about his novel *Annie Kilburn* (1888) in a letter (quoted by Michael Elliott in this volume),[a] he concludes: "[I]f you read it to

a Michael Elliott, "Realism and radicalism: the school of Howells," chapter 17 in this volume, 298.

the end, you'll see that I solve nothing . . . The most that I can do is perhaps to set a few people thinking."[7] In his most impassioned novel, *The Hazard of New Fortunes* (1890), he shows both the deep human folly and the fundamental decency of industrialists, artists, anarchists, capitalists, the bourgeoisie, reformers, editors, Southerners, Midwesterners, Northerners, Bostonians, New Yorkers, Bohemians, and the rest of his diverse cast of characters.

This omnidirectional critique and survey, this refusal to take sides on the part of Howells, Cather, Faulkner and the other great regionalists, this pointed engagement combined with suspension of judgment, I have described as "literary cosmopolitanism."[8] Literary cosmopolitanism is not specific to regional texts – it is central to American literary assessment since the Civil War – but regionalist texts are where this ethos got its first wide airing. Regional literature, in short, is cosmopolitan literature, and the more cosmopolitan, the more literary. In making this argument I explicitly take issue with Bruce Robbins's piece in this volume, which argues that the American novel is insufficiently "worlded," attending to Main Street *instead* of the larger world.[b] In making his argument, however, Robbins is directly in the mainstream of American literary criticism: the question of sufficient "worlding" or breadth of perspective is the frame for critics examining everything from the earliest examples of regionalist fiction to postcolonial literature. Lawrence Buell notes that this criterion animates the debate about romance and realism, that John De Forest, for instance, understood the Great American Novel to be one that, in Buell's approving words, "was to provide a recognizable portrait of the nation in all its geographic and social diversity."[c] Contemporary critics, whether prizing the inclusivity of past writers or condemning their lack thereof, maintain the values already in practice in the late nineteenth century.

Those texts to which literary readers and critics return again and again are texts that represent Main Street through reference to a larger world. In *Main Street* (1920), Sinclair Lewis, who Carl Van Doren claimed was promulgating a revolt from the village,[9] presents a protagonist obsessed with broadening her own horizon, and the reader–writer compact that animates the novel relies on an understanding of the comically limited "worlding" that she and the other characters can manage. But the provincial tales of tiny Dunnet Landing, Maine in *The Country of the Pointed Firs* (1896) and related stories by Sarah Orne Jewett constantly refer to the larger world, too, to global commerce, to thousands of

b Bruce Robbins, "The worlding of the American novel," chapter 66.
c Lawrence Buell, "Theories of the American novel in the age of realism," chapter 19 in this volume, 333.

years of world literature, to polities, social schemes, economics, and cultures from China to England to Greece and beyond. Regionalism was already in revolt from the village in its classic phase, and in cosmopolitan fashion, equally in revolt against the metropolis.

In one of the best-known anecdotes about literary regionalism, Jewett, already enthroned as one of regionalism's leading lights by the turn of the century, read Cather's early Nebraska stories at Cather's request. Almost twenty years later, in a preface to a 1922 edition of her first novel, *Alexander's Bridge* (1912), Cather recounted some of the advice that Jewett gave her: "One day you will write about your own country," Cather says Jewett told her. "In the meantime, get all you can. One must know the world *so well* before one can know the parish."[10] In Cather's first collection of stories, *The Troll Garden* (1905), she at least partially follows this advice, with stories set in cities among worldly, well-traveled, well-heeled characters, some with provincial pasts, some experiencing other forms of cultural dislocation, and Nebraska stories with a strong metropolitan perspective. But Jewett counseled even more emphasis on the perspective of the world in developing characters from the parish: "You don't see them yet quite enough from the outside," Jewett wrote in a letter. "You stand right in the middle of each of them when you write, without having the standpoint of the looker-on who takes them each in their relations to letters, to the world."[11] This I take to be one of the explicit theorizations of regionalist cosmopolitanism: the point is not just to get inside the local world, but to do that while at the same time standing outside, and outside not just in relation to New York or Boston, but to the world, and not just to the material world, but to letters – that is, the point is not simply one of attaining the proper sociological distance but of engaging the broadest, the most global ethical issues, which is, from this perspective, the fundamental business of the literary.

Cather has emerged as the paradigmatic regionalist in part because she perfected the regionalist novel, rather than the short story. Unlike Mary Wilkins Freeman, who was very successful (critically and commercially) in the magazine world, but less so as a novelist, Cather produced a string of bestselling novels, and she continues to attract a broad readership to this day. But more important, she managed, despite or perhaps aided by Jewett's criticisms, one of the most thoroughly cosmopolitan (in my sense of the word) bodies of work in the canon.

Cather's first published story, or sketch, really, was already deeply involved with cosmopolitan issues. "Peter" is about a family in "the dreariest part" of southwest Nebraska. The adult son wants to sell his father's fiddle, since the old man is too infirm to play it. But the instrument is a potent symbol for the father, endowed with the romance of his life as a violinist in Prague. These images of art contrast directly with the social and aesthetic aridity of the plains, the mundane materiality of no-nonsense farmers, and the heedless rapacity of the man's own go-getter son. In the end, at least in part due to grief about his lost ability to play and in part because of his son's terrorizing practicality, he breaks the fiddle over his knee and then shoots himself in the mouth with a shotgun. The editors of *The Mahogany Tree*, the journal that published "Peter," argued repeatedly that realism was the antithesis of art. They recognized in Cather's fiction not an embrace of frontier people but a rejection of American mores, not a portrayal of the way life is, but of the way it shouldn't be. And one senses that Cather might have agreed, that in this case perhaps Jewett was right.

But in her other early stories, like "On the Divide" (1896), published in *Overland Monthly*, a San Francisco regionalist journal founded by Bret Harte, and "Eric Hermannson's Soul," published another four years later in 1900 in *Cosmopolitan* (I can't resist noting the journal's title), Cather provides a more balanced introduction to Nebraska's immigrant populations. In the latter story, a classic urban interloper interacts with a frontier local, a standard organizing device, and an almost schematic technique for the literary examination of the relation of center to regional periphery. In the global reach of their plots and balanced representation of the competing claims of the world and the parish, these stories already express the cosmopolitan commitments Cather would continue to maintain as an author, often marked by a breadth of explicit reference. In the course of one story she refers to the wastes of Iceland, the jungles of Africa, islands in the Pacific, New York, Montana, Kansas, gypsies, Nero, Harvard, the Black Hills, Rossetti, Grieg, Schubert, Puvis de Chavannes, the Miller of Hofbau, upper and lower classes, Valkyries, Newport, Bourget, the Thebaid, Troy, Algiers, the Arctic, Siegfried, Tennyson – and on and on. Jewett couldn't have wanted more than that.

The novels *O Pioneers!* (1913), *My Ántonia* (1918), *The Professor's House* (1925), *My Mortal Enemy* (1926), *Death Comes to the Archbishop* (1927), and *Lucy Gayheart* (1935) all fulfill the promise of that commitment. The first paragraphs of *O Pioneers!* set up a series of central cultural debates – about modernity and tradition, city and country, nature and culture, gender, work, and religion – and the plot offers balanced, competing representations of the available positions: the competing claims of city, town, and country, diverse discourses on ethics, religion, and responsibility, arguments for and against innovation, progress, stability, and convention all get their due. And in each case, resolution is undercut: Alexandra is right to break the gender mold, but she goes too far, and loses touch with her sexuality altogether. Carl is not enough of a man, and a little bit too much like one. The city is a place of anomie, but the country is worse. The country teaches one about life, but not as well as the city. The city, though, seems to teach nothing worth knowing.

To take a specific example: the mortgage was used in regionalist texts as a symbol of modernity's destruction of traditional rural values, but Alexandra's decision to remortgage the family farm and buy up neighboring farms through the use of further mortgages (what is today called "leveraging") makes her success possible. Lest we think, however, that this relation to capital is the right one, we have the example of her disgustingly bourgeois brothers. The constant oscillation between competing ideologemes is the essence of Cather's art.

Alexandra is our heroine not because of what she accomplishes in her life or doesn't, but because of the breadth of her comprehension, the open-minded understanding that includes sympathy for even the murderer of her best friend. But despite her position as the text's model for comprehensive understanding, she often falls short – "her personal life, her own realization of herself, was almost a subconscious existence; like an underground river that came to the surface only here and there, and then sank again under her own fields." As we see Alexandra's blindness, and see her alone with her problems, we realize the limitations of Alexandra's family and culture, especially compared to the culture we share with Cather. No one in the novel understands Alexandra, and yet we do. The characters are self-interested, while we have a Kantian disinterested interestedness. Our aesthetic relation to these human problems is a form of broad understanding, our understanding both the means and the end of our aesthetic experience. Alexandra is represented as almost an artist, her farm not just a business but an aesthetic accomplishment made possible by the breadth of her vision, but the cosmopolitanism of the novel is wider still.

In *My Ántonia* (1918), Cather again represented a near-artist as her protagonist. "She was one of the truest artists I ever knew," Cather told an interviewer about the model for Ántonia, "in her keenness and sensitiveness of her enjoyment, in her love of people and in her willingness to take pains."[12] Cather uses a double frame: the opening narrator, who has a wicked wit and functions at least at first almost like an implied author, and Jim Burden, who this first narrator doesn't think much of, and who is classically unreliable, full of blind spots and evasions. This unreliability helps set up the text's cosmopolitanism, as does a sprinkle of classical and literary allusions. The novel activates many of the same dichotomies as *O Pioneers!* – foreigner/native, local/national, traditional/modern, nature/culture, young/old – with the same basic technique of oscillation. The critical debates since – for instance, whether the novel is nostalgic, finding the past both "precious" and "incommunicable," as the famous last line has it, or vehemently modern and forward-looking – are kept alive by those who make the mistake of seeing one half or the other of the argument the text makes.[13]

In *Death Comes to the Archbishop*, the missionary bishop considers irreconcilable difference explicitly, never questioning his guide Jacinto's beliefs: "There was no way in which he could transfer his own memories of European civilization into the Indian mind," the bishop thinks, "and he was quite willing to believe that behind Jacinto there was a long tradition, a story of experience, which no language could translate to him." These novels, though, refute the impossibility of understanding. They compare past cultures to present, indigenous to European, professional cultures to those of the lay people around them. They play the local microcultures scattered through Nebraska, the Midwest, and the Southwest against others differentiated by class, nationality, taste, and trajectory, including some in New York, San Francisco, Washington, DC, and further-flung metropolises. They counter men's perspectives by women's, young and old, religious and secular, heterosexual desire and homosexual, and weigh the representational capacity of the various arts against each other. In all cases except the last, Cather refuses to endorse one side over the other. She remains catholic in her sympathies, uninterested in adjudicating the claims and committed to portraying the full range of them.

The other major regionalist authors all managed some version of this cosmopolitan juggling act in their best work, and those that did it most successfully – that is, those who represented the widest array of social positions and problems, who exercised the widest sympathy (along with the most widely spread criticisms), who gave voices to the most and the most significant competing ideologies – are the writers who are, like Cather, in everyone's canon: Jewett, Twain, Chesnutt, Chopin, Dunbar, and Norris, for instance.[14] And within each writer's corpus, the more cosmopolitan texts are more often taught, more often discussed in the criticism, more often anthologized, more often included on comprehensive exams – they activate all the machinery of the canon, while the more parochial texts do not. Norris's *McTeague: A Story of San Francisco* (1899) and *The Octopus: A Story of California* (1901) touch on many of the pressing debates of their day about evolution, class, politics, capital, science, art, and gender in a wide survey of positions, while *Moran of the Lady Letty* (1898), *Blix* (1899), and *A Man's Woman* (1900) more clearly side with particular gender and racial ideologies of their day, all featuring male characters, for instance, who are led to full masculinity through experiencing their own animality before being tamed by the civilizing influence of women. These latter texts are correspondingly read only by the most devout specialists.

The writers who are less successful, who can't refrain from the soapbox, whose biases interrupt their literary presentation – these are in some second tier. María Amparo Ruiz de Burton, although she consciously strove in *The Squatter and the Don* (1885) to build bridges between Anglo and Hispanic Californians, did so only at the top of the class system, never acknowledging the cultures of the Indians, the settled and itinerant laborers, the servants, the smaller homesteaders and their families.[d] Many readers today are put off by what strikes them as her very limited cosmopolitanism. Mary Hallock Foote wrote a few stories that manage the cosmopolitan view, and these can be found in recent anthologies, but the mass of her work is deadeningly partisan to blindered bourgeois values. And I defy anyone to find literary value in the many books of ardent women's suffrage opponent and popular author Adeline D. T. Whitney.

This greatly oversimplifies things, of course. Hamlin Garland was championed by Vernon Parrington and Henry Nash Smith as a progressive propagandist, one whose broad sympathies justified his art, but he was rejected by the New Critics of the postwar era for his didacticism – one of their kinder assessments was that he was "a sensitive observer and chronicler rather than a great artist."[15] More recently, Judith Fetterly and Marjorie Pryse have used Garland as a prime example of a writer who holds his rural characters up for urban ridicule while Bill Brown, Stephanie Foote, Nancy Glazener, and Philip Joseph have all produced more nuanced evaluations, each taking his Midwestern populist sympathies seriously.[16] I have tried to show that even in his most politically engaged stories, like "Up the Cooley," he demonstrates understanding for both the Midwestern farmer and the Eastern sophisticate, an understanding of the populist position and that of the disengaged aesthete, and, in his best work, rigorously exercises a literary refusal to take sides.[17]

During the 1920s, "revolt from the village" writers like Edgar Lee Masters, Sherwood Anderson, Sinclair Lewis, and Ruth Suckow, achieved their cosmopolitanism more through universally applied disdain than a universally

d For more on Burton, see Gretchen Murphy, "The hemispheric novel in the post-revolutionary era," chapter 33, 567 in this volume.

applied sympathy, but they wrote much more in continuation of than in reaction against earlier local color writers. Anderson's *Winesburg, Ohio* (1919) is the story of George Willard's attempt (admittedly failed) to understand the full range of people in his town, framed by the tale of a writer who is himself insufficiently cosmopolitan. The characters who think they are sophisticated are not, those that think they are well traveled are not, those that think they comprehend human variety do not. Sinclair Lewis attempts an encyclopedia of human types and occupations in his novels of the 1920s, and George Babbitt, Carol Kennicott, Martin Arrowsmith, Elmer Gantry, and Samuel Dodsworth are all marked by their failure to comprehend their worlds, as are all of the supporting characters in different ways. The writers of the twenties make their argument for the cosmopolitan vista by cataloguing failures to achieve it.

Hum Ishu Ma, Anzia Yezierska, and the Harlem Renaissance and Southern Renaissance writers, too, tend to exercise balance through critique, but they too recognized that they were successful as literary writers to the extent that they exercised the cosmopolitan overview, and to this day the level of critical acclaim accorded individual authors and works from this group is directly related to the achievement of that balance. *Cogewea* (1925), for instance, by Hum Ishu Ma (also known as Mourning Dove), is a literary novel with regular, if heavy-handed, oscillations of perspective and value (and references to Longfellow and other literary lights), in which the Eastern whites are blind to the values of the West, the Indians to the whites, and both Indians and whites to the special perspective of the "half-bloods." It is, finally, however, what a character calls a "meller-dramy," in which the good-hearted but humble suitor and the rich nasty suitor fill their respective roles, both receiving their just rewards. The book resolves when the "half-blood" protagonist and her "half-blood" fiancé, unfairly ostracized by both whites and Indians, get together in a "zone of [their] own," inherit a pile of money, and face an exceedingly bright future. The literary problem is not just the neatness of the plot resolution, but the fact that Hum Ishu Ma claims this "zone" is inaccessible to anyone else, whether primitive, modern, Indian, or white, and the melodramatic conclusion is of a piece with this ideological decision.

Although Jessie Redmon Fauset was often explicit about her cosmopolitanism– *Plum Bun* (1928), is significantly subtitled *A Novel without a Moral* – her political commitment to portraying positive rather than negative images of African American life nevertheless limited her ability to live up to it. As a result, few would now argue that she is as great a novelist as Nella Larsen or Zora Neale Hurston, to take the two women to whom she is most often compared. Valerie Babb's chapter in this volume is a perfect example of the kind of assessment I am making here: Babb surveys the strengths and shortcomings of the major novelists of the Harlem Renaissance (like most critics, saying very little about the novels of W. E. B. Du Bois, who believed that "all art is propaganda") by praising "variety," the "multifaceted," and noting the problems of didacticism and narrowing proscriptions.[e] Larsen, Hurston, Jean Toomer, Claude McKay, Langston Hughes, Ellen Glasgow, Faulkner – these are all writers critically acclaimed exactly to the extent that they manage to portray the complexities and conundrums of their characters in ways that reference the widest variety of stratified and heteroglot languages – commercial, professional, artistic, generic, scientific, political, and so on – that take into account the most angles, that use the most lenses. Glasgow, for instance, in *Barren Ground* (1925) voices the languages of the Old South, the New South, the Northeast, patriarchy, matriarchy, scientific farming, witchcraft, religious mania, medicine, psychiatry, aesthetics, primitivism, Puritanism, progressivism, and evolution, while working in the styles of realism, gothic, romance, and the ghost tale. This was her way, as she claimed in her autobiography, to "write of the universal, not the provincial."[18]

Cather said that what was great about Henry James was the sheer number of sidelights he shone upon his subject, that Jewett was a great writer because she described Maine "in the light of wide experience, from near and from afar," that Norris in his "Story of California" was great because "his horizon is wide" and "not limited by literary prejudices," and that Walt Whitman was a great poet because he was morally "neither good nor bad."[19] Throughout the last 150 years of American literary history, and very much up to the present day, one finds praise for writers using these same criteria, and criticisms for failures to achieve the cosmopolitan ideal – failures of sexism, racism, classism, and all the other sins against the widest forms of sympathy and understanding.

If this all sounds too idealistic, I should say that of course it is. The central ethos of American literary culture as I'm defining it is one that is humanistic, Enlightenment-forged, progressive, hopeful, and thus, like all of those things, it is perhaps woefully wrong-headed and doomed by the forces of capital and power to have no real impact on the most fundamental facts of human life. As I finished writing this piece I was in Kiev, Ukraine, where in the main square I watched a group of young local dancers breakdancing on a mat, MTV-Jams-hip-hopped to the hilt, doing moves that originated in the projects of Brooklyn, breaking to James Brown and German robo-techno and

e See Valerie Babb, "Wright, Hurston, and the direction of the African American novel," chapter 42.

contemporary Russian hiphop, a perfect example of the global flow of culture in our hypermediated world, and a scene that is replicated by Korean b-boys in Seoul and street kids in São Paulo.

On the other side of the square was something much more local: a trio of middle-aged Ukrainian performers wearing versions of traditional peasant dress were singing folksongs with gusto to a fairly large crowd, although not as large as the one for the breakdancers. This made me think of the preservationist impulse of literary regionalism: "One January day, thirty years ago," begins Cather's *O Pioneers!*, "the little town of Hanover, anchored on a windy Nebraska tableland, was trying not to be blown away." Writing about local folkways was important, according to some local colorists and regionalists, because regional differences were disappearing, erased by a standardizing modernity, and Cather's near-past time frame, twenty to thirty years before the present, is very common in such writing, a recognition that what was being preserved was already past, that actual preservation was impossible. These Ukrainian folksingers were also trying to capture a bit of culture already largely blown away – a peasant culture erased as a way of life by new economic and cultural forms – and they shared the American literary regionalists' conviction that in that perishing particularity something important for collective understanding was housed. In regionalist nonfiction, from John Muir to Mary Austin to the Southern Agrarians to Aldo Leopold to Wendell Berry to Annie Dillard to Gretel Ehrlich, this preservationist impulse has always been explicit, and regionalist fiction has often eloquently, if implicitly, made the case for a conservatory relation to the land and cultures they describe – one way to honor difference is to not let it die.

Some aspects of the scene in front of me also reminded me of why at least a few critics of American regionalist fiction have found it reactionary and even politically offensive.[20] Standing just to the right of the performers, practically sharing the stage with them, was a group of young men, flush with feeling, roused by the music to an oddly angry sense of pride and community, almost daring passersby to ignore the significance of this performance. They were in their twenties and thirties, their heads very closely shorn, with a few tattoos and facial scars, defiantly wearing these and the sartorial marks of the hooligan, and in this land of genocide it was hard to miss the historical echoes: these young men were finding in this rehearsal of their regional folk culture an ideal image of their own place in history, as have many angry young men around the world in the last century – the American Ku Klux Klan, the Nazi party, Neo-nazi groups, the Taliban – young men who embraced right-wing nationalisms, resenting the impositions of modernity and blaming their own plight on it. This is our culture, these young men seemed to be saying, and in celebrating it we reject yours.

This isolationist, nationalist impulse is the opposite of that shared by the literary regionalists, for whom the ongoing conflicts among populations were the source and stuff of their fiction, but whose ethos was one of inclusiveness, of equal attention to the world and the parish, of support for both preservation and progress. It was an ethos that always argued for the value of seeing, in the knotty mesh of relation in their society, not a salvational image, not an identity to be adopted, but instead, for what it was worth, an irresolvable complication, something Cather calls, in the last line of "Paul's Case," the final story in *The Troll Garden*, "the immense design of things."

Notes

1. I refer primarily to Josephine Donovan, *New England Local Color Literature: A Women's Tradition* (New York: Frederick Ungar, 1983); Louis Renza, *"A White Heron" and the Question of Minor Literature* (Madison: University of Wisconsin Press, 1984); David M. Jordan, *New World Regionalism: Literature in the Americas* (Toronto: University of Toronto Press, 1994); Kate McCullough, *Regions of Identity: The Construction of America in Women's Fiction, 1885–1914* (Stanford, CA: Stanford University Press, 1999); Judith Fetterly and Marjorie Pryse, *Writing Out of Place: Regionalism, Women, and American Literary Culture* (Urbana: University of Illinois Press, 2005) and works by Kaplan, Foote, Brown, Joseph, and Dainotto cited below. For a more complete bibliography see Tom Lutz, *Cosmopolitan Vistas: American Regionalism and Literary Value* (Ithaca, NY: Cornell University Press, 2004).
2. See Ramón Saldívar, "The American borderlands novel" (chapter 62 this volume), and Rob Wilson and Wimal Dissanayake, eds., *Global/Local: Cultural Production and the Transnational Imaginary* (Durham, NC: Duke University Press, 1996).
3. The telephone reference is to the opening of Gale's *Friendship Village* (1908).
4. Amy Kaplan, "Nation, Region, Empire," in *The Columbia History of the American Novel*, ed. Emory Elliott *et al.* (New York: Columbia University Press, 1991); Richard Brodhead, *Cultures of Letters: Scenes of Reading and Writing in Nineteenth-Century America* (Chicago: University of Chicago Press, 1993).
5. Judith Fetterley and Marjorie Pryse, "Introduction," in *American Women Regionalists, 1850–1910: A Norton Anthology* (New York: Norton, 1992).
6. William Dean Howells, *Criticism and Fiction, and Other Essays 1837–1920* (New York: New York University Press, 1959), 20–21.
7. Howells to Hale, August 30, 1888, in William Dean Howells, *Selected Letters, Volume 3: 1882–1891*, ed. Robert C. Leitz III *et al.*, vol. XIX of *A Selected Edition of William Dean Howells* (Boston: Twayne, 1980), 228–229.

8. Lutz, *Cosmopolitan Vistas*, 3.
9. Carl Van Doren, "Contemporary American Novelists: x. The Revolt from the Village: 1920," *Nation* 113 (October 12, 1921), 407–412.
10. Preface to *Alexander's Bridge* (1922), rpt. in *Alexander's Bridge*, ed. Marilee Lindeman (New York: Oxford University Press, 1997), 95.
11. Sarah Orne Jewett, *Letters*, ed. Richard Cary (Waterville, ME: Colby College Press, 1967), 248.
12. L. Brent Bohlke, ed., *Willa Cather in Person: Interviews, Speeches, and Letters* (Lincoln: University of Nebraska Press, 1986), 44.
13. Cf. Glen A. Love, "Jim Burden: A Rare Modern," in *Approaches to Teaching Cather's "My Ántonia,"* ed. Susan J. Rosowski (New York: MLA, 1989), 146–149.
14. For discussions of these authors elsewhere in this volume, see Andrew Lawson (Twain, chapter 21), Robert Reid-Pharr (Chesnutt, chapter 28), Barbara McCaskill (Chesnutt, Dunbar; chapter 29), Elizabeth Nolan (Chopin, chapter 34), Donna Campbell (Dunbar, Norris; chapter 30), and Tim Prchal (Cather, chapter 25).
15. Robert E. Spiller *et al.*, *Literary History of the United States*, vol. II,, 3rd rev. edn. (New York: Macmillan, 1963),1017.
16. Fetterly and Pryse "Introduction," xi–xii; William Brown, "The Popular, the Populist, and the Populace: Locating Hamlin Garland in the Politics of Culture," *Arizona Quarterly* 50 (Autumn 1994): 89–110; Stephanie Foote, *Regional Fictions: Culture and Identity in Nineteenth-Century American Literature* (Madison: University of Wisconsin Press, 2001); Nancy Glazener, *Reading for Realism: The History of a U.S. Literary Institution, 1850–1910* (Durham, NC: Duke University Press, 1997); Philip Joseph, *American Literary Regionalism in a Global Age* (Baton Rouge: Louisiana State University Press, 2007).
17. Lutz, *Cosmopolitan Vistas*, 65–78.
18. Meredith Nicholson, "Edward Eggleston," *Atlantic Monthly* 90 (December 1902): 804–809; J. H. Morse, "The Native Element in American Fiction," *Century* 4 (June 1883): 288–298.
19. Quoted in Sharon O'Brien, ed., *Willa Cather: Stories, Poems, and Other Writings* (New York: Library of America, 1992), 925, 931, 905, 854, 855, 902–903.
20. This is a very easy charge to make against a pro-regionalist text like Twelve Southerners, *I'll Take My Stand* (New York: Harper, 1930), in which agrarian, anti-industrialist rhetoric shares the page with thoroughgoing racism. Cf. also Roberto Maria Dainotto, "'All the Regions Do Smilingly Revolt': The Literature of Place and Region," *Critical Inquiry* 22 (Spring 1996): 486–505.

27

Wharton, marriage, and the New Woman

JENNIFER L. FLEISSNER

"When a girl leaves her home at eighteen," writes Theodore Dreiser at the outset of *Sister Carrie* (1900), "she does one of two things. Either she falls into saving hands and becomes better, or she rapidly assumes the cosmopolitan standard of virtue and becomes worse." We see encapsulated here the two dominant plots for women over the first century of the American novel. In the one case, a laborious program of self-improvement, culminating in marriage; in the other, a swift fall into seduction, terminating in death.

Both of these denouements, scholars have suggested, may be read in broader historical terms, as attempts to manage the crises of modern individualism via the marriage plot. When a young woman seeks to chart the course of her own life, guided by her own desires rather than inherited norms, what results? For its proponents, modernity's freedoms – as represented by the founding of liberal democracies like the USA – offered unprecedented opportunities for the progressive betterment of *all* human beings, loosed at last from the dead weight of tradition. Detractors feared the opposite, a universe evacuated of meaning or purpose, with human activity reduced to an unending, chaotic struggle among atomized, pleasure-seeking selves.[1] In the wake of the French Revolution, this dystopic vision loomed largest. Thus, in the 1790s, heroines like Eliza Wharton of *The Coquette* (1797) appear dangerously "volatile" (ever-changing, unstable) in their insistent "pursuit of happiness"; by killing them off, the novel imposes moral closure on a journey of desirous self-exploration that otherwise threatens to defy all limits.[a] By the 1850s, in contrast, modern individualism is not so much curtailed as shown

a Anna Mae Duane, in "Susanna Rowson, Hannah Webster Foster, and the seduction novel in the early USA," chapter 2 in this volume, casts this denouement less as the result of individualism taken to an extreme than as the triumph of its opposite: submission to a force external to the self, whether one's own body, the will of another, or the will of God, 39–40, 44–47.

willing and able to manage its own potential excesses from within.[2] Hence, we see far greater confidence in the workability of "self-government": heroines learn the appeal of reining in their unruly impulses, by yoking individual desire to the civic end of marital stability.[b]

By 1900, however, a dramatic change occurs. Despite Dreiser's rehearsal of these two familiar options for the novelistic heroine, they prove remarkably inadequate to the narrative arc of his own ingénue, Carrie Meeber. Nor can they account for the trajectory of Selma White, the ambitious antiheroine of one of the biggest US bestsellers of the same year, Robert Grant's *Unleavened Bread*. In both novels, the modern commitment to ongoing self-making and -remaking is neither curbed nor chastised; rather, the women's plots simply go on and on, narratively fueled by the persistence of desire rather than by the aim to contain it. In the case of the single and seduced Carrie, "coquetry" paves the way not to ruin but to recognition – a shift made possible by replacing the goal of marriage with that of paid employment as an actress. Lacking in clear signposts of achieved success, this career-governed narrative leaves our heroine on the final page still rocking onward to ever-new dreams. If Carrie thus defies the fatal finale of seduction fiction, we might say Grant's Selma rewrites the domestic novel in similar terms, by refusing to see marriage as any sort of brake on her ongoing "drama of social aspiration."[3] Rather than conclude her story, Selma's nuptials occur in the book's opening chapter, initiating a cycle that continues throughout the text as she whips through three husbands in a ceaseless attempt to find the proper setting for what she loftily calls her own "development."

If we now tend to read Dreiser's work as defining of modern American subjectivity,[c] readers in 1900 responded to *Unleavened Bread* in similarly allegorical terms. Hence, by focusing on a figure like Selma, one wrote, Grant had produced the first "broadly and significantly American" rather than simply regional novel.[4] In the era of the Robber Baron, excess ruled the day, and, thus, so did Selma. As with Carrie, her raging ambitions brought her not censure but success – even though the book's readers found her uniformly appalling.

Indeed, the same reviewer opined, Selma specifically embodied "the strange *restlessness* that has got possession of so many women at the present

b As Cindy Weinstein's essay "Sentimentalism," chapter 12 in this volume helpfully makes clear, self-government here is often explicitly opposed to an unwilled submission to a tyrannical spouse; 212–217.

c See, in this volume, Jude Davies, "Dreiser and the city," chapter 22, and David Zimmerman, "Novels of American business, industry, and consumerism," chapter 24.

time." This oft-used idiom of "restlessness" made the era's feminist "New Women," as they were deemed in the periodicals, seem symbolic of a modern America that, in its very hunger for growth and change, had begun to lose its essential moorings. "[I]n great hotels, on mammoth steamers and luxurious trains," wrote the novelist Robert Herrick in *Together* (1908), "emancipated woman" could be found, "rushing hither and thither." "The woman had been set free," decided Henry Adams, "volatilized like Clerk Maxwell's perfect gas; almost brought to the point of explosion, like steam."[5] Grant had captured some essence of the "weightlessness" of turn-of-the-century experience by focusing on such a "volatile" woman, all agreed – even Theodore Roosevelt, who called *Unleavened Bread* as a result "the strongest study of American life that has been written for many years."[6] Despite such accolades, however, we have largely forgotten Grant today. If recalled at all, his work is deemed of interest chiefly for having inspired the much more gifted and prolific Edith Wharton to create her protagonist Undine Spragg in *The Custom of the Country* (1913).[7] As Wharton's title suggests, she, too, saw her consummately self-interested, compulsively divorcing heroine as standing at the whirling core of early twentieth-century American life.

Why, though, would Edith Wharton choose to "add her voice," by satirizing such a heroine, to what the pioneering Wharton scholar Blake Nevius calls the "general indictment" of the "'new woman'" in turn-of-the-century American fiction?[8] As a professional writer – one, notably, whose own termination of a sexless marriage brought forth a "more than customary restlessness" – Wharton herself has appeared the very model of the ambitious, liberated *fin-de-siecle* woman.[9] Yet she typically mocked organized feminism, at one point noting "with satisfaction" that "the leaders of the movement, judging from their photos," appeared "unfitted" for both of women's primary "functions" – that is, for "pleasure and procreation."[10]

Particularly when coupled with some of Wharton's other less than progressive views, such remarks could easily seem to reduce her to the outmoded elitist many critics had deemed her decades ago, prior to her feminist reclamation.[11] Wharton was, in fact, quite relentless in her critique of the modernizing USA, which seemed to her a cultural and spiritual wasteland; like her friend Henry James, she eventually sought refuge in the Old World, moving permanently to France in 1911. Several recent critical studies thus consider her less a feminist avatar than an "antimodern" thinker, in Jackson Lears's term.[12] Jennie Kassanoff emphasizes the conservative dimensions of Wharton's distaste for modern America, seeing her as chiefly appalled by the rise of "vulgar" parvenus like the Jewish Rosedale in *The House of Mirth* (1905) – hence, in

Kassanoff's depiction, by a more bustlingly "democratic" social landscape – and thus as lamenting the decline of the Anglo-Saxon elite to which her own family belonged.[13] In distinct contrast, Dale Bauer in *Edith Wharton's Brave New Politics* (1995), focusing on Wharton's less critically studied later novels of the 1920s and 1930s such as *Twilight Sleep* (1927), treats her scorn for mass culture in politically opposite terms, as akin to that of Marxist theorists who saw it as a path toward increased standardization of human beings.[14]

Kassanoff and Bauer agree, however, that Wharton's politics may be salvaged if we see them as gradually "progressing," from the 1890s to the modernist 1920s, toward positions more akin to the critics' own. Yet to treat Wharton's aghast view of the social landscape *circa* 1900 as merely that of a dying breed, a threatened elitist, may too readily adopt the era's own discourse of social evolution, at the cost of exploring the actual complexity of her stance. Certainly Wharton was capable of a patrician nostalgia. Yet one may believe her prone to over-romanticizing a lost world of *noblesse oblige* and still share her chagrin – as, say, W. E. B. Du Bois might have – at the replacement of sentimentally construed relations between classes with a Darwinian jungle of unrestrained greed. Applying a discourse of progress to Wharton's thought is especially problematic because of its susceptibility to one of her own core critiques. Specifically, Wharton persistently takes issue with a markedly American tendency that, for her, showed how *similar* the Progressive Era and the Jazz Age in fact were: a tendency to imagine – naïvely, in her view – that what sociologist Emile Durkheim termed the "liberation of desires" could result not in a centrifugal anomie but simply in the sunny forward march of enlightenment.[15]

Wharton's multifaceted critique of American modernity can be evaluated only if we read her once more in the company of the contemporaneous novelists she herself admired, or to whom her work was often compared at the time – from Grant, Dreiser, and Herrick to Frank Norris, Sinclair Lewis, and David Graham Phillips.[16] While traditional scholarly boundaries have tended to separate Wharton as a "novelist of manners" *or* as a feminist from these masculine "naturalists" or critics of capitalist culture,[d] those boundaries fail to grasp how central the critique of New Womanhood was to fiction's broader exploration of modernizing America from the 1890s through the early decades of the twentieth century. Importantly, as we will see, to emphasize the perspective of Wharton – the only writer of those mentioned whose work

d Donna Campbell's chapter in this volume, "The rise of naturalism" (chapter 30) presents a more capacious and flexible account of the naturalism that encompasses Wharton. See esp. 505–506.

spans this entire era – is to encounter a New Woman at once more demonized, *and* more radically steeped in an unknowable potentiality, than accounts of this period's writing have yet conceived.

Materialism, morality, and the modern woman

For years, Edith Wharton was viewed as simply too much a child of privilege to generate meaningful social commentary through her fiction. Feminist critics played a crucial role in reconstructing her as acute cultural critic, precisely by reading her through gender more than class. Wharton re-emerged as the woman writer most able to develop and sharpen the critical revisions of the seduction and marriage plots already starting to be produced by, most notably, Henry James.[17] In these revisions, the premarital "fallen woman" story becomes the exposé of society's destruction of an actual sexual innocent (as in James's "Daisy Miller" [1878], or Wharton's *The House of Mirth*, with Lily Bart). Alternatively, wifehood appears as not a reward but a trap for a free-spirited heroine (James's Isabel Archer of *The Portrait of a Lady* [1882], and Verena Tarrant of *The Bostonians* [1886]; and arguably Wharton's Undine Spragg, as well as Charity Royall of *Summer* [1917]).[e]

More significantly still, feminist criticism enabled Wharton's portrayal of women's "primitive" status as jewel-laden symbols of masculine wealth to resonate anew. Novels like *Custom* and *The House of Mirth* were reinterpreted as part of the contemporaneous critique of bourgeois marriage as thinly veiled prostitution or chattel slavery by economists like Thorstein Veblen, novelists like Kate Chopin, and, most sweepingly, the feminist intellectual and fiction writer Charlotte Perkins Gilman.[18] Unprecedented feminine inroads into education and non-menial paid employment, as well as agitation for rights within marriage such as liberal divorce laws and sexual "self-ownership," seemed to portend an evolutionary elevation of womanhood, one that could simultaneously bring "the race" as a whole to a new plane of cooperation and shared achievement. New Women, in other words, appeared uniquely positioned to save a materialistic modern world from its own

e As Carrie Tirado Bramen's essay in this volume, "James, realism, and the pragmatist ideal" (chapter 18), makes clear, however, the shift of culpability from the heroine herself to the society that constrains her need not imply a progressive critique; rather, Jamesian realism (like Wharton's) typically presented such constraints as the inevitable (if nonetheless lamentable) byproduct of "sociality" itself. This fact can result in the surprising similarities between Isabel Archer as Bramen depicts her and a seduced heroine like Charlotte Temple; both imagine real life might take the exalted form they've learned from reading novels; 310–311.

vices, by bringing their maternal status as selfless advocates for others to bear on public life.[19]

If this was so, however, then how to account for the perspective we have already begun to see in many of the novels of this era, from Wharton's own to those of Herrick, Dreiser, and Grant? Blake Nevius writes that "one of the truisms of American fiction after 1890" held that "the 'new woman' was *the chief vessel of the materialism* which threatened the values of the older society."[20] How could the New Woman, often within the same texts, stand for the forward march of moral progress and the spread of compassless self-indulgence? What we need to grasp is the way these opposed narratives of modernity actually began, over the course of the nineteenth century, to become conflated – a conflation in which "restless" public women played a central role.

The key here lies in the rise of consumer culture. In a late eighteenth-century novel like *The Coquette*, the heroine's desire to delay marriage by flitting about in fashionable society appears as a form of "egotism," a selfish, punishable flouting of communal norms. Subsequent mid-century domestic novels share an opposition between the stable comforts of a privatized domesticity and the "volatility" of fashionable, market-driven lives aimed at public display. Already in the mid nineteenth century, however, in works like Herman Melville's "I and My Chimney" (1856) and Harriet Beecher Stowe's *House and Home Papers* (1865), we see the glimmerings of a new kind of story, one in which the battle between fashionable society and domestic life happens *within* the marital home – and fashion even starts to win the day. Once this shift has occurred, it becomes newly possible to begin to imagine a plot of feminine desire that, undampened by the traditional forms of narrative closure, simply goes on and on.

What enables this importation of such a plot of desire into the postmarital landscape? In America, the answer is not adultery, but home improvement. A fashionable wife wants to redo the house. Specifically, she wants to render it at once more public and more modern and stylish. In these tales – as well as in Stowe's later novels, such as *Pink and White Tyranny* (1871) – the beleaguered husband, not the "domestic" woman, attempts fruitlessly to stand up for the virtues of tradition, stability, and, indeed, that of domestic space as a privatized haven in a heartless world.[21]

In many ways, then, the divorce novels of the turn of the century merely take the consumerist marriage plot to its logical conclusion, with the husbands themselves now appearing as last year's discards. Moreover, the restless wife begins to be joined by the single "woman adrift," like Dreiser's Carrie, whose equally open-ended storyline has also been understood – both then and now – as merely the regrettable result of a consumerist sensibility.[22] The urban working girl's "passion for independence" thus appeared inseparable from a "love of luxury"; like the social-climbing wife, girls like Carrie sought employment, it was argued, chiefly in order to "decorate themselves beyond their needs and station."[23] As with the wives, however, heroines like Carrie are rewarded for their desires with social success.

In sum, a wildly unfettered plot of female desire no longer looks antithetical to progress, as in earlier novels that reassured readers by curtailing that desire or sublimating it within domestic life. Desire becomes, instead, the very motor of progress. This argument began to be made quite literally in the 1890s by the new consumer-based economics, which portrayed consumption not as a parasitical indulgence in luxury, but rather the underpinning of a healthy American nation. Abundance, argued the influential Wharton School professor Simon Nelson Patten, would lead not to excess but to moderate, intelligent choices on the part of sated consumers.[24] Those consumers, preeminently women,[25] arrived at a new cultural centrality in which the indulgence and the restraint of their desires could no longer be distinguished from one another.

The same might be said, interestingly, of another turn-of-the-century development: the rise of New Thought or "mind cure," a home-grown breed of spiritualism that emphasized the mind's power to shape personal and social circumstances. As Beryl Satter has shown, the New Thought movement shared many tenets with the era's "social-purity" feminism; mind-cure advocates like Emma Curtis Hopkins similarly conceived of a beneficent American future guided by women's unique ability to maintain a "balanced," selfless internal state.[26] As with consumerism, however, New Thought's emphasis on a healthy feminine relation to desire eventually became hard to disentangle from an affirmation of the naturalness and, hence, goodness of desire as such. By the 1930s New Thought had morphed into the philosophy behind such materially minded success manuals as *Power Through Constructive Thinking* (1932) – the precursors of the "pray for wealth" guides still popular today.[27]

This distinctively American (and feminized) "*marriage* of material and spiritual progress," then, offered an irresistible target for turn-of-the-century social critics, Edith Wharton among them.[28] To attack such a union, however, writers could not simply uphold the values of progress through moral virtue, because the latter discourse had already been co-opted by the materialism they sought to critique. Hence, they took a different tack. If heroines such as

Grant's Selma White or Wharton's Pauline Manford (in *Twilight Sleep*) symbolize their moment in believing a frankly materialist outlook to be compatible with virtue and enlightenment, the novels that portray them undermine that outlook by exposing it as materialist through and through. Rather than imposing a progressive plot, that is, they expose a plot that believes itself progressive as a narrative of terminal dissatisfaction.

Has such a critique simply given up on imagining an alternative to the modern landscape it surveys with such horrified fascination? Not simply, as we shall see; sometimes, as in the figure of the put-upon husband, a clear nostalgia will rear its head. Yet this glance backward to a happier, stabler time represents only one of three responses to the new feminine plot of ongoing desire. The second response, in many ways more typical of Wharton's work, refuses nostalgia because, in what might be termed a "tragic" vein, it is predicated on the belief that human beings have always foundered in their quests for ideal contentment, then and now.

Finally, we will see, Wharton and other writers she admired began to explore a third response, in which the plot of endless desire turns out not to be tragic at all. Refusing the grand historical narratives of progress and decline alike, such works substituted something closer to a comic alternative: a tale of the ordinary life of the public woman in mundane new spaces such as the office. Replacing consumption with production, they recast the seeming abyss of endlessness simply as the calendrical time of the modern everyday.

Progress, nostalgia, and tragedy

In order to critique heroines for conflating discourses of moral and material progress, novels such as Grant's *Unleavened Bread* depend on key terms that can refer to either realm. For the newly married but still ambitious Selma White, the prospect of childbearing appears "impersonal and vaguely disgusting," entailing, in her view, "interference with everything elevating." While Selma herself means *elevation* as "spiritual development" to "a higher plane of existence," the book treats this lofty talk as window dressing for a no-holds-barred pursuit of social ascent – of becoming ever "more 'modern'" by keeping up in purchasing power with the stockbroker's wife down the block. Hence, while Selma appears to achieve her life goals by novel's end, the book's structure – in which she vacillates constantly between two "American" extremes of conceiving virtue as a "sober, simple life" and viewing it as wealth and social prominence – emphasizes the likelihood that she will always yearn for an end as yet unreached.

Wharton's *Custom* makes this point more strongly, as Undine Spragg discovers on the book's final page that, as a thrice-divorced woman, she can never be an ambassador's wife – and yet, darn it all, "it was the one part she was really made for!" The later *Twilight Sleep*, however, most clearly works to update Grant's conception of the strenuously "modern" woman's conjunction of material and spiritual aims. In the 1920s, however, the key concept yoking the two realms is not elevation but purity, understood in combined moral and hygienic terms – in her ex-husband's words, Pauline Manford "would like to teach the whole world to say its prayers and brush its teeth." This reduction of moral uplift provides the gateway to an infinite optimism, in which all the world's ills can be chalked up to mere "dyspepsia or want of exercise," or simply to negative thinking. And yet Pauline, too, tellingly finds herself unable to escape a persistent anxiety, despite – or because of – all "her breathless pursuit of repose."

The suspicion of "the modern project" as "both vulgar and excessively utopian," as Robert Pippin has put it, places Wharton in the company of many of the most enduringly relevant thinkers of her time. Like William James, who feared a modern world with "no suffering and no dark corners," Pauline's husband Dexter yearns at his desk for a lost world where he might use "his muscles . . . to do real things, instead of all this . . . spinning around faster and faster in the void . . ."[29]

In some of the novels of Wharton's contemporaries, this Rousseauian nostalgia dominates. Robert Herrick's *Together*, an epic exposé of American marriage *circa* 1908, portrays wives as bent as Selma and Pauline on achieving their most "perfect development," and diagnoses this highly "developed" state as decadence: too "finely organized" for the "plain animal duties" of child-bearing, the wives do not ascend to a higher intellectual plane but collapse into "Americanitis" or neurasthenia, their very "restlessness" a sign of exhausted "race vitality." The main character, Isabelle, comes to imagine "freedom" very differently, as the "open air" of life in a small western town. "[I]n the dumb animal hordes, who labor and breed children," Herrick intones, "lies the future."

Herrick thus propounds what Jackson Lears identifies as the most common reaction against American modernity in this era, the bourgeois quest for a more "authentic," "vital" relation to existence, often embodied in manual labor for men and childbearing for women.[30] It is surprising how susceptible to the latter, at least, Wharton could sometimes be. An exalted maternity (whether fantasized or actual) serves as the eventual antidote to modern "rootlessness" for Wharton heroines as otherwise distinct as *House of Mirth*'s

Lily Bart and Charity Royall in *Summer*.[31] Such rhapsodies can easily sound sentimental beside the radical admission of the tug-of-war between children's needs and maternal desires in a novel like Kate Chopin's *The Awakening* (1899) (to say nothing of the even grimmer depictions of serial childbearing as gothic trap in Nella Larsen's *Quicksand* [1928] and Edith Summers Kelley's *Weeds* [1923]). In place of an apotheosized maternity, Chopin offers what could be termed a New Woman's vitalism, in which a constrained wife's forthright pursuit of her "animal" desires – for multiple sexual partners, food, even sleep – signals not decadence but its opposite, a romanticist escape from society's artificial demands.[f]

In the "progressive" reading of Wharton, wherein the *grande dame* gradually wakes up to the dynamic power of modernity, mid-career works such as *The Reef* (1912) and *Summer* often serve as central exhibits linking her project to Chopin's. In their direct exploration of female passion, both can be read as the fruit of Wharton's own delayed erotic awakening in the brief but intense adulterous liaison she shared with the journalist Morton Fullerton in 1909. Yet Wharton seems finally as dubious as William James that a meaningful freedom might result simply from allowing "animal" passions their full rein. *The Reef* dwells almost masochistically on the pain such passions turn out to entail. Undine of *The Custom of the Country*, moreover, a creature of pure "primitive" appetites, leaves chaos in her wake as surely as does her counterpart in *Twilight Sleep*, Lita, whose "animal sincerity" charms the nostalgic Dexter.

Given her unwillingness simply to embrace a vitalist nostalgia – even in its feminist "free love" mode – Wharton's anti-modern critique tends more often to take a tragic form. Against the notion that "human beings can orchestrate their own happiness," that is, she emphasizes the limits imposed on that dream not simply from without but from within.[32] *Summer*, while refusing to kill off its promiscuous heroine Charity, does make clear the fleetingness of the erotic idyll she enjoys; her lover's flight leaves her the stunned wife of the male guardian from whose home she had always fantasized escape. Given the novel's Shakespearean mapping of desire's path onto the changing seasons, however, this denouement reads less as a nostalgic rebuke to modernity's promises of liberation than as a mere cold statement of what Frank Norris might have called "the existing order of things": summer gives way to winter in the end.[33]

f See Elizabeth Nolan's essay in this volume, "The woman's novel beyond sentimentalism" (chapter 34), for a longer discussion of Chopin's work that places it in conversation with that of other women writers exploring naturalist modes around the turn of the century as a way to counter sentimental forms; 572–581.

If Charity's denouement thus possesses a certain formal "rightness," however, it still affects many readers as tragic in a more visceral sense. Here more of Wharton's real ambivalence about the modern dream of self-realization comes into play. If she saw that dream as often deluded, she also knew what it felt to be a woman trapped by marriage, and hence to see the modern escape hatch of divorce as a godsend. She likely knew – years before Freud would express as much – that the postmarital neuroses evident in women like Norris's Trina McTeague might result less from the immutable facts of human sexuality than from the sheltered Victorian upbringing that produced Wharton's own famously "disas[trous]" wedding night.[34] The main point for Wharton, as always, was simply that the Progressive critique of Victorianism could be as blinded by "innocence" about tragic realities as the world it replaced.[35] Hence, her portrayal (in *French Ways and Their Meaning* [1919]) of American New Women, "noisily develop[ing] their individuality" in "the most improved hygienic surroundings," as akin to cosseted infants in a "Montessori-method baby-school." For all their determined modernity, they appeared to her far less sophisticated than the women to whom she contrasts them, the *salonnières* of the eighteenth century, who like Wharton herself preferred to enjoy the nonromantic company of men.

The most complicated test-case for these issues in Wharton's major fiction may be *The Reef*'s orphaned governess, Sophy Viner. In many ways, Sophy, too, appears mostly naïve as she pronounces, "with youthful finality," "Oh, I never mean to marry . . . You see I'm all for self-development and the chance to live one's life. I'm awfully modern, you know." Shedding the last vestiges of family support when her appointed guardian dies, Sophy views herself not as the easy prey for opportunists of both sexes that she arguably becomes, but as enjoying a "plunge into the wide bright sea of life" after years of "captivity." And yet Wharton seems not untaken by Sophy's exuberance. Her determined optimism, her "restless" nature, even her "frank greed" for the good life ("clothes and fun and motors . . . admiration and yachting and Paris!") are too lusty to be mistaken for social-purity feminism, yet also lack the "hard edge" of Undine Spragg. Perhaps it is not surprising, then, that Wharton gives her an ending with all the open-ended ambiguity of Dreiser's Carrie's; in the book's final scene, she is simply nowhere to be found.

History "adrift"

What Sophy perhaps most shares with Carrie and Undine, as well as with *House of Mirth*'s Lily Bart, is a need, given absent or hapless parents, to rely solely on her own charms to navigate the "whirling waters" about her. Wharton's nautical language for the modern urban landscape echoes that of many of the era's writers, who tended to refer to such untethered feminine figures as "women adrift."[36] This notion of "drift" makes clear the plot of indeterminate ongoingness these heroines share with the ambitious wives discussed earlier. For Lily Bart in particular, the result seems only chaos: she becomes "mere spin-drift of the whirling surface of existence, without anything to which the poor little tentacles of self could cling before the awful flood submerged them." Dreiser's Carrie, too, can appear a perilously "lone figure" amid the "tossing, thoughtless sea" of Chicago. Portrayed as an ever-shifting ground, the city demands an ability to continually shift direction and even identity, if need be, on the part of its inhabitants. Lily, Carrie, and Sophy all share this actress-like mutability, this responsiveness to their environments and to the social cues of those around them.

Many have read this ever-changing self simply as a commodity. Yet this prevalent view cannot account for the qualities of warmth and sympathy that consistently distinguish Lily, Carrie, and Sophy from, say, Undine; nor can they explain comments such as Dreiser's that Carrie remained "too full of wonder and desire to be greedy." Dreiser and Wharton themselves, that is, appear to have understood their heroines' changeability not simply as consumerist, but more in the terms of the pragmatist philosophers of the era – from William James to John Dewey and Jessie Taft – who championed what they called the "social self" as a distinctively feminine alternative to the modern liberal subject.[37] In its deep, embodied attunement to the desires of others, such a self was not an isolated, fully autonomous man of reason but could only be thought, for better and worse, as in constant relation to its world.[38]

Lily Bart's tragic end, then, might be said to result not from her absence of a stable, core self – as many have argued – but from her excess of self-control. Her face lacks sufficient "plastic possibilities," as an observer puts it, limiting her capacity for "expression"; Sophy, in contrast, is characterized above all by her "changing face and flexible fancies," the "incessant come-and-go of her sensations." As with Carrie, these qualities enable a supreme adaptability, which is also the Darwinian virtue finally missing in Lily; when the single Miss Bart attempts belatedly to earn her own wage, she finds she is "an organism as helpless out of its narrow range as the sea-anemone torn from the rock."[g]

g See Campbell's essay in this volume (chapter 30), for a similar depiction of the evolutionary contrast between Lily and Carrie; 505–506.

Lacking rootedness, set "adrift," Lily must perish – an ending that saves her "whole" from the fate assigned to Sophy and Carrie, that of simply going on and on, ever-changing. And yet it is hard to see their unfinished stories simply as tragic or pathetic ones. In the end, they may share less with Lily or Undine than with Susan Lenox, the heroine of one of the novels of this period that Wharton most consistently praised, David Graham Phillips's *Susan Lenox: Her Fall and Rise* (1917). Susan runs through even more names, lovers, and dwelling-places than Undine, Carrie, or Grant's Selma White; like Carrie, moreover, she is a literal actress, concretizing her plot of endless self-transformation by finding fame playing role after role onstage. Yet Phillips takes an even more Darwinian stance toward his heroine than Dreiser, his narrative expressing nothing but admiration for Susan's outsized will to live. "You love dresses – and jewels – and luxury?" one admirer asks a newly well-provided-for Susan. "As a starving man loves food," she replies. Susan has, in fact, literally faced starvation; in one scene, she delightedly devours an entire pie. Hence, "material" concerns in a consumerist and a more basic, embodied sense are both central to her character. While she enjoys the "freedom [from] ties" of being a woman adrift, Phillips's two-volume tome finally defines being "forever free" for Susan in economic terms: as the bequest she receives from her dying beloved mentor, which allows her at last to pursue a theatrical career.

"I love money," wrote the renegade New Thought speaker Helen Wilmans in 1901, "and the reason I love it is because money has another name and that name is freedom."[39] We can glimpse a novelistic expression of this stance not only in Phillips, but in nonwhite and non-bourgeois women writers from the early twentieth century as well. In all cases, it remains startling – whether the "wolf[like]" hunger for food and experience alike that drives Sara Smolinsky in Anzia Yezierska's *Bread Givers* (1925), or the characterization of the women's club speaker Mrs. Willis in Pauline Hopkins's *Contending Forces* (1900) (both novels are discussed elsewhere in this volume).[h] Hopkins, who once wrote of her fear that black New Womanhood might amount to nothing more than a desire to emulate *Unleavened Bread*'s Selma White,[40] seems to embody that danger in the opportunistic Willis, who sees in the "advancement of the colored woman" a topic "that should float her upon its tide into the prosperity she desired." And yet, Hopkins writes, "Trivialities are not to be despised.

h See Tim Prchal, "New Americans and the immigrant novel," chapter 25, 432–433, and Barbara McCaskill, "The African American novel After Reconstruction," chapter 29, 487–493.

Inborn love implanted in a woman's heart for a luxurious, esthetic home life may be the means of . . . freeing a race from servitude."

Creating a direct continuum from consumerist adornment to aesthetics to political freedom, Hopkins thus renders moot the critique whereby modernity's lofty goals of progress founder on the shoals of luxury and self-indulgence. In turn, women, with their purported love of beauty and talent for the pleasures of civilized life, become – as perhaps in the days of salons – not the engines of decadent enervation but the guiding spirits of an enlightened age.[41] Such a possibility might well have pleased Wharton, who often feared that progressive reform would mean an end to loveliness. No wonder, then, that she praised alongside the works of Dreiser and Phillips Sinclair Lewis's 1920 *Main Street*, in which Carol Kennicott's spirited (albeit endlessly thwarted) projects of village reform blend aesthetic and political ends.

Like Undine Spragg and Susan Lenox before her, Carol asserts that all she wants is "everything." Unlike them, she – and *Main Street*'s narrator – states that she is not alone in wanting it, that one can find "the same discontent in women with eight children and one more coming – always one more coming! And you find it in stenographers and wives who scrub, just as much as in girl college-graduates . . . All we want is – everything for all of us! . . . So we shan't ever be content –" This discourse gives the impossibility of "contentment" for such a heroine quite a different ring from the consumerist version we see at the end of, say, Wharton's *Custom of the Country*.

Consumer culture and what Lawrence Birken has called the "democratization of desire" it brings with it are often cast as a new breed of seducer, doling out a new form of punishment – perpetual discontent, rather than pregnancy and death – to the heroine who wants too much.[42] In *Main Street*, *Contending Forces*, *Bread Givers*, and *Susan Lenox*, by contrast, the heroine's lack of contentment, her "restlessness," is a sign not of the futility of her quest, but of its vitality. Whether through images of heroines "adrift" on ships and trains, or simply through the dogged repetition of the phrase "I'll go on," these books insist on the endlessness of their stories in order not to give the lie to a belief in triumph, but to militate against the ever-present possibility of a final defeat.[43]

Beginning in the 1910s with Edna Ferber's Emma McChesney books, and continuing with Sinclair Lewis's *The Job* (1917) and Booth Tarkington's *Alice Adams* (1920), all the way through to Christopher Morley's *Kitty Foyle* (1939), an even more resolutely undramatic story begins to be told. The heroine's job wears her out, she yearns a bit for the comforts of husband and home – but she then gets distracted again. Prince Charming proves a dud, or the work more interesting than she had expected. Or she simply – Lily Bart-like – can't make up her mind. In the interim, she flirts a little, reads, stays up late with female friends, and ponders the pioneer spirit of "the woman of the covered typewriter," in Kitty Foyle's words.

A few of these "white-collar-girl" books – particularly the earlier ones, like Ferber's and Lewis's – allow their heroines to find love in the workplace, imagining that the old and new feminine plots might form a whole.[44] Yet the marital end seems, increasingly over time, not quite the point of these texts. In 1929, one observer described the newly gender-integrated office in rather different terms, as a space enabling "the unprecedented mingling of the sexes within an unsentimental ... environment, hostile to romance and the dream life, most congenial to comradeliness and a sort of flirtatious friendliness."[45] Could this be, against all odds, a peculiarly American resurgence of the social space Edith Wharton most mourned (in *French Ways*) from the first Revolutionary era – the salon, a site peopled by "intelligent men and women who see each other often enough to be on terms of frank and easy friendship"? If there might be a comic, even a farcical (rather than tragic) narrative for an age of corporate capitalism, perhaps these are the stories in which it could be found.[46]

Notes

1. On laudatory vs. critical accounts of modernity, see Robert B. Pippin, *Modernism as a Philosophical Problem* (Malden, MA: Blackwell, 1999), and, on the US context specifically, T.J. Jackson Lears, *No Place of Grace: Antimodernism and the Transformation of American Culture* (Chicago: University of Chicago Press, 1994), e.g., 12.
2. Canonical examples for the two sides of this shift would include, for the seduction novel, Susanna Rowson, *Charlotte Temple* (1791) and Hannah Webster Foster, *The Coquette* (1797), and for the domestic novel, Susan Warner, *The Wide, Wide World* (1850) and Maria Cummins, *The Lamplighter* (1854). A pertinent account of the transition from the one mode to the other appears in Winfried Fluck, "Reading Early American Fiction," in *The Literatures of Colonial America: An Anthology*, ed. Susan P. Castillo and Ivy Schweitzer (London: Blackwell, 2001).
3. Blake Nevius, *Edith Wharton: A Study of Her Fiction* (Berkeley: University of California Press, 1961), 61.
4. Harry Thurston Peck, "Unleavened Bread," *The Bookman* 11.5 (July 1900): 464. For a different argument about the cultural work of regionalism, see Tom Lutz, "Cather and the regional imagination," chapter 26 in this volume.
5. Peck, "Unleavened Bread," 465 (emphasis mine). For more on modern women's "restlessness," see Ella Wheeler Wilcox, "The Restlessness of the Modern Woman," *The Cosmopolitan* 31.3 (July 1901): 314–317, and Margaret Deland, "The

Change in the Feminine Ideal," *The Atlantic* 105 (March 1910): 290–291. Henry Adams, *The Education of Henry Adams* (New York: The Modern Library, 1931 [1918]), 444.

6. Quoted in Hermione Lee, *Edith Wharton* (New York: Vintage, 2007), 156. On modern urban "weightlessness," see Lears, *No Place of Grace*, 32–47.
7. On the relationship between Grant and Wharton, and between *Unleavened Bread* and *Custom*, see Ellen Dupree, "Jamming the Machinery: Mimesis in *Custom of the Country*," *American Literary Realism* 22.2 (1990): 5–16.
8. Nevius, *Edith Wharton*, 91.
9. R. W. B. Lewis, *Edith Wharton: A Biography* (New York: Harper, 1975), 339, 247.
10. Lee, *Edith Wharton*, 611–612.
11. For an overview of Wharton's shifting scholarly reputation, see Millicent Bell, "Introduction: A Critical History," in *The Cambridge Companion to Edith Wharton*, ed. Bell (Cambridge: Cambridge University Press, 1995), 1–19.
12. See Lears, *No Place of Grace*.
13. Jennie Kassanoff, *Edith Wharton and the Politics of Race* (New York: Cambridge University Press, 2000).
14. Dale Bauer, *Edith Wharton's Brave New Politics* (Madison: University of Wisconsin Press, 1995).
15. Emile Durkheim, *Suicide: A Study in Sociology* (1897; New York: The Free Press, 1951), 256.
16. Both in her autobiography *A Backward Glance* (1933) and in her essay "The Great American Novel" (*The Yale Review* 16 [1927]: 646–656), Wharton singles out for praise Grant's *Unleavened Bread*, Dreiser's *American Tragedy* (1925), Norris's *McTeague* (1899), Lewis's *Main Street* (1920), and Phillips's *Susan Lenox: Her Fall and Rise* (1917). Contemporary reviews of *The Custom of the Country* typically compared it with the novels of Herrick, such as *One Woman's Life* (see James Tuttleton, Kristin O. Lauer, and Margaret P. Murray, eds., *Edith Wharton: The Contemporary Reviews* (Cambridge: Cambridge University Press, 1992), 199–218.
17. See, for example, Elizabeth Ammons, *Edith Wharton's Argument with America* (Athens: University of Georgia Press, 1980); Judith Fetterley, "The Temptation to be a Beautiful Object: Double Standard and Double Bind in *The House of Mirth*," *Studies in American Fiction* 5 (1977): 199–211; and Elaine Showalter, "The Death of the Lady (Novelist): Wharton's *House of Mirth*," *Representations* 9 (Winter 1985): 133–149. The Wharton biographies published in the 1970s by R. W. B. Lewis (*Edith Wharton*) and Cynthia Griffin Wolff (*A Feast of Words: The Triumph of Edith Wharton* [New York: Oxford University Press, 1977]) also played a crucial role in restoring Wharton's faded reputation.
18. See Thorstein Veblen, *The Theory of the Leisure Class* (New York: Macmillan, 1899). See Elizabeth Nolan's essay in this volume, "The woman's novel beyond sentimentalism" (chapter 34), for more on Chopin, and on Gilman's treatises and her fiction.
19. See Carroll Smith-Rosenberg, "The New Woman As Androgyne: Social Disorder and Gender Crisis, 1870–1936," in *Disorderly Conduct: Visions of Gender*

in Victorian America (New York: Oxford University Press, 1985), 245–296, and William Leach, *True Love and Perfect Union: The Feminist Reform of Sex and Society* (New York: Basic Books, 1980).

20. Nevius, *Edith Wharton*, 91, emphasis mine.
21. See Milette Shamir, *Inexpressible Privacy: The Interior Life of Antebellum American Literature* (Philadelphia: University of Pennsylvania Press, 2006) and Debra Ann MacComb, *Tales of Liberation, Strategies of Containment: Divorce and the Representation of Womanhood in American Fiction, 1880–1920* (New York: Garland, 2000).
22. See, e.g., Blanche Gelfant, "What More Can Carrie Want? Naturalistic Ways of Consuming Women," in *The Cambridge Companion to American Realism and Naturalism*, ed. Donald Pizer (New York: Cambridge University Press, 1995).
23. Mrs. John and Marie van Vorst, *The Woman Who Toils: Being the Experience of Two Ladies as Factory Girls* (New York: Doubleday, 1903), 82; Alice Kessler-Harris, *Out to Work: A History of Wage-Earning Women in the United States* (New York: Oxford, 1982), 100.
24. See Simon Nelson Patten, *The Consumption of Wealth* (Philadelphia, University of Pennsylvania Press, 1889).
25. On women and consumerism, see Rita Felski, *The Gender of Modernity* (Cambridge, MA: Harvard University Press, 1995).
26. See William Leach, *Land of Desire: Merchants, Power, and the Rise of a New American Culture* (New York: Pantheon, 1993), 231–244, and Beryl Satter, *Each Mind a Kingdom: American Women, Social Purity, and the New Thought Movement, 1875–1920* (Berkeley: University of California Press, 1999).
27. Not to mention such popular ephemera as Elbert Hubbard's lists of tips for "self-improvement," which Edith Wharton clipped ads for in 1928 as examples of the absurdity of American culture. The indexes of Hubbard's works tellingly combined such topics as "Ambition, attainment of," "Goodness, power of," "Life, sacredness of," "Success, secret of," and "Woman, uplift of." Quoted in Lee, *Edith Wharton*, 609.
28. Lears, *No Place of Grace*, 4, emphasis added.
29. Pippin, *Modernism as a Philosophical Problem*, 21; William James, "What Makes a Life Significant," in *On Some of Life's Ideals* (New York: H. Holt and Company, 1912).
30. See Lears, *No Place of Grace*, 57, 30–31.
31. Adams, *Education*, 379–390.
32. Rita Felski, "Introduction," in *Rethinking Tragedy* (Baltimore: Johns Hopkins University Press), xii.
33. Frank Norris, "Fantaisie Printaniere," in *Frank Norris of "The Wave"* (San Francisco: Westgate, 1931).
34. Lewis, *Edith Wharton*, 53.
35. See Nevius's discussion of *The Age of Innocence* in *Edith Wharton*, 180–189. Carrie Tirado Bramen's essay in this volume, "James, realism, and the pragmatist ideal" (chapter 18), presents James's *Portrait of a Lady* and other works as similarly critiquing the optimistic American attempt to avoid suffering; 310–311.

36. On the nautical metaphor, see Jennifer Fleissner, *Women, Compulsion, Modernity: The Moment of American Naturalism* (Chicago: University of Chicago Press, 2004), chapter 4. On women adrift, see Joanne J. Meyerowitz, *Women Adrift: Independent Wage Earners in Chicago, 1880–1930* (Chicago: University of Chicago Press, 1988).
37. For more on pragmatist selfhood in the work of William James, see Carrie Tirado Bramen's essay in this volume, "James, realism, and the pragmatist ideal" (chapter 18). In *Edith Wharton and the Politics of Race*, Jennie Kassanoff usefully reads Sophy in relation to pragmatism. Yet Kassanoff seems undecided as to whether Wharton's ambivalent embrace of a kind of vitalism in Sophy represents a nostalgic anti-modernism or a laudable embrace of "the gritty realities of twentieth-century life" (110).
38. On pragmatism and the social self, see James Livingston, *Pragmatism, Feminism, and Democracy: Rethinking the Politics of American History* (New York: Routledge, 2001).
39. Quoted in Satter, *Each Mind a Kingdom*, 176.
40. Pauline E. Hopkins, "Women's Department," *Colored American Magazine* (June 1900): 118–123, 121, quoted in Martha H. Patterson, *Beyond the Gibson Girl: Reimagining the American New Woman 1895–1915* (Urbana: University of Illinois Press, 2005), 70.
41. For a provocative argument connecting early republican fears about the effeminizing effects of trade to the demonization of *fin-de-siècle* consumerism as the "primal scene" of American historiography, see Livingston, *Pragmatism, Feminism, and Democracy*.
42. Lawrence Birken, *Consuming Desire: Sexual Science and the Emergence of a Culture of Abundance* (Ithaca, NY: Cornell University Press, 1988), 141.
43. *Contending Forces* leaves its heroine Sappho aboard a ship; in *Carrie* and *Susan Lenox*, the train comes to stand for the story that, promisingly or frighteningly, simply goes "on and on." "I'll go on" is Carol Kennicott's mantra throughout *Main Street*, and it is repeated regularly by Sara Smolinsky of *Bread Givers* as well.
44. For more, see C. Wright Mills, *White Collar: The American Middle Classes* (New York: Oxford University Press, 1956).
45. Samuel D. Schmalhausen, "The Sexual Revolution," in *Sex in Civilization*, ed. V. F. Calverton and Schmalhausen (Garden City, NY: Garden City Publishing Co., 1929): 349–436, 359, quoted in Livingston, *Pragmatism, Feminism, and Democracy*, 179–180.
46. See Livingston, *Pragmatism, Feminism, and Democracy*, 19, 29.

28

The postbellum race novel

ROBERT F. REID-PHARR

Perhaps the most pressing matters to which students of the rather large body of so-called "race literature" produced during and immediately after the Civil War and Reconstruction must attend are simple questions of periodization and genre. In works ranging from Frances Harper's *Iola Leroy* (1892) to Mark Twain's *Pudd'nhead Wilson* (1894), and from Thomas Dixon's *The Leopard's Spots* (1902) to Sutton Griggs's *The Hindered Hand* (1905), one is confronted with what seems at times a shockingly discordant cacophony of form, theme, content, and style. "Old-fashioned" sentimental and gothic modes sit uncomfortably with modernist preoccupations with science and technology. The romance attempts valiantly, if quixotically, to regain ground long since lost to realism. And American writers of the late nineteenth and early twentieth centuries appear strangely preoccupied with race and racialism in a manner that many may find to be juvenile, if not downright embarrassing.

Indeed, the period, if one might call it that, seems so very unsettled as to make many otherwise rather generous scholars and critics throw up their hands in frustration. One may assume, with several notable exceptions, that the awkwardly named "postbellum race novel" is so very "undercooked" that we need pay little attention to it and then only as part of our ever so dull antiquarian duties. We might set sail from the eloquent creations of Melville, Hawthorne, Emerson, Stowe, Douglass, and Dickinson, make a picturesque stop or two along the way, dipping our toes into the warm shallows of the major works of the minor Chesnutt or the minor works of the major Twain, only to finally regain our way, a strong wind at our backs, as we attend to the well-wrought, well-considered novels, essays, poetry, and criticism of modernism, black, white, and otherwise.

Irritation, shock, discordance, cacophony, discomfort, disaster, childishness, embarrassment, frustration, and awkwardness, might all, in other contexts, be recognized as key elements within complicated, thoughtful, even great literature. The most interesting aspect of the postbellum race novels, however, is how they represent a profound transitional moment of cultures and societies both within and without the United States. As literary and cultural critic Amy Kaplan usefully reminds us, the period during which these texts were being written and published was a moment in which the country was asserting itself as both a military *and* an imperial power with the quick acquisition of Puerto Rico and Guam, the further "domestication" of the American West and Hawaii, not to mention heavy – and heavy-handed – passes at Cuba, the Philippines, and Mexico. It was also apparent that (domestic) forms of white supremacy and imperialism were being re-articulated through both the imposition of state-sponsored segregation/racial terror "at home" and bold, bare-knuckled imperialism "abroad."[1]

This chapter suggests that the word "imperialism" does not fully articulate the changes in society and culture that were taking place from roughly the 1870s to the 1920s, changes that have profound resonances in contemporary life. Instead, as the nineteenth century struggled through bloody labors to give birth to the twentieth, the country witnessed progressions in not only questions of racial ideology but also matters of science and technology, class consciousness, religious thought, sexuality, gender relations, communications, and travel – all seasoned by a healthy dose of fear that the national body, hard on the heels of the Civil War, might just pull itself apart again. One might rightfully argue then that the (re)turn to forms of virulent racialism, white supremacy if you will, as well as forms of seemingly positive – and perhaps positivistic – racial solidarity (black pride) bespoke a certain nostalgia for an uncomplicated body politic, based on universal religious, scientific, political, and sociological truths. The racialism of the post-war period was at once underwritten and challenged by deep and complex processes of structural – and infra-structural – change. Thus the awkwardness of the postbellum race novel was both an uneasy acknowledgment of the fact that the nation's founding ideologies were turned in upon themselves as well as an attempt to deny, or perhaps resolve, this difficult recognition.

Continuing this line of thought, it is perhaps best that we omit, at least for the moment, consideration of what we might think of as the most well-wrought and progressive texts of the period. Indeed unlike Barbara McCaskill, who elsewhere in this collection rightfully offers a largely celebratory survey of post-Reconstruction African American novels and novelists, I have chosen instead to look a bit more closely at the complex, contradictory, and oftentimes vulgar ideologies of race that many late nineteenth- and early twentieth-century writers confronted.[a] I hope, that is, to demonstrate that the work of white and black postbellum novelists cannot be fully appreciated unless one pays particular attention to the fact that they were first and foremost designed to reestablish ideological order by both memorializing the presumed passing of stable narratives of race, nation, class, and gender while also helping to bring into focus new ways of imagining subjectivity and community in the context of a quickly modernizing American culture.

I would suggest, therefore, that the difficulty that the novels of this period pose for current generations of students, scholars, and critics is that while they speak directly to many of the underlying assumptions about race, community, and national identity that continue to bedevil the USA, they do so from within a context in which Americans were intensely aware of the stresses attending the basic social and cultural structures of their nation. Thus the "bad" postbellum race novel is not difficult for us because it is so ancient, strange, or "obscene," but, on the contrary, because it represents such an unseemly beginning to our own beliefs (compulsions, one is wont to say) about the "essence" of race and nation. Indeed, the "romantic racialism" that suffuses many of the texts from the period was designed to help alleviate the tension produced by the fast-paced changes in the economic, social, and political life of much of the nation, changes with which we are intimately familiar today.

We will begin, therefore, with a romance that is among the clumsiest and most embarrassing texts of the period: Thomas Dixon's *The Leopard's Spots: A Romance of the White Man's Burden, 1865–1900* (1902). This first work within Dixon's so-called *Reconstruction Trilogy* (which also included *The Clansman* [1905] and *The Traitor* [1907]) is extremely difficult to read. The text, part of which was adapted for the screen by D. W. Griffith in *Birth of a Nation* (1915), reeks of white supremacy, anti-black racism, and a puerile disdain for the impressive gains of Reconstruction. What surprises then, what causes the critic to sputter and gasp, is how very interesting the novel can actually be.

The work is an obvious retort to Harriet Beecher Stowe's *Uncle Tom's Cabin*, complete with the resurrection of Simon Legree, and George Harris, the near-white child that young Eliza carried with her as she ran from Kentucky across the ice of the Ohio River to the relative freedom that awaited her on the other side. It begins at the close of the Civil War with the pitiful image of a poor white soldier, tellingly named Tom, who with a "Minie ball" embedded in his shoulder and a wooden peg embedded in the remains of his ruined leg, returns to his North Carolina home. Thus like many of the novels

a See Barbara McCaskill, "The African American novel after Reconstruction," chapter 29.

of the period *The Leopard's Spots* begins with consideration of the war that marked a transition – not always willing – from one period of national development to another.

It is with this in mind that we ought to approach the fact that Tom is a profound racist, one who cannot explain his sentiments even to himself. Tom's racism speaks not so much to the personal "failings" of his character (nor those of Dixon) but instead to the more difficult to discern reality that Tom, both in his weakened, dependent state, as well as in many matters of culture, particularly his speech, cannot easily be distinguished from the blacks who for the most part act as bit players in the drama that Dixon creates. Indeed Tom's anti-black racism marks his interstitial status, the fact that he stands, bitter and disabled, between the comfortable "certainty" of the antebellum period and the exciting adventure of a quickly modernizing America. This racial antipathy demonstrates, then, exactly the difficulty faced by Americans in the postbellum period as they attempted to negotiate the vertigo caused by the obvious losses the Civil War brought about (remember Tom's missing leg) as well as the profound turn toward fast-paced technological, economic, ideological, and cultural change that the war represented.

> Every time I'd go into battle and hear them Minie balls begin to sing over us, it seemed to me I could see their black ape faces grinnin' and makin' fun of poor whites. At night when they'd detail me to help the ambulance corp carry off the dead and the wounded, there was a strange smell on the field that came from the blood and night damp and burnt powder. It always smelled like a nigger to me! It made me sick . . . I hate 'em! I can't help it any more than I can the color of my skin or my hair.

Dixon's prose is extremely clever here. For though Tom's poverty and his dialect directly link him to readily available representations of scores of black characters, suggesting that he should by rights be the first to understand the black's (enforced) inability, he falls back on seemingly inexplicable and deeply imbedded psychological ("grinnin' and makin' fun") and biological ("ape faces" "strange smell") narratives that belie the much more obvious realities of war ("night damp and burnt powder").

This move is particularly important, as Dixon is clearly aware that even among the white population itself there were potent forces at play that might threaten the hierarchies of the so-called Old South. One is stunned while reading *The Leopard's Spots* to find Dixon continually mentioning the white Farmers' Alliance, a group of small landowners committed to joining with their black countrymen in order to break a tiny white oligarchy's stubborn hold on both land and capital during the 1880s. We also find upper-class white women struggling to gain space in the public sphere through their ministrations to the recently enslaved. Moreover, Dixon goes so far as to draw attention to quickly developing ideas that challenged the very notions of courtly love that helped to cement the ideological structures underwriting the slaveocracy's hold on economic and social power.

The point is that the world that Dixon (and even more important, his readers) inhabited was one whose very modernity bespoke a constant assault on ideas – and ideology – that many took to be fixed and stable matters of truth. Indeed, with regard to sexuality and desire alone, Dixon alludes to prostitution, bastardy, marital infidelity, and most especially incest, forced interracialism, and rape even as he breathlessly extols the depth and virtues of romantic and courtly love. What one witnesses then is a work that rather clearly looks both backward and forward; backward to the brutalities of slavery and the reality of earlier forms of interracial intimacy *not* wholly dependent upon the institution of slavery for their maintenance[2] and forward to the decline, if not exactly the demise, of proscriptions against non-hierarchical interracial social contact and other forms of "illicit" sexuality.

Before leaving this point I would like to at least gesture toward the works of authors such as Joel Chandler Harris and Thomas Nelson Page. Like Dixon, both Harris and Page were (white) Southern racialists. Nonetheless, their writings, though often controversial, have not attracted the same criticism as their fire-breathing contemporary. Harris, the author of such texts as *Uncle Remus, His Sayings and His Songs: The Folklore of the Old Plantation* (1880), *Nights with Uncle Remus* (1881, 1882), *Uncle Remus and His Friends* (1892), and *Uncle Remus and the Little Boy* (1905), became in his lifetime a celebrated "local colorist" who was rightly praised as one of the first US writers to consistently make use of American dialect. Indeed, Harris's works were so popular that they formed the basis for the wildly successful 1946 Walt Disney film, *Song of the South*. Page, who published nearly two dozen works of fiction and history, including *Marse Chan* (1884), *In Ole Virginia* (1887), *Befo' de War* (1888), *The Negro: The Southerner's Problem* (1904), and *Robert E. Lee, The Southerner* (1908), was closer to Dixon in his unapologetic defense of the "culture" of the South. That said, it is important to note that in both cases the authors continued the struggle with social, technological, and cultural change that I have associated with Dixon. Moreover, the often farcical use of black dialect in their texts demonstrates just how closely these writers' efforts dovetailed with much of the racist nonsense that defined American minstrelsy. Indeed, though we see in Dixon, Harris, and Page a quite understandable concern with the speed with which the United States was establishing itself as a technologically and economically advanced nation, we also see their working to restrict their black characters from fully enjoying the gains that attended the country's modernization. Harris's Uncle Remus might have been a lively, delightful, witty character who reminded readers of both a "simpler" past and the ways that African traditions were expressed within slave communities. It is quite difficult, however, to imagine such an individual functioning well in either government or industry.

Here one begins to see the interrelationships among cultural and social intercourse in the postbellum era. Eric Sundquist reminds us that the Supreme Court's infamous *Plessy v. Ferguson* decision of 1896 came in reaction to Homer Plessy's "deliberately staged" challenge to the segregation of New Orleans streetcars, an action that was itself the culmination of "Supreme Court decisions, legislative maneuvers, and developments in sociological theory" that created an atmosphere of excitement, expectation, misplaced nostalgia, and dread within the US public.[3] Sundquist goes on to argue that Mark Twain's celebrated novel, *Pudd'nhead Wilson* (1894), in which the slave, Roxy, who like Homer Plessy was "near white," exchanges her own newborn son for the son of her master, was produced within this same milieu. I would add that though Twain's novel is on its surface an allegory of the oftentimes ridiculous obsession that Americans had – and have – with never quite properly established racial distinctions it is also a clear demonstration of Twain's fascination with the ethical and cultural difficulties posed by rapidly developing technologies and forms of thought.

Moreover, Twain evinces in *Puddn'head Wilson* a profound interest in the technologies of policing, detection, and investigation, particularly fingerprinting, that were becoming increasingly common aspects of American society. Thus for Twain the "bizarre" spectacle of a mother substituting her own child for another resonated with the equally strange reality of a world that had become advanced enough to allow for the survival of conjoined twins and sophisticated enough to solve matters of crime and identity with only the faintest "physical" evidence (prints). The problem was that such advances in science and technology could not speak to the questions of ethics, morality, community, and identity that many, including Twain, assumed to be the stitching that bound the nation together. The "elegance" of novelists like Dixon, Harris, Page, and Twain turned then on the ability of these authors to embrace this promising future while doggedly maintaining a grip on the (false) memory of a noble past.

It is this aesthetic/ethical phenomenon that underwrites Dixon's depiction of one of the key black characters in *The Leopard's Spots*. Dark and burly, Nelse is the faithful retainer of the Gaston family whose son, Charlie, orator, lover, lawyer, co-founder of the Klan, and governor of North Carolina is the hero of the novel. For his part, Nelse establishes once again the figurative procedures that were set loose when Stowe gave light unto Tom. Profoundly loyal, militantly protective, and self-denying unto death, he is the very "old Negro" who gives definition to the new. And like Uncle Tom before him, his passing portends the coming of an era of (necessary) separation between black and white, a separation that Dixon, strangely enough, bemoans.

Writing of Nelse's skillful deployment of his banjo as he accompanies his Confederate master during the war, Dixon provides an image of national community and goodwill that is frankly breathtaking, coming from this scion of white supremacy:

> Lawd child, we's allers slippin' out twixt de lines atter night er carryin' on wid dem Yankees. We trade 'em terbaccer fur coffee en sugar, en play yards, en talk twell mos' day sometime. I slip out fust in er patch er woods twix' de lines, en make my banjer talk. En den yere dey come! De Yankees fume one way en our boys de yudder. I make out lake I doan see 'em tall, des playin' ter myself. Den I make dat banjer moan en cry en talk about de folks way down in Dixie. De boys creep up closer en closer twell dey right at my elbow en I see 'em cryin', some un 'em – den I gin 'er a juk! En way she go pluckety plunck! en dey gin ter dance and laught! Sometime dey cuss me lak dey mad and lam me on de back. When dey hit me hard den I know dey ready ter gimme all dey got.

What we see here is nothing less than Dixon's perhaps cynical, but still compelling, nostalgia for "ancient" forms of comportment that not only allowed for the maintenance of racial hierarchies, that telltale "lamming on the back," but also worked to bring together disparate, indeed warring, elements within white America. Or to put the matter more straightforwardly still, when the Negro exits from his traditional place on the bottom, this does more than destroy the social contract that holds together white supremacy and black abjection: it also disrupts the variety of both implied and openly articulated assumptions regarding how the various racialized, gendered, and classed communities of this country might come together to form a single national body. In a sense then, the Negro acts as the conduit, the synapse, that allows one part of America to communicate with the other without reference to profound forms of violence. Dance, backslaps, the moans and jerks of the Negro's banjo stand in for the interactions that might motivate war. This explains why elsewhere in the novel Reverend Durham, another white supremacist and Klan leader, bemoans the fact that his black congregants who before had sat in their segregated balcony pews "colorcolorlaborspell-bound" by his sermons have all exited the church to form their own congregations. The point is that, as this nonsensical neologism suggests, the tensions of race and class that did, in fact, bring the country to its knees were not simply matters that black persons witnessed and suffered through. Instead they operated for centuries as the very means by which these tensions were both relieved and turned into something like an American culture.

Here one ought to consider again the arguments of scholars like Eric Lott and Shelley Fisher Fishkin that turn on the idea that part of what the gimmicky, malapropism-filled depictions of black culture in nineteenth- and early twentieth-century America that spilled over from the minstrel stage onto the pages of such artists as Mark Twain, William Dean Howells, and Paul Laurence Dunbar did for the general American populace was to provide a medium by which "we" might feel and imagine something approaching a genuinely original American culture, a profound, "pre-literate," "extra-logical" conception of the relation of self to other that denied the necessity of European, African, Asian, and aboriginal knowledges in the production of the American citizen/subject/self.[4] Thus, when Reverend Durham's black congregants came down from their segregated pews, what they accomplished, like Richard Allen and Absalom Jones more than a century before, was not only the creation of the contemporary black American church, but in a sense, the white church as well. Their departures, their removals, their efforts to place their hands on that complex of institutions and forms self-consciously utilized by all Americans in their attempts to define and utilize "blackness" in the postbellum public sphere, did not excise race from the national picture, but instead gave to it the particular valences with which we are familiar today.

This might help to explain why in 1900, in a three-part series entitled "The Future American," no less a light than Charles Chesnutt argued in the pages of the *Boston Evening Transcript* that the answer to racism and white supremacy was the fusion of races through intermarriage and miscegenation. This logic, which would be repeated later by Jean Toomer in the groundbreaking novel, *Cane* (1923),[b] was for Chesnutt at once both practical and romantic. He wanted not only to end racial strife, but to help (re)establish the promise of American culture. He wanted to turn the country toward the type of seamless supra-racial, multiclassed, and homoerotic vision of national unity announced by Nelse with his moaning, crying, jerking banjo. The problem of course was that

b Valerie Babb provides a sustained reading of *Cane* elsewhere in this volume, in "Wright, Hurston, and the direction of the African American novel," chapter 42, 701–702.

the straightforwardly heterosexual and reproductive miscegenation that Chesnutt undoubtedly imagined seemed for many black intellectuals, and perhaps eventually even Chesnutt himself, as simply far too close to the backward-looking, bacchanalian, and recidivist version of fellowship that Dixon imagined, a form of fellowship that, when all the merrymaking came to an end, would leave class, race, and sex exploitation securely in place.

Chesnutt became a celebrity with the 1899 publication of the extremely well-received short story collections, *The Conjure Woman* and *The Wife of His Youth*. These were followed in 1900 by *The House Behind the Cedars*; in 1901 by the *Marrow of Tradition*, and finally *The Colonel's Dream* in 1905. Thus within a six-year period he not only wrote and published prodigiously but also became a financial and critical success, among the most gifted and celebrated black American writers of his time.

There are many obvious similarities between the aesthetic and cultural, if certainly not the political, practices of Chesnutt and his contemporary, Dixon. Most obviously, both spotlight North Carolina – with its pretensions of having established cooler, more moderate versions of slavery and segregation – in their literature. Both sought what some in our own time might call the "creative center" of American culture and politics, that place where the material realities of modernity (trains, telephones, journalists, doctors, politicians, would-be socialites and industrialists) are met by the South's presumably profound sense of history and tradition. And to his credit, part of what makes Chesnutt an interesting figure for contemporary readers is that he does not shy away from the complexity of what he is after.

In his masterful novel, *The Marrow of Tradition* (1901), the work that fictionalized the complex of political and cultural explosions that resulted in the Wilmington Race Riot of 1898 – a rising of white supremacists that killed twenty-two blacks and white Republicans, overturned the municipal government, and helped to deliver the state legislature to the Democrats, effectively ending Reconstruction in North Carolina and establishing Jim Crow there – Chesnutt wryly presents us with a tableau of female characters, fussing over a newborn baby. These women, even in the domestic, apolitical confines of the nursery, precisely represent the tensions that would be unleashed in Wilmington on that fateful November day in 1898. In attendance are Mrs. Cartaret, white, privileged, haughty, and stunningly needy after giving birth to her first son; Mammy Jane, a figure like Dixon's Nelse, who represents the white's fantasy of the "Old Negro;" and most interestingly, a well-trained, and race-conscious black nurse "standing, like most young people of her race, on the border line between two irreconcilable states of life."[c]

Here Chesnutt clearly articulates the complexities of transition that so overdetermined the postbellum race novel. The young nurse, sprawled between two "irreconcilable states of life," represents precisely the tension inherent in the process of modernization that I have been at pains to represent. She is not like Tom, Nelse, or Mammy Jane in their acceptance of "traditional" racial hierarchies. At the same time, she has not yet established herself as a truly modern subject, self-aware and confident as she struggles to gain a place for herself within the national culture. The great difficulty facing Chesnutt, then, was his recognition (at least on what Ralph Ellison would later term the lower frequencies) that the future of the black American community and indeed the future of the nation as a whole rested on exactly the type of "less than agreeable," "chip on the shoulder" figures represented by the nurse. Indeed the "interracialism" that Chesnutt imagined in "The Future American" would have to be put on hold if the promises of American technological, industrial, and cultural progress were to be realized.

It is important to remember that post-Reconstruction Wilmington was not, as one might imagine, a simple Southern backwater in which hateful attitudes toward black persons were so ingrained that they erupted into racial violence. Instead, this port city had in the years since the Civil War grown exponentially, attracting both white and black immigrants from rural parts of North Carolina and elsewhere. Moreover, it was one of the most economically integrated locations in the South prior to the 1898 riot. A vibrant black middle class of barbers, restaurant owners, teachers, tailors, grocers, government employees, physicians, *and* nurses was quite apparent on its streets. The tension that Chesnutt demonstrates in his fine novel turned not so much, then, on whites' being stunned by the "onslaught" of blacks. Instead, what Chesnutt demonstrates is that these same whites could not accept the reality that the logic of innate and irreconcilable differences between "races" of people was crumbling. That is to say, Wilmington (or Wellington in Chesnutt's novel) was becoming (politically, economically, socially, culturally, and racially) a modern American city.

One of the things that I have attempted to argue in this chapter is that both black and white authors of the post-Reconstruction period utilized the theme of "racial anxiety" in their works to comment upon the stress produced by the

c McCaskill also discusses *Marrow*, as well as other fiction by Chesnutt, in chapter 29, 486–491.

fact that the United States, and particularly the South, was quickly modernizing during this period. I have also suggested that this modernization process demonstrated quite clearly that there was not, in fact, any clear distinction between black and white persons. I do not mean to suggest, however, that all black writers found the presumed "lessening" of the social distance between groups more palatable than did their white counterparts. On the contrary, many black writers of the era eagerly appropriated the so-called "one drop rule" as part of their rhetorical arsenals. Unlike Chesnutt they were often quite eager to resist the attractions of racial amalgamation or "social" equality. "Black" individuals, no matter how light or dark, rich or poor, were all taken to represent a single unified community. Nonetheless they quite often understood themselves as a distinct or peculiar community with a special mission to perform for the country and the world.

This explains why in the fiction of Pauline Hopkins, former slaves, victims of rape, abandoned children, prostitutes, the fair-skinned, and the coal-black are resuscitated for the sake of the ethnic/national project. It is interesting to note in this regard that in all of her works, most significantly her novels, *Contending Forces* (1900), *Hagar's Daughter* (1901–1902), *Winona* (1902), and *Of One Blood* (1902–1903), Hopkins worked to direct the attentions of the developing black middle class toward the black (African) community from which presumably they sprang. She did so, however, not by altogether breaking down the inter-group barriers that separated some parts of the black community from others. Instead, following Chesnutt's form if not his politics, she focused most specifically on that community of "middle-class" black individuals whom she took to be most susceptible to dreams of racelessness. Thus Hopkins attempted consistently to demonstrate a noble lineage of gifted black individuals who stood solidly *within* their racial community but who nonetheless remained distinct from many of their black compatriots. Black elites were just that, both black *and* elite. The black doctors, lawyers, ministers, attorneys, and teachers who would come to dominate the modern black community did not simply spring into existence through happenstance or sheer luck. Instead, like Reuel Briggs in *Of One Blood* they were the last in a long line of black (African) nobility, one rightly destined to dominate the affairs of their equally black but less (genealogically/genetically) gifted black peers.[d]

Black American intellectuals did reject blatant white supremacy. At the same time many – indeed most – would (much like their white counterparts)

d McCaskill discusses Hopkins in chapter 29, 487–492.

continue to support the notion that each race had some special gift to give to the country and to the world. These gifts would inevitably be bestowed, moreover, by the most "advanced" members of the black community, as in Frances E. W. Harper's 1892 novel, *Iola Leroy*, a text that is treated extensively in this collection by Barbara McCaskill. Thus, even as the lived reality of many "black" persons might have been that they were in fact the offspring of both "blacks" and "whites" and the putative heirs of a nascent (mulatto) American culture, they nonetheless continually demonstrated in the literature that they produced a preference for clear articulations of so-called racial distinction. The point is that racial belonging was not understood by Harper, or the writers whom she represents, as "simply" a two-dimensional phenomenon. Instead, the refusal of the whitening/brightening version of interracialism that is on display here was both a positive articulation of "black pride" as well as a rejection of the lack of sentiment and loyalty that many postbellum intellectuals felt underwrote the United States' scientific, imperialist, and to an extent, anti-racialist projects.

Before leaving this matter I would like to make two more points. First, it is important to note that this belief that so-called "racial equality" did not necessitate racelessness or "color-blindness" *per se* can be found in the work of even a liberal white writer like George Washington Cable, who in novels like *Old Creole Days* (1879), *The Grandissimes* (1880), and *Madame Delphine* (1881) decried the systematic oppression of (Southern) blacks even as he continued to celebrate the very cultural and social traditions of the antebellum South that underwrote this reality. Second, is the important fact that while I must point out that many black writers reiterated the racialist claims of their white peers, I do not want to suggest that this political/aesthetic stance did not provoke what we might think of as ethical vertigo.

Sutton Griggs, the Texas-born essayist and novelist who published such key texts as *Imperium in Imperio* (1899) and *The Hindered Hand* (1901), was intensely concerned with the ways that the proto-nationalism that seemed so logical to many of his black contemporaries might ultimately work against the best interests of both black and white communities. In both novels much of the dramatic action takes place because of disagreements between black male intimates, all of whom have the best interests of the black community at heart. In *Imperium* we are introduced to dark, working-class Belton Piedmont and his light-skinned and middle-class friend, Bernard Belgrave. The two are key members of a secret black organization, The Imperium, that is established to support black American communities. Belton ends up betraying the organization, however, as he becomes increasingly frightened by the separatism and militancy most consistently expressed by his elite doppelgänger, Bernard. In *The Hindered Hand*, again we have two friends, Ensal and Earl, the one seeking to change the fate of black Americans through moral suasion, the other committed to violent conflict.

The point is that some black writers, especially Griggs and Chesnutt, remained aware of the political and ethical pitfalls inherent in the belief that the logical "modern" response to white racist oppression was to utilize whatever means necessary (including the dominance of black elites over the rest of the community) to advance black civil rights. Indeed, for all of the black writers whom we have examined here, the major question seems to have been how to fully enjoy the fruits of modernization: (advances in technology, positive changes in attitude toward race, class, and gender) while holding on to the sentimental and romantic ethical safeguards established within and in relation to the cauldron of slavery. How was the black community to advance while remaining ethically, politically, economically, and culturally "whole"?

Though this brief treatment of the postbellum race novel has been an essentially recuperative affair I have little interest in separating "the good" works of the period from "the bad." Instead, the chapter was written as part of the ongoing efforts of critics and historians who wish to be a part of the re-evaluation of literature that has been figured as irritating, shocking, discordant, cacophonous, discomforting, disastrous, childish, embarrassing, frustrating, and awkward. And perhaps to make the taste left in its readers' mouths even worse, this chapter has been largely structured around an at least somewhat sympathetic reading of Thomas Dixon's *The Leopard's Spots*. We have seen, in fact, that the style and structure of Dixon's romance might be taken to be illustrative of the engagement of both black and white postbellum US authors with not only the country's imperial ambitions but also questions of racial ideology, science and technology, class consciousness, religious thought, sexuality, gender relations, communications, and travel. Moreover, Dixon's white supremacist text is not read so much against the tradition of black American literature to which it spoke *as* directly *into it*. In fact, a consistent claim of this chapter has been that black American and "racist" or white supremacist writing are both motivated by similar anxieties and possibilities. Thus, with several notable exceptions, many disparate authors, holding many different positions in relation to the so-called "racial divide," have come to essentially quite similar conclusions. While there would never be a return to the absolute domination of black persons and communities by self-categorized whites, the vision of an inter- or supraracial America would have, it seems, to be put on hold. It is to precisely this now somewhat less than fresh conundrum of race, nation, and culture that our own generation of critics and creative writers have been led by those late nineteenth- and early twentieth-century intellectuals who preceded us. Hopefully, then, these brief comments will make somewhat easier the considerable work that still remains.

Notes

1. Amy Kaplan, *The Anarchy of Empire in the Making of U.S. Culture* (Cambridge, MA: Harvard University Press, 2002).
2. See Martha Hodes, *White Women, Black Men: Illicit Sex in the Nineteenth Century South* (New Haven: Yale University Press, 1997); Werner Sollors, *Interracialism: Black–White Intermarriage in American History, Literature and Law* (New York: Oxford University Press, 2000).
3. Eric J. Sundquist, *To Wake the Nations: Race in the Making of American Literature* (Cambridge, MA: Harvard University Press, 1993), 227.
4. See Eric Lott, *Love and Theft: Blackface Minstrelsy and the American Working Class* (New York: Oxford University Press, 1995); Shelley Fisher Fishkin, *Was Huck Black? Mark Twain and African American Voices* (New York: Oxford University Press, 1993).

29

The African American novel after Reconstruction

BARBARA McCASKILL

From the 1880s to the 1920s, African American novels explore what W. E. B. Du Bois identified in his *Souls of Black Folk* (1903) as the new century's dominant crisis: "the problem of the color-line – the relation of the darker to the lighter races of men."[1] Such novels also incorporate, and at times revise, influential elements from existing African American expressive, performative, and narrative traditions. Recalling the concerns of pre-Civil War African American novelists, the post-Reconstruction works retain a focus on the South, with its landscape, idioms, religions, rituals, and historical connections to slavery and the slave trade. As other authors in this volume note, the South and Southern slavery haunt the imaginations of the earliest American writers. John Ernest, for example, connects "the emergence of African Americans in American novels" to early national debates about meanings of race and the morality of the traffic in human bodies. Robert S. Levine identifies "cultural discourses" of Southern slavery in early novels such as William Wells Brown's *Clotel; or, The President's Daughter* (1853), while Jennifer Greeson considers the South as a touchstone which enables American novelists to critique the nation's march toward modernity.[a]

I would add to this conversation that, rather than romanticize or demonize the region, African American novelists of the transitional, post-Reconstruction generation portray the South as a complex, multifaceted place: as a symbol of the former slaves' contested claims to citizenship and equality; as America's violent, fratricidal shadow; as source of a dynamic black culture grounded in an African heritage; as a potentially powerful nexus of African American educational, political, and economic achievement. The novels of Frances

a John Ernest, "Stowe, race, and the antebellum American novel," chapter 15, 255; Robert S. Levine, "The early African American novel," chapter 16, 272; Jennifer Rae Greeson, "Imagining the South," chapter 14.

Ellen Watkins Harper, Charles Waddell Chesnutt, Pauline Elizabeth Hopkins, Paul Laurence Dunbar, Sutton Griggs, Du Bois, Oscar Micheaux, and James Weldon Johnson innovatively combine African American oral and vernacular features (such as sermons, spirituals, and blues) with the regional and realistic elements that, in this volume, the essays of Michael A. Elliott and Tom Lutz examine in white American writings.[b] Even as these novels turn toward new possibilities and nascent politics, they imagine the faith, courage, struggles, and indignities that shaped the race before the Civil War – as readily apparent in the so-called free North as in the rice and cotton plantations of Southern bondage.

Frances Harper's best-known novel, *Iola Leroy; or, Shadows Uplifted* (1892), announces a major concern of post-Reconstruction African American novelists: to articulate their people's struggle for race uplift – for political enfranchisement, educational and economic opportunities, and pride in African heritage and ancestry. The uplift project challenged the disfranchisement of blacks during Redemption with the notion that, in Harper's words, "the color of a man's skin has nothing to do with the possession of his rights," and it championed pursuits that would gradually raise the former slaves to citizenship such as "education, temperance, and good home-building, industry, morality, and the like." The novel's initial nine chapters are set in and around a North Carolina plantation, where the restive slaves anticipate a rout of "the Secesh" and an imminent liberation by oncoming Yankee soldiers. Characters with names like Uncle Daniel and Aunt Linda relate doleful tales from bondage featuring mothers forced to neglect their babies and young men facing beatings for trying to learn how to read.[2] Yet the story of African America that emerges is not one of victimhood under slavery's deathly shadow, but of resisting oppression and resurrecting a mighty nation within a nation, where "the blood of [a] strong race" manifests in black people's Christian principles of love and forgiveness of enemies, devotion to family and home, community service, and other qualities that would become synonymous with the work of race uplift.

Harper's novel reverses aspects of the classic fugitive slave's story, while looking backward and retaining familiar plot conventions, dramatic symbols, and character descriptions from African American written and oral literature before Emancipation. The heroine Iola, the long-haired, blue-eyed, white-skinned daughter of a white Creole planter and a quadroon slave, in the

b Michael A. Elliott, "Realism and radicalism: the school of Howells," chapter 17; Tom Lutz, "Cather and the regional imagination," chapter 26.

tradition of the century's sentimentalized tragic mulatta tales, is enslaved when her father dies, due to a loophole in her manumission papers. As she is saved in the nick of time from rape by a lascivious master by other slaves on their way to joining the Union army, Iola's release depicts the once-enslaved as participants in their own deliverance and as revolutionaries who launched insurrections in spite of threats of brutal reprisals. Her liberation counters condescending perceptions of blacks as helpless and dependent. It also underscores the tension between nationalism and racial autonomy on the one hand, and patriotism and interracial alliances on the other, which the members of her race confronted as they carved out political, economic, and cultural roles in the new postwar society.

Post-Reconstruction novels such as *Iola Leroy* revisit the condemnation of slavery typical of the tragic mulatta story, while updating the old tragic mulatta plotlines for a new era and a liberated people.[c] Post-Reconstruction novels revisit and revise the tragic mulatta to enlarge debates about citizenship and assertions of racial solidarity and pride, and to rethink what is lost and gained by African Americans' self-critiques of their communities and institutions.

In Charles W. Chesnutt's first novel, *The House Behind the Cedars* (1900), a decision to work for the advancement of her people comes late for the racially mixed Rena Walden. Following her brother's example, she initially rejects the life of a "poor girl in an obscure part of the old town," in order to pass into the "new conditions" of wealth, pedigree, and power that white privilege bestows. After her white husband uncovers the secret of her ancestry, she returns to black society to dedicate herself to teaching and the task of "lifting the black mass still floundering in the mud where slavery had left it." Unable to shake her feelings for the white man whom she truly loves, and whose love spurs him to try and reunite with her in spite of social taboos, she recedes into the black community, where she faces loneliness, confusion, illness, and death. Her tragic demise highlights the limitations of race work and nationalism as paths to progress and fulfillment, rather than presenting racial solidarity as an antidote to the inequality, oppression, and disrespect that African Americans negotiated. Rena's saga exposes the

c In this volume, Robert S. Levine's literary history of early African American novels examines how the figure of the tragic mulatta enabled writers like William Wells Brown, Harriet Wilson, Frank J. Webb, and Martin Delany to move beyond a critique of slavery and racism, and to destabilize perceptions about genre, gender, and racial and national identity. Levine, chapter 16 in this volume, esp. 271–272, 274, 277–280.

fissures among African Americans which had widened since Emancipation and divided them on the basis of race, class, education, and skin color.

In other post-Reconstruction novels featuring tragic mulattas, such fatalism is supplanted by a rosier conclusion to their sacrificial efforts in aid of the most downtrodden descendants of the slaves. In contrast to Chesnutt's Rena Walden, Harper's Iola Leroy – named for the anti-lynching crusader Ida B. Wells, who occasionally used "Iola" as a pseudonym – commits herself to her people. Rejecting a chance to pass out of blackness and live comfortably up North by marrying the proud and wealthy white Dr. Gresham, she instead marries the black Dr. Latimer. To paraphrase Booker T. Washington's later Atlanta Exposition address, she casts down her bucket with him in the segregated South to elevate the poorest of their people to secure, stable, self-determining lives.

In Pauline Hopkins's *Contending Forces: A Romance Illustrative of Negro Life North and South* (1900), the brutality and violence of the slavery past haunts the sewing circles and teas of the women of Boston's proud black enclaves, where they discuss such topics as "The place which the virtuous woman occupies in upbuilding a race." They attend public debates where speakers denounce lynchings of African Americans in the South as "subterfuge for killing men." They learn how the accusation of raping white women is the Southern mob's coded excuse for murdering black men who vote, amass property, and attempt to marry outside of the race. As proof that the post-Reconstruction South destroys the black woman's innocence and despises the black man's self-respect, the upstanding, well-bred Sappho Clark harbors a sad secret of her past sexual slavery and the murder of her father. Fearing the judgment of the Northern black community should her shameful Southern memories become public, Sappho nearly sabotages her chance to marry an educated African American man who is not repelled by her history. He understands that the traumas experienced by Sappho and other black women like her are outcomes of living in a "savage and barbarous country" of lynchers and rapists whom black intellectuals like Ida B. Wells struggle to bring to justice.

The political divisions that existed among the era's African American leadership both reflected and affected the various ways in which post-Reconstruction novels articulated the project of the race's advancement. Although they responded to the new challenges of freedom, they also evoked pre-Emancipation times when eighteenth- and nineteenth-century anti-slavery activists took opposite sides on such questions as whether African Americans should form communities in the North or colonize other countries, or if gradual or immediate freedom of the slaves would be more effective. Published at the dawn of the twentieth century, Hopkins's *Contending Forces* explores both poles of the agenda for educational and economic progress which Booker T. Washington and W. E. B. Du Bois, the race's most prominent spokesmen, offered as an alternative to stagnation and oppression. Washington advocated a gradualist approach that emphasized vocational and agricultural skills to create a productive, employed, assimilated citizenry. Du Bois, on the other hand, took issue with what he perceived as overly conciliatory aspects of Washington's pragmatic blueprint. He argued for ambitiously cultivating an elite, professional class of African Americans, and for bringing unrelenting pressure on the legal and judicial systems in order to accomplish the swift enfranchisement of their people. Characters in Hopkins's novel represent both of these points of view, and their conflict reflects debates about uplift within the race.

Post-Reconstruction African American novels also address the racial prejudices of whites that caused what Du Bois called a collective double consciousness, or "a sort of dual personality" as James Weldon Johnson described it in *Autobiography of an Ex-Colored Man* (1912), within African Americans. This duality combines an American perspective with an "outlook on all things, not from the viewpoint of a citizen, or a man, or even a human being, but from the viewpoint of a *colored* man." By "*colored*" Johnson is referring more to a worldview than a skin tone, to a viewpoint of America derived from the position of an outcast and marginalized race, of a nation-within-a-nation whose centuries of struggle have infused the American experience with both hopefulness and desperation. In the dignified, sympathetic renderings of the Southern black characters in *Iola Leroy*, *Contending Forces*, Chesnutt's *The House Behind the Cedars* and *The Marrow of Tradition* (1901), Harper's serialized *Hagar's Daughter: A Story of Southern Caste Prejudice* (1901–1902), and other post-Reconstruction African American novels, it is not difficult to recognize a response to the racist ideologies expressed by writers such as Thomas Dixon and represented in material artifacts such as postcards, stereoviews, sheet music, and engravings and photographs in the popular press. They pandered to white readers' nostalgia for "happy, carefree . . . days on the plantation,"[3] an idyllic fiction featuring benevolent, affable masters and their obedient, tractable slaves, cooperatively building a plantation paradise under sunny Southern skies. Such texts and material objects harbored an unconcealed antipathy for the dreaded "new issue"[4] Negro, who called for immediate equality as Emancipation's birthright. The "new issue" Negro also commanded the respect customarily reserved for the slaveholding class which had once commodified black bodies into paradoxical "God-breathing machines" of capitalism, "no more, in the sight of their masters, than the cotton they plant, or the horses they tend."[5] Post-Reconstruction African American novels expose this seeming nostalgia as a cover for an abiding sense of white supremacy.[d]

Consistent with many realist writers of their generation, Harper, Chesnutt, Johnson, and other post-Reconstruction African Americans employ dialect in their novels to signal illiteracy and country ways among their black characters. Their use of such speech recognizes slavery's history, but it also refutes the notion of the race as collectively inferior and ignorant, a byproduct of the pro-slavery rhetoric that lingered in plantation fiction. In *Iola Leroy*, for example, dialect among Harper's African Americans is a barometer of the common sense and calculation that shrewd slaves conceal from their owners. Within their dialect, they develop a secret language to communicate news of Yankee victories, and organize furtive meetings. Novels such as *Iola Leroy* and *The Marrow of Tradition* also introduce their plots with dialogues between illiterate, dialect-speaking Southern black servants and educated, proper blacks or whites. The vernacular in such examples denotes the bygone divisions of slavery days, even as it acknowledges the blood connections and shared ancestries that unite Southerners across distinctions of class and race. Given slavery's aftermath – the tangled family genealogies and brutal violence of the Jim Crow era – dialect in these novels finally serves as a reminder that, as Chesnutt writes in *The Marrow of Tradition,* "The habits and customs of a people were not to be changed in a day, nor by the stroke of a pen."

Also in order to combat popular perceptions about blacks' backwardness and savagery, and in resistance to the cultural erasure that slavery and the slave trade had attempted, post-Reconstruction novels describe and celebrate African cultural practices that survived four centuries of bondage. These enduring African American contributions to American culture and aesthetics emerge in the literature decades before the Harlem Renaissance, and they anticipate Valerie Babb's analysis in this volume of African Americans' attraction during the Harlem Renaissance to art, literature, and music as useful mechanisms for counteracting and complicating white society's negative perceptions.[e] For example, to

d For a discussion of the ways postbellum novels address white supremacy and black racial solidarity against a backdrop of disintegrating racial categories, see Robert Reid-Pharr, "The postbellum race novel," chapter 28 in this volume.

e Valerie Babb, "Wright, Hurston, and the direction of the African American novel," chapter 42, esp. 700–701.

James Weldon Johnson's ex-colored man, the "barbaric harmonies" and "audacious resolutions" of ragtime, "the abrupt jump from one key to another, the intricate rhythms in which the accents fell in the most unexpected places," could never be the affirmations of black inferiority that they might sound like to uninitiated or hyper-educated ears. Instead, he writes: "One thing cannot be denied; [ragtime] is music which . . . appeals universally; not only the American, but the English, the French, and even the German people find delight in it. In fact, there is not a corner of the civilized world in which it is not known, and this proves its originality." This universal influence of African American culture – a vindication after the cultural death that slavery attempted to enact – is a literary theme that resonates during the post-Reconstruction era.

Some novels occasionally express skepticism about appropriations of such African retentions and selectivity about which ones the world should value. In Hopkins's *Contending Forces* one character blasts "the pretensions of those" placing merit in "spells and charms." She denigrates "the occult arts which were once the glory of the freshly imported African" by accusing the slaves of directing them against their own people rather than their more deserving owners. Criticism of the ex-slaves' African-derived superstitions is not uncommon during this era. Yet blame leveled against the blacks themselves, with little acknowledgment of slavery's role in the matter, is exceptional.

In Hopkins's *Hagar's Daughter*, the conjuring and goophering that the slaves practice comment on the codes of honor and chivalry that their Southern masters have abdicated by buying and selling other human beings. Aunt Henny, a turbaned, fat, "coal black" cook who is the physical foil to the tragic mulatta Hagar, relies on omens and visions, her protective charms forged from the skins of various reptiles, rabbits' feet, and serpents' teeth, and her spells to keep the Devil at bay – all regularly punctuated by Christian hymns and prayers. They symbolize the peculiar institution's failures and the planter aristocracy's lies and self-delusions. While the slaveholders inaugurate the Confederacy and move to secede from the Union, Aunt Henny mumbles and hums her spells, as if in recognition of another new folly. Her superstitions suggest the pretensions and emptiness of a society in which a mere "drop of the accursed blood of the Negro slave" can up-end everything. Aunt Henny's Afrocentric rituals do not vindicate her humanity and intelligence: they validate how slavery stupefies all races and classes of humanity in its grip. Kristina Brooks identifies a character like Henny as inspired by minstrelsy, enabling Hopkins to make clear that "it is not her *nature* that unfits her for subjectivity and the reader's identification but her *nurture* under the southern system of slavery that overrides 'natural' maternality and renders her an object."[6]

In contrast, Chesnutt's *Marrow of Tradition* presents the spells, charms, omens, and "witchcraft and conjuration" from the slaves' African past as powerful and effective weapons against white supremacy. Similarly, as Iola Leroy's mission to uplift her people unfolds, Harper celebrates the community-building enabled by cultural productions that survived the journey from the African continent through the Middle Passage and the New World: the spirituals, shouts, and sermons inspired by earnest spirits; the sewing, cooking, and constructing of churches and schools outpoured from roughened hands. The protagonist of Johnson's *Ex-Colored Man* adds to the catalogue of African American artistic contributions the dialect spoken by working-class black Southerners, and the call-and-response patterns, three-part harmonies, and stirring tempos of the church-going and camp-meeting crowd's spirituals. In addition to ragtime music, he identifies the spirituals or "Jubilee songs," folktales, and the cake-walk as "four things which refute the oft-advanced theory that [African Americans] are absolutely an inferior race, which demonstrate that they have originality and artistic conception, and, what is more, the power of creating that which can influence and appeal universally."

Going even further, Hopkins's magazine novel *Of One Blood; Or, The Hidden Self* (1902–1903), credits the wisdom, science, and arts of the inhabitants of Western civilization to primal African sources, when the mixed-race hero traces the cradle of human history and his own personal ancestry to Meroe, "the ancient Ethiopian capital." Hazel V. Carby writes that in its theme "that contemporary black Americans are Ethiopians," the novel "is an early fictional response to the philosophy of Pan-Africanism in the United States, a philosophy that was always thought to have lain dormant until W. E. B. Du Bois revived it and organized the first Pan-African Congress to address the Peace Conference at Versailles after World War I."[7]

African American women's post-Reconstruction novels respond to national debates about the woman question by exploring the theme of "education of the race through its motherhood," as Harper writes in *Trial and Triumph* (1888–1889). They assess the era as a period when both marriage and activism competed as viable choices for African American women, and, as Paula Giddings writes, "both their ability to establish a traditional home life and their achievements in the public sphere were seen as bright markers of racial progress."[8] Harper and Hopkins demonstrate the value of women's education through depictions of black mothers and grandmothers and aunts, as well as nurses and teachers and clubwomen, who advise their communities and families on the virtues of morality and temperance.

By training in manual labors, educated black male characters in their novels acknowledge the racism of society and the doors of opportunity that close before them because of their color. Educated black women in these books preempt such disappointments by channeling their intellectual gifts into building happy, Christian homes and similar domestic spaces in churches, hospitals, and schools. This bifurcation of black male characters into competitive, public workspaces and black female characters into nurturing, domestic ones, on the one hand reflects received gender conventions that rigidly demarcated men's and women's roles in society. However, since African American women endeavor to prepare community members both for family life and the expanding opportunities and responsibilities of citizenship, such characters provide a platform for the novelists to present female education as a means of merging domestic reform with social activism, and what Claudia Tate termed a "new domestic pedagogy" wherein a woman might occupy dual roles "as the authority of her own ego reformation as well as the instigator of similar reform in her community."[9]

For example, the gifted character Annette Miller of Harper's *Trial and Triumph*, who loves literature and wins high academic distinctions, refutes detractors of female education by demonstrating that a woman's "intellectual growth" need not come at the expense of "the moral life of the race." As the novel concludes she is called to teach and use her mind to uplift her people everywhere – even "street gamins knew her as their friend." Similarly, the rich widow Mrs. Willis in Hopkins's *Contending Forces* transforms the domestic space of the sewing circle into a forum for discussing educated African American women as models of morality and virtue.

Arnold Rampersad writes that Du Bois's novel, *The Quest of the Silver Fleece* (1911), advances an even more radical idea about educated women: that they "are the superior sex in terms not only of morality but also of intellect and leadership."[10] In the character of the dark-skinned Alabama schoolteacher Zora Creswell, Du Bois suggests that this perfection in self-mastery and self-help arises because of rather than in spite of African ancestry. Although Zora debuts in the novel as a "bold, godless thing," as "a heathen hoyden of twelve wayward, untrained years," her lying, stealing ways prove not racial inferiority but the peonage, criminality, and sexual abuse that seem to comprise the only future for poor, rural black girls like her living during Jim Crow. Du Bois offsets her poverty and ignorance by characterizing her as curious, ambitious, and imaginative. After obtaining employment and expanding her social and cultural horizons up north, Zora returns south in the footsteps of the fictional Rena Waldens and Iola Leroys before her. As a bulwark against the "cruelty, poverty, and crime" that ruin African American girls, she founds a boarding school for orphans, and purchases land to liberate their families from the sharecropping cycle of debt and surrogacy.

Published one year after Du Bois's novel, Johnson's *The Autobiography of an Ex-Colored Man* returns to many themes and structures that characterize earlier novels of the post-Reconstruction period, even as it inspires the Harlem Renaissance productions of the 1920s and 1930s. The *Ex-Colored Man*'s nameless protagonist is an African American pianist and Everyman. His decision to pass for white reinforces what other post-Reconstruction novels had promised about whiteness as a symbol of privilege, a way to affluence and entitlement, and an escape from the racist hands hindering the progress of ambitious and talented African American youth. In earlier post-Reconstruction novels like *Iola Leroy* and *The House Behind the Cedars*, characters who contemplate passing may find themselves confronting the moral bankruptcy of white America and concluding that selfless service to the race is the higher calling to which they can channel their gifts. Yet the protagonist of Johnson's *Ex-Colored Man*, characterized by what William L. Andrews calls an "almost Olympian detachment from racial loyalties,"[11] does not in his passing recognize such a clear selection between blackness and race loyalty or whiteness and race betrayal. When the ex-colored man blames Americans for placing "a greater premium on color, or better, lack of color, than anything else in the world," his accusation goes for his black peers as well as his white ones.

Themes of white racism – and blacks' internalization of it through feelings of shame, inferiority, and self-loathing – persist among the post-Reconstruction African American novelists. Ma Smith's warning to her daughter Dora in *Contending Forces* to beware of the "sectional prejudice" that can "stifle natural feelings of brotherly love" between Northern and Southern African Americans suggests the self-destructiveness of internalized racism. Some of the works of this era offer outcomes such as economic security, increased educational prospects, and better advantages for black children as understandable reasons for passing, even as they mutter against the prejudice that warrants such desperate moves, and mourn the selfishness – often rewarded – that motivates the decision to pass in the first place. Discussions of passing in later post-Reconstruction books like Johnson's *Ex-Colored Man* do not so much comment on racial authenticity as they contest the grounds on which a character like Iola Leroy can say, "The best blood in my veins is

African blood." Such works foreground challenges to most Americans' claims to pure European or African bloodlines, and confront the hybrid outcomes of centuries of interracial encounters.

In addition to its bloodlines, the America of Johnson's ex-colored man is culturally, socially, and linguistically "colored."[12] The protagonist discovers ragtime, which blends classical European counterpoints with syncopated African rhythms. The Tenderloin district of lower Manhattan where he makes and loses his fortune was at the time of Johnson's writing the locus of the city's bohemians, "an organic culture" where, as in Harlem a few years later, "male and female, established and transient, black and white"[13] collided, amused themselves together, and pushed the boundaries of social custom and convention. Like the Native/English expressions and phrases of the nineteenth century's frontiersmen, explorers, and cowboys, the cool slang of the *Ex-Colored Man's* hep cats and hipsters is another American hybrid, that demonstrates the formation of a unique and Creole language with roots in the speech and folkways of more than one racial group.

Looking back as well as forward once again, post-Reconstruction black novelists return their readers to the antecedents of the genre: the fugitive slave narratives. Constructing Southern African American communities as culturally generative, spiritually grounded spaces, their denizens poised to do battle for the beacon of freedom that blazed ahead, the post-Reconstruction novelists take a page from the earlier fugitive slave narratives of the eighteenth and nineteenth centuries. Like the most memorable fugitive slave narrators, they explore the complexities of the South's relationship to generations of African Americans who toiled in servitude there: the region had come down to them simultaneously as a hell and a haven, a destroyer and a crucible for dreams, a casket yet also a cradle.

African American characters recall the slave narratives by lashing out against the false Christianity of whites who yoked them to bondage and who used the Good Book to justify the satanic system they created. In *Hagar's Daughter*, for instance, a white "reverend gentleman" in "the gospel ministry" is as hypocritical as any plantation owner when he boasts of converting a trader so that "now he won't sell a man from his wife if he can get anyone to buy them together." And where the slave narrators before them criticized black preachers in the master's pocket who only quoted sacred texts on obedience and surrender, *Trial and Triumph* and other African American novels after Reconstruction also look down on African American ministers who "love the fleece more than the flock" and who allow their selfish desperation for money and respect to override their sincerity and compassion.

One convention of the slave narrative genre is to attack the capitalistic underpinnings of slavery through auction block scenes where family members are cruelly separated. In post-Reconstruction African American novels, on the other hand, it is the emancipated slaves' refusal to abandon their mothers, or, as in Iola's case, the persistent quest to reunite with them, which stands as a recurring theme. This theme of reunion anticipates the rhetoric of other post-Reconstruction novelists, for whose characters the reconstruction of slave families can symbolize the reconciliation of Northern abolitionists and former Southern slaveholders, or of slaveholders and their former slaves. Johnson's ex-colored man observes an authentic, "affectionate relation between the Southern whites and those blacks who come in close touch with them" which "has not been overdrawn even in fiction." And perhaps this rhetoric serves another function. To retrieve the mother, "and bind anew the ties which slavery had broken," to quote Iola, also may represent a rededication to the motherland: not to the literal African continent, but to the Southern landscape which all descendants of American slaves claimed as their cultural and spiritual birthplace, and where the major work of uplift waited to be done.[14]

Dunbar's *The Sport of the Gods* (1902) also depends on a structure that retraces the runaway's movement from south to north, to venture that "the small villages and country districts of the South" are more hospitable for "untrained negroes" than "the pernicious influence of the city." When their innocent father Berry Hamilton, a faithful servant to his white Southern employees, is wrongfully imprisoned for theft, his wife Fannie and children Kit and Joe attempt to start over in New York's Tenderloin. Ragtime music and sporting men and social clubs populate the stage of Dunbar's novel (as in the lower Manhattan of Johnson's *Ex-Colored Man*), and they herald the family's descent into such vices as murder and adultery. Dunbar lifts the scrim on the post-Reconstruction North to expose the "false ideals and unreal ambitions" of "the stream of young negro life . . . up from the South," as if to render them equivalent to the segregated trolley cars and substandard housing and "nigger" pews that greeted and trapped unwitting antebellum fugitives.

The ex-colored man's swift-footed ascent from Southern obscurity to Northern wealth and privilege, culminating in his marriage to a white woman, recalls the transformative process of freedom that stood as a stock plot element in the ex-slaves' autobiographies. Yet he has traveled some distance from the latter century's fiction. Instead of "publicly fighting the cause of [his] race," the self-described "small and selfish" ex-colored man terminates his story from the disappointed standpoint of "an ordinarily successful white man who has made a little money."

Like the ex-slave writer separated from parents, siblings, and home by the traumas of slavery, the ex-colored man initiates his narrative with the rhetoric of omission. Born in the South "in a little town of Georgia," he can give "only a faint recollection" of the landscape of his birthplace; its name is one he "shall not mention"; he insists upon concealing even the names of town residents he can recall, including those of his parents. The phrase "The Autobiography" that announces Johnson's novel lays claim to the black man's humanity, imagination, and autonomy, as did the subtitle "Written by Himself" of the previous century's slave narrators. *The Autobiography of an Ex-Colored Man* is a product of the 1900s, not the 1800s, yet in the context of what befalls Johnson's character, what remains the same is African Americans' struggle for equality. Where the fugitive slave narratives were earnest in their belief that they could use their master's tools – education, mobility, suffrage – to dismantle the institution of slavery, post-Reconstruction novels like the *Ex-Colored Man* could find this formula wanting. Yet, at a bittersweet and often contentious moment in the nation's history, African American novelists did stand united and hopeful on at least one point: the Reconstruction and its aftermath were not failures. Divisive and unifying, conciliatory and acrimonious, the occasionally explosive post-Reconstruction years pointed semi-emancipated African Americans down the messy, meandering road toward freedom. African American novelists of these years invent a literature whose legacy extends beyond mere documentation of the era's debates or reactions to its racism. Though they acknowledge a debt to previous generations writing during bondage, they are ultimately not practitioners of the past but foragers of the new. From their alchemy of African and European sources, they introduce original ways of imagining and expressing what it means to be an African American.

Notes

1. W. E. B. Du Bois, *The Souls of Black Folk*, ed. Henry Louis Gates and Terri Hume Oliver (New York: W. W. Norton & Co., 1999), 5.
2. Frances Smith Foster notes how, modifying "standard depictions" of enslaved African American women "as victims of physical cruelty and especially of sexual violation," Harper's abolitionist poetry included portrayals of slave mothers separated from their children. Such poetic themes also appear in Harper's post-Reconstruction fiction. See Frances Smith Foster, "Introduction," in *A Brighter*

Coming Day: A Frances Ellen Watkins Harper Reader, ed. Foster (New York: Feminist Press, 1990), 31–32.

3. I am quoting from the ex-slave Annie Louise Burton's post-Reconstruction discussion of her early years in Alabama. As Elizabeth Keckley demonstrates in her fond reminiscences of her former owners the Garlands, such pastoral descriptions of bondage and expressions of attachment to their masters from the mouths of former slaves were by no means limited to the first fleeting years of childhood innocence. Annie Louise Burton, *Memories of Childhood's Slavery Days* (1909), in *Six Women's Slave Narratives*, ed. Henry Louis Gates, Jr. (Oxford: Oxford University Press, 1988), 3; and Elizabeth Keckley, "Old Friends," chapter 14 of *Behind the Scenes, or, Thirty Years a Slave, and Four Years in the White House* (1868), ed. Henry Louis Gates, Jr. (Oxford: Oxford University Press, 1988), 238–266.
4. Du Bois uses this term in his landmark sociological study *The Philadelphia Negro* (1899), where he identifies and challenges white perceptions of "new issue" black youth, the first generation born after Emancipation, whose allegedly uppity attitudes and laziness rendered them unfit for domestic service. See Barbara Ryan, "Old and New Issue Servants: 'Race' Men and Women Weigh In," in *Post-Bellum, Pre-Harlem: African American Literature and Culture, 1877–1919*, ed. Barbara McCaskill and Caroline Gebhard (New York: New York University Press, 2006), 89.
5. Harriet Brent Jacobs, *Incidents in the Life of a Slave Girl* (1861), ed. Nellie Y. McKay and Frances Smith Foster (New York: W. W. Norton, 2001), 12.
6. Kristina Brooks, "Mammies, Bucks, and Wenches: Minstrelsy, Racial Pornography, and Racist Politics in Pauline Hopkins's *Hagar's Daughter*," in *The Unruly Voice: Rediscovering Pauline Elizabeth Hopkins*, ed. John Cullen Gruesser (Urbana and Chicago: University of Illinois Press, 1996), 141–142.
7. Hazel V. Carby, "Introduction," *The Magazine Novels of Pauline Hopkins* (New York and Oxford: Oxford University Press, 1988), xlv.
8. Paula J. Giddings, *Ida – A Sword among Lions: Ida B. Wells and the Campaign against Lynching* (New York: Amistad, 2008), 357.
9. Claudia Tate, *Domestic Allegories of Political Desire: The Black Heroine's Text at the Turn of the Century* (New York: Oxford University Press, 1992), 141.
10. Arnold Rampersad, "Foreword" to *The Quest of the Silver Fleece* (1911), by W. E. B. Du Bois (Boston: Northeastern University Press, 1989), 9.
11. William L. Andrews, "The Representation of Slavery and the Rise of Afro-American Literary Realism, 1865–1920," in *African American Autobiography: A Collection of Critical Essays*, ed. Andrews (Englewood Cliffs, NJ: Prentice Hall, 1993), 88. This essay originally appeared in *Slavery and the Literary Imagination: Selected Papers from the English Institute, 1987*, new series, no. 13, ed. Deborah E. McDowell and Arnold Rampersad (Baltimore and London: Johns Hopkins University Press, 1989), 62–80.
12. Robert M. Dowling analyzes contemporaneous discussions of *fin-de-siècle* New York as a microcosm of American "interethnic experiences." See "Marginal Men

in Black Bohemia: Paul Laurence Dunbar and James Weldon Johnson in the Tenderloin," chapter 3 of his *Slumming in New York: From the Waterfront to Mythic Harlem* (Urbana and Chicago: University of Illinois Press, 2007), 80–82.

13. *Ibid.*, 83; Robert M. Dowling, "A Marginal Man in Black Bohemia: James Weldon Johnson in the New York Tenderloin," in McCaskill and Gebhard, *Post-Bellum, Pre-Harlem*, 124.
14. In *Trial and Triumph*, set in the North, Harper takes a similar approach to this conflation of motherhood and motherland. An argument occurs between the African American teacher Mr. Thomas and his former student Charley Cooper, who is considering going away and passing for white in order to get better-paying jobs. To convince the young man to stay, Mr. Thomas warns him that he will never be able to see his mother again. Encouraging Charley to "stand in your lot without compromise or concealment, and feel that the feebler your mother's race is the closer you will cling to it," Mr. Thomas casts devotion to the race in the language of filial loyalty.

30

The rise of naturalism

DONNA CAMPBELL

In "The Naturalism of Mr. Dreiser" (1915), the critic Stuart P. Sherman found nothing to praise in Theodore Dreiser's naturalism, which, Sherman complains, "drives home the great truth that man is essentially an animal" impelled by a "jungle-motive," with protagonists that acquire not wisdom but "sensations." Treating morality as an innate feature of human nature, Sherman singled out as unrealistic the idea that Dreiser's Jennie Gerhardt would feel not "sin or shame or regret" at bearing a child out of wedlock. He concludes that, unlike realism, which relies on a theory of human behavior, naturalism is "based upon a theory of animal behavior" and lacks the "moral value" and "memorable beauty" of true art.[1] Naturalism had weathered similar charges of indecency, crudity, and a lack of decorum since its appearance on the American literary scene in the mid-1890s. Late nineteenth-century theories of Darwinian evolution had not only undercut the supposedly "natural" division between humans and animals but had also questioned the "natural" itself. Was morality "natural," or love, or duty? Or were they all simply socially acceptable manifestations of human drives such as fear, desire, and self-preservation? Conservative critics like Sherman were understandably worried by the work of Dreiser and others like him, for American naturalism, in applying scientific principles to the medium of fiction, threatened to strip the conventional pieties from the façade of the social order.

Naturalism in the United States had no unifying school, no group of disciples, and no formal manifesto. Except for Frank Norris, who proclaimed himself the "boy Zola," its practitioners described their work simply as writing about what was true or real.[2] Dreiser, for example, described his practice as simply giving a "true picture of life," and Stephen Crane maintained that he was following in the footsteps of W. D. Howells.[3] In a more dramatic description of naturalism's purposes, Frank Norris declared that "Terrible things must happen to the characters of the naturalistic tale. They must be twisted from the ordinary, wrenched out from the quiet, uneventful round of every-day life, and flung into the throes of a vast and terrible drama that works itself out in unleashed passions, in blood, and in sudden death."[4] Naturalism is thus a term more often applied after the fact to a type of fiction that shares a particular set of features than a category used by the novelists themselves. Characteristics of naturalism observed by later critics include a deterministic philosophy that challenges the idea of individual free will; the belief that forces of environment and heredity shape human lives; a quasi-scientific perspective on characters, who are often defined by their race- and class-based traits rather than by their individual natures; and an interest in what reviewers of the day saw as low and sordid subjects, such as sex and violence in working-class lives.

But naturalism remains easier to recognize than to define. June Howard notes that after George Becker's frequently cited description of naturalism as "pessimistic materialistic determinism," "the next most frequently made observation about naturalism must surely be that it is *not* pessimistic determinism."[5] Yet definitions such as Becker's continue to limit the canon of naturalism. For example, Norris's *The Pit* (1903) and Edith Wharton's *The House of Mirth* (1905) incorporate biological and deterministic themes, but they are rarely defined as naturalistic because of their upper-class milieux. In addition, although Norris saw naturalism as an expansive and inclusive type of romanticism, given its sensational and melodramatic elements, some contemporary reviewers contended that naturalism was simply a narrower version of realism, a view that continued into the 1990s with Michael Davitt Bell's *The Problem of American Realism* (1993). In his extensive work on naturalism, Donald Pizer adopts a formalist approach, identifying two fundamental tensions within naturalistic works: first, the opposition between limited characters and the "heroic or adventurous" acts they perform; and second, the contrast between the deterministic universe of naturalistic fiction and the "compensating humanistic value" that readers and characters find within it.[6] Howard likewise sees a series of contradictions or "antinomies" as constituting naturalism.[7] Naturalism should thus be considered not as a monolithic whole but as *naturalisms*, a series of sometimes contradictory narrative practices based in theories of evolution, psychology, race, and Social Darwinism.

Two key characteristics illustrate the kinds of tensions within naturalism. Despite its supposed objectivity, naturalism is a particularly self-referential genre, calling attention to its impersonal pose, and thus to the presence of the author, in language that inserts the author-as-scientific observer into the flow of narrative.[8] In analyzing George Hurstwood's middle-aged loss of vitality in *Sister Carrie* (1900), for example, Dreiser's narrator explains that he is afflicted with "katastates," or poisons in the blood that cause feelings of depression, a now discredited theory that lent an aura of scientific credibility to the representation of Hurstwood's emotional state. The self-referentiality of the explanatory author-scientist is also evident in a related characteristic of naturalism, the figure of the spectator, whose intellect differentiates him from the lower-class characters and aligns him with the reader.[9] A second feature of naturalism is its theme of a divided self torn between rationality and animality, often expressed through the plot of the "brute within" breaking through the veneer of civilization and overpowering the "better self." For example, when Norris's character McTeague is aroused by the sight of an unconscious woman, "[T]he animal in the man stirred and woke" but "another better McTeague rose with the brute . . . It was the old battle, old as the world." In Norris's *Vandover and the Brute* (composed 1895; published 1914), college man and aesthete Vandover loses this battle as he runs "[n]aked, four-footed" back and forth in his room, crying "Wolf – wolf!" Indeed, the "brute within" is, as Charles Child Walcutt points out, an inverted image of the transcendentalist idea of the god within, just as the naturalistic vision of a powerfully indifferent and hostile nature inverts the transcendentalists' idea of a beneficent nature.[10] Naturalistic writers saw that the untrammeled nature within human beings – sometimes selfish, often violent, and always driven by desire – made "devolution" (a scientifically dubious concept suggested by the connotations of progress within the word "evolution") and atavism as likely as the transcendentalists' vision of human perfectibility.

Both the scientist-observer and the dualism of the "brute" versus the "better self" originated in theories of evolution and Social Darwinism. As historian Robert C. Bannister explains, Darwin provided the principal but by no means the only theories of evolution. Although Darwin had laid out the principles of natural selection and sexual selection in *Origin of Species* (1859) and *The Descent of Man* (1871) respectively, naturalistic writers like London and Dreiser gravitated toward the ideas of Herbert Spencer, especially that of "the survival of the fittest," an idea often erroneously attributed to Darwin. Spencer's philosophy had a teleology that Darwin's lacked; as Spencer explains in *Social Statics* (1851), a "fatal maladaptation" means that if organisms "are not sufficiently complete to live, they die, and it is best that they die" to "purify society."[11] A vivid example of this principle unfolds early in Dreiser's *The Financier* (1912) when the young Frank Cowperwood watches a lobster snip off pieces of a squid in a fish tank as the helpless squid darts about its confined space until its inevitable demise. "Things lived on each other – that was it," concludes Cowperwood, and "men lived on men," a philosophy that informs his ruthless rise to power as a businessman. A more optimistic aspect of Spencer's theory, according to Richard Lehan, is the idea that "mankind was advancing even as the individual was circumscribed by physical limits."[12] Spencer's mechanism for this forward movement was the evolution of "the moral sense" through adaptation, a process that would move human beings from the "barbarous selfishness" that gave rise to colonialism and slavery to a perfected condition of "greatest mutual dependence."[13] According to historian Carl Degler, evolutionary ideas were thus employed equally by reform Darwinists, who drew on scientific rationales to promote agendas ranging from government regulation to eugenics, and by laissez-faire or conservative Darwinists, who argued that the natural order should not be regulated.[14]

Just as recent reconsiderations of modernism have pushed the definitional boundaries of classic modernism, a reconsideration of naturalism requires exploring the roughly simultaneous incarnation of several naturalisms, each of which established a context of ideas from which writers constructed their texts and through which they anticipated being read. Such an investigation also suggests the possibilities of expanding the canon to include later authors as well as those marginalized by race, gender, or socio-political agendas. For example, as Lisa Long asks, "Would 'African American' practices remain outside the purview of traditional (read: white) literary genealogies" if works like Paul Laurence Dunbar's *The Sport of the Gods* (1902) were considered integral, rather than peripheral, to the strategies of naturalism?[15] To investigate naturalisms, then, requires an examination not only of "classic" naturalism but also of its later twentieth-century manifestations in the eras of reform fiction and modernism.

Classic naturalism

The true subject of the naturalistic text is the human body, the battleground upon which the clash of external and internal forces is waged. Dissociated from its connotations of transcendent humanity, the body becomes one more machine in a mechanistic universe or one more organism within a hostile ecosystem. Whether machine or organism, the human body is governed by the laws of nature, but it is also endowed with consciousness and the ability to suffer.[16] Violent acts pervade classic naturalism, ranging from the beatings that Trina receives in Norris's *McTeague* (1899) to the fistfights that characterize life in the lower-class New York of Crane's *Maggie* (1893), to the brutality on board Wolf Larsen's ship *The Ghost* in Jack London's *The Sea-Wolf* (1904). Whether their lives play out on a stage as inhumanly large in scale as London's Yukon, Crane's West, or Norris's Death Valley, or the equally impersonal and vast urban spaces of Dreiser, Upton Sinclair, or Henry Blake Fuller, naturalistic characters have a dual existence: their bodies live and die within the relentlessly material realm of the present, but their souls or spirits are caught between a primitive past inscribed in their genes and a future signified by urban modernity. The focus on the body is also important because the human organism was, after all, the most fraught testing ground for the evolutionary theories of Spencer and Darwin.

Given its preoccupation with violence, physical force, and testing the self against extreme conditions, naturalism has traditionally been seen as a masculine genre, featuring what John Dudley calls a "hypermasculine definition of the writer," and an "anti-aesthetics" of masculinity in keeping with Theodore Roosevelt's embrace of the strenuous life.[17] The "strenuous life" ideology fit well with Spencer's dictum of "survival of the fittest" and was applied on a grand scale to the future of races as well. With the frontier no longer available as a testing ground, Norris's and London's Anglo-Saxon ideal man could recover masculinity only by triumphing within a brutal and primitive masculine culture or by dominating the men of "effeminate" races through imperial ventures.[18] Norris's *Moran of the Lady Letty* (1898) and London's *The Sea-Wolf* exemplify these oppositions, for both depict overcivilized men being brought to masculine vigor after surviving a hostile environment. With its subject transposed from men to dogs, the same plot also plays out in London's *The Call of the Wild* (1903), in which Buck, a healthy but pampered pet, is kidnapped and sold into bondage during the Yukon gold rush, where he learns that "his moral nature" was a hindrance in "the ruthless struggle for existence . . . under the law of club and fang." Only by killing "man, the noblest game of all" can Buck break his ties to human beings, and only by yielding to the atavistic call of his ancestral wolf pack, the "call of the wild," can he regain masculinity and independence. As James R. Giles points out, however, in killing the tribe of Yeehats that have murdered his beloved master John Thornton and owning the space that they occupied, Buck, like Norris's idealized Anglo-Saxon, embarks on an imperial venture.[19]

As Frank Norris's *McTeague* illustrates, the modern city is dangerous in the naturalistic novel: both adaptation to the urban environment and resistance to it can prove fatal. A dentist who serves the working-class inhabitants of Polk Street lives in brutish contentment until Trina Sieppe enters his life, bringing with her not only the catalyst of sexuality but also the dream of a middle-class existence. For McTeague, as for other characters in naturalism, an awakening to sexuality, class mobility, and modernity signals a crisis. McTeague cannot make the full transition to a modern society: despite his experience as a dentist, he lacks a diploma and is forced to give up his practice.[20] As the couple sink into poverty, McTeague regresses from the orderly life he had learned with Trina. Hard liquor awakens "the brute in the man," this time with violence toward Trina. The second stage of his atavism occurs after he murders Trina and retreats to the mining country of his youth, becoming a natural man in a natural landscape that he understands preternaturally well. Carrying Trina's gold becomes McTeague's downfall in the searing desert of Death Valley, where the novel ends with him handcuffed to his rival's body, and thus to the past he had left behind.

Many naturalist novels are driven by a fear of and fascination with women's bodies, not simply the "figure of the compulsive modern woman" that Jennifer Fleissner analyzes, but also, as Mark Seltzer argues, the figure of the "fallen girl" and the "monstrous mother of the slums."[21] In *Maggie: A Girl of the Streets*, Crane presents the twinned bodies of fallen woman/monstrous mother. As Maggie Johnson progresses from her first love affair into a descent into prostitution and death, the narrator emphasizes that her painted and debased body becomes an object of spectacle for prospective clients as for the reader. Maggie begins as a "flower who blossomed in a mud puddle," with a rare individuality and sensitivity to beauty, but she loses her identity when she becomes first "a little pale thing with no spirit" and then "a girl of the painted cohorts of the city." In his vividly expressionistic style, Crane renders the contrasts between the bodies of characters in *Maggie* as a series of extremes of color and size: for example, the pale and "painted" body of Maggie contrasts with the "red, writhing body" of her mother, Mary Johnson. Grotesque and terrifying, Mary is the monstrous mother of the slums whose body suggests the violence of childbirth as well as the fecundity that populates the violent streets of New York. Set in the same slum neighborhood and even the same building as *Maggie*, *George's Mother* (1896) likewise features a terrifying maternal figure: Mrs. Kelcey, who also drives her child into the streets, this time through her nagging. Lacking the physical bulk of Mrs. Johnson, even Mrs. Kelcey's "little" body with its "dwindled muscles" provokes anxiety in George. The mother is not monstrous because of her body, although the grotesque Mrs. Johnson comes close; rather, she is monstrous because of the power she wields over her children. When Mrs. Kelcey finally lies on her deathbed, George sits motionless in a chair, staring at the walls, his stillness suggesting the way his life has also ground to a halt. (A similar sort of paralysis in the presence of death strikes Henry Fleming of *The Red Badge of Courage*, when he is "turned to stone" before the sitting corpse of a soldier in a forest clearing, and he watches "spellbound" as the tall soldier dies "danc[ing] a sort of hideous hornpipe.")[a] The mother–son dynamic illustrates how naturalist characters are most fully alive only when resisting the biological and social forces that seek to constrain them, yet if these forces prove either overpowering or absent, the result is, as in Kelcey's case, stasis, the "stuckness in place" that Jennifer Fleissner sees as an essential feature in naturalism.[22]

Along with decline and stasis, a third naturalist plot is inspired by Darwin's theory of sexual selection. Since *Descent of Man* had established sexual selection as the province of the female of the species, novelists influenced by Darwin, including Kate Chopin, Edith Wharton, and Theodore Dreiser, rewrote the courtship plot common to realism into novels about sexual choice.[b] As Bert Bender shows, these writers followed closely Darwin's observations about animal courtship behavior, including the role of such secondary sexual characteristics as prehensile hands, body adornment, and the power of music to influence the selection of a mate.[23] In Harold Frederic's *The Damnation of Theron Ware* (1896), Theron experiences Celia Madden's playing Chopin for him on the piano in her private studio as powerfully erotic.[c] A similar process of female sexual selection operates in Hamlin Garland's *Rose of Dutcher's Coolly* (1895), which was criticized in its time for its sexual frankness. As Rose progresses from an admiration of a circus acrobat's naked athleticism to the intellectual charms of the man who becomes her lover, Garland emphasizes the extent to which Rose makes her own choices: her last words in the novel are "I realize it all, and I choose it." Yet Rose's choices are possible in part because she has left the countryside behind, and with it the biological and economic forces that trap the prairie farmers and their wives in *Main-Travelled Roads* (1891).

When the heroine's biological choice is disrupted by the dictates of society, the result is predictably disastrous. Edith Wharton presents that scenario in *The House of Mirth* (1905), in which the poor but well-born Lily Bart is unable to survive because she fails to adapt to the exigencies of the marriage market, as Jennifer Fleissner contends in her essay in this volume (chapter 27). Lily must

a In his discussion of *The Red Badge of Courage* in this volume, Lawrence Buell relates similar moments of sensorial disorientation to naturalism's "destabilization of the convention of character coherence," chapter 19, 330. John Carlos Rowe also discusses *The Red Badge of Courage* in "US novels and US wars" (chapter 49), focusing on Crane's avoidance of racial and political contexts (817–818).

b Elizabeth Nolan discusses naturalistic elements in Chopin's *The Awakening* and Wharton's *Ethan Frome* in "The woman's novel beyond sentimentalism," chapter 34.

c Amy Hungerford traces the waning political power but enhanced aesthetic position of religion in *The Damnation of Theron Ware* in "Religion and the twentieth-century American novel," chapter 44, 732–735, in this volume.

repeatedly choose between Lawrence Selden, the man to whom she is attracted, and a series of more powerful potential mates whom she rejects, until it is too late. Wharton casts Lily's fate in specifically Darwinian terms: although Lily often sees herself as pursued by the Furies of the *Oresteia*, the narrator renders her not as a tragic character but as a figure at the end of an evolutionary cycle, a "mere spin-drift of the whirling surface of existence." In evolutionary terms, Lily is an anomaly because unlike most of the women around her, she lacks the power of suppressing her feelings adequately, prizes freedom above submission, and does not select powerful men. By contrast, Undine Spragg of Wharton's *The Custom of the Country* (1913) is an evolutionary success story, her entire absence of scruples and finer feelings enabling her rise in the world through successive divorces, each time adapting so perfectly that her triumph is inevitable. Carrie Meeber of Dreiser's *Sister Carrie* – discussed in more detail elsewhere in this volume – likewise adapts easily to each of her surroundings in turn, demonstrating a chameleonlike quality that Dreiser emphasizes by making her discard first one lover and then another before becoming a successful actress.[d]

Despite the illusion of choice that the doctrine of sexual selection implies, naturalistic novels rarely feature successful and procreative unions, in large measure because social forces interfere with the process. As courtship, not marriage, is the focus of realist novels, so the process of sexual selection, not its results, is the focus of naturalist ones.

Naturalism and reform

Naturalist authors strove for objectivity in presenting their work, a principle set forth in Zola's "The Experimental Novel" (1883) but violated to varying degrees by Zola and every subsequent writer of naturalism. Most classic naturalists drew the line, however, at the overt promotion of a specific social agenda, a distinction that traditionally separates nineteenth-century reform fiction from naturalism. In naturalistic novels, the solution to social problems exists outside the story itself; by contrast, reform fiction advocates a solution. For example, although *McTeague* depicts alcoholism, compulsive hoarding, domestic violence, and three murders, the narrative voice remains detached (sometimes ironically or bemusedly so) from the events it describes and never

d Further discussion of *Sister Carrie* may be found in Jude Davies, "Dreiser and the city" (chapter 22) and Jennifer L. Fleissner, "Wharton, marriage, and the New Woman" (chapter 27).

argues for changing conditions. In the Progressive era, protest novels like Upton Sinclair's *The Jungle* (1906) and David Graham Phillips's *Susan Lenox: Her Fall and Rise* (1917), both often grouped with naturalist novels, moved the focus from the individual- and religion-based action sought by earlier novels of industrial reform to the collective responsibility of social groups.[e]

Born out of wedlock and forced into marriage, Phillips's Susan Lenox runs away to the city and is drugged, raped, beaten, and forced into prostitution. Like Crane's Maggie, Susan can escape from her miserable surroundings only by selling herself, and Phillips presents her decision as a rational choice. Like Dreiser's Carrie Meeber, Susan turns to acting as a way out, creating herself as a spectacle that she can control. But the novel shows its roots in protest fiction through its treatment of Susan's plight. Whereas Crane indicts the hypocrisy of the social system but proffers no solution, Phillips makes a strong case for women's education and professional training, since as Susan tells various confidants, her upbringing as a lady unfitted her for survival. Unlike benevolence novels, which rely on a sympathetic narrative voice or a character with whom the reader can identify, or earlier naturalistic novels, which employ the figure of a spectator or narrator to translate the feelings of their inarticulate subjects, *Susan Lenox* features a modern heroine who recognizes her plight yet can still do little to change it. As such, she represents what Donald Pizer has called the "mature phase" of naturalism, in which a character's intelligence allows a level of self-awareness inaccessible to the less reflective figures of early naturalism.[24]

The distinction between the earlier and more mature phase of naturalism with its self-aware characters is most evident in two naturalistic novels focusing on race, Paul Laurence Dunbar's *The Sport of the Gods* (1902) and Ann Petry's *The Street* (1946). In *The Sport of the Gods*, Berry Hamilton, the respected African American butler of a white landowner, is unjustly imprisoned for theft, after which his wife and two children move to New York. Dunbar combines two common plots of the naturalist novel in tracing the children's fates in the city: like Carrie Meeber, Kitty becomes a musical comedy star, but her success is purchased at the cost of her innocence; and Joe, like Crane's George Kelcey, is seduced by drink and the pleasures of the city, after which he kills his mistress and is sent to prison. After a white newspaperman proves his innocence, Berry is released and returns to the South with his wife, but his

e Cecelia Tichi discusses Sinclair more extensively in "Novels of civic protest," chapter 23, 393–397 in this volume; for a further discussion of Phillips and reform fiction, see David Zimmerman's "Novels of American business, industry, and consumerism," chapter 24, 418–419.

life and family have been destroyed. In this manner, *The Sport of the Gods* follows the naturalistic plot of decline, but its catalyst resides in social, not primal, forces, beginning with racism. In this way, Dunbar remaps the naturalistic landscape as the dangerous terrain of a racist nation. Neither city nor country provides a safe space in a racist culture, for, as the narrative voice concludes, "Down there, the bodies were restrained, and they chafed; but here the soul would fester."[f]

Ann Petry's *The Street* (1946) likewise presents a naturalistic landscape from which escape is impossible. Like Susan Lenox, Petry's Lutie Johnson struggles to preserve a sense of dignity and to make a living amidst the poverty, violence, and filth of New York, but her attempts are thwarted by racism and sexism. Avoiding the easy option – and, in naturalism, the conventional choice – of prostitution, and trying to keep her son safe from the poisoned charms of the street, Lutie tries to escape by pursuing a singing career. But unlike Carrie Meeber and Susan Lenox, Lutie can find no way to avoid the clutches of predatory men like Junto, the white nightclub owner who seeks sexual favors, and Jones, the black superintendent whose desire for Lutie curdles into hatred once she rejects him. Lutie, a self-aware character in the mature phase of naturalism, reflects that her life has been spent within an "ever-narrowing space" and that the streets of Harlem are "the North's lynch mobs." When Lutie bludgeons her one-time suitor Boots Smith to death, she "was striking at the white world which thrust black people into a walled enclosure from which there was no escape." Lutie, like McTeague, lashes out violently and then flees, a pattern that Bigger Thomas also follows in Richard Wright's *Native Son* (1940).[g]

Naturalism in the era of modernism

Modernism seems at first antithetical to naturalism: where naturalism uses the accumulation of details woven into a narrative to represent reality, modernism employs fragments; where naturalism adheres to an empirical method and a positivistic belief in knowable causes, modernism denies such ultimate beliefs; and whereas the hallmark of naturalism is objectivity, that of

f Barbara McCaskill contrasts Dunbar's vision of the city with that of James Weldon Johnson's *Autobiography of an Ex-Coloured Man* in "The African American novel after Reconstruction," chapter 29 in this volume (493–496)

g Valerie Babb discusses Wright's racial outrage and Petry's use of place in "Wright, Hurston, and the direction of the African American novel," chapter 42, 710–712 in this volume.

modernism is subjectivity, the representation of interior states of consciousness not solely through a reliance on external symbols but through techniques such as stream of consciousness and free indirect discourse.[h] But naturalism endures into the period of modernism and, in keeping with this move toward interiority, often explores the internal compulsions explained by Freud, whose writing Dreiser called "a strong, revealing light thrown on some of the darkest problems that haunted and troubled me and my work."[25] Psychoanalytic theory, particularly concerning the unconscious and repression, added another dimension to the deterministic philosophy of naturalism. According to Freud, seemingly accidental incidents could actually be attributed to the eruption of previously repressed thoughts, memories, or desires, thus further tightening the deterministic net. The naturalisms of the twentieth century retain the focus on determinism and the body that marks the classic phase of naturalism, now infused with psychological determinism, as in Sherwood Anderson's *Winesburg, Ohio* (1919), Dreiser's *An American Tragedy* (1925), and Henry Roth's *Call It Sleep* (1934), and by modernist techniques of representation, as in John Dos Passos's *U.S.A.* (1938) and James T. Farrell's *Studs Lonigan* (1935).

Anderson and Roth use the theme of concealment and exposure to suggest an awakening to consciousness that would have been impossible for early naturalist protagonists. *Winesburg, Ohio*, a novelistic sequence of short stories linked by the character George Willard, features the social and psychological repression inflicted by the small town and its residents. Its preface, "The Book of the Grotesque," explains that those who cling to a truth and allow it to dominate their lives become "grotesques," a concept that David T. Mitchell and Sharon Snyder read elsewhere in this volume as projecting the "shadowy substance of characters" onto "the unique physiognomy of bodies recognizable as disabled."[i] As the characters attempt unsuccessfully to communicate their truths, the result is a series of naturalistic epiphanies in which each character gains both illumination and disillusionment about the possibility of change, with George, a reporter, usually acting as both auditor and catalyst.

The naturalist epiphany undergoes a transformation in *Call It Sleep*. Roth combines a naturalistic setting – a loud, gritty, poverty-stricken lower East Side neighborhood – with modernist techniques to capture the confusion of his young protagonist. David Searle is caught between the competing choices

h Peter Nicholls analyzes modernist prose technique in "Hemingway, Stein, and American modernisms," chapter 37 in this volume.

i David T. Mitchell and Sharon L. Snyder, "Disability and the American novel," chapter 60 in this volume, 1006.

typical of what Tim Prchal calls the "narrative of immigrant adjustment": Yiddish and English; an abusive father and a protective mother; and the book-learning of the *cheder* and the experiential knowledge of the streets. [j] David tries to reproduce the story of Isaiah's purification by a piece of burning coal by thrusting a milk ladle into the electrified fork of the tracks. The blinding bolt of electricity that surges through him, and the *Waste Land*-like cacophony of voices and fragmented images he experiences as he lies in the street, constitute a epiphany that nearly kills him, but he emerges with the power to shape words instead of being shaped by them. In deciding that he will "call [his state of awareness] sleep," David prefigures his potential career as a writer much as George Willard's recollections of Winesburg stories prefigure his.

Dreiser's *An American Tragedy* also depicts the interplay of social and psychological forces. Based on a 1906 murder case, in which Chester Gillette was convicted of drowning his pregnant lover, Grace Brown, *An American Tragedy* shows the results of internalizing the values of a social system permeated by capitalist models of success – or, to put it another way, dreaming the American dream.[k] Dreiser uses free indirect discourse to render the characters' thoughts, notably those of Clyde and his lover Roberta, a technique especially suited to capturing the novel's themes of vacillation and indeterminacy. Dreiser also describes Clyde's psychological processes through his dreams. In the crucial scene of Roberta's drowning, in contrast to other naturalistic characters who act impulsively and disastrously, Clyde takes scarcely any action at all, and, goaded by the "Efrit" of his unconscious, kills her by inanition and indecision, swimming away from her when their small boat overturns. Clyde's passive killing of Roberta and his subsequent vacillation over whether he is to blame create an indeterminacy about his motives, moral culpability, and legal responsibility in keeping with modernist skepticism about determining the nature of truth.

Farrell and Dos Passos present two sides of a naturalist panorama, with *Studs Lonigan* focusing on his protagonist's inner life in the context of ethnic tensions in Chicago's changing Irish-American neighborhoods and *U.S.A.* tracing events in US culture and world history through a handful of protagonists. Farrell's trilogy, which consists of *Young Lonigan* (1932), *The Young Manhood of Studs Lonigan* (1934), and *Judgment Day* (1935), follows William

j See Tim Prchal's "New Americans and the immigrant novel," chapter 25, 435. Andrew Hoberek also discusses Roth's novels in "The Jewish great American novel," chapter 54 in this volume.

k David Schmid calls *An American Tragedy* a "hybrid nonfiction novelistic text" in his discussion of the novel in "The nonfiction novel," chapter 59 in this volume, 988.

"Studs" Lonigan from 1916 until his death in the early years of the Depression. Like Crane's George Kelcey, Studs flees from the nagging religiosity of his home to the vitality of the streets. He gains there a perspective circumscribed by drinking and fighting, with the added complications of racial and ethnic hatred against African Americans and Jews. Studs falls into a long addiction to the city and its pleasures, with each bout of drinking, fighting, or sex being an attempt to stop feeling "trapped like a rat in a cage." His futility is epitomized by his abortive pursuit of Lucy Scanlan, who represents the "something more he wanted than the glory" of the football game that marks the high point of his life. "He wanted things, wanted something, wanted his luck to change," Studs reflects at one point, and, because he "couldn't stand this, he quickened his steps to get home and read the newspaper, listen to the radio, do anything to get those thoughts out of his head." If Clyde Griffiths's flaw is that he has absorbed socially approved aspirations, Studs's flaw is that he can articulate no aspirations at all.

Dos Passos uses not a single character but a dozen in *U.S.A.*, which consists of *The 42nd Parallel* (1930), *1919* (1932), and *The Big Money* (1936). Their stories are refracted through a series of biographies of American industrialists, idealists, and inventors; fifty-one stream-of-consciousness Camera Eye sequences reflecting the author's perspective; and sixty-eight newsreels that reproduce snippets of newspaper headlines, popular songs, current events, and catch phrases. The always apposite and often ironic juxtaposition of elements underscores Dos Passos's acerbic vision of the American dream. For example, the earnest, idealistic, and hardworking Mary French meets only sexual betrayal and failure in her relationships with men in the labor movement, but J. Ward Moorehouse, who marries the boss's daughter, and Margo Dowling, who, like Dreiser's Carrie Meeber, trades on her sexuality as a means to stardom, both succeed because of adaptability. Notwithstanding the modernist techniques of pastiche and stream of consciousness, *U.S.A.* is also naturalistic, not only in its accretion of mundane details but also in Dos Passos's recognition that individuals as well as governments and peoples are governed by forces and movements beyond their control. The limited choices that result from those constraints range from the repetitively stupid and individually self-destructive (recalling Trina McTeague's hoarding of gold or Studs Lonigan's sexual encounters) to the violent and widely destructive rage against an entire system, such as we see in the murder of Boots Smith in *The Street*, and, in *The Big Money*, the rigged trial and unjust execution of Sacco and Vanzetti, which also became the subject of Upton Sinclair's *Boston* (1928).[1]

Often dismissed as a short-lived blip on the radar screen of literary history, naturalism – or as I have been suggesting, naturalisms – constitute a sustained and nuanced approach to representing the pressures of cultural conditions, hereditary traits, historical forces, and environmental pressures on the human body. As Dos Passos, Farrell, Dreiser, and Roth demonstrate, the narrative methods of naturalism need not follow the conventional dictates of realism. Nor, as Phillips, Petry, and Dunbar show, do certain varieties of naturalism require abandoning social conscience in the service of accurate representation. Existing on the interstices – or, as Howard put it, the antinomies – between absolute determinism and humanistic free will, a belief in social progress and a scientific objectivity, and a shifting constellation of cultural criteria, naturalist novels share a set of defining interests, among them determinism, evolution, and materialism; plots of stasis, decline, and sexual selection; and themes of sexuality, atavism, addiction, and desire. Hovering above all is the threat of Norris's "terrible things," the turns of fortune or sudden bursts of violence that pervade naturalistic texts and make them, in all senses, "twisted from the ordinary."[26]

Notes

1. Stuart P. Sherman, "The Naturalism of Mr. Dreiser" (1915), 188–196, in *Documents of American Realism and Naturalism*, ed. Donald Pizer (Carbondale: Southern Illinois University Press, 1998), 192, 195, 194, 196.
2. Frank Norris to Isaac Frederick Marcosson, June 9, 1901, in *Frank Norris: Collected Letters*, ed. Jesse S. Crisler (San Francisco: Book Club of California, 1986), 160.
3. Theodore Dreiser, "True Art Speaks Plainly" (1903), 179–180, in Pizer, *Documents of American Realism and Naturalism*, 180. In an 1894 letter to Lily Brandon Munroe, Crane wrote, "Later I discovered that my creed was identical with the one of Howells . . . ." Stephen Crane to Lily Brandon Munroe, March–April 1894, 62–64, in *The Correspondence of Stephen Crane*, ed. Stanley Wertheim and Paul Sorrentino (New York: Columbia University Press, 1988), 1: 63.
4. Frank Norris, "Zola as a Romantic Writer" (1896), 1106–1108, in *Frank Norris: Novels and Essays*, ed. Donald Pizer (New York: Library of America, 1986), 1107.
5. June Howard, *Form and History in American Literary Naturalism* (Chapel Hill: University of North Carolina Press, 1985), 36, 40, 30.
6. Donald Pizer, *Realism and Naturalism in Nineteenth-Century American Literature*, rev. edn. (Carbondale: Southern Illinois University Press, 1984), 11, 12.

1 For a discussion of Dos Passos's modernist techniques in relation to forms of mass media, see Mark McGurl's essay in this volume (chapter 41, "The novel, mass culture, mass media," 689–690).

7. Howard, *Form and History*, 36, 40, 30.
8. For an explanation of the observer in naturalism that predates Howard's, see Georg Lukács's "Narrate or Describe?" in *Writer and Critic and Other Essays*, ed. and trans. Arthur Kahn (London: Merlin Press, 1970), 110–148.
9. See Howard's *Form and History* for a discussion of the spectator in naturalism. For Dreiser's debt to Freud, as well as to scientist Elmer Gates's theories of brain chemicals, see Louis J. Zanine, *Mechanism and Mysticism: The Influence of Science on the Thought and Work of Theodore Dreiser* (Philadelphia: University of Pennsylvania Press, 1993).
10. Charles Child Walcutt, *American Literary Naturalism, a Divided Stream.* (1956; Westport, CT: Greenwood Press, 1973).
11. Robert C. Bannister, *Social Darwinism: Science and Myth in Anglo-American Social Thought* (Philadelphia: Temple University Press, 1979); Herbert Spencer, *Social Statics: Or, the Conditions Essential to Human Happiness Specified, and the First of Them Developed* (1851; New York: D. Appleton and Company, 1890), 415.
12. Richard Lehan, *Realism and Naturalism: The Novel in an Age of Transition* (Madison: University of Wisconsin Press, 2005), 104.
13. Spencer, *Social Statics*, 446, 456, 482.
14. Carl N. Degler, *In Search of Human Nature: The Decline and Revival of Darwinism in American Social Thought* (New York: Oxford University Press, 1991), 14.
15. Lisa A. Long, "Genre Matters: Embodying American Literary Naturalism," *American Literary History* 19.1 (2007): 171. See also Elizabeth Ammons's call for an expanded definition of realism in *Conflicting Stories: American Women Writers at the Turn into the Twentieth Century* (Oxford: Oxford University Press, 1991). Kenneth Warren argues for the importance of considering race in realism in *Black and White Strangers: Race and American Literary Realism* (Chicago: University of Chicago Press, 1993).
16. The idea that man is a type of machine has a long history in naturalism. For an extended discussion, see Mark Seltzer's *Bodies and Machines* (New York: Routledge, 1992).
17. John Dudley, *A Man's Game: Masculinity and the Anti-Aesthetics of American Literary Naturalism* (Tuscaloosa: University of Alabama Press, 2004), 5. Theodore Roosevelt's essay "The Strenuous Life," originally given as a speech before the Hamilton Club in Chicago on April 10, 1899, endorsed not only the testing of masculinity in the West but military intervention in international affairs as a moral duty (*The Strenuous Life: Essays and Addresses* [New York: The Century, 1903], 1–21).
18. For the connections between masculinity and empire, see Amy Kaplan, *The Anarchy of Empire in the Making of U.S. Culture* (Cambridge, MA: Harvard University Press, 2002).
19. James R. Giles, "Assaulting the Yeehats: Violence and Space in the Call of the Wild," in *Twisted from the Ordinary: Essays on American Literary Naturalism*, ed. Mary E. Papke (Knoxville: University of Tennessee Press, 2003), 188–201, esp. 192.

20. See Walter Benn Michaels's influential reading of the distinction between the symbolic economy of paper and representation and the material significance of gold in *The Gold Standard and the Logic of Naturalism* (Berkeley: University of California Press, 1987). David Zimmerman discusses Michaels's theories of consumer capitalism in "Novels of American business, industry, and consumerism" chapter 24 in this volume, 422–423.
21. Jennifer Fleissner, *Women, Compulsion, Modernity: The Moment of American Naturalism* (Chicago: University of Chicago Press, 2004); Seltzer, *Bodies and Machines*, 98. For the "fallen woman" in naturalism, see Laura Hapke, *Girls Who Went Wrong: Prostitutes in American Fiction, 1885–1917* (Bowling Green, OH: Bowling Green State University Popular Press, 1989).
22. Fleissner, *Women, Compulsion, Modernity*, 9.
23. Bert Bender, *The Descent of Love: Darwin and the Theory of Sexual Selection in American Fiction, 1871–1926* (Philadelphia: University of Pennsylvania Press, 1996).
24. Donald Pizer, "American Naturalism in Its 'Perfected' State: *The Age of Innocence* and *An American Tragedy*," in *Edith Wharton: New Critical Essays*, ed. Alfred Bendixen and Annette Zilversmit (New York: Garland, 1992), 127–141. Jennifer Fleissner discusses *Susan Lenox* briefly in "Wharton, marriage, and the New Woman," chapter 27 in this volume, 464–465. On Wharton's *House of Mirth* and *Susan Lenox*, see also Donna M. Campbell, "The 'Bitter Taste' of Naturalism: Edith Wharton's *The House of Mirth* and David Graham Phillips's *Susan Lenox*," in *Twisted from the Ordinary: Essays on American Literary Naturalism*, ed. Mary E. Papke (Knoxville: University of Tennessee Press, 2003), 237–259.
25. Remarks" (1931), in *Theodore Dreiser: A Selection of Uncollected Prose*, ed. Donald Pizer (Detroit: Wayne State University Press (1977), 263–264. For Freud's influence on Dreiser, see Zanine, *Mechanism and Mysticism*; Ellen Moers, *Two Dreisers* (New York: Viking Press, 1969); Thomas P. Riggio, "The Dream Life of Theodore Dreiser," *Dreiser Studies* 28.2 (1997): 3–21; Frederic E. Rusch, "Dreiser's Introduction to Freudianism," *Dreiser Studies* 18.2 (1987): 34–38; and John Clendenning, "Desire and Regression in Dreiser's *An American Tragedy*," *Dreiser Studies* 25.2 (1994): 23–35.
26. Frank Norris, "Zola as a Romantic Writer," in *Frank Norris: Novels and Essays*, ed. Donald Pizer (New York: Literary Classics of the United States, 1986), 1106–1108, quotation at 1107.

31

Imagining the frontier

STEPHANIE LE MENAGER

When Wallace Stegner writes of Susan Burling Ward, the heroine of his magisterial Western novel, *Angle of Repose* (1971), "she knew it was a deficiency in herself that her imagination was so controlled by *things,*" he offers a key insight into frontier aesthetics. Like Susan, who "was often unable to get expressiveness and individuality into figures and faces" until she placed them in some setting, writers of the frontier tend to derive character, or even the category of the human, from landscape and spatial metaphor. Defined as "the line of most rapid and effective Americanization" by Frederick Jackson Turner,[1] the frontier has functioned as a grand spatial metaphor, the line between civilization and so-called savagery, Old World and New.[a] In the collective imaginings of the United States, the frontier has also functioned to separate the USA from global imperial history, marking it as an exceptional national experiment.

In the heyday of Euro-American Manifest Destiny, Henry David Thoreau defined the frontier as wherever we front a fact. While Thoreau appreciates the non-human aspects of the environment, including what we might call *things*, his gloss upon the frontier considers it as a problem of human imagination and cognition. Thoreau writes in *Walden* (1854) that to "stand right fronting and face to face with a fact" would be the equivalent of the sacrifice of the self to fact's "sweet edge"; fact is so radically unlike the self, in other words, that truly to comprehend a fact amounts to self-negation. Such confrontations with non-identity dramatize the frontier experience. The frontier, calcified by mid-twentieth-century historians and literary critics into a "grand obsession," in Annette Kolodny's wry

a In this volume, Timothy Sweet expands upon the relationship of the material facts of setting to foundational spatial metaphors in US literature, highlighting the troubling political potentiality that antebellum authors associated with "transitional" or incompletely settled, post-frontier landscapes ("American land, American landscape, American novels," chapter 5, 88–92).

phrase,[2] has figured complexly in North American fictions, where it functions as a means by which Euro-American writers remark and cannily evade recalcitrant facts, such as the presence of indigenous American nations and the aridity of lands west of the hundredth meridian.

If there is a single metanarrative that can be derived from the diverse iterations of frontier experience in US literature, it is that the frontier performs the settler culture's failure of thought, the paralysis of its imagination in the face of facts too threatening, experiences too rare. Like the sublime, the frontier could be described in terms of "the aestheticization of fear," although it also enacts, as I've suggested, a drama of thinking.[3] From the detailed scientific accounts of western lands by the US Army Corps of Topographical Engineers, to the blood and thunder sensationalism of the late Victorian dime novel and the senseless brutality of the anti-Western films of the 1960s, a tension between wonder and horror, thinking and the foreclosure of thinking in violence or ideology, marks the frontier as the site where facts shimmer temptingly but are never *fronted*.

The exceptional as failure of thought

The exception is by definition unique, theoretically outside of time. The frontier problem that Stegner identified as that of establishing "a continuing human pattern" in a "country that changes as fast as the West" has been solved by exceptionalist thinking. The exception is a happier name for aberration, a challenge to the essentially Victorian notion of history as meaning that accumulates in sequential layers, over time. Frederick Jackson Turner, the late Victorian historian who more than any single person might be called the creator of the frontier idea, was an advocate of presentism who recognized the frontier as a useable past because it could be severed from the complex skein of history – because it had *no place* in history.[4]

Appropriately, Turner's famous lecture, "The Significance of the Frontier in American History" (1893), was first delivered at the Chicago World's Fair, an exhibition highlighting the United States' exceptional position on the world stage. On a city lot adjacent to the fair, *Buffalo Bill's Wild West* show attracted fair-goers who recognized the West as informing the unique civilization represented only partially by the *beaux-arts* "White City" within the fairgrounds. American exceptionalism showed itself more readily in the upstart city of Chicago, a former frontier trading post that within half a century had become the nation's railroad hub, home to the Board of Trade that Frank Norris takes as a metaphor for modern *anomie* in *The Pit: A Story of Chicago*

(1903) and whose commodification of life is more brutally enacted in the slaughterhouses of Upton Sinclair's muckraking *The Jungle* (1906). *The Pit* and *The Jungle* are novels of industrial frontierism, indicative of the close and vexed relation between the frontier and modernity. Stephen Crane's turn-of-the-century short stories "The Blue Hotel" (1899) and "The Bride Comes to Yellow Sky" (1898) similarly offer up "modern" frontier towns crowded with urban drummers and factory-made Western costume. As the so-called gateway to the West, Chicago encapsulated such awkward juxtapositions. It was, in the later nineteenth century, world capitalism's raw edge.

Chicago, Buffalo Bill, the frontier, and the fair delivered complementary performances of the United States' distinctiveness. Each promoted the argument that America represented the new, but this rupture with history that marked international modernist sensibility was cast, in the US context, as an improbably future-oriented primitivism. Turner describes frontier time in terms of the "recurrence of the process of evolution," "a return to primitive conditions," "continually beginning over again."[5] The germ of this frontier thesis already was present in American letters as early as the seventeenth century, in captivity narratives such as Mary Rowlandson's *The Sovereignty and Goodness of God* (1682), wherein the settler culture strengthens itself by surviving abduction and torture at the hands of indigenous "savages" in the New World wilderness.

The repeating process of regression and regeneration signified in the term "frontier" is complemented by the fantasy of a vast interior space to be settled, what Henry Nash Smith described as the Edenic West's "virgin land."[6] Turner would argue that there were no "growing peoples" in the way of US settlement, and by this logic, the nations of Native America could be justifiably eliminated. Theodore Roosevelt's multi-volume epic *The Winning of the West* (1889–1896), in close dialogue with Turner, places the conquering of American Indian nations at the foundation of the nationalizing movement that came to be known as Progressivism. Those who warred against Native Americans saw their efforts as spurring social evolution rather than making history, because they saw the so-called Indians as pre-historical. Unlike Roosevelt, Turner scarcely mentions the Indian Wars, absorbing them in the vaguer necessity of mastering an anonymous forcefield that he calls "the wilderness" or "the environment."[7] The frontier thesis – hence the American thesis – gains much of its symbolic potency by association not with history but with the a-historical concept of nature.

James Fenimore Cooper, who has been recognized as the figure who put into play the conventions of thought that Turner would later conceptualize as "the frontier," had a more difficult time than Turner in representing North America as divorced from world history. Sandra M. Gustafson's careful reading of Cooper's *oeuvre* in this volume argues that a proto-cosmopolitan "worlding" of US national narrative can be discovered in Cooper's fictions of early national frontiers.[b] Yet Cooper's meticulous pursuit in the 1820s to 1840s of a set of key terms by which to describe US national culture facilitated the economy of style that characterizes later and more ideologically foreclosed frontier representation.[8] Cooper's genre, the historical novel, promised, like the frontier thesis, to create a useable past, but the historical novel also demanded complicated and credible depictions of specific contexts – Cooper 's concern with the latter feature of the genre makes him sometimes more interesting than those we might consider his successors.[c] The first three novels of Cooper's Leatherstocking series nonetheless do what historical novels in the tradition of Sir Walter Scott typically do, which is to restage a historical drama in such a way as to resolve contemporary cultural anxieties contingent upon that earlier conflict.

The first novel in the Leatherstocking series, *The Pioneers* (1823), is a post-frontier text insofar as it describes the development of a thinly disguised Cooperstown, New York, one generation after settlement by Europeans. In its emphasis on the rise of a democratic, if mercenary, US community in the wake of the colonial culture of the Dutch patroons, this novel uses beginnings to disguise endings in a way that Philip Fisher recognizes as prevalent in frontier narratives from the era of Jacksonian Indian Removal.[9] Even in the 1820s, prior to Removal, it had become possible to visualize a future that included the near-total destruction of Native America, and artists within the settler culture scrambled to capture this sweeping violence as their own origin story, less a genocide than a birth. In *The Pioneers*, Oliver Edwards, who throughout much of the novel is mistaken for a "half-breed," inherits the extensive land rights of the town's aging baron, Judge Temple. Though Edwards turns out to be white, his performance as half-Indian still covers the problem of Native American disenfranchisement that also troubles Cooper, most famously in his sentimental depiction of the death of the sachem Chingachgook.

b Sandra Gustafson, "Cooper and the idea of the Indian," chapter 6.

c Winfried Fluck remarks in this volume that "historical novels . . . aim at a reality-effect produced by claims of accuracy in historical reference and verisimilitude in the description of customs and locales" ("The nineteenth-century historical novel," chapter 7, 122).

The urgency of rendering an ending as a beginning, for the purpose of nation-building, suggests one practical use of the repeating time scheme of Turner's frontier; "continually beginning over again" makes little room for unhappy conclusions, tilting national time ever forward. (That Mark Twain misnames Chingachgook "Chicago" in his 1895 essay "Fenimore Cooper's Literary Offenses" points to a remarkably dynamic play amongst frontier icons, in which the old/defunct can immediately summon the raw and the new.) However, Cooper, unlike later writers, elaborates upon the more traditional, Anglo-European definition of the frontier as a specific term of war, "the front line of an advancing army."[10] This military-historical recognition of the frontier figures prominently in the second Leatherstocking novel, *The Last of the Mohicans* (1826), where Cooper declares in his very first sentence that "the colonial wars of North America" are his pre-eminent topic. As Russ Castronovo suggests elsewhere in this volume, Cooper's relegation of frontier warfare to the colonial period also serves the purpose of "gentrifying" nineteenth-century US imperialism.[d] The final two novels in the Leatherstocking series, *The Pathfinder* (1840) and *The Deerslayer* (1841), return to colonial conflict with a symbolic economy made possible by their time of composition, near the conclusion of Jacksonian Removal and the wider visibility of US military triumph which would receive the name of "Manifest Destiny." Turning toward violence as the primary structuring agent of culture, Cooper hypothesized a distinctly American theory of identity that would be played out in the stripped-down, stylized genre of the Western.

Cooper's frontier novels are troubled by domestic arrangements in a way that many Westerns are not. He struggles awkwardly to reconcile marriage, and its promise of cultural continuity through time, to the disruption of continuity sought in war. Cooper typically rules out the possibility of marriage between enemies in, for example, the failed romance of Cora and Uncas in *The Last of the Mohicans*. Yet he allows for a range of homosocial and even homoerotic relationships among warring races.[e] Consider his narrative of the Pawnee Hard Heart's "adoption" of Natty Bumppo as his fictive father in the third Leatherstocking novel, *The Prairie* (1827).[11] The scout's entrance into the Pawnee family makes possible a death scene at the conclusion of *The Prairie* where Native and European America come together to agree upon a nonviolent historical succession. "Go, my children," intones a Pawnee elder to the youth. "Remember the just chief of the palefaces, and clear your own

d Russ Castronovo, "Imperialism, Orientalism, and empire," chapter 32, 538.
e See Gustafson in this volume, chapter 6.

tracks from briars!" In its fantasies of conquest as a tacit agreement between rising and dying nations, as in its fantasies of the settler becoming "native" without reproductive sex or the crossing of blood, the Leatherstocking series betrays the deep wishes and fears of a settler culture faced with unthinkable facts, such as its own violence.

The desire to think outside of history is most fully satisfied by Cooper in the exceptional figure of the scout Leatherstocking. This legendary character, also known as Hawkeye, Natty Bumppo, and the Deerslayer, made conventional the American exception to world history – the nation's so-called natural conquest. The scout is the white pathfinder so versed in Native "gifts" that with the noninvasive skill of a surgeon he opens the North American continent for the settler culture.[12] Natty Bumppo, Kit Carson, Buffalo Bill Cody, and Wild Bill Hickock were all scouts, and susceptible to similar fictional treatment. In De Witt Peters's *The Life and Adventures of Kit Carson, the Nestor of the Rocky Mountains* (1858), Carson appears as part of an "almost extinct race" to which Euro-Americans owe an unspeakable debt. The scout performs advance work in the contact zone on behalf of the American experiment, and he does it in such a way as to suggest that cultural transgressions such as miscegenation or murder have been unique sacrifices enacted by extraordinary individuals. The scout thus absorbed the unassimilable experiences of first contact for the settlement culture, becoming the convenient repository and mask of its collective trauma.

"US settlement culture" is a term of art that refers to the culture of Euro-Americans who settled or, more bluntly, who colonized North America. Historians once referred to these settlers as "pioneers" or simply Americans. In fact, US settlement culture was far from homogeneous. It was at once postcolonial and imperialistic, fretful and aggressive, a fledgling nation an ocean away from Europe and eager to expand still farther from metropolitan London.[13] The grand gesture of the Louisiana Purchase by Thomas Jefferson that could be said to have birthed the idea of the American West was an unconstitutional gamble; Jefferson had only the sketchiest sense of the limits of the territory that he had bought from Napoleon. The Purchase opened a space of combined desire and mystery. As Washington Irving acknowledges in his *Tour on the Prairies* (1835), arguably the first narrative to showcase the misadventures of "the tenderfoot," Euro-American bodies were overwhelmed in the undefined – unthinkable – spaces beyond the so-called jumping-off towns of Missouri. Irving depicts his own traveling party as a ship of fools, objects of Native "comic humor and dry satire." It is interesting to speculate upon what would have become of the frontier idea if the comic had remained the settlement culture's preferred mode of self-representation, but few western travelers maintained Irving's equanimity.

More typically, the settlers' debility produced compensatory theories of racial mastery. Francis Parkman's evolutionary framing of westward migration in *The Oregon Trail* (1849) provides a clear example of how Euro-American weakness could bear an inverse relationship to boasts of continental mastery. Parkman acknowledges his virtual emasculation in the oceanic landscape of the Plains, where he often traveled while half-blind and diarrheic. At the same time, he imposes himself upon an Oglallah village, callously remarks its poverty, and proceeds to measure "the position of Indians among the races of men."[14] Parkman's grandiosity can be attributed to a post-regional rather than postcolonial problem. He was a Harvard man come west for his health, unwittingly speaking for the waning of New England as a cultural force and the manner in which this regional loss could be recouped by transforming oneself into a Westerner.

Perhaps the most famous elaboration of the frontier as therapy for northeastern regional malaise is Owen Wister's novel *The Virginian, a Horseman of the Plains* (1902). The renowned physician and novelist S. Weir Mitchell prescribed Wyoming as a cure for Wister's chronic illness,[f] and as Wister wrote to his mother, the great West struck him "like Genesis," inspiring a personal rebirth far from the oppression of an unwanted business career and the niceties of Philadelphia manners.[15] The hijinks of cowboys in the bunkhouse reminded Wister of his Harvard fraternity, except that the cowboys' rough play need not be identified with a finite or feckless adolescence. "The cow-puncher's ungoverned hours did not unman him," Wister asserts in his first preface to *The Virginian*, citing Wall Street and Newport, his social milieux, as antagonists to a ludic masculinity grounded in the "chance to live and play as [you] would like." An anachronism and, of course, an exception, the cowboy represents a "brief epoch" and "complete picture," the beloved if not entirely assimilable supplement to the industrial modernity Wister recognizes as *his* time. *The Virginian* offers essentially two kinds of commentary on modernity: first, there is the novel's manifest plot of upward mobility, wherein the cowboy becomes a corporate rancher and coal baron; second, there are the novel's highly visual, filmic moments, where the sequential progression of plot is abandoned to the pure pleasure of dwelling

f Elizabeth Young's discussion of S. Weir Mitchell in this volume offers rich contexts for this frontier remedy in Mitchell's fictional response to Civil War injuries to the male body and in his experiments with rest cures for female hysteria ("Supernatural novels," chapter 13, 226).

upon charismatic images. Taken together, these narrative modes suggest the restructuring of everyday life into labor-time and leisure-time, with leisure, like a new frontier, offering a safety-valve for men who felt themselves diminished by increasingly efficient bureaucratic regimes.

Wister's snapshots of the cowboy, framed by the window of a Pullman car or by the gaze of his Eastern dude narrator, prepare the way for numerous cinematic cowboys whose comfortable masculinity pleased moviegoers through the mid-twentieth century. Described as "a slim young giant, more beautiful than pictures" with "the cartridge belt that slanted across his hips" suggesting phallic danger counter-balanced against the almost feminine "face" that "shone . . . as . . . ripe peaches," the Virginian is unveiled for scopophilic pleasure. As surrogate viewer, the dude eagerly imagines himself the cowboy's "bride." Such homoerotic desire is divorced from the sexual acts that could not be spoken in Victorian fiction.[16] As Annie Proulx would write almost a century later in the most fully realized gay Western, "Brokeback Mountain" (1999), "there was some open space between what he knew and what he tried to believe." Wister's final, oblique reference to the Virginian's marriage, that he proved "able to give his wife all and more than she asked or desired," is perhaps as close as he comes to talking about sex, and yet the desired object referred to here is money.

What strikes many contemporary readers as wrong with *The Virginian* is precisely its interest in production, its complicity with the industrialization of agriculture and the subordination of the everyday to corporate structures that are supposed to be antitheses of frontier primitivism. The hero's willingness to lynch his former best friend and potential lover, Steve, as a rustler, suggests a stark betrayal of the little man for the comforts of corporate patronage. The lynching also raises specters of the Jim Crow South, the Virginian's birthplace, that are typically banished from frontier narrative. Finally, the novel's complete denial of Native American history, as Louis Owens has argued, robs it of even the mythic resource of "the Indian," the figure who informs the anarchic tendencies of the fictional cowboy.[17] Yet these disappointments also reveal what Jane Tompkins has called "the cost of being a [Western] hero" (in her view, the repudiation of the man you love) and the strange kinship of American exceptionalism to the modernization of time and affect.[18]

Popular and frontier affects

What did the frontier feel like? Many scholars see this as an ideological question. Patricia Nelson Limerick critiques the "persistently happy affect" of the frontier, arguing that "in popular culture it carries ... a tone of adventure, heroism, and even fun" and denies "the sometimes bloody and brutal realities of conquest."[19] Bret Harte's depictions of the mining frontier in widely read short stories such as "The Luck of Roaring Camp" (1868) indicate a relatively early refusal of the facts of conquest in favor of the popular sentimental mode of the Victorian era. In the twentieth century, the simply structured, rhythmic prose and triumphant Euro-American survivalism that mark the fiction of Louis L'Amour, who with over one hundred published novels remains the master of the "popular" frontier, seem to confirm Limerick's accusation. Yet even within L'Amour's *Hondo* (1953), his novelization of a film starring John Wayne and the basis for a 1960s television series, thematic iterations of sexual loneliness, the injury wrought upon Native nations, and the urgency of environmental stewardship suggest defiant counternarratives and uncomfortable emotional registers. Theorists of popular culture would caution us not to conceive of a single frontier affect disseminated or imposed by the forms of industrial leisure.[20] Modern technological innovations in printing, film, and television have offered specific structures, if not specific feelings, to consumers of the frontier.

It could be argued that the frontier was born on the back of industrial popular culture, as the arts began to sift into "high" and "low" forms and toward distinct classes of audience in the later decades of the nineteenth century.[g] Bill Brown implies as much in his study of the dime Western, noting that mid-nineteenth-century technologies such as the steam-powered cylinder press and the interstate railroad networks made it possible for the New York publishing house of Beadle, home to the famous *Deadwood Dick* series, to hold a standing order of 60,000 copies for any new novel.[21] As reading in the 1860s became a "genuine act of consumption," in Brown's terms, publishers perfected the marketing strategy of the series, wherein novelty is promised within a familiar horizon of expectation.[22] The tempo of heightened expectation and predictable, comforting resolution structures series as well as individual texts within series. As sensational novels, series Westerns generally seek to heighten arousal, generating and releasing tension through frenetic repetition of crises and denouements.

Brown, Michael Denning, and others have written of the anarchic appeal of dime fiction to working-class readers, the capacity of such fiction to model a

g Nancy Glazener's "The novel in postbellum print culture," chapter 20 in this volume, addresses the sometimes oversimplified notion of mass culture to delineate the varied ways in which forms of production and distribution proved constitutive of the novel from the late nineteenth through the twentieth centuries. See also Ronald J. Zboray and Mary Saracino Zboray, "The novel in the antebellum book market," chapter 4.

healthy rage against the new managerial class that sought to define US manhood in the Progressive era.[23] Yet it is impossible to approach the dime Western without confronting the recurrent figure of rape, white women humiliated, tied to trees, and stripped by the same male outlaws and Indians who might also represent the critical consciousness of the working class. Why female victimization should figure as surrogate or appeasement to male rage involves questions larger than the dime Western. Yet the dime Western's utilization of male rage and female terror offers insights into the fragile hegemony of American exceptionalism. Ideologies could be sustained and undone in a dynamic popular culture where, in Shelley Streeby's terms,[24] "cheap literature responded to and shaped changing configurations of gender, race, and sexuality."[h]

In the first installment of the Deadwood Dick series, *Deadwood Dick, The Prince of the Road* (1877), we encounter a female victim, improbably "stripped to the waist" by the Lakota leader Sitting Bull. This woman is rescued by the white outlaw Fearless Frank before she can be penetrated by "the fiend incarnate" who tied her; the rescue is so prompt and the violation so incomplete that the scene acts as a kind of ideological candy. Whether a sign of the settler culture's impenetrability at the time of the Great Sioux War or a plug for masculine outlawry in a year of brutal corporate retaliation against striking railroad workers, the (white, working-class male) consumer's satisfaction appears guaranteed. In the denouement of this single episode, at least, the frontier maintains a happy affect. A later dime novel, *Saved by Buffalo Bill! From the Ghost Dancers, Wild Indians of the Dakotas!* (1892), offers a similar scene of female ravishment and male heroism. Though the Buffalo Bill novel appears in a series unrelated to *Deadwood Dick*, their distinct treatments of a stock scene engaging the figure of Sitting Bull betray the complexity of the dime novel's relation to settlement history. The cover art for the later novel features a white woman tied to a tree, with one breast peeking out from beneath a ragged Indian blanket. We will learn that this image depicts "the horrible condition in which Buffalo Bill found the lovely and refined Pauline. The sight unmanned him for a moment, but only for a moment." To be unmanned "only for a moment" represents a peculiar pleasure of Western serial fiction. However, in *Saved by Buffalo Bill!*, there are specters other than castration. There are the Ghost Dancers who have kidnapped Pauline, and more importantly, there is Sitting Bull, who has been assassinated by the Pawnee police because Buffalo Bill arrived in the Dakota Territory too late to save him.

h Shelley Streeby, "Dime novels and the rise of mass market genres," chapter 35, 593.

While Sitting Bull's real-life murder is recounted with relative accuracy, the many melodramatic episodes that structure the novel distract from this central, unhealable wound: Buffalo Bill failed to rescue the Indian man he loved. "Colonel Cody would have brought Sitting Bull in safely, quietly, and without bloodshed without war and without fuss and boasting." The unpunctuated, paratactic list-structure of this sentence that names all of the elements which would *not* have been present had Cody arrived in time serves to underline how the scene is in fact crowded with these same elements: bloodshed, war, fuss, boasting, noise, danger. "Contemptible enem[ies]," including bureaucratic Indian agents and corrupt army officers out to win "brevet grades," are to blame. Cody, poised against the institutions of military-industrial capitalism, "has always been the Indians' friend" and had he been Commissioner of Indian Affairs "we venture to predict that within a very few years the Indians would become American citizens voting and doing their full part for civilization and progress." Here are many shades of frontier affect: guilt, shame, despair at what might have been but what can never be, even though Buffalo Bill utilized all of the precise tools of industrial modernity ("the empress steamer," "the train for Chicago") to get to Dakota in time. While it is impossible to know what readers in 1892 felt, the ironically titled *Saved by Buffalo Bill!* telegraphs a problem about progress, and a desire to bring back the frontier so that it might be done over, and better, without the blood and noise. The ravished Pauline represents a female sexual vulnerability that stimulates masculine aspiration.

The new opportunities for violence and heroism offered by the ravished woman suggest, too, a rehearsal for what William Handley has characterized as the movement of frontier violence away from the externalized "meeting place of savagery and civilization" into the domestic space of the family in twentieth-century Western fiction.[25] Zane Grey's novel *Riders of the Purple Sage* (1912), hailed as "the most famous of all Western novels,"[26] brings the problem of sexual violence together with a historical border war in a turgid, imperfectly resolved plot that signals the twentieth-century Western's inward turn. Grey's male protagonists, the gunslinger Lassiter and the "rider" Venters, prove equally incapable of living through the cultural conflicts that characterized Mormon–Gentile relations in southern Utah in 1871, the novel's setting. Each male protagonist opts to leave "this wild country" for a safe haven, for Venters the "great world" and for Lassiter the secluded Surprise Valley, which is far removed from the social complexities of cultural contact and indeed, of the historical novel itself. Yet the "mad" sexual jealousies ascribed to the male and female principals (whose coupling imperfectly concludes Grey's story) presage psycho-sexual conflicts of the future. *Riders* plays out these conflicts with polygamous Mormons, who are uniquely unassimilable frontier figures. But absent such conveniently polarizing villains, such conflicts eventually define the Western's version of modern heterosexuality. As Freudian psychology began to leak into US public consciousness in the early twentieth century, heterosexuality itself approaches the status of a final frontier or unconquerable, self-annihilating fact.

In more restrained prose that marks a transition within the formally ambitious twentieth-century Western toward the sparer style of Hemingway, Willa Cather charts the social and sexual jealousies within small, post-frontier communities in her Great Plains novels *O Pioneers!* (1913), *My Ántonia* (1918), and *A Lost Lady* (1923). Cather also demonstrates the desire to redo conquest from the point of view of women and intellectuals who must go on living with their regret about what might have been – figures such as Jim Burden in *My Ántonia* and Professor Godfrey St. Peter in *The Professor's House* (1925) forecast the (literal) burden of revisionist Western historians in the later twentieth century. The psychological Western receives its most extraordinary elaborations on film, as in John Ford's classic *The Searchers* (1956), with its plot of interracial rape, revenge, and reintegration into the settler homestead. The film's brilliant riff upon the original frontier genre, the captivity narrative, reveals the apparent refuge of the white, patriarchal home as a site of danger that competes with the externalized wilderness. Here what Herman Melville theorized as "the metaphysics of Indian-hating" in his *The Confidence-Man* (1856) links tellingly to the settler's loss of self-mastery. *The Searchers* predicts the birth of the anti-Westerns of the 1960s and 1970s, films which Will Wright defines as essentially parodic insofar as they exaggerate the plots and aesthetics of earlier Westerns.[27] Directors such as Sergio Leone and Sam Peckinpah recovered the impact of the once-naturalized violence at the core of frontier ideology through a new visual vocabulary of shock.[28]

The anti-Western novel developed concurrently alongside the great anti-Western films. Larry McMurtry, a prolific screenwriter and a novelist, has shown more eloquently than any author of Western "bestsellers" how the popular novel can rethink and debunk the Old West in terms similar to the revisionist project begun in the 1980s under the now familiar name of the New Western History. McMurtry's best early novels, such as *Horseman, Pass By* (1961), basis for the film *Hud* (1963), and *The Last Picture Show* (1966), made the fictional Thalia, Texas, the site of an aestheticized disappointment. In the sparely written, deliberately narrow settings of these novels, "the beautiful thing" almost never comes and the power of the hot, dry land lies precisely in its withholding of answers to human desire. Oil riches may flow into the coffers of ragged cowboys and farmers, but these fluid monies separate human effort from value, confirming the reign of dumb luck and the equal worth of Thalia's two favorite past-times, "readin' the Bible" and "jackin' off." As Lois Farrow remarks in *The Last Picture Show*, "everything's flat and empty, and there's nothing to do but spend money." Lois's observations prophesy the radical acts of consumerism and renunciation that structure *Texasville* (1987) and *Duane's Depressed* (1999), the second and third novels in McMurtry's *Last Picture Show* trilogy.

McMurtry's morally bleak New West erupts in everyday violence, from child molestation to murder, that receives a deep history in his epic novel of the waning frontier of the 1880s, *Lonesome Dove* (1985). The popular complement to Cormac McCarthy's challenging revisionist novel *Blood Meridian* (1985), published in the same year, *Lonesome Dove* offers a comic pastiche of Western narrative forms and intertextual reference, including captivity narratives, cattle drives, naïve sheriffs, Sioux Wars, the Comanche slave trade, Mexican border lore, and Western "town stories" of gamblers and whores. The lynching of Jake Spoon by his old friends, the Texas Rangers Gus McCrae and Woodrow Call, recalls the lynching of the rustler Steve by his friend "Jeff" in Wister's *The Virginian* (1902); Gus's (and McMurtry's) language play suggests Twain's anti-referential slang in *Roughing It* (1872); Captain Call's refusal "to use names for females" points to the blockage of male speech and female agency in mid twentieth-century Western film and even to the woodenness of Cooper's women, who Twain disdainfully noted were described by the generic moniker, "females." Ideological readings of *Lonesome Dove* tend to settle around a point made midway through the novel by Gus McCrae, who is arguably the primary focalizing subject, that "everything we done [settling the frontier] was probably a mistake." The US public's enthusiasm for this essentially anti-imperialist critique, which swelled after *Lonesome Dove* became a television mini-series in 1989, can be credited to McMurtry's consistently avuncular, even Reaganesque, narrative tone. In addition, his rich scatological humor and reiteration of Gus's "favorite subject," marriage, insure that *Lonesome Dove* returns to the generic conventions of comedy.

A savvy footnote to the late twentieth-century moment of the anti-Western, Sherman Alexie's short story "Dear John Wayne" (2000) furthers the deconstruction of the Old West and the cowboy persona with a fictional account of John Wayne's breakdown on the set of *The Searchers*. Alexie's "John Wayne" eagerly confides his real name, Marion Morrison, and his fear of horses to a Spokane extra with whom he falls in love. Weeping in the arms of an Indian, John Wayne embraces the opportunity that many frontier heroes recognize as irrevocably lost. A Spokane / Coeur d'Alene author, Alexie signals his distance from the tradition of the settlement culture primarily by the fact that in his story John Wayne is not the rescuer. Generously, Alexie allows Wayne to desire surrender to an Indian woman. The desire to be overwhelmed, by pleasure or death, may be the most foundational and taboo of frontier affects.

The return of unassimilable facts

Three years before he died in 1910, Mark Twain published a short story in *Harper's* in which the inevitable fact of death offers a keen critique of frontier ideology. Twain's "Extract from Captain Stormfield's Visit to Heaven" (1907) represents the misadventures of a dead Mississippi River pilot in a Heaven that replicates the contours of the known world at a grossly magnified scale, such that this Heaven–Earth holds all peoples who have lived throughout time. Twain's Heaven deflates Turner's idea of the United States as "the land which has no history." Since Heaven contains all time, it contains world histories that demystify the so-called natural conquest of North America by the United States. Stormfield complains, "I notice that I hardly ever see a white angel; where I run across one white angel, I strike as many copper-colored ones – people that can't speak English." The waves of colonial warfare indicated by so many "copper" angels, proof that "America was occupied a billion years and more, by Injuns and Aztecs," form only part of the captain's history lesson. Heaven also refutes the bold future-orientation built into US nationhood as "continually beginning over again" by previewing the diminishment of Euro-American global prominence for eternity. The future of the future of humanity will be non-English-speaking, and brown.

Twain's satiric send-up of frontierist regeneration in this story indicates his broad anti-imperialist commitments by the early twentieth century, but the tale (which he began nearly forty years earlier, in 1868) also designates the American West as the United States' point of entrance into world imperial conflict. California, site of the most complete genocide of Native America, is singled out as an especially bad district of Heaven "for whites": "it swarms with a mean kind of leather-headed mud-colored angels." These mud angels offer a spectral return of the California Paiutes whom Twain degradingly labeled "the despised Digger Indians of California" in his western memoir

Roughing It (1872).[29] Unlike "Heaven," the California and Nevada of *Roughing It* don't predict postcolonial revenge. These imagined territories do suggest the unstable reality of the mining frontier that Twain joined in the 1860s – and the difficulty of finding the words to capture such a frontier when it is in the process of booming.

Gavin Jones and other scholars have noted how western slang destabilizes US national realities in *Roughing It*, a problem signaled in the assaults of an "uneasy" Dictionary of Standard English that literally bruises Twain and his fellow emigrants as they travel overland by stage.[30] The dictionary's inability to sit still with the travelers' other baggage proves prescient, as "slang was the language of Nevada," Twain's destination, where "such phrases as 'You bet!' 'Oh no, I reckon not!' 'No Irish need apply,' and a hundred others, became so common as to fall from the lips of a speaker unconsciously . . . and consequently failed to mean anything."[31] The booming of a mining town results in an instantly urban culture where regional and international argots compete with each other. Moreover, tall tales and lies printed in local newspapers to trump up mining stock fuel the boom, such that the public is fed on wonders unmoored from the ores in the ground.

Twain's frontier illustrates the idea that language is disarticulated from fact and sets its own standard of value. Such a revelation would have been rather stunning in the era of US realism, when William Dean Howells urged that the novelist might craft reality itself through "detailed, careful, distanced observation," as Michael Elliott argues in this volume.[i] Twain's fictive memoirs of the far West are among his most stridently anti-realist efforts. In them he foregrounds the incongruities that inform his humor, he breaks his narrative frame with unabashedly insincere asides, and he revels in the fractured temporality of the same slapdash, episodic structures that can be seen as formal weaknesses in his Mississippi River novels, which attempt a more deliberate coherence. In a sense Twain pushes the frontier idea's rupture with history and realism to a radical conclusion, such that it breaks upon its own semantic logic.

The kinship that critics have noted between Twain and the contemporary author Cormac McCarthy typically begins in a discussion of McCarthy's *Blood Meridian, or the Evening Redness in the West* (1985), which has been widely considered as a definitive treatment of the frontier idea. Susan Kollin describes

i See Michael Elliott (291) and throughout "Realism and radicalism: the school of Howells," chapter 17.

McCarthy's protagonist in this novel, the fourteen-year-old "kid" who travels from Tennessee into Texas and Mexico in the 1840s, as "a corrupted reversal of Huck Finn."[32] This child who is nearly immune to both conscience and wonder betrays the brutality of a westering settler culture that was also mindless and adolescent. Like Twain, McCarthy began conceiving the American project through Southern regionalism, which grants him recourse to the grotesque and to a stylization of talk that has its roots in Mississippi Valley humorists like Johnson Jones Hooper, creator of the frontier trickster "Simon Suggs."[j]

Blood Meridian has been described as both a parody and a satire of the traditional Western. The novel can be seen as an anti-Western that plays with recognizable formulae of the genre, such as the male protagonist's pursuit of self-realization in the vast open spaces of the West, while at the same time undermining such tropes by embedding them within the violent history of global imperialism. The keen awareness of international history that informs *Blood Meridian* makes it an apt successor to *Moby-Dick* (1851), where the necessarily global oceans invite the US imagination beyond oppositional self-making. McCarthy's kid travels in the company of white supremacist filibusterers and, later, with mercenary scalp-hunters who wantonly murder Mexican villagers to increase their bounties. In a world where peaceful Mexicans can be passed off as "Apaches," the Anglo frontiersman also loses authenticity. Here cowboys are "violent children orphaned by war"; war disrupts the possibility of culture at the edges of US colonization and covers the "despair" motivating imperial desire. McCarthy's riders head toward a "naked horizon," an uncertain boundary suggestive of the postmodern disavowal of all epistemological horizons, those metanarratives that frame experience.[k] In *Blood Meridian*, there is no faith in providential destiny, nor even a stable point of origin from which to measure human progress. The novel's crisis of faith is so acute that we might question whether it can function

j To a degree, Suggs's savvy suggests the cosmopolitan competency that Tom Lutz broadly attributes to the American regional imagination of the late nineteenth and twentieth centuries in "Cather and the regional imagination," in this volume (chapter 26). For a reading of *Blood Meridian* focused on its borderland themes, see Ramón Saldívar's essay in this volume (chapter 62, "The American borderlands novel"). For more on the hoaxes and exaggerations Twain published as a Nevada Territory journalist, see Andrew Lawson, "Twain, class, and the Gilded Age" chapter 21 in this volume, esp. 366–367.

k For a complete account of the deployment of theories of postmodernity within the novel, see Ursula Heise, "Postmodern novels," chapter 58 in this volume.

effectively as parody or satire, since both genres depend upon implicit norms to ground their imitative play.

Each novel in McCarthy's *The Border Trilogy* mourns some foundational source of value which might restore the frontier to moral significance: in *All the Pretty Horses* (1992) the lost source of value is cattle ranching, in *The Crossing* (1994) it is an older nature, a pre-human wildness, and in *Cities of the Plain* (1998) it is an Edenic sex untainted by the commercial exploitation that marks twentieth-century border cultures. Kollin describes *The Border Trilogy* as "end-of-the-West" novels, nostalgic elaborations of the dying Western genre.

Throughout *The Border Trilogy* the figure of the red sun, receding beyond the horizon, naturalizes the waning of the West as a site of cultural importance. At the conclusion of *All the Pretty Horses*, for example, the hero, John Grady Cole, rides through an industrial Texas where "there were few cattle ... because it was barren country indeed yet he came at evening upon a solitary bull rolling in the dust against the bloodred sunset like an animal in sacrificial torment." This blood-red sun acts as the objective correlative to piercing grief for an apparently exceptional human experiment that has ended or become decadent. It is as if in moving farther from Southern regionalism toward the Western in *The Border Trilogy*, McCarthy tamed his historical consciousness. *Blood Meridian* wildly burlesqued nostalgia for the Old West. The earlier novel shows us the same sun that sets upon John Grady Cole rising upon the project of US nationhood in the 1840s and 1850s, rising "out of nothing like a great red phallus until it cleared the unseen rim and sat squat and pulsing and malevolent." Here nature loses its common function as legitimizing figural ground. *Blood Meridian* reassembles the Western back into the starker historical definition of the frontier as the front line of (colonial) war that Cooper posed as American literature's original problem. But one would have to live through the great wars of the twentieth century, particularly Vietnam, to propose a malevolent penis as metaphor for the culture's horizon of meaning.[33]

What appears as the diminishment of meaning in the Anglo-European frontier tradition as it culminates in Cormac McCarthy has been re-evaluated in twentieth- and twenty-first-century Native American and Latino/a literatures. Ramón Saldívar notes that Native and Latino/a authors experiment with an anti-dualistic "border thinking" that aspires to the decolonization of knowledge.[1] McCarthy's Western novels, located at the US/Mexico border, also embrace such challenging border thought. Yet McCarthy's aestheticization of

1 Saldívar, chapter 62, 1040.

frontier violence has proven ethically muddy in a way that Native and Latino/a authors' more direct indictments of dispossession and genocide have not.

In her now classic *Borderlands/La Frontera* (1987), Gloria Anzaldúa defines a borderland as "a vague and undetermined place created by the emotional residue of an unnatural boundary." Anzaldúa offers an eloquent alternative to the frontier thesis that rejects Turner's spatial fantasy of a west-facing "line" for the more anthropologically sound concept of the contact zone, where the USA and Mexico uncomfortably intermingle – economically, culturally. Anzaldúa's revision away from US westward expansion toward expansion into the hemispheric South reflects contemporary imperial realities, but her emphasis on the psychological experience of the borderlands is certainly applicable to Western American history.[m] She describes her project as an attempt to think through the "blocks" imposed by more traditional and US-centered modes of frontier imagining. *La Frontera* dramatizes the struggle of an autobiographical speaker deemed impossible by the frontier thesis, a queer/mestiza who holds within herself the contradictory forces of "the line." "Every step forward is a *travesia*, a crossing. I am again an alien in new territory . . . 'Knowing' is painful because after 'it' happens I can't stay in the same place and be comfortable." This willingness to be uncomfortable with the new is what the frontier thesis disavowed, and why many frontier narratives have avoided or masked recalcitrant facts, such as the presence of indigenous American nations and prior Mexican settlers.

Beginning with an invocation to the Laguna deity Thought-Woman, Leslie Marmon Silko's novel *Ceremony* (1977) also recognizes the revisionary effort from *el otro lado* as an experiment with a new kind of thinking. Silko reincorporates facts that have been deemed abject, unworthy of recognition by the dominant culture, into the pan-American repertoire of stories. She achieves this recuperative project by interweaving traditional Pueblo story and ritual with Euro-American modernist narrative modes. *Ceremony* maintains multiple perspectives and an open frame, concluding with the hopeful invocation "Sunrise, / accept this offering, / Sunrise." Here begins an effort of coalition across tribal, national, ethnic, and aesthetic boundaries, a transnational aspiration that recognizes its own potential for failure in its literal invitation to the reader to accept it, to heed its call.

m In chapter 14 of this volume, Jennifer Greeson offers a compelling gloss, drawing from historical literary archives, on how the contemporary global South has been prepared by earlier regional representations of the South and West ("Imagining the South," esp. 236–237).

The fragility of border thinking, the possibility that it might remain an unfulfilled project, has inspired novels that foreground inconclusiveness. Unsolvable or half-resolved mysteries, such as Linda Hogan's *Mean Spirit* (1990) and Louis Owens's *Bone Game* (1994), speak eloquently for the post-colonial West.[34] At the end of *Bone Game*, a banished but still present Ohlone ghost looks out over the University of California at Santa Cruz, which is built upon his ancestral homeland. The ghost repeats a judgment about his colonizers that could not be assimilated into the novel's more superficial denouement, the solving of some campus murders. The final words of the novel are the reason the ghost remains, his reflection upon his trauma: *"Eran muy crueles"* ("They were very cruel").

The frontier, as a metaphor and theory of nationhood, enacts a grand obsession, a drama by and about US settlement culture and its coming to power in North America. I see no reason to limit the creative destruction that border studies and gender studies have wrought upon the frontier by loosing "the frontier" from its cultural limitations, such that "the frontier" could be used interchangeably with newer concepts like Anzaldúa's "borderlands" or José David Saldívar's nuanced "transfrontera contact zone."[35] The frontier marks a centuries-long effort of complex, blocked, anxious, and destructive thinking, and it still lives, as a cultural narrative or myth. Novels such as T. C. Boyle's *Tortilla Curtain* (1995) and Toni Morrison's *Paradise* (1997) reflect the persistence of the frontier in sterile socio-cultural forms such as the gated community and the so-called moral majority.[n] Frontierism likewise persists in the rhetoric of US foreign policy. Yet it also has produced cultural forms, such as novels, that express multiple and contradictory structures of feeling. The frontier demands serious study. Not looking at it would represent a failure of thought complicit with the worst of its own logic.

Notes

1. Frederick Jackson Turner, "The Significance of the Frontier in American History," in *History, Frontier, and Section: Three Essays by Frederick Jackson Turner* (1893; Albuquerque: University of New Mexico Press, 1993), 59–92: 61.
2. Henry David Thoreau, *Walden* (1854; New York: Signet NAL, 1960), 70; Annette Kolodny, "Letting Go Our Grand Obsessions: Notes Toward a New Literary History of the American Frontiers," *American Literature* 64 (March 1992): 1–18.

n As Catherine Jurca remarks in this volume, since the 1990s "the polymorphous suburbs of condos, malls, office parks, and McMansions have yielded new opportunities for exploring alienation" ("The American novel and the rise of the suburbs," chapter 53, 884).

Though I agree with Kolodny's reconceptualization of US/American Studies, I do not see the wisdom of reinstating the term "frontier" at the center of her comparatist project.

3. Philip Fisher defines the sublime as "the aestheticization of fear," in Philip Fisher, *Wonder, the Rainbow, and the Aesthetics of Rare Experience* (Cambridge, MA: Harvard University Press, 1998), 2.
4. On Turner and presentism, see Patricia Nelson Limerick, "Turnerians All: The Dream of a Helpful History in an Intelligible World," in *Something in the Soil: Legacies and Reckonings in the New West* (New York: W.W. Norton, 2001), 141–165; see also Turner, "The Significance of the Frontier," 39–58.
5. Turner, "The Significance of the Frontier," 60.
6. Henry Nash Smith, *Virgin Land: The American West as Symbol and Myth* (Cambridge, MA: Harvard University Press, 1950), 3–12.
7. Turner, "The Significance of the Frontier," 61.
8. Slotkin offers the definitive treatment of Cooper's role in establishing frontier iconography, as well as the importance of the historical novel in this effort, in Richard Slotkin, *The Fatal Environment: The Myth of the Frontier in the Age of Industrialization, 1800–1890* (Middletown, CT: Wesleyan University Press, 1985), 81–106.
9. Philip Fisher, *Hard Facts: Setting and Form in the American Novel* (New York: Oxford University Press, 1985), 26.
10. *The Compact Oxford English Dictionary*, 2nd edn., s.v. "frontier."
11. Leslie Fiedler's famous exploration of the "pseudo-marriage of males" that structures US fiction appears in *Love and Death in the American Novel* (New York: Anchor Books, 1966), 366.
12. Slotkin discusses Cooper's theory of racial gifts in *Fatal Environment*, 88.
13. Lawrence Buell, "American Literary Emergence as a Postcolonial Phenomenon," *American Literary History* 4 (October 1992): 411–442.
14. Francis Parkman, Jr., *The Oregon Trail* (1849), ed. David Levine (New York: Penguin, 1982; rpt. New York: Penguin Classics, 1985), 168. Citation is to the 1985 edition.
15. The quotation from Wister's letters to his mother comes from Jane Tompkins, *West of Everything: The Inner Life of Westerns* (New York: Oxford University Press, 1992), 137.
16. My insistence on the presence of homoeroticism in *The Virginian* represents less a difference of opinion than a different degree of emphasis with William R. Handley, "Wister's Omniscience and Omissions," in *Reading The Virginian in the New West*, ed. Melody Graulich and Stephen Tatum (Lincoln: University of Nebraska Press, 2003), 39–72.
17. Louis Owens, "White for a Hundred Years," in Graulich and Tatum, *Reading The Virginian*, 72–89.
18. Tompkins, *West of Everything*, 149.
19. Patricia Nelson Limerick, "The Adventures of the Frontier in the Twentieth Century," in *The Frontier in American Culture: Essays by Richard White and Patricia*

Nelson Limerick, ed. James R. Grossman (Berkeley: University of California Press, 1994), 67–102: 75.

20. Stephen Tatum's discussion of popular culture within the framework of Western literary studies is especially helpful. See Stephen Tatum, "The Problem of the 'Popular' in New Western History," *Arizona Quarterly* 53 (July 1997): 153–190.
21. Bill Brown, "Reading the West: Cultural and Historical Background," in *Reading the West: An Anthology of Dime Westerns*, ed. Bill Brown (New York: Bedford Books, 1997), 20–21. On Beadle, see Shelley Streeby, chapter 35 in this volume ("Dime novels and the rise of mass market genres").
22. Brown, "Reading the West," 20, 22.
23. Michael Denning, *Mechanic Accents: Dime Novels and Working-Class Culture in America* (London: Verso, 1987).
24. For a thoroughgoing discussion of the relation of sensational literature to discourses of sex, race, and empire, see Shelley Streeby, *American Sensations: Class, Empire, and the Production of Popular Culture* (Berkeley: University of California Press, 2002).
25. William R. Handley, *Marriage, Violence, and the Nation in the American Literary West* (Cambridge: Cambridge University Press, 2002).
26. Tompkins, *West of Everything*, 164.
27. Will Wright, *Six Guns and Society: A Structural Study of the Western* (Berkeley: University of California Press, 1975).
28. For discussion of the evolution of the Western film through the twentieth century, see Jim Kitses and Gregg Rickman, eds., *The Western Reader* (New York: Limelight, 1998); David Lusted, *The Western* (London: Pearson/Longman, 2003); Edward Buscombe, ed., *The BFI Companion to the Western* (New York: Da Capo Press, 1988).
29. Mark Twain, *Roughing It* (1872; New York: Penguin, 1981), 166.
30. Gavin Jones, *Strange Talk: The Politics of Dialect Literature in Gilded Age America* (Berkeley: University of California Press, 1999), 60.
31. Twain, *Roughing It*, 337.
32. Susan Kollin, "Genre and the Geographies of Violence: Cormac McCarthy and the Contemporary Western," *Contemporary Literature* 42 (Autumn 2001): 566.
33. Slotkin marks a crucial change in the tone of the Western in the Vietnam era, specifically after Mylai, in Richard Slotkin, *Gunfighter Nation: The Myth of the Frontier in Twentieth-Century America* (New York: Harper Perennial, 1992), 578–623.
34. The unsolvable or imperfectly resolved mystery falls into the rubric of the "forensic aesthetic" that Stephen Tatum recognizes as permeating contemporary cultural production in and about the American West. See Stephen Tatum, "Spectral Beauty and Forensic Aesthetics in the West," *Western American Literature* 41 (July 2006): 123–145.
35. Saldívar elaborates, "This zone is the social space of subaltern encounters, the Janus-faced border line in which peoples geopolitically forced to separate

themselves now negotiate with one another and manufacture new relations, hybrid cultures, and multiple-voiced aesthetics." In José David Saldívar, *Border Matters: Remapping American Cultural Studies* (Berkeley: University of California Press, 1997), 13. Annette Kolodny, Jane Tompkins, Melody Graulich, and Krista Comer have been pivotal figures in the transformation of Western literary history through gender studies.

32

Imperialism, Orientalism, and empire

RUSS CASTRONOVO

The foreign locales that crop up in US literature show that only rarely could a history of "the American novel" claim to be a story, to borrow a title from Mark Twain, of "innocents abroad." For what invocations of Havana, Constantinople, Cuba, and Peking – just to mention a few of the geographically far-flung sites that reappear throughout the literature of the nineteenth and early twentieth centuries – make clear is that white Americans were hardly guiltless when it came to imperial adventures. For quite a long time, however, accepted historical narratives cast the USA as a nation without an imperial tradition, one whose hands were unsullied by the sort of history that bloodied traditional European powers.[1] In early examples of imperial romances from the first half of the nineteenth century, dashing heroes and sentimental heroines embody this uncomplicated history, their sexual innocence and purity expressive of a fantasy that white subjectivity could remain untainted by the stain of moral, political, and cultural complications that US culture inevitably confronted as white men and women courted one another on the slave-trading African coast, the exotic climes of the Levant, or other presumably romantic backdrops. Examples from later in the nineteenth century and continuing into the first decades of the twentieth lend a scientific hue to this fantasy, rooting the quest for cultural purity in biology as part of an effort to control the linkages among race, sexuality, and empire that empowered but also potentially jeopardized white subjects. As the forces of imperialism, Orientalism, and empire combined to push US influence into ever-widening spheres, the preoccupation with innocence – understood in terms that were corporeal, moral, and national – impelled American literature increasingly inward as well, deep into the haunted chambers of the self.

It might be said that American literature begins its nationalist phase with protestations of sexual innocence, as Thomas Paine in 1776 deplored the British government as a corrupting force comparable to a "prostitute" that ensnares unsuspecting young men.[2] But this fantasy proved difficult to maintain, and not only because US incursions in Texas, Cuba, the Philippines, and Native American lands posed contradictions for a nation that had declared itself dedicated to liberty – a paradox summed up by Thomas Jefferson's famous comment about the USA as an "Empire of Liberty."[3] The fantasy also presented more visceral elements: a combination of intimate violence and barely repressed desire that confronted white bloodlines with the dangerous sexuality found in the African or South American jungle, the Orientalist harem, and the tropical allure of the Caribbean or Pacific Rim, to say nothing of the Southern slave plantation, which, for many writers, seemed to distill all these foreign contexts into a particularly potent homegrown concoction of race and sex. The threat was not merely limited to an exotic background: whether white men and women traveled abroad or stayed home on the plantation, they flirted with miscegenation, creating the risk of breeding the very otherness that they so feared. Both the foreign backgrounds and exoticism that made the imperial novel so distinctive also implied the precarious global reach of white male sexual desire. Although designed to confirm American readers' sense of self-mastery, the primitive settings, sultry women, and jungle escapades common to fictions of empire also raised the possibility that white superiority and control were being stretched to their limits.

In the nineteenth-century American novel, this unsteady mixture of desire and danger is often represented elliptically so that impolite suggestions do not disrupt genteel tastes. Novelistic devices such as allegory manage – but also engage – the unruly contexts of empire and expansion. When the hero of James Fenimore Cooper's *The Last of the Mohicans* (1826) contemplates a waterfall, the forest guide is disturbed by the different shades of the water chaotically blending in ways that foreshadow the repressed anxieties over racial mixing that are at the center of the novel. "Look at the perversity of the water," Natty Bumppo observes. "It falls by no rule at all . . . in one place 'tis white as snow, and in another 'tis green as grass." Written in 1826 but set in 1757 and thus before the founding of an independent American nation, *The Last of the Mohicans* gentrifies imperialism by relegating frontier warfare to a thing of the past despite the fact that the forced removal of Native Americans by the USA continued steadily throughout the nineteenth century. The waterfall presents a disconcerting allegory no matter the historical epoch: the "perversity" of mixing threatens each foray into foreign territory. As the different streams of water mingle, so too, are different bloodlines brought into promiscuous contact with one another in the pages of Cooper's novel. Lily-white maidens become smitten with noble but dark savages. Meanwhile, other white maidens are revealed not to be as white as meets the eye. The daughter of the English colonel bears the taint of an earlier imperial history in the Caribbean, having inherited African ancestry from her mother. Natty's discomfort in watching the waterfall registers the risk of miscegenation that the nation invites with its expansive military policies.[a] Edgar Allan Poe featured the same topos in *The Narrative of Arthur Gordon Pym* (1838) when a group of American explorers in the South Seas comes across a stream "made up of a number of distinct veins, each of a distinct hue" and observes with fascination "that these veins did not commingle." The water's anatomy makes clear that the subject here is not only aqueous but human. Nature here is not the organic system that Winfried Fluck (in his contribution to this volume) identifies as providing an intuitive hierarchy and order for the world of the historical novel.[b] Instead, water, the indispensable element of all life, presents a scene of chaos. Where Cooper blends allegory into a historical novel to express his consternation about racial mixing, Poe incorporates the fantastic into his narrative to deny the real fluidities of race that underlie imaginaries of exploration and empire.[c]

Like proponents of Manifest Destiny who were no respecters of borders, the American imperial novel overrode the cultural borders that separated respectable literary works from their "lower-class" cousins such as the dime novel. The same anxieties over miscegenation and foreign contagion that crop up in leather-bound books emerge in starker relief in the tales spun in the cheap story papers.[4] Writing under the nom de plume "Lieutenant Murray," Maturin Murray Ballou churned out stories for *Gleason's Pictorial Drawing-Room Companion* and other venues for popular fiction that frankly dripped of sexuality, white seduction, and foreign intrigue. Not only are his novels of swashbuckling and romance far-fetched, but even his career as a writer for popular tastes seems improbable. Son of the famous New England minister Hosea Ballou, he is credited with "crush[ing] the foreign domination of proletarian literature" in the United States by writing fiction for widely circulating periodicals that filled their columns with talk of Manifest Destiny.[5] Despite his familial inheritance of probity and virtue, Ballou soon displayed a knack for turning out steamy tales of white slaves, cannibalism, and military derring-do. Unlike Cooper or Poe, he did not treat the threat of commingling aroused by empire and imperialism obliquely. Instead, his

a For treatment of Cooper's novels, see Sandra Gustafson's essay in this volume (chapter 6, "Cooper and the idea of the Indian").
b Winfried Fluck, "The nineteenth-century historical novel," chapter 7 in this volume.
c See Elizabeth Young's reading of Poe in the context of the supernatural (chapter 13, "Supernatural Novels," 223–225).

stirring romances of the 1850s confronted sexuality head-on in settings that ranged from the slave-trading African coast to colonial Cuba to Turkish harems. The common thread connecting these geographically disparate locales is that sexuality in each is available for global profit. But such narrative globetrotting always returns home, specifically to the US South and the plantation economies of the Americas.

Ballou's *The Sea-Witch, or, The African Quadroon* (185?) and its circum-Atlantic plot offers a veritable lesson on the interconnections created by the global system of Anglo-American empire. In her schemes to seduce the American captain of a slave ship, the title character exposes the captain and a British maiden to attacks from African natives, poison darts from a blow gun, and British naval officers charged to mete out death to anyone participating in the illegal international slave trade. Her unrequited love is hardly poetic or pitiable; its threat can be expressed only through a comparison to another imperial frontier: "No one, save a North American Indian, can hold and nourish a spirit of revenge like a Quadroon. It seems to be an innate trait of their nature, and ever ready to burst forth in a blaze at any moment." Ballou's "shilling novelettes" draw together various imperial scenes, foreign as well as domestic, upon a single stage.[6] The effect is paradoxical, as the outward energies of US slave-trading in the Atlantic basin and encroachment upon Native American lands in the West create an inward crisis for the white male subject. Luckily, a white woman is on hand, not only to win the captain's affections, but also to reform him into renouncing human piracy. White female sexuality, as opposed to the unregulated, "tiger-like" passion of the African, restores moral order, allowing the couple to return to Britain in a married bliss that is all the more blissful because it seals them off from the dangerous associations of empire.

So, too, the novel tries at the outset to sequester American readers so that the connections between imperialist adventure and domestic slave-trading will not surface. A preface from the editor of *The Flag of Our Union* (no doubt written by Ballou himself) proclaims that his story paper's publication of *The Sea-Witch* should not be read as a "pro-slavery or anti-slavery tale." According to the paper's editor, slavery, insofar as it appears in the ensuing pages, offers little more than scenic ambience and is "not . . .. a *feature* of the story." Neither this narrative framing nor the happy conclusion can gainsay antebellum contexts: domestic slavery is always a constitutive feature of the landscape, no matter if the South's "peculiar institution" seems remote from the romantic fantasy of imperial adventure. This interconnection is illuminated from the other side, as it were, in domestic portraits of US slavery, in which imperial and orientalist accents add color to the scene. In Harriet Beecher Stowe's *Dred; A Tale of the Great Dismal Swamp* (1856), plantations are lined with trees imported from "the banks of the Amazon," worked by African slaves who evoke the "fiery glories of a tropical landscape," and adorned by quadroon women of "African and French blood" who give an "impression of brilliancy and richness that one receives from tropical insects and flowers." Although Stowe's setting never reaches beyond US borders and although Ballou's captain never returns to New Orleans with his shipment of slaves, these contexts each mingle with their repressed foreign counterpart, creating unsettling connections between domestic homelands and imperial spaces. Whereas William Faulkner once said that the "past is never dead, it is not even past," readers of the American novel might say that South is never just the South or the merely regional but, as Jennifer Greeson argues in her essay in this volume (chapter 14), is always bound up with the wider geography of US imperial ambitions.[7] The tenacious cultural fiction, one maintained for decades by American historians, that the USA lacked an imperial tradition of the sort that blemished traditional European powers, is dispelled by this literary archive, which reveals how a supposedly innocent nation waged a program of empire that was both internal and external, encompassing the South and the "Indian territory" alongside more geographically far-flung sites in the Caribbean, Latin America, and the Pacific Rim.[d]

White subjects, especially in the intimate spaces of sexuality and femininity, became tangled up in this convergence of inner and outer empire. What became difficult to sort out was white women's moral and ideological position in a climate bordered by associations with license, seduction, and rape. Ballou was one of the first to profit from this anxiety by lavishing attention on the fiction of "white slavery" in his alternately lurid and high-toned periodical novel of 1851, *The Circassian Slave, or, The Sultan's Favorite*. Also ready to cash in on the melodramatic plight of the white harem slave was P.T. Barnum, who exhibited a "Circassian Beauty" in his museum. The image of pure white women from the Caucasus region being sold into Eastern slavery "had special significance to pseudoscientific, anthropologically minded Americans" since, as the source of the word "Caucasian," this landscape evokes an ancient whiteness whose significance echoes to this day.[8] The fascination with seraglios, odalisques, and captive white women represents both a displacement

d This diverse geography is often one of war. For more on this point, see John Carlos Rowe's contribution to this volume, "US novels and US wars," chapter 49.

of and a deep attraction to the enslaved sexuality that was a quotidian fact in US plantation economy. Although Edward Said states that nineteenth-century discourse about the Orient – its fading grandeur, its despotism, its otherness – was mainly a product of European colonialism, American writers also discovered the usefulness of the East, especially as a screen for understanding as well as obscuring race relations at home.[9] On the one hand, interest in the Ottoman harem pushes the South's peculiar institution to the background by lamenting the plight of the white slave. On the other, the frequency with which sultans' palaces turned up in American writing suggests the everyday popularity of male mastery over powerless women.

Helpless women, of course, require bold men to rescue them. This scenario appears as a stock formula in US travel writing and the fictions it inspired. In "An American in Constantinople," a contributor to *Harper's* describes "the romance of the harem," depicting British and American vacationers in Istanbul who flank a procession of white-looking Turkish women in an attempt to see beyond their veils.[10] The male tourist condemns the traffic in women even as he cannot refrain from talking about the delicate hands, ruby lips, and allure of "Eastern ladies' eyes."[11] But this obsession with near-white sexuality threatens to make white men as helpless as the women they have come to protect, appraise, and judge. *The Circassian Slave* presents scene after scene, each more erotically charged than the last, for voyeuristic consumption: "The picturesque and lovely groups of female slaves . . . laughed and toyed with each other" while clad in "rich though scanty dress" – such descriptions are a fair specimen of the eye candy conjured up by Ballou. Can white men resist the sexuality that is freely offered to them in these pages? Might bold men themselves prove helpless in the presence of exotic, heavily sexualized women? These are not idle questions, even for white Americans who would never leave home to travel to the "Orient." As the Orientalist gestures of plantation romances unavoidably suggest, white men had the opportunity to sexualize women in one of the mainstays of the antebellum economy. When *The Circassian Slave* describes a white-skinned woman of "ravishing loveliness . . . led forth to the auctioneer's stand," the setting might just as well be antebellum New Orleans or Charleston as the Middle East.

Although the Civil War put an end to the legal traffic in women, the fear that white men could be led astray by foreign beauty remained an abiding concern. Even novels that portrayed American men traveling to exotic landscapes for the noblest purposes confronted this danger. John William De Forest, best known for his romances of Reconstruction, showed that even Christian soldiers ran the risk of foreign temptation. In *Irene: The Missionary*

(1879), De Forest's narrator follows a group of modern-day crusaders to Syria who, propelled by zeal to convert young Arab women to Christianity, get caught in the Druze–Maronite conflict of 1860. While overt violence is certainly a threat, it is covert sexuality that most confounds this group from the American Board of Foreign Missions. The novel's title character, proclaimed "the finest girl at this end of the Mediterranean," attracts the amorous attention of diplomats, doctors, and amateur archaeologists throughout the region; the conflict revolves around the question of whether her beauty can compete with the allure of veiled women. For her white admirer, who is excavating ancient sites to prove various ethnological assumptions, the skin of Syrian women has a "color" that might be seen in "a handsome brunette from Louisiana or Cuba." In his better moments – of which there are not many – he is sure that he loves Irene, spiritual and refined though she is, but for a good part of the novel he flirts with young native girls. When Irene learns of her suitor's indiscretion in kissing Saada, a fourteen-year-old convert to Christianity, she is forced to question whether white men view white and Arab women similarly – that is, as sexual objects.

Left unchecked, white male sexuality imperils the gendered and racial distinctions crucial to the civilizing mission that justified both cultural and military imperialism. Desire is indeed the problem of the imperial novel, as the exotic setting and racy content show that the sexualized other is never too far from white heroes and heroines. In fact, such otherness may be lodged in the internal conception of those subjects. As De Forest implies, white women would do well to worry that they are no different from palace slaves, while white men seem to find this problematic convergence titillating.

This convergence supplied a different sort of crusader with fodder for a critique of US internal racism. Like novelists who warily linked desire and race relations, civil rights activist Ida B. Wells also examined the associations between interracial sex and lynching. Rather than accept the "old threadbare lie that Negro men rape white women," Wells in 1892 lodged the counteraccusation that many lynching victims were black men who had accepted the advances of white women.[12] She drew together imperial and domestic contexts to indict the ritual mutilation, burning, and murder of black persons in both the South and North. In invoking "the wilds of interior Africa" or "the cannibals of the savage Indians" as points of comparison for lynching, Wells had a dual purpose: to convince reformers not to deplore foreign conditions while ignoring barbarism at home, and to show that American civilization was not as civilized as it pretended to be. Her pamphlet, *Mob Rule in New Orleans*, concludes that black victimization within US borders was "even worse" than any atrocities committed by the " 'unspeakable Turk.' "[13] By using scare quotes, Wells acknowledges the fictive nature of this Orientalist epithet even as she calls upon its rhetorical force at a moment when she is writing about the protections afforded white womanhood. Drawn from the pages of popular periodical fiction, the topos of the harem recirculates to position white men as cruel and despotic. The effect of Wells's invocation of imperial imaginaries is to unsettle race, sexuality, and civilization at home.

The lethal associations between black men, white sexuality, and savage contexts were not put to rest by Wells's activism. Edgar Rice Burroughs achieved tremendous popularity by playing upon these charged associations in *Tarzan of the Apes* (1914), the first in a series of two dozen novels detailing white civilization's "emphatic embrace of racially motivated violence."[14] Although set in the wilds of Africa, this violence has a haunting familiarity, as Tarzan terrorizes black tribesmen with a lynching campaign that bears all the punitive stamps of stateside American racism. In one scene, Tarzan lies in wait for passing black hunters and slips a rope noose about their necks and then hangs them from trees. The question raised by Burroughs's drama is whether a human being raised in the jungle by apes will claim his human inheritance. By killing blacks, Tarzan proves that he is not just a man but a white man. Even as Tarzan claims this fundamental distinction, one that is surely more important than the aristocratic title associated with his true identity as Lord Greystoke, his desire for Jane Porter – that is, his own awakening sexuality – threatens to reintroduce the primal contexts that he tries to master with clothes, literacy, and other trappings of civilization. The geography of this threat encompasses the African interior, but it is also psychological, located deep within white interiority itself. Can Tarzan tame the animal-like passions that draw his body toward Jane Porter? This struggle is not Tarzan's alone: even Jane, a civilized American girl, must battle what Burroughs describes as the "primal woman in her" as she likens Tarzan to a "stalwart forest god."

In contrast to Wells's pamphlets and Burrough's fictions of tropical bloodlust, De Forest's novel seems a rather safe affair, filled with descriptions of Eastern decline that are an abiding feature of Orientalism. While the Near East figures as a sort of erotic quicksand for white men, the overall message is that manly Western civilization can easily overpower a feminized Oriental culture. Yet the domestic contexts that intrude upon the foreign mission dispel this comfortable conclusion. Fleeing ethnic violence in Syria and Lebanon, De Forest's title character and her male protectors are seemingly transported into an anti-miscegenationist's nightmare: "Of a sudden, a gigantic negro sprang forward after the passing travelers." Adding that "this black monster" is likely to "commit outrages," De Forest leaves little doubt that this fanatic Arab is really a black rapist. The global East and the US South collide at the point of sexualized racial threat. Even as the conjunction of internal and foreign empire poses a danger, racist practices at home come to the rescue. After the assassin is disarmed of his "rusty khanjar, or large dagger" (just the sort of exotic detail to interest readers), one man in the party confides, "we Americans do quite right in thrashing negroes. I wish an able South Carolina paddler had our misbelieving friend in hand." At one moment fueling white supremacy's deepest fears and at the next promising a solution of which the Ku Klux Klan could be proud, the American Orientalist novel manages the very dangers that it invites.

The inseparability of foreign and domestic spaces suggests two competing corollaries: on the one hand, domestic gender ideals for white manhood and womanhood are lured toward unsettling connotations of global otherness; on the other, figures embodying racial difference are drawn into the intimate recesses of white personhood. This entangling of race and sexuality at once expands and contracts the imaginative scope of US imperialist writing so that its capacity to provide cultural reassurance is alternately stretched and relaxed. By these novels' last pages, however, this tension dissipates when white men and women leave a seductive foreign setting and return home snugly wrapped up in heterosexual romance.

Except that these men and women often return only to find that they themselves bear the taint of their foreign interludes, or else that foreignness is lodged at home. De Forest's Irene and her archaeologist boyfriend sail back from a civil war in Syria to encounter a civil war in the United States, suggesting that tribal warfare at the antipodes is not all that different from internecine conflict at home. Even Ballou's formulaic novels have an unstable reagent mixed in the formula. The liberated harem girl of *The Circassian Slave* returns to the Caucasian homeland where "daughters still dream of a home among the Turks." If slavery represents a desirable lot for white women halfway across the globe, the accusation also attaches itself to white women at home – whether New England girls aspiring to Victorian gender conventions or the fetishized "fancy girls" of the domestic slave trade. Jumping back to the western hemisphere in *The Heart's Secret, or, The Fortunes of a Soldier* (1852), a novel set in Cuba, Ballou describes how the coquette and young adventurer call off their sparring long enough to get engaged or, as the hero puts it, "we are 'to bury the hatchet,' as the American orators say." The comparison between romantic union and racial warfare suggests how domestic accord in one spot of colonial imagination recalls settler–native conflicts in another.

The most incendiary foreign import appears in a text whose white characters never leave home. In *Dred*, Stowe's vision of biblical redemption meets up with an Africanist presence to produce an unstable amalgam: "When this oriental seed, an exotic among us, is planted back in the fiery soil of a tropical heart, it bursts forth with an incalculable ardor of growth." At one level, Stowe is talking about New World Africans, stereotypically referencing the putative religious enthusiasm of blacks. At another level, however, her subject is texts, as the "oriental seed" refers to the Bible's eastern origins. This association between enslaved body and sacred text points to more than the powerful Orientalist undertow running through the plantation and other American hierarchies. It might also be taken as a larger reflection of the way that nineteenth-century novelistic fiction – in its need for adventure, use of exotic settings, absorption in romance, and, finally, devotion to white subjects – demands *other* contexts, places, and people that ultimately require exclusion.[e]

Within Stowe's purple prose lies a metaphor of seeds, soil, and tropical fecundity, which anticipates the way in which biology and eugenics drove the contradictions of imperialism deeper into what Said calls the "underground self" of the Western subject.[15] As the US redoubled its empire-building efforts in the late nineteenth and early twentieth centuries, the paired antinomies of territorial expansion and white psychological contraction became more sexually charged. Problems of breeding, blood, and race even crept into utopian visions of white civilization.

Stowe remains important to this story also because for a short time she took in and provided for the family of her young niece, Charlotte Perkins Gilman, left destitute by a father's abandonment. Critics suggest that Stowe's feminism played a role in Gilman's development, and the fruits of that reform thinking can be seen in *Herland* (1915), although, as Elizabeth Nolan suggests elsewhere in this volume, Gilman also radically revised the ideals of domesticity envisioned by Stowe.[f] Starting with the conceit that a highly advanced but undiscovered race of women flourishes in the South American jungle,

e For more on white interiority, see John Ernest's observations in this volume about black characters in Stowe's *Uncle Tom's Cabin* in particular (chapter 15, "Stowe, race, and the antebellum American novel").

f Elizabeth Nolan, "The woman's novel beyond sentimentalism," chapter 34, 572–574.

Herland offers a wry commentary on the "primitive" gender practices found everywhere in American civilization. So far, so good: this novel of a feminist utopia moves beyond US borders, not to invade and exploit, but to offer a pacific alternative to a society based on sexual conquest. And yet, this imaginary land of pure women requires imperial notions of whiteness.[16] The search for an ideal women's world begins as an imperial expedition among "savages" – and, as becomes clear by the novel's end, those "savages" include white men from the civilized Western world.

Utopia is predicated upon the distinctions of imperialist ethnography. The male narrator and his buddies are emboldened by their desire to journey to a land of available women, ripe for the taking, as though in the tropical climate they could discover a female sexuality free from Victorian inhibitions. But this desire also needs to be repressed lest the men be seen longing for the natives of South America. They want jungle love, yet with all the trappings of the genteel parlor. By classifying people into savage and civilized types, the imperial vision of these men at once gives them access to a region of untapped sexuality and preserves that zone as pure and refined.

But Gilman is not about to give these men what they want. The ironic joke she plays on her male characters is that the "ultra-women" of *Herland* are chaste vessels who reproduce by parthenogenesis, that is, asexually without input from men. Gilman's male narrator admits that he "had not come to the country with any Turkish-harem intentions." He invokes, if only to reject, the Orientalist topos common to American writing about the Middle East as well as the American South. *Herland* is not just a novel about utopia then; it is also an attempt to make the novel utopian, freeing it from the expectation that romance and reform require allusions to exotic backgrounds in which women are held in thrall. Gilman's amalgam of utopia and colonialism retains its sexual innocence precisely because there is no sex. No one gets lost in the dark continent of sexuality because cross-racial desire never poses a problem in a land whose women possess no sexual desire. With white men denied an outlet for their more "primitive" urges, the erotic attractions of colonial contact are kept safely under wraps. And were desire an issue, the potential complications of racial hybridity never become a problem, since the inhabitants of "Ma-land" (*sic*) have preserved the purity of their race.[17] "There is no doubt in my mind that these people were of Ayran stock," the narrator assures himself. This encounter between Western white men and civilized white women seems like the ideal colonial situation: desire has been rendered safe by the eugenic surety of whiteness.[18]

The fantasy of recovering a pure white civilization in the heart of the Amazon jungle crumbles with the rude realization that white men remain "savages" after all. When the most impetuous of the narrator's companions tries to rape one of the girls of "Woman Country," the unavoidable suggestion is that white masculinity lodges a primitive otherness at its core. Evicted from paradise, the men nonetheless talk of a return trip to the Amazon and "civilizing – or exterminating – the dangerous savages" as part of a plan to make Herland accessible to the outside world. Killing and rape remain just below the surface of even the most civilized and utopian renditions of imperialism. While this accusation seems mainly directed at white men, the taint of untamed desires lurks beneath the outer refinement of white womanhood elsewhere in Gilman's *oeuvre*.

Even Gilman's domestic novella about a young woman "cured" into madness, "The Yellow Wallpaper" (1892), contains tropical contexts that overtake the white subject so fully that the final sentences of the novella depict the narrator in an animalistic posture, creeping over the prostrate form of her husband. Long before Burroughs ever dreamed up *Tarzan of the Apes*, Gilman has her protagonist down on all fours against a background as dense as any jungle, reversing gender roles by clambering on top of a man. As colonial suggestions are localized in domestic sexuality, the overextensions of empire stretch the white subject perilously thin, exposing the cracks in the veneer of civilized ideologies of gender. Men also slide down the evolutionary ladder in Frank Norris's *Vandover and the Brute* (1914), which ends with the title character on the floor, eyeing the food going into a little boy's mouth. Thus despite the wisdom that eugenic science would make white civilization as impregnable as Gilman's utopia of women secluded in their mountain fastness, turn-of-the-century fiction voiced anxieties that reproduction would endanger, not purify, the race. At risk are not only the sensualists or the hysterics of Norris's and Gilman's novels. Even men as virtuous as Dolly Haight in *Vandover* (though his feminized nickname is a tip that something is amiss) are enervated by the collision of empire and sexuality.[19] When peer pressure gets the better of Dolly and he allows himself to be dragged into a bar named "The Imperial," a prostitute plants a wet kiss on his mouth. Nothing more than that ensues – but by the end of the novel, Dolly is a ghost of his former self, his body ravaged by the syphilis he contracted on that one ill-fated occasion. Neither *Herland* nor *Vandover* offers an overt critique of imperialism, but each novel sexualizes foreign affairs in ways that speak to the uncertainty that lingers – despite the bravado and triumphalism associated with the Spanish–American War of 1898 and other colonial adventures – in this era of expansion into Latin America and the Pacific Rim. Do military and economic activities conducted outside the borders of the white republic threaten the wholesomeness of US life?[20] Might it even be said that the USA suffers from imperial promiscuity?

If to many novelists the answer seemed "yes," one consolation was that this *mésalliance* made for stirring storylines. At least that is how one reader, President Teddy Roosevelt, responded to the work of Richard Harding Davis, a war correspondent who converted his experiences into fiction. Reminiscing about Davis's pluck as an embedded journalist with the Rough Riders during the Spanish–American War, Roosevelt praised Davis for supplying the regiment with key tactical information. So, too, in the president's opinion did Davis deserve honors for advancing US interests on the ideological battlefield: "His writings form a text-book of Americanism which all our people would do well to read at the present time."[21] Davis's characters literally love nationalism. As the hero of Davis's *Captain Macklin: His Memoirs* (1902) announces, "A soldier cannot devote himself both to a woman and his country . . . The flag is a jealous mistress." This comparison between national loyalty and heterosexual devotion resonates with the larger cultural anxieties that American innocence is strained by interventions into colonial locales. In a parallel to the sexual adventurer who risks blood contamination, the military adventurer threatens to introduce contagion into the body politic of white civilization. Royal Macklin's interest is excited by popular press reports about "The Revolt in Honduras" and so he joins a group of filibusters whose plan is to carve the "United States of Central America" out of the several countries of the isthmus. But this plan is politically and morally suspect; the foreign cause he fights for is symbolized by a "strange flag of unknown, tawdry colors, like the painted face of a woman in the street." What sort of moral pollution might the American male contract from his prostituted patriotism?

Imperial adventure exposes national loyalty to the threat of ideological miscegenation. As an American mercenary supporting a French general's coup in Honduras, Macklin trades what should be the spontaneous feelings of patriotism for mere profit. He and his compatriots, to use a term made famous by the title of Davis's 1897 bestseller, are *Soldiers of Fortune*.[g] Such wavering national affection invites the bugbear of racial mixing. The flag of the legionnaires that has been compared to a painted woman is encircled by "menacing negro faces," its wanton appeal to disgraced Americans, profiteering Europeans, and native blacks creating a mongrel assemblage that seems a hideous mockery of Gilman's eugenic white Eden. If Roosevelt testified that Davis "was as good an American as ever lived," Macklin, by

g For more on *Soldiers of Fortune*, see Gretchen Murphy's "The hemispheric novel in the post-Revolutionary era," chapter 33, 559–560.

contrast, seems hell-bent on an imperial dalliance that encourages American masculinity to consort with some questionable influences.[22] The Honduras scheme ends in a debacle, but no matter since an opportunity to join the "Tonkin Expedition" allows Macklin to play his colonial hand in South Asia. If Cooper and Poe each advised that the metaphoric waters of whiteness be kept pure, by the start of what would be called "the American century" Davis sees that the currents of American innocence have become muddied.

The interlacing of imperialism, empire, and sexuality did not die out with these turn-of-the-century novels. In *Dark Princess* (1928), W. E. B. Du Bois proved himself an astute contributor to this body of work by invoking the lush exoticism of Orientalist fiction in his own romance about anti-colonial struggle. Like his predecessors, Du Bois commingles domestic and international contexts, as his tale oscillates between homegrown US racism and the colonial policies of Western powers in India, Ethiopia, and elsewhere. In focusing on what his journal *The Crisis* called "the darker races" and sexuality amid the contexts of Asia, Africa, and the USA, Du Bois returned to persistent anxieties at once erupting from and repressed within the history of the American novel from the nineteenth to the early twentieth century. For Du Bois, however, this hybridity is cause for jubilation.

Dark Princess embodies in flesh and blood Stowe's airy predictions in *Dred* about an "oriental seed" mixing with the "tropical" passion of Africa. The novel's hero, Matthew Towns, and heroine, Princess Kautilya, heir to a small Asian kingdom, defy the forces that keep them apart. The result of their union is a male child who will be the salvation of both the Third World and oppressed minorities in the West. Interracial sex will redeem a world ravaged by colonialism and slavery, thanks to the new "Messenger and Messiah to all the Darker Worlds!" Lest this honorific seem to repeat the crusading bent that poses Western Christians as saviors of benighted "Orientals," Du Bois endows the boy with a pan-religious destiny for Muslims, Hindus, and Buddhists. It is a conclusion that suggests something of a revelation for the American novel as well: any image of cosmopolitan hope and global collectivity depends on earlier imperial imaginaries of empire.[h]

h Does *Dark Princess* represent a high-water mark of cosmopolitan thinking that is at low ebb in the contemporary American novel? Readers interested in this question will find it useful to consult Bruce Robbins's essay in this volume ("The worlding of the American novel," chapter 66).

Notes

1. Malini Johar Schueller shows how this view was challenged in the 1960s by William Appelman Williams and R. W. Van Alstyne. See *U.S. Orientalisms: Race, Nation, and Gender in Literature, 1790–1890* (Ann Arbor: University of Michigan Press, 1998), 18–20. See also Amy Kaplan, "'Left Alone with America:' The Absence of Empire in the Study of American Culture," in *Cultures of United States Imperialism*, ed. Amy Kaplan and Donald E. Pease (Durham, NC: Duke University Press, 1993), 3–21.
2. Thomas Paine, *Common Sense*, in *The Thomas Paine Reader* (New York: Penguin, 1987), 71.
3. Jefferson to George Rogers Clark, December 25, 1780, in *Papers of Thomas Jefferson*, 35 vols., ed. Julian P. Boyd *et al.* (Princeton: Princeton University Press, 1951), IV:237–238.
4. For the relationship of the popular press and story papers to the imperialist contexts created by the Mexican–American War of 1846–1848, see Shelley Streeby, *American Sensations: Class, Empire, and the Production of Popular Culture* (Berkeley: University of California Press, 2002). Streeby's contribution to this volume, "Dime novels and the rise of mass market genres" (chapter 35), explores the popularity of dime novels, noting the diversity and longevity of the form.
5. Ralph Admari, "Ballou, Father of the Dime Novel," *The American Book Collector* 4 (September–October 1933): 123.
6. Mary K. Edmonds, "Maturin Murray Ballou," in *American Travel Writers, 1850–1915*, ed. Donald Ross and James J. Schramer (Detroit: Gale Research, 1998), 22.
7. William Faulkner, *Requiem for a Nun*, in *William Faulkner: Novels, 1942–1954: Go Down, Moses, Intruder in the Dust, Requiem for a Nun, A Fable* (New York: Modern Library, 1994), 535. See Jennifer Greeson, "Imagining the South," chapter 14 in this volume.
8. Linda Frost, "The Circassian Beauty and the Circassian Slave: Gender, Imperialism, and American Popular Entertainment," in *Cultural Spectacles of the Extraordinary Body: Freakery*, ed. Rosemarie Garland Thomson (New York: New York University Press, 1996), 250.
9. Edward W. Said, *Orientalism* (New York: Vintage, 1978), 2–4.
10. "An American in Constantinople," *Harper's New Monthly Magazine* 26 (February 1858): 300.
11. *Ibid.*
12. Ida B. Wells-Barnett, *On Lynchings* (Amherst, NY: Humanity Books, 2002), 29.
13. *Ibid.*, 203.
14. William Gleason, "Of Sequels and Sons: Tarzan and the Problem of Paternity," *Journal of American Culture* 23.1 (Spring 2000): 41.
15. Said, *Orientalism*, 3.
16. Colleen Lye notes a similar dimension to Jack London's utopian socialism, which requires the invocation and "defeat of the 'yellow peril'" (*America's Asia: Racial Form and American Literature, 1893–1945* [Princeton: Princeton University Press, 2005], 39).

17. Gail Bederman discusses the interplay of race and sex in Gilman's thinking in *Manliness and Civilization: A Cultural History of Gender and Race in the United States, 1880–1917* (Chicago: University of Chicago Press, 1995), 121–169. See also Thomas Peyser, *Utopia and Cosmopolis: Globalization in the Era of American Literary Realism* (Durham, NC: Duke University Press, 1998), 64–82.
18. For Gilman, the cure for the ills of modern civilization lies in a eugenic solution that links social virtues to biological notions of race.
19. On Norris's imperialist aesthetics, see Russ Castronovo, *Beautiful Democracy: Aesthetics and Anarchy in a Global Era* (Chicago: University of Chicago Press, 2007), 180–211.
20. On the idea of a white republic, see Alexander Saxton, *The Rise and Fall of the White Republic: Class Politics and Mass Culture in Nineteenth-Century America* (New York: Verso, 1990).
21. Theodore Roosevelt, "Davis and the Rough Riders," in Richard Harding Davis, *Captain Macklin: His Memoirs* (New York: Charles Scribner's Sons, 1916), vii. Although Roosevelt holds up Davis as an exemplar of "Americanism," the satire and irony in his fiction undercuts that evaluation. See Davis's collection, *The Exiles and Other Stories* (1916).
22. Roosevelt, "Davis and the Rough Riders," vii.

33

The hemispheric novel in the post-revolutionary era

GRETCHEN MURPHY

During the first quarter of the nineteenth century, revolution swept much of the Western Hemisphere. By 1825, Brazil had freed itself from Portugal, and Spain had lost wars of independence to former colonies Argentina, Bolivia, Chile, Columbia, Guatemala, Ecuador, Mexico, and Peru. (Haiti had also liberated itself from France, but as the only independent black state in the New World, it had a more strained relationship to the shared revolutionary moment.) The revolutionaries leading these independence movements were, like the founders of the United States, influenced by European political philosophy and the Enlightenment, and their nationalisms can be viewed as part of a larger transnational liberal movement in Europe and America. Yet the spatial construct they more frequently employed to illustrate what had happened described a separation from Europe: the New World had radically broken ties with the Old to start over in a land naturally destined for democracy. In the Latin American republics, in remaining Spanish colonies such as Cuba, and in the United States, broad identification with the Western Hemisphere as a space of democratic difference from European monarchy became a key component of national mythologies expressed in cultural forms including poetry, painting, and the novel.[1]

However, this utopian conception of hemispheric destiny existed alongside a number of factors dividing the Americas North and South. Religious and racial prejudices and intra- and international factions tied to particular economic interests such as plantation slavery, transatlantic trade, or agrarian territorial expansion all arrayed against the political idealism of hemispheric identification, offering competing geographies for the new republics. An 1821 commentary published in the *North American Review* offers an example. As a Whiggish journal published in mercantile New England, the *North American Review* viewed Spanish American democracy decidedly more coolly than did publications from more southern US states, hearkening instead to enduring commercial bonds with Europe: that "Buenos Ayres and Mexico are a part of our continent may suggest fine themes for general declamation and poetry is true," the writer grants, but transatlantic trade and civilized sympathies suggest a future in which "South America will be to North America, we are strongly inclined to think, what Asia and Africa will be to Europe." Thus while some geographic forms of identification such as the 1823 Monroe Doctrine declared hemispheric solidarity in the struggle against European monarchy, other colonial structures of thought created divisions and hierarchies within the Americas.[2]

This sense of hemispheric solidarity and its opposing strains of racial and imperialist thought form a central object of the newly emerging study of nineteenth-century "transamerican literary relations."[3] US and Latin American novels, particularly historical romances in the tradition of Sir Walter Scott, are an important component of this new scholarship, and this chapter offers a synthetic view of some of the English- and Spanish-language novels that participated in national and transnational conversations about revolutionary New World identity. (Thus in part this chapter explores some further consequences of the international success of Scott's *Waverley*, mentioned by Winfried Fluck elsewhere in this volume.[a]) The first section discusses a series of historical novels that envision New World colonial history – especially Hernan Cortés's conquest of Mexico – in order to project hemispheric unity as well as US imperialism, demonstrating the ambivalence at the heart of the hemispheric project. The second section introduces novels that replace the sweeping scope of hemispheric political idealism with more local affiliations formed to chart the future of slavery in the New World. These novels, written in Cuba and the United States, tell stories about interracial romances and feature US–Cuban political, economic, and social relationships as a means of reckoning with slavery and racial difference in Cuban and US nationalisms. Finally, the chapter concludes with a discussion of late nineteenth-century border romances of California. Highlighting their relationships with transnational political thought and cultural exchange, I consider what it means to label these novels "hemispheric," with all that the term can signify.

An early example of hemispheric literary imagining can be found in *Jicoténcal* (1826), a Spanish-language novel about Cortés's conquest of Mexico. Both *Jicoténcal*'s publishing history and its plot suggest hemispheric political bonds. Printed by the William Stavely Publishing House in Philadelphia, the novel is believed to have been authored by one or more

a See Winfried Fluck, "The nineteenth-century historical novel," chapter 7, 118.

Cuban and/or Central American dissidents who gathered in Philadelphia to support Cuban independence through publishing and organizing efforts. The novel's readership was also international and multilingual: it was reprinted in Mexico, and William Cullen Bryant reviewed *Jicoténcal* for the *United States Review and Literary Gazette*, comparing it to works by "the author of Waverly" (that is, Walter Scott) and using the occasion to comment on the interrelatedness of recent American independence movements and the obligation of the United States to aid fellow nations fighting for freedom.

Beyond scenes of writing, publication, and reception, transnational collectivity is an ideal clearly promoted within the novel's plot, where the fracturing among various indigenous tribes, referred to generally by the narrator as "Americans," leads to their downfall in a clear warning to nineteenth-century American revolutionaries. Like Cuban revolutionary José Martí's 1891 essay "Our América," with its later call for an "urgent, wordless union of the continental soul," *Jicoténcal* calls for transamerican unity.[4] The novel embellishes upon real colonial records (primarily Antonio de Solís's *Historia de la conquista de Méjico* [1685]) to tell a fictional story that includes as main characters historical figures such as Cortés, his translator Doña Marina (the infamous *la Malinche* of Mexican cultural traditions), and Xicoténcatl the Younger, an indigenous warrior whose hispanicized name provides the book's title.[5] The plot follows Jicoténcal's failed effort to rally his people, the Tlaxcalans, against Cortés's invading Spanish army, a struggle made to symbolize the American wars of independence through a number of obvious devices. The narrator describes the Tlaxcalans' government as a "republic" ideally ruled by reason and natural law, but undermined by superstition, passion and greed, all flaws embodied in the treacherous villain Magiscatzin, who secretly engineers the Tlaxcalans' doomed alliance with the Spaniards. The indigenous characters' speeches on reason, religion, and self-rule echo Enlightenment philosophy, and at key moments the narrator breaks out of the historical frame to explicitly deliver the moral of the story in relation to current political crises: "I call on all nations! If you love your freedom, gather together your interests and your forces and learn that, if there is no power that will not fail when it collides against the immense force of your union, neither is there an enemy so weak that it will not defeat and enslave you when you are disunited."

As proponents of Enlightenment reason and neoclassical restraint, the Tlaxcalans are characterized less through ethnographic efforts to portray indigenous responses to colonialism and more through what Debra Castillo calls "straightforward homologies" with popular notions of Greek and Roman antiquity.[6] The effect resembles but falls short of Martí's postcolonial historical imagination in "Our América," where he insists that "The history of America from the Incas to the present must be taught in its smallest detail, even if the Greek Archons go untaught. Our own Greece is preferable to the Greece that is not ours; we need it more."[7] While Martí calls for both historical study of and political coalition with Indians, *Jicoténcal* looks to Europe's originary sites of ancient democracy as historical models, relocating them in the New World in a move that displaces living Indians with a European tradition of romantic primitivism.

However, *Jicoténcal*'s version of romantic primitivism contrasts interestingly with the familiar model found in James Fenimore Cooper's *The Last of the Mohicans* (1826), published the same year as *Jicoténcal*. Like *Jicoténcal*, *The Last of the Mohicans* depicts national bonds forming out of a historical moment of tragic Indian demise, but it racializes those national bonds quite differently. (See the chapters in this volume by Sandra Gustafson, Jennifer Rae Greeson and Russ Castronovo for further discussion of Cooper's racial politics.[b]) Both novels (and, indeed, most of the novels that I discuss in this chapter) could be classified as what Doris Sommer has called "foundational fictions" in that they use romantic heterosexual relations to form unions symbolizing newly forming national identities, but while *Jicoténcal* redeems its mixed-race unions by allowing the partners to live and suggesting that their offspring will carry forward the national spirit, Cooper's novel draws firm lines between fertile white unions that will create an American future and doomed mixed-race unions.[8] Indeed, as Anna Brickhouse has suggested, the death of Cooper's Cora, whose Afro-Caribbean blood makes her an "embodiment of the novel's anxious diagnosis of Caribbean history," signals a kind of hemispheric anti-imagining that affirms white racial purity rather than sharing geopolitical identity with the too-fluid racial mixing of the West Indies.[9] In contrast, at the end of *Jicoténcal*, the call for political unity is left to be carried out by the children of Doña Marina, Cortés's mistress and interpreter, who atones for her betrayal of her people, transforming from the sexualized symbol of American infidelity to a redeemed mother of New World colonial resistance.[10]

While we might anticipate that the conquest of Mexico would provide a historical setting for fictional explorations of Mexican national identity, the notion of a hemispheric novel allows us to recognize that this history also

b Sandra Gustafson, "Cooper and the idea of the Indian" (chapter 6); Jennifer Greeson, "Imagining the South" (chapter 14); Russ Castronovo, "Imperialism, Orientalism, and empire" (chapter 32).

provides a rich site for fictional constructions of an interconnected New World identity. Cuban works such as Gertrudis Gómez de Avellaneda's novel *Guatimozín* (1846; translated into English by Mrs. Wilson W. Blake in 1898) continue the tradition, as do a series of historical novels written by United States authors. For these US authors, such stories of originary New World identity negotiate a number of tensions about the role of the United States in partnering with or leading Mexico and other Spanish American democracies, as well as about the ongoing relationship of the United States to violent Indian removal policies.[11] A series of US-authored historical romances set in Mexico offer similarly sympathetic portrayals of indigenous Americans beset by cruel Spanish conquistadors, supporting for US readers the black legend of unjust Spanish conquest and identification with New World liberation from Spain.[12] Examples from this tradition are Robert Montgomery Bird's *Calavar, or, The Knight's Conquest: A Romance of Mexico* (1834) and its sequel *The Infidel, or The Fall of Mexico: A Romance* (1835), the anonymously published novella "Chalcahual" (printed in the 1848 *Democratic Review*), and Lew Wallace's *The Fair God, Or, The Last of Tzins: A Tale of the Conquest of Mexico* (published in 1872, but begun while Wallace served as a soldier in the Mexican–American War). These works reveal a perception in the United States that Mexican history *was* a part of United States history, an idea that drew the artist Emanuel Leutze (of *Washington Crossing the Delaware* fame) to this subject matter for his 1848 painting *The Storming of the Teocalli by Cortez and His Troops*. In all of these works, identification is suspended between the barbarous European invaders and the noble indigenous American defenders, creating a sense of obligation to right the wrongs of Spanish colonialism and to perfect the civilizing mission in the New World.

The introduction to Bird's *Calavar* signals this ambivalent identification by positioning the United States as a kind of executor to the fallen Aztecs, whose political will was thwarted by Spanish colonization. In the tradition of historical romances such as Hawthorne's *The Scarlet Letter* (1850) or Lydia Maria Child's *Hobomok (1823)*, *Calavar*'s introduction claims that the novel is based upon a recovered historical document – in this case, one created by a lineal descendent of the Aztec emperor Montezuma and entrusted by him to an American traveler (referred to only as "the American"), who promises to translate the work into English and publish it. The American proves his worthiness for this task by praising pre-Columbian civilizations and declaiming the lack of civilized improvements that Spanish rule brought to the Americas, even after the war of independence made Mexico a democracy. (Montezuma's descendant calls the Mexican democratic presidents "viceroys" in a confusion that emphasizes the continuation of Spanish failures in the Mexican republic.) It is the duty of the American, by virtue of his "intellectual as well as political independence" to convince the world of untapped American potential, once freed from Spanish tyranny *and* Mexican disorder.[13]

Lew Wallace, author of the bestselling *Ben-Hur* (1880), employs a similar framing device in *The Fair God* (1873), which begins with a preface representing the story as a lost colonial document, one supposedly written by an early sixteenth-century Tezcucan who wrote the story of Spanish conquest from his own perspective "to rescue his race from oblivion." Like *Calavar* and *Jicoténcal*, *The Fair God* portrays its Aztec heroes as proto-democrats. Its hero, the Aztec leader Guatamozin (whose name invokes a real-life historical figure central to Mexican national narratives), uses reason to conquer superstition in defending his people from Cortéz. While the weak-willed Montezuma encourages his people to submit to the conquerors, (because he believes that the light-skinned Cortés is Quetzalcoatl, the "fair" god), Guatamozin convinces the Aztec "nation," as he repeatedly calls it, to use "the judgment and the will of many to elect a new king and expel the invaders." Readers know Guatamozin will fail, but are reassured by the dying Montezuma's prophecy that someday the United States will take a role in carrying out his unfinished business of democracy: Montezuma looks eight generations into the future and sees the New World "tribes newly risen, like the trodden grass, and in their midst a Priesthood and a Cross. An age of battles more, and lo! The Cross but not the Priests; in their stead Freedom and God!"[14]

But if *The Fair God* encourages identification with lost Aztecs to authorize United States control of Mexican territory or resources, it does so in part by employing US racial prohibitions and the fear of sexual impurity that Russ Castronovo argues elsewhere in this volume accompanied US imperial fantasies. [c] Following the conventions of earlier historical novels, Wallace creates a variation on the la Malinche story of a native woman who acted as an interpreter and adviser to Cortés by designating an Aztec woman as the symbol and agent of American failure; in *The Fair God*, it is Montezuma's daughter Nenetzin who falls in love with a Spaniard, betrays her people unwittingly, loses her virginity, and dies soon thereafter. A clear example of what Sandra Messinger Cypress calls the "Malinche paradigm" of equating fallible female purity with compromised national integrity, Wallace's swift punishment of Nenetzin in the narrative also denies racial mixing: the imagined Aztecs to be aided by future US Americans are not the offspring of this

c See Castronovo, chapter 32.

tragic mixed-race union but remain instead in the fertile realm of historical imagination.[15] It is possible that Wallace read *Jicoténcal*; he researched *The Fair God* for over twenty years in English and in Spanish, traveling to the Library of Congress and to Mexico City.[16] But his vision of transamerican unity and of the racial character of the Americas contrasts clearly with *Jicoténcal*, demonstrating the ambivalence with which many US Americans regarded the notion of shared hemispheric identity.

This ambivalence is stretched to its limit by the end of the century, as we see in Thomas Janvier's *The Aztec Treasure-House: A Romance of Contemporaneous Antiquity* (1890), a fantasy adventure in which contemporary American scientists and treasure hunters join a Mexican priest in search of a lost city of Aztecs who have remained hidden from European colonization since Cortés's invasion. The plot allows the Americans to re-enact Spanish conquest by plundering a kingdom filled with Indian treasure, while also acting as agents in a narrative of hemispheric liberation – the Americans set off a "revolution" in the lost kingdom, ensuring a more just society free from the tyranny of its priests. Reckoning with these dual impulses toward revolution and material gain, late nineteenth-century authors began to take the contradiction between hemispheric political idealism and US imperial destiny as their topic. They devised plots that look not to a mythic, proto-democratic indigenous past but to the commercial present as a setting for transamerican relations. Richard Harding Davis's *Soldiers of Fortune* (1897) and O. Henry's *Cabbages and Kings* (1904) both take place in present-day imaginary contemporary Latin American republics. Called "Olancho" and "Anchuria," these states are generic spaces that typify a generalized sense of Latin American political corruption and instability; a character in *Soldiers of Fortune* calls Olancho "one of those little republics down there." The two texts differ in tone (the best-selling *Soldiers of Fortune* is a romance while O. Henry's composite novel of interlinked stories is a satire), but both contend with the perception that hemispheric political solidarity is an outdated notion unsuited to the modern world. In both works, US Americans aid in deposing governments unfriendly to US economic interests. The hero of Davis's *Soldiers of Fortune* manages simultaneously to secure the interests of the US mining company he represents and to restore democracy by placing power in the hands of old General Rojas, the leader who, the Americans say, would be chosen as president by the Olanchans "if they were ever given a chance to vote for the man they want."[17] In *Cabbages and Kings*, the Vesuvius Fruit Company aids a revolution against a government that threatens its profits by raising the taxes on exported bananas. When a character naïvely protests that "a business firm does not go to war with a nation," a fruit company representative explains, "Oh, it is only a matter of business . . . and that is what moves the world of to-day." While Davis reassures readers that the United States can foster both democracy and development in its dealings with its southern neighbors, O. Henry's novel satirically mixes the language of business and the language of democracy to show the reader a new, politically unstable (as in the "world-moving" Vesuvius), but perhaps inevitable state of affairs wherein democracy takes the back seat to informal commercial empire. Coining the now familiar phrase "banana republic" and ironically naming a US insurance company that benefits from Anchurian revolution the "Republic Insurance Company," O. Henry's novel underscores the new brand of neoliberalism guiding US perceptions of the hemisphere.[18]

But to view hemispheric novels as pitting Martí's transnational "Our América" against the homogeneous colossus of US commercial and territorial expansion would be too limiting. Within the Americas, economic and racial formations created cultural circuits and regional links that surpass or blur this sense of binary conflict. One example is the geographic formation that Philip Curtin calls the "plantation complex," which linked the Southern antebellum United States with Caribbean agricultural slaveholding economies, producing narratives of transnational coalition that regionally and racially divided the United States rather than binding them together.[19] (Jennifer Greeson discusses this transnational association of the US South with the Caribbean elsewhere in this volume.[d]) US–Cuban writings about slavery and race provide a revealing case study wherein the larger political ideal of New World democracy fades behind these alternate regional identifications and disidentifications.

Louisa May Alcott critiques Cuban slavery in her first novel, *Moods* (1864), where the transcendentalist hero Adam Warwick reclaims his individualism by rejecting the seductive Cuban beauty Ottilla, who has tricked him into marriage. He leaves her, announcing his intention to return "Straight to the North. The luxurious life enervates me; the pestilence of slavery lurks in the air and infects me; I must build myself up and find again the man I was." For Alcott, the lucrative sugar-producing colony of Cuba serves as a geographic shorthand for the social and material connections that prevent a New Englander's self-reliance.

For Mary Peabody Mann, whose 1887 novel *Juanita: A Romance of Real Life in Cuba Fifty Years Ago* was based on her 1833–1835 stay at a Cuban plantation, Cuba similarly represents a space of oppression threatening to disturb New

d See Greeson, chapter 14, 239, 249.

England political and philosophical notions of nation and selfhood. *Juanita* tells the story of Helen Wentworth, a New England schoolteacher visiting her old boarding school friend Isabel Rodriguez, now the wife of a wealthy Cuban sugar plantation owner. Horrified by the brutality and inhumanity of slavery she sees on the plantation, Helen is thrown into self-doubt about her own complicity with slavery. Her crisis is both individual and regional; as a representative New Englander, she is shocked by Cuban slavery into a recognition of slavery in the Southern United States and of the unequal status of free people of color in the Northern states. This recognition also sends her into repeated speculations about the relationship of slavery to Unitarian and transcendentalist conceptions of nature and to cherished traditions of New England liberty. Mann visited Cuba with her sister Sophia, Nathaniel Hawthorne's bride-to-be, and while Sophia's "Cuba Journals" were widely circulated in transcendentalist circles and admired for their philosophical treatments of nature, Mann's treatment of nature in *Juanita* is less optimistic than her sister's, darkened by uncertainty about the coexistence of slavery and tropical natural beauty.

Torn between a moral obligation to bear witness to slavery's wrongs and a desire to protect herself from the discomfort of confronting slavery, Helen finally decides to leave Cuba, after telling Isabella that her "knowledge of slavery was getting to be unbearable." Here Helen embodies the prevailing New England preference for disassociation with the problematic slaveholding colony. While Helen and other characters discuss the possibility that the United States will annex Cuba, liberating it from Spanish control and improving the condition of its slaves through gradual reform, the narrator, speaking with decades of hindsight, reminds readers that in practice, annexation would only have "extend[ed] the area of slavery" under the US flag.

Mann's anxiety about the corrupting influence of Cuban slavery also encompasses a fear of racial mixture, an element that makes *Juanita* an interesting counterpoint to Cuban-authored novels about race and slavery during the same period. Gertrudis Gómez de Avellaneda's novel *Sab* (1841) features a number of similar plot elements, similarities that could be parallel development or literary influence, since it is entirely possible that Mann read *Sab*. (Fluent in Spanish, Mann was a correspondent with the Argentinian novelist and soon-to-be president Domingo Faustino Sarmiento; in 1868 she translated into English his famous novel *Facundo*, which, interestingly for my purposes here, was inspired by Cooper's Leatherstocking tales.[20]) Both *Juanita* and *Sab* feature enslaved, mixed-race title characters who serve in positions of authority and who fall in love with whites brought up alongside them in the household they serve, only to die tragically. In Mann's novel, Juanita is a mixed-race Moor who is treated more as a family member than a servant; her room is filled with books, her paintings line the walls of the home, and she works in the Rodriguez household by helping the white governess in the nursery, a highly segregated space that Isabella will not allow other slaves to enter. Raised side by side with the eldest Rodriguez son, Ludvico, Juanita falls in love with him only to have her heart broken when he marries the frivolous US-educated Cuban heiress Carolina. In de Avellaneda's novel, Sab is also an ancillary member of Don Felix de B—'s family circle (and a literal but unacknowledged relative as the illegitimate son of Felix's brother); Sab works as the plantation overseer and has been educated along with his young mistress, Don Felix's beautiful daughter Carlotta de B—, who is the object of Sab's affections and who naïvely trusts her heart to an avaricious Anglo-American suitor, Enrique Otway.

However, these parallel plots convey quite different conceptions of Cuban nationalism. In *Sab*, Sab's unrequited love for Carlotta seems an early articulation of the interracial alliances that fueled Cuban nationalism later in the century, as Carlotta's misplaced affection for the blond but heartless Enrique instead of the sensitive, romantic Sab reveals the error of arbitrary racist social divisions and the interference of Anglo-American interlopers preventing Cuban interracial national bonds. Caught between her father's financially failing, genteel slaveholding regime and the heartless US and British commercial interests represented by Enrique, Carlotta is tragically flawed in her inability to choose Sab, her cousin and her slave, the one character capable of sharing in her passionate identification with the romantically portrayed Cuban landscape and indigenous history. In a nationalist move similar to those seen in *Jicoténcal*, *Calavar*, and *The Fair God*, Sab's symbolic association with Cuban nationalism is secured by his relationship with pre-Columbian Cuban indigeneity, embodied in his adopted Indian mother Martina. The novel ends after Sab's death with the repentant Carlotta joining Martina's spirit to honor Sab's grave in a belated act of Cuban multiracial national love.[21]

Mann's *Juanita* is much less concerned with Cuban nationalism, finding in Ludvico's and Juanita's tragic interracial romance reason to steer clear of slavery – and of racial difference – altogether. Isabella tries desperately to segregate her children from their African slaves and "the contamination of Cuban life," hoping that they will grow up to someday move away from the island altogether and make Cuba "more of a dream than a reality." Although sympathetically portrayed, the tragic mulatta Juanita is a contaminant that slips past Isabella's boundaries. While Isabella trusts that Juanita's presence in the household is safe because both Ludvico and Juanita "know completely their positions in society forbid anything like marriage between them," the New Englander Helen warns, "You sleep on a volcano. May it never burst forth into flame!" The volcano is not slave rebellion, but the "chaos" of an interracial society that Mann cannot reconcile with either US annexation or Cuban independence.

Slave rebellion, feared especially in nineteenth-century Cuba because of its large black population's rapid growth through the illegally continuing Atlantic slave trade, haunts both *Juanita* and *Sab*, through references to the feared precedent of Haitian revolution and descriptions of the brutal repression required to maintain white power in Cuba. But unlike in Martin Delany's novel *Blake* (1859–1862), where blacks in Cuba and the United States coordinate a hemispheric slave rebellion,[e] Mann and de Avellaneda's novels explore the social transgressions of love and sex more than the possibility of violence.

Another Cuban novel that explores cross-racial love is Cirilo Villaverde's novel *Cecilia Valdéz: La Loma del Angel* (1882), which like *Sab* and *Juanita* features a tragic interracial romance between individuals with ambiguous family bonds, and which, like *Sab*, promotes "*la Cuba mulata*," the idea of a Cuban national identity generated in racial mixing. The title character, Cecilia, is a mulatta who does not know her father's identity and thus unwittingly falls in love with her white half-brother. Here the implicit story of incest between pseudo-foster siblings in *Sab* and *Juanita* becomes literal. The narrator melodramatically withholds knowledge of Cecilia's true relation to her lover until late in the novel, long after most readers have guessed the secret. Their incest implies the blindness of a society that officially prohibits miscegenation, showing that when kinship between people of different races is denied, true identities are buried and kinship prohibitions cannot stand. However, as Wernor Sollors has pointed out, incest and miscegenation were complex tropes for figuring racial meanings in nineteenth-century literature, and we can also see a positive meaning for Cecilia and Leonardo's relationship: love between white and black Cuban brothers and sisters conveys a longed for but as yet imperfect fraternal unity.[22]

Perhaps a better US corollary to *Cecilia Valdéz* is not *Juanita* or earlier antislavery novels such as *Uncle Tom's Cabin* (1852), but rather the tradition of post-emancipation novels exploring mixed-race identity. For example, Pauline Hopkins's novel *Of One Blood; Or, The Hidden Self* (1903) also offers complex,

e For more detailed discussion of *Blake*, see Robert S. Levine, "The early African American novel," chapter 16, 275–277, in this volume.

multiple meanings for a situation of incest and miscegenation. There, on the one hand, the mixed-race illegitimate children of slave and slaveowner, Reuel and Dianthe, commit the horror of incest, tricked by slavery's secrets into thinking that they are not brother and sister – "of one blood." And yet, on the other hand, the biblical notion that blacks and whites are "of one blood" also carries positive connotations in Hopkins's novel, as the fraternal bonds of shared humanity unite all the black and white main characters of the novel.[23]

As Spanish-language Cuban novels, *Sab* and *Cecilia Valdéz* offer rich comparisons to US melodramas of miscegenation, but their printing histories remind us that the hemispheric approach tends to perforate national borders rather than reinforcing them. Villaverde wrote and published *Cecilia Valdéz* in New York, and Rodrigo Lazo has demonstrated that the author's long exile in New York and his involvement in movements for US annexation of Cuba influenced his writing of the novel, an influence that emerges in the novel's oblique references to the United States.[24] *Sab* was first published in Spain, where de Avellaneda lived most of her adult life, but copies smuggled past Spanish censors circulated in Cuba, and the novel later appeared as a serial in a New York Spanish-language periodical, suggesting its role in the Cuban exile's revolutionary activities. For Lazo, such transnational publication histories suggest the necessity of separating literary history's typical conflation of space, nation, and language.[f] Study of these and other multilingual and transnational print cultures complicates Benedict Anderson's familiar claim about nationalism following from closed circuits of printed narratives in the form of newspapers and novels, suggesting a more interconnected emergence of New World nationalisms.[25]

What, then, is a hemispheric novel? Is it one that references inter-American relations in its plot or thematic content? One that engages transnational phenomena like revolution, slavery, or the literary device of the tragic mulatta? One that crosses national borders in its history of publication, distribution, translation, or reception? If a hemispheric novel is all of these things, then the category is potentially limitless, including any work that influences or is influenced by texts from other places in the Americas. Certainly it would include Helen Hunt Jackson's *Ramona* (1884), a tragic romance of cross-racial Mexican–Spanish and Indian love set in post-1848 California. José Martí translated *Ramona* into Spanish, adapting Jackson's critical exploration of the effects of US expansion on Indians and Mexican culture into what he called "our novel," and described it as "a work that in

f See Rodrigo Lazo, "Hemispheric American novels," chapter 65 in this volume.

our countries of America could be a true resurrection."[26] Read in the context of US regionalism and sentimental reform, Jackson's novel is remarkable for its assimilationist portrayal of Native Americans and its characteristically US American ambivalence about race mixing. Although it takes Aunt Ri's "hit-er-miss" pattern rag rug, with its "indiscriminately mixed tints" and "unexpectedly harmonious blending of colors" as a metaphor for a desired multiracial US society, the plot takes care that colors are not too indiscriminately mixed, allowing Ramona's marriage to the Indian Alessandro because she is part Indian herself, and, after Alessandro's murder, sending Ramona and Felipe Moreno, her Spanish-blooded foster-brother and second husband, to Mexico to raise their family, an ending that symbolically leaves California and its race relations for the white American settlers to sort out.[27]

Yet in Martí's interpretation, *Ramona* articulates a New World mestizo identity that unites Spanish and Indian heritage and is beset by Anglo-American imperialism in a cultural context that extends beyond the borders of the United States. Like *Sab* and *Juanita*, *Ramona* is named for a racially mixed title character who lives as an ancillary member of the pure-blooded Spanish family, one that paternal authority in the form of Señora Moreno would keep segregated. Before Ramona marries her white foster-brother Felipe, she falls in love with and marries a man of her mother's Indian race, making her less an impurity than a cultural conduit, one that Jackson ultimately removes from US borders, but that Martí nevertheless integrates into his own conception of the new American family.

However, it is also possible that we could call *Ramona* a hemispheric novel even if Martí had never assigned such importance to it, given its setting in the California borderlands. Like María Amparo Ruiz de Burton's *The Squatter and the Don* (1885) and Gertrude Atherton's *The Californians* (1898), both regional novels written in the wake of the bestselling *Ramona*, such stories have the potential effect of denationalizing simplistic conflations of English language, US territorial statehood, and American culture by showing the legacies of military violence, territorial claims, and multiple languages and cultures contending within the perceived space of national culture. Similar claims have been made for a number of US novels that render various historical frontiers and peripheral regions of the United States as cultural borderlands, including Cooper's *The Prairie* (1827) or George Washington Cable's *The Grandissimes* (1880). Less Frederick Jackson Turner's limit between civilization and savagery and more a multipolar space for contending Euro-American articulations of New World identity,[g] the frontiers and peripheries in these fictions exhibit a terrain that cannot provide a regenerative escape from global forces because those global forces shape the stories set there.[28]

But perhaps defining or labeling a hemispheric American novel should not be our goal, since scholars pursuing transamerican literary relations have been less interested in identifying a genre or canon than in revealing circuits of meaning that revise nationalist conceptions of culture. One would be more likely to describe a hemispheric *approach* rather than a body of work called hemispheric novels. Yet the form of the nineteenth-century novel, particularly the genre of heterosexual romance binding together and/or excluding disparate elements into a historically symbolic family, must be recognized as a key tool for figuring the racial and international conflicts that accompanied New World nationalisms and their various visions of hemispheric identity. My focus in this chapter has been on these competing and interconnected familial national narratives, but a few words are required here about my conception of hemispheric studies, which is admittedly more historically contingent than that of some other critics working in the area, and certainly narrower than one might expect upon hearing the geographically expansive term "hemisphere." While some critics have called for an American studies that covers the space it purports to name, decenters the United States, and captures the perspectives of "a polycentric American hemisphere with no dominant center," the hemispheric concept's historical association with specific nineteenth-century American revolutions makes it an awkward tool for framing globalized cultural studies of the Americas from Greenland to the Falkland Islands.[29] To reject dominant centers, one would need to look beyond the various colonialist, nationalist, and transnational interests that deployed the geographic frame, and at the same time justify dividing the hemisphere from the rest of the globe, a division that makes no sense without those partial views. As a concept, the Western Hemisphere bears the historical traces of political projects that defined the Americas through a social and spatial binary separating Europe from America, and as such the very term connotatively fortifies a duality of Old and New Worlds existing in different times and spaces, making it an unlikely device for challenging border effects in literary studies. While I agree with Rodrigo Lazo's statement in this volume that a hemispheric approach pertains not to a literal geographic area but to "a set of relationships that cross time and space in a variety of ways," I would warn that

g On Turner's conception of the frontier, see Stephanie LeMenager, "Imagining the frontier," chapter 31 in this volume, 515–516.

the binary division at its foundation can conceal global relationships as much as reveal them.[h]

In other words, one must not buttress the spatial binary of Old and New Worlds by overlooking narratives of the Americas that contest notions of New World difference and project other kinds of global geographies. For example, Ruiz de Burton has been labeled a hemispheric writer, but her first novel *Who Would Have Thought It?* (1872) is far more invested in a cosmopolitan, transatlantic social sphere than in any conception of New World difference, especially one that – like Martí's – uses interracial bonds with Indians to naturalize and sustain transamerican political projects.[30] In another variation on the "racially ambiguous foundling in the family" narrative in *Juanita, Sab, and Ramona*, Ruiz de Burton's Mexican heroine Lola de Medina is rescued from captivity with Indians and adopted by the Norval family in New England, where she falls in love with the eldest brother Julian, much to Mrs. Norval's disapproval. Mrs. Norval considers Lola to be "black," but the reader is reassured of not only her whiteness but also of her ties to a civilized, European cultural authority: the de Medinas prefer the restoration of monarchy in Mexico rather than any hemispheric bond either with presumptuous Anglo-American imperialism or with Indians and New World Africans. When Lola marries Julian, she is not symbolically inducted into a broadened US national family, because the couple instead move to Mexico to live with the Europeanized de Medinas, safely returning to a stable scene of patriarchal authority, purified of the traumatic threat of New World hybridity. If we recognize *Who Would Have Thought It?* as a commentary on post-revolutionary conceptions of the hemisphere, we also see that it rejects the revolutionary territorial frame of the hemisphere in favor of a transatlantic mapping of white cosmopolitanism.

Where the project of hemispheric American studies will take us is not yet known. Is it an end unto itself or an intermediate step toward a more globalized literary study? How will institutional roadblocks to multilingual and comparative cultural criticism be surmounted, and will the project's ideal of decentering the United States extend to scholarly engagement with critics writing outside of the United States academy? Will it lead us away from our dependence upon nation as the fundamental unit of cultural analysis or only return us to a more complicated sense of interconnected nationalisms? And perhaps most important for this volume, to what extent can hemispheric American studies supplement a history of the United States novel, when some

h Lazo, chapter 65, 1091.

of its theoretical underpinnings call into question the very existence of something called "the United States novel"? These remain points of controversy, but to ask them is to take a step toward redefining the spatially and linguistically isolated conception of "culture" that has grounded traditional versions of literary history.

Notes

1. On the historical evolution of the Western Hemisphere as a geographic and political concept, see Arthur P. Whitaker, *The Western Hemisphere Idea: Its Rise and Decline* (Ithaca, NY: Cornell University Press, 1954).
2. On the Monroe Doctrine as a cultural expression of both solidarity and division, see Gretchen Murphy, *Hemispheric Imaginings: The Monroe Doctrine and Narratives of U.S. Empire* (Durham, NC: Duke University Press, 2005).
3. This phrase is most notably used by Anna Brickhouse in her groundbreaking *Transamerican Literary Relations and the Nineteenth-Century Public Sphere* (Cambridge: Cambridge University Press, 2004).
4. José Martí, "Our América," in *José Martí: Selected Writings*, ed. and trans. Esther Allen (New York: Penguin Books, 2002), 296. Martí is a key figure for recent scholarship on inter-American studies.
5. Guillermo I. Castillo-Feliú took the liberty of re-indigenizing the title's spelling in his translation of the novel, *Xicoténcatl: An Anonymous Historical Novel about the Events Leading Up to the Conquest of the Aztec Empire* (Austin: University of Texas Press, 1999). In general, in this chapter, I retain the spellings for Aztec historical figures used in the literary works even when they are not currently preferred (for example, *Montezuma* instead of *Moctezuma*).
6. Debra Castillo, *Redreaming America: Toward a Bilingual American Culture* (Albany: State University of New York Press, 2005), 22.
7. Martí, "Our América," 291.
8. Doris Sommer, *Foundational Fictions: The National Romances of Latin America* (Berkeley: University of California Press, 1991).
9. Brickhouse, *Transamerican Literary Relations*, 61.
10. For critical readings of *Jicoténcal* in the context of transamerican literary relations, *ibid.*, 37–83; Castillo, *Redreaming America*,1–54; and Jesse Alemán, "The Other Country: Mexico, the United States and the Gothic History of Conquest," in *Hemispheric American Studies*, ed. Caroline F. Levander and Robert S. Levine (New Brunswick, NJ: Rutgers University Press, 2008), 75–95.
11. See Eric Wertheimer, *Imagined Empires: Incas, Aztecs, and the New World of American Literature* (Cambridge: Cambridge University Press, 1999).
12. Julian Juderías coined the term "black legend" in his *La leyenda negra y la verdad histórica* (1914), to describe depictions of Spain and Spaniards as cruel and intolerant in Protestant anti-Spanish literature since the sixteenth century. On

the black legend in the United States, see María DeGuzmán, *Spain's Long Shadow: The Black Legend, Off-Whiteness, and Anglo-American Empire* (Minneapolis: University of Minnesota Press, 2005).

13. On *Calavar* and *The Infidel*, see Alemán, "The Other Country," Castillo *Redreaming America*, and Nancy Buffington, "Conquering Histories: The Historical Romances of Robert M. Bird," *Modern Language Studies* 30.2 (Autumn 2000): 87–117.
14. On *The Fair God*, see Murphy, *Hemispheric Imaginings*, 97–118.
15. See Sandra Messinger Cypess, *La Malinche in Mexican Literature from History to Myth* (Austin:University of Texas Press, 1991) and Rolando Romero and Amanda Nolacea Harris, eds., *Feminism, Nation, Myth: La Malinche* (Houston, TX: Arte Público Press, 2005).
16. See Robert Morsberger and Katherine M. Morsberger, *Lew Wallace: Militant Romantic* (New York: McGraw-Hill, 1980).
17. On *Soldiers of Fortune* see Murphy, *Hemispheric Imaginings*, 119–144.
18. On *Cabbages and Kings*, see Kirsten Silva Gruesz, "The Mercurial Space of 'Central' America: New Orleans, Honduras, and the Writing of the Banana Republic," in Levander and Levine, *Hemispheric American Studies*, 140–165.
19. Philip Curtin, *The Rise and Fall of the Plantation Complex: Essays in Atlantic History* (New York: Cambridge University Press, 1990).
20. On Mann's relationship with Sarmiento, see Patricia M. Ard, "Introduction: Mary Peabody Mann's Juanita: A Historical Romance of Antillean Slavery," in *Juanita: A Romance of Real Life Cuba Fifty Years Ago*, ed. Patricia M. Ard (Charlottesville: University Press of Virginia, 2000), xiv–xv. On Sarmiento and Cooper, see Sommer, *Foundational Fictions*, 52–82.
21. On *Sab*, see Sommer, *Foundational Fictions*, 114–137 and Brickhouse, *Transamerican Literary Relations*, 173–179.
22. Wernor Sollors, *Neither Black Nor White Yet Both: Thematic Explorations of Interracial Literature* (Cambridge: Cambridge University Press, 1997), 316–318.
23. On the multiple meanings of blood in Hopkins's novel, see Jennie A. Kassanoff, "Fate Has Linked Us Together: Blood, Gender, and the Politics of Representation in Pauline Hopkins's *Of One Blood*," in *The Unruly Voice: Rediscovering Pauline Hopkins*, ed. John Cullen Gruesser (Urbana: University of Illinois Press, 1996), 16.
24. Rodrigo Lazo, *Writing to Cuba: Filibustering and Cuban Exiles in the United States* (Chapel Hill: University of North Carolina Press, 2005), 169–192. On *Cecilia Valdéz*, see also Brickhouse, *Transamerican Literary Relations*, 153–160.
25. Benedict Anderson, *Imagined Communities: Reflections on the Origin and Spread of Nationalism* (London: Verso, 1983).
26. José Martí, "Prologue," in *Ramona: Novela Americana*, trans. José Martí (New York: [s.n.], 1888), v, iv. On Martí's translation and transculturation of *Ramona*, see Susan Gillman, "Otra Vez Caliban/Encore Caliban: Adaptation, Translation, American Studies," *American Literary History* 21.1–2 (2008): 187–209.

27. On Aunt Ri's rug as a symbol, see John M. Gonzales, "The Warp of Whiteness: Domesticity and Empire in Helen Hunt Jackson's *Ramona*," *American Literary History* 16.3 (2004): 437.
28. For examples of this approach, see Stephanie LeMenager, *Manifest and Other Destinies: Territorial Fictions of the Nineteenth-Century United States* (Lincoln: University of Nebraska Press, 2004); and Jennifer Rae Greeson, "Expropriating The Great South and Exporting Local Color," *Hemispheric American Studies* 18.3 (2006): 116–139.
29. Caroline F. Levander and Robert S. Levine, "Introduction: Essays Beyond the Nation," in Levine and Levander, *Hemispheric American Studies*, 7.
30. In "The Squatter, the Don, and the Grandissimes in Our America," in *Mixing Race, Mixing Culture: Inter-American Literary Dialogues*, ed. Debra Rosenthal and Monica Kaup (Austin: University of Texas Press, 2002), Susan Gillman assigns to Ruiz de Burton an "incipient, hemispheric vision" expressed in her novels and in her letters, one that Gillman claims "saw the Californios as part of a larger international collectivity or 'raza,' Spano-Americans, like the race-family-nation of Nuestra América that Martí identified as distinct from the American which is not ours" (157). I contend that this is a mischaracterization of Ruiz de Burton's view of *la raza*, which is decidedly more transatlantic and less tied to the revolutionary space of New World identity and race mixing than Martí's. In *Hemispheric Imaginings* (97–118), I argue that Ruiz de Burton opposed Martí's racial and spatial conception of "Our America."

34

The woman's novel beyond sentimentalism

ELIZABETH NOLAN

In her autobiography, *A Backward Glance* (1934), Edith Wharton cites her inspiration for the gritty realism of her 1911 novel, *Ethan Frome,* as a desire to revise the depiction of the New England landscape as seen through the "rose-coloured spectacles" of her predecessors, Sarah Orne Jewett and Mary Wilkins Freeman. In so doing, she appears to cast these regional artists, somewhat inaccurately, as sentimentalists. Elsewhere in the memoir she comments on the "laxities of the great Louisa" May Alcott, a writer to whom that epithet might more appropriately be applied, since contemporary responses to her work tended to note the "limited field" of her "charming and homely" domestic settings, whilst praising the "moral purpose" of the simple, straight-forward stories "which her own sex find especially delightful."[1] Wharton's interpretation of the generic affiliations of her antecedents may be inconsistent, but her disparagement of the achievements of these "authoresses" and her determination to distinguish her work from theirs speaks clearly of the burden placed upon a generation of artists by the legacy of a by then widely discredited tradition. Writing in the wake of sentimentalism, Wharton and many of her female contemporaries faced a particular challenge – how to negotiate a marginalized female literary tradition in order to establish a credible presence in the artistic life of the nation?

Women with literary ambition recognized that asserting the aesthetic value of their work depended on refusing what was perceived as the narrow, sentimental focus on home, hearth, and virtue under threat as exemplified in the "cosey parlor" of the "gentle and womanly" Mrs. Bird in Harriet Beecher Stowe's *Uncle Tom's Cabin* (1852), in the extended, tortuous trials of Ellen Montgomery, the heroine of Susan Warner's *The Wide, Wide World* (1850), and in the novels of numerous other women whose prolific output is discussed by Cindy Weinstein elsewhere in this volume. Women of Wharton's generation often sought to distance themselves from a huge body of fiction, which although incredibly popular, was derided by dominant critical discourse as limited, trivial, and formulaic, marred by an excess of feminine feeling and divorced from the serious business of articulating the American condition.[a] In attempting to establish their artistic credentials, many defined themselves against and in opposition to sentimental conventions and those of other marginalized, "feminine" narratives, including local color and regionalist traditions.[b] Instead they located their work within traditionally male forms. Willa Cather's fiction foregrounds her education in the classics and reveals her appropriation of the pastoral mode and the heroic pioneer narrative. Kate Chopin's work, like Wharton's, is informed by readings in the social sciences and engages with literary realism and naturalism discussed elsewhere in this volume (see especially Elliott, Bramen, and Campbell[c]). All three looked beyond female and, indeed American models, to situate their art in relation to a wider, more cosmopolitan European context, their stated literary influences including Flaubert, Maupassant, Eliot, and Proust.

As they sought to establish their own foothold in the literary marketplace, some women reinforced their identification with male-oriented traditions by adopting the tone of gender-biased critiques which denied the female-authored text the status of "literature." Others went further, their determination to distinguish their art from "inferior" feminine modes leading them to abjure the identity of woman writer altogether. Chopin biographer Emily Toth notes that as a fledgling author, her subject read widely in women's fiction, Warner's *Wide, Wide World* being among the titles in her library. Later, in attributing her artistic awakening to Guy de Maupassant, in whose psychological realism she recognized the potential to escape "tradition," Chopin would seem to denigrate the literary value of her early reading matter.[2] Similarly, although in more emphatic language, social reformer and activist Charlotte Perkins Gilman derided the emotional excesses of the traditional sentimental heroine and the legions of fictional women engaged in "screaming, fainting, or bursting into floods of tears."[3] In her autobiography, Wharton notes that during her own lifetime she only respected the intellectual capacity of three women and attributed the development of her own artistic

a See Cindy Weinstein's essay, "Sentimentalism," chapter 12 in this volume, 209.

b Tom Lutz, in "Cather and the regional imagination," chapter 26 in this volume, notes that for many critics the identification of writing as regionalist indicated limitation, provincialism, and a lack of national and international significance (438).

c See, in this volume, Michael Elliott, "Realism and radicalism: the school of Howells" (chapter 17); Carrie Bramen, "James, pragmatism and the realist ideal" (chapter 18); and Donna Campbell, "The rise of naturalism" (chapter 30).

sensibilities to the mentorship and guidance of an intimate group of male writers and intellectuals. In her reflections on matters of literary composition, a subject that occupied her throughout her career, Wharton gendered her work male: "I conceive of my subjects like a man – that is, rather more architectonically & dramatically than most women."[4] Willa Cather's critical appraisal of women writers was similarly damning. "I have not much faith in women in fiction," she said. "They have a sex consciousness that is abominable." Whilst acknowledging the craft of a select group of authors, including George Eliot and George Sand, and giving a nod to Charlotte Brontë for keeping her "sentimentality under control," Cather declared that "When a woman writes a story of adventure, a stout sea tale, a manly battle yarn, anything without wine, women and love, then I will begin to hope for something great from them, not before."[5]

And yet, despite the clamor of these women to embrace the authoritative, critically acclaimed principles of male narrative, such principles do not translate into their fiction. It is not the "manly battle yarn" and the tale of daring on the high seas that characterize the novels of Cather, Chopin, Gilman, and Wharton, but rather the domestic elements rooted in the discredited narratives of their female predecessors. Images of home and family abound in their work, as do tropes of maternity, community, and depictions of women's culture. Indeed, throughout their literary careers, the women discussed here enact frequent literary returns to what I will term "the local." Traditionally, of course, matters of scope have been a key determinant in the value and significance of art – the weighty universalism of stereotypically masculine literature opposed to the conventionally diminutive female narrative, bounded by particular spatial and geographic limits. But a localized focus does not have to suggest a limited artistic range, nor does it preclude serious literary engagement with the American condition. In *Cosmopolitan Vistas*, Tom Lutz places the regionalist voice at the center of important debates about "city and country, nature and culture, centre and periphery, tradition and modernity, high and low."[6] In so doing, he articulates a version of the local which is attuned to concerns of a global or universal nature, providing a useful framework through which the woman's novel of the post-sentimental era can be read. As Lutz notes, to write from the sensibility of a particular locale or cultural position is to be neither provincial, minor, nor marginal, epithets which, of course, commonly attach to women's writings.

Writing beyond sentimentalism, it would seem, depends less on a comprehensive eschewal of all that is "feminine" in art than on a radical reimagining of aspects of the domestic and the local. The 1890s to the 1920s witnessed a range of innovative twists on the local, all of them articulating particularly female artistic visions. Sustaining a dialogue with the traditions of a previous generation, the works discussed here demonstrate a remarkable range of artistic innovation. Chopin, Wharton, Cather, and Gilman variously invoke the conventions of the sentimental in order to expose their limitations; they rework and extend the thematic and stylistic range of local narratives to articulate universal concerns; and fuse the apparatus of marginalized modes with elements of mainstream literary currents including naturalism, transcendentalism, and utopian fiction. Their experiments in the novel participate in the creation of sophisticated hybrid forms and contribute to complex evolutions of genre, taking them beyond the limits of sentimentalism and enabling them to assert an aesthetic presence that is both credible and distinctly female.

Kate Chopin's novelistic career was over before any of the other women under discussion began theirs, and so it is not surprising that *The Awakening* (1899) is contiguous with nineteenth-century sentimental traditions. The work demonstrates a canny understanding of its sentimental progenitors and is punctuated with references and allusions to the conventions of domestic and local color fiction. But if Chopin evokes features of the sentimental, her lyrical, experimental narrative with its sensuous prose, unusual circular structure, and its focus on the inner consciousness of the heroine, subverts the underlying domestic ideology of the tradition at every turn, posing serious questions about the fundamental principles of family life – particularly marriage and motherhood. In stark contrast to the self-sacrificing mother figure of the domestic tale, the novel's heroine comes to view her children as "antagonists who had overcome her; who had overpowered and sought to drag her into the soul's slavery for the rest of her days." The apparatus of "feminine" fiction is used here as a foil for a woman's quest for an individual existence beyond female roles sanctioned by patriarchy and by conventional narrative.

Edna Pontellier, the novel's heroine, is an indifferent wife and an ambivalent mother. Although, like the sentimental heroine, she is prone to frequent weeping and experiences extremes of emotion from despair to euphoria, these bouts – and the heightened, dramatic language in which they are often rendered – reflect less on feminine fragility than on the momentous shift taking place as the middle-class wife and mother begins to realize the possibility of an autonomous existence: "She felt as if a mist had been lifted from her eyes, enabling her to look upon and comprehend the significance of life, that monster made up of beauty and brutality." The spatial imagery of *The Awakening* also palpably invokes the locations of earlier feminine modes – much of the action takes place on Grand Isle, where woman's culture dominates as wives and children take refuge from the stifling heat of New Orleans in midsummer. But again, *The Awakening* unsettles expectations, framing domesticity and maternity as restrictive and confining for women. Symbols of entrapment abound, and the novel's demarcation of gendered spaces serves merely to provide a series of boundaries for its transgressive heroine to exceed. Edna is often to be found in the liminal space of the porch, a site from which she mounts small rebellions against her husband's authority, on one occasion refusing to retire to the marital bedroom for the night, making it plain that she will not heed his demands for her to do so: "I mean to stay out here. I don't wish to go in, and I don't intend to."

By far the most contentious challenge to the domestic aesthetic that Chopin stages in this narrative is her separation of female sexuality not only from the sanctity of marriage and the function of motherhood, but also from any kind of moral framework. Edna's extramarital dalliance with Alcée Arobin, a man who elicits her desire but to whom she has no emotional attachment, is presented without authorial intervention or censure, a detail which provoked a flurry of outraged reviews and cost Chopin her literary reputation and her career. But, contemporary commentators responded only to *The Awakening*'s supposed immorality and did not comprehend the complex interplay of genres enacted by this groundbreaking novel. For in addition to its keen interrogation of female traditions, the narrative makes bold interventions into more authoritative forms. Notable amongst these is literary naturalism, a category informed by the work of the social scientists and generally understood as centering on the representation of human beings governed by instincts and passions who are conditioned and controlled by environment, heredity, economics, or chance. And it is in Chopin's engagement with naturalism that her revisioning of the local is most striking. Key naturalistic texts including Stephen Crane's *Maggie: A Girl of the Streets* (1893) and Frank Norris's *McTeague* (1899) employ equally tight locations, sharing a focus on the grim fight for survival in the brutal, often violent, city environment. Chopin, however, leaves behind the impoverished, urban, industrial setting and transplants the naturalistic imperative to the milieu of the middle class, the elegant drawing rooms of New Orleans' French Quarter and particularly to a genteel Louisiana summer retreat. Making selective use of the standard conventions of the genre, she moderates their effects to suit her purpose, which is to free her protagonist from the socially imposed roles of wife and mother that circumscribe her existence.

Chopin recognizes the potential of naturalistic narrative conventions to challenge social definition of the individual. Following the naturalist lead, Chopin figures Edna as a natural creature, emphasizing the drives and impulses that determine her heroine's unconventional behavior. Edna is depicted as a "beautiful, sleek animal waking up in the sun" and the manner in which she satisfies her basic appetite for food is primal rather than polite; she takes to "tearing" bread with her "strong white teeth." In extending the range of animal instincts that direct Edna, Chopin claims powerful sexual urges for her, and in so doing, she creates the controversial figure of the sexualized mother which places her in direct opposition to the values of domestic fiction. Her eroticization of Edna also indicates her difference from a masculinized literary naturalism informed by the tenets of Social Darwinism, which assign the woman a passive role in sexual selection.

Chopin's hybrid version of naturalism is further differentiated from mainstream currents by its lack of interest in heredity as a determining factor in human behavior. But if inherited factors are muted here, environment is pivotal, especially to the narrative's refiguring of the local aesthetic.

Up until publication of *The Awakening*, Chopin had been recognized as a practitioner of local color fiction, a relatively conventional genre, rich in the language and culture of a specific locale, offering nostalgic sketches of regional life. And, although she had often made use of this conservative frame to articulate subtle social critiques, her earlier collections of short stories were generally well received and celebrated for their "quaintness." In *The Awakening*, however, she evokes the familiar rural landscape, using it not as the setting for a "charming" tale of southern life, but for her frank exploration of female sexual desire and revolt against maternal self-sacrifice. In doing so, she refutes the reductive interpretations of the "local" in the local color fiction on which her literary reputation was based.

In her novella, *Ethan Frome* (1911), Wharton also engages naturalist themes while locating her tale in the regional, rural space. As in Chopin's text, environment is key, but the "mute melancholy landscape" of Starkfield, Massachusetts is remote from the exotic heat of Grand Isle, and awakening characters to their natural impulses and desires is not Wharton's primary concern. In Wharton's brand of naturalism, the imagery of disabling, smothering winter and snow conveys the role of determinism in human existence and the frustration of unfulfilled lives. Ethan Frome, a "ruin of a man," is victim to a range of external forces: familial obligation, grinding poverty, and a hostile environment render him incapable of directing his fate. Even his attempt to escape his misery through suicide with Mattie, his wife's young cousin and the woman he loves, is thwarted by a chance swerve of the sled they had hoped would take them to their deaths together. In Wharton's bleak treatment of the local scene, Mattie and Ethan survive, damaged and disfigured, trapped in a mutually helpless and dependent state with the differently defeated wife, Zeena. Donna Campbell has discussed at length Wharton's fusion of naturalism and local color fiction and her borrowing from and subversion of elements of female traditions in the novella. She notes, for example, the choice of a male rather than female perspective for the standard framed narration and explores the ways in which the professional, outsider figure "interrogates and implicitly condemns such standard local color myths as those of cohesive community, of healing, and of preserving and self-denial."[7] But, as well as participating in innovative experimentation with form and genre, Wharton's treatment of the New England scene can be read as an important reimagining of the local aesthetic to engage in debates of national and international significance.

Catharine Maria Sedgwick's earlier *New England Tale* (1822) is a "domestic tale" from the "female pen," described by one commentator as "a beautiful little picture of native scenery and manners, composed with exquisite delicacy of taste."[8] But *Ethan Frome* and its companion piece *Summer* (1917), whose protagonist, Charity Royall, represents a version of the sentimental heroine – to all intents and purposes an orphan, seduced, abandoned and pregnant with an illegitimate child when she is rescued by marriage to her much older guardian – have a thematic range which looks well beyond that of Sedgwick. Both novels exceed their immediate setting, transcending the concerns of the domestic, the local community, and the region. Their shared concern with the pessimism and isolation of small town life offers a bleak meditation on American modernity. Starkfield, a "dead" community from which "most of the smart ones get away" and *Summer*'s North Dormer, "a weather-beaten sunburnt village of the hills, abandoned of men, left apart by railway, trolley, telegraph, and all the forces that link life to life in modern communities," indicate the impact of the modern world on New England communities. Both are failing, dying towns.

Written in France during the First World War, *Summer* is undoubtedly informed by Wharton's experiences at the European front. The language Wharton employs to describe the desolate landscape of North Dormer, littered with ruined buildings, broken and decrepit architecture, resonates with her *Fighting France* (1915), for vivid descriptions of France's wartime wasteland. In Charity Royall's environs one house "looked singularly desolate. The paint was almost gone from the clapboards, the window-panes were patched with rags, and the garden was a poisonous tangle of nettles." In the Argonne that Wharton visits there is a similar "spectacle of ... tragic desolation ... fragments of masonry, bits of shop-fronts" and the ruins of "handsome doorways" and "the colonnaded court of a public building." A committed Francophile, much of Wharton's war writing rails against the ongoing destruction of a model society by an overdeveloped and mechanized modernity, and laments the passing of a superior culture. Janet Beer has noted that the narrative of *Summer* suggests a similar loss of a once admirable civilization: "everywhere there are traces of a time when a different kind of community spirit had been in evidence. From the quality of the now mouldy books in the town library to the vestiges of architectural refinement in the crumbling fabric of the once fine houses."[9] And dark and violent episodes disrupt the narrative of *Summer*, including the death of Charity's estranged mother, whose carelessly positioned body, with limbs splayed and clothes torn, has been interpreted as suggesting a battlefield corpse.[10] This is not a "manly battle yarn" but it is a war story and a reflection on the nature of civilization itself, and whilst it shares features with the journalism/travel writing genre of *Fighting France* it is mediated through the local aesthetic and the framework of female literary traditions. Far from the sentimentality of the local sketch, Wharton articulates in *Summer* a literary response to international conflict. To do so, however, she both locates herself in and speaks out of the regional frame.

Similarly, in spite of her outspoken critique of women's fiction, Willa Cather's most accomplished work employs the settings and apparatus of discredited female modes. Her first novel, *Alexander's Bridge* (1912), is transatlantic in scope and Jamesian in style, set in the elegant drawing rooms of Boston and London, but her mature artistic vision relies on envisioning matters of national and cross-cultural significance through the lens of the immediate and the personal, as Tom Lutz has discussed. But as well as focusing on the regional, Cather's writing is often informed by gendered concerns and she frequently places women's culture at the heart of her fiction, using the motifs of food and cooking, quilting and sewing, communal activity, conversation, and storytelling in her explorations of cultural and national history. Particularly in her early prairie novels, accounts of epic snowstorms, small town scandals, shared hardships, and neighborly cooperation become the stuff of legend. In *My Ántonia* (1918), for example, the woman-centered domestic space of Mrs. Harling's kitchen, where people gather to wait for the "cookies to bake or the taffy to cool," is the site in which Ántonia, the symbolic "founder of races," is coaxed to "tell her stories." As Susan J. Rosowski and

Ann Romines have noted, Cather's female-centered aesthetic and domestic subject are expansive, looking beyond the local to participate in significant debates about society and nation.[11]

In the expression of her aesthetic principles, Cather appears to have heeded the advice of Sarah Orne Jewett, whose work she admired greatly even if Edith Wharton did not, to address the bigger picture from the "quiet center of life." Recognizing the importance to the artist of the everyday routines, memories, oral traditions, and lived experiences of that "quiet center," Cather claimed that, "Art must spring out of the fullness and richness of life . . . out of the very stuff that life is made of."[12] And in terms of formal structure, she commented on the relationship between this "everyday" aesthetic and the wider reach it can attain.

The Professor's House (1925) serves as a useful illustration of Cather's application of these artistic principles and brings together the key strands of this discussion – the refiguring of the local aesthetic and experimentation with the novel form. In this narrative, again, the motifs of the domestic proliferate. The opening section foregrounds the "house" of the title, offering a detailed description of a well-worn, rather ramshackle dwelling and the familial and domestic routines that have characterized life within its walls. But the home presented is a far cry from Mrs. Harling's kitchen in *My Ántonia*, from which narratives of an emerging nation emanated. In this house, Godfrey St. Peter, his wife Lillian, and their adult children lead thwarted and unfulfilled lives in a modern America bereft of moral or spiritual worth and driven by shallow materialistic values. In this climate, human relationships are dysfunctional and unsatisfactory, marriage stagnates, and the family home is a negative, non-productive environment. As Chopin does in *The Awakening*, Cather establishes a sense of claustrophobia and confinement through the metaphor of houses, architecture, and indoor spaces. She too uses elements of the domestic tradition to address wider issues, in this case to ask how societies develop over time and to express a sense of ambivalence about the civilizing process. In common with those of Chopin and Wharton, Cather's novel also engages in formal innovation, fusing new elements into a version of the domestic tale. And she relates her experimentation – the inclusion of a separate, self-contained story within the main narrative frame – to her central philosophy of artistic transcendence:

> In my book I tried to make Professor St. Peter's house rather overcrowded and stuffy with new things; American proprieties, clothes, furs, petty ambitions, quivering jealousies – until one got rather stifled. Then I wanted to

> open the square window and let in the fresh air that blew off the Blue Mesa, and the fine disregard of trivialities which was in Tom Outland's face and in his behavior.[13]

Combining "Tom Outland's Story" of the discovery of an ancient, highly developed but long-lost cave-dwelling civilization on the Southwestern Mesa with the stifling portrait of the family in modern America, Cather again reaches beyond the immediate to gain access to alternative possibilities and visions.

Of the authors discussed here, Charlotte Perkins Gilman has the most direct relationship to sentimentalism. As the great-niece of Harriet Beecher Stowe and Catharine Beecher, the doyennes of American domesticity, she could be considered an inheritor of the tradition. But she revises her legacy in radical fashion, and her confrontations with the local or domestic aesthetic are the most forthright of all the post-sentimental authors discussed. A prolific writer of fiction, fable, poetry, and treatise, Gilman had political rather than aesthetic ambitions for her writing. She articulates the philosophies underpinning her social reform agenda in major theoretical works including *The Home: Its Work and Influence* (1903) and *Women and Economics* (1898), which identifies the private family home and the societal apparatus that supports it as the site and source of women's oppression. According to this thesis, women's economic dependence on men, their exclusion from the public realm, and the separation of space along gendered lines lie at the root of the inequality between the sexes that she seeks to reform. To Gilman, the complex ills of society originate in and proceed from the ideology of separate spheres, which of course, is foundational to sentimentalism. According to Gilman, the woman's ancillary, dependent status necessitates the development of excessive sex characteristics to conform to ideals of femininity in order to attract a mate to maintain her. She blames the self-contained model of the home, in which children are raised in isolation, for promoting selfishness and insularity, creating successive generations who will continue to neglect the common good of society. Her theories constitute a fundamental rejection of the domestic-centered vision of the prominent women from whom she was descended and their idealization of domesticity and motherhood is ruthlessly undermined across the body of her work.

Gilman's critique of domestic ideology finds expression in her fiction, where some rather unpleasant domestic arrangements are presided over by male figures who, at best, maintain paternalistic relationships with the women in their lives and, at worst, abuse them. Debilitated by postpartum depression, the narrator of the decidedly anti-sentimental "The Yellow Wallpaper" is confined by her doctor husband to a country estate which is part prison, part asylum with "barred windows . . . hedges and walls and gates that lock." And the women in *Unpunished*, the satirical detective novel published after Gilman's death, are tyrannized by the villainous patriarch, Wade Vaughn. But much of Gilman's writing, both fiction and non-fiction, pursues an ambitious and optimistic plan for social reform, with solutions that radically reconfigure domestic architecture and reimagine domestic culture. Her work is didactic in tone, relentlessly proffering practical alternatives for women limited by the expectations of traditional domestic roles in a patriarchal society.

This vision is articulated most boldly in her utopian narratives. Carol Farley Kessler, who has discussed Gilman's belief in the transformational power of literature, defines the author's notion of utopia not as "fantastic," but rather as an achievable blueprint for social improvement.[14] Chris Ferns describes Gilman's engagement with utopian fiction as an appropriation of "a genre overwhelmingly dominated by men" – an exercise that aligns her with the practices of Chopin, Wharton, and Cather. Noting that, typically, it is possible for "utopian bliss to be attained only through the imposition of a distinctively male hierarchy," he suggests that in locating "knowledge and power" with the woman and affirming the values of an all-female society, Gilman manipulates form to articulate a particularly female vision.[15]

In *Herland* (1915) Gilman offers a fictional reordering of society through a radically different take on female community, a staple of the sentimental narrative. Here, she realizes the theories of *Women and Economics* and presents the solution to the disabling environment suffered by the narrator of "The Yellow Wallpaper," an inventive variation on "the local" where Herland provides an isolated rural environment, a "regional" alternative to the mainstream, with a clear focus on women's culture. In *Herland*, women are self-sufficient. Sexual reproduction has been circumvented by the development of parthenogenesis and the women have strong, healthy bodies, "athletic . . . and powerful." Because there are no men and the women do not need to attract a mate for economic survival, artificial sex distinctions are irrelevant. Clothes are "simple in the extreme and absolutely comfortable" – practical rather than ornamental – enabling the land's inhabitants to engage in worthwhile, productive work according to their individual talents. In this alternative world, the spatial conventions of the traditional family home are overturned; the architecture is designed by women for women. The individual kitchen, the centerpiece of domestic fiction, is rendered redundant in Herland, where meals are taken in the communal dining room, fostering the community spirit essential to Gilman's grand plan of social reform. Not defined in relation to husbands or children, but recognized as autonomous individuals, the Herlanders' "sense of personal privacy" is accommodated by an allocation of their own space – "two rooms and a bathroom." Herland's children, all girls, are taken out of the environment of the private home and raised communally in a balanced, stimulating environment.

Each of Gilman's targets for reform is addressed and resolved in the narrative of *Herland*, and the fantastical space is practical and asexual (indeed passionless), conceding no ground to romance and sentiment, but the domestic-centered ideology of her Beecher ancestors does remain as a clear touchstone. Some readers have taken this as an indication of her acceptance of their philosophies and have questioned the extent to which she successfully distinguishes herself from previous traditions. Monika Elbert has suggested that Gilman "waxes poetically about a future race of perfect mothers and the contemporary woman's ultimate happiness being linked to maternal duty."[16] Whilst I would disagree with Elbert's assessment, it is fair to say that in Herland, motherhood is afforded great reverence, and elsewhere Gilman does tend toward evangelical rejoinders to the "world's" mother to exert a presence in the public realm. There is a certain ambiguity in her treatment of maternity, and often her maternal discourse frames the conservative, reactionary rhetoric that exists, paradoxically, alongside Gilman's progressive radicalism. Often, for example, she espouses eugenic theories, discussing the mother's duty to the "race." But her discourse repeatedly wrests the "natural" maternal role away from the individual woman, and is oriented toward a more abstract concept in which superior female values will benefit wider society. Gilman consistently contradicts the sanctification of the mother/child relationship by an androcentric ideology that contains women within prescribed boundaries. In *Herland*, only those who demonstrate competence in the "highly specialized craft" of mothering are permitted to care for the children. Gilman envisions practical mothering in the public realm, not sentimental mothering in the private.

Hildegard Hoeller similarly suggests that Wharton brings together disparate, traditionally oppositional forms, including the sentimental, with such fusions providing her with a vehicle for the expression of intense passions.[17] *The House of Mirth* (1905), discussed elsewhere in this volume by Jennifer Fleissner in the context of the figure of the New Woman, serves as illustration of how Wharton draws on Darwinian theories, in this case to offer a sophisticated study of New York social groupings as a competitive system that slowly crushes the heroine, Lily Bart.[d] But in a narrative in which children and maternity are remarkable mainly by their absence, as she cradles another woman's baby to her breast, Lily is "thrilled" by "a sense of warmth and returning life," and it is into this particular scene that some critics have read a problematic regression to sentiment. In a novel otherwise recognized as a complex literary achievement, Wharton's Lily, who experiences a moment of communion with a working-class girl and her child, manages to raise, however briefly, the specter of "natural" maternal instinct and its attendant limitation of women. As Suzanne Clark has reminded us, as literary critics we "still respond to the way the word *sentimental* is loaded,"[18] and nowhere are these critical sensitivities more heightened than around the genre's central trope of maternity.

In recent years, of course, there has been a critical re-evaluation of the sentimental genre itself and its significance to American literary and cultural history. Feminist scholars have reread the conservative values apparently promoted by sentimentalism as transgressive and anti-patriarchal. Jane Tompkins suggests that sentimental novels frequently offered "devastating" critiques of the culture: Stowe's *Uncle Tom's Cabin* (1852), she notes, appropriates and revises central cultural myths – of religion and motherhood – to intervene in public debates about slavery, "the nation's greatest political conflict."[19] Subsequent studies have extended Tompkins's thesis. Joanne Dobson, for example, shifts focus away from the sentimental novel as cultural artifact, calling instead for a rigorous literary critical approach to the tradition,[20] and in this volume Cindy Weinstein offers a re-evaluation of the work of E. D. E. N. Southworth. However, as some feminist scholars seek to redeem nineteenth-century sentimentalism by identifying subtexts of subversion, others stigmatize those who seek to get beyond the tradition, by rooting out evidence of the sentimental to undermine significant literary achievements. In so doing, they fail to recognize the potential for women of the amalgamation and evolution of form and genre and the reimagining and refiguring of the local aesthetic.

Notes

1. Edith Wharton, *A Backward Glance* (New York: Charles Scribner's Sons, 1964), 293, 51. See reviews of *An Old Fashioned Girl* (1870): *Richmond Whig and Advertiser* 49.40 (May 20, 1870): 4; *Worcester Evening Gazette* 27.79 (April 4, 1870): 2.1, in *Louisa*

d See, in this volume, Jennifer Fleissner, "Wharton, marriage, and the New Woman," chapter 27, 462–464.

May Alcott: The Contemporary Reviews, ed. Beverly Lyon Clark (Cambridge: Cambridge University Press, 2004), 97–109.

2. Emily Toth, *Unveiling Kate Chopin* (Jackon: University Press of Mississippi, 1999), 17. See Kate Chopin, *The Complete Works of Kate Chopin*, 2 vols., ed. Per Seyersted (Baton Rouge: Louisiana State University Press, 1969): 700–701.
3. Charlotte Perkins Gilman, *Women and Economics: A Study of the Economic Relation Between Women and Men* (1898; New York: Prometheus Books, 1994), 150.
4. R. W. B. Lewis and Nancy Lewis, eds., *The Letters of Edith Wharton* (New York: Scribner's, 1988), 124.
5. William M. Curtin, ed., *The World and the Parish: Willa Cather's Articles and Reviews, 1893–1902* (Lincoln: University of Nebraska Press, 1970), 276–277.
6. Tom Lutz, *Cosmopolitan Vistas: American Regionalism and Literary Value* (Ithaca, NY: Cornell University Press, 2004), 31.
7. Donna M. Campbell, *Resisting Regionalism: Gender and Naturalism in American Fiction, 1885–1915* (Athens: Ohio University Press, 1997), 168.
8. William Howard Gardiner, *North American Review* (July 1822), quoted in Lucinda L. Damon-Bach and Victoria Clements, eds., *Catharine Maria Sedgwick: Critical Perspectives* (Lebanon, NH: University Press of New England, 2003), 37.
9. Edith Wharton, *Fighting France* (New York: Charles Scribner's Sons, 1915), 82; Janet Beer, *Edith Wharton: Writers and Their Work* (Tavistock, Devon: Northcote House, 2003), 47–48.
10. See Julie Olin-Ammentorp, *Edith Wharton's Writings from the Great War* (Gainesville: University Press of Florida, 2004).
11. Lutz, *Cosmopolitan Vistas*; Susan J. Rosowski, *Birthing a Nation: Gender, Creativity and the West in American Literature* (Lincoln: University of Nebraska Press, 1999); Ann Romines, *The Home Plot: Women, Writing and Domestic Ritual* (Amherst: University of Massachusetts Press, 1992).
12. *Letters of Sarah Orne Jewett*, ed. Annie Fields (Boston: Houghton Mifflin, 1911), 249; Willa Cather, Interview with *Lincoln Sunday Star*, November 6, 1921. Reprinted in L. Brent Bohlke, ed., *Willa Cather in Person: Interviews, Speeches, and Letters* (Lincoln: University of Nebraska Press, 1986), 47.
13. Willa Cather, *On Writing* (Lincoln: University of Nebraska Press, 1988), 31–32.
14. Carol Farley Kessler, *Charlotte Perkins Gilman: Her Progress Toward Utopia* (Liverpool: Liverpool University Press, 1995), 2.
15. Chris Ferns, "Rewriting Male Myths: *Herland* and the Utopian Tradition," in *A Very Different Story: Studies on the Fictions of Charlotte Perkins Gilman*, ed. Val Gough and Jill Rudd (Liverpool: Liverpool University Press, 1998), 24–37.
16. Monika Elbert, "The Sins of the Mothers and Charlotte Perkins Gilman's Covert Alliance with Catharine Beecher," in *Charlotte Perkins Gilman and her Contemporaries*, ed. Cynthia J. Davis and Denise D. Knight (Tuscaloosa: University of Alabama Press, 2004), 103–126.
17. Hildegard Hoeller, *Edith Wharton's Dialogue with Realism and Sentimental Fiction* (Gainesville: University Press of Florida, 2000).

18. Suzanne Clark, *Sentimental Modernism: Women Writers and the Revolution of the Word* (Bloomington: Indiana University Press, 1991), 11.
19. Jane Tompkins, *Sensational Designs: The Cultural Work of American Fiction, 1790–1860* (New York: Oxford University Press, 1986), 124, 134.
20. Joanne Dobson, "Reclaiming Sentimental Literature," *American Literature* 69 (1997): 263–288.

35

Dime novels and the rise of mass-market genres

SHELLEY STREEBY

Written and marketed for a wide audience, dime novels are often remembered as escapist formula fiction for boys that presented few opportunities for authorial innovation. A longer history of the dime novel, however, complicates this memory by revealing an immense body of popular literature, written and read by both women and men, which mediated the conflicts of its era in diverse ways rather than ignoring them. Many dime novel authors started out as contributors to the story papers and other periodicals that emerged in the wake of the late 1840s print revolution.[a] In the first dime novels of the 1860s, they adapted familiar genres, including captivity and seduction narratives; stories of scouts, white settlers, and Indian fighting; mysteries of the city; historical and international romances; and pirate, crime, and war stories. These genres, along with new ones, flourished in the last part of the dime novel's heyday, when the production of cheap literature more closely resembled the fiction factories of dominant memory. This last era witnessed a transformation in the meaning of authorship as characters became trademarks owned by publishing companies, which also controlled house names such as Bertha M. Clay, under which Street and Smith published the stories of several different writers. The publishers and editors of this period often came up with titles, characters, and plots and then asked authors, who were poorly paid and had to write very quickly, to invent stories based on those ideas, thereby making the dime novel a more standardized literary commodity. At the same time, beginning in the 1870s and 1880s publishers began to target boys as a privileged audience for dime novels and to offer girls distinctly different fare, especially romances, even as they changed the names of female writers to disguise their gender and radically cut down on stories

a For a quantitative and qualitative analysis, see Ronald Zboray and Mary Saracino Zboray, "The novel in the antebellum book market," chapter 4, esp. 68–71.

written by women in dime novels that were aimed at boys. This shift both responded and contributed to what historian Gail Bederman calls the remaking of manhood in the late nineteenth century, which involved an emphasis on a new masculinity that was defined more in opposition to the feminine and the sentimental and that was different from earlier models of manliness that emphasized self-restraint and other qualities shaped by the influences of mothers, sisters, and wives.[1]

This chapter traces a pre-history of the dime novel in the popular sentimental and sensational literature of the late 1840s and 1850s; charts the proliferation of the dime novels introduced by Beadle and Company in the 1860s and 1870s; and finally examines the dime novel's twilight era around the turn of the century, when it both competed with and inspired early cinema, comics, and pulp magazines. Although dime novels have frequently been derided and are rarely read today, they helped to shape some of the most important genres of US mass culture, including the romance, the detective story, the Western, science fiction, and stories of war and imperial adventure, as new media adapted and transformed their stories for the twentieth century.[b]

In 1860, Erastus and Irwin Beadle issued the very first dime novel, Ann Stephens's *Malaeska; The Indian Wife of the White Hunter*. The Beadles were printers who ran a stationery shop and published books and periodicals in Buffalo, New York until 1856, when they moved to New York City, where they issued songbooks and handbooks as well as the dime novels that made them famous. Beadle's new novels were distinguished by the trademark dime on their bright-orange covers, along with their small size, portability, and length of around 100 pages. Inside the covers, readers found sentimental and sensational stories of adventure and romance, capture and rescue, and hidden and exposed identities. But the term has come to signify a much larger body of popular literature that sold for different prices (especially a nickel or a quarter) in a variety of formats, including the paper-covered novel, the cheap library, the thick book, and the oversized, illustrated pages of the story paper. As Michael Denning observed in his classic 1987 study *Mechanic Accents*, early collectors preferred novels that showcased the "pioneer spirit of America,"

b While Mark McGurl's "The novel, mass culture, mass media" (chapter 41) begins in the early twentieth century, he observes in passing that the connections between industrial modernity and mass culture have a much longer history. For comparative analyses of other mentioned categories of "genre fiction," see chapters in this volume by Anna Mae Duane (2), Pamela Regis (51), Jan Baetens (69), Sean McCann (48), Stephanie Le Menager (31), and John Carlos Rowe (49).

and this preference shaped the construction of the dime novel as a critical object, since most of the dime novel archives available in research libraries were based on these collections.[2] Because of this selective ideological focus on patriotic Westerns written by men, other genres were often forgotten, along with the fact that many women, such as Metta Victoria (Fuller Victor) and Ann Stephens, authored Westerns. Judging from readers' letters, as well as comments made by publishers, women also made up a significant proportion of the audience. By the early 1880s, however, publishers more strongly distinguished between male and female readers of dime novels, as well as between children and adults. These distinctions partly resulted from the dime novel industry's efforts to invent and capture new markets as rival firms competed for readers. They also responded to emergent ideas about the perceived need to police children's reading in order to protect them from dangerous forms of popular culture, as well as to turn-of-the-century ideas about manliness and civilization, which presumed that healthy boys were uninterested in the romances and sentimental fiction that had been avidly consumed by both male and female readers throughout much of the century and that continued to be marketed to girls.

Mary Andrews Denison's dime novels remind us of women's significant participation in this new culture industry and of the permeability of the boundary between sensational literature and the culture of sentiment[c] in the early period of dime novel production, for she not only wrote for Beadle but also contributed to *Godey's Lady's Book* and the Boston *Olive Branch* and edited the *Lady's Enterprise*.[3] In the seven dime novels that she authored she adapted a range of genres, including stories of the American Revolution and colonial times, mysteries of the city and romance, and narratives of captivity and imperial adventure. Her books apparently appealed to a wide audience that included women of all ages as well as the men and boys who are more often imagined as typical dime novel readers. During the years when dime novels were a central form of mass entertainment, stories of imperial adventure such as Denison's *The Prisoner of La Vintresse; or, The Fortunes of a Cuban Heiress* (1860) remained incredibly popular.[4] Denison's novel, which was one of the first to be published by Beadle, is about a Cuban heiress who falls in love with a Connecticut farmer's son, who is arrested and accused of being a spy for US

c Although Cindy Weinstein does not directly address the permeability of this boundary in her essay on "Sentimentalism" (chapter 12) her astute analysis of E. D. E. N. Southworth's "conflicted relation to sentimentalism" (216) opens up space to consider how the sensational erupts from within the sentimental in much of Southworth's fiction in ways that shadow or make impossible sentimental closure.

filibusters. He remains a prisoner on a remote Cuban plantation until the heroine returns to save him after experiencing a series of thrilling adventures in the USA. By posing the question of whether the heiress's beloved is a filibuster, Denison alludes to the many expeditions to "liberate" Cuba that flourished in the 1850s, notably including the plans to purchase or forcibly annex Cuba that were outlined in the Ostend Manifesto, a secret official document that was made public and that caused an outcry among Northern Republicans about Southern efforts to annex Cuba for the purposes of extending slavery's sway.

In response to these debates over slavery and US empire, Denison turned to the already familiar subgenre of international romance. A variation on the national romances that were published throughout the Americas, these novels translated questions about international relationships into melodramas of seduction, endangered virtue, gender and racial masquerade, love, and sometimes, marriage.[d] During the US–Mexico War, international romance was the most common mode through which story paper novelists imagined a relationship between the United States and Mexico. In novels such as Charles Averill's *The Mexican Ranchero; or, The Maid of the Chapparal* (1847), Ned Buntline's *Magdalena the Beautiful Mexican Maid: A Story of Buena Vista* (1846), and George Lippard's *Bel of Prairie Eden: A Romance of Mexico* (1848), international romances, usually between US soldiers and Mexican women, who sometimes masquerade as men and fight for Mexico, condense volatile, still open questions about future US–Mexico relations. More than a decade later, Denison imagined a romantic relationship between a Cuban heiress and a Northern US farmer's son partly in response to debates about the desirability of annexation. Although the romance ends in marriage, Denison invokes without resolving anxieties about the extension of slavery and the debilitating effects of US empire-building on American manhood. Denison's *Prisoner* thereby endorses a Northern Republican outlook on slavery, US expansion, and Southern dreams of empire, which is not surprising since, as Alexander Saxton suggests, dime novel entrepreneurs "maintained a linkage to the Republican party comparable to that of the impresarios of blackface minstrelsy to the Jacksonian party."[5]

These anxieties and debates over slavery, empire, and white manhood also shape the popular sensational novels of the late 1840s and 1850s, including crime literature, mysteries of the city fiction, and the stories of labor and

d For a discussion of international romances in hemispheric novels, see Gretchen Murphy, "The hemispheric novel in the post-revolutionary era," chapter 33, esp. 556–557.

capital that Denning suggested were "marked by the imprint of their working-class audience."[6] Emphasizing increases in literacy and attending to narratives about working-class reading practices, Denning opposed the view that dime novels were simply a part of an expansive, middle-class culture. Mysteries of the city and frontier/imperial adventure were not entirely separate genres, either, for many dime novels connect cities to empires, and many popular authors, including George Lippard and Ned Buntline, wrote both kinds of fiction. Lippard wrote two US–Mexico war novels along with numerous city stories, while Buntline authored urban novels as well as two US–Mexico war novelettes and several Westerns, including plays and the first dime novels about Buffalo Bill.[e] Lippard's *Bel of Prairie Eden* begins on the prairies of Texas, shifts to Veracruz, Mexico, and winds up in Philadelphia as his story of the US–Mexico war morphs into a mysteries of the city novel. Buntline's *Mysteries and Miseries of New Orleans* (1851), on the other hand, begins in the city but quickly turns into an imperial adventure novel about filibustering in Cuba. Denison's *Prisoner* is also a generic hybrid in which scenes of international romance and danger are juxtaposed to the heroine's efforts to negotiate the perils of New York City. In all of these novels, city and empire are complexly entangled, but they imagine diverse symbolic resolutions to conflicts over empire and the urban transformations wrought by industrial capitalism rather than speaking with one voice. And while much of this literature responds to emerging class antagonisms, many novels struggle to suppress such conflicts within narratives of fraternity, patriotism, and white manhood and womanhood.

When Beadle and Company marketed the first dime novels in the 1860s, the firm hoped to appeal to "all classes, old and young, male and female," as the Publisher's Notices that preceded *Malaeska* reveal. The company also promised that there "shall not be a line or a sentiment in any of these books which may not be placed in the hands of a child, or be uninteresting to the grandmother of a family."[7] Although publishers imagined the audience for dime novels in expansive terms, however, the sectional conflict that would soon culminate in the Civil War increasingly divided the nation, and it is not surprising that the dime novel, as a largely Northern institution, responded to this emergent split. As Saxton suggests, in the 1850s white egalitarian heroes in earlier story paper fiction moved "decisively in an anti-slavery direction,"

e In "Melville and the novel of the sea" (chapter 9), Hester Blum includes Buntline's nautical fiction in her analysis of mid nineteenth-century popular fiction that found a large audience with actual sailors (154).

defining free labor and free soil in opposition to chattel slavery and the Southern plantation.[8] Such a white egalitarianism partly leveled the playing field among whites of different classes, but hatred of slavery was often quite compatible with a disdain for African Americans or with a romantic racialism that sympathized with slaves but kept traditional hierarchies intact. Although it is sometimes assumed that the dime novel effaced the ongoing trauma of the Civil War, dozens of novels published between 1860 and 1865 respond to the crisis from Northern Republican perspectives along this spectrum. N. C. Iron's *The Two Guards* (1863) and Metta Victor's *Maum Guinea and Her Plantation "Children": A Story of Christmas Week with the American Slaves* (1861) and *The Unionist's Daughter: A Tale of the Rebellion in Tennessee* (1862) are arguably the most critical of slavery, although they combine sympathy with a condescending paternalism. Historian Alice Fahs has shown that dime novels were popular with soldiers and that a number of publishers issued cheap fiction designed to appeal to them, such as Charles Alexander's *Pauline of the Potomac; or, General McClellan's Spy* (1862), Buntline's *The Rattlesnake; or The Rebel's Privateer* (1862), and Wesley Bradshaw's *The Angel of the Battlefield: A Tale of the Rebellion* (1865). As Fahs observes, the ubiquitous stories about "women spies, scouts, and cross-dressing soldiers" not only imagined "a more active – and transgressive – women's role in the war" but also sometimes "allowed for expressions of autoeroticism and homoeroticism not socially acceptable within the confines of heterosexual culture." On the other hand, the few cheap novels about the war that were published in the South invented threats to white women's honor, including black men and Yankees, in ways that anticipate the postwar white supremacist literature of Thomas Dixon as well as the infamous film it spawned, D. W. Griffith's *Birth of a Nation*.[9]

Like Beadle's Civil War dime novels, the early Westerns and novels of imperial adventure also manifest Northern Republican, free soil, and white egalitarian sympathies.[10] Many female authors of Beadle's dime Westerns focused on white settlers: Ann Stephens wrote two novels about white women in the West: *Sybil Chase; or, The Valley Ranche. A Tale of California Life* (1861) and *Esther: A Story of the Oregon Trail* (1862); Frances Fuller Victor explored conflicts among whites over land in *Alicia Newcome, or The Land Claim: A Tale of the Upper Missouri* (1862); and Metta Victor authored *The Two Hunters; or, The Canon Camp. A Romance of the Santa Fe Trail* (1865), which placed a wealthy Mexican woman within the boundaries of whiteness by marrying her to a New York merchant's son, who defends her from the Comanches. While Stephens's novels betray fears that the lure of gold and easy money, encounters with nonwhites in the borderlands, and movement away from white civilization might imperil free labor and white egalitarian ideals, Frances and Metta Victor's Western fiction is mostly devoid of nonwhite characters and struggles to imagine borderlands spaces as sites where free soil and free labor ideals may be tested and reaffirmed.

But although all of these stories were popular and *Malaeska* was a major success, the biggest hit among the earliest dime novel Westerns was Edward Ellis's *Seth Jones; or, The Captives of the Frontier* (1860), a historical novel set in frontier New York in the late eighteenth century. The eponymous hero, who we learn at the end is actually a gentleman, is a Yankee and Indian fighter whose battles are in some ways reminiscent of Cooper's Leatherstocking novels, but who exhibits more of what Saxton calls "the hard side of white egalitarianism," which imagines "Anglo-Saxon" solidarity and brotherhood through scenes of gory violence directed at Indians and other nonwhites.[11] Ellis would go on to write over a hundred dime novels, including at least ninety-one for Beadle. Dozens of other Westerns, set in both historically remote and proximate eras, were published by Beadle during the 1860s, as were many novels of imperial adventure beyond the borders of the nation, such as land reformer A. J. H. Duganne's two "Yankee in Mexico" novels, *The Peon Prince; or, the Yankee Knight-Errant. A Tale of Modern Mexico* (1861) and *Putnam Pomfret's Ward; or, A Vermonter's Adventures in Mexico* (1861).

In 1877, Beadle introduced Deadwood Dick, one of the most popular of the new dime novel outlaw characters that would soon provoke a moral panic among middle-class reformers. At the same time, the firm began to distinguish between stories for adults and younger readers by publishing two new series of cheap stories that inaugurated what would come to be known as Beadle's Dime and Half-Dime Libraries. The latter was aimed at boys, and the very first novel in the series was Edward Wheeler's *Deadwood Dick, The Prince of the Road (1877)*, a sensational story that would spawn thirty-two sequels and that was part of a larger resurgence of outlaw stories in this tumultuous era of conflict between labor and capital. These stories inspired many imitations, such as Street and Smith's Diamond Dick, the hero of dozens of novels, and Beadle even produced a Deadwood Dick, Jr. series after Wheeler's death, which the firm tried to hide from the public by employing others to write novels that were published under his name for years to come. The Half-Dime Libraries and the Deadwood Dick type of story drew the ire of reformer Anthony Comstock, who in his 1883 *Traps for the Young* deplored the "coarse, slangy story in the dialect of the barroom, the blood and thunder romance of border life, and the exaggerated details of crime, real and imaginary."[12] During the years Wheeler wrote scores of successful novels for Beadle, editor Orville

Victor "begged in the interests of morality" that Wheeler "make the stories less terribly forcible in the language of his rougher characters" and diminish "the torrents of liquor that flowed like rivers," and eventually Wheeler responded by "curbing" the "language" and "whisky-drinking."[13] Perhaps even more disturbing than Wheeler's slang and his use of barroom settings, however, was the reversal in his early stories whereby, in Comstock's words, "crimes are gilded; and lawlessness is painted to resemble valor, making a bid for bandits, brigands, murderers, thieves, and criminals in general."[14]

Many other outlaw stories that flourished during this period, including Joseph Badger's about the California bandit Joaquín Murrieta, as well as dozens of stories about Jesse and Frank James, offer similarly critical views of industrial and finance capitalism, provoke sympathy for criminals, feature rich non-producers and other powerful men as villains, and question the justice of law. Beadle did not publish any James brothers stories, presumably because the firm considered the men poor role models for young boys, and Orville Victor worked hard to control Wheeler, eventually taking credit for Deadwood Dick's "reform" from "the outlawed terror of the law-abiding" into "the deadly foe of the law-breaker."[15] But although the 1873 Comstock Law,which banned the mailing of obscene material, as well as Comstock's own efforts as an agent of the Post Office, at times scared publishers into toning down or eliminating outlaw stories, their abiding popularity and their populist anger suggest that efforts to resolve class antagonisms through appeals to white fraternity and national belonging might be imperiled at times of economic crisis, when the interests of elites and non-elites could not be so easily harmonized.[16]

That the first Deadwood Dick story was published in a new Beadle series for boys raises questions about how cheap literature responded to and shaped changing configurations of gender, race, and sexuality. As it had been long before and would be long after, the melodramatic triangle of male villain/captor, female victim/captive, and male hero/rescuer is foundational here. The endangered women of captivity narratives, Leatherstocking tales and their successors, seduction novels, stories of the US–Mexico war, mysteries of the city fiction, and working-girl romances also turn up in many dime outlaw stories, sometimes in lurid scenes such as one in *Deadwood Dick, The Prince of the Road*, when Fearless Frank rescues the beautiful Alice Terry from the "fiend incarnate – Sitting Bull" after he finds her "stripped to the waist" and with welts upon her "snow-white back." Centering emotion and drama around the figure of threatened white womanhood and imagining the Indian as a diabolical villain are familiar from earlier forms of both elite and popular frontier literature.[f] But the novels also contain some surprises, such as Calamity Jane, who appears in the nick of time to lead the way to save the hero from the white villains. She is first introduced to the reader as a ruined woman who was "set adrift upon the world, homeless and friendless" but who has "bravely fought her way through the storm." After she saves Deadwood Dick, she turns down his offer of marriage, replying sternly that she "has had all the *man*" she cares for, but she continues to play a prominent role in many of the sequels. Comstock probably had characters like Calamity Jane in mind when he warned that the Half-Dime Library novels were bad for girls because they showcased the "violation of marriage laws" and "cheapen[ed] female virtue."[17] In addition to offering seductively ambivalent models of female vice, the novels also unsettle a stark binary opposition between male and female: Calamity Jane's "trim boyish figure" and Deadwood Dick's fingers, which are "as white and soft as any girl's," as well as the many scenes of gender masquerade in dime novels, remind us how fluid and theatrical gender and sexuality may be in popular literature.[g]

An overt shift in the gendering of Beadle's audience took place in 1882, when *Beadle's Weekly* began to cut down dramatically on novels by women and to use initials to disguise female authorship. Since publishers were part of a culture that was increasingly redefining manhood to emphasize a masculinity defined in opposition to the feminine and the sentimental, it is not surprising that, more and more, they assumed that only men could write stories that would appeal to boys by modeling the red-blooded masculinity that was viewed, in the 1880s and after, as an essential part of white manhood. But a change is already apparent in the list of novels published in the Half-Dime Library in the late 1870s, which are almost all written by men and which are frequently about boys, as in Wheeler's *Wild Ivan, the Boy Claude Duval; or, The Brotherhood of Death* (1878) or Ellis's *The Boy Miners; or, The Enchanted Island* (1879). The 1882 policy of disguising female authorship and the shift to male writers as well as the success of a Beadle's series for boys mark sea changes that help to explain why the dime novel is remembered as a boys' cultural form and why women's considerable participation is often overlooked.

f In "Imagining the frontier" (chapter 31), Stephanie Le Menager focuses on how such scenes of female victimization in the Deadwood Dick series offer a kind of "ideological candy" for "the (white, working-class male) consumer's satisfaction" (524).

g For more recent examples, see Elizabeth Freeman's analysis of the gay and lesbian pulp novels that she argues peaked in the 1930s and 1960s, in "Reimagining genders and sexualities," chapter 57, 947–948.

Although girls and women no doubt read Beadle's story papers and dime novels of this era, during the 1880s and 1890s publishers made distinctions, more and more, between male and female periodicals and genres.[h] By marketing popular literature in these ways, they redefined the romance as a female genre and as antithetical to the world of boys, even though romances were integrated as subordinate parts into genres that the industry increasingly aimed at boys, such as Westerns, detective novels, and stories of science, war, and imperial adventure.[i] Street and Smith became a major purveyor of cheap romances for girls at the same time that the firm also continued to publish cheap literature for a general audience and stories for boys, such as the Buffalo Bill novels written by Buntline, Prentiss Ingraham, and others beginning in 1869, as well as the Frank Merriwell and Nick Carter detective stories that were massively popular from the 1890s through the early twentieth century. Francis Smith's 1871 story *Bertha the Sewing Machine Girl; or, Death at the Wheel* inspired a host of plays and novels about working girls, while Street and Smith's flagship story paper, the *New York Weekly* (1859–1910), featured the work of women writers alongside novels by prominent men. Street and Smith was also one of six publishers to issue books by Laura Jean Libbey, one of the most popular writers of the era. Libbey wrote more than eighty novels about working girls, secret identities, cross-class romance, reversals of fortune, rapacious men, frightening marriages, and female adventure, with titles such as *Little Leafy, the Cloakmaker's Beautiful Daughter: A Romantic Story of a Lovely Working-Girl in the City of New York* (1891).

The incorporation of romance into a genre that also appealed to men is apparent in the title of the very first Beadle dime novel about a detective, Metta Victor's *The Dead Letter: An American Romance* (1866). Victor's novel reveals how the detective story emerged from within the mysteries of the city genre. Her detective investigates the shocking murder, like those narrated in sensational penny papers, of a New York banker who is engaged to an heiress. Despite the prominence of romance and sentiment and the morally exemplary characters that connected this novel to the world of respectable white middle-class womanhood, Victor or her publishers decided to affix the pseudonym

h See Barbara Hochman's astute observation, in "Readers and reading groups" (chapter 36), that "formal separation of readerships for didactic and marketing purposes is a very partial index of how people actually read" (600).

i In "Female genre fiction in the twentieth century" (chapter 51) Pamela Regis suggests that in the last three decades of the twentieth century the marketing of romances specifically to women perhaps reached its zenith, making romance novels arguably "the dominant form of American fiction" (847).

Seeley Regester to the story, and her authorship was not revealed until much later.

If Victor imagines the detective as a sentimental gentleman whose ability to feel makes him a masterful agent of justice, the only known African American writer of dime novels, Philip Warne, responds to the emerging myth of the genius detective in his 1881 Beadle dime novel *Who Was Guilty?* by making the detective's voice one among many, featuring a different first-person narrator in each chapter, and asking the reader to decide who is the criminal. Instead of encouraging respect for the law and those who enforce it, Warne's novel suggests that law does not protect the poor, that poor people are the victims of rich men's abilities to manipulate the law, and that the detective, who "initially received the homage of the gaping crowd as if he were something superhuman," cannot necessarily solve the crime, and may be too eager to accuse the poor.

Beadle published Warne's fiction, which consisted mostly of Westerns in addition to a few mystery novels, from 1875 to 1894, but some time near the end of that period, according to a letter written by dime novelist Gilbert Patten, Warne appeared in Orville Victor's office to introduce himself, to the latter's "amazement and dismay." Patten claimed Victor advised Warne to "get out of New York and never appear in the office again," although he had thought enough of Warne's talent to publish dozens of his novels during the previous two decades. Victor's response, as well as those of other dime novel authors who used racist epithets to refer to Warne and who resented his presence in their ranks, suggests that dime novels were aggressively defined as a field of white endeavor despite the Northern Republican sympathies of many of their producers.[18] Nonetheless, Warne sent his work to Beadle from afar for almost twenty years before encountering a representative of the firm face to face, and it is possible that other writers found ways to circumvent the industry's unspoken rule that only whites could author dime novels. By the turn of the twentieth century, however, the conditions and meaning of dime novel authorship had changed, and it was much more difficult for authors to evade the direct oversight and control of editors and publishers.

The long, uneven shift to a more industrial mode of dime novel production, which was part of what Bill Brown refers to as "the rapid reorganization of consumer culture" at the end of the nineteenth century, coincided with the ascendancy of the detective story as arguably the most popular dime novel genre.[19] Old Sleuth, Young and Old King Brady, Cap Collier, Nick Carter, and other detectives of the era were trademarks owned by publishers who exerted considerable control over the authors they hired to pen the stories. John

Coryell wrote the first Nick Carter story, which appeared in Street and Smith's *New York Weekly* in 1886, but the character's popularity probably peaked after 1891, when publisher Ormond Smith revived the character for a weekly library. Although more than twenty writers contributed to the library, Frederic Dey wrote the most memorable of hundreds of stories. But according to a company history, Smith closely supervised Dey and others in order to keep "the character of Nick Carter just as he wished it."[20] Nick Carter became the most popular and long-lived dime novel detective. Street and Smith issued a Nick Carter weekly until 1915, when they changed the title to *Detective Story Magazine* and turned it into a pulp publication that continued until 1949. And throughout the early twentieth century, Nick Carter stories proliferated in other forms, including plays, early films, comic books, and a radio drama.

The proliferation of dime novel series aimed especially at boys and publishers' preference for exemplary male characters also shaped other genres that are still popular today, including science fiction and stories of imperial adventure. The Frank Reade series combined both of these genres as the wealthy main character, his son, and his grandson and granddaughter devised marvelous inventions and traversed the globe. Frank Tousey published hundreds of Frank Reade stories by several different writers, most notably Cuban immigrant Luis Senarens, who devised adventures for Frank Reade, Jr. all over the world but especially throughout the Americas. Whether he was using his new torpedo boat to make war on Brazilian rebels, searching the Yucatán channels with a submarine yacht, doing secret service work for Uncle Sam in Havana harbor, driving an electric moto-van through Venezuela, or using his airship to find lost races in Peru, Frank Reade, Jr. was a patriotic youth always eager to use the latest technology to assist the state and the police. The same was true of the boy heroes of the military adventure stories of this era, who were sometimes involved in contemporaneous US wars in Cuba and the Philippines. Street and Smith's Red, White, and Blue Library, *Army and Navy Weekly*, *Starry Flag Weekly*, and *True Blue*, all of which featured young men in military institutions, were wildly popular at the turn of the century, and Upton Sinclair wrote several stories for these weeklies under the pseudonyms Lt. Frederic Garrison and Ensign Clarke Fitch.

The most famous boy character of this period, Frank Merriwell, was also initially imagined by publisher Smith as a young man in a military school, but as he was brought to life in 1896 by former Beadle's author Gilbert Patten, he became instead a student at a New England academy and then Yale's most famous athlete before experiencing numerous thrilling adventures in the US West and Mexico. Patten blamed the motion picture industry for the decline of the dime novel, even though he had sold a few stories to the movies himself and the Merriwell character was featured in more than one early film.[21] Wishing for greater success in the movie industry, Patten was gently told by his agent that the screen rights to his stories could not be sold because the motion picture business had been built on them. Although this was little comfort to Patten, it suggests that the dime novel did not really disappear, for the mass market genres and new media of the twentieth century adapted and transformed the most popular products of the nineteenth-century's major culture industry.

Notes

1. Gail Bederman, *Manliness and Civilization: A Cultural History of Gender and Race in the United States, 1880–1917* (Chicago: University of Chicago Press, 1995), 16.
2. Michael Denning, *Mechanic Accents: Dime Novels and Working-Class Culture in America* (London: Verso, 1987), 13.
3. Two useful resources are the American Women's Dime Novel Project at http://chnm.gmu.edu/dimenovels and The House of Beadle and Adams Online at http://www.ulib.niu.edu/bandp/bibindex.html.
4. See the five narratives, including Denison's *Prisoner*, Lippard's *Bel*, and Buntline's *Magdalena*, collected in Shelley Streeby and Jesse Alemàn, eds., *Empire and the Literature of Sensation: An Anthology of Nineteenth-Century Popular Fiction* (New Brunswick, NJ: Rutgers University Press, 2007). See also Russ Castronovo, "Imperialism, Orientalism, and empire," chapter 32, 537–542 for a discussion of popular antebellum literature about empire.
5. Alexander Saxton, *The Rise and Fall of the White Republic: Class Politics and Mass Culture in Nineteenth-Century America* (London and New York: Verso, 1990), 322.
6. Denning, *Mechanic Accents*, 5.
7. Ann Stephens, "Malaeska; or The Indian Wife of the White Hunter," in *Reading the West: An Anthology of Dime Westerns*, ed. Bill Brown (Boston and New York: Bedford Books, 1997), 59, 57. See Yu-Fang Cho, "A Romance of (Miscege) Nations: Ann Sophia Stephens' Malaeska: The Indian Wife of the White Hunter (1839, 1860)," *Arizona Quarterly* 63.1 (Spring 2007): 1–25, and Christine Bold, "Malaeska's Revenge: Or, the Dime Novel Tradition in Popular Fiction," in *Wanted Dead or Alive: The American West in Popular Culture*, ed. Richard Aguila (Urbana: University of Illinois Press, 1996), 21–42.
8. Saxton, *Rise and Fall of the White Republic*, 196.
9. Alice Fahs, *The Imagined Civil War: Popular Literature of the North and South, 1861–1865* (Chapel Hill and London: University of North Carolina Press, 2001), 231, 240, 249–255.
10. For a comprehensive discussion of the popular literary Western, see Christine Bold, *Selling the Wild West: Popular Western Fiction, 1860–1960* (Bloomington: Indiana University Press, 1987). For a classic American Studies discussion of the

dime novel Western, see Henry Nash Smith, *Virgin Land: The American West as Symbol and Myth* (Cambridge, MA: Harvard University Press, 1950), 99–135.

11. Saxton, *Rise and Fall of the White Republic*, 198.
12. Anthony Comstock, *Traps for the Young* (New York: Funk and Wagnalls, 1883), 21.
13. Cited in E. F. Bleiler, "Introduction," in *Eight Dime Novels*, ed. Bleiler (New York: Dover, 1974), ix.
14. Comstock, *Traps for the Young*, 21.
15. Bleiler, "Introduction," x.
16. On outlaw stories and dime novel populism, see Denning, *Mechanic Accents*, 157–166, and Richard Slotkin, *Gunfighter Nation: The Myth of the Frontier in Twentieth-Century America* (Norman: University of Oklahoma Press, 1998), 125–155. See Nancy Glazener's account of the Comstock laws in her essay in this volume, "The novel in postbellum print culture," chapter 20, 344–345.
17. Comstock, *Traps for the Young*, 22.
18. Quoted in Marlena Bremseth, "Introduction," in Philip Warne, *Who Was Guilty? Two Dime Novels*, ed. Bremseth (Norfolk, VA: Crippen and Landru, 2005), 20. On the racist epithets, see 13–14.
19. Brown, *Reading the West*, 14.
20. Quentin Reynolds, *The Fiction Factory; or From Pulp Row to Quality Street* (New York: Random House, 1955), 67.
21. Gilbert Patten, *Frank Merriwell's Father: An Autobiography*, ed. Harriet Hinsdale (Norman: University of Oklahoma Press, 1964), 243. The fact that a successful comic strip was based on the Merriwell series suggests that the dichotomy between character and action in popular culture was perhaps less absolute than Patten imagined.

36

Readers and reading groups

BARBARA HOCHMAN

In an 1873 "Introduction" to *A Library of Famous Fiction*, Harriet Beecher Stowe recalled that while she was growing up "novels were considered a dangerous indulgence, and in our youth one of the stock themes for composition-writing was 'On the disadvantages of novel-reading.' "[1] Stowe's comments and the *Library of Famous Fiction* itself endorse the novel as a literary form; but the declaration of victory over the lingering resistance to fiction was premature.[2] The "rise" of the novel in the United States was uneven.[3] Until well into the twentieth century fiction-reading was an extremely popular but still contested social practice – entertaining, useful, and important for some, disturbing and potentially dangerous for others. The modern novel, Thomas Wentworth Higginson wrote in 1896, "is to this generation what drama was to the Elizabethan age; we must simply accept it as the now recognized mould, into which the brightest contemporary intellect is cast."[4] A certain reluctance, evident in Higginson's "we must simply accept it," is often salient in commentaries of the period. Anxiety about fiction-reading as destructive and addictive lingered in many quarters.

This chapter addresses changes in the status of fiction between the 1870s and the 1920s by examining its cultural meaning for several discrete reading publics: cultural insiders (authors and literary commentators; educators and newly professionalized librarians) but also cultural outsiders (African Americans, immigrants, and children). The formal separation of readerships for didactic and marketing purposes is a very partial index of how people actually read. Over the last twenty-five years historians, media specialists, literary scholars, and others have honed and combined methodologies in an effort to refine the idea of the reader and the reading public.[5] Drawing on methods from social science, ethnography, history, and literature, scholars have conducted surveys, compiled statistics, pored over private letters and diaries alongside printed texts, analyzed the institutional practices of publishers, schools, libraries, and book clubs.[a] Despite much collaborative interdisciplinary research, questions proliferate. What shall we consider useful evidence of reading? How are comments in letters and diaries different from published accounts? How can library records suggest what books meant to individuals and communities of readers? To what extent is response shaped by cultural as well as personal history?

In what follows, I consider the representation of reading in several contexts – including fiction itself. Throughout, I seek a balance between the individual reader and the cultural group, the compliant or resisting reader and the text. I aim to create a fluid rather than a stable image of readers and reading groups. I assume that any one particular reader may be part of many groups, that readers may be inconsistent in their tastes and that readers' claims about reading may – or may not – accurately reflect their experience.

The novel was increasingly prominent in literary culture toward the end of the nineteenth century – it was the most popular genre in both the marketplace and the library.[6] But for diverse social groups as well as individuals, the meaning and value of fiction was in flux. Late nineteenth-century discourse celebrated the "reading habit" in newspapers, magazines, and lectures. Publishers, editors, and educators offered advice about how to select books, how to read them, where to put them.[7] While commentators solemnly asserted that "reading is a very serious affair,"[8] a growing mass of readers avidly consumed dime novels, detective fiction, and Westerns (all genres considered elsewhere in this volume). The meaning and impact of reading is elusive. The "Great Gatsby" owns a library with books that are "absolutely real – . . . pages and everything," as one drunken visitor exclaims. But Jay Gatsby himself does not read in the course of the novel; *Hopalong Cassidy* may be the only book he ever opened.[9] Owning books, even owning a library, is one thing. Reading is another.

In the course of the nineteenth century the profession of authorship became both more honorable and more lucrative in the United States. While the novel was already "improbably" thriving in the antebellum period, even in the absence of effective copyright laws or a unified national market, fiction became big business in the 1890s.[b] The term "bestseller" was coined in 1892;[10] passage of an international copyright law in 1896 was partly designed

a On contemporary book clubs see DeNel Rehberg Sedo, "Twentieth- and twenty-first-century literary communities," chapter 70 in this volume.

b See Ronald Zboray and Mary Saracino Zboray, "The novel in the antebellum book market," chapter 4 in this volume, 73.

to encourage and protect US authors. As the reading public grew, and as technological developments dramatically increased the ease and speed with which fiction could be produced, advertised, and distributed, cultural commentators hotly debated the pros and cons of fiction.[c] Novelists themselves participated in this conversation, contributing reviews and essays to the periodical press while punctuating their fiction with scenes of reading (see below). Librarians evaluated and categorized texts – differentiating the worthy from the "dangerous."[11] But as guidelines and warnings about fiction-reading proliferated, readers had ever more books to choose from and often ignored the recommendations of professionals.[d] Cultural guardians themselves did not always toe the line. Henry Ward Beecher's sermons against pernicious reading reflect his intimate familiarity with Eugene Sue's *The Mysteries of Paris* (1842),[12] which provided a template for dozens of racy and violent antebellum "mysteries of the city."[e] Like Beecher, Hamlin Garland's grandfather denounced cheap fiction, but read it himself. (When found reading "a very lurid example of 'The Dammable Lies'" he explained that he "was only looking into it to see how bad it was."[13])

As fiction gained respectability, commentators sought candidates for the "Great American Novel."[14] By the 1890s some novels had even gained the status of "classics." Fiction had become a genre with a respectable history as well as a future. But despite numerous attempts to categorize and evaluate specific works, readers of all ages and backgrounds read books that were not designed for them. They read "bad" books as well as "good," and appropriated fiction for multiple ends.

The novel and the reading habit

> We are not all expected to be musicians . . . why should we all be readers?
> (Edith Wharton [1903])[15]

Toward the end of the century, the "reading habit" was regularly invoked as a key to individual and national progress. Periodicals, advice books, and public lectures drew attention to rising literacy levels and praised book production as

c See Robert Coover, "A history of the future of narrative," chapter 71 in this volume, on the relation between new technologies, new literary forms, and new audiences.

d Sedo explores current debates that surround "what constitutes 'good' literature," and who has the authority to classify it as such (chapter 70, 1154).

e For more on mysteries of the city, see Shelley Streeby, "Dime novels and the rise of mass market genres" (chapter 35) and Sean McCann, "The novel of crime, mystery, and suspense" (chapter 48).

a measure of America's cultural coming-of-age. Educators and librarians enthusiastically embraced what Lee Soltow and Edward Stevens have called "the ideology of literacy" – the notion that a love of books and reading would foster aesthetic taste, worldly success, and civic responsibility.[16] Across the country, children and immigrants were particular targets for a reformist zeal that took reading as an indispensable step in the ongoing development of the individual, the nation, and "the race."

There were two competing scripts in the narrative of cultural uplift through reading. For some, reading was valuable in and of itself – more important than the content of any particular book. "Better bad books than no books," Frank Norris claimed.[17] Not everyone agreed, however. Many educators and librarians saw it as their mission to shape and control what was read, especially by "new" readers – women, immigrants, young people. (African Americans were conspicuously absent in much of this debate – a point to which we will return.) Fiction gained considerable legitimacy by the turn of the century, but it still occupied only a small segment of "high" literary culture. If great literature ("the best which has been thought and said in the world," in Matthew Arnold's much-cited phrase[18]) could inculcate respect for virtue, literary language, and democratic ideals, the "wrong" book could be harmful, especially to impressionable and inexperienced readers. According to editor and child-development expert Millicent Shinn, "poor books lessen . . . rather than develop . . . the power of coming to like good ones."[19] Fiction seemed particularly dangerous insofar as naïve readers might read for reality – taking fiction as truth – disregarding style or moral sentiments.

Members of the conservative elite were skeptical about the "reading habit," directed or undirected. For James Russell Lowell, Edith Wharton, and others, the ideology of literacy stirred anxiety. Too much reading was seen as a threat to the "aristocracy of thought," and a menace to "true culture."[20] It was often the very readers not "born" to the practice who were most enthusiastic about literacy. Prominent African Americans strongly advocated the reading habit. In a much reprinted passage from *The Souls of Black Folk* (1903), W. E. B. Du Bois includes Balzac and Dumas on the short list of authors with whom he imagines walking "arm in arm."[21]

Booker T. Washington is more cautious than Du Bois when he speaks of reading: he claims to care "little" for fiction, preferring newspapers or biography: "I like to be sure that I am reading about a real man or a real thing."[22] This view fully harmonizes with longstanding concerns that the lure of fiction might elicit fantasy and stimulate impossible dreams. Elizabeth McHenry's account of nineteenth-century African American literary societies confirms the predominant emphasis in the black community on reading as moral and intellectual education, not escape, subversion, or play.[23] Since at least as far back as Frederick Douglass's *Narrative* (1845), African American stories of reading display the author's familiarity with the "right" books. As Karla F. C. Holloway observes, black autobiographies invariably include a "book list" that testifies to the author's cultural authority and literary sophistication.[24] In the late nineteenth and early twentieth century, American fiction makes only a modest appearance on booklists by African Americans (as on recommended reading lists generally).

African American fiction of the period, however, complicates the story of reading and often projects a dystopian version of the characteristic script. In James Weldon Johnson's fictionalized *Autobiography of an Ex-Colored Man* (1912), the narrator recalls that Harriet Beecher Stowe's *Uncle Tom's Cabin* (1852) "opened my eyes as to who and what I was and what my country considered me." This is reading "for reality," with a vengeance, appropriating fiction for purposes unanticipated by proponents of the reading habit. In Charles Chesnutt's *The House Behind the Cedars* (1900) Rena, a mulatto, wonders whether she can believe what she has read. As she contemplates marrying a white man without revealing her origins she reflects: "But would her lover still love her if he knew all? She had read some of the novels in the bookcase in her mother's hall . . . She had read that love was a conqueror, that neither life nor death, not creed nor caste, could stay his triumphant course." The "novels in the bookcase" tell compelling tales, but do not stand the test of social reality. As a child, Rena's brother John also finds solace in the "quaintly carved black walnut bookcase" with its "remarkable collection of books." This perfectly typical book collection includes Fielding's complete works, Bulwer's novels, *Clarissa*, *Tristram Shandy*, *Robinson Crusoe*, *Don Quixote*, and the *Arabian Nights*. The bookcase contains no slave narratives, no novels about life in the United States.

Taken together the classic volumes in the walnut bookcase offer diverse plots and themes, but provide no guidelines for African Americans living in North Carolina at the end of the nineteenth century. Reading seems to open "a new world" to Rena's brother, but "long before he had read . . . all [the books] – he . . . had tasted of the fruit of the Tree of Knowledge: contentment took its flight." Rejecting these books, John becomes skeptical, savvy, and cautious but his sister, tempted to believe in "the triumphant course of love," is disastrously misled. By depicting the false promise of the bookcase, Chesnutt exposes the limits of reading and indicts the ideology of literacy.

(Not surprisingly several versions of *The House Behind the Cedars* were rejected for publication by Houghton Mifflin in the 1890s.[25])

Librarians: inviting the "people" but guarding the gates

> "Father said it used to be a gentleman was known by his books; nowadays he is known by the ones he has not returned."
>
> (William Faulkner, *The Sound and the Fury* [1929])

When books were available mainly to those who had inherited them or could afford them, "a gentleman was known by his books." In letters and autobiographies by women from Harriet Beecher Stowe or Margaret Fuller to Charlotte Perkins Gilman and Edith Wharton, a father's library endows books with a seductive, near-magical, aura. Viewed from outside the family, a man's library indicated social status; it was also presumed to reflect character. Owning goods implied class position, but owning books was believed to mean more: "Show us the man at work in his library, and we view him in his essence, not in his seeming."[26] Similar maxims had long suggested that a good book, like a valuable friend, provided companionship and counsel while reflecting the intellectual and moral condition of the reader.[27] Late nineteenth-century advice books such as Lyman Abbott's *Hints for Home Reading* (1880) asserted that no home was too humble for a bookshelf. As one guide to "House and Home" suggests in 1896, "the requirements of a [home] library . . . may be considered almost canonical. It is reposeful and dignified in color . . ."[28] Yet as print culture expanded, books were increasingly imagined not as somber, exclusive possessions of a "man at work in his library" but as inviting, welcoming: "cheerful" books beckon to "the family."[29]

Public libraries of this period made books increasingly available but, like the idea of the home library and the "reading habit" itself, the public library was caught between the goals of study and recreation, exclusion and inclusion. The driving force behind the establishment of public libraries in the last quarter of the nineteenth century was its proposed function as the spearhead in a "democratic extension of education."[30] "The best reading for the greatest number at the least cost," John Dewey's motto, was adopted by the American Library Association in 1879. Janice Radway notes that the design of grand public libraries funded by Andrew Carnegie and reproduced in small local structures across the country was, like the Dewey decimal system, partly intended to make books accessible.[31] Yet, as Radway suggests, the large circulation desk at the center of these libraries must have seemed forbidding, especially to new readers unaccustomed to striding into a public place and asking a stranger for advice.

While public libraries of the Progressive era were committed to disseminating books and fulfilling readers' wishes (up to a point), they also had a clear pedagogic purpose: libraries were to be a moral force in the community. Librarians would "help the reader to advance from one stage of literature to another." "The reader" was someone who did not have a library at home and who would benefit from instruction in the matter of taste – the child or the "poor immigrant."[32] African Americans are rarely included in this script. For Richard Wright, growing up in the 1920s, the majestic public library (for "whites only") in Memphis Tennessee was a site of exclusion, shame, and subterfuge.[33] As long as segregation was the law of the land and industrial training the primary goal of black education, institutions financed or run by white boards of trustees placed no premium on more varied uses of literacy for African American readers. Immigrants were more commonly taken as proof-texts for the idealized story of the reading habit and the library. The Boston Public Library plays a key role in the autobiography of the immigrant Mary Antin. *The Promised Land* (1911) was widely read as testimony to the transformation of a "born ... alien" into a patriotic and literate "citizen." Unlike the *Autobiography of an Ex-Colored Man*, or *The House Behind the Cedars*, Antin's autobiography was a bestseller. Although the narrative is something of a fairy tale, designed to conceal the ambivalence and failure that marked and marred Antin's transformation from a Russian girl to "an American," *The Promised Land* was read as truth, not fiction, and offered as a model to others.[f] It continues to be read as an endorsement of the melting pot and the progressive goals of the library.[34]

Educators and commentators encouraged "men and women everywhere ... to acquire books of the right sort and to make the right use of them."[35] But would the availability of books – even books of "the right sort" – guarantee "right use"? The "how" of reading is notoriously difficult to assess. One way that turn-of-the-century librarians selected "good" novels was by their endings: sinners needed to get their just deserts.[36] Such a strategy relies on a dubious assumption about how reading works: the moral at the end of a story is likely to be forgotten while more compelling features of the

f Immigrant novels of this period reflect the controversies surrounding "soaring immigration figures, nativist rhetoric, and legislative action." See Tim Prchal, "New Americans and the immigrant novel," chapter 25 in this volume (quotation at 427).

narrative are retained. Reading practices are both culturally inflected and personal; what a reader takes from a text is colored by what he or she already brings to it. Educators, librarians, and parents could promote the reading habit and limit access to "dangerous" texts, but they could neither anticipate nor legislate the effects of reading.

Reading fables

"Oh, I hoped there would be a Lord; it's just like a novel!"
(Henry James, *The Portrait of a Lady* [1881])

The representation of reading was a staple in fiction of this period. Sometimes, as noted, fictionalized scenes of reading cut across the dominant cultural consensus. Serious fictional challenges to the promise of literacy, however, tend to appear in marginalized texts such as *The House Behind the Cedars* or Edith Wharton's *Bunner Sisters* (1916), where the sisters' naïve equation of literacy with virtue leads to seduction, death, and despair.[37] Though fictionalized scenes of reading do not generally have such dire consequences, cautionary tales of "bad" reading are woven into both popular and critically acclaimed novels of the period. In *The Portrait of a Lady*, Isabel Archer's undirected childhood reading prefigures her disastrous marriage. William Dean Howells's *The Rise of Silas Lapham* (1885) targets the devastating effects of sentimental fiction by staging an argument about *Tears, Idle Tears* (a novel invented by Howells for the occasion). The wrongheaded characters are exposed by their defense of what the more sophisticated characters describe as "slop silly slop." In *Sister Carrie*, (1900), Theodore Dreiser makes Carrie's marginal class status and lack of refinement apparent in her taste for the bestselling fiction of Bertha Clay.[38] Carrie's reading of Balzac's *Père Goriot* (1835) at the end of Dreiser's novel might seem to signify progress, but her susceptibility to French realism confirms the social marginality already suggested by her sexual behavior and her acting career. In Owen Wister's *The Virginian* (1902) the cowboy hero who marries the schoolteacher falls asleep when Molly reads aloud from Jane Austen's *Emma*, but his appreciation of Shakespeare reveals his "natural" taste and anticipates the novel's happy ending. In Edith Wharton's *Summer* (1917), by contrast, Charity Royall reads nothing – the library where she works is a closed book to her – and her deepest desires are, predictably, thwarted. When Helga Crane reads Marmaduke Pickthall's *Said the Fisherman* (1903) in the first scene of Nella Larsen's *Quicksand* (1928), because she "wanted forgetfulness, complete mental relaxation, rest from thought of any kind," she takes the first step on a predictable road to disaster. Along the way, the New York Public Library rejects her application for a job.

Fiction of the period repeatedly rewards the good readers and punishes the bad. Scenes of reading also serve to justify the existence of the "host" novel, proclaiming its suitability as serious reading – reading for moral edification, intellectual benefits, and aesthetic pleasures. Yet images of reading are often mere cameos in long works of fiction. To interpret diverse texts via such moments is to be as shortsighted about the pleasures of novel-reading as the librarians who measured literary value by whether or not sinners are punished. Scenes of reading cannot tell us how novels were actually read.

In the course of the late nineteenth and early twentieth century, novels became increasingly legitimate as recreational reading. Middlebrow institutions such as the Book-of-the-Month Club emerged alongside modernism,[39] yet modernist fiction was elitist in its ethic, its aesthetic, and its intended audience – not designed for an expanded reading public. As Hugh Kenner notes, "you cannot skim a Faulkner novel."[40] The most widely read novels of the period, those with deep roots in popular culture, were rarely celebrated as important literature, for "the serious reader."[g] James, Howells, Wharton, Wister, Hemingway, Larsen, and others sought legitimacy for their work in a culture that privileged critical and purposive reading – novel-reading as uplift, art, moral philosophy, social criticism. But a unified narrative of readers and reading groups is misleading. I end this chapter by looking briefly at some responses by both informed and untrained novel-readers in order to pull out some loose threads from the tightly woven fabric of the "rise of the novel."

Novel-reading: work or play?

"A Mere Boy stood on a pile of blue stones. His attitude was regardant. The day was seal brown. There was a vermillion valley containing a church. The Church's steeple aspired strenuously in a direction tangent to the earth's center . . ."[41] With these lines, Frank Norris mocks Stephen Crane's distinctive prose, collapsing *Maggie: A Girl of the Streets* (1893) into *The Red Badge of Courage* (1895) and satirizing Crane's aesthetic pretensions. Parody overturns expectations, but must rely on them to do so. Publishing in *The Wave*, a small

g Coover expresses postmodern skepticism about what counts as the "serious reader" in his essay for this volume (chapter 71, 1178).

regional weekly in San Franciso, Norris assumes a community of readers with shared tastes – and texts.[42]

In a letter of 1905, the neurologist and popular novelist S.Weir Mitchell addresses a still smaller interpretive community in order to lampoon Henry James's "late" style: "James has been the presiding social center here," Mitchell writes to his friend Owen Wister, "and has been a source to me of curious interest . . ." Mitchell proceeds to explain the favorite game of "a retired old gentleman."

> "I take," he says, "Some cards and I write James on one and John, which is my name on another, then I read sentence by sentence a page by Henry James and if I understand it I put down one on the card for James, and if I do not, I put down one for John, and when I have finished the page I see whether James or John has won the game."[43]

Like Norris's send-up of Crane, this passage displays the writer's cultural competence (and perhaps a bit of envy); it also blurs the distinction between "high" and "low" fiction. Wister considered himself a serious author; he denounced what he called "quack-novels" – books with widespread appeal and false pretenses to "literature."[44] Yet *The Virginian* was a runaway best-seller, and Mitchell took it for granted that his friend would appreciate a joke aimed at Henry James's long sentences and esoteric allusions.

Mitchell's account of the "old gentleman's" game raises questions about what novels are for. Reading was a "serious affair" in public discourse by cultural guardians. But in private, writers and sophisticated readers could laugh at high seriousness and enjoy "quack-novels" themselves. Early in Ernest Hemingway's *The Sun Also Rises* (1926), Jake says of Robert Cohn that "for a man to take [W. H. Hudson's *The Purple Land* (1885)] at thirty-four as a guide-book to what life holds is about as safe as it would be for a man of the same age to enter Wall Street direct from a French convent, equipped with a complete set of the more practical Alger books." *The Sun Also Rises* posits a reader familiar with Alger and Hudson as well as James. Jake calls James "a good writer" and rereads Turgenev – but while waiting for his friend Bill after an idyllic morning catching fish he also reads: "a wonderful story about a man who had been frozen in the Alps and then fallen into a glacier and . . . his bride was going to wait twenty-four years exactly for his body to come out on the moraine, while her true love waited too, and they were still waiting when Bill came up." Poking fun here at A. E. W. Mason's "The Crystal Trench" (from *The Four Corners of the World* [1917]), Jake confirms his credentials as a sophisticated reader. But Jake's distaste for romantic illusion does not mar his pleasure in Mason's "wonderful story," which he has carried with him on a bucolic jaunt that marks the high point of Jake's experience in the novel. Many modes of reading coexist within a single reader, and across the reading public.

Didactic accounts cannot tell us how reading proceeds and what it means to readers variously situated in US society with respect to race, class, gender, or age. Psychologist G. Stanley Hall's "A Study of Dolls" (1896) includes a girl who reads Longfellow's *Hiawatha* to her doll. *Hiawatha* was one of the most celebrated poems of the period, much used to instill respect for great authors in schoolchildren.[45] In *The Promised Land* Antin reads Longfellow to her sister. Such moments confirm widely shared notions of what reading *should be*. But diverse representations of reading tell alternative stories, especially when examined and analyzed in relation to one another.

Frances Hodgson Burnett describes her childhood reading of *Uncle Tom's Cabin* in terms that initially confirm the cultural consensus about a well-known book – one, Burnett writes, that "marked an era in my existence." However, Burnett's account departs radically from familiar scripts for responding to *Uncle Tom's Cabin*, whether grounded in sentimental or historical appreciation: Burnett reports her mother's alarm at finding little Frances, red in the face, whipping a doll she has tied to the candelabra stand. Thus the author who created the extraordinarily popular *Little Lord Fauntleroy* (1885) implies that childhood reading may elicit ideas and emotions rarely recommended to little girls.[46]

Children, immigrants, African Americans, but also popular (or elite) authors reading each other – these are only some of the disparate groups that consumed fiction as the novel came into its own. In their reading, multiple communities and individuals diverge occasionally or consistently, slightly or dramatically, from the consensus. The full story of reading requires attention to multiple responses – and to the representation of reading in fiction itself.

Notes

1. The *Library of Famous Fiction* reprints "9 Standard Masterpieces" ranging from *The Pilgrim's Progress* to the *Arabian Nights* (New York: J. B. Ford, 1873), vi. The collection includes fiction, but no American texts.
2. In the 1880s and 1890s, lists of recommended reading still kept American fiction to a minimum. See Frederic Beecher Perkins, *The Best Reading* (New York: G. P. Putnam's Sons, 1880); Noah Porter, *Books and Reading: What Books Shall I Read*

and How Shall I Read Them? (New York: Charles Scribner's Sons, 1883); Lyman Abbott, *Hints for Home Reading: A Series of Chapters on Books and Their Use* (New York: G. P. Putnam's Sons, 1880, 1892). Writers of realism presented their work as socially, morally, and aesthetically significant, but sentiment remained popular. See also Elizabeth Nolan (chapter 34); Nancy Glazener (chapter 20); Cindy Weinstein (chapter 12).

3. The classic account of the "rise of the novel" is Ian Watt, *The Rise of the Novel* (Berkeley: University of California Press, 1957). Assessments differ regarding the novel's arrival at full generic respectability in the West: as Robert Darnton notes, "the novel, like the bourgeoisie, always seems to be rising" (*The Kiss of Lamourette: Reflections in Cultural History* [London: Faber & Faber, 1989], 159). Useful accounts of the American context include Cathy Davidson, *Revolution and the Word: The Rise of the Novel in America* (New York: Oxford University Press, 2004); Richard Brodhead, *Cultures of Letters: Scenes of Reading and Writing in Nineteenth-Century America* (Chicago: University of Chicago Press, 1993); Joan Shelley Rubin, *The Making of Middlebrow Culture* (Chapel Hill and London: University of North Carolina Press, 1992); Janice Radway, *A Feeling for Books: The Book-of-the-Month Club, Literary Taste, and Middle Class Desire* (Chapel Hill and London: University of North Carolina Press, 1997).
4. Thomas Wentworth Higginson, "Books and Reading," in *The House and Home: A Practical Book*, ed. Lyman Abbott *et al.*, 2 vols. (New York: Charles Scribner's Sons, 1896), 1:364.
5. For a small sample see James L. Machor and Philip Goldstein, *New Directions in American Reception Study* (New York: Oxford University Press, 2008); Barbara Ryan and Amy Thomas, eds. *Reading Acts: U.S. Readers' Interactions with Literature: 1800–1950* (Knoxville: University of Tennessee Press, 2002); Patricinio Schweickart and Elizabeth Flynn, eds., *Reading Sites: Social Difference and Reader Response* (New York: MLA, 2004); Ronald J. Zboray and Mary Saracino Zboray, *Everyday Ideas: Socioliterary Experience among Antebellum New Englanders* (Knoxville: University of Tennessee Press, 2006).
6. Toward the end of the century, patrons of public libraries "borrowed novels more than any other kind of reading, and did so at a rate that far exceeded the percentage of fiction held by collections" (Thomas Augst and Kenneth Carpenter, eds., *Institutions of Reading: The Social Life of Libraries in the United States* [Amherst: University of Massachusetts Press, 2007], 176).
7. Advice books address topics ranging from the choice of books to library "décor." On the importance of books and reading to the Victorian middle class, see Louis L. Stevenson, *The American Homefront: American Thought and Culture, 1860–1880* (Ithaca, NY: Cornell University Press, 2001); Barbara Sicherman, "Reading and Middle-Class Identity in Victorian America: Cultural Consumption, Conspicuous and Otherwise," in Ryan and Thomas, *Reading Acts*, 137–160.
8. "Reading and Education," *The Dial* (February 16, 1895): 102.
9. F. Scott Fitzgerald, *The Great Gatsby* (1925). Gatsby's boyhood list of goals (which includes the injunction to "read one improving book or magazine a week") is

inscribed in his well-worn copy of *Hopalong Cassidy* (1904). The juxtaposition of Gatsby's Franklinesque "schedule" and the popular cowboy novel encapsulates some of the tensions I explore in this chapter.

10. James Hart, *The Popular Book* (New York: Oxford University Press, 1950), 184.
11. According to Dee Garrison, "there were still locked-away collections" in public libraries as late as 1922, despite "a widespread acceptance of mass reading demands" (*Apostles of Culture: The Public Librarian and American Society 1876–1920* [Madison: University of Wisconsin Press, 2003], 100, 271 n. 66).
12. See Henry Ward Beecher, "The Strange Woman," in *Lectures to Young Men* (Salem, MA: John P Jewett & Co. 1846), 214.
13. *A Son of the Middle Border* (1917), cited in Christine Pawley, *Reading on the Middle Border: The Culture of Print in Late-Nineteenth-Century Osage, Iowa* (Amherst: University of Massachusetts Press, 2001), 13.
14. The term "Great American Novel" was coined by J. W. De Forest, himself a novelist, in "The Great American Novel," *The Nation* (January 9, 1868): 27–9. Lawrence Buell considers this search for the "Great American Novel" in chapter 19 in this volume, "Theories of the American novel in the age of realism."
15. Edith Wharton, "The Vice of Reading," *North American Review* 177 (1903): 514.
16. Lee Soltow and Edward Stevens, *The Rise of Literacy and the Common School in the United States: A Socioeconomic Analysis to 1870* (Chicago: University of Chicago Press, 1981).
17. Frank Norris, "The American Public and 'Popular' Fiction" (Syndicated, 1903.) Rpt. in Donald Pizer, ed., *The Literary Criticism of Frank Norris* (New York: Russell & Russell, 1976), 127.
18. Matthew Arnold, *Culture and Anarchy*, ed. J. Dover Wilson, (1869; London: Cambridge University Press, 1960), 6.
19. Millicent W. Shinn, "Concerning School Libraries," *Overland Monthly* 27.162 (June 1896): 646. http://quod.lib.umich.edu/m/moajrn/. Path: Browse, Overland Monthly.

    Shinn was editor of the *Overland Monthly* from 1883 to 1895. She earned a PhD in child development from the University of California at Berkeley in 1898, and published several well-respected works on early childhood.
20. James Russell Lowell, "The Five Indispensable Authors," *Century Magazine* 47 (April–November 1893–1894): 223–224; Wharton, "The Vice of Reading," 519. See Robert Coover in this volume on "the booming democratizing print era, so receptive to the novel form" ("A history of the future of narrative," chapter 71, 1173).
21. W. E. B. Du Bois, *The Souls of Black Folk* (New York: Penguin, 1995), 139.
22. Booker T. Washington, *Up From Slavery* (1901; New York: Dover, 1995), 129.
23. Elizabeth McHenry, *Forgotten Readers: Recovering the Lost History of African American Literary Societies* (Durham, NC: Duke University Press, 2002), 172, 173.
24. Karla F. C. Holloway, *Bookmarks: Reading in Black and White* (New Brunswick, NJ: Rutgers University Press, 2006), 9.

25. Brodhead, *Cultures of Letters*, 207–209. On Chesnutt and other African American novelists in the post-Civil War period see also Barbara McCaskill, "The African American novel after Reconstruction", chapter 29 in this volume. On the "complex, contradictory, and oftentimes vulgar ideologies of race" confronting writers of the period see Robert Reid-Pharr, "The postbellum race novel" chapter 28 in this volume, 471–472.
26. "Reading and Education," 102.
27. On the trope of books as friends see Barbara Hochman, *Getting at the Author: Reimagining Books and Reading in the Age of American Realism* (Amherst: University of Massachusetts Press, 2001).
28. Mary Gay Humphreys, "House Decoration and Furnishing," in Abbott *et al.*, *The House and Home*, II:132, 135.
29. *Ibid.*, 135.
30. Garrison, *Apostles of Culture*, 13.
31. Janice Radway, "The Library as Place, Collection, or Service," in Augst and Carpenter, *Institutions of Reading*, 246.
32. William Foster, "Where Ought the Emphasis be Placed in Library Purchases," *Library Journal* 29 (1904): 236–237; quoted in Garrison, *Apostles of Culture*, 99. Garrison speaks of the librarian as "missionary" (*Apostles of Culture*, 99, 37). "Like . . . museums, concert halls and parks," Thomas Augst writes, ". . . public libraries became spaces of civic devotion, where even poor immigrants might pursue the self-transformation and social mobility that continue to define the ethos of liberal individualism" (*Institutions of Reading*, 11).
33. Richard Wright describes his encounter with the library in his fictionalized autobiography *Black Boy* (1945).
34. On the book's enormous popularity see Werner Sollors, "Introduction" to *The Promised Land* (New York: Penguin, 1997), xxxii and Hana Wirth-Nesher, *Call it English: The Languages of Jewish American Literature* (Princeton: Princeton University Press, 2006), 54. Both discussions also complicate the ideal narrative.
35. "Reading and Education," 102.
36. Garrison, *Apostles of Culture*, 100. Even outlaw novels, such as those of Edward Wheeler, which aimed to attract readers with crime and "whisky-drinking," sought to avoid Comstock's condemnation of stories in which "crimes are gilded; and lawlessness is painted to resemble valor" (Shelley Streeby, "Dime novels and the rise of mass market genres," chapter 35, 593).
37. In 1892 *Bunner Sisters* was rejected by *Scribner's Magazine*. It first appeared in Wharton's collection *Xingu* (1916). On the allure of "literature" in *Bunner Sisters* see Barbara Hochman, "The Good, the Bad, and the Literary: Edith Wharton's *Bunner Sisters* and the Social Contexts of Reading," *Studies in American Naturalism* 1.1–2 (Summer–Winter 2005): 128–144.
38. Bertha M. Clay (pen name of Charlotte M. Brame) was a popular writer of dime novels, mostly romances, that appeared primarily in story papers. Her best-known work of fiction was *Dora Thorne* (1880).

39. On the history of the Book-of-the-Month-Club see Radway, *A Feeling for Books*.
40. Hugh Kenner, *A Homemade World: The American Modernist Writers* (New York: Knopf, 1975), 205.
41. Frank Norris, "Perverted Tales," *The Wave* 16 (December 18, 1897); rpt. Pizer, *The Literary Criticism of Frank Norris*, 172.
42. Norris worked at *The Wave* as both editorial assistant and regular staff writer from 1896 to 1898. Founded as a kind of society journal in the 1880s, by the mid-nineties *The Wave* expanded its coverage to general affairs of the San Francisco area (Donald Pizer, "Introduction," *The Literary Criticism of Frank Norris* [xix]). On Norris and *The Wave* see also Joseph R. McElrath, Jr., *Frank Norris Revisited* (New York: Twayne Publishers, 1992), 13–21; McElrath, *Frank Norris and "The Wave": A Bibliography* (New York: Garland, 1988); McElrath and Jessie S. Crisler, *Frank Norris: A Life* (Chicago: University of Illinois Press, 2006).
43. S. Weir Mitchell to Owen Wister, January 26, 1905. Manuscript Division, Library of Congress.
44. Owen Wister, "Quack Novels and Democracy," *The Atlantic Monthly* (June 1915): 721–734.
45. Elementary schools throughout the United States taught Longfellow as a "civilizing force" in the late nineteenth and early twentieth century (Angela Sorby, *Schoolroom Poets: Childhood, Performance, and the Place of American Poetry, 1865–1917* [Lebanon, NH: University of New Hampshire Press, 2005], 29). American schoolchildren continued to read and recite "large quantities of Longfellow" until the middle of the twentieth century (Joan Shelley Rubin, "Poetry Recitation and American Readers," in Ryan and Thomas, *Reading Acts*, 260).
46. Frances Hodgson Burnett, "The One I Knew Best of All: A Memory of the Mind of a Child," *Scribner's Magazine* 13 (January–June 1893): 76. Until recently children's literature and child readers have been neglected in history, criticism, and pedagogy. See Julia Mickenberg, "Children's novels," (chapter 52, 861).

PART THREE

*

MODERNISM AND BEYOND

Introduction: modernism and beyond

CLARE VIRGINIA EBY

Literary history is a messy business. Novels refuse to stay contained within categories, and periodization – that other stock in trade of literary history – is often necessary, yet invariably contingent. Examining very different terrains, John Carlos Rowe and Elizabeth Freeman reflect on the consequences of imposing ideas of order on the disarray of literary texts. Rowe shows how the category "war novel" obscures internal conflicts in the US that culminate in military action and how "recognized 'wars'" shape literary history by determining its "periodizing" markers – and so we have antebellum literature, literature between "the wars," and so on. Freeman demonstrates how "male-dominated, nationalist military history or presidential policy" can dictate the periods of literary history, obscuring as much as they reveal. She argues that "gender/sexual dissidents" challenge "even the principal terms that organize this volume: 'History,' 'American,' and 'Novel.'"

This section of *The Cambridge History of the American Novel* especially chafes against literary-historical period markers and labels: it centers on the period from the 1920s through the 1970s but spills out chronologically in both directions and mingles discussion of internationally acclaimed innovators with accounts of formula-driven popular practitioners. Thus the "beyond" in the title describes this section's contents as much as does the leading term, "modernism."

The chapters here illustrate that the practitioners of popular forms – as much as the towering innovators whom Ezra Pound had in mind when he urged writers to "make it new" – respond creatively to modernity. Imposing a bit of that contingent literary-historical order, we can term these two responses "popular mass-market modernity" and "high literary-philosophical modernism" – as long as we acknowledge at the outset that they become utterly entangled in practice.

This section opens with Peter Nicholls's analysis of two influential strands of literary modernism inaugurated by one of the US's pre-eminent sexual dissidents, Gertrude Stein, and one of its most ardent (if not always convincing) defenders of heterosexual masculinity, Ernest Hemingway. While both provide "radical alternatives to the novelistic realism" on which the previous section of *The Cambridge History of the American Novel* centers, Stein and Hemingway develop opposed "stylistic economies": her "lavish expenditure" and his "poetics of omission." Robert Chodat examines American novelists' engagement with high modernism via their responses to European philosophers such as Sartre, Heidegger, and Kierkegaard (as well as to homegrown philosophers such as William James), while Maria Farland demonstrates how mid-century women writers sought to move beyond such architects of modernity as Freud and Marx.

The more self-conscious among the literary modernists regarded mass-market modernity warily, as Sean McCann illustrates with the example of F. Scott Fitzgerald. What Mark McGurl terms "industrial modernity" upset the traditional role of the novelist – whether "literary" or popular – and challenged ideas about inviolable (and authoritative) authors. Some writers sought to establish their own relevance by engaging interpretive systems far older than the novel, such as religion, philosophy, and the law. Amy Hungerford considers the literary engagement with religion in terms of the "modernist analysis of consciousness that . . . drove formal innovation." Robert Faggen illustrates the "transcendent, if not religious aims" of the Beats and their search "for some kind of liberation toward a better and spiritual plane of existence." Priscilla Wald probes the philosophical depths of science fiction, showing its investment in "ethical inquiry," particularly in "reimagining the category of 'the human.'" Gregg Crane emphasizes how American novelists' engagement with law – another authoritative "storytelling enterprise"– allows them to dramatize meta-legal questions such as whether "law [is] capable of justice." Scrutinizing another dimension of justice, Lovalerie King shows how Ralph Ellison and James Baldwin lovingly challenged America to live up to its own founding principles.

Novelists were also tested by the explosion of new forms of mass media, particularly the cinema and television. What, asks McGurl, does the "triumph of spectacle mean for the viability of the printed novel as a cultural form?" And how would popular modernity's "onslaught of entertaining images" affect novelistic realism? Among possible answers explored here, Alan Wald discusses John Steinbeck's filmic techniques; James L. W. West III, Candace Waid, and McGurl consider the screenwriting of Fitzgerald, Nathanael West, and especially William Faulkner; Kirk Curnutt looks at Rudolph Valentino's role in establishing the 1920s' characteristic sexual style; and Priscilla Wald and

Rowe discuss influential cinematic adaptations of science fiction and war novels, respectively. Other chapters assess the impact of television, radio, newspaper, and advertising. Yet despite the mass media's ubiquity, folk culture and an emphasis on orality persist in, and beyond, modernism, as Valerie Babb shows in her discussion of African American fiction of the 1920s and 1930s, and Nicholls by tracing the influence of Stein's prose rhythms on Hemingway, while Waid describes Southern literature in general and Faulkner in particular as finding their "impetus in orality." (Ursula Heise and Sean Kicummah Teuton also take up the persistence of orality in their chapters on postmodern novels and Native American fiction in Part Four.)

Chapters earlier in *The Cambridge History of the American Novel* establish that the US novel has always been a business proposition, but the scale of that business – and of the markets it pursued – changed early in the twentieth century. The publishing industry shifted from an entrepreneurial to an increasingly rationalized corporate proposition.[a] West tracks this "new business model" emerging in the 1920s, based on "a more competitive, frontlist-oriented style of publishing, with emphasis on sales, advertising, and promotion," and fueled by book clubs, paperbacks, and literary agents. With the rise of a model of "corporate authorship" (McGurl), novels become as much "commercial possibilities" as literary works (West). Yet these changes in the book industry could benefit writers. As television and film provided enhanced options for the time-honored practice of "adaptations and recyclings" of novels, unprecedented incomes could result, as West shows. Electronic publishing has extended the reach of the female romance (whose history is traced by Pamela Regis), and children's literature flourished, as Julia Mickenberg demonstrates, once publishers started carving out juvenile divisions and promoting series such as Nancy Drew. Some novels ruminate on their own conditions of production: thus for McCann, the crime story "was both a product of the commercialization of literature and . . . a means to understand the social and cultural consequences of the discipline of the market." Other new forms, such as proletarian fiction (Alan Wald) and the suburban novel

a On the entrepreneurial model of publishing, see Ronald Zboray and Mary Saracino Zboray, "The novel in the antebellum book market," chapter 4; on the history of publishing and reading groups more broadly, see also Nancy Glazener, "The novel in postbellum print culture," chapter 20; Shelley Streeby "Dime novels and the rise of mass market genres," chapter 35; Barbara Hochman, "Readers and reading groups," chapter 36; DeNel Rehberg Sedo, "Twentieth- and twenty-first-century literary communities," chapter 70; and Robert Coover, "A history of the future of narrative," chapter 71, all in this volume.

(Catherine Jurca), are direct and self-conscious responses to the increasingly corporate and commercial market.

As *The Cambridge History of the American Novel* does not privilege high or mass modernism – seeing both as responding creatively to the mass market – it also rejects unidirectional arguments about the novel critiquing, competing with, or capitulating to the mass media or any other interpretive systems. Rather, the chapters in this section emphasize symbiotic relationships among novelists and other media. Indeed for West, a distinguishing feature of the twentieth-century book industry is a new "[e]mphasis . . . on subsidiary rights and on tie-ins with other forms of public entertainment." Steinbeck owes his success in part, according to Alan Wald, because he incorporated popular culture into *The Grapes of Wrath* (1939). Curnutt establishes Fitzgerald's productive disagreement with contemporary sexology in *The Great Gatsby* (1925), while Farland shows the inspiration that mid-century women writers found in Betty Friedan's *The Feminine Mystique* (1963). As McGurl says, "The story of the modern novel's relation to mass culture and mass media is . . . not simply one of hostile status differentiation . . . but of an intimacy that keeps asserting itself even when the writer attempts to hold it at bay."

As the novel's success in the corporate market allowed established forms to flourish and new ones to emerge, the proliferation of subgenres led to the segmentation of readers into subgroups, many identifying themselves by religion, politics, gender, ethnicity, race, or sexual orientation. One result is an increasing inclusiveness; for instance, Babb shows how African American novels at mid-century "gave voice to those who had always been spoken for." According to King, Ellison and Baldwin sought more than a voice, enlisting aesthetics to political ends in advancing strong critiques of race relations at the dawn of the Civil Rights Movement. For Farland, another dimension of the segmentation of reading publics resulted from "the widening of feminism's purview to a set of diverse alliances – or from the opposed perspective, fragmentations – Chicano-feminist; black-feminist; eco-feminist; materialist-feminist." However one interprets the trend, it sets the stage for the proliferation of identity-based fictions that, as Andrew Hoberek writes in his discussion of the Jewish novel, "pos[e] the formal problem of how to foreground marginality in a culture where difference has become an increasingly mainstream value."

While the final section of *The Cambridge History of the American Novel* will trace the proliferation of identity-based novels into the twenty-first century, this section has a great deal to say about gender and sexuality as one such identity category. Masculine hegemony, the bourgeois family, women's subordinate position, and presumptive heterosexuality come in for questioning. Curnutt argues that the iconic Jay Gatsby "defied the dominant paradigm of masculine sexuality" and that Fitzgerald's literary analogues are thus Stein, Djuna Barnes, and others who reframed the heterosexual love story. Tracing a gay and lesbian literary tradition, Freeman also emphasizes the queerness of such exemplars of high modernism as *Absalom, Absalom!* (1936), concluding that "even the most canonical history of the American novel is already a queer one." Mickenberg shows how the neglected field of children's literature provides alternatives to the familiar canonical trope of boy-as-national-representative. Other contributors insist on the significance of women even when their subject is ostensibly male. Waid, for instance, stresses the importance of Faulkner's writings about masculinity while arguing that his "work is central to the continued force of the female-dominated mainstream" of twentieth-century American literature. Farland identifies new mid-century subgenres such as "women's mental breakdown novels" which focus on elite college graduates, while Regis demonstrates the flexibility of the most ubiquitous of popular genres, the female romance, in incorporating lesbian couples and even a bisexual marriage *à trois*. And so the American novel, canonical and popular, continues to reconfigure a shifting set of identities during – and beyond – the era of modernism.

37

Stein, Hemingway, and American modernisms

PETER NICHOLLS

The emergence of a reading public for American fiction was, as chapter 36 shows, a gradual and often contested one. And even as audiences for novels and short stories grew, continuing worries about the moral "dangers" of fiction were compounded by the appearance of new modernist forms which called in question the most fundamental conventions of imaginative narration. Modernism would mean many things, but in its deepest impulse it sought radical alternatives to the novelistic realism that by the beginning of the new century had become fiction's dominant mode.[a] Gertrude Stein, born one year after the publication of Harriet Beecher Stowe's *A Library of Famous Fiction*,[b] would lead a modernist assault on familiar notions of character and action in the novel that would also shape the hugely influential but very different writing of her most famous pupil, Ernest Hemingway.

Stein's principal complaint about nineteenth-century fiction was that it made narration the creature of memory; as she put it in a 1934 lecture called "Portraits and Repetition":

> slowly I realized this confusion, a real confusion, that in writing a story one had to be remembering, and that novels are soothing because so many people one may say everybody can remember almost anything. It is this element of remembering that makes novels so soothing. But and that was the thing that I was gradually finding out listening and talking at the same time that is realizing the existence of living being actually existing did not have in it any

a As noted in Michael Elliott, "Realism and radicalism: the school of Howells", chapter 17, 290, William Dean Howells had memorably declared that realism was "the only literary movement of our time that has any vitality." On the nineteenth-century "Realism–Romance Debate", see Lawrence Buell, "Theories of the American novel in the age of realism" (chapter 19).

b Barbara Hochman, "Readers and reading groups", chapter 36, 600, observes that Stowe's work endorsed the novel as a literary form, but "the declaration of victory over the lingering resistance to fiction was premature."

element of remembering and so the time of existing was not the same as in the novels that were soothing.[1]

The traditional novel, according to Stein, is "soothing" because it strives to present us with a world that is familiar and recognizable. It spirits us into a time frame which is safe because everything has already happened and can be comfortably negotiated from the vantage point of the present. By way of contrast, Stein says, the time in which we actually live is one of risk and surprise; it is anticipatory rather than reflective, more concerned with what is happening and about to happen than with what has already happened. We may note parenthetically that Stein's repudiation of the novel on these grounds represents only one strand of modernism, as the case of Proust magnificently illustrates, but it is nonetheless a strong strand which variously contrasts the representational conventions of "literature" with forms of writing which cultivate an immediacy of presentation (so Hemingway describes himself "trying in all my stories to get the feeling of the actual life across – not to just depict life – or criticize it – but to actually make it alive").[2] Stein's time of "actually existing" is, of course, hard to confine within the grammar of conventional narration, as it strains against the habitual ordering of events in the past tense and demands an often breathless urgency to convey the unpredictable rhythms of "living." Stein's sentences constantly exceed their anticipated boundaries, with more and more clauses added to defeat our well-trained attempts to bring their elements into a familiar order (note how the sheer momentum of the writing overrides the commonsense ban on the coupling of two conjunctions, "but and").

The projective quality of Stein's writing informs her thoughts on all subjects, even her assessment of her own car driving skills: "She goes forward admirably, but she does not go backwards successfully."[3] Stein is not surprised to find that she is hopeless at reversing her car, for her deepest aesthetic impulse is always to "go forward" rather than to go backward, into memory. So she rejects "the fact that knowledge is acquired, so to speak, by memory", arguing that "when you know anything, memory doesn't come in. At any moment that you are conscious of knowing anything, memory doesn't come into it. You have the sense of the immediate."[4] This repudiation of memory also goes to the heart of what Stein means by "identity." How do I know who I am? asks Stein: "I am I because my little dog knows me but, creatively speaking the little dog knowing that you are you and your recognizing that he knows, that is what destroys creation."[5] Identity in this sense connotes a fixed and closed self that Stein's little dog will never fail to recognize. But time,

Stein insists, is not continuity but difference, and narration, far from simply reporting on the past, always changes its object: "No matter how often what happened had happened any time any one told anything there was no repetition. This is what William James calls the Will to Live. If not nobody would live."[6] Not repetition, then, but "insistence" is the force of desire within language as it is within life: "there can be no repetition because the essence of that expression is insistence, and if you insist you must each time use emphasis and if you use emphasis it is not possible while anybody is alive that they should use exactly the same emphasis."[7] In writing there must be "neither memory nor repetition,"[8] but instead a present whose continuity is a product of differences: "each sentence is just the difference in emphasis," Stein observes,[9] and "insistence," which, like desire, goes on and on and is never completely satisfied, yields a model for a writing which similarly adds but does not conclude ("After all the natural way to count is not that one and one make two but to go on counting by one and one"[10]).

How might such ideas relate to the production of fiction? At first sight they seem to run counter to all claims the novel might so far have made to create a coherent and recognizable world. Indeed, it is notable in the passage quoted above that Stein has nothing to say about the creation of plot and character in fiction but speaks rather of sentences, thereby displacing emphasis from the traditional devices of storytelling to the medium of writing itself. In her long career she would work in many forms, producing novels, short stories, lectures, plays, operas, and poems, but always she would consider these primarily as types of writing rather than as discrete rule-governed genres. The effects of this perspective are immediately apparent in her earliest works. Take, for example, the following passage from *Three Lives* (written 1904–1905, published 1909): "Jeff Campbell was never any more a torment to Melanctha, he was only silent to her. Jeff often saw Melanctha and he was very friendly with her and he never any more was a bother to her. Jeff never any more now had much chance to be loving with her. Melanctha never was alone when he saw her." The sentences are short and declarative, and the simplicity of the syntax may give the impression of *faux naïveté*. But observe in even this brief extract the subtlety of implication: while the word "never" provides a sort of ground bass to these four sentences its reappearance amounts, as Stein has said, to something more than mere repetition, the word subtly shifting its meaning each time that it is used. While "never" declares that something won't happen now or later, the sinuous logic of the passage suggests that Jeff probably *would* be a bother to Melanctha if he ever had the chance to be alone with her. How, too, do we calibrate the distinction between being "very friendly" and being "loving"? The two terms are set off clearly against each other as apparently antithetical, but the reader is induced to weigh them very carefully and thereby to find what is actually an underlying proximity between them. Again, transparently "simple" words conceal a larger complexity which is governed by change and contingency.

Commenting in a lecture on *Three Lives* and on her next novel, *The Making of Americans* (written 1906–1908, but not published until 1925), Stein observed that "In these two books there was elaboration of the complexities of using everything and of a continuous present and of beginning again and again and again."[11] The second of these books runs to almost a thousand pages and takes much further the use of a "continuous present" (which may, contrary to expectation, actually deploy a past tense). Again, Stein is not interested in the intricate psychology of her characters but in their typicality, which can be grasped by discerning what she calls their "bottom nature." People, she finds, say the same things over and over again, "with infinite variations," and what is important is not so much what they say "but the movement of their thoughts and words endlessly the same and endlessly different."[12] Stein's novel proceeds less like fiction than like a scientific experiment (she had studied with William James at Radcliffe College), and the fact that everyone is "always repeating the being in them" allows her third-person narrative to discover the pattern of this "being" in the texture of phrasal repetition. The narrative method of *The Making of Americans* is exhaustive and exhausting, for its guiding belief "that it was possible to describe every kind there is of men and women" produces an emphatic attention to "types" which we tend to associate more with traditional allegory than with the social and psychological complexities of the conventional novel. For Stein, the hallmark of literary modernism is that "the novel which tells about what happens is of no interest to anybody. It is quite characteristic that in *The Making of Americans*, Proust, *Ulysses*, nothing much happens. People are interested in existence. Newspapers excite people very little."[13]

"Interesting": an overused word, often deployed when the speaker is reluctant to issue a real value-judgment. In Stein's usage, however, the word appears to be synonymous with "exciting," something capable of causing arousal. We notice, too, that "People are interested in existence," so this interest is not personal and idiosyncratic but universal, shared by all and comparable, perhaps, to James's "Will to Live." It is with this particular sense in mind that Stein in the last year of her life responded when asked about her attitude toward the atomic bomb:

> They asked me what I thought of the atomic bomb. I said I had not been able to take any interest in it. What is the use, if they are really as destructive as all that there is nothing left and if there is nothing left and if there is nothing there is nobody to be interested and nothing to be interested about.[14]

Characteristically, Stein's words do double duty here: to say that the atomic bomb is uninteresting is, on the face of it, absurd, but Stein thinks of "interest" rather as James does when he defines "interesting" objects as "those which appeal most urgently to our aesthetic, emotional, and active needs."[15] What, then, is genuinely interesting turns out to be the local textures of a shared everyday life, where James's spectrum of "needs" is vividly engaged. We are "interested" in what currently involves us, not in what we remember ("a thing is interesting that you see happening," says Stein[16]) and it is therefore not especially surprising that as she became increasingly fascinated by her "continuous present," so her writing moved farther away from the usual temporal perspectives of fiction.[17] From *Tender Buttons* (1914) to the last book published in her lifetime, *Wars I have Seen* (1945), Stein lingers over the detail of daily life, seeking to present it not as the backdrop for some significant action but to celebrate its self-sufficiency as it makes its appearance in writing. In *Wars I Have Seen*, for example, the rhythms and detail of domestic routine displace the conventional narratives of war in a way which acknowledges that this particular war has "put an entire end to the nineteenth century," with its conception of conflict as the stuff of "legendary" stories.[18] If, finally, we have "killed" the nineteenth century, as Stein puts it, this means that we are also free of the conventions of literary realism and can begin to understand that "life is not real it is not earnest, it is strange which is an entirely different matter."[19] Stein's allusion here to Longfellow's "A Psalm of Life" flattens out the original's exclamatory rhetoric ("Life is real! Life is earnest! / And the grave is not its goal") and in doing so replaces the conception of the afterlife with the more immediate pleasures of an ordinary life valued now for its paradoxical "strangeness."

The radicalism of Stein's break with realism is clear if we compare Hemingway's use of the same quotation. In *Death in the Afternoon* (1932), he remarks that "Someone with English blood has written: 'Life is real; life is earnest, and the grave is not its goal.' And where did they bury him? And what became of the reality and the earnestness?"[20] Hemingway's attitude is toughly realistic in its acknowledgment of death as "the unescapable reality" – he brashly ignores the actual sense of Longfellow's lines – and where Stein holds out the promise of a tantalizing "strangeness" Hemingway's realism amounts to little more than the lugubrious "great common sense" he attributes to the people of Castilla. This realistic attitude is, however, significantly complicated by Hemingway's stylistic debt to Stein. In his first years in Paris, he was a devoted admirer, and in typing up and proofing the gargantuan *The Making of Americans* he immersed himself in the rhythms of her prose, learning the crucial lesson that the modernist writer "did not describe reality" but "made up" something "round and whole and solid."[21] This "making up" followed Stein's writing practice in its attention to the rhythms of "beginning again and again and again" and "counting one by one," as in this passage from the short story "Up in Michigan," published in Hemingway's first book *Three Stories and Ten Poems* (1923):

> Liz Coates worked for Smith's. Mrs Smith, who was a very large clean woman, said Liz Coates was the neatest girl she'd ever seen. Liz had good legs and always wore clean gingham aprons and Jim noticed that her hair was always neat behind. He liked her face because it was so jolly but he never thought much about her.

As in Stein's early work, statement stands in for description. There is no attempt to be psychologically "inward" with the characters in the story, and instead repetition focuses attention on the words that are used ("Liz" three times in three sentences, for example).The vocabulary is painstakingly modest ("good," "neat," "jolly") in its avoidance of "literary" and dramatic effect. The rhythms of Stein's "Melanctha" haunt this story and much of Hemingway's work to come:

> Melanctha Herbert was beginning now to come less and less to the house to be with Rose Johnson. This was because Rose seemed always less and less now to want her, and Rose would not let Melanctha now do things for her. Melanctha was always humble to her and Melanctha always wanted in every way she could to do things for her.

In Hemingway's story, as in Stein's, simplicity frequently intimates a greater complexity. In the passage quoted above, for example, Jim notices the neatness of Liz's hair and her "jolly" face, "but he never thought about her." This problematic relation of "noticing" yet "not thinking" will quietly prepare us for Jim's cruelly thoughtless sexual assault on Liz which provides the mordant ending of the story.

Stein, as it happened, was the first to review *Three Stories*, commending its "poetry and intelligence," but also advising Hemingway to "eschew the hotter emotions and the more turgid vision."[22] In "Up in Michigan," though, the real implications of the story – that men don't "think" of women, that sexuality always entails loss and damage – are still deftly understated: "There was a mist coming up from the bay. She was cold and miserable and everything felt gone," and the final sentence of the story smoothly transfers the woman's coldness to the whole landscape, "A cold mist was coming up through the woods from the bay." In the larger reaches of Hemingway's novels, however, the sense of inevitable and irredeemable loss that is the crucial component of his tragically inflated or "turgid" vision becomes far more obtrusive. In *A Farewell to Arms* (1929), for example, Stein's rhythm of repetition remains much in evidence, though it is often used to register a failure of order and rationality: "I tried to tell about the night and the difference between the night and the day and how the night was better unless the day was very clean and cold and I could not tell it; as I cannot tell it now."

This failure to "tell" can produce a powerful poetics of omission – Hemingway's famous "iceberg" principle[23] – but it can also lead to an unfocused fatalism that becomes tiresomely portentous in his later fiction. It is there in germ in *A Farewell to Arms*: "They threw you in and told you the rules and the first time they caught you off base they killed you." In the posthumously published *Islands in the Stream* (1970) such "great common-sense" frequently courts bathos: "I do feel better, Thomas Hudson thought. That is the funny part. You always feel better and you always get over your remorse. There's only one thing you don't get over and that is death." Stein's phrase "turgid vision" goes to the heart of the problem, since protagonists like Thomas Hudson or the Colonel in *Across the River and into the Trees* (1950) express an overblown masculinity which is heroic only insofar as it is thrives on a "tragic" recognition that the odds are finally stacked against it. To borrow Hemingway's title for his 1933 volume of short stories, the winner takes nothing and this rule is at once an "ethical" injunction and an acknowledgment that winning is finally impossible.[24] The vision is falsely "turgid," inflated not by belief – witness Jake's ill-defined sense of himself as "a rotten Catholic" in *The Sun Also Rises* (1926) – but by pervasive superstition.[25] Writing itself is prized as a gamble, formal and existential, a craft requiring "luck as well as discipline" and "For luck you carried a horse chestnut or a rabbit's foot in your right pocket."[26] Yet talisman or no, one's luck is rationed – as the character David Bourne remarks of his own fiction in the posthumously edited *The Garden of Eden* (1986), "You can't believe you did it. When it's once right you never can do it again. You only do it once for each thing. And you're only allowed so many in your life."

For all the things that Stein and Hemingway share we can detect here a fundamental difference between them which might signal the emergence of two differently inflected forms of modernism. Where the fatalistic "vision" of Hemingway is reflected in the "luck" required to produce the "true sentence," for Stein the process of writing produces a supreme contentment. It is a difference between them of which Hemingway was acutely aware: "It makes us all happy to write," he observed in a letter written after Stein's death, "and she had discovered a way of writing she could do and be happy every day . . . When I can't write (writing under the strictest rules I know) I write letters; like today. She found a way of writing that was like writing letters all the time."[27] Stein's sublime confidence that she is "the most important writer writing today" allows her simply to invent the "rules" that suit her,[28] a move that, for Hemingway, trivializes the real drama of writing as an endless struggle with "the strictest rules." Stein – scandalously in his terms – just does what she wants. Partly for this reason, she is never unhappy – "I never had an unhappy anything," she says,[29] and "No song is sad," because "In the midst of writing there is merriment."[30]

The differences between the two writers are perhaps deliberately registered in the title Stein chose for a wartime memoir, "The Winner Loses," which seems to allude to Hemingway's *Winner Take Nothing*.[31] The titles might seem to say the same thing, but in fact Stein's refers to Germany, the power which seems to be winning but which in fact will lose. Like Hemingway, Stein was deeply superstitious, a devotee of fortune-telling and hand-reading,[32] and "The Winner Loses" makes regular reference to what she calls "the Bible," Leonardo Blake's astrologically based *The Last Year of War – and After*, published in 1940.[33] Blake's predictions pinpoint periods in which significant events might take place, but his chronology of Hitler's downfall, of course, proves quite wrong. Stein, however, happily accepts this extraordinary miscalculation: "The book of prophecy once more gave the significant days for June and they were absolutely the days that the crucial events happened, only they were not the defeat of Germany but the downfall of France."[34] Prophecy for Stein, we conclude, doesn't actually have to come true. Rather, it is the sheer pull of the future – the certainty that something *will* happen – that interests her and excites her superstitiousness: "Because it is certain that superstition means that what has been is going on. I always rightfully believe and believed in every superstition . . . Seeing superstition has nothing to do with believing anything except what anybody is seeing."[35] Whether or not it's actually possible to believe in *every* superstition is less important to Stein than the claim made here for the generality of what "anybody is seeing" (and seeing, here, is certainly not believing). As she puts it in *How Writing is Written*, "What is the use of knowing what has happened if one is not to know what is to happen. But of course one is to know what is to happen because it does. Not like it might not happen as of course it does."[36]

All this is remote indeed from the dark fatalism of Hemingway's "the cards we draw are those we get" which keeps the probability of losing constantly in view.[37] By way of contrast, for Stein, writing is always a winning, a lucky progress that in moving forward extinguishes any sense of lack or loss. Writing is like breathing for her – she "disliked the drudgery of revision," Hemingway notes wryly[38] – and she sees thinking itself as an obstacle to composition, claiming that "in a real master-piece there is no thought, if there were thought then there would be what you thought not what you do write."[39] Doing "right" is to write, not to think, and there is no Hegelian anxiety here about the word destroying what it names; to the contrary, nothing is ever lacking in Stein's world because there are always more words. By way of contrast, for a lot of authors, writing actually seems to threaten or degrade the things and events that are written about – Hemingway's Nick Adams, for instance, worries that writing "kills" the real things it names.[40] Stein, however, can remark of old friends that "Having written all about them they ceased to exist"[41] and any possible pathos here is quickly extinguished by the wry intimation that her friends' disappearance is simply due to their not being interesting enough to provoke more writing.

The cavalier tone of that comment is telling, though, and Stein's intense rivalries with her friends did indeed make them frequently "cease to exist" for her. Hemingway was one such casualty, with Stein becoming deeply resentful of his success with *A Farewell to Arms* (1929). For his part, Hemingway attributed the rift to a baffling conversation he overheard between her and Alice: "Then Miss Stein's voice came pleading and begging, saying 'Don't pussy. Don't. Don't. Don't, please don't. I'll do anything, pussy, but please don't do it. Please don't. Please don't pussy.' "[42] Exactly what the stakes of this sexual game might have been neither we nor Hemingway ever get to know, but Stein at this moment is clearly the loser, willing or not, something which we might surmise completely unsettles Hemingway's fantasy of lesbian oneness and his image of Stein as the perpetual winner and maker of the rules.[43] Hemingway retained his admiration for her person and her work, however: Stein would be a model for the powerful figure of Pilar in *For Whom the Bell Tolls* (1940), and in a story called "On Writing" Nick Adams "could see the Cézannes. The portrait at Gertrude Stein's. She'd know if he ever got things right."[44]

For her part, Stein produced "Evidence," a series of prose pieces, parts of which seem to refer to a 1929 meeting with Hemingway. The tone is rather different from Stein's first portrait of "He and They, Hemingway," warning darkly that "Ernest should beware of succeeding to bewildering."[45] These personal differences are not important in themselves but they do indicate an awareness of diverging aesthetics, something that Stein retrospectively introduced into her account of their meeting in *The Autobiography of Alice B. Toklas* (1933). It was at a time, she recalls, when all young men seemed to be twenty-six, and then she continues: "So Hemingway was twenty-three, rather foreign-looking, with passionately interested, rather than interesting eyes. He sat in front of Gertrude Stein and listened and looked."[46] The contrast in their relative positions in this vignette nicely encapsulates the striking contrasts in their modes of writing. To compare the immense productivity of Stein's prose with the spare, stripped-down quality of Hemingway's early fiction is to see how his verbal precisions are always won in the face of disasters that *will have* happened in the future, of things that *will have* ended, while the rich continuous present tense of Stein's writing promises endless plenitude, an almost orgiastic fullness of experience to come.[47]

The anticipatory drive of Stein's writing and the deceptively bland optimism it seemed to imply made her a contradictory influence for the younger modernists who admired her experimentalism. While writers such as Sherwood Anderson, William Faulkner, and Scott Fitzgerald relished her thoroughgoing commitment to the craft of writing, their work was less able to slip the burdens of history or to avoid Fitzgerald's sense that the present was always in some way "cracked." It was thus that Fitzgerald recalled his period of great success in New York City, for example: "from that period," he writes, "I remember riding in a taxi one afternoon between very tall buildings under a mauve and rose sky; I began to bawl because I had everything I wanted and knew I would never be so happy again."[48] The "single gorgeous moment," as he calls it in an essay called "Early Success," is, in contrast to Stein's "continuous present," never adequate in itself, always "cracked" by a darker, retrospective knowledge of what will have happened afterwards.[49] For Hemingway, it would ultimately be Stein's great limitation that "she wanted to know the gay part of how the world was going, never the real, never the bad."[50]

That future anterior tense had been experienced with great immediacy by Hemingway in a way that made it impossible for him, at any rate, to pass over the "real" and the "bad." His wartime wounding at Fossalta had left him decorated as a war hero but damaged as a survivor – both winning and losing, we might say. For the condition of survival, whatever myths Hemingway wove around it, is one which is somehow poised between anticipation – the end must come – and the altogether stranger awareness that the end has already happened even as we survive and live on. Here the open tense of Stein's "continuous present" is ominously blocked, with narrative time seeming to recoil upon itself. As Maurice Blanchot puts it in his unsettling *récit The Instant of My Death* (1994), where the protagonist is spared from death at the very last moment, after this "unexperienced experience" of death, all that remains is "the instant of my death henceforth always in abeyance."[51] It is this idea of a reprieve that hangs heavy over much of Hemingway's fiction – in *Islands in the Stream*, for example: "Then, later, had come the feeling of reprieve that a wound brings. He still had the feeling of the bad dream and that it had all happened before. But it had not happened in this way and now, grounded, he had the temporary reprieve. He knew that it was only a reprieve but he relaxed in it." For the survivor, then, death comes to be that which will have taken place, suggesting too the failure of any futural perspective, the end always announced proleptically in the beginning. Stein's jubilant sense of anticipation and "beginning again" here mutates into a darker sense of endings always known in advance, a fatalistic sense that haunts Hemingway's longer fictions.

The whole dynamic of winning and losing is thus vitiated at its core for the survivor – "The position of the survivor of a great calamity is seldom admirable," Hemingway commented in the manuscript of *A Farewell to Arms*[52] – and it's here that we can grasp the full import of his pursuit of the "true sentence" which replaces the relations between people by a powerfully stoical and essentially closed version of the self.[53] Indeed, the survivor becomes the very model of the writer: "the writer must be intelligent and disinterested and above all he must survive . . . The hardest thing, because time is so short, is for him to survive and get his work done."[54] The writer-survivor cannot afford to "let go," as Hemingway puts it in the famous story "As I Lay Me," where the war-damaged soldier cannot risk falling asleep, lest he never wake again.

Here we may see a fundamental difference between the writings of Hemingway and Stein, and perhaps, too of variant strands of literary modernism. The difference is analogous to a distinction Freud makes when he is discussing the function of word-play in jokes. Such play, he says, focuses "our psychical attitude upon the *sound* of the word instead of upon its *meaning* – in making the (acoustic) word-presentation itself take the place of its significance as given by its relations to thing-presentations." We experience a particular pleasure on such occasions, Freud observes, and "It may really be suspected that in doing so we are bringing about a great relief in psychical work and that when we make serious use of words we are obliged to hold ourselves back with a certain effort from this comfortable procedure."[55] Freud implies that a "serious use of words" always entails a kind of repression, that if words are savoured in the mouth rather than being put swiftly to work, meaningful tasks will never be accomplished. Stein's writing, we might say, seeks always to lift this repression, abolishing the lack on which a descriptive language is founded and thereby discovering a poetry in which the mind, like Melanctha in *Three Lives*, can freely "wander." Hemingway, in contrast, is at once drawn to and repelled by such "wandering" (aesthetic and erotic), and the Steinian rhythms and repetitions of his early prose are ultimately constrained by a "holding back" that is both formal and thematic, a discipline of craft and attention which allows the writer to "survive."[56] Two different stylistic economies are at work, then, one entailing a lavish expenditure, with no sense that the largesse will exhaust itself, while the other is dependent on a more straitened husbanding of restricted resources in light of inevitable losses to come.

The two would have very different legacies. For some modernist poets – William Carlos Williams and Mina Loy, for example – it was Stein's achievement, as Williams, put it, to give words "a curious immediate quality quite apart from their meaning" and this "placed writing on a plane where it may deal unhampered with its own affairs, unburdened with scientific and philosophic lumber."[57] Loy similarly emphasized that "There is no particular advantage in groping for subject matter in a literature that is sufficiently satisfying as verbal design,"[58] and this celebration of purely formal values perhaps explains why few novelists would find in Stein's absorbed attention to the rhythms of "verbal design" a directly helpful model for their own modernism. Stein, after all, had consistently valued "writing" above any particular genre, and it was not until the arrival of what is now called Language writing, with its own disregard of generic boundaries and its attention to "A semantic atmosphere, or milieu, rather than the possessive individualism of reference,"[59] that Stein's work acquired the exemplary status she herself had wished for. In contrast, Hemingway's legacy for American novelists has been far more extensive, informing a whole range of "hard-boiled" styles, from the proletarian realism of the thirties, through "noir" writers such as Raymond Chandler and Dashiell Hammett, on into the "tough" existential fictions of Norman Mailer, all writers for whom it has been the winning punch of Hemingway's work rather than its losing streak that has been most commonly emulated.[c]

Yet style is a curiously insubstantial thing when deprived of the world which sponsors it, as the fiction of our own time never fails to remind us. Don DeLillo's recent novel *Cosmopolis* (2003), for example, immerses us in the cyber-world of advanced capitalism in which winning and losing take place on a global scale. Here the market contains every thing, there is no "outside," no space untouched by economic forces.[60] This world is "full," like Stein's, though it is "full" of the abstracted movements of money, rather than of sensuous human activity; and while, like Stein's world, it is one for which "The future becomes insistent," it is no longer the horizon of possible experience that is the issue here but rather the position of the futures market. In the following passage from *Cosmopolis*, the main protagonist, Eric, remembers a one-time friend, Nikolai, with whom he had once taken a memorable hunting trip: "They'd seen a tiger in the distance, a glimpse, a sting of pure transcendence, outside all previous experience ... The sight of the tiger aflame in high snow made them feel bound to an unspoken code, a brotherhood of beauty and loss." The mention of the hunters' shared "unspoken code" alludes directly to Hemingway and probably to his story "The Snows of Kilimanjaro," which has the following epigraph:

> Kilimanjaro is a snow-covered mountain 19,710 feet high, and is said to be the highest mountain in Africa. Its western summit is called the Masai "Ngàje Ngài," the House of God. Close to the western summit there is the dried and frozen carcass of a leopard. No one has explained what the leopard was seeking at that altitude.

Here the leopard dies in its futile quest for God, a quest so futile yet so fundamental that it cannot be "explained" or even named as such; indeed, the fact of its existence is highly equivocal: the reader seems to see it, but by implication the narrator probably has not. In contrast, in Eric's account the "sting of pure transcendence" is felt with apparent immediacy by the two men, but this is subtly undermined by DeLillo's broad allusions to Hemingway's story which actually render the "sting" a purely aesthetic one of "beauty and loss." These are not, in Hemingway's terms, "true sentences," dressed

c For thirties realism, see Alan Wald, "Steinbeck and the proletarian novel," chapter 40. Sean McCann, "The novel of crime, mystery, and suspense", chapter 48, 807–811, discusses the "hard-boiled" fiction of Chandler and Hammett. Andrew Hoberek, "The Jewish great American novel", chapter 54, 896, interestingly proposes that Mailer "turns to consciousness as the anti-Hemingwayesque site on which to claim Hemingway's mantle."

deliberately as they are in another man's clothes, nor do their poeticisms qualify as Stein's "winning language." In the endlessly mediated world of *Cosmopolis*, writing can no longer aspire to be anything but "literature," a conclusion rendered the more powerful by DeLillo's artful bracketing of an earlier modernism.

Notes

1. Gertrude Stein, *Look at Me Now and Here I Am: Writing and Lectures 1909–45*, ed. Patricia Meyerowitz (Harmondsworth: Penguin Books, 1984), 108–109.
2. Carlos Baker, ed., *Ernest Hemingway: Selected Letters 1917–1961* (New York: Granada Publishing, 1981), 153.
3. Gertrude Stein, *The Autobiography of Alice B. Toklas* (Harmondsworth: Penguin Books, 1977), 189.
4. Gertrude Stein, *How Writing is Written*, ed. Robert Bartlett Haas (Los Angeles: Black Sparrow Press, 1974), 155.
5. Stein, *Look at Me Now*, 149.
6. *Ibid.*, 101.
7. *Ibid.*, 100.
8. *Ibid.*, 107.
9. *Ibid.*, 119.
10. *Ibid.*, 136. Jean-François Lyotard, *The Differend: Phrases in Dispute*, trans. Georges Van Den Abbeele (Manchester: Manchester University Press, 1988), 68, observes that "In Stein's text, a phrase is one time, an event, it happens. The anxiety that this will not start up again, that Being will come to a halt, distends the paragraphs."
11. Stein, *Look at Me Now*, 26.
12. *Ibid.*, 86.
13. Stein, *How Writing is Written*, 158. Cf. Stein, *Look at Me Now*, 114–115: "All this time I was of course not interested in emotion or anything that happened. I was less interested then in these things than I had ever been. I lived my life with emotion and with things happening but I was creating in my writing by simply looking."
14. Gertrude Stein, *Reflection on the Atomic Bomb*, ed. Robert Bartlett Haas (Los Angeles: Black Sparrow Press, 1973), 161.
15. William James, *The Principles of Psychology*, 2 vols. (New York: Dover, 1950), II: 312 (italics in original). Cf. *ibid.*, I:402: "Millions of items of the outward order are present to my senses which never properly enter into my experience. Why? Because they have no *interest* for me. *My experience is what I agree to attend to.* Only those items which I *notice* shape my mind – without selective interest, experience is an utter chaos. Interest alone gives accent and emphasis, light and shade, background and foreground – intelligible perspective, in a word."
16. Gertrude Stein, *Everybody's Autobiography* (New York: Vintage Books, 1973), 263.

17. On the relation of narrativity to "interest" and Freud's reality principle, see Leo Bersani and Ulysse Dutoit, *Arts of Impoverishment: Beckett, Rothko, Resnais* (Cambridge, MA: Harvard University Press, 1993), esp. 89.
18. Gertrude Stein, *Wars I Have Seen* (New York: Random House, 1945), 20.
19. *Ibid.*, 44.
20. Ernest Hemingway, *Death in the Afternoon* (St. Albans: Triad/Panther, 1977), 234. "Englishness" usually connotes for Hemingway a certain effeteness and lack of "realism."
21. Ernest Hemingway, *By-Line: Ernest Hemingway* (New York: Charles Scribner's Sons, 1967), 216. In a letter to Sherwood Anderson, Hemingway described Stein's novel as "one of the very greatest books I've ever read." *Ernest Hemingway: Selected Letters, 1917–1961*, ed. Carlos Baker (New York: Granada Publishing, 1981), 206.
22. The review appeared in the *Chicago Tribune* (European edition) in November 1923. It is reprinted in Scott Donaldson, "Gertrude Stein Reviews Hemingway's *Three Stories and Ten Poems*," *American Literature* 53.1 (March 1981), 114–115.
23. See *Death in the Afternoon*, 170–171: "If a writer of prose knows enough about what he is writing about he may omit things that he knows and the reader, if the writer is writing truly enough, will have a feeling of those things as strongly as though the writer had stated them. The dignity of an iceberg is due to only one-eighth of it being above water."
24. Hemingway, *Winner Take Nothing* (1933) has an epigraph which purports to be from an old gaming manual: "Unlike all other forms of lutte or combat the conditions are that the winner shall take nothing: neither his ease nor his pleasure, nor any notions of glory; nor if he win far [*sic*] enough, shall there be any reward for himself." Carlos Baker notes that Hemingway "composed the passage in what he took to be the true seventeenth-century manner" (*Ernest Hemingway: A Life Story* [Harmondsworth: Penguin Books, 1972], 366).
25. The following exchange is indicative of Jake's sense of his Catholicism: " 'Listen, Jake,' he said, 'are you really a Catholic?' 'Technically.' 'What does that mean?' 'I don't know.' " For Hemingway's own wavering Catholic convictions, see Scott Donaldson, *By Force of Will: The Life and Art of Ernest Hemingway* (Harmondsworth: Penguin Books, 1978), 225–229.
26. Ernest Hemingway, *A Moveable Feast* (1936; London: Arrow Books, 1994), 12, 79. See also the discussion of superstition in Donaldson, *By Force of Will*, 230–34.
27. Hemingway, *Selected Letters*, 650. Cf. *Garden of Eden*: "It had gone so simply and easily that he thought it was probably worthless."
28. Stein, *Everybody's Autobiography*, 28.
29. *Ibid.*, 75.
30. Stein, "Rooms," in *Look at Me Now*, 198; Stein, "Lifting Belly," in *The Yale Gertrude Stein*, ed. Richard Kostelanetz (New Haven and London: Yale University Press, 1980), 54.
31. Noted by Ann Douglas, *Terrible Honesty: Mongrel Manhattan in the 1920s* (New York, Farrar, Strauss, and Giroux, 1995), 142–143.

32. See Ulla Dydo, *Gertrude Stein: The Language That Rises 1923–1934* (Evanston, IL: Northwestern University Press, 2003), 411 n. 12. Cf. Stein, *Everybody's Autobiography*, 155: "It is natural to believe in superstitions and hand-reading and predictions. I like hand-reading better than predictions, predictions are a little more frightening."
33. *The Winner Loses: A Picture of Occupied France*, in *Selected Writings of Gertrude Stein*, ed. Carl Van Vechten (New York: The Modern Library, 1962), 616.
34. *Ibid.*, 622. On Stein and Blake, see also John Whittier-Ferguson, "Stein in Time: History, Manuscripts, and Memory," *Modernism/Modernity* 6.1 (January 1999): 129–130.
35. Stein, *Everybody's Autobiography*, 116.
36. Stein, *How Writing is Written*, 30.
37. Hemingway, *Across the River and into the Trees* (1950).
38. Hemingway, *A Moveable Feast*, 16.
39. Gertrude Stein, *The Geographical History of America* (1936), quoted in David Kaufmann, "Desperate Seriousness and Avant-Garde (Mis)Recognition in some of Stein's Sentences," *Modern Philology* 97.2 (November 1999): 223.
40. Hemingway, "On Writing," in *The Nick Adams Stories*, introd. Philip Young (New York: Scribner, 1972), 237. See also *The Garden of Eden* (1986), where David Bourne observes of his writing that "It had gone so simply and easily that he thought it was probably worthless."
41. Stein, *Everybody's Autobiography*, 119.
42. Hemingway, *A Moveable Feast*, 104. See also in Dydo, *The Language That Rises*, 243 n. 41, Stein's notebook reference to Toklas: "she listens, she is docile, stupid but she owns you . . ."
43. See Hemingway, *Selected Letters*, 795, which records Stein's lecture to him on the virtues of lesbian sex. A slightly different version of the story appears in *A Moveable Feast*, 18.
44. On Stein as a model for Pilar, see Nancy R. Comley and Robert Scholes, *Hemingway's Genders: Rereading the Hemingway Text* (New Haven and London: Yale University Press, 1994), 46–49; Hemingway, "On Writing," 239.
45. Gertrude Stein, "Evidence" (1930), in *Stein: A Reader*, ed. Ulla Dydo (Evanston, IL: Northwestern University Press, 1993), 544. For "He and They, Hemingway" (1923), see *Reader*, 450. Dydo, *The Language That Rises*, 382 describes "Evidence" as "a malicious, personal attack on Hemingway."
46. Stein, *Autobiography*, 230.
47. To take one of many examples in Hemingway's work: " 'My,' she said. 'We're lucky that you found the place,' I said and like a fool I did not knock on wood. There was wood everywhere in that apartment to knock on too" (*A Moveable Feast*, 33). See also *The Sun Also Rises* (1926), on "the feeling of going through something that has all happened before" and "an ignored tension, and a feeling of things coming that you could not prevent happening."
48. F. Scott Fitzgerald, "My Lost City," in *The Crack-Up*, ed. Edmund Wilson (New York: New Directions, 1945), 28–29.
49. Fitzgerald, "Early Success," in *The Crack-Up*, 90.

50. Hemingway, *A Moveable Feast*, 23.
51. Maurice Blanchot/Jacques Derrida, *The Instant of My Death* and *Demeure: Fiction and Testimony*, trans. Elizabeth Rottenberg (Stanford, CA: Stanford University Press, 2000), 47, 11. Blanchot's text was first published as *L'instant de ma mort* (Paris: Fata Morgana, 1994).
52. Quoted in Michael S. Reynolds, *Hemingway's First War: The Making of* A Farewell to Arms (Princeton: Princeton University Press, 1976), 60.
53. See *A Moveable Feast*, 12: "All you have to do is write one true sentence. Write the truest sentence that you know." Fredric Jameson, *Marxism and Form: Twentieth-Century Dialectical Theories of Literature* (Princeton: Princeton University Press, 1971), 410, observes a related opposition in Hemingway's thinking "between life among things and life with other people, between nature and society."
54. Ernest Hemingway, *Green Hills of Africa* (London: Arrow Books, 1994), 19.
55. Sigmund Freud, *Jokes and Their Relation to the Unconscious* (1905), *Pelican Freud Library*, vol. VI, trans. James Strachey (Harmondsworth: Penguin Books, 1983), 167–168.
56. The consequences of "letting go" are grim indeed, as we see from the fullest expression of Hemingway's life-long fascination with androgyny and lesbianism, *The Garden of Eden*. Here the "wandering" which Stein exemplifies as woman and as writer is seen to issue in insanity and the destruction of artistic talent. It is generally felt that the ending chosen by the publisher from the mass of manuscript is far more anodyne than Hemingway intended. See Comley and Scholes, *Hemingway's Genders*, chapter 3; Mark Spilka, *Hemingway's Quarrel with Androgyny* (Lincoln and London: University of Nebraska Press, 1995), chapter 11; and Robert Fleming, "The Endings of Hemingway's *Garden of Eden*," *American Literature* 61.2 (May 1989): 261–270.
57. William Carlos Williams, "The Work of Gertrude Stein," in *Selected Essays* (New York: New Directions, 1969), 114, 116.
58. Mina Loy, "Gertrude Stein," in *The Last Lunar Baedeker*, ed. Roger L. Conover (Highlands, NC: The Jargon Society, 1982), 294.
59. Bruce Andrews, "Text and Context," in *The L=A=N=G=U=A=G=E Book*, ed. Andrews and Charles Bernstein (Carbondale and Edwardsville: Southern Illinois University Press, 1984), 36. See also Peter Nicholls, "Difference Spreading: from Gertrude Stein to L=A=N=G=U=A=G=E Poetry," in *Contemporary Poetry Meets Modern Theory*, ed. Anthony Easthope and John Thompson (London: Harvester-Wheatsheaf, 1991), 116–127. Lyn Hejinian's "Two Stein Talks," reprinted in *The Language of Inquiry* (Berkeley and Los Angeles: University of California Press, 2000), offer the most subtle reading of Stein's work in relation to the evolving Language tendency.
60. In *Cosmopolis*, DeLillo explains that "This is the free market itself. These people are a fantasy generated by the market. They don't exist outside the market. There is nowhere they can go to be on the outside. There is no outside."

38

The Great Gatsby and the 1920s

KIRK CURNUTT

At a pivotal moment in *The Great Gatsby*, Nick Carraway traces the genesis of the accelerating tragedy to a kiss that Jay Gatsby bestowed upon Daisy Fay in 1917 as he prepared to depart for the Great War. "One autumn night," Nick writes, his ostentatious West Egg neighbor – then a lowly infantry lieutenant – suddenly awoke to the ritualistic importance of this most deceptively simple of sensual exchanges: "He knew that when he kissed this girl, and forever wed his unutterable visions to her perishable breath, his mind would never romp again like the mind of God. So he waited, listening for a moment longer to the tuning fork that had been struck upon a star. Then he kissed her. At his lips' touch she blossomed for him like a flower and the incarnation was complete."

The interlude is the most famous kiss in a corpus that contains so many that a contemporary once congratulated F. Scott Fitzgerald for cataloguing "the osculatory habits of the flapper."[1] A more generous appraisal would argue that the tableau epitomizes Fitzgerald's talent for dramatizing the poignancy of romance in a gossamer style composed of equal parts enchantment and lachrymosity. And yet, curiously, few critics talk about *The Great Gatsby* as a love story anymore. While the novel frequently tops polls of great American romances, its popular reputation exists independently of its academic import. When commentators do invoke the word "love," it tends to follow the prefix "self-" to reaffirm the conventional wisdom that Gatsby's "unutterable visions" have less to do with winning the object of his affection than with selecting her to embody his "platonic conception of himself." In this view, the kiss marks the moment at which Gatsby invested in an otherwise unremarkable eighteen-year-old Louisville belle his certainty that he was not the anonymous son of "shiftless and unsuccessful farm people" but a *Somebody* – a desire that renders Daisy almost tangential to the "ineffable gaudiness" of the former James Gatz's aspiration. As critics have insisted since the novel's canonization in the 1950s, Gatsby's relentless drive to transcend the "indiscernible barb wire" of social class is itself emblematic of the American urge to affirm the plasticity of the individual self, the myth of entrepreneurial self-perfection that insists the only barriers preventing one from "doing great things" are failures of imagination. With Nick Carraway alternately dismissing and lionizing the naïveté of Gatsby's faith in the national ideology of boundless opportunity, *The Great Gatsby* is both a critique of and a tribute to the power of America as an ideal to inspire "dreams . . . commensurate to [one's] capacity for wonder."[2]

Without rejecting this standard interpretation, rereading *Gatsby* for its depiction of love and sex is important for understanding how Fitzgerald differed from his contemporaries – and the 1920s in general – when treating these concerns. Every bit as much as the fabled 1960s, the decade was obsessed with eros and eroticism. As John D'Emilio and Estelle B. Freedman note, "American society was moving by the 1920s toward a view of erotic expression that can be defined as sexual liberalism – an overlapping set of beliefs that detached sexual activity from the instrumental goal of procreation, affirmed heterosexual pleasure as a value in itself, [and] defined sexual satisfaction as a critical component of personal happiness and successful marriage."[3] Fiction was a medium of this amelioration, with writers across a range of genres – from literary modernism to romance to hard-boiled detective fiction to fantasy / adventure – often walking a thin line between exploration and exploitation as they mapped the consequences of "pleasure as a value in itself." Provocative novels such as Joseph Hergesheimer's *Cytherea* (1922), Maxwell Bodenheim's *Replenishing Jessica* (1925), and Frances Newman's *The Hard-Boiled Virgin* (1926) – not to mention the more notorious examples of James Joyce's *Ulysses* (1922) and D. H. Lawrence's *Lady Chatterley's Lover* (1928) – stoked outrage and redrew the boundaries of obscenity. Less famously, they helped shape reader perceptions of how one should experience passion by stylizing an erotic repertoire of gestures, from kisses to caresses to coitus itself.[a]

Compared to the explicitness of these contemporaries, Fitzgerald's treatment of eros can seem downright demure if not quaint; his interest lay less in sexual passion than in what might be called "romantic performance" – i.e. the art of falling in love, not bed. Nevertheless, from his debut, *This Side of*

a In her discussion of the generation preceding Fitzgerald's, Barbara Hochman notes that in Dreiser's *Sister Carrie* (1900), Carrie Meeber's taste for French literature "confirms the social marginality already suggested by her sexual behavior and her acting career" ("Readers and reading groups," chapter 36, 607). When Fitzgerald himself mocks a "racy" novel in *Gatsby*, he selects an English example comparable to E. M. Hull's *The Sheik*: Robert Keable's *Simon Called Peter* (1921).

Paradise (1920), to *The Beautiful and Damned* (1922) and the charming stories collected in *Flappers and Philosophers* (1920) and *Tales of the Jazz Age* (1922), his depiction of modern romance as a gaudy game of pursuit revolving around disguises, poses, and outlandish plots hatched to win the heart of an intended both reflected and influenced how his generation publicized sex. Yet in *The Great Gatsby*, Fitzgerald created a tragic lover with a surprising lack of erotic presence. In doing so, he defied the deterministic ideals of gender beneath the era's conception of romance in a way that, once properly appreciated, urges us to qualify our historical inclination to celebrate 1920s literature as sexually progressive.

A notable measure of the increasing prominence of eroticism in the 1920s was the emerging concept of sex appeal. First coined around 1919 and sometimes politely referred to as "S.A.," the term was used interchangeably with romance novelist and screenwriter Elinor Glyn's famously epigrammatic pronoun "It" to dramatize the allure of movie stars like Rudolph Valentino and Clara Bow. The trait was hardly exclusive to the cinema. Glyn, Ethel M. Dell, and Edith Maude Hull were but three bestselling authors to avail themselves of the concept to depict a new type of literary hero. No longer the "unsuitable men" of the eighteenth-century seduction novel, neither the predatory Gilbert Osmond of James's *The Portrait of a Lady* (1888) nor the opportunistic Alcée Arobin of Chopin's *The Awakening* (1900), these fictional lovers did not threaten to ruin heroines' reputations by seducing them. Rather, throughout a slew of now-forgotten romance novels with titles such as *The Little French Girl, Bad Girl, Love's Ecstasy*, and *Bandit Love*, they initiated partners into previously taboo amatory knowledge.

Among this new breed of lover, the most famous was Ahmed Ben Hassan, the hero of Hull's *The Sheik* and the role that rocketed Valentino to fame. The popularity of both the novel – it was among the top ten bestsellers in America in both 1921 and 1922 – and George Melford's film adaptation made the character a simultaneous style icon and stock character. An amazing diversity of ethnic cultures, from African American to Italian to Mexican American, appropriated the *faux* Middle Eastern trappings of Hull's fantasy, while the storyline of an orientalized foreigner seducing a repressed Westerner became an almost instantly hackneyed formula.[4] The Sheik proved a particularly resonant image in the Harlem Renaissance, with several authors finding the figure's exotic eroticism a complement to the movement's faddish primitivism.[5] Wallace Thurman's *The Blacker the Berry* (1929), for example, includes a secondary character, Braxton, who fancies himself "a golden brown replica of

Rudolph Valentino." Braxton is such a poseur that he not only frequents the movies to study the charisma of the "late lamented sheik" – Valentino died in 1926 – but he also practices "Rudy's poses and facial expressions" in the mirror, learning "how to use his eyes in the same captivating manner," though his charms are transparently contrived and therefore ineffectual.

The Sheik and *The Blacker the Berry* offer important contrasts for appreciating something often overlooked in *The Great Gatsby*: when compared to such figures, Jay Gatsby does not strike one as particularly sexy. The point is easily missed even though Fitzgerald alludes twice to Hull's hero. The first reference occurs when Nick Carraway describes his incredulity at Gatsby's claim to have "lived like a young rajah" after being orphaned in childhood: "The very phrases were so threadbare," Nick says of the preposterous tale, "that they evoked no image except that of a turbaned 'character' leaking sawdust at every pore."[6] The second is more explicit. As Nick and his sometime love interest Jordan Baker promenade through New York City, they overhear "The Sheik of Araby," the risqué 1921 hit song written to cash in on the character's notoriety.[7] These references serve a dual function. On the one hand, they urged original readers to equate Gatsby's pursuit of Daisy with *The Sheik*'s chase-and-conquer formula. At the same time, they would call attention to how artificial or "threadbare" its seduction motifs had become by virtue of their repetition in books and films.

Gatsby does not emulate the Sheik's orientalized fashion as literally as Braxton does, but his self-presentation is as contrived. While Thurman signals Braxton's artificiality by parodying his propensity for affectation, Fitzgerald calls attention to his character's lack of genuineness through a curious exclusion. Although described as an "elegant young roughneck," Gatsby makes no effort to exude Braxton's uninhibited animalism – an animalism that, for romance writers, was the *sine qua non* of a lover's authenticity.

Gatsby's deficiency is most glaring during the central seduction scene, which takes an inexplicable slapstick turn at the precise moment that the lover's sex appeal ought to excite a swoon. Meeting Daisy for the first time in a half-decade, Gatsby strikes such a ridiculous pose by reclining against Nick's mantelpiece in "a strained counterfeit of perfect ease, even of boredom" that he accidentally knocks over a clock. Shortly afterward, he is so "dazed" escorting Daisy through his mansion that he almost falls down his own stairway. In such passages, Fitzgerald nearly turns his hero into a Chaplin rather than a Valentino, a figure of comedic pathos rather than romantic passion. Daisy is the one who kisses *him* on the mouth.

Gatsby's comparative lack of sex appeal comes into even greater relief when compared to the one male character that does seem to possess the will to erotic power of the Sheik: Tom Buchanan, Daisy's husband and the villain of the novel. In Daisy's own words, Tom is "a brute of a man," a "great, big hulking specimen" whose blunt physicality is the antithesis of Gatsby's dapper if studied reserve. At two points, Fitzgerald even describes Tom's abusiveness: first when Daisy displays a knuckle bruised during an argument with her husband, and second and more dramatically, when Tom breaks the nose of his mistress, Myrtle Wilson, after she demands a bit too insistently that he leave his wife. For most readers, such cruelty makes Tom wholly despicable, and yet such aggression was apiece with the masculine sexuality that Sheik-style heroes embodied. What Dorothy Parker noted in her acidic *New Yorker* assessment of Glyn's *It* is true of 1920s romance fiction in general: the genre's conception of an appealing male lover "interestingly entangle[s] his It with sadism." [8] This is the kind of lover who, invariably, "takes" his woman.

I want to suggest that Gatsby's lack of sexual animalism reflects Fitzgerald's disenchantment with the gender determinism that lay beneath the 1920s' conception of true romance. For all the decade's self-congratulatory claims to have freed eroticism from Victorian prudery, the majority of Jazz Age discourse – scientific and self-improvement discourse as well as fiction – refortified rather than challenged conventional assumptions about masculine and feminine difference. Glyn, the indefatigably prolific author of *It* offered a reductive delineation of these assumptions in *The Philosophy of Love* (1923), one of her many nonfiction attempts to extrapolate from her romance novels practical advice on attaining and sustaining romantic felicity: "Woman's ideal man is always rather masterful . . . It is he who always holds the reins in the relations with him, never [her]."[9]

One might dismiss such rhetoric as hyperbole if variations on its essentialism did not appear in a range of period advice guides, from imposing scientific efforts such as the Dutch gynecologist Theodoor Van de Velde's *Ideal Marriage: Its Physiology and Technique* (1926) to Ben Lindsey's *Companionate Marriage* (1927) and Floyd Dell's *Love in the Machine Age* (1930). Van de Velde is typical of such discourse when he casually notes that men are "*naturally* educators and initiators of their wives in sexual matters" and that romance fails because "they often lack . . . the qualifications of a leader and initiator." [10] An often surprising cast of women writers likewise endorsed this opinion. Even birth-control pioneer Margaret Sanger in *Happiness in Marriage* (1926) counseled female readers to allow husbands to "dominate" sexual relations because women were likely limited in erotic expertise.[11] While "sexual modernization" conceded that women were perfectly capable of enjoying erotic pleasures, it had not yet extended to them the privilege of being "sexual subjects" with the authority to define and act upon their own amorous intent.[12]

No tableau in 1920s fiction illustrates the supposed "mastery" of male sexuality more dramatically than the one that made *The Sheik* notorious – namely, the tent scene in which Ahmed Ben Hassan for all intents and purposes rapes kidnapped heroine Diana Mayo:

> Stooping he disengaged her clinging fingers from the heavy drapery and drew her hands slowly together up to his breast with a little smile. "Come," [the Sheik] whispered, his passionate eyes devouring her.
>
> She fought against the fascination with which they dominated her, resisting him dumbly with tight-locked lips till he held her palpitating in his arms.
>
> "Little fool," he said with a deepening smile. "Better me than my men."
>
> The gibe broke her silence.
>
> "Oh, you brute! You brute!" she wailed, until kisses silenced her.

It may well be, as Karen Chow argues, that this oft-imitated scenario became "a common trope in romance novels" because the "forced" seduction allows Diana "to lose her inhibitions without taking moral responsibility for doing so" and "consequently . . . to express herself sexually." Yet that argument is far more problematic when "purple passages of submission and domination" do not culminate in the voicing of feminine sensuality.[13]

Of course, not all era fiction condones this aggression. Djuna Barnes's *Ryder* (1928) is but one work in which the masculine sex drive is a rapacious force against which women have little legal or even linguistic recourse. In satirizing her polygamist father, Wald Barnes, the author rejected polyamory as a rather transparent excuse for male opportunism and irresponsibility. At the same time, the novel's allusive, parodic style rhetorically redressed whole traditions of fable and folklore for sensationalizing sexual assault as "a woman's quickest way of laying herself open to Legend." But while *Ryder* is thoroughly modernistic in technique, the depiction of men as "Cock[s] o' the Walk" has more in common with the Victorian stock character of the sexual brute rather than the 1920s' lover whose aggression is a natural expression of his sex drive. Indeed, male virility is more often depicted in post-Victorian novels as threatened rather than a threat. As evidence, one might simply point to the long list compiled by Sandra M. Gilbert and Susan Gubar of "maimed, unmanned, victimized" male characters, including "the eunuch Jake Barnes in Hemingway's *The Sun Also Rises*, the paralyzed Clifford Chatterley in *Lady Chatterley's Lover*, the gelded Benjy in Faulkner's *The Sound and the Fury* as well as the castrated Joe Christmas in *Light in August*." One could add the impotent rapist Popeye in Faulkner's *Sanctuary* (1931); the repressed-by-mechanization Hugh McVey in Sherwood Anderson's *Poor White* (1920); and the depleted-by-senescence hero of Maxwell Bodenheim's *Naked on Roller Skates* (1930) who cannot satisfy his wife's masochistic desire to be "punched in the face" by "an A number one, guaranteed bastard" before "creep[ing] in [his] arms." As Gilbert and Gubar note, the "sexual anxieties" of these dysfunctional males imply fear that the "feminine potency" attending sexual liberalism would unleash an "emasculat[ing]" force.[14]

One sees this fear across a striking variety of genres. To cite what may be the oddest example, in the 1920s' pulp realm of science fiction/fantasy, Amazonian myths are frequently reconstituted as battles between the sexes in which a male hero "saves" either an unsexed woman warrior or a subjugated male from a matriarchal culture whose inverted gender hierarchy dooms it to decay. In the sixth installment of Edgar Rice Burroughs's Tarzan series, *Tarzan and the Ant Men* (1924), the Lord of the Jungle inspires fellow males enslaved by the Alalus, a tribe of ape-like women, to rise up and restore the "natural" order of the sexes. Burroughs's expository description of this loveless culture includes lines that, stripped of their fantastic trappings, sound as if they could come straight from Van De Velde or Glyn: "The hideous life of the Alalus was the natural result of the unnatural reversal of sex dominance. It is the province of the male to initiate love and by his masterfulness to inspire first respect, then admiration in the breast of the female he seeks to attract. Love itself developed after these other emotions."

For sheerly illustrative purposes, no genre of 1920s' fiction demonstrates the insistence upon male "masterfulness" better than the so-called "sex novel," a grab-bag classification that included any work, popular or experimental, that veered toward the graphic – including *Ulysses* and *Lady Chatterley's Lover*. Stephen Kern has argued that sexual explicitness enabled Joyce and Lawrence to recontextualize eroticism out of Victorian standards of "normality" and into the discourse of the "real" simply by allowing characters to reflect upon the meaning of sensuous gratification in the privacy of their own uninhibited thoughts.[15] What Kern fails to question, however, is whether sex scenes might uphold gendered power hierarchies rather than transcend them as fictional lovers act out the supposedly innate roles of "taker" and "taken." Consider the infamous passage in which Oliver Mellors sodomizes Lady Connie Chatterley:

> She had to be a passive, consenting thing, like a slave, a physical slave . . . She would have thought a woman would have died of shame. Instead of which, shame died . . . routed by the phallic hunt of the man.

Against this backdrop, *The Great Gatsby* is all the more striking for its seeming aversion to what Van De Velde called the "essential force of *maleness*." For some critics – Leslie Fiedler, most notably – Gatsby is so "unmanned" that his lack of sexual initiative, combined with the absence of any overt "consummated genital love" in the novel, can only suggest Fitzgerald's immaturity: "The adolescent's 'kiss' is the only climax his imagination can really encompass . . . [I]t is the only climax he ever realizes in a scene."[16] But while biographers readily admit that Fitzgerald was personally prudish, *Gatsby* is not a prudish novel – at least, not in the way that Percy Marks's *The Plastic Age* (a bestseller in 1924) can seem nearly ninety years later. In this campus romance inspired by Fitzgerald's own *This Side of Paradise*, Marks's desire to caution against Jazz Age permissiveness results in a veritable shaming of protagonist Hugh Carver's sex drive: "He was lashed by desire; he was burning with curiosity – and yet, and yet something held him back. Something – he hardly knew what it was – made him avoid any woman who had a reputation for moral laxity. He shrank from such a woman – and desired her so intensely that he was ashamed."[17] The "something" that Hugh fears, frankly, is female sexuality, embodied by an undergraduate vixen named Cynthia. Hugh's overwrought efforts to protect himself from seduction have caused subsequent commentators to chide him in terms that perpetuate the equation between masculinity and sexual aggression: R. V. Cassill, for instance, dismisses Hugh as a "ninny."[18]

Gatsby precludes any similar accusation against its hero with a detail introduced late in the narrative that forces a wholesale re-estimation of its hero's aloof asexuality. In chapter 8, after Daisy accidentally mows down Myrtle Wilson in Gatsby's roadster while speeding away from a confrontation between her husband and lover, Nick Carraway flashes back to 1917. Significantly, this is not the same flashback that culminates in the incarnating kiss by which Gatsby idealizes Daisy as the embodiment of his ambition. In this second description of the couple's courtship, Fitzgerald reveals that Daisy is far from Gatsby's first lover. Indeed, we learn that Gatsby once radiated a sex appeal that gave him great mastery over his conquests: "He knew women early. Since they spoiled him he became contemptuous of them." This is language straight out of a 1920s' romance novel, surprisingly reminiscent of the florid descriptions of John Gaunt's sway over women in *It*.[19]

That Gatsby was once sexually assertive is only the preliminary revelation, however. Fitzgerald next reveals that his hero and Daisy were sexually active before the apotheosizing kiss, at a time in their relationship when Gatsby's intent was mastery, not romance: "He *took* what he could get, ravenously and unscrupulously – eventually he *took* Daisy one still October night, *took* her because he had no real right to touch her hand" (emphasis added).

Although the use of two separate flashbacks clouds the precise chronology of Gatsby and Daisy's 1917 romance, the kiss seems to be the mechanism that frees him from the masculine urge to "take," for it marks the moment at which his desire for Daisy transcends the merely physical: "He had intended, probably, to take what he could and go – but now he found that he had committed himself to the following of a grail . . . When they met again, two days later, it was Gatsby who was breathless, who was, somehow betrayed." Such transformations in men are far from unusual in romance novels of the era – indeed, they are mandatory. Both *The Sheik* and *It* conclude with Hassan and Gaunt on their knees, overwhelmed by emotion as they beg their lovers not to leave them. As Patricia Raub has argued, such endings mark a role reversal in gender dynamics through which the heroine "acquires power over the hero" by subordinating male sexuality to feminine love.[20] Far from challenging gender determinism, however, such tableaux merely perpetuate it by insisting that sex is a male prerogative while emotional gratification is a woman's. By contrast, Fitzgerald's inclination in this second flashback is toward a romantic mutuality that eludes these categories.

In Gatsby, then, Fitzgerald created a lover who defied the dominant paradigm of masculine sexuality. For this reason, he deserves to be counted alongside Gertrude Stein and Djuna Barnes, whom Elizabeth Freeman in her chapter in this volume calls the "gender/sexual dissidents" of the 1920s who "interrogated the heterosexist paradigm" of the conventional love story. While *Gatsby* may not have "pushed the genre to its limits" as "Melanctha" or *Nightwood* do, it does rewrite from within the idea of what a heterosexual man's vision of love and romance can be.[b]

While Gatsby's characterization is unusual, however, Daisy's sexuality is disappointingly conventional. If Fitzgerald divested his hero of the romantic role of sexual aggressor, he was apparently incapable of imagining any comparable alternative for her. As a result, his heroine embodies the passivity of the "taken" in a manner that inadvertently illustrates how little self-determination the 1920s' conception of love actually offered women. The

b Elizabeth Freeman, "Reimagining gender and sexualities," chapter 57, 942.

two flashes of initiative Daisy demonstrates toward Gatsby – taking his arm in his garden and later kissing him – are tentative exertions of sexual sovereignty, yet the era's dominant ideology of romance did not extend much agency to women beyond such provisional gestures. Instead, as the examples of Diana Mayo in *The Sheik* and Ava Cleveland in *It* suggest, love happened *to* women, usually in inverse proportion to their resistance to a man's sex appeal.[21]

The theme is hardly limited to romance novels; it constitutes the dilemma of many a 1920s' literary heroine. One of the more surprising manifestations may be found in the femme fatale in the emerging school of hard-boiled detective fiction. The prototypical Brigid O'Shaughnessy in Dashiell Hammett's *The Maltese Falcon* (1930) may seduce men whose criminal assistance she desperately needs, but she does so impulsively rather than willfully – which is why she falls for the coolly unemotional Sam Spade instead of merely using him. While sleeping with Brigid provides Spade a lesson in how to avoid ending up a dangerous woman's "sap," she can only feel betrayed by his unwillingness to help cover up her murder of Spade's own business partner: "You've been playing with me? Only pretending you cared – to trap me like this? You didn't – care at all? You didn't – don't – l-love me?" The novel even ends with a coda reasserting this lack of rationality in female love as Spade's loyal secretary, Effie Perine, questions how the detective could "take" Brigid and then callously turn her over to the police: "You did that, Sam, to her?"[22]

Complementing this inability to muster romantic self-control is a promiscuity coded as irrationality in many female characters, from Brett Ashley in Hemingway's *The Sun Also Rises* to Caddy Compson in Faulkner's *The Sound and the Fury* (1929). Women's chaotic sexual energy is present in comedy as well as tragedy: the humor in Anita Loos's *Gentlemen Prefer Blondes* (1925) arises from the fact that Lorelei Lee moves from affair to affair through serendipity and happenstance, not by intention. In the end, for many of these characters, the only way to control unruly yearnings is by abnegating desire. Frances Newman's *The Hard-Boiled Virgin* thus ends with Katharine Faraday eschewing sex for writing; while her choice is often read as a triumphant assertion of female autonomy, it also demonstrates the difficulty for heroines of satisfactorily integrating sexuality within their personality.

Daisy Buchanan's passivity must be read as indicative of this insistence upon female "prostration." Her acquiescence is evident in Fitzgerald's explanation for her marriage to Tom Buchanan: "All the time [that Gatsby was abroad in the war] something within her was crying for a decision. She wanted her life shaped now, immediately." That same desire to be "shaped" explains why, during the climactic confrontation between Gatsby and Tom, Daisy cannot act: she expects the decision to be made for her. Pressured by Gatsby to tell her husband that she never loved him, the best she can offer is that she "did love him once – but I loved you too." Fitzgerald goes so far as to hint that Daisy realizes she lacks the agency to decide which man is her "true" love. Whereas Gatsby needs Daisy to take the initiative to choose him to validate his sense of self, Tom decides the issue simply by asserting his mastery and informing his wife that her lover's "presumptuous little flirtation is over," effectively snuffing any will on her part: "Her frightened eyes told that whatever intentions, whatever courage she had, were definitely gone." Daisy thus represents a conundrum too few authors interrogated: if a woman is taught to be "taken" by love, how can one expect her to exert initiative and define her own romantic agency?

Fitzgerald believed that by making Daisy so passive he failed to grant her sympathy. Upon *The Great Gatsby*'s publication, he feared – as it turns out, correctly – that the novel would prove a commercial disappointment because it "contains no important woman character and women controll [*sic*] the fiction market at present."[23] He likewise fretted that *Gatsby* lacked the appeal of a passionate love story: "The worst fault in it, I think is a BIG FAULT: I gave no account (and had no feeling about or knowledge of) the emotional relations between Gatsby and Daisy from the time of their reunion to the catastrophe."[24] Fitzgerald's anxiety suggests doubts about whether he could render their intimacy more explicitly without perpetuating instead of questioning the gendered "taker" and "taken" roles. The 1920s' notion of romance simply did not offer many alternatives.

Over the next decade, as Fitzgerald labored through divergent drafts of his fourth novel, his view of the relationship between love, sexuality, and gender grew darker.[25] *Tender Is the Night* finds its main characters, Dick and Nicole Diver, hopelessly locked in sex roles whose inequalities are dramatized through inappropriate dependencies that doom mutuality from the start. Dick is Nicole's doctor; she was her own father's lover; he suffers from a need for young women to admire him as a parental figure. Such emotional complications inspire a will to power among partners that turns romance violent. Accordingly, love is no longer a pursuit – it is war. This is one way in which late Fitzgerald differs from Hemingway, whose *A Farewell to Arms* (1929) and *For Whom the Bell Tolls* (1940) both posit love as a respite from the naturalistic battles of existence – a tragically short-lived respite, but a respite nonetheless. For Fitzgerald, by contrast, romance can only recapitulate power struggles. Thus, Dick's adulterous attraction to Hollywood ingénue

Rosemary Hoyt is dramatized through a military motif: "Though he thought [Nicole] was the most attractive creature he had ever seen, though he got from her everything he needed, he scented battle from afar, and subconsciously he had been hardening himself and arming himself [to pursue Rosemary], hour by hour." Frequently, the equation between romance and violence is literal. A flashback to the Divers' courtship finds their first kiss interrupted by cannon fire, while in another episode, they witness a woman with "helmet-like hair" shoot a former lover dead. Fitzgerald's decayed hero is left struggling to emulate that blunt force in a fruitless effort to recoup masculine power. Dick's farewell to Nicole as she leaves him for another man are the most vicious words Fitzgerald ever wrote: "I never did go in for making love to dry loins," he tells her.

Such a line is inconceivable in Gatsby's world. That it is not only spoken so bluntly but put in the mouth of a man with whom readers are intended to sympathize reveals how, despite *Gatsby*'s best efforts, Fitzgerald could find nothing tender in the art of love.

Notes

1. Alexander Boyd, "Mostly Flappers," *St. Paul Daily News* (December 26, 1920): 4:6; rpt. in Jackson R. Bryer, ed., *F. Scott Fitzgerald: The Critical Reception* (New York: Burt Franklin, 1978), 48.
2. For representative examples, see the essays collected in Arthur Mizener, ed., *F. Scott Fitzgerald: A Collection of Critical Essays* (Englewood Cliffs, NJ: Prentice-Hall, 1963).
3. John D'Emilio and Estelle B. Freedman, *Intimate Matters: A History of Sexuality in America* (New York: Harper and Row, 1988), 241. See also Paula S. Fass, *The Damned and the Beautiful: American Youth in the 1920s* (New York: Oxford University Press, 1977), 260–290; Steven Seidman, *Romantic Longings: Love in America, 1830–1980* (New York: Routledge, 1991), 65–91.
4. See Laura Frost, "The Romance of Cliché: E. M. Hull, D. H. Lawrence, and Interwar Erotic Fiction," in *Bad Modernisms*, ed. Douglas Mao and Rebecca L. Walkowitz (Durham, NC: Duke University Press, 2006), 94–118.
5. For example, *The Sheik of Harlem* was a popular 1923–1924 musical comedy.
6. *The Young Rajah* was the name of Valentino's follow-up to *The Sheik*, based upon the 1895 novel *Amos Judd* by John Ames Mitchell (1844–1918).
7. "The Sheik of Araby" was written by Harry B. Smith, Francis Wheeler, and Ted Snyder. Fitzgerald quotes the chorus, which alludes to Hull's rape scene: "I'm the Sheik of Araby. / Your love belongs to me. / At night when you're asleep / Into your tent I'll creep."

8. Dorothy Parker, "Madame Glyn Lectures on 'It,' with Illustrations," in *The Portable Dorothy Parker*, ed. Brendan Gill (New York: Penguin, 1973), 467.
9. Elinor Glyn, *The Philosophy of Love* (Auburn, NY: Authors Press, 1923), 225. See also 78 and 107 respectively on gender determinism: "Woman is as willing to be ruled as she ever was – she always adores a master"; "Man was meant to be strong . . . and women have remained such primitive, unspoilt darlings, that they can still be dominated by these qualities when they have a chance to see them!"
10. Theodoor H. Van De Velde, *Ideal Marriage: Its Physiology and Technique* (New York: Random House, 1930), 7, emphasis added. For a fuller discussion, see Michael Melody and Linda Peterson, *Teaching America about Sex: Marriage Guides and Sex Manuals from Late Victorians to Dr. Ruth* (New York: New York University Press, 1999), 72–114.
11. Margaret Sanger, *Happiness in Marriage* (New York: Brentano's, 1926), 6.
12. Pamela S. Haag, "In Search of 'The Real Thing': Ideologies of Love, Modern Romance, and Women's Sexual Subjectivity in the United States, 1920–1940," *Journal of the History of Sexuality* 2.4 (April 1992): 556.
13. Karen Chow, "Popular Sexual Knowledges and Women's Agency in 1920s England: Marie Stopes's *Married Love* and E. M. Hull's *The Sheik*," *Feminist Review* 63 (Autumn 1999): 71–72.
14. Sandra M. Gilbert and Susan Gubar, *The War of the Words*, vol. 1 of *No Man's Land: The Place of the Woman Writer in the Twentieth Century* (New Haven: Yale University Press, 1988), 36.
15. Stephen Kern, *The Culture of Love: Victorians to Moderns* (Cambridge, MA: Harvard University Press, 1998), 5.
16. Van De Velde, *Ideal Marriage*, 158–159; Leslie Fiedler, *Love and Death in the American Novel* (New York: Criterion Books, 1960; rev. edn., Stein and Day, 1966), 314.
17. Percy Marks, *The Plastic Age* (New York: Century, 1924), 165.
18. R. V. Cassill, Afterword to *ibid.*, 337.
19. See Glyn, *It*:

> Early in his career [Gaunt] had grown to know women – and what they meant to men . . . From his fifteenth year, when the saloonkeeper's wife at the corner of his street grovelled before his six feet of magnificent stripling strength, to his fortieth birthday, females of all types and classes had manifested ardent passion for him.
>
> "Must be his smell," one refined lady of the gutter said to another, once, – "'cause darn me if I can see any beauty in him!"
>
> There was not any beauty in him, she was right, but there was some strange magnetism, and perhaps it was augmented by his absolute indifference.

20. Patricia Raub, "Issues of Passion and Power in E. M. Hull's *The Sheik*," *Women's Studies* 21.1 (1992): 126.
21. Daisy's passivity is in marked contrasted to later heroines of novels such as Joan Didion's *Play It as It Lays* (1967), Marge Piercy's *Woman on the Edge of Time* (1976),

and many other explicitly feminist fictions that appropriate, as Maria Farland says in her essay in this volume, "traditionally male patterns of exploration and self-assertion to create stories of women's liberation from the spatial confines of home and marriage" ("Literary feminisms," chapter 56, 931).

22. Apropos of Sean McCann's essay in this volume ("The novel of crime, mystery, and suspense," chapter 48), this callousness can be interpreted as a class-based response to the efforts of clients to civilize and therefore domesticate hard-boiled men such as Spade: "Like their dime novel predecessors, the *Black Mask* writers [the school to which Hammett belonged] eschewed the intellectual pretensions of the classic detective story and instead made their heroes shrewd craftsmen, skilled above all as hunters and combatants. Indeed, they intensified the populist intimations of the dime-novel detective, making their protagonists impudent tough guys who often speak the vernacular of the working-class city while repeatedly baffling the impositions of their wealthy clients and the bureaucratic demands of the police" (807–808).
23. *Dear Scott/Dear Max: The Fitzgerald–Perkins Correspondence*, ed. John Kuehl and Jackson R. Bryer (London: Cassell, 1971), 101.
24. *The Letters of F. Scott Fitzgerald*, ed. Andrew Turnbull (New York: Scribner's, 1963), 341–342.
25. The biographical reasons for Fitzgerald's bitterness are well known. By 1926, his alcoholism was severely affecting his marriage. Strained relations between the couple were compounded further in 1930 with the onset of Zelda's mental illness, which required long stays in sanitariums in Europe and America. As the possibility of romantic mutuality grew increasingly remote in his eyes, the dynamics of power imbalances between lovers in his fiction overwhelmed the chivalric idealism of *Gatsby*.

39

Philosophy and the American novel

ROBERT CHODAT

Plato's banishment of the poets didn't prevent a number of subsequent thinkers, over an enormous period of time, from drawing intimate connections between literature and philosophy. "Poetry," said Aristotle – by "poetry" he meant "the making of plot-structures" – "is both more philosophical and more serious than history, since poetry speaks more of universals, history of particulars."[1] Philosophy and poetry involve comparable sorts of knowledge: they investigate kinds or types of characters and actions, and thus provide, for Aristotle, a key to the world's purposeful order. For the romantics and idealists at the end of the eighteenth century, purposeful orders belonged less to the world than to the generative human mind. But while this shift in emphasis represented a critical moment in the history of Western thought, it led them nevertheless to suggest, like Aristotle, that literature plays a central role in human understanding. "Only poetry," said Friedrich Schlegel, approaches "the sublime urbanity of the Socratic muse," and in the "The Oldest System-Program of German Idealism" (1796) we find the claim – attributed variously to Hölderlin, Hegel, Schelling, or all three of them – that "the supreme act of reason" is an "aesthetic act." Via Coleridge, Carlyle, and others, such ideas receive their American expression in Emerson, for whom "the true philosopher and the true poet are one," each assigning "the apparent order and relations of things to the empire of thought."[2]

On the face of it, no new Athens or Jena or Concord arose in American culture in the half-century after World War I, and the ancient quarrel between literature and philosophy seems to have grown as heated as Plato wished. A number of historical factors contributed to this situation. One is the long-standing American distrust of philosophical speculation. Writing in 1940, and extending the by-then common debates about the distinctive character of the

American novel,[a] Philip Rahv argued that the "morality of abstention" descending from Puritanism and frontier culture had engendered a "cult of experience" among American novelists, a "vast phenomenology swept by waves of sensation and feeling." For Rahv, this left them unequipped to handle the range or depth of themes that European authors addressed instinctively: "Everything is contained in the American novel except ideas."[3]

A second contributing factor was literary modernism. Modernists were certainly motivated by deeply philosophical questions about meaning and selfhood, and some of them, such as T. S. Eliot and Gertrude Stein, even studied under philosophers. And it isn't hard to name theoretical figures who permanently shaped the modernist sensibility: Nietzsche, Bergson, Freud, William James, Spengler. Yet some of modernism's best-known pronouncements discourage the idea that discursive and literary texts should be understood side by side. If the great failure of Victorian writing was its baggy generalizations and didacticism, then a truly "modern" art required a more austere, less edifyingly abstract mode. Hence, for example, Eliot's famous praise of Henry James's "escape" from "Ideas": "He had a mind so fine that no idea could violate it." Hence, too, the equally famous dictum of William Carlos Williams, who disagreed with Eliot about so much else: "No ideas / but in things."[4]

A third factor contributing to the renewed tensions between philosophy and literature came from within philosophy. An American college student after the Civil War would everywhere have encountered Scottish Common Sense philosophy, which dominated American educational institutions for much of the nineteenth century, and if adventurous enough, he may have confronted the American Hegelians, who in 1867 started *The Journal of Speculative Philosophy*, the first English-language philosophical journal. By the end of the century, this same student would have been reading American pragmatism.[5] The differences between these various schools shouldn't be underestimated, but they all shared the traditional ideal of philosophy as an investigation of both theoretical reason (metaphysics, logic, science) and practical reason (ethics, politics). By the mid-1930s, however, many Vienna School positivists had fled Hitler into American exile and the divide between "analytic" and "continental" philosophy, which had opened at the start of the century, began to harden institutionally. In the

a For a sense of the major themes of these debates in the years before Rahv's remarks, see Lawrence Buell's essay in this volume, "Theories of the American novel in the age of realism," chapter 19.

words of W. V. O. Quine, the American most responsible for importing the new thinking, philosophy of science was increasingly regarded as "philosophy enough." From this perspective, questions about beauty, divinity, or moral evaluation – concerns that literature and philosophy had traditionally shared – could be dismissed as non-factual matters of "value"; judgments like "good" or "beautiful," as A. J. Ayer said, simply "express certain feelings and evoke a certain response."[6] Broadly speaking, most American philosophers in the next several decades affirmed this ideal and, as part of a rapidly professionalizing discipline, ignored the messy domains of history, art, and politics. Young American writers with a speculative turn of mind would find little sustenance in Quine, Ayer, or their colleagues, and would have to look elsewhere for inspiration.

The fifty years after World War I, then, seem a particularly tense moment in the ancient quarrel, and an unlikely period for any productive relationship between philosophy and the novel. Yet the divisions I've just sketched are too simple, for a couple of reasons. One is that Aristotle and the romantics were right: *any* literary text can be understood as having a philosophical dimension. This basic intuition informed New Critics such as I. A. Richards and John Crowe Ransom, who had extensive backgrounds in philosophy, and has been even more vigorously reinforced in the literary theory of the last forty years. Literary theory is, after all, largely an outgrowth of post-Hegelian philosophy, and most of its major figures, from Bakhtin and Lukács to Butler and Žižek, trained primarily as philosophers. Deconstruction in particular emphasized the fluidity between literature and philosophy, but even since the death of Paul de Man, critics have regularly made implicit or explicit claims about language, meaning, moral identity, justice, and other broad concepts traditionally associated with philosophy. Indeed, this receptiveness to philosophical themes has arguably made contemporary literary studies, more than philosophy itself, one of the most fertile places for the reintegration of analytic and continental traditions.

Emphasizing the gulfs between philosophy and fiction is misleading, moreover, because, despite the cultural and institutional obstacles I've described, a number of American novels were quite directly engaged with philosophical questions from the 1920s onwards. Some, in fact, are among the bestselling novels of the century: Ayn Rand's *The Fountainhead* (1943), for example, or Robert Heinlein's *Stranger in a Strange Land* (1961). But it wasn't only relatively marginal philosophical ideas like Objectivism and neo-hedonism that captured the novelistic imagination in this period, and in the best cases, an engagement with philosophy didn't entail – as it generally did with Rand and Heinlein – sacrificing the heteroglossia and irony that have long been associated with the novel as a genre. To be sure, such aspirations occasionally put American authors at odds with the cultural traditions that Rahv identified. Saul Bellow once remarked that his own fiction was criticized for being "a hybrid curiosity, neither fully American nor satisfactorily European."[7] Such criticism would probably be less frequently heard, and would certainly have less intellectual credibility, in countries where literature and philosophy are taught together in schools and where writers and philosophers regularly publish in the same periodicals. Yet some American novelists, Bellow included, risked hearing such criticism, and we can identify a few different philosophical traditions that provoked and animated American novelists in significant ways.

One is American pragmatism, which by the early twentieth century was recognized as *the* distinctly American contribution to Western philosophy. Pragmatism's roots are twofold. From Darwin it inherited a view of human beings as creatures actively coping with their environments through probabilistic and eminently human reasoning. From Emerson it inherited a moral commitment: a belief that, as John Dewey said in his 1903 essay on Emerson, knowledge is gained not in palaces and schoolrooms, but "in the highway, in the untaught endeavor," and that democracy need not entail a gray, leveling conformity.[8] Building on these dual sources, pragmatists acknowledged that modernity's scientific revolutions had shaken the moral and cognitive certainties of the past. But they insisted, too, that modernity's experimental spirit be extended to selves and society, that we were not contemplative observers beholden to some greater Being. In recent decades, the influence of these pragmatist ideas on modern American poetry has received considerable attention.[9] But its influence can be felt on at least some prose writers as well, and recent critics have persuasively identified its impact not only on William James's brother Henry,[b] but also on Gertrude Stein, W. E. B. Du Bois, and Zora Neale Hurston.[10]

One useful way to understand the full range of pragmatism's relation to twentieth-century fiction is to consider two novels by authors explicitly indebted to it: Kenneth Burke's *Towards a Better Life* (1932) and Ralph Ellison's *Invisible Man* (1952). Burke's novel is noteworthy because he is one of the major figures of twentieth-century criticism, an Emersonian autodidact occasionally credited with anticipating most developments in later literary

b On the relation between William and Henry James, see also Carrie Bramen's essay in this volume, "James, pragmatism, and the realist ideal" (chapter 18); and Amy Hungerford's essay in this volume, "Religion and the twentieth-century American novel," chapter 44, 734–735.

theory. But *Towards a Better Life* is largely forgotten. Burke was an editor for *The Dial* in the 1920s, and his novel's plot turns on a tension familiar from the European modernists he was publishing: namely, the conflict between the morally and financially precarious world of the bohemian and the comfortable, complacent world of the bourgeois. John Neal is an outcast who writes a series of baroque, bitter letters to his more charming, untroubled friend Anthony, a man who, John says, "drew forth the good things in life like a magician pulling rabbits out of a hat." In his own self-commentaries, however, Burke repeatedly claimed that his novel was something other than a modernist dirge. He had, he said, a fondness for the *Erziehungsroman*, the Goethian novel of education, and to this end his text is built not on plot and character, but a web of philosophical maxims, a form that sometimes recalls Nietzsche's *Thus Spoke Zarathustra* (1883–1885), to which Burke also compared his novel.[11] Most of the speech acts Burke identified in his novel are ripe for modernist expressions of loss: "lamentation, rejoicing, beseechment, admonition, sayings, and invective." But he insisted that the discordant elements of the work "fall together clearly enough if we see in the *book a ritual of rebirth* (the paradoxical use of *grotesquely tragic* devices to solemnize the emergence of *comedy* as a 'doctrine')," [12] and as evidence he cited an aphorism near the novel's end: "One sneers by the modifying of a snarl; one smiles by the modifying of a sneer. You should have lived twice, and smiled the second time." What Burke says about his book *Attitudes Toward History* (1937) is thus meant to be applicable to his novel as well: "It operates on the miso-philanthropic assumption that getting along with people is one devil of a difficult task, but that, in the last analysis, we should all want to get along with people (and do want to)."[13]

But it's not clear that Burke's after-the-fact interpretations fully capture the novel itself. Burke claimed to have written a piece of rhetoric that will purge the reader of John Neal's poisonous attitudes, yet the novel gives few signs of what purgation actually entails. John Neal begins and ends a spiteful man, and his first-person narration grows alarmingly unstable and unreliable as the text progresses. What starts as a series of meditative letters ends with a final chapter of "jottings," half-intelligible fragments about spiritual exile and the limits of language. "Henceforth silence," reads the final Eliotic sentence, "that the torrent may be heard descending in all its fullness."

Invisible Man arguably expresses a more consistently Burkean-pragmatist attitude than Burke's own novel. Like many writers who came of age in the 1930s, Ellison's earliest philosophical inclinations were toward Marxism, which he encountered at Tuskegee and more fully in New York in the mid-1930s.[c] In the mid-1940s, however, Ellison grew dissatisfied with Marxism's scientific aspirations, and came to regard Burke as "the liberator!" – to the point even of writing Burkean slogans in the margins of his work-in-progress.[14] Ellison, who had trained as a musician, associated Burke's ideals with the African American tradition of the blues, which expresses the hope, he said, to keep comedy and tragedy in dual suspension: to retain "brutal experiences," and also to "transcend" them, "squeezing" from them "a near-tragic, near-comic lyricism."[15] To be sure, Ellison's recourse to the blues indicates the extent to which he never responded to Burke uncritically.[16] But it was through Burke's theorizing that Ellison came to see how he could reject his early mentor Richard Wright's claims about "the cultural barrenness of black life" without in turn falling into mere aestheticism.[d] It allowed him to create a narrator who is "a blues-toned laugher-at-wounds,"[17] a character who extends the black tradition – embodied in the novel by Louis Armstrong – of making "poetry out of being invisible." As in Burke's novel, Ellison's text is rife with aphorism, but nowhere does it evoke the same overriding sense of paralysis. Moral and linguistic ties collapse at the end of *Towards a Better Life*, but Ellison's narrator concludes by asking if, despite the humiliations that have driven him underground, he might still have "a socially responsible role to play." In this capacity to "emerge less angry than ironic," in this effort to construct what Ellison called a "raft of hope" moving us toward "the democratic ideal,"[18] *Invisible Man* enacts a Burkean "ritual of rebirth," and in doing so anticipates the complex patriotism of later philosophical pragmatists like Richard Rorty and Hilary Putnam.[e]

Pragmatism's reach didn't end with Burke and Ellison. As Ellison was collecting honors for *Invisible Man*, pragmatist philosophers also captivated his Southern contemporary, Walker Percy. Percy had studied medicine, but in the early 1940s read extensively in modern fiction and philosophy. And among the theorists he came most to admire was C. S. Peirce, the figure widely credited with having founded pragmatism as a school of thought. What captivated Percy was Peirce's capacity to appreciate modern science while also resisting its reductivist impulses. In the mid twentieth century, reductivism was most famously pursued – as Thomas Pynchon was later to exploit in

c For a sense of this philosophical, literary, and cultural background, see Alan Wald's essay in this volume, "Steinbeck and the proletarian novel" (chapter 40).

d See Lovalerie King's essay in this volume, "Ellison and Baldwin: aesthetics, activism, and the social order" (chapter 43).

e For more on the relation between Burke and Ellison, see Gregg Crane's essay in this volume, "Law and the American novel," chapter 46, 768.

Gravity's Rainbow (1973) – by behaviorists, for whom, as Percy says, words are simply stimuli that "call forth responses."[19] Peirce's theories offered a philosophical justification for a distinction between physical and intentional descriptions. A sound is a "wave disturbance in the air" and travels "through the solids of the middle ear, as afferent nerve impulse, as an electrocolloidal change in the central nervous system." But it becomes a *word* only when it is, as Peirce says, "connected with its object by virtue of the idea of the symbol-using mind, without which no such connection would exist." Communication, that is, consists not merely of causal motions, but of purposeful actions and social practices, practices that Percy and Peirce both associate with religious communion.[20]

Percy's early novels evoke these visions of communication and communion, dramatizing, like *Invisible Man*, a movement toward comic reconciliation. The epilogue of *The Moviegoer* (1961) shows the narrator, Binx Bolling, marrying his cousin Kate and agreeing to enroll in medical school. And toward the end of *The Last Gentleman* (1966), the nihilistic and alcoholic Sutter Vaught, having isolated himself in New Mexico, considers returning home to the South, reconciling himself with his family, and renewing his medical practice. In each case, much as the narrator of *Invisible Man* asks whether he still has "a socially responsible role to play," these protagonists pursue the "misophilanthropic assumption" underlying Burkean Pragmatism, asking how they can "make a contribution," end their isolation, and reintegrate themselves into a wider community.

Unlike in *Invisible Man*, however, Percy's comic rebirths appear abruptly, and the optimism of his novels remains muted. The tentativeness of these conclusions reflects not only the sense of mourning characteristic of much twentieth-century white Southern writing,[21] but also a second, more obvious philosophical influence on Percy's work – namely the Christian existentialism of Kierkegaard and Gabriel Marcel. As in Kierkegaard and Marcel, communication remains only an ideal in Percy's novels, and amelioration is available only through divine grace.[22] Whatever its ending implies, *The Moviegoer* is dominated by Binx's affectless speculations on "the malaise" and his entrapment in what Kierkegaard's *Either/Or* (1843) called the "aesthetic stage," where his surroundings – his job, his girlfriends – are treated as crops to be rotated whenever boredom hits. Most memorable in *The Last Gentleman* are, similarly, the picaresque crises of young Will Barrett and the remarkable passages he reads from Vaught's diary, which recall the most illusion-stripping moments of Dostoevsky. Percy himself converted to Catholicism in the 1940s, and it's telling that, in both novels, regeneration is available only after the death of a long-suffering youth: Binx's half-brother Lonny, Vaught's brother Jaimie. Isolation is, for Percy, "a falling-away from an earlier communion," but this communion cannot be restored in this life, and as John F. Desmond has said, "catastrophe" in his novels seems "preferable to spiritual dry rot."[23] Thus whereas Ellison's novel ends with the secular Deweyan hope to "affirm the principle on which the country was built," the persistent mood of Percy's work is encapsulated in the deeply un-Deweyan question that opens his essay "The Delta Factor" (1975): "Why does man feel so sad in the twentieth century?"[24]

As Amy Hungerford demonstrates in this volume, Percy was hardly the only novelist to engage religious themes and languages in the postwar decades,[f] and he was hardly alone in turning to Christian Existentialism specifically. The young John Updike, for instance, sometimes regarded his own early novels like *Rabbit, Run* (1960) as "illustrations of Kierkegaard." Others, however, were attracted to the more humanistic Existentialism of Jean-Paul Sartre, Simone de Beauvoir, and Albert Camus, who also emphasized unbridgeable human alienation, but in a decidedly more worldly – even Promethean – idiom. While Updike was discovering Kierkegaard and Karl Barth, Norman Mailer's *Advertisements for Myself* (1959) rowdily celebrated the "American existentialist" known as the "hipster" – the man (and for Mailer it was usually a man) who "knows that if our collective condition is to live with instant death by atomic war," then the only "life-giving answer" is to "divorce oneself from society," "to set out on that uncharted journey into the rebellious imperatives of the self."[25] Such panegyrics to existentialism struck some commentators as being preposterously at odds with the naïve idealism of American culture.[26] But if, as Dewey's student Sidney Hook complained, existentialism's origins in war-torn Europe made it universalize the logic of extreme situations at the expense of ordinary practical intelligence, Mailer's remarks indicate how in fact much of existentialism converges closely with American antinomianism.[g] A "touch of Emersonianism" runs through Sartre's early work, said the philosopher Roy Wood Sellars in 1947, and it is perhaps unsurprising that postwar commentators were quick to compare Hemingway and Camus and to recognize the influence of Faulkner on twentieth-century French fiction.[27]

f Hungerford, chapter 44, esp. 737–747.

g Andrew Hoberek captures these connections in slightly different terms in his description of Mailer's relation to Hemingway; see his essay in this volume, "The Jewish great American novel," chapter 54, 896–897.

Among Americans, the most sustained novelistic treatment of this humanistic existentialism was Richard Wright's *The Outsider* (1953). Wright's *Native Son* (1940) and *Black Boy* (1945) had presented powerfully naturalistic depictions of African American life, and extended the tradition of radical reformism evident among many earlier literary naturalists.[h] In the mid-1940s, however, Wright grew disillusioned with Marxism and expatriated to Paris, befriending Sartre and de Beauvoir, and *The Outsider* exemplifies this intellectual evolution.[28] The novel portrays an intellectually ambitious but troubled black postal worker in Chicago, Cross Damon, who is presumed to have died in a horrible subway accident, and who seizes the opportunity to cast aside the burdens of his life and create himself anew. Within days he has turned to gruesome violence, murdering first a postal colleague and later, after escaping to New York City, killing both a communist leader and his fascist neighbor. At the end of the novel, the hunchbacked district attorney Ely Houston accuses Damon of the crime, but refuses to prosecute, preferring instead for Damon to suffer in his own self-created existence. "You are going to punish yourself, see?" says Houston. "You are your own law, so you'll be your own judge . . . I wouldn't *help* you by taking you to jail."

What's notable in *The Outsider* is how, with the murders of Gil and the communist and fascist, the novel allegorizes existentialism's deep ambivalence about politics – an ambivalence that, for many postwar American intellectuals, seemed to offer an alternative to the Cold War's nuclear-armed monoliths.[29] What's also notable is just how far the text stands from, say, Sartre's *Nausea* (1938), often considered the paradigm of the secular existential novel. Sartre's text consists entirely of diary entries, meandering speculations on the falsity of concepts and bourgeois existence, whereas Wright's third-person narration has the air of a potboiler, crowded with fast-paced action, improbable coincidences, and terrible violence. This isn't to deny that the novel is soaked in Sartrean terminology. Most of its five parts are given suitably existentialist titles ("Dread," "Despair," "Decision") and Damon is as preoccupied as Sartre himself about bad faith and self-consciousness. Houston solves the murder only when he learns that Damon has read Jaspers and Heidegger, and in a remarkable scene, Damon delivers a twenty-page Sartrean lecture on the "power-hungry heart" underlying all political systems. It was these existentialist elements that drew fire among Wright's critics, both political and

h On the naturalist tradition, see Donna Campbell's essay in this volume, "The rise of naturalism," chapter 30, 506–508. On Wright's early work, see also Wald, chapter 40, 680.

aesthetic.[30] But to single out these features is to consider what the text says at the expense of what it does, and to miss how, despite Damon's protracted monologues, the style and form of the text depart very little from Wright's earlier naturalistic work. As much as in *Native Son*, the tightly wound plot of *The Outsider* implies a world in which characters' lives are overwhelmingly shaped by circumstances beyond their control. Damon doesn't create his own narrative, and whatever Wright's own stated beliefs, the limitations of existentialism grow increasingly evident in the text itself. When in the final pages Damon, gunned down by an unknown assailant, mutters to Houston, "The search can't be done alone," we glimpse, as in Burke's novel, a moment where philosophical idea and literary vision generate productive tension rather than provide mutual reinforcement.[31]

A sign that existentialism had lost its early oppositional edge came when, in the mid-1960s, advertisers began using Mailer's hipster to sell soda and cigarettes.[32] But among writers, cracks began showing a decade earlier, even beyond Wright's ambiguous novel. Halfway through Flannery O'Connor's "Good Country People" (1955), the platitudinous Mrs. Hopewell peeks into one of the intimidating tomes owned by her daughter, who holds a PhD in philosophy but is consigned to living at home due to physical ailments. "Science, on the other hand," the mother perplexedly reads, "has to assert its soberness and seriousness afresh and declare that it is solely concerned with what-is . . . If science is right, then one thing stands firm: science wishes to know nothing of nothing." The passage is culled directly from Heidegger's 1929 lecture "What is Metaphysics?", and the fact that the bitter, pretentious daughter eventually loses her artificial leg to a con man posing as a traveling Bible salesman suggests how, for the Catholic O'Connor, secular existentialism represented merely a fashionable version of humanist hubris. A decade later, Donald Barthelme – who had studied with Maurice Natanson, a key figure in the American reception of continental philosophy – offered more radically comic deflations in "A Shower of Gold" (1964), a story featuring an existentialist game show called "Who Am I?", and *Snow White* (1967), where existentialism is just one of the dozens of discourses offered up for delicious parody. As a literary and philosophical vision, existentialism had become, as the historian Tony Judt puts it, merely "a general-purpose catchword," one more stylish commodity, and had started giving way to something else.[33]

One term for this "something else" is, of course, postmodernism. Commentators have debated the meaning of "postmodernism" in a variety of domains,[i] but given the context sketched here – and bearing in mind that I'm simplifying an immensely complex history – the term can be said to mark, in both fiction and philosophy, a growing resistance to postwar existentialism and especially to its father figure, Sartre. Sartre's name is seldom mentioned in what is today called "French theory," but we shouldn't forget that figures such as Foucault and Derrida were originally inspired to write, as the latter put it, "thanks to him but especially against him."[34] For all their important differences, the starting point for these and other French thinkers of the 1960s was a belief that the "free and lonely self" that Iris Murdoch identified in Sartre is a misleading fiction, and that selves are constructed by the linguistic and cultural forces governing a particular time and place.[35]

The cultural traditions and institutional arrangements marking French intellectual life meant that novelists and philosophers there played roughly equivalent roles in developing such anti-humanistic claims. The death of the author, the constructedness of narrative forms, the perspectival nature of knowledge: these themes pervaded French fiction and philosophy alike in the 1960s – so much so that these generic distinctions yielded for a time to blurrier terms like "text" and "writing." In the USA, by contrast, the lingering gulf between literature and philosophy made for some lag-time between early postmodern fiction in the 1960s and its theoretical justification (and institutionalization) in the 1970s. Pynchon and William Gaddis were notoriously silent about the experimental novels they were publishing, and even John Barth's "The Literature of Exhaustion" (1967), often cited as a manifesto of postmodern fiction, contains little of the extended philosophical reflection one finds everywhere in his French contemporaries.

Two exceptions to this generalization are William Gass and Susan Sontag. Gass is one of the few American novelists to have actually worked professionally as a philosopher, and the essays in *Fiction and the Figures of Life* (1970) not only anticipate the preoccupation with language that dominated critical discussions of the 1970s, but also thematize the aesthetics pursued in his own early novels *Omensetter's Luck* (1966) and *Willie Master's Lonesome Wife* (1968). Sontag was a far more public figure than Gass, and her work more deliberately sounded the *Zeitgeist*. As a student at the University of Chicago and Harvard in the 1950s, Sontag studied not only under Kenneth Burke, but also with the political philosopher Leo Strauss and the theologian Paul Tillich, and under the latter began a doctoral dissertation on "the metaphysical presuppositions

i For an overview of these interdisciplinary debates, see Urusula Heise's essay in this volume, "Postmodern novels," chapter 58, 964–966.

of ethics."[36] Her mature work, however, is defined far less by these teachers than by the avant-garde movements she discovered in Paris in the late 1950s. Throughout the 1960s, Sontag was not only a tireless commentator on the rapidly changing New York art scene, but also an early conduit for French *écriture*, most visibly in her admiring preface to the English translation of Roland Barthes's *Writing Degree Zero* (1968). Like Barthes and many of his contemporaries, Sontag was primarily a theorist of anti-theories, and her work was treated with suspicion by the older generation of New York intellectuals, who regarded her celebration of the erotic surfaces of art as self-indulgent, even reactionary.[37] Sontag's doubts about Marxist and Freudian literary interpretation anticipate Lyotard's criticism of *grands récits*, and she chastises novelists especially for retaining a commitment to discursive rationality. Literature, she claims, was traditionally valued for its "reportage and moral judgment," but the "model arts of our time are actually those with much less content, and a much cooler mode of moral judgment": music, film, dance, architecture, painting. "The basic unit for contemporary art," she writes, "is not the idea," but "the analysis and extension of sensations," "the representation of (new) modes of vivacity."[38]

Such polemics didn't prevent Sontag from writing novels herself. But it is telling that the protagonists of her two novels from the 1960s show less of an explicit interest in ideas and theories than most of the other characters I've described here. Hippolyte of *The Benefactor* (1963) wrote a philosophical article as a young man but later in life loses whatever conventional intellectual ambitions he had, and Diddy of *Death Kit* (1967) designs brochures for microscopes. Indeed, the modification of Descartes in the epigraph to *The Benefactor* – *"Je rêve donc je suis"* ("I dream therefore I am") – establishes the theme of each novel. Both dramatize a Cartesian withdrawal from the sociocultural world, but instead of moving toward clear and certain knowledge, these withdrawals move the characters, as *Death Kit* says, "away from all coherent rational spaces." Hippolyte identifies his entire life with his dreams, with all their capacity for surprise and sensual fullness, and *Death Kit* records Diddy's final extended hallucinations after he has committed suicide. Both of these novels received mixed praise and abuse when they appeared, and for some readers it was precisely Sontag's talent for assertion that caused friction. Benjamin DeMott, for instance, lauded the "impulse to rage" in Sontag's essays, but also claimed that such impulses are "thwarted by fictional form," which requires a "forgiving fullness of view, obligations of understanding and compassion."[39] Yet it is Sontag's drive both to create art and to reflect upon it, and her wish to bring these new arts and theories to a broad audience, that gives her an important if underappreciated role in what Ursula Heise, in her chapter in this volume, identifies as the first, metafictional wave of postmodern fiction.[j] With Sontag, the philosophical novel moves away from the realist modes dominant in postwar existentialist fiction and toward the self-reflexive forms more fully explored in the 1970s and 1980s by Pynchon, Don DeLillo, and Paul Auster – novels in which, as Brian McHale has argued, the dominant philosophical question is less about epistemology, what characters or readers know, than about ontology, the nature of reality itself.[40]

The relationship between fiction and philosophy is always immensely complex, and this complexity is especially illuminating when the fiction is American. As I noted at the start, the novel is a deeply polyphonic genre, and a thorough discussion of the texts mentioned here would detail not only the philosophical voices they orchestrate, but also the variety of speech genres – descriptive, narrative, metaphoric, meditative – pulling them centripetally away from assertion and argument. The ambivalence of the novel as a form is perhaps best exhibited in the figure often cited as the most accomplished American novelist of ideas, Saul Bellow, whose sense of himself as a "hybrid curiosity" I mentioned earlier. Philip Rahv, who lamented the paucity of ideas in American fiction, singled out Bellow's *Herzog* (1964) for its "intellectual mastery,"[41] and it's not hard to see why. In Moses Herzog's obsessive letter-writing, Bellow demonstrates a remarkable feel for the texture of modern intellectual history. *"Dear Professor Doktor Heidegger,"* goes one representative epistle, *"I would like to know what you mean by the expression 'the fall into the quotidian' . . . Where were we standing when it happened?"* Rahv's comment could equally well characterize Bellow's other novels, from the existentialist meditations of *Dangling Man* (1944) to the post-Nietzschean psychology of *Henderson the Rain King* (1959) to the fictionalized response to the New Left in *Mr. Sammler's Planet* (1970). And yet at the same time, Bellow's novels are also deeply suspicious of the intellect's ambitions. His focus is less on what his 1976 Nobel Speech ironically called "the most serious thoughts" than the intellectual's frequently comic belief that "serious thoughts" are an adequate response to the simultaneously threatening and intoxicating modern environments around us. As Louis Menand has written of *Ravelstein* (2000), whose title character is based on the Straussian political philosopher Allan Bloom, Bellow "is not a theorist" but "a novelist fascinated by theorists," characters (almost uniformly male) who are prone to building "mad theoretical tree houses."[42]

j See Heise, chapter 58, 968–975.

The particular social institutions and cultural traditions that have typically shaped American writers mean that even the most highly educated novelists have tended to be philosophical autodidacts. Readers like Rahv see this as a burden, but from another perspective, it might also be a boon. As Herzog's letter to Heidegger suggests, particular philosophies always emerge in midstream, from lived experience and within particular cultural environments, and insofar as they have recognized this, American novelists may be driven less by naïveté than a principled urge – attributed sometimes to their philosophical compatriots – to "evade" philosophy's traditional aspirations, deformations, and blindspots.[43]

The mention of *Ravelstein* is apt here, for it suggests some of the ways American novels have continued an engagement with philosophy since the late 1960s. One is that, as intellectual life in American culture has grown increasingly confined to the universities, the philosophical novel has begun to merge with the campus novel. Whatever the differences between Binx Bolling, Cross Damon, and other protagonists noted here, none has a PhD But by the end of the twentieth century, the phrase "public intellectual" had begun to sound antiquated (Sontag is frequently cited as the last) and college campuses became one of the few believable settings for a depiction of serious intellectual debate, as well as the white-collar workplace for an increasing number of novelists.[44] This shift is registered not only in *Ravelstein*, with its descriptions of university life and academic rivalries, but even more explicitly in, say, Richard Powers's *Galatea 2.2* (1995), in which a novelist participates in a group researching artificial intelligence.

Ravelstein and *Galatea* are notable, moreover, because they mark an evolution in the kinds of philosophical ideas informing contemporary fiction. As I've suggested, the analytic/continental rift in twentieth-century philosophy has importantly determined the kinds of philosophical ideas available to twentieth-century novelists. But with the work of Iris Murdoch, Richard Rorty, Stanley Cavell, Charles Taylor, and other thinkers, the last thirty years have seen growing commerce between philosophical traditions, and this has opened up a greater range of philosophical themes to novelists who are paying attention.[45] The power of post-Hegelian philosophy has hardly diminished, of course. Consider, for instance, Cormac McCarthy's *Blood Meridian* (1985), the dialogue of which sometimes sounds like an exegetical commentary on Nietzsche's *Genealogy of Morals*; or the fiction of Charles Johnson, who in *Middle Passage* (1990) and elsewhere draws heavily on his extensive formal training in phenomenology. But an ambitious talent such as Powers's is as liable nowadays to explore "analytic" theories of mind in *Galatea* or *The Echo Maker* (2006) as he is to cite the "continental" writings of Walter Benjamin, as in *Three Farmers on Their Way to a Dance* (1985), and a high-level philosophical education in logic and mathematics did not prevent David Foster Wallace from becoming perhaps the most prominent novelist and essayist of his generation. Indeed, it may be no accident that Wittgenstein, the figure who most conspicuously straddles analytic and continental traditions, has over the last quarter-century been a source of fascination to a number of American novelists, including not only Wallace, but also David Markson, Bruce Duffy, and R. M. Berry.[46] A new Athens, Jena, or Concord would be a lot to expect. One hopes nevertheless that these developments help us recognize why poets and philosophers, if not exactly "one" as Emerson believed, are often products of the same muse, and that, if the relationship between them is a quarrel, the quarrel takes place among friends.

Notes

1. *The Poetics of Aristotle*, trans. Stephen Halliwell (Chapel Hill: University of North Carolina Press, 1987), 41.
2. Friedrich Schlegel, *Philosophical Fragments*, trans. Peter Firchow (Minneapolis: University of Minnesota Press, 1991), 5; "The Oldest System-Program of German Idealism," in *Friedrich Hölderlin: Essays and Letters on Theory*, trans. and ed. Thomas Pfau (Albany: SUNY Press, 1988), 154–156; Ralph Waldo Emerson, *Essays and Lectures*, ed. Joel Porte (New York: Library of America, 1983), 36. Nothing I've said here is meant to deny, of course, that the relationship between literature and philosophy was the topic of many discussions in the two millennia between Aristotle and the Romantics.
3. Philip Rahv, "The Cult of Experience in American Writing," in *Literature and the Sixth Sense* (Boston: Houghton Mifflin, 1970), 22–25.
4. T. S. Eliot, "Henry James," in *Selected Prose of T. S. Eliot*, ed. Frank Kermode (London: Faber, 1975), 151; William Carlos Williams, *Selected Poems*, ed. Charles Tomlinson (New York: New Directions, 1985), 145.
5. On Scottish Common Sense philosophy in the USA, see Bruce Kuklick, *A History of Philosophy in America, 1720–2000* (New York: Oxford University Press, 2002), chapters 3–4. On the American Hegelians, see *The American Hegelians: An Intellectual Episode in the History of Western America*, ed. William H. Goetzmann (New York: Knopf, 1973). The history of pragmatism has been more richly documented than these other movements, with extensive treatments by such scholars as Kuklick, Louis Menand, John Patrick Diggins, Cornel West, David Hollinger, and James T. Kloppenberg.
6. W. V. O. Quine, *The Ways of Paradox and Other Essays*, rev. edn. (Cambridge, MA: Harvard University Press, 2006), 151; A. J. Ayer, *Language, Truth, and Logic* (1936; New York: Dover, 1952), 113.

7. Saul Bellow, "Foreword" to *The Closing of the American Mind*, by Allan Bloom (New York: Schuster and Schuster, 1987), 14–15.
8. John Dewey, "Emerson – The Philosopher of Democracy" (1903), in *The Essential Dewey, Volume 2: Ethics, Logic, Psychology*, ed. Larry A. Hickman and Thomas M. Alexander (Bloomington: Indiana University Press, 1998), 369.
9. See, e.g., Joan Richardson, *A Natural History of Pragmatism: The Fact of Feeling from Jonathan Edwards to Gertrude Stein* (New York: Cambridge University Press, 2007), chapter 6; Andrew Epstein, *Beautiful Enemies: Friendship and Postwar American Poetry* (New York: Oxford University Press, 2006); Richard Poirier, *Poetry and Pragmatism* (Cambridge, MA: Harvard University Press, 1992).
10. On Henry James and pragmatism, see Ross Posnock, *The Trial of Curiosity: Henry James, William James, and the Challenge of Modernity* (New York: Oxford University Press, 1991); Richardson, *Natural History*, chapter 5. On Stein and pragmatism, Richardson, *Natural History*, chapter 7. On Du Bois's fiction and pragmatism, see Ross Posnock, *Color and Culture: Black Writers and the Making of the Modern Intellectual* (Cambridge, MA: Harvard University Press, 2000), chapter 5. Hurston's reaction to pragmatism is more ambivalent than these other figures, as David Kadlec has argued in his *Mosaic Modernism: Anarchy, Pragmatism, Culture* (Baltimore: Johns Hopkins University Press, 2000), chapter 6.
11. Kenneth Burke, *Here & Elsewhere: The Collected Fiction of Kenneth Burke* (Jaffrey, NH: Black Sparrow, 2005), 414–415.
12. *Ibid.*, 8, 406.
13. Kenneth Burke, *Attitudes Toward History*, third edn. (Berkeley: University of California, 1984), "Introduction."
14. Arnold Rampersad, *Ralph Ellison: A Biography* (New York: Knopf, 2007), 286, 205–206. For more on Burke and Ellison, see Gregg Crane, "Ralph Ellison's Constitutional Faith," in *The Cambridge Companion to Ralph Ellison*, ed. Ross Posnock (New York: Cambridge University Press, 2005), 104–120; Beth Eddy, *The Rites of Identity: The Religious Naturalism and Cultural Criticism of Kenneth Burke and Ralph Ellison* (Princeton: Princeton University Press, 2003); Timothy L. Parrish, "Ralph Ellison, Kenneth Burke, and the Form of Democracy," *Arizona Quarterly* 51 (1995): 117–148.
15. Burke, *Attitudes Toward History*, 12–13; Ralph Ellison, *Shadow and Act* (New York: Random House, 1972), 78.
16. See Donald E. Pease, "Ralph Ellison and Kenneth Burke: The Nonsymbolizable (Trans)Action," *boundary* 2.30 (2003): 65–96.
17. Ralph Ellison, "Introduction" to *Invisible Man* (1952; New York: Vintage, 1990).
18. *Ibid.*, xviii, xxi.
19. Walker Percy, *The Message in the Bottle: How Queer Man Is, How Queer Language Is, and What One Has to Do with the Other* (New York: Noonday, 1975), 194.
20. Percy's remark about "wave disturbance" appears in *Message in the Bottle*, 194; Peirce's remark about the "symbol-using mind" is found in *Philosophical Writings of Peirce*, ed. Justus Buchler (New York: Dover, 1955), 114. On Peirce's religious underpinnings, see Douglas Anderson, "Peirce's Common Sense Marriage

of Religion and Science," in *The Cambridge Companion to Peirce*, ed. Cheryl Misak (Cambridge: Cambridge University Press, 2004), 175–192. On Percy and Peirce generally, see John F. Desmond, *Walker Percy's Search for Community* (Athens: University of Georgia Press, 2004).

21. On Southern mourning, see Richard Godden, *William Faulkner: An Economy of Complex Words* (Princeton: Princeton University Press, 2007).
22. Percy remarked that the epilogue of *The Moviegoer* was also meant to evoke *The Brothers Karamazov*. See *Conversations with Walker Percy*, ed. Lewis A. Lawson and Victor A. Kramer (Jackson: University of Mississippi Press, 1985), 66.
23. Percy, *Message in the Bottle*, 283; Desmond, *Walker Percy's Search*, 9.
24. Percy, *Message in the Bottle*, 3.
25. John Updike, *Odd Jobs* (New York: Knopf, 1991), 844; Norman Mailer, *Advertisements for Myself* (1959; Cambridge, MA: Harvard University Press, 1992), 339.
26. See, for instance, Kingsley Widmer, "The Existential Darkness: Richard Wright's *The Outsider*," *Wisconsin Studies in Contemporary Literature* 1.3 (Autumn 1960): 13.
27. See Sidney Hook, "Pragmatism and Existentialism," *The Antioch Review* 19 (1959): 151–168. On the overlap of existentialism and American antinomianism, see George Cotkin, *Existentialist America* (Baltimore: Johns Hopkins University Press, 2002), 8. Sellars's remark is in his review of Sartre's *Existentialism*, *American Sociological Review* 12 (1947), 726. For some postwar discussion of Hemingway, Faulkner, and French fiction, see Albert J. Guérard, "French and American Pessimism," *Harper's Magazine* (August 1945): 267–272; Harry R. Garvin, "Camus and the American Novel," *Comparative Literature* 8 (1956): 194–204; Richard Lehan, "Camus and Hemingway," *Wisconsin Studies in Contemporary Literature* 1.2 (Winter 1960): 37–48.
28. On Wright's relationships with these figures, see Michel Fabre, "Richard Wright and the French Existentialists," *MELUS* 5.2 (Summer 1978): 39–51.
29. This political ambivalence was most famously expressed in Sartre's 1946 lecture "Existentialism is a Humanism"; see his *Essays in Existentialism* (New York: Citadel, 1993), 31–62.
30. Reviewing the novel in 1953 for Paul Robeson's newspaper *Freedom*, Lorraine Hansberry criticized Wright for exalting "brutality and nothingness" over and above the African American struggle for freedom; see her "Review of *The Outsider*," in *The Critical Response to Richard Wright*, ed. Robert J. Butler (Westport, CT: Greenwood Press, 1995), 109. More recently, and from a different direction, Dan McCall has complained that Wright's late fiction is marred by "disastrous metaphysical harangues and socio-historical tirades"; see his "Wright's American Hunger," in *Richard Wright: Critical Perspectives Past and Present*, ed. Henry Louis Gates, Jr. and K. A. Appiah (New York: Amistad, 1993), 367.
31. Mae Henderson, for one, has suggested that the naturalistic form of the text was a deliberate decision, since in his earlier writings Wright was not shy about using experimental, even surrealistic, forms. See her "Drama and Denial in *The*

Outsider," in Gates and Appiah, *Richard Wright: Critical Perspectives Past and Present*, 388–408.

32. See Thomas Frank's *The Conquest of Cool: Business Culture, Counterculture, and the Rise of Hip Consumerism* (Chicago: University of Chicago Press, 1998).
33. Tony Judt, *Postwar: A History of Europe since 1945* (New York: Penguin, 2005), 400. The passage O'Connor takes from Heidegger can be found in Heidegger's *Basic Writings*, ed. David Farrell Krell (New York: Harper & Row, 1977), 98.
34. Jacques Derrida, *Points ... : Interviews, 1974–1994* (Stanford, CA: Stanford University Press, 1995), 122.
35. Iris Murdoch, *Existentialists and Mystics: Writings on Philosophy and Literature*, ed. Peter Conradi (New York: Penguin, 1999), 104, 149.
36. On Sontag's early intellectual influences at Chicago and Harvard, see Carl Rollyson and Lisa Paddock, *Susan Sontag: The Making of an Icon* (New York: Norton, 2000), 29–42.
37. Irving Howe's 1969 essay "The New York Intellectuals," for instance, describes Sontag as "a highly literate spokesman" for people "who have discarded or not acquired intellectual literacy." See his *Selected Essays 1950–1990* (New York: Harvest, 1990), 240–280.
38. On Freud and Marx, see Susan Sontag, *Against Interpretation* (New York: Farrar, Straus and Giroux, 1966), 6–7. On the novel's anachronism relative to other arts, *ibid*., 298–301.
39. Benjamin DeMott, "Diddy or Didn't He?", review of *Death Kit* by Susan Sontag, *New York Times* (August 27, 1967): B2.
40. Brian McHale, *Postmodern Fiction* (London: Routledge, 1987).
41. Rahv, "Saul Bellow's Progress," in *Literature and the Sixth Sense*, 393.
42. Louis Menand, "Bloom's Gift," review of *Ravelstein*, *New York Review of Books* (May 25, 2000): 17.
43. See Cornel West, *The American Evasion of Philosophy* (Madison: University of Wisconsin Press, 1989).
44. The idea of a merger between the philosophical and campus novel was suggested to me by Ben Roth. On creative writing and universities, see Mark McGurl, *The Program Era: Postwar Fiction and the Rise of Creative Writing* (Cambridge, MA: Harvard University Press, 2009).
45. One shouldn't exaggerate the degree to which these figures – or Ian Hacking, Alasdair MacIntyre, Hilary Putnam, Martha Nussbaum, or Cora Diamond – have actually softened the analytic/continental divide. Indeed, the rise of cognitive science and related fields has in some ways made analytic philosophy an even more specialized domain than it ever has been, and certainly the desire to make philosophy into a professional discipline hasn't abated. Still, the critique of analytic philosophy voiced by Murdoch, Rorty, *et al.* has remained powerful, and will continue to provoke responses and exert influence.
46. See Wallace, *The Broom in the System* (1987), Duffy, *The World as I Found It* (1987), Markson's *Wittgenstein's Mistress* (1988), and Berry's *Dictionary of Modern Anguish* (2000).

40

Steinbeck and the proletarian novel

ALAN M. WALD

When John Steinbeck's masterwork *The Grapes of Wrath* was published in 1939, the Communist Party's *Daily Worker* applauded it beneath the headline, "The *Grapes of Wrath* is a Great Proletarian Novel." The reviewer's uncritical admiration was effusive:

> It is at once a monumental protest against the horrors of a profit system whose high priests oppose the New Deal, unionization, and relief, and an infinitely compassionate portrait of the masses who suffer under the system. But out of their suffering, Steinbeck shows, will grow a great movement to restore the land to the people ... It is hard to think of a more satisfying proletarian novel in America.[1]

A few weeks later, the Party-sponsored weekly magazine *New Masses* put forward a more systematic appraisal by Granville Hicks, a public member of the Party and author of the notable Marxist critical study *The Great Tradition: An Interpretation of American Literature since the Civil War* (1933; revised 1935). Hicks's verdict was identical:

> Hitherto, whenever anybody asked us what we meant by proletarian literature, we had to say, "Well, it ought to have this quality that you find in so-and-so's work, and that quality so exemplified by the other fellow, and such-and-such found in somebody else" ... We shan't have to offer that kind of composite illustration any more. We can now say, "Proletarian literature? Oh, that means a book like John Steinbeck's *The Grapes of Wrath*."[2]

In the estimation of Hicks, who had previously co-edited the groundbreaking anthology *Proletarian Literature in the United States* (1935), the traits of proletarian fiction illustrated by Steinbeck encompass imaginative power, knowledge of the life experience depicted, characters who are individual yet representative, and a long-term optimistic view of the triumph of determined working people over the exploitative economic forces. From a present-day point of view, Hicks's characterization suggests that the concept of the proletarian novel should be understood in the manner that the architect Philip Johnson defined other styles and genres: it is less "a set of rules or shackles," and more "a climate in which to operate, a springboard to leap further into the air."[3]

Yet the twenty-first-century reader is scarcely equipped to appreciate or assess the claims of seventy years ago that a bestseller by John Ernst Steinbeck epitomized the genre of the proletarian novel. Today, in general literary scholarship about the United States, the proletarian novel is mostly ignored or mentioned vaguely; when defined, it is presented as an aberrant sideshow, mostly limited to a phenomenon of the early 1930s exemplified in little-known books of uneven quality that feature strikes and Communist sentiments, such as Jack Conroy's *The Disinherited* (1932), Grace Lumpkin's *To Make My Bread* (1932), Robert Cantwell's *The Land of Plenty* (1934), William Rollins's *The Shadow Before* (1934), and Clara Weatherwax's *Marching! Marching*! (1935).[4] Too often unseen, even in the early 1930s, are novels written in the climate of proletarianism that deal with situations apart from union organizing, such as Erskine Caldwell's poor tenant farmers in *Tobacco Road* (1932), Guy Endore's Haitian rebels in *Babouk*, Nelson Algren's criminal outcasts in *Somebody in Boots* (1934), and H. T. Tsiang's experimental narrative in *The Hanging on Union Square* (1935).

A constriction of meaning of the category of proletarian novel over the decades is principally a result of the difficulty of translating a complex politico-cultural phenomenon from one distinct historical era to another. The term "proletarian" itself seems dated, even foreign, and any notion that a Communist movement might inspire creative literature of national import and aesthetic merit was crushed by US Cold War propaganda combined with the repressive practice of self-proclaimed Communist regimes abroad. Nevertheless, scholars who are specialists in cultural radicalism have established that what is called "proletarian literature" gained a foothold, principally in the Great Depression, due to a combination of three factors: a longer tradition of at least five decades of writing about working-class experience from a sympathetic, quasi-socialist perspective; the objective conditions of the deep and widespread economic crisis after 1929; and the contentious tutelage of writers and activists in and around the Communist movement, who since the 1920s promoted – in some cases with the authority of Party titles or editorial positions – what they believed to be Marxist notions of cultural commitment and aesthetics.

After the Great Depression, Steinbeck would be increasingly depicted as a thinker always at odds with the Communist movement, while the ideology of

The Grapes of Wrath became treated in the post-World War II era as purely New Deal liberalism and "Jeffersonian."[5] A small group of experts in left-wing fiction, many stirred by the phenomenon of the New Left in the 1960s, have been more accurate in granting the magnetism of the Communist movement and its ideals for major as well as minor writers of the 1930s, including Steinbeck; but even they usually draw back from identifying *The Grapes of Wrath* as typical, and certainly not as the pinnacle, of the proletarian tradition.[6] This wavering about embracing Steinbeck as a paradigmatic figure of proletarian literature is the result of a perfect storm attributable not only to the Cold War containment of proletarian literature to minor and ideologically explicit works, but also to two major quandaries in Steinbeck scholarship.

One involves a tendency to give too much weight to the poetic and visionary themes of Steinbeck's early writing – *Cup of Gold* (1929), *The Pastures of Heaven* (1932), *To a God Unknown* (1933) and *Tortilla Flat* (1935). As Sylvia Jenkins Cook has remarked, these books reveal that Steinbeck was fashioned as a writer by mystical and pagan feelings about the relationship of people to the land they tend, and by early readings in Xenophon, Herodotus, Plutarch, and Sir Thomas Malory. Moreover, as Ann Loftis observes, the last of these books presented an "interpretation of Hispanic culture through comic stereotypes" that now seems quite patronizing; in 1937 Steinbeck expressed regret about any misunderstanding that this might have caused.[7] Coincidentally, inspired by the tide pools of the Pacific, Steinbeck reached some expertise in marine biology under the tutelage of his friend Edward Ricketts, which added to a desire to express his own scientific philosophy in his fiction. [8] Such a backdrop prepared Steinbeck for sympathy with the struggle of agrarian workers, and surely such formative influences, along with the impact of his family and youthful experiences, did not evaporate from his creative writing and political thought when he turned to the novels now regarded as his Worker Trilogy – *In Dubious Battle* (1936), *Of Mice and Men* (1937), and *The Grapes of Wrath*.[9] But increasingly after 1935 there are notable mutations in his outlook, choice of subject matter, and style, that show his movement toward the general outlook of the 1930s Left.

A second block to placing Steinbeck at the center of a Left tradition is the steady growth of anti-radical sentiment he expressed in the post-World War II years, climaxing in vitriolic attacks on the anti-Vietnam War movement of the 1960s. Of course, a political move to the Right was characteristic of a substantial portion of Steinbeck's literary generation (James T. Farrell, John Dos Passos, Grace Lumpkin, Albert Halper, Ralph Ellison, and Robert Cantwell followed a similar trajectory).

Steinbeck is also sometimes singled out for exhibiting elements of romanticism and mysticism; but these are easily found in others on the pro-Communist literary Left.[10] A celebrated instance is that of Meridel Le Sueur, whose writings, such as *The Girl* (written in the 1930s, published in novel form in 1978), were as much influenced by D. H. Lawrence as by Karl Marx. Le Sueur recurrently attributes essentialist qualities of reason to male and emotion to female characters, yet she is invariably classified among the proletarians in part due to her open Communist membership.[11] A case by case study is required to understand the politics of authors in the mid twentieth century inasmuch as a writer could well be part of a broad pro-Communist movement without Party affiliation or a declaration of faith in "Marxism–Leninism"; the term "Progressive" was frequently used as a bridge between liberalism and Communism, further confounding the attribution of a political identity without prudent research.

Only after the 1930s, and above all during the Cold War era, did literary criticism register the urgency to set Steinbeck decisively apart from Far Left politics and ideology – with historic penalties for the overall treatment in scholarship of the proletarian novel. At that time, from the early 1940s through the 1960s, the era of the political demonization of Communism was in full force.[12] The combination of the consolidation of Steinbeck's reputation as a major author – due to the long-lasting fame of *The Grapes of Wrath* and the popularity of *East of Eden* (1952) – along with the drifting of his politics away from the Left, encouraged a tendency to counterpoise Steinbeck to the cultural trend with which he originally appeared to have most affinities.[13] After all, if Steinbeck was a principal American novelist, due either to high quality or mass popularity, how could he exemplify proletarian literature, increasingly regarded as a hothouse movement inspired by an alien ideology? As a result of this apparent contradiction, Steinbeck criticism began to stress his allegedly universal, mythic, and even pro-capitalist themes, while the genre of the proletarian novel became a more restricted and artistically suspect phenomenon.

This scholarly effacement of what was most certainly a deep affinity between Steinbeck and the rising tide of class rebellion in the 1930s is thus symbolic of potential misapprehensions about many novels and novelists in the mid twentieth century forged in the climate of proletarianism, and the sundry means by which writers are affected by social movements. That is why Steinbeck criticism must be rooted intimately in the context of the culture of the Great Depression, not forced to conform to the ideological oversimplifications, apologies, and cover-ups of the post-World War II era.

In the reflections of Malcolm Cowley in a November 8, 1939, essay, "A Farewell to the 1930s," we can see the crystallization of several facets of the troubled affiliation of the proletarian novel to Steinbeck. Cowley insists, on the one hand, that the term "proletarian writing" has now become identical to "a milder academic term . . . the literature of social protest."[a] But he also assigns economically based strike action as a central element in this type of literature to the degree that proletarian novels in the 1930s "began to follow a pattern almost as rigid and conventional as that of a Petrarchan sonnet. The hero was usually a young worker, honest, naïve and politically undeveloped. Through intolerable mistreatment, he was driven to take part in a strike. Always the strike was ruthlessly suppressed, and usually its leader was killed. But the young worker, conscious now of the mission that united him to the whole working class, marched on toward new battles."[14] According to Cowley, this core narrative persisted throughout the decade.

Most notably, it persevered in modified appearance beyond the influential 1935 turnabout in the Communist policy of the Popular Front, after which revolutionary trade unions were abandoned for the Congress of Industrial Organizations (CIO) and the earlier attacks on liberalism were softened. According to Cowley, one major effect of this political swing in regard to the proletarian novel was to promote an expansion of literary form, such as "collective" novels (those with group heroes); another was to amplify the range of experiences dramatized by writers, encouraging novels in which the strike action itself is not present and explicit class struggle recedes into the background. John Dos Passos's *U.S.A.* (*The 42nd Parallel*, 1930; *1919*, 1932; and *The Big Money*, 1936), and Josephine Herbst's Trexler Family Trilogy (*Pity is Not Enough*, 1933; *The Executioner Waits*, 1934; *Rope of Gold*, 1939) were part of this evolving trend in mid decade. Cowley also notes the development of the genre from margin to center of the national culture. Despite the hostility of conservative critics and even dissident Marxists such as James T. Farrell (in *A Note on Literary Criticism* [1936]) to proletarian literature in the early and mid Depression, the situation dramatically shifted in 1939: "A proletarian novel, *Christ in Concrete*, received an almost official recognition by being chosen as Book of the Month. Another proletarian novel, *The Grapes of Wrath*, was not only a bestseller but the most widely-read book of the year."[15] The first began as a short story by Pietro Di Donato in *Esquire* magazine, and was

a For a broader analysis of "Novels of civic protest" in the late nineteenth and twentieth centuries, see Cecilia Tichi's essay in this volume (chapter 23).

issued by Bobbs-Merrill publishers. The second, published by Viking Press with much advance publicity, created a firestorm of controversy with its harsh criticisms of agricultural working conditions in California, and won the Pulitzer Prize.

What is eye-catching in this summary is that Cowley's core plot for the proletarian novel, even though rather blown up, oversimplified, and sensationalized in journalistic style ("a pattern almost as rigid and conventional as that of a Petrarchan sonnet"), captures the central narrative of *The Grapes of Wrath*. Tom Joad, Jr., a rural worker who has served a prison sentence for a murder in self-defense that he freely acknowledges, discovers that his family has been dispossessed of its land due to dust bowl conditions in Oklahoma. Teaming up with Jim Casy, a country preacher who has lost his religious faith, Joad reconnects with his extended family as it travels to California. In the course of a series of labor struggles pitting migrant workers against growers, vigilantes, and law enforcement, Casy evolves into a union organizer who is assassinated by the police. Tom then pledges himself to take Casy's place as a traveling agitator, willing to use any means necessary to defend and unite workers until economic justice and human dignity are achieved. If one foregrounds this essential narrative, *The Grapes of Wrath* is indubitably an expression of the proletarian literary movement.

Yet the novel additionally suggests features of the Popular Front expansion of that tradition, perhaps most conspicuously through its refusal to name Communists as providing any part of the socio-economic way out, or including any consideration of Communism as the solution. Like much of the Popular Front ethos itself, *The Grapes of Wrath* tends to be fuzzy about long-term solutions, blending ideas of reform and revolution, and to give special emphasis to the "Americanness" (in the ethnocentric sense of the protagonists being born in the United States with a white Protestant identity) of those engaged in the battle to survive exploitation and eventually triumph. What we see is that the proletarian novel was produced by a convergence between a writer and a fundamental socio-political vision of working-class and then anti-fascist struggle that was promoted aggressively by Communists but was by no means reducible to a Communist program or a particular version of Marxist theory.

Still, *The Grapes of Wrath* conveyed in its pages far more than this primary story of the tradition of the proletarian novel, pioneered by such personal narratives as Agnes Smedley's *Daughter of Earth* (1929) and Michael Gold's *Jews Without Money* (1930), and then succeeded by the wave of strike novels emphasized by Cowley. By the late 1930s, the national climate had moved to the political Left, due to the success of the CIO and fear of growing fascism, and Steinbeck managed to find a blend of popular culture and biblical symbols that allowed the book to rise to the center of American culture. Thus *The Grapes of Wrath* has remained canonical while several hundred novels that diversely relate to the genre lag behind, unknown to the general reading public. A list of neglected works from the same period includes not only the above-mentioned *Christ in Concrete*, but also fine novels such as William Attaway's *Blood on the Forge* (1941), with its dazzling use of black folk culture to address complications of race and class, and Thomas Bell's *Out of This Furnace* (1941), which felicitously merges family and labor history over several generations.

Steinbeck is consistent with the radicalism of the late 1930s in amalgamating select patriotic themes with a Left viewpoint. His "Okies," a term generally used for migrants from the mid-West, are white and native-born, yet are subject to discrimination in a manner that recalls racial chauvinism. (Steinbeck's references to people of color in *The Grapes of Wrath* are few, and mainly confined to historical allusions to Western conquest in the inter-chapters that alternate with his narrative of the Joad family.)[16] Steinbeck's women can be tough and independent, providing leadership as commanding as that of any male, yet are profoundly committed to the family, even as the family itself embodies a kind of extended proletarian community.[17] Steinbeck's workers clearly face all-encompassing oppression orchestrated by a capitalist system bolstered by state power, yet the owners themselves are never revealed (operating through surrogates, sometimes mechanized), and there is an episode of respite in a government-administered camp run by a kindly manager.[18]

One might choose to regard Steinbeck's Worker Trilogy as an expression of the proletarian literary movement, or, alternatively, "universally," as a parable of the human condition. The latter evolved to the prevailing view after the early Steinbeck was assessed through the prism of Cold War critical precepts. Either route has dramatic consequences for interpreting Steinbeck's fiction, as can readily be seen even in books sharply critical of the Cold War repressive environment. An example is the otherwise compelling intellectual history, *Radical Visions and American Dreams* (1973), where Richard Pells ascribes Steinbeck's success to his tapping into the era's fascination with biological themes of humanity as part of the animal condition, which seemed apropos in light of the harsh Depression conditions. Besides, Steinbeck excelled in the adaptation of the 1930s techniques of film and documentary through the novel's interchapters, journalistic observations of speech and mores, and the priority given to dialogue and action over introspection.[b] What is more, the book imaginatively transcended the local situation by creating an aura of nostalgia for agrarian ideals and love of the land, biblical references (especially the search for the Promised Land), and Jim Casy's Emersonian oversoul ("all men got one big soul ever'body's a part of"). By focusing on these secondary features, Pells is able to conclude that *The Grapes of Wrath* "was not really a political novel at all." Instead, the triumph of goodness (as opposed to "adherence to specific program or ideology") and the love of ordinary folk were crucial to the Joads becoming "mythic creations" who "spoke for no particular class or economic doctrine but for all humanity." Thus Pells insists that the novel is actually about "patience" and "tradition."[19]

The effort to place Steinbeck in opposition, as opposed to in independent critical proximity, to Communism, is also evident in critical debates about *In Dubious Battle*, which is the narrative of Jim Nolan, the son of a murdered worker. By joining the Communist Party, Jim hopes to regenerate himself; he becomes the sidekick of Mac, an experienced Party cadre who brings him to an apple pickers' strike in the Torgas Valley. During a vicious battle with the owners, Mac promotes the view that he and Jim must "use everything" to win, and they consistently devote themselves to that objective. Much of the time Mac's philosophy sounds brutal: "A tough strike is good. We want the men to find out how strong they are when they work together." Although completely devoted to the working-class cause, Mac makes statements such as "We can't waste time liking people," and gradually Jim begins to emulate and then out-distance his mentor. Among those who join the encampment of striking workers is Doc Burton, a physician who argues with both men about the possibility of an authentic victory. As the book moves to its violent climax, Doc disappears, Jim is killed by a shotgun blast to the face, and Mac declares to the workers over Jim's corpse: "This guy didn't want nothing for himself . . ."

Much of the postwar scholarship about *In Dubious Battle* views Mac and Jim as diabolical; the "dubious" in the title, from Milton's *Paradise Lost*, is taken to mean, more or less, that partisanship for the strike is an unworthy commitment rather than one that is necessary but complicated or problematic.[20] During the 1930s, however, critics did not think the reader had to choose between the two Communists and Doc. The reviews take for granted that Steinbeck is in complete sympathy with the cause of the landless migrants; after all, the opponents of the workers are depicted as the perpetrators of a

b See Mark McGurl's essay in this volume, chapter 41, "The novel, mass culture, mass media," 693–695, on the film adaptation of *The Grapes of Wrath*.

terrorist violence that unambiguously recalls fascism, while the positive characters in the middle class are won to the workers' side. It is predominantly later scholars who insist pointedly that Steinbeck was speaking through Doc, reinforced by the evidence that many of Doc's philosophical opinions echo those of Steinbeck's friend and mentor, Edward Ricketts. Only a rare commentator took note that Doc was an unlikely role model for Steinbeck's point of view inasmuch as Doc is merely a passive onlooker who vanishes (most likely kidnapped and killed by vigilantes, a fate that Steinbeck feared if he were identified as a Communist).[21] In contrast, a few months after *In Dubious Battle* appeared, Steinbeck himself launched his career as a crusading journalist on behalf of the migrants and passed several years of political activity in collaboration with Communists.

The most likely explanation for the tough talk of Mac and Jim, beyond Steinbeck's insistence that he was representing authentic speech, is that Steinbeck remained committed to what he called his "non-teleological" perspective[22] and wished to present the revolutionary project, especially when it involved the creation of the masses as "group man," as dangerous and problematic. A sensible conclusion is that Steinbeck himself was observing the events depicted, hearing both the arguments of Doc as well as viewing the role played by Mac, the only survivor among the three protagonists of *In Dubious Battle*. It is not Doc's ultimate stance as a bystander but his compelling argumentation that attracts Steinbeck:

> Listen to me, Mac. My senses aren't above reproach, but they're all I have. I want to see the whole picture – as nearly as I can. I don't want to put on the blinders of "good" and "bad," and limit my vision. If I used the term "good" on a thing I'd lose my license to inspect it, because there might be bad in it. Don't you see? I want to be able to look at the whole thing.

The battle is "dubious" because the struggle of the workers has thorny features that need to be recognized and studied, not because it is an unworthy effort to fight the greedy exploiters.

Recognizing the centrality of Steinbeck's Worker Trilogy to the tradition of the proletarian novel leads us to an expansion of a notion of the genre, even while acknowledging that a part of its roots lies in sectarian discussions among ideologues and that many works of proletarian fiction are primarily of interest for historical reasons. The proletarian novel was not an ideology put into dramatic form, but the creation of a tradition of individualized writers drawn diversely toward real social movements and a special vision that emerged in the 1930s. Marxism and the Communist Party were part of the mix, but clear-cut affiliations and protestations of political faith were hardly decisive. Here it is instructive to compare the literary trajectory of Richard Wright, an avowed Marxist and open member of the Communist Party, with the career of Steinbeck. Although Wright was African American, six years younger, and did not commence publishing until the early 1930s, there are prominent similarities. Most significant, the stories that became *Uncle Tom's Children* (1938) began to appear in print just after Steinbeck's *North American Review* story about two Communists, "The Raid" (1934), and around the time of *In Dubious Battle*. Like Steinbeck, Wright took his materials from oral histories with Communist militants, at least one of whom was a political dissident, and early on Wright fell under suspicion of some Party ideologues while ultimately receiving overwhelming approval.[23] Like Steinbeck, many of Wright's stories had a rural setting and several involved saint-like Communist martyrs to violence at the hands of vigilantes and police.

Nevertheless, when the two men produced their major novels at the end of the 1930s, Steinbeck opted for a classical conversion narrative to radical commitment in the case of Tom Joad, while Wright's *Native Son* presented its protagonist, Bigger Thomas, as a failed convert who murders one of those who proselytize him (Mary) and frames another (Jan). Moreover, Steinbeck, the non-Party member, chose to present a de-ethnicized class-against-class perspective, while Wright the Marxist elevated the race question to center stage; Steinbeck made the case for organized workers, while Wright presented oppressed characters with a marginal relation to the work force; and Steinbeck depicted a noble proletarian family, while Wright created a destitute mother in the grip of religious delusion and a son who was a hoodlum. All in all, putting public statements and biographical identifications aside, Steinbeck's literary trajectory in the late 1930s appears far closer to what one would imagine a pro-Communist writer to produce if literature were the direct transcription of ideology rather than the outgrowth of the individual artist in a social context.

We began with Granville Hick's observation that the form and content of one work, *The Grapes of Wrath*, trumped all other efforts to define the proletarian novel. One might conclude that such a novel was quintessentially the organic outgrowth of the mainstream experiences of the twentieth-century United States as the events of the 1930s unfolded. A wide swath of writers of the time, from the outstanding to the mediocre, were attracted to a specific radical interpretation of the Great Depression: one that was militantly class-conscious, hostile to the abuses of capitalism, in favor of industrial union efforts such as the CIO, anti-fascist with a readiness to identify the US racist

Right with the German Nazis, sympathetic to African Americans and other minorities, and inclined toward collectivist solutions including the view of the Soviet Union as an ally of positive social change. A New Deal liberal could embrace such views in partial or tepid form, but the Communists were widely understood and admired as the most militant, courageous, and self-sacrificing in fighting for the entire vision.

As literature is wont to do, the impulse of the proletarian novel was communicated in diverse degrees and forms, although rarely did the core story appear in as complete and successful a rendition as in *The Grapes of Wrath*. Yet it is harder to demonstrate when and where the tradition ended, a subject of considerable debate during the recent decades.[24] Inasmuch as the genre was produced, and with such monumental impact, in the Great Depression, the most reasonable approach is to recognize that the genre has continued, even if in new and sometimes seemingly "marginal" areas. Particularly tricky is that, starting in the late 1930s, there are many novels which, while variously bonded in their origin to the proletarian perspective, go so far afield in subject matter as to mask their guiding sensibility. A preliminary list might include Millen Brand's novel of mental illness, *The Outward Room* (1937); John Sanford's hard-boiled novel about upstate New York, *Seventy Times Seven* (1937); William Blake's historical narrative, *The World is Mine* (1938); Stuart Engstrand's depiction of Swedish immigrants, *They Sought for Paradise* (1939); W. L. River's epic, *The Torguts* (1939); Benjamin Appel's novel of gangster fascists in Harlem, *The Dark Stain* (1943); Howard Fast's fictionalized biography, *Citizen Tom Paine* (1943); Vera Caspary's *noir* classic, *Laura* (1943); Ira Wolfert's crime thriller, *Tucker's People* (1943); Mark Harris's anti-racist story, *Trumpet to the World* (1946); and Jo Sinclair's exploration of Jewish identity, *Wasteland* (1946).[25]

Naturally, the tradition of the proletarian novel also persists in novels more overt in dramatizing in contemporary life the vision of society that took shape in the Depression. In discussing these works, critics sometimes employ terms such as the revolutionary novel, the radical novel, the novel of the Left, and the novel of social commitment, but a key reference point is always the climate of the proletarian novel in the early 1930s. This more explicit tradition appears robustly in certain World War II fictions, such as Norman Mailer's *The Naked and the Dead* (1948) and Stefan Heym's *The Crusaders* (1948). It is also evident in postwar novels that urge the continuation of political struggles in the mold of the Great Depression vision, such as Carlos Bulosan's semi-autobiographical *America is in the Heart* (1946), Willard Motley's *Knock on Any Door* (1947), and Alexander Saxton's *The Great Midland* (1948).[26]

However, there is a twist in some expressions of the genre. Writers can prefer, like Richard Wright, to rework and comment ironically on certain elements of the proletarian novel for artistic and other reasons. Carson McCullers, in *The Heart is a Lonely Hunter* (1940), uses characters who articulate versions of class struggle, black nationalism, and anti-fascism but who never connect; and Norman Mailer, in *Barbary Shore* (1951), features a proletarian veteran with no memory and a Communist mentor who has collaborated with the FBI. This reminds us that even John Steinbeck, who, in contrast and without irony, crafted a straightforward class struggle narrative in *The Grapes of Wrath*, nevertheless forged his art through previously formed emotions and structures of thought. In Steinbeck's ultimately heterogeneous blending of the political and personal, his amalgam of the anxieties shared by the nation with feelings that were particularized and eccentric, he resembled the majority of aspiring writers working in the climate of proletarian literature in his own time as well as in later decades.

Notes

1. Joseph Davis, "The *Grapes of Wrath* is a Great Proletarian Novel," *Daily Worker* (April 4, 1939): 9.
2. Granville Hicks, "Steinbeck's Powerful New Novel," *New Masses* (May 2, 1939): 22–24.
3. Quoted in Witold Rybczynski, *The Look of Architecture* (New York: Oxford University Press, 2001), xii.
4. Most literary reference books, such as Jack Salzman, ed., *The Cambridge Handbook of American Literature* (Cambridge: Cambridge University Press, 1986), do not have an entry under "proletarian novel" or "proletarian literature," even when they cover other movements such as "Transcendentalism" and "Imagism." The rare entry in the revised edition of James D. Hart, *The Oxford Companion to American Literature* (New York: Oxford University Press, 1995), "Proletarian literature," p. 536, focuses on writers publishing in the early 1930s and states that they embrace "Marxist theory." On the other hand, among specialized studies there are sophisticated treatments such as Caren Irr, *The Suburb of Dissent: Cultural Politics in the United States and Canada during the 1930s* (Durham, NC: Duke University Press, 1998).
5. For instance, in Emory Elliot, ed., *The Columbia Literary History of the United States* (New York: Columbia University Press, 1988), Daniel Aaron argues on p. 754 that *The Grapes of Wrath*

   > aroused humanitarian indignation in the teeth of a conservative reaction without undermining confidence in the redeemable republic . . . it binds the Depression . . . to America's democratic heritage . . . *The Grapes of*

Wrath was New Deal ... art ... It owed more to the evangelical progressivism of nineteenth century reformers than to Karl Marx. Even the novel's symbolism was New Dealish (the migrants' only place of refuge is a government camp) . . .

6. Walter Rideout's influential study, *The Radical Novel in the United States, 1900–1954: Some Interrelations of Literature and Society* (Cambridge, MA: Harvard University Press, 1956), p. 288, states that, while influenced by the proletarian novel, Steinbeck was "not a 'proletarian novelist' " because he allegedly sought to integrate migrant families into the existing system, not exacerbate class antagonisms. In her formidable *Radical Representations: Politics and Form in U.S. Proletarian Fiction, 1909–1941* (Durham, NC: Duke University Press, 1993), 416–419, Barbara Foley regards *The Grapes of Wrath* as part of the tradition and devotes several pages to analyzing it as a "collective novel." Michael Denning's brilliantly innovative reading of the era, *The Cultural Front: The Laboring of American Culture in the Twentieth Century* (London: Verso, 1996), 259–276, removes the organized pro-Communist social and cultural movement from the center of the 1930s Popular Front, yet also argues that *The Grapes of Wrath*, despite popular success," is "not a true exemplar of the cultural politics and aesthetic ideologies of the Popular Front" partly due to its "racial populism." One of most constructive additions to scholarship in this area is M. Keith Booker, *The Modern American Novel of the Left* (Westport, CT: Greenwood Press, 1999). As one of those who made recommendations to Booker for his choice of exemplary texts, I wholeheartedly endorse the preponderance of his selections. Moreover, his handling of radical themes in *The Grapes of Wrath* is persuasive, and he cites additional scholarship from that angle. My own research documenting Steinbeck's alliance with the Communist movement in the 1930s will appear in a forthcoming essay.
7. Ann Loftis, *Witnesses to the Struggle* (Reno: University of Nevada Press, 1998), 54.
8. Sylvia Jenkins Cook's "Steinbeck, the People, and the Party," in *Literature at the Barricades: The American Writer in the 1930s*, ed. Ralph Bogardus and Fred Hobsen (Tuscaloosa: University of Alabama Press, 1982, 82–95, is one of the finest studies of the ideology of the text in Steinbeck's 1930s writings.
9. This term is used on p. xix in Tetsumaro Hayashi, ed., *John Steinbeck: The Years of Greatness, 1936–39* (Tuscaloosa: University of Alabama Press, 1993). Other scholars use similar terms to describe his major writings of the era.
10. Waldo Frank, Henry Roth, Guy Endore, and Fielding Burke immediately come to mind.
11. See the discussion of Le Sueur's work in Alan M. Wald, *Exiles from a Future Time: The Forging of the Mid-Twentieth Century Literary Left* (Chapel Hill: University of North Carolina Press, 2003), pp. 95–100.
12. The landmark discussion of political demonization as the attribution of sinister and pervasive power to a conspiratorial center of evil, is Michael Rogin, *Ronald Reagan: The Movie* (Berkeley: University of California Press, 1988).

13. One of the fullest cases for detaching Steinbeck from the proletarian literary movement appears in Warren French, *The Social Novel at the End of an Era* (Carbondale: Southern Illinois University Press, 1966), in chapter 2, "A Troubled Nation," pp. 42–86. French draws upon a series of earlier arguments for a reading of Steinbeck that affiliates him with "Chestersonian Distributivism" and "Jeffersonian Agrarianism."
14. Cowley's entire essay was reprinted in Henry Dan Piper, ed., *Think Back on Us . . . The Literary Record* (Carbondale: University of Southern Illinois Press, 1967), pp. 347–354.
15. *Ibid.*
16. See Lewis Owens, "Writing in Costume," in *John Steinbeck: The Years of Greatness, 1936–39*, ed. Tetsumaro Hayashi (Tuscaloosa: University of Alabama Press, 1993), pp. 77–94.
17. See the chapters in "Part 1: Steinbeck's Women," in Hayashi, *John Steinbeck: The Years of Greatness*, 3–74.
18. See Charles Cunningham, "Rethinking the Politics of *The Grapes of Wrath*," *Cultural Logic* 5 (2002), http://clogic.eserver.org/2002/cunningham.html.
19. Richard Pells, *Radical Visions and American Dreams: Culture and Social Thought in the Depression Years* (New York: Harper and Row, 1973), pp. 218–219.
20. "Mac is a vicious exponent of Machiavellian opportunism, a supporter of lost causes, a leader of the dispossessed," writes John L. Gribben in "Steinbeck and John Milton," in *Steinbeck's Literary Dimension: A Guide to Comparative Studies*, ed. Tetsumaro Hayashi (Metuchen, NJ: The Scarecrow Press, 1973), p. 103.
21. Of the several essays that argue for Steinbeck's overall sympathy with Mac, the most impressive is Jerry H. Wilson, "*In Dubious Battle*: Engagement in Collectivity," *Steinbeck Quarterly* 13 (1980): 31–42.
22. Steinbeck, influenced by marine biologist Edward Ricketts, used this term to indicate the aim of observing scientifically, without moral judgment or the expectation of change.
23. These details are available in several biographies of Wright, most recently Hazel Rowley, *Richard Wright* (New York: Henry Holt, 2001).
24. This is far from the only debate about proletarian literature that has attracted attention in the past twenty years. Another is the relationship between gender and the proletarian novel, launched most brilliantly in Paula Rabinowitz, *Labor and Desire: Women's Revolutionary Fiction in Depression America* (Chapel Hill: University of North Carolina Press, 1991).
25. I have identified and discussed these and many other titles in Alan M. Wald, *Writing From the Left: New Essays on Radical Culture and Politics* (New York and London: Verso, 1994).
26. In the scholarship of the twenty-first century, explorations of the legacy of the tradition have advanced into two additional areas. One is the post-1930s expansion of mass culture, especially children's literature, science fiction, and detective fiction. The other is the relation of the proletarian novel to multiculturalism. An excellent study of the first area has been published as

Julia L. Mickenberg, *Learning from the Left: Children's Literature, the Cold War, and Radical Politics in the United States* (New York: Oxford University Press, 2006). (See also Mickenberg's essay in this volume [chapter 52, "Children's novels"].) For an overview of the other mass culture fields, see the two entries by Alan Wald in *Encyclopedia of the American Left*, ed. Mary Jo Buhle *et al.*, 2nd edn. (New York: Oxford University Press, 1998): "Science Fiction," pp. 724–726, and "Popular Fiction," 620–627. In regard to multiculturalism, Timothy Libretti has been among the most prolific scholars. See, for instance, "The Other Proletarians: Native American Literature and Class Struggle," *Modern Fiction Studies* 47.1 (Spring 2001): 164–189. Other examples include Jamil Khader, "Transnationalizing Aztlan: Rudolfo Anaya's *Heart of Aztlan* and U.S. Proletarian Literature," MELUS (Spring 2002): 1–13, and Eric Schocket, "Redefining American Proletarian Literarure: Mexican Americans and the Challenge to the Tradition of Racial Dissent," *Journal of American and Comparative Studies* 24.1–2 (2001): 59–62.

41

The novel, mass culture, mass media

MARK McGURL

Already by 1917, if not earlier, the key elements of an agonized preoccupation with mass visual culture in modern American fiction were in place. What would the triumph of spectacle mean for the viability of the printed novel as a cultural form? What would the onslaught of entertaining images do to the reality referenced by novelistic realism? What narrative techniques could the novel borrow from the cinema or television or, barring that, what could it offer in lieu of sights and sounds? What, finally, does the difference between a reader and spectator portend for modern political subjectivity and the forms of cultural authority to which it may respond?

All of these questions are compressed into a fleeting moment in Edith Wharton's short novel, *Summer* (1917), where the issue is, indeed, on any number of levels, compression. Venturing forth from Nettleton, the tiny New England village of her upbringing, to the larger town a buggy and then train ride away, Wharton's protagonist Charity Royall enters what appears to be a movie house, though neither it nor the popular medium for which it provides the setting have yet, for her, acquired their familiar names. The young librarian's experiences there as a consumer of culture could hardly be more distinct from those of the reader of a rigorously realistic novel like *Summer* itself, with its inexorable progression of eminently probable events. The movie house is

> a glittering place – everything she saw seemed to glitter – where they passed, between immense pictures of yellow-haired beauties stabbing villains in evening dress, into a velvet-curtained auditorium packed with spectators to the last limit of compression. After that, for a while, everything was merged in her brain in swimming circles of heat and blinding alternations of light and darkness. All the world has to show seemed to pass before her in a chaos of palms and minarets, charging cavalry regiments, roaring lions, comic policemen and scowling murderers; and the crowd around her, the hundreds of hot

> sallow candy-munching faces, young, old, middle-aged, but all kindled with the same contagious excitement, became part of the spectacle, and danced on the screen with the rest.

Here is one version, among many, of the early twentieth-century trope that would find its most complex and prominent expression in Walter Benjamin's 1936 account of cinema as the shock of the new.[1] For the dazzled bumpkin Charity the palms and minarets and policemen on the screen cause a profound disorientation: how has "all the world has to show" found its way into this one crowded space in the backwater town of Nettleton? And what strange process of agglomeration has beset the individuals among whom she sits?

A creature of Wharton's condescension, Charity isn't equipped to say, but we latter-day sophisticates can supply the analytical term she needs: it is industrial modernity that has occasioned this compression of time and space and identity in the movie house. Unbeknownst to her, the train that carried her to the city with "the descending mob caught . . . on its tide" was already complicit in her cinematic bewilderment, hooking her into a modern communications system, in the broadest sense, extending in all directions across the girth of the globe. As Wolfgang Schivelbusch, Leo Marx, and others have shown, the train had since the mid nineteenth century been the very image of the machine in the garden, the loud smoking harbinger of an ambiguously improved future.[2] In an early instance of the literal kinship of modern cinema to modern travel, Jon Lewis describes how early twentieth-century enterprises like Hale's Tours and Scenes of the World would "contextualize cinema as something of a theme-park ride. Patrons of Hale's Tours paid a uniformed 'train conductor' and entered a theater designed to look like a railroad car. Films displayed by rear-screen projectors played at the front as the cars rocked to simulate an actual train ride."[3] It makes sense that the iconography of train travel – from Lumière's *Arrival of a Train at the Station* (1895) and Edwin Porter's *The Great Train Robbery* (1903) to Buster Keaton's *The General* (1927) and beyond – would frequently be featured in early film as content. The train moves persons and things across the landscape at unprecedented speed, and movie reels do the same, metaphysically.

But in truth, to judge from Charity's reaction to a pious lecture on some paintings she once attended, or to the written notes she receives from her urbane lover Lucius Harney – alike in being utterly "bewildering" to her – it would seem that anything we could plausibly designate as a communication medium might contribute to her existential unsettling. This would accord with a tendency in media theory, in particular the strands emanating from

Marshall McLuhan, to grant any technology the status of "medium" insofar as it becomes the material underpinning, or substrate of, meaningful human experience.[4] As the novel opens Charity is standing at the door of her home looking down the "grassy road that takes the name of street" when it passes through her village. Spotting a strange young man in city clothes walking her way, she turns away from him and "look[s] critically at her reflection" in the hallway mirror, a spasm of vanity that underlines how she, too, no less than any city girl, will be susceptible to a world that produces modern subjectivity in, and as a process of, mediated self-alienation. As Mark Seltzer has noted, it had long been the vocation of the novel genre to "acclimatize" the individual to the "social demands of reflexivity," and *Summer* does this both for its main character and its readers.[5]

Perhaps the movies are distinct from other media forms, including roads and mirrors and novels, only in the intensity and novelty of their unsettling technical operations. Michael North has shown that the flickering of light and dark in the theater (the result of a mismatch between recording and hand-cranked projection frame-rates in the silent era) is compellingly, if metaphorically, continuous with the black and white issue of print technology and also, ultimately, with the binary processes underlying contemporary digital media.[6] All of them present the existential problem of mechanism, which for modern intellectuals such as Lewis Mumford marks an alien (and alienating) industrial systematicity at the very foundation of modern life.[7] Ever after, if only at the margins of our rapt admiration of the power of technology to reshape the world, we catch glimpses of the disquieting specter of a being Mumford called "Post-Historic Man," but which we have recently been wont to call the posthuman.[8] This, put simply, is the human being stripped of his or her metaphysical apartness from and elevation over the natural and technological worlds.

Low-tech literature most often forgets its implication in this techno-mediatic system, understanding itself instead – and this is particularly true of the project of literary regionalism of which *Summer* is a semi-dissident instance – as a therapeutic antidote to modern ills.[a] The technologies upon which literature depends were developed so long ago as to have become entirely naturalized, if not simply invisible, hiding from us the truth that a book, no less than a cell phone or PDA, is a kind of meaning-bearing gadget.[b]

a For a more thorough account of the purposes of literary regionalism, see Tom Lutz, "Cather and the regional imagination," chapter 26 in this volume.

b For more on the book as one form of technology among others, see Robert Coover, "A history of the future of narrative," chapter 71 in this volume.

True, the novel is consumed privately and quietly, and the images in which it traffics can only be produced with the individual reader's help. In this sense, the ideology of individualism to which the novel has been so largely dedicated is reinforced in phenomenological practice. And yet the standardized print on the page, put there by Gutenberg's machine, points to the systems that have defined, in advance and from without, the readerly interiority activated by the book.

The story of the modern novel's relation to mass culture and mass media is therefore not simply one of hostile status differentiation, although there has been plenty of this, but of an intimacy that keeps asserting itself even when the writer attempts to hold it at bay. It is an intimacy sustained by the writer's dependency on the technical, economic, and social system underlying his or her endeavor. This system presents a permanent, if maddeningly polymorphous, challenge to the writer's individual authority and even, ultimately, his or her professional existence. However briefly, Charity meets modernity. She meets movies, and in meeting movies meets the possible obsolescence of the printed texts whose moldering she oversees – with no interest at all in reading them – as the village librarian. Without necessarily knowing it, she witnesses a challenge to one print genre in particular, the one that contains her, which had once upon a time seemed quite modern enough.

In themselves there is nothing "modernist" about the images Charity sees – they are hackneyed clichés, exactly the kind of thing literary modernism would want to ironize if not abolish – but the technical means of their presentation makes them inadvertently avant-garde. It is indeed as though Wharton has discovered the experiential datum that, combined with any number of other motives, drives the experimental impulse in modern literature. The irony is that, for all that Wharton was a champion of modern improvements, and unusually unsentimental about the backwardness of people like Charity (this is what made Wharton a dissident regionalist), she would live to see her own literary techniques, and to some extent her own cultural authority, outmoded. A decade or so later a self-consciously avant-garde writer, John Dos Passos, would attempt to replicate the hypermediated quality of modernity in works like the *U.S.A. Trilogy* (1930–1936), where an energetic jumble of narrative elements, including sections called "camera eye" and "newsreels," mimes the infestation of history and identity by mechanical media. And this was only the most literal registration of the industrial modern in the form of narrative fragmentation. But even Dos Passos was not content to let chaos have the last word. Part of his inspiration for the techniques used in his quasi-cinematic novels was none other than filmmaker D. W. Griffith, and as did the latter in *Birth of a Nation* (1915), Dos Passos aspired ultimately to synthesize the diversity of narrative elements in his text in a unified epic-novelistic portrait of the United States of America.

Does Dos Passos "critique" the mass media whose forms he borrows, or do his works amount to capitulations to the new technical regime? His highly critical depiction, in the third novel of the trilogy, *The Big Money* (1936), of the career of Margo Dowling in Hollywood would suggest a continuing sense of critical distance. As summarized by Donald Pizer, "Dos Passos's Hollywood consists of megalomaniacal directors with phony foreign backgrounds, reluctant upper-class stars, and dumb studlike leading men, all of whom are committed to kinky sex and studio double-dealing politics while purveying on screen a world of never-never romance."[9] But perhaps, even despite this theme-based critique, Dos Passos's technical borrowings from film attest to the existence of a system of cultural representation that now includes literary modernism as one of its charmingly obstreperous subsystems.

Consider, for instance, Nathanael West's *The Day of the Locust* (1936), a quintessentially modernist text, but also one that seems, to many of its critics, to have absorbed more than a little of the cinematic into its storytelling form.[10] Is this absorption a one-way affair? For American writers of the 1930s, Hollywood loomed large as a powerful competitor in the business of storytelling, representing the final triumph of mass taste, sentimentality, and factory production over the higher forms of narrative art. At the same time – never mind the simple act of selling the rights to one's novels to Hollywood, which few could resist – venturing into the camp of the enemy as a highly paid screenwriter became a strong temptation for the likes of William Faulkner, F. Scott Fitzgerald, Dos Passos, and West himself. The Yale-trained protagonist of *The Day of the Locust*, Tod Hackett, is a painter who has come to Los Angeles to work on movie sets, but he is an obvious stand-in for the squads of British and American novelists and playwrights who were recruited to the dream factory upon the sudden advent of the talkies in the late 1920s, when the number of scripted words needed to make a movie exponentially increased.

Taking up residence in what Faulkner, with acid irony, called the "Golden Land," they were subjected to a profoundly different model of authorship – corporate authorship – than the unitary one to which they had always been accustomed.[11] If the novelist was an autonomous craftsman or professional, the screenwriter was an industrial employee, and no less alienated than the factory worker from the product of his labor. Tragicomic tales of the indignities attendant to this highly paid proletariat were legion. The effect of the movie on the audience in Wharton's Nettleton is one of literal massification – "young, old, middle-aged, but all kindled with the same contagious excitement" – and the same is true, although now conflictually, of a form of authorship in which the individual signature is submerged in a collective scripting process. This process was managed from without by the director and producer, in whom is vested the executive authority once claimed by the writer. As Monroe Stahr, the title character of F. Scott Fitzgerald's *The Last Tycoon* (1940) puts it, "I'm the unity." But even he, as the title makes clear, is the last of a dying breed. The future belongs to crowds.

On one level the contempt *The Day of the Locust* displays for the capital of twentieth-century mass culture, Los Angeles, could hardly be more intense. L.A. stands accused, first of all, of being tacky, a supreme violation of modernist urges toward aesthetic purity and medium specificity. Charity's movie house condenses a riot of unrelated images, and so, according to West, does the real place called Hollywood, California: as though in sympathy with the exotic inauthenticities of the studio lots themselves, the neighborhoods beyond their gates are a jumble of "Mexican ranch houses, Samoan huts, Mediterranean villas, Egyptian and Japanese temples, Swiss chalets, Tudor cottages and every possible combination of these styles . . ." The lots themselves amount to what West memorably calls a "dream dump," a junkyard of the imagination. Crucial to both the cinematic and architectural versions of cultural condensation is a certain "weightlessness" of the medium of expression: the plaster and paper that make up the houses of Hollywood "know no law, not even that of gravity." If literary realism in the Jamesian tradition can be understood as a kind of submission to the burdens of natural and social law, popular culture has no such limits. It goes wherever it wants to, even into space, probability and physics be damned.

Benjamin describes the purpose of the new medium of film in surprisingly functional terms as "*to train human beings in the apperceptions and reactions needed to deal with a vast apparatus*" – modern industrial technology – "*whose role in their lives is expanding almost daily.*"[12] The fear held by people like Lewis Mumford and Nathanael West was that this adaptation was making people into machines. Tod is surrounded in *The Day of the Locust* by characters like the movie cowboy Earle, who is handsome like a "mechanical drawing," and Homer, who ends up walking around "like a badly made automaton," but most importantly by Faye Greener, the femme fatale wannabe movie star whose very interiority seems to have become mechanized. As she tells Tod, it is her habit to sort through her stock of fantasies like a pack of cards until she finds one that suits her mood, a process she admits is "too mechanical for the best results" but which she must execute anyway, having no access to "natural" dreams. As Mumford would one day put it, "Even a large part of our fantasies are no longer self-begotten: they have no reality, no viability, until they are harnessed to the machine."[13]

Even more troubling is the way the aggregate of these mechanical people, these desiring machines, can so easily become a violently frustrated mob. The biblical "day of the locust" of West's title is of course the era of the modern crowd. This is the time of the masses who, as Benjamin had it, will no longer stand for the "distance" that facilitates and maintains the artwork's aura. As in Charity's movie house, all that the world has to show must be brought home, made familiar; otherwise things could get ugly. The association of mass culture with the fascist mob would endure in the widespread hostility on the part of 1950s intellectuals even to the quieter forms of mass culture, like paperback genre fiction.[c] It was on these grounds that book reviewers could describe the detective-vigilante novels of Mickey Spillane as "Gestapo" training manuals.[14] In West's novel the inability of mass culture to deliver on its promises of transcendence leads finally to an explosion of rage in the form of a riot, as the audience of a movie premiere "realize that they've been tricked and burn with resentment . . . Nothing can ever be violent enough to make taut their slack minds and bodies. They have been cheated and betrayed."

Not surprisingly, one of the victims of this riot is the high culture figure, Tod. Radicalizing the image of the absorption of the artist by Hollywood, he is swept up in a rush of bodies that seems simultaneously an advance and a regression in both a literal and figurative sense. His predicament at the movie premiere is a parable, almost, of the loss of a natural reference point for the artist as well as the loss of his artistic autonomy: "He was within a few feet of the tree [he was trying to grab] when a sudden, driving rush carried him far past it. He struggled desperately for a moment, then gave up and let himself be swept along . . . [H]e was turned again and again, like a grain between millstones." A scene like this suggests why, as Thomas Strychasz has convincingly shown, the novel is not most powerfully read either as a simple rejection of mass culture by modernism or a gleeful participation in its phantasmagoria.[15] Instead, in his account, it must be read as an agonized meditation on the always potential collapse of the critical distance between the modern artist and the mass culture he inhabits.

c Sean McCann is able to offer a much richer account of the complex relations between modernism and genre fiction in "The novel of crime, mystery, and suspense," chapter 48 in this volume. For a broader account of the rise of paperback fiction, see also James L. W. West III, "Twentieth-century publishing and the rise of the paperback," chapter 47.

As Tod is carried along in excruciating pain, he begins to imagine that he can escape his situation and return to work on his painting, his would-be apocalyptic masterpiece, "The Burning of Los Angeles." He has been working on this work of high art for so long that "the way to it in his mind [has] become almost automatic." Here, on one level, is an image of the transcendence of mass culture by high culture, which presumes to include mass culture in its Bosch-like apocalyptic designs; but on another level this is an image of the triumph of mechanism (note that his path has become "automatic," just as Faye's fantasies had been), which now puts a high art option in the vending machine of cultural escapism.

West's was of course not the only iteration of the vexed relation of modern literature to mass culture in the 1930s, and *Locust* does not begin to exhaust the implications of that relation. A substantially different version of the literary struggle with the mass media is enacted in John Steinbeck's *The Grapes of Wrath*, which he wrote at precisely the moment he was becoming fascinated by the storytelling possibilities of film. The novel was published in April of 1939, and within a week film rights to the story had been purchased by Darryl Zanuck of Twentieth Century Fox for the considerable sum of $75,000. After just nine months for scripting, casting, set design, shooting, editing, packaging, and promotion, the film premiered in January 1940, while the novel was still on the bestseller list. The film, too, directed by John Ford, became a critical and popular hit. The success, simultaneity, and, to a certain degree, shared identity of the two works assured that the relation of one to the other would be a matter of some dispute.

At issue, foremost, was the political relation of the two works: how would a protest novel – Malcolm Cowley called it one of the "great angry books," the sort that "rouse" a "people to fight against intolerable wrongs"[16] – fare in its translation to the screen?[d] (Among those who thought there might be a problem with this translation (including the author himself), thinking took two interestingly complementary forms. Conservatives like Martin Quigley worried that movies are "no place for social, political, and economic argument."[17] Spokesmen for the California corporate agriculture interests, who were already waging a campaign against the novel, seconded this view. On the left, conversely, the worry was that Steinbeck's justly wrathful novel would be watered down by Zanuck on its way to the screen. Rumors circulated that he had

d A longer history of the protest novel as an important form in American literary history is available in Cecelia Tichi, "Novels of civic protest," chapter 23 in this volume. See Alan Wald, "Steinbeck and the proletarian novel," chapter 40 in this volume, for a more thorough account of Steinbeck's political commitments.

bought the story on orders from the banks in the East that controlled the major studios, including his own Twentieth Century Fox, merely to shelve it. After all, the film industry had consistently aligned itself with its fellow California corporate entities, most notoriously through a studio-produced media smear campaign to defeat the candidacy of Upton Sinclair, running on the End Poverty in California (EPIC) platform, for California governor. Steinbeck himself, at any rate, thought the threat of sanitization by Hollywood great enough that he held Zanuck's $75,000 in escrow with the threat to use it to sue the studio in the event that the novel's message was distorted.

Steinbeck never did file suit, even though several structural changes were made to his story that could be said to blunt its messages. Besides the expected omission of materials from the long novel, they mainly take the form of a reordering of its events. For example, the novel does not end, as the film does, with the optimistically eugenic populism of Ma Joad (played by Jane Darwell): "That's what makes us tough. Rich fellas come up and they die and their kids aint no good and they die out, but we keep a' comin'. We're the people that live. They can't wipe us out, they can't lick us. We'll go on forever, Pa, 'cause we're the people." Granted that "the people" of this novel are a far more noble instance of the social aggregate than Nathanael West's mob, but this hardly seems a plan for political action. Ma Joad's words visually echo in the movement of the truck across the screen. As much a symbol of mechanical motion as the railroad train, the truck will apparently continue to drive onward indefinitely, though the credits now begin to roll. Some of the significance of this final image of movement becomes obvious when we place it next to Tom Joad's famous final speech, which in the novel, though not in the movie, comes very near its conclusion, there to operate (or so it might appear) as a declaration of radical political intent:

> "Well, maybe like Casy says, a fella ain't got a soul of his own, but on'y a piece of a big one – an' then – "
>
> "Then what, Tom?"
>
> "Then it don' matter. Then I'll be all aroun' in the dark. I'll be ever'where – wherever you look. Wherever they's a fight so hungry people can eat, I'll be there. Wherever they's a cop beatin' up a guy, I'll be there . . . I'll be in the way guys yell when they're mad . . ."
>
> "I don' un'erstan'," Ma said. "I don' really know."
>
> "Me neither," said Tom. "It's just stuff I've been thinkin' about. Get thinkin' a lot when you ain't movin' aroun'."

By way of this speech, one could say, the selfish individual of classical, free-market liberalism is threatened with the collective action of a proletariat

Oversoul. But note Tom's opposition, here, of "movin' aroun'" to political "thinkin'," the latter understood to be a product of stasis. In the context of an unsettling industrial modernity, this opposition suggests that the film has ceded the activist symbolism of "social movement" in favor of a submission to the law of technological mobility. That the film ends not with this speech but with a more open-ended vision of "movin' aroun'" might seem further to support the argument that the film de-radicalizes the book.

If so, this wasn't noticed by the book's author. In fact, he thought it a "hard, straight picture" in which no "punches were pulled" and a "harsher thing than the book, by far."[18] Edmund Wilson offers one way of explaining this equanimity. In his study of California writers, *The Boys in the Back Room* (1941), he argues that

> Since the people who control the movies will not go a step of the way to give the script writer a chance to do a serious script, the novelist seems, consciously or unconsciously, to be going part of the way to meet the producers. John Steinbeck, in *The Grapes of Wrath*, has certainly learned from the films – and not only from the documentary pictures of Pare Lorentz [director of *The Plow that Broke the Plains* (1936), a documentary about the Dust Bowl], but from the sentimental symbolism of Hollywood. The result was that *The Grapes of Wrath* went on the screen as easily as if it had been written in the studios.[19]

Wilson claims not that the film was faithful to the novel, but that the book was prospectively faithful to the film that would be made from it. In this view, the novel's "sentimental symbolism," its imbrication in a modern economy of emotions, is legible as an imperative to be moving in still another sense. This is the sense referenced in the title of Ben Singer's study of early film, *Melodrama and Modernity*, where there is no contradiction between modern technology and human emotion – where, indeed, one is the medium of the other.[20] Perhaps, then, it is not simply that Steinbeck's novel has absorbed some of the storytelling techniques of Hollywood, as Dos Passos's *U.S.A.* Trilogy and *West's Day of the Locust* had. It has also absorbed some of its technicity – its thoroughgoing commitment to the merging of modern identity in and with modern technology.

Returning to the beginning of the novel with this in mind, the novel's technicity becomes visible even before the arrival in California. A crucial turn in the westward career of the Joads occurs somewhere in Texas, when the strong thematic link the novel has drawn between uprooting and death is reversed and modern deracination becomes, instead, a new way of life: "Two days the families were in flight, but on the third the land was too huge for them and they settled into a new technique of living; the highway became their home and movement their medium of expression." So recently evicted from the land they have inhabited for generations, the Joads can't quite be said to be getting their kicks on Route 66, but they do seem to be undergoing a profound change of sensibility there. Back on the farm it had seemed that life and identity were only thinkable as stasis. This is the stasis of stable traditions, but it is also the retrospective siting of individual memory, where personhood is constituted in relation to the stable objects in one's environment: "I've been goin' aroun' the places where stuff happened," says Tom Joad's erstwhile neighbor Muley soon after Tom returns to a home that has been emptied of his family and literally knocked askew from its foundation by a corporate-owned tractor. "Place where folks live is them folks. They ain't whole, out lonely on the road in a piled-up car. They ain't alive no more."

But now it appears, on the contrary, that even "movement" can be "settled into," as a once-murderous mobility becomes, instead, the body's new routine. Families like the Joads want a home, too, or so we are led to assume, but as the story progresses the notion of their final "arrival" there grows increasingly hard to imagine. The phrase "technique of living" should prick the ears of readers of Steinbeck, an author we tend to think of as offering organic rather than technical-artificial metaphors for the, say, turtle-like struggle of human life. The conceptualization of mechanized movement as itself a "medium of expression" twists the narrative upon itself in such a way as to produce a seam through which we can glimpse a primitive affinity between the novel's form as linear narrative and its many moving themes. John Steinbeck is in other words a practitioner of what we might call, although it seems like it should be a contradiction in terms, the posthuman sentimental, where systems and affects come intimately together. The "ever-onward" sentiments of the movie version simply make this truth about the novel all the more visible.[21]

The term that best expresses this complex of interactions across the nature/artifice divide is the one that Marshall McLuhan and Neil Postman used to describe their respective research programs: "media ecology." This term would break down the distance between natural systems, or ecosystems, and artificial ones like the railway or the highway or cinema and television. A media ecology – literally – is what Chance the gardener inhabits in Jerzy Kosinski's *Being There* (1971), certainly the best-known literary critique of a culture enframed, not by movies, but by television. This is a culture, more precisely, of "vidiocy," in which the television has succeeded the movies as the primary challenger to the cultural authority of the novel, which now indeed could align itself with movies against the new scourge. Movies might make the novel look small, but the television encroached upon the inviolate domestic sphere where the novel had always ruled more or less unchallenged. As the novel opens, Kosinski's illiterate simpleton is enjoying life in the walled garden he has inhabited his entire life, never once venturing into the city outside. His innocence and isolation are even more extreme than Charity's, but they have been subjected to an interesting shift. Charity had to travel quite a ways to encounter the modernity of the movies. In the village her thrills had been restricted to lying on the grass of a summer's day, "her face pressed to the grass and the warm currents of the grass running through her." Chance by contrast lives with an electrical current and even has a television; watching it is the only thing he does besides working in the garden.

Both the garden and the television provide forms of domestic enclosure – "environments" in the strict sense – but the television is if anything more edenic than the garden in its ability to triumph over natural and social law: "Chance went inside and turned on the TV. The set created its own light, its own color, its own time. It did not follow the law of gravity that forever bent all plants downward." Here again is the modern compression of time and space and identity: "By changing the channel he could change himself," and just like those transported moviegoers in Wharton's Nettleton he can "spread out into the screen without stopping, just as on TV people spread out into the screen." There are no pockets of premodernity in the world of *Being There*: media are everywhere, and the regionalist paradigm of rural removal toward authenticity is no longer viable, if it had ever been.

The collapse of the distinction between nature and media in *Being There* becomes clear when the Old Man who has kept Chance in the garden his whole life (we suspect that Chance is his unmentionable lovechild) suddenly dies and the house is sold. Expelled from Eden, Chance now becomes subject to the uncertainties of the modern, and indeed is immediately hit by a limousine in the street. Since, having borrowed his clothes from the Old Man, he looks the part of a prosperous businessman, this accident of fate begins his rapid ascent as a conservative culture hero. Within days he has the ear of the President, and his homilies on the seasonal cycles of his garden are taken, instead, as optimistic pronouncements on the cyclical nature of the market.

Kosinski's point would seem to be that the regime of vidiocy, in which the novelist is an anachronism, extends far beyond the boundaries of the box and the living room in which it is watched. In *Being There* all the world has become TV, and traditional distinctions – not only between nature and artifice, reality and fiction, but also between the abjectly ignorant and the knowledgeable – have been "smoothed out."[e] Rather than personifying uncertainty, the man named "Chance" personifies a paradoxically ambient improbability, the rise of a really unrealistic world. This is a world in which an illiterate simpleton, knowing nothing but what he has seen on TV, can be asked (as it seems certain Chance will be at the novel's close) to run for Vice President. His rapid ascent to power comments most directly on the fate of political authority in the day of the locust, but it has unmistakable implications for the cultural authority of the novelist as well. It is perhaps only natural that, faced with constant intimations of his irrelevance to the wider culture, he might seek to transform himself, as Jerzy Kosinski himself notoriously did, into a celebrity looking forward to the next of his many appearances on the *Tonight Show*.

And is that the end of it? Will the novel finally be swallowed by the mass media systems whose spread it has both exemplified and analyzed? Perhaps, although the frequency with which critics, like End-time prophets, have been wont to pronounce the imminent "death of the novel" over the course of the twentieth century might well give one pause. As a form, the novel is nothing if not adaptable – in many senses, including the film adaptation – and there still seem to be a great many of them being written.

Notes

1. Walter Benjamin, "The Work of Art in the Age of Its Technological Reproducibility," in *The Work of Art in the Age of Its Technological Reproducibility and Other Writings on Media* (Cambridge, MA: Harvard University Press, 2008).
2. See Wolfgang Schivelbusch, *The Railway Journey: The Industrialization of Time and Space in the 19th Century* (Berkeley: University of California Press, 1986); Leo Marx, *The Machine in the Garden: Technology and the Pastoral Ideal in America* (New York: Oxford University Press, 1964).
3. Jon Lewis, *American Film: A History* (New York and London: Norton, 2008), 16.
4. See Lance Strate, *Echoes and Reflections: On Media Ecology as a Field of Study* (Cresskill, NJ: Hampton Press, 2006), 23.
5. Mark Seltzer, *True Crime: Observations on Violence and Modernity* (New York and London: Routledge, 2007), 69.
6. See Michael North, *Camera Works: Photography and the Twentieth Century Word* (New York: Oxford University Press, 2007).

e While I have been arguing for the importance of other media to twentieth-century fiction more broadly, see Ursula Heise's "Postmodern novels," chapter 58 in this volume, for a discussion of the importance of television and other visual media to postmodern fiction in particular. See especially 973–978.

7. See for instance Friedrich Kittler, trans. Michael Metteer, *Discourse Networks: 1800/1900* (Stanford, CA: Stanford University Press, 1990).
8. Lewis Mumford, *Art and Technics* (New York: Columbia University Press, 2000), 84.
9. Quoted in Justin Edwards, "Man with a Camera Eye: Cinematic Form and Hollywood Malediction in John Dos Passos's The Big Money," *Literature Film Quarterly* (January 1, 1999): 6. Edwards argues that the stronger influence on Dos Passos than Griffith was Sergei Eisenstein.
10. See Thomas Strychacz, *Modernism, Mass Culture, and Professionalism* (Cambridge: Cambridge University Press, 1993), 188.
11. William Faulkner, "Golden Land," in *Collected Stories of William Faulkner* (New York: Vintage, 1995), 701–726.
12. Benjamin, "The Work of Art in the Age of Its Technological Reproducibility," 38, italics in original.
13. Mumford, *Art and Technics*, 6
14. Quoted in Jesse Berrett, "Gresham's Law of Culture: The Case of Mickey Spillane and Postwar America," in *Scorned Literature: Essays on the History and Criticism of Popular Mass-Produced Fiction in America* (Westport, CT: Greenwood Press, 2002) 3.
15. Strychacz, *Modernism, Mass Culture, and Professionalism*, 194.
16. Quoted in Jay Parini, *John Steinbeck: A Biography* (New York: Henry Holt, 1995), 269.
17. Quoted in Warren French, ed., *A Companion to The Grapes of Wrath* (New York: Viking, 1963), 164.
18. Parini, *John Steinbeck*, 288.
19. Edmund Wilson, *The Boys in the Back Room: Notes on California Novelists* (San Francisco, Colt Press, 1941), 61.
20. Ben Singer, *Melodrama and Modernity: Early Sensation Cinema and Its Contexts* (New York: Columbia University Press, 2001).
21. Michael Szalay has argued for an updated, New Deal sentimentalism in *The Grapes of Wrath*; see *New Deal Modernism: American Literature and the Invention of the Welfare State* (Durham, NC: Duke University Press, 2000), chapter 4.

42

Wright, Hurston, and the direction of the African American novel

VALERIE BABB

In *New Masses* Richard Wright reviewed Zora Neale Hurston's *Their Eyes Were Watching God* (1937) and observed, "The sensory sweep of her novel carries no theme, no message, no thought . . . She exploits that phase of Negro life which is 'quaint,' the phase which evokes a piteous smile on the lips of the 'superior' race." In the *Saturday Review of Literature* Hurston responded in kind six months later, characterizing Wright's *Uncle Tom's Children* (1938) as "a book about hatreds . . . His stories are so grim that the Dismal Swamp of race hatred must be where they live . . . Since the author is himself a Negro, his dialect is a puzzling thing . . . Certainly he does not write by ear unless he is tone-deaf."[1] The polarity of writerly visions implied in these reviews provides a useful way of examining the contentious issues of appropriate racial representation and artistic choice engaging African American novelists from the 1920s to the 1950s. Wright's concern with a white audience reveals the tremendous pressure placed on writers to portray the race in a "proper" light; Hurston's mention of Wright's awkward dialect shows respect for indigenous black forms as legitimate sources for literary art.[2] One vision stresses the imperative of literature to transform social opinion; the other, the imperative to be true to cultural spirit; and both stress the need to adopt and adapt strategies to craft a literature revealing the worth of black existence and the beauty of black art.

The validity of black being was by no means a given in a United States less than four score beyond slavery. Cultural discourse still included debates over whether blacks were fully human and deserving of equal rights. In this climate, literature and art were drafted to prove black merit. In an 1880 journal entry, for example, Charles Chesnutt argued that "The subtle almost indefinable feeling of repulsion toward the Negro, which is common to most Americans . . . cannot be stormed and taken by assault." Instead, "their position must be mined . . . The negro's part is to prepare himself for social recognition and equality; and it is the province of literature to open the way for him to get it."[3] Shortly after Chesnutt, thinkers such as Alain Locke and W. E. B. Du Bois would reassert the role of the arts as a means through which white America's negative perceptions of African Americans could be changed.

Locke, the first African American to receive a Rhodes scholarship, was guest editor for the *Survey Graphic* special edition, *Harlem: Mecca of the New Negro* (1925). For the issue he gathered articles, poems, fiction, and art of the leading talents of the time. Less than a year later, he republished much of the content as *The New Negro* (1925), an anthology that became one of the most influential products of the New Negro movement and the Harlem Renaissance.[4] In his introductory essay Locke wrote, "Our greatest rehabilitation may possibly come through . . . the revaluation by white and black alike of the Negro in terms of his artistic endowments and cultural contributions."[5] In "Criteria of Negro Art" (1926) W. E. B. Du Bois more strongly stated the expectation that art should be engaged in social change. "All art is propaganda," he wrote, "and ever must be, despite the wailing of the purists."[6] Locke and Du Bois express the desire for an African American artistic tradition that would make self-evident the equality of the culture producing it. For them and others, then, it was crucial that African American writing reflect the "best" of the race.

Contending conceptions of what constituted the "best" made their way into the themes and textures of the major novels of this period as writers extended the stylistic innovations first seen in the post-Reconstruction novel. According to Barbara McCaskill, "Such novels . . . incorporate, and at times revise, influential elements from existing African American expressive, performative, and narrative traditions" while they argue for racial equality.[a] By the 1920s these traditions had evolved into a variety of artistic strategies. One group, including Claude McKay, Langston Hughes, and Zora Neale Hurston, celebrated black vernacular material as an appropriate means of portraying black life, precisely because the sources were indigenous. Other authors such as Richard Wright and Ann Petry saw realism and an urban naturalism as vehicles for their themes. Jessie Fauset and Nella Larsen redacted existing literary forms such as the Austenesque novel of manners to black life, while Jean Toomer (who rejected racial categorization, preferring to identify himself simply as an American) used memory and place to create *Cane* (1923), a genre-defying tribute to African American rural and urban life.

a Barbara McCaskill, "The African American novel after Reconstruction," chapter 29, 484.

It may seem odd to include Toomer's *Cane* in a history of the American novel because it does not conform to the sustained narrative generally associated with traditional novelistic structure; instead, it replicates communal narrative through pieces that reference one another and characters that appear in more than one segment. *Cane* mixes poetry, prose, elements of drama, African American work songs, and spirituals to present a spectrum of African American responses to removal from Africa, the legacies of enslavement, and the re-creation of African-derived culture in the United States. The book's three parts reflect a classic black migratory pattern, from rural South to urban North, and, in its ending, back to rural South. Inspired by Toomer's sojourn in Sparta, Georgia, *Cane* is elegiac. By creating a call and response between black past and present, it laments a "sun . . . setting / on a song-lit race of slaves." In "Song of the Son" and "Georgia Dusk" undercurrents of past enslavement undulate through verses memorializing the beauty of rural black life, while the urban landscape of "Seventh Street" starkly draws the city as anti-pastoral. Combining prose, dramatic form, and a plot of reverse migration "Kabnis" intertwines all of Toomer's themes – the importance of cultural memory, legacies of race, and the confluence of space and identity. *Cane*'s dialogue between the natural and the social landscapes of black life, its meshing of orality and written traditions, make it one of the most stylistically innovative works of the early twentieth century, lying squarely within the emerging tradition of modernist experimentation.[b]

Walter White's *The Fire in the Flint* (1924) appeared a year after *Cane*, but the renderings of the South in these two works could not be more different. *Cane*'s impressionistic imagery expresses "rememory" of the black South while White's verisimilitude urges transformation of it.[7] *Cane* presages novels such as Hurston's that mined the black Southern past for rich vernacular discoveries, while *Flint* foreshadows works such as Wright's that cast the region as a painful locus to escape. From 1918 to 1928, as then assistant field secretary for the National Association for the Advancement of Colored People (NAACP), White traveled extensively and often passed as white to chronicle race riots as well as lynchings.[8] *The Fire in the Flint* gave fictive form to the brutality he witnessed. Though very didactic, it nonetheless powerfully evokes the confinement and arbitrary abuse of African Americans in the segregated South. Using African American veterans as symbols of the United States' hypocrisy in

b For a discussion of the impact modernism would have on novelistic fiction in the United States, see Peter Nicholls, "Hemingway, Stein, and American modernisms," chapter 37 in this volume.

asking black Americans to fight for a democracy in which they could not share – a theme that would recur in subsequent novels of the time – White tells the story of Kenneth Harper, a graduate of Atlanta University and an unnamed northern medical school whose attendance at the Sorbonne and European military service mean nothing when he returns to his segregated Georgia. White's investigative reporting influences his detailed portrayals of the lynchings at the novel's core and the perversity of a practice in which a twelve-year-old boy darts into dying flames to emerge "laughing hoarsely, triumphantly exhibiting a charred bone" the family would later display on the mantle.

White's second novel, *Flight* (1926), is the story of Mimi Daquin, the daughter of Louisiana *gens de couleur libre*, who ultimately realizes the costs of passing as white and reclaims her black antecedents. *Flight* displays conventions that might be termed tropes in 1920s-era novels treating black subject matter. Often in these works there is a journey motif, from south to north, reflecting the Great Migration, or from the United States to Europe, reflecting increasing black expatriatism. Black character types – the entertainer, the intellectual, the returning WWI soldier, the black striver – represent varying facets of race progress. Characters' discussions of racism, the aesthetics of European versus African art, and "high" versus "low" culture replicate debates of the time. These novels invariably reference the iconic significance of Harlem, variously referred to as the City of Refuge, the Cultural Capital of African America, the Mecca of the New Negro, the City within a City. In addition to providing a backdrop against which to conjure modern black life, Harlem offered writers the opportunity to vivify black cultural contributions to distinctly American culture, among these jazz, dances such as the Charleston and the Lindy, and the blues.

Ironically, one such novel that took Harlem as its core inspiration became a lightning rod for controversy, raising questions of cultural ownership, appropriation, and representation. Carl Van Vechten's *Nigger Heaven* (1926) clearly reflects a love of things black and things urban, but many complained that the prolific output of this white American writer sensationalized black life and glamorized black decadence. Through urban settings, period details, and characters that often represented actual individuals, Van Vechten fashioned entertaining portraits of what was popularly termed the Jazz Age.[9] His *Nigger Heaven* did the same for 1920s African American cultural life. Characteristic of the Harlem novel, it contains long digressions into aesthetics and philosophies of racial uplift. Harlem's local color is represented through cabarets, street corners, and exquisitely appointed black salons.[10] In the treatment of its material, *Nigger Heaven* seems a novel with a split personality. On the one hand it embraces the sensational and sexually explicit; on the other hand, it reveres African American art of the time. Van Vechten portrays African Americans as having a "primitive birthright . . . that all the civilized races were struggling to get back to"; yet, amid what may be viewed as a fetishizing of the primitive is also thoughtful aesthetic admiration. The 1926 edition featured cover art by Aaron Douglass, and the seventh printing published in 1927 included "songs and snatches of Blues" by Langston Hughes.[11] Nonetheless, because Van Vechten was a white author his novel is often viewed as an act of cultural appropriation in which an outsider poses as an authority explaining the significance of things black.

Nigger Heaven was caught in the middle of the presentation/representation contention. Anticipating later writers such as McKay, Hughes, and Hurston, Van Vechten desired a celebration of black vernacular elements, but with such a provocative title and content, his novel inevitably became the target of criticism addressing not only cultural representation, but also cultural ownership. Should Van Vechten, as a white man, have presumed to take liberties with content he may know well but is nevertheless not his own? W. E. B. Du Bois clearly thought not. In a review of the novel for *Crisis*, he referred to its portraits of black life as a "blow in the face."[12] In his memoir *Along This Way* (1933), James Weldon Johnson identified the novel's major problem as its title: "Most of the Negroes who condemned *Nigger Heaven* did not read it; they were stopped by the title."[13]

Van Vechten was not the only writer to be sharply criticized for his portrayal of black life. Another was the black Jamaican Claude McKay. Well known for his poetry, McKay also authored three novels, *Home to Harlem* (1928), *Banjo* (1929), and *Banana Bottom* (1933). In a review of *Home to Harlem* W. E. B. Du Bois wrote, "It looks as though . . . McKay has set out to cater for that prurient demand on the part of white folk . . . He has used every art and emphasis to paint drunkenness, fighting, lascivious sexual promiscuity and utter absence of restraint in as bold and as bright colors as he can."[14] What Du Bois read as negative, McKay's novel presents as a positive celebration of the folk elements of Harlem. The protagonist Jake returns from World War I, a deserter not because of cowardice but because he can no longer tolerate the racism and hypocrisy that existed amidst an ostensible fight for democracy. His return to Harlem unifies McKay's picaresque plot while offering vignettes of the Harlem landscape. For McKay, folk material made black literary art unique, and he would return to it in his next novel, but this time he would take the action abroad.

Banjo, with multiracial, multinational, multi-ethnic content, expresses the global dimensions of black experience. Harlem is replaced by Marseilles, France, which McKay describes as a place of "picturesque proletarians from far waters whose names were warm with romance: the Caribbean, the Gulf of Guinea, the Persian Gulf, the Bay of Bengal, the China Seas, the Indian Archipelago." Like all port cities, Marseilles is a center of cultural hybridity, and with this setting, McKay shows black identity to consist of more than African American elements. Though *Banjo*'s celebration of the vagabond life ran counter to New Negro themes of racial uplift, it nonetheless provided a unique showcase for the richness of African-derived cultures. Unabashed by criticism that he was not representing the "best elements" of black life, McKay once again embraced this content in his next, perhaps most masterful novel, *Banana Bottom*. Set in turn-of-the-century Jamaica, *Banana Bottom* has a post-colonial emphasis, examining racial legacies of the colonial and imperialist systems. In the novel a young woman, Bita Plant, is informally adopted by white missionaries who sent her to England for education. She returns home and finds herself an oddity to her people and an experiment to her white sponsors. She is torn between what McKay casts as an atavistic yearning to be part of her traditions and the obligation she feels to live the well-structured life her benefactors have planned for her, right down to the selection of a prospective spouse. Bita's homecoming allows McKay to display cultural forms devalued under colonialism and argue for their validity. Both *Banjo* and *Banana Bottom* show the range of indigenous elements available to those writers across the black diaspora who were less concerned with transforming social opinion than with being true to cultural spirit.[15] *Banana Bottom* thus expands the novel of this period to include black diasporic dimensions.

As the African American novel continued to evolve through the 1930s, black novelists' increasing desire to control literary portraiture of the race became more evident. Jessie Fauset, for example, began her writing career with *There is Confusion* (1924), a novel written in response to Thomas Sigismund (T. S.) Stribling's *Birthright* (1922).[16] Holding degrees from Cornell and the University of Pennsylvania, Fauset served as editor for *Crisis* magazine from 1919 to 1926, encouraging and publishing writers such as Hughes, McKay, and Nella Larsen. Feeling the need for a more realistic commentary on black life, Fauset employed traditional novelistic forms to her own ends. She made frequent use of images of domesticity, love, and marriage to critique the perversion of human relations by societal racism, classism, and colorism. Her focus on the interior lives of middle-class African Americans along with the employment of traditional novelistic genres often led to Fauset's being perceived as emblematic of an old guard too concerned with white acceptance. Wallace Thurman characterized her as a writer who presents black characters "in all their virtue and glory with their human traits, their human hypocrisy and their human perversities glossed over."[17] Yet Fauset's novels are more complex than this characterization suggests. Her narratives embody all manner of African American experience – promiscuity, economic and sexual exploitation, the ill treatment of World War I veterans, racial progress or the lack thereof, and passing as the forfeiture of a valuable birthright, a theme she returned to frequently.[18]

All of Fauset's novels rework traditional genres. In her second, *Plum Bun* (1929), the theme of passing shapes the novel of manners to African American experience. The main character passes for white and turns giddy with a freedom that includes attendance at white leftist salons and a marriage proposal from the scion of a wealthy family. Her giddiness ends when she is chagrined at having to "cut" her own sister rather than risk discovery. Fauset's *Comedy American Style* (1933) recasts the elements of traditional comedy – the presence of lovers, an outsider figure who might subsequently be restored to the social structure, the ethos of survival in the face of challenges, and a character with shortcomings patently ludicrous – into a story in which a mother's desire to eradicate all evidence of her black heritage leads to tragedy. Fauset's *The Chinaberry Tree* (1931) may be read as a novel of domesticity denied. Set just after slavery, the work focuses on the Edenesque home of former slave Sarah Strange, her daughter Laurentine, and the way their idyll is menaced by Sarah's once being the beloved mistress of the town's most prominent slaveholder and Laurentine their daughter. Amidst all the tensions of her novels, however, Fauset still manages to show the lives of African Americans "drylongso" (a term meaning something that has become customary or ordinary), to give an interior vision of African American life not always obsessed with oppressive racism.

Like Fauset, Nella Larsen appears to be concerned with portraying African Americans in the best light possible. Larsen depicts middle-class identity and mobility, but the themes of alienation and rootlessness along with the questioning of traditional values give her works a modernist perspective that questions the idea of a racial self. In *Quicksand* (1928), the main character, Helga Crane, might be viewed as the epitome of a modernist heroine of the post-World War I lost generation, constantly seeking for she knows not what. Larsen casts her as a child of mixed parentage to explore the idea of belonging, and Helga's fretful traveling symbolically recapitulates African American migratory journeys from south to north and from the United States to

Europe in search of a dream deferred. In her second novel, *Passing* (1929), the main character's decision to pass has made her, to borrow Toni Morrison's phrase, "dangerously free," to break not only rules of racial confinement, but also rules of friendship and marital fidelity.[19] One reviewer of *Passing* observed that Larsen, "Unlike other negro novelists, and white novelists who write about negroes . . . does not give her following a bath in primitive emotionalism."[20] The review reveals as much about the prevailing voyeurism and demand for literary exoticism as it does about Larsen's going against type to create complex portraits of 1920s African American life.

Larsen's writing complicates the binary implied by the Hurston–Wright example. On the one hand, her educated and upwardly mobile characters fit the standards of New Negro representation; but on the other hand, her use of passing and mixed-race characters deconstruct these standards and reveal identity and race pride to be far more complex concepts than New Negro paradigms might suggest. Essentially, Larsen subverts New Negro notions with the very representations that New Negro criteria advocated. In *Quicksand*, an educated schoolteacher, rejected by her white family and feeling like an outsider in her own race, is intellectually and sexually stagnated and begins a self-destructive odyssey; in *Passing*, a middle-class wife is so concerned with caste comfort that her response to the adultery that threatens her domestic idyll sets tragedy in motion. Larsen's characters are certainly "of the better classes," but their lives are frayed by struggles between personal and racial identities.[21]

In a letter to Langston Hughes congratulating him on the publication of *Not Without Laughter* (1930), Larsen wrote, "You have done what I always contended impossible. Made middle class negroes interesting (or any other kind of middle class people)."[22] The portraits in *Not Without Laughter* range from church to bordello, and interspersed throughout the text are fond evocations of vernacular culture: snippets of blues lyrics, a dance hall where "Easy Rider [a popular song of the time] filled every cubic inch," "lies," "the dozens," and "sayings."[23] A *Bildungsroman* based loosely on Hughes's own experiences in his hometown, Lawrence, Kansas, the novel draws African American identity as a complex of interior lives and not as racial principle. Rather than packaging philosophical discussions as long dialogues, Hughes renders major political issues and events of the time – World War I, passing, discrimination – in personalized terms. Hughes's second novel, *Tambourines to Glory*, published much later, in 1958, continues this tradition as it explores two key elements of African American life, religion and spirituality. His two main characters, Essie and Laura, live on welfare in kitchenette apartments until Laura jokingly hits on the idea of their becoming street ministers. Essie takes the mission to heart while Laura sees it as an opportunity for material gain. Their contrasting views satirize the commercialization of religion, and their enterprise evokes charismatic leaders of the time such as Bishop Ida Bell Robinson, who began houses of worship to satisfy needs not met by orthodox churches.[24] As in other Hughes fiction, vernacular traditions hold a position of prominence, and their presence reflects his view that these forms are the wellspring for a distinctly African American literary expression. Hughes's novels are devoid of the *White Man, Listen!* (1957) polemics of Richard Wright and manifest instead "lives . . . so diversified, internal attitudes so varied, appearances and capabilities so different," that nothing covers them all except Hurston's rhapsodic "My people! My people!"[25]

As an anthropologist and folklorist, Zora Neale Hurston devoted most of her professional life to retrieving an African American cultural past. Hurston easily moved in "high" and "low" circles, and she was thus able to create a body of fiction that transformed written form with elements of orality to craft a literary voice more in keeping with the expressive style of the communities she portrayed. In her first novel, the semi-autobiographical *Jonah's Gourd Vine* (1934), Hurston introduces readers to the porch of Joe Clarke's store and with it the powerful oral forms that would shape her canon – sermons, call and response, "lies," the unerring rendering of regional dialect, and the liberal use of free indirect discourse to vivify folk portraits. By reproducing these forms in her writing, Hurston argues for the validity of oral culture as a means of artistic expression; but she goes further and constructs thematic metaphors that equate orality with sense of self. In *Their Eyes Were Watching God* (1937), for example, characters affirm their worth through speech. As they talk, they regain humanity, transforming themselves from "tongueless, earless, eyeless conveniences" to "lords of sound and lesser things." The central character Janie's independence as a woman is symbolized through her hard-won battle to tell her own "lies." Through Nanny, Janie's grandmother and a former slave, the desire to "preach a great sermon about colored women sittin' on high" represents potential thwarted by racial and gender subjugation. For most of the town, verbal contests on the porch of Joe's store are measures of social and often masculine power.

The overlaying of orality onto written expression is evident in all Hurston's novels. *Moses Man of the Mountain* (1939) retells the biblical legend of the Exodus, using Southern African American cadences to create a subtext conjuring black life during and after slavery. *Moses* provides views of culture sustained within enslavement that pointedly abolitionist nineteenth-century slave narratives did not or could not. It anticipates later neo-slave narratives such as Sherley Anne Williams's *Dessa Rose* (1986) and Toni Morrison's *Beloved* (1987) that give imagined voice to those who could not tell their own story. In *Seraph on the Suwanee* (1948), Hurston takes white characters as her subjects, but the emphasis on Southern voice, and on the power of language, continues in the story of a beautiful poor white woman who must overcome insecurity and reticence to find her voice and save her marriage. Hurston's employment of white characters stresses her position that culture is as much a part of group identity as race is. *Seraph* moves beyond phenotypic definitions of a people and considers the relationship of shared ritual and memory.

In a literacy-centric culture and often against the strictures set forth by the New Negro movement, Hurston's novels boldly redefined the terms of racial representation. Acceptable content in her work included the folk, unsensational denizens who speak in dialect and lay bare intraracial content such as colorism and race-envy. Acceptable forms included narrative voice imbued with orality. For some, however, this content and form were too precious. African American novelists of the 1940s, influenced by realism, naturalism, and leftist politics, were more concerned with revealing the socio-economic struggles of black life than expressing racial uniqueness.[26] Richard Wright was a prime example. It was precisely Hurston's emphasis on the colloquial that drove him to demean her work as "quaint." In his work the folk is the marker of a racial past that mires black progress. Dialect is not an artistic form but a mark of inferiority; vernacular traditions represent desperation and ignorance; and the South is a place to flee even though flight to imagined Northern idylls often trades a rural hell for an urban one.

Much of what characterizes Wright's canon can be seen in nascent form in his first foray at novel writing, *Lawd Today*. Crafted in 1935 and originally titled "Cesspool," it was rejected by publishers and published posthumously in 1963. The novel follows a day in the life of Jake Jackson, a postal worker who feels entrapped and dreams of "doing things."[27] Its images of predestined black male failure, stultifying environments, and stifling black women are elements present in most of Wright's works, along with many of the strategies of 1920s novels that take snapshots of African American existence – journey motifs, urban vignettes, discussions of racial relations, and references to iconic figures (in this case Father Divine and Marcus Garvey).[28] Scenes featuring numbers playing and "lies" told in a black barbershop illustrate Wright's limited evocation of the vernacular, but none of this material is drawn with affection; rather, it is cast as the creation of a desperate people whose portrayals are crafted to unveil the "whole panoply of rules, taboos, and penalties designed . . .

to insure complete submission" of African Americans.[29] Some viewed Wright's literary mission as artistically flawed. James Baldwin, for instance, described him as "the most eloquent spokesman" of the African American experience whose "work . . . is most clearly committed to the social struggle"; but Baldwin goes on to observe that an "artist is strangled who is forced to deal with human beings solely in social terms."[30] The style that Baldwin deemed as sacrificing art for social propaganda, however, made Wright one of the most influential writers of American literature.

The novel that secured Wright's place in the American literary canon, even before the canon became more racially inclusive, was *Native Son* (1940). Its protagonist, Bigger Thomas, imaginatively transforms his accidental suffocation of Mary Dalton, his white employer's daughter, into a willful act of murder. Taking ownership of a white heiress's death makes Bigger social actor, not social victim, and he experiences a freedom he has never known: "He felt that he had his destiny in his grasp. He was more alive than he could ever remember having been." Though *Native Son* is fiction, Wright underscores the reality of its vision. In the 1940 essay "How Bigger Was Born," he describes the real-life inspirations for the character. Extracts replicating coverage of the notorious Robert Nixon murder case lend verisimilitude to sections of the novel describing Bigger as a fugitive.[31] *Native Son* communicates the entrapment of predestined black failure, and Wright offers no remedy. Only by an act sealing his death does Bigger achieve a brief illusory autonomy.

As concerned as Wright was with having readers see racial truth, he was more concerned with having them see themselves in that truth. He emphasizes the Americanness of Bigger through the title of the novel, and in its closing court scenes Bigger's attorney Max shows him to be the yield of "a soil plowed and sown by all our hands." Wright fixes Bigger firmly in the American literary tradition, later declaring that we

> have in the Negro the embodiment of a past tragic enough to appease the spiritual hunger of a James; and we have in the oppression of the Negro a shadow athwart our national life dense and heavy enough to satisfy even the gloomy broodings of a Hawthorne. And if Poe were alive, he would not have to invent horror; horror would invent him.[32]

Wright's comments expose the traditional neglect of African American experience as a literary source, a practice challenged by the African American literary flowering of this period.

Wright's next two novels, *The Outsider* (1953) and *Savage Holiday* (1954) can best be described as novels of ideas.[c] *The Outsider*'s protagonist, Cross Damon, an intellectual by nature and an outsider even among his friends, becomes a mouthpiece for Wright's disaffection with the Communist Party.[33] Though racism looms large in the novel, so too do Wright's views on ineffectual religion and the relationships of man to man, man to woman, and man to larger human community. *Savage Holiday* (1954) marks a departure for Wright in that his main character is white, with race rendered only through rare tangential descriptions of black workers. Combining elements of determinism and existentialism, as in *The Outsider*, Wright explores the ensuing tragedy once a character is unmoored from the safety of his professional identity and forced to face his repressed sexuality and fear of female sexuality. *Savage Holiday* and *The Outsider* are excursions through philosophical dilemmas of alienation. With his last published novel, *The Long Dream* (1958), Wright returns to the familiar ground of the segregated South. The protagonist Rex "Fishbelly" Tucker, the son of a prosperous undertaker, comes of age by learning that his existence is threatened each time he crosses the boundary between the "black belt" of Clintonville, Mississippi and the town's white world. His lessons in segregationist ideology foster not his submission, but rather his falling "fatally in love with that white world . . . in a way that could never be cured." His father's death and Rex's own arrest drive home the unremitting nature of his subjugation, and he ultimately seeks solace in Paris.

Richard Wright's literary vision, particularly as manifested in *Native Son*, influenced a generation of writers including James Baldwin, Ralph Ellison, and Gwendolyn Brooks. Many critics add Ann Petry to this list, and indeed her first novel *The Street* (1946) exhibits a Wrightian determinism. The main character, Lutie Johnson, is a study in environmental victimization. Her job as a domestic in a wealthy Connecticut home fuels her longing for an idealized domesticity her means will never satisfy. She must live in a Harlem that has gone from New Negro Mecca to ghetto. While walking its streets looking for an apartment for her and her son, she conjures the rags-to-riches rise of Benjamin Franklin to give her fortitude. The novel develops the irony of a poor, black, single mother aspiring to the same goals as a founding father, and inevitably Lutie and her son are crushed by an America far from the more perfect union signified by Franklin. Petry's female protagonist genders determinism and expands Wright's masculinist vision of racial and class constriction. Lutie's fate

c For a discussion of this novel as an allegory of existentialism see Robert Chodat, "Philosophy and the American novel," chapter 39, 661–662 in this volume.

is both to be denied full social enfranchisement and to be objectified because of her sex.

The titles of all of Petry's novels indicate the importance of place and suggest that it as well as race, gender, and class define character. *Country Place* (1947) treats the difficult re-entry of a returning white veteran into the toxic suffocation of a small town.[34] *The Narrows* (1953) uses Dumble Street to tell the story of Link Williams, a black man who becomes involved with a married white heiress. Site becomes symbol for Petry. Her brand of spatial determinism is more New Left than New Negro, revealing the limitations of art to effect social change. Continued poverty, continued discrimination in housing and employment, and the increasing presence of pro-labor, pro-black Communist Party ideology in black discourse influenced Petry, and her novels consistently engage racial, sexual, and class politics. As late as 1988 Petry would note, "The sad truth about *The Street* is that now forty-one years later I could write that same book about Harlem or any other ghetto."[35] Petry's comment casts literature in a limited role to effect change for African Americans, and seems to imply that the New Negro hope that art would provide social redemption was unrealized. I would suggest, however, that subsequent movements in African American literature have revised this concept, and continued to embrace art as a vehicle for social change. In the 1960s, for example, the Black Arts movement, the artistic arm of the Black Power movement, viewed art not as a way to prove the worth of blackness to white America, but as a way to create a black nationalism which would connect to other anti-racist, anti-colonial, and anti-imperialist initiatives on the international stage. The relationship of art and social agency would be reassessed yet again with the advent of the New Black Aesthetic movement, in which cultural hybridity complicates essentialist notions of the what and why of African American writing.[d]

While the arguments of art versus agency have been constants in African American literary history, to view African American literature solely within this dyad gives too narrow a scope to its interpretation. To return to the Hurston–Wright example that began this chapter, while these two writers might be said to represent contrasting views of how a novel should be written, both share a hyper-awareness of the racial implications of their writings during a time when black writers began to construct an *ars poetica* for black literature. Both ask, who is the audience for this literature? What should constitute its

d For more on these later movements, see Michael Hill's essay in this volume, "Toni Morrison and the post-civil rights African American novel," chapter 64, esp. 1079.

content? What compositional strategies should shape its form? As Robert S. Levine points out in "The early African American novel," elsewhere in this volume, these are questions that dogged the earliest African American novelists and still engage authors today.[e] As different as Hurston's and Wright's approaches might have been, once their novels became part of the public sphere both authors' writings were variously enlisted to change white American perceptions of African Americans, whether to illuminate racial injustice or to reveal humanity.

African American novelists from the 1920s to the 1950s bore the torch of an African American literature that was no longer solely a "literature of necessity," to borrow the phrase of Sterling Brown, but also a canon creatively drawing upon the rich cultural legacies of black expression.[36] Their innovative strategies reshaped traditional novelistic content: salons were to be found in the drawing rooms of elegant Harlem homes, on the front porches of rural Southern towns, or on the modest verandas of Caribbean bungalows; prose enriched with orality gave voice to those who had previously been spoken for; and multifaceted characterizations replaced racial caricature. The aesthetic debates embedded in these novels recapitulated the first consciously articulated self-examination of African American literary form. Perhaps the most significant contribution of the novel during this time is its beginning a consideration of race versus Race, where the latter term refers to blackness defining itself not solely in contestation with whiteness, but rather as a reservoir of indigenous material capable of producing a variety of appropriate racial representations and a unique literary canon.

Notes

1. Richard Wright, "Between Laughter and Tears," review of *Their Eyes Were Watching God* by Zora Neale Hurston, *New Masses* (October 5, 1937): 23; Zora Neale Hurston, review of *Uncle Tom's Children* by Richard Wright, *Saturday Review of Literature* (April 2, 1938): 32.
2. In the chapter I have used "African American" to describe Africanist content and experience indigenous to the United States and "black" to describe broader diasporic content.
3. *The Journals of Charles W.* Chesnutt, ed. Richard H. Brodhead (Durham, NC: Duke University Press, 1993), 140.
4. I use "New Negro" here to denote a movement consciously advocating the use of art and social sciences to remake cultural conceptions of African Americans. I use

e For Levine's discussion of the intertextual strategies of the early African American novel, see "The early African American novel," chapter 16 in this volume (esp. 268–269).

"Harlem Renaissance" to characterize a more popular cultural movement that saw a flowering in African American art, music, literature, and cultural performance. For a recent discussion of the distinctions between these terms, see George Hutchinson, Introduction, *The Cambridge Companion to the Harlem Renaissance*, ed. George Hutchinson (Cambridge: Cambridge University Press, 2007), 1–10.

5. Alain Locke, "The New Negro" (1925), in *The Norton Anthology of African American Literature*, ed. Henry Louis Gates, Jr. and Nellie Y. McKay (New York: W. W. Norton, 1997), 969.
6. W. E. B. Du Bois, "Criteria of Negro Art" (1926), in Gates and McKay, *The Norton Anthology of African American Literature*, 757.
7. Here I borrow Toni Morrison's term. In her novel *Beloved* "rememory" implies the lack of a hard and fast demarcation between past and present, memory and actuality.
8. The riots White investigated included those of the Red Summer of 1919, a period so named by James Weldon Johnson to describe particularly violent race strife erupting in several cities including Chicago, Washington, DC, and Elaine, Arkansas. These three riots in particular were noted for black revolt against white-initiated violence. See Robert Whitaker, *On the Laps of Gods: The Red Summer of 1919 and the Struggle for Justice That Remade a Nation* (New York: Random House, 2008) and William Tuttle, *Race Riot: Chicago in the Red Summer of 1919* (Champaign: University of Illinois Press, 1996). From 1929 to 1955 White covered forty-one lynchings. He wrote of his anti-lynching work in a disturbing essay "I Investigate Lynchings" (1929) and then in *Rope and Faggot* (New York: Knopf, 1929), which is still held as one of the most authoritative analyses of the history and causal factors of lynching.
9. Some of those peopling Van Vechten's novels include Edward Arlington Robinson as himself and Mabel Dodge appearing as "Edith Dale." In *Nigger Heaven* the character Adora Boniface was based on A'Lelia Walker, the only child of Madam C. J. Walker, the nation's first self-made woman millionaire. A'Lelia's townhouse, known as "The Dark Tower," was the most famous salon of the Harlem Renaissance. For more information see A'Lelia Bundles, *On Her Own Ground: The Life and Times of Madam C. J. Walker* (New York: Simon & Schuster, 2002).
10. That the cabaret appears in Harlem novels urging new racial relations in United States society is not a coincidence. Cabarets have often been characterized as places of democracy, where races, classes, and genders could mix in a social space. See Stephen Kern, *The Culture of Time and Space, 1880–1918* (Cambridge, MA: Harvard University Press, 2003).
11. Van Vechten's acknowledgment following the glossary of the 1927 edition of *Nigger Heaven*.
12. W. E. B. Du Bois, review of *Nigger Heaven* by Carl Van Vechten, *Crisis* (December 1926): 81.
13. James Weldon Johnson, *Along This Way* (1933; New York: Penguin, 1990), 382.

14. W. E. B. Du Bois, review of *Home to Harlem* by Claude McKay, in Gates and McKay, *The Norton Anthology of African American Literature*, 760.
15. In situating Claude McKay beyond the Harlem Renaissance and in the tradition of Caribbean writers, Carl Pedersen reads McKay's novels as a trilogy examining black life in the diaspora. See "The Tropics in New York: Claude McKay and the New Negro Movement," in *Temples for Tomorrow: Looking Back at the Harlem Renaissance*, ed. Geneviève Fabre and Michel Feith (Bloomington: Indiana University Press, 2001), 259–269.
16. Known more for adventure stories designed to teach proper morals, Stribling departed from form with *Birthright*. The novel criticized the racial segregation and values of the South through the story of a Harvard-educated African American who struggles tragically to improve the life of his community.
17. Wallace Thurman, "Fire Burns," *Fire!! A Quarterly Devoted to the Younger Negro Artists* 1.1 (1926): 47. *Fire!!* was designed to showcase the work of younger Harlem Renaissance writers. Wallace Thurman (editor), Richard Bruce Nugent, Zora Neale Hurston, and Langston Hughes were contributors. Critiquing what they saw as the absurdity of the New Negro movement's seeking white approbation of black culture, they sought instead to weave "vivid hot designs upon an ebon bordered loom" and satisfy "pagan thirst for beauty unadorned" (*Fire!!*, Foreword).
18. Two works attempting to read Fauset as more than a formulaically conservative writer or the midwife of the Harlem Renaissance are Jacquelyn Y. McLendon, *The Politics of Color in the Fiction of Jessie Fauset and Nella Larsen* (Charlottesville: University of Virginia Press, 1995) and Carolyn Wedin Sylvander, *Jessie Redmon Fauset, Black American Writer* (Boston: G. K. Hall, 1980).
19. Morrison uses this phrase in *The Bluest Eye* to describe her character Cholly's disavowal of the social rules governing a society that devalues him.
20. Anonymous, "Beyond the Color Line," review of *Passing* by Nella Larsen, *The New York Times Review of Books* (April 28, 1929): n.p.
21. Larsen's reputation was marred by a plagiarism scandal in which she was accused of lifting materials from Sheila Kaye-Smith's "Mrs. Adis" (1922) to create her short story "Sanctuary" (1930). Larsen would deny the charge, stating that she heard the story from an older black woman, sometime between 1912 and 1915, and subsequently discovered it was common in the tradition of African American folklore, thus predating Kaye-Smith's 1922 story and giving the original anecdote no ownership.
22. Undated letter to Langston Hughes, in Nella Larsen, *Passing*, ed. Carla Kaplan (New York: W. W. Norton, 2007), 168.
23. Part of the African American vernacular tradition, "lies" are stories told in boasting; the "dozens" is a competitive system of insults and implied allusions; and "sayings" are kernels of folk wisdom.
24. In 1924 Bishop Ida Bell Robinson founded the Mount Sinai Church of America, which grew to eighty-four churches from New England to Florida. Initially she pastored in the United Holy Church of America, but when she discovered that

women pastors were treated unequally, she formed her own church to offer women the opportunity to minister. Of the 163 ministers she ordained, 125 of them were women. See Priscilla Pope-Levison, *Turn the Pulpit Loose: Two Centuries of American Women Evangelists* (New York: Palgrave Macmillan, 2004).

25. *White Man, Listen!* (New York: HarperCollins, 1995) is a series of essays in which Wright touches on topics including the Cold War and East–West relationships, tribal Africa versus industrializing Africa, and the effect of postcolonial concerns on African American experience; Zora Neale Hurston, *Dust Tracks on a Road: An Autobiography* (Urbana: University of Illinois Press, 1984), 237.
26. Works examining the growing influence of the Left on African American creators include Bill Mullen and Sherry Linkon, eds., *Radical Revisions: Rereading 1930s Culture* (Urbana: University of Illinois Press, 1996); William J. Maxwell, *New Negro, Old Left: African-American Writing and Communism between the Wars* (New York: Columbia University Press, 1999); and James Edward Smethurst, *The New Red Negro: The Literary Left and African American Poetry, 1930–1946* (New York: Oxford University Press, 1999).
27. Wright himself was a postal worker, and this figure will reappear in *The Outsider*.
28. For more on Father Divine's Peace Mission, which aggressively attempted to desegregate all aspects of American society during the 1920s and 1930s, see Robert Weisbrot, *Father Divine* (New York: Chelsea House, 1992).
29. Richard Wright, "How Bigger Was Born" (1940), in *Richard Wright: Early Works: Lawd Today!, Uncle Tom's Children, Native Son* (New York: The Library of America, 1991), 857–858.
30. James Baldwin, *Nobody Knows My Name: More Notes of a Native Son* (New York: Dial, 1961), 188–189. For a discussion of the relationship between Wright and Baldwin see Maurice Charney "James Baldwin's Quarrel with Richard Wright," *American Quarterly* 15.1 (Spring 1963): 65–75.
31. Robert Nixon was one of two young African American men accused of murdering a white woman by crushing her skull with a brick. Though no evidence of sexual assault was discovered, the murder was publicized as a sex crime. See "Sift Mass of Clews [*sic*] for Sex Killer," *Chicago Tribune* (May 28, 1938):1; "'Somebody Did It,' So 2 Youths Who 'Might Have Done It' Are Arrested," The *Chicago Defender* (June 4, 1938): 24; Charles Leavelle, "Brick Slayer is Likened to Jungle Beast," *Chicago Sunday Tribune* (June 5, 1938): sec. 1, 6.
32. Wright, "How Bigger Was Born," 881.
33. Wright broke with the Communist Party in 1944. In "I Tried to be a Communist" he would explain why. This essay appeared in the *Atlantic Monthly* seven moths prior to *Black Boy*'s publication in 1945. It derives from the second part of Wright's autobiography, not published until its appearance as *American Hunger* in 1977. The two parts of Wright's life story are now published together as *Black Boy (American Hunger)*. The essay is reprinted in *The God that Failed*, ed. Richard H. S. Crossman (New York: Columbia University Press, 1949), 115–164.

34. Laura Dubek describes *Country Place* as belonging "to a group of 'white life' novels published by black writers in the years following World War Two." In continuing her analysis she notes that the novel subverts "the sentimentality of postwar white family narratives such as William Wyler's award-winning film *The Best Years of Our Lives* (1946)." See "White Family Values in Ann Petry's *Country Place*," *MELUS* 29.2, *Elusive Illusions: Art and Reality* (Summer 2004):55.
35. "Ann Petry," *Contemporary Authors Autobiography Series* 6 (Detroit: Gale Research, 1988), 265. Petry was also a contributor to the *People's Voice*, a radical periodical founded in 1942 by New York congressman Adam Clayton Powell, Jr. For further information on Petry's participation in leftist politics see Alex Lubin, ed., *Revising the Blueprint: Ann Petry and the Literary Left* (Jackson: University Press of Mississippi, 2007).
36. Sterling Brown, "A Century of Negro Portraiture in American Literature" *Massachusetts Review* 7.1 (Winter 1966):73–96.

43

Ellison and Baldwin: aesthetics, activism, and the social order

LOVALERIE KING

Ralph Waldo Ellison and James Arthur Baldwin fused the warring emotions of love and anger in order to draw out the complexities of black American experience and subjectivity. While both Ellison and Baldwin were (like many black Americans) angry about their country's failure to live up to its promise, to its democratic ideals,[1] they also expressed love for America. Their attempts to reconcile the tension between loving America and being angry about its failings on racial matters link two central interrelated themes in their work: the quest for American identity and the myth of the American Dream. In exploring these overarching themes, they used aesthetic approaches that allowed them to focus on the importance of self-definition and personal responsibility while also exploring the relationship between democracy and love.

While both authors criticized America, Baldwin was more open and public in making extra-literary political commentary. Indeed, Baldwin, the Harlem-bred poet/prophet/philosopher, was as interested in critiquing American identity as he was in embracing it.[2] He produced most of his novels while living abroad, where he fled early and often. Writing in 1986, the year before his death, of the betrayal of Martin Luther King, Jr.'s "dream," Baldwin emphasized America's betrayal of its own ideals: "I think it [King's dream] was manipulated, as were we, and that it was never intended that any promise made would be kept. In any case, and incontestably, we are certainly no better off in 1986 than we were that day in Washington, in 1963," the year of King's historic march on Washington.[3] Ellison avoided such harsh public critiques, refusing an activist role during the Civil Rights Movement and denigrating the vociferous calls for cultural nationalism during the Black Arts Movement.[4] For Ellison, the highly disciplined and philosophical Oklahoma-bred, self-proclaimed Renaissance man, political detachment paralleled a rigid dedication to form in crafting impressionist work that is rife with symbolism. Yet, based on Ellison's work and the way he lived his life, it is difficult to imagine anything more important to him (or his protagonists) than American identity.

Ellison's seemingly apolitical stance in fact allows him to fashion a powerful aesthetic that fuses searing criticism with soaring idealism. Alan Nadel perceptively terms Ellison "one of American literature's most sophisticated naïfs," noting that "Only someone naïvely seduced by the propaganda of the American Dream and an essentialist notion of individualism could articulate some of the positions that Ellison held. But only by assuming that naïve role and rhetoric could Ellison put himself in the position to make so fully visible the contradictions between the imagined (or imaginary) America and its lived practice."[5] Ellison represents that simultaneous (and paradoxical) affirmation and rejection of America in the prologue to *Invisible Man* (1952) by referencing and thereby embracing so much that is American even as the complaint raised by Louis Armstrong echoes in the background. In his 1953 speech accepting the National Book Award for *Invisible Man*, Ellison claimed that "the way home we seek is that condition of man's being at home in the world, which is called love, and which we term democracy."[6] In other words, if love can be expressed via politics, then that expression comes with the achievement of true democracy in the United States.

Baldwin articulates a similar understanding of the relationship between love and democracy in the familiar closing lines of "Down at the Cross" in *The Fire Next Time* (1963). He writes, "If we – and now I mean the relatively conscious whites and the relatively conscious blacks, who must, like lovers, insist on, or create, the consciousness of the others – do not falter in our duty now, we may be able, handful that we are, to end the racial nightmare, and *achieve our country*, and change the history of the world."[7] Ten years later, in an interview with *The Black Scholar*, Baldwin would present a decidedly prescient and modified vision for change that would be facilitated not by progressive intellectuals but by the everyday working class in their steadfast resistance to a corrupt and decaying social order.[8] Yet his work illustrates a fundamental difference from that of Ellison: whereas Ellison envisions love and brotherhood flowing from the achievement of democracy, Baldwin's work suggests that it is through love and brotherhood that democracy can be achieved. Love, in other words, will redeem America's promise of democracy.

The historical context for Ellison's and Baldwin's literary careers spans several decades beginning with the 1940s and the period surrounding World War II. Though the war eventually brought the United States into full economic recovery from the Great Depression of the 1930s, Jim Crow segregation remained in effect – a situation that Ellison tackled head-on in several well-examined early scenarios in *Invisible Man*: the Battle Royal, the Trueblood incident, and its related Golden Day event. World War II had been a test for African Americans, many of whom had served (or had family members who had served) in a major war yet still found themselves begging for full citizenship rights. By the middle of the 1950s, organized social protest was gaining momentum that would ultimately lead to changes in the social order. The ensuing Civil Rights Movement – which had evolved into the Black Power Movement by 1968 – generated the cultural energy for the Black Arts Movement (BAM).[9] While much of the creative energy of the BAM was directed toward poetry and drama, African Americans published a number of distinguished novels from World War II to the early 1970s.

Several African American novels published in the 1940s – which originate in very different emotional spaces – serve to spotlight the originality of Ellison's and Baldwin's emphasis on love. Richard Wright, Ann Petry, Chester Himes, and Dorothy West trace justifiably pessimistic trajectories in which the dream of middle-class stability entices but excludes blacks while short-circuiting any enduring love. Two of the best-known novels from this period, Wright's *Native Son* (1940)[10] and Petry's *The Street* (1946), exemplify the protest literature written in the naturalist vein that was then popular among African American writers. Wright and Petry serve up harsh critiques of the urban North in the 1930s and 1940s, representing it not as a promised land but rather as a socio-economic straitjacket for protagonists Bigger Thomas (of *Native Son*) and Lutie Johnson (of *The Street*). As Wright's title emphasizes, Bigger's problem is precisely that he is *native*, defined by American values; the rape and murders he commits conform to white expectations, while his poverty is depicted as part of a socio-economic straitjacket that leaves him no meaningful alternatives to the situations that lead to these acts. Petry is sharply critical of her protagonist's absorption of American beliefs in upward mobility. At the end of both novels the protagonists are alone and doomed, with Bigger sentenced to death and Lutie on the run, having abandoned her child after committing manslaughter and larceny. Himes's *If He Hollers Let Him Go* (1945) displays similar pessimism. With a plot that moves from the urban North into the open West, with its mythic connotations of open frontiers and infinite possibilities, the novel tracks protagonist Bob Jones's quest to be seen as "just a simple Joe walking down an American street." This modest wish yields heartbreak and disillusionment. West's *The Living is Easy* (1948) focuses on status-obsessed Cleo Judson, whose early experiences of poverty and servitude give birth to her unbridled pursuit of property, an acquisitiveness that undermines her capacity for love. In all four novels the quest for the American Dream obscures love and its nurturing potential.

Later African American novels brought further explorations of American identity and the dream of socio-economic advancement. Gwendolyn Brooks's often overlooked and semi-autobiographical gem, *Maud Martha* (1953), offers a more hopeful ending. Appearing the year after Ellison's *Invisible Man* and the same year as Baldwin's semi-autobiographical *Go Tell It on the Mountain*, Brooks's novel features a poetic representation of black female consciousness in protagonist Maud Martha Brown's journey to self-discovery. Dark-skinned, nappy-haired, female, and poor, Maud's progress depends on her capacity to imagine herself as a subject worthy of love. Her daughter's birth provides the impetus for her transformation. John Oliver Killens's *Youngblood* (1954) and Paule Marshall's *Brown Girl, Brownstones* (1959) both examine the harmful effects of racism and unequal economic opportunity access on black family dynamics. Chester Himes's crime novels (including *A Rage in Harlem* [1957], *The Real Cool Killers* [1959], The Big *Gold Dream* [1960], *All Shot Up* [1960], *Cotton Comes to Harlem* [1965], *The Heat's On* [1966], and *Blind Man with a Pistol* [1969]) riff on the standard detective story formula in order to illustrate the dynamic relationship between oppression, criminalization, and the social order – along with the elusiveness of justice in a system tilted against the black community.[a] "I couldn't name the white man who was guilty," said Himes in his autobiography, "because all white men were guilty."[11] John Alfred Williams published several novels, including *One for New York* (1960), *Sissie* (1963), and *The Man Who Cried I Am* (1967), with its thinly disguised portraits of Baldwin, Wright, Himes, Malcolm X, and others. Kristin Hunter's *God Bless the Child* (1964) satirizes the protest tradition of the 1940s, as protagonist Rosie Fleming literally and figuratively succumbs to consumption in this pathological portrait of urban Americans in pursuit of property by any means.[12] Hunter's novel serves as the anti-type for Ellison's epic *Invisible Man*, which appeared on the eve of the Civil Rights Movement.

Wedged between the protest tradition and the BAM, *Invisible Man* was not immediately appreciated by many in the black literary community as an appropriate representation of black American experience, but Ellison was much more interested in representing what he felt than what others thought it appropriate for him to feel. He attributed his literary awakening to T. S. Eliot's *The Waste Land* (whose influence is apparent in both *Invisible Man* and

a For a reading of Himes's crime fiction focused on *Run Man Run* (1966), see Sean McCann's essay, "The novel of crime, mystery and suspense," chapter 48 in this volume, 799.

the posthumously published *Juneteenth* [1999]), and this interest underpinned his concern with the interplay between African American and European American culture.[13] His work goes right to what he believes is the heart of America: the innocence and promise of its founding moments.

Invisible Man explores the American condition through the consciousness of an unnamed black male narrator. The novel captures the uniqueness of black experience while also holding it up as a universal human experience. With references to Louis Armstrong, the prologue immediately establishes a blues mood, while hallucinatory memories of the protagonist's grandfather and others recall the legacy of slavery. The subsequent narrative unfolds as reflections from the previous two decades of the narrator's life. In the epilogue, we return to the basement hole where the narrator remains in hibernation – but preparing for "more overt action" and, implicitly, interaction with others. Like Petry's Lutie Johnson and Himes's Bob Jones, Ellison's protagonist initially believes innocently in a Booker T. Washington-inflected version of the Horatio Alger rags-to-riches story.[14] He believes that education and hard work are the keys to success for black Americans.

An excellent student whom whites call a *"credit to his race,"* the narrator receives as reward a scholarship to a specifically Negro college.[15] Before he receives the scholarship, however, he is forced to compete in a humiliating and bloody ritual of (literally) blind capitalist pursuit – a "Battle Royal" – as entertainment for the town's white leaders. The initiation ritual, complete with a blonde stripper placed to entice the black youths, reminds the participants of their subordinate place in the social order. After delivering a speech that follows the Washingtonian model of humility, invisible man is awarded his scholarship and a briefcase. This early scene establishes the problem that must be resolved concerning his passive acceptance of external circumscription of his life's potential. That is, invisible man must master self-definition by rejecting the constraints that the briefcase (and its externally imposed contents) symbolizes. Thus, the novel traces the narrator's journey from naïve faith to enlightenment (symbolized by his well-lit basement hole), whereupon he is able to affirm self and society. But before attaining enlightenment, the narrator's pursuit leads him from one potentially self-destructive encounter to the next. He lacks what some would call "mother-wit" because he not only puzzles over his grandfather's cryptic advice to don the mask of acquiescence, he also does not see beneath the mask of accommodation worn by his early mentor, the black college president Bledsoe.

When he is expelled from school for trying to do what he thinks he is supposed to do – give white people what they want – he moves to New York

City, a journey that parallels the move of African Americans from the South to the urban North (the Promised Land) during the Great Migration years of the early twentieth century. Employed at a paint factory specializing in "optic white," the narrator's job is to mix a small amount of black paint into a white base to create the signature shade – thus conveying Ellison's symbolic critique of the American myth of racial purity. Just as he had wandered off the prescribed path while at school and exposed the deliberately innocent trustee Mr. Norton to the realities of black life through the spectacle of the incestuous Jim Trueblood, the narrator veers from formula. Indeed, wherever he goes, his inability to adhere to prescription sends him off on another adventure. Just as turning down the wrong road leads to his expulsion from college, his divergence from the formula for optic white leads ultimately to the accident that causes his hospitalization; his divergence from the rules of the ironically named Brotherhood will finally send him into hibernation.[16] Invisible man is finally driven underground during the violent Brotherhood-orchestrated race war (modeled after the real-life Harlem riot of 1943) near the end of the novel. He finds himself alone there with only the self he managed to rescue. While the narrator fails to gain the socio-economic advances that he originally sought, Ellison makes it clear that he learns the far more important value of self-definition.

Linked forever to predecessor texts such as Frederick Douglass's *Narrative of the Life of Frederick Douglass* (1845), James Weldon Johnson's *The Autobiography of an Ex-Coloured Man* (1912), and Wright's *Native Son* and *Black Boy* (1945), *Invisible Man* also serves as a point of reference for numerous subsequent novels including Randall Kenan's *A Visitation of Spirits* (1989), Charles Johnson's *Oxherding Tale* (1982) and *Middle Passage*(1990), Percival Everett's *Erasure* (2001), and others. Johnson in particular expands on Ellison's prototype via his *Middle Passage* protagonist, Rutherford Calhoun, who achieves significant spiritual growth during the course of his reverse Middle Passage. Like Melville's Amasa Delano in *Benito Cereno* (1855), whom Johnson references, Ellison's invisible man and Johnson's Rutherford Calhoun suffer from limited perception, a condition significantly lessened by the end of all three stories.

Invisible Man became a touchstone for a number of African American women's novels, as well. Toni Morrison's *The Bluest Eye* (1970) signifies heavily on the Trueblood incident and extends Gwendolyn Brooks's treatment of black female subjectivity within American culture, while setting the stage for numerous subsequent deliberately and explicitly gendered explorations of African American identity, including Alice Walker's *The Color Purple* (1982),

Gloria Naylor's *The Women of Brewster Place* and *The Men of Brewster Place*, and Alice Randall's *The Wind Done Gone* (2001). Just as Alice Randall uses Ellison's *Invisible Man* as a touchstone for her treatment of invisibility, subjectivity, and the achievement of self-definition and love in *The Wind Done Gone*, her exploration of black political conservatism and racialized American identity in *Rebel Yell* (2009) owes much to the overriding themes of *Juneteenth* (1999).

If *Invisible Man* offered a critique of ideological zealotry from a black cultural perspective, *Juneteenth* offers a similar critique via a conversation between the racially ambiguous and politically ultra-conservative symbol of America, Senator Sunraider, and his adoptive black father, A. Z. Hickman. Ellison returns to the American identity theme with a vengeance in the allegorical *Juneteenth* through the race-baiting Senator Sunraider, formerly known as Bliss. In one of the more astute commentaries on the novel so far, Alan Nadel suggests that,

> While the problem for the invisible man was to be seen, the problem for Bliss is to remember. He must take himself – and us – to the depths of that American unconscious where the contradictions that undermine democracy can be confronted. Pursuing that search from Bliss's and Hickman's perspectives makes clear that Bliss is not only Christ but also America, both the sacrificial spirit and the historical embodiment of democracy.[17]

It follows from Nadel's point that Ellison's most important goal in *Juneteenth* is to undermine the racialization of American identity, which stands as a barrier to the achievement of true democracy – and love.

Juneteenth's themes, plot, and narrative strategies – including its use of flashbacks in the service of spiritual reinvigoration and the memory and recollection of essential history, sermons, and lengthy prayer passages – recall not only *Invisible Man* but also Faulkner's *Absalom, Absalom!* (1936) and *Light in August* (1932), as well as Baldwin's *Go Tell It on the Mountain* and *Just Above My Head* (1979). The primary setting is Sunraider's bedside, and the characters offer a composite of the America that Ellison loves. The reader learns via flashbacks that Sunraider had been raised by Hickman in the black community and the black church. Born of a woman identified as white and an unidentified father, Bliss had once been a spiritual leader in that community. Most telling, he understands the nuanced relationship between African American and Anglo-American culture in a way that allows him to appreciate the ties between their folk traditions; yet, he chooses to deny that shared past and instead promote segregation based on the myth of racial purity. He leaves his early life behind and becomes one of the most rabidly conservative senators in

Congress. Clearly, the racial ambiguity of America's past parallels Bliss's own. In a passage that speaks to the nation's originating promise of democracy, Hickman prays over Bliss's – that is, America's – wounded body: "Maybe that was our mistake, we just couldn't surrender everything, we just couldn't manage to burn out the memory and cauterize the wound and deny that it had ever happened . . . Remember the promising babe that he was and the hope placed in him . . ." In other words, in the earliest moments of the national experiment, there was the possibility for a definition of national identity that did not adhere to rigid racial categories and boundaries, and that was a moment of potential for community, fellowship, and democracy.[18] Here, as in *Invisible Man*, Ellison uses the novel form to express hope that America will return to that founding promise.

If Ellison asserted that democracy had the potential to produce love, Baldwin felt that love was the only redemptive power; for him, love had the power to produce democracy. He situates love's redemptive power within human beings and their relationships to one another. He makes love (the quest for love, the absence of love, love as salvation, and so on) a key and recurring concern in his six novels: *Go Tell It on the Mountain* (1953), *Giovanni's Room* (1956), *Another Country* (1962), *Tell Me How Long the Train's Been Gone* (1968), *If Beale Street Could Talk* (1974), and *Just above My Head* (1979). While Ellison's work served primarily to obliterate the notion of a segregated past that supports a false myth of racial purity, Baldwin's work sought to obliterate such attempts at easy categorization and separation. As Baldwin brilliantly suggests in his third novel, *Another Country*, with its demographically diverse cast of characters trying but failing on many levels to achieve a democratic community, such efforts actually work against the achievement of democracy.

Baldwin felt that a preoccupation with race often obscured the impact of other oppressive forces that could serve as impediments to the expression of individual subjectivity, and he was committed to representing individual subjectivity in all its complexity.[19] Baldwin's work took on the topic of sexual identity and its relationship to individual subjectivity and American identity in ways that Ellison's did not.[20] If Baldwin were to adhere to his own dictum in *Notes of a Native Son* – to write from his own experience and to force from that experience the "last drop, sweet or bitter," then he had to make questions about sexuality and sexual identity as important as those about race, class, and gender.[21] Baldwin experienced sexuality as fluid, without the bipolar prefixes hetero- or homo-. This perspective is evident from his first novel forward. He daringly and explicitly explored homoerotic desire and the destructive potential of homophobia as early as 1956 in *Giovanni's Room*, which has become a central text in contemporary queer and gender-oriented literary history; however, Baldwin had already alluded to homoeroticism in *Go Tell It On the Mountain* via the main character's attraction to another man. Indeed, *Giovanni's Room* begins an expansion of Baldwin's examination of artificial barriers and divisions that close off possibilities for love, community, and democracy, an examination he began in *Go Tell It on the Mountain*.

Part spiritual autobiography and part neo-freedom narrative, *Go Tell It on the Mountain* tells the story of a young man whose options for self-realization are miserably circumscribed. Baldwin's initiation novel represents the emotional and economic struggles of an African American family living in Harlem in the middle of the Great Depression, but more crucially it also explores the personal, philosophical, and political effects of being black, poor, and gay in America.[22] The autobiographical essays in *Notes of a Native Son* (1955), along with "Down at the Cross" from *The Fire Next Time* (1963), provide essential information for understanding the ambiguity of John's/Baldwin's religious conversion, as well as its temporariness as a remedy for what he seeks: self-acceptance, subjectivity, and love.[23]

Baldwin expands his focus on sexual identity and his concern with complex subjectivity in *Another Country*, which features an array of characters from various ethnic and economic backgrounds whose friendships and sexual relationships criss-cross boundaries of race, class, gender, and (of course) national identity. Postmodernist in its approach, the novel resists plot closure as well as temporal and spatial boundaries and offers a critique of an America that considers itself both democratic and moral while fostering its plethora of highly destructive prejudices that close off possibilities for love. In this kind of critique, we can see some of the nuanced differences between the aesthetic approaches and choices that Baldwin and Ellison made and especially the difference between their political stances toward America. With *Another Country*, Baldwin critiques not only heteronormativity but also homogeneity. Various pairs in the novel – Rufus and Leona, Vivaldo and Ida, Cass and Richard, Yves and Eric – engage in relationships that cross boundaries of race and sexual identity. The problematic effects of buying into the divisive politics of America are evident in each character's life, but the most detrimental effect can be seen in Rufus's suicide, which serves as a warning to an America that hates, and wants to erase, part of itself.[24]

One thread of the story follows the heterosexual relationship between Rufus (a black American jazz musician) and Leona (his much-abused Southern white American lover). The question asked by the song title "Do

You Love Me?" reverberates throughout the tale. Black and gay, Rufus channels his own self-hatred into his physical and emotional abuse of Leona, who in the end returns mentally broken to her family in the South. As with other relationships in the novel, love's potential is undermined because the players are psychically constrained by the effects of false barriers that forestall expressions of complex subjectivity – exemplified most decidedly in Rufus's suicide. Thus, following one of the major storylines in *Invisible Man*, *Another Country* explores the benefits of self-definition (or the peril in the lack thereof). If Rufus's suicide represents the peril, the benefits are clearly exemplified through Eric, a white bisexual actor who avoids being limited by an externally imposed model of homogeneous humanity. He achieves the important feat of self-definition that others among the cast of characters do not achieve. In turn, he is able to engage in loving, healing relationships. He prefigures black actor Leo Proudhammer of *Tell Me How Long the Train's Been Gone*, whose capacity to transcend socially constructed racial and sexual boundaries is represented by his friendships; his two closest friends and lovers are a Southern white woman from a racist family and a younger and very militant black male Northerner.

Latent homoeroticism in *Go Tell It on the Mountain*, homosexual self-loathing in *Giovanni's Room* (a novel discussed by Elizabeth Freeman elsewhere in this volume),[b] and the problems attendant to crossing socially constructed boundaries and categories in *Another Country* are all topics revisited in *Tell Me How Long the Train's Been Gone*, a novel that illustrates the potential rewards of resisting sexual and racial divisions through the depiction of intraracial and homosocial love relationships. *Tell Me How Long the Train's Been Gone* centers on the relationship between protagonist Leo Proudhammer, his white Southern friend and lover Barbara, and black, Northern, would-be revolutionary Christopher. Here, Baldwin further develops his argument that enduring love is produced within human interactions, while challenging homophobic notions of black manhood that were part of Black Nationalist discourse of the time. In general, the novel offers a critique of racism, sexism, the racialization of crime, the criminalization of race, and heteronormativity by depicting loving, nurturing bisexual relationships among a black artist, his white female confidante and friend, and his militant young black male lover.

Baldwin's fifth novel focuses primarily on heterosexual relationships, with the redemptive power of love serving as his overarching theme. Published after the peak of the Civil Rights Movement, *If Beale Street Could Talk* represents his vision of cooperation among everyday working people as a

b Elizabeth Freeman, "Reimagining genders and sexualities," chapter 57, 954–955.

powerful force for change that can assist in the achievement of democracy. Baldwin writes as if in drag, with the mostly first-person narrative unfolding through the female voice of Tish Rivers, who is three months pregnant by her wrongly incarcerated lover Fonny. The imprisonment of Fonny, a gentle artisan, speaks to the myriad ways that America's unrealized democracy maintains the intellectual, psychological, and emotional imprisonment of African Americans. Baldwin's account of Tish's family's efforts to secure Fonny's freedom highlights the failures of America in the aftermath of the Civil Rights and Black Power movements while commenting on what would come to be called "America's Prison Industrial Complex."

Baldwin's final novel, *Just above My Head*, spans several decades of the pursuits of the four main characters, two pairs of siblings who split into matched couples: Arthur Montana, his brother Hall, Hall's lover, Julia, and her brother Jimmy, who is Arthur's lover. Hall's voice narrates Arthur's rise and fall. Mobility once again serves as a central goal, as the novel spans many locales, including the American South, San Francisco, Harlem, Paris, Abidjan, and London. Baldwin's story of Arthur's rise to fame as a singer and his subsequent reversal of fortune after losing his connection with the community that gave him the gift of song shares the theme of cultural betrayal that Ellison depicts in the character of Senator Sunraider in *Juneteenth*. In *Just above My Head*, Baldwin also revises Leo Proudhammer's story in *Tell Me How Long the Train's Been Gone*, but more importantly in his final novel he is able to conceive of the black church and its music in a broader context.[25] He makes liberal use of familiar African American cultural materials (including spirituals and sermons) in exploring the theme of love and commitment through the various relationships among the central characters. If a much younger Baldwin could declare that there was no love in the church (which he suggests in John Grimes's story in his first novel and also in the first essay of *The Fire Next Time*), then an older Baldwin acknowledges that the church can and does serve as a site for developing love. The gift of song that the church and community bestow upon Arthur most notably expresses that love, and he must pay it forward by sharing it in concerts across America and abroad. Arthur's tragic fall results from a disruption of that implied covenant and it underscores Baldwin's concern with the importance of self-definition.

When Ralph Ellison and James Baldwin emerged on the literary scene, they were both considered to be *Negro* writers who were also American. As such, they were part of a continuing tradition of African American literature deeply engaged with protesting the legacies of slavery and unequal economic opportunity, even as their work (Ellison's in particular) marked a distinct aesthetic turn within that tradition. Their characters, plots, and themes advanced an agenda of hope, rather than the dead-end of bitterness and nihilism. They fused the warring emotions of love and anger in the historical response of black Americans to America in order to draw out the complexities of black American experience and subjectivity. Both authors committed themselves to the eradication of artificial barriers and racial stereotypes in American life, and both expressed the desire for the achievement of a true brotherhood. They readily combined art with politics to fashion an aesthetic appropriate to the task before them, and they understood that there is no necessary dichotomy between art and politics. It was Baldwin, after all, who asserted that the artist's only real concern is "to recreate out of the disorder of life that order which is art."[26] Both he and Ellison were highly successful.

Notes

1. Baldwin once noted that Ellison was "as angry as a black man can be and still be alive." See Avon Kirkland, producer/writer/director, *Ralph Ellison: An American Journey*, video-recording (California Newsreel, 2001). Baldwin, of course, credited fear of the potential consequences of his own anger and rage for his initial flight from America. See James Baldwin, "Notes of a Native Son" (1949), rpt. in *Notes of a Native Son* (Boston: Beacon, 1984), 85–114.
2. See Baldwin, "A Question of Identity" (1955), rpt. in *Notes of a Native Son*, 124–137; "The Discovery of What It Means to Be an American" (1961), in *Nobody Knows My Name: More Notes of a Native Son* (New York: Vintage International, 1993), 3–12; "The American Dream and the American Negro" (1965), rpt. in *Baldwin: Collected Essays*, ed. Toni Morrison (NewYork: Library of America, 1998), 714–719.
3. Baldwin, "Introduction," in Michael Thelwell, *Duties, Pleasures, and Conflicts* (Amherst: University of Massachusetts Press, 1987), xvii–xxii; xviii.
4. See, for example, Arnold Rampersad, *Ralph Ellison: A Biography* (New York: Knopf, 2007), 381–441.
5. Alan Nadel, "Ralph Ellison and the American Canon," *American Literary History* 13.2 (Summer 2001): 393–404: 403.
6. Ralph Ellison, "Brave Words for a Startling Occasion" (January 27, 1953), rpt. in *The Collected Essays of Ralph Ellison*, ed. John F. Callahan (New York: The Modern Library, 1995), 151–154; esp. 154.
7. James Baldwin, "Down at the Cross," in *The Fire Next Time* (1963), rpt. in *James Baldwin: Collected Essays*, 291–347; esp. 346–347, emphasis mine.
8. James Baldwin, interview by *The Black Scholar* (1973), rpt. in *Conversations with James Baldwin*, ed. Fred L. Standley and Louis H. Pratt (Jackson: University Press of Mississippi, 1989) 157–158.

9. Amiri Baraka's staging of his play, *Dutchman*, in 1964 is often cited as the inaugural event of the BAM.
10. Both Wright and Baldwin produced most of their fiction while living away from the United States; both proved much more prolific than Ralph Ellison in that regard.
11. Chester Himes, *My Life of Absurdity* (1976; rpt. New York: Thunder's Mouth Press, 1995), 102.
12. Killens contributed several other works including *And Then We Heard the Thunder* (1963), *Sippi* (1967), *The Cotillion; or, One Good Bull is Half the Herd* (1971). Celebrated contemporary author John Edgar Wideman published his first novel, *A Glance Away*, in 1967, partly as an attempt to distance himself from the Black Arts Movement. Subsequent works have reflected a shift in this early strategy. Ishmael Reed, who is as much a critic as he is a brilliant and innovative novelist, published *The Freelance Pallbearers* and *Yellow Back Radio Broke-Down* (which parodies the American Western) in 1967 and 1969, respectively. The multi-talented Clarence Major is an incredibly important author whose novel *All-Night Visitors* (1969) falls within this period, as does the important essay, "A Black Criterion" (1967). Major, who is also an accomplished visual artist, is best known for his metafiction, and produces poetry and short fiction as well. Other novels appearing during this roughly twenty-year span include Samuel R. Delany's *Jewels* (1963), *The Fall of the Towers* trilogy (1963–1965), *The Ballad of Beta-2* (1965), *Babel 17* (1966), *The Einstein Intersection* (1967), and *Nova* (1968). Delany's later works of the 1970s and 1980s are deemed superior to these early offerings.
13. Ellison also notes the influence of James, Joyce, Malraux, Faulkner, Hemingway, Dostoevsky, and others.
14. See Richard Yarborough, "The Quest for the American Dream in Three Afro-American Novels: *If He Hollers Let Him Go*, *The Street*, and *Invisible Man*," *MELUS* 8.4 (Winter 1981):33–59: 47. Yarborough explores the effect of Washingtonian discourse which translated the Horatio Alger story into an African American story of self-help.
15. This is a reference to one of the HBCU's (Historically Black Colleges and Universities) that were established for black Americans before 1964. For a complete listing, see www.ed.gov/about/inits/list/whhbcu/edlite-list.html.
16. Ellison uses characters and organizations such as Bledsoe, Ras the Exhorter/Destroyer, and The Brotherhood to represent ideological solutions available to African Americans coping with the social, economic, and political conditions of early Cold War America.
17. Nadel, "Ralph Ellison and the American Canon," 402.
18. Toni Morrison's *A Mercy* (2008) eloquently captures this moment in America's infancy.
19. Lynn Scott, *James Baldwin's Later Fiction: Witness to the Journey* (East Lansing: Michigan State University Press, 2002), xxviii.

20. Several critics have noted Ellison's muted engagement with homoeroticism. See Daniel Y. Kim, "Invisible Desires: Homoerotic Racism and Its Homophobic Critique in Ralph Ellison's *Invisible Man*," *Novel: A Forum on Fiction* 30.3 (1997): 309–328; Alan Nadel, "Invisible Man, Huck, and Jim," in *Invisible Man: Modern Critical Interpretations*, ed. Harold Bloom (Philadelphia: Chelsea House Publishers, 1999), 153–177; and David Wright, "No Hiding Place: Exile 'Underground' in James Baldwin's 'This Morning, This Evening, So Soon,'" *College Language Association Journal* 42.4 (1999):445–461.
21. Baldwin, "Autobiographical Notes," rpt. in *Notes of a Native Son*, 7.
22. Randall Kenan casts John Grimes's dilemma in a Southern rural setting in *A Visitation of Spirits* (1989). Kenan's protagonist, the doomed Horace Cross, is an African American teenager who has grown up as a bastard child in a Southern black religious dynasty. He is already dead when the novel opens; however, his spirit hovers over the community and much of the story is filtered through his consciousness. Love within his community is conditioned upon a rigid adherence to homogeneity; there is little space for contemplation and no space for expression of any sexual identity other than heterosexual. Horace's attempt to transform himself into something more acceptable – a bird native to that area – results in his suicide.
23. See Baldwin, "Down at the Cross: Letter from a Region in My Mind," in *The Fire Next Time* (1963), rpt. in *James Baldwin: Collected Essays*, 296–347.
24. Adrienne Kennedy's play, *Funnyhouse of a Negro* (1964; New York: Samuel French, 1997), brilliantly executes this idea via a schizophrenic central character named Sarah who tracks the black part of her identity to the jungle to kill it and, in doing so, commits suicide.
25. Though he was very critical of the church, the church and its music were enduring elements of Baldwin's personal experience.
26. See Baldwin, "Autobiographical Notes," 3–9: 7.

44

Religion and the twentieth-century American novel

AMY HUNGERFORD

One of realism's founding fathers – Gustave Flaubert – proclaimed that "the artist in his work should be like God in the universe, present everywhere and visible nowhere."[1] Whatever god-like status turn-of-the-century American realists cherished with respect to their creations, the more mundane aspects of religion also appeared occasionally in their works. Religious practice was part of the landscape of social life that concerned novelists such as Theodore Dreiser, Edith Wharton, Henry James, and Sinclair Lewis. A signal – and early – example is Harold Frederic's *The Damnation of Theron Ware* (1896), which stands out for its dramatic focus on religious change at the end of the nineteenth century and for its simultaneous critique of and respect for the religious worlds embedded in American society. *The Damnation of Theron Ware* announces the continuing significance of the American novel's relationship with religious life and religious discourse throughout the twentieth century and into the twenty-first, even while it registers changes in emphasis – from Protestant to Catholic models of religious thought, from moral message to ritual form, from sectarian conviction to pluralist doubt, from catechism to mysticism.[2]

The changes in emphasis on display in *Theron Ware*, already palpable in the early century, solidify into a dominant strand of American fiction after 1960. In that strand of fiction, religious thought entwines in new ways with the highest ambitions of literary art. In this chapter I suggest that religious understandings of the literary come to motivate some of the most prominent novelists in the latter part of the century – writers such as Cormac McCarthy, Thomas Pynchon, Marilynne Robinson, Don DeLillo, and Toni Morrison – whose work ultimately constitutes an argument for the novel's continuing relevance to American life into the twenty-first century.

Harold Frederic wrote several novels, but only *Theron Ware* achieved critical success.[3] Even so, it never made its way firmly onto the syllabi of American literature courses. This is a shame, in part because of the novel's accomplishment as an example of American realism, but the book's continuing obscurity may register how religion has been considered marginal to the literature of this period. Once the moralizing Christianity of Harriet Beecher Stowe is displaced by the high art of Henry James, or the by the moral ambiguities of Theodore Dreiser, a novel about the religious crisis of a Methodist minister seems difficult to integrate into the literary history of the period.

One way to integrate *Theron Ware* is to see in it a reflection of the secularizing forces at work in American culture after the Civil War – at work even in the backwater towns of upstate New York where Methodist ministers may be sent to preach. The eponymous minister, a fine young preacher who falls into consumer debt in his first post after seminary, is sent for chastening to one of those backwater towns. His misery is leavened, however, by a chance encounter with the Roman Catholic Irish of the town: he is swept up one day in a procession bearing an injured workingman home, where the fallen man receives the sacrament of extreme unction. Through this incident an intellectual and sensual world opens up for Theron which leads him away from his pretty wife Alice, away from his faith, and finally away from his ministry altogether. Theron's new Roman Catholic friend, Father Forbes, is steeped in the intellectual advances of Europe; and the beautiful Celia Madden, Father Forbes's suspiciously constant companion and the daughter of the local industrial magnate, practices a Dionysian feminism in her private chambers within her father's mansion.

The Madden mansion is a figure for the church to which these characters belong. When Celia returns from her education at "a distant convent," her father cedes a suite of rooms entirely to her in which she creates a pagan temple to art that nevertheless teems with the iconic trappings of her church – candles, gilt, perfume, music, paintings of mother and child. These rooms become the den in which the flames of Theron's growing desire for Celia are fanned during a private Chopin recital to which Celia invites him – she plays passionately, her red hair and loose nightgown flowing free. As Celia's dying brother Michael explains to Theron late in the novel, Celia and Father Forbes are safe because, for all their provocative behavior and beliefs, "they are held up by the power of the true Church, as a little child learning to walk is held up with a belt by its nurse. They can say and do things, and no harm at all come to them, which would mean destruction to you, because they have help, and you are walking alone."

This exhortation to keep among his own people comes too late for Theron: he makes the mistake of taking seriously, or rather, Protestantly, the intellectual modernity of Celia and Father Forbes. Theron sees in their professed unbelief the call to conversion: the call to abandon his own belief. He sees in their sophistication, and in Celia's money and sensual freedom, the image of his own desires, the grand projection of the upwardly mobile acquisitiveness that got him into trouble before the novel opens. This liberating modernity feeds his desire for Celia, too (fueled in turn by jealous fantasies about her relations with the priest); at the same time, he feels a growing attraction to Father Forbes, an attraction Frederic sets in homoerotic terms.[4] The novel implies that the aesthetic structures of ritual – evident in those first enchanting Latin prayers for the dying man, sublimated into Celia's music and into the sensual raptures of the liberated Theron – represent the real persistence of religious life in a modern world.

When Theron abandons the ministry for a career in politics, we know he has found an analogous profession – making empty speeches that move crowds. Frederic seems to suggest that unlike Celia's secularized Catholicism, Theron's sublimation of the religious act of preaching reveals not the persistence of religion but its original bankruptcy. Frederic ensures that we have this distance from Theron, despite the narrative voice's identification with him, by periodically allowing us to see him as others see him and thereby ensuring that we see how ridiculous he has become. Max Weber's analysis a decade later of secular capitalism as an outgrowth of Protestantism takes a more generous view of secularized Protestantism than Frederic does, but had Frederic lived (he died in 1898), he might well have found Weber a natural ally for his thought.[5] Still, *The Damnation of Theron Ware* is so sympathetic to Catholic aestheticism and its human complexity that the damnation at issue is of American Protestantism more than it is a damnation of just one man or of religion wholesale. This is not a novel about the waning of religious power in the face of scientific advance and historical critique, but about its aesthetic future in plural America.

Two Americans, William and Henry James, are importantly responsible for how that future evolved. William James, in *Varieties of Religious Experience: A Study in Human Nature* (1902), aimed to be scientific about religion in the mode of the newly emerging social sciences, but left unanswered the question of whether religious experience reflects religious realities. He refused the stance of the nineteenth-century atheist "man of science" – who was sure God did not exist – in favor of suspending both belief and disbelief in the religious truth of the experiences he described. If the approach owed something to his family history – his father was a believer in the doctrines of Swedenborg, and wielded a powerful influence over both William and his brother Henry – it also owed something to the techniques Henry was developing in fiction.

The rigorously limited psychological point of view through which Henry James came to focalize the third-person narrative (apparent most dramatically in the child Maisie's consciousness in *What Maisie Knew* [1897]) is a literary form of William James's suspension of the very question of belief. As Pericles Lewis has pointed out, Henry James's interest in the reality of the unseen (as in *The Turn of the Screw* [1898]) and his characters' returns to the near-empty churches of Europe, suggest in broader terms this modernist's literary engagement with questions that had long been the province of religion.[6] The sometimes fatal, always tragic misunderstandings of James's Americans in Catholic Europe (we might think of Lambert Strether's fascination with the Catholic aristocracy of France in *The Ambassadors* [1903], or Daisy Miller, catching her death while out and about with an Italian man in Rome in *Daisy Miller* [1878]) echo Theron Ware's inability to understand Celia Madden and her world. James's characters misunderstand with a good deal more tact than the Rev. Ware, and thus balance more equitably the two kinds of religious subjectivity William James laid out: the healthy-minded (which he identified with Catholicism and the idea of grace through works) and the sick souls (those Protestant types who live with the tragedy of original sin, the worry of a constantly examined conscience, and salvation by the unpredictable grace of an unknowable God).

Back on American soil – indeed, deeply embedded in that soil – the question of faith and belief is more broadly, but no less passionately, pursued by William Faulkner. What William James had called "the will to believe" (in his 1896 essay of that name) becomes the unifying refrain of *Light in August* (1933), where the capacity – or the desire – to believe, even in the absence of evidence, defines both the most tragic and the most redemptive elements of the novel's vision. On the one hand we are given Joe Christmas, whose uncertain racial parentage dooms him to what Faulkner represents as a spiritual homelessness. On the other hand, the young unmarried woman Lena Grove, wandering at the end of the novel with her newborn baby and her face "calm as a church," becomes the image of the Madonna. She believes that all will be right with the world in the wake of the baby's birth. This is the apotheosis of her more specific belief, throughout the novel, that the father of her baby, the scoundrel Lucas Burch, will welcome her and the child when she finally tracks him down. Her faith in the goodness of this particular bad man becomes a redemptive faith in the renewal of the world. The blossoming of this faith is chronologically simultaneous in the narrative with racial catastrophe: the death and castration of Joe Christmas.

Like Lena's, the face of Joe Christmas's murderer, a self-appointed keeper of public order named Grimm, is said to be "serene" with the "unearthly luminousness of angels in church windows," suggesting the unstable moral charge of religious imagery.[7] Like Frederic's vision of Protestantism, Faulkner's in this novel is deeply critical. The disgraced Rev. Hightower sees the church destroyed by "the professionals who control it and who have removed the bells from its steeples." He sees those steeples as "empty . . . bleak, skypointed not with ecstasy or passion but in adjuration, threat, and doom." That threat is manifested memorably in the novel by Christmas's adoptive father, McEachern, who teaches Christmas Presbyterianism with the strap and prays to "a Presence who could not even make a phantom indentation in an actual rug." And the boy ends up in McEachern's hands as an indirect consequence of Christmas's grandfather Hines's fanatical religious hatred; Hines was first to accuse the child of having "nigger blood," saw him as the "devil's spawn," God's curse on the world for women's "bitchery." Lena's baby is born in the cabin where Christmas has lived. The horror-filled life of Christmas prepares a place – a humble shed, a manger – for the holy child. Between them the two messianic figures condense the life of Christ into a single paroxysm of violence: as Christmas is sacrificed, Lena's child is born.

If Lena's serenity is genuinely redemptive, while Grimm's is undercut by the horror of what he does to Joe Christmas, this redemptive quality is partly attributable to the difference between her Catholic penumbra and the bell-less "steeples" of Protestant churches. Although the "angels in church windows" to which Grimm's face is compared are from a Catholic decorative vocabulary, his name and his "professional" administration of order in the town associate him most strongly with the novel's Protestant elements. But Faulkner pushes his meditations on belief well beyond these sectarian registers, to explore, as the James brothers had, how belief informs individual perception, and how the isolation of one mind from another produces divergent but autonomous understandings of the world. The narrative itself advances formally on the basis of these philosophical questions, with its repeated deferrals of revelation and the strategy of returning to the same stretch of time so that it can be narrated through different characters and thus known beyond the limitations of individual belief. These writers' meditations on religion thus cannot be separated from the modernist analysis of consciousness that, for so many writers, drove formal innovation; indeed, my point reinforces, from another perspective, the claim Robert Chodat makes that fiction and philosophy are closer to one another than we might think in the American tradition.[a] The ambivalence about religion evident thematically in Faulkner and Henry James translates into supremely successful literary strategies.

As complex as religion appears in the novels of the early twentieth century, religion was an even more various affair in American life at large. The pointless carnage of the First World War challenged the resources of religion and literature alike, and a frank American secularism flourished in the 1920s, as we see, for example, in F. Scott Fitzgerald's novels *The Great Gatsby* (1925) and *Tender is the Night* (1934). While some intellectuals (such as T. S. Eliot, who converted to Anglo-Catholicism in the mid-1920s) found a satisfying spiritual response to the modern world among the world's store of religious traditions, others turned to religion for more secular purposes. Walter Benn Michaels has argued, for example, that religion becomes a flexible technology for nativist racial logic in Faulkner's *The Sound and the Fury* (1929) and Willa Cather's *Death Comes for the Archbishop* (1927).[8] Side by side with these modernist engagements with religion, popular religion continued to flourish in America: the American Pentecostal church was born in revival meetings led by the African American preacher William J. Seymour at the Azuza Street Mission in Los Angeles (1906); black churches flowered alongside the arts in the Harlem Renaissance; immigrant religious communities – mainly Jewish and Catholic – thrived in urban enclaves; the Protestant Establishment retained its hold on the elite strata of American social life.

This variousness never went away, though it was eclipsed in civic life at mid-century by a blander public piety that was the counterpart to the patriotism required by America's entrance into the Second World War. After the war, that piety came to be conflated with the values of American democratic capitalism – values newly labeled "Judeo-Christian" – in order to morally distinguish the American way of life from "godless" Communism. As the journalist William Lee Miller wrote, Americans at mid-century were "very fervent believers in a very vague religion."[9] The sometime-sociologist Will Herberg in his famous *Protestant, Catholic, Jew* (1955) described religion in America as a function of wanting to belong to an American way of life.[10] Indeed, integrating Jewishness into American culture depended upon its being seen as a "religion" on the model of Christianity – a model that was not a

a See Robert Chodat, "Philosophy and the American novel," chapter 39 in this volume.

natural fit, given Judaism's emphasis on practice and on questioning, over internalized belief in the Protestant sense. In the fifties and into the mid-sixties, the Civil Rights Movement brought religious leaders to the center of the American political stage, but their religious credentials mainly underwrote a moral message of tolerance that unified a powerful coalition that included liberal Protestants, Catholic leftists, and Jewish humanists.

The work of James Baldwin in the 1950s and 1960s exemplifies these cross-currents in American religious life – the simultaneous importance of sectarian intensity and an often homogenizing religious pluralism. In his 1963 diatribe, "The Fire Next Time," Baldwin gives a disillusioned account of his conversion to evangelical Christianity at the age of fourteen. He calls the church a "gimmick" on a par with the other gimmicks – pimping, gambling, doping, and stealing – that blacks "on the Avenue" chose as a strategy for survival in the white world.[11] Baldwin abandoned anything resembling Christian belief of an orthodox sort not long after his conversion and brief career as a boy preacher. But his work is God-haunted from beginning to end.[12] In his first and most critically successful novel, *Go Tell It on the Mountain* (1953), he imagines a version of religion that solves all the problems with Christianity that he lays out in the later essay – problems he already saw when working on the novel, which he wrote well after leaving the church. The key term in this fictional truce with Christianity is ecstasy: the peculiar qualities of the ecstatic state – its physicality and the community's need to interpret it – allow the novel to reconfigure themes of politics, sexuality, and religion in relation to one another.

In *Go Tell It*, the young Brother Elisha is the object of the protagonist John Grimes's erotic fascination and love. John and Elisha arrive early to clean the church, but end up in a wrestling match that brings John thrillingly close to his friend's body. Most critics read the novel's erotics as evidence of the contradiction between John Grimes's awakening sexuality and the strictures of the black church.[13] I would argue that the religious ecstasy in *Go Tell It* has precisely the opposite effect. It brings those religious and sexual impulses inside the circle of the black church, into the company of the saints; what is more, this novel posits same-sex desire as the very version that can best be welcomed by the church itself.

Baldwin's counterintuitive move emerges in the way Elisha figures in John's ecstatic conversion. When John, slain in the spirit, cries out to the Lord, he hears a voice that turns out to be Elisha's bidding him to "Go through." When John comes to, reborn in Christ, he sees just above him Elisha "smiling; and behind him were the saints – Praying Mother

Washington, and Sister MacCandless, and Sister Price. Behind these, he saw his mother, and his aunt; his father, whom he despises, "for the moment, was hidden from his view." In short, he wakes to the perfect revision of the black church: a church where his father is excluded and his pairing with Elisha is smiled upon by his mother and by the singing saints. In the aftermath of John's ecstasy, Elisha gives him a "holy kiss." The doomed heterosexual pairing of John's mother and stepfather led them into the compromised institution of the church; by contrast, the pairing of John and Elisha becomes an entrance to the city of God, suddenly made radiant in the morning sun.

The sixties were a time not just of religious critique of Baldwin's sort or of the universalist ethics of the Civil Rights Movement; as Baldwin's interest in religious ecstasy suggests, the decade was also a time of religious revival in its most dramatic forms. This was evident in the counterculture's turn towards Eastern religions, and in the Jesus freaks and Hare Krishnas who became part of the countercultural scene. The Charismatic movement was sweeping through mainline denominations, starting in 1960 in an Episcopal church in California where the priest, Dennis Bennett, received the baptism in the Holy Spirit and, to his congregation's surprise, spoke in tongues. And in what at first seems like a more staid example, the Roman Catholic Church in the sixties undertook a major renewal in the wake of the Second Vatican Council – a renewal first expressed in the widespread abandonment of a ritual form that many thought completely exhausted: the Latin Mass. These religious developments had their literary counterparts, novels where the very genre was imagined in religious terms that echoed some of the religious thought on display in the so-called "Age of Aquarius."

J. D. Salinger, for instance, merged formal concerns with religious ones in a way that used the notion of literary *style* as a solution for the tensions between the attraction of religious intensity and the constraints of religious prejudice. Salinger was the son of a Jewish father and a Catholic mother, and he crafted his own syncretic spiritual practices throughout his life. The question of religion crops up throughout his work, but the most sustained meditation on the subject, and what I would call his manifesto on religion and fiction, comes in *Franny and Zooey* (1961). The novel tells the story of the young Franny Glass's religious crisis, brought about by her effort to follow the Russian Orthodox religious classic *The Way of the Pilgrim* (1884) in its admonition to "pray without ceasing." Returning home to the Glass family apartment on the Upper West Side after a nervous collapse, she receives the philosophical ministrations of her brother Zooey, a struggling actor living at home with their parents, former vaudevillians whose theatrical bent has been fully realized in their two youngest children. Zooey both chastises Franny for going about her prayer the wrong way and reminds her of the religious training they had both received from their beloved older brothers.

Zooey urges Franny to "know the Jesus to whom she is praying" – arguing for the crucial specificity of the religious tradition she has turned to in her spiritual crisis. The work of the novel is to show how this is not at odds with a thoroughly syncretic spirituality Franny and Zooey share as the legacy of their brothers' teaching. Like ecstasy for Baldwin, acting – the very idea of performance – becomes the solution to that tension. Zooey tells his sister that "acting is the only truly religious thing" she can do; to reach the humble human listener in the audience is, Zooey believes, to reach "Christ himself." Zooey insists that Franny must be truly Christian in her practice of prayer because it is a mode of sacred performance. The essence of acting, for Salinger, is to inhabit a voice, something that Salinger himself amplifies in the novel's style. His mannered prose and the relentless dialogue that fills the Glass apartment enact a belief in the human voice as the locus of divine presence. No matter what one is saying, to inhabit such voices fully (as actor or as the writer of fiction) is to be one with the verbal creativity of God.

Salinger's understanding of language as ritual form echoes in the work of writers well into the 1980s. For example, the work of the first literary-scholar-turned-media critic, Marshall McLuhan, reveals how Catholic conceptions of language pervaded American culture at that time.[14] In *Understanding Media* (1964), McLuhan argued that dramatic changes in media – from oral to written culture in the wake of the printing press, from written to aural and visual culture in the age of radio, television and film – changed cultures not through the ideas they disseminated but because the new media created new formal and abstract structures of meaning. That is, McLuhan claimed that the new media transformed not only what people thought about but more fundamentally, *how* they thought. McLuhan's famous formula, "the medium is the message," had a fundamentally Roman Catholic logic that was not lost on his critics. Not surprisingly, given his formalism, McLuhan lamented the demise of the Latin Mass.

The connection between language and the Mass has persisted in the imagination of Catholic writers for decades. Don DeLillo has a novelist in *Mao II* (1991) call his chosen genre "the Latin Mass of language, character, occasional new truth." DeLillo doesn't confine the mystical formalism of language to either the Mass or the novel, though. In novel after novel we see instances of ritual speech, sometimes emanating from cults (as in *The*

Names [1982]), sometimes from expatriates in Greek cafés (also in *The Names*), sometimes from Marxist theory or the Marine Corps manual (*Libra* [1988]), sometimes from the television (*White Noise* [1985], *Underworld* [1997]). Ritual language is, for DeLillo, everywhere, but he is not thus imagining a secular religion. For the redemptive reality of ritual language consists in its ability to access something like divine presence on the Eucharistic model, without requiring either traditional belief in religious doctrine or the violence associated with cult practice. Language can do this, DeLillo suggests, precisely insofar as it becomes pure form.[15]

Such large-scale and self-reflexive forms are something of a convention among novels aiming to be "literary" in the second half of the twentieth century and into the twenty-first century. Examples include William Gaddis's *The Recognitions* (1955), which has been used by the deconstructive theologian Mark C. Taylor as the literary paradigm for truly postmodern faith, and Thomas Pynchon's work, from *V.* (1963) through *Gravity's Rainbow* (1973) and beyond, which returns to formal pattern as the source of mystical transcendence, as in the mandala structures that repeat themselves in *Gravity's Rainbow*, or when Oedipa Maas looks down on the lights of San Narciso in *The Crying of Lot 49* (1966), seeing in them the pattern of an electrical circuit laid out on the land and at the same time experiencing what she thinks of as a "religious instant."[16] Denis Johnson invokes the similarly unknowable abstract pattern of history's particulars in *Tree of Smoke* (2007), as Skip Sands, the scion of a Boston Catholic clan, endlessly reorganizes a CIA file of all known intelligence on Vietnam under the charismatic direction of his uncle, Colonel Francis Xavier Sands. The file is known to the Colonel and his disciples as "the tree of smoke," the worldly site of something like the overwhelming, and ultimately divine, Real embodied in the fecund lands and violent conflicts of Southeast Asia. Johnson's is ultimately an unknowable Hebraic God – not just in *Tree of Smoke* but also in the earlier *Resuscitation of a Hanged Man* (1991), and perhaps less obviously, his celebrated short story collection *Jesus' Son* (1992).[17]

The novels I have been discussing craft, in literary form, models of religious mysticism, but there are other religious discourses at work in the contemporary novel as well. In this vein we might identify, finally, a few writers who belong to a prophetic tradition. For these writers it is the power of the literary voice rather than mystical structure that is imagined in religious terms. Two contemporary writers working in the idiom of Faulkner, Toni Morrison and Cormac McCarthy, use biblical or preacherly cadences to figure the authority not only of characters but – more importantly – of their own narratives.

Morrison's *Song of Solomon* (1977) appropriates the very name of a canonical text of the Old Testament, and in the character of Pilate she imagines a supernaturally powerful woman who leads the central protagonist, Milkman, to inherit the supernatural power of flight that legendarily belonged to his African ancestor Solomon. Morrison leaves it as an open question whether flight is just a figure for empowerment or something we are meant to accept as part of the fictional world she creates, and thus as a testament to the truths of the African folklore from which she is drawing. Either way, the supernatural returns in *Beloved* (1987), where the past is imagined as having a supernatural power over the present that goes far beyond the genealogical cursedness represented by Faulkner's Joe Christmas.[b] The reincarnated ghost of Sethe's murdered baby, Beloved terrorizes not only her mother (with the voraciousness of her desire for her) but also serves to remind the community of women around Sethe of the evils they have each had to banish. More generally, the past of slavery continues to exist in the form of "rememory," disembodied experience of the slave past that, Sethe warns her daughter Denver, can repossess even those who "never were there." At the close of the novel one of the narrative voices tells us that the story of Beloved, finally vanquished by the community of women, is not a story to "pass on." It means both that this is not a story that should be communicated, given the suffering it confers on the listener, and that it is a story that will never die. The ghost Beloved doubles the novel of the same name, and *Beloved*, like Beloved, is imagined as a supernaturally persisting narrative, a story with a life of its own.

For Cormac McCarthy the cadence of scripture and of religious poetry (especially *Paradise Lost*) permeates the very fabric of his novels' sentences, most notably in his masterpiece, *Blood Meridian* (1985). Practicing a version of parataxis common in biblical Hebrew – linking elements in a sentence using "and" rather than subordinating grammatical structures like "if," "until," or "because" – McCarthy represents the US–Mexico border in the late 1840s as a space of ultimate metaphysical truths.[c] The scriptural sound of this novel is so convincing that the biblical and literary scholar Robert Alter cites McCarthy's English (along with that of Gertrude Stein and Faulkner) as proof that an English translation of the Pentateuch (the first five books of the Bible) that honors the sound of the Hebrew is, after the literary advances of the twentieth

b For more on *Beloved* in the context of supernatural fiction, see Elizabeth Young, "Supernatural novels," chapter 13, 232–233.

c For a reading of *Blood Meridian* as a "borderland novel," see Ramón Saldívar, "The American borderlands novel," chapter 62, 1036–1038; Stephanie Le Menager reads it elsewhere in the volume as a frontier novel (see "Imagining the frontier, chapter 31, 530–531).

century, within reach.[18] The central character of *Blood Meridian*, the evil and charismatic Judge Holden, speaks with a voice similarly biblical in cadence; the moral emptiness of his rhetorical power suggests a hollowed-out shell of religiously inflected authority – an authority to be prophetic without having anything to prophesy. McCarthy's late novel, *The Road* (2006), set in a similarly violent and apocalyptically devastated landscape (Appalachia ten years into an apparent nuclear winter) gives us a more sympathetic version of such authority. The father and young son who make their way from Tennessee to the Gulf survive on the conviction that they are "carrying the fire." This Promethean image goes beyond the moral – it does not only mean that they are "the good guys," people who have refused to turn to cannibalism to survive. It means, more importantly, that the father has reason to preserve the son, and himself as the boy's protector, even in a world completely without hope of reconstruction. The transcendent quality of that fire persists even though it refers to nothing within or beyond the ruined world; the fire is best understood, then, as a figure for the luminous quality of the novel's prose, which like the boy's spirit persists despite the utter absence of social life and of natural and built worlds upon which to base it. The destroyed world allows McCarthy to imagine a language that by definition transcends all its possible objects.

In terms of style and religious preoccupation the writer working closest to McCarthy at the end of the century is Marilynne Robinson, though as an avowed Christian her version of religious imagination seems to promise specific substance in contrast to McCarthy's hollowed-out prophecy. But her Calvinism – which for Robinson is summed up in the twinned facts of God's radical freedom to extend grace, and humanity's fundamental difference from God – results in an equal emphasis on the voice as the locus of the transcendent. Robinson is more various in her narrative practice, inhabiting the lyric voice of a young girl's consciousness in her first novel, *Housekeeping* (1980), the voice of a minister at the end of his life in *Gilead* (2004), and the free indirect discourse focused through the consciousness of a woman at midlife in *Home* (2008). Her narrative voices, to put it generally, are the voices of thought, and part of what her characters think about is explicitly religious – as when the minister John Ames reflects upon theology and forgiveness in *Gilead*, or when Ruth compares herself to Lot's wife or imagines the resurrection of the saints in *Housekeeping*. But the way they are imagined to live these rich internal lives suggests the human value that Robinson elsewhere, in her many essays on religious subjects, grounds in the Calvinist understanding of God's grace as it reaches toward inevitably flawed human beings.[19] The formal commitments of Robinson's narratives, then, are grounded in her religious worldview precisely because they so powerfully communicate human thought within God's world.

Robinson's work represents a convergence of the religious currents I have been tracking in twentieth-century American fiction. Hers is a stance – and a formal strategy – both intensely religious and fully pluralist, the pluralism underwritten by the religious belief in God's radical freedom. And her work reminds us that for all the more sublimated forms of religious imagination in American fiction of the twentieth century I have been discussing, there are also those more obvious examples of religiously inspired fiction. For example, we might think of the Catholic fictions of Flannery O'Connor as a counterpoint to Robinson's pluralist emphasis on God's freedom. In *Wise Blood* (1952) both major characters – Haze Motes and Enoch Emery – are utterly at the mercy of a Catholic understanding of metaphysical truth, even if they are not at the mercy of the church's worldly authority. In Haze Motes's case, he simply cannot escape Christ as a bodily reality no matter how hard he tries to be a flamboyant apostate, founder of the "Church Without Christ" (he looks like the minister his father was no matter what clothes or hats he buys for himself). In Enoch's case, his "wise blood" prompts him – against his will, even – to complete outlandish and opaque rituals, many of which approximate Catholic rituals, that have the effect of driving Haze (whom Enoch dragoons into participating) to the spiritual extreme of self-mutilation. In blinding himself with lye Haze fully reveals his inability not to believe in Christ. His lack of freedom to avoid God is epitomized when his car – the embodiment of American freedom, the one thing Haze truly desires – is pushed over an embankment by a police officer who has stopped him for reckless driving. Haze's effort not to believe is good only for the junkyard in the wake of Christ's inexorable truth. The failure of Haze to leave his Protestant upbringing (he makes clear, at one point, that he is no Catholic) proves the underlying failure of Protestantism in general in the novel: he can protest all he wants, but he cannot leave Christ's real presence, the foundation of the one true church.

This novel and her famous short stories have made O'Connor perhaps the best-known Catholic writer of the century, but among novelists focused thematically on religion we might also think of her contemporary Walker Percy, or Thomas Keneally, an Australian Catholic writer working slightly later in the century who was responsible for the nonfiction novel *Schindler's List* (1982), the film version of which – directed by Steven Spielberg (1993) – is probably the most famous Holocaust film ever made. Similarly, we find a WASPy Protestantism on display in John Updike's novels. Religion, an intermittent concern in Updike's famous Rabbit novels, becomes the central subject of *Roger's Version* (1986), a retelling of *The Scarlet Letter*, where a young man trying to use computer modeling to prove the existence of God faces off, theologically and amorously, against a smug and unbelieving professor of religion. Beyond these Christian examples, we find the Jewish fiction of writers such as Cynthia Ozick, Bernard Malamud, Myla Goldberg, and Anita Diamant. Diamant's novel *The Red Tent* (1997), the fictionalized story of the biblical Dinah, was widely popular, but she built her career writing self-help books on living a contemporary Jewish religious life. Major Native American novelists have been consistently interested in religion – both in recuperating tribal religions and in mounting sustained critiques of the forced Christianization of Indian children. Leslie Marmon Silko mounts some of the most searing of such critiques, while, in her novel *Ceremony* (1977), she imagines a version of Native religion powerful enough to heal the compounded scars of reservation life and the Vietnam war. Louise Erdrich manages in her novels – especially the gorgeous *Last Report on the Miracles at Little No-Horse* (2001) – to imagine a synthesis of Catholicism and Native spirituality, suggesting how the peculiarly vague qualities of the American religious imagination as I have described it can serve the more specific purposes of what Sean Kicummah Teuton describes elsewhere in this volume as assimilationist narratives.[d] In the most popular vein of religious fiction, we might note the runaway success of novels such as Tim LaHaye and Jerry B. Jenkins's *Left Behind* series and its spinoffs (1995–), about the seven years of Tribulation on Earth following the "rapture," in which all true Christian believers are gathered up bodily into Heaven, or the word-of-mouth/internet marketing phenomenon, William P. Young's *The Shack* (2007), an allegorical novel about a father meeting God's incarnations when he goes to visit the remote shack where his daughter was murdered.

I group these works together, despite their obvious diversity as examples of the genre and in the range of their ambitions as literature, because their engagements with religion are mostly thematic rather than formal – that is, the authors do not see religion so much as a force shaping what literature is and does than as a force literary discourse reflects upon or with which it wrestles. While a writer such as Flannery O'Connor might be said to embrace a Catholic quality in the New Critical understanding of literature that guided her composition process, the fiction's main religious investment is to be found more in her stories' allegorical punch than in their New Critical sense of form

d See Sean Kicummah Teuton, "The Native American Tradition," chapter 67, 1109–1111.

and structure.[e] These remain works that are important to the history of how American religion and literature speak to one another in the twentieth and into the twenty-first century, for they testify both to readers' and writers' interest in thinking about religion and to the continuing American belief – most evident in the overtly evangelical fiction – that novels are an effective vehicle for delivering spiritual messages.

Mystical structure or divine voice or scriptural authority or religious themes: through these modes of religious discourse American fiction navigates the twentieth century's various and vibrant religious landscape. Since the terrorist attacks of 2001 both the interest in religion and the status of mysticism in particular have changed. The dominant strain of literary engagement with religion had been Christian, with Jewish fiction an identifiable but more prominently humanist, parallel strain, with a syncretic engagement with Asian religion and philosophy overlaying both and reaching back to the American transcendentalists of the nineteenth century. Interest in Islam among American writers can be found as early as Royall Tyler's *The Algerine Captive* (1797), and reappears in the twentieth century in William Burroughs's writing from Tangier in the 1950s and 1960s, in Paul Bowles's *The Sheltering Sky* (1949) and *Let it Come Down* (1952), and in Baldwin's critiques of an American offshoot, the Nation of Islam. It is only just emerging as a sustained concern in American writing.[20] For Burroughs, though he found international Tangier a liberating space and was inspired by certain aspects of Muslim culture, Islam was another monotheism out to exert its control over the individual mind; for Baldwin, the Nation of Islam substituted racism against whites for racism against blacks under the guise of religion – no improvement, in Baldwin's view. Like many of the post-9/11 books on Islam, Azar Nafisi's bestselling *Reading Lolita in Tehran: A Memoir in Books* (2003), though written by an "insider" to Muslim culture, attempts to understand what is presented as a sharp divide between Islam and Western culture. She casts the difference in political terms even when the subject is literature, though as Bruce Robbins argues in this volume, the more common way to face that divide is simply to

e See Gregory S. Jackson, "Religion and the nineteenth-century American novel" (chapter 10). Jackson's essay demonstrates how realism in the novel emerges in tandem with the desire to make the sermon a more powerful instrument of religious instruction that would not lay out doctrines so much as make its hearers experience religious feelings, and help them imagine how to – and how not to – live as Christians. In this sense religious themes did have a profound formal impact on what Jackson calls "homiletic novels" of the nineteenth century. By the twentieth century the realism borrowed from the homily was no longer a new development in the novel.

retreat from it into the domestic, or make the foreign into a genre of nothingness. The latter solution (as in *Tree of Smoke*, an example Robbins and I both invoke) has something in common with the empty religion I have spoken of here.[f]

A notable exception to this preoccupation with Islamic authoritarianism and difference can be found in Robert Stone's *Damascus Gate* (1998), a mystical thriller featuring a skeptical reporter, Christopher Lucas, son of a Jew and a Catholic, at home in neither faith, and a peaceful American Sufi, Sonia Barnes, teaming up to foil American fundamentalist Christians and extremist Israeli Jews plotting to blow up the Temple Mount and thus usher in the Armageddon. *Damascus Gate* epitomizes the closing movements of the mystical turn in American fiction that I have been tracking in this chapter, a turn palpable in both high- and low-culture novels. In the mystical tradition of Sufism Stone finds an acceptable version of the Islam so persistently imagined as anathema to religious pluralism. (It is telling, too, that the Sufi must be American – as if to say that an acceptable form of Islam must somehow be made into an American form.)

After 9/11 comes a less mystical and utopian religious sense; the vagueness of DeLillo, McCarthy, Johnson, or Pynchon, or the utopianism of Erdrich, looks less powerful as religious imagination in the present moment than visions of religion both darker and more traditional. The most compelling of such visions, for this reader, is the one we find in the fiction of Edward P. Jones, a writer working in the African American tradition mined by Toni Morrison. An omniscient but uncaring God is mirrored in the omniscient narrative of his Pulitzer Prize-winning epic novel *The Known World* (2004) (about the fictional Manchester County, Virginia and its black and white slaveholders). In his story collections, *Lost in the City* (1992) and *All Aunt Hagar's Children* (2006), satanic figures show up to harass women on the street, in the supermarket, in their very beds. Jones's God is largely silent and complicit with the violence of history. His devil is alive and well, intimate and scary.

Notes

1. Gustave Flaubert, letter to Louise Colet, December 9, 1852. I am indebted to Pericles Lewis's *Religious Experience and the Modernist Novel* (Cambridge: Cambridge University Press, 2010) for the quotation.

f Bruce Robbins considers post-9/11 novels' attempts to represent confrontations between the USA and the Islamic world in "The worlding of the American novel," chapter 66. For his discussion of *Tree of Smoke*, see 1103–1104.

2. An essential pre-history to Catholicism's increasing importance in twentieth-century American literature can be found in Jenny Franchot's *Roads to Rome: The Antebellum Protestant Encounter with Catholicism* (Berkeley: University of California Press, 1994).
3. Stanton Garner gives a detailed history of the novel's composition and publication in England and America in "History of the Text," included in *The Harold Frederic Edition*, vol. III, *The Damnation of Theron Ware or Illumination*, text established by Charlyne Dodge (Lincoln: University of Nebraska Press, 1985), 353–415.
4. Several critics have discussed the erotics of the novel. See Thomas Ferraro, "Of 'Lascivious Mysticism' and Other Hibernian Matters," *U.S. Catholic Historian* 23.3 (Summer 2005): 1–17; John W. Crowley, "The Nude and the Madonna in *The Damnation of Theron Ware*," *American Literature* 45.3 (November 1973): 379–389; Fritz Oehlschlaeger, "Passion, Authority, and Faith in *The Damnation of Theron Ware*," *American Literature* 58.2 (May 1986): 238–255; Lisa Watt MacFarlane, "Resurrecting Man: Desire and *The Damnation of Theron Ware*," *Studies in American Fiction* 20.2, (Autumn 1992): 127–143.
5. Max Weber, *The Protestant Ethic and the Spirit of Capitalism* (1905), trans. Talcott Parsons (London and Boston: Unwin Hyman, 1930).
6. See Pericles Lewis, " 'The Reality of the Unseen': Shared Fictions and Religious Experience in the Ghost Stories of Henry James," *Arizona Quarterly* 61.2 (Summer 2005): 33–66. Carrie Bramen, in this volume, sees James's relation to religion as one primarily of rejecting his father's spiritual worldview in favor of an "indeterminate" world of social relations. See "James, pragmatism, and the realist ideal," chapter 18, 309.
7. For an important early treatment of religion in the novel, see C. Hugh Holman, "The Unity of Faulkner's Light in August," *PMLA* 73.1 (March 1958): 155–166.
8. See Walter Benn Michaels, *Our America: Nativism, Modernism, and Pluralism* (Durham, NC: Duke University Press, 1995), esp. 1–15 (Faulkner), 78–82 (Cather).
9. William Lee Miller, *Piety Along the Potomac: Notes on Politics and Morals in the Fifties* (Boston: Houghton Mifflin, 1964), 33.
10. Will Herberg, *Protestant, Catholic, Jew: An Essay in American Religious Sociology* (Garden City: Doubleday, 1955).
11. James Baldwin, *The Fire Next Time* (c.1963; New York: Vintage, 1993), 24.
12. See, for example, Shirley S. Allen, "Religious Symbolism and Psychic Reality in Baldwin's *Go Tell it on the Mountain*," in *James Baldwin: A Critical Evaluation*, ed. Therman O'Daniel (Washington, DC: Howard University Press, 1977), and Clarence E. Hardy III, *James Baldwin's God: Sex, Hope, and Crisis in Black Holiness Culture* (Knoxville: University of Tennessee Press, 2003).
13. In *James Baldwin's God* Clarence E. Hardy III argues that Elisha's eroticized ecstasy represents the tension between the church – with its sexual repressiveness – and the "dangerous" impulses of the black male body. Csaba Csapó reads the novel's ending, where Elisha gives the newly converted John the "holy kiss,"

as demanding a trade-off between homoerotic love and Christian faith. See "Race, Religion and Sexuality in Go Tell It on the Mountain," in *James Baldwin's Go Tell It on the Mountain: Historical and Critical Essays*, ed. and introduction Carol E. Henderson (New York: Peter Lang, 2006), 57–74.

14. American Catholic culture in the fifties and sixties had attained celebrity status. In addition to the prominence of McLuhan in public life, one of the first – and most popular – television series was Bishop Fulton Sheen's "Life is Worth Living," which ran with great success from 1951 to 1957 (and for decades afterwards in the form of reruns); and Catholic writers like Flannery O'Connor, Graham Greene, and Walker Percy were well known to general readers.
15. For the full analysis of DeLillo's relation to the Latin Mass, see my "Don DeLillo's Latin Mass," *Contemporary Literature* 47.3 (2006): 343–380.
16. For Taylor's reading of Gaddis, see *Confidence Games: Money and Markets in a World Without Redemption* (Chicago: University of Chicago Press, 2004). On the mandala, see Steven Weisenburger, *A Gravity's Rainbow Companion: Sources and Contexts for Pynchon's Novel* (Athens: University of Georgia Press, 1988); for an early and influential reading of *Lot 49*'s religious structures, see Edward Mendelson, "The Sacred, the Profane, and *The Crying of Lot 49*," in *Pynchon: A Collection of Critical Essays*, ed. Edward Mendelson (Englewood Cliffs, NJ: Prentice Hall, 1978). See also John McClure's discussion of Pynchon and other contemporary writers in *Partial Faiths: Postsecular Fiction in the Age of Pynchon and Morrison* (Athens: University of Georgia Press, 2007).
17. For a more extensive discussion of religion in Johnson's work, see my "Fiction in Review," *The Yale Review* 97.1 (January 2009): 155–162.
18. See the introduction to Robert Alter, *The Five Books of Moses: A Translation with Commentary* (New York: W. W. Norton, 2004). See my fuller discussion of biblical style in chapter four of *Postmodern Belief: American Literature and Religion since 1960* (Princeton: Princeton University Press, 2010).
19. See, for example, her essays on John Calvin and on her childhood experience of religion in the collection *The Death of Adam: Essays on Modern Thought* (Boston: Houghton Mifflin, 1998).
20. The best work so far on the Arab world in the American imagination is being done by Brian T. Edwards. His book *Morocco Bound: Disorienting America's Maghreb, from Casablanca to the Marrakech Express* (Durham, NC: Duke University Press, 2005) has excellent chapters on Bowles and Burroughs.

45
Faulkner and the Southern novel

CANDACE WAID

Penning his infamous critique of the state of art, letters, and literacy in the cultural desert he dubbed "The Sahara of the Bozart," H. L. Mencken quotes a "true poet," one J. Gordon Coogler, whom he calls "the last bard of Dixie": "Alas for the South! Her Books have grown fewer. / She was never much given to literature." According to Mencken, with the single exception of James Branch Cabell, "you will not find a single southern prose writer who can actually write."[1] Soon after Mencken wrote these words in 1917, the region he had defined as a desert would become home to an unparalleled concentration of the most gifted writers in the history of the United States.

The Southern Renaissance has been declared by critics as having begun in 1929, the year that saw the publication of major works by Robert Penn Warren, Thomas Wolfe, and William Faulkner. From the outset, poet and sometime novelist Allen Tate questioned the appropriateness of the word "renaissance," concluding that this literary outpouring "was more precisely a birth, not a rebirth." Building on Tate's insights, historian C. Vann Woodward concluded that "nothing comparable had happened before in the South that could conceivably be said to have been reborn in the twentieth century." Introducing "[t]he second and more common historical usage of [the term] 'renaissance' " to refer to "the evocation of the ghost of a dead civilization, as the ghost of Hellenic culture was evoked in thirteenth to fifteenth-century Italy," Woodward insisted that "surely nothing of that sort took place in the South." However, this Southern literary emergence is indeed based on "the ghost of a dead civilization," the vital and haunting specter of slavery recorded and recounted in the slave narrative and slave novel.[2]

While Louis Rubin notes that critics could "justly feel uncomfortable . . . talking about an entity known as 'Southern Literature,' " as opposed to individual authors, he insists on the necessity of addressing this phenomenon, placing Faulkner as only "the most distinguished" of what he recognizes as "a galaxy of accomplished literary artists."[3] If the quantity of literary production is impressive in the twentieth-century South, the quality is shocking. Amid a region known for its illiteracy, the power of orality and the story cycle has been central to twentieth-century Southern literature. Arguably, this literature has created the South, and page by page it both answers and begs the question of Southern distinctiveness.

William Faulkner (who once, while quite drunk, resisted going further north than he had already been on the subway system in Manhattan) had an unerring sense of direction. Faulkner never denied being Southern and he was among the first to acknowledge the existence of Southern literature as a phenomenon. African American writers and Harlem Renaissance figures such as Zora Neale Hurston and Alice Dunbar-Nelson also chose to identify themselves as Southern. Dunbar-Nelson (best known for her New Orleans stories in *The Goodness of St. Rocque* [1899]) enunciated the grounds of her own race-blind ambition, expressed in her desire to surpass George Washington Cable as a great "Southern writer."[4] Jean Toomer, the most influential ancestor of Southern modernism, published *Cane* (1923), a prose poem cycle that has increasingly been understood as a highly experimental novel. This lyrical masterpiece, seen as a culmination of the experimental promise of the Harlem Renaissance and the African American exploration of the collage form, was written by an author who pleaded unsuccessfully with his publisher, Horace Liveright, to keep *Cane* from being marketed as a work by an African American. Toomer claimed that he was a new American, and wanted to be true to all of the bloods that ran in his veins.[a]

Alice Walker, recalling a course on Southern literature that consisted of works by Faulkner, Welty, McCullers, and O'Connor, remembers reading Flannery O'Connor at Sarah Lawrence in the 1960s, and has acknowledged O'Connor's fiction as the reason that she had no desire to live and write in a segregated literature. Born in a sharecropper's shack, Walker was capable of imagining a literary estate that did not cede territory. Able to distinguish "Southern" from "white," Walker noted that there were no black Southern writers taught in the racially focused course she took.[5] While C. Vann

a See also Valerie Babb's essay in this volume, "Wright, Hurston, and the direction of the African American novel" (chapter 42), which reads *Cane* as "reflect[ing] a classic black migratory pattern, from rural South to urban North, and, in its ending, back to rural South" (702).

Also in this volume, Barbara McCaskill's "The African American novel after Reconstruction" (chapter 29) examines figurations of the South "as a complex, multi-faceted place: as a symbol of the former slaves' contested claims to citizenship and equality; as America's violent, fratricidal shadow; as source of a dynamic black culture grounded in an African heritage; as a potentially powerful nexus of African American educational, political, and economic achievement" (484).

Woodward would understand that the region would come of age when the adjective "Southern" referred to blacks as well as whites, Woodward and others continued to see the emergence of the Renaissance as a white mystery, rather than the progeny of aesthetic miscegenation inherent in William Faulkner's work as well as Alice Walker's literary genealogy.

Even the most conservative conception of the Southern Literary Renaissance, one that names a figure such as William Styron as Faulkner's heir, necessitates a consideration of the formal influence of Robert Penn Warren, finally placing both Warren and Styron in the tradition of the slave narrative. Styron's first novel, *Lie Down in Darkness* (1951) has been understood as being Faulknerian in theme while being indebted in formal terms to Warren's *All the King's Men* (1946), the most successful of his ten novels. Warren's fifth novel, *Band of Angels* (1955), concerns an elite light-skinned woman who discovers that she is a slave at the time of her father's death. Here, Warren rewrites the story of the "tragic mulatta" told in slave novels such as William Wells Brown's *Clotel; or The President's Daughter* (1853) and Frances E. W. Harper's *Iola Leroy; or Shadows Uplifted* (1892), to give the heroine of color a voice as the narrator, rather than as a victim.

A dozen years after Warren published his fictionalized slave narrative, William Styron penned a first-person account that gives voice and interiority to the most feared black revolutionary in US history. It speaks to the origins and materials of Southern literature that Styron's *Confessions of Nat Turner* (1967), recognized as his most successful work, is written in the threatening voice of a resisting slave, a character whose motivations include psycho-sexual torments in the form of fantasies about white women. *William Styron's Nat Turner: Ten Black Writers Respond* (1968) documents the Black Power movement's entry into the literary landscape as contested political ground, rejecting Styron's first-person foray into the experience of black masculinity. Styron, who would later speculate that he had "unwittingly created one of the world's first politically incorrect texts,"[7] had written a novel that revealed the heightened racial tensions over black masculinity that had reached a white heat in the late 1960s. The neo-slave narrative, often in novels set in the United States or the Caribbean, forms a suggestive parallel to the Southern novel as it continues to be developed as a site of political fiction that addresses race in narratives that use the past to reflect on problems in the present. In many ways, Faulkner's controversial *Light in August*, as it located this crisis of masculinity and incarceration within a body defined by race rather than color, provided a crucial turning point for writing about the violence inherent in the enforcement of race. The embodied conflict of Joe Christmas ignited political writers, often male, across the wavering and full spectrum of the color line.

The Southern Literary Renaissance began in a decade also known for its nostalgic idealizations of a plantation South, a mythology canonized in Margaret Mitchell's bestseller *Gone with the Wind* (1936) and given heft in over seventy Hollywood films trading on the "Old South." Mitchell's novel, which contains only one mixed-blood character, Dilsey (a name perhaps borrowed from Faulkner), avoids issues of race while promoting regeneration through capitalism. Faulkner's *Absalom, Absalom!*, published the same year as *Gone with the Wind*, places race and miscegenation at its center. In fictions that usually did not provide solutions or consolations, Faulkner created a world that could not satisfy programmatic Depression-era desires, but would inspire later writers of varying colors and classes to create their own complexly articulated versions of Faulkner's fictional Yoknapatawpha County.[8]

From the 1970s to the present, critics have touted the New Regionalism, a literary movement that continues, in the culturally deep tracks of Faulkner and Eudora Welty, to represent regions within the region that continues to be the most distinctive, productive, and accomplished literary area of the United States. Raymond Andrews was forty-four when he published *Appalachee Red* (1978), which chronicles life in his fictional Muskhogean County after World War I, a world that he examines in more depth in *Baby Sweet's* (1983), a novel set in a local brothel during the era of the Civil Rights Movement. More political, and situated in a plantation past, Ernest Gaines's eight novels take place in the fictional environs based on the actual River Lake Plantation, where his once enslaved family has continued to live for seven generations. The author of a work that narrates a woman from slavery into the twentieth century, *The Autobiography of Miss Jane Pittman* (1971), Gaines, like Faulkner, is known for multivocal narrations, in particular *A Gathering of Old Men* (1983), a work, which like Faulkner's *As I Lay Dying*, is presented through the first-person accounts of fifteen named narrators. Faulkner remains similarly recognizable as a formal presence for Randall Kenan in his creation of Tims Creek, a community whose fictional template includes layered stories, letters, and journal entries to build a Yoknapatawpha in the contemporary Carolina Piedmont.

Faulkner's work can be seen as one of the primary sources of this creative outpouring, the wellspring of a region whose narrative desire and accomplishment remain unabated. In terms of ethnic and race-based fictions, Faulkner is likewise a major influence. The only one of his novels that Faulkner himself felt was hopeless and that he had no desire to rewrite was his wonderfully offensive *Mosquitoes* (1929), which features artists, their would-be patrons, and hangers-on, talking about aesthetics and sex (often at the same time) while addressing such pressing questions as the development of advertising schemes for selling a good laxative.[9] Faulkner's most popular novel (arguably his only work that could merit classification as "popular" at all), *Sanctuary* (1931), was initially considered to be a work that could – with its lurid brothel and courtroom revelations (most shockingly the rape of a judge's daughter named "Temple" with a corn-cob) – land both its author and publisher in jail. Simultaneously deified and damned, Faulkner was an author of continued influence, but was nevertheless (with the exception of his "corn-cob book") out of print by 1946. Faulkner's own assessment of his career in 1945 is telling: "My books have never sold . . . the labor (the creation of my apocryphal country) of my life, even If I have a few things to add to it, will never make a living for me."[10]

Faulkner's need for money led him to take a job as a writer for Hollywood, where he worked intermittently on screenplays (1932–1953), most notably adaptations of Chandler's *The Big Sleep* and Hemingway's *To Have and Have Not.*[11] The Warner brothers would brag that they had the best writer in America on contract for slave wages. Critics have primarily seen this period when he worked as a writer for the film industry as a fallow time during which Faulkner's creative resources were sapped for lesser purposes.[12] While Faulkner did produce fewer and less critically celebrated works during the fifteen years between the publication of *Go Down, Moses* (1942), his powerfully experimental story cycle, and his return to the Snopes trilogy, any in his nineteen novels (*Soldier's Pay* [1926], *Mosquitoes* [1927], *Sartoris* [1929], *The Sound and the Fury* [1929], *As I Lay Dying* [1930], *Sanctuary* [1931], *Light in August* [1932], *Pylon* [1935], *Absalom, Absalom!* [1936], *The Unvanquished* [1938], *The Wild Palms* [*If I Forget Thee, Jerusalem*] [1939], *The Hamlet* [1940], *Go Down, Moses* [1942], *Intruder in the Dust* [1948], *Requiem for a Nun* [1951], *A Fable* [1954], *The Town* [1957], *The Mansion* [1959], *The Reivers* [1962]) would garner him a place in the history of the novel.[13] Taken together, the Snopes trilogy is the great, late Faulkner. Beginning with *The Hamlet* (1940), Faulkner traced the Snopes family's descent into spiritual vapidity through materialism in *The Town* (1957) and *The Mansion* (1959).

Responding to the interest of the French intelligentsia and other dedicated readers, Malcolm Cowley in 1946 brought Faulkner's immense accomplishments back before the American public in the form of *The Portable Faulkner* (1946). Cowley's visionary edition achieved what Faulkner had not; *The Portable Faulkner* made the US's most aggressive experimentalist readable and even palatable for generations. Ironically, the reputation of Faulkner's post-World War II work has suffered because of his earlier virtuosity. Critics have compared the late Faulkner with the iconic Faulkner, rather than seeing his late novels as works with a different purpose. Had Faulkner narrated nothing else concerning the dramatic changes precipitated by the war, his *Intruder in the Dust* (1948) would constitute a literary landmark for its treatment of black masculinity and manhood, presenting the threat of lynching through the constant odor of gasoline to reveal a United States where men of color cannot expect justice. If in 1948 the United States was not ready to acknowledge that there was a race problem in the South, if not in the whole country, the reception in 1960 of Harper Lee's only novel, *To Kill a Mockingbird*, suggests the importance of history to fiction and fiction to history.

In his hand-drawn map of Yoknapatawpha County, which initially appeared in *Absalom, Absalom!* (1936), Faulkner signs himself in as "sole owner and proprietor" by locating and listing characters and events from what critics have increasingly recognized as one long novel. Faulkner's long novel begins in 1929 with the publication of *Sartoris* and *The Sound and the Fury*, works that introduced the world that he would come to call his "own little postage stamp of native soil."[14] Short of Faulkner's own exclamation of pride to Ben Wasson that he had written a novel that was "a real son of a bitch," David Minter provides the most succinct assessment of Faulkner's departure from novelistic as well as psychological norms, concluding that "*The Sound and the Fury* is thematically regressive, stylistically and formally innovative."[15]

Faulkner's experimentalism was inspired by Edith Wharton's and Willa Cather's innovations in voice in their regional novels *Ethan Frome* (1911) and *The Professor's House* (1925).[b] *The Sound and the Fury* and *As I Lay Dying* descend directly from Wharton's and Cather's experiments in framing first-person narration. Tom Outland is a precursor for the Quentin Compson of *The Sound and the Fury*, as well as for Addie Bundren of *As I Lay Dying*. Like Outland, Quentin speaks directly despite his death in a narrative that is somehow both embedded and literally outside of time. Arguably, the novel originates from

b In "Cather and the regional imagination," chapter 26 in this volume, Tom Lutz insists on the cosmopolitanism of Faulkner and other regionalist authors who, in his reading, "assume specifically local mores and folkways are significant frames for their characters' understanding of the world and each other," while they also "take … for granted that elsewhere people and their doings are understood somewhat dissimilarly" (439–440). Significantly, both Jewett and Cather, as they focused on the similarities in domestic cultures devoted to fulfilling basic human needs, wrote about the relationship of localism, of regionalism, to an internationalism that crosses the boundaries of national literatures and national enmities based on the artificiality of politically mandated borders.

questions about time raised by Edith Wharton in a 1925 diatribe against modernism, condemning this movement for being located in a "pathological world where the action, taking place between people of abnormal psychology, and not keeping with our normal human rhythms becomes an idiot's tale, signifying nothing."[16]

Faulkner's breakthrough, as he described it in his two 1933 "Introductions" written for (but not used in) the Modern Library edition of *The Sound and the Fury*, grew out of rejection. Arthur Kinney has argued persuasively that Faulkner's manuscript version of *Flags in the Dust* is a carefully balanced work of art that was chopped into an inferior product.[17] Seen as too long, with too many storylines, the manuscript that Ben Wasson would edit into *Sartoris* tried the patience of those who had not yet become accustomed to Faulknerian prose. That *Flags in the Dust* ([1929, 1973]) was rejected for publication some eleven times caused Faulkner to return to first terms. There has been controversy over how Faulkner has presented his creative development, a questioning of his own mythologizing of the place of *The Sound and the Fury* as a point of origins that begins with a primal scene.[18] The novel's regressive theme of genital sexuality and procreation is a fundamental site of modernism, a movement that is itself profoundly concerned with origins. To extend Minter's insight, the brilliance of *The Sound and the Fury* is that Faulkner's formal innovation *is in itself* regressive. According to Faulkner, the novel "began with the picture of the little girl's muddy drawers, climbing that tree to look in the parlor window" onto a scene of death.[19] As Caddy views the body of "Damuddy," a word that is a seamless syllabic joining of daddy and mother and that refers to the novel's character of the grandmother, she reenacts a primal scene of language for Faulkner himself: "Damuddy" is the first of many words invented by Faulkner, that name that he as the first grandchild gave to his mother's mother.

In an act that underlines the centrality of primal language, *The Sound and the Fury* joins the mute and seemingly languageless (literally "infantile") Benjy, a thirty-three-year-old "idiot," to the crescendo of the black chorus of Dilsey's church on Easter morning, as they shout together and are made one by spiritual ecstasy. The call offered up to God in the novel's fourth section is the primal sound for food: "mmmmmmmmmmmmmmmmm." Moreover, the only language that Benjy understands is not the word "Caddy," but the primal sound for fear: "shhh" or in its English form: "hush."[20] Primal sounds that range across the northern continents of Europe and Asia, these human articulations for food and fear speak to the idea of universal utterance. The water-splashing scene, viewed widely as a microcosm of the novel as a whole, reveals this return to first terms that is so telling in what must be read as Faulkner's striking intentionality. Primal language is crucial to Benjy's version of the children playing in the branch. Initially, this scene (at least to the uninitiated) seems to suggest that Benjy may understand language:

> "I'll run away and never come back," Caddy said. I began to cry.
> Caddy turned around and said "Hush." So I hushed . . . Caddy was all wet and muddy behind, and I started to cry and she came and squatted in the water.
> "Hush now," she said. "I'm not going to run away." So I hushed. Caddy smelled like trees in the rain.

Deceptively simple, this passage reveals the control that underwrites the novel as a whole. The appearance that Benjy understands Caddy's threat gives way to the more plausible claim that Benjy may be responding to Caddy's tone of voice. Caddy's "hush" combines with the removal of the visual disturbance of her soiled drawers to silence her "bellering" brother. Speaking in first terms and concealing the harbinger of her coming "change," Caddy reveals the complexity within Benjy's seemingly simple perceptions.

Stating the "worst case," Eric Sundquist argues, "[T]here is reason to believe that without Faulkner's work of the next ten years *The Sound and the Fury* would itself seem a literary curiosity, an eccentric masterpiece of experimental methods and 'modernist' ideas."[21] But it must be argued (as Faulkner himself did argue) that his work of the next ten years would not have been conceivable without his having written *The Sound and the Fury*. Louis Rubin contends that in writing *The Sound and the Fury* Faulkner "extended and expanded" "his own sympathies," "eliminating . . . any elements of local color quaintness and folksy caricature,"[22] a transformation that would enable him to write about race and miscegenation. While scholars have been critical of Dilsey's larger-than-life status as a monumental and fallen "ruin," as she fills the door at the start of the closing section of *The Sound and the Fury*, she is a force of culture rather than nature, and as such counterbalances the goddess-like fecundity suggested by Caddy Compson, and also embodied by Eula Varner of *The Hamlet* (1940), a seductress who commits suicide in a Jefferson that has no place for a promiscuous daughter of the white elite.

The gentle ethnographic impulses recording and preserving a disappearing Southern past can be said to have returned with a vengeance in Toni Morrison's love-hungry and dissatisfied baby ghost who comes back in *Beloved* (1987) with a woman's appetites, remembering the "sixty million and more" who suffered and died during the Middle Passage.[c] As it rose to the highest level of articulation, Southern local color became political local color. Voice itself was the bearer of culture and the only way that people who had been legally established as things could assert their humanity. As local color became regionalism, this literature revealed cultural rules encoded in language, offering worlds to be decoded by readers who could find in fiction what Franz Boas termed "cultural relativism." The most famous of Boas's students in terms of her literary accomplishments, Alabama-born Zora Neale Hurston, returned to the South as a participant observer. Hurston wrote in folk voice, transcribing and commenting upon the vital oral cultures of turpentine camps and voodoo parlors, as well as the thriving African rituals of Haiti, where she wrote *Their Eyes Were Watching God* (1937).[d]

Faulkner's contribution to the ethnographic novel of manners is to expose a world that is highly nuanced and less genteel than the gentle analyses of culture characteristic of local color. Faulkner's work considers individuals, families, and communities in his Yoknapatawpha County as sites and subjects of anthropological inquiry. Just as John Galsworthy's Forsytes and Edith Wharton's Marvells and Dagonnets, and her Archers and Wellands, represent complex cultures, provincial aristocracies that can degenerate, Faulkner's Compsons, Sartorises, Sutpens, and McCaslins generate and degenerate from their cobbled-together self-fashionings as biblical patriarchs in plantation fictions. The Snopeses, the Gibsons, and the Beauchamps in their endurance could have provided mere grounds for local color, but instead these families introduce and frame the presence of the disinherited of the earth. Faulkner's Mink Snopes, his Ryder, and his Dewey Dell Bundren are feeling subjects who might have remained unexamined because each is (in Patricia Yaeger's moving term) a "throwaway body."[23] These detailed cultures – exposed by figures such as Toomer and Faulkner – open the sluice for George Wylie Henderson, Hurston, Richard Wright, and Eudora Welty: ethnographers all. The best of the Southern writers understand the crucial quality of the grotesque in a world where people are categorized as animals, brutes defined by their race and

c Michael Hill's essay on "Toni Morrison and the post-Civil Rights African American novel," chapter 64 in this volume, sees *Beloved* as emblematic of late twentieth-century African American novels in its "capacity to address the historical residue that informs a contemporary reality" (1078).

d Babb notes in this volume that in *Their Eyes Were Watching God* and other novels, Hurston demonstrates "the validity of oral culture as a means of artistic expression" and also "constructs thematic metaphors that equate orality with sense of self" (chapter 42, 708).

class.[24] The poor, the black, the pregnant, the female, the insane, the suicidal, the homicidal, and even the speechless idiots of Faulkner's Yoknapatawpha occupy and witness a complex, multivalenced and multivocal world that has been rendered through writing. This sensitivity to the "wretched of the earth" primed the pump for the least expected of voices in the tradition of Carson McCullers and Flannery O'Connor. While emerging from what are ultimately very different works, the voices of teenage protagonists from Bobbie Ann Mason's *In Country* (1985) and Dorothy Allison's *Bastard Out of Carolina* (1993) carry the burden of Dewey Dell Bundren into the final decades of the twentieth century.

In formal terms, the Southern novel is birthed by the major nineteenth-century tradition of African American letters in which the slave narrative gave rise to the slave novel, establishing a direct line of descent that leads to Mark Twain's *Adventures of Huckleberry Finn* (1885), Jean Toomer's *Cane* (1923), Faulkner's *Light in August* (1932), and his *Absalom, Absalom!* (1936). These last are the most Southern of Faulkner's novels, because they are both continuations of and inversions of the slave narrative, sending protagonists South toward a fatal knowledge of the racial secrets that have imprisoned them. While Kate Chopin's *The Awakening* (1899) and Zora Neale Hurston's *Their Eyes Were Watching God* present this journey toward racial knowledge as one of sexual epiphany, Faulkner's *Light in August* serves as a renewed point of origins for mid twentieth-century narratives that turn to the South to explore the violent narrative of black masculinity. Seen from this perspective, Richard Wright's most Southern novel is his memoir, *Black Boy* (1945), narrating his psychological journey South to his childhood as he writes his run toward freedom.

A novel for which Faulkner expressed his unqualified admiration, the culminating work in this tradition of the journey into the psychological heart of darkness, to know and experience the prison of race for whites as well as blacks, is Ralph Ellison's *Invisible Man* (1952). While *Invisible Man* clearly riffs on Faulkner's *As I Lay Dying* through the life story of a character named Trueblood, who dreams he is having relations with a woman in white in a grandfather clock, Ellison's man of color recalls waking to discover that he is violating his own daughter. The lives of Faulkner's poor whites are first the dream, then the nightmare come true for Ellison's blacks. *Invisible Man* identifies the source of enslaved minds in the Southern history of incarceration, but this self-confinement, like the potential for liberation, takes place underground in Harlem, suggesting that invisibility may cease through the Harlem, rather than the Southern, Renaissance.[e] All of these works involve the story of a journey South toward a fatal identity that lies at the crossroads of art and race. While this tradition includes *Absalom, Absalom!*, *Light in August* is clearly Faulkner's signifying novel in terms of presenting the crisis of black manhood. Joe Christmas can only be confirmed in his otherwise unknown and unknowable racial identity at the moment that his manhood is sacrificed, literally cut away in an act of actual castration.[25]

In addition to his influence on writing about masculinity, Faulkner's work is central to the continued force of the female-dominated mainstream in the history of the twentieth-century US novel. These headwaters do not only flow from the regionalist fictions of Wharton and Cather; they also pour from authors who focus on female cultures and the paradoxical necessity of a matriarchy that assigns a patriarchy its place by defining the terms of male protection and predation. To understand this period in Southern letters and in the development of the novel, it is necessary to introduce another innovator who was coeval with Faulkner. Katherine Anne Porter was most successful in her development of what she, eschewing the femininity of words such as "novella" and "novelette," called the "short novel," most notably *Old Mortality* (1937), *Noon Wine* (1937), and *Pale Horse, Pale Rider* (1939).[26] Written before *Absalom, Absalom!* was published, Porter's work anticipated the startling lyricism of Faulkner's *The Hamlet*, which along with *Absalom, Absalom!* opened the world for Carson McCullers and Eudora Welty, as well as the later mythopoetical, post-Weltian Yoknapatawphas of Toni Morrison and Louise Erdrich.

William Styron and Walker Percy are Faulkner's primary heirs in relation to a nationalist conception of Southern literature proceeding from a notion of "Southern" as white and male, and predicated on the existential narrative that attends the Southern male's self-immolation because of the failure of aristocratic honor.[f] Yet, in many ways, Welty and Morrison are Faulkner's strongest and most direct heirs because they are relentlessly experimental and because they (like Faulkner himself) descend from so many mythologies and literatures, so many voices and published volumes. Welty's work is most like

e Elsewhere in this volume Lovalerie King finds a positive trajectory in *Invisible Man*, which she reads as concluding in the attainment of subjectivity and the American Dream. (See "Ellison and Baldwin: aesthetics, activism, and the social order," chapter 43).

f Elsewhere in this volume, Robert Chodat discusses the tentatively optimistic conclusions of Percy's novels, reading them as typical of "the sense of mourning characteristic of much twentieth-century white Southern writing" ("Philosophy and the American novel," chapter 39, 659).

Faulkner's in its search for articulating experiences and knowledge that are difficult to express in words and not spoken by a single individual, but which become audible if the listener and reader arrive at the very scene of the multivocal. Morrison, fearless in her own encyclopedic creativity, draws from the spoken and the written, but she reserves her most lyrical prose for the diabolical beauty of the pastoral from hell: a past that is not Africa, but rather is located in the environs of the violent and still violating remains of a slave South.

Although there are specific riffs that indicate a Faulknerian presence or, at least, provocation in Morrison's fiction[27] (she wrote her master's thesis at Cornell on suicide in the fiction of Virginia Woolf and Faulkner), Morrison most resembles Faulkner in her epic portrayal of multigenerational family narratives, most notably *Sula* (1973), *Song of Solomon* (1977), and *Beloved* (1987), works which radically shift the focus to the development of female identity in families dominated by women. Faulkner's *Absalom, Absalom!*, with its narrative of female isolation that places the novel's childless women as "unsistered Eve[s]," contains his most detailed (albeit vague) account of women and daughters in the female household of Judith, Clytie, and Rosa. These weird sisters gather together in silent survival to demarcate a significant set of relationships that are rare in Faulkner's extensive treatment of Southern life and culture, a territory which Morrison and Welty own.[28] If Quentin Compson, like the young Richard Wright, makes his journey South through remembering words and scenes from the perspective of his young manhood, *Absalom, Absalom!* reveals another aspect of this journey southward toward the place of a mystery whose solution may be fatal. While *Light in August* centers on literal journeys that are racial, sexual, and psychological, *Absalom, Absalom!* insists on the centrality of language in a narrative journey: the unraveling of a mystery contained in versions of the past, the novel's "might-have-been which is more true than truth."

The Southern novel, defined here as a journey into the past that is located in the South, achieves its Faulknerian apotheosis, the fusion of the family saga with an experimental form devoted to orality, in Eudora Welty's *Losing Battles* (1970). In this last, longest, and most experimental of her novels, Welty accomplishes the most radically innovative work in this tradition by setting it not just in the past, but in the isolated and preserved past of the Mississippi mountains during the Great Depression. With its over thirty-five named speakers, *Losing Battles* is arguably the most insistently oral novel in the history of the English language. Created entirely from the spoken word and descriptions of the physical world, *Losing Battles* conveys interiority through the relentless portrayal of what can be heard and seen. Realism with a narrative vengeance, *Losing Battles* provides absolutely no access to any character's interior thoughts, and yet this is a work of remarkable emotional depth. It is no accident that the reader is invited to the family reunion that comprises *Losing Battles* in the antagonized position of a reluctant participant, more precisely, as an in-law. Welty's novel provides a taxonomy of language, denoting the incursions of modernity not only through the diction of advertising, but also by distinguishing listeners and tellers according to the degree to which they need to be offered a moral for every story.

In a definition that still works, Allen Tate defined Southern letters as a literature "conscious of the past in the present."[29] And how could it not be? In his effort to explain Southern identity, Woodward insists on "the burden of Southern history," and he, like Faulkner, is clearly aware of the black man's burden within it. From the beginnings of this "world the slaves made," men and women were not free.[30] Founded upon the history of slavery, the South was defined by race and the very American struggle for freedom through literacy that generated one of the great literary lineages of the nineteenth century: the slave novel. Framed by fictions of race, this crossing of the written and the oral marks the origniary point for any claim to a peculiarly Southern tradition of letters. Variously defined through a delineation of dialectics: rural versus urban, agrarian versus industrial, past versus future (with contentions over the present), the major claim for Southern distinctiveness is found in its complex and complexly interrelated multivocal literary tradition amid a heightened consciousness of the coloring of class.

The fact of William Faulkner lay at the core of the defining debate between the fugitives (the poets of Vanderbilt University that included Tate and Warren) and the culture-rooted regionalists (the sociologists of the University of North Carolina in Chapel Hill, including Rupert Vance and Howard Odum). These noted figures engaged in a debate centered on the question of "Why William Faulkner?" or, more to the point, "How could William Faulkner exist?" While the Vanderbilt poets took a belletristic position that touted the concept of genius, the social scientists, joined by then-graduate student in history, Woodward, argued that a William Faulkner was created, made possible, by social conditions. After his belated recognition, Faulkner himself speculated on the origins of his art:

> And now I realize for the first time what an amazing gift I had: uneducated in every formal sense, without even very literate, let alone literary, companions, yet to have made the thing I made. I don't know where it came from. I don't know why God or gods or whoever it was, selected me to be the vessel. Believe me, this is not humility, false modesty: it is simply amazement.[31]

Wherever he came from, William Faulkner, to borrow a phrase from *Absalom, Absalom!* did not come out of nowhere, "out of the soundless Nothing." Rather, he was spawned by a world that was like William Shakespeare's, a world where variants of Elizabethan English were still spoken and where the heightened narrative intelligence of those who were not readers and writers, but listeners, talkers, and tellers, generated a story-centered world. This orality arising from the conditions that made speech itself essential to proving the humanity of people who were sold as things is key to Faulkner and Faulkner's contribution to the history of the novel.

Notes

1. H. L. Mencken, "The Sahara of the Bozart," in *Prejudices: A Selection* (New York: Vintage Books, 1955), 69, 71. "Sahara" was originally published as a newspaper article in 1917. According to Richard Wright, Mencken's *Prejudices* taught him the use of published words as weapons.

   When Mencken published "The Sahara of the Bozart," Ellen Glasgow, considered to be the pre-eminent Southern novelist, had written eight of her seventeen novels, which would culminate with her Pulitzer Prize-winning *In This Our Life* (1941).
2. Allen Tate, "A Southern Mode of the Imagination," in *Studies in American Culture: Dominant Ideas and Images*, ed. Joseph J. Kwiat and Mary C. Turpie (Minneapolis: University of Minnesota Press, 1960), 96; C. Vann Woodward, "Why the Southern Renaissance?" *Virginia Quarterly Review* (Spring 1975): 222–239.
3. Louis Rubin, "The Dixie Special: William Faulkner and the Southern Literary Renascence" (1982), in *The Mockingbird in the Gum Tree: A Literary Gallimaufry* (Baton Rouge: Louisiana State University Press, 1991), 39.
4. Elizabeth Ammons, *Conflicting Stories: American Women Writers at the Turn into the Twentieth Century* (New York: Oxford University Press, 1992), 125.
5. Alice Walker, "Beyond the Peacock: The Reconstruction of Flannery O'Connor," in *In Search of Our Mothers' Gardens* (New York: Harcourt Brace Jovanovich, 1983), 43.
6. The rapidly assembled book (Boston: Beacon Press, 1968) was edited by John Henrik Clarke. This moment is interesting in itself because it reveals some of the sources of rage that have fueled essentialist criticism. Like many Southern novels not even mentioned in this chapter, Styron's controversial *Confessions of Nat Turner* won the Pulitzer Prize. Notably, Faulkner won the Pulitzer Prize for *A Fable* (1954) and *The Reivers* (1962), Harper Lee received it for *To Kill a Mockingbird* (1960), Welty was awarded it for *The Optimist's Daughter* (1972), and Alice Walker won it for *The Color Purple* (1982).
7. Styron quoted in Tony Horwitz, "Untrue Confessions," *The New Yorker* (December 13, 1999): 84. Horwitz also notes the revisionary readings of Cornel West and Henry Louis Gates, Jr. (86).

8. Faulkner's *As I Lay Dying* (1931) was compared unfavorably with Erskine Caldwell's salaciously saleable depiction of Southern poverty in *Tobacco Road* (1932), which devoted part of its *mélange* to the potential uplift for blacks as well as whites in the form of agricultural cooperatives. Caldwell, author of some twenty-five novels, only five of which were published in the 1930s, produced twenty novels in the 1940s.
9. While *Requiem for a Nun* was written as a play by Faulkner with his protégée, Joan Williams, this work's extravagant stage directions push the boundaries of drama toward the expanded definition of the novel insisted upon by Jean Toomer in *Cane* (1923), a prose poem cycle that incorporates the alternating dialogue of a play as part of its experimental form.
10. Faulkner quoted in Thadious Davis, *Games of Property: Law, Race, Gender, and Faulkner's* Go Down, Moses (Durham, NC: Duke University Press, 2003), 241.
11. Faulkner, who appears not to have cared whether or not his name was listed as a contributing writer, received credit for his work on *Today We Live* (1933), *The Road to Glory* (1936), *Slave Ship* (1937), *Gunga Din* (1939), *To Have and Have Not* (1940), *The Big Sleep* (1946), and *Land of the Pharaohs* (1955).
12. Joseph Urgo has gone against this commonly held view by pointing out that *Absalom, Absalom!*, composed during Faulkner's tedious tenure as a scriptwriter, can be seen as a narrative form that was enriched by Faulkner's participation in the storyboard phase of film production that consists of the meeting of a group of writers who propose alternate and additional plotlines for shaping the narrative of a film. Urgo, "*Absalom, Absalom!* The Movie," *American Literature* 62.1 (1990): 56–73.
13. In quantity, quality, and diversity, the critical work on Faulkner is second only to that on Shakespeare. Nevertheless, Lawrence Schwartz's *Creating Faulkner's Reputation: The Politics of Modern Literary Criticism* (Knoxville: University of Tennessee Press, 1988) provides a template for understanding the complexities of the critical responses to Faulkner. Cleanth Brooks has written over a half dozen major works on Faulkner, among them *William Faulkner: The Yoknapatawpha Country* (Baton Rouge: Louisiana State University Press, 1963), while Peter Brooks has also transformed Faulkner criticism through the single article, "Incredulous Narration: *Absalom, Absalom!*" in *Reading for the Plot: Design and Intention in Narrative* (New York: A. A. Knopf, 1984). A truncated list of Faulkner critics of magnitude includes: Andre Bleikasten, Thadious Davis, Susan Donaldson, Doreen Fowler, Richard Godden, John Irwin, Anne Goodwyn Jones, Donald Kartiganer, Barbara Ladd, John Matthews, Noel Polk, Carolyn Porter, Panthea Reid, Diane Roberts, Theresa Towner, Philip Weinstein, and Joel Williamson. This list obviously leaves out dozens of major scholars and biographers, a few of whom have their own footnotes.
14. James B. Meriwether and Michael Millgate, eds., *Lion in the Garden: Interviews with William Faulkner, 1926–1962* (Lincoln: University of Nebraska Press, 1980), 255.

15. David Minter, *William Faulkner: His Life and Work* (Baltimore: Johns Hopkins University Press, 1980), 94.
16. Edith Wharton, *The Writing of Fiction* (New York: Scribner's, 1925), 27–28.
17. Forthcoming essay in *Faulkner and Yoknapatawpha: The Returns of the Text.*
18. See Eric J. Sundquist, *Faulkner: The House Divided* (Baltimore: Johns Hopkins University Press, 1983).
19. Frederick L. Gwynn, Joseph Blotner, and Douglas Day, eds., *Faulkner in the University* (Charlottesville: University Press of Virginia, 1959), 1.
20. See Roman Jakobson, "Why 'mama' and 'papa?', " in *Selected Writings, Volume 1: Phonological Studies* (The Hague: Mouton, 1962), 538–545, and Maurice N. Walsh, "Explosives and Spirants: Primative Sounds in Cathected Words," *The Psychoanalytic Quarterly* 37 (1968): 199–211 for respective discussions of these sounds. While linguists have long been concerned with speculations about primal language and have come to some consensus on the "mmmmmmmmmmmmmmm" sound, Faulkner's use of these sounds in *The Sound and the Fury* demonstrates his concern with sound and his own theories of primal speech as early as 1928.
21. Sundquist, *The House Divided*, 3.
22. Louis Rubin, "The High Sheriff of Yoknapatawpha County: A Study in the Genius of Place," in *The Mockingbird in the Gum Tree: A Literary Gallimaufry* (Baton Rouge: Louisiana State University Press, 1991), 80.
23. See Katherine Berry Frye's " 'Washed Up and Wiped Out': Addie Bundren," delivered at "Backwoods, Backwater: Bartering Social Identities in Faulkner's South," University of California, Santa Barbara, 2008. The concept of "throw-away bodies" comes from Patricia Yaeger's *Dirt and Desire: Reconstructing Southern Women's Writing, 1930–1990* (Chicago: University of Chicago Press, 2000), 11.
24. Philip Fisher, *Hard Facts: Setting and Form in the American Novel* (Oxford: Oxford University Press, 1985).
25. See Jay Watson's article "Writing Blood: The Art of the Literal in *Light in August*," in *Faulkner and the Natural World: Faulkner and Yoknapatawpha*, ed. Donald M. Kartiganer and Ann J. Abadie (Jackson: University Press of Mississippi, 1999), 66–96.
26. These works were published under the title *Pale Horse, Pale Rider: Three Short Novels* (1939).
27. Two of the major volumes treating the relationship between Faulkner and Morrison's fiction are Carol A. Kolmerten, Stephen M. Ross, and Judith Bryant Wittenberg, eds., *Unflinching Gaze: Morrison and Faulkner Re-envisioned* (Jackson: University of Mississippi Press, 1997), and Philip Weinstein, *What Else But Love? The Ordeal of Race in Faulkner and Morrison* (New York: Columbia University Press, 1996).
28. Words such as "stertorious," describing the deep and resonant lowing of the bovine, and "ammoniac" (both in *As I Lay Dying*), to describe the specificity of a barn's urine-soaked floor, articulate the knowledge of the senses that is not

limited by knowing the words. The vocabulary of Faulkner's novels nevertheless reveals his archival knowledge of nineteenth-century domesticity that includes the genteel concept of the "cup towel" among the more lowly appurtenances of dish rags and drying cloths.

29. Allen Tate, "The Profession of Letters in the South," *Virginia Quarterly Review* 11 (April 1935): 161–176.
30. C. Vann Woodward, *The Burden of Southern History* (Baton Rouge: Louisiana State University Press, 1960); Eugene Genovese, *Roll, Jordan Roll: The World the Slaves Made* (New York: Vintage, 1974).
31. See Joseph Blotner, *Faulkner: A Biography*, 2 vols. (New York: Random House, 1974), II:1457. This was an undated letter from Faulkner to Joan Williams written in the spring of 1934.

46
Law and the American novel

GREGG CRANE

From Hugh Henry Brackenridge's *Modern Chivalry* (1792–1815) to William Gaddis's *A Frolic of His Own* (1994), legal figures and themes are nearly ubiquitous in American fiction. Similarities between the two discourses suggest a reason why. Law and fiction both use narrative form to establish or challenge values, norms, and ideas of order.[1] As Robert Cover, a legal scholar, observes, "No set of legal institutions exists apart from the narratives that locate it and give it meaning."[2] Allan Hutchinson expands on Cover's theme: "We are never not in a story. History and human action only take on meaning and intelligibility within their narrative context and dramatic settings." As storytelling enterprises, law and fiction offer ways to "mediate our engagement in the world with others," providing "the possibilities and parameters of our self-definition and understanding."[3] Given the overlap between law and fiction as normative and narrative projects, the presence of law in literary narratives and of literary narratives in legal reasoning seems unsurprising, even inevitable. Because of the heterogeneity and changing composition of the American populace, legal and literary narratives provide particularly important means of formulating fundamental values, such as equality and justice.

Novelists are also plainly drawn to the peculiarities of the law: its forms, specialized rules and vocabulary, as well as its need to be predictable and to furnish a degree of certainty in its results. Law novels often feature descriptions of the formalities of courtroom procedure and specialized concepts and phrases (e.g., the title of Gaddis's *A Frolic of His Own* points to doctrine limiting the liability of a master for the wrongful behavior of a servant acting outside the scope of his agency). And law novels often derive their plots from the processes of investigation and trial – their climax being furnished by the chilling or liberating certainty of a verdict.

Not needing to be predictable, certain, or safe, fiction can also become, for the legally minded novelist, an opportunity for jurisprudential experiment and critique. For Kenneth Burke, the power of Ralph Ellison's *Invisible Man* (1952) derives in large part from the constitutional experiment it performs – its insistence that, despite all present and past facts to the contrary, the US Constitution is more than an expression of political power and racial bias, that its ethical values are real and that it "holds out the same promise to us all."[4] The conclusion of *Invisible Man* affirms through pretense and speculation that the principles of democracy can and should be severed from the nation's racist history and that democracy need not boil down to oppression. After all it seems to the protagonist that his grandfather "mean[t] to affirm the principle" of democracy even though it had been "compromised to the point of absurdity." Dreamed into existence "out of the chaos and darkness of the feudal past," the ideals of the Constitution, like Ellison's novel itself, offer a way of imagining a reality that remains only a possibility. Though "corrupt," this imaginative vision can, by saying "as if," bring something new into the world.[5] For Ellison, the function of writers in "the tradition of Mark Twain, Emerson, and Thoreau" includes disruption, "yell[ing] 'Fire' in crowded theaters," and, by pushing forward American democracy, such artists become "an irreplaceable part of the social order."[6]

The law offers American novelists a particularly attractive and iconic complex of meaning which is simultaneously historically particular and ethically universal. To inhabit the drama of the American law novel is to travel to a specific and detailed moment in history, but it is also to participate vicariously in an ethical drama that resonates beyond the confines of the particular moment. The classic example of this duality is Herman Melville's *Billy Budd* (*c.*1886–1891; published 1924).[7] On the one hand, Melville's novel seems as archetypal as a Greek tragedy (indeed, many have compared *Billy Budd* to Sophocles's *Antigone*). The dilemma it raises is eternal: when can one legitimately defy the law for the sake of contrary moral obligations? On the other hand, *Billy Budd* engages history in considerable detail, referring to notable mutinies, the war between the British and the French, the American Revolution, the slavery crisis, as well as contemporary concerns about the appropriateness of capital punishment.[8] The historically specific issues raised by the trial of Billy Budd simultaneously register a more abstract question – is law capable of justice?

Across two centuries, this fundamental query has driven the American law novel. Some novelists, such as Harriet Beecher Stowe and Harper Lee, believe that the law can be made to serve justice. Other novelists, from Melville to E. L. Doctorow, agree with the first line of Gaddis's *A Frolic of his Own*: "Justice? – you get justice in the next world, in this world, you have the law." In this chapter, I describe the ebb and flow of novelistic attempts to imagine American law as potentially serving the interests of justice. I begin with the various conceptions of the moral foundation of law from the early republic to the Civil War. Next, I look at fictional depictions of law as power from the late nineteenth century to World War II. Then I take up the resurgence of a moral conception of law in the Civil Rights era. I conclude with fiction after the 1960s which seems deeply skeptical that the law refers to anything outside of itself.

The moral authority of law

Novels in the early republic confronted the question of whether the people should judge for themselves the ethical legitimacy of legal and social norms. According to republican theory, aren't the people the ultimate arbiters of what is just and proper? State a moral case to a ploughman and a professor, said Thomas Jefferson, and "the former will decide it as well, and often better than the latter, because he has not been led astray by artificial rules."[9] The nation's first novelists worried that such independence of judgment could prove destructive to individuals and society. Seduction novels, such as William Hill Brown's *The Power of Sympathy* (1789), Susanna Rowson's *Charlotte Temple* (1791), and Hannah Foster's *The Coquette* (1797) present cautionary tales for those inclined to break rules in pursuit of their own inclinations.[a] Hugh Henry Brackenridge's picaresque, *Modern Chivalry* (1792–1815), recommends not an unqualified deference to tradition and social hierarchy but a balance between forces for and resistant to social and legal transformation. In Captain Farrago's kindly but critical responses to his servant Teague O'Regan's ambitious antics, Brackenridge creates a synecdoche for the dual pressures shaping and informing American democracy: the upward force of those seeking to advance and the downward exertions of those seeking to regulate the lower orders.[b] In *Wieland* (1798), Charles Brockden Brown uses the conventions of the gothic novel to depict the danger of heeding one's inner voice instead of social convention and law. In the novel's climactic catastrophe, Wieland murders his wife and four children in the belief that he is obeying a divine commandment. Set in the decade before the Revolution, *Wieland* warns of the danger involved in claiming the kind of absolute insight

a Anna Mae Duane, "Susanna Rowson, Hannah Webster Foster, and the seduction novel in the early USA," chapter 2, 37–38, 43–44.

b Paul Giles, "Transatlantic curents and the invention of the American novel," chapter 1, 25–26.

entitling one to defy law and longstanding custom. Brown's warning does not reject the republican ethos so much as highlight the difficult questions about legal and ethical authority the Revolution has unleashed.[c]

The relation of law to ethical principle was a central issue in the slavery crisis. In "Resistance to Civil Government," Henry David Thoreau puts the moral basis of legal legitimacy in the form of a question: "Can there not be a government in which majorities do not virtually decide right and wrong, but conscience?"[10] For Thoreau, the possession of a moral sense licenses individuals to exercise independent judgment as to the validity of any given piece of legal doctrine. This theme was taken up by a wide array of nineteenth-century novels (e.g., Catharine Maria Sedgwick's *Hope Leslie* [1827], Frederick Douglass's "The Heroic Slave" [1853], William Wells Brown's *Clotel* [1853], Lydia Maria Child's *A Romance of the Republic* [1867], and Helen Hunt Jackson's *Ramona* [1884]).

Among these fictional arguments for the interconnection of law and morality, Harriet Beecher Stowe's *Uncle Tom's Cabin* (1852) was the most famous and influential. In a well-known scene, Stowe uses a dialogue between an Ohio Senator and his wife to illustrate how conscience can and should be brought to bear on questions of legitimate pubic policy and law. When Mary Bird argues to her husband that the Fugitive Slave Act of 1850 is plainly immoral, Senator Bird replies, "Your feelings are all quite right, dear . . . I love you for them; but . . . we mustn't suffer our feelings to run away with our judgment; you must consider it's not a matter of private feeling, – there are great public interests involved." Mrs. Bird replies, "I don't know anything about politics, but I can read my Bible; and there I see that I must feed the hungry, clothe the naked and comfort the desolate." Her religious and moral convictions ("Obeying God never brings on public evils") cannot be confined to the private sphere of the home. In positing self-evident moral truths, Mary Bird's argument recalls the republican belief in a legal system grounded in virtue and sanctioned by the citizenry's moral sense.

In *The Scarlet Letter* (1850), Nathaniel Hawthorne is reluctant either to endorse or reject the type of independent moral insight represented by Stowe's Mary Bird and many other abolitionists. Set in the Massachusetts Bay Colony of Hawthorne's Puritan forebears, Hester Prynne's drama speaks to the revolutionary ferment sweeping Europe in 1848 as well as the slavery controversy.[11] Standing on the scaffold before the community, Hester is

c For a more detailed reading of *Wieland*, see Bryan Waterman, "Charles Brockden Brown and the novels of the early republic," chapter 3, 55–57.

pained by her public exposure but not submissive. Her "haughty smile" and "glance that would not be abashed" as well as the "gorgeous luxuriance" of the "A" she has embroidered signify continued defiance of her society and its law. Hester's defiance, like Hutchinson's, raises the question of whether the social order can coexist with dissent.[d]

After the Civil War and the failure of Reconstruction, the quest to ground the nation's legal system in a universal morality came to seem quixotic – a fool's errand.[12] American society had grown too big to be swayed by its Mrs. Birds or Hester Prynnes, and the populace's increasing heterogeneity made the idea of a moral consensus like that symbolized by Mrs. Bird and Hester (at the end of Hawthorne's novel) distinctly unlikely. In addition, religious doubt (at least in certain sectors of American society) complicated notions that morality could be invoked to decide the legitimacy of any given law.

While *Huckleberry Finn* (1884) is not deaf to the appeal of a Stowe-like conception of the moral foundation of law, Twain's novel evinces considerable skepticism about the practicability of this vision, a skepticism informed at least in part by the nation's abandonment of Reconstruction.[13] Unlike Stowe's good-natured housewife or Hawthorne's rebellious heroine, who are both firmly located in broader communities, Huck and Jim are outcasts from their society and its legal, political, and economic institutions. They establish the rules and values that govern their life on the raft without the aid of organized religion, social institutions, or legal doctrine (for example, when Jim reprimands Huck for a juvenile and thoughtless prank, he can only appeal to their mutual affection as a basis for a rule of consideration between them). Expressed as religious impiety to distinguish it from the religious, moral, or legal orthodoxies of his society, Huck's choice to "go to hell" rather than return Jim to slavery elevates their friendship over the imperatives of social milieu, tradition, and law. However, the separation from society enabling Huck's independent moral judgment also means that his civil disobedience will move neither senator nor community. His moral triumph will have no public or doctrinal impact (indeed, Huck's civil disobedience is rendered risk-free and ineffectual by Miss Watson's prior freeing of Jim).[e]

d For a more detailed reading of *The Scarlet Letter*, see Jonathan Arac, "Hawthorne and the aesthetics of American romance," chapter 8, esp. 140–143.

e For a more detailed reading of Twain's novel, see Andrew Lawson, "Twain, class, and the Gilded Age," chapter 21, 370–374.

The law as power

The rise of Jim Crow measures, such as mandatory segregation in railroad cars (*Plessy v. Ferguson* [1896]) and in public schools (*Cummings v. Richmond* [1899]) and the struggle between the haves and have-nots in the last decades of the nineteenth century revealed the law to be an instrument, a tool or weapon, animated by the interests, desires, hostilities, and beliefs of those wielding it. In the 1886 case of the Haymarket anarchists, for instance, the law seemed to be characterized by fear, xenophobia, class animus, and corruption, and not by anything resembling ethical principle. The patent injustice of the prosecution of the Haymarket defendants inspired William Dean Howells's *A Hazard of New Fortunes* (1890),[f] Robert Herrick's *The Memoirs of an American Citizen* (1905), and Frank Harris's *The Bomb* (1908).[14] The evidence against the defendants was so weak as to make the guilty verdict and execution tantamount to mob rule thinly disguised as law. For these and many other novelists, there proved to be something horribly fascinating in observing the interplay of bias, fear, and self-interest in the supposedly neutral processes of legal judgment – the close proximity of the fury of the mob and the formal procedures of a trial.

Trying to examine the law honestly, even scientifically, Oliver Wendell Holmes, Jr. cautions his readers in "The Path of the Law" (1897) not to mistake law for morality. To understand the law, Holmes argues, "you must look at it as a bad man, who cares only for the material consequences which such knowledge enables him to predict, not as a good one, who finds his reasons for conduct, whether inside the law or outside of it, in the vaguer sanctions of conscience."[15] Holmes's "bad man" perspective is realistic in the sense that it seeks to know what the law *is*, not what it *should* be. This type of realism accepts the fact that, as a human-made instrumentality and expression of political power, the law can be used for any end.

While earlier fictions, such as Herman Melville's *Benito Cereno* (1855) and Martin Delany's *Blake* (1859–1862), anticipated the conception of law as power, this perspective became more prevalent in fiction at the end of the century. Novels with varied political and jurisprudential positions focused on the determinative role of power in the shape, effect, and meaning of the law. Of course, for members of a discrete political minority such as African Americans, the conception of law as power was not particularly helpful or hopeful. Charles Chesnutt's *The Marrow of Tradition* (1901), James Weldon

f David Zimmerman discusses *Hazard* in "Novels of American business, industry, and consumerism," chapter 24, 416.

Johnson's *The Autobiography of an Ex-Coloured Man* (1912), and Pauline Hopkins's *Contending Forces* (1900), all discussed elsewhere in this volume, continued to make the higher law argument that ethical principles should ground and limit the laws enacted by the majority.[g]

For progressive novelists, the problem was not that the law was an expression of power but that a corrupt judiciary was bent on substituting its will and the will of its wealthy masters for that of the democratic majority. A spate of now-forgotten novels, such as David Graham Phillips's *The Fashionable Adventures of Joshua Craig* (1909), Isaac Kahn Friedman's *The Radical* (1907), Henry O. Morris's *Waiting for the Signal* (1897), Frederic Upham Adams's *President John Smith* (1897), and Robert Herrick's *A Life for a Life* (1910) depicted judicial nullifications of progressive legislation as part of the plutocratic oppression of the working class.[16] For novelists inclining toward a deterministic vision of society (whether progressive in their political views or not), the idea that law was, in Holmes's words, merely a supple tool of power, came as no surprise. Frank Norris, Theodore Dreiser, Jack London, Upton Sinclair, John Dos Passos, John Steinbeck, Richard Wright (all discussed elsewhere in this volume) and many others wrote fictions depicting law as an implement used by the bourgeois and elite classes to consolidate and protect their interests. Many of these works include fictionalized versions of actual cases or legal controversies (e.g., Dreiser's *An American Tragedy* [1925], Sinclair's *Boston* [1928], and Wright's *Native Son* [1940]), and some were aimed at inspiring a particular legal reform or advancing a political position (Sinclair's *The Jungle* [1906]).

Having seen the government's reach extended by such measures as the Sedition Act of 1918 and the Supreme Court's decision in *Olmstead v. United States* (1928) permitting the use of wiretaps by the FBI, many novelists and other Americans came to view law as nothing more than an instrument of political power. In the first half of the twentieth century, these writers turned from questions about the ethical foundation of legal authority to consideration of whether the instrumentality of law might not, on occasion, furnish some form of leverage for those seeking justice or truth. The courtroom scenes in Wright's *Native Son*, for instance, show that the law can be a maze of rules, procedures, and tactics that can ensnare the weak, yet elements of this apparatus such as the right of cross-examination, can also be used to resist the workings of power and prejudice.

g See Barbara McCaskill, "The African American novel after Reconstruction," chapter 29, and Robert F. Reid-Pharr, "The postbellum race novel," chapter 28.

Repeatedly, though with varying degrees of optimism, novels in the twentieth century, such as William Faulkner's *Intruder in the Dust* (1948), Harper Lee's *To Kill a Mockingbird* (1960), Bernard Malamud's *The Fixer* (1966), E. L. Doctorow's *The Book of Daniel* (1971), and Tom Wolfe's *The Bonfire of the Vanities* (1987), seek in the ostensibly neutral rules of investigation, criminal procedure, and evidence some means of distinguishing the law from the will and self-interest of the political majority. In many twentieth-century novels, these rules seem to hold out the possibility that the law might be used to uncover the truth if not to achieve an ethically satisfying vision of justice. While their detective-protagonists often operate on the margins of the law, the novels of Dashiell Hammett, Raymond Chandler, Walter Mosley, and others are driven by a belief that the truth of a particular crime can be uncovered, despite the fact that justice may prove unattainable. Even a hellishly opaque and tortuous legal process, such as that described by Malamud in *The Fixer*, may provide the means to reveal the truth, a possibility embodied in Investigating Magistrate Bibikov's commitment to honest inquiry and due process. The fact that so many of these novels have downbeat endings makes the renewed novelistic search for the means of justice and truth in the law all the more striking. From Erle Stanley Gardner to Scott Turow and John Grisham, the subgenre of the courtroom thriller offers its audience the satisfaction of exposing the facts of a case, if not always of putting things right. The underlying causes of the crime are often not resolved or addressed in any substantial way, but the law works at least to reveal, finally, who did what to whom.[h] In the true crime or "non-fictional" crime novel, such as Truman Capote's *In Cold Blood* (1966) and Norman Mailer's *The Executioner's Song* (1980), the novelist in effect becomes a master investigator,[i] offering a better and more complete version of actual criminals and crimes than the legal process itself.[17]

The resurgence of the moral argument

The kind of hopeful speculation about the law we see so faintly in *Native Son* becomes stronger and more prevalent in fiction the nearer we get to the Civil Rights era. In a letter characterizing the Civil Rights Movement and *Brown v. Board of Education* (1954), Ralph Ellison expresses guarded optimism about the

h For more on fictional crime solvers and their complex, often ambivalent relationship to the crimes they investigate, see Sean McCann, "The novel of crime, mystery, and suspense," chapter 48, 805–806, 808–811.

i David Schmid, "The nonfiction novel," chapter 59, 991–997.

utility of the law, seeing it as "something solid" that can be used by the "nimble" and "willing."[18] In Ellison's *Invisible Man* (1952), the unnamed narrator shows similar agility to find freedom in the realization that certainty is an illusion. If he rejects a vision of "the world [as] nailed down" and the false certainties of "rank" or "limit," Ellison's protagonist discovers, his world can "become one of infinite possibilities," a surprising and ironic outcome for a black man living in a racist society. But such fluidity is not by itself sufficient, without some bit of ethical and legal certainty, so the protagonist ends underground.

From the late 1940s on, many novels (like William Faulkner's *Intruder in the Dust* [1948], Elizabeth Spencer's *The Voice at the Back Door* ([1956], Carson McCullers's *Clock without Hands* [1961], Alice Walker's *Meridian* [1976], and Ernest Gaines's *A Gathering of Old Men* [1983]) return to the possibility that human law might be grounded in or regulated by the principles of a higher law. Harper Lee's *To Kill a Mockingbird* (1960) [j] is a representative example of this resurgence of higher law reasoning in American fiction, illustrating both the kind of leverage and flexibility Ellison describes.[19]

Leverage, in Lee's novel, comes from the seeming certainty of particular legal/ethical ideals, such as the ideal of fair procedure which requires treating all alike without regard to background or condition. The all-white jury, Atticus Finch argues, has a legal duty (which the reader recognizes as ethical as well) to judge accused rapist Tom Robinson on the basis of the evidence, not the self-serving racist creed that "*all* Negroes lie, that *all* Negroes are basically immoral beings, that *all* Negro men are not to be trusted around our women." In a court (if not outside it) equality is the mandate: "in our courts all men are created equal." Of course, complying with notions of fair and equal procedure is not unalloyed altruism. It can tangibly benefit those in power, protecting them when they are no longer part of a political majority.[20] The norm of procedural fairness provides the advocate with a solid basis for pushing the law toward something better and nobler than the majority's bias and will.

For Lee, flexibility comes into the law through the processes of judgment which determine when one bends, modifies, or ignores a rule, including the rule that the law treats all alike (the cornerstone of Atticus's closing argument). Judgment, for Lee as for Stowe, includes the act of sympathetic identification. Early in the novel, Atticus instructs his daughter, Scout, "You never really understand a person until you consider things from his point of

j Candace Waid, "Faulkner and the Southern novel," chapter 45, 755.

view . . . until you climb into his skin and walk around in it." When Scout, wanting to stay home from school, brings up the fact that Burris Ewell doesn't go to school and scoffs at the truancy law, Atticus responds that the law blinks at Burris's case because those enforcing the law have a sympathetic understanding of his family's situation. "Sometimes it's better to bend the law a little in special cases," Atticus says, but "[i]n your case, the law remains rigid. So to school you must go." As modeled by Atticus, good judgment involves balancing the need for order, deference to legitimate authority, with other values and interests. The result is a fluid, pragmatic approach to social and legal norms. The most dramatic instance of this approach comes at the end of the novel when Atticus allows himself to be persuaded that an investigation of the reclusive Boo Radley's involvement in the death of Bob Ewell is not in the interest of justice. It would, as Scout says, having well learned her father's lesson that sympathetic identification must at times temper the application of the law, be "like shootin' a mockingbird."

Lee's novel manifests considerable confidence in the epistemological promise of the law: the conviction that the law can reveal the truth through logical argument and dispassionate examination of the evidence. The courtroom scene in *To Kill a Mockingbird* climaxes in Atticus's demolition of the prosecution's key witnesses, Bob Ewell and his adult daughter Mayella. The excitement of this scene derives from the way the evidence snaps shut on the mind like a trap, forcing one to see the truth regardless of the pull of prejudice and self-interest.[21] Careful investigation, an open-minded examination of the evidence, and fair trial procedure allowing Atticus to cross-examine the prosecution's witnesses make it possible to prove Tom's innocence. While the jury willfully rejects this proof, there is some hope in the fact that the process could be used to prove the truth of the event. Atticus, like Bigger Thomas's lawyer Boris Max in *Native Son*, is determined to make the trial serve the truth, if not justice: "that boy might go to the chair," says Max, "but he's not going till the truth's told."

The law as echo-chamber

In the latter decades of the twentieth century, many law novels doubt the law's capacity for truth as well as justice. In his blunt satire, *The Bonfire of the Vanities* (1987), Tom Wolfe portrays the courtroom as a carnival of competing self-interests, farcical theatrics, and futile assertions of procedural regularity and consistency. One senses that the mechanisms of the law could be used to find the truth (e.g., Judge Kovitsky's setting aside the Grand Jury indictment against Sherman McCoy would seem to be a partial step in the right direction though even this decision is based on manipulated evidence and perjury), but the instrument of law cannot overcome the corruption of the society manipulating it. Wolfe compares the New York elite to the gathering described in Edgar Allan Poe's "The Masque of the Red Death": "bound together, [they] whirl about one another, endlessly, particles in a doomed atom . . ."

While very different in tone and intent from Wolfe's novel, E. L. Doctorow's *The Book of Daniel* (1971) also invokes Poe as a symbol of the darkness at the heart of the American nation and its law. Doctorow's protagonist, Daniel Isaacson, finds in Poe an oracle of the history of injustice shadowing the egalitarian and democratic promise of the nation's foundational principles. Doctorow's novel portrays the government's prosecution of Paul and Rochelle Isaacson (loosely modeled on Julius and Ethel Rosenberg) as a politically motivated witch-hunt. The government's fevered desire to make an example of this couple motivates a grotesque exaggeration of whatever subversive activity may have occurred, and this exaggeration renders the death penalty absurdly disproportionate. It is additionally clear that Rochelle Isaacson is electrocuted despite having committed no crime (as apparently was the case with Ethel Rosenberg). Understandably, Daniel comes to see the law as existing only to protect privilege and to exercise its dominion.

But Doctorow's novel does not simply indict the injustices manifest in the Isaacson/Rosenberg case. It also critiques the law's reliance on simple and absolute distinctions such as guilt or innocence, suggested by the law's requirement that the core question of betrayal (have the Isaacsons betrayed their country?) be answered yes or no. Doctorow's novel takes pains to complicate such categories. Betrayal proves to be neither so simple nor so exceptional to fit an either/or determination. In the novel's climactic trial scene, Rochelle glares at Mindish, wanting to catch his eye, but, when Mindish looks "for one fraction of a second into her eyes," his expression does not indicate shame or a sense of guilt. Instead, his glance expresses "the private faith of a comrade, one to another, complicitors in self-sacrifice," a look Paul "did not have to return." What precisely this exchange means is not clear. It cannot mean that Paul, the radio repair man, was instrumental in providing the Soviet Union with the atom bomb, but it does indicate that Paul and Mindish have shared a secret unknown to Rochelle. In some fashion, Paul has betrayed Rochelle. He has gambled with both of their lives and lost. As the journalist Jack P. Fein recognizes, the Isaacsons had to "have been into some goddamn thing," and this humble, commonsensical truth is particularly wrenching to Daniel because, given the practical insignificance of whatever they were "into," it illuminates the profligacy of their sacrifice of each other and their family. The very commonness and complexity of betrayal (the government betrays its citizens, the Communist Party betrays its members, Mindish betrays his friends, Daniel betrays his wife, sister, and his foster-parents, Paul betrays Rochelle, and both parents betray their children) argues against the fantasy of absolute categories, and it casts doubt on absolutists of all stripes, including Daniel's parents as well as the government. Such doubts greatly complicate the effort to make the kind of categorical distinctions fundamental to the law.

Daniel describes the courtroom as a "large shadowed hall" where "[v]oices echo." This aptly figures the postmodern assessment of law as an endlessly recursive and reverberating stream of language, "a constant feedback of human multiplicity." Or as a lawyer in William Gaddis's *A Frolic of his Own* (1994) puts it, "What do you think the law is, that's all it is, language . . . language confronted by language turning language itself into theory till it's not about what it's about it's only about itself." In Gaddis's novel, as in Doctorow's, different vantage points on the law are taken up in turn – the moral argument, the idea of law as power, and the epistemological promise that law might prove capable of revealing the truth of complex events – but in the end it all threatens to collapse into language. Yet both Doctorow and Gaddis leave the reader with the possibility of meaning which comes in their novels not from the match between some legal signifier and some idealized ethical referent but by virtue of the multiple and varied interactions of the human players in these dramas. Meaning and value turn out to be a matter of human effort, human constructions. The language of law, like other languages, provides us with a means of imagining meaning, positing human connection, defining its terms and conditions and limits. Looking back over the history of the American law novel, one is struck by the genre's investment in this project of narratively imagining the nexus between particular histories and larger values such as justice and fair play. Even when the task seems impossible, it proves an irresistible subject.

Notes

1. See Richard Weisberg, "Coming of Age Some More: 'Law and Literature' beyond the Cradle," *Nova Law Review* 13 (1988): 121.
2. Robert Cover, "Nomos and Narrative," in *Narrative, Violence, and the Law: The Essays of Robert Cover*, ed. Martha Minow, Michael Ryan, and Austin Sarat (Ann Arbor: University of Michigan Press, 1992), 95–96.

3. Allan Hutchinson, *Dwelling on the Threshold: Critical Essays in Modern Legal Thought* (Toronto: Carswell, 1988), 13–14. See also, Richard Delgado and Jean Stefanicic, "Norms and Narratives: Can Judges Avoid Serious Moral Error?" *Texas Law Review* 68 (1991): 1929–1960.
4. Kenneth Burke, "Ralph Ellison's Trueblooded *Bildungsroman*," in *Speaking for You: The Vision of Ralph Ellison*, ed. Kimberly Benston, (Washington, DC: Howard University Press, 1987), 353.
5. Ralph Ellison, *The Collected Essays of Ralph Ellison*, ed. John Callahan (New York: Modern Library, 1995), 482.
6. *Ibid.*, 773.
7. The first issue of *Cardozo Studies in Law and Literature* (1989) was dedicated to discussions of *Billy Budd*.
8. See, e.g., H. Bruce Franklin, "*Billy Budd* and Capital Punishment: A Tale of Three Centuries," *American Literature* 69 (1997): 337–359.
9. Gordon Wood, *The Radicalism of the American Revolution* (New York: Vintage, 1993), 240.
10. Henry David Thoreau, "Resistance to Civil Government," in *Walden and Civil Disobedience* (New York: Signet, 1960), 223.
11. See Larry J. Reynolds, "The *Scarlet Letter* and Revolutions Abroad," *American Literature* 57 (1985): 44–67; for a discussion of elements of criminal law in Hawthorne's novel, see Laura Hanft Korobkin, "The *Scarlet Letter* of the Law: Hawthorne and Criminal Justice," *Novel* 30 (1997): 193–217.
12. See, e.g., Comfort Servosse's many critical discussions of the failure of the law and government to do the right thing by protecting the rights of the freedmen and women of the South in Albion W. Tourgée's Reconstruction novel, *A Fool's Errand* (1879).
13. The classic essay on Huck's moral crisis is Laurence B. Holland's "A 'Raft of Trouble': Word and Deed in *Huckleberry Finn*," *Glyph* 5 (1979): 69–87; for a useful discussion of the figure and theme of citizenship in Twain's novel, see Brook Thomas, *Civic Myths: A Law-and-Literature Approach to Citizenship* (Chapel Hill: University of North Carolina Press, 2007), 125–176.
14. See Robert A. Ferguson's fine discussion of these books in *The Trial in American Life* (Chicago: University of Chicago Press, 2007), 196–227.
15. Oliver Wendell Holmes, Jr., "The Path of the Law," in *The Essential Holmes*, ed. Richard Posner (Chicago: University of Chicago Press, 1997), 161–162.
16. Maxwell Bloomfield, "Constitutional Ideology and Progressive Fiction," *Journal of American Culture* 18 (1995): 77–85.
17. See Ann M. Algeo, *The Courtoom as Forum: Homicide Trials by Dreiser, Wright, Capote, and Mailer* (New York: Peter Lang, 1996) and Simon Petch, "Norman Mailer, Gary Gilmore, and the Untold Stories of the Law," *Heat* 3 (1997): 147–160.
18. Letter dated March 16, 1956, from Ralph Ellison to Albert Murray, in *Trading Twelves: The Selected Letters of Ralph Ellison and Albert Murray* (New York: Vintage, 2000), 116–117.

19. For an apt discussion of the contradictions in Atticus Finch as an icon of the ideal lawyer, see Tim Dare, "Lawyers, Ethics, and To Kill a Mockingbird," *Philosophy and Literature* 25 (2001): 127–141.
20. As Bibikov, the investigating magistrate, tells Yakov, the accused, in Malamud's *The Fixer*, "if your life is without value, so is mine. If the law does not protect you, it will not, in the end, protect me."
21. Though Colonel Bodyansky, in *The Fixer*, would clearly like to charge Yakov with sexual assault on Zinaida Lebedev, Bibikov has come into possession of a letter from her, written after the alleged assault, that utterly contradicts her assertions, stymieing at least that part of the wrongful prosecution.

47

Twentieth-century publishing and the rise of the paperback

JAMES L. W. WEST III

American novelists and their publishers faced a rapidly changing professional situation during the middle decades of the twentieth century, from approximately 1920 to 1970. By the end of the First World War, it had become apparent to US book-publishing houses that they could no longer operate in the nineteenth-century fashion – an approach, developed by leading British firms, that had emphasized low overhead, a limit on new titles, modest advertising, controlled print runs, and distribution through established bookshops.[a] Such strategies had worked reasonably well in the USA during the late 1800s and early 1900s but, by 1920, no longer served the interests of most American publishers. The key issues were distribution and price maintenance: British publishers could market their books through an established network of bookshops and send them virtually anywhere in Great Britain through an efficient railway system; they could also maintain retail prices, and thus avoid price-cutting and loss-leadering, owing to the Net Book Agreement, a measure they had agreed upon in 1899 to create a loose monopoly among themselves over book pricing. British publishers depended on the home island for most of their sales and got rid of slow-selling titles and remaindered stock in the colonial trade. These strategies were effective. The major publishing firms in Great Britain, all of them based either in London or Edinburgh, controlled the book business, kept the booksellers under tight rein, and prospered.

American publishers attempted these same methods, adopting their own Net Book Agreement in 1901 in an attempt to bring order to a chaotic book-pricing system in the USA. These publishers sold most of their books in the urban Northeast (with its concentrated markets, its bookshops, and its good railway connections) and treated the South and Midwest as colonial markets,

a Nancy Glazener traces the prequel to these developments in "The novel in postbellum print culture," chapter 20 in this volume.

areas in which they had to be careful not to overextend themselves.[b] The US version of the Net Book Agreement, however, was quickly challenged in the courts by Macy's department store, whose attorneys argued that any attempt at price control amounted to collusion and restraint of fair trade. This was the era of Teddy Roosevelt and trust-busting; Macy's received a sympathetic hearing in court. The publishers and booksellers were declared to be in violation of the Sherman Anti-Trust Act of 1890 and were assessed some $140,000 in damages, the money to be paid to Macy's jointly by the American Publishers Association and the American Booksellers Association. US firms now saw that the British model of book-publishing would not work for them. They would have to do business in a fashion better suited to the laws and demographics of their own country.[1]

Fortunately for these publishing houses, new and more populous areas for sales were opening up, printing technology was improving, and literacy levels were rising. A new business model was very much possible. American publishers therefore developed a more competitive, frontlist-oriented style of publishing, with emphasis on sales, advertising, and promotion. They issued numerous books, hoping that one bestseller, or a handful of strong sellers, would cross-subsidize the rest of the list and cover losses on titles that had not performed up to expectations. The backlist (which, under the old business model, had generated a steady flow of operating capital) now became less important. Emphasis was placed instead on subsidiary rights and on tie-ins with other forms of public entertainment – especially the stage and the moving picture business.[c]

These developments had a pronounced effect on American novelists, putting them more closely in touch with market pressures and holding out to them the possibility of significantly greater earnings. Industrialization, urbanization, and improved transportation systems were creating new outlets and classes of readers. Book-publishing was becoming more sophisticated; mail-order book clubs were sending books to customers in remote places; paperback houses would soon make books available to almost everyone at affordable prices. American authors began to see that they might reach readers heretofore unavailable to them and collect advances and

b For a fuller account elsewhere in this volume of these early bookselling practices, see Mary Saracino Zboray and Ronald Zboray, "The novel in the antebellum book market," chapter 4, esp. 75–76.

c For other instances of this tendency, see Glazener, chapter 20, 352–353; Barbara Hochman, "Readers and reading groups," chapter 36, 601–602; and Robert Coover, "A history of the future of narrative," chapter 71, 1172–1173, in this volume.

royalties that were much more generous than those paid a few decades before.

Several new and more adventurous literary firms were founded and came to prominence during the first three decades of the twentieth century: Knopf, Liveright, Random House, Simon and Schuster, and Viking, for example. Older firms, such as Scribner, Putnam, Harper, and Appleton, continued to publish but began to adopt more energetic methods of promotion and sales. This changed landscape provided authors with options when choosing their publishers. Most writers of the period switched houses at least once during their careers, motivated usually by a desire for more attention and higher sales. F. Scott Fitzgerald was an exception: he stayed for his entire career with Charles Scribner's Sons, in part because of his loyalty to the Scribner editor Maxwell Perkins; but Ernest Hemingway moved from Liveright to Scribner, Edith Wharton from Scribner to Appleton, Sinclair Lewis from Harcourt to Doubleday to Random House, Thomas Wolfe from Scribner to Harpers, Willa Cather from Houghton Mifflin to Knopf, Sherwood Anderson from B. W. Huebsch to Liveright to Scribner; and William Faulkner from Liveright to Smith & Haas to Random House.

In discussions of the literary marketplace one often encounters the term "professional authorship," meaning full-time writing meant to provide the author with a living. But an author, even in a materially advanced society such as the United States, is not truly a "professional," as a sociologist would define that term. Even when authors enjoy high cultural status and earn large sums of money, the conditions of their labor are altogether different from those of genuine professionals such as attorneys, physicians, and academics. Candidates for the true professions are trained for entry. They earn advanced degrees and undergo apprenticeships (as medical interns, for example, or untenured professors) before they are admitted permanently into the profession. Often they are required to pass qualifying tests – the bar exams, for example – and are issued licenses to practice. Each profession has its own hierarchies and status levels, signified by titles and ranks. Members of professions form associations and develop written codes of ethics; they also acquire specialized vocabularies and command fields of expertise beyond the knowledge of their clients – who, typically, assume subordinate roles in all dealings. A profession is in effect a legal monopoly on a particular kind of work. True professionals are thus insulated from the pressures of the capitalistic marketplace. They retain the power to admit or (very rarely) to expel workers from their professions; they fix fees and minimize competition.[2]

Authors enjoy almost none of these advantages. Aspiring writers, no matter what country they live in, require no special degrees or qualifications, need not pass examinations, and are not issued licenses to practice. There are no ranks or titles within the field of authorship; writers' associations come and go, but they tend to be loosely organized and to wield no power with legislatures or the courts – unlike, for example, the American Bar Association and the American Medical Association. The language that authors use in their writing might be experimental or stylish, but it is not usually beyond the understanding of the educated layman. Indeed it is publishers, a quasi-professionalized class, who command a specialized language – the terminology of production, printing, and distribution – and who regard authors as *their* clients, not the other way around. Authorship in all societies can therefore be said most nearly to approximate cottage labor. Authors produce craft goods and deliver them to publishers and editors, the middlemen in the trade who convert the handiwork into saleable merchandise.

Authors, in consequence, need their own representatives, their own allies who are loyal to them and can insulate them from the impersonality and bureaucracy of trade publishing. During the twentieth century in America, literary agents have come to occupy this role. Agents, or "authors' representatives," can usually sell articles and stories to magazines and can place novels with appropriate book-publishing houses more successfully than authors can. And good agents know the market intimately and are experienced at negotiating – unlike authors, who are sometimes taken advantage of in contractual dealings.

Literary agents first appeared in the USA during the 1890s and early 1900s: they functioned at the intersection between authorship and the marketplace, giving advice on prices and contracts, selling stage and movie rights, collecting and distributing royalties, and advising on translations and British editions, an important area after the advent of the first international American copyright law – the Chace Act, passed by the US Congress in 1891.[d] These agents took 10 percent of authorial earnings; they justified this share by negotiating for higher prices and looking after reprint requests, lecture invitations, and other chores that took up valuable writing time.[3]

The first influential agent in America was Paul Revere Reynolds, a Boston native who opened an office in New York City in 1891 and represented many of the important English-language writers of his time. His American clients included Stephen Crane, Frank Norris, Booth Tarkington, and Zona Gale;

d Glazener makes a similar point; see chapter 20, 343.

among his British writers were Oscar Wilde, Joseph Conrad, H. G. Wells, and George Meredith.[4] Other agents followed: Harold Ober, who began in the business as one of Reynolds's employees, became one of the most visible agents in the New York literary marketplace; he left Reynolds to strike out on his own in 1929 and eventually represented F. Scott Fitzgerald, William Faulkner, and Agatha Christie among many others.[5] The field of agenting was an early and important mode of entry into the literary world for women: Flora May Holly, Mavis McIntosh, Elizabeth McKee, and Elizabeth Nowell became authors' representatives, sometimes associating themselves with large literary agencies such as Curtis Brown and Brandt & Brandt and sometimes establishing independent firms. At first some of the old-line American publishers, Henry Holt and Charles Scribner especially, resented the insertion of the agent into their dealings with authors. But eventually most US publishers came to see that agents could be useful, winnowing out inferior writing, running errands, performing research work, answering mail, renewing copyrights, and helping authors with their tax returns. Agents such as James B. Pinker in England and Carl Brandt in the USA even functioned as informal bankers, advancing money to writers on unsold work and paying bills and insurance premiums for them from royalties received.[6]

Literary agents understood that, in producing a work of fiction, an author was creating an array of commercial possibilities. A novel, for example, might be serialized over a period of weeks or months in a major national magazine, then published in a clothbound edition, offered in a book-club reprint, recycled as a cheap hardback, offered again as a paperback, and finally published as a volume in a collected edition. A novel might be adapted for the stage or made into a movie; in the 1930s and 1940s popular novels and stories were sometimes turned into radio scripts and, in the 1950s and 1960s, into television shows. A British edition might bring further returns; translations into other languages could yield additional money. None of these subsequent forms of publication or adaptation required further creative labor from the novelist. The emoluments that came to the author, with the agent's help, were similar to dividend money arriving regularly from a well-chosen stock investment or rent collected each month from a solid real-estate property.[7]

Fitzgerald's *The Great Gatsby*, published by Scribner's in 1925, is a good example of a novel that generated significant money from subsidiary rights after initial publication. Fitzgerald was disappointed in the sales of the clothbound edition – only about 21,000 copies – but in 1926 Harold Ober sold stage rights to the Broadway producer William A. Brady and cinema rights to the

Famous Players studio. These two sales generated some $26,000 of additional income for Fitzgerald, money that he collected with no additional work. In 1934 *The Great Gatsby* was reprinted by the Modern Library; in 1945, five years after Fitzgerald's death, the novel became one of the first titles on the Bantam paperback list. In 2000 *Gatsby* was turned into an opera; two years later it was issued in an unabridged audio version, read by the actor Tim Robbins. Fitzgerald did not live to enjoy the income from these subsequent incarnations of his novel, but his heirs received significant amounts of money from them.[8]

Willard Motley's tough-guy novel *Knock on Any Door*, published by Appleton-Century in 1947, is a second example of a novel that generated significant subsidiary money. After its initial hardback publication it became a selection of the Fiction Book Club, was turned into a "picture dramatization" for *Look* magazine, appeared in condensed form in *Omnibook* magazine, was condensed again as a newspaper serial for King Features, and was reprinted as a Signet paperback. Columbia Pictures acquired the movie rights soon after publication, for $65,000, and turned *Knock on Any Door* into a successful film starring Humphrey Bogart. All of these adaptations and recyclings stimulated the sales of the original clothbound edition, keeping it on the *New York Times* bestseller list for eight months in 1947 and 1948.[9]

As one final example, two chapters from William Styron's 1979 novel *Sophie's Choice* were pre-published in *Esquire*. The clothbound edition from Random House was a bestseller; Book-of-the-Month Club chose the novel as a featured selection; Bantam paid $1.5 million for paperback rights; motion picture rights sold for $650,000 to the producer Keith Barish; Jonathan Cape in London acquired British rights for $200,000; and Gallimard in Paris paid the same figure for French rights. In December 2002, an opera version of *Sophie's Choice* by the composer Nicholas Maw premiered at the Royal Opera House, Covent Garden, and has since been performed at the Kennedy Center in Washington, DC, and the Sydney Opera House in Australia. Styron's initial creative investment in the novel has yielded forms of income that he, working alone on the manuscript during the mid-1970s, could scarcely have predicted.[10]

The Great Depression of the 1930s was ruinous to the American economy as a whole, but the book business held steady and even expanded. Bennett Cerf, one of the founders of Random House, would later remark: "During the Depression we were sitting in clover. In fact, every year we went a little bit ahead, and there was never one when we went backward."[11] The only major publisher to go under during the 1930s was Horace Liveright, but his failure was caused more by his tendency to gamble on the stock market and on

Broadway shows than by a slowdown in book sales.[12] Publishing, as a business, can adjust quickly to lean economic times by cutting back on new titles, reducing staff, minimizing overheads, and concentrating on reprints. Most American publishers followed these strategies during the 1930s and survived the decade in reasonably good condition.

The market for books expanded significantly during the Second World War and in the years immediately afterward. The publisher William Jovanovich, who served as a naval officer during the war, remembered that "publishers were able to sell practically everything to war-workers, who had plenty of money and not much to spend it on."[13] Nonfiction bestsellers such as *Thirty Seconds over Tokyo* by Ted W. Lawson and *Guadalcanal Diary* by Richard Tregaskis, both published in 1943, were enormously popular. Military novels topped the sales lists after the war: Irwin Shaw's *The Young Lions* (1948), Norman Mailer's *The Naked and the Dead* (1948), and James Jones's *From Here to Eternity* (1951) enjoyed long runs at the bookshops and established their authors, all three of them veterans, as writers to watch. Many of the returning servicemen took advantage of the G. I. Bill of Rights to attend college at government expense; this stimulated the college textbook market and provided publishers with steady classroom sales, thus providing capital for more risky ventures in fiction.

Of the several forms of republication that developed in the USA during the middle decades of the twentieth century, the book-club edition was one of the most important. Executives in book clubs saw that the US postal service, an existing mode of distribution, could be used to reach readers who had no access to standard urban bookshops. The first American book club, the Book-of-the-Month Club (BOMC), was founded by Harry Scherman and Maxwell Sackheim in 1926; later that year Nelson Doubleday began a rival club called the Literary Guild.[e] Both ventures were successful, and numerous smaller clubs followed, usually specializing in a particular form of literature – the detective novel, for example, or the romance. The clubs advertised for members in magazines and newspapers; they sent monthly catalogues to their subscribers, who could select any book from the catalogue or could simply wait and allow the main selection for that month to be mailed to them. Initially book clubs purchased printing overruns and remaindered stock from trade publishers; later they began to lease printing plates from these publishers

e Also see Hochman, chapter 36, 608; and DeNel Rehberg Sedo, "Twentieth- and twenty-first-century literary communities," chapter 70, 1162, in this volume.

and to manufacture their own editions, which mimicked the casings and jackets of the original editions but were made from cheaper paper and binding cloth.

American publishers were skeptical about book clubs at first. Because the clubs sold their books at less than the full retail price, they were seen as price-cutters. Owners of independent bookshops particularly resented the clubs, arguing that customers who would normally be drawn into their shops to purchase popular bestsellers would now simply order the same books at reduced prices through the US mails. The clubs, however, were so successful in reaching a "hidden public" of new readers that established publishers eventually fell into line and began to angle for book-club adoptions. Bookshop owners too learned that the massive advertising campaigns mounted by the book clubs actually stimulated the sales of their own stocks of bestsellers.[14]

Such American novelists as Sinclair Lewis, Ernest Hemingway, Marjorie Kinnan Rawlings, John Steinbeck, James Gould Cozzens, and John O'Hara benefited greatly from the clubs. Six of Steinbeck's books, for example – *Of Mice and Men* (1937), *The Red Pony* (1937), *The Moon Is Down* (1942), *The Wayward Bus* (1947), *Sweet Thursday* (1954), and *The Short Reign of Pippin IV* (1957) – were primary selections or alternates for BOMC. Having even a single volume selected by a major club could provide an extraordinary boost to a writer's career. The book-club edition of Stephen Vincent Benét's long narrative poem *John Brown's Body*, for example, sold so briskly that his income jumped by over 10,000 dollars in 1928; Eugene O'Neill's *Nine Plays*, published originally by Liveright in 1932, sold over 97,000 copies in its book-club edition during the late 1930s.[15]

Members of the club selection juries exercised influence on the cutting and editing of a few novels, still in proof, which they were considering for adoption. Robert Trumbull made excisions in the galleys of his novel *The Raft* (1942) in order to please the BOMC juror Henry Seidel Canby; Ross Lockridge, Jr., consented to bowdlerizations in *Raintree County* (1948) in order to win adoption of that novel by BOMC.[16] In what is probably the best-known instance of such influence Richard Wright, at the urging of BOMC, transformed his heavily autobiographical novel *American Hunger*, in which he had traced the progress of the protagonist from an oppressed childhood in Mississippi to involvement with the Communist Party in Chicago, into a simplified story of racial prejudice set entirely in the South. Wright shortened the novel by approximately one-third, wrote a new ending for what remained, and gave the book a new title: *Black Boy*. He also consented to the alteration of two sexually charged passages. The novel, published in its first trade edition by Harper in 1945, was known only in this abbreviated, sanitized, and retitled form until 1991, when a restored text of the original *American Hunger* was published by the Library of America.[17]

Another important outlet for novelists was the Modern Library, a reprint series that traced its descent to the Little Leather Library, which had been issued by the publishers Charles and Albert Boni during the first two decades of the twentieth century. The name of the series was changed to the Modern Library after the Boni brothers merged with Horace Liveright in 1917 to form the firm of Boni & Liveright. Titles in the Modern Library, issued in small clothbound format, were available in most independent bookshops and at the book counters of department stores. Many popular novels were reprinted in the Modern Library, along with out-of-copyright classics.

Bennett Cerf and his friend Donald Klopfer acquired the Modern Library from Horace Liveright in 1925 for 200,000 dollars. Cerf and Klopfer advertised the series energetically, building up a nationwide distribution system and establishing good relationships with book retailers outside the urban Northeast. Thus when Cerf and Klopfer began to publish their own new titles during the early 1930s under an imprint that they called Random House, they already had in place an extensive network for advertising and selling their books. And in the days before paperbacks were widely available in the American trade, the Modern Library editions were often used as textbooks in college courses, providing more income for Random House and its authors.[18]

By far the most important development in American book-publishing during the middle decades of the twentieth century was the rise of mass-market paperback houses. Paperback publishing was not new to the US book trade: twice before, once during the 1840s and again from about 1880 to 1893, paperback publishers had experimented with the sale of cheaply produced softbound books. The first such venture, which lasted from 1840 until 1845, was pursued by price-cutters such as Park Benjamin and Rufus W. Griswold, who took advantage of the absence of an international copyright law in the USA to pirate the works of established British writers.[f] These early speculators, called "yellowback publishers," created chaos in the American trade by

f The pervasive effect of international copyright (primarily of its absence) is discussed elsewhere in this volume by Zboray and Zboray, chapter 4, 73; Glazener, chapter 20, 343; and Hochman, chapter 36, 601–602.

their underselling; soon they fell into competition amongst themselves and eliminated each other by uncontrolled price-cutting. The second US experiment in paperback publishing encountered similar difficulties. Such publishers as Erastus Beadle, John W. Lovell, and Frank Leslie issued enormous "libraries" of fiction (again, much of it pirated from Great Britain) during the 1880s and early 1890s. These cheap paperbound editions were meant to undercut the market for traditional clothbound books, and for most of the 1880s they did so. Eventually, however, these publishers succumbed to the lure of overproduction, producing far more books than the market would bear. They were also confronted after 1891 with the Chace Act, the international copyright statute (mentioned earlier in this chapter) that put an end to the worst forms of overseas piracy. The paperback publishers of the 1880s had been in business for quick profits. Their methods had caused much consternation among the established firms, who did not lament their demise.

The third experiment in US paperback publishing began cautiously, with the establishment of Pocket Books in 1939. Six years later Ian Ballantine, who had apprenticed in the book trade with Penguin publishers in England, founded a second major paperback house: Bantam Books. Both Pocket Books and Bantam Books were successful, this time because prices and production were carefully monitored by the established American houses, whose owners had invested in the new paperback houses in order to control their pricing and print runs. These American publishers also limited the royalties of authors initially to 4 percent on sales up to 150,000 and 6 percent thereafter, this to maximize profits. Even with this relatively low share of the proceeds, many writers enjoyed great increases in their overall earnings from paperback sales.[19]

During the Second World War a group of American publishers (W. W. Norton, Malcolm Johnson, and John Farrar among them) established the Council on Books in Wartime. Its purpose was to provide free reading matter for Americans serving in the armed forces. The format of these wartime editions was revolutionary: small rectangular paperbacks, approximately 5½ × 4 inches, with the type in double columns, and secured by a heavy staple through the spine, the book designed to fit into the breast pocket of a military fatigue jacket. The Council published hundreds of titles in its Armed Services Editions for the troops during the early 1940s; after victory on the European front in 1945, they issued hundreds more in a similar series called Overseas Editions in English, these meant to be distributed in occupied countries. In all some 123.5 million copies of 1,324 titles were issued, an enormous stimulus for reading and a strong indication to American

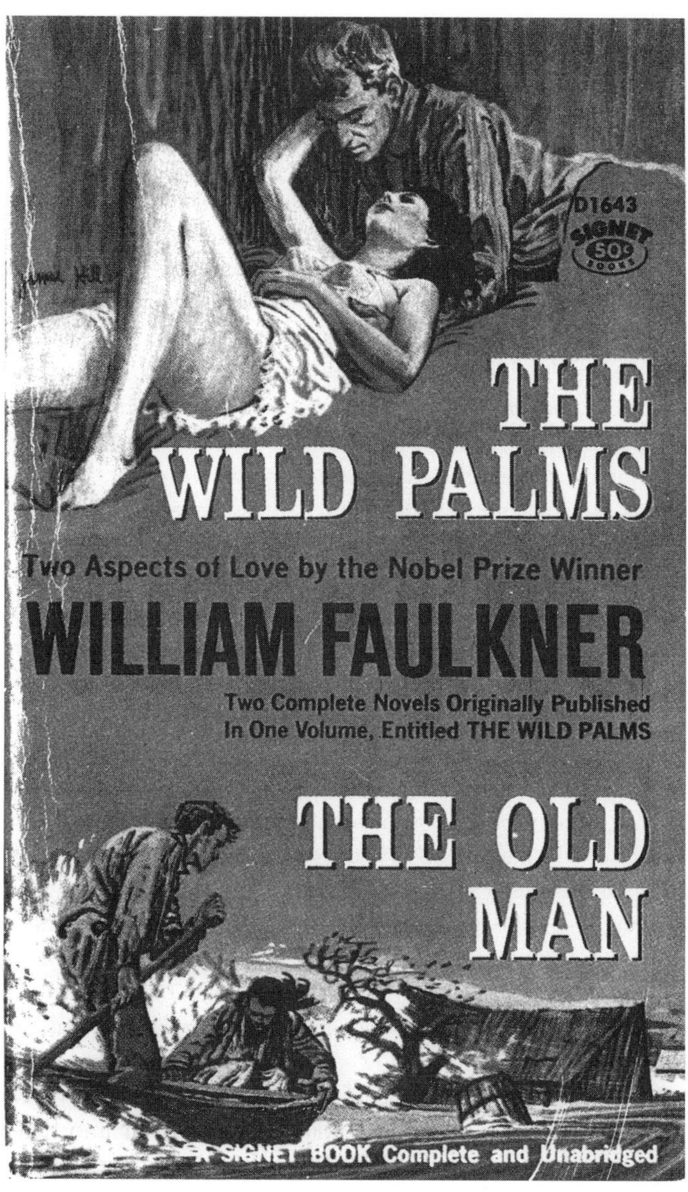

4 Front cover illustration to the 1959 Signet Paperback Edition of William Faulkner's *"The Wild Palms* and *The Old Man."*

publishers that paperback books might finally work on the domestic market.[20] As a consequence several new paperback imprints appeared in the USA during the 1940s – Avon, Dell, Popular Library, and New American Library among them.

The great insight for these publishers was that paperbacks could be distributed through the same outlets as popular magazines. Paperbacks could be sold (most of the early ones for twenty-five cents each) from revolving wire racks in tobacco shops, newsstands, pharmacies, and grocery stores. The storeowners did not choose the titles; that work was done on a weekly basis by the distributors, who removed slow-selling stock for pulping and replaced it with recent strong sellers. The covers of these early paperbacks often featured lurid artwork and sexually suggestive blurbs – so much so that Willa Cather, for one, refused to allow her novels to go into paperback editions. But most writers looked the other way, conscious of how many readers they were reaching and how much money they stood to receive from sales.

Of the major novelists of the period, perhaps none benefited so much from paperback sales as did William Faulkner. Certainly he needed the income. During the 1930s and early 1940s he relied on the magazine market as his major source of money, but his stories did not sell consistently to top-paying outlets such as the *Saturday Evening Post* and *Collier's*, and he did not use an agent, instead attempting to sell the stories himself from his home in Oxford, Mississippi. Faulkner's most dependable markets during the first fifteen years of his career were magazines like the *American Mercury*, *Forum*, and *Scribner's*, all of which had much more modest circulation figures than the *Post* and paid correspondingly lower prices. In 1932 Faulkner began to write for the movie industry, and he proved to be adept at it. He worked in Hollywood most frequently with the director Howard Hawks, who valued his aptitude for writing dialogue and his ability to improvise on the set. By 1936 Faulkner was earning $1,000 a week from Twentieth Century Fox, but he hated the atmosphere of Hollywood and showed a tendency, whenever he lived there for extended periods, to drink heavily. He was chained to Hollywood, however: his novels did not generate enough income to support his many dependents, who during these years included a wife, a child, two stepchildren, his mother, an aunt, his brother's widow and her child, and several aged family retainers.

By 1940 Faulkner was laboring under heavy debts and unpaid taxes; in 1942 he found himself nearly insolvent. In desperation he signed a contract with Warner Brothers at $300 a week – a much lower figure than a writer of his stature and experience should have received. Furthermore, the contract put Faulkner on a tether, allowing the movie studio to call him to Hollywood whenever it wished. Faulkner worked under these conditions until 1946, when Bennett Cerf, his publisher, and Harold Ober, whom he had by now engaged as his agent, managed to extricate him from the contract. By this time Faulkner's books had begun to sell briskly in paperback. New American Library (NAL) brought out four Faulkner titles in the late 1940s and reprinted three more in the early 1950s, paying Faulkner modest advances but, more importantly, generating significant continuing royalties.[21]

An internal office memorandum, reproduced below, records the sales figures and financial details of Faulkner's relationship with NAL through mid-May 1951. The most popular of Faulkner's titles was *Sanctuary* (originally published in 1931), with over a million softcover copies in print, generating total royalties of a little over $13,000. Following behind were *The Wild Palms*

The New American Library
OF WORLD LITERATURE, INC.
INTER-OFFICE MEMO

TO: VW
DATE 5/14/51
cc: AJP
FROM: drd drd
RE: William Faulkner--titles published by and under contract to NAL

No. & Title	Original Publisher	NAL pub. date	Advance paid	Royalties paid as of 12/31/50--incl. adv.	as of 5/51 No. copies printed	No. of printings
#632 SANCTUARY	Random	4/47	$2250	$13,174.34	1,103,424	12
#659 THE WILD PALMS	Random	1/48	$1000	$10,911.48	998,505	6
#692 THE OLD MAN	Random	11/48	$1000	$2,151.25	245,940	1
#743 INTRUDER IN THE DUST	Random	9/49	$3000	$3,000.00	357,040	3
#825 KNIGHT'S GAMBIT	Random	12/50	$2000	$2,145.12	289,640	1
#863 PYLON	Random	4/51	$2000	$2,000.00	303,240	1
#887 SOLDIERS' PAY	Liveright	8/51	$1000 ($500 to be paid on pub.)	$1,000.00		
SARTORIS	Harcourt		$1000	$1,000.00		

5 "New American Library" Interoffice Memo, May 14, 1951.

and *The Old Man* – the two interleaved novellas that Faulkner had first published as a single novel in 1939. Then came *Intruder in the Dust* (1948), *Knight's Gambit* (1949), and *Pylon* (1935). The memo shows that NAL had already acquired the paperback rights for Faulkner's earlier novels *Soldiers' Pay* (1926) and *Sartoris* (1929) and had scheduled publication for the first of these books in August 1951. Total paperback royalties for Faulkner from NAL stood at over $33,000 – the approximate equivalent of $260,000 in buying power in 2007.[22] Faulkner had also benefited from the sale in the mid-1940s of movie rights to three of his short stories and to *Intruder in the Dust* for a total of $60,000. In 1950 his volume of *Collected Stories* was adopted by Book-of-the-Month Club; in that same year he was informed that he was to receive the Nobel Prize for Literature, and the attendant publicity further stimulated the sales of his paperback editions. Finally he was able to feel some financial ease, thanks to the marketing of his subsidiary rights and to his great popularity on the paperback market.[23]

In 1961, the year before Faulkner's death, Random House went public with its first issue of stock on the New York Stock Exchange. Five years later the firm was acquired by Radio Corporation of America (RCA) for approximately forty million dollars. This sale inaugurated a period during the 1970s and 1980s when several major trade houses in the USA were sold to investment conglomerates. These conglomerates, often with ties to the entertainment and education industries, were in search of synergy between (for example) a trade house and a television network. The principal duty of the conglomerate was to stockholders; its purpose was to generate profit. The entry of conglomerates into publishing caused much unease among literary people – writers, critics, editors, and the publishers themselves – about whether the quality of American literature might be negatively affected. Would experimental fiction still have a place in the offerings of major houses? What would happen to midlist authors, whose novels and other writings generated only modest returns? Would book publishing be transformed into a headlong pursuit of lucre by corporate business types with no literary taste? Would publishers still function as intellectual gatekeepers and cultural arbiters?[24]

Some of those fears were well founded, but big-money conglomerates quickly discovered that book-publishing was resistant to bottom-line economics. The people in publishing, from executives to editors to rank-and-file laborers, worked to preserve its character, sometimes through simple inertia, sometimes by complaint and rebellion. Serious novelists and nonfiction writers continued to be published; margins of profit remained predictable but low, causing many of the conglomerates eventually to sell their publishing holdings. Novels in particular remained a chancy form of publishing, occasionally yielding high profits but usually failing to earn out advances and editorial costs until many years after initial publication, if then. Literary houses were not ruined by conglomerate ownership. In fact, the infusion of new capital helped book publishers to grow, to increase the numbers of titles they published, to move into new fields, and to reach out to different markets.[25]

American novelists between 1920 and 1970, with help from their agents and advice from their editors and publishers, were able to adapt to the changing conditions of authorship in the USA. New publishing houses, more vigorous marketing, successful distribution through paperback houses and book clubs, adaptation of writings for the stage and screen, and exploitation of subsidiary rights helped authors to acquire a greater share of the profits of publishing and made available new audiences for serious literary work.

Notes

1. Charles A. Madison, "The Macy Suit," in *Book Publishing in America* (New York: McGraw-Hill, 1966), 158–160. See also James L. W. West III, *American Authors and the Literary Marketplace since 1900* (Philadelphia: University of Pennsylvania Press, 1988), 32–33.
2. The classic study of the rise of professionalism is A. M. Carr-Saunders and P. A. Wilson, *The Professions* (Oxford: Clarendon, 1933). See also Burton J. Bledstein, *The Culture of Professionalism* (New York: Norton, 1976); and Christopher P. Wilson, *The Labor of Words: Literary Professionalism in the Progressive Era* (Athens: University of Georgia Press, 1985).
3. For the history of the literary agent in Great Britain, see James Hepburn, *The Author's Empty Purse and the Rise of the Literary Agent* (Oxford: Oxford University Press, 1968); and Mary Ann Gillies, *The Professional Literary Agent in Britain, 1880–1920* (Toronto: University of Toronto Press, 2007). For the agent in the USA, see West, *American Authors*, pp. 77–102.
4. Frederick Lewis Allen, *Paul Revere Reynolds* (New York: privately published, 1944).
5. An account of Ober's career can be found in the introduction to *As Ever, Scott Fitz – Letters between F. Scott Fitzgerald and His Literary Agent Harold Ober, 1919–1940*, ed. Matthew J. Bruccoli and Jennifer McCabe Atkinson (Philadelphia and New York: J. B. Lippincott Co., 1972), xvii–xxii.
6. Some publishers and authors remained unconvinced of the usefulness of the agent. For a famous publisher's jeremiad see Henry Holt, "The Commercialization of Literature," *Atlantic Monthly* 96 (November 1905): 577–600. For an author's (dyspeptic) view see Raymond Chandler's "Ten Percent of Your Life," *Atlantic Monthly* 189 (February 1952): 48–51.

7. This strategy was not new among American authors, but agents helped to perfect it. See the chapters "Longfellow" and "Longfellow's Income from His Writings, 1842–1852," in William Charvat, *The Profession of Authorship in America, 1800–1870* (Columbus: Ohio State University Press, 1968), 106–167.
8. A useful source for information about Fitzgerald's literary earnings during his lifetime is *F. Scott Fitzgerald's Ledger: A Facsimile* (Washington, DC: NCR/ Microcard Editions, 1972).
9. Craig S. Abbott, "Versions of a Best-Seller: Motley's *Knock on Any Door*," *Papers of the Bibliographical Society of America* 81 (June 1987): 175–185.
10. James L. W. West III, *William Styron: A Life* (New York: Random House, 1998), 424.
11. Bennett Cerf, *At Random: The Reminiscences of Bennett Cerf* (New York: Random House, 1977), 77.
12. Two accounts of Liveright's career are Walker Gilmer, *Horace Liveright: Publisher of the Twenties* (New York: David Lewis, 1970); and Tom Dardis, *Firebrand: The Life of Horace Liveright* (New York: Random House, 1995).
13. William Jovanovich, *Now Barabbas* (New York: Harper and Row, 1964), 123.
14. Studies of BOMC include Charles Lee, *The Hidden Public: The Story of the Book-of-the-Month Club* (Garden City, NY: Doubleday, 1958); Joan Shelley Rubin, *The Making of Middlebrow Culture* (Chapel Hill: University of North Carolina Press, 1992); and Janice A. Radway, *A Feeling for Books: The Book-of-the-Month Club, Literary Taste, and Middle-Class Desire* (Chapel Hill: University of North Carolina Press, 1997).
15. West, *American Authors*, 126.
16. Lee, *The Hidden Public*, 122–123.
17. The restored text of *American Hunger* appeared first in Richard Wright, *Later Works* (New York: Library of America, 1991). See Arnold Rampersad, "Too Honest for His Own Time," *New York Times Book Review* (December 29, 1991): 3; and James W. Tuttleton, "The Problematic Texts of Richard Wright," *Hudson Review* 45 (Summer 1992): 261–271.
18. Gordon B. Neavill, "The Modern Library Series and American Cultural Life," *Journal of Library History* 16 (Spring 1981): 241–252.
19. Madison, "The Paperback Explosion," in *Book Publishing in America*, 547–556; also Frank L. Schick, *The Paperbound Book in America* (New York: Bowker, 1958); Thomas L. Bonn, *Under Cover: An Illustrated History of American Mass-Market Paperbacks* (New York: Penguin, 1982); and Robert Dahlin, "Men (and Women) Who Made a Revolution," *Publishers Weekly* 244 (July 1997): 51–60.
20. Madison, "The Paperback Explosion," 548; also Daniel J. Miller, *Books Go to War: Armed Services Editions in World War II* (Charlottesville, VA: Book Arts Press, 1996).
21. Lawrence H. Schwartz, "The Commerce of Culture: Publishing Faulkner in the 1940s," in *Creating Faulkner's Reputation: The Politics of Modern Literary Criticism* (Knoxville: University of Tennessee Press, 1988), 38–72.
22. A useful website for making these comparisons is www.measuringworth.com/.

23. The memorandum is preserved among the Random House collections at the Butler Library, Columbia University, Box 18, folder N.
24. For a book-length expression of these apprehensions, see Thomas Whiteside, *The Blockbuster Complex: Conglomerates, Show Business, and Book Publishing* (Middletown, CT: Wesleyan University Press, 1981).
25. A recent account of the book trade after the Second World War is Al Silverman, *The Time of Their Lives: The Golden Age of Great American Book Publishers, Their Editors and Authors* (New York: St. Martin's Press, 2008).

48

The novel of crime, mystery, and suspense

SEAN McCANN

About a third of the way through *Tender is the Night* (1934), as Dick Diver is about to begin the precipitous decline that is the subject of Fitzgerald's novel, the young psychiatrist encounters a displaced American veteran in a neighborhood on the outskirts of Paris. The man reminds Dick of

> a type of which he had been conscious since early youth ... [i]ntimate to garages, where he had vague business conducted in undertones, to barber shops, to the lobbies of theaters ... Sometimes the face bobbed up in one of Tad's more savage cartoons – in boyhood Dick had often thrown an uneasy glance at the dim borderland of crime on which he stood.

This scene plays a minor yet structurally significant role in Fitzgerald's novel. The unnamed veteran – who provides a "menacing," working-class counterpoint to Dick's romantic memories of the war and to his visions of personal and national destiny – will return in the novel's final pages as a reminder of Dick's fateful collapse. But he is also more broadly representative of some of the salient qualities of American literary modernism, which is full of similarly menacing marginal figures. Meyer Wolfshiem in *The Great Gatsby* (1925), Sam Cardinella in Hemingway's *In Our Time* (1925), Faulkner's Popeye (in *Sanctuary* [1929]) or Joe Christmas (in *Light in August* [1932]) – all are, like the nameless veteran of *Tender is the Night*, examples of the ambivalent fascination with which the modernists regarded the development of a transient urban working class.

Indeed, it is striking how many of the major works of American modernism are, at their core, crime narratives in which violence becomes the index of corrosive economic modernization. But Fitzgerald's unnamed man is important not only as a figure of the menacing underside of the industrial economy; he is equally important as a representative of its popular culture. The Tad to whom Fitzgerald alludes in this passage is Thomas Aloysius Dorgan, a sportswriter and pioneering cartoonist for William Randolph Hearst's *New York Journal American* who reputedly coined many memorable slang phrases of the early twentieth century, including "cat's pajamas" and "hard-boiled." Fitzgerald underscores the significance of his allusion to this figure by making his anonymous veteran an aggressive newspaper vendor. The veteran thus marks not only the periphery of Dick Diver's professional milieu, but also of the mass cultural entertainment that was the rival and trading partner of literary modernism. He brings the news to Dick Diver, and the content of his message is the imagery and language of popular journalism itself.

Three decades later Chester Himes made a similar point from a reverse angle. In *Run Man Run* (1966), Himes, who had become a renowned crime novelist after abandoning his efforts to write social protest fiction in the style of Richard Wright, created a variation on the detective thrillers that brought him fame. After witnessing a random police killing, Harlem porter Jimmy Johnson must flee for his life through the obscure warrens of a racially segregated city, struggling to evade the homicidal policeman who is determined to hunt him down. At one moment in his travels, Jimmy stands before the bookstore in the Hotel Theresa ("the Waldorf Astoria of Harlem") and observes its showcase: "*Black No More*, by George Schuyler, he read; *Black Thunder*, by Arna Bontemps; *The Blacker the Berry*, by Wallace Thurman; *Black Metropolis*, by Cayton and Drake; *Black Boy*, by Richard Wright . . . Suddenly he felt safe. There, in the heart of the Negro community, he was lulled into a sense of absolute security."

That illusion of safety does not last, of course – which is Himes's point. Jimmy's brief vision of racial community does not stand a chance before the racist violence of the police or before the class and gender divisions that fracture Harlem society. Like Himes himself – with whom he shares some significant biographical details – Jimmy is implicitly capable of greater achievements, but remains bound by racial oppression to menial labor. ("He worked with his hands," [but] "his mind was crowded with numerous thoughts.") And he will soon be reminded that he has little in common with the "prosperous people" catered to by elite Harlem institutions like the Hotel Theresa. In effect, Himes's intimation is similar to Fitzgerald's. In *Run Man Run*, the image of serious literary expression briefly interrupts a pulp crime narrative rather than vice versa. But for both Himes and Fitzgerald, literary art is associated with superiority to the accidents of a violent, unpredictable, and erotically perilous social order. The pulp crime story, by contrast, looks like that society's most typical expression.

Taken together, those brief moments in Himes's and Fitzgerald's novels mark out the distinctive and remarkably durable niche that crime fiction has tended to occupy in the larger ecology of American letters. Since the dawn of commercial mass culture in the United States nearly two hundred years ago, stories of crime and violence have been the most prominent face of popular entertainment, and they have been consistently understood not only to depict, but also to elicit, dangerous forces of appetite, desire, violence, and fear. In this way, crime fiction has been taken often to exemplify the seductive powers of commercial entertainment in particular, and sometimes to illuminate the manipulative, or coarsening, or exploitative nature of capitalist society in general. Understood to be both the product and on occasion the symptom of a troubled and unjust social order, the crime novel has mattered most to the history of the American novel in the way it has been used to define and redefine the highly charged border marking serious literary artistry. As the eminent critic Clive James once suggested of the novels of Raymond Chandler, crime fiction in the USA signifies because it is "almost literature."[1]

That liminal status reaches back to the market revolution of the antebellum era and to the emergence during the 1830s and 1840s of the elements of both a viable American book and magazine publishing industry and of a booming, commercial mass culture built especially on cheaply priced pamphlets and newspapers.[a] The consequences of the latter were, in Edgar Allan Poe's view, "beyond all calculation."[2] Turning out a vast wave of sensational writing focused especially on tales of crime and violence, the cheap publishing of the antebellum years produced a literature that both its critics and its defenders took to be the mark of a new, democratic culture. In the view of Alexis de Tocqueville, for instance, the "literary industry" of the antebellum USA shared little with "the art of literature" that had been cultivated by the aristocratic systems of patronage he knew in France. But in that very way it was an illuminating sign of the dynamics of a commercial society. "Accustomed to the struggle ... of practical life," Tocqueville explained, democratic audiences "require strong and rapid emotions ... to rouse them up and to plunge them at once, as if by violence, into the midst of the subject."[3] The sensation story, in short, was both a product of the commercialization of literature, and, at least potentially, a means to understand the discipline of the market itself.

a See the discussion by Ronald Zboray and Mary Saracino Zboray in chapter 4 of this volume, "The novel in the antebellum book market."

We can understand much of the subsequent history of American crime fiction if we see it in the light of the response to this potential made by two seminal figures – Poe and his admirer and sometime friend George Lippard. Each drew on the central elements of the antebellum era's new culture industries and sought to use the subjects of crime and violence to develop a vantage from which to view the economic development that had transformed their world. Their approaches to this effort were finally quite different, but Poe and Lippard each forged a powerful narrative paradigm built around the revelation and control of crime, and the story forms they established would exercise enduring influence over generations of writers to come.

Of these two writers, Lippard is the far less familiar. But if he has been forgotten by all but cultural historians, Lippard was once an outsize figure – renowned in his own day not only for his enormously popular novels, but also for his work as a crusading journalist and for his impassioned advocacy on behalf of workers and the poor. His most important book, *The Quaker City, or The Monks of Monk Hall* (1844–1845), was the bestselling American novel before the publication of *Uncle Tom's Cabin*, selling upward of 200,000 copies during the first decade following its publication and going through some twenty-seven printings.[4] An object of intense public controversy, Lippard's novel became a sensation at least in part because of the way it used the materials of the era's popular journalism and fiction to dramatize the "festering corruption" that had accompanied the commercial expansion of the first decades of the nineteenth century. His novel was intended, Lippard remarked, to depict "the colossal vices and the terrible deformities . . . in the social system" of contemporary Philadelphia and to reveal the way that system denied "the great idea of Human Brotherhood."

In particular, Lippard's Philadelphia conceals beneath its ostensibly democratic exterior the aristocratic vices of debauchery and sexual corruption, given free rein in an economic system that rewards greed and ambition. Although the novel's elaborately tangled narrative is difficult to summarize, its main plotlines all hinge on the greed and vice of Philadelphia's mercantile elite, and they all contribute to the novel's controversial ability to combine political indignation with voyeuristic titillation. The entire web of corruption circles about the dark and mysterious mansion of the novel's title – a secretive club on the outskirts of the city where the local elite engage in lurid pleasures beneath the guidance of a demonic and racially indeterminate master of ceremonies named Devil-Bug.

To construct this nightmarish image of the commercial city, Lippard drew on a wide range of influences. *The Quaker City* is indebted to the gothic novels of Matthew Lewis and Charles Brockden Brown (to whom the book is dedicated) and to Eugène Sue's *Mysteries of Paris* (1842), whose peripatetic revelation of urban vice it imitated and intensified. Above all, Lippard, took inspiration from the sensationalism of the flourishing antebellum press. The vision of urban crime Lippard proposed – in which the dark places of the city conceal licentious desires, irrational passions, and the threat of racial corruption – had been brewing in popular journalism for the previous several decades. The wide popularity of cheaply produced criminal biographies and trial reports, published in the hundreds throughout the antebellum era, had tutored readers to a new fascination with violence and sexual deviance, displacing earlier, theological understandings of crime and punishment. In this newly secular understanding of crime, violence and disorder were understood not in terms of sin and providence but, rather, in their relation to social norms of cooperation and self-discipline. The result was the gradual emergence of a distinctly "gothic" sensibility in which violence and cruelty were understood to be marginal to the order of liberal society. Crime in this view was the consequence of illicit and unbounded passions and could be best conceived as "mystery" – that is, as an epistemological and moral puzzle that presented a challenge to the authority of reason and law.[5]

Lippard's novel contributed significantly to that gothic view of the nineteenth-century metropolis as a place of moral peril, where individuals freed of the guidance of custom might indulge their destructive desires. In *The Quaker City*, as in the era's trial pamphlets and criminal biographies, crime and deviance are above all erotic and typified by the sexual abuse of nubile young women.[b] As in the era's sensational journalism, moreover, the crimes that excite Lippard's outrage emphasize not only injustice and inequality, but – as Tocqueville very nearly implies – the failure to maintain the self-control valued by market society. To this gothic view of crime, however, Lippard brought a republican complaint against social corruption that enabled him to weave his images of cruelty and vice into a larger, political narrative. Where the popular press circulated tales of individual abuse and personal failure, Lippard created an encompassing narrative of social decline in which the virtues of American democracy were threatened by an economic system that encouraged predation and license.

That vision of the criminal city would exercise enduring influence over the development of American crime fiction. During Lippard's own day, *The*

b See Milette Shamir, "Manhood and the early American novel," chapter 11 in this volume, for a discussion of the way the antebellum era's emergent ideology of self-control was figured especially through stories of sexual transgression and erotic violence.

Quaker City encouraged countless imitations which aimed to explore the decadent, undemocratic city. Lippard himself followed *The Quaker City* by bringing a similar treatment to another locale in *New York: Its Upper Ten and Lower Million* (1853), and he was imitated by countless pamphlet fiction writers working in an industry that flourished in the middle decades of the century, many of whom shared little of his political conviction but who were eager to exploit his vision of the vice-ridden city. Ned Buntline's *Mysteries and Miseries of New York* (1848), for example, reached a mass audience by imitating Lippard's depiction of the nineteenth-century city as a den of hidden corruption and elite predation. Virtually every one of the era's new urban centers came in for the same treatment in some fifty *Mysteries of . . .* novels published between 1844 and 1860 – the *Mysteries of Troy*, for instance, or *The Mysteries and Miseries of San Francisco*. The result was the establishment of a robust set of conventions for conceiving the urban landscape that would persist through many subsequent generations in popular storytelling.

But Lippard's gothic city was only one of the significant legacies of antebellum crime literature. Still more influential would be Poe's creation of the detective story, an invention that we can understand best as an alternative to Lippard's vision of the criminal metropolis. Like Lippard, Poe was fascinated by the materials of popular journalism – the medium, as he put it, of "the excitable, undisciplined and child-like popular mind."[6] He, too, would draw on those materials for his own fiction, most famously in the use of the scandalous death of the cigar girl Mary Rogers to create his second detective story, "The Mystery of Marie Rogêt" (1842). But Poe sought to carve out a literary position quite unlike the one created by his contemporary. Lippard conceived himself as a popular tribune whose bestselling works articulated the demands of an unrepresented majority of workingmen, and he embraced the popular press as means of speaking to a mass audience. Poe, by contrast, was primarily a magazine writer and editor, seeking to reach an emerging audience of middle-class readers whose tastes would fall between the sensationalism of the penny press and the cultural eminence of the New England quarterlies like the *North Atlantic Review*, both of which he excoriated.

The aesthetic convictions to which Poe devoted extensive theorizing were thus in part a direct repudiation of the values Lippard emphasized. Lippard embraced both the eroticism and the anti-formalism of the sensational press. To capture the sheer upheaval of the capitalist city – a world where, as he puts it in *Quaker City*, "every thing [is] fleeting and nothing stable" – his fiction would need to be equally outlandish, embracing "extravagant views of life" that were at odds with "mathematical probability."[7] Poe's romantic aesthetics, with their emphasis on the design of plot ("that in which no part can be displaced without ruin to the whole"), leaned in the opposite direction, seeking to combine sensation literature's emphasis on astonishment with a "sculptural" artifice that would reward "cultivated thought in the reader."[8] Indeed, Poe criticized sensation fiction like Lippard's for the way its proliferating examples of violence and intrigue submerged "the soul of the plot" beneath the "multitudinous outrage and horror" of the modern city, thereby sacrificing the potential for "poetical justice."[9]

The detective story, by contrast, allowed Poe to imagine outrage and horror submitted to the order of plot, and by extension it enabled him to proffer in the person of the detective something near to his ideal vision of the man of letters – neither a "wealthy gentleman of established leisure" nor "the poordevil author" who struggled to survive in the vertiginous literary marketplace of the antebellum era, but rather a freelance intellectual whose intelligence brought him stature and security and whose abilities allowed him to perceive meaning where others saw confusion.[10] A declassé aristocrat and an eccentric intellectual in a mass society, Poe's detective C. Auguste Dupin manages to be in, but not wholly of, market society, and he is therefore able to discover within the seemingly random actions of city life, the formal patterns that provide a sense of order beneath apparent chaos.

In this manner, Poe's detective story offered not only the aesthetic pleasure of form, but a reassuring image of civic life. Lippard depicted the city as a Hobbesian universe of predation and universal competition, "where no man has a friend." Poe, by contrast, envisioned his detective as a solitary man, who is nevertheless able to forge a friendship with the stories' unnamed narrator – they met by chance in a bookstore – and to provide services valued by his rival the Prefect of Police. Where Lippard viewed the capitalist city as inimical to brotherhood, then, Poe's detective story imagines that friendships and agreements can be established amid the competition and accidents of market society.

In the decades after the Civil War, as American industrial capitalism underwent an extended period of growth and the US publishing industry experienced dramatic expansion, Poe's vision became a commonplace, and the detective story he invented emerged as a developing taste of the growing middle-class public. Even before Arthur Conan Doyle created renewed enthusiasm for the detective story at the turn of the century, a native tradition of the genre flourished in the work of women writers who used the detective story to explore and defend domestic ideology. In the work of Metta Victor (the pseudonym of Metta Victoria Fuller) – author of *The Dead Letter* (1866), the first American detective novel – and of subsequent, bestselling writers like Anna Katherine Green and Mary Roberts Rinehart, the potential implicit in Poe's form was brought to realization in stories that focus on "the domestic spaces of the wealthy professional and mercantile classes."[11] A hybrid of the sentimental fiction discussed by Cindy Weinstein in this volume[c] and of the elements of the popular crime story, these novels used the instruments of the detective story to explore the tensions that in ostensibly rare circumstances threaten the sentimental relations of the middle-class home. The sources of crime and injustice in these novels are variously greedy husbands, intolerant fathers, dishonest suitors, and untrustworthy servants, all of whom are shown to betray the bonds of affection that should guide their conduct. As Catherine Nickerson points out, moreover, the perils they represent are understood to reflect qualities associated with the market – ambition, desire, cunning, self-interest – intruding on a domestic sphere that is supposed to be immune to them. Much as in Poe's less fully elaborated model, in sum, the work of the detective comes in protecting the nurturing institutions of the capitalist world from the pathological aberrations they seem inevitably to produce.

That vision of the detective as a reassuring counter to the dangers of the Gilded Age economy became widely popular during the latter decades of the nineteenth century, the era when the detective first became an American culture hero. Analogues to the domestic detective were popularized, for instance, by Allan Pinkerton, whose series of novels – beginning with *The Expressman and the Detective* (1874) – advertised the accomplishments of the Pinkerton Agency in controlling the dangers that accompanied the rise of an industrial economy. Celebrating the "professional labors" of the skilled detective (as he put it in *Expressman*), Pinkerton depicted his agency vanquishing the threat of greedy clerks and resentful employees, as well as the more serious dangers of organized labor and political subversion. An equally important role was played by Julian Hawthorne (son of Nathaniel), who created a popular series of fictionalized accounts of the adventures of Inspector Thomas Byrnes, the creator of New York City's "detective bureau" and the coiner of the phrases "deadline" (the boundary around New York's financial district, which criminals were forbidden on Byrnes's order from crossing) and "the third degree" (Byrnes's highly touted means of interrogation). Indeed, most of the qualities that would later be identified as central to the "police procedural" novel – popularized by Ed McBain in the 1960s and 1970s and echoed

c See Cindy Weinstein, "Sentimentalism," chapter 12.

in countless movie and television police dramas – were anticipated in Hawthorne's fiction. Like Pinkerton, Hawthorne highlighted the teamwork of detectives whose mastery of the routine tasks of surveillance, investigation, and interrogation enabled them to keep the criminal underworld under control. To the antebellum picture of the city as a place of dangerous passions and hidden vices, Hawthorne and Pinkerton thus added a new emphasis on the importance of skill, management, and organization – qualities approved by Pinkerton's and Byrnes's clients in the nation's new financial elite. Hawthorne himself was perhaps the paradigmatic example of the era's professional writer, the new vocational figure memorably described by William Dean Howells in his account of "The Man of Letters as the Man of Business" (1893).[12] As Howells did, Hawthorne earned a comfortable living and a prominent public reputation by turning out books and magazine stories, and his detective fiction emphasized the qualities necessary to his own success – intelligence, discipline, industry – casting them in opposition to a criminal underworld whose reckless improvidence represented those qualities of market society about which Hawthorne, like Howells, was most ambivalent. Anna Katherine Green's hugely successful *The Leavenworth Case* (1878) offered a similar intimation. Allying her police detective Ebenezer Gryce to Raymond Everett, "a rising young lawyer," Green sets the pair in opposition to a fecklessly greedy merchant and his unscrupulous secretary and emphasizes the way the detective and the lawyer share an ability to decipher the novel's many mysterious documents. Intelligence and training allow Green's professionals to counter their rivals' criminal duplicity. As Nickerson points out, the novel – fittingly subtitled "A Lawyer's Story" – hinges above all on the skills and the status concerns of the professional and makes them the occasion for a middlebrow defense of literary accomplishment.[13]

By the end of the century, the figure of the professional detective was so familiar that Mark Twain could burlesque the image of the clue-spotting crime solver in *Tom Sawyer, Detective* (1896) and make it the target of a darker satire in *Pudd'nhead Wilson* – in which neither the professional's ability to ferret out crime nor his ideological opposition to decadent elites and dependent workers serves the interest of justice (1894). With the arrival of Sherlock Holmes in US mass-market magazines like *Collier's* during the last years of the 1890s and the first decade of the twentieth century, the popular enthusiasm for the detective would take on intense new life, prompting the first public definitions of detective fiction as a distinct novelistic genre and inspiring a vast wave of Holmes-inspired knock-offs. In the decades just before and after World War I, "slick" magazines and the booklists of mainstream publishing houses were full of increasingly mannered renditions of eccentric detectives, genius detectives, and scientific detectives – a trend that culminated with the success in the late twenties of S. S. Van Dine's refined aesthete Philo Vance and, slightly later, with Rex Stout's still more popular Nero Wolfe.[14]

While the middlebrow image of the professional detective was taking form during the late nineteenth century, a different version of the detective story emerged in the era's story papers and dime novels. In these low-cost publications, the vogue for the detective story was combined with remnants of the urban landscape fostered by Lippard and his followers among the mysteries of the city writers. The very names of the most prominent dime-novel detectives – Old Sleuth and Old Cap Collier – indicate their distance from the professional figures celebrated by Hawthorne and Green. Neither distinctive as individual personalities, nor particularly skilled at interpretation, analysis, or management, the dime-novel detectives are rather figures of the crime solver as craftsman. Their most important vocational skills are those of disguise and combat, and their significant narrative functions concern their ability to move unobserved through the multiple levels of the city, illuminating the dimensions of status and revealing the hidden corners and concealed vices of a hierarchical society. Where the detectives of Green, Pinkerton, and Hawthorne typically subdue criminal insubordinates, the dime-novel detective tends to be, as Michael Denning notes, a "mechanic hero" whose most important task is to shield the vulnerable from exploitation and abuse.[15]

Those qualities percolated through the dime novels and then the pulp magazines that displaced them in the early part of the twentieth century, passed on from Old Sleuth to his heir Young Sleuth and then to the more widely remembered detective Nick Carter.[d] But they did not come to broader public attention and cultural legitimacy until the 1920s, when Dashiell Hammett and Carroll John Daly led the *Black Mask* school of crime writers (so named for the era's most ambitious and renowned pulp magazine) in refashioning the conventions of the dime-novel detective story into a new, "hard-boiled" variety of crime fiction. Amid the crime wave that accompanied Prohibition, the dime-novel detective story's episodic narrative method and peripatetic rendition of social geography assumed fresh relevance, and Daly, Hammett, and their peers updated the style to fit the dimensions of the new metropolis. Like their dime-novel predecessors, the *Black Mask* writers eschewed the intellectual

d See Shelly Streeby's discussion in chapter 35 of this volume, "Dime novels and the rise of mass market genres," 595–596.

pretensions of the classic detective story and instead made their heroes shrewd craftsmen, skilled above all as hunters and combatants. Indeed, they intensified the populist intimations of the dime-novel detective, making their protagonists impudent tough guys who often speak the vernacular of the working-class city while repeatedly baffling the impositions of their wealthy clients and the bureaucratic demands of the police.

The audience for that populist image of the detective burgeoned during the twenties and thirties, as first the Prohibition-induced crime wave and then the Depression focused popular attention on the still uncharted conditions of the industrial metropolis. In this respect, the sudden vogue for the hard-boiled detective paralleled the contemporaneous emergence of gangster films and novels, such as W. R. Burnett's *Little Caesar* (1925), which offered readers a handle on the recent explosion of organized crime. The gangster novel of the twenties was perhaps the first prominent example of the crime story as social problem novel. Its use of the rise and inevitable fall of the gangland kingpin to dramatize broader concerns about the role of bureaucratic institutions and urban society would make it the forerunner to many subsequent crime novels. Burnett's own *High Sierra* (1940), for example, or Ira Wolfert's *Tucker's People* (1943), William McGivern's *The Big Heat* (1953), Mario Puzo's *The Godfather* (1969), Richard Price's *Clockers* (1992) along with its sequels, and the most accomplished crime stories of our own era, the HBO television dramas *The Sopranos* (1999–2007) and *The Wire* (2002–2008) – all of these, as well as countless similar though less impressive works, use the crime story in the manner Burnett pioneered in the twenties, as a seismographic measure of shifts in the social order. All, too, offer visions of the criminal metropolis that descend recognizably from the mysteries-of-the-city narrative that Lippard and his followers popularized. A realm of ruthless competition and dark impenetrability, the criminal city of the gangster saga appears, in the title of one of Burnett's novels, as an *Asphalt Jungle* (1949).

The hard-boiled crime story, which emerged contemporaneously with the gangster novel, offers a similar vision of the criminal metropolis. Among the most striking characteristics of the *Black Mask* school is the way the hard-boiled writers resuscitated the labyrinthine image of the city that had descended from antebellum sensation fiction, restoring to prominence the very "multitudinous" landscape of crime and injustice that the professional detective was created to keep under control. Dashiell Hammett at one point considered naming his first novel – eventually titled *Red Harvest* (1929) – "The 17th Murder" in order to indicate the sheer multiplicity and confusion of the city he depicted. The Los Angeles traversed by Raymond Chandler's Philip Marlowe is a dark maze whose proliferating scenes of aristocratic license and sexual cruelty rival Lippard's gothic city. The world that Chester Himes, a later master of the style, created in Harlem similarly amounted to a remarkable re-invention of the urban terrain that had been painted by the mysteries and miseries writers of the mid nineteeth century. Himes's detective heroes Coffin Ed and Gravedigger Jones repeatedly plunge into a Harlem underworld where brute racial injustice has elicited carnivalesque extremes of vice and violence.

In one of the traditions of popular storytelling that descended from the *Black Mask* school, the hard-boiled private eye contends with and masters that landscape in a fashion that makes him reminiscent of the detective created by Edgar Allan Poe. This hard-boiled tradition of streetwise mastery begins with Carroll John Daly, whose protagonist Race Williams employs his knowledge of the metropolis, along with his skills in physical and verbal combat, to bring corrupt elites and the lawless denizens of the city's tenements to heel. It continued in both the vigilantism that Mickey Spillane popularized in the decades after World War II and, in a somewhat more refined form, in Ross Macdonald's contemporaneous vision of the detective as psychoanalyst and man of sorrows. Indeed, in some respects, Macdonald, who sought to bring emotional depth and literary sophistication to the hard-boiled detective story, became Poe's truest heir. Like Poe, Macdonald aimed to elevate the materials of pulp fiction by emphasizing the power of intelligence to discover deep patterns of order amid the apparent accidents of social competition, and like Poe, he cast his detective hero as a figure whose intellectual sophistication shielded him from the irrational desires that waylaid the criminals and victims of his fiction.

The more significant tradition of hard-boiled writing, however, cast itself in almost direct opposition to this version of the detective story. In *Red Harvest* and his subsequent novels, Dashiell Hammett did not so much elevate as ironize the conventions of the detective story, treating them as a kind of fiction that revealed the arbitrariness of every aspiration to justice or order. That theme was brought to fullest realization in Hammett's most celebrated work *The Maltese Falcon* (1930), a novel that used the conventions of the detective story to set up an irreconcilable tension between the detective's coldly amoral professional skill and the potent, yet irrational allure of love and belief. Though Sam Spade can reveal the novel's eponymous statue, thought to conceal fabulous wealth beneath its blank façade, to be a valueless fake – a "dingus" – he can do little to curb the irrepressible desire the object calls forth in all its pursuers, even himself. Though he similarly reveals the novel's femme fatale, Brigid O'Shaughnessy, to be a murderer and unhesitatingly turns her over to the police, he is unable to deny his love for her or to present a simple account of his motivations. The detective story, whether in the version of Poe or Hawthorne or Macdonald, traditionally used the tale of investigation and apprehension to present a drama of emancipation, in which the detective's professional abilities allowed him to free himself from the desires and compulsions that controlled other people. Hammett, by contrast, who referred to his detective as a "dream man," left his protagonist stranded, and suggested that his pursuit of autonomy was a fantasy and itself a form of constraint.[16]

In his determination to "make literature" of it, Hammett in effect treated his genre as a kind of pastoral literature (in the sense of pastoral proposed by his contemporary William Empson), casting it as a kind of naïve and limited form of life whose constraints his writing would probe and explore and strain against.[17] The detective story as it descended from Poe thus became the epitome of middlebrow culture, constantly reaffirming the moral that literature improved and elevated, and that professional intelligence could serve to harmonize the operations of an otherwise perilous economic system. In Hammett, that hope is at once alluring and absurd. The villain of his second novel, *The Dain Curse* (1929) offers a sly self-portrait of the writer himself as a failed novelist who compensates for the loss of his ambitions by fabricating myths that entrap the novel's naïve ingénue and ultimately the villain himself. Here and throughout his work, the pathos of Hammett's fiction stems from the way it imagines the author, like the detective, as the prisoner of fictions each would like to believe he controls.

That self-reflexive treatment of the detective story as form would become the central device of the most celebrated hard-boiled crime fiction. "If a man writes as well as I do," Hammett's follower Raymond Chandler explained, "he creates a schism between the melodramatic exaggeration of his story and the way he writes about it."[18] Chandler would treat that schism in a manner quite opposed to the cool detachment Hammett favored, making the gulf between form and aspiration the occasion not for stories of ironic self-subversion, but for tales of longing and nostalgia. (The difference is evident both in the romantic persona of Chandler's detective hero Philip Marlowe and in the renowned baroque style through which Chandler records the detective's poetic sensitivity to his world.) But like Hammett, Chandler transformed the detective story by self-reflexively dramatizing its limitations and by foregrounding the pathos of his own unsuccessful efforts to transcend them.

The manner in which their fiction explored that schism explains why hard-boiled writers like Hammett and Chandler were so appealing to modernist artists and critics, and why the elements of their style would prove to be lastingly resonant. The classic detective story, as it was invented by Poe and refined by his successors, was a myth of liberal society – of the way, despite inevitable aberrations, a market of free agents could produce a decent and harmonious social order. But it was by the same token also a fantasy of literary recognition in which the gifts of critical intelligence become indispensable to middle-class society. The hard-boiled writers' determination to undermine that myth explains why their vernacular was the perfect device for Fitzgerald to use in puncturing the self-deceptions of Dick Diver. It explains as well why many writers who sought to criticize liberal society forcefully from the right or the left – William Faulkner and Richard Wright, for example – would be repeatedly drawn to versions of the hard-boiled story, and why elements of the form would be endlessly appealing to later writers (e.g., Patricia Highsmith, Thomas Pynchon, Joyce Carol Oates) who would be still more cutting in mocking the pretenses of middlebrow culture. All these writers share the sense adumbrated by Tocqueville that the crime story epitomizes the crassest features of market society, and all would practice variants on the strategy outlined by Hammett and Chandler, generating pathos out of the inevitably failed effort of serious literary expression either to control or transcend it.

Notes

1. Clive James, *Reliable Essays: The Best of Clive James* (London: Picador, 2001), 291.
2. Edgar Allan Poe, "Richard Adams Locke" (1846), in *Essays and Reviews* (New York: Library of America, 1984), 1214.
3. Alexis de Tocqueville, *Democracy in America* (1835, 1840), trans. Henry Reeve, rev. Francis Bowen, ed. Phillips Bradley, 2 vols. (1945; New York: Vintage, 1990), II:59.
4. David S. Reynolds, *Beneath the American Renaissance: The Subversive Imagination in the Age of Emerson and Melville* (Cambridge, MA: Harvard University Press, 1988), 207.
5. Daniel A. Cohen, *Pillars of Salt, Monuments of Grace: New England Crime Literature and the Origins of American Popular Culture, 1674–1860* (New York: Oxford University Press, 1993); Karen Halttunen, *Murder Most Foul: The Killer and the American Gothic Imagination* (Cambridge, MA: Harvard University Press, 1998).
6. Poe, review of *Mosses from an Old Manse*, by Nathaniel Hawthorne (1847), *Essays and Reviews*, 579.
7. Lippard, quoted in Reynolds, *Beneath the American Renaissance*, 207.
8. Poe, review of *Night and Morning*, by Edward Lyton Bulwer (1841), *Essays and Reviews*, 148, 151. On Poe's relation to antebellum popular culture, see especially

Terence J. Whalen, *Edgar Allan Poe and the Masses: The Political Economy of Literature in Antebellum America* (Princeton: Princeton University Press, 1999).

9. Poe, review of *Barnaby Rudge*, by Charles Dickens (1842), *Reviews and Essays*, 238–239.
10. Poe, "Anastatic Printing" (1845), quoted in Whalen, *Edgar Allan Poe and the Masses*, 54.
11. Catherine Ross Nickerson, *The Web of Iniquity: Early Detective Fiction by American Women* (Durham, NC: Duke University Press, 1998), xi; see Shelley Streeby's discussion in this volume for an illuminating account of the way Victor revised the features of antebellum sensation fiction, replacing the populist emphasis of sensation fiction with a vision of the detective as "sentimental gentleman" ("Dime novels and the rise of mass market genres," chapter 35, 596).
12. In the campaign biography of Lincoln which launched Howells's career, Howells defended Lincoln from suspicions of ignorance by emphasizing the politician's reading habits, in particular his taste for "the absolute and logical method of Poe's tales . . . in which the problem of mystery is given, and wrought out . . . by processes of cunning analysis." Quoted in Neil Harris, *Humbug: The Art of P. T. Barnum* (Chicago: University of Chicago Press, 1981), 86.
13. Nickerson, *The Web of Iniquity*, 65, 70–96.
14. *The Benson Murder Case*, the first novel by S. S. Van Dine (the pseudonym of art critic Willard Huntington Wright) was published by *Scribner's Magazine* in 1926 and went on to become a bestseller in book form. It was followed by ten subsequent murder mysteries, though Van Dine's popularity waned during the thirties. Rex Wolfe published the first Nero Wolfe novel, *Fer-de-Lance*, in 1934 with dozens of sequels appearing over the subsequent four decades.
15. Michael Denning, *Mechanic Accents: Dime Novels and Working-Class Culture in America*, rev. edn. (London: Verso, 1998), 204.
16. Dashiell Hammett, "Introduction," *The Maltese Falcon* (New York: Modern Library, 1934), viii,
17. See Mark McGurl, "Making 'Literature' of It: Hammett and High Culture," *American Literary History* 9.4 (1997): 702–717 and William Empson, *Some Versions of Pastoral* (London: Chatto & Windus, 1935).
18. *Selected Letters of Raymond Chandler*, ed. Frank McShane (New York: Columbia University Press, 1981), 194.

49

US novels and US wars

JOHN CARLOS ROWE

Traditional approaches to the "war novel" and "the literature of war" have focused mostly on cultural reactions to specific wars, accepting a causal relationship that privileges the historical event over its representation. The Civil War takes place, and we have the cultural "response." Edmund Wilson's famous *Patriotic Gore: Studies in the Literature of the American Civil War* (1962) is a good example of this approach.[1] Since Paul Fussell's *The Great War and Modern Memory* (1975), however, the relationship between "war literature" and the "event" of warfare has been treated in a more dialectical manner.[2] Literature and other cultural production may predict war, warn us away from it, prepare us emotionally for it, even help legitimate warfare. Cultural work may also help us understand certain social and political issues as inextricable from violent conflict, even when not identified as specific wars. In focusing only on the Haitian Revolution or the American Civil War, for example, we tend to ignore the long histories of struggle against colonialism and slavery that culminated in warfare. In considering only those wars officially recognized by the US government, we forget the military campaigns waged by the US against native peoples in the course of westward expansion. In thinking conventionally about warfare in political and strategic ways, we also tend to ignore the consequences for non-combatants. In historical periods when women participated in warfare primarily in supporting or defensive roles, their experiences of war were often ignored. By the same token, children and the elderly and other non-combatants figure only in the backgrounds of many classic "war novels."

In broadening the scope of this relation, I hope to open up the category from the relatively restricted genre of the "war novel" to a much broader range of prose fiction that addresses organized state violence in US history. The recognized "wars" (even if the Vietnam War was technically "undeclared") are conventional means of "periodizing" literary, as well as much social and political, history: the American Revolution, the Civil War, the

Spanish–American War, World War I, World War II, and the Vietnam War. Forgotten utterly or neglected significantly are the "other," sometimes referred to as "little" wars: the War of 1812, the Plains Wars, the Philippine–American War, the Korean War, the "Cold War," and the two "Gulf Wars." Taking just one literary example for each of these fourteen different wars (others could be mentioned, of course) in the traditional manner, I would be hard pressed to say much about any of those texts, except the usual platitudes about just what qualities makes a single text truly representative of a particular war.

Instead, I will consider "war in American culture" as the expression of deep internal divisions. These fissures have been manifest in pre-existing racial/ethnic, class, and gender/sexual conflicts and have helped shape foreign policies that have defined "foreign" cultures, often to the point of military and other violent conflicts. I will thus be extending my own earlier efforts to link internal and external imperialisms in US history, understanding the internal "wars" – the Revolution, War of 1812, Civil War, Plains Wars, Cold War – in relationship to the "foreign" conflicts – Spanish–American and Philippine–American Wars, World Wars I and II, Vietnam, and the Persian Gulf. The governing assumption of this approach is that warfare brings to the historical and existential surface long-simmering conflicts, whose importance literature often identifies in advance of actual warfare and in some cases excavates from the ruins of war.

Charles Brockden Brown's *Edgar Huntly* (1799) reveals the dialectical process whereby literature discloses a collective unconscious of national fears in its representation of recent wars. Addressing the violence of the American Revolution, *Edgar Huntly* also draws on specific details from the French and Indian Wars, confusing the conflict between the British and French with the rebellion of British colonists in the American Revolution. The general term "French and Indian Wars" refers broadly to conflicts between the British and French dating from King William's War (1689–1697) to the French and Indian War (1755–1763), the North American portion of the Seven Years War. In one sense, Brown, whose Quaker merchant family remained neutral during the Revolution, seems to understand the Revolution as a consequence of the colonial violence in North America and its close relationship to continental wars. As the protagonist, Edgar Huntly, violently sleepwalks through hostile Indian country, struggles to solve the mysterious murder of his friend, Waldegrave, and is shadowed by the insane Clithero Edny, Brown represents the new nation as unstable, full of warring factions, and on the verge of anarchic collapse.

The historical confusions and conflations in Brown's fiction are typical of much popular cultural work from the Revolution to the first decades of the nineteenth century. In one of his most bizarre sleepwalking adventures, Huntly awakens to a confrontation with a live panther in a cave, kills it, and eats it raw, gaining strength to defeat two powerful Delaware (Lenni-Lenape) males guarding the entrance to the cave. Scholars have long interpreted this episode as an allusion to the infamous "Abraham Panther Narrative," published in 1769 as anti-British propaganda during the Revolution, even though the woman in the narrative, Jane McCrea, was a British partisan,[3] and Huntly's political loyalties are not specified. The "Panther Narrative" also transforms the Wyandots who mistakenly killed her into a single enormous "black man" with violent sexual intentions. An early advocate of US annexation of French Louisiana territory, Brown does not criticize the USA for continuing European imperialism, but instead suggests merely that the new nation take the lead in North America. Brown argues in his fiction that the USA needs to identify its proper "citizens" and distinguish them from a variety of enemies, including Native Americans – especially the Delaware (Lenni-Lenape) living around Philadelphia – and Catholics, as well as those from Spain, France, and Germany.

Like Brown, James Fenimore Cooper folds North American colonial conflicts into the historical watershed of the American Revolution, suggesting that its emancipatory and democratic purposes enabled the new nation to transcend the endless cycle of warfare typical of the "Old World." Cooper's Natty Bumppo fights for the British in the French and Indian War represented in *The Last of the Mohicans* (1826), but Cooper's readers knew that he was really writing about the American Revolution, exemplified by the self-reliant frontiersman at home in the woods who is able to distinguish good, assimilated Indians like Chingachgook from bad renegades, like the murderous Magua.[a]

The ideological line from Brown to Cooper is fairly clear: both novelists help legitimate the new nation by identifying foreign "threats," justifying violence against indigenous peoples as "self-defense," and privileging certain white racial and Protestant religions over the full demographic diversity of the US nation.[4] Several antebellum novelists bring to light this generally unconscious imperial and inherently violent narrative of US ideology. In *Typee: A Peep at Polynesian Life* (1846), Melville implicates the USA in the European colonial battles for the Pacific islands from the very beginning of the novel,

a Sandra Gustafson offers a nuanced treatment of Cooper's use of Good Indian–Bad Indian tropes in "Cooper and the idea of the Indian," chapter 6 in this volume.

reminding us that Captain David Porter attempted to annex the Marquesas islands to the United States while he pursued his US naval orders to harass British shipping in the area during the War of 1812. Linking Hawaii with the Marquesas, Melville calls attention to US expansionist interests in the Hawaiian islands, where as early as the 1830s the USA had established whaling supply stations and in 1898 would annex the islands, in part to provide supply routes to the gold fields in the Yukon. In many other works, Melville satirizes US democratic aspirations by reminding his readers how thoroughly the nation perpetuates European colonial power. *Israel Potter: His Fifty Years of Exile* (1855) traces the picaresque adventures of a Revolutionary War soldier through transatlantic adventures and long residence in London, peregrinations that testify to continuing US dependence on Europe. *Pierre, or The Ambiguities* (1852) recalls the bloody battles fought by Pierre's ancestors, the Dutch Patroons, against Native Americans in upstate New York while reminding us of the profound class distinctions still governing the apparently "classless" democracy of nineteenth-century America.

Few scholars would dispute the claim that the Mexican–American War (1846–1848) is a blatant instance of US imperialism, contending with a nation that only twenty-five years earlier had thrown off Spanish colonial rule and was still struggling with post-revolutionary instability. Despite its historical importance for increasing US territory by more than one third, testing military strategies that would be used in the Civil War, and deploying racial stereotypes of Mexicans that would persist to the present day, the Mexican–American War has been given relatively little attention by cultural historians. Yet as Shelley Streeby has pointed out, this war established such types as the Mexican *bandido*, popularized the Western "dime novel,"[b] and contributed to strategic confusions between Mexican and Native Americans.[5]

Often forgotten in such discussions are the many Native American peoples who were displaced first by the Spanish, then by Mexicans, and finally by the conflict between Mexican and US colonialisms in California and the Southwest.[c] John Rollin Ridge's (Yellow Bird's) popular novel, *The Life and Adventures of Joaquín Murieta* (1854) helps focus all of these issues, even if Ridge was not writing specifically to indict US imperialism in AltaCalifornia. Ridge's Sonoran bandit incorporates many of the author's concerns about the mistreatment of the Cherokee by the US government in the 1830s, but

b See also Shelley Streeby's analysis of dime novels in this volume, "Dime novels and the rise of mass market genres," chapter 35.

c Sean Kicummah Teuton traces this tension in the development of the novel in Native American literature in chapter 67, "The Native American Tradition."

Ridge – himself a Cherokee - strictly distinguishes the Cherokee and other tribes east of the Mississippi from the California tribes, such as the Tejon, who are represented in the novel as primitive and savage. Ridge's version of the historical bandit who raided shipments leaving the California gold fields is a master of disguise who adapts easily to the new social circumstances in California after the Mexican–American War. His lawlessness is a consequence of the anarchy in postwar California, where the provisions of the Treaty of Guadulpe-Hidalgo protecting Californios' civil and property rights were repeatedly abrogated by new laws, frontier violence, and mob rule.

The Civil War looms, of course, as the central military event in the nineteenth-century USA, but its battles are represented in fiction well in advance of the actual hostilities. Fugitive slave narratives and novelistic neo-slave narratives, many published by anti-slavery societies, revolve around both the violence of the slavocracy and the forms of resistance employed by African Americans. Frederick Douglass's *Narrative of the Life of Frederick Douglass, an American Slave, Written by Himself* (1845) turns crucially on the moment in which the young Frederick Bailey defends himself successfully against the slavebreaker Edward Covey. Martin Delany's protagonist, Blake, travels from the US South to Canada and then to Cuba, plotting a hemispheric revolution against slavery in *Blake, or The Huts of America* (1861–1862).[d] Harriet Beecher Stowe's *Dred, A Tale of The Great Dismal Swamp* (1856) represents the maroon community led by the fugitive slave, Dred, as the site of a planned, albeit abortive, revolution against slavery.[6]

The fiction directly representing the actual Civil War is vast, ranging from John William De Forest's *Miss Ravenel's Conversion from Secession to Loyalty* (1867), which attempts to work through the sectional differences of the Civil War, to the long list of postbellum popular works exemplified by Margaret Mitchell's Pulitzer Prize-winning *Gone with the Wind* (1936), which sentimentalizes the "gracious" culture of the white South while preserving its strict racial hierarchies in the manner of antebellum "plantation romances," which rationalized slavery as a benign despotism.[e] It is interesting that in the long list of novels written about the Civil War, Stephen Crane's *The Red Badge of*

d Robert S. Levine treats *Blake* at greater length elsewhere in this volume. See "The early African American novel," chapter 16, 275–277.

e The sequence that runs in this volume from the essays by Jennifer Rae Greeson (chapter 14, "Imagining the South") through Barbara McCaskill (chapter 29, "The African American novel after Reconstruction") and Robert Reid-Pharr (chapter 28, "The postbellum race novel") and Candace Waid (chapter 45, "Faulkner and the Southern novel") traces the contradictions that attend the effort to portray slavery in this positive light.

Courage (1895) should stand out as the canonized American literary classic, despite Crane's deliberate effort to treat the Civil War merely as a metaphor for warfare and violent conflict in general.

Yet Crane's avoidance of the racial, sectional, and political issues of the Civil War may be the reason that *The Red Badge of Courage* has achieved such canonical status. Psychologizing the macropolitical issues of the Civil War in the experiences of Henry Fleming, who initially flees from battle to face existential dread and then returns curiously transformed into a daring leader of his Union regiment, Crane stresses an archetypal education of an American confronting the ineluctable adversities of existence. Published as the USA rose to global power in the years leading up to the Spanish–American and Philippine–American wars, *The Red Badge of Courage* envisions warfare as essential to the human condition, hardly pausing to discuss the Civil War's unique qualities, and offers a model for heroic individuals overcoming their fears of battle not for the sake of military glory but for manhood and maturity.[7]

The Spanish–American War began with the sinking of the USS *Maine* in Havana Harbor (February 15, 1898), an event newspaper tycoon William Randolph Hearst attributed to a Spanish bomb in order to drive the USA into war with Spain. The war is full of fictional events of this sort, including Theodore Roosevelt's mythologizing of the US military charge up San Juan Hill in his memoir, *The Rough Riders* (1899), and the news coverage by such notable fiction writers as Crane, Frank Norris, and Richard Harding Davis.[8] The historical leap from the Civil War to the Spanish–American War is typical of many cultural and political histories focused on military conflict, with the unfortunate consequence that the Plains' Wars and ongoing frontier violence between Native Americans and the US government is either neglected or treated separately.

Manifest Destiny created political instabilities all across the western territories. Ridge's complaints about injustice in California during the 1850s could be applied as well to the Southwest, the Great Basin, the Rockies, and the Plains, where the displacement of native peoples from traditional regions of hunting and gathering and the arrival of settlers in large numbers produced unavoidable conflicts. Increasingly after the Civil War, when the USA military concentrated on troubles in "Indian country," genocidal attacks on native peoples and their food sources, especially the American bison, became standard policy. Native Americans who refused to report to reservations were declared "hostiles," hunted, and killed. The massive scholarship and literature representing Custer dwarfs the many other conflicts native peoples endured in this period. Few people have heard of the Pyramid Lake War, the Muddy Lake

War, the Bannock War, or the Nez Perce War, but each of these conflicts had enduring consequences for Paiutes, Bannocks, and Nez Perce in California, Oregon, Nevada, Utah, and Idaho. The Blackfeet writer James Welch asks in *Killing Custer* (1994) why Custer's Last Stand has occupied such a major place in US cultural history, when so many massacres of native peoples are largely forgotten.[9] The answer to his rhetorical question is in many respects self-evident: Custer's and Major Reno's defeat at the Little Bighorn was a pyrrhic victory for Native Americans, who may have won the battle but were subsequently targeted by an angry population for total control on reservations and in prisons, as well as outright extermination.

Admiral Dewey's sailors in Manila Harbor and US troops in the Philippines during the Philippine–American War (1899–1902) referred to Philippine citizens as "Indians," as if this were the "new" frontier in an ever-expanding frontier now stretching across the Pacific. The war the USA waged against Philippine republicans after having helped defeat Spanish colonialism is a largely forgotten story, thanks to how it contradicts US foreign policy rhetoric of "emancipation" and "democracy." Yet the legacy of Philippine insurgency against both the colonialism of Spain and the USA is represented well in Carlos Bulosan's two novels, *America Is in the Heart: A Personal History* (1946) and his unfinished novel about the Huk rebellion at the end of World War II, *The Cry and the Dedication* (1995). Despite Bulosan's deep commitment to US democracy and its cultural heritage, exemplified in such figures as Emerson, Thoreau, and Whitman, he was also a powerful critic of US failures to deliver its democratic promise. *America Is in the Heart* dramatizes the disappointment of *Piñoys* (Philippine-American immigrants), like Bulosan himself, with US democracy and its exclusionary qualities. *The Cry and the Dedication* is a more radical indictment of US imperialism, beginning with the betrayal of republican hopes when the US annexed the Philippines at the end of the Philippine–American War and extending up to the ethnic Huk efforts to regain indigenous control of the Philippines at the end of World War II. Instead, the USA suppressed the Huk rebellion and installed as a puppet-ruler President Ferdinand Marcos, who served US interests while suppressing and robbing his own people.

From Melville's Marquesas and Hawaii to Bulosan's Philippines, the Euro-American imperial path reaches all the way to Japan and China, inevitably involving violent conflicts.[f] The search for a literary representation of the

f Russ Castronovo analyzes the fictions of American imperial adventure in chapter 32, "Imperialism, Orientalism, and empire."

Taiping Rebellion (1850–1864) in China may take us as far as Amy Tan's *The Hundred Secret Senses* (1995), but US involvement in the suppression of this rebellion against Manchu rule has much larger cultural connotations. The Taiping Rebellion was an internal rebellion against the tottering Manchu dynasty in China, a dynasty which had failed to modernize, resulting in much of the individual misery that drove Chinese males to seek employment on "Gold Mountain" – that is, the United States. The Boxer Rebellion of 1900 was an anti-imperialist movement of the Secret Society of "Boxers," who wanted to drive out the British-controlled opium trade and convince Chinese converts to renounce Christianity. The USA supported British influence in China and sent troops to help quell the Boxer Rebellion, creating political instability that drove rural males to the United States in quest of work. This emigration produced the conditions that created "Chinese-American culture," including literature, which also resulted specifically from the anti-immigration laws and policies generally gathered under the heading of "the Chinese Exclusion Laws."

Do the experiences of the Chinese in the USA under the strict anti-immigration rules of various Exclusion Laws qualify as material for "the war novel"? To which war are we referring – the Taiping Rebellion, the Boxer Rebellion, or the many violent acts or "driving outs" by which Chinese were persecuted and in many cases murdered in the USA during Exclusion? Maxine Hong Kingston's *China Men* (1980) is a fictional memoir that expresses quite effectively the complex imbrication of political persecution in the USA with the consequences of foreign, colonial wars. Kingston notes that despite stereotypes of Chinese immigrants as premodern, rural peasants unsuited to the rapid industrialization of post-Civil War America, they were in fact the workers who helped build railroad networks all over the USA, often performing the most specialized and dangerous jobs, thus contributing directly to US modernization.[g]

The traditional "war novels" from World War I are surprisingly critical of the war itself. Desertion from military service in Europe often stands as a badge of honor, claimed by such characters as Frederic Henry in Ernest Hemingway's *A Farewell to Arms* (1929), John Andrews in John Dos Passos's *Three Soldiers* (1921), and Joe Williams in Dos Passos's *1919* (1932), the second volume of his *U.S.A.* trilogy (1938). All of these characters are white, American males, and their disillusionment with war confirms their American goodness

g Susan Koshy traces the development of this literature, including *China Men*, elsewhere in this volume, in "The Rise of the Asian American Novel," chapter 63 esp. 1055–1056.

and idealism. The liberal, self-reliant, exceptionalist US individual declares a separate peace in these novels.

World War I continues to be represented throughout twentieth-century US literature as an illegitimate war whose US involvement is questionable. Ralph Ellison barely refers to World War II in *Invisible Man* (1952), despite his claim in 1981 that the book "had been conceived as a war novel."[10] He does pay special attention to World War I, however, by introducing a veteran in the "Golden Day," the local juke-joint where early in the novel the narrator takes Mr. Norton. The speech of Ellison's mad veteran expresses African Americans' anger about the nation's failure to reward their military service, but his "madness" – a disorder clearly attributable to US racism rather than to shell-shock – renders ambiguous Ellison's criticism of World War I. Ellison's use of World War I in the novel makes his neglect of the more recent war even more disturbing. After all, the riots in Harlem that conclude *Invisible Man* – based on those that occurred in real life in 1943 – were prompted in large part by African American veterans' anger about their reception at the end of World War II, but Ellison elides these issues.

Literary modernism generally protested the folly of warfare, even though the movement's own stance often prevented its practitioners from explicitly connecting twentieth-century warfare with the European imperialism that fostered much modernist cosmopolitanism. The solution for many writers in the USA and Europe was to treat war in existentialist terms, reducing it to a metaphor for human alienation and absurdity. Hemingway's Frederic Henry takes the sheer contingency and death of warfare as an occasion to choose his own destiny, abandoning warfare first for the woman he loves, Catherine Barkley, and finally accepting her death (and that of their unborn child) with the sort of stoicism Hemingway endorsed as a masculine value. The existentialist solution persisted into the US fiction produced in response to World War II, with two disturbing consequences: it depoliticized specific wars, universalizing them as inevitable consequences of "bad faith"; and it treated reductively different experiences of war by presenting everyone's experience as similarly absurd, thereby trivializing genocide, holocaust, and other civilian casualties. Colonial subalterns, ethnic minorities, women, children, and the elderly tended to be transformed merely into minor characters highlighting the central disillusionment of the white, male soldier, whose conduct toward these same minorities was often excused on account of the extreme conditions of warfare.

The grand narrative of the world wars reinforced the primarily white masculine features of US ideology from Manifest Destiny to the Cold War.

Many violent conflicts or "little wars," usually waged against minoritized peoples, were conveniently overlooked. The late eighteenth-century revolution of slaves against their French colonial rulers in Haiti was the first successful slave rebellion, and it led the USA to marginalize Haiti. Melville's *Benito Cereno* (1856), which resets a real-life 1804 rebellion on a slave ship to 1799 in order to position it within the scope of the Haitian revolution, may be considered a novel of this conflict.[11]

In a similar vein, we can consider the "Cultural Front" of the Communist Party of the USA (CPUSA) and socialist activism stretching from the Wobblies (Industrial Workers of the World or "I.W.W.") through the 1930s to constitute "combat" against a capitalist system intent on exploiting workers at home and abroad. Michael Denning's monumental *The Cultural Front: The Laboring of American Culture in the Twentieth Century* (1996) demonstrates the scope and variety of the Left's political struggles and their cultural means.[12] "Class warfare" is often invoked by CPUSA, as in the title of Clara Weatherwax's proletarian novel, *Marching! Marching!* (1935), which mobilizes workers in struggles with capital and Communist internationalism.[h] CPUSA members and fellow travelers were also active in the Russian Revolution, as John Reed's eyewitness account, *Ten Days That Shook the World* (1919) narrates, and in the Spanish Civil War, which Hemingway's *For Whom the Bell Tolls* (1940) curiously represents in the love story of Robert Jordan and Maria, its anti-Communist sentiments, and its transformation of anti-fascism into a mirror of US democracy.

Such little and "alternative" wars should not, of course, distract us from the vast literature produced in response to World War II. The dustjacket of Martha Gellhorn's *The Wine of Astonishment* (1948), suggests a delay in the postwar fictional response to World War II: "When World War II came to an end, novels and plays reflected a change in the mood of the public by turning away from military themes. Now, three years later, the world conflict is beginning to emerge again, in fiction and on stage."[13] Between 1948 and 1961, many of the canonical novels about World War II were published, including Norman Mailer's *The Naked and the Dead* (1948) and Joseph Heller's *Catch-22* (1961). Mailer's psychological realism in his account of soldiers fighting on the fictional Pacific Island of Anopopei works to personalize and Americanize the War in the Pacific. His "Time Machine" device, in which Mailer flashes back to his characters' previous lives at home,

h Alan Wald traces the development of the proletarian novel in greater detail in chapter 40, "Steinbeck and the proletarian novel."

reinforces the humanity of the US soldiers in opposition to the "foreignness" of the enemy. Asked to explain the suicide missions of Japanese soldiers, the Japanese-American translator, Wakara, remains baffled. Reading a dead Japanese soldier's diary, Wakara wonders: "A thinker, a poet; there were many Japanese like him. And yet they died like anything but poets, died in mass ecstatic outbursts, communal frenzies." Thirteen years later, Heller's *Catch-22* invokes the absurdist qualities of war by focusing on US Air Force bombing runs over Italy at the end of the war, long after such air cover is really needed, criticizing the military bureaucracy as the precursor of post-war capitalism and what President Eisenhower later termed "the military-industrial complex." Despite its nihilist pessimism, *Catch-22* locates humanity in individual characters like Yossarian, who find in the absurdity of war some motivation for compassionate behavior. Despite a cosmopolitan aura and skepticism regarding patriotism, Yossarian still represents the "American individual," whose libertarian contempt for government of all kinds anticipates the John Rambo character of the Vietnam era (whose enduring cinematic presence was inspired by David Morrell's 1972 novel, *First Blood*).

Many novels of popular male bonding and heterosexual romance were published during and after World War II, in an effort to normalize warfare while at the same time glamorizing its horrors. James Jones's *From Here to Eternity* (1952) is perhaps the most memorable work in this mode, both because of its technical sophistication and because it was made into an extremely popular film directed by Fred Zinnemann in 1953.[14] Set in 1941 Hawaii and encompassing the Japanese attack on Pearl Harbor, the novel mythologizes US entry into the war in terms of its characters' star-crossed destinies. Indeed, Mailer's and Jones's melodramas of war and reinforcement of certain stereotypes of American (male) individualism would often be cited as motives for enlistment by US soldiers from Korea to the Second Gulf War and Afghanistan.

John Hersey's war fiction, such as *Men on Bataan* (1942), also mythologizes military combat, especially the horrors of the unsuccessful US battle for Bataan and the Bataan death march by prisoners of war ordered by the Japanese. But Hersey was also capable of representing the other side of the war, as he does in *Hiroshima* (1946), which follows six people who survived the explosion of the atom bomb on August 6, 1945. Hersey incorporates interview testimony of these survivors into his own narrative, anticipating the genre of docudrama while drawing on the conventions of the war novel.[i]

i David Schmid analyzes the unstable boundaries between fact and fiction in the novel in chapter 59, "The nonfiction novel."

Published in the same year as *Hiroshima*, Miné Okube's *Citizen 13660* (1946) offers another docudramatic response to Japanese internment in the "Relocation Camps" mandated by President Franklin Roosevelt's Executive Order 9066. *Citizen 13660* locates absurdity not in a metaphysical condition but squarely with the US government, which was incapable of distinguishing between its own Japanese-American citizens (many of whom fought courageously for the USA) and its Japanese enemy.

Social problems at home were also addressed in wartime works like Carson McCullers's *Reflections in a Golden Eye* (1941), the macabre story of relations between members of a small Southern town and the local army base. Set before the entrance of the USA into the war, the novel nevertheless anticipates how wartime America would be changed by the rapid military expansion around the globe, a subject McCullers would address obliquely in *The Member of the Wedding* (1946).

Postwar America turned almost immediately to new conflicts at home and abroad, only some of which are properly classified as part of the "Cold War." The new global order determined largely by the Allied nations at the Yalta and Potsdam conferences called for long-term decolonization even as the USA, Great Britain, and Russia specifically *recolonized* the globe in ways that would help precipitate a series of formal and undeclared wars for the next six decades. Much of the American literature about these postcolonial and neocolonial wars is short on political analysis and long on drama and melodrama. Once again, writers tended to personalize the experience of warfare in order to give a human face to the impersonal forces of military conflict. In doing so these novelists furthered a wider cultural dynamic in which the combat soldier gains authority as an "expert" on foreign policies and politics about which he knows little. This rhetorical position turns veterans into "war heroes," and their judgments about how to conduct "just wars" and avoid unnecessary ones assume more significance than the views of policymakers, scholars, and public intellectuals.

Donald McCann argues that US writers did not respond to the Korean War, because it was forgotten amidst efforts by US culture to address World War II.[15] I think there are other reasons for the American literary neglect of the Korean War, especially confusion regarding issues created by US, UN, Chinese, and Russian involvement in what was originally a civil war between capitalist and communist interests in Korea. The Korean-born writer Richard E. Kim described the political and ethical confusions of the war in his novel, *The Martyred* (1964). Assigned to investigate the deaths of twelve Christian ministers at the hands of the Communists, Kim's protagonist, Captain Lee, a South Korean Intelligence Officer, discovers that these "heroes" betrayed others. Outraged, Lee wants to expose the twelve "martyrs" for their cowardice, but in the end recognizes the political consequences and ends up preserving their lies. By rendering ambiguous the moral issues involved on both sides of the Civil War in Korea, Kim helps explain why other US writers, unfamiliar with Korean history and culture, might have avoided the subject. He also warns those seeking simple solutions to Cold-War problems, just one year before major US troop build-up in Vietnam.

Interest in the current geopolitical confrontation between the USA and North Korea has certainly spurred interest in fiction and memoirs by Korean Americans. Helie Lee's novel, *Still Life with Rice: A Young American Woman Discovers the Life and Legacy of Her Korean Grandmother* (1996) and her memoir, *In the Absence of Sun: A Korean American Woman's Promise to Reunite Three Lost Generations of Her Family* (2002) recall the Japanese occupation of Korea before and during World War II, the subsequent civil war, and the geopolitical partition of the Korean Peninsula. She focuses on the recent past and the dictatorship in North Korea, complementing other immigrant narratives about the journey from a repressive homeland to relative freedom in the USA. Books like Khaled Hosseini's *The Kite Runner* (2003), Azar Nafisi's memoir *Reading Lolita in Tehran: A Memoir in Books* (2004), Ayaan Hirsi Ali's *Infidel* (2007), and Lee's narratives tend to support US militancy with regard to their respective home countries: Afghanistan, Iran, Somalia, and Korea. The literature of diaspora is politically as well as culturally diverse and can often serve the neo-imperial interests of one state that may have provided protection and aid to an exilic community from another one. By the same token, the writer in exile often strengthens the US state's foreign policies with regard to that writer's "homeland."

US fiction and memoir in response to the Vietnam War (1965–1975) constitute a large field of study with its own interpretive problems. The political and aesthetic diversity of these representations cannot be explained simply by the deeply divided public positions on this war, or its moral ambiguities. It is tempting to claim Vietnam as a "unique" war in US history: the first the nation clearly lost; the first "undeclared" war; the first war to be routinely covered in real time on the evening news. Yet the Vietnam War is in many respects a continuation of US neo-imperialism from Captain Porter's early bid to annex the Marquesas, through Manifest Destiny to the Spanish–American, Philippine–American, and Korean wars. In all of these military ventures, the USA sought to impose its will on less powerful nations. Well in advance of major American troop build-ups in Vietnam, William Lederer and Eugene Burdick effectively represent the contradiction of US rhetoric and actual foreign policies in *The Ugly American* (1958), a novel anticipated by the British novelist Graham Greene's *The Quiet American* (1955). Kim represents the moral ambiguities in the Korean War, but Greene and Lederer and Burdick stress the hypocrisy and self-delusion in US foreign policies and failed diplomacy in Southeast Asia.

Numerous as the US novels, short stories, poems, and plays about the Vietnam War are, the most influential literary forms centering on the conflict were memoirs, autobiographies, documentaries, and docudramas. Troubled by contradictions between news and official government statements, the US public wanted the "real" and "true" Vietnam.[16] As a consequence, eyewitness reports, firsthand memoirs, and other direct reports were especially popular, even though they often confirmed public perceptions that the war was out of military or diplomatic control. In 1961, Philip Roth complained in "Writing American Fiction" that the artist was hard-pressed to compete with a social reality that outdid the most inspired imagination. The Vietnam War carried Roth's concern to an extreme unmatched in previous US cultural experience. For example, following advice from Southeast Asian specialists to "modernize" South Vietnam and thus ally rural peasants with the US puppet government, the USA shipped countless electrical appliances to rural villages that lacked electricity.[17]

Many novels and memoirs exploit the fantastic characteristics of US military and foreign policies in Vietnam, offering readers a new kind of "realism" that was based on the representation of fantasy, delusion, and contradiction. Helicopter gunships swoop down to kill elephants in Tim O'Brien's *Going after Cacciato* (1978). Using techniques of magic realism to underscore the insanity of the war, O'Brien stages a fictional desertion, in which his characters simply abandon the war and walk to Paris via Tehran, which was under the Shah's terrorist rule. Robert Stone uses a drug deal gone awry to symbolize US involvement in Vietnam in *Dog Soldiers* (1974), a book that culminates in a surreal solo death march that mixes gutty determination with Eastern philosophy, seen from the inside of the dying character's head. Philip Caputo's *A Rumor of War* (1977) is a memoir, "not a work of the imagination."[18] Nevertheless, Caputo represents a fantastic world of combat, remote from "the World" (the United States) and the "air-conditioned headquarters of Saigon and Danang," which "might well have been on another planet." Michael Herr's hip, stoned-out style in his *Dispatches* (1977) challenges the boundary between fiction and fact, once again by stressing the ideological production of contradictions in the military and foreign policies of the USA in Vietnam.

"Vietnam Vietnam Vietnam, we've all been there," Herr famously chants in the last line of *Dispatches*, but in truth few Americans were ever *there*. CBS journalists were sent to the war with specific instructions *not* to learn much about the history and culture of Vietnam, so that they could send back fresh impressions. US diplomats and generals rarely learned Vietnamese or made efforts to understand the region's complex political history. As the list of novels, memoirs, films, and other cultural responses to the war grew, US ignorance repeated itself in works representing primarily American, not Vietnamese, suffering.

A few scholars and artists attempted to change that situation. Frances FitzGerald's *Fire in the Lake: The Vietnamese and the Americans in Vietnam* (1972) appeared in the last years of the war. Criticized by some as an Orientalist interpretation, dependent as it was on the French Sinologist Paul Mus's work on Indochina, *Fire in the Lake* at least opened public debates regarding Vietnamese history and culture. Le Ly Hayslip's *When Heaven and Earth Changed Places* (1989), popularized in Oliver Stone's film, *Heaven and Earth* (1993), not only challenged Americans to recognize the impact of the war on the Vietnamese, but also to recognize the impact of Southeast Asian immigrants in the USA. Hayslip's memoir and its sequel, *Child of War, Woman of Peace* (1993), also challenged the growing list of "coming home" novels and memoirs, which previously had focused almost exclusively on US veterans of the war, including USA nurses, as in Lynda Van Devanter's *Home before Morning* (1983). Caputo hopes vainly that *A Rumor of War* might "prevent the next generation from being crucified in the next war," then changes his mind: "But I don't think so." Since the USA lost the Vietnam War, Americans have done little to address directly the country's imperial ambitions, from westward expansion to our current wars in Afghanistan and Iraq. As terrible as the events on September 11, 2001 were, this attack on the USA by a non-state organization, al Qa'eda, had at least something to do with the global perception by many that the USA is the major neo-imperial power in the post-Cold War era.[j]

Despite its reputation as a capacious form, including very diverse materials in heteroglossic ways, the novel is also historically specific to nationalism, dependent on its middle-class origins, and conventionally tied to a dominant

j Bruce Robbins's analysis of "The worlding of the American novel" in chapter 66 of this volume includes a section on post-9/11 novels.

language. US literary responses to post-Vietnam era wars and global conflicts often betray these limitations. John Updike's final novel, *Terrorist* (2006), bravely attempts to personalize the terrorist by imagining a young man's gradual initiation into and eventual repudiation of a terrorist plot to bomb the Lincoln Tunnel, but Updike's necessary focus on his protagonist excludes broader analyses of global politics. Philip Roth's *American Pastoral* (1997) criticizes internal problems in the USA, especially those that led to such radical anti-war groups as the Weathermen, but tells us little about the international problems provoked by one-way globalization. Roth's *The Plot against America* (2004), nominally a counterfactual World War II-era novel in which Charles Lindbergh is elected President in 1940, is actually an allegory about the rise of fascism and intolerance in the USA after 9/11. Insightful as Roth's critique of the Bush administration is, it focuses on anti-Semitism, side-stepping the so-called "clash of civilizations" pitting Western societies against global Islam. It is possible that Roth hopes to suggest some analogy between the persecution of Jews in Lindbergh's and Muslims in George W. Bush's America, but if so, the parallel is insufficiently developed. Similarly, Don DeLillo's *Falling Man* (2007) tries to assess the personal consequences of 9/11, but the representative lives in New York City he imagines are too conventionally American to address the complex transnational questions posed by 9/11. DeLillo's earlier *Mao II* (1991) is more convincingly transnational in its treatment of US neo-imperialism's destabilization of the Middle East, particularly during Israel's occupation of Lebanon between 1982 and 1985. Of a piece with this novel is DeLillo's broad critique of US global capitalism in *Underworld* (1997) and *Cosmopolis* (2003).

In *Mao II*, Bill Gray is a novelist who discovers in the course of the narrative that fiction's challenge to the nation can no longer compete with terrorism's assault on the state. Like the Vietnam-era literary authors and memoirists incapable of challenging the fantasmatic ideology of the US war-machine, DeLillo despairs of influencing the historical juggernaut of US neo-imperialism and hypercapitalism's drive toward one-way globalization.

Perhaps the only US novelist to have attempted to assess the full historical and geopolitical scope of such neo-imperialism is Thomas Pynchon, whose entire body of work focuses on the development of postmodern, neo-imperial power out of modern imperialism and nationalism. Pynchon's first major novel, *V.* (1963), tracks global imperialism from the seventeenth-century Dutch and British up to the end of World War I; he continues his analysis in *Gravity's Rainbow* (1973) by focusing on the post-World War I rise of National Socialism in conjunction with German imperialism in Southwest

Africa and the global ambitions of the Third Reich. When Pynchon's V-2 rocket descends at the end of the novel, it heads straight for the theater in which his readers are imaginatively seated, chanting for the show to begin, and prepares us for Pynchon's connection of the Nazis' imperialism, racism, genocide, and technological obsessions with US neo-imperialism in Vietnam. Pynchon's *Vineland* (1990) interprets US government efforts to crush the Old and New Left (especially by means of Cointelpro and other subversive governmental activities) as extensions of imperialism, now waging undeclared wars against the counterculture, Native Americans, Asian business, and global Communism. In *Mason and Dixon* (1997), Pynchon suggests that US neo-imperialism is by no means a recent, postmodern, exceptional phenomenon, but rather the consequence of the European imperialism that sought to impose its values on the Western Hemisphere. Mason's and Dixon's "surveying" provides the controlling metaphor, suggesting that the mapping of sectional divisions and, of course, private property mark the beginnings of the entropic tendency of the modern world toward its destruction. The long, complex, but eminently clear argument Pynchon has made about US neo-imperialism is extended in *Against the Day* (2006), a novel set in the World War I era and elaborating how the US rise to global power in that era continues to shape its contemporary foreign policies and international relations.

Pynchon is not alone in his criticism of US neo-imperialism as the source of the ceaseless wars that have defined national history and identity. Gore Vidal's *Empire* (1987) returns to the McKinley and Theodore Roosevelt administrations to warn Americans of their long history of imperialism. We must add to this list the many contemporary Native American, Asian American, Chicano/a and Latino/a, and African American writers who have written powerfully about how US mistreatment of its minority populations reflects its global, extraterritorial *hubris*.

Toni Morrison's *Beloved* (1987) is a particularly good reminder that US domestic policies and external warfare are inextricably linked. Morrison's controversial dedication, "Sixty Million and more," has drawn considerable criticism, especially from survivors and scholars of the Holocaust. In my view, Morrison links slavery and the Holocaust, as well as the genocide against Native Americans, in order to suggest the much broader context in which we must understand modern injustice and warfare. Slavery, Morrison argues convincingly, was warfare, as was the genocide of the Holocaust and against Native Americans. If we look only at discrete "wars" and consider merely literary efforts to represent those wars, then we will never comprehend the historically connected and deeply buried causes of human suffering and injustice in the modern world. Every effort to conquer another is a war; each refusal of basic human rights is violent.

Notes

1. Edmund Wilson, *Patriotic Gore: Studies in the Literature of the American Civil War* (New York: Atheneum, 1962).
2. Paul Fussell, *The Great War and Modern Memory* (New York: Oxford University Press, 1975).
3. John Carlos Rowe, *Literary Culture and U.S. Imperialism: From the Revolution to World War II* (New York: Oxford University Press, 2000), 48.
4. This cultural narrative is carefully worked out in Richard Slotkin, *Regeneration through Violence: The Mythology of the American Frontier; 1600–1860* (Middletown, CT: Wesleyan University Press, 1973).
5. Shelley Streeby, *American Sensations: Class, Empire, and the Production of Popular Culture* (Berkeley: University of California Press, 2002). Robert Johannsen's *To the Halls of the Montezumas* (1985) offers a comprehensive cultural history of how literature and visual art justified the US invasion of Mexican territory by demonizing Catholic Mexicans, especially men, and its *mestizo* culture.
6. See John Carlos Rowe, "Stowe's Rainbow Sign: Violence and Community in *Dred: A Tale of the Great Dismal Swamp* (1856)," *Arizona Quarterly* 58.1 (Spring 2002): 37–55.
7. See Gail Bederman, *Manliness and Civilization: A Cultural History of Gender and Race in the United States, 1880–1917* (Chicago: University of Chicago Press, 1995).
8. Crane's dispatches from the Spanish–American War were published in New York newspapers and *McClure's* magazine, and collected in *The War Dispatches of Stephen Crane*, ed. R. W. Stallman and E. R. Hagemann (New York: New York University Press, 1964). Richard Harding Davis, *Cuba in War Time* (New York: R. H. Russell, 1899); Frank Norris's pieces in *Century Magazine*, the *Atlantic Monthly*, and his pamphlet *The Surrender of Santiago*, in *Collected Writings, Hitherto Unpublished in Book Form*, vol. x (Garden City, NY: Doubleday, Doran and Co., Inc., 1928).
9. See Michael A. Elliott, *Custerology: The Enduring Legacy of the Indian Wars and George Armstrong Custer* (Chicago: University of Chicago Press, 2007), which offers a thorough cultural history of this issue.
10. Two-thirds of Ellison's "Introduction" focuses on World War II, as if thirty years later Ellison feels compelled to explain why he shifted his focus from the setting of his original plans for the novel to the "narrative that was upstaged by the voice which spoke so knowingly of invisibility" to him.The use of an inspiring muse or genius to explain literary decisions has, of course, a long literary heritage, to which Ellison appeals in other respects in this introduction, but it is also a notoriously unconvincing way to account for such changes.
11. See Robert S. Levine, *Conspiracy and Romance: Studies in Brockden Brown, Cooper, Hawthorne, and Melville* (Cambridge and New York: Cambridge University Press,

1989), chapter 4, "'Follow Your Leader': Captains and Mutineers in Herman Melville's *Benito Cereno*," 165–230.

12. Michael Denning, *The Cultural Front: The Laboring of American Culture in the Twentieth Century* (London: Verso, 1997).
13. Martha Gellhorn, *The Wine of Astonishment* (New York: Charles Scribner's Sons, 1948), dustjacket.
14. *From Here to Eternity*, directed by Fred Zinnemann, starring Burt Lancaster, Deborah Kerr, Montgomery Clift.
15. Donald McCann, "Our Forgotten War: The Korean War in Korean and American Popular Culture," in *America's Wars in Asia: A Cultural Approach to History and Memory*, ed. Jackie Hiltz, Steven I. Levine, and Philip West (Armonk, NY: M. E. Sharpe, 1998), 65–83.
16. John Carlos Rowe, "Eye-Witness: Documentary Styles in the American Representations of Vietnam," in *The Vietnam War and American Culture*, ed. John Carlos Rowe and Rick Berg (New York: Columbia University Press, 1991), 148–174.
17. George C. Herring, *America's Longest War: The United States and Vietnam, 1950–1975*, second edn. (New York: Alfred A. Knopf, 1986), 43–73, 95–96, 100, 243.
18. Philip Caputo, *A Rumor of War* (New York: Holt, Rinehart, and Winston, 1977), xix.

50

Science fiction

PRISCILLA WALD

Stories of warning and wonder

The mutant mind-reading robot in Isaac Asimov's "Liar!" (1941) wants to know about the human world that so puzzles him. Accordingly, as he explains to robopsychologist Susan Calvin, science books "just don't interest me. There's nothing to your textbooks. Your science is just a mass of collected data plastered together by make-shift theory . . . It's your fiction that interests me. Your studies of the interplay of human motives and emotions." As Asimov (and his robot) knew, there was much to learn from fiction about the laboratory of life. "Science fiction," as the genre was defined and developed in the early to mid twentieth century, grew out of a faith in the revelatory and speculative power of fiction, which could help to fathom and probe the scientific discoveries and technological innovations that lay beyond contemporary understanding. Its initial proliferation in popular culture made it a "pulp" genre appealing more to devoted fans than to literary critics, but increasingly science fiction has drawn attention both from literary critics and from scientists intrigued by the unique formulations, speculations, and theories offered by the most sophisticated examples of the genre. As the titles of the early magazines devoted to science fiction make clear, amazement, wonder, and awe are key words of the genre, but it is wonder inspired by the possibilities of science that distinguishes science fiction from the literature of fantasy. The speculation associated with the genre emerges from cognitively plausible – if sometimes far-reaching – scenarios that imaginatively engage and potentially challenge the most unquestioned scientific assumptions about human capacity and the world.

Definitions and precedents

Hugo Gernsback, an immigrant from Luxembourg, founded the first English-language science fiction magazine, *Amazing Stories*, in 1926. Coining the term "science fiction," he inspired the growth of the genre in the U.S. Since that time, definitions have proliferated, but they generally include some kind of literary engagement with science and technology and with the effect of developments in those areas on social relations and the physical world. The science fiction writer Robert Heinlein proposed "speculative fiction" to describe the genre because of its focus on possible futures, and that term is often used to encompass the literature of fantasy as well. But others, including Asimov, rejected Heinlein's suggestion because it blurred the distinction between plausible scenarios and wholly fantastic ones. The power of the genre, such critics argue, lies in what the science fiction critic Darko Suvin calls its "cognitive estrangement," which works only when the scenarios have some connection to empirical knowledge; that connection promotes speculation about received wisdom only insofar as it can persuasively defamiliarize experience by stretching the imagination through reason.[1]

Where Gernsback's taste was for the sensational and technological, his editorial successor, John W. Campbell, was more literary, and it was he who ushered in "the Golden Age" of science fiction in the late 1930s, as war was spreading throughout Europe and beyond. Campbell's editorial influence facilitated the emergence of three prolific authors who significantly shaped the genre: Asimov, Heinlein, and Arthur C. Clarke. The writing of this period matured stylistically, and writers showed a greater interest than their predecessors in what science fiction could contribute to understanding human being and humanity.

Asimov, Heinlein, and Clarke were all especially prolific writers, which certainly contributed to their influence, but all three also took literary style and content as well as science seriously, and their work set new standards for the genre. All three wove their considerable knowledge of science into well-crafted and well-developed tales of futuristic adventure that served equally as social commentary. While their combined influence is evident in the development of the genre, each had a set of concerns that was individually influential as well. Asimov explored geopolitical change on a large scale; his Foundation series (1942–1993), for example, chronicles the fall and re-emergence of a galactic empire. Heinlein was primarily concerned with the nature of individualism and with threats to personal liberty. Including novels as different as the militaristic *Starship Troopers* (1959) and the countercultural *Stranger in a Strange Land* (1961), both of which won Hugo awards, his diverse body of work has led to his characterization as an advocate of both militarism and free love. Clarke's most influential works, such as *Childhood's End* (1953) and *2001: A Space*

Odyssey (1968, based on the short story, "The Sentinel"), infuse "hard science fiction" with mysticism.[2]

The influence of the Second World War and its aftermath is obvious in the changing terms of the genre. The war had accelerated scientific discoveries in such areas as cell biology, genetics, and cybernetics, leading to new questions about the biological nature of human being, as the atrocities of the war prompted introspection about the future directions of humanity. Postwar geopolitical realignments resulting from large-scale immigration and migration and the shifting borders of decolonizing nations further exacerbated the sense of disequilibrium. These concerns came together in the emerging genre, and they have remained at its core, even (perhaps especially) as science fiction found its way into avant-garde, mainstream, and highbrow literary circles.

The alternative histories, dimensions, and worlds depicted in science fiction constitute its overlap with utopian fiction and fantasy, but science fiction focuses on the effect of scientific discoveries and technological innovations on human experience generally. Dr. Jaunte's discovery of the human capacity for teleportation in Alfred Bester's 1956 *The Stars My Destination*, for example, causes the economy to collapse and affects social and biological evolution accordingly. Such projections put the genre continually at the service of ethical inquiry, as authors tease out the potential implications of scientific and technological change and the challenges posed when people must collectively question the assumptions through which they experience the world. The ethical dilemma that the Nazi-hunting protagonist faces at the end of Ira Levin's 1976 novel about an elaborate plot to clone Adolf Hitler, *The Boys from Brazil*, for instance, concerns the fate of the unwitting teenaged Hitler clones and turns on the uncertainties not only of cloning, but also of the biological dimensions of human character. The overly deterministic belief that genes can forecast a person's future has been an increasingly common science fiction theme since the formal beginning of the US Human Genome Project in 1990. Challenges to androcentrism are also especially common in science fiction works that present the human species through the eyes of aliens or of human beings traveling from the future or from another dimension – as in Philip K. Dick's 1966 *The Crack in Space* or Philip Pullman's *Dark Materials* trilogy (1995–2000) – who may look upon the human population with disgust, pity, or perhaps the indifference of predators for whom such inferior species are most valued as means to an end: as bodily hosts, pets, or food, for example.

The genre has its most obvious literary historical roots in such writers as the French Jules Verne and the British H. G. Wells. It flourished, however, in the twentieth-century U.S. According to critics such as H. Bruce Franklin and

David Ketterer, the U.S. provided an especially receptive environment for the genre since science fiction was a kind of romance, which also characterizes the nineteenth-century American novel.[3] Underscoring the discontinuities between twentieth-century science fiction and its predecessors, Gary Westfahl persuasively argues for Gernsback's considerable influence on the genre, noting that the founding of the journal greatly shifted the production of the kind of writing that Gernsback dubbed "science fiction" from Europe to the U.S.[4]

It is also significant that in the twentieth century the U.S. became the indisputable leader in the production of another genre that had emerged in England: the comic book.[a] The culture of the U.S. in the first half of the twentieth century seems to have encouraged the development of stories populated by aliens, mutants, space travelers, superheroes, and others who transcend the known limits of the human body and challenge the allegedly immutable laws of space and time.

Those who came of age during the First World War witnessed the lost promise of science and technology, the failure of the utopian dreams of self-making and social perfecting that flourished at the dawn of "The American Century," when Edward Bellamy's 1888 novel, *Looking Backward*, spawned utopian societies across the nation and industrialization and urbanization fueled the emerging world power's imperial aspirations. Nick Carraway, the protagonist of a novel that appeared one year before Gernsback founded his new journal, typified this generation, as did its young author, F. Scott Fitzgerald. *The Great Gatsby* (1925) chronicles the war-weary Nick's fascination with the self-made Jay Gatsby, whose "heightened sensitivity to the promises of life . . . an extraordinary gift for hope, a romantic readiness" distinguishes him, for Nick, from the rest of humanity.[b] Gatsby's self-invention makes him a figure almost larger than life, a romantic superhero trapped in a realist novel and chafing at its limitations. While Nick's generational cohort watched the instruments of promise and prosperity transformed into weapons of war, finding the world they inherited curiously haunted by the Gatsbys of their imaginations, Ernest Hemingway's Nick Adams sought recovery from his war-inspired breakdown in the devotional adherence to the repetition of everyday ritual, and the ghosts of failed dreams and uncertain futures peopled the landscapes of T. S. Eliot's *Waste Land* and William Faulkner's post-slavery

a On the history of comic books, see Jan Baetens's essay in this volume ("Graphic novels," chapter 69).

b For an extended discussion of *The Great Gatsby* in relation to its moment, see Kirk Curnutt's essay in this volume, "*The Great Gatsby* and the 1920s," chapter 38.

South. Their unmitigated nostalgia – Nick Carraway laments that the Dutch sailors' first apprehension of the New World represents "man['s coming] face to face for the last time in history with something commensurate to his capacity for wonder" – was what science fiction refused from the outset, as it took up that capacity, seeking new frontiers in the limitlessness of the human imagination.

The capacity for wonder included a near-mandate to speculate. Writers used science fiction to imagine the bleakest dystopias and the most glorious utopias, the possibilities of space travel and alien contact and the terrors of superpowers, diseases, and instruments of mass destruction unleashed upon a population. The future was as uncertain for the mutants and aliens, space travelers and superheroes as for the "Lost Generation," but the threats that loomed on their horizons were balanced by possibilities. These works envisioned properties of time, space, and matter, depicting mutations that ranged from the grotesque to the marvelous, a distinction they often refused. It was a fiction of warning as well as wonder, chronicling the dangerous power of the imagination and the greater danger posed by its absence. The world of science fiction moved resistlessly into the future even while science fiction authors looked backward through a nostalgia tempered by the acknowledged limitations of the past.

The orientation of science fiction toward the future might help to explain why it is often theoretically avant-garde – that is, why it often anticipates, perhaps even influences, theoretical as well as social and cultural concerns and scientific developments. The physicist Leó Szilárd worked out the idea of nuclear chain reaction in 1933, a year after reading H. G. Wells's 1914 novel, *The World Set Free*, in which Wells coined the term "atomic bomb" and described a version of nuclear warfare on a global scale.[5] More generally, the familiar preoccupations of science fiction in the mid twentieth century anticipated the widespread concerns of the 1970s, including anxieties about environmental exhaustion, widespread species extinction, and an uncertain global future. It is not surprising that critical interest in science fiction proliferated in the late 1960s and 1970s; the genre, which had had half a century to mature by then, had shown itself to be diagnostic, if not prophetic.

Estrangement and global transformation

Change characteristically evokes anxiety, and both are staples of science fiction, which emerges from the understanding that organisms that do not change can only stagnate and die. Science fiction mines the processes of change for what they can reveal about the present as well as possible futures. Asimov glossed that function in his Foundation series, which began in the early 1940s in the form of short stories that revolved around the concept of "psychohistory," an imaginary science that builds on history, sociology, and statistics to predict the future of large collectivities. While the science of psychohistory is not an exact analogue for science fiction, the uncertain future of the species and the role of prediction based on observation are recurring themes of the genre. Unpredictability feeds the human spirit, nourishing creativity, awakening possibility, and inspiring growth. Utopian societies viewed through the lens of science fiction frequently prove as dangerous as their dystopic counterparts. Perfectibility may remain a distant ideal, but science fiction concerns itself more with variability. In Asimov's cosmic vision, human beings have colonized the many planets of the galaxy, and not only has each established its own social and political system, but evolution has worked differently in each case as well. A society that emphasizes technology, for example, discovers new ways of manipulating time and space, while one that follows the teachings of psychohistory develops powerful mechanisms of mind control. Yet another world, settled by inhabitants who prioritize personal freedom, evolves into a society of isolated hermaphrodites who procreate through a kind of natural cloning. The universes depicted in science fiction are strange and familiar, populated by creatures who, even if they are human, challenge the contemporary definition of human being as well as the temporal and spatial coordinates that circumscribe human existence. Such is the "cognitive estrangement" through which Suvin defines science fiction.

Suvin derives this concept from the Russian formalist Victor Shklovsky's idea that art should "defamiliarize" the world: that it should break the habits of understanding and make the familiar strange. While Shklovsky coined the term "defamiliarization" (*ostranenie*) in his 1917 essay, "Art as Technique," related ideas were emerging in other contexts. The late nineteenth-century work of philosopher William James in the nascent field of psychology displayed a particular interest in the ideas of attention and habits of consciousness.[c] His student Gertrude Stein, working in a laboratory with the German psychologist Hugo Münsterberg, experimented with devices designed to draw attention to those habits. Her influential poetics came out of this interest, and similar concerns motivated the artistic experiments of the

c Carrie Bramen analyzes Jamesian philosophy in "James, pragmatism, and the realist ideal," chapter 18 in this volume.

Dadaists and Surrealists. Freud, whose ideas infuse those experiments, offered an aesthetic theory of defamiliarization in his 1919 essay, "The Uncanny" (*Das Unheimliche*), in which he explored the disturbing sensation that arises either when something strange should be familiar or, conversely, when something familiar seems strange.

For the German sociologist Georg Simmel, the concept of "estrangement" was central to the process of social transformation. As the transmitter of new ideas, the stranger was at once necessary for the development of a group and disturbing in its disruption of the group's coherence. In an interesting turn, Simmel suggests that the "estrangement" effected by the stranger is more the result of similarity than of difference. The familiarity of the stranger complicates a group's sense of its own uniqueness, prompting group members to recognize that what they thought distinguished them from others is a fiction. Estrangement thereby heralds the expansion of the contours of a group. Emerging at the turn of the twentieth century, these overlapping concepts evince the changes that accompanied the new social relations of an increasingly global world. The emerging genre of science fiction registered the fear and fascination attending these transformations. It therefore makes sense that cognitive dissonance would become a defining feature of the genre and that science fiction might be, as I have suggested, theoretically avant-garde.

Nothing more profoundly defamiliarized the social, political, and cultural landscape and reshaped human existence than the decolonization movements that proliferated in both postwar periods.[6] Artistic expression in all forms was central to decolonization, as the broadly influential Négritude movement illustrates. With its roots in the short-lived journal *L'Etudiant Noir*, founded by Aimé Césaire, Léopold Senghor, and Léon Dumas in Paris in the early 1930s, the movement spawned manifestos and extended analyses calling for the necessity of a new consciousness to complete the long-awaited political transformation worldwide. Oppression, they argued, was a state of mind as well as of body, and the arts had to fashion new ways of thinking and express a new culture to accompany the new political system. These works maintained that only a radical conceptual shift in perceptions of the physical as well as the social and political world could decolonize the mind and therefore complete the project of decolonization. The estrangement that accompanied these changes was especially compatible with the aesthetics – if not always the politics – of science fiction; a focus on the liberation of human consciousness as well as on intergalactic colonization, which are consistent themes of the genre, registers the impact of the decolonization movements. Such themes allowed science fiction writers and filmmakers of the mid twentieth century to explore the new world order, in which, as political scientist Harold Isaacs observed, "some 70 new states carved out of the old empires since 1945 [are] made up of nonwhite peoples newly out from under the political, economic and psychological domination of white rulers" with people "stumbling blindly around trying to discern the new images, the new shapes and perspectives these changes have brought, to adjust to the painful rearrangement of identities and relationships which the new circumstances compel."[7]

The relative newness of science fiction, the consequent self-consciousness of its most prominent authors, and the importance of science and technology to the social changes worldwide combined to weave the geopolitical and racial concerns of the moment into the fabric of the genre itself. The potential implications of geopolitical transformations, for example, find ready expression in the alien encounters that proliferate in science fiction works. Space travelers may find themselves facing insurmountable communication barriers, sometimes because of radical differences between them and the cultures they encounter and sometimes because they cannot see through their own expectations. In Ray Bradbury's "The Earth Men" (from *Martian Chronicles*, 1950), for example, the space travelers' problem is not that they are too strange, but not strange enough; they cannot make meaningful contact because their claim to be travelers from Earth mimics the most common form of Martian insanity. Intergalactic encounters have enabled science fiction writers to defamiliarize social relations, human being, and the world generally. The alienness of these encounters enfranchises speculation by complicating readers' preconceived perspectives; they often do not map neatly onto recognizable power relations. They are characteristically disorienting, offering readers multiple perspectives from which to consider the themes of power, dehumanization, and collective interactions and the interarticulation of science and social forms with which science fiction is concerned.

Human being and humanity

Robots, androids, and other constructed beings that populate the science fiction world prompt ongoing speculation about the boundaries and meaning of the human. From the earliest works of the Golden Age, these constructed beings raised questions that were surfacing as well in the emerging field of cybernetics, which studied the regulatory mechanisms of both living organisms and machines. While machines constructed by human beings might seem incontrovertibly nonhuman, these entities nevertheless run the gamut from loving caretaker and companion to formidable enemy, and are endowed with human characteristics even when they are ostensibly depicted in contradistinction to human beings. Czech Cubist painter Josef Capek coined the word "robot," which first circulated in his brother Karel's 1920 play, *R.U.R.* (or, *Rossum's Universal Robots*). Deriving the term from the Czech noun *robota*, meaning *labor*, the Capeks intended to convey the idea of an indentured servant, but the term quickly overlapped with "android" and other variants of constructed beings.[8] Like all technology, robots were designed to extend the capacities of and otherwise assist human beings, and they typically evoke a confused sense of mastery and servitude, possibility and limitation.

No one has done more to develop the concept of these artificial beings and their complicated relationships to human beings than Asimov, who began his robot stories in 1939–1940, eventually collecting them in *I, Robot* (1950), which in turn spawned a series of novels and stories that he augmented throughout his prolific writing life. In these stories, Asimov developed the science of robotics (a term he coined) and endowed his creations with "positronic brains" (another coinage, from positron, a newly identified particle). Asimov's robot writings interweave elaborate attention to the technology and science of robotics with an equally focused account of its social impact. In response to human anxiety about the potential danger of robots, for example, Asimov's scientists hard-wired them according to the Three Laws of Robotics, which specify that robots cannot harm and indeed must protect human beings, that they must obey human commands that do not conflict with the first law, and that they must protect themselves in all cases that do not conflict with the first two laws. In spite of these laws, however, human dependence on robots proves a danger in Asimov's fictional world, and they are eventually banned on Earth and many other colonized planets.

Perhaps guilt resulting from the human history of oppression infuses the fear of dependence on robots to produce the irrepressible anxiety evident in most robot stories that these created beings will revolt violently against their (inferior) masters and creators. That enduring anxiety motivates Philip K. Dick's human characters to hunt the human-appearing androids in *Do Androids Dream of Electric Sheep?* (1968) and its cinematic adaptation, *Blade Runner* (1982), in which human cruelty and aggression turn the "replicants" violent – and thus, the story suggests, human. In Dick's novel, as in numerous other robot stories, the androids pose a particular danger because they are indistinguishable from human beings. The difficulty of distinguishing between the "natural" and created humanoids in terms of psychology and emotion, not just physical appearance, is a pervasive theme in science fiction.

It motivates the action in Dick's *Electric Sheep*, as the characters hunting the androids work to perfect tests that can reliably identify an android. Increasingly sophisticated androids have mastered the art of "passing" for human, but as the novel makes clear the ability to pass attests to the irrelevance of the distinctions between androids and human beings. That lack of distinction underlies the most profound anxiety these beings generate, not only because their indistinguishability makes them an invisible threat, but primarily because of what they reveal about human beings as they mirror them. One of the chief architects of the field of cybernetics, Norbert Wiener, wrote in his 1950 popular account of the science, *The Human Use of Human Beings*, that artificial intelligence did not so much show the humanity of machines as it did the mechanistic quality of human beings.[9] Neither that similarity, nor the mechanistic qualities of human beings troubled Wiener, who refused to lament what he saw as a false sense of human uniqueness. Others were less sanguine. Concern about human automatism became more pronounced in science fiction following the Second World War not only because of cybernetics, but also because of a general introspection generated by the techno-scientific atrocities and philosophical horrors of that war.

Accompanying the quest for a universal and transcendent definition of human being that could make human life sacrosanct were new discoveries about the biological nature of human being and the physical universe. Atomic research as well as the medical problems that emerged from exposure to radiation accelerated the insights of genetics, which blossomed in the postwar period. Insights from that field rapidly found their way into science fiction in the decades following the war, as is evident in the proliferation of stories about genetic engineering, especially cloning, including A. E. Van Vogt's *The World of Null-A* (1945), Poul Anderson's *Un-Man* (1953), Theodore L. Thomas's "The Clone" (1959) – which Thomas expanded into a novel in 1965 in collaboration with Kate Wilhelm, who would author her own clone novel, *Where Late the Sweet Birds Sang*, in 1976 – Theodore Sturgeon's "When You Care, When You Love" (1962), the film *The Human Duplicator* (1965), and Ursula Le Guin's *Nine Lives* (1969). These works further troubled the distinction between "natural" and "created" beings and registered the disturbances caused by emerging social, psychological, and biological theories that destabilized conventional ideas about the nature of human being.

Science fiction also explored the social construction of gender and sexuality. Well in advance of the development of reproductive technologies that allowed eggs to be fertilized outside of the uterus, science fiction space travelers routinely encountered external wombs, cloning mechanisms, hermaphrodites, and multiple genders in worlds with social orders that varied accordingly. Social critique rather than science is the primary concern of novels such as Joanna Russ's *The Female Man* (1975), which dramatizes the meeting of protagonists from alternative dimensions (including an all-female world) that allows her to depict the impact of a woman's environment on her psychological development. While Russ cursorily explains reproduction in the all-female world, works that attend more carefully to the mechanisms of alternative genders and reproduction offer a radical inquiry into how biological assumptions naturalize social relations.[d] Le Guin explores the social institutions that androgynes might produce in *The Left Hand of Darkness* (1969), while Asimov, in *Foundation and Earth*, shows how a culture based on an ideal of extreme personal independence might yield, through a combination of engineering and evolution, a world of hermaphrodites. Similarly, in Nicola Griffith's *Ammonite* (1993), the female survivors of a virus that has killed much of the population of the planet Jeep, including all of the men, discover a capacity for parthenogenetic reproduction that they learn to develop cooperatively. In her xenogenesis trilogy (1987–1989), Octavia Butler introduces the concept of a third gender with the ooloi, the "treasured strangers" who genetically engineer progeny even beyond their own species. As they pushed at biological as well as social and cultural definitions of personhood, these science fiction works registered the fears but also hopes that suffused debates concerning race, gender, sexuality, and social change as well as new reproductive techniques such as in *vitro* fertilization.[10]

Central to the biological changes imagined in these works was the assumption that human beings might one day be able to control biological evolution through mental forces alone. In turn, that assumption generated anxieties about human susceptibility to mind control. The identifiable mechanisms of human automatism that formed the basis of cybernetics were complemented by the possibilities and implications of mental conditioning that the Russian physiologist and psychologist Ivan Pavlov had explored at the turn of the twentieth century. Mental susceptibility and determinism in any form created anxiety in the West, especially in the US, where individualism, free will, and the ideology of independence suffused expressions of national identity.

d Elizabeth Freeman sees Charlotte Perkins Gilman's depiction of an all-female world in her 1915 *Herland* as "the forerunner of feminist speculative fiction," in her discussion of the relationship of science fiction and narrative experimentation to gender-bending and sexual experimentation in chapter 57 of this volume, "Reimaging genders and sexualities, 950–951. For Maria Farland, *The Left Hand of Darkness* "embodies the radical utopian possibility of feminists' innovative appropriations of the narrative devices of science fiction in these years" ("Literary feminisms," chapter 56, 934).

Anxieties about mind control informed the almost obsessive fear of brainwashing, accounts of which circulated in media reports alleging a new form of torture practiced on American prisoners in Korean POW camps as well as by China and other communist governments on their own citizens. Psychiatrists and social psychologists saw such mind control as the extreme form of social conditioning, and studies proliferated. Science fiction anticipated and subsequently registered this concern in depictions of alien possession of human beings in such works as John W. Campbell's *Who Goes There?* (1938), Heinlein's *The Puppet Masters* (1951), the film *Invasion from Mars* (1953), Philip K. Dick's "The Father Thing" (1954), and Jack Finney's *The Body Snatchers*, a 1954 *Collier's* serial, which became a novel (1955) with multiple cinematic spin-offs.[11]

Toward a cultural mythology

The danger of mental control shaped writers' attitudes toward language and found expression in the stylistic experimentation associated with such movements as Beat literature and postmodernism. The avant-garde writer William Burroughs confessed that he lived "with the constant threat of possession, and a constant need to escape from possession, from Control."[12] Seeking to provoke his readers into distrusting language itself – the word as virus – Burroughs explored compositional techniques that would promote speculation by forcing readers to become conscious of the elements of communication and of their own longing for the comfort of conformity.[e] With roots in the Beat Movement, Burroughs wrote consistently about addiction and counterculture, turning to aesthetic experimentation with *Naked Lunch* in 1959 and eventually to science fiction in his Nova trilogy (1961–1964), a saga about viral space invaders that he called a "mythology for the space age."[13]

With his use of "mythology," Burroughs named a theme that would intrigue postmodern writers, whose break with narrative realism and whose radical skepticism in some cases led to an interest in dream visions and myths. That interest formed one of the meeting points of science fiction and postmodernism. Suvin concedes that the estrangement he associates with science fiction is an attribute of myth as well, yet he sees the two as diametrically opposed: the difference between changeable norms (science fiction) and cultural verities (myth).[14] While individual works of science fiction are not characteristically

e For a more detailed reading of Burroughs, see Robert Faggen, "The Beats and the 1960s," chapter 55.

mythic (excepting some of the works that border on fantasy), collectively the genre manifests many conventional features of myth, including a preoccupation with distant origins and heroes, a connection with divinity or the supernatural or fantastical, and a prevailing sense of the imminent possibility of apocalypse; myths are also stories that, according to mythographer Bruce Lincoln, "possess both credibility and *authority*," which they derive from their expression "of paradigmatic truth" and through which they "evoke the sentiments out of which society is actively constructed."[15] They characteristically accompany and promote large-scale social transformations.

Beginning in the Golden Age, science fiction collectively manifested an interest in reimagining the category of "the human" in both philosophical and biological terms in correspondence with dramatic geopolitical transformations and against the continual possibility of species extinction through human or natural (including evolutionary) causes. While myths summon a hazy, almost-forgotten past, the temporal setting of science fiction is anticipatory, imparting the sense that contemporary readers are themselves being left in that prehistoric past: we are the figures of our distant descendants' myths, or perhaps of the myths of a conquering culture. It is unclear in Asimov's *Foundation's Edge* (1982) and *Foundation and Earth* (1983), and throughout most of the popular twenty-first-century television series *Battlestar Galactica* (2004–2009), for example, whether the planet Earth belongs to myth or to a history so distant that it is practically indistinguishable from myth.[16] That indistinction is an intriguing dimension of much science fiction, which shows contemporary readers what our own moment might look like from the perspective of a distant future, thereby illustrating how history bleeds into myth.[17]

Postmodernism encouraged a kind of generic promiscuity; in fact, the work of writers such as Burroughs, Thomas Pynchon, Samuel Delany, Harlan Ellison, and Thomas Disch blurs the distinction between science fiction and experimental postmodern writing in the 1960s.[f] Michael Moorcock, who assumed editorship of the English science fiction journal *New Worlds* in 1964, encouraged that trend as he enjoined writers to pay increased attention to literary style and sophisticated plot. The term "New Wave" described the increasing interest in literary style and experimentation, thematic as well as stylistic attention to language, and concern with social critique and the "soft"

f In the opening to chapter 58 in this volume, Ursula Heise dubs postmodern "without question the most important organizing category for a wide spectrum of debates about contemporary society and culture" in the last quarter of the twentieth century ("Postmodern novels," 964). For her discussion of science fiction and postmodernism, see especially 967.

sciences (psychology, sociology) in science fiction. Delany's *Babel-17* (1966), for example, explores the power of language to control thought when the poet, linguist, telepath, and starship captain Rydra Wong gradually finds herself becoming a traitor as she unwittingly learns the language, Babel-17, being transmitted by enemy agents. The interest in the mythic registered in many postmodern works complemented the tendency toward epic sagas and origin stories that science fiction had manifested at least since its Golden Age.

The increasing popularity of science fiction, the opportunity for visual wonders that it offered, and the aptness of the genre for reflection on new media and other technologies made science fiction an irresistible subject for film and television, which greatly expanded the audience for the genre. Film and television variants, including *Star Trek* and *Star Wars*, often exceeded the popularity of such mythic sagas as Asimov's Foundation books, Le Guin's Earthsea novels, and Marion Zimmer Bradley's Darkover and Avalon series even as they built on their literary foundations. Their popularity makes them especially important in the production of a mythology for the contemporary moment, a project that is central to the evolution of the genre.

In the many literary, cinematic, and televisual sagas, humanity can see itself reflected in the magnitude of its defining journey. Heroes and demons populate these stories, and even the most scientifically rigorous stories cannot fail to capture the magic of science and technology, which is to say the magic of our contemporary moment. Science fiction registers the uncertainty of what it means to be human in a simultaneously expanding and contracting world and against the looming threat of extinction. The genre as a whole transcends the specific politics of an author or a work – progressive, conservative, or reactionary – to register the resistances and resistlessness of geopolitical and biological transformation.

Notes

1. Darko Suvin, see especially *Metamorphoses of Science Fiction: On the Poetics and History of a Literary Genre* (New Haven: Yale University Press, 1979) and *Positions and Presuppositions in Science Fiction* (New York: Macmillan Press, 1988).
2. "Hard science fiction" refers to science fiction that is centrally engaged with the details of science and technology and, sometimes, with the more quantitative sciences (such as physics and chemistry).
3. See H. Bruce Franklin, *Future Perfect: American Science Fiction in the Nineteenth Century* (Oxford: Oxford University Press, 1966; revised and expanded 1995) and David Ketterer, *New Worlds for Old: The Apocalyptic Imagination, Science Fiction, and American Literature* (Bloomington: Indiana University Press, 1974).

4. See Gary Westfahl, *Mechanics of Wonder: The Creation of the Idea of Science Fiction* (Liverpool: Liverpool University Press, 1999) and *Hugo Gernsback and the Century of Science Fiction* (Jefferson, NC: McFarland & Company, 2007).
5. Richard Rhodes, *The Making of the Atom Bomb* (New York: Simon and Schuster, 1986), 24.
6. For a discussion of the impact of colonialism on the emergence of science fiction, see John Rieder, *Colonialism and the Emergence of Science Fiction* (Middletown, CT: Wesleyan University Press, 2008).
7. Harold R. Isaacs, "Color in World Affairs," *Foreign Affairs* 47.2 (January 1969): 235–250: 235.
8. http://capek.misto.cz/english/robot.html
9. Norbert Wiener, *The Human Uses of Human Being: Cybernetics and Society* (Garden City, NY: Doubleday Anchor Books, 1954 [1950]), 96.
10. Louise Brown, the first "test tube baby," was born in England in July 1978.
11. I have written elsewhere of the appeal of this story into the present, which is evident in the numerous retellings in both novelistic and cinematic form. See chapter 4 of Priscilla Wald, *Contagious: Cultures, Carriers, and the Outbreak Narrative* (Durham, NC: Duke University Press, 2008).
12. William S. Burroughs, *Queer* (New York: Viking Press, 1985), xxii.
13. William Burroughs, quoted in Eric Mottram, "Rencontre avec William Burroughs," in *Conversations with William Burroughs*, ed. Allen Hibbard (Jackson: University Press of Mississippi, 1999), 11–15: 11. For expanded discussions of Burroughs (as well as Meerloo), see Wald *Contagious*, chapter 4.
14. "SF is defined by its estranged techniques of presenting a cognitive norm." It is not "a thin disguise for the expression of eternal mythical human-cum-cosmic verities." Suvin, *Positions and Presuppositions in Science Fiction*, x, xi.
15. Bruce Lincoln, *Discourse and the Construction of Society: Comparative Studies of Myth, Ritual, and Classification* (New York and Oxford: Oxford University Press, 1989), pp. 24–25, italics in original.
16. The series ends with a twist in which the human and hybrid human/cylon survivors of the human/cylon wars turn out to be the progenitors rather than the descendants of contemporary human beings, and the contemporary planet Earth is named for an earlier planet of that name.
17. The historian Joseph Mali uses the term "mythistory" to convey the mythic nature of history. See Mali, *Mythistory: The Making of a Modern Historiography* (Chicago: University of Chicago Press, 2003).

51

Female genre fiction in the twentieth century

PAMELA REGIS

American women write and read all of the genres that constitute "genre fiction": the mystery, detective fiction, science fiction and fantasy, the Western, horror fiction, thrillers, spy fiction, and romance novels. The romance is the most gendered of all these genres – it is *the* female genre, both written and read largely by women.[1] The romance novel is also the most popular of these genres. In 1999, for example, more than 2,500 romances were published in North America, accounting for 55.9 percent of mass market and trade paperbacks sold.[2] In the twentieth century alone, thousands of American authors wrote and published tens of thousands of romance novels. In 2007, the latest year for which there are data, the number of romance titles published in North America had risen to 8,090.[3]

In the last three decades of the twentieth century market forces coalesced that would lead to this remarkable output, and that would make romance novels the dominant form of American fiction. By 1971 Harlequin Books,[a] founded in Canada in 1949 as a paperback reprint publisher, had devised an extensive, efficient distribution system for their romances, written almost wholly by British and Commonwealth authors, as well as by their single American author, Janet Dailey.[4] Throughout the 1970s, Harlequin dominated the American romance market for short contemporary romances (so-called "category" romances). In 1980, American publisher Simon & Schuster entered this market by creating Silhouette Books, whose editors tapped the backlog of manuscripts by American writers rejected by Harlequin, most notably, Nora Roberts (about whom more later).[5] Other publishers soon followed, and by 1985 more than eighty new romances were published each month.[6]

a It is important to emphasize that Harlequin did not invent the popular romance. See Shelley Streeby's discussion of the late nineteenth-century marketing strategies for story paper and dime novel romances, "Dime novels and the rise of mass market genres," chapter 35, 595.

Name-brand, short romances set in contemporary times fueled this romance boom, together with long historical novels, released as single titles, beginning with *The Flame and the Flower* (1972) by the American author Kathleen E. Woodiwiss.

This growth in romance writing, publishing, and reading attracted the attention of critics,[7] who typically viewed the novels as sub-literary.[b] Feminist cultural critics, most notably Janice A. Radway, analyzed romances published in the 1970s and 1980s, concluding that the ending in marriage, as well as the capitalist motives behind the publication and distribution of romances, was at best suspect, and at worst coercive, perpetrators of restrictive heteronormative patriarchal ideologies.[8] Romance authors themselves replied that the novels' typically free and active heroines uplift and empower readers.[9] Recent post-feminist considerations of the benefit or harm in reading romance often revise the earlier condemnation[c] of the form.[10]

In evaluating the romance as a contemporary cultural artifact, critics isolate it from its literary history. They obscure the relationship between contemporary romance novels and texts written as long ago as the colonial period, novels whose central action is a courtship, the essential feature of what we now call a romance novel. As a result, identification of a romance canon has barely begun. Cultural criticism of the romance novel also bypasses traditional formalist analysis. As a result "romance novel" has neither a widely agreed-upon definition nor a set of accepted (or even disputed) categories to employ in analyzing it.[11] Some analysis of the romance traditions of individual nations has begun, but the American romance has not been studied as a body of texts separate from romances written in English by UK and Commonwealth writers.

I offer in this chapter a definition of the romance novel, some categories to advance its literary analysis, and a first effort to place it in literary history, especially in foundational relation to the sentimental literature of the nineteenth century. I will then identify and analyze seven twentieth-century American romances dating from both before and after the 1980s boom in romance publishing. Brief analysis of these seven novels will demonstrate the continuity of the romance form, the persistence of sentimental values, as well

b Contrast the critical assessment of crime fiction as "almost literature" in Sean McCann, "The novel of crime, mystery, and suspense," chapter 48, 800.

c Other forms of women's writing have undergone post-feminist re-evaluation as well. Elsewhere in this volume see Elizabeth Nolan's discussion of the sentimental in "The woman's novel beyond sentimentalism," chapter 34, 583; for a succinct review of the critical literature of the sentimental, see Cindy Weinstein, "Sentimentalism." chapter 12, note 3 (219–220).

as the variety of protagonists created and issues addressed by the twentieth-century American romance novel.

All romance novels end with the protagonist's choice of union with a partner or partners. The protagonist of the typical American romance novel wishes to be as free as possible in all aspects of life. As a result, American romances typically depict the tension between freedom and companionate union. Definitions of the romance novel can be too broad (a love story) or circular (a novel published and marketed as a romance). A more useful definition begins by noting that every text now called a romance novel is a courtship narrative, a form of fiction which has been written in English for at least two and a half centuries. Formally speaking then, a romance novel is "a work of prose fiction that tells the story of the courtship and betrothal of one or more heroines."[12] However, as we shall see, some of the more recent romances feature a courtship between two heroines, between two heroes, or among two heroes and a heroine. Thus we can define the genre by saying if the focus of the book is courtship and the outcome betrothal, the novel is a romance.

The romance novel form is a subset of comedy, depicting the characteristic movement from a disordered society to an ordered one. Early romance novels, however, replace the usual comedic hero with a heroine. For heroes in older comedies, such as those of Shakespeare, courtship issues are usually just one symptom of the disorder of society perpetrated by an older generation that the hero must overthrow. For a protagonist in a romance novel, courtship is the central concern, and consequently the reader's as well. The barriers to courtship, therefore, form the central conflict of the work, and the happy ending in betrothal creates the new, closer-to-ideal society that replaces the disordered, dysfunctional one at the novel's start. Betrothal for most of the history of the romance novel has meant marriage, but by the end of the twentieth century it suffices for the heroine and hero (or other combination of lovers) to promise themselves to each other – in other words, to betroth themselves – whether or not that union is recognized under the law.

Defining the romance novel as a narrative about courtship, rather than as a story about love or a book industry marketing decision, enables identification of eight essential narrative elements: *identification of the disorder of the society* in which the courtship transpires, the *meeting* between the courting characters, the *barrier* to their union, their *attraction* to each other, the *point of ritual death* (or the moment in the narrative – echoing the death and restoration myth of Persephone – at which the wished-for union of the courting characters seems impossible), their *declaration* of love for each other, their *recognition* of the reasons that the barrier should not stand, and their *betrothal*.[13] The romance novel's progression from disorder to order typically depicts a protagonist who begins the novel constrained by society's barriers to companionate union, but who ends the novel freed from them. Freedom is essential to the new order at the romance novel's end.

Romance authors have deployed the elements with considerable flexibility, and in every possible order. Elements may also be doubled and tripled, permitting the author to mirror and echo, for emphasis or irony, any given thematic element. In addition, they may be dramatized or happen offstage, as it were, with the results merely reported. Although the ending in marriage, also known as the happily-ever-after, has received a fair amount of critical attention from scholars,[14] the novel's issues have been presented and resolved by the time it occurs. The barrier to betrothal is typically a much richer repository of meaning in the romance novel than the happily-ever-after.

The romance novel originates from and is still centered in a fact of female life unchanged for centuries: most women marry. At the beginning of the final decade of the twentieth century, 98.7 percent of American women had been or were married by age 45.[15] Yet each woman courts and is courted uniquely. This individual experience helps explain the proliferation and variety of romances within the larger structure of the genre. Any issue can form a barrier to betrothal, from life-threatening disaster to amusing miscommunication, and the sheer variety yields romances that range from dark explorations of life's worst problems to witty romps.

The first novel printed in America was a bestselling British courtship narrative: *Pamela: or, Virtue Rewarded* (1741) by Samuel Richardson, published in Philadelphia in 1742–1743 by Benjamin Franklin. Although Paul Giles places *Pamela* in the context of both captivity and seduction narratives,[d] it is important to note that B's failed "seduction" of the eponymous heroine is actually a courtship that ends in betrothal. Indeed, *Pamela* is widely regarded as the first popular romance novel in English.[16] Franklin's edition was not a publishing success, but the novel was abridged early and often, and in their small size and brevity the abridged volumes resemble nothing so much as a short contemporary romance novel such as those published by Harlequin.[17] The abridgements retain the eight narrative elements of the romance novel outlined above. Pamela's story, if not Richardson's actual telling of it, was readily available in early America and so we may fairly consider it the country's first

d Paul Giles, "Transatlantic currents and the invention of the American novel," chapter 1, 24.

romance novel. In addition, *Pamela* inaugurates in America a second literary tradition that by the middle of the nineteenth century would dominate American fiction: the sentimental novel,[18] whose re-evaluation is carried forward elsewhere in this volume.[e] Jane Tompkins has argued that "the popular domestic novel of the nineteenth century represents a monumental effort to reorganize culture from the woman's point of view" and that it "elaborated a myth that gave women the central position of power and authority in the culture."[19] The site of that power was the home. Sentimental values included affection, connection, family and kinship, sympathy, and emotion – especially love. Religious belief, generally a nondenominational, evangelical Christianity, was an important element in these narratives. These values, with the single exception of the effacement of an overtly Christian belief system in most twentieth-century romances, still inform all romance novels. Belief in Christianity survives, meanwhile, as the defining value in the romance subgenre known as "inspirational romance."

Many nineteenth-century sentimental novels focus on courtship and betrothal and employ the eight essential elements of a romance novel as defined above.[20] Indeed, elsewhere in this volume Cindy Weinstein notes the "low tolerance for sentimental plots that did not end in marriage."[f] Some of the major parallels between sentimental fiction and the romance novel are therefore worth noting. The household is the natural setting of sentimental fiction, while a romance novel – a narrative of a courtship – recounts the origin of a new household. The family is the social unit that forms the natural setting of sentimental fiction, while the romance novel ends with the founding of a new family. Love is the core emotion linking people in the sentimental novel, while love for a companionate partner is the core emotion of the romance novel. The homemaker, a woman, is the locus of power in the sentimental novel, while the heroine who is in the process of becoming a homemaker is the most powerful character in a romance novel. There she exercises her power in choosing the hero and making a companionate marriage. As romance writer Jayne Ann Krentz has observed, "with courage, intelligence, and gentleness she brings the most dangerous creature on earth, the human male, to his knees. More than that, she forces him to acknowledge her power as a woman."[21]

e Anna Mae Duane in "Susanna Rowson, Hannah Webster Foster, and the seduction novel in the early USA," chapter 2, explores issues of "self-possession" that accompany the earliest American sentimental novels, 38–39, while Weinstein, in chapter 12, discusses less frequently analyzed sentimental novels.

f Weinstein, chapter 12, 210.

A comparison of Richardson's *Pamela* with *Vivia; or The Secret of Power* (1857) by E. D. E. N. Southworth, one of the most successful of the nineteenth-century sentimental novelists, will contrast a representative English romance heroine with her American counterpart, Vivia LaGlorieuse. Like *Pamela*, *Vivia* tells the story of the courtship and betrothal of a heroine. Like *Pamela*, *Vivia* contains the eight essential elements of the romance novel. Analysis of the barriers to their unions will provide a look at the sentimental values at work in both romances, especially, in the case of Southworth, religion.

Richardson, Southworth, and the rest of the romance novelists I will be examining reflect three sweeping, transgenerational changes in society, changes that began as far back as the early modern period and extend through the twentieth century. First, the romance heroine illustrates the importance of property rights, including *self*-ownership. Second, she pursues companionate, as opposed to dynastic, marriage. Third, she exercises her liberty to pursue her own happiness, as opposed to living for or at the direction of family, society, the state, or the church.[22] The barriers between the courting couples in *Pamela* and *Vivia*, like all romance barriers, reflect the protagonists' struggle with property and with the conflict between liberty and companionate marriage. Looked at in this way, the contrasting barriers of the English and the American text indicate the direction the romance novel takes in America and set the stage for the twentieth-century works examined in this chapter.

Richardson's Pamela Andrews, like many eighteenth-century English female servants, has been sent into service as a lady's maid by her impoverished parents. At first the would-be victim of a seduction perpetrated by her employer, called in the novel Mr. B—, finally she is courted by and marries him. The barriers to this union reflect class differences – B's assumption that he, in effect, owns Pamela, and her assertion of her rights to self-ownership, to her personal property, and to her freedom of movement. Pamela's life is at stake when she contemplates suicide to escape imprisonment, her liberty is at stake when B imprisons her physically and attempts to force her to marry against her will, and her property is at stake both when B confiscates her money and when he threatens her livelihood. Thus, with life, liberty, and property in peril, the novel's issues are Lockean. Companionate marriage triumphs as B comes to love Pamela, and she reciprocates. Pamela is B's wife for the last quarter of the novel, but so great is the difference in their social classes that she must work hard to establish around herself the improved society that romance promises.

Unlike Pamela, Southworth's Vivia begins the novel parentless. Unlike Pamela, Vivia's liberty is unconstrained and her property rights are secure (she is revealed as an heiress midway through the novel). Companionate marriage seems easily within her reach as well: she loves Wakefield, the hero, and he loves her. By the time he proposes (she had designated him "her champion" and bestowed on him "her colors" when they were both children), he has achieved literary fame, yet Vivia has twice refused to betroth herself to him. He asks for her reasons, declaring that his "inspiration" has long been "your crowning love." Vivia explains that such love is a perversion of morality unless subordinate to one's love for God. Before commanding Wakefield to "[w]ithdraw your self . . . from me . . . and turn to the Lord," Vivia explains that "[t]o live from the Creator is freedom, individuality, life indeed, and life eternal!" When Wakefield frees himself from this perversion of his faith, Vivia makes the courtship's third and final proposal.

Unlike the English Pamela, the American Vivia faces no issues of class or property in her courtship. Unlike Pamela, who in the eyes of society will always be the servant who became the lady of the manor, and unlike B, who will always be branded as a member of a privileged class who married his own servant, the American heroine and hero easily leave their origins behind to better themselves in the world. Vivia is deserving, in true sentimental fashion, through her good works and superior morals. For Southworth, true liberty includes the attainment of Christian virtue and the ultimate, eternal happiness promised to those who exercise such virtue. Vivia, in demanding that Wakefield meet this highest standard for liberty, acts in accord with that primary sentimental tenet – that the woman occupy the moral center of the home, or, in the case of this novel, the prospective home. The romance form makes the heroine a protagonist and the sentimental tradition reinforces the role of the heroine as a moral force. Southworth creates an internal barrier – a matter of belief and of a choice that her hero, and most particularly her heroine, may freely make.

In choosing Wakefield, Vivia must reconcile liberty with companionate marriage. Although American romances would later be written about all manner of external barriers, an internal barrier – a matter of the beliefs, attitudes, and morals of the heroine and hero, requiring the reconciliation of liberty and companionate marriage – is typical of American romances. "Inspirational" (i.e., Christian-themed) romance novels have been a constant presence in the genre and remain popular. Grace Livingston Hill, for example, wrote more than ninety novels, most of them during the first half of the twentieth century, with an evangelical message. More recently, Robin Lee Hatcher won the 2001 Nora Roberts Lifetime Achievement Award from the Romance Writers of America for her Christian romances.[23]

Two twentieth-century romance novelists who began writing in the first third of the century, Kathleen Thompson Norris and Faith Baldwin, may have read Southworth, whose serialized novels continued to be issued in single volumes as late as 1910. Their belief in the values of the home, its primacy and importance, and of the wife's key role in that institution reflect the strong influence of the sentimental novel. Like many romance novelists, both Norris and Baldwin had long, productive careers. Between 1911 and 1955 Norris wrote more than seventy-five novels, publishing three novels a year at her commercial peak. Baldwin wrote more than eighty novels between 1931 and 1977. Both Norris and Baldwin deploy the romance form to launch sober, clear-eyed investigations of the state of women's happiness, recording the difficult reconciliation by their heroines of liberty and companionate marriage. In Norris's *Rose of the World* (1923), companionate marriage has eluded the heroine, but liberty in the form of "self-expression … contentment" and "satisfaction," has not. Her values are sentimental: her daughter and the home she makes for her family provide her with self-expression and satisfaction despite her husband's controlling, disapproving view of her. Rose finds liberty but not love within her first marriage. In her eventual betrothal to Jack, freedom and love yield the happily-ever-after, and a glimpse of a society reordered by these values intrinsic to every romance novel.

In Baldwin's *Week-End Marriage* (1931) the primary barrier to the true union of heroine Lola and her husband Ken is Ken's drift toward dissipation when Lola leaves their home in Brooklyn to accept a promotion in St. Louis. Locating the marriage before the true betrothal, Baldwin exploits the flexibility of the genre's essential elements. Lola desires "a fifty-fifty marriage … an American marriage" but Ken becomes unmoored by her departure, losing a job, drinking in speakeasies, and even escorting a woman "friend" on outings with another couple. In true American romance fashion, the barrier to betrothal finally proves interior. Lola overcomes her reluctance to give up her career and goes into business with Ken, and the importance of making a home together thus trumps the very American virtue of earning your own keep. The uneasy compromise between companionate marriage and the heroine's freedom reflects the power of sentimental values.

Companionate marriage is not possible for the two female protagonists of *The Price of Salt* (1952), an early lesbian romance novel.[24] Patricia Highsmith employs the love-at-first-sight trope at the meeting of the two heroines in a New York department store. Within a few pages, Therese says to Carol, "'I think you are magnificent' … not caring how it might sound, because she knew the woman knew anyway." The barrier to the union of these two heroines includes Carol Aird's husband, who hires a private detective to gather evidence to use against her in the custody battle over their daughter, and Therese's boyfriend, who finally rejects her as "sordid and pathological."

Recognition, and with it the union of heroine and heroine, follow upon Carol's divorce. The romance novel is often derided as having an unsatisfactory ending that is too neat and unbelievably happy. But, because she refuses to renounce Therese, Carol loses custody of her daughter. In a 1990 afterword, Highsmith describes the novel's outcome, despite Carol's loss of custody, as a "happy ending for [the] two main characters .... Prior to this book, homosexuals male and female in American novels had had to pay for their deviation by cutting their wrists, drowning themselves in a swimming pool, or by switching to heterosexuality (so it was stated), or by collapsing – alone and miserable and shunned – into a depression equal to hell."[25] Marriage is not possible for these women. Yet in the closing pages of the book the sentimental tradition, with its emphasis on the home, is just visible in Carol's proposal to Therese: "I've taken an apartment up on Madison Avenue ... I was hoping you might like to come and live with me ..."[g] But in writing a romance novel whose protagonists are a same-sex couple, Highsmith demonstrates that companionate union is possible, and she vindicates the values of the two heroines – their love and their choice to be together. Highsmith complicates the neat ending by her sexually revolutionary message, and then tempers it with Carol's loss of custody of her daughter.

Same-sex romances, both lesbian and gay, are a growing area of romance publishing today. Among the new publishing ventures that constituted the boom in twentieth-century romance was Naiad Press, established in 1971 as a publisher of lesbian romance novels.

Historical romance fiction, with the heroine as the focus of third-person limited point of view, typically depicts a companionate quest set in a society that practices and values dynastic marriage for kinship, political, or economic goals. In many novels, the hero must overcome these dynastic beliefs. Historical romances, which remain popular, return to its once-revolutionary status what historian Stephanie Coontz has called "the radical idea of marrying for love" as the twenty-first-century reader experiences the difficulties of a woman whose striving for companionate marriage is questioned by at least part of the society in which the books are set.[26] Heroines in historical romances often seek and

g Elizabeth Freeman places *The Price of Salt* in the context of Highsmith's career as a writer of crime fiction in "Reimagining genders and sexualities," chapter 57, 948.

exercise an anachronistically wide-ranging freedom. In 1986, soon after the Romance Writers of America was founded, Roberta Gellis was recognized for her historical romances, most of which she set in medieval England.

Two notable American bestsellers, *Gone with the Wind* (1936) by Margaret Mitchell and *Forever Amber* (1944) by Kathleen Winsor, were forerunners to the late century historicals such as Woodiwiss's *The Flame and the Flower*. Both of these precursors were historical novels and passionate love stories. Woodiwiss's book, however, is a romance novel, while Mitchell's and Winsor's are not. Scarlett O'Hara Hamilton Kennedy marries Rhett Butler for reasons other than love, and when she finally comes to love him, he no longer loves her, so there is no betrothal. In the final action of *Forever Amber*, Duchess of Ravenspur Amber St. Claire leaves her husband to follow her love, the Duke of Carleton, to America. In neither case does the barrier to betrothal fall. Neither hero declares his love for the heroine at a time when she reciprocates. There are no betrothals and no true companionate unions.

In *The Flame and the Flower*, on the other hand, the barriers to the union between Brandon Birmingham and Heather Simmons do fall. The novel begins with the sort of unpromising meeting typical of historical romances of this era when Brandon mistakes Heather for a prostitute he has asked for, and he deflowers and impregnates her. They marry, sail from London to Charleston, she gives birth, and slowly the barriers to companionate union are overcome. Woodiwiss's novels have the explicit, lengthy sex scenes that gave this subgenre its "bodice-ripper" epithet, but they might more accurately be described as long, sensual, historical romances. Sex with the hero begins on his terms, and part of the barrier to betrothal is the working out of a mutually satisfying sexual relationship.

Works by three post-boom romance writers illustrate the persistence within the genre of sentimental concerns and the conflict between liberty and companionate marriage around the turn of the twenty-first century. These works also illustrate the inclusiveness and power of the genre.

Jennifer Crusie regards romance writing as a feminist response to canonical, literary novels. Of the books she read to earn advanced degrees in literature (she left unfinished her dissertation on romance novels to become a romance writer), Crusie notes, "I spent years reading about miserable women like the one who pursued the life she wanted, had lousy sex with a masochistic dweeb, and spent the rest of her endless life atoning by doing good works in a letter sweater." She adds that when she writes a sex scene, she thinks, "In your ear, Hawthorne."[27] Crusie, who published her first novel in 1993, displays this irreverent excess in her fiction. The heroine of *Bet Me* (2004), Min Dobbs, receives a betrothal ring in the form of a chocolate iced doughnut, the surest sign that her intended is comfortable with her Rubenesque body. This excess is comic, but nonetheless endorses sentimental domesticity.

From 1995 to the present, Beverly Jenkins has written twenty-one African American romance novels, most of them historical fictions. Among her nineteenth-century sources for *Indigo* (1996), set in 1858–1859, is a true account of a free African American man selling himself into slavery to marry the enslaved woman whom he loves. Hero Vashon courts this couple's daughter, Hester. The barriers to their betrothal combine the political and the personal, including Underground Railroad activities that place them in danger. The happy ending – Hester's rescue, her pregnancy, Vashon's discovery and purchase of Hester's mother from slavery (his Christmas present to Hester) – takes place in the shadow of John Brown's execution for his raid on Harpers Ferry. The marriage creates and repairs family ties: it establishes a new family with its promise of a next generation, and it also enables the reunion of the living members of Hester's family of origin, torn apart by slavery. This sentimental outcome echoes the values of a work like *Uncle Tom's Cabin*. In most historical romances, freedom, love, family, and companionate union contrast with the repressive conditions created by the institutions and practices of the past. In African American historical romance novels, including those by Shirley Hailstock and Roberta Gayle, this contrast is extreme.[28]

The first novel of Ann Herendeen, *Phyllida and the Brotherhood of Philander* (2005), is a Regency romance, with a bisexual hero who courts and marries both a heterosexual woman, and, with her consent and the help of a "molly chaplain" (a term for a cleric who performs mock weddings for gay men), a homosexual hero.[29] To create a companionate union, the hero must recognize his love for his wife (in addition to, not instead of, his long-acknowledged love for the man he will also marry), he must learn techniques appropriate for sex with a female partner, and he must revise his idea of "family" to include two spouses. Herendeen, who has named as her literary forebear Georgette Heyer, the mother of the Regency romance, explains in the preface to *Phyllida and the Brotherhood of Philander* (2008) that she consciously adopted the typical Regency tone, "blithe comedy with sparkling dialogue" and the subgenre's typical characters, aristocrats who were "the ultimate in glamorous sophistication." In this novel, sentimental values domesticate sexual practices and family structures that were (and in some cases still are) against the law. Novels like *Phyllida* show that the romance novel, once derided for its heteronormative ideology, is proving more inclusive than society at large.

Nora Roberts's first novel, *Irish Thoroughbred* (1981), was published by Silhouette after being rejected by Harlequin, which was surely one of the shortest-sighted editorial decisions of all time. Nearly thirty years later, Roberts's new releases and reprints of her extensive backlist routinely appear on the bestsellers lists. By the turn of the twenty-first century more than fifty of her novels had appeared on the *New York Times* bestsellers list. A Roberts romance is intense and deftly plotted, focusing on what she perceives as the heart of the romance genre – the "one man/one woman love story" given "a very modern and very American spin" with "stronger heroines, less domineering heroes, [and] more contemporary themes" than the Harlequins of the 1960s and 1970s.[30] Unlike the subordinate, often passive heroines of many earlier romances, Adelia Cunnane of *Irish Thoroughbred* has a hair-trigger temper, great physical courage, and the resourcefulness to make a new start when she emigrates to America. Roberts's strong heroines, are, however, no stronger than Vivia, Lola, Rose, and Carol, the pre-boom heroines examined above.

In American hands, the romance novel has always favored strong heroines. Post-boom protagonists such as Heather, Min, Hester, Phyllida, and also the men at the center of recent romance novels, still do what American romance protagonists have always done. They pursue companionate union that permits them to retain their freedom.

Notes

1. "Industry Statistics," Romance Writers of America, www.rwanational.org.
2. *Ibid.*
3. *Ibid.*
4. Joseph McAleer, *Passion's Fortune: The Story of Mills and Boon* (Oxford: Oxford University Press, 1999), 139.
5. Paul Grescoe, *The Merchants of Venus: Inside Harlequin and the Empire of Romance* (Vancouver: Raincoast, 1996), 157.
6. Carol Thurston, *The Romance Revolution: Erotic Novels for Women and the Quest for a New Sexual Identity* (Urbana: University of Illinois Press, 1987), 62.
7. Rachel Anderson, *The Purple Heart Throbs: The Sub-literature of Love* (London: Hodder and Stoughton, 1974).
8. Janice Radway, *Reading the Romance: Women, Patriarchy, and Popular Literature*, 2nd edn. (Chapel Hill: University of North Carolina Press, 1991); Tania Modeleski, *Loving with a Vengeance: Mass-Produced Fantasies for Women* (Hamden, CT: Archon, 1982); Ann Barr Snitow, "Mass Market Romance: Pornography for Women Is Different," *Radical History Review* 20 (1979): 141–161.

9. Jayne Ann Krentz. ed., *Dangerous Men and Adventurous Women: Romance Writers on the Appeal of Romance* (Philadelphia: University of Pennsylvania Press, 1992).
10. See, for example, Deborah Lutz, "The Haunted State of Mind: The Revival of the Gothic Romance in the Twenty-first Century," in *Empowerment Versus Oppression: Twenty-First Century Views of Popular Romance Novels*, ed. Sally Goade (Newcastle: Cambridge Scholars Publishing, 2007), 81–92.
11. See Sally Goade, "Introduction," in *ibid.*, 2–5 for a recent recitation of the various definitions of "romance."
12. Pamela Regis, *A Natural History of the Romance Novel* (Philadelphia: University of Pennsylvania Press, 2003), 19.
13. *Ibid.*, 27–45.
14. Rachael Blau DuPlessis, *Writing Beyond the Ending: Narrative Strategies of Twentieth-Century Women Writers* (Bloomington: Indiana University Press, 1985) provides an early, excellent critique of the happily-ever-after.
15. Joan Hoff, *Law, Gender, and Injustice: A Legal History of U.S. Women* (New York: New York University Press, 1991), 278.
16. Kristen Ramsdell. *Romance Fiction: A Guide to the Genre* (Englewood, CO: Libraries Unlimited, 1999), 5.
17. See, for example, *The History of Pamela, or Virtue rewarded/Abridged from the works of Samuel Richardson* (Philadelphia: M. Carey, 1808).
18. Leo Braudy, discussing the form of the English sentimental novel, claims that "the true heir of the eighteenth-century novel, and its sentimental and gothic offspring, is not the nineteenth-century English novel but that great stepchild – the American novel." "The Form of the Sentimental Novel," NOVEL*: A Forum on Fiction* 7 (1973): 13.
19. Jane Tompkins, *Sensational Designs: The Cultural Work of American Fiction 1790–1860* (New York: Oxford University Press, 1986), 124–125.
20. See Karen Tracey's account of the nineteenth-century American double-proposal novel, *Plots and Proposals: American Women's Fiction, 1850–90* (Chicago: University of Illinois Press, 2000).
21. Krentz, *Dangerous Men*, 7.
22. Regis, A *Natural History of the Romance Novel*, 55–59.
23. www.rwanational.org.
24. Highsmith, writing as Claire Morgan, published this novel as *Carol* in Great Britain.
25. Patricia Highsmith, "Afterword," in *The Price of Salt* (New York: Norton, 1990), 261.
26. Stephanie Coontz, *Marriage, a History: How Love Conquered Marriage* (New York: Penguin, 2005), 15.
27. Jennifer Crusie, "Glee and Sympathy," Jenny Crusie website, http://www.jennycrusie.com (accessed July 24, 2008).
28. Rita B. Dandridge argues that Jenkins, Hailstock, and Gayle work "with/in discourses of race and gender to construct [heroines who live] romantic lives as fulfilled women and public lives as agents for ethnic advancement." "The Race,

Gender, Romance Connection," in *Doubled Plots: Romance and History* (Jackson: University of Mississippi Press, 2003), 201.

29. Regency romances are set between 1811 and 1820, the period of English history during which the Prince of Wales ruled England as regent for the incapacitated King George III.
30. Kay Mussel, "*Paradoxa* Interview with Nora Roberts," *Paradoxa* 3 (1997): 155.

52

Children's novels

JULIA MICKENBERG

Children's literature holds an odd and uncomfortable place within the canon of American literature. As Lynne Vallone has noted, "the history of the novel and the history of 'adolescent' or 'children's' literature are inextricably linked. In general, however, histories of the development of the novel fail to include children's literature, or refuse to see the implications for the novel of an adolescent ... [or child] readership."[1] Children's literature is essentially ignored in all American literature anthologies, and it is rarely taught in literature surveys; only recently have English departments begun to hire children's literature specialists. When children's literature *is* recognized as significant to the larger scheme of literary production, this entire category, comprising a multiplicity of genres, is usually lumped together: hence a single entry in this volume. The exemption of "juvenile literature" from the American literary canon points to children's historical marginality as audiences and as social actors. But the effacement of children's literature from the canon can be rationalized apart from its devaluation, and tied more to the fact that "the novel" and "children's literature" might be seen as exclusionary categories.

The novel as a category, however fluid, usually presumes a level of complexity and depth and an engagement with serious social issues, such that it might be said to preclude a child reader. Indeed, the "virtually unanimous injunction against novel reading found in conduct literature, periodicals, and didactic fiction for girls and young women from the seventeenth to the twentieth century" points to what Vallone describes as "that readership's literary 'hunger,'" that is, young people's desire for rich, relevant reading material. It also highlights the fact that children and youth were, historically, both avid readers of novels and an explicitly unintended audience – or, at any rate, an audience that reformers wished to steer elsewhere.[2] But just as the novel's potentially explosive, real-world content is a specter lurking at the boundaries of children's literature, threatening to strip the child of his or her innocence and thus deprive him or her of childhood, the child is a specter haunting the novel's subject matter and its potential readership. The history of works for children – of a length and complexity such that they might be called "novels" – adds an important dimension to the history of the novel in general.

My focus in this chapter will be upon the ways in which "social significance" emerged as an emphasis in children's fiction, beginning in the 1930s and 1940s, and culminating in the 1970s; that is, upon literature that speaks to children precisely because it explodes preconceived notions about childhood, and children's literature. By 1970, children's novels focused not on protecting children's innocence, but on preparing them for a reality once thought incompatible with childhood. Thus, it is only with what Neil Postman has called the "disappearance of childhood" (in an era of media saturation, high divorce rates, and a general waning of adult authority) that the "children's novel" came of age.[3] The increasing intrusion of pressing social issues, and the development of realistic child characters, points, on the one hand, to what some critics decried as the "adult-eration" of children's literature. Seen in more positive terms, it also marked the children's novel's increasing relevance and centrality as a literary form in contemporary American culture.

A secondary thread running throughout this chapter concerns parallel developments in children's literature and in the novel more generally. An array of movements such as abolitionism, feminism, civil rights, and environmentalism, and an array of literary trends such as the novel of the frontier, the proletarian novel, the regional novel, the mass market paperback, the African American novel, and the Jewish novel, among others (all considered elsewhere in this volume), can likewise be tracked within the development of children's fiction. There is much in the canon of American literature, from captivity narratives to *Huckleberry Finn* to *Catcher in the Rye*, that crosses over to the category of children's literature, whether by inadvertently attracting a large child readership, or by design. Indeed, Leslie Fiedler argues that "boyish" adventure stories were a central, if not *the* central narrative form in classic American fiction. (Yet he also made clear that labeling such works "children's literature" was an insult to their quality and significance.)[4] While it is beyond the scope of this chapter to trace the image of the child in the American novel (another direction in which this chapter could be taken), one might fruitfully think about the function of children as characters within almost the complete range of "grown-up" novels discussed in this volume: whether they function as protagonists, as absent or minor figures who are central to the narrative drive, or as intended or unintended audiences of the works.[5] To take one typical paradigm, if the child – usually a boy – of the predominantly male-authored canonical American novel stands in for the developing nation itself, in children's literature (where women have historically held pre-eminent roles as authors and as mediators of children's reading), men, and male characters, never had the same overwhelming dominance. As such, the "melodramas of beset manhood" that appear throughout the history of the American novel do not have quite the same prevalence in children's literature.[6] Other paradigms similarly need readjustment.

A religious, didactic, and moralizing impulse predominated in American children's literature prior to the mid nineteenth century, although fairy tales and nonsense literature as well as suspenseful captivity narratives and even biblical-based works like John Bunyan's *The Pilgrim's Progress* (1678) showed sensitivity to children's desire for entertainment. Beginning in the mid nineteenth century, emphasis moved away from molding the child's mind and instilling virtuous habits and beliefs to stimulating the child's imagination; in other words, writers were beginning to recognize childhood not simply as a prelude to adulthood, but as a thing in itself to be treasured.[7]

This new perception of childhood precipitated what has come to be known as the "Golden Age of children's literature," stretching roughly from 1865 to 1920.[8] This era saw the publication of classic works such as Louisa May Alcott's *Little Women* (1869), Mark Twain's *The Adventures of Tom Sawyer* (1876), Margaret Sidney's *Five Little Peppers and How They Grew* (1881), L. Frank Baum's *The Wonderful Wizard of Oz* (1900), Kate Douglas Wiggin's *Rebecca of Sunnybrook Farm* (1903), Jack London's *The Call of the Wild* (1903), and Frances Hodgson Burnett's *A Little Princess* (1905). The "Golden Age" was an era, as Henry Steele Commager famously noted in 1968, "when majors wrote for minors"; moreover, adults and children read many of the same books and authors.[9] Writers such as Mark Twain, Harriet Beecher Stowe, and William Dean Howells often wrote explicitly for children, but their adult writings were also, in many cases, adopted by the young. Other canonical or semi-canonical nineteenth-century American authors such as James Fenimore Cooper, Nathaniel Hawthorne, and Susan Warner either wrote works specifically for children or found an avid audience in children; Hawthorne's *A Wonder Book for Girls and Boys* (1852) was one of the first American books to be written chiefly for children's entertainment, and Susan Warner's *Wide, Wide World* (1850), written originally for girls, is now often taught as a representative example of nineteenth-century women's writing, especially in the sentimental genre, as Cindy Weinstein points out in this volume.[10]

Although works by Twain, Alcott, and others showed young people who were fallible and sometimes even naughty in settings that felt true to life, the protagonists in these books are nearly always "good," even when they are "bad." Huck Finn's famous comment, "All right, then, I'll *go* to hell," represents a critique of unjust laws and religious hypocrisy – he would sooner go to hell than betray Jim, the runaway slave – and thus the comment suggests that children's righteous convictions supercede any false notions of propriety. (The lovable "bad boy" tradition, established by writers such as Twain and Thomas Bailey Aldrich, continued with comic book characters from the Katzenjammer Kids to Dennis the Menace, and in series like the *Our Gang/Little Rascals* films. But the "bad girl" tradition, which we see beginning with Jo March's character in *Little Women*, is more ambivalent: what Anne Scott MacLeod refers to as the "Caddie Woodlawn" syndrome, in which girls trade in freedom, independence, and feistiness as they move from "asexual childhood" into true [young] womanhood, seems to have been the norm.[11]) In all cases, these children are innocent of sexual knowledge. In *Little Women*, even as war, death, and the specter of female sexual desire mark the course of the story, the text itself feels like a space of refuge: Mr. March comes home from the Civil War alive; sexual desire is never labeled as such; and even Beth's death, for which readers are long prepared, and which she awaits "cheerfully," is painted in sentimental and religious terms: "Like a confiding child she asked no questions but left everything to God and nature, Father and mother of us all."[a] Historian Steven Mintz argues that children's literature of the Golden Age is nostalgic at its core, offering "fantasies of escape and empowerment" and "adventures and challenges no longer attainable in real life," especially as actual children's lives became more regimented.[12]

Despite their romantic image of childhood, books of the Golden Age *are* informed by social and ideological conflicts. Horatio Alger's *Ragged Dick* is often read as a kind of Ur-text of social Darwinist ideology, and scholars have documented ways in which nationalism, abolitionism, feminism, and educational reform entered *Little Women* and other work by Alcott.[13] *The Adventures of Huckleberry Finn* grapples with the essential moral dilemmas around race

a As the reference to God would suggest, *Little Women* is also deeply informed by religious traditions, and owes an explicit debt to John Bunyan's Christian allegory, *The Pilgrim's Progress*, as Gregory S. Jackson points out in chapter 10 in this volume, "Religion and the nineteenth-century American novel" (172–173). Jackson also discusses the religious influence upon other canonical texts of children's literature, ranging from Susan Warner's *Wide, Wide World* (1850) to Madeline L'Engle's *A Wrinkle in Time* (1962). Indeed, apart from the current discussion, Jackson's essay contains the most explicit acknowledgment and discussion in *The Cambridge History of the American Novel* of literature for children and the close relationship between literary texts aimed at juvenile and adult audiences. For Jackson's explicit discussion of religious literature aimed at young adults, see 176–179.

and class in the second half of the nineteenth century; Frances Hodgson Burnett's *A Little Princess* is a product of the imperial era in which it was published;[14] Gene Stratton Porter's *A Girl of the Limberlost* (1909) speaks to an eco-feminist consciousness born out of the developing conservationist ethic and also shows a growing tension between rural and urban regions; and Jean Webster's *Daddy Long Legs* (1912), in addition to depicting the young New Woman, likewise highlights class divisions and the growing popularity of socialism.[15] L. Frank Baum's *Wizard of Oz* has repeatedly been discussed as a commentary on the political issues of its day, from populism to race relations and sectional differences.[16] This period produced enduring works of children's literature, certainly, but today the portrayals of children and of adult–child relations in these books, especially those featuring female protagonists, often seem oversentimentalized and unrealistic.[17]

The "sacralization" of childhood by the early twentieth century has been amply documented by historians of childhood. Children's sentimental value increased at the very moment their utilitarian value decreased, as child labor was condemned and ultimately outlawed, and as schools rather than workplaces became childhood's spaces for nearly all classes and races.[18] Birth rates declined at the turn of the century, and new methods of birth control meant that every child could be, in theory, a wanted child. New professions (such as pediatrics), social movements (such as the campaign against child labor), and institutions and organizations (from the Children's Bureau to the Boy Scouts) arose in the name of child protection and child development. In many ways, the actual lives of children improved in the early twentieth century: fewer went to work; more went to school; many had access to better nutrition and health care; and infant mortality declined. A new consciousness of childhood's "stages" produced the "adolescent" (G. Stanley Hall's *Adolescence* was published in 1904) and, likewise, led to increasing segmentation of the children's literature marketplace according to age as well as gender.[19]

Children's reading rooms in libraries, and children's librarians, began to appear in the late nineteenth century, and offered professional opportunities to a new class of women with higher education.[20] Children's librarians strenuously worked to keep dime novels and other sensational literature away from their shelves, but children not surprisingly managed to read them all the same.[b] Anne Lundin refers to the earliest and most influential

b For further discussion of the perceived dangerousness of dime novels, see Shelley Streeby, "Dime novels and the rise of mass market genres," chapter 35 in this volume, 588.

children's librarians as "library matriarchs," whose romantic bias left a lasting legacy upon children's literature and the process of canon formation. [21] But the romantic image of childhood continually butted against real-world experiences of children, and became difficult to sustain.

A series of efforts to professionalize children's literature and to promote children's reading emerged in the early twentieth century. In 1913, Franklin K. Mathiews, the Chief Librarian of the Boy Scouts, called for a Children's Book Week to highlight good literature for children (as opposed to the trash his charges read). Mathiews's project, which depended upon the expertise of specialists to identify the "right" books for children, was a huge success, and by 1919 Book Week was a full-fledged institution, repeated annually. Journals such as *Booklist* (established in 1905) and the *Horn Book* (established in 1924) became important forums for reviewing children's books, and librarians began publishing lists of recommended children's books. Macmillan established the first separate "juvenile" division in an American publishing house in 1919, and by the end of World War II, thirty-two publishers had juvenile divisions – all, incidentally, headed by women. (While this can be read as a mark of the field's "coming of age," some scholars have interpreted the establishment of separate juvenile divisions as evidence of the field's marginalization from the literary mainstream.[22]) Finally, the Newbery and Caldecott Awards, established in 1922 and 1937 respectively, set the terms for the construction of a modern children's literature canon.[23]

Such professionalizing kept mass-market fiction away from library shelves, but mass market publishing for children continued unabated, gaining momentum with the establishment of the Stratemeyer Syndicate in 1904. Its series included The Bobbsey Twins (1904–1979), Tom Swift (1910–1941, with later variations), the Hardy Boys (1927–1979), and Nancy Drew (1930–2003, with continuing variations). Stratemeyer inspired a host of other series, almost none of which were carried by libraries, but which still succeeded because of their affordability. The characterization and plots of these series tends to be conventional, but "social significance" occasionally intrudes upon these texts. There is the familiar example of Nancy Drew's feminist proclivities; later in the twentieth century, the Troy Nesbit series (1962–1964) offered subtle commentary on environmental issues and nuclear proliferation, and the Kathy Martin series (1959–1965) commented on a host of issues, from racism to youth rebellion.[24] As quickly produced and debased works, series books were a form ripe for social commentary, precisely because they moved outside the view of cultural watchdogs.[25]

The shunning of dime novels and then series books by librarians was essential to the boundary-drawing and professionalizing process that marked the emergence of children's literature as a distinctive field of publishing, but developments in education were also key, and certainly helped bring real-world issues into children's literature by the 1940s. While children's librarians tended to privilege imaginative literature, seeing work that was too bound up with the "real world" as inappropriate for the young, educators, particularly those under the influence of John Dewey, increasingly called for both non-fiction and fiction that would equip children to participate in society. With children's books more frequently incorporated into school curricula, educators gained a stronger voice, as did their calls for books engaged with the real world. In Dorothy Canfield Fischer's *Understood Betsy* (1913), one sees the tension between a sentimental view of childhood and progressive educators' emphasis on fostering children's autonomy. The book contrasts a nine-year-old girl's upbringing by overprotective New England aunts against the practices of Vermont relatives and a country schoolteacher who foster "Betsy's" independence and, consequently, her self-confidence. *Understood Betsy* was somewhat unusual for its time, but its underlying ethic would gain a significant following in coming decades.

The 1920s and 1930s were notable for expanding the scope of American children's literature to include foreign cultures, as well as (to a more limited degree) minority cultures in the United States, with Newbery Medals going to Charles Finger's *Tales from Silver Lands* (1924), which dealt with the South Seas; Dhan Gopal Mukerji's *Gay Neck: The Story of a Pigeon* (1927), focusing on India's culture; Eric P. Kelly's *The Trumpeter of Krakow* (1928), portraying medieval Poland; Elizabeth Coatsworth's *The Cat Who Went to Heaven* (1930), dealing with the Far East; and *Young Fu of the Upper Yangtze* (1932), dealing with China. Certainly, an Anglo-American norm pervades children's literature of the early twentieth century, but the early dominance of the British book marketplace and the attention to foreign lands, especially in the 1920s and 1930s, suggests a certain cosmopolitanism.[26] Even so, portraits of the American minority experience were at best limited, and, at worst, strikingly racist. Laura Adams Armer's attempt to write from a Native American point of view in *Waterless Mountain* (1931) sharply contrasted with the majority of works that depicted American Indians either as wild savages or as relatively harmless curiosities, but rarely as fully developed human beings. Such negative images of Indians were so pervasive as to be unremarkable: indeed, a recent commentary upon Laura Ingalls Wilder's decision to leave white vigilante violence out of her *Little House* books (1932–1943) notes: "It is 'fit' for children to read about 'wild Indians' but not serial killers who are white." Even contemporary children's books often indulge in stereotypes about American Indians.[27]

The African American experience was likewise distorted in mainstream children's literature. In 1932, Langston Hughes emphasized "the need . . . for books that Negro parents and teachers can read to their children without hesitancy . . . books whose dark characters are not all clowns, and whose illustrations are not merely caricatures."[28] Popular books such as Rose B. Knox's *Miss Jimmy Deane* (1931) showed an old South in which loyal Negroes knew their place, and racist imagery in works ranging from the Newbery Medal-winning *Voyages of Doctor Doolittle* (1923) to *The Bobbsey Twins* books reveals the pervasiveness of stock stereotypes and racist caricatures. Even books written with an explicitly anti-racist intent such as Hildegarde Hoyt Swift's *Railroad to Freedom: A Story of the Civil War* (1932) delicately avoided offending Southern readers. Swift's book emphasizes Harriet Tubman's deep affection for the master and mistress who had been consistently cruel to her in her lifetime. (An older tradition of abolitionist children's literature following from Harriet Beecher Stowe's *Uncle Tom's Cabin* [1852] likewise portrayed African Americans in sentimentalized and one-dimensional terms.[c])

African American authors' entry into the mainstream children's literary marketplace helped produce more humanized and realistic depictions. Hughes and his friend Arna Bontemps, both participants in the Harlem Renaissance, were the first black writers to break into trade children's literature.[29] As Katharine Capshaw Smith has elegantly chronicled, children were emblematic figures in the Harlem Renaissance, with writers and publishers sharing the goal of "building racial pride in a child audience."[30] Hughes and Bontemps's work, perhaps most notably their co-authored novel *Popo and Fifina, Children of Haiti* (1932), concerns itself less with uplifting young black readers than with cultivating a black aesthetic within mainstream children's literature and combating the racist imagery consumed by white readers. A story of a brother and sister in a small fishing village in Haiti who barely subsist but whose life is defined more by sensual, poetic experience than by the numbing effects of poverty, the book also contains a veiled protest against the American occupation of Haiti and a subtle critique of American values and working conditions. The book was hailed by reviewers and remained on

c For further discussion see John Ernest, "Stowe, race, and the antebellum American novel," chapter 15.

Macmillan's prestigious list for two decades, and both authors continued to publish fiction, poetry, and nonfiction for children throughout their careers.

Although some scholars have argued that the Great Depression and Second World War barely registered in juvenile literature, they were in fact central to the development of "socially significant" literature for children, a term that begins to appear in children's literature discourse in the late 1930s.[31] While historical novels such as Laura Ingalls Wilder's *Little House in the Big Woods* (1932) and Carol Ryrie Brink's *Caddie Woodlawn* (1935) suggest a desire to retreat into a pre-industrial past, one can also find in the 1930s and 1940s conscious efforts to expose children to the pressing issues of the day.[32] Lavinia Davis's *Adventures in Steel* (1938) is an example of what Michael Denning calls the "laboring of American culture," emphasizing the dignity of labor and promoting ethnic and working-class unity and unionization.[33] Regionalism, another trend in fiction of the 1930s, entered children's literature most visibly through Lois Lenski's regionalist (and realist) novels such as *Bayou Suzette* (1943) and *Strawberry Girl* (1945, winner of the Newbery Medal).[d] Lenski's extensively researched books tend to focus upon poor whites in rural regions, like the Cajun Bayou Suzette or the "Florida Cracker" family in *Strawberry Girl*.

The Great Depression, the rise of fascism, and the Second World War convinced many librarians and educators that children needed greater preparation to fully participate in a society that offered unprecedented challenges. Janey Larkins, the protagonist in Doris Gates's Newbery-winning *Blue Willow* (1940) – a book sometimes referred to as the "juvenile *Grapes of Wrath*" – became emblematic of a new kind of character and of storylines in children's literature that were increasingly attuned to the serious issues of the day,[34] although happy endings still prevailed.[e] The Intercultural Education movement grew out of wartime efforts to challenge the racist and nationalist ideology of fascism, and that movement promoted books emphasizing American cultural diversity. Eleanor Estes's *The Hundred Dresses* (1944) highlights the poor, Polish, and Catholic Wanda Petronski's struggles with her middle-class, Protestant classmates. Florence Crannell Means became well

d On trends in regionalism leading up to and including this period, see Tom Lutz, "Cather and the regional imagination," chapter 26 in this volume.

e The expectation of happy endings meant that the children's "protest novel" differs from the protest novel as Cecelia Tichi describes it in this volume. In addition, juvenile authors' resistance to the dire, "manichean" model Tichi describes (at least prior to the late 1960s), makes them, perhaps, more "susceptible to wide-ranging inquiry in search of nuance, subtlety, ambivalence, ambiguity, and so on." See "Novels of civic protest," chapter 23, 400).

known and respected for her books dealing with American racial minorities: *The Shuttered Windows* (1938), for instance, deals with African Americans and racial segregation, and *The Moved Outers* (1945), a Newbery Honor book, was essentially the only children's book of the time to deal with the Japanese internment experience. And Sydney Taylor's *All-of-a-Kind Family* books, published beginning in the 1950s, suggest that war's discrediting of anti-Semitism finally made possible mainstream children's books portraying Jewish life. Perhaps not surprisingly, this occurred at the same moment that Andrew Hoberek identifies elsewhere in this volume as defining for the twentieth-century Jewish-American novel more generally.[f] Esther Forbes's Newbery-winning historical novel about the American Revolution, *Johnny Tremain* (1943), has been called "the most important book of the war," as it implicitly linked the struggle for American independence to the Allied struggle against fascism.[35] Such work offers evidence of the ways in which a broad-based popular front against fascism inflected children's literature along with popular culture more generally.[36]

More radical impulses made their way into children's literature as well. The proletarian novel had its counterpart in children's literature, although only a few full-length children's novels of a political nature were published in the USA, and most of these in the 1940s rather than the 1930s. If, as Alan Wald suggests in this volume, the proletarian novel has been seen as vaguely "un-American" and marginalized in American literary history,[g] proletarian fiction for children – much of which never reached beyond the children of socialists and communists, but some of which attracted a significant audience – would be entirely forgotten were it not for several recent works that give new attention to the genre.[37] Working under the guidance of Theodore Dreiser, Ruth Epperson Kennell published two novels portraying child life in the "New Russia," *Vanya of the Streets* (1931) and *Comrade One Crutch* (1932); the books were widely reviewed and well received in their time, but are forgotten today. Margaret Thomsen Raymond's *A Bend in the Road* (1934), a story geared toward older girls, included romance, labor struggle, and generational / ethnic conflict in an American factory town suffering under the weight of the Depression. Jay Williams's medieval-themed *The Sword and the Scythe* (1946) uses a fourteenth-century peasants' rebellion to comment on the nature of class struggle. International Publishers, the Communist Party publishing house, published several children's novels on historical and contemporary

f Andrew Hoborek, "The Jewish great American novel," chapter 54 in this volume.
g Alan Wald, "Steinbeck and the proletarian novel," chapter 40 in this volume.

subjects between 1945 and 1952, including Eric Lucas's *Swamp Fox Brigade: Adventures with General Francis Marion's Guerillas* (1945) and Jean Karsavina's *Tree By the Waters* (1948), which deals with a silverware factory strike in New England.

While the period of McCarthyism that followed World War II limited such open political expression, the postwar period brought profound changes in the popular image of childhood and in the actual experiences of children. Children's literature experienced something of a cultural lag in response to such changes, but by the end of the 1960s it had undergone a sea change. Two books published in the early 1950s, J. D. Salinger's *Catcher in the Rye* (1951) and E. B. White's *Charlotte's Web* (1952), point to the tectonic shifts in American childhood. The first, which would have a transformative effect on children's literature, was not actually written for children; indeed, *Catcher in the Rye* was widely banned from schools.[38] Censors cited the book's foul language, but the very real teenage protagonist, with whom millions of young people identified, was himself threatening because of his contempt for adults and adult institutions. Holden Caulfield is not a juvenile delinquent *per se*, but his alienation mirrors that of iconic movie characters like Marlon Brando's in *The Wild One* (1953) and James Dean's in *Rebel Without a Cause* (1955), and evoked the specter of real juvenile delinquents.[39] Even today the name Holden Caulfield remains recognizable as a symbol of the alienated youth of the 1950s ("they knew . . . Holden Caulfied would found SDS," muses the narrator of E. L. Doctorow's *The Book of Daniel* [1971], seeking to explain the rise of the New Left). Holden's frank, stream-of-consciousness language would become the norm for the young adult "problem novels" that began to be published in the late 1960s.

Charlotte's Web was actually written for children and attracted younger readers than those who read *Catcher in the Rye*. *Charlotte* portrays a rural scene evocative of a bygone era, and its talking spider, pig, and rat seem unlikely vehicles for realism or social significance. But the deep feeling of loss that pervades the book – the threat of Wilbur's death, the imminence of Charlotte's, the fleeting nature of childhood, and the rural idyll that readers sense is rapidly disappearing – makes it an apt marker for a lost American innocence following World War II. Jill Lepore says that the publication of White's prior novel for children, *Stuart Little* (1945), can be read as "an indictment of both the childishness of children's literature and the juvenilization of American culture." Moreover, she argues, the failure of the *grande dame* of children's librarians, Anne Carroll Moore, to halt the book's publication and to keep it out of libraries – because it involved a woman giving birth to a mouse – indicated a dramatic shift in standards of literary quality and acceptability in children's literature.[40]

Tom Engelhardt argues that the dropping of atomic bombs on Hiroshima and Nagasaki in 1945 marked the end of American innocence, and by extension, childhood innocence (this association between the bomb and imperiled child innocence was reinforced in 1964 with Lyndon Johnson's infamous "Daisy" ad, showing a young girl threatened by the nuclear holocaust that his rival, Barry Goldwater, might launch).[41] Films of the 1950s and 1960s show a tension between between the Disney model of childhood innocence (expressed in movies like *Treasure Island* [1950] and *Old Yeller* [1958]) and a darker image of childhood, communicated perhaps mostly starkly in *The Bad Seed* (1954) (subsequently produced as a Broadway show and a movie), which portrays a child murderess.

Despite fears about racial mixing following the *Brown v. Board of Education* verdict in 1954, children's novels remained relatively free of references to desegregation until the 1960s. Notable exceptions include Lorenz Graham's *South Town* (1958), which won the 1958 Child Study Award for realistically dramatizing problems confronting young people, and Dorothy Sterling's *Mary Jane* (1959), which directly addressed school desegregation.

The rejection of adult authority and bleak view of childhood and youth which would come to dominate in the 1970s do not visibly surface in children's literature until the late 1960s, but earlier books begin to grapple with moral ambiguity or to critique the conformity and repressive politics of the Cold War. Henry Felsen's 1952 novel *Two and the Town* deals with teenage pregnancy, and Madeline L'Engle's Newbery-winning fantasy novel, *A Wrinkle in Time* (1962), sharply critiques conformity. Two historical novels, Elizabeth George Speare's *The Witch of Blackbird Pond* (1958) and Ann Petry's *Tituba of Salem Village* (1964), used the Salem witch trials (as Arthur Miller did in *The Crucible* [1953]) to comment upon McCarthyism and the repressive atmosphere of the Cold War; Petry's novel brings in a racial dimension by focusing on the slave woman, Tituba Indian, who was said to have bewitched several young girls.

The publication of Louise Fitzhugh's *Harriet the Spy* (1964) marked a kind of break, as it placed a jaded, alienated, Holden Caulfield-esque character in a book that was actually intended for children. The story portrays a streetwise, independent, eleven-year-old Manhattanite who barely interacts with her wealthy parents and who spends her days spying on neighbors. The matter-of-fact language and disdainful image of adults also owes a debt to *Catcher in the Rye*. The book's queer aesthetic, perhaps most evident in Fitzhugh's illustrations of a boyish-looking Harriet, operates, according to Robin Bernstein, as a powerful, even "magical" subtext that many readers have found empowering.[42] Rejecting chronologies of gay and lesbian literature that mark the 1969 Stonewall Rebellion as a point of origin, Elizabeth Freeman's essay in this volume encourages us to take more seriously the queer subtext in a work such as *Harriet the Spy*.[h]

More than anything, *Harriet* challenged the stability of adult–child, and particularly parent–child relations, as well as adult authority, which had previously remained remarkably stable in children's literature. As Anne Scott MacLeod notes, "Without breathing hard about it, Louise Fitzhugh discarded several cherished children's literature taboos, producing a book that I think of as a major breach in the protective walls around children's books."[43] The book was immediately challenged for its "unlikable characters and moral ambiguity," but it struck a chord with many child readers, and it remains popular today.[44]

Other child characters emerged around this time who also broke the children's literature mold. Ramona Quimby, introduced in 1955 in Beverly Cleary's *Beezus and Ramona*, came into her own in the revolutionary year of 1968 with *Ramona the Pest*. Like Harriet Welsch, Ramona feels qualitatively different from child protagonists of an earlier era; she is a clever, strong-willed, and sensitive child who is aware of but does not accept adult assumptions about children. In succeeding *Ramona* books, the character also shows awareness of her parents' money concerns (challenging an upper-middle-class norm in much of children's literature), and recognizes that not all adults (including teachers and caretakers) like all children.

But Ramona's deep affection and respect for her own parents contrasts with characters in books that began to be published in the late 1960s and 1970s, books that definitively mark the end of childhood as a protected and innocent realm. Geared mostly toward adolescents, their portraits of childhood tend toward bleakness, and adults – parents or otherwise – are often rendered as incompetent, absent, negligent, or outright evil. These books touch on topics that would have been beyond the pale just a few years earlier: S. E. Hinton's *The Outsiders* (1967), written when Hinton herself was a teenager, portrays gang violence; in Paul Zindel's *The Pigman* (1968) a childish prank ultimately results in an old man's death; the anonymously authored *Go Ask Alice* (1971) deals with drug abuse; Alice Childress's *A Hero Ain't Nothin' but a Sandwich* (1973) features a thirteen-year-old drug dealer; Rosa Guy's *Ruby* (1976) deals with homosexuality; and Judy Blume's *Forever* (1975) shows teenagers having sex,

h Elizabeth Freeman, "Reimagining genders and sexualities," chapter 57 in this volume.

enjoying it, and not getting punished for it (or getting married). Such works point to ways in which literature for young people marked not only the generational tensions of the 1960s and 1970s but also a more sweeping reassessment of children's literature as a form. Critics at the time complained about the "adult-eration" of children's fiction, but they recognized that a fundamental shift had taken place.[45]

Perhaps one of the most significant changes was that children's literature was no longer an "all-white world," as critic Nancy Larrick had called it in 1965.[46] In 1969, Julius Lester's nonfictional *To Be a Slave* (1968) was named a Newbery Honor Book, and in 1977 *Roll of Thunder, Hear My Cry* (1976) by Mildred Taylor was the first book by an African American to be awarded the Newbery Medal (2010 was the first year the Caldecott went to an African American illustrator, however). By the late 1970s children's literature had become more relevant to the actual lives of children and to the problems facing society, and more representative of ethnic, racial, religious, and even sexual diversity. This shift has not only kept children reading books, in spite of increased competition from television, movies, the internet, and video games; it has also drawn adult readers to books written for children and adolescents.

Indeed, today the "children's novel" is often as popular with adults as with young people: witness the bestseller status of J. K. Rowling's *Harry Potter* series (1997–2007) and the popularity of Philip Pullman's *His Dark Materials* trilogy (1995–2000), which, along with graphic novels and other works in the fantasy genre, have led the trend in "crossover" fiction, prompting some publishers to print parallel editions of the same books to more effectively market them.[47] Arguably, then, we are in a new "Golden Age," one in which, once again, adults and children are reading many of the same books, but in which an innocent, protected world is no longer available – and, perhaps, is not even attractive – to either.

Notes

1. Lynn Vallone, *Disciplines of Virtue: Girls' Culture in the Eighteenth and Nineteenth Centuries* (New Haven: Yale University Press, 1995), 4.
2. *Ibid.* For related discussions of how such trends affected the book market and patterns of reading, see Ronald Zboray and Mary Saracino Zboray, "The novel in the antebellum book market" (chapter 4 in this volume) and Barbara Hochman, "Readers and reading groups" (chapter 36 in this volume).
3. Neil Postman, *The Disappearance of Childhood* (New York: Vintage Books, 1982; rpt. 1994).

4. Leslie Fiedler, *Love and Death in the American Novel* (New York, Criterion Books, 1960), 180–182; Fiedler, "Second Thoughts on *Love and Death in the American Novel*: My First Gothic Novel." *Novel: A Forum on Fiction* 1.1 (Autumn 1967): 9.
5. For an example of work that reads children's literature in conjunction with literature for adults that projects particular images of childhood; see, for instance, Joseph L. Zornado, *Inventing the Child: Culture, Ideology, and the Story of Childhood*, 1st paperback edn. (New York: Garland, 2006).
6. The phrase is from Nina Baym, "Melodramas of Beset Manhood: How Theories of American Fiction Exclude Women Authors," *American Quarterly* 33.2 (1981): 123–139.
7. Roger Lancelyn Green, "The Golden Age of Children's Books," in *Only Connect: Readings on Children's Literature*, ed. Sheila Egoff, G. T. Stubbs, and L. F. Ashley (New York: Oxford University Press, 1980), 12.
8. See, for instance, a special issue of the *Children's Literature Association Quarterly* devoted to the Golden Age (26.1 [Spring 2001]) and Jerome Griswold, *Audacious Kids: Coming of Age in America's Classic Children's Books* (New York: Oxford University Press, 1992). Works published during this time are generally seen as the "classics" of children's literature and appear frequently on course syllabi.
9. Henry Steele Commager, *The Commonwealth of Learning*, 1st edn. (New York: Harper & Row, 1968), 69.
10. Comment on Hawthorne's *Wonder Book* is from Marjorie Allen, *One Hundred Years of Children's Books in America* (New York: Facts on File, 1996), 2. For further discussion see Gillian Avery, *Behold the Child: American Children and Their Books, 1621–1922* (London: Bodley Head, 1994), 114–131. See Cindy Weinstein's "Sentimentalism," chapter 12 in this volume.
11. Anne Scott MacLeod, *American Childhood: Children's Literature of the Nineteenth and Twentieth Centuries* (Athens: University of Georgia Press, 1994), 3–29.
12. Steven Mintz, *Huck's Raft: A History of American Childhood* (Cambridge, MA: Belknap Press of Harvard University Press, 2004), 186.
13. See Janice M. Alberghene and Beverly Lyon Clark, *Little Women and the Feminist Imagination: Criticism, Controversy, Personal Essays* (New York: Garland, 1999); Beverly Lyon Clark, *Kiddie Lit: The Cultural Construction of Children's Literature in America* (Baltimore: Johns Hopkins University Press, 2003), 102–127. Also see *Children's Literature* 34 (2006) for a special issue devoted to Alcott.
14. See Mavis Reimer, "Making Princesses, Re-making *A Little Princess*," in *Voices of the Other: Children's Literature and the Postcolonial Context*, ed. Roderick McGillis (New York: Garland, 1999), 111–134; and Manisha Mirchandani, "Colonial Discourse and Post-Colonial Negotiations: *A Little Princess* and Its Adaptations," *New Literatures Review* 33 (Summer 1997): 11–24.
15. Janet Malcolm argues that *A Girl of the Limberlost* is not an environmentalist novel at all, but is rather obsessed with the idea of mining natural resources for profit; in that sense it may more aptly be called "conservationist" than environmentalist. See Janet Malcolm, "Capitalist Pastorale," *New York Review of Books* 56.1 (January 15, 2009). www.nybooks.com/articles/22243, accessed May 30, 2009.

16. See Henry M. Littlefield, "The Wizard of Oz: Parable on Populism," *American Quarterly* 16.1 (Spring 1964): 47–58, and Gretchen Ritter, "Silver Slippers and a Golden Cap: L. Frank Baum's *The Wonderful Wizard of Oz* and Historical Memory in American Politics," *Journal of American Studies* 2 (August 31, 1997): 171–202.
17. On the subject of historical children's literature and its relevance for contemporary child readers, Peter Hunt notes two quite different studies operating: "the study of books that *are* for children, and the study of books that *were* for children." Peter Hunt, "Passing on the Past: The Problem of Books that Are for Children and that Were for Children," *Children's Literature Association Quarterly* 21.4 (Winter 1996–1997): 200.
18. See Viviana Zelizer, *Pricing the Priceless Child: The Changing Social Value of Children* (New York: Basic Books, 1985).
19. For a recent exploration of the roots of teenage identity, see Sarah Chinn, *Inventing Modern Adolescence: The Children of Immigrants in Turn-of-the-Century America* (New Brunswick, NJ: Rutgers University Press, 2008).
20. See Kay Vandergrift, "Female Advocacy and Harmonious Voices: A History of Public Library Services and Publishing for Children in the United States," *Library Trends* 44.4 (1996): 683–718. The essay is part of a special issue entitled *Female Advocacy and Harmonious Voices: A History of Public Library Services and Publishing for Children in the United States*.
21. Anne H. Lundin, *Constructing the Canon of Children's Literature: Beyond Library Walls and Ivory Towers* (New York: Routledge, 2004), 8.
22. For the argument that the field gained from this separation see Jacalyn Eddy, *Bookwomen: Creating an Empire in Children's Book Publishing, 1919–1939* (Madison: University of Wisconsin Press, 2006); for the opposing argument see Griswold, *Audacious Kids*, viii. Also see Clark, *Kiddie Lit*, 48–76.
23. On the relationship between prizing and the formation of a children's literature canon, see Kenneth Kidd, "Prizing Children's Literature: The Case of the Newbery Gold," *Children's Literature* 35 (2007): 166–190.
24. See Julia Mickenberg, "Nursing Radicalism: Some Lessons from a Post-War Girls' Series," *American Literary History* 19.2 (2007): 491–520.
25. For a related argument about dime novels, see the now-classic study, Michael Denning, *Mechanic Accents: Dime Novels and Working-Class Culture in America* (London: Verso, 1987).
26. See Charles C. Alexander, *Here the Country Lies: Nationalism and the Arts in Twentieth-Century America* (Bloomington: Indiana University Press, 1980).
27. For the discussion of Wilder, and for more on images of American Indians in children's literature, see http://imagesofindiansinchildrensbooks.blogspot.com/. Accessed August 17, 2008.
28. Langston Hughes, "Books and the Negro Child," *Children's Library Yearbook* 4 (1932): 109.
29. On the history of African American children's literature, see especially Michelle H. Martin, *Brown Gold: Milestones of African American Children's Picture Books, 1845–2002* (New York: Routledge, 2004).

30. Katharine Capshaw Smith, *Children's Literature of the Harlem Renaissance* (Bloomington: Indiana University Press, 2004), 164.
31. See, for instance, Helen Hoke, Leo Lerman, and Evelyn Hamilton, "The Problem Book," *Publishers' Weekly* (October 18, 1941): 1550.
32. On this interest in the roots of American culture, see Warren Susman, "The Culture of the Thirties," in *Culture as History: The Transformation of Tradition in the Twentieth Century* (New York: Pantheon, 1984). For an interpretation of Depression-era children's literature as the "Pollyanna Syndrome," see Allen, *One Hundred Years of Children's Books in America*, 73–84. On the argument that World War II had little impact on children's literature, see William Tuttle, *Daddy's Gone to War: The Second World War in the Lives of America's Children* (New York: Oxford University Press, 1993), 156.
33. Michael Denning, *The Cultural Front: The Laboring of American Culture in the Twentieth Century* (London: Verso, 1996), xvi.
34. Vernon Ives, "Children's Books and the War," *Publishers' Weekly* 144 (1943): 1592–1593; Julia Sauer, "Making the World Safe for the Janey Larkins," *The Library Journal* 66.22 (1941): 49–53; Flora Straus, "Let Them Face It: Today's World in Books for Boys and Girls," *The Horn Book* 21 (January 1945): 63–64; Jean Van Evera, "They're Not What They Used to Be!," *Parents* 21.10 (1946): 28–29ff.
35. Gillian Avery *et al.*, "Children's Literature in America, 1870–1945," in *Children's Literature: An Illustrated History*, ed. Peter Hunt (New York, Oxford: Oxford University Press, 1995), 250.
36. On the Popular Front see Denning, *The Cultural Front*. For a fuller discussion of how the Popular Front influenced children's literature, see Julia Mickenberg, *Learning from the Left: Children's Literature, the Cold War, and Radical Politics in the United States* (New York and Oxford: Oxford University Press, 2006).
37. Recent work that considers proletarian literature for children includes Paul Mishler, *Raising Reds: The Young Pioneers, Radical Summer Camps, and Communist Political Culture in the United States* (New York: Columbia University Press, 1999); Mickenberg, *Learning from the Left;* and Julia Mickenberg and Philip Nel, eds., *Tales for Little Rebels: A Collection of Radical Children's Literature* (New York: New York University Press, 2008).
38. For an extended discussion of censorship controversies surrounding Salinger's book, see Pamela Hunt Steinle, *In Cold Fear: The Catcher in the Rye Censorship Controversies and Postwar American Character* (Columbus: Ohio State University Press, 2000).
39. On postwar fears about youth and juvenile delinquency see James Gilbert, *A Cycle of Outrage: America's Reaction to the Juvenile Delinquent* (New York: Oxford University Press, 1986).
40. Jill Lepore, "The Lion and the Mouse: The Battle that Reshaped Children's Literature," *The New Yorker* (July 21, 2008): 66–73, quotation at 72.
41. See Tom Engelhardt, *The End of Victory Culture: Cold War America and the Disillusioning of a Generation* (New York: Basic Books, 1994).

42. See Robin Bernstein, " 'Too Realistic' and 'Too Distorted': The Attack on Louise Fitzhugh's *Harriet the Spy* and the Gaze of the Queer Child," *Critical Matrix: Journal of Women, Gender, and Culture* 12.1–2 (2000–2001): 28.
43. MacLeod, *American Childhood*, 199.
44. Bernstein, "Too Realistic," 26.
45. Elaine Moss, "The Adult-eration of Children's Books." *Signal* 14 (May 1974): 65–69; Sheila Egoff, "The Problem Novel," in *Only Connect: Readings on Children's Literature*, 2nd edn., ed. Sheila Egoff (Toronto and New York: Oxford University Press, 1980), 360.
46. Nancy Larrick, "The All-White World of Children's Books," *Saturday Review* (September 11, 1965): 63–65, 84–85.
47. Jasper Rees, "We're All Reading Children's Books," *Daily Telegraph*, London (November 17, 2003). www.telegraph.co.uk/arts/main.jhtml?xml=/arts/2003/11/16/borees.xml&page=1. Accessed June 22, 2008.

53

The American novel and the rise of the suburbs

CATHERINE JURCA

The suburb has been an important setting and subject of the American novel since the 1920s, with its ascendance as the residential environment of choice for the white middle class. Until recently, the suburban novel has received little attention from literary scholars; analysis of canonical American literature has focused instead on the wilderness and the frontier, on the isolated landscapes and folkways that are the province of regionalism, and on the cities that ground realism and modernism as well as ethnic and African American writings. One of the earliest treatments of the suburb in literature established the terms on which it could be discounted. In "The Great American Novel" (1927), Edith Wharton lamented her fellow writers' preoccupation with "the little suburban house at number one million and ten Volstead Avenue."[1] Wharton noted the "material advantages" such a house provided but deplored the spiritual and aesthetic deficiencies of "the safe and uniform life" found within it. A poor stimulus for "the artist's imagination," it helped to foster the "middling," "middle class" existence that writers purported to condemn.[2] The suburban literary tradition has flourished in spite of Wharton's effort to derail it; indeed, her essay did not so much describe an existing literature as provide a blueprint for it. The suburban novel continues to privilege analysis and assessment and to focus on the banal, the mediocre, and the conventional, even as the suburbs themselves have radically changed. Far from representing the threat to American letters that Wharton railed against, however, suburban novels have been showered with accolades and prizes and gained a popular audience. In recent decades they have achieved increasing recognition for literary merit while continuing to stake a claim to sociological significance, as reviewers routinely celebrate this work for speaking deep truths about the manners and mores of the middle class.

The "truth" that this literature attests to is that despite the material advantages that suburban house ownership has historically afforded so many of its middle-class residents – the comforts and conveniences of the prosperous "good life," the chance to escape the problems of the city while remaining close enough to enjoy its attractions, financial rewards in the form of tax deductions and rising property values – the characters who reside in these houses seldom enjoy any of its fruits. In novels by Sinclair Lewis, Sloan Wilson, Richard Yates, John Updike, Rick Moody, Richard Ford, and David Gates, among others, the story the suburban novel tells over and over again is one of white middle-class spiritual and cultural impoverishment, of disappointment, despair, and failure, as though there has been no worse fate in our society than to own a fully loaded split-level within forty miles of New York City. With a few important exceptions, this literature treats its characters as the victims of their affluence. Discontent and self-pity are the mainstays of the literary suburbanite's psychic life and come to seem virtually constitutive features of white middle-class identity and experience. As the names above suggest, in many instances it is male writers who have found the idea of alienation from the suburb and suburban house (what I have elsewhere described as the feeling of *homelessness*) particularly compelling.[3] But sentimental attachment to the idea of home is no less pronounced for the impossibility of achieving it, and these writers become the unexpected heirs to a domestic literary tradition, addressed in this volume by Cindy Weinstein, once associated almost exclusively with feminine values and aesthetics.[a]

Wharton could so accurately anticipate almost a century of writing about the suburb because it is so deeply indebted, consciously or not, to Sinclair Lewis, a writer whose talents she admired even as she strived to redirect them. With *Babbitt* (1922), which he dedicated to Wharton, Lewis created the prototype of the suburban novel and its main character. Babbitt, the paradigmatic middle-class man, is not only the "materialist, self-complacent business man" who loses his way in a culture of abundance, but rather he is a self-loathing malcontent as well.[4]

Lewis's creation of this type placed Babbitt squarely in the suburbs, as both a resident of the Floral Heights subdivision and self-employed realtor of suburban properties. Babbitt's occupation is significant, for historians have seen the 1920s as a turning point in the development and marketing of the suburb. At this time the population at the periphery of cities began to increase faster than in their cores. Advertisements, articles, and an "Own Your Own

a As Cindy Weinstein notes in "Sentimentalism" (chapter 12, 209–211) the tradition of domestic writing by women in the nineteenth century was disparaged, rather than praised, by their male counterparts and subsequent generations of literary scholars.

Home" campaign sponsored by government and business promoted the single-family, freestanding suburban house as the natural home of the white middle class and associated it with the prolific consumption of mass-produced commodities.[5] Lavish descriptions of Babbitt's suburban house and contents – the "triumphant modern mattresses," "standard electric bedside lamp," "real or imitation" mahogany tables, and so on – provide much of the novel's documentary texture. These details also support Lewis's most basic critique of Babbitt's debilitating way of life: "There was one thing wrong with the Babbitt house. It was not a home." Babbitt's so-called rebellion from the constraints of Zenith and the de-individuating forces of standardization drive him to find those places where he can achieve the emotional satisfaction his house does not provide. First Babbitt attempts to "beautifully come home" in the apartment of an attractive Bohemian widow, and later, during a camping trip, he seeks "his real home" with a "half Yankee, half Indian" guide. Babbitt's trip to the Maine woods for a little interracial bonding looks a lot like the masculine flight to freedom that Leslie Fiedler described almost forty years later, but Babbitt strives not to flee the home but to reclaim it for an emotionally disenfranchised middle-class man.[6]

Babbitt's rebellion, then, is predicated on his recognition of his homelessness, which is based on the idea that affluent suburban lifestyles entail emotional and spiritual impoverishment, that such things as comfortable beds and *faux* wood furniture destroy middle-class well-being and constitute reasonable grounds for dissatisfaction. Babbitt, who has also benefited both professionally and personally from the rise of the suburbs, is the primary casualty of them. Moreover, it is his growing awareness of his suffering and resultant efforts to cope with it that are supposed to be the most attractive thing about him, the sign that he repudiates the conformity on which his identity has hitherto depended, however temporarily, as he and Lewis tiptoe toward reform. It would not be until the postwar period, and the nationwide proliferation of subdivisions and the onslaught of fiction dealing with their inhabitants, that Lewis's prototypical suburbanite would become the stereotypical suburbanite, and discontent and self-pity would emerge as the sine qua non of suburban middle-class experience.

The evolution of the suburban novel directly reflects the changes suburbs themselves underwent after the war, as new techniques of house construction, economic incentives for builders and veterans, and high wages made suburban house ownership possible for most white middle-class and many working-class families for the first time.[7] The construction of houses such as Babbitt's maligned Dutch Colonial, built singly on spacious lots, was supplanted by large-scale developments. Enthusiasts interpreted the opportunities for ownership of mass-produced houses in places such as Levittown, and the goodies to fill them, as evidence of the democratic erasure of class boundaries. Millions of working-class families could finally "enjoy what has been traditionally considered a middle-class way of life."[8] For the middle class, however, the stakes of this transformation were somewhat different. Novelists and sociologists became preoccupied with the deterioration of the status of the middle class. White-collar employment in the modern corporation was thought to replicate the demeaning conditions of blue-collar labor; suburban house ownership within "rank after rank of little boxes stretching off to infinity" likewise marked the descent of "the next managerial class" into an undifferentiated and inglorious mass.[9]

So intent were novelists on representing and condemning the effects of these changes in the 1950s that some of them adopted the language of the social sciences to make their case. They substituted typical for individual characters to the extent that Babbitt seemed, in retrospect, an exemplar of uniqueness, not to mention the product of a once unique authorial vision. John and Mary Drone, in John Keats's *The Crack in the Picture Window* (1957), stand in for the whole category of degraded suburbanite and office worker; the claim for representativeness suggested by their names is bolstered by empirical data on the economics and politics of suburban development. Each chapter of David Karp's *Leave Me Alone* (1957) begins with an epigraph from a fictional sociology of suburban life that the novel then dramatizes. In Charles Mergendahl's *It's Only Temporary* (1950), mass housing yields mass behavior – for example, in one development "some five thousand automatic stoves were switched on while some five thousand wives cooked dinner for some five thousand returning husbands." In the drive to prove the massification of the middle class, these writers concerned themselves rather less with how the suburban novel itself began to feel as mass-produced as the housing and characters it described.

Their approach runs exactly counter to John Cheever's short stories, the gold standard of suburban fiction in this period. Cheever's stories feature conspicuously distinctive characters such as Johnny Hake, the housebreaker of Shady Hill, an older, upper-middle-class suburb, and responses to suburban life that are idiosyncratic in the extreme, as if his characters refuse to participate in the literary stereotype of the suburbanite as mid-century mass man. Cheever's stories insist on "the complexity of life," in the words of "The Wrysons" (1958), but rather like the over-simplification of life that is found in suburban novels of the period, the effect of such calculated differentiation could be a certain repetitiveness as well.

The most important literary icon of postwar corporate-suburban life is Tom Rath, the protagonist of Sloan Wilson's bestselling *The Man in the Gray Flannel Suit* (1955). Wilson's novel too was a quasi-sociological project. Tom, one of "half a million other guys in gray flannel suits," was touted on its book jacket as "a fairly universal figure in mid-twentieth-century America," although Wilson eschewed the cruder techniques of the novels cited above and strived to create psychologically authentic characters. Reviewers thought the novel captured "the panicky quality of the lives of so many of those commuters in gray flannel," even if the problem of surviving on $7,000 a year, which opens the novel, was "less than heartbreaking to the average reader" and thus a trifle less "universal" than the publicity department of Simon and Schuster claimed.[10] But the title points to a new model of middle-class identity, in which the business suit, once a symbol of respectable affluence and autonomy, becomes instead the uniform that symbolizes the wearer's subordination, the loss of his privilege. The affect that goes with the suit is a powerful feeling of alienation from the institutions that were seen as central to the middle class in the postwar years. The very first thing we learn about Tom and his wife, Betsy, is that they loathe their "little house" in Westport, Connecticut, which is "almost precisely like the houses on all sides." Ownership of a suburban house is associated here, as in so many other novels of the 1950s, with the outright failure of their dream rather than its achievement. The Raths take no pleasure in his job in the amorphous world of a corporate public relations department, and even when the corporation's president selects Tom as his successor, almost his son, it merely increases Tom and Betsy's already profound self-pity. Hardly mindless conformists, the Raths are their own most vehement and unhappy critics.

Along with other postwar novels, *The Man in Gray Flannel* articulates a new cornerstone of white middle-class identity. The Raths are invested in the idea that their discontent is exceptional and thus makes them unique – nothing, that is, like their dull, satisfied neighbors – despite evidence that their neighbors feel the same anxieties and longings and eagerness to move. The Raths, in other words, don't simply feel bad about being middle class, as Babbitt did; they want to deny that they even belong to the middle class. Other suburban characters share this denial and try to establish their individuality in an environment that is, unlike the frontier or the metropolis, perceived as wholly unexceptional. In Richard Yates's *Revolutionary Road* (1961), set in 1955, Frank and April Wheeler have no desire to fit in: they hate "having to *live* among all these damn little suburban types." They befriend another couple, with whom they exchange tales of their benighted neighbors' "extreme suburban smugness," thereby distinguishing themselves as an "embattled, dwindling, intellectual underground." But eventually even this community of four proves too large, too compromising to the Wheelers' sense of their exceptionalness, and they decide (but never manage) to run away to Paris to prove that they really are "special and superior to the whole thing." These novels portray the suburbanite as "the anti-suburbanite," whose status derives not from economic superiority to the working class but from the fantasy of cultural superiority to people who are like them.[11]

Suburbanization in the United States has continued apace, and by 1990 more Americans called the suburbs home than they did cities and rural areas combined.[12] And more novelists have called these demographic changes into question, as the polymorphous suburbs of condos, malls, office parks, and McMansions have yielded new opportunities for exploring alienation. Recent suburban novels are routinely marketed and treated by reviewers as contributions to the sociology of suburban life, even as they garner prestigious literary prizes. When Sinclair Lewis won the Nobel Prize in 1930, it seemed clever to think of the award as a recognition from grateful Europeans for fulfilling their impressions of the banality and bankruptcy of the dominant American culture.[13] Pulitzer and National Book Award prizes for John Updike's *Rabbit is Rich* (1981), *Rabbit at Rest* (1990), Richard Ford's *Independence Day* (1995), and Jonathan Franzen's *The Corrections* (2001), along with other nominations, suggest the continuing literary cachet of similar themes and the white middle-class discontent and self-pity they give rise to. Recent suburban novels are credited with exposing the conditions of contemporary American life: with directing "penetrating looks under the suburban veneer" in the case of Rick Moody's *Purple America* (1997); with "strip[ping] bare the cultural and moral universe of a suburb" in James Kaplan's *Two Guys from Verona: A Novel of Suburbia* (1998); with "challeng[ing] the facades of mundane and contemporary existence" in A. M. Homes's *Music For Torching* (1999), which "torches a whole genteel tradition of suburban fiction."[14] These and similar comments are often used to sell such novels, as though the suburban novel had not been going beneath the surface of the superficial good life and exposing the hollowness of its premises for eighty years. Most Americans may choose to live in suburbs, but the suburbs are readily advertised to readers as the place they love to hate.

This is not, of course, to say that the suburban novel remains unchanged since men in gray flannel suits and their wives wrung their hands over houses that all looked alike. A new generation of literary suburbanites inhabits a world of much greater peril. With the exception of John and Mary Drone in Keats's *Picture Window*, characters in 1950s novels worried obsessively about dismal outcomes but did not experience them. For all their anxiety about the future, Tom and Betsy Rath emerge not only with a renewed commitment to their marriage but also with a seaside estate within easy commuting distance of New York City which they plan to subdivide into eighty houses. Disaster averted. Things have already begun to change by the end of *Revolutionary Road*, when April Wheeler, the mother of two children, dies while trying to induce an abortion so that the move to Paris need not be cancelled and they can escape the diminished existence of mid-century suburbanites. April's recognition of the relationship between her maternity and her place in the suburbs is not a feminist insight – not even as much so as Myra Babbitt's own "small . . . rebellion" against the boredom of her domestic routine, a lament that matters primarily as yet another claim on Babbitt and stimulant to his dissatisfaction. April's impulses are instead governed by the overweening desire to rise above a banal middle-classness.

By contrast, a feminist critique of the suburbs drives Marilyn French's best-selling novel, *The Women's Room* (1977). The novel moves between the fictional narrative of another Mira and authorial reflections on the instability of a social order that depends upon the unpaid and isolated labor of women. For French the lie of the suburbs is that unskilled and under-educated women ever really enjoy the security of their husbands' paychecks and house ownership, for which they give up the prospect of interesting and autonomous lives. The standardization that matters in the novel is not that of suburban houses and furnishings but of suburban husbands, who almost without exception cruelly abandon wives and children at the same moment, resulting in suicide, suicide attempts, mental illness, and poverty for most of the women, a pattern Maria Farland traces in other 1970s feminist novels and memoirs, and carefree affluence for the men.[b] *The Women's Room* thus bears a certain family resemblance to Ira Levin's cult classic, *The Stepford Wives* (1972), the novel of suburban conformity par excellence. To a man, the robotic husbands of Stepford, Connecticut cannot abide the independence of their feminist wives and so murder them, building perfect audioanimatronic versions that never complain or make demands or need replacement.

Women are not the only ones endangered in the suburban novel since the 1970s. Rising inflation, recession, and the energy crisis during that decade

b See Maria Farland's essay in this volume, "Literary Feminisms," chapter 56, 930, 932–934.

squeezed the middle class along with other workers; since then, globalization and corporate downsizing, as well as the growth of low-wage service jobs, have prompted numerous articles and books that continue to ponder the question of whether the American middle class is "doomed."[15] The prior worry that secure, well-paid corporate employment might suppress individuality comes to seem decidedly quaint. Suburban protagonists of this later generation typically inhabit a panicky world where, as Jimmy Carter tells the public in John Updike's *Rabbit Is Rich*, Americans "think things are going to get worse instead of better." And this time the characters are right, at least about themselves. A decade earlier, in Updike's *Rabbit Redux* (1971), Harry (Rabbit) Angstrom lives in Penn Villas, an ugly subdivision of "identical houses." To the dismay of his neighbors, after his wife, Janice, leaves him, he takes in a couple of unconventional roommates – a white runaway teen and a black man – by which Rabbit reduces the "intensity of duplication" in his community and makes a small, ambivalent strike on behalf of his individuality and autonomy. When neighbors join forces to burn the house down, he experiences freedom, not regret. In *Rabbit Is Rich*, he has no room for such sentiments. He now runs a Toyota dealership that Janice inherited at a time when the "fucking world is running out of gas," but he is displaced from it by his son, a cocaine addict who embezzles more than $200,000. Toyota revokes the dealership, and to repay their debts, Janice, a budding realtor, sells their house in the toney suburb of Penn Park, "the only place," we learn in *Rabbit at Rest*, where Rabbit "has ever felt at home." In contrast with Babbitt, who embarks on a leisurely quest for spiritual fulfillment, homelessness here means losing an actual house.

The precariousness of middle-class existence is a constant theme in recent suburban novels. Most protagonists are afraid of falling, and sometimes they actually do. The title character of David Gates's *Jernigan* (1991) enjoys his ironic relation to the suburb. He is "into the degradation" of his "shitbox house" until he is fired from his job, when he tells himself "Hey, you always said you were into degradation: dig it now." One of Kaplan's two guys from Verona, New Jersey, experiences a standard middle-class malaise in which he wonders about the "goodness of the good things," until he loses his company, house, and family in a millennial stock market crash. Even suburbanites who don't lose jobs, houses, and status see themselves, as the title of one Ann Beattie novel indicates, as "falling in place," their mobility one way or another simply arrested, which produces its own emotional and spiritual crises. *Falling in Place* (1980) is one of the few suburban novels of more recent vintage in which characters really do not worry about their financial future and have no reason to, although John Knapp believes that his meaningless work in advertising is "silly," and his wife Louise acknowledges that "it doesn't seem to help us be happy" to live in such a "beautiful" place, before she asks her son whether he thinks she "make[s] a good adult." Competent adults are usually in short supply in these novels, which are dedicated to describing the numerous ways that families, not simply marriages, fall apart. Satisfaction in the suburb proves virtually inconceivable as well as unachievable.

The word "dysfunction" does not begin to describe the problems depicted in later suburban novels. Adultery and divorce and mental illness are only the most mundane difficulties; in addition to freak accidental deaths of parents and children, suicide, murder, and, in the case of Joyce Carol Oates's *Expensive People* (1968), even matricide loom large. At the cusp of the trend, Cheever's *Bullet Park* (1969), a fable of the suburbs, features a blissfully happy family that discovers it is not. Eliot Nailles adores his wife, son, and life, believing that "purpose and order underlay the roofs, trees, river and streets." But then his teenage son, Tony, decides he is too sad to get out of bed and Nailles needs drugs to make it through his commute. Lest we think Cheever has produced a novel of ordinary suburban discontent, a man named Paul Hammer inexplicably moves to Bullet Park for the sole purpose of crucifying Nailles, before just as randomly deciding to murder Tony instead. This literally senseless violence is thwarted in the act, and "everything was as wonderful, wonderful, wonderful, wonderful at it had been," which is to say, contra this mantra against despair, not so wonderful at all.

Mostly what has changed since Cheever is the idea that white middle-class people think they like their lives, that the suburbs provide them with something like "purpose and order," before the killing begins. The Knapps' ten-year-old son shoots his sister in Beattie's *Falling in Place*, and the family stops falling in place long enough for Louise finally to ask for that divorce. Paul and Elaine Weiss, in Homes's *Music for Torching*, live in a kind of ecstasy of despair, recrimination, and failure. "You can't control everything," Paul says in the beginning of the novel, after they set their house on fire to start a new life, only to come right back to the old one. Indeed, they control nothing: the novel ends with an eight-year-old sociopath loose in a school with a gun, and Paul and Elaine's younger son is killed. Violence fulfills rather than challenges the trajectories of these plots.

An exception to the narrative of suburban discontent would seem to be Richard Ford's widely acclaimed trilogy: *The Sportswriter* (1986), *Independence Day*, and *The Lay of the Land* (2006), which ends with narrator Frank Bascombe wounded by a couple of gun-wielding teens on a killing spree. Unlike most of the characters who populate suburban novels, Frank is determined, as many reviewers have observed, to take pleasure in the quotidian and to revel in its mysteries. Frank's self-conscious appreciation of a very comfortable suburban life is much harder work than his actual job in real estate. Recalling the *faux*-upbeat ending of Cheever's *Bullet Park*, Frank's life is somewhat desperately "wonderful, wonderful, wonderful, wonderful" rather than wonderful.

Discontent also remains as a constitutive feature of Gloria Naylor's *Linden Hills* (1985), a series of vignettes about a prosperous, exclusively African American suburb that traces the spiritual and cultural bankruptcy of its residents who, Babbitt-like, cannot "transform" their well-appointed houses "into that nebulous creation called a home." Linden Hills outdoes white suburbs on the scale of soullessness as measured by the residents' deracination and the scandal of their inauthenticity. "Linden Hills wasn't black; it was successful," as though the term "black bourgeoisie" were an oxymoron and one kind of class identity necessarily trumps, is intrinsically incompatible with, an inflexible racial identity.[c] If black suburbanites are contaminated by Linden Hills in this novel, it is because the place makes them virtually indistinguishable from white suburbanites, and so the residents are left with nothing but the misery of affluence.

Different demographics do produce different narratives, however, and suburbs can look rather better to those used to being outside them. In Philip Roth's *Goodbye, Columbus* (1959), Neil Klugman of Newark enjoys the privileges of suburban Short Hills during a summer romance with Brenda Patimkin, the daughter of a wealthy Jewish manufacturer. If *Linden Hills*, following Dante's *Inferno*, takes readers and residents on "a journey down to the lowest circle of hell," as proclaimed on the back cover, the 180 feet that Short Hills rises over Newark "brought one closer to heaven." Mr. Patimkin is a deeply contented man, in part because he is not a white-collar drone, engaged in meaningless work, like the male breadwinners in virtually all 1950s suburban novels, but instead a successful entrepreneur. He cannot express in words "all the satisfaction and surprise he felt about the life he had managed to build for himself and his family." Indeed, surprise as well as self-making may be a condition of his satisfaction. The second generation takes everything for granted, as part of the novella's "generational drama of assimilation," and thus can indulge in a little of the suburban discontent that

c On the substitution of racial identity and cultural difference for class identity, especially for affluent minorities, see Walter Benn Michaels's essay in this volume, "Model minorities and the minority model – the neoliberal novel," chapter 61.

Brenda's father cannot conceive of.[16] Neil is sure that Brenda's "life, which ... consisted to a large part of cornering the market on fabrics that felt soft to the skin, took on the quality of a Hundred Years' war." Neil is ironic about Brenda's sense of entitlement, but he takes the privileges themselves seriously and enjoys every piece of fresh Patimkin fruit while it lasts. Meanwhile, an African American boy in the Newark library looks at reproductions of Gauguin paintings and dreams of Tahiti, a destination hardly less attainable for him than Short Hills, which Neil knowingly approaches "at dusk, rose-colored, like a Gauguin stream."

Some forty years later Roth would devote an entire novel to probing the psyche of an almost preternaturally contented man. No one was ever less alienated from his advantages than Seymour (Swede) Levov in *American Pastoral* (1997). Swede is the Newark Jewish community's golden boy, "as close to a goy as we were going to get," a handsome star athlete who marries a former Miss New Jersey and takes over his family's glove manufacturing business. If relocation to the suburbs becomes a vehicle of assimilation for Jews and other ethnic Europeans (the Patimkin children of *Goodbye, Columbus* being a case in point), the Swede aspires to nothing less than the transcendent origins of American experience. He lives with his family on one hundred acres of pure Revolutionary War history, "out past the suburbs" in Old Rimrock, the pinnacle of his achievement, the bedrock of his complacency. The narrator, Nathan Zuckerman, a childhood Swede-worshiper, initially sees him as a man without subjectivity, whose perfect life granted him immunity from even routine disappointments and precluded self-questioning. Then Zuckerman discovers that in the 1960s the Swede's beloved daughter Merry had turned radical, blown up a general store in town, killing a man, and then gone into hiding. The novel imagines Swede's attempt to process "the worst lesson that life can teach – that it makes no sense." He is unable to believe and unable to deny what happened, that for all of his efforts and advantages life was "uncontrollable," and it shatters him.

Franklin Hata, the Korean-Japanese-American protagonist of Chang-rae Lee's *A Gesture Life* (1999), reassembles the shards of his life in the suburban town of Bedley Run, where he has lived for thirty years in one of the nicest houses and enjoys "an almost Oriental veneration as an elder." He has taken his racially appointed role to heart among the familiar strangers who are his white neighbors and friends, while also refusing the commitment to cultural difference that is central to Walter Benn Michaels's reading of the obfuscatory class politics of Lee's previous novel, *Native Speaker* (1995).[d] Franklin's

d For a reading of *Native Speaker*, see Michaels, chapter 61.

ambition is to become an exemplary suburbanite, to be "the living, breathing expression of what people here wanted – privacy and decorum and the quietude of hard-earned privilege." It separates him from other residents as well as from his suburban literary predecessors. He knows there are worse things than living in a suburb because in World War II, as a medical officer, he fell in love with a "comfort woman." He could not protect her, either from his own ambivalent desire or from the Japanese soldiers who brutally gangraped and murdered her, as we learn in flashbacks. Franklin's well-regulated life in Bedley Run is built not so much on a lie as on the American promise of second chances, an opportunity he is too "grateful" to disdain. Where others in the community feel "insecure and threatened," he embraces "the good and decent living, a cloister for those of us who are modest and unspecial." Franklin's past may raise questions about whether he deserves the privileges he enjoys, but the novel rejects the premise that there may be an ethical pay-off to not enjoying them. As the town's "primary citizen," he sees belonging not as a scourge of the soul, but as the privilege it is.

These writers and their ethnic protagonists help to clarify that suburban alienation is a luxury of racial as well as class advantages. That is, affluent white characters can indulge in the experience of spiritual homelessness in the suburb and the attendant feelings of superiority it often confers on them because no one challenges their right to be there. Belonging is something to cherish if you have actually had to earn it. Even after decades in his town, Franklin is only "ever securing" his position, not "secure in" it. This insight into the limits of homelessness predates Roth and Lee. In fact, Sinclair Lewis developed it in *Kingsblood Royal* (1947), a novel that asks to be read in light of *Babbitt*. Neil Kingsblood is a Babbitt-y, "one-hundred per cent. normal, white, Protestant, male, middle-class" Midwesterner, until he discovers a remote black ancestor and understands himself to be, by the logic of the one-drop rule, black himself. Neil is at first dismayed but soon excited, as he learns that African American culture is much cooler than his own. He is less thrilled when he loses his job and neighbors learn his secret; the Kingsbloods think their home in Sylvan Park, a "picture-window real-estate development," is "sacred and secure," but then neighbors try to kick them out, invoking racial covenants. Even the most ordinary house in an ordinary subdivision turns into an "extreme symbol of dignity and independence" in this novel, and the Kingsbloods defend themselves against the hostile mob. Neil may no longer be a fan of the culture of the white middle class, but he develops an acute appreciation for its other prerogatives, as have his neighbors. When it comes to race, spiritual homelessness is quite beside the point; it is all about the right to live where you want.

The late twentieth-century version of the house as castle is the subdivision as gated fortress. T. Coraghessan Boyle's *Tortilla Curtain* (1995) addresses how far affluent suburbanites will go to secure their well-being and property values. Delaney Mossbacher and his wife, Kyra, live in a subdivision in Topanga Canyon, where the houses are uniform but worth protecting against the encroachments of Los Angeles: "the gangbangers and taggers and carjackers they read about in the metro section over their bran toast and coffee." The novel describes how Delaney's conservative fear of gangbangers comes to overwhelm his liberal values. Over his initial protests, their subdivision builds first a gate and later a wall to enclose the whole community. The big bad city that the wall keeps at bay is represented by a hapless Mexican couple, illegal immigrants who are living down in the nearby canyon. The novel begins with Delaney's car striking Cándido Rincón, injuring him severely and endangering América, his wife, who must now work under unhealthful conditions to support them. The Rincóns can't afford a wall to protect them from Delaney, and they do want what he and his neighbors have: a "clean white house." Delaney becomes obsessed with Cándido, who makes him feel like "a victim." LA's definitive outsiders, impoverished illegal aliens, are the absurd focus of wealthy white neighbors' hysterical fears. As his liberal guilt gradually gives way to illiberal rage, Delaney becomes a proponent of the wall, willingly exchanging the "extreme symbol of dignity and independence" for maximum security, even though the wall does not keep out the real "tagger," the white neighbor's son who writes graffiti on it. Once again, the racial plot proves incompatible with the alienation plot. The white middle-class community is something to embrace rather than resist or deny.[17] *Tortilla Curtain* thus is a kind of parodic extension of the premise operating in suburban novels that deal explicitly with questions of race: revolt from the suburb only makes sense when no one else, not even the least plausible of usurpers, is threatening to take your privileges from you.

Notes

1. Edith Wharton, "The Great American Novel," *Yale Review* 16 (July 1927): 655, 646.
2. *Ibid.*, 650, 651.
3. See Catherine Jurca, *White Diaspora: The Suburb and the Twentieth-Century American Novel* (Princeton: Princeton University Press, 2001), 4–5.
4. This definition of "Babbitt" is from the online *Oxford English Dictionary*.

5. See Mark Foster, *From Streetcar to Superhighway: American City Planners and Urban Transportation, 1900–1940* (Philadelphia: Temple University Press, 1981), 47; Kenneth T. Jackson, *Crabgrass Frontier: The Suburbanization of the United States* (New York: Oxford University Press, 1985), chapter 10; Margaret Marsh, *Suburban Lives* (New Brunswick, NJ: Rutgers University Press, 1990), 129–181; Gwendolyn Wright, *Building the Dream: A Social History of Housing in America* (New York: Pantheon, 1987), chapter 11; Roland Marchand, *Advertising the American Dream: Making Way for Modernity, 1920–1940* (Berkeley and Los Angeles: University of California Press, 1985), 77–80.
6. See Leslie Fiedler, *Love and Death in the American Novel* (New York: Criterion Books, 1960).
7. See Jackson, *Crabgrass Frontier*, 203–218, 231–245, and Wright, *Building the Dream*, 240–261.
8. Frederick Allen, *The Big Change: America Transforms Itself, 1900–1950* (New York: Harper, 1952), 213.
9. William H. Whyte, Jr., "The Transients," *Fortune* 47 (May 1953): 113. See also Whyte, *Organization Man* (New York: Anchor, 1957); C. Wright Mills, *White Collar: The American Middle Classes* (New York: Oxford University Press, 1951); and David Riesman, "The Suburban Dislocation," *Annals of the American Academy of Political and Social Science* 314 (Fall 1957): 123–146.
10. "Slipped Disk," *Time* 66 (July 18, 1955), 102; "Tom Rath, Commuter," *New York Times* (July 17, 1955): sec. 7, p. 18.
11. Jurca, *White Diaspora*, 148.
12. See Kenneth T. Jackson, "America's Rush to Suburbia," *New York Times* (June 9, 1996): sec. 1, p. 15.
13. See Mark Schorer, *Sinclair Lewis: An American Life* (New York: McGraw-Hill, 1961), 553.
14. Gary Williams, review of *Purple America*, cited in Moody, *Purple America*; Kaplan, *Two Guys from Verona: A Novel of Suburbia*, back cover; reviews of *Music For Torching*, *New Orleans Times Picayune* and *Newsweek*, cited in Homes, *Music For Torching*.
15. Barbara Ehrenreich, "Is the Middle Class Doomed?" *New York Times Magazine* (September 7, 1986): 44.
16. Andrew Hoberek, *Twilight of the Middle Class: Post-World War II American Fiction and White-Collar Work* (Princeton: Princeton University Press, 2005), 90.
17. For a more utopian reading of this novel in the context of suburban racial politics, see Kathryn Knapp, " 'Ain't No Friend of Mine': Immigration Policy, the Gated Community, and the Problem with the Disposable Worker in T. C. Boyle's *Tortilla Curtain*," *Atenea* 28 (December 2008).

54

The Jewish great American novel

ANDREW HOBEREK

In his 1957 essay "The University as Villain" Saul Bellow, an inveterate critic of academia, surprisingly affirms the university employment of writers. Arguing against the cult of "Experience" which declares, "Writers have always come out of the gutter. The gutter is their proper place," Bellow contends, "The life of a civilized man is, increasingly, an internalized one, and towards this internalized life writers have been encouraged to take a gross and foolish attitude." Thus, the university-based author "may find a Whitehead or an Einstein as well worth writing about as saloon-keepers or big game hunters."[1] This should remind us that not only have many of Bellow's protagonists – Moses Herzog, Albert Corde, Abe Ravelstein – been academics, but even the most active ones – Augie March, Eugene Henderson – have been decidedly introspective. More than a surprising amendment to Bellow's anti-academic stance, his comments limn the formal program of what might be called the Jewish great American novel: the transition from the cult of experience identified with Ernest Hemingway and its replacement by a form of realism grounded in the representation of characters' cognitive and emotional states. In the hands of Bellow, Norman Mailer, and Philip Roth, the American novel abandoned an increasingly stereotyped realm of manly action and renewed itself via the sweepingly ambitious depiction of what Amy Hungerford calls, with reference to Bellow's books, "the thinking, self-contradicting, peculiar mind of a particular individual."[2] At the same time these authors reject modernist subjectivism, foregrounding instead the mind's relationship to the external world and to other minds. Bellow's and Roth's delight in urban description; Mailer's pioneering contribution to the nonfiction novel (as discussed by David Schmid elsewhere in this volume[a]); the concern with intersubjectivity that runs from Augie March's role as "a sort of Columbus of those near-at-hand" to Roth's recent use of quotation and self-conscious acts of

a David Schmid, "The nonfiction novel," chapter 59, 993–997.

imagination to expand first-person narration;[3] all these features mark postwar Jewish American writers' efforts to assimilate the lessons of the Jamesian psychological novel (whose surface decorum masks, as Carrie Bramen suggests elsewhere in this volume, a profound engagement with the material and psychic limitations on human happiness[b]) to the great American novel's traditional project of sweeping social representation. They can pursue this ambition in part because the shift from action to introspection within their fiction exemplifies a widespread postwar concern with consciousness as the site of tension between individual and society.

Bellow announces this shift from action to introspection in the opening paragraph of his first novel, *Dangling Man* (1944). "[T]his is an era of hardboiled-dom," Bellow writes:

> Today, the code of the athlete, of the tough boy . . . is stronger than ever. Do you have feelings? There are correct and incorrect ways of indicating them. Do you have an inner life? It is nobody's business but your own. Do you have emotions? Strangle them. [This code] does admit of a limited kind of candor, a closemouthed straightforwardness. But on the truest candor, it has an inhibitory effect. Most serious matters are closed to the hardboiled. They are unpracticed in introspection, and therefore badly equipped to deal with opponents whom they cannot shoot like big game or outdo in daring.

This passage remains a trial run at Bellow's signature style. Despite the all but explicit critique of Hemingway, the passage's short, declarative sentences and its blend of tough-guy vernacular ("nobody's business"), faint Anglicisms ("the truest candor"), and vaguely scientific-sounding prose ("an inhibitory effect") mimic the stoic language it decries. Tentatively introspective, it remains bound to a dour, Dostoevskean alienation with which Bellow would later express dissatisfaction, calling *Dangling Man* and *The Victim* (1947) "my M.A. and . . . my Ph.D.," apprentice books constrained by a "proper" European modernism.[4]

Bellow's true breakthrough, what Norman Podhoretz called "a new prose style, the first attempt in many years to experiment with the language in fiction,"[5] came with his third novel, the 1954 National Book Award Winner *The Adventures of Augie March* (1953). The opening sentence of *Augie March* is as distinctively Bellovian as the prose of *Dangling Man* is derivatively Hemingwayesque: "I am an American, Chicago born – Chicago, that somber city – and go at things as I have taught myself, free-style, and will make the record in my own way: first to knock, first admitted; sometimes an innocent

b Carrie Bramen, "James, pragmatism, and the realist ideal," chapter 18.

knock, sometimes a not so innocent." Here the declarative sentences of *Dangling Man* survive only as a scaffold on which Bellow erects a superstructure using participles, hyphens, colons, and semicolons. In marked counterpoint to the "somber" Chicago they invoke, these sentences are relentlessly cheerful: as peripatetic as the protagonist, the product of a mind disorganized but unwilling to be bound by a "closemouthed" hard-boiled style. They are introspective without being brooding.

Early critics of *Augie March* praised the novel as a distinctively American departure from an institutionalized, European modernism: a turn from "the well-made novel" of "Flaubert, Kafka, Gide, Henry James"[6] to the spirited vernacular of Twain's *Adventures of Huckleberry Finn* (1885).[7] But Bellow also drew upon the pre-modernist canon of European realism: as he later wrote Bernard Malamud, "I backed away from Flaubert, in the direction of Walter Scott, Balzac, and Dickens."[8] Traces of these models appear in the picaresque structure indebted to Fielding,[9] the Dickensian descriptions of Chicago, and the quirky characters that Augie meets in his adventures.[10] In neither case, however, does Bellow simply reproduce earlier literary models. Rather, he draws on both American vernacular narrative and European realism in the service of a new form able to comprehend the "internalized life" of modern man.

The opening of chapter 16 of *Augie March* dramatizes Bellow's progression toward this new form. Set in the midst of a distinctly Hemingwayesque episode – Augie's Mexican trip with his wealthy lover Thea Fenchel, who hopes to write a magazine article about training an eagle – the chapter begins with a brief (and, one wants to say, self-conscious) paragraph in Hemingway's style: "We found Thea's house ready. If it was her house. Perhaps it was Smitty's. I thought I'd find out in due time. There was no rush about it." It then segues into a longer paragraph describing the village in which Augie and Thea are to take up residence, the house in which they have rented rooms, the mother and son who serve as "cook and houseboy." This leads to a fully Bellovian paragraph in which Augie describes not his surroundings but the vacillating thoughts and feelings they provoke:

> Yes, for all my opposition and dread of the bird, wishing him a gargoyle of stone or praying he would drop dead, I saw the other side of it, and what was in it for [Thea], that she was full of brilliant energy. But I thought, What was wrong with the enjoyment of love, and what did there have to be an eagle for?

In its movement from Hemingwayesque terseness to realist description to the delineation of Augie's mental processes, this passage recapitulates Bellow's stylistic evolution, culminating in a new realism focused on the individual mind's interaction with the world. As James Wood notes, Bellow's "prose is densely 'realistic'" but departs from "the usual conventions of realism" to offer the world as "filtered through a remembering mind": "a kind of emotional cubism, whereby the mind returns repeatedly, but with variations, to the same details, and ponders and reponders."[11] Podhoretz was thus wrong to claim that the novel falls short of psychological realism, that Augie is "a character who is curiously untouched by his experience, who never changes or develops, who goes through everything yet undergoes nothing."[12] If *Augie March*, like all of Bellow's work, eschews the psychologization that Bellow associated with modernist orthodoxy and postwar therapeutic culture, it attends to individual psychology via "thick descriptions" of consciousness related to those of Wittgensteinian philosophy and the French *nouveau roman*'s phenomenologically inflected narratives.[13]

Despite his seemingly greater commitment to Hemingway, Bellow's contemporary Norman Mailer similarly turns to consciousness as the anti-Hemingwayesque site on which he will claim Hemingway's mantle. Following his much-lauded first book, the 1948 war novel *The Naked and the Dead* (discussed by John Carlos Rowe elsewhere in this volume[c]), Mailer produced *Barbary Shore* (1951), a commercial and critical failure that draws the residents of a Greenwich Village rooming house into a heavy-handed allegory of Cold War politics. While just as poorly received by readers and critics, *The Deer Park* (1955) takes malaise and failure as its subjects in a manner that anticipates Mailer's subsequent turn – in *Advertisements for Myself* (1959) and afterward – towards chronicling his own career's ups and downs. *The Deer Park* raises the specter of Hemingway via its obvious revision of *The Sun Also Rises* (1926). Mailer's narrator Sergius O'Shaugnessy, a former Air Force officer rendered psychologically impotent by the trauma of flying bombing missions in Korea, spends his time drinking with the Hollywood aristocracy and their bohemian hangers-on in the California resort town of Desert D'or. O'Shaugnessy's affair with an actress cures his impotence but ends unhappily. He studies bullfighting in Mexico, then returns to the USA to write a novel about his experiences, giving up when he realizes his prose "was inevitably imitative of that excellently exiguous mathematician, Mr [*sic*] Ernest Hemingway." Mailer himself escapes this trap, however, in the same way Bellow had, by narrating his characters' cognitive and emotional processes. Mailer of course cultivated a reputation as a man of action, and in his

c See John Carlos Rowe, "US novels and US wars," chapter 49, 822–823.

controversial essay "The White Negro" (1957) he celebrated "the psychopath" who "knows instinctively that to express a forbidden impulse actively is far more beneficial to him than merely to confess the desire in the safety of a doctor's room."[14] Mailer's writing, however, suggests that inaction can be just as useful aesthetically, since it is not action but the fluctuating mental processes of the active and the inactive alike that provide his subject matter.

Another typically Maileresque aspect of *The Deer Park*, its non-Jewish protagonist, raises the question of what exactly is Jewish about the Jewish great American novel. In her account of Bellow's repudiation of Hemingway in *Dangling Man*, Ruth Wisse describes Bellow's style in identitarian terms: "Just as Isaac Babel had felt that an Odessan Jew could release untapped energies of Russian literature, Bellow knew he had something joyous to add to American literature by talking as demonstratively – as Semitically – as he knew how."[15] It is more useful, however, to identify the Jewish great American novel's emergence at the specific moment in Jewish American history when declining anti-Semitism and an expanding white-collar workforce allowed Jews, like other white ethnics, to enter the middle-class mainstream.[16] Although we refer to the postwar decades as a time of Jewish "assimilation," postwar representations of Jews ambivalently emphasized both their newly mainstream status and their valuable resistance to the putatively homogenizing tendencies of white-collar middle-class life. In Jonathan Freedman's formulation, Jews exemplified a new form of white ethnicity "shaped not only by . . . ethnics themselves . . . but by nonethnic white people who came to those ethnics for specific things they came to feel were missing in their own increasingly anomic postwar experience."[17] Thus the Jewish great American novel departs from what Tim Prchal, in his chapter in this volume, identifies as the "immigrant adjustment novel" of the early twentieth century, in which authors like Anzia Yezierska and Abraham Cahan addressed the process (and in some cases the costs) of immigrants' successful adaptation to American life.[18] The protagonists of Bellow, Mailer, and Roth, by contrast, are American-born Jews – and sometimes not even Jews at all – whose increasingly taken-for-granted Americanness allows them to not only affirm but also question mainstream values.

While novels such as Herman Wouk's *Marjorie Morningstar* (1955), which Leslie Fiedler called "the first fictional celebration of the mid-twentieth-century *détente* between the Jews and middle-class America,"[19] took the Jewish movement into the mainstream as their subject matter, the Jewish great American novel went beyond this concern with content. In their detailed exposition of characters' mental and emotional lives Bellow, Mailer, and Roth found the perfect formal vehicle for transforming marginality into an aesthetically generative condition. In 1964 the social scientist Milton Gordon's *Assimilation in American Life* offered an account of the immigrant as "marginal man" who "Frustrated and not fully accepted by the broader social world he wishes to enter ... and beset by conflicting cultural standards" exhibits "personality traits of insecurity, moodiness, hypersensitivity, excessive self-consciousness, and nervous strain."[20] In the current context Gordon's formulation seems less like a description of immigrant identity than of the Jewish American fiction by which, one suspects, he may have been influenced. Foregrounding their protagonists' simultaneous immersion in and dissent from social constraints, the architects of the Jewish great American novel turned marginality to advantage by making it the matrix of an interior form of individualism appropriate to a world of putative "organization men."[21]

The Jewish great American novel ultimately became the dominant form for Jewish American fiction, beating out its postwar competitor, Malamud's American reinvention of classical Yiddish fiction by authors like Sholem Aleichem and Isaac Bashevis Singer. Malamud's first novel, *The Natural* (1952), clearly stakes a claim to great American novel status with its story of baseball player Roy Hobbs's checkered career. There are intimations of the Jewish great American novel in Hobbs's likeable unlikeability, his ambivalent deliberations about the women competing for his affections, and his final capitulation to pressure to betray his talent, but Malamud's preferred mode is less psychological realism than symbolism. He limns Hobbs's character through outward signs such as his superstitious attachment to his homemade bat, Wonderboy, and his unrealistically insatiable appetite. Moreover, Malamud's work tends toward nostalgia, whether the heartland nostalgia of *The Natural* or the nostalgia for the vanishing urban, ethnic milieu of his short fiction and *The Assistant* (1957).[22] Malamud's fabulistic form has exerted an important influence on subsequent novelists, most notably Cynthia Ozick and most recently Michael Chabon. But it did not come to exemplify American fiction as such the way the work of Bellow, Mailer, and Roth did.

Both Malamud's fiction and the Jewish great American novel seek to make their characters' dilemmas representative of universal, and not simply ethnic, concerns, but the latter more successfully exploits the thematic and formal opportunities posed by postwar Jews' historical situation. Consider Roth's first book, the short story collection *Goodbye, Columbus* (1959). The title novella – with protagonist Neil Klugman ambivalently positioned between the earlier generation represented by his working-class aunt and uncle and the businessman Ben Patimkin, on one hand, and the well-off Patimkin children, on the other – can convincingly be read as a parable for suburban Jewish assimilation (as discussed also by Catherine Jurca in her chapter in this volume[d]). But Ross Posnock argues that Roth treats the "essentialist melodrama of assimilation" as "irrelevan[t]" to what really interests him: Klugman's romance with the wealthy Brenda Patimkin and, even more importantly, "the messy Americanness of appropriation and self-(re)invention" that marks Klugman's trajectory through and beyond this romance.[23] *Goodbye, Columbus* might thus be read as Roth's allegory of the genesis of the Jewish great American novel itself. Klugman rejects both nostalgia and deracination for the role of the marginal man, whose "excessive self-conscious" Roth, like Bellow and Mailer, sees not as a social-scientific pathology but as a formal opportunity.

Bellow's books following *Augie March* similarly treat postwar Jews' insider/outsider status both concretely and as a metaphor for broader, at times existential concerns. *Seize the Day* (1956) follows failed actor Tommy Wilhelm through a series of encounters with his ex-wife, his disappointed father, and his spiritual (and, disastrously, financial) adviser Dr. Tamkin, culminating with Wilhelm sobbing inarticulately – "past words, past reason, coherence" – at a stranger's funeral. A brief return to the tighter structure of his pre-*Augie* novels, *Seize the Day* nonetheless provides a forum for self-exploration in Wilhelm's conversations with those close to him, while the final scene foregrounds both the desirability and the difficulty of intersubjective communication. *Henderson the Rain King* (1959) returns to *Augie March*'s first-person narration and picaresque style for the story of the wealthy, Gentile Eugene Henderson's adventures in Africa. As Henderson's initials hint, the novel offers yet another revision of Hemingway. While Henderson might seem like the antithesis of Tommy Wilhelm, he too bemoans his ineffectuality. His trip to Africa provides an opportunity not for manly display (in his effort to destroy the frogs fouling one tribe's cistern, he blows up the cistern itself) but for self-exploration, alone and with the African philosopher-king Dahfu. In *Herzog* (1964) Bellow alternates the story of his title character, a professor of romantic literature still reeling from the collapse of his second marriage, with the philosophizing letters that he writes to the famous living and dead.

At the start of the 1960s, Joseph Heller's *Catch-22* (1961) provided a kind of hinge between the Jewish great American novel and the anti-realistic, self-referential narratives that would, as Ursula Heise notes in her chapter in this volume, constitute the first wave of

d See Catherine Jurca, chapter 53, "The American novel and the rise of the suburbs."

postmodernism.[e] While Heller's introspective protagonist Yossarian bears the imprint of the Jewish great American novel – a style Heller would embrace more fully in first-person works like the story of middle-class alienation *Something Happened* (1974) and the King David-narrated *God Knows* (1984) – *Catch-22*'s dark, absurdist humor and vision of society itself as a conformist organization more clearly anticipate the work of Thomas Pynchon and other nonrealist experimental novelists.

But Bellow and his compatriots experimented in this period as well. *Herzog*'s turn to the epistolary exemplifies these authors' mid to late-sixties exploration of different forms of first-person monologue. Mailer's contribution to this trend is *Why Are We in Vietnam?* (1967), a novel about a wealthy young Texan named DJ whose story of enlisting in the army following a disillusioning Alaskan hunting trip with his father may, Mailer leads us to believe, be just the late-night patter of a literal African American disc jockey. But while *An American Dream* (Mailer's 1965 novel about an ex-congressman who murders his wife) and *Why Are We in Vietnam?* restored Mailer's reputation as a novelist in the eyes of some critics, he became increasingly known as a writer of books that straddled the line between fiction and nonfiction. In founding examples of the New Journalism like *The Presidential Papers* (1963) and *The Armies of the Night* (1968), Mailer seems motivated not only by the desire to bring novelistic techniques to writing about current events, but also by the realization that he himself might provide better grist for self-exploration than any invented protagonist. Mailer makes the masculinist ethos he imbibed from Hemingway – drafting *The Deer Park*, he notes, "I was more tired than I had ever been in combat"[24] – a subject for self-examination. *Armies of the Night* –subtitled "History as a Novel, the Novel as History" – likewise puts on display the decidedly nonheroic participation of the character "Norman Mailer" in the 1967 Pentagon protest.

Roth's experimentation with the monologue, meanwhile, produced his first novelistic masterpiece, *Portnoy's Complaint* (1969). Roth's earlier novels, *Letting Go* (1962) and *When She Was Good* (1967), were, as Morris Dickstein notes, "still written under the sign of Henry James."[25] We should not underestimate the role of James's writing as a model for Roth, a body of work that for all its un-Rothlike decorum is committed to the same "relaxing of defenses . . . surrender of control, [and] immersion in intense experience" that drive Roth's fiction at its most excruciatingly revelatory.[26] But in a by-now familiar pattern, Roth arrives at *Portnoy*'s idiosyncratic style in reaction to a canonical

e See Ursula Heise, chapter 58, "Postmodern novels," 968–974.

version of the well-made novel. As Roth subsequently claimed, *Portnoy* emerged from several pieces, including "several thousand words on the subject of adolescent masturbation" rescued from an experimental monologue in the style of a traveling lecture accompanying a "slide show [depicting] full-color enlargements of the private parts, fore and aft, of the famous."[27] The "psychoanalytic monologue" that ultimately provided *Portnoy*'s form lays the groundwork for Roth's subsequent work in two important ways: by giving shape to Roth's brilliant set-pieces on childhood and sex and by allowing him to combine "the fantastic element" with "realistic documentation."[28]

Despite scenes like the protagonist's threesome with his model girlfriend and a prostitute in Rome, moreover, the novel is hardly the simple expression of countercultural values of sexual liberation that proponents and detractors alike declared it to be. This reading underplays the obviously conflicted nature of the book's sex scenes and ignores the sections devoted to Alexander Portnoy's New Jersey boyhood. Portnoy fantasizes, for instance, having grown up to become not New York's swinging Assistant Commissioner of Human Opportunity but a happily married, softball-playing man of the old neighborhood who "cannot imagine myself living out my life any other place but here." Far from ironic, this passage reflects *Portnoy*'s true innovation, which is to take the characteristic fifties conflict between individual desire and social constraints and effectively double each of its terms: family becomes a site of sensual fulfillment as well as repression; sex a site of constraint as well as license. "The joke on Portnoy," Roth remarked in a 1969 interview, "is that for him breaking the taboo turns out to be as unmanning in the end as honoring it."[29]

Roth's ambivalent relationship to both sides of the cultural conflict emerging in the 1960s proves immensely productive for his subsequent career, and can be usefully contrasted with Bellow's response to the counterculture in *Mr. Sammler's Planet* (1970). Critics generally take this novel – with its story of Holocaust survivor Artur Sammler's encounters with promiscuous and irresponsible younger relatives, a black pickpocket who threateningly exposes himself to Sammler, and a campus activist who interrupts Sammler's Columbia lecture on British intellectuals of the 1930s to call him an "effete old shit" whose "balls are dry" – as marking Bellow's shift into reaction. It is perhaps more revelatory, however, to consider the novel as posing the formal problem of how to foreground marginality in a culture where difference has become an increasingly mainstream value. Echoing his earlier reaction against modernism, Bellow has Sammler call for a renewed classicism – "Make peace therefore with intermediacy and representation. But choose higher representations" – even as he defines such classicism as the site of true creativity in a society characterized by the paradoxically conformist pursuit of originality. In this way Bellow reorients the Jewish great American novel's traditional interplay of transgression and self-examination, of individual desire and social constraints, around opposition to what he characterizes as the new conventionality of the counterculture.

Bellow's critique of the counterculture anticipates his subsequent objection to what Walter Benn Michaels describes, in his chapter in this volume, as the contemporary novel of identity, an objection based not only on the fact that such fiction privileges the group over the individual but also, perhaps even more centrally, on its status as prepackaged pseudo-individualism.[f] Bellow's redefinition of conservatism as a form of besieged true individualism, which heralded his emergence as the laureate of neoconservatism, allowed him to maintain his characteristically fifties sense of embattled individuality in the face of what seemed like the sixties endorsement of his position. But the increasingly explicit politics that accompanied this move came at some cost to the flexibility and open-mindedness central to the Jewish great American novel's dramas of consciousness.[30] Bellow's great late books, such as *Humboldt's Gift* (1975), *The Dean's December* (1982), and *Ravelstein* (2000), work primarily as novels of ideas that are, as Robert Chodat says elsewhere in this volume of all Bellow's novels, "deeply suspicious of the intellect's ambitions."[g] At their best these books still frame their intellectual debates as conflicts among believable, self-questioning characters. *Humboldt's Gift*, for instance, mounts a critique of liberalism as the realm of abstract ideas through the medium of a protagonist, Charlie Citrine, who himself professionally propagates such ideas. Once much given to abstractions ("Brutal Wall Street stood for power, and the Bowery . . . was the accusing symbol of weakness"), Citrine finds himself increasingly drawn to the concrete, an attraction that emerges among other places in frequent nostalgic catalogues of double decker buses, hot fudge sundaes, and vaudeville seals. More than just adept characterization, such passages dramatize the way in which Bellow's paradoxical position (a novelist of ideas opposed to ideas) breaks down the novel's traditional ability to contain such details in a meaningful form. Here Bellow, who began his career transcending Hemingway, ironically produces something not too

f See Walter Benn Michaels, chapter 61, "Model minorities and the minority model – the neoliberal novel," 1017.

g Robert Chodat, "Philosophy and the American novel," chapter 39, 665.

distant in its nostalgic way from the Hemingway-inflected minimalism then appearing from writers like Joan Didion and Raymond Carver.

Where Bellow in the late 1960s recasts the conflict between individual and society as a narrative of embattled conservatism, Roth rejects the simple form of this dichotomy and in the process redoubles the Jewish great American novel's capacity for self-interrogation. Despite its conclusion, with the heretofore-invisible analyst delivering the "PUNCH LINE" "Now vee may perhaps to begin. Yes?," *Portnoy's* lesson does not take root immediately. Roth's next few novels explore the free-play aspect of *Portnoy* in ways that make him seem like both a budding postmodernist and a neo-Malamudian fabulist: *Our Gang* (1971) offers a surreal satire of the Nixon administration; *The Breast* (1972) rewrites Kafka as the story of a man transformed into a giant mammary; and *The Great American Novel* (1973) (in which, Roth would write, "the tendency to comedy that's been present even in my most somber books and stories was allowed to take charge of my imagination"[31]) tells the mythic and frequently unrealistic tale of a fictional World War II-era baseball team. *My Life as a Man* (1974) and *The Professor of Desire* (1977) return to the more realistic treatment of sexually conflicted intellectual protagonists. But it is *The Ghost Writer* (1979) – featuring the first appearance of Roth's great alter ego Nathan Zuckerman (a somewhat different character with the same name had appeared in *My Life as a Man*) – that marks the emergence of Roth's mature style, blending autobiographical realism with postmodern or fabulistic touches. Thus in *The Ghost Writer* a young Zuckerman with similarities to a young Roth meets and stays with his literary idol E. I. Lonoff, meeting in Lonoff's home a young woman whom he imagines, in a section of the novel, as an Anne Frank who has secretly survived the Holocaust. A similar elaboration of alternate histories distinguishes *The Counterlife* (1987), which imagines diverging lives and deaths for Zuckerman and his brother Henry; *Operation Shylock: A Confession* (1993), in which Philip Roth travels to Israel and meets another Philip Roth who claims to be a Mossad agent; and *The Plot Against America* (2004), about a young Philip Roth's experiences under the Nazi-friendly presidency of Charles Lindbergh. These alternate realities clearly register Roth's impatience with the assertion that fiction with autobiographical elements is simply autobiography – with the misreading of *Portnoy* as "a confession in the guise of a novel" rather than "a novel in the guise of a confession."[32]

Where Mailer recreates his career by bringing to nonfiction the techniques of the novel, then, Roth reanimates the traditional novel by splicing it with autobiography – albeit autobiography spiked with liberal doses of pure imagination. Thus in *Zuckerman Unbound* Roth's protagonist confronts readers of his novel *Carnovsky* who "had mistaken impersonation for confession" and family members angry at what they perceive as the public airing of private conflicts. Through this device Roth brings the artist's prerogative into play alongside sex and family as another fruitful site for exploring the interplay between transgression and constraint.

At its best, the Jewish great American novel understands the tension between individual and society not as existential dilemma but as formal opportunity: the interface that renews the novel's vocation as a medium for comprehending both consciousness and the external world. Thus Mailer, in many ways the most solipsistic of writers, achieves arguably his greatest triumph with *The Executioner's Song*, his 1979 book about the condemned Utah murderer Gary Gilmore. Although this book contains numerous excerpts from documentary materials – Gilmore's letters to his girlfriend Nicole Baker, records of jailhouse interviews, and so forth – it is far from a simple transcript. For one thing, Mailer is twice distanced from these materials since they are the product not of his research but that of his collaborator Lawrence Schiller; for another the book self-consciously exploits the form of the "true crime" genre which despite its déclassé status harkens back to the English novel's emergence from broadsheets and other popular genres dedicated to representing crime. If *The Executioner's Song* shares what David Schmid identifies elsewhere in this volume as the nonfiction novel's constitutive interest in "the relationship between violence and American reality,"[h] its power stems from a fundamentally novelistic source: the "empathetic identification with people very different from himself" that, as Dickstein notes, enables Mailer to set aside "ego" and "pet ideas" and treat his favored themes immanently.[33] While almost hyperbolically drawn to protagonists unlike their author – the pharaonic Egyptians of *Ancient Evenings* (1983), Jesus Christ in *The Gospel According to the Son* (1997), Adolf Hitler in *The Castle in the Forest* (2007) – Mailer's late works seldom reach the heights of *The Executioner's Song*, largely because they fail to achieve this quality of immersion.

Roth's genius, by contrast, is the ability to transform even the most autobiographical of materials into subjects for "empathetic identification" – to transform himself into a character, as he does literally in novels like *Operation Shylock* and *The Plot Against America*, as well as in *The Facts* (1988), the memoir whose afterword features Nathan Zuckerman's critical dissection of his creator's recounting of events. Roth has, however, been accused of his own form of solipsism, of being unable to write about characters unlike

h Schmid, chapter 59, 996.

himself – especially women. The female characters of *The Human Stain*, for instance, tend with periodic exceptions toward caricature: Faunia Farley is an erotic fantasy, Delphine Roux a stereotype of intolerant feminism, Ernestine Silk an icon of dignified black womanhood.[34] Roth's inability to supply some characters with the kind of rich, self-contradictory detail that gives the illusion of reality does not necessarily indict the form of the novel of consciousness, however.

Indeed, Erica Jong's unfortunately underread 1973 novel *Fear of Flying* tackles precisely the issues of familial conflict, sex, and individual creativity that preoccupy Roth's great characters from Portnoy to Zuckerman to Mickey Sabbath of *Sabbath's Theater* (1995), and with no less sexual frankness. Like a Roth character, Jong's protagonist engages in a comic (and ultimately fruitless) quest for "the zipless fuck" that will be "free of all remorse and guilt." And like all her male colleagues, Jong evinces a cold-eyed skepticism about psychoanalysis and therapeutic culture – which unlike them she understands as means of enforcing patriarchal social codes. Jong's example suggests that behind their mutual antagonism the Jewish great American novel and feminism actually share a number of preoccupations.

In his most recent novels, moreover, Roth has found a way to link his characters' private or personal concerns with broader historical themes. Roth has, in the past, held strong and publicly articulated political positions, although his early political pieces such as the Swiftian essay "Cambodia: A Modest Proposal" (1970) or *Our Gang* seem outside the main line of his writing. While he found a model for connecting the political with the personal in the work of the authors – Witold Gombrowicz, Danilo Kiš, Milan Kundera, and others – whom he has published in his "Writers from the Other Europe" series for Penguin, this model has limited use in the US context: Portnoy, Zuckerman, and Sabbath may experience tension between themselves and society, but never outright state oppression. The recent Zuckerman novels known as the American Trilogy, however – *American Pastoral* (1997), *I Married a Communist* (1998), and *The Human Stain* – repeatedly return to the decades of the Jewish great American novel's nascence to offer a retrospective history of personal life as filtered through such phenomena as McCarthyism, the counterculture, and the postwar intellectual cult of individualism.[35] An important predecessor of these works is E. L. Doctorow's *The Book of Daniel*, which in 1971 inaugurated a new, retrospective phase of Jewish American fiction by making its sixties radical protagonist the son of a fictionalized Julius and Ethel Rosenberg. But whereas Doctorow's subsequent historical fictions tend toward the flat characterization and other stylistic qualities of postmodernism,[36] Roth's historicist turn enlarges and deepens his realist commitments. The American trilogy both expands the novel of consciousness outward to encompass a new strain of Dreiserian realism (visible in the stories of American success, failure, and unhappiness to which Zuckerman serves as witness) and spurs it on to the self-conscious investigation of its own history, and the larger histories with which it intersects. From this retrospective vantage point, it becomes that much clearer that the Jewish great American novel emerges from the same climate of commitment to the personal that drove such contemporaneous phenomena as psychoanalysis, the counter-culture, and feminism. While the authors I have been describing generally depict these phenomena as the antitheses of their work, we may perhaps more accurately describe them as competitors.

Notes

1. Saul Bellow, "The University as Villain," *The Nation* 185.16 (November 16, 1957): 362–363.
2. Amy Hungerford, *The Holocaust of Texts: Genocide, Literature, and Personification* (Chicago: University of Chicago Press, 2003), 135.
3. On the "aesthetic of quotation and conversation" in the novels of Roth's American trilogy – *American Pastoral* (1997), *I Married a Communist* (1998), and *The Human Stain* (2000) – see Robert Chodat, "Fictions Public and Private: On Philip Roth," *Contemporary Literature* 56.4 (2005): 690; on their narrator Nathan Zuckerman's imaginative reconstruction of others' lives via acts of "evocative guesswork" see Ross Posnock, *Philip Roth's Rude Truth: The Art of Immaturity* (Princeton: Princeton University Press, 2006), 104, 206–219.
4. Maggie Simmons, "Free to Feel: Conversation with Saul Bellow" (1979), in *Conversations with Saul Bellow*, ed. Gloria L. Cronin and Ben Siegel (Jackson: University Press of Mississippi, 1994), 161.
5. Norman Podhoretz, "The Adventures of Saul Bellow" (1959), in *Doings and Undoings: The Fifties and After in American Writing* (New York: Noonday, 1964), 216.
6. *Ibid.*
7. R. W. B. Lewis, *The American Adam: Innocence, Tragedy, and Tradition in the Nineteenth Century* (Chicago: University of Chicago Press, 1955), 198.
8. Quoted in James Atlas, *Bellow: A Biography* (New York: Random House, 2000), 177.
9. *Ibid.*, 175.
10. Joyce was also a model for Bellow, but Joyce as bard of Dublin and its larger-than-life inhabitants rather than as modernist experimentalist (*ibid.*, 170–171).
11. James Wood, "Give All," review of James Atlas, *Bellow: A Biography*, *The New Republic* 223.20 (November 13, 2000): 37.

12. Podhoretz, "The Adventures of Saul Bellow," 218.
13. Robert Chodat, "Beyond Science and Supermen: Bellow and Mind at Mid-Century," *Texas Studies in Language and Literature* 45.4 (Winter 2003): 395, 391–425 throughout. See also Chodat, *Worldly Acts and Sentient Things: The Persistence of Agency from Stein to DeLillo* (Ithaca, NY: Cornell University Press, 2008), 89–119.
14. Norman Mailer, *Advertisements for Myself* (1959; Cambridge, MA: Harvard University Press, 1992), 346.
15. Ruth R. Wisse, *The Modern Jewish Canon: A Journey through Language and Culture* (New York: Free Press, 2000), 297.
16. See Ira Katznelson, *When Affirmative Action Was White: An Untold History of Racial Inequality in Twentieth-Century America* (New York: Norton, 2005), 103.
17. Jonathan Freedman, *Klezmer America: Jewishness, Ethnicity, Modernity* (New York: Columbia University Press, 2007), 138. See also see my chapter " 'The So-Called Jewish Novel'," in *The Twilight of the Middle Class: Post-World War II American Fiction and White-Collar Work* (Princeton: Princeton University Press, 2005), 70–94.
18. Tim Prchal, "New Americans and the immigrant novel," chapter 25, 431. See also Freedman, *Klezmer America*, 168–169.
19. Leslie A. Fiedler, *Love and Death in the American Novel* (1966; New York, Stein and Day, 1959), 258.
20. Milton M. Gordon, *Assimilation in American Life: The Role of Race, Religion, and National Origins* (New York: Oxford University Press, 1964), 57; see also Freedman's discussion of Gordon's intellectual cohort and this passage, *Klezmer America*, 136, 273–274.
21. William H. Whyte, *The Organization Man* (1956; Garden City, NY: Anchor, 1957). The classic reading of post-World War II US fiction in these terms is Tony Tanner, *City of Words: American Fiction 1950–1970* (New York: Harper & Row, 1971). Timothy Melley provides a theoretically and historically informed update of Tanner's argument in *Empire of Conspiracy: The Culture of Paranoia in Postwar America* (Ithaca, NY: Cornell University Press, 2000).
22. Cf. Wisse, *The Modern Jewish Canon*, 292.
23. Posnock, *Philip Roth's Rude Truth*, 101.
24. Mailer, *Advertisements for Myself*, 243.
25. Morris Dickstein, *Leopards in the Temple: The Transformation of American Fiction 1945–1970* (Cambridge, MA: Harvard University Press, 1999), 218.
26. Posnock, *Philip Roth's Rude Truth*, 121, 118–124 throughout.
27. Philip Roth, *Reading Myself and Others* (New York: Farrar, Straus and Giroux, 1975), 36.
28. *Ibid.*, 41.
29. *Ibid.*, 19.
30. Cf. Dickstein, *Leopards in the Temple*, 176.
31. Roth, *Reading Myself*, 75.
32. *Ibid.*, 218.
33. Dickstein, *Leopards in the Temple*, 160.

34. For a dissenting view, see Posnock, *Philip Roth's Rude Truth*, 229–233. In my view Posnock too readily applauds the elements of interiority Roth gives these characters, while disregarding the way Roth uses the feminist Roux – whose chief sin is her own "addict[ion] to caricature" (231) – to preemptively thwart his own potential critics.
35. As Posnock pithily puts it, in the American trilogy "Schtick recedes, history enters" (*ibid.*, 46).
36. Fredric Jameson famously describes Doctorow's *Ragtime* (1970) as an exemplar of postmodern "pastiche," in *Postmodernism, Or, The Cultural Logic of Late Capitalism* (Durham, NC: Duke University Press, 1991), 21–22. For a more positive account of *Ragtime* as an example of postmodern style, see Hillary Chute, "*Ragtime, Kavalier & Clay*, and the Framing of Comics," *Modern Fiction Studies* 54.2 (Summer 2008): 268–301.

55

The Beats and the 1960s

ROBERT FAGGEN

The history of the "Beat" novelists and their descendants in the 1960s really begins somewhere in mid nineteenth-century American fiction and poetry, particularly with Melville and Whitman. The seemingly autobiographical invocations to the self and a sprawling, erotic landscape found a willing ear in both Jack Kerouac and Allen Ginsberg. Kerouac's empathy with seekers, wanderers, and outcasts hearkens to Melville's turning to "mariners, renegades, and castaways," as he called his characters in *Moby-Dick* (1851); all of Kerouac's writing has the force of being a new "Song of the Open Road," if not, more accurately, songs of the open *roads*. The analogies between the nineteenth-century American writers and the Beats – both in style and thought – also reveal the extent to which all had, though in different ways, transcendent, if not religious aims. Any notion that the Beats were merely about being "rebels" or "cool" or "counterculture" ignores the fundamental positive aim apparent in almost all their writing – a desire for some kind of liberation toward a better and spiritual plane of existence. However much that vision became denigrated, parodied, or sold out, it was a fundamental part of the writing from the beginning – even in the very conception of Beat. Whether Kerouac was writing about his perennial muse Neal Cassady, or Burroughs was writing about "junk," the inscrutable things, the ultimate things of life, remained in the forefront of their most outrageous visions.

Because the publications of Ginsberg's *Howl*, (1956) Kerouac's *On the Road* (1957), and Burroughs's *Naked Lunch* (1959) span the second half of the 1950s, it is too easy to locate the context of Beat writing in McCarthyism and the putative suburban optimism of that moment. Kerouac and Ginsberg were boiled much longer in the cauldron of the late Depression 1930s and the postwar 1940s; certainly this context pertains to Burroughs as well. The world that went into the making of the signal work of Beat literature, *On the Road*, was 1940s America. And we are now well aware that Kerouac's more spontaneous version of it – the scroll version – emanated from his typewriter in 1951, not 1957.[1] A novel with a less innovative style, *The Town and the City*, also appeared in 1951, but it already reveals some of Kerouac's deeper concerns about Beat life and oscillations.

Kerouac did not often reflect on the writing process, and he was not given to pronouncements about writing. Nor did he live long enough to become an elder statesman of letters. Unlike the rather brilliantly self-promoting Ginsberg, Kerouac remained private, sensitive, suffering, and quick to capitulate to the demons that drove him deeper into drink. But when he did reflect about what "Beat" meant – it was a word he had used in *On the Road* and even earlier – Kerouac could be precise and revealing:

> The Beat Generation, that was a vision that we had, John Clellon Holmes and I, and Allen Ginsberg in an even wilder way, in the late forties and early fifties, of a generation of crazy, illuminated hipsters suddenly riding and roaming America, serious, curious, bumming and hitchhiking anywhere, ragged, beatific in an ugly graceful new way – a vision gleaned from the way we had heard the word "beat" spoken on streetcorners on Times Square and in the Village, in other cities in the downtown city night of postwar America – beat, meaning down and out but full of intense conviction . . . It never meant juvenile delinquent, it meant characters of special spirituality who didn't gang up but were solitary Bartlebies staring out the dead wall wind of our civilization – the subterranean heroes who'd finally turned from the "freedom" machine of the West and were taking drugs, digging bop, having flashes of insight, experiencing a "derangement of the senses," talking strange, being poor, and glad, prophesying a new style for American culture.[2]

In the rhythmic stream typical of his most successful writing, Kerouac succinctly covers the landscape here – from the idea of "Beat" as "down" but also – *pace* Yeats – positively full of "intense conviction." And the origin was very much Times Square (so different from the post-Giuliani sanitized version of the twenty-first century), filled with drifters, dope addicts, grifters, and jazz improvisers. But Kerouac's play on "Beat" and "beatific," his commingling of the downtrodden and the spiritual (particularly as he envisions it in Bartleby, Melville's remarkable figure of suicidal stoicism), gives a sense of the complexity of the idea as it informed his and his cohorts' fiction. It was a vision of hope and despair inextricably mixed.

On The Road was not the first Beat novel, even if Kerouac first drafted it in a three-week fit of typing on a single scroll in 1951, for the novel was not published until 1957. John Clellon Holmes's *Go* (1952) can probably lay some claim to that distinction, certainly in content, if not in any kind of indelible or highly influential style. A *roman-à-clef*, *Go* revolves around the fragile young marriage of Paul Hobbes (a thinly disguised version of Holmes himself) and his wife Kathryn as they whirl in the orbit of Gene Pasternak (Jack Kerouac), David Stofsky (Allan Ginsberg), and Hart Kennedy (Neal Cassady). We witness the scene through the eyes of one of its more skeptical participants. Ginsberg's ecstatic, visionary moments and excesses form the core of the book, but Pasternak, the Kerouac character, gives what was almost certainly the first expression of the Beat vision as "a sort of revolution of the soul."

This existential vision has the quality of Dostoevsky. And Kerouac and Holmes were both immersed in the Russian novelist at the time. *Go* has some of the quality of narrative polyphony characteristic of Dostoevsky's novels, avoiding landing on a single defining voice. Hobbes's "rationalism" is but that of one character. Each character appears to be one of the "devils" caught in the whirlwind of Pasternak's vision.

Holmes depicted the fervor of the "something" that was happening in terms of music. Bop became the music of the Beats and hipsters, and the quintessential subterranean Times Square jazz spot was the "Go Hole," where

> in this modern jazz, [young people] heard something rebel and nameless that spoke for them, and their lives knew a gospel for the first time. It was more than music; it became an attitude toward life, a way of walking, a language and a costume, and these introverted kids (emotional outcasts of a war they had been too young to join, or in which they had lost their innocence), who had never belonged anywhere before, now felt somewhere at last.

Holmes sees a new kind of Jazz Age, perhaps less innocent, more rebellious, more introverted, more "outcast" than the previous one. Here, as throughout, Holmes narrates wild excesses of emotion that crash and dissipate:

> When the music began, silence swept the room as if by command. As the sound built slowly from an eerie, beautiful geometry of ensemble phrases to the wild tumult of some tenor sax solo, the hushed attention of the audience would be split by the thud-thud of stamping feet, an occasional "go" would signify approval and finally, during a piercing trumpet chorus, two enthusiasts in the rear would become totally "gone" and start to babble and laugh.

What Hobbes (Holmes) sees and hears at the "Go Hole" is embodied in Hart Kennedy, the representation of Neal Cassady, a man who "move[s] with itchy calculation and whose reddish hair and broken nose gave him an expression of shrewd, masculine ugliness." Hart's hard-core, Western masculinity combines with his frenetic movement to make him the authentic demiurge to whom everyone turns. Stofsky and Pasternak (Ginsberg and Kerouac) become, as they did in life, entranced by the dancing devil Hart (Cassady). Capturing precisely Kerouac's deep preoccupation with Dostoevsky in the 1940s, Holmes reveals the analogies young Kerouac made between Cassady and the mad, suicidal Kirilov of Dostoevsky's *Devils* (1872), who "couldn't stand ecstasy for more than a split second." Hart/Cassady "can stand it all the time, and all of life is ecstasy to him!"

Go is both a Beat novel and a novel about the "Beats." It is an interesting and well-executed novel about fascinating characters; it provides a lucid glimpse into the ferment of the Beat world as it had been developing in the late 1940s. Norman Mailer, in his provocative 1959 essay *The White Negro*, described the Beat and the hipster as American existentialist keyed into the fear of instant death from either the atom bomb or slow death from conformity or genocide. But their common way of understanding connected them deeply to black culture: "So there was a new breed of adventurers, urban adventurers who drifted out at night looking for action with a black man's code to fit their facts. The hipster had absorbed the existentialist synapses of the Negro, and for practical purposes could be considered a white Negro."[3] Along with existential fear, the wild energy and invention of post-war jazz, particularly bebop, from Miles Davis to Thelonius Monk to Charlie Parker, became an essential part of Beat culture. Mailer pointed out that "go" was a hot word in the "hip" lexicon,

> with its sense that after hours or days or months of monotony, boredom, and depression one has finally had one's chance, one has amassed enough energy to meet an exciting opportunity with all one's present talents for the flip (up or down) and so one is ready to go, ready to gamble. Movement is always to be preferred to inaction.[4]

Go was published in 1952, a rich year in American letters: Flannery O'Connor's *Wise Blood*, Ernest Hemingway's *The Old Man and the Sea*, the young Kurt Vonnegut's *Piano Player*, and James Baldwin's *Go Tell it On the Mountain* all appeared. Perhaps most remarkable was Ralph Ellison's *Invisible Man*, a *Bildungsroman* that plays strongly on the ambiguities of social revolt and the power of music and jazz on the conscience of an individual. J. D. Salinger's *The Catcher in the Rye* had appeared the preceding year, received as a brilliant portrait of a young man coming to terms with innocence and experience in the city. One year later, in 1953, William S. Burroughs would publish *Junky*, his novel of descent into the abyss of heroin, Other books, now long forgotten, also explored the drift into an unconventional world within American life, including George Mandel's *Flee the Angry Strangers* and Chandler Brossard's *Who Walk in Darkness*, both published in 1952 as well.

Anyone exploring the "neon wilderness" within the dark, wild side of city life already owed much to the stories and fiction of Nelson Algren. Algren's 1950 *The Man with the Golden Arm*, the first winner of the National Book Award, had depicted the heroin addict as something other than a fiend (beating William Burroughs to it). His vision of life in that world and in the seedy one of New Orleans in *A Walk on The Wild Side* (1956) could not be rivaled as a tough arena to become a better human being. But Kerouac was hard at work developing his own Beat vision of American life before Holmes gave it a voice in 1952, both in *Go* and his now famous essay "This Is the Beat Generation," published in the same year in *The New York Times Magazine*.[5] Kerouac's early work, particularly *The Town and the City* and the early scroll version of *On the Road*, as well as his working journals from the late 1940s and early 1950s, bears out a great deal of what Holmes depicted in his novel. As Kerouac worked energetically in 1947 and 1948 on *The Town and The City*, he had in mind Dostoevsky's model of the sprawling polyphonic novel. But he also felt that he was not yet channeling his own, more personal inspirations:

> the greatest writing, the *unconscious*. Someday I'll learn . . . I wish I could write from the point of view of one hero instead of giving everyone in the story his due value – this makes me confused, many times disgusted. After all, I'm human, I have my beliefs, I put nonsense in the mouths of characters I don't like, and this is tedious, discouraging, disgusting. Why doesn't God appear to tell me I'm on the right track? What foolishness![6]

Herman Melville, Dostoevsky, Thomas Wolfe, and Walt Whitman all inspired Kerouac as he tried to imagine what he considered "the Alpha and Omega of riddles": "My kingdom is not of this world."[7] For Kerouac, the mystery or riddle Christ articulated in the Sermon on the Mount was how to see all the suffering on earth and yet to confound it, to remain even ecstatic in the midst of it.

The Christ of Dostoevsky's "The Grand Inquisitor" (from *The Brothers Karamazov* [1880]) fascinated Kerouac, as did the ever-searching characters of *Moby-Dick* and persistent souls of Melville's *Piazza Tales* (1856), to whom he refers often in his notebooks and his novels. It should be no surprise that Melville – who was rediscovered in the 1920s and thus still fresh to the reading public – would have had a particularly strong hold on Kerouac's imagination. Kerouac shared his Melville reading with his close friends; in a letter to Ginsberg from early 1952, Kerouac asks, "will you please be kind and return my Melville to me,"[8] referring to his copy of Henry Murray's 1949 edition of *Pierre, or the Ambiguities* (1852). Murray, a prominent psychologist at Harvard, had developed a strong interest in Melville not long after the novelist's rediscovery, and his reading in Melville became a part of the development of his ideas about personality. In his elaborate and nuanced introduction to *Pierre*, Murray makes the point – one that no doubt resonated with Kerouac – that Melville "purposed to write his spiritual autobiography in the form of a novel, that is to say that he was experimenting with the novel and incidentally making use of some personal experiences."[9] The particular case of *Pierre*, mentioned specifically in Kerouac's letters and journals, may be significant. As Murray points out in his introduction, the story suggests the Thomas Wolfe-like odyssey of returning to the idyll of one's youth in order to shed it. Wolfe also haunted Kerouac's imagination, no doubt, for the same reason. Kerouac's agonized sense of rootlessness could always be traced to his longing for home and his failure to recapture it. Like Melville's Pierre, Kerouac remained deeply tied to his mother, so much so that the rest of the world seemed a sad falling from her love.

The strong gnostic forces in Melville, the struggle between light and darkness, the tendency to contemplate the world as both wonderful and the irredeemable work of an evil demiurge, appealed to Kerouac. If anyone could rival Dostoevsky for plumbing the darkest aspects of human psychology and the wildest pursuits of divine inscrutability, it was Melville.

Kerouac squeezed considerable Melvillean juice into the partly autobiographical *The Town and the City*. The book owes much to *Pierre* (as well as to Wolfe's *You Can't Go Home Again*, a *Bildungsroman* about a young writer transformed by his travels and his vision of America). The character most biographically akin to the author in Kerouac's novel is Peter, one of several siblings, who grows up in a small town (Galloway, which resembles Kerouac's hometown of Lowell, Massachusetts) and winds up in New York City. The basic plot structure follows *Pierre* (another Peter); both young men move from the rural and the innocent world to the city – in fact, New York. And the movement mirrors a move from innocence to experience. Kerouac's Peter, like Melville's *Pierre*, becomes deeply disturbed by a change in the way he views his father (which parallels the tragic difficulties Kerouac experienced with his own father). Kerouac's Peter also becomes entranced with his mysterious sister, Liz, the only person in whom he feels comfortable confiding. Peter helps Liz elope one evening with her boyfriend Buddy, and she disappears for years; Peter finds her again as a loner and drifter living in New York City as "one of the many girls in America who flit from city to city in search of something they hope to find and never even name, girls 'who know all the ropes,' know a thousand people in a hundred cities and places, girls who work at all kinds of jobs, impulsive, desperately gay, lonely hardened girls." Liz anticipates Neil Cassady before Cassady emerges in full force as Dean Moriarty in *On the Road*. A true hipster who is also reading *Moby-Dick*, she challenges her brother: "Can anyone be anything but a rebel in a conventional world like this?" Peter's moral agonies just seem to be Beat ups and downs corresponding to the life of his sister. Peter's pain at the loneliness and moral ambiguity of life adrift in the city and the country after the war haunts the book and gives it its Beatness and its longing for a broader vision. At its conclusion, we find Peter "on a highway," "on the road again, traveling the continent westward, going off to further and further years . . ."

Though Kerouac thought " 'true thoughts' abound in Town & City," by 1948, near its completion, he was ready to move on. "Now I'll sharpen things," he wrote in his working journals. "I have another novel in mind – 'On the Road' – which I keep thinking about: about two guys hitchhiking to California in search of something they don't really find, and losing themselves on the road, and coming all the way back hopeful of something *else*. Also, I'm finding a new principle of writing."[10] After Mark Van Doren and Robert Giroux saw *The Town and the City* through to publication at Harcourt (it would appear in 1950), Kerouac contemplated pushing his prose and his vision toward something more open and lyrical. He wanted more than a *Huckleberry Finn*-like buddy narrative:

> Not a river-like novel; but a novel like poetry, or rather, a narrative poem, an epos in mosaic, a kind of Arabesque preoccupation . . . free to wander from the laws of the "novel" as laid down by the Austens and the Fieldings into an area of greater spiritual pith (which cannot be reached without this technical device, for me anyway) where the Wm. Blakes & Melvilles and even short-chaptered Celine, dwell. I want to say things that only Melville has allowed himself to say in "The Novel." And Joyce.[11]

Part of what Kerouac sought in *On the Road* was the "inscrutable thing" that Melville wrote of in *Moby-Dick*; he had been firing himself toward the three-week fit of nonstop writing that produced in 1951 the famous first draft on an unbroken paper scroll. His attitude toward writing was completely lyrical, itself a fiery hunt and a journey, very much inspired by the "go" demiurge of Cassady, who wrote rambling, ten-thousand-word letters to him. What inspired Kerouac was the mad intensity of both Cassady and Ginsberg, lovers who represented Manichean forces of light and darkness and two kinds of spiritual – not only intellectual – powers that would free him from the shackles of fear and sadness.

The frequently quoted passage early in *On the Road* announcing Sal Paradise's passion for the "mad ones" is so often taken out of context that it bears remembering that it comes in the middle of a discussion of the figures of Carlo Marx (Allen Ginsberg) and Dean Moriarity (Neal Cassady). It's worth noting, too, the Christian emphasis that Kerouac gives to his own name as narrator: someone taken with salvation and paradise. Sal sees himself as somehow behind or less than these two entirely blessed visionaries, or "holy con men," with all of the Melvillean play on "confidence man," with its ambiguity of faith and trickery:

> A tremendous thing happened when Dean met Carlo Marx . . . Their energies met head-on, I was a lout compared, I couldn't keep up with them. The whole mad world swirl of everything that was to come began then; it would mix up all my friends and all I had left of my family in a big dust cloud over the American Night . . . They [Carlo and Dean] rushed down the street together, digging everything in the early way they had, which later became so much sadder and perceptive and blank. But then they danced down the streets like dingledodies, and I shambled after them as I've been doing all my life after people who interest me, because the only people for me are the mad ones, the ones who are mad to live, mad to talk, mad to be saved, desirous of everything at the same time, the ones who never yawn or say a commonplace thing, but burn, burn, burn like fabulous roman candles exploding like spiders across the stars and in the middle you see blue centerlight pop and everybody goes "Aww!"

Kerouac demonstrates what Emily Dickinson had a century earlier: that "much madness is divinest sense."[12] Or that the crazy ones on deck, like Melville's Pip, had really seen the depths. Kerouac set himself up as a follower and a seeker, looking to get lost in the wilderness.

The 1950 scroll version of *On the Road* makes its underlying Melvillean mythology more explicit than the later version. In the first few pages, Kerouac writes: "I left with my canvas bag in which a few fundamentals things were packed, left a note for my mother, who was at work, and took off for the Pacific Ocean like a veritable Ishmael with fifty dollars in his pocket."[13] Cassady was many things: a Queequeg, a Gene Autry, and even, in the 1957 edition, Ahab, for as he barrels eastward with Dean at the wheel, Sal is reminded of his days in rough seas in the merchant marine – and of Melville's timeless mariner:

> "Hee – hee-he!" tittered Dean and he passed a car on the narrow bridge and swerved in dust and roared on . . . As a seaman I used to think of the waves rushing beneath the shell of the ship and the bottomless deep thereunder – now I could feel the road some twenty inches beneath me, unfurling and

> flying and hissing at incredible speeds across the groaning continent with that mad Ahab at the wheel.

On the Road begins and ends with Sal's (or really, Kerouac's) dream of Dean. Kerouac's posthumously published *Visions of Cody* (1973) was an extensive set of meditations on his faithless friend and muse, Neal Cassady.

From the scroll version of 1951 to its final version as a *roman-à-clef, On the Road* went through many revisions (despite the popular conception that it was purely spontaneous) and six rejections before Viking published it in 1957. It received what has become a legendary laudatory review in *The New York Times* by Gilbert Millstein, who called it "the most beautifully executed, the clearest, and the most important utterance yet made by the generation Kerouac himself named years ago as 'beat,' and whose principal avatar he is."[14] Kerouac was already ahead of Norman Mailer, who would describe within a year the idea of "the white Negro" as one who had "to live with death as immediate danger, to divorce himself from society, to exist without roots, to set out on the uncharted journey with the rebellious imperatives of the self."

Viking would reject a number of Kerouac's other novels, but in 1958 they accepted *The Dharma Bums*, another road novel. From 1957 to 1960 Kerouac would write, in addition, three other "road" novels, *The Subterraneans* (1958), *Tristessa* (1960), and *Lonesome Traveler*(1960). Being on the road became his most powerful figure for seeking, and in *The Dharma Bums*, located in California and breathing deeply of his experiences of west coast Zen Buddhists (including the poet Gary Snyder), Kerouac explores more deeply than he had before the mysteries of unworldly and worldly passion and learning to live with both in balance.

Although Kerouac, Ginsberg, and Burroughs were originally either from or associated with New York and the east coast, their writing and their scene departed quickly for the west. Whether settling, as Ginsberg and Kerouac did, in San Francisco, or creating a fantastic, utopian psycho-scape, as Burroughs did, the American West became once again the frontier of possibility for the Beat writers and their followers.[a]

Burroughs became a more outlandish exile, living – if one could call it that – and eventually writing in a room in Tangier. His subjects were addiction, junk, and homosexuality, particularly as they were demonized by society. His weapon was outrageous satire. As someone who did not need money and had apparently slipped into addiction for no ascertainable reason, he wrote about it

a Here is another version of the imagined frontier that is discussed by Stephanie Le Menager in chapter 31 of this volume, "Imagining the frontier."

and society's perception of it with an eerie, sometimes frightening satirical detachment.

Burroughs had met Ginsberg and Kerouac at Columbia through another student, Lucien Carr. Carr subsequently murdered his obsessed mentor, David Kammerer, and Burroughs's and Kerouac's involvement in the cover-up led to their collaboration on a novel based on the murder, *And the Hippos Were Boiled in their Tanks* (1945, 2008). Burroughs fell in love with Ginsberg, who returned the affection only to the extent of serving as his agent and editor, and in 1953, with Ginsberg's help, Burroughs published *Junky*, a novel based on his heroin experience. The book was more sensational for its content than for its form. But nine years of heroin addiction and loveless wandering, some of those in Tangier, eventually produced *Naked Lunch*, published by Olympia Press in 1959. Encouraged greatly by Kerouac, who provided the title, and Ginsberg, who helped him with the form, Burroughs insisted emphatically in a 1960 letter to Irving Rosenthal, "THE BOOK IS NOT A NOVEL" (though critics have seen it differently).[15] Burroughs instead saw it very much as a satire; the "naked lunch" being what one ultimately sees on the end of one's fork but really an unmasked vision of what we digest. The style of the book is in every way "cut-up," moving swiftly from one strange vision to the next, with chapters arranged in an order that defies linear narrative. But the elusive narrator is in every way a lurid cut-up mocking a society that tortures and executes people for their sexual practices and pleasures; one of the most strikingly pornographic chapters, "A. J.'s Annual Party," fuses both homosexual gratification and graphic depiction of execution by hanging.

In contrast to Kerouac's visionary passion, Burroughs depicts the world through themes of possession, confinement (such as the *Interzone* [1989]), parody, satire, and paranoia. The surreal quality of Burroughs would resonate with Ken Kesey, Thomas Pynchon, Kurt Vonnegut, and others who would render their own paranoid visions of a controlled, hyper-real world, confused by addiction and misguided psychiatric views of human nature. When the US postmaster attempted to suppress the publication of *Big Table I*, a journal that would later excerpt *Naked Lunch* in early 1958, Burroughs caught the attention of a Stanford writing fellow named Ken Kesey.

From his youth, Ken Kesey would seem to be the least likely figure to become one of the renegades of literature and culture by the time he reached his mid twenties. The son of a successful Oregon dairy farmer, Kesey did not study much literature as an undergraduate at the University of Oregon, but he did encounter the novelist James B. Hall, who brought the technique of Hemingway and

Faulkner's fiction (especially the short fiction) alive for him[16]. With his raw ability, ambition, and the support of Hall, Kesey won a Woodrow Wilson fellowship to study at Stanford and wound up in classes in 1958 taught by Wallace Stegner, Richard Scowcroft, and Frank O'Connor. His classmates included Larry McMurtry, who was already on his way to becoming an important new voice of the American Western with *Horseman, Pass By* (1961), Wendell Berry, Gurney Norman, Peter Beagle, and Tillie Olsen.

Kesey wrote two novels in the 1950s that remain unpublished; "End of Autumn," about his college experiences, and "Zoo," about the San Francisco North Beach Beat scene. The latter Kesey tried hard to get published, and it won him an additional fellowship from Harcourt. Its hero resembles Kesey himself: caught between two worlds, neither of which he finds true to himself. It also reveals the Kesey now sympathetic to the hipster side of San Francisco, the world of black jazz musicians, unorthodox marriages, and wild Kerouackian road adventures into Mexico.

In the early months of 1960, largely out of the need for cash, Kesey signed up for drug tests at the local Veterans Administration hospital in Menlo Park. The test turned out to be part of MK-ULTRA, a CIA-sponsored program testing psychotomimetic drugs on highly intelligent Stanford graduate students. The government had hoped that these drugs might be used in the Cold War against the Soviets to control minds. Instead, the tests became a grand study in cultural irony – the losing control of minds.

Kesey took a variety of drugs, and at around the same time took a job as a nurse's assistant in the summer of 1960 on the psychiatric ward of the Veterans Hospital. At night he started to write *One Flew over the Cuckoo's Nest*. Kesey has described rewriting the first few pages of the book on peyote. But the important point of Kesey's story has to do with the structure of the novel. At some point, he changed the point of view. What had been a third-person narrative about a renegade named McMurphy who comes into the hospital mental ward and shakes things up became a first-person narrative through the very strange first-person perspective of an unspeaking American Indian named Bromden, who has been diagnosed as a schizophrenic. Kesey had conceived of the book, which he wrote in just a few intense months in 1960, partly as a Western in which the cowboy (McMurphy) rides into the corrupt town (the mental ward) to clean it up and then departs.[b] But the perspective of Bromden changed everything, bringing the Indian consciousness, as Kesey saw it, to bear upon the white American world.

b Le Menager traces the development of this idealized cowboy figure in chapter 31.

Kesey did not see Bromden as clinically "schizophrenic." In fact, *Cuckoo's Nest* became important for the way in which it challenged abuses (including the regular use of lobotomies and shock treatments) in the hitherto much-lauded world of psychiatric treatment.[17] But Kesey did not really view the novel as an indictment of the system of psychiatric treatment, although his work on the ward combined with his own use of LSD gave him a strong sense of the inner humanity of even those deemed the most chronically ill. Madness, Kesey thought, was a condition of all human suffering; the ward a metaphor of the attempt to control and a place for those broken by its worst effects.[c] Unlike in the subsequent play by Dale Wasserman and the highly successful 1972 film of *Cuckoo's Nest*, Kesey's "windmill," his "whale," his evil, was not "Big Nurse" at all but the inscrutable "Combine," a grim mechanical, bureaucratic, impersonal reaper that encompassed the nuthouse within which Nurse Ratched was just one cog. The sense of the individual facing immense machinery lies at the center of what some consider Kesey's paranoid vision, while others saw it as a defining glimpse into the dehumanizing environment that man had created for himself.

Kesey read portions of *Cuckoo's Nest* in the fall of 1960 to Malcolm Cowley's Stanford writing seminar. Cowley recognized its potential and took it to Viking; by March 1961, Kesey had a contract and was editing a final version of what would become one of the hit books of 1962. The year 1961 was an extraordinary one for American fiction. In taking a backward glance at American institutional madness, Joseph Heller's *Catch -22* became an instant cultural institution itself. Richard Yates's *Revolutionary Road* presented a beautifully written, tragic look at the failure of American suburban dreams of the 1950s. Walker Percy's *The Moviegoer* also presented a finely wrought vision of the dissatisfactions of American working life.

One Flew over the Cuckoo's Nest was met with almost universally positive criticism upon its publication. Kerouac heralded Kesey as a major new novelist.[18] Many would see *Cuckoo's Nest* on one level as the final blow against American repression in many forms, especially McCarthyism. It was written in the midst of the immense success of Harper Lee's *To Kill a Mockingbird* (1960), a work that dealt with racial injustice in the South; Kesey's novel – though many critics have somehow missed it – centered on making a broken American Indian "large" again. It also signaled a uniting of the surreal world of

c For a fuller account of this narrative type, see Maria Farland's discussion of what she calls "the mental breakdown novel" elsewhere in this volume ("Literary feminisms," chapter 56, 932–933).

the psychedelic with the defiant world of the American West. Kesey sought to extend that vision further in his second novel, an epic about the logging industry called *Sometimes a Great Notion* (1964).

A sprawling, multivocal work, *Sometimes a Great Notion* followed in the tradition of Faulkner's great Yoknapatawpha novels. But Kesey had decided to be much more controlled than Faulkner. The narrative is told from the perspective of Viv Stamper, the family patriarch's wife, as she reflects on a photo album. She is the force that drives the novel, which deftly moves in and out of numerous voices and perspectives in a drama of conflict as the Stamper family defies a union that tries to usurp its hold on the logging business. "The "Combine" here encompasses both the trade union and the fictional Waconda Auga River – in Kesey's vision, everything that conspires to crush the individual. In addition to the Stamper family's struggle against the river, there is a fraternal conflict within the family that threatens to tear it apart: rough-necked Hank Stamper and Yale-educated Leland Stamper fight over Hank's wife, Viv. At the root of their characters are two different attitudes toward a nihilistic vision of the universe: one defiant and one suicidal. At times the two merge. And hence the Huddie Ledbetter (Leadbelly) song, "Good Night Irene," from which Kesey took his title:

> Sometimes I live in the country
> Sometimes I live in the town
> Sometimes I get a great notion
> To jump in the river and drown

Quizzing the universe on every level, Kesey sought in his greatest novel to find a way out of *that* notion. His answer eventually was that the novel was not enough of an answer. He preferred to become a lightning rod rather than a seismograph. Upon the publication of *Sometimes a Great Notion*, Kesey decided to travel to New York with a group of his friends to celebrate a new chapter in his life. Perhaps not surprisingly, one of the main influences on his shift was Kerouac's *On the Road*. "(I) read it three times before," recalled Kesey in a 1992 interview, "hoping to sign on in some way, to join that joyous voyage, like thousands of other volunteers inspired by the same book and its vision."[19] He took to the road in 1964 in a 1939 Harvester school bus called "Furthur," which was painted psychedelic colors. And at the wheel was Neal Cassady.

Kesey's universe was governed by large, inhuman forces, both manmade and natural: the "Combine" and the river. Thomas Pynchon, who studied under Vladimir Nabokov at Cornell in the late 1950s, further extended Kesey's exploration of the paranoid vision. In *V.* (1963), Pynchon examines a mystery, a "dream of annihilation." The quest is to understand in the strange interchange of public and private events whether there is a symbolic and metaphysical meaning to the denigration of life in the twentieth century. Is conspiracy real or is it merely an illusion? Pynchon pursues the possibility of conspiracy with greater vigor and humor in *The Crying of Lot 49* (1966). Set in the postmodern landscape of southern California and Los Angeles – a pasteboard façade since Nathanael West's *Day of the Locust* – the plot quickly becomes a *noir* mystery and a conspiracy: Oedipa Maas has become the executor of a former's lover's labyrinthine estate. She soon discovers (or thinks she discovers) that her dead lover's estate was deeply connected to a centuries-old postal society that may have been trying to infiltrate the US postal system since the time of the Pony Express. Oedipa resists the insane suggestions of her psychoanalyst, but she is taken with all manner of edgy hipsters and rockers, including a rock band called the Paranoids.

The menacing sense of large-scale control reaches apocalyptic heights in Kurt Vonnegut's first major novel, *Cat's Cradle* (1963), a book that takes its title from an almost universal children's game of creating a web of forms with a loop of string held by two people. The narrator, John, begins with an amusing allusion to *Moby-Dick* and its mythic antecedent: "Call Me Jonah. My parents did, or nearly did. They called me John." Like Ishmael and Jonah, John – along with the children of a cold-blooded scientist and co-inventor of the atomic bomb – will journey to the belly of beast: in this case, an island created and ruled in an anthropological game of religion and dictatorship – and threatened with apocalyptic doom. Paradise becomes nothing more than a site of social control – and of satire – and the countercultural cool religion of Bokononism nothing more than part of the woven game of social control on the island.

Kesey's impact on the 1960s continued well beyond his literary fiction; his 1964 summer psychedelic bus trip with his Merry Pranksters and the subsequent acid tests in California (featuring the mass distribution of LSD) fueled a large part of the psychedelic movement on the west coast. But Kesey had little patience for campus or other protest movements; he also fled to Mexico briefly to avoid prosecution on drug possession charges. Kesey's and Pynchon's literary legacy can be felt in Richard Fariña's 1966 *Been Down So Long It Looks Like Up to Me*, a title that Fariña took from a Furry Williams blues song that was subsequently covered by The Doors in 1971. Fariña's protagonist, Gnossos Pappadopoulous, is a young but somewhat jaded Odyssyean wanderer who returns to his upstate New York college. Well read and on a profound search for truth, Gnossos, like Kesey's Leland Stamper or McMurphy, is a shapeshifter, fashioning himself after such cartoon characters as Plastic Man and Captain Marvel. His stance of cool detachment falters when a sinister dean named Oeuf tempts him to join a cabal of mystery and conspiracy related to a campus uprising.

Fariña was a student at Cornell in the late 1950s, the moment at which the novel is set. (He and Pynchon were classmates and friends.) Campus sex, drugs, and protests – mostly involving control of students' sex lives – pale in comparison to Gnossos's experience in revolutionary Cuba. There Gnossos confronts death and loses his trivial sense of exemption.

Fariña wrote most of *Been Down So Long* in 1963, but it was not published until 1966; days after its publication, he was killed in a motorcycle accident. The allusive and complex novel paints an amusing as well as dark portrait of the Beat and hipster scene as it unfolded in the 1960s: the alienated, brooding figure on the road, in an inchoate, inarticulate search amid a whirl of sex and drugs, and a deepening sense of upheaval and conspiracy, and, ultimately, a more profound, if not liberating confrontation with mortality. Yet there remained always the hope and possibility of transcendence: in the very first sentence of *Been Down So Long*, Gnossos is also called "furry Pooh Bear," and we can't help but smile at the beatific vision in the last paragraph of *On the Road*: "and don't you know that God is Pooh Bear?"

Notes

1. As the editors of the scroll edition have pointed out, Kerouac actually started drafting *On the Road* in the late 1940s.
2. Jack Kerouac, "About the Beat Generation," in *The Portable Jack Kerouac*, ed. Ann Charters (New York: Penguin, 2007), 559. Previously published as "Aftermath: The Philosophy of the Beat Generation," in *Esquire* 49.3 (March 1958).
3. Norman Mailer, "The White Negro," in *Advertisements for Myself*, (Cambridge, MA: Harvard University Press, 1992), 341.
4. *Ibid.*, 350.
5. John Clellon Holmes, "This Is the Beat Generation," *The New York Times Magazine* (November 16, 1952): 10.
6. Jack Kerouac, *Windblown World: The Journals of Jack Kerouac 1947–1954*, ed. Douglas G. Brinkley (New York: Penguin, 2006), 9.
7. *Ibid.*, 16.
8. *Kerouac: Selected Letters: Volume 1, 1940–1956*, ed. Ann Charters (New York: Penguin, 1995), 310.
9. From Henry Murray's introduction to Herman Melville, *Pierre* (New York: Hendricks House, 1949), xxiv.
10. Kerouac, *Windblown World*, 123.

11. *Ibid.*, 242.
12. Emily Dickinson, "Much Madness is divinest Sense (Poem 435)," *c.*1862, in *The Complete Poems of Emily Dickinson*, ed. Thomas H. Johnson (Boston: Little, Brown and Co., 1960), 209.
13. Jack Kerouac, *On The Road: The Original Scroll*, ed. Howard Cunnell, (New York: Viking, 2009), 115.
14. Gilbert Millstein, review of *On The Road*, *The New York Times* (September 5, 1957): 27.
15. William S. Burroughs to Irving Rosenthal, 1960, in *Naked Lunch, The Restored Text*, ed. James Grauerholz and Barry Miles (New York: Grove Press, 2001), 249.
16. This information has been compiled from extensive personal interviews with Hall.
17. For an account of what would become the "anti-psychiatry" movement, see Paul S. Appelbaum, *Almost a Revolution: Mental Health Law and the Limits of Change* (New York: Oxford University Press, 1994).
18. In a blurb solicited by Kesey's publisher, Viking, for *One Flew over the Cuckoo's Nest*, Kerouac called Kesey "A great new American novelist."
19. Ken Kesey, unpublished interview with the author, May 1992.

56

Literary feminisms

MARIA FARLAND

The decades 1945–1965 have appeared to mark an intermission in the unfolding history of US feminisms – a period of stasis or even retrogression following the gains of the New Women of a half century earlier, and the Rosie the Riveters of the previous decade.[1] By the twentieth century's end, earlier feminisms appeared classist, racist, and overly universalizing in their conception of the category of "woman," so that the period between World War I and Vietnam might be seen to epitomize the prevalence of consensus culture within feminism itself. This chapter aims to counter this periodization of US feminisms through a re-examination of mid-century women's literature, focusing on three pivotal texts: Mary McCarthy's *The Group* (1962), Sylvia Plath's *The Bell Jar* (1963 UK, 1971 USA); and Betty Friedan's *The Feminine Mystique* (1963). Published between the first wave of liberal feminism (dating to the late nineteenth and early twentieth centuries), which largely focused on legal and political equality, and second wave feminism (dating to the 1960s and 1970s), these texts recapitulate some of the signal concerns of early twentieth-century feminism: the concern with the milieu of higher education; the depiction of the diminished options for women in the workplace; and the celebration of potential freedoms gained through sexual expression. Yet they also articulate the shared sense that women at mid-century had failed to progress sufficiently, and thus begin to point forward to many of the concerns of feminism's second wave, especially its attention to the psychological implications of sexist stereotypes; the failed promise of sexual liberation for women's liberation; and the repressive character of institutions such as psychiatry.

Mid-century feminist fictions also witnessed a surprisingly rich engagement with what historians have termed "Freudo-Marxism": "the effort to bridge the gap between the two dominant intellectual traditions of the nineteenth and twentieth centuries." If political and sexual radicals in these decades frequently defined themselves in terms of "a synthesis of Marx and Freud," their feminist counterparts displayed an increasingly antagonistic indebtedness to Marxian and Freudian concepts and categories.[2] Figures like Marx and Freud are best understood as "founders of discursivity"; they assume significance not merely as "the authors of their own works," but as the "produce[rs] of something else: the possibilities and rules for the formation of other texts."[3] Writing in the period between World War II and Vietnam, feminist writers confronted the powerful influence of these transdiscursive figures, contesting the earlier generation's assumption that Marxian and Freudian models of social transformation would advance the cause of women's liberation, and attempting to modify concepts drawn from Marx and Freud to fit their own ends.

Wildly popular at a time when feminism was in abeyance, *The Group*, *The Bell Jar*, and *The Feminine Mystique* reflect mid-century intellectuals' growing disenchantment with many strands within the Old Left, where Marx and Freud remained the chief arbiters of discursive possibilities. In the wake of Stalinism and World War II, US intellectuals began to challenge the socialist party organization many earlier feminists – such as Emma Goldman, Agnes Smedley, and Tillie Olsen – had embraced.[4] Their strongest retort to Old Left feminism's Marxist leanings can be seen in their choice of a new protagonist for women's liberation fictions: the bourgeois college graduate. Friedan's *The Feminine Mystique*, which famously called the reduction of women to full-time homemakers "the problem that has no name," brought to the fore the plight of the overeducated suburban housewife "afraid to ask even of herself the silent question: Is this all?" For Friedan, Plath, and McCarthy, as for the New Left in the years that immediately followed, the college graduate, rather than the proletarian worker, was understood to play a key role in social transformations. This emphasis on the college experience as integral to women's coming-of-age narratives would reappear in later novels like Joyce Carol Oates's *Marya: A Life* (1986), whose female protagonist moves through college, graduate school, and a post-academic career in journalism.

While mid-century fictions like *The Bell Jar* and *The Group* mirrored Friedan's focus on the narrowing of opportunities for women, they diverged from her emphasis on traditionally liberal-feminist benchmarks of equality in the workplace and political sphere. Though Plath and McCarthy did not identify themselves as feminists, their novels contain many elements of incipient second-wave feminism, most notably the emphasis on the personal and cultural dimensions of women's liberation, discussed in more detail below. Both novels explore the control of the body – and especially the reproductive body – as a key component of women's liberation, with frank discussions of abortion and birth control.[a] (Saul Bellow complained that *The Group* had "too many pessaries.")[5] Both novels anticipate feminism's growing concern with lesbianism, and while *The Bell Jar*'s depiction of its lesbian character Joan is ambivalent, *The Group* offers a wholly affirmative vision of Lakey's lesbian expatriation to Paris. In their attention to the personal dimension of oppression, these fictions deflect attention away from classical Marxism's emphasis on private property as the root of women's oppression; indeed, they frequently embrace the private sphere's values of interiority, privacy, and introspection as the preferred vehicles for imagining women's liberation.

Strikingly, both novels indict the oppressive leanings of psychiatry – especially Freudian psychiatry – and the ways in which patriarchal societies equate female independence and forms of madness. In this indictment of psychiatry, they also share a concern with the imposition of sexist stereotypes upon the female psyche as a primary mechanism for women's oppression. For Plath and McCarthy, the psychiatric institution presents itself as the figure for sexist institutions writ large. Plath's Esther Greenwood and McCarthy's Kay Petersen undergo psychiatric hospitalization as a consequence of their failure to conform to gender role expectations. This narrative of psychiatric incarceration appears across a range of feminist fictions of the period.

Finally, as Lisa Hogeland compellingly shows, feminist fictions enjoyed an ambivalent relationship to the sexual revolution, at times linking greater sexual freedom to female self-determination, and at times viewing sexuality as an inherently limiting arena for women.[6] For many mid-century intellectuals anchored firmly in Freud, sexual repression appeared "to create the character structure necessary for the preservation of an authoritarian social regime."[7] Typifying this view, Wilhelm Reich's popular *Sexual Revolution* denounced the patriarchal family as a "*factory for authoritarian ideologies* and conservative structures."[8] The movement for sexual liberation seemed to point beyond the sexist norms of the traditional family, to a world of greater openness and freedom for women. Landmark feminist fictions like Erica Jong's *Fear of Flying* (1973) – and popular works like Diane di Prima's *Memoirs of a Beatnik* (1969), Helen Gurley Brown's *Sex and the Single Girl* (1962), and Judith Rossner's *Looking for Mr. Goodbar* (1975) – continued this exploration during the decades of the sixties and seventies. But the feminist

a On ownership of the body in earlier women's fiction, see Anna Mae Duane, "Susanna Rowson, Hannah Webster Foster, and the seduction novel in the early US" (chapter 2, esp. 38–42).

interrogation of Freudo-Marxian conceptions of repression and liberation is likewise visible in the earlier texts of McCarthy and Plath, just as the preoccupation with women's embodiment can be seen in their ambivalent depictions of "pessaries" and sexual initiation and adventuring.

Gradually, as feminism assumed new momentum and urgency in the early 1970s, the homogeneous white affluence of *The Group* and *The Bell Jar* – along with that of Friedan – would come to epitomize what many feminists began to see as the too-narrow perspective of earlier movements. As literary feminisms loosely grouped together under the rubric "third wave" emerged in the 1980s and 1990s to challenge and complicate the homogeneity of their predecessors, their literary counterparts increasingly devoted themselves to the dynamics of plurality and difference within the category of "women," bringing the emergence of new voices of plurality in the early 1980s (most notably, *This Bridge Called My Back: Writings by Radical Women of Color*, edited by Cherrie Moraga and Gloria Anzaldúa in 1981). Echoing the second wave's signature claim that "the personal is political," feminists of the third wave articulated a dual direction for US feminism: a continued emphasis on the personal dimensions of women's oppression; and a newfound skepticism toward the political system (whether communist or capitalist) as a vehicle for women's liberation.[9] Such tensions epitomized the way in which literary feminisms consistently absorbed an adjacent set of debates within feminist theory and activism, with feminist novelists often shaping their plots and characters around the dynamics of conformity and difference internal to the feminist movement itself.

"The problem that has no name"

The years 1962–1963 marked a watershed for mid-century feminisms. In 1963, Betty Friedan's *Feminine Mystique* took aim at the "problem that has no name," exposing the desperate dissatisfaction of millions of American housewives – many of them college graduates – trapped in tidy family homes.[10] In the realm of fiction, Mary McCarthy's bestselling 1962 novel *The Group* had brought attention to a related milieu. *The Group*'s depiction of affluent postwar women captured the popular imagination with its stylish portrait of sophisticated Vassar graduates living in New York City in the 1930s. Though more urbane than Friedan's housewives, these women followed a similar trajectory: underemployment, boredom, and existential malaise. The year 1963 also brought the British publication of another novelistic depiction of America's recent female college graduates, Sylvia Plath's *The Bell Jar*. While the settings of these three works vary, they share a common element: a newfound concern with the plight of the moderately affluent college-educated woman, stranded in a world where career opportunities remained limited and marriage persisted as the primary vehicle for female identity. Such plotlines posed a loud retort to the postwar period's cultural glorification of the family unit, dubbed by historian Elaine Tyler May "the domestic version of containment."[11] They also posed an implicit corrective to Old Left feminists, for whom heroines like Plath's would have seemed problematically aligned with bourgeois institutions and aspirations.

The first of these works to see publication, *The Group* set its temporal frame in the milieu a *New York Times* reviewer termed "Manhattan's Bohemia of the Depression Years," an era of "furtive, feral wars of the Trotskyites and the Stalinists, the rear-guardists and the avantists."[12] Contrasting with these largely male struggles within the Old Left, *The Group* portrays a world in which highly educated women study art history (Lakey); pursue pregnancy and motherhood (Priss); perform clerical/editorial work (Libby); selflessly devote themselves to nursing (Polly); and pick out draperies at Macy's (Kay). In *The Bell Jar*, by contrast, Esther Greenwood explicitly disavows such second-rate career alternatives, rejecting her mother's suggestion that she attend secretarial classes. Esther proclaims that she "hate[s] serving men in every way," invoking a preferred scenario of female authorship and authority: "I wanted to dictate my own thrilling letters." Considering the prospect of marriage and family, she deplores the sexual division of labor in the American home: "and then when he came home after a lively, fascinating day he'd expect a big dinner, and I'd spend the evening washing up even more dirty plates until I fell into bed, utterly exhausted. This seemed a dreary and wasted life for a girl with 15 years of straight A's, but I knew that's what marriage was like." Like her counterparts in other feminist fictions, the character of Esther confronts women's vexed choices in the arenas of career and family.

In their attention to the confinement of domestic life, Friedan, McCarthy, and Plath set the terms for feminist novels' approaches to setting, while also reinventing narrative traditions of domestic and sentimental fiction discussed elsewhere in this volume.[b] Sue Kaufman's 1967 novel *Diary of a Mad Housewife* depicted a trophy wife in a loveless marriage who seeks relief in an extramarital affair and in psychotherapy, the latter employing formulaic elements of the feminist mental-breakdown narrative, a popular novelistic depiction of psychiatric illness that would become popular in 1970s fiction, as I discuss

b See especially Duane, chapter 2; Cindy Weinstein, "Sentimentalism" (chapter 12); Jennifer Fleissner, "Wharton, marriage, and the New Woman" (chapter 27).

below. Alix Kate Shulman's *Memoirs of an Ex-Prom Queen* (1972), widely considered one of the first major novels to emerge from the women's movement, chronicles its protagonist's escape from a drab existence "cooped up" in "one of those post-war windowless houses six blocks beyond the last stop of the streetcar line." The trials of domestic confinement, though especially acute among Friedan's suburban women, could also be found in literary chronicles of women living in poverty, whether in Ann Petry's surprisingly graphic *Country Place* (1947), Lorraine Hansberry's drama *A Raisin in the Sun* (1959), or Sandra Cisneros's later *House on Mango Street* (1984), where confinement within the home appears to afflict females even prospectively, in girlhood. Soon the imagined escape from such limitations began to lead to direct political action; in Marilyn French's *The Women's Room* (1977) Val is a militant feminist whose ties to the Boston women's liberation movement advance Mira's transformation from housewife to feminist, while also setting the terms for a new subgenre within the era's feminist fiction. In the years that immediately followed, entire novels devoted to women living within the movement – such as Alix Kate Shulman's *Burning Questions* (1978), Marge Piercy's *Vida* (1979), and Alice Walker's *Meridian* (1976) – emerged to make the New Left an important setting for literary feminism in its own right.

If women's imagined escape from domestic settings and duties provided one impetus for narrative possibilities, female escape from biological determinism provided a second narrative element.[c] It was as a story about a birth control clinic that portions of *The Group* first saw publication in 1954 under the title "Dottie Makes an Honest Woman of Herself." Similarly, *The Bell Jar* features frank discussions of contraception. Beyond these bold depictions of reproductive technologies, novels of the era also took on abortion, with the publication of texts like Linda Bird Francke's *The Ambivalence of Abortion* (1978), and more cautionary tales such as Joan Didion's *Play It as It Lays* (1970), in which protagonist Maria Wyeth is coerced into aborting her pregnancy.[13]

Notable for its frank depiction of issues surrounding pregnancy and abortion, Didion's *Play It as It Lays* signaled a third kind of divergence from stable domesticity seen in many feminist fictions of the period: the lure of the road.[d] The heroine of *Play It as It Lays* takes to the freeways, compulsively roving

c On flight and feminists' narrativization of escape from normativity, see Elizabeth Freeman, "Reimagining genders and sexualities," chapter 57 in this volume, esp. 943–944.

d On the masculine road novel during this period, see Robert Faggen, "The Beats and the 1960s" (chapter 55) in this volume. Faggen does not mention the much-debated issue of women writers within the Beat movement, but my discussion of feminist writers' place in the tradition of road narratives complements his essay.

through motels and truck stops, drunk sexual encounters and anonymous bars, and even incarceration for car theft and drug possession. Such wandering is often associated with Beat-generation novels like *On the Road*, where geographic mobility appears to be a masculine prerogative.[14] Numerous postwar women writers adapted the form and themes of the male road narrative, though for female authors the fantasy of escape assumed somewhat different dimensions. Whether in the time travel of Piercy's *Woman on the Edge of Time* (1976) and Ursula LeGuin's *Left Hand of Darkness* (1969); the European tours seen in Jong's *Fear of Flying* and Shulman's *Memoirs of an Ex-Prom Queen*; the urban *flâneuses* cruising the New York streets in di Prima's *Memoirs of a Beatnik* or Rossner's *Looking for Mr. Goodbar*; or the Kesey-esque Mexican sojourns of Bonnie Bremser's *Troia: Mexican Memoirs* (1971); these women's travel narratives borrow from traditionally male patterns of exploration and self-assertion to create stories of women's liberation from the spatial confines of home and marriage.[15] While some of these female journeys highlight the vulnerability of the female body – through depictions of rape, for example – they nevertheless celebrate the possibilities of increased physical mobility for female readers.

These diverse texts suggest literary feminism's adoption of traditionally male settings, yet as historian Alice Echols has observed, feminists in these years questioned whether "transcendence of gender or the affirmation of femaleness" would better advance women's emancipation.[16] The competing lure of female-centered modes of experience and representation drew attention to French feminists like Hélène Cixous and Luce Irigaray, who posited a distinctive "*écriture féminine*" grounded in the female body. Within activist circles, feminists established lesbian communities, and some joined lesbians in embracing women-identified communities as the ultimate challenge to patriarchal authority. The figure of the lesbian appears in earlier novels like *The Bell Jar* and *The Group*, though Plath anticipates Betty Friedan's early antipathy to lesbianism in the character of Joan, who commits suicide near the novel's end. Gradually, feminist fictions moved beyond Friedan's conception of the "lavender menace," which came to appear retrograde, to celebrate lesbian protagonists and communities, and this celebration extended to writers of color such as Audre Lorde, Gloria Anzaldúa, and Ana Castillo. Rita Mae Brown's 1973 *Rubyfruit Jungle* contains distinct echoes of Friedan's "problem with no name," when its protagonist Molly insists she "didn't want a split-level home with a station wagon, pastel refrigerator, and a houseful of children spread evenly through the years." Like di Prima and Bremser, Brown's autobiographical protagonist takes to the road, eschewing conventional models of lesbian relationship, and later confronting the threat of psychiatric incarceration common in feminist fictions in these years. Though writers like Audre Lorde (in *Zami: A New Spelling of My Name* [1983]), and Lisa Alther (in *Kinflicks* [1975]) offered competing visions of lesbian community and solidarity, tensions between minoritizing and universalizing conceptions of lesbian identity emerged at the center of the pluralizing currents within feminist theory and fiction in the 1980s and 1990s.[e]

Feminist anti-psychiatry

Novels like *The Bell Jar* and *The Group* laid the groundwork for explorations of private life and relationships as new focal points for feminism. But the emphasis on gender norms also brought a competing investigation of their inverse: the abnormal or psychologically aberrant individual, embodied in what might be called the mental breakdown novel. Mid-century mental breakdown novels and memoirs frequently feature an affluent, college-educated protagonist – or set of protagonists – whose intellect, career ambitions, and professional accomplishments leave her dissatisfied in the home or thwarted in a hostile workplace. In *The Bell Jar*, perhaps the landmark twentieth-century novel of mental breakdown, the pressures of conformity to gender norms lead to depression and madness. In *The Group*, the threat of female assertiveness causes Harald Peterson to commit his wife to an asylum. These narratives typify the images of women – the neurotic or the hysteric for example – common in popular mental breakdown novels in these decades. Yet these stories also indict psychiatric categories – including Freudian categories – as they embody gender conformity. For many mid-century feminists, this demand for conformity to the "feminine role" had emerged as perhaps the most formidable impediment to women's advancement.

The limitations of the feminine role figure prominently in the well-known mental breakdown plot of *The Bell Jar*, so that Esther Greenwood's descent into madness stems from sexist social norms and then confronts them in the context of institutionalization and recovery. Esther's rejection of traditional models of femininity – embodied in the figures of Dodo Conway, JayCee, and Mrs. Willard – led some readers to see the novel as misogynist, and others to see it as an emblematic text of 1970s feminism. Charting its protagonist's

e Lesbianism also provided an alternative to traditional conceptions of marriage / happiness and seduction / death as the dominant plot elements for female lives, as discussed by Fleissner in chapter 27 of this volume. For further discussion of resistance to heteronormative institutions, see Freeman, chapter 57 in this volume.

descent into madness, the novel foregrounds the loss of self that occurs with the failure to conform to social expectations for middle- and upper-class female identity. At the same time, as I have argued elsewhere, novels like *The Bell Jar* and *The Group* draw a stark contrast between lower- and middle-class psychiatric institutions, so that for *The Group*'s Kay Peterson, the psychiatric hospital is seen as part prison and part luxurious spa.[17] Spanning these contradictory arenas, the mental institution becomes the fictionalized embodiment of complete social dispossession, as well as the possession of the ultimate middle-class entitlement and privilege, psychological depth and complexity. Through their intricate elaborations of status markers, fictional representations of mental breakdown and recovery frequently inscribe class-based hierarchies and distinctions.

As literary feminists of the succeeding generation continued to work within this highly popular set of narrative conventions, they expanded their representations of mental breakdown beyond the narrow social purview of Plath and McCarthy, as seen in the neglected 1976 novel by Marge Piercy, *Woman on the Edge of Time*. The novel's Chicana protagonist, Consuela Ramos, is wrongly committed to a psychiatric institution when she defends her pregnant niece Dolores from her fiancé's physical attacks. Connie confronts the institutionalized sexism of social services and psychiatry, making clear that asylum inmates face rituals of gender normalization as integral to their hospitalization. Piercy even compares psychiatric incarceration to warfare, citing the army of specialists who work to ensure patient conformity: "all the caseworkers and doctors and landlords and cops, the psychiatrists and judges and child guidance counselors, the informants and attendants and orderlies, the legal aid lawyers copping pleas, the matrons and EEG technicians, and all the other flacks who had . . . locked her up and medicated her and condemned her." Psychiatry's violence to the self frequently figures as physical rather than mental. When a "cure" seems to elude her, Connie is selected for an experimental "amygdalotomy" – a "neuroelectric experiment" performed on the hospital's indigent patients – which she ingeniously escapes.

Though threats to the body abound in feminist mental breakdown narratives, it is the mind that becomes the preferred vehicle of female escape in many novels of the period.[18] *Woman on the Edge* employs a time travel plot reminiscent of Kurt Vonnegut's *Slaughterhouse Five* (1969); like Billy Pilgrim in *Slaughterhouse*, Connie finds herself swept into a utopian future world in which social ills like imperialism, environmental pollution, and homophobia no longer exist. In the decades after mid-century, feminist time travel fictions emerged as a fascinating subgenre, ranging from Ursula LeGuin's *The Left Hand of Darkness* and *The Dispossessed* (1974) to Margaret Atwood's *Handmaid's Tale* (1985) and Octavia Butler's *Kindred* (1979). With its pathbreaking images of a society in which gender differences are obliterated, LeGuin's novel embodies the radical utopian possibility of feminists' innovative appropriations of the narrative devices of science fiction in these years. While Piercy's *Woman on the Edge* stands out for its unusual melding of anti-psychiatry and science fiction, its time travel subplot provides an escape valve for forms of virulent sex oppression that are imagined as residing in the recesses of the mind, rather than the surfaces of the body.

Novels like *Woman on the Edge*, with its grab-bag of utopian visions, set into motion the widening of feminism's purview to a set of diverse alliances – or from the opposed perspective, fragmentations – Chicano-feminist, black feminist, eco-feminist, materialist-feminist, etc. Later twentieth-century feminist fictions thus gradually extended the observations of the previous generation's predominantly white, middle-class feminism to encompass more diverse identities and perspectives. The anti-institutional strain in women's mental breakdown and time-travel fictions, while initially keyed to the affluent milieu of Esther Greenwood's Smith College or Kay Peterson's Vassar College, could be equally effective in the indictment of institutions such as the welfare state, allowing feminist writers to extend a set of essentially bourgeois narrative conventions to reach beyond their class-specific origins. Writers of color like Toni Morrison began to employ features of the popular mental-breakdown narratives in novel ways, as seen in the vivid depiction of Pecola's descent into madness in *The Bluest Eye* (1970). In these ways, women's mental breakdown novels emerged as an additional site of feminism's highly generative relationship to Freudo-Marxist concepts and categories. But they also began to challenge the presumed unity of the category of "women," a challenge that would come to dominate feminist theory in the eighties and nineties.

Women's liberation, sexual liberation

While feminist mental breakdown novels emphasized scenes of women's oppressive incarceration, other feminist fictions of the era adopted the inverse strategy, exploring the liberatory possibilities of the sexual revolution for a new generation of women. Though frequently linked to the decade of the 1970s, fictions of sexual independence began to appear in the 1950s and 1960s, with the publication of texts like Helen Gurley Brown's *Sex and the Single Girl* (1962) and Diana di Prima's *Memoirs of a Beatnik* (1969), a semi-autobiographical novel which paid homage to sexual experimentation in the milieu of 1950s bohemian New York. Modeled on Jack Kerouac's *On the Road*, where manic travel, drug use, criminality, and erotic deviance were standard fare, di Prima's protagonist's sexual adventures range from lesbian and group sex to anal intercourse and *ménage à trois* with a father–son duo. Works like *Memoirs* were explicitly marketed to "Adult Readers," a designation made possible by the same loosening of censorship that spawned *Playboy* and *Penthouse*. For many feminists in these years, especially those indebted to Freudo-Marxian thinkers like Wilhelm Reich, these trends appeared to hold liberatory promise for women. In a 1968 speech at Columbia University, "Sexual Politics: A Manifesto for Revolution," Kate Millett optimistically called for "the end of sexual repression – freedom of expression and of sexual mores."[19] Yet Millett also warned that sexual liberation could easily devolve into "exploitative license for patriarchal and reactionary ends."[20] This fear of co-optation was to characterize feminism's largely antagonistic posture toward the sexual revolution and many of the feminist fictions to arrive on the scene during the 1970s and 1980s.

Almost immediately, feminist critics moved to dismiss their contemporaries' too-easy equation of women's freedom with erotic experimentation, noting that the sexual revolution, in the words of feminist Dana Densmore, continued to view women as "purely sexual beings, and sensual fucking machines."[21] Second-wave manifestos urged women to declare "Independence from the Sexual Revolution," and in Ana Castillo's *Mixquiahuala Letters* (1986), the protagonist joins a feminist group which imposes celibacy as a requirement for membership.[22] Mirroring these trends, feminist literary critics complained that newly popular female novelists like di Prima, Brown, and later Erica Jong were flawed in their equation of women's freedom with sexual freedom. Similarly, Robin Morgan deplored what she called the "epidemic of male style" in the women's movement, referring primarily to a male-gendered sexual aesthetic – especially those indebted to Beat-era writers like Mailer and Kerouac – centered on promiscuity, conquest, and individualism.[23] Still other critics like Millett and Elaine Showalter condemned literary culture as masculinist, singling out "phallic" writers like D. H. Lawrence and Norman Mailer. Reflecting this growing skepticism toward sexual liberation, many 1970s feminist fictions began to note the erasure of female subjectivity from popular images of erotic experimentation.

They also frequently critiqued psychoanalysis, chastising the implicit sexism of such concepts as penis envy and the Oedipus complex.

In the effort to move beyond masculinist elements of the sexual revolution, many writers turned to female sexuality as an avenue for liberation from patriarchal sensibilities. Perhaps the earliest of the era's works to emphasize female sexuality was Anaïs Nin's *Diary*, which sold out within four weeks of its first printing in 1966.[24] Nin's vivid portraits of a woman artist's attempts to secure a foothold in literary culture – coupled with her vivid portraits of female sexual experience and fantasy – found a receptive audience among readers who catapulted the book to bestseller status within weeks of its publication. Even Kate Millett, who was often skeptical of the sexual revolution, praised Nin for providing "the first real portrait of the artist [as] a woman that we have ever had."[25] If Millett's endorsement seems surprising in light of many feminists' mistrust of the mainstreaming of sexual experimentation in the 1960s and 1970s, it is crucial to remember the intense interest in the question of female fantasy in these years. While some feminists dismissed Nin's stereotyped images of femininity, her ability to embody a female image of a creative artist – akin to that of Kerouac, Ginsberg, and the popular Beat generation – would continue to draw female readers into the 1970s and beyond. Ginsberg had termed the Beats the "libertine circle," and with the addition of writers like di Prima and Nin, female bohemians and artists joined the decade's vivid representations of sexual transgression (on the Beats broadly, see Faggen's chapter in this volume[f]).

Soon after, female sexual fantasy again made its mark on the bestseller list with the publication of Nancy Friday's compilation *My Secret Garden* (1973), recently dubbed "the first comprehensive exploration of women's fantasies."[26] In the same year, *My Secret Garden* was joined by Erica Jong's *Fear of Flying*, a novelistic exploration of female sexual self-expression that would go on to sell more than 12 million copies around the world. The novel joined the ongoing feminist revaluation of Freud, while also incorporating elements of anti-psychiatry discussed above. *Fear of Flying* charts the gradual disaffection of its protagonist Isabel Wing from Freudian psychoanalysis, a movement allegorized in her disintegrating marriage to a prominent psychoanalyst, whom she abandons in favor of a follower of R. D. Laing, the celebrated prophet of the anti-psychiatry movement. Isabel's embodiment of Freudian conceptions of identity locates the novel

f Faggen, chapter 55.

at the cusp of spirited feminist interrogations of Freud during the post-1945 decades.

Though *Fear of Flying* has repeatedly been dismissed by readers and critics who have seen it as naïvely embracing what Rita Felski derisively termed "the values of a male dominated society," the novel registers considerable ambivalence toward its heroine's quest for erotic adventure.[27] As Lisa Hogeland has noted, Jong's controversial novel clearly points to the perils of sexual adventuring, and thus parallels feminism's ambivalent relationship to the sexual revolution in the same period. The novel's signature fantasy of the "zipless fuck" revolves around a predictable Friday-esque scenario of anonymous sex between a soldier and a woman on a train, but *Fear of Flying* repeatedly repudiates these fantasies. Indeed, at the conclusion of her search for self, Isabel withdraws from sexuality altogether, leaving her various lovers for solitary contemplation in her hotel room, and finally recanting the novel's initial erotic euphoria when she rebuffs a sexually aggressive train conductor. While *Fear of Flying* rose to prominence as a chronicling of its protagonist's erotic experimentation, the novel ultimately rejects the liberatory promise of sexual adventures, cautioning readers of the vulnerability of the female body to rape, exploitation, and appropriation. Novelist Joyce Carol Oates, who like Jong has faced ambivalent responses from feminist critics, also depicts violence against the female body, in works like *The Wheel of Love* (1970), or later novels that focus on questions of female autonomy, such as *Do with Me What You Will* (1973), *The Assassins* (1975), *Childwold* (1976), *and Unholy Loves* (1979).[28]

The protagonist of *Fear of Flying* avoids sexual violence, but contemporary novels like Judith Rossner's *Looking for Mr. Goodbar* (1975) showed readers that erotic escapades could lead to bodily danger and even death. At *Goodbar*'s conclusion, the independent female sexual adventurer meets her end at the hands of drifter Gary Cooper White, who stabs her while repeatedly raping her when she refuses to spend the night with him. The novel's rape and murder mirrored the warnings expressed by contemporary theorists such as Andrea Dworkin, who argued that male rage in the wake of women's advancement would bring new acts of sexual and social violence against women. Feminists like Dworkin and Catherine MacKinnon cautioned that the perceived waning of masculine social power could lead men like White, an unemployed Vietnam vet, to see themselves as the victims of a situation like *Goodbar*'s. This intensified attention to violence against women shapes texts as varied as Toni Morrison's *The Bluest Eye* (1970) and Sandra Cisneros's *House on Mango Street* (1984), where the threat of violence against women crosses boundaries of race and class.

The rape-crisis theory that emerged in the 1980s was the logical extension of feminism's ambivalent relationship to the sexual revolution, seen in both theory and fictions of the era. When radical feminist Ti-Grace Atkinson proclaimed that "the institution of sexual intercourse is anti-feminist," she was echoed by feminist fictions like Marilyn French's *The Women's Room*, which baldly stated that "all men are rapists," boldly adding "They rape us with their eyes, their laws, and their codes."[29] While representations of rape remained relatively rare in US fiction during these years, they emerged as another locus through which feminists began to take their distance from the vestigially Freudian optimism about the liberatory potential of sex.[30] Surprisingly varied in their appeal, these cautionary tales of female vulnerability to sexual predators found resonance within emerging writings by African American and Latina feminist authors, ranging from Lucille Clifton and Audre Lorde, to Morrison, Cisneros, and Ana Castillo.

In the sheer multiplicity of these writers, we see the wider expansion of feminist concerns about the female body, identity, and sexuality, as the more timid explorations of earlier writers like Plath, McCarthy, and Friedan began to make their way into ever more diverse literary venues and circles. Mid-century female writers, often considered isolated from the dynamics of first- and second-wave feminisms, mark the gradual transition from early to later twentieth-century concerns, as seen in their engagement with the Freudo-Marxist traditions of an earlier generation, and their anticipation of the younger generation's preoccupation with the incarcerating effects of gender norms, psychiatry, and sexual roles.

Notes

1. On feminism broadly see Ruth Rosen, *The World Split Open: How the Modern Feminist Movement Changed America* (New York: Viking, 2000); on feminism in the sixties and seventies decades see Alice Echols, *Daring to Be Bad: Radical Feminism in America 1967–1975* (Minneapolis: University of Minnesota Press, 1989).
2. Paul Robinson, *The Freudian Left: Wilhelm Reich, Geza Roheim, Herbert Marcuse* (New York: Harper & Row, 1969), 40, 5.
3. Michel Foucault, "What is an Author," in *The Foucault Reader*, ed. Paul Rabinow (New York: Pantheon, 1984), 113, 114.
4. For an overview see Ellen Kay Trimberger, "Women in the Old and New Left: The Evolution of a Politics of Personal Life," *Feminist Studies* 5 (Autumn 1979): 431–450.
5. Quoted in Nancy K. Miller, "Women's Secrets and the Novel: Remembering Mary McCarthy's *The Group*," *Social Research* 68 (Spring 2001): 173–199.

6. Lisa Maria Hogeland, *Feminism and Its Fictions: The Consciousness-Raising Novel and the Women's Liberation Movement* (Philadelphia: University of Pennsylvania Press, 1998).
7. Robinson, *The Freudian Left*, 50.
8. Wilhelm Reich, *The Sexual Revolution: Toward a Self-Regulating Character Structure*, trans. Theodore P. Wolfe (New York: Orgone Institute Press, 1945), 72.
9. See Echols, *Daring to Be Bad*.
10. Betty Friedan, *The Feminine Mystique* (New York: Norton, 1963), 26.
11. Elaine May, *Homeward Bound: American Families in the Cold War Era* (New York, HarperCollins, 1988), xxiv.
12. Charles Poore, "Books of the Times," *The New York Times* (August 29, 1963): 22.
13. On abortion see Judith Wilt, *Abortion, Choice, and Contemporary Fiction: The Armaggedon of the Maternal Instinct* (Chicago: University of Chicago Press, 1989).
14. On the male road narrative see Rowland A. Sherrill, *Road-Book America: Contemporary Culture and the New Picaresque* (Chicago and Urbana: University of Illinois Press, 2000).
15. Deborah Paes de Barros, *Fast Cars and Bad Girls: Nomadic Subjects and Women's Road Stories* (New York: Peter Lang, 2004).
16. Echols, *Daring to be Bad*, 287.
17. See Maria Farland, "Sylvia Plath's Anti-Psychiatry," *Minnesota Review* 55–57 (November 2002): 245–256.
18. For an insightful discussion of this important issue see Carolyn Dever, *Skeptical Feminism: Activist Theory, Activist Practice* (Minneapolis: University of Minnesota Press, 2004). For a fascinating contemporary discussion, see Meredith Tax, "A Woman and Her Mind," in *Radical Feminism*, ed. Anne Koedt, Ellen Levine, and Anita Rapone (New York: Quadrangle Books, 1973), 23–35.
19. Kate Millett, *Sexual Politics* (Urbana: University of Illinois Press, 2000), 366.
20. *Ibid.*
21. Dana Densmore, "Independence from the Sexual Revolution," in Koedt, Levine, and Rapone, *Radical Feminism*, 111.
22. See Echols, *Daring to be Bad*, 158.
23. Robin Morgan, "Three Articles on WITCH," in *Going Too Far: The Personal Chronicles of a Feminist* (New York: Random House, 1978).
24. Helen Tookey, *Anais Nin, Fictionality and Femininity: Playing a Thousand Roles* (New York: Oxford Press, 2003), 190.
25. Quoted *ibid.*
26. Jeffrey Escoffier, *The Sexual Revolution* (New York: Running Press, 2003), 156.
27. Rita Felski, *Beyond Feminist Aesthetics: Feminist Literature and Social Change* (Cambridge, MA: Harvard University Press, 1989), 14.
28. Hogeland, *Feminism and its Fictions*, 73. Elaine Showalter describes Oates as a feminist who "has never had the acknowledgment from feminist readers and critics that she deserves," whereas Gayle Green dismisses Oates as "not a feminist." Quoted in Brenda Daly, "Sexual Politics in Two Collections of

Joyce Carol Oates's Short Fiction," *Studies in Short Fiction* 32 (Winter 1995): 83–93: 83.

29. Ti-Grace Atkinson, *Amazon Odyssey* (New York: Links Books, 1974), 86.
30. See Sabine Sielke, *Reading Rape: The Rhetoric of Sexual Violence in American Literature and Culture, 1790–1990* (Princeton: Princeton University Press, 2002).

57

Reimagining genders and sexualities

ELIZABETH FREEMAN

From its earliest instances in Anglo-American literature, the novel questioned prevailing gender and sexual norms. Beginning in the eighteenth century, this genre challenged the primacy of the aristocracy, for it figured the rising middle class and its worldview through the lens of virtuous womanhood. In novels such as *Pamela* (1740) and *Clarissa* (1748), pious female servants resisted rapacious lords, and bourgeois marriages of true minds overcame the power-consolidating arrangements of upper-class families. Feelings trumped force; housewifery trumped high birth. As a literary form, then, the novel was already radical in the way it reconceived power relations with feminine subjectivity at the core. But it was also what we might now call conservative in its championing of consensual heterosexual relations as the supreme achievement of social being.[1] In later years, women and gay men wishing to write *beyond* the conventionally heterosexual ending therefore had to retool the bourgeois domestic novel.

This work was well underway by the mid nineteenth century, at least in Anglo-US writing, so that later writers already had a novelistic, sexually experimental tradition to draw upon. The American Renaissance had produced works that challenged the British model and offered new formations of sex and gender, particularly the marital "closure" readers of the novel had come to expect. Hawthorne's *The Scarlet Letter* (1850) showcased an adulterous heroine; Melville's *Moby-Dick* (1851) depicted a microcosmic all-male world on a whaling ship; Thoreau's *Walden* (1854) extolled the virtues of bachelorhood in the wild. The later nineteenth century produced novels of withdrawal from the dominant social world, and these withdrawals were often figured as flights from marriage and family. Sarah Orne Jewett's *The Country of the Pointed Firs* (1896), for instance, was the masterpiece of a New England women's tradition that celebrated spinsters and female eccentrics living in rural towns. In Mark Twain's *The Adventures of Huckleberry Finn* (1885), another famous example of non-heteronormative love, a black man and a white boy escape the civilizing influence of women. But it was Henry James who most systematically deranged both social and literary form: from his open depiction of misdirected female eroticism in *The Turn of the Screw* (1898) and of a quasi-marital relationship between two women in *The Bostonians* (1886), to the most opaque masterpieces of his late period, Jamesian novels are marked by plots that seem to go nowhere or end in bad marriages. They also closely track the interior psychological states of characters who have failed to develop into heteronormative adulthood, and play with point of view, perspective, and narratorial persona in ways that highlight the textual and constructed nature of identity. In sum, even the most canonical history of the American novel is already a queer one, if by queer we mean imaginatively and stylistically committed to a multiplicity of alternative gendered and sexualized subject-positions.[2]

But once depicting gender and sexual experimentation became increasingly risky as the twentieth century saw increasing crackdowns on public gay life, many authors muted explicit homoeroticism. Eschewing realism, many challenged prevailing styles and plot structures, produced works that muddled traditional ways of categorizing literature, and bent the novel to new social purposes. To track the way that American novels have reimagined genders and sexualities in a given period, then, involves more than producing a timeline of works that feature strange new bodies and relations, or those authored by people we now recognize as gay, lesbian, or queer. It means tracking the way gender/sexual dissidents have questioned and recalibrated even the principal terms that organize this volume: "History," "American," and "Novel." Accordingly, this entry will focus on three ways that, as thinking about genders and sexualities changed from the early twentieth century to the dawn of second-wave feminism and gay liberation in the 1970s and beyond, writers transformed the novel's forms and functions. Some questioned the heterosexist paradigm of the bourgeois domestic novel itself and pushed the genre to its limits. Others embraced formulaic popular literature in ways that demand a rethinking of received literary histories and of what counts as literature. And still others used the novel not to build up a sense of national identity, as some have argued was the mission of the American novel, but instead to invent post-national ways of belonging, both critiquing "America" and imagining modes of social life that superseded the physical and conceptual limits of the United States.

Sexing the novel: gender and genre

Traditional literary history centers on events to which women and queers have a skeptical and/or marginal relation. Conventional periodization is based on male-dominated, nationalist military history or presidential policy, resulting in categories such as "colonial, "antebellum," "Progressive-era," and "postwar" literature. Even standard accounts of modernism, whether optimistic or pessimistic, figure a world whose master narratives had been fractured by the Great War. Modernism's supposed successor, postmodern literature, is highly self-reflexive in ways that turn history into pure, depthless textuality, mimicking the process of late capitalism and commodity culture. Thus the explicitly feminist and queer novelistic traditions that have emerged alongside and within these masculine, nationalist, and macroeconomic conceptual categories seem to be of merely sociological rather than literary interest. But modernism and postmodernism actually look more alike than different in their concern with the contingency of supposedly timeless and natural narratives if we examine sex, gender, and sexuality in these two literary movements. Both led to new ways of breaking the rules of form that – in a dialectic with content – reimagined gender and sexuality as resoundingly cultural and multiple, that is, as socially constructed and culturally and historically specific.

Among US white women authors, Gertrude Stein and Djuna Barnes stand out as the most original practitioners of formal techniques that transgressed both genre and gender norms.[a] Each understood that the bourgeois novel of manners was simply not capacious enough to figure (rather than merely represent) the dynamics of a lesbian relationship. Both experimented with multiple or "misassigned" first-person voices, episodic plots, and seemingly endless sentences, Stein's marked by repetition and juxtaposition and Barnes's by spirals of subordinate clauses. Stein's first novel, *Q.E.D.* (written in 1903, published in 1950 as *Things As They Are*), is a fairly straightforward depiction of a lesbian love triangle. She seems to have reworked *Q.E.D.* into a story of interracial, possibly bisexual love in "Melanctha," the first part of her triptych *Three Lives* (1909). Her *Autobiography of Alice B. Toklas* (1933) both portrays her productively symbiotic relationship with Toklas and belies the realist premises of autobiography. The narrator, supposedly Toklas, speaks only through an

a Peter Nicholls (in this volume) gives an especially nuanced and detailed account of Stein's experimental prose and its epistemological stakes, without connecting her stylistic particularities to her gender or sexual orientation (chapter 37, "Stein, Hemingway, and American Modernisms").

"I" that is clearly Stein's. In revealing more about Stein and her circle of fellow geniuses than it does about her beloved life partner, the novel implicitly critiques the notion of a singular subject in ways that have proved particularly important to feminist theory. Djuna Barnes's *Ladies' Almanack* (1928) is part book of days, part gossip tabloid, and part utopian lesbian fantasia; this hilarious portrait of a women's community consists of a sequence of loosely connected, bawdy episodes involving caricatures of Barnes's friends thinly disguised as quarrelling medieval wenches. *Nightwood* (1936), Barnes's masterpiece of formal innovation and gender and sexual imagination, tells of several doomed love affairs involving, among others, a German-Jewish aristocrat, an Irish-American gynecologist, a circus performer, and an American expatriate obsessed with a lost lover. The novel suspends plot, narrator, and action, unfolding through somewhat disjunctive scenes recounted in long hallucinatory monologues by a shifting first-person narrator, who speaks in sentences that practically collapse under the weight of their nested grammatical structures. These recursive techniques suspend not only the sentence but also social convention: in *Nightwood*, desire is never resolved into easy couplehood, nor will identity consummate in self-presence and self-understanding.

Stein's and Barnes's most obvious inheritor of formal innovations that mirror or perform new understandings of gender and sexuality is Bertha Harris, whose novel *Lover* (1976) challenges readerly expectations on almost every front. Five generations of women shift positions on the family tree in *Lover*, in episodes that double back upon themselves and change, as told by a first-person narrator so shifty as to be unlocatable in time and space. Harris wrote *Lover* in explicit homage to *Nightwood*, to what she called its "vaudeville atmosphere" of circus, opera, and theater. While Stein and Barnes variously dismantle the subject-verb-object sentence, the marriage-driven plot, and the naturalized first-person narrator, Harris also skews the logic of generational succession and celebrates the theatricality of all identities in ways that anticipate recent theories of queer time and performativity.[3]

Gay male authors also undertook formal and generic experiments. Like Barnes, several were clearly influenced by the European Decadents, such as Baudelaire and J. K. Huysmans, who celebrated all things unnatural, decaying, and nonfamilial as well as cherishing the gratuitously ornamental. For example, Charles Henri Ford and Parker Tyler's *The Young and the Evil* (1933) gleefully portrays the romps of a couple of Southern men in bohemian and queer New York. This novel is marked by a strangely flat, minimally punctuated, Stein-like prose peppered with aphorisms – such as "A doll does not believe in itself he thought only in its dollness." In its melodramatic embrace of the trivial and its arch tone, *The Young and the Evil* epitomizes the era of high camp that succeeded Decadence.

But *The Young and the Evil* also occasionally lurches into the sort of monologic free verse that Allan Ginsberg would later use in his long poem *Howl* (1955). In this sense, Ford and Tyler's novel anticipates some of the sexual and narrative energies of the more earnest Beat movement of the 1950s. For all its machismo, Beat literature was extraordinarily queer. For instance, William S. Burroughs's *Queer* (written 1951–1953, published 1985) features heroin addicts in pursuit of drugs and sometimes other men, while his more formally experimental *Naked Lunch* (1959) chops up and remixes plot, shifting time and space in imitation of a psychedelic high, and introduces nonhuman characters such as the Mugwumps. Explicitly depicting non-heteronormative sex and extreme bodily experiences, Burroughs's work also echoes Kerouac and Ginsberg's "beat" cadences (units of sense marked off more by breath than by conventional grammar) and even Walt Whitman.[b] Though the gay Chicano author John Rechy had only occasional contact with the Beats, his *City of Night* (1963) shows a clear Beat influence: it depicts a nameless "youngman" wandering the streets looking for sex and encountering hustlers, invalids, transsexuals, cast-off actors pursuing ephebes, and homophobic cops who have sex with men. Rechy too abandons plot for vignette, and his prose imitates both the meanderings of his characters and their everyday speech. In sum, Beat literature offered a poetics of the body, of breath, sensation, and the breaking of physical and cognitive boundaries, that openly confronted the pieties of bourgeois existence, including middle-class gender and sexual norms. These authors and the lesbian ones cited above set the stage for the New Narrative movement of the 1970s and 1980s, in which high critical theory and a poetics of the body collided in highly experimental prose.

Just as mainstream literary history often focuses on battles, traditional gay and lesbian literary history has often used the Stonewall rebellion of 1969, in which LGBT people fought a police raid, to mark the advent of a more "liberated" gay literature. The all-male Violet Quill Club of 1980–1981 – Robert Ferro, Andrew Holleran, Felice Picano, and Edmund White, among others – is sometimes given credit as the first important "post-Stonewall" gay literary coterie.[4] The work that emerged from these men's time as a writing group is beautifully written and autobiographical enough to give a nuanced picture of gay white male life in the mid- to late-twentieth century. These

b For a related reading of Burroughs, and of the "Beat" concept generally, see Robert Faggen's essay in this volume, "The Beats and the 1960s," chapter 55, esp. 917–918.

authors offered complex depictions of gay issues, rather than homosexuality *as* an issue. For instance, Ferro's *The Family of Max Desir* (1983) explores the balance between life in the gay ghetto and an Italian American's wish to honor and participate in extended family relations. White's novels *A Boy's Own Story* (1982) and *The Beautiful Room Is Empty* (1988) chronicle the coming out of an unnamed narrator from his 1950s childhood to the Stonewall rebellion, but in a nonsequential and elliptical fashion that belies the teleological structure of "coming out" itself. The Violet Quill club writers and their colleagues – Andrew Holleran (*The Dancer from the Dance*, 1978), Larry Kramer (*Faggots*, 1978), Felice Picano (*Ambidextrous: The Secret Lives of Children*, 1985), David Plante (The Francoeur Family trilogy, 1978–1982), Armistead Maupin (the *Tales of the City* novels, 1978–1987), and David Leavitt (*The Lost Language of Cranes*, 1986) – offered new possibilities for understanding gay male life and new subject-positions to novel readers. Though the club was short-lived, its project of producing an artistic literature that cherished the ordinary as well as extraordinary facets of gay lives culminated, in many ways, with successor Michael Cunningham's Pulitzer Prize-winning *The Hours* (1998), a structurally and stylistically complex rewriting of Virginia Woolf's 1925 novella *Mrs. Dalloway*.

But arguably, these authors' status as a "circle" or "school" of writing in which gay life and letters merged was anticipated by the 1920s Left Bank lesbian writers who surrounded Djuna Barnes and Gertrude Stein, the mid-century Beat movement that influenced Burroughs and Rechy, and the 1970s feminist small press writers among whom Bertha Harris circulated. These circles of authors were equally daring, and their works generally more stylistically innovative. Read alongside works written before the 1970s, the post-Stonewall novels produced by the Violet Quill authors can look somewhat conventional, somewhat more like a return to realism. They do substitute plots of sexual experimentation, journeys toward gay identity, and subcultural formation for the traditional bourgeois novel's hackneyed love plot, but until Cunningham they are less interested in the question of how aesthetic technique itself can mirror and/or transform consciousness. To capture the ways that novelists reimagined gender and sexuality, we need to bend the timeline of lesbian and gay literature to include both works that challenge the conventions of the novel in avant-garde ways, and the "rearguard" works of popular culture that until recently have not been counted as artistic enough to merit study.

Letting loose the canons: reimagining literary history

The feminist and LGBT literary history of the nineteenth and twentieth centuries has conventionally focused on so-called "high literature": works published by elite small presses or magazines and aimed at a highly educated readership. Yet not all literature that reimagined gender and sexuality appeared in these venues. A history of how American authors reimagined gender and sexual norms also demands consideration of popular genres. Indeed, many feminist, queer, and otherwise sexually adventurous works of the twentieth century blend the formally innovative work of the high art novel with the formulaic pleasures of genre fiction. The "pulp," the gothic, the crime novel, the Western, and science fiction all offered possibilities for rethinking dominant codes of masculinity, femininity, and heteronormativity. While the sexual imagination of bohemian or avant-garde artists appears in breakdowns of novelistic and grammatical structures, in popular literature it often appears in more literal reconfigurations of space and time, in queer elsewheres. We might think of these elsewheres as a queer frontier literature, marked not by the terrifying confrontations with nonidentity that mark traditional frontier literature, as Stephanie LeMenager characterizes the category in her chapter for this volume, but by a surplus of possibilities for thinking beyond the hetero-gendered here and now.[c]

Gay and lesbian pulp novels, which peaked in popularity between the 1930s and the mid-1960s, are perhaps the most recognizably queer mass genre. Pulps exposed the salacious details of sexually adventurous straight women, gay men, lesbians, and other denizens of "the underworld," titillating a reader usually addressed as normatively male and straight. But these novels were marketed to the masses and, as James L. W. West, III argues in his chapter in this volume, "American authors began to see that they might reach readers heretofore unavailable to them," an audience of outsiders for whom the trope of the underworld figured the tensions of leading a double life.[d] In pulps these readers found women who were sexually active outside of marriage, gay and lesbian relationships, manly women and queeny men, and kink-lovers of various stripes. However exaggerated or stereotyped these images were, they reflected aspects of real experience outside of monogamous heterosexual

c Stephanie Le Menager, "Imagining the frontier," chapter 31 in this volume, 515.
d James L. W. West III, "Twentieth-century publishing and the rise of the paperback," chapter 47 in this volume, 782.

marriage. Marijane Meaker, writing as "Vin Packer," launched the genre with her 1952 novel *Spring Fire*, a lesbian drama set in a sorority – and Meaker went on to author, as Ann Aldrich, five documentary tales depicting the lesbian underground in all its sordid glory. As M. E. Kerr, Meaker also penned a couple of young adult novels treating the theme of homosexuality (*Is That You, Miss Blue* in 1975 and *Deliver Us from Evie* in 1994). Ann Bannon's *Beebo Brinker* chronicles (1957–1962), which the author claims were inspired by Meaker, have been read by generations of lesbians because Bannon offered up a somewhat more sympathetic vision of lesbian love. Out of a formula designed both to arouse and to police the desires of supposedly straight readers, Meaker and Bannon crafted little romances rather less decorous than Jane Austen's, but with some of the same concerns: how was a lesbian to earn a living? What did she need to sacrifice to survive? And how might she speak over oblivious straight people to get her meaning to other lesbians?

The crime genre, which reworked pulp novels' depictions of "criminal" sexual dissidents into tales of literal lawbreaking and justice, also offered new identities and erotic possibilities. Sean McCann, in his chapter for this volume, argues that even for major writers of the early to mid twentieth century, the intuitive language of social disorder and social injustice was crime.[e] But that language also provided an imagistic register for the experience of being homosexual in America. Crime fiction usually features romantically unattached protagonists moving through the secret parts of a city, seeking clues (often unwittingly clues about themselves as well as about external events) and so allegorizes the experience of homosexuality as a painstaking search for self-understanding in hostile conditions. Patricia Highsmith, for instance, wrote crime thrillers with homoerotic twists: her one lesbian romance, *The Price of Salt* (1952), reflects her more general interest in the psychodynamics of same-sex attraction, but she figured its legally criminal status in novels like *Strangers on a Train* (1950) and *The Talented Mr. Ripley* (1955), both of which feature lawbreaking men playing erotically charged cat-and-mouse games with one another. By the late twentieth century, gay male and lesbian mystery fiction, authored by popular writers such as Sandra Scoppetone and Michael Nava, would become a subgenre.

Related to the mystery and the thriller in its appeal to extreme emotions and uncanny spaces, the gothic has been another productively queer lowbrow genre. Not only does the Romantic-era British gothic trade on the irrationality

e Sean McCann, "The novel of crime, mystery, and suspense," chapter 48 in this volume, esp. 798.

eventually attributed to sexual minorities, but its vampires and ghosts are also notable for their gender ambiguity and ability to penetrate or inhabit other bodies. Popular American horror and ghost fiction has tended to follow British gothic conventions, but the work of US author Anne Rice deserves special mention for the way it brings out the latent queerness of vampires and ghosts.

More recognizably a US genre, the Southern gothic merged elite late-nineteenth-century regionalism with British gothic tropes to produce overtly queer imaginings, as in William Faulkner's novels, which contain any number of ambiguously gendered, incestuous, and otherwise nonnormative characters, and whose prose plays with revelation and secrecy, withholding and overexposure, in ways that reflect modern understandings of homosexuality as an open secret – and serve as a searing rebuke of racialized heteronormativity. Faulkner's *Absalom, Absalom!* (1936) is perhaps the finest critique of the racial politics of the US sex/gender system. In this novel, two young male Harvard students, obviously invested erotically in one another, recount and reconstruct the story of a bisexual white man, Henry Sutpen, whose passion for a college friend, later revealed to be his illegitimate half-brother through his father's disavowed marriage to a black woman, destroys the legacy of his white supremacist family. The story is passed from unmarked narrator to unmarked narrator in an intricate frame structure, and the secrets revealed include not only erotic attraction between men, but also the interracial heritage of all "white" Americans.

Other authors extended Faulkner's topics and techniques. Carson McCullers exploited the conventions of the gothic – old houses, desolated and ruined places, characters on the verge of madness – in *The Heart is a Lonely Hunter* (1940), *The Ballad of the Sad Café* (1943), and *The Member of the Wedding* (1946). She peopled these novels with characters variously infirm, disabled, transgender, bisexual, and triangular in their desires, which often play out in monologue, dream, or fantasy rather than in action. And Truman Capote's *Other Voices, Other Rooms* (1948) resembles not only Faulkner but also McCullers in its dense, hallucinatory prose, and its haunting portrayal of unmoored characters loosely conglomerated into a family – here a prepubescent boy, his grim stepmother, his dying father, his reclusive dandy of an uncle, and a black servant, all trapped in a decaying mansion in the deep South. Probably the most famous contemporary novel inheriting the gothic's queer energies is Dorothy Allison's *Bastard Out of Carolina* (1992), the story of a young proto-lesbian Appalachian girl who is raped by her stepfather, yet survives her brutal upbringing with a fierce mixture of shame and pride in her heritage.

Writers interested in rethinking gender and sexuality have turned not only south but also west. Ostensibly a macho genre, the Western nevertheless, in its exclusion of women, hinted at the joys of same-sex erotic encounters. Jack London's *Call of the Wild* (1903), an anthropomorphized dog's story of hardship under various masters in the Klondike, explores this possibility through interspecies love. Willa Cather's *The Professor's House* (1925) and *Death Comes for the Archbishop* (1927) offer up the wide open, arid spaces of New Mexico, where women seem to fade away: these landscapes are not reproductive in any heteronormative sense, but suggest alternative sites of inculcation, mentorship, and other passionate relations between men. Capote's *In Cold Blood* (1966), while more famous as a hybrid of fiction and crime journalism, also depicts two desperate men with queer backgrounds and desires in a desolate Kansas landscape.[f] And as an experiment in pushing the sexual envelope – here toward heterosexual pedophilia – Vladimir Nabokov's *Lolita* (1955) camped heavily on the Western. As Humbert Humbert and his preteen stepdaughter Lolita, with whom he is having an affair, take a frantic road trip across the country, they are pursued by Lolita's other lover, the eccentric bisexual Clare Quilty. Nabokov consummates Humbert's obsession with Quilty in a ludicrous send-up of the Western's "money shot," a gunfight between an enraged Humbert and a drunk Quilty. Jane Rule's *The Desert of the Heart* (1964), the story of two divorcées who fall in love in Reno, brought out the lesbian possibilities inherent in a genre that so resolutely refuses domestic femininity, and eventually, overtly gay male Westerns appeared (the 2005 film *Brokeback Mountain*, based on a story by E. Annie Proulx, being perhaps the most recent).

Speculative fiction, also called science fiction, offers perhaps the freest rein for reimagining gender and thereby sexuality. Speculative fiction's technique of "cognitive estrangement," or defamiliarization, relies particularly on the reorganization of sensory and bodily experiences, which has had powerful resonance for a population already estranged from dominant culture and engaged in new ways of experiencing erotic and bodily pleasure.[g] Charlotte Perkins Gilman's *Herland* (1915), about three men who blunder into an all-female society in which parthenogenetic motherhood is the highest social

f In "The nonfiction novel" (chapter 59 in this volume), David Schmid argues that *In Cold Blood* must be read as a critique of interpersonal violence (993); however, it is equally well read as a queer critique of the Cold War-era nuclear family and the blending of fiction and documentary that produced it as a norm.

g For a detailed description and examples of speculative fiction's cognitive estrangement, see Priscilla Wald, "Science fiction," chapter 50 in this volume.

value, is in some ways the forerunner of feminist speculative fiction, though Gilman skirts the obvious possibility of lesbian love. Marge Piercy's *Woman on the Edge of Time* (1976) offers a similar all-female utopia, this time with lesbianism a viable option as, in a different way, does Joanna Russ's experimental *The Female Man* (1975), which stages a meeting between four women living in four different historical times and places.[h] Samuel Delany is surely one of the most important and prolific writers of the genre, producing a highly conceptual *oeuvre* that queries conventional gender, sexual, and racial constructions while inventing new ways of being. Scholars of gender and sexuality in speculative fiction single out as especially innovative Delany's *Equinox* (originally titled *The Tides of Lust*, 1973), which features a shipful of sexual daredevils; *Dhalgren* (1975), in which a young biracial drifter undergoes various permutations of time, space, and sexual congress in a ruined city; and *Triton* (1976), whose characters live on a planet where the possibilities for psychological and physical self-modification are infinite.[5] In all of these works, differently gendered and sexualized bodies and/or extreme sexual experiences are templates for and reflect social critique and/or liberation.

While utopia and dystopia may be the "final frontier" for speculating on gender and sexuality in genre fiction, some writers were much less sanguine about American literature's connection between illicit eroticism and foreign expansion. As Russ Castronovo argues in this volume, the "exotic" settings and enticingly different cultural norms of both frontier literature and the novel of empire "implied the precarious global reach of white male sexual desire," and thus were a means of contesting its dominance.[i] Thus for many authors, reimagining gender and sexuality meant neither simply reconstituting the novel as a form, nor muddling neat generic or period distinctions, but rather staging a critique of "America" and its imperial project.

"The More Profound Nationality of Their Lesbianism":[6] reimagining "America"

Traditionally, the divide between Europe and America that structures the field of English literature reinforces gendered and sexualized conceptions of nationhood. Throughout the literary and cultural history of the United States, "America" itself has been imagined in patriarchal and heterosexist terms –

h Maria Farland also considers utopian feminist literature that addresses homophobia in "Literary feminisms," chapter 56 in this volume.

i Russ Castronovo, "Imperialism, Orientalism, and empire," chapter 32 in this volume, 538.

variously, as England's rebellious offspring, a republic founded on the principles of conjugality, a "house divided" by Civil War, a product and scene of white masculine frontier adventure, an Anglo-Saxon territory threatened by women's sexual activity, a bastion of family values threatened by communists or terrorists, and so on – and these terms have been elaborated in and by the novel.[7] Additionally, several influential critics have argued that the novel itself has been a means for consolidating the time, space, and emotions proper to nationality, as well as for the overt promotion of national culture.[8] But the literature of gender and sexual dissidents has always been more cosmopolitan, more engaged with connections across the boundaries of nation-states, more critical of the sexual politics of empire, than the official category "American literature" generally allows for.

In the aftermath of World War I, a coterie of wealthy, mostly white writers went to Paris, and from that vantage point they envisioned themselves as part of a cosmopolitan elite, freed from both the stylistic norms and the social strictures of the United States. The aforementioned Stein and Barnes were two such authors. Among the work of "Sapphic" modernists, H.D.'s *HERmione* (written 1927, published 1981), is an extraordinary example of a bisexual aesthetic: this thinly disguised fictionalization of H.D.'s simultaneous affairs with Frances Gregg and Ezra Pound features interior monologues that mimic imagist poetry. *HERmione* suggests that both hetero- and homosexual relations are linguistic performances. And indeed, as Kirk Curnutt argues in his chapter for this volume, the sexual liberation so vaunted by this era entailed a certain theatricality, a flaunting of the sexual self, that contradicted a newly celebrated heterosexual intimacy.[j] Attention to the performativity of straight sex characterizes both *The Great Gatsby* (1925), where Nick Carraway'a homoerotic obsession with the theatrical Gatsby offers a more authentic passion precisely because it must articulate itself through indirection and disavowal rather than through flamboyant display, and Ernest Hemingway's *The Sun Also Rises* (1926), which follows an impotent man, Jake Barnes, and his androgynous, polyamorous girlfriend, Brett Ashley, as they move through the expatriate social scene. In the latter novel, wounded heterosexual masculinity offers a vantage point from which to recognize and critique the rampant materialism of Americans, and the way it structures and scripts heterosexual courtship.

Within the corpus of Harlem Renaissance novels, a dialectic between a primitivism looking south, and an urban cosmopolitanism looking north, emerges in the work of African American authors: Zora Neale Hurston,

j Kirk Curnutt, "*The Great Gatsby* and the 1920s," chapter 38 in this volume.

Langston Hughes, Claude Mc Kay, and Jean Toomer celebrated the vernacular and indigenous, while Richard Wright, Nella Larsen, and Ann Petry explored the complexities of metropolitan life.[k] For these authors nature and the city, alternately liberated and oppressive in various works, become landscapes of the mind for which the US nation-state cannot serve as a legitimate horizon of gendered, sexualized, and otherwise social belonging. James Weldon Johnson's *The Autobiography of an Ex-colored Man* (1912) anticipates both the boom in African American writing and Gertrude Stein's later play with fictional autobiography. But this novel also figures some central concerns of the Harlem Renaissance, particularly interracial marriage, the way racial stereotypes are intertwined with sexual ones, and the analogies and disjunctions between passing as white and passing as straight. Johnson's unnamed narrator, a parody of the "tragic mulatto," is feminized by his racial ambiguity, and the novel concerns itself as much with the homoerotics of white patronage as with interracial heterosexual marriage.[9] Nella Larsen's *Passing* (1929) is particularly astute about the erotics of crossing the color line; its main character Irene Redfield obsessively envies and judges, while also fiercely desiring, her friend Clare Kendry, who passes as white in public. More openly than Irene, the main character of Larsen's earlier novel *Quicksand* (1928), Helga Crane, yearns for sexual fulfillment as she withers under the protocols of racial uplift; her move to Denmark to be with her white relatives, however, belies any easy turn to cosmopolitanism, for there she is merely seen as an exotic object.[l] Perhaps the most damning vision of the nation's impossibility as a horizon of belonging for black people is Richard Wright's *Native Son*, expurgated and published for the Book-of-the-Month Club in 1940. Upon the publication of the restored edition in 1991, *Native Son* became even more legibly an indictment of the conditions that distort black male sexuality – segregation, the overvaluation of white femininity, and the long history in which black men were cast first as docile children and later, after slavery, as animals bent on raping white women.

Zora Neale Hurston's *Their Eyes Were Watching God* (1937) is much more optimistic about black sexuality, at least that of women, and re-envisions the black female experience within and through the post-Reconstruction South. Hurston's novel reads interestingly in juxtaposition not only with Larsen but also with Jamaican immigrant Claude McKay's *Home to Harlem* (1928): both

k For a fuller discussion of the rural/urban dialectic and nuanced discussions of these authors, see Valerie Babb, "Wright, Hurston, and the direction of the African American novel," chapter 42.

l See Barbara McCaskill, "The African American novel after Reconstruction," chapter 29.

authors reimagine sexuality by imagining relocation. While Larsen hints that urban milieux offer possibilities for a more fluid sexuality and McKay depicts New York as a scene of sexual and racial transformation, Hurston celebrates African Americans who stay in place and revel sensuously in nature and the "folk," with Janie's physical, possibly even masturbatory transport before a luscious pear tree figuring the possibility of autonomous, self-pleasuring black womanhood. Even this novel's structure – Janie narrates the tale to her friend Pheoby in what Carla Kaplan has called an "erotics of talk" – figures sensuality between women.[10]

In the generation succeeding the Harlem Renaissance, James Baldwin is pivotal to the project of understanding how American nationalism and imperialism rely on both the racialization of sex and the sexualization of race. In Baldwin's *Giovanni's Room* (1956), a novel ostensibly about a love affair between white men in Paris, the American David represents his Italian lover Giovanni in consistently racist terms: as "insolent and dark and leonine," a "valuable racehorse," as a body for sale on an auction block. In fact, though David tells Giovanni he has never before slept with a man, as a boy he had sex with a friend, a black child whose "body suddenly seemed the black opening of a cavern in which I would be tortured till madness came, in which I would lose my manhood." Here the black rectum, reiterating David's vision of his mother as a "body so putrescent . . . that it opened, as I clawed and cried, into a breach so enormous as to swallow me alive," is the feminized grave of white manhood. While David, affianced to Hella, comes to Paris for the usual sensual delights, he clearly brings American racism and sexism with him. The décor of Giovanni's room, where the two men stay during their affair, serves to metaphorize whites' imprisoning vision of African American gender and sexuality far more than it does the erotic freedom supposedly available in Paris. The dim room's windows are painted white, and look out upon a courtyard troped as a "jungle"; its wallpaper depicts heterosexual lovers promenading in a rose garden. These images foreshadow Giovanni's eventual imprisonment and execution for the murder of an openly gay Parisian. Ironically, Giovanni dies as any black man in the early twentieth century USA might have died for killing a white one. David tears up the letter announcing Giovanni's sentence and throws it to the wind, but the pieces insistently blow back upon him, implicating him as a representative of white masculine privilege and more broadly of "America." In this novel, "gay" Paris and the fiction of sex liberated by crossing international boundaries mask a scathing critique of the sexual politics of racism, as well as implicitly questioning the ability of even gay white Americans to expatriate themselves from the history of race in the USA by simply going somewhere else, imaginatively or otherwise.[m]

Baldwin and his successors, the anti-racist, anti-imperialist, feminist and queer novelists of the 1970s and beyond – such as Audre Lorde, Melvin Dixon, Arturo Islas, Achy Obejas, Merle Woo, Jessica Hagedorn, and many others – suggest that an imagination transgressive of gender and sexual norms must necessarily confront, critique, and redress a legacy of national and imperial violence. Often, this violence has been enacted in the explicit name of pure womanhood, aggressive masculinity, heteronormative racial purity, and more recently, even liberal sexual freedom – as in the post-9/11 vision of Afghan women liberated from their burquas by US bombs. These contemporary writers suggest that any supposedly radical queer/feminist imagination, whenever it isolates gender, sexuality, and even literary form and history as vectors separate from and innocent of the racialized politics of empire, will fail to liberate the global majority. In other words, for doubly and triply minoritized American novelists, it is not enough to transgress in the name of gender and sex alone, because these too are implicated with imperial power. But violence has also been enacted in terms that mask any connection with gender and sexuality, such as free trade, personal responsibility, and immigration reform: thus these writers demonstrate that no liberatory project can simply jettison bodily and aesthetic experimentation as white middle-class concerns. In form and content, their works argue that we must reimagine sex, gender, and literature as intertwined means by which empires subordinate populations and reproduce themselves, whether in the name of racial superiority, or of democracy's triumph, or of capitalism's inexorable movement forward. We must also, in turn, reimagine race, nation, and empire as simultaneously gendered, sexualized, and aesthetic techniques of power. No smaller vision will do.

Notes

1. See Nancy Armstrong, *Desire and Domestic Fiction: A Political History of the Novel* (New York: Oxford University Press, 1987).
2. A particularly useful account of the gendered and sexualized project of writing beyond the bourgeois novel is Joseph Allen Boone, *Tradition Counter Tradition: Love and the Form of Fiction* (Chicago: University of Chicago Press, 1987).

m For a reading of *Giovanni's Room* in the inverse context of American belonging, see Lovalerie King, "Ellison and Baldwin: aesthetics, activism, and the social order," chapter 43 in this volume, 725–727.

3. For example, one of the main characters, Veronica, is a forger of paintings for which the originals do not exist, anticipating Judith Butler's concept of gender as a copy without an original. See Judith Butler, *Gender Trouble: Feminism and the Subversion of Identity* (New York: Routledge, 1990).
4. For a typical example of this progress narrative, see www.glbtq.com/literature/am_lit3_gay_post_stonewall.html.
5. See Eric Garber and Lyn Paleo, eds. *Uranian Worlds: A Guide to Alternative Sexuality in Science Fiction, Fantasy, and Horror*, 2nd edn. (Boston: G. K. Hall, 1990).
6. This section's title is borrowed from Bertha Harris, "The More Profound Nationality of Their Lesbianism: Lesbian Society in Paris in the 1920s," in *Amazon Expedition* (New York: Times Change Press, 1973), 77–88.
7. On revolutionary rhetoric, see Jay Fliegelman, *Prodigals and Pilgrims: The American Revolution against Patriarchal Authority, 1750–1800* (Cambridge: Cambridge University Press, 1982); on republican conjugality see Shirley Samuels, *Romances of the Republic: Women, the Family, and Violence in the Literature of the Early American Nation* (New York: Oxford University Press, 1996); allegories of the Civil War in familial terms may be traced to Lincoln's "A House Divided" speech of 1858; on frontier masculinity see Richard Slotkin, *Regeneration Through Violence: The Mythology of the American Frontier, 1600–1860* (Norman: University of Oklahoma Press, 2000); on homophobia and anticommunism, see David K. Johnson, *The Lavender Scare: The Cold War Persecution of Gays and Lesbians in the Federal Government* (Chicago: University of Chicago Press, 2004).
8. See Benedict Anderson, *Imagined Communities: Reflections on the Origin and Spread of Nationalism* (New York: Verso, 1991); Homi K. Bhabha, "DissemiNation: Time, Narrative, and the Margins of the Modern Nation," in *The Location of Culture* (New York: Routledge, 1994), 139–170; and Doris Sommer, *Foundational Fictions: The National Romances of Latin America* (Berkeley: University of California Press, 1991).
9. See Siobhan Somerville, "Double Lives on the Color Line: 'Perverse' Desire in *The Autobiography of an Ex-Coloured Man*," in *Queering the Color Line: Race and the Invention of Homosexuality in American Culture* (Durham, NC, Duke University Press, 2000), 111–130.
10. Carla Kaplan, *The Erotics of Talk: Women's Writing and Feminist Paradigms* (New York: Oxford University Press, 1996).

PART FOUR

*

CONTEMPORARY FORMATIONS

Introduction: contemporary formations

BENJAMIN REISS

Mikhail Bakhtin wrote almost a century ago that "the novel is the sole genre that continues to develop, that is as yet uncompleted. The forces that define it as a genre are at work before our very eyes."[1] But even Bakhtin would have been surprised by some of the changes the novel has undergone in recent years. In the volume's final section of dealing with contemporary formations of the American novel, Robert Coover sees video games marching forth from the arcade and the ones and zeros of executable code spilling out from the computer to transform our sense of what literary narrative can do. DeNel Rehberg Sedo examines how mass media and the internet (as well as government-sponsored reading groups) have helped form new kinds of interactive reading communities; some of these are beginning to shape what gets published, how it gets marketed, and to whom. And Jan Baetens shows how even such a low-tech phenomenon as comics – the most sophisticated of which have been "knocking on literature's door" for decades – have now found an unlikely welcome in the house of the novel, in the process subtly eroding our baseline sense of the novel as "a narrative work of verbal fiction between two covers."

Despite all of these changes, the novel's extraordinary powers of absorption and formal flexibility allow it to continue to perform its traditional function: to picture and reflect upon the broader transformations of the world surrounding it. The dizzying proliferation of information technology; globalization and the rise of a "neoliberal" economic order; world populations linked but also profoundly threatened (ecologically and otherwise) by technology and the transnational flow of capital; the countervailing assertion of ethnic identity and its discontents; the related revising and fracturing of grand national narratives; new forms of violence that make traditional state warfare almost obsolete; the precarious status of books in a world of digitization; and the persistence of old forms of narrative within a changed media landscape: these are some of the key themes running through novels discussed in the following chapters. These developments have also spawned new categories of critical analysis, which are highlighted most clearly in chapters in this section.

Many prominent recent changes to narrative art and to novel-making are referred to under the heading of "postmodernism," a term for which Ursula Heise provides a typology and developmental narrative in relation to the novel. She tracks four linked movements in postmodern novels since the 1960s: "metafiction" (or fiction acutely aware of its own artifice); the fictional reconstruction of previously ignored or forgotten histories; "cyberpunk" narratives engaging virtual realities and human bodies hybridized by technology; and narratives representing "global scenarios by means of innovative fictional forms." Linking each of these, in her account, is a sense of the "crisis of representation: a deeply felt loss of faith in our ability to represent the real." Indeed, that felt crisis of representation neatly frames almost all of the chapters in this section and helps to explain some of the formal upheavals mentioned above. David Schmid attributes it to the unprecedented forms of mass violence that became so pervasive in the twentieth century: death camps, atomic bombs, and other horrors that defied traditional modes of representation. The nonfiction novel, he argues, arose as a mode of understanding "the stakes of representing reality, especially when that reality seems disturbed or distorted by violence." Not surprisingly, that newest variant of the novel, the graphic novel, troubles the fact/fiction divide as insistently as it does the divide between verbal and visual arts. This refusal to conform to established representational modes allowed its first canonical practitioner, Art Spiegelman, to suggest powerfully the unrepresentability of the real-life horrors of the Holocaust.

Re-narrating the past in order to reveal the violence and subjection ordinarily repressed in nationalistic narratives is an important part of Toni Morrison's method in *Beloved* (1987), the most canonical American novel of the late twentieth century. Centering on the career of Morrison, Michael Hill charts the recent movement of African American literature from a strong strain of minority writing to a position of national, even international, preeminence. The now-regular garnering of major critical prizes (headed by Morrison's Nobel Prize, but including major laurels for John Edgar Wideman, Ishmael Reed, Charles Johnson, Paule Marshall, and others) signifies not only a shift into the literary mainstream, but also the ability of African American writers to re-direct that stream. Like African American writers, Native American authors have long struggled, according to Sean Kicummah Teuton, with the need "to meet the demands of a mainstream reading audience" without acceding to their stereotypes and misrepresentations.

Shrugging off the powerful myth of the Vanishing Indian, novelists of the Red Power era (including N. Scott Momaday, James Welch, and Leslie Marmon Silko) elucidate "how American Indian people can awaken politically, reclaim a history, and build a community."[a] And yet, especially in recent years, Native American writers have boldly moved their protagonists into more postmodern geographical, thematic, and formal terrains: city spaces, openly gay relationships, and metafictional and fantastical styles where identity is slippery and the hold of the past begins to weaken.

Even as old identity categories begin to fragment, new ones cohere. Susan Koshy outlines a literary tradition associated with a racial category of younger provenance than African American or Native American. In contrast to African American literature, which "has gathered historical density and coherence over time and built a continuous tradition," many novels now classified as Asian American were written before the category existed. This tradition, then, constitutes an "invented" lineage, rather than a "found" history, along the lines sketched out by Leonard Cassuto in his general introduction to this volume. (In another respect, though, Asian American writers such as Chang Rae Lee and Maxine Hong Kingston update an old literary American literary tradition of narratives of immigration and uneasy belonging.) Similarly, disability is a concept that can unify a broad range of experiences and representations stretching back to a time well before the category was created. In their chapter, David Mitchell and Sharon Snyder trace a long history of narratives of disability, up to the point at which "disabled people begin to find themselves identified as the bearers of an experience akin to other minority communities."

According to Walter Benn Michaels, however, the attention we give in our schools and in volumes such as this one to "novels of identity" – those in which the central drama involves defining "who we are" rather than "how much (or little) we own" – is profoundly misguided. Such critical attention helps maintain a picture of "the USA as a country composed of many different minorities rather than of a large majority falling further and further behind the one minority that matters most – the rich." Michaels's essay exemplifies the way in which this volume questions (sometimes aggressively) the methods and underlying assumptions of literary history as it is practiced today. Not surprisingly, several contributors in this section take explicit issue with

a The pervasiveness of the Vanishing Indian myth is chronicled in essays by Timothy Sweet (chapter 5), Sandra Gustafson (chapter 6), Winfried Fluck (chapter 7), and Stephanie LeMenager (chapter 31) earlier in this volume.

Michaels's plea to move beyond race as a critical category. Michaels and Rodrigo Lazo offer competing readings of Francisco Goldman's *The Ordinary Seaman* (1997). Michaels sees it as a novel that interrogates identity categories, revealing that our neoliberal economic order uses race as a kind of smokescreen to hide the more fundamental economic inequalities that keep the American economic system working for the rich. Lazo, on the other hand, points to *The Ordinary Seaman*'s portrayal of the continuing effects of racial categories on labor relations. Similarly, instead of attempting to reveal an economic structure obscured by an obsessive focus on race, Ramón Saldívar sees multiple racial and class-based categories in fluid interaction with each other in borderlands novels by authors such as Américo Paredes, Cormac McCarthy, and Leslie Marmon Silko.

The chapters by Saldívar and Lazo return us to questions of region, setting, and spacialization that have framed a number of previous chapters in the volume.[b] Saldívar reads the US border regions as contested spaces where different cultural and linguistic traditions come into often violent conflict. Lazo turns to novels that take "the Americas," rather than any particular region or nation within them, as their setting. With examples ranging from the first novelistic travel narratives written by European explorers through contemporary works by Junot Diaz and E. Annie Proulx, he sketches a tradition of novels that "call attention to complex settings that include people from various parts of the hemisphere who must negotiate power imbalances that have roots in the colonial history of the Americas."[c] Pushing beyond even this hemispheric perspective, Bruce Robbins finds the much-trumpeted global consciousness in post-9/11 novels to be – for the most part – quite thin. He charges recent literary fiction with failing to "get inside foreign minds in the midst of foreign histories," and argues that popular modes like science fiction and the political thriller have for some time been more worldly than even the globe-trotting narratives of much highbrow work. A more successful engagement with the "world" as system, according to Jonathan Levin, comes in the eco-novels that have proliferated and gained maturity since the 1970s. Recent novels like Don DeLillo's *Underworld* (1997), he argues, have moved well

b See particularly the essays by Timothy Sweet (chapter 5), Hester Blum (chapter 9), Jennifer Rae Greeson (chapter 14), Stephanie LeMenager (chapter 31), Tom Lutz (chapter 26), Jude Davies (chapter 22), Gretchen Murphy (chapter 33), Candace Waid (chapter 45), and Catherine Jurca (chapter 53).

c Gretchen Murphy's essay earlier in this volume (chapter 33) considers the emergence of "hemispheric solidarity and its opposing strains of racial and imperialist thought" in nineteenth-century postcolonial writing from the Americas (554).

beyond the themes of wilderness preservation and attachment to the land prevalent in earlier works by writers like Edward Abbey and Barbara Kingsolver to portray a "postnatural" landscape in which not a square inch of the globe is uncontaminated by human activity. Nonetheless, Levin sees these writers as linked by a "sense of reverence and wonder before the natural world, whether that world is regarded as a wilderness, a farm, or a more elaborately engineered hybrid."

Finally, Robert Coover's chapter offers a sort of global positioning system (GPS) for the narrative arts as we find them now, one that might help us see pathways into the future. It is fitting that the final word of *The Cambridge History of the American Novel* go to Coover, a major novelist (whose *The Public Burning* [1977] is discussed by several contributors here[d]) and one of our most trenchant observers of the new media ecology in which the novel now finds itself embedded. His chapter situates the tentative attempts of contemporary narrative artists to grapple with digital technology within a vast historical frame that arcs well beyond the temporal and geographic confines of "the American novel," reaching back to the invention of cuneiform in ancient Sumer and moving through Gutenberg's invention of movable type to show how the novel was born out of the technological innovations of several millennia. Although Coover foresees that the novel – at least in its centuries-old "monomedia" form –will begin to be replaced by other narrative forms, he asserts that "there remains through all generations a desire for literary art that is intellectually and aesthetically written, organic, intentional, speculative, beautiful, entertaining, evocative, innovative if possible, a witness to the times." The chapters in this section show how complicated a job it is to witness these particular times, and how boldly the novel is rising to the challenge.

Notes

1. Mikhail Bakhtin, *The Dialogic Imagination: Four Essays*, ed. Michael Holquist, trans. Caryl Emerson and Michael Holquist (Austin: University of Texas Press, 1982), 3.

d See essays by Winfried Fluck (chapter 7), Ursula Heise (chapter 58), and David Schmid (chapter 59).

58
Postmodern novels

URSULA K. HEISE

Anatomies of postmodernism

During the last quarter of the twentieth century, the concept of the "postmodern" was without question the most important organizing category for a wide spectrum of debates about contemporary society and culture. As a fulcrum of discussions that ranged from philosophy, language, and literature all the way to questions of the human body, identity, political subjecthood, social inequality, science, technology, and economic structures, its implications became necessarily diffuse. Postmodernism was maligned for having too many meanings by some and for having no meaning at all by others, ridiculed by some as the epitome of pointlessly arcane and convoluted academicism and by others as a synonym for hopeless intellectual befuddlement. If the concept proved to have considerable staying power in spite of such attacks, critiques, dismissals, and jokes, it is undoubtedly because it did provide a convenient shorthand for wide-ranging debates about the legacies of modernity. Questions such as whether the worldwide spread of capitalism implied the globalization of Western modernity or its obsolescence, whether Enlightenment ideas of individual identity and political subjectivity were necessary tools or conceptual obstacles in struggles for gender or race equality and colonial independence, and what role science and technology should play in a pluralist and cross-cultural context of competing theories and practices of knowledge were debated across a wide variety of political, cultural, and academic venues.

The "modern" implicit in such debates was often the philosophical, political, and cultural legacy of a modernity whose most important roots were perceived to lie in the eighteenth century, but a somewhat different notion of the modern informed parallel conversations about literature and the arts. In seeking to understand the influences behind the fundamental innovations that transformed architecture, the visual arts, fiction, and film in the 1960s, critics referred to the aesthetic modernisms of the early twentieth century as much as they did to the broader philosophical issues of Enlightenment modernity. But, as theorists such as Hans Bertens, Steven Connor, and Steven Izenour have lucidly demonstrated, the implications of the postmodern moment differ widely in different artistic practices. In architecture, local, vernacular, and pop-cultural elements of the kind described by Robert Venturi and Denise Scott Brown emerged as a new formal idiom radically different from the functionalism of Bauhaus and International-Style architecture.[1] Historical pastiche also formed part of this new style, as the playful Chippendale finish atop Philip Johnson's AT&T Building (1984) in New York demonstrated.[2] Painters and sculptors similarly turned away from modernist high-cultural autonomy and abstraction toward popular culture (as in the works of Andy Warhol or Claes Oldenburg), or toward the reintroduction of narrative structures and historical elements (as in many of Robert Rauschenberg's paintings). But fiction and photography, at the same moment, began to prefer anti-realist and anti-narrative styles, while other art forms such as film, theater, dance, and poetry included both realism and anti-realism, narrative and its fragmentation. According to Bertens,

> [i]f there is a common denominator to all these postmodernisms, it is that of a crisis in representation: a deeply felt loss of faith in our ability to represent the real, in the widest sense. No matter whether they are aesthetic, epistemological, moral, or political in nature, the representations that we used to rely on can no longer be taken for granted.[3]

This sense of a representational crisis explains why concerns about language, rhetoric, and figuration surface consistently across debates that in very different ways engage with the question of how "reality" and "facts" are defined, accessed, and communicated in contemporary society. Many of the most important theories of the postmodern engage with concepts of discourse, narrative, metaphorization, and performance to explain fundamental structures of contemporary societies: Jürgen Habermas's theory of a "crisis of legitimation" that affects modern political, social, and scientific concepts and institutions; Jean-François Lyotard's outline of a crisis of the "metanarrative" templates that had shaped Western thought since the Enlightenment; Jean Baudrillard's postulation of a shift into a "hyperreal" culture of simulation in which apparent copies or imitations have lost their ties to authentic originals; Andreas Huyssen's and Fredric Jameson's descriptions of a weakening sense of historicity both among artists and in Western cultures at large; Michel Foucault's and Jacques Lacan's theories of selves constructed through discourse; and Judith Butler's approach to gendered identity as a kind of performance, to name only a few of the most influential approaches.[4] But even if such issues constitute a leitmotif that reappears across otherwise widely varying bodies of theory, calling such perspectives "postmodernist" highlights one of the additional complications of the term. At one level, as we have seen, the designation "postmodernist" can refer to a characteristic of artworks for the most part created after 1960 in a variety of countries. But at another level, certain sets of postmodernist theories and philosophical perspectives (usually, but not always, influenced by one of several strains of French poststructuralism) could and were brought to bear on texts and artworks not necessarily associated with this period, which justifies a title such as *Postmodernism Across the Ages*. And finally, "postmodernist" has often been used as a term describing properties of late twentieth-century societies and cultures in general.[5]

A large number of introductions and anthologies dedicated to postmodernism have explored these issues in detail.[6] In the more specific context of developments in the late twentieth-century North American novel, additional complexities arise. If postmodernism indeed involves fundamental changes in the understanding of narrative and historicity, one would naturally expect it to transform the shape of fictional texts; but between the 1960s and the early twenty-first century, the meanings of the phrase "postmodern fiction" repeatedly shifted grounds as it was used to refer to thematically and formally quite different types of novels and short stories. As I will show in more detail below, postmodern novels fall into at least four different categories. During the 1960s and 1970s, postmodernism was most centrally associated with an extremely self-referential and often openly anti-realist type of narrative also called "metafiction," in which the conditions and articulations of textuality itself take precedence over the novel's relation to its extratextual referents. Metafictional novels tend to involve arbitrary formal constraints (such as the omission of certain letters); elaborate textual embeddings and *mises en abîme*; explicit references to processes of writing, storytelling, publishing, and reading; logically contradictory plotlines; characters conceived in active disregard of principles of psychological plausibility; narrators whose identities remain ambiguous; mosaics of quotation, parody, and pastiche of other texts (sometimes to the point of downright plagiarism); linguistic patchworks of different styles; and experimental typographies. During the later 1970s and the 1980s, however, "postmodern fiction" also began to include less experimental novels concerned with unearthing histories forgotten or ignored by mainstream culture, often those of women, immigrants, and racial or ethnic minorities.

Some of these novelists show an intense awareness of the constructedness of history and the blurry boundaries between history and fiction, but they are far less committed to an anti-realist agenda. Instead, they carve out new fictional territory in between histories of oppression and the complex socio-cultural conditions of narrative and textuality.

In a third wave of postmodernist novels, science fiction texts associated with the "cyberpunk" movement of the 1980s came to add another layer of resonance to the term. Combining their fascination with the cutting edge of digital technology with a deep investment in the oppositional socio-cultural stance of punk rockers, authors such as William Gibson, Bruce Sterling, and Pat Cadigan reimagined the near future under the rule of global computer networks. By and large conventionally realist in their narrative idiom, these novels nevertheless came to be perceived as quintessentially postmodern in their explorations of new virtual spaces and technologically reconfigured bodies.[a] Their persistent portrayals of a thoroughly globalized world in the economic and technological spheres prepared the way for the fourth wave of postmodernist novels. In the 1990s and early 2000s, an increasing number of writers thematized globalization and its relation to modernity and postmodernity in novels that combine elements of the earlier waves of postmodern narrative, from metafictional elements and the foregrounding of different gendered, national, racial, and ethnic communities to the emphasis on new technologies. But the deepening interest in how to represent global scenarios by means of innovative fictional forms also points to the weakening hold that the concept of postmodernism has on analyses of contemporary culture. Discussions about transnationalism, internationalism, and globalization, which took on increasing importance in the social sciences from the early 1990s, and in the humanities from the mid-1990s onward, continue to address fundamental questions about the political, social, economic, and cultural forms of modernity in the contemporary world. But their focus on issues of geopolitics, the risk society, environmental crisis, the renewed importance of nationalisms and religious beliefs, and the definition of cultural identities in a global field of media connections also marks shifts of emphasis that may well imply the obsolescence of the idea of the "postmodern" in the sense of the 1970s and 1980s.

Criticism since the 1980s has proposed a variety of useful perspectives on postmodern fiction. To name only a few of the most influential, Christopher

a For a history of the genre in its conception of the human body, see Priscilla Wald, "Science fiction," chapter 50.

Butler and Brian McHale have analyzed the transformations of high-modernist aesthetic templates in postmodern narrative; Allan Thiher has linked postmodern narrative experiments to currents in twentieth-century language philosophy; Fredric Jameson, Margaret Rose, and the novelist Raymond Federman have theorized their forms of parody, pastiche, and intertextual quotation; Linda Hutcheon and Amy Elias have foregrounded the connections and disjunctures between postmodern fiction and the writing of history; and Mark McGurl has approached post-1960s fiction (somewhat more broadly understood) in its growing associations with the academy.[7] I will have occasion to refer to many of these theories here, but will focus them through a somewhat different, media-theoretical approach to postmodern fiction that surfaces in the work of Joseph Tabbi, Michael Wutz, N. Katherine Hayles, and Kathleen Fitzpatrick.[8] One way of understanding the continuity of postmodern fiction across its very different articulations during the last half-century, I will argue, is to understand its narrative innovations as varying attempts to resituate print narrative in a changing media landscape increasingly dominated by the moving image and by digitization.

Metafiction and its transformations

In the 1960s and 1970s, postmodernist fiction meant above all the highly self-referential and "metafictional" work of writers who took to their logical extreme modernist and avant-garde techniques of literary experimentation, in the process displaying a new awareness of the materiality of print and its functions. Indeed, the first wave of postmodernist fiction was accompanied by a host of publications pronouncing dire warnings about the death of the novel and the demise of reading in the age of film and especially television: Leslie Fiedler, Susan Sontag, Louis Rubin, and John Barth, for example, all declared themselves pessimistic about the novel's possibilities for cultural survival.[9] In this context of conscious self-scrutiny, the first wave of postmodernist fiction shifts from what Brian McHale has called the "epistemological dominant" of high-modernist fiction to an "ontological" orientation designed to explore the nature of textuality and the cognitive making and unmaking of narrative worlds. Modernist fiction such as that of Joseph Conrad, Ford Madox Ford, James Joyce, Virginia Woolf, or William Faulkner, McHale suggests, seeks to explore the real through its varied perceptions, memories, anticipations, and translations into story by a variety of characters. The resulting juxtaposition of different perspectives highlights how reality is refracted through individual minds without completely destabilizing its factuality; in most modernist novels, the different perspectives share enough material to make it clear that all the characters do in fact experience the same basic reality. Postmodernist narrative strategies, by contrast, work to undermine the sense of a shared and coherent fictional universe in a variety of ways – by exposing their own constructedness, or by violating conventions of narrative logic and causality, for example. In so doing, they force readers to consider what constitutes the reality or plausibility of a narrative universe, how textual worlds are made and unmade, and by extension, how we construe the reality of the extratextual world. The underlying concern shaping narrative experimentation, in other words, is no longer the representation of the world refracted through a human mind and again through language, but ontological questions about the nature of textuality, observation, inference, coherence, and the real.[10]

The emphasis on the figure of the artist and his (mostly his) development in novels by Thomas Mann, Marcel Proust, or James Joyce had already begun to transform, in the 1940s and 1950s, into more radical reconsiderations of the conditions of textuality and the materiality of print in the short stories of the Argentinian writer Jorge Luis Borges, the *nouveaux romans* of French novelists such as Alain Robbe-Grillet and Nathalie Sarraute, and the novels of Vladimir Nabokov. In one of his most famous short stories, "La librería de Babel" [The Library of Babel, 1941], Borges had imagined the entire universe consisting of a library that contains books with all possible words in all possible combinations. Postmodernist writers took up this challenge of imagining the world as a game of linguistic and textual recombinations by adopting formalist generative procedures that, by constraining selection and combination, gave rise to new novelistic forms. In this vein, Walter Abish's *Alphabetical Africa* (1974) follows strict rules as to which letters of the alphabet can appear in which book chapters, just as French novelist Georges Perec's novel *La disparition* (1969) entirely omits the letter "e." William Burroughs, in *Naked Lunch* (1959), but particularly in *The Soft Machine* (1961), *The Ticket That Exploded* (1962), and *Nova Express* (1964), uses bits and pieces of previous texts (his own as well as other authors') cut up and reassembled into a new textual whole whose fractures and seams remain clearly visible and define the fictional text as a portal to other texts rather than a self-contained whole. Gilbert Sorrentino's *Mulligan Stew* (1978), going one better than Joyce's *Finnegans Wake* (1939), consists of a patchwork of different generic and historical styles in a narrative with only marginal plot coherence, the whole preceded, in a self-deprecatory gesture, by reproductions of a whole set of publishers' rejection letters.

This shift of emphasis from the author or artist to the text also makes itself felt in the recurring concern of postmodernist artworks in general and novels in particular with issues of originality, imitation, and quotation. Donald Barthelme's novel *Snow White* (1967), for example, humorously retells the well-known fairy tale as a 1960s counterculture story of a woman who routinely has sex in the shower with the seven dwarves. Her "prince," Paul, in the meantime, meditates self-consciously on his blue blood and the role he is expected to take, enters a monastery, and travels around the world before setting up an elaborate surveillance system for Snow White and finally drinking the poison destined for her. In a similar vein, "Dunyazadiad" (1972), one of three novellas by John Barth that reappropriate some of the most time-honored myths in the Western canon, retells the *1001 Nights* from the viewpoint of Sheherazade's younger sister, Dunyazade. Sheherazade, it turns out, quickly runs out of stories and is incapable of making up any others until she succeeds, by pure chance, in conjuring up a genie from the twentieth century – transparently Barth himself. He is only too delighted to report to her what stories she is supposed to tell according to the text of the *1001 Nights*, a twist that locks the two authors into a circuit of transmission in which no originality is possible. In a very different narrative idiom, many of Kathy Acker's novels reappropriate male pornographic discourse for feminist purposes, but at the same time allude to some of the classics of Western literature, from Miguel de Cervantes (in her *Don Quixote*, 1986) and Charles Dickens (in her *Great Expectations*, 1983) to her contemporary William Gibson, whose cyberpunk novel *Neuromancer* (1984) she quite ostentatiously rewrites at the beginning of *The Empire of the Senseless* (1988). In novels such as these, as Raymond Federman programmatically declared in his essay, "Plagiarism as Imagination," the point is precisely not any pretense of authorial originality (for many postmodernists a post-Romantic myth in the first place), but the creative reappropriation of already existing texts and discourses.[11]

In another variant of texts that open out on other texts rather than on references to the "real world," some postmodernist novels are in fact texts about other texts which the reader may or may not get to see. Charles Kinbote, the protagonist of Nabokov's *Pale Fire* (1962), engages in an extended experiment of reading when he appends to the long poem "Pale Fire" a critical and interpretive apparatus that recasts it as the story of his own life. In a somewhat different vein, Federman's *Double or Nothing: A Real Fictitious Discourse* (1971) tells the story of a writer who locks himself up to write a novel, with every page of the resulting metanovel typographically configured in a different way, and Ishmael Reed's *Mumbo Jumbo* (1972) revolves around the search for a fragmented and dispersed piece of scripture that is definitively lost by the end, in a novel supplemented with photos, handwritten letters, and a bibliography. In texts such as these, the attention to the development of the artist is replaced by the metafictional focus on the text itself, with the author just another one of the fictions produced by the text: in Barth's "Dunyazadiad" and Coleman Dowell's *Island People* (1976), the authors themselves appear as characters called up or written into existence by other characters.

Quite obviously, in texts that are either patchworks of narrative styles or obvious rewritings of earlier texts, the narrative voice loses much of the authority and central structural function it still possessed in the architecture of high-modernist novels. Fictional characters become similarly modular, composite, or indeterminate in metafiction. The characters of Ronald Sukenick's *Out* (1973), for example, change their names, appearance, and even gender from chapter to chapter, to the point where it is difficult to say whether they are indeed the same characters; and even in Sukenick's late and most autobiographical novel, *Mosaic Man* (1998), the first-person protagonist turns out to be more of a patchwork of different literary prototypes and discourses (as the title with its double allusion to the form of the mosaic and to the protagonist's Jewish origins already suggests) than a realistically conceived character. The implausible names and even more implausible psychologies of many of Thomas Pynchon's characters have been commented on in detail; in one of the most influential novels in the postmodernist canon, *Gravity's Rainbow* (1973), the protagonist, Tyrone Slothrop, not only goes through a series of disguises and assumed identities but gradually becomes unrecognizable to his friends and in the end simply disperses into the landscape. Other characters in *Gravity's Rainbow* as well as in Pynchon's earlier novels *V.* (1963) and *The Crying of Lot 49* (1965) are constituted and arranged in patterns of correspondence and contradiction with each other that seem to obey an underlying structural principle more than any imperative of psychological realism.[12] Novels such as these translate into fictional form concerns about the coherence and constructedness of human identity that have been articulated in different ways by theorists such as Lacan, Foucault, and Butler, and thereby form part of the dialogue between the American novel and continental philosophy explored in greater detail by Robert Chodat in this volume.[b]

The same skepticism toward what is usually conceived to be the real makes itself felt in some kinds of postmodern plots. The parallax juxtapositions of different memories or perceptions of reality in the novels of such authors as Joseph Conrad, William Faulkner, or Virginia Woolf give way in many postmodernist texts of the 1960s and 1970s to juxtapositions of plotlines so

b Robert Chodat, "Philosophy and the American novel," chapter 39.

incompatible with each other that they can no longer be construed as forming part of a consistent narrative universe. Again, Borges had anticipated such fictions in his short story "El jardín de senderos que se bifurcan" [The Garden of Forking Paths, 1941], which proposed a labyrinthine vision of real and textual temporalities constantly bifurcating into alternative universes. Barth took up this vision in his seminal essay "The Literature of Exhaustion" (1967) and the title story of his collection *Lost in the Funhouse: Fiction for Tape, Print, Live Voice* (1968), as did French novelist Alain Robbe-Grillet in a whole range of novels published in the 1960s and 1970s that revolve around repeated scenes just dissimilar enough from each other that they might in fact not be repetitions but different scenes. But the idea that narrative plots might no longer add up to any coherent presentation of reality also haunts postmodernist texts in other forms. One of the characters in Clarence Major's *Reflex and Bone Structure* (1975), for example, is found murdered in her apartment in Harlem, but later dies in a plane crash on her way to a concert in Russia, in a contradiction the novel leaves deliberately unresolved. Almost all of the protagonists of Philip K. Dick's science fiction novels, from *Martian Time Slip* (1964) and *The Three Stigmata of Palmer Eldritch* (1965) to *Flow My Tears, The Policeman Said* (1974) and *VALIS* (1980), suffer from serious ruptures in their experience of reality that seem at first induced by schizophrenia or drugs, but in the end remain inexplicable both to them and the reader.

Some postmodernist texts, especially from the 1970s, take such reflections on coherence and the real, along with the high-modernist interest in the workings of memory and temporality, one step further by reflecting in a highly self-referential fashion on American history. Reed's *Mumbo Jumbo*, Pynchon's *Gravity's Rainbow* and Robert Coover's *The Public Burning* (1977), for example, all reflect on the politics of the 1950s, 1960s, and the Nixon era through a combination of facts and fictional events and characters, and a profusion of plots and narrative modes whose satirical edge can never be quite disentangled from their realism. Reed reflects on the Civil Rights Movement through a narrative ostensibly set in the 1920s, but ends up rewriting all of Western history from Ancient Egypt to the Middle Ages and twentieth-century America as a recurring conflict between factions that are ultimately distinct mainly by virtue of their race. Pynchon situates *Gravity's Rainbow* in a post-World War II Germany that at times resembles the 1960s USA more than 1940s Europe so as to consider whether the counterculture really did open up any new paths for American culture or simply reconfirmed already existing political tendencies. Coover, revisiting the Cold War, the 1958 execution of Julius and Ethel Rosenberg, and Nixon's gradual ascent to power, adopts a partly allegorical and partly satirical mode to explore the complex relationship between facts, their political and journalistic transformations, and the role fiction might play in representing them. Linda Hutcheon has coined the term "historiographic metafiction" to describe such novelistic engagements with history that do not fit easily into the established genre of the historical novel, in that history is questioned in terms of its textual constructedness even as its facts are invoked.[13]

If such metafictional experiments respond to broad cultural changes in the experience of temporality, causality, and historicity, as a number of studies have suggested, they also reflect on the altered status of literary narrative in the changing mediascape of the 1960s.[14] One of the characters in Barth's epistolary novel *LETTERS* (1979) remarks that

> [n]owadays the [novel] is so fallen into obscure pretension on the one hand and cynical commercialism on the other, and so undermined at its popular base by television, that to hear a young person declare that his or her ambition is to be a capital-*W* Writer strikes me as anachronistical, quixotic, as who should aspire in 1969 to be a Barnum & Bailey acrobat, a dirigible pilot, or the Rembrandt of the stereopticon.

The fear that the novel – and perhaps, literature more broadly – might become obsolete in the age of film, television, and the computer, which is palpable in these as well as many other statements surrounding the alleged "death of the novel," is, however, less relevant for a historical account of postmodern fiction than the fact that Barth invokes pressure from other media as one significant cause for changes in the structure of fiction: metafiction, in his argument, arises out of an awareness of the altered status of the novel.[15] If, as Mark McGurl argues in this volume, American novels from the 1910s onward have at times reflected on their relationship to television and the mass culture it represents, novelists after 1960 increasingly translate this engagement into novelistic form itself.[c] While it would no doubt be reductive to explain the many facets of first-wave postmodernism exclusively by reference to the altered media ecology that begins to unfold with the rise of television in the 1950s, it is obvious that a new consciousness of the novel as printed text does inform many fictional experiments that involve novels-within-novels, typographical configurations, and the integration of visual material such as photographs, paintings, and handwritten letters into the narrative. In addition, at a thematic level, the predicament of novel writers and readers, as well as the presence of television sets, films, and computers often form a crucial part of

c Mark McGurl, "The novel, mass culture, mass media," chapter 41.

novels from the 1950s onward, from the B-movies in William Burroughs's *Naked Lunch* and Jerzy Kosinski's illiterate, TV-watching protagonist in *Being There* (1970) all the way to the televisions and computers that figure prominently in the novels of Pynchon, Don DeLillo, and Richard Powers.

In a letter to the author-in-the-text, one of the characters of Barth's *LETTERS* suggests to him that "you do not yourself take with much seriousness those Death-of-the-Novel or End-of-Letters chaps . . . you *do* take seriously the climate that takes such questions seriously; you exploit that apocalyptic climate . . . to reinspect the origins of narrative fiction in the oral tradition." While in Barth, this turn to the oral tradition manifests itself in rewritings of Greek myth and Homeric epic, it assumes a different shape in many of the novels by women and minority writers who came to be associated with the label of "postmodernism" from the 1970s onward. Many of the novels frequently classified as postmodern from the 1970s and 1980s, by such authors as Bharati Mukherjee, Maxine Hong Kingston, Toni Morrison, Alice Walker, Amy Tan, Leslie Marmon Silko, Sandra Cisneros, and Gloria Anzaldúa highlight histories that the dominant culture had forgotten or deliberately ignored – stories of women, of immigrants, of racial and ethnic minorities, of colonized peoples, and of the gay underground.[d] The most innovative fictions in this second wave seemed to oppose metafictional self-referentiality in that they return to more or less realist modes of narration, with an emphasis on narrative voice and plausible character construction, well-formed if often open-ended plots, an interest in oral storytelling rather than the materialities of print, and an eagerness to convey precisely the facts and realities of lives not earlier considered worthy of literature. The seriousness and urgency of the political issues involved, many of them the great social issues of the 1960s and 1970s – women's emancipation, civil rights, decolonization – seemed difficult to square with the playful, text-oriented and self-referential techniques of postmodernist novels of the 1960s and 1970s. In quite a few accounts of the contemporary novel, therefore, these writers come to represent a highly political, oppositional postmodernism dominated by women and minority writers that contrasts with the textual self-absorptions of the mostly white and male writers of first-wave postmodernism. Just as academic postmodernism gradually shifted from textually dominated poststructuralism to the psychoanalytically and historically inflected poststructuralisms of Jacques Lacan and

d The modalities of these stories are explored in more detail in essays by Walter Benn Michaels ("Model minorities and the minority model – the neoliberal novel," chapter 61), Ramón Saldívar ("The American Borderlands novel," chapter 62), Susan Koshy ("The rise of the Asian American novel," chapter 63), and Elizabeth Freeman ("Reimagining genders and sexualities," chapter 57).

Michel Foucault, postmodernism in the novel seemed to shift from metafiction to identity politics.

But to accept such a dichotomy would be to ignore the important continuities between first- and second-wave postmodern fiction.[16] "Identity politics" formed part of the postmodernist project insofar as it sought to rethink and renarrativize Enlightenment notions of self, individuality, and subjecthood that had implicitly been based on white, heterosexual European masculinity. That so many of the thinkers and writers involved in this debate were women of color was not accidental, since their particular critique of patriarchy often highlighted at the same time some of the limitations of first-wave, mostly white, middle-class and First-World feminism. In important ways, therefore, the cutting-edge novelists of the 1980s participated in and continued the postmodernist critique of Enlightenment modernity even when they adopted realist narrative idioms despised by the earlier generation of postmodernists.

Equating 1960s postmodernism with experimental anti-realisms and the literary identity politics of the 1970s and 1980s with a return to realism also misstates the case from a narratological perspective. African American writers such as William Demby, Clarence Major, and Ishmael Reed had already demonstrated in the first wave of postmodernist fiction that an interest in questions of racial equality and in the real living conditions of blacks in the United States, for example, does not require reliance on conventionally understood realism. On the contrary, fragmented narrative structures and discontinuous characters can forcefully highlight the contradictions and paradoxes of discrimination and disenfranchisement and foreground the constructed and shifting nature of racial and ethnic distinctions. Similarly, the early work of Kathy Acker, Marguerite Young's monumental *Miss MacIntosh, My Darling* (1965), Barbara Guest's *Seeking Air* (1977), and the work of women writers outside the USA – Christine Brooke-Rose's *Between* (1968), Brigid Brophy's *In Transit* (1970), or Monique Wittig's *Les guerrillères* (Women Warriors, 1969) – had pointed the way toward articulations of feminism in distinctly anti-realist narrative idioms. For these reasons, 1980s women and minority novelists who view the novel as a medium for articulating alternative identities and histories, precisely because they mistrust dominant forms of narrative, often do not return to realism in either its nineteenth-century or its high-modernist guise, but instead selectively integrate some of the metafictional and anti-representational strategies of earlier postmodernists. Leslie Marmon Silko's *The Storyteller* (1981), for example, strains conventional genre definitions through its eclectic mix of prose and poetry, its episodic explorations of Laguna Pueblo myth and present-day Native American encounters with racial discrimination, and its inclusion of photographs whose function is often something other than documentary, inciting the reader to reflect on the very nature of realism. Gloria Anzaldúa's *Borderlands/La Frontera* (1987) similarly defies genre expectations as it blends historiography with autobiography and poetry. Toni Morrison's *Beloved* (1987) and Maxine Hong Kingston's *The Woman Warrior* (1976) include important elements of the supernatural whose relation to the "real" histories these novels tell invites questions about the foundations of historical storytelling. While texts such as these undoubtedly differ fundamentally from the elaborate textual games of Reed or Pynchon, they nevertheless share with them a deep-seated wariness of established historical narratives and a high degree of self-referentiality in their attempts to create new templates.

As hinted in the earlier quotation from Barth's *LETTERS*, the prominence of oral storytelling in many of the postmodernist novels of the 1970s and 1980s might also be understood as an alternative way of resituating the novel in a visually dominated media context. When omnipresent visual media such as television, film, and the computer dominate, the novel stages more unmediated, face-to-face storytelling as a means of re-establishing community and the connection with the past. Oral storytelling and oral traditions figure prominently in Native American and Asian American novels of the 1970s and 1980s – most obviously as a way of laying claim to ignored and oppressed cultural legacies, but also, I would argue, as a way of regrounding the novel as a medium for perpetuating oral narratives that might otherwise be lost. Without question, this ambition leads to media-theoretical paradoxes and textual play in many ways similar to those of the metafictionalists. In a short story by Anishinaabe novelist Gerald Vizenor entitled "Shadows" (1992), for example, the university-educated Native American narrator encounters an old storyteller of his tribe who shares some of her oral traditions with him on the condition that he never put them in print – a condition the narrator violates by publishing the short story we read. Such tensions between oral and printed storytelling and the cultural conventions that surround them inform a wide range of Native American, Chicano, and Asian American novels. As Sean Kicummah Teuton suggests in his chapter on the Native American novel in this volume, many of these texts seek to engage with "colonialism and the power of oral traditions to resist it."[e] The tension between oral and written narrative that often surfaces in this context suggests that the novel, in its

e Sean Kicummah Teuton, "The Native American Tradition," chapter 67, 1111.

confrontation with other media, may well continue to invent new uses for itself. Robert Coover, in this volume, sees fiction being inexorably pulled toward the new, interactive modes of computer games and immersive virtual realities. But some dimensions of postmodern fiction suggest that the novel might also function as the space in which older communication modalities are represented and remembered. What Coover calls "monomedia" may in this context be less dated than they appear.[17]

Some second-wave novels push questions about orality and print toward a more complex media-theoretical engagement that clearly draws on the self-referentiality of first-wave postmodern fiction. Korean American writer Theresa Hak Kyung Cha's *Dictée* (1982), for example, links the story of a Korean woman's emigration to the United States with her mother's displacement to Japanese-occupied Manchuria decades earlier, in an exploration of superimposed oppressions and estrangements that become quite common in novels of the 1980s and 1990s. But Cha's use of dictation as a device of transition from orality to writing, her mix of French and English text with Chinese characters, her inclusion of photos drawn from her autobiography, from Korean history, and from Western film, her organization of the narrative by means of Eastern and Western myths as structuring devices, and her integration of novelistic, cinematographic, and lyrical idioms raise many of the same questions about individual identity, its roots in familial, national, and ethnic histories, the role of language(s) and storytelling in cultural oppression and liberation that the novels of many Asian American and other minority writers raise. The experimental, media theory-inflected narrative strategies destabilize any firm foundation for such histories and identies no less radically than many of the historiographic metafictions of the 1960s and 1970s.

The rise of identity politics as a dominant concern of American novels, therefore, by no means implies any simple return to narrative realism; at the same time, some of the 1980s texts usually perceived as paradigmatically postmodernist are not as anti-realist as the texts of William Burroughs, John Barth, or Kathy Acker. Don DeLillo's *White Noise* (1985) is the most famous example of a novel that is often understood as a portrait of the quintessentially postmodern society of the late twentieth-century United States, inauthentic and deeply invested in simulacra, consumer commodities, and media that have come to replace any immediate access to the real. "For most people there are only two places in the world. Where they live and their TV set," one of the characters sums up a social landscape shaped by media as much as by lived experience. Yet with the exception of DeLillo's skillful deployment of satirical elements that leave the reader in doubt as to how seriously to take some elements of this social portrait, *White Noise* proceeds by and large in realist fashion: its humor, its philosophical depth, and its biting social critique all rely on the reader by and large believing in the narrative world she is shown. Hyperself-aware though the characters may be, they are not implausible, and the plot has a good deal more coherence and resolution than a novel by, say, Gilbert Sorrentino or Harry Mathews. *White Noise*, therefore, portrays by mostly realist means the kind of hyperreal world theorized by Jean Baudrillard without translating the critique of realism into its narrative form.[18] Contrary to the simplistic oppositions that are often drawn in accounts of 1970s and 1980s fiction between a predominantly white male postmodernism and a return to realism in the writings of women and minority novelists, it turns out that some of the white males are not as anti-realist and some of the minority writers not as realist as is commonly alleged.

In the 1980s, the postmodern novel shifted into yet another dimension: its association with science fiction and its portrayal of emergent technologies in the biological and above all the digital realms. Long reliant on conventional narrative techniques, science fiction had already undergone fundamental changes in the 1960s through the so-called New Wave, somewhat differently articulated in Britain and the US. This movement introduced greater attention to social and cultural issues, increased character depth, and sophisticated psychological portrayals, as well as narrative techniques borrowed from high-modernist novels and the *nouveau roman* to a once formally traditional genre. By the 1980s, science fiction had exploded into a whole range of different subgenres and styles of writing ranging from "hard" science fiction, with its realistic portrayals of science and technology, to feminist novels and fantasy. Priscilla Wald, in this volume, comments on the "generic promiscuity . . . [that] blurs the distinction between science fiction and experimental postmodern writing in the 1960s."[f] Writers such as Philip K. Dick and Thomas Pynchon had succeeded in blurring the boundaries between mainstream literary fiction and science fiction[19] in part because they, like other first-wave postmodernists, had taken a deep interest in film and television as part of a changed media landscape in which the novel had to redefine itself. This consciousness of the crucial influence exerted on literature by rapidly changing mediascapes took a new shape in the emergence of cyberpunk, a brand of science fiction that was intensely concerned with

f Priscilla Wald, chapter 50, 844.

computers and international digital networks as potential new spaces and new forms of community.

The concept of the "cyborg," an intimately fused combination of biological and technological body parts that had first appeared in the early 1960s, was given wide publicity by Donna Haraway's "Cyborg Manifesto" (1984) as a figure with utopian potential, and appeared as the logical human counterpart to the "cyberspace" first named by novelist William Gibson in 1982.[20] The new medium of the computer, in Gibson's novels as well as those of other cyberpunk writers, replaced television as the alternate imaginary space humans inhabit. Rejecting a futuristic version of multisensory television called "SimStim," Gibson's hackers in *Neuromancer* (1984) instead reside in cyberspace, their "distanceless home, [their] country, transparent 3D chessboard extending to infinity." Human bodies and the environments they inhabit emerge as irreversibly reconfigured by both digital and biotechnologies in these visions, and the ensuing "posthumanism" – the reimagination of the human as a hybrid of biology and technology rather than the organic whole envisioned during the Enlightenment – now became an integral part of "postmodernism." If reality and textuality had informed first-wave postmodernism as the opposing poles implicit in multiple novelistic games and negotiations, and second-wave postmodern fictions were re-introducing oral forms of storytelling as a means of capturing alternate histories, cyberpunk novels in the third wave of postmodern fiction shifted to a media-based dialectic of reality and virtuality constituting each other in the emergence of new spaces and bodies.

From postmodernism to globalization

The 1990s and early 2000s saw continuations and transformations of all the different modes of postmodern narrative, from metafiction to ethnic writing and technologically inflected visions. The legacies of metafiction are most obvious in monumental novels such as David Foster Wallace's *Infinite Jest* (1995) and Mark Danielewski's *House of Leaves* (2000). While Wallace makes ample use of game structures in organizing a narrative world in which entertainment in various forms predominates, Danielewski takes to new extremes the postmodernist strategies of embedded narrative, self-referentiality, and experimental typography in a novel in which print, film, and architecture all play against each other. Implicitly or explicitly, the question of the relationship between literature and other media surfaces as a recurrent concern in these novels: "teleputers," combinations of television and computers, signal an omnipresent entertainment industry and culture in the lives of Wallace's characters; and in Danielewski's plot, an intricately layered narrative of embedded texts and readings revolves centrally around an imaginary film, *The Navidson Record*, which the reader comes to know about through a mosaic of letters, interviews, poems, and other written materials. Richard Powers, in a realist style more reminiscent of DeLillo than Barth, explores the relationship of computers and virtual reality to legacies of literature, painting, and architecture in novels such as *Galatea 2.2* (1995) and *Plowing the Dark* (2000). Similarly, Paul Auster's intensely media-aware novel *The Book of Illusions* (2002) portrays a Comparative Literature professor's discovery of the films of Hector Mann, a silent-film actor and director who mysteriously disappeared decades before the onset of the narrative. As the professor researches Mann's films, discovers he is still alive, and delves ever more deeply into his life, work, and eventual death, he gives detailed shot-by-shot descriptions and interpretations of several of Mann's films. Auster here goes even further than Danielewski in turning the novel into a verbal transliteration of film, acknowledging the central importance of the moving image but also – through his exclusive engagement with the obsolete medium of silent film – the ways in which verbal narrative might still be film's necessary complement and mouthpiece, and perhaps its means of perpetuating itself into the future.[21]

While authors such as Wallace, Danielewski, and Auster redeploy the strategies of first-wave postmodern fiction, other novelists combine some of the dimensions of second- and third-wave postmodern novels with a new awareness of a rapidly globalizing world. Bruce Robbins's chapter in this volume explores in more detail the narrative plots, political implications, and imaginative shortfalls of such "worldly" novels, so a few examples of texts that clearly build on various dimensions of the postmodernist legacy may suffice here.[g] Neal Stephenson, in his cyberpunk novel *Snow Crash* (1992), develops further the 1980s vision of a world dominated and divided by corporations and their franchises more than by nation-states, but complemented by a virtual world in which the power of hackers supercedes that of executives. More than his predecessors, Stephenson foregrounds the ethnic, racial, and cultural multiplicity of this world, even as he also suggests that this multiplicity is itself endlessly reproducible and commodifiable. In one scene, Stephenson's main character, the aptly named Hiro Protagonist, an American of mixed Asian and African extraction, is momentarily surprised to encounter a receptionist with the same racial make-up – only to discover that in the

g Bruce Robbins, "The worlding of the American novel," chapter 66.

virtual space in which he finds himself at that moment, software automatically produces receptionists who are ethnically and racially identical to the arriving customer.

Japanese American novelist Karen Tei Yamashita rewrites Stephenson's fictional equation from the other end in her novel *Tropic of Orange* (1998). Set in a thoroughly multicultural Los Angeles populated not only by African Americans, Asian Americans, and Latinos but also immigrants from Asia and Latin America, Yamashita turns the postmodern metropolis into a node in a global network of economic, cultural, and media interchanges. As she tells a story inflected by Latin American magical realism as much as by North American ethnic writing, *film noir*, and techno-postmodernism, media emerge as virtual spaces that at the turn of the millennium define identities as much as geographical places do: her multiracial characters include an avid radio listener, a TV reporter, and a Chicano print journalist who by the end of the novel turns into a cyberspace-based private eye, a "neuromancer of the dark," as he calls himself in a direct allusion to Gibson's cyberpunk classic. Both Stephenson and Yamashita, then, outline panoramas of global identities in which media become as crucial as nations, races, or ethnicities in shaping individuals and communities; while Stephenson draws on science fiction, Yamashita redeploys magical realism to portray the emergence of global spaces that no longer seem representable by realist means.

William Gibson himself completed this picture in one of his most recent novels, *Pattern Recognition* (2003), whose protagonist, an international cool hunter for the advertising industry, travels around the globe from New York to London, Tokyo, Moscow, and Paris, but feels most at home in an internet-based fan community. "It is a way, now, approximately, of being at home. The [on-line] forum has become one of the most consistent places in her life, like a familiar café that exists somehow outside of geography and beyond time zones," Cayce Pollard reflects on her virtual travels. But in a multi-medial twist, it turns out that this fan community has emerged around fragments of alluring but mysterious film footage that periodically appear on the web and seem for a time to hold out the promise of a realm of pure creativity and true art dissociated from the world of commodities and advertising. As the film is disseminated through the internet and both media are rendered verbally in Gibson's novel, *Pattern Recognition* seems less anxious about the possible competition between different media than fascinated by their new synergies.

Whether the term "postmodern" adequately describes novels such as *Snow Crash*, *Tropic of Orange*, and *Pattern Recognition* is an open question, considering that the term "postmodernism" itself has begun to be replaced by other concepts such as "transnationalism" and "globalization" since the mid-1990s. But undeniably, in both these novels and the new discussions around the interrelation of globalization and culture, many of the same concerns persist about the legacies of modernity that shaped debates about postmodernism. Questions about the ties of modernity to its European and North American origins, about the ongoing relevance or the demise of its central philosophical assumptions and social institutions, about the spread of modernity and/or its exhaustion inform discussions about globalization, even as geopolitical and economic dimensions tend to assume greater centrality in these debates than in those about postmodern culture. Finding appropriate narrative forms for articulating these questions about the legacy of the modern in a thoroughly global and media-connected world is the challenge that recent novels have begun to address by drawing eclectically on modernist and postmodernist narrative strategies from Europe, the Americas, and other parts of the world.

Notes

1. Robert Venturi, Denise Scott Brown, and Steven Izenour, *Learning from Las Vegas: The Forgotten Symbolism of Architectural Form* (Cambridge, MA: MIT Press, 1972).
2. After AT&T sold the building to Sony in 2002, it was renamed Sony Tower.
3. Hans Bertens, *The Idea of the Postmodern: A History* (London: Routledge, 1995), 5, 11. For discussions of postmodernism as it manifested itself in different artforms, see also Christopher Butler, *After the Wake: An Essay on the Contemporary Avant-Garde* (Oxford: Clarendon, 1980); Steven Connor, *Postmodernist Culture: An Introduction to Theories of the Contemporary*, 2nd edn. (New York: Blackwell, 1997), chapters 3–6; Steven Connor, ed., *The Cambridge Companion to Postmodernism* (Cambridge: Cambridge University Press, 2004), chapters 2–5.
4. Jürgen Habermas, *Legitimationsprobleme im Spätkapitalismus* (Frankfurt: Suhrkamp, 1973); Jean-François Lyotard, *La condition postmoderne: Rapport sur le savoir* (Paris: Minuit, 1979); Jean Baudrillard, *Le miroir de la production: Ou, l'Illusion critique du matérialisme historique*, 2nd edn. (Paris: Casterman, 1977), and *Simulation et simulacres* (Paris: Galilée, 1981); Andreas Huyssen, *After the Great Divide: Modernism, Mass Culture, Postmodernism* (Bloomington: Indiana University Press, 1986); Fredric Jameson, *Postmodernism, Or, The Cultural Logic of Late Capitalism* (Durham, NC: Duke University Press, 1991). Foucault's and Lacan's theories of self are articulated across a variety of texts; as representative examples, see Michel Foucault, *Surveiller et punir: Naissance de la prison* (Paris: Gallimard, 1975); Jacques Lacan, *The Talking Cure: Essays in Psychoanalysis and Language*, ed. Colin MacCabe (London: Macmillan, 1981) and Jacqueline Rose's introduction to *Feminine Sexuality: Jacques Lacan and the Ecole Freudienne*, ed. Juliet Mitchell and Jacqueline Rose, trans. Jacqueline Rose (London: Macmillan, 1982);

Judith Butler, *Gender Trouble: Feminism and the Subversion of Identity* (New York: Routledge, 1990).

5. Bertens, *Idea of the Postmodern*, 3–18; Bill Readings and Bennet Schaber, eds., *Postmodernism Across the Ages: Essays for a Postmodernity that Wasn't Born Yesterday* (Syracuse, NY: Syracuse University Press, 1993).
6. See Steven Best and Douglas Kellner, *Postmodern Theory: Critical Interrogations* (New York: Guilford, 1991); Patricia Waugh, ed., *Postmodernism: A Reader* (London: E. Arnold, 1992); Thomas Docherty, ed., *Postmodernism: A Reader* (New York: Columbia University Press, 1993); Joseph Natoli and Linda Hutcheon, eds., *The Postmodern Reader* (Albany: State University of New York Press, 1993); Nicholas Zurbrugg, *The Parameters of Postmodernism* (Carbondale: Southern Illinois University Press, 1993); Steven Best and Douglas Kellner, *The Postmodern Turn* (New York: Guilford, 1997); Christopher Butler, *Postmodernism: A Very Short Introduction* (Oxford: Oxford University Press, 2002); Connor, *The Cambridge Companion to Postmodernism*, chapters 1 and 6–10.
7. Butler, *After the Wake*; Brian McHale, *Postmodernist Fiction*, 2nd edn. (London: Routledge, 1991); Allan Thiher, *Words in Reflection: Modern Language Theory and Postmodern Fiction* (Chicago: University of Chicago Press, 1984); Jameson, *Postmodernism*, 16–19; Margaret A. Rose, *Parody: Ancient, Modern, and Post-Modern* (Cambridge: Cambridge University Press, 1993); Raymond Federman, *Critifiction: Postmodern Essays* (Albany: State University of New York Press, 1993); Linda Hutcheon, *A Poetics of Postmodernism: History, Theory, Fiction* (London: Routledge, 1988); Amy Elias, *Sublime Desire: History and Post-1960s Fiction* (Baltimore: Johns Hopkins University Press, 2001); Mark McGurl, *The Program Era: Postwar Fiction and the Rise of Creative Writing* (Cambridge, MA: Harvard University Press, 2009).
8. Joseph Tabbi and Michael Wutz, eds., *Reading Matters: Narrative in the New Media Ecology* (Ithaca, NY: Cornell University Press, 1997); N. Katherine Hayles, "Print Is Flat, Code Is Deep: The Importance of Media-Specific Analysis," *Poetics Today* 25.1 (Spring 2004): 67–90; Kathleen Fitzpatrick, *The Anxiety of Obsolescence: The American Novel in the Age of Television* (Nashville, TN: Vanderbilt University Press, 2006).
9. Leslie Fiedler, "Cross the Border, Close the Gap," in *The Collected Essays of Leslie Fiedler*, 2 vols. (New York: Stein and Day, 1971), II:461–485; Susan Sontag, "Against Interpretation," in *Against Interpretation* (New York: Anchor Books, 1990), 3–14; Louis Rubin, *The Curious Death of the Novel: Essays in American Literature* (Baton Rouge: Louisiana State University Press, 1967); John Barth, "The Literature of Exhaustion," *The Atlantic* (August 1967): 29–34. Concerns about the fate of print culture have persisted over the 1980s and 1990s; see Neil Postman, *Amusing Ourselves to Death: Public Discourse in the Age of Show Business* (New York: Viking, 1985); Alvin Kernan, *The Death of Literature* (New Haven: Yale University Press, 1990); Robert Coover, "The End of Books," *New York Times Book Review* (June 21, 1992): 1, 23–25.

10. McHale does not suggest that all experimental twentieth-century novels neatly fit one pattern or the other, but rather that this distinction points to a broad watershed in relation to which the critic can situate individual textual projects.
11. Raymond Federman, "Plagiarism as Imagination [An Unfinished Paper . . .]," *New Literary History* 7.3 (Spring 1976): 563–578.
12. Pynchon continues such experimentation in his more recent work. *Against the Day* (2006) features characters that appear to be pastiche figures from popular fiction genres such as the Western or the spy thriller. One group of characters, the crew of an 1890s airship, are indeed simultaneously characters from a boys' adventure series and "real" individuals in the novel, flipping back and forth from one identity to the other.
13. Hutcheon, *Poetics of Postmodernism*, chapters 6, 7, and 8. See also Elias's elaboration of Hutcheon's theory in *Sublime Desire*. For a discussion of historiographic fiction in the context of the long history of historical fiction, see Winfried Fluck, "The nineteenth-century historical novel," chapter 7 in this volume, 131–132.
14. For analyses of historicity, temporality, and postmodern fiction, see Jameson, *Postmodernism*; Elizabeth Ermarth, *Sequel to History: Postmodernism and the Crises of Representational Time* (Princeton: Princeton University Press, 1991); Joseph Francese, *Narrating Postmodern Time and Space* (Albany: State University of New York Press, 1997); Ursula K. Heise, *Chronoschisms: Time, Narrative, and Postmodernism* (Cambridge: Cambridge University Press, 1997).
15. I am indebted to the lucid analyses of Barth's work and the question of media in Fitzpatrick's *Anxiety of Obsolescence* (23–25) and Joel Burges's "The Uses of Obsolescence: Historical Change and the Politics of the Outmoded in American Postmodernity," PhD diss., Stanford University, 2007, chapter 3. Burges also discusses the fact that, starting in the 1950s, film manifests its own obsolescence anxieties vis-à-vis television.
16. For discussions and attempts to overcome these binary oppositions, see Francese, *Narrating Postmodern Time and Space*, and Wendy Steiner, "Postmodern Fictions, 1970–1990," in *The Cambridge History of American Literature*, vol. VII, ed. Sacvan Bercovitch (New York: Cambridge University Press, 1999), 425–538. See also the discussion in Amy Hungerford, "On the Period Formerly Known as Contemporary," *American Literary History* 20.1–2 (Spring/Summer 2008): 410–412.
17. Robert Coover, "A history of the future of narrative," chapter 71, 1180. Indeed, there are signs that print fiction is exerting a reverse pull on digital technologies, forcing them to simulate monomediatic forms of reading. The popularity of audiobooks, for example, predates digitization, but has immensely increased through the rapid spread of MP3 mediaplayers such as the iPod, which allows for easy download of even extremely long novels read aloud in their unabridged versions (from nineteenth-century novels, which can run to over thirty listening hours, all the way to Pynchon's *Against the Day*, which totals fifty-three hours). At the same time, hand-held electronic reading devices such as the

Sony e-Reader and Amazon's Kindle reinstate conventional print appearance (with some modifications such as adjustable font size) on a digital basis, without the game-style or virtual-reality environments Coover foregrounds.

18. But DeLillo's innovative uses of satire should be noted as a constraint on his realism: see the analyses by N. H. Reeve and Richard Kerridge, "Toxic Events: Postmodernism and Don DeLillo's *White Noise*," *Cambridge Quarterly* 23 (1994): 305, and Ursula K. Heise, *Sense of Place and Sense of Planet: The Environmental Imagination of the Global* (New York: Oxford University Press, 2008), 167–169.
19. On the connections between mainstream fiction and science fiction, see Brian McHale, "POSTcyberMODERNpunkISM," in *Storming the Reality Studio: A Casebook of Cyberpunk and Postmodern Science Fiction*, ed. Larry McCaffery (Durham, NC: Duke University Press, 1991), 308–323; Joseph Tabbi, *Postmodern Sublime: Technology and American Writing from Mailer to Cyberpunk* (Ithaca, NY: Cornell University Press, 1995); Veronica Holllinger, "Science Fiction and Postmodernism," in *A Companion to Science Fiction*, ed. David Seed (Malden, MA: Blackwell, 2005).
20. Donna J. Haraway, "A Cyborg Manifesto: Science, Technology, and Socialist-Feminism in the Late Twentieth Century," in *Simians, Cyborgs, and Women: The Reinvention of Nature* (New York: Routledge, 1991), 149–81.
21. See also Ruth Ozeki's *My Year of Meats* (1999): far less metafictional than Auster's *Book of Illusions*, this novel nevertheless revolves around the creation of a television series in the USA that is to be broadcast in Japan, and includes detailed descriptions of individual episodes.

59

The nonfiction novel

DAVID SCHMID

> Nicholas Branch sits in the book-filled room, the room of documents, the room of theories and dreams. He is in the fifteenth year of his labor and sometimes wonders if he is becoming bodiless. He knows he is getting old.

Anyone writing about the nonfiction novel will sympathize with Nicholas Branch, the retired CIA analyst in Don DeLillo's *Libra* (1988) who has been hired to write the definitive history of the Kennedy assassination. The problem facing the student of the nonfiction novel is not only ontological but also practical: like Branch, one faces a mountain of material that grows bigger all the time, because in both theory and practice it is difficult to write about the nonfiction novel without also discussing a range of associated discourses and genres, including the fictive novel, the documentary novel, the historical novel, historiographic metafiction, and (New) journalism. In order to avoid the entropy that threatens to overwhelm Branch, I want to propose that (1) these genres are all concerned with what it means to represent reality; (2) these genres often express this concern with reality through attempts to give narrative form to that which is violent and/or traumatic; and (3) that the nonfiction novel genre has proven itself particularly adept at exploring the impact of violence on the representation of reality. My intent is less to define a genre in narrow terms and more to anatomize the attitudes and anxieties about the relation between fact and fiction in narrative that have collected around the term "nonfiction novel."

Does the representation of violence provide the nonfiction novel with an opportunity to distinguish itself, to establish its own specificity in relation to other forms of prose narrative? In his essay on the Kennedy assassination, "American Blood," DeLillo argues that "violence itself seems to cause a warp in the texture of things."[1] Perhaps the nonfiction novel is better equipped than other prose genres to delineate the shape of that warp?

To answer these questions, I want to suggest that the nonfiction novel participates in what Alain Badiou has called "the passion for the real." According to Badiou, this passion, which is distinguished by the desire to penetrate behind the deceiving appearance of what ordinarily passes for reality, provides "the key to understanding the [twentieth] century."[2] For Badiou, the "passion for the real" is practically defined by excessive violence and by the effort to represent that violence. The nonfiction novel participates in the same conjunction of violence and representation that defines Badiou's passion for the real; the nonfiction novel similarly tries to understand the stakes of representing reality, especially when that reality seems disturbed or distorted by violence.[3]

One way in which the novel has responded to these opportunities and challenges is by combining fictional and nonfictional discourses. In *Factual Fictions*, Lennard Davis argues that a readerly uncertainty about "the factual or fictional reality of the work" defines the early novel, an exemplary case being Daniel Defoe's *Roxana* (1724).[4] Defoe is a key figure in the pre-history of the nonfiction novel, not only for the way that his readers were unable to take for granted whether the information they read in his novels was fictional or factual, but also because their confusion had much to do with Defoe's dual identity as a journalist and novelist. In both the history of the novel in general and the history of the twentieth-century American novel in particular, journalism plays a key role, and its significance for the American nonfiction novel cannot be overstated. In *From Fact to Fiction* (1985), Shelley Fisher Fishkin discusses the influence that their early experience as journalists had on the work of a number of major American creative writers, including Mark Twain, Walt Whitman, Theodore Dreiser, and Ernest Hemingway. The case of Dreiser is especially interesting, because Fishkin argues that his career as a newspaperman gave Dreiser an acute sensitivity to the developing social realities around him, as well as an appreciation of just how well violence and scandal sold with the American public.[5]

Dreiser would put these influences and experiences to work most effectively in *An American Tragedy* (1925). This novel, inspired by the real-life murder of Grace Brown by Chester Gillette in 1906, constitutes a major pretext for the American nonfiction novel. Before discussing *An American Tragedy* in more detail, however, it is worth noting that Dreiser's choice of subject matter as much defines the novel as does his blending of fiction and fact or the influence of journalism. From the earliest days of the genre, the novel was closely associated with criminality, not only because its powerful influence was seen as potentially inciting readers to commit crime, but also because the novel routinely represented crime. As Davis has argued, "The move from newspaper to history to novel was easily accomplished with the recording of the lives of various criminals."[6]

Many journalists and novelists had trodden the path Dreiser followed in developing *An American Tragedy*. But quite apart from his familiarity with such cases, Dreiser had other reasons for wanting to explore violence in such a long novel, and those reasons make *An American Tragedy* even more relevant to the nonfiction novel genre. In a 1927 letter, Dreiser explains the inspiration behind *An American Tragedy*:

> I had long brooded upon the story, for it seemed to me not only to include every phase of our national life – politics, society, religion, business, sex – but it was a story so common to every boy reared in the smaller towns of America. It seemed so truly a story of what life does to the individual – and how impotent the individual is against such forces. My purpose was not to moralize – God forbid – but to give, if possible, a background and a psychology of reality which would somehow explain, if not condone, how such murders happen – and they have happened with surprising frequency in America as long as I can remember.[7]

Dreiser here demonstrates with both economy and power how the details of contemporary social realities that he came across routinely in his work as a journalist can shape the form of a novel both inspired and closely influenced by actual events.

An American Tragedy's post-publication history amplifies its role as a central pre-text for the nonfiction novel. In 1931, the New York Supreme Court ruled against Dreiser, who had complained about Paramount's film adaptation of the novel. The court ruled that because *An American Tragedy* clearly followed the story of Chester Gillette, it therefore lay in the public domain. Perhaps irritated by the implication that he had simply transliterated actual events into novel form, Dreiser subsequently wrote several articles about the philosophical and historical sources of the novel, culminating in a long article entitled "I Find the Real American Tragedy," first published serially in *Mystery Magazine* in 1935.

These articles elaborate what nonfictional materials Dreiser used in composing *An American Tragedy*, and also clarify how he transformed those materials to develop a hybrid nonfiction novelistic text. Dreiser borrowed many details from the Gillette case, including the characters, plot, and setting of the murder. He also borrowed whole passages from newspaper accounts of the trial, along with quotations from the attorneys, excerpts from Grace

Brown's letters, and Gillette's final written statement. Although many of these materials appear verbatim in *An American Tragedy*, in another sense they merely constitute Dreiser's raw materials. What he added to them was the detailing of the environmental pressures that made Clyde Griffiths commit the crime. The cultural representativeness of the crime, in other words, its ability to throw light on American culture, was all Dreiser's invention. The nonfictional materials provided a crucial ingredient in making *An American Tragedy*, and in particular its famous trial scenes, an epochal judgment on so many aspects of American reality, but it was the way in which Dreiser combined those materials with fictional techniques that both gives the text its power and makes *An American Tragedy* such a landmark in the history of the nonfiction novel.

Dreiser brought his extensive experience as both a journalist and a novelist to bear on the composition of *An American Tragedy*, and this overlap between journalism and fiction has important ramifications not only for understanding his work, but also for the study of the nonfiction novel as a whole, as we can see if we turn to the example of John Hersey, a writer known as both a novelist and a literary journalist, and therefore someone whose career can be located within that hazy borderland between fact and fiction that is the special preserve of the nonfiction novel.[8] In "The Novel of Contemporary History," an article published in the *Atlantic Monthly* in November 1949, Hersey states: "among all the means of communication now available, imaginative literature comes closer than any other to being able to give an impression of the truth."[9] Much of Hersey's most important work, in both fiction and nonfiction, attempts to discern the outlines of that truth in the context of war, when the question of truth – what it is, who defines it – becomes especially tortured. In *A Bell for Adano* (1944) and *The Wall* (1950), Hersey provided successful novelistic treatments of the damage done by war, but his most enduring work came when he combined fictional and nonfictional techniques to treat a subject that had never before been addressed adequately: the atomic explosion at Hiroshima.

Hersey wrote *Hiroshima* for *The New Yorker*, and it first appeared as the full text of the August 31, 1946 issue. The response was intense and immediate, and the vast majority of the reviews agreed that the power of *Hiroshima* came from Hersey's decision to relay the terrible facts of the bombing and its aftermath in flat, simple terms. Bruce Bliven's review in *The New Republic* (1946) is representative: "Hersey does no editorializing, passes no judgments; he does not try to say whether the atomic bombing of Japan was justified . . . He just tells the story."[10] In fact, what Bliven describes as just telling the story was a method developed carefully by Hersey in order to achieve a desired effect, namely, to communicate to an American audience exactly what had been done in their names in order to win a war.

Hersey's most important tactic in achieving this aim was to focus on the stories of six survivors of the blast: Toshiko Sasaki, Dr. Masakazu Fujii, Hatsuyo Nakamura, Father Wilhlem Kleinsorge, Dr. Terfumi Sasaki, and the Reverend Mr. Kioshi Tanimoto. These individuals become characters in a narrative in which Hersey seemingly allows the facts to "speak for themselves," while in fact directing the readers' sympathies. His own description of the common thread in his work suggests his purpose in *Hiroshima*: "I have been obsessed, as any serious writer in violent times could not help being, by one overriding question, the existential question: What is it that, by a narrow margin, keeps us going, in the face of our crimes, our follies, our passions, our sorrow, our panics, our hideous drives to kill?"[11]

In order to understand why the combination of fictional and nonfictional techniques provided Hersey with a more satisfying answer to this question, consider his description of what happened to Toshiko Sasaki at the moment the bomb exploded:

> Everything fell, and Miss Sasaki lost consciousness. The ceiling dropped suddenly and the wooden floor above collapsed in splinters and the people up there came down and the roof above them gave way; but principally and first of all, the bookcases right behind her swooped forward and the contents threw her down, with her left leg horribly twisted and breaking underneath her. There, in the tin factory, in the first moment of the atomic age, a human being was crushed by books.

The matter-of-fact description of the bomb's impact satisfies the reader's desire to know "what happened," while the individual caught in the middle of the wreckage also gives the reader a focus for her emotions, especially important when we consider how the Japanese were routinely portrayed at this time as figures with whom it was impossible to identify or empathize.[12] Such passages contradict the claim that Hersey's objectivity is too flat and depersonalized for the reader to fully appreciate the devastating impact of the bomb on the citizens of Hiroshima. Hersey's use of fictional and nonfictional techniques in *Hiroshima* conveys the enormity of an atomic explosion in a double register: the facts of the bomb's impact are relayed with the authority of nonfiction, while the tragic dilemmas of the survivors are told with the emotive power of fiction. It is this combination that leads Mas'ud Zavarzadeh to describe the nonfiction novel as possessing "the shapeliness of fiction and the authority of reality usually reserved for factual narrative."[13]

Nonfiction novelistic techniques are effective in dealing with violence on a number of different scales, whether it be war, murder, or simply a generalized sense of conflict or turmoil, in all of which the sense of what we generally perceive as "reality" may be disturbed. For example, in the Preface to *Slouching Towards Bethlehem*, Joan Didion explains her title as reflecting a sense that reality has become warped. She explains that one piece in the book, deriving from time she spent in the Haight-Ashbury district of San Francisco, reflects "the first time I had dealt directly and flatly with the evidence of atomization, the proof that things fall apart."[14] The first piece in *Slouching*, "Some Dreamers of the Golden Dream," is not coincidentally about a murder.

Didion provides an important counter-tendency to the otherwise strongly masculinist bias of the nonfiction novel. Any explanation of this bias must remain speculative at this point, but perhaps it has something to do with the often highly gendered presence of egotism in nonfiction novelistic texts (Mailer, of course, would be the classic example) an egotism that gives these writers a sense of entitlement in commenting about public events, often through the use of an autobiographical persona. In this sense, it is symptomatic that Didion tends to work on a smaller, more intimate canvas, creating sketches rather than large synthetic narratives.[a]

Why did so many American writers during the post-World War II period, including Didion, Truman Capote, and Norman Mailer, choose to follow Hersey's lead and work in both fictional and nonfictional genres? Or, to put the same question in a slightly more pointed form, why did so many of these writers start off as fictionists, achieve great success in this genre, but then devote themselves more and more to hybrid forms of writing that blended fictional and nonfictional techniques and materials? A possible answer emerges from an article by Philip Roth entitled "Writing American Fiction" that appeared in the March 1961 issue of *Commentary*, in which Roth complains that the contemporary American novelist faces a very difficult and perhaps even insoluble problem "in trying to understand, and then describe, and then make *credible* much of the American reality . . . [t]he culture tosses up figures almost daily that are the envy of any novelist."[15] It was the murder of two

a For related discussion of women writers using intimate canvases to address broadly social questions, see Elizabeth Nolan's essay in this volume, "The woman's novel beyond sentimentalism," chapter 34.

teenage girls, Pattie and Babs Grimes, in Chicago in the late 1950s, and the ensuing media circus that surrounded the investigation of that crime, that made Roth throw up his hands in despair. Roth's discouragement by this incident is symptomatic of the traditional novelist's difficulty in making sense of and rendering into satisfying narrative form so many aspects of post-World War II American reality.

At around the same time that Pattie and Babs Grimes were being dispatched, Truman Capote read the following headline in the *New York Times*: "Wealthy Farmer, 3 of Family Slain."[16] When Capote saw this headline he could not have known where it would lead him, but he had been looking for some time for a suitable subject that would help him explore certain theories: "It seemed to me that journalism, reportage, could be forced to yield a serious new art form: the 'nonfiction novel,' as I thought of it."[17] What was it about murder that suggested itself as the subject for which he had been looking? Although Dreiser answered this question by emphasizing murder's cultural representativeness, Capote instead stressed pragmatic matters of scale and sales: "[A]fter reading the story it suddenly struck me that a crime, the study of one such, might provide the broad scope I needed to write the kind of book I wanted to write. Moreover, the human heart being what it is, murder was a theme not likely to darken and yellow with time."[18] In the murder of the Clutter family, in other words, Capote had found the ideal subject: it possessed all of the immediacy and impact of a headline case, but Capote also saw in it a way to transcend the temporal limitations of traditional journalism and create something that was more permanent. The nonfiction novel was the genre that allowed Capote to avoid a Roth-like despair.

In Cold Blood (1965) is a landmark in the development of the nonfiction novel for many reasons, not the least of which is Capote's unabashed declaration that the form began with him, and that consequently he was the inventor of a new genre. For this reason, a large part of his 1966 interview with George Plimpton consists of Capote disposing of various pretenders to the throne, including not only Hersey's *Hiroshima*, which Capote describes as nothing more than "a strict classical journalistic piece," but also Oscar Lewis's *Children of Sanchez* (1961), Meyer Levin's *Compulsion* (1956), and the New Journalism as practiced by Jimmy Breslin and Tom Wolfe. Whether or not one agrees with Capote's patriarchal claim on the genre, there is no doubting the fact that *In Cold Blood*, or more precisely, the welter of publicity that accompanied its publication, put the nonfiction novel unequivocally on the map.[19]

Why would Capote and other practitioners of the nonfiction novel want to blur the categories of fiction and nonfiction? The answer, at least in Capote's case, is because he wants to address a problem of scale. In *Hiroshima*, Hersey was faced with the challenge of how to personalize an event as enormous as an atomic explosion. His solution was to concentrate on the stories of a few individuals, thus reducing the immense to a human scale. Capote was faced with the opposite problem (and one already faced by Dreiser): how to take a crime that seemed merely sordid and unexceptional and make it meaningful on a large scale, beyond the immediate circumstances of the crime. In both cases, the combination of fictional and nonfictional techniques gave Hersey and Capote the flexibility they needed to achieve their aims: Capote was able to take two small-time hoods and turn their pathetic lives and eventual executions into something like tragedy, while at the same time taking the utter normality of the Clutter family and making that the foundation for their stoic heroism. Although Capote suggests to Plimpton that his reasons for writing *In Cold Blood* were thoroughly pragmatic, ultimately (and perhaps not surprisingly) his aims seem quite similar to those of Dreiser in *An American Tragedy*, namely, to examine the ways in which postwar America mythologizes interpersonal violence, a mythology in which both victims and perpetrators occupy positions that resonate with larger, practically archetypal significance. Of course, many would argue that *In Cold Blood* does much more to contribute to this mythology than to analyze it critically, but nevertheless Capote's text constitutes an enduring example of how the nonfiction novel uses fictional and nonfictional techniques to explore the complexities of American violence from a variety of points of view.

One of the most striking features of *In Cold Blood*, the fact that Capote appears nowhere in it, also provides us with a way of distinguishing him from the other giant of the American nonfiction novel, Norman Mailer. Capote considered his decision to keep himself out of the book at all times absolutely essential: "My feeling is that for the nonfiction-novel form to be entirely successful, the author should not appear in the work. Ideally. Once the narrator does appear, he has to appear throughout, all the way down the line, and the I-I-I intrudes when it really shouldn't."[20]

It is impossible to imagine Mailer, whose work is defined by the constant presence of his own ego, making such a statement, and yet in works such as *The Armies of the Night* (1968) and *The Executioner's Song* (1979), he makes contributions to the nonfiction novel that are just as important as *In Cold Blood*. Beginning with his phenomenally successful first novel, *The Naked and the Dead* (1948), and continuing in such works as *Barbary Shore* (1951) and *An American Dream* (1965), Mailer built a formidable reputation for himself as a novelist particularly interested in exploring the relationship between violence and American reality.[21] But Mailer's reputation is based just as much, if not more, on his nonfiction writing as on his fiction. Both his Pulitzer Prizes were for nonfiction novels (*The Armies of the Night* and *The Executioner's Song*) and, by and large, critics were usually disposed much more kindly to Mailer's nonfiction than to his novels.

Mailer had a number of reasons for beginning to write nonfiction (on this subject, see Andrew Hoberek, who argues elsewhere in this volume that Mailer preferred himself to any invented protagonist[b]), not the least of which was his grappling with the same problems described so vividly by Philip Roth. In a 1979 interview that Mailer gave while finishing *The Executioner's Song*, he reflects on how the nonfiction novel helps to address those problems: "I found here the perfect social novel and, as Kissinger once said, 'It has the added advantage of being true.'"[22] The nonfiction novel helped Mailer get over a block he had developed in writing traditional novels; it gave him the ability to continue to use fictional techniques, but to combine them with factual accuracy and an engagement with American reality that he felt he could not achieve through traditional fictional prose narrative.

The key point to emphasize here, and the quality that distinguishes Mailer's use of the nonfiction novel from that of Capote, is that Mailer never felt that he was creating a new genre; similarly, and again unlike Capote, he felt no particular sense of loyalty to or ownership of the nonfiction novel form. For Mailer, nonfiction novels were just ways of revivifying and redefining the novel form, in order to make it possible to write about subjects that he felt at the time could not be addressed in other, more conventional, ways. These emphases can be seen in *The Armies of the Night*, Mailer's treatment of the October 1967 March on the Pentagon, which he divides into two halves titled "History as a Novel" and "The Novel as History" (see Cecelia Tichi's essay in this volume for a fuller discussion of the Manichean structures of *Armies*[c]). Although it seems as if *Armies* treats both the novel and the writing of history as kinds of discourse, neither of which has a more persuasive truth claim than the other, Mailer never really relinquishes the priority of the novel, as these remarks from late in the book indicate:

> [A]n explanation of the mystery of the events at the Pentagon cannot be developed by the methods of history – only by the instincts of the novelist . . . the novel must replace history at precisely that point where experience is sufficiently emotional, spiritual, psychical, moral, existential, or supernatural

b Andrew Hoberek, "The Jewish great American novel," chapter 54, 900.
c Cecelia Tichi, "Novels of civic protest," chapter 23, 399.

> to expose the fact that the historian in pursuing the experience would be obliged to quit the clearly demarcated limits of historic inquiry.

Although it is purchased at the price of an insufficiently nuanced view of historical writing, Mailer outlines a very expansive definition of the novel here that includes information and techniques usually identified with the writing of history; in essence, he defines the nonfiction novel from within a nonfiction novel. His unwillingness to identify with this form in the explicit manner that distinguishes Capote's *In Cold Blood* comes partly from Mailer's oft-stated low opinion of journalism, but more crucially from his continued reliance on ego, which Capote professed to relinquish in *In Cold Blood*, and which Mailer defends quite explicitly in *Armies*:

> [I]t is fitting that any ambiguous comic hero of such history should be not only off very much to the side of the history, but that he should be an egotist of the most startling misproportions, outrageously and often unhappily self-assertive, yet in command of a detachment classic in severity, for he was a novelist and so in need of studying every last lineament of the fine, the noble, the frantic, and the foolish in others and in himself . . . Once History inhabits a crazy house, egotism may be the last tool left to History.[23]

The consistent presence of Mailer's ego leads him to play down the obvious break between *Armies* and his previous work. Instead, he insists on continuity, represented by the priority he gives to the novel form. In this respect, *The Executioner's Song*, Mailer's 1979 book about the life and execution of Utah murderer Gary Gilmore, is much more experimental than *Armies*. Although it shares the earlier text's skepticism about the possibility of arriving at an authoritative version of events, in *The Executioner's Song*, Mailer finally lets go of the safety net of his own ego[24] and opens himself up to the possibility that he is writing something that bears formal resemblances to a novel, even as it allows him to explore new ground: "[I]f I'd written it as a novel, I would have made every effort to understand him and to explain him to the reader. I began to feel that it was more interesting not to. I began to feel that I had to change some of my ideas about what literature should consist of."[25] Perhaps because, as Hoberek notes, the power of *The Executioner's Song* derives from a fundamentally novelistic source (namely, empathetic identification with people different from oneself), Mailer remains unwilling to call his work a "nonfiction novel."[d] Nevertheless, the experience of writing this book opened up the territory for him, because it pursues what is simultaneously one of

d Hoberek, chapter 54, 904.

Mailer's enduring themes and the privileged subject of the American nonfiction novel: the relationship between violence and American reality. If Mailer once felt, along with Philip Roth, that the traditional novelist's ability to understand American reality was seriously challenged by the 1960s, writing *The Executioner's Song* convinced him that it was still possible to come to know that society through examining its relation to violence.[26]

The echoes here of Dreiser's reasons for writing *An American Tragedy* are not at all accidental, for the two books have much in common. Like Dreiser, Mailer was attracted to a murder case because of the window it gave him on life in America, and like his predecessor, he worked with an enormous variety of materials (including interviews, letters, and other documents, some of which had been gathered before Mailer became involved in the case, and some of which he gathered himself). Unlike Dreiser, however, Mailer is not especially interested in understanding why the protagonist of his narrative killed, or in establishing his protagonist as a kind of representative American. In this sense, despite sharing certain techniques and concerns with Dreiser's *American Tragedy*, what Mailer does in *The Executioner's Song* is more monumental and more ambitious; by recreating the murderer's life before he became a national celebrity (the beginning of the book, which discusses the early life, is necessarily the most novelistic) and then analyzing the ways in which Gilmore became the calm center of a media storm after his arrest and trial, Mailer attempts nothing less than his own mythology of American violence, a mythology underpinned by fact but carefully structured through the manipulation of many different points of view, giving *The Executioner's Song* both multiplicity of tone and a singularity of purpose.

The range of the book is suggested by its division into two halves, "Western Voices," which concentrates more closely on the world from which Gilmore came, and "Eastern Voices," whose focus is on the rapidly developing and remarkably intense media circus that surrounds him and continues beyond his eventual execution. As Gilmore transforms from person to icon and becomes absorbed into various American popular cultural industries, Mailer grows more involved with the issue of what genre can best tell this complex story, an issue greatly complicated by his highly developed self-consciousness about his own participation in the dynamic he is anatomizing. The end result, not surprisingly, is a paradox, a "true-life novel," the original subtitle of *The Executioner's Song*, dropped from later editions, perhaps because of its ability to remind us that the light the nonfiction novel can throw on the cultures of violence in contemporary America can be uncomfortably revealing.

Many of the issues I have been discussing in this chapter – the relation between journalism and literature, the novelty of hybrid forms of prose narrative such as the nonfiction novel, and in particular, the feeling that traditional forms of prose narrative, especially the novel, had become exhausted and unable to represent accurately the peculiar dimensions of contemporary American reality – come together in Tom Wolfe's celebration of the "New Journalism." Wolfe's audacious claim that the novel was in the process of being eclipsed by journalism, because only journalism was true to the legacy of nineteenth-century novelistic realism, crystallized the emerging sense that the relative amount of cultural capital possessed by fiction and nonfiction in American literature was in the process of shifting decisively, and perhaps permanently.[27]

At the time Wolfe published *The New Journalism* in 1973, his braggadocious tone seemed justified; indeed, when Mailer published *The Executioner's Song* to great acclaim in 1979 the triumph of the nonfiction novel seemed complete. And yet, if one surveys the contemporary American literary landscape in the opening years of the twenty-first century, it is striking just how few people refer to New Journalism or the nonfiction novel as anything else than a historical curiosity, as something that used to be a benchmark, but which has now been superseded.

The apparent transience of the nonfiction novel should come as no surprise. Even Mas'ud Zavarzadeh, possibly the genre's most enthusiastic champion, has acknowledged its fragility: "The nonfictional novel with its balance of the actual and the fictional is a very vulnerable genre. Lack of compositional equilibrium can easily turn a nonfiction novel into an unsuccessful historical novel, an unimaginative fictive narrative, a book of routine reportage, or some other form of mono-referential narrative."[28]

Given this unpredictability, what does the future hold for the nonfiction novel? Throughout this chapter, I have examined the way in which the nonfiction novel has responded to the challenge faced by other genres of American prose narrative with increasing regularity over the course of the twentieth and twenty-first centuries: how to represent both large- and small-scale violent or traumatic events. The most recent example of this challenge erupted on 9/11, and the responses to the events of that day illustrate the continuing urgency of the imperative to represent, to make sense of, to cast into narrative form, the relationship between violence and reality. Given that the genres I have discussed in this chapter have all been engaged, to a greater or lesser degree, with the issue of how best to represent reality, the question then becomes: what is the best way to embrace it?

We can return to Don DeLillo in search of an answer, because his belief that the Kennedy assassination constitutes an "aberration in the heartland of the Real" could serve as an apt description for that violent warp in reality that the nonfiction novel attempts to respond to and narrativize.[29] In an essay written in response to the events of 9/11 entitled "In the Ruins of the Future" (2001), DeLillo explains, "The writer wants to understand what this day has done to us . . . But language is inseparable from the world that provokes it." DeLillo notes that the "writer tries to give memory, tenderness and meaning to all that howling space" and in doing so adds his narrative to many thousands of others, none of which will contain the single truth about such an event, all of which will constitute a valid response to that violence.[30]

In his essay "False Documents" (1983), E. L. Doctorow famously states that "I am thus led to the proposition that there is no fiction or non-fiction as we commonly understand the distinction: there is only narrative."[31] At one time, this statement might have seemed to promote the epistemological authority of the nonfiction novel, but it could just as easily be taken as its epitaph. Even if this is the case, there is no reason to mourn, for surely the lesson to be drawn from the nonfiction novel is that, even if the division between fiction and nonfiction remains extraordinarily persistent, the hybrid and impure status of the nonfiction novel points the way both to the past and to the future of the novel genre itself.

Notes

1. Don DeLillo, "American Blood," *Rolling Stone* (December 8, 1983): 23.
2. Alain Badiou, *The Century*, trans. Alberto Toscano (Oxford: Polity, 2007), 32, 48.
3. For this reason, the nonfiction novel does not follow the path suggested by Barbara Foley's fear that debates concerning the inability to distinguish fact and fiction have led to a situation where, "The 'power of freedom,' it appeared, consisted in fiction's release from any obligation to offer determinate statements about reality." Barbara Foley, *Telling the Truth: The Theory and Practice of Documentary Fiction* (Ithaca, NY and London: Cornell University Press, 1986), 16. According to Foley, the documentary novel can be read as a response to the troubling of the boundary between fact and fiction (25). While the documentary novel is much more dedicated to accuracy and veracity, the nonfiction novel is more experimental and skeptical about the prospect of accurately representing events.
4. Lennard Davis, *Factual Fictions: The Origins of the English Novel* (New York: Columbia University Press, 1983), 9. I should make clear that I have no intention of contributing to the vexed question of the origins of the nonfiction form. For a representative example of such debates, see Robert Augustin Smart, *The*

Nonfiction Novel (Lanham, MD, and New York: University Press of America, 1985). For an account of the slipperiness of the fact/fiction divide in early American novels, see Paul Giles's essay in this volume, "Transatlantic currents and the invention of the American novel," chapter 1, esp. 22–23.

5. Shelly Fisher Fishkin, *From Fact to Fiction: Journalism & Imaginative Writing in America* (Baltimore: Johns Hopkins University Press, 1985), 112–113.
6. Davis, *Factual Fictions*, 134.
7. Quoted in Fishkin, *From Fact to Fiction*, 112–113.
8. In concentrating on Hersey, I unfortunately but necessarily pass over other writers whose work is perhaps just as important for a full understanding of the nonfiction novel, such as James Agee's *Let Us Now Praise Famous Men* (1941), and John Dos Passos's *U.S.A.* trilogy (1938). On the former, see Smart, *The Nonfiction Novel;* on the latter, see Foley, *Telling the Truth* and "From U.S.A. to Ragtime: Notes on the Forms of Historical Consciousness in Modern Fiction," *American Literature* 50.1 (March 1978): 85–105.
9. John Hersey, "The Novel of Contemporary History," *Atlantic Monthly* (November 1949): 80–84: 80.
10. Bruce Bliven, Review of *Hiroshima, The New Republic* 115.10 (September 9, 1946): 300–301: 301.
11. Quoted in Michael J. Yavenditti, "John Hersey and the American Conscience: The Reception of *Hiroshima*," *Pacific Historical Review* 43.1 (February 1974): 24–49: 33.
12. For far more radical American texts about war that also use nonfiction novelistic techniques, see Art Spiegelman's *Maus* (1996), discussed by Jan Baetens in "Graphic novels," chapter 69 of this volume, and Michael Herr's *Dispatches* (1977).
13. Mas'ud Zavarzadeh, *The Mythopoeic Reality: The Postwar American Nonfiction Novel* (Urbana: University of Illinois Press, 1976), 57. Importantly, however, Zavarzadeh argues that the combination of fiction and reality goes on to make something qualitatively different from either fiction or nonfiction. For a nuanced recent argument for why it might be important to keep insisting on some working distinction between fiction and nonfiction, see Daniel W. Lehman, *Matters of Fact: Reading Nonfiction Over the Edge* (Columbus: Ohio State University Press, 1997).
14. Joan Didion, "Preface," in *Slouching Towards Bethlehem* (New York: Dell, 1968), xi.
15. Philip Roth, "Writing American Fiction," *Commentary* (March 1961): 223–233: 224, emphasis in original.
16. George Plimpton, "The Story Behind a Nonfiction Novel," *New York Times* (January 16, 1966). www.nytimes.com/books/97/12/28/home/capote-interview.html. Downloaded May 3, 2008. This long interview played a crucial role in establishing the legend of *In Cold Blood* and the status of the nonfiction novel.
17. *Ibid.*
18. *Ibid.*
19. Unfortunately, much of the publicity around *In Cold Blood* missed what was most important about Capote's work because of its preoccupation with the issue

of whether the book was strictly factual or contained certain invented details. Such criticisms illustrate a tendency to think of narrative in mutually exclusive bipolar terms, and thus miss the opportunity to think of the nonfiction novel as a qualitatively new genre. The problem, as Robert Siegle has identified it, is the tendency to think of the nonfiction novel as an oxymoron; the solution, he says, is to think of the genre as a tautology ("Capote's *Handcarved Coffins* and the Nonfiction Novel," *Contemporary Literature* 25.4 (Winter 1984): 437–451.

20. Plimpton, "The Story Behind a Nonfiction Novel."
21. In a 2006 interview, Mailer discussed what he sees as the relationship between novel-writing and violence in his work: "The excitement that violence offered me in the earlier books, particularly in *An American Dream*, was that no one else was doing it . . . Violence was the new frontier, then." John Whalen-Bridge, "The Karma of Words: Mailer Since *Executioner's Song*," *Journal of Modern Literature* 30.1 (Fall 2006): 1–16: 11–12.
22. Melvyn Bragg, "A Murderer's Tale: Norman Mailer Talking to Melvyn Bragg," in *Conversations with Norman Mailer*, ed. J. Michael Lennon (Jackson: University Press of Mississippi, 1988): 252–261:260.
23. It is, in part, Mailer's egotism that Zavarzadeh has in mind when he describes *Armies* as a prime example of the testimonial nonfiction novel, a "narrative of encounter between the author – the historical person whose name appears on the title page, not a fictional 'second self' – and the brute physic or physical facts" (*The Mythopoeic Reality*, 130).
24. Mailer had considered including in *The Executioner's Song* a figure who would represent himself so that he could comment on the action, but then decided, "You have to be brave enough to write this book without putting yourself in it at all." Quoted in William F. Buckley, Jr. and Jeff Greenfield, "Crime and Punishment: Gary Gilmore," in *Conversations with Norman Mailer*, 228–251: 251.
25. *Ibid.*, 234.
26. *Ibid.*, 238.
27. See Tom Wolfe, "The New Journalism," in *The New Journalism*, ed. Tom Wolfe and E. W. Johnson (London: Picador, 1973), 15–68; 48. Wolfe covers much of the same ground, but this time in the middle of writing *The Bonfire of the Vanities*, in "Stalking the Billion-Footed Beast: A Literary Manifesto for the New Social Novel," *Harper's Magazine* (November 1989): 45–56.
28. Zavarzadeh, *The Mythopoeic Reality*, 112.
29. Don DeLillo, *Libra* (New York: Viking Penguin, 1988), 15. See Baetens, chapter 69, 1151–1152, in this volume, for a perceptive analysis of a key post-9/11 text with strong connections to the nonfiction novel, namely, Art Spiegelman's comic/graphic novel, *In The Shadow of No Towers* (2004).
30. Don DeLillo, "In the Ruins of the Future," *Guardian* (December 22, 2001). http://books.guardian.co.uk/departments/generalfiction/story/0,,623732,00.html. Downloaded June 3, 2008.

As a number of critics have pointed out, DeLillo's nonfictional pronouncements on the power and influence of writers tend to be considerably more optimistic than those in his fiction. See for instance, the disparity between the hopefulness of DeLillo's article "In the Ruins of the Future" and the pessimism of the novelist Bill Gray in *Mao II* (1991), who is condemned to write a narrative that can never be completed.

31. E. L. Doctorow, "False Documents," in *E. L. Doctorow: Essays and Conversations*, ed. Richard Trenner (Princeton: Ontario Review Press, 1983), 16–27:26.

60

Disability and the American novel

DAVID T. MITCHELL AND SHARON L. SNYDER

The origins of imperfection

In an ancient Pima Indian creation story about the origins of the first people, three gods apply their creativity to the sculpting of prototypical human physiques. As the gods hold up their creations for inspection, they exchange critiques regarding imperfections in the models. Ee-ee-toy queries Jahwerta Mahkai and Toehavs about their "queer dolls" by pointing out that Jahwerta's dolls have only one leg and Toehavs's dolls have webbed fingers. Both gods respond to the critiques by claiming alternative capacities for their dolls and consequently for the value of bodily difference. Ee-ee-toy rejects these alternative explanations and throws the dolls away to install his models as the standard. The result of Ee-ee-toy's destructive act is that "sickness and disease" enter into the world.[1]

The origin myth has a double-edged moral for the Pima and contemporary readers. Audiences may imagine themselves as descendants of a "perfect first people," while also receiving a warning about the disastrous consequences of the devaluation of difference. Pointedly, the exclusion of bodily variation results in vulnerability to decay. The myth also premises the critical role that disability plays in American literary traditions: when human differences of body and mind are rejected, literary narratives often indict the social context of suppression – rather than people with disabilities – as the source of the problem.

Our objective here is to demonstrate a history of variations in disability-based representations particular to American novels. Within this history we find literary formulae of embodiment that ground fantasies of American exceptionalism through the installation of normative schemes of national belonging. Such expressions inevitably prove finite, narrow, and unnecessarily confining. They also, at times, prompt violent responses to individuals and communities that fail to meet socially derived expectations of human acceptability – particularly those regarding significant variations in appearance, functionality, and sensory/cognitive capacity. The rejection of bodily differences justifies cultural disqualification of individuals from access to: (1) social institutions and the privileges of citizenship and (2) a broader recognition of disability as integral to experiences of human embodiment.

Without deformity of body

Like the Pima creation myth, the first European travel narratives premise the location of an "undiscovered" utopic landscape recognized by the absence of bodily "blight." Mirroring Judeo-Christian stories of prelapsarian worlds unspoiled by human infirmity, early European narrative depictions of the New World detail a landscape of unparalleled perfection. In one of Columbus's letters to the sovereigns of Spain, the explorer portrays native peoples encountered on the island of Hispanolá in idyllic terms as "the best people under the sun" who "are all well formed" without "any deformity of body."[2] Here disability is conjured up by the presence of its culturally desired illusory antithesis – the perfect body – in order to sell the value of future colonial ventures to European financial sponsors. This fantasized bodily perfection becomes a commonly repeated pattern in early travel narratives. John Winthrop's sermon, "A Model of Christian Charity" (1630), exhorts the new English immigrants aboard the *Arbella* to recognize that "[l]ove is a bond of perfection" which must knit their social body together in the likeness of Christ's body: "the most perfect and best proportioned body in the world."[3] In order to enforce this ideological rhetoric, New World immigration policy would bar people with disabilities from immigrating to the colonies, and later the United States, well into the first half of the twentieth century.

As the American novel tradition develops at the end of the eighteenth century one witnesses the impact of travel narrative portrayals of embodiment on gothic characterization strategies. Writers such as Charles Brockden Brown, William Montgomery Bird, James Fenimore Cooper, Edgar Allan Poe, and others populated their narratives of American manifest destiny with a range of unsettling bodies to achieve heightened sensations in their reading publics. In doing so, early novelists employ disability as the threatening underbelly of otherwise presumably stable social institutions such as family, church, community, and work. The cumulative effect of this early representational history tends to locate disability as an increasingly feared occurrence outside of normative human experiences. Disabled, racialized, ethnic, sexualized, and gendered bodies were often presented as visibly disabled to middle-class European reading sensibilities. As Leonard Cassuto argues, the formation of the "racial grotesque" demonstrates that "whites tried hard to imagine nonwhites as non-people as part of the justification for slavery and Indian removal."[4] This literary practice established a naturalized equation that linked bodily, sensory, and cognitive differences as symptoms of immoral character. In doing so writers of the early republic adopted a normative national form that enshrined a narrow bourgeois aesthetic as the appropriate measure of American belonging.

Alternatively, writers of the American Romantic tradition increasingly portrayed disability not as the faulty embodiment of marginalized peoples but rather as characteristic of the deforming precepts of social elites espousing bodily perfection schemes. Nathaniel Hawthorne's writings address stigmatizing attitudes on the part of those who believe themselves capable of improving upon an imperfect (often physical) Nature. *The Scarlet Letter* (1850) follows the exploits of the physician, Chillingworth, who walks with a limp as he oversees the destruction of the Puritan minister, Dimmesdale, by exploiting his thematically resonant heart condition. Likewise, in "The American Scholar" (1837) Ralph Waldo Emerson employs a metaphorics of truncated humanity (that which he terms "inverse cripples") to critique parochial beliefs about human dominion over Nature promoted by popular philosophy. In *Narrative of the Life of Frederick Douglass, An American Slave* (1845) the narrator describes the abominations of the American slave system in terms of disfigurements inflicted upon his body and those of other slaves by cruel overseers who resorted to lash and gun as the instruments of racial superiority. Rebecca Harding Davis's *Life in the Iron Mills* (1861) narrates a story of capitalist labor exploitation from the point of view of Deborah Wolfe, a hunchbacked female narrator whose bodily condition exposes the ravages of unsafe working conditions in a Virginia iron forging factory. In "The Yellow Wallpaper" (1892), Charlotte Perkins Gilman exposes the politics of patriarchal medicine by connecting the "rehabilatory" incarceration of women within domestic spaces as a putative antidote to female hysteria. In these ways nineteenth-century novelistic traditions turned fantasies of bodily perfection upside down by disabling those promoting bodily norms that would exclude people with disabilities alongside other cultural minorities.

The overarching result is that American gothic and romantic writers set a dialectic of disability into motion. Explorations of disability resulted in the crafting of a novelistic tradition that offered a more varied menu of disability representations beyond grotesque caricatures. Increasingly, American novelists probed the productive value of disability as a device of characterization that equated conditions of physical and mental impairment with the symptoms of social abuse rather than fallen humanity. This more nuanced approach gradually politicized disability by making it resonate with larger social causes.

Perhaps the most significant nineteenth-century example of disability as a sign of social ills can be found in the novels of Herman Melville. In *Moby-Dick* (1850), Melville delves into the tormented psychology of Captain Ahab, a one-legged monomaniacal sea captain. Ahab pursues a world-ranging vengeance quest in which he tracks the white whale responsible for disabling him. Along the way Ahab modifies the *Pequod*, his favored whaling boat, to accommodate a prosthetic leg in rather innovative ways. Yet, his creativity in transforming a hazardous life at sea for one with mobility difficulties is ultimately used as evidence of the extent to which he will go to avenge his disablement through a crazed pursuit.

In *The Confidence-Man: His Masquerade* (1857), Melville presents a novelistic universe that would "anatomize the wise man's folly, and cleanse the body of the infected world if it would but patiently receive his medicine." Conceiving of the world as an infected host gave Melville the means to position disability as a central image in a scathing critique of American economic disparities.[5]

The setting for *The Confidence-Man* is a Mississippi steamboat upon which a group of disabled con-artists bilk unwary able-bodied passengers out of their fortunes. Cripples, spastics, blind, deaf-and-dumb characters appeal to sentiments of pity that other passengers heap upon them. Melville seeks to diagnose the inappropriateness of pity toward disability as a false projection of the able-bodied perceiver: "whether the alleged hardships of that alleged unfortunate ["the negro cripple"] might not exist more in the pity of the observer than the experience of the observed." In response one passenger observes that, "He knew nothing about the cripple," and speculates that if one could "get at the real state of his heart, he would be found about as happy as most men, if not, in fact, full as happy as the speaker himself."

The Confidence-Man unveils how US capitalism masquerades as a system of exchanges motivated by charity to alleviate human afflictions. Ultimately Melville exposes such undertakings as devaluing the humanity of those marginalized individuals/communities they claim to assist. By turning the tables on a common sentiment (pity) directed at disabled people in the nineteenth century, *The Confidence-Man* demonstrates that the system of charity is a well-greased track upon which social inequities are justified and the guilt of the prosperous appeased. The critical insight of Melville's "masquerade" is that bodily incapacity cannot be located outside of, or as a perversion of, the range of embodied experiences that comprise "suffering humanity."

Insufficiencies of the social body

Rather than referencing social disorder by populating literary worlds with disabled bodies, twentieth-century American novels increasingly referenced disability – particularly cognitive disability – through an exposé of the social violence that figures disabled people as aberrant. Rather than use disability as symptomatic of social upheaval, the signification of disability as deviance becomes a marker of an insufficiency in the social – rather than individual – body.

One early example of this rhetorical strategy can be found in Sherwood Anderson's experimental novel, *Winesburg, Ohio* (1919). The work begins with a dream sequence wherein the protagonist, an unnamed writer who is physically infirm, old, and bedridden, conjures up a curious "procession of grotesques." Instead of being terrified by this nightmarish vision, a response encouraged of late eighteenth- and early nineteenth-century audiences, the writer leaves his bed to compose stories about these "grotesques" that "represented all the men and women he had ever known."

Significantly, it is in this dream-like state that the writer first encounters figures that compel him to recognize the makings of a story. Anderson's depiction of small-town Midwest life features an array of character tics that act as symptomatic expressions of social repression. Grotesque bodies connect the "deformities" of a secret life (homosexuality, incest, licentiousness, spiritual infidelity, etc.) with differences primarily associated with disabled bodies. The writer's dream provides an opportunity for fantastic transmutations of what he might otherwise find banal human traits; the shadowy substance of characters takes shape in the unique physiognomy of bodies recognizable as disabled. Bodily anomalies command the attention of the writer, who then transforms them into grotesques – characters that are extravagant, irregular, or fantastic in form.[6] Anderson argues that what "made the people grotesques" is not their physical properties but their commitment to deforming personal "truth[s]." While the narrator's fascination with bodily distortion threatens to overcome him – even "becoming a grotesque" himself – he is saved from such a fate. "The young thing inside him" preserves his sense of integrity and non-misshapenness. In other words, he resists his own distorting system by virtue of mastery over the creative process.

This exoneration of the artist from implication in his own artistic landscape of grotesques suggests a reconsideration of definitions of disability operative in early twentieth-century industrialized culture. As modernist writers sought symbols to represent a degraded social milieu, disability provided opportunities to explore neglected experiences of embodiment. This effort at literary rehabilitation tends to pathologize deforming cultural beliefs rather than aberrant bodies themselves. Such a tendency continues in other notable works of the period, including William Faulkner's tale of Southern family collapse in *The Sound and the Fury* (1929).[a]

The Sound and the Fury begins with the point of view of thirty-three-year-old Benjy who has a developmental disability – he is what Shakespeare called "an idiot . . . full of sound and fury." While for Shakespeare the tale of an "idiot" signifies nothing, Faulkner finds great meaning embedded in Benjy's perspective as a person with a developmental disability. Most of the criticism of Faulkner's novel to date promotes Benjy to the status of a symbolic representative of mute, human tragedy. Yet, on closer reading, the novel provides a scathing exposé of the social reception of people with cognitive disabilities during the eugenics era.

Eugenicists (*c.*1880–1945) portrayed individuals with cognitive disabilities as incapable of living a fully human life. Diagnostic categories such as idiot, imbecile, moron, and subnormal were predicated on scientific beliefs that people with developmental disabilities arrived at plateaus of mental development. No matter how much care, training, support, or education they received, feebleminded people could not transcend their inbuilt limitations. Such individuals were characterized as the hereditary victims of "bad seed" – despite the positive emphasis on "good genes" in the original definition of the Greek work "eugenics" – and various kinds of family debauchery (alcoholism, infidelity, kleptomania, poverty, etc.) resulted in generational layers of incompetence, invalidity, and incapacity.

In essence, eugenicists applied concepts of better breeding technologies for plants and livestock to human beings. A eugenic diagnosis of deficiency led perforce to the surrender of rights to basic citizenship. Disabled people targeted during the eugenics era found themselves deprived of social mobility, human connectedness, and family belonging. Those identified as "mentally defective" were identified as sexual menaces that degraded the country's hereditary stock. In order to prevent inferior genes from spreading, people with severe disabilities were subject to sanctioned forms of social violence such as permanent institutionalization, sterilization, and, in Nazi Germany, extermination.

a For further commentary on *The Sound and the Fury*, see Candace Waid, "Faulkner and the Southern novel," chapter 45 in this volume, 756–757.

All of the Compson family members in *The Sound and the Fury* are explicitly evaluated according to their ability to imagine Benjy's humanity. Benjy's difficulties in leading a socially productive life result in his castration, segregation, and denial of access to public schooling – essentially the refusal of his right to the dignity of an interdependent life. The critical tendency to cast Benjy as a literary symbol in *The Sound and the Fury* overlooks the novel's scathing critique of the dehumanizing environment of the eugenics period. Ultimately, Faulkner presents Benjy's experience not as a sign of wider cultural collapse, but rather as a limited measure of just how far the social fabric has unraveled around him.

As the atrocities of Nazi Germany were publicized in the US after World War II, it became known "mercy death" solutions for disabled people resulted in the government-ordered slaughter of nearly 300,000 people in German psychiatric institutions. Such extermination practices included starvation, gassings, and planned overdoses by physicians as "medical interventions" in what Henry Friedlander calls "the origins of Nazi genocide."[7] The mass murder of people with disabilities between 1939 and 1946 shows how degrading concepts of human variation often lead to inhuman practices.

Awareness of the deadly outcomes produced by Nazi operators of eugenic murders under the T4 "euthanasia" program had significant consequences for writing practices regarding people with disabilities.[8] Disabled author Flannery O'Connor critiqued the widespread tendency to represent disability as an object of sentimentality in the immediate aftermath of World War II. In her 1961 introduction to *A Memoir of Mary Ann*, O'Connor discusses the dangers of hiding suffering from popular audiences and inserting pity in its place: "When tenderness is detached from the source of tenderness, its logical outcome is terror. It ends in forced labor camps and the fumes of the gas chamber."[9] O'Connor's observation links a genocidal mindset to depictions that efface pain and bodily difference too easily. For O'Connor this practice is a dangerous convention contributing to further social violence, and one she diagnoses throughout her novels.

At the conclusion of her first novel, *Wise Blood* (1952), O'Connor's protagonist, Hazel Motes, the ex-preacher of the Church without Christ, decides to blind himself in order to combat excessive religious sentimentality toward the "poor and needy." Ironically, blindness turns Motes into an object of charity himself rather than combating commonly held assumptions about disabled people as requiring excessive care. Yet, in the place of this social myth, the novel portrays blindness as the inexhaustible exploration of a vantage point that can contain "the sky and planets and whatever was or had been or would be."

O'Connor's initial exploration of Christian redemption in *Wise Blood* is taken up and more fully explored in later works such as *The Violent Bear It Away* (1960). In both novels O'Connor exposes the Christian tradition of the miraculous alleviation of bodily suffering by Christ as a belief that results in violence toward disabled bodies. The would-be preacher, Tarwater, rejects redemption, based on his non-sentimental approach to being born again: "You're only born once," as he matter-of-factly states to one truck driver. Standard biblical exegesis recognizes baptisms, miracle cures of cripples, and raisings from the dead as increasing evidence of Christian tolerance for the insufficiencies of the flesh – particularly with respect to the bodies of those who are "unfortunate," "afflicted," and "sickly." Such a logic for O'Connor sits at the heart of cultural endorsements of euthanasia according to which people with disabilities would be better off dead than supported in their efforts to navigate environments not made to accommodate a range of differences. We can recognize in this critique one important eruption of the increasingly serious political undercurrents in disability narratives that inform post-World War II literary depictions.

Disability-based critiques of trite formulas of narrative resolution can also be found at key points in J. D. Salinger's *Catcher in the Rye* (1951). The narrator, Holden Caulfield, hates those who cry their "goddamn eyes out over phony stuff in the movies" largely because popular films perpetuate myths about certain rehabilitation and easy cures for people with disabilities. Such popular narrative conventions of disability signify a dangerous binary determinism for Salinger as they rush to solve the problem of disability through a "kill or cure" approach.

The eugenic logic of sentimental storylines interrogated in *Catcher in the Rye*, also surfaces in Harper Lee's *To Kill a Mockingbird* (1960). Lee's story connects the experiences of a physically disabled African American man, Tom Robinson, to the fate of a cognitively disabled Caucasian man nick-named, Boo, "whose mind was bad." Whereas in *The Sound and the Fury* the local African American church supplies Faulkner's Benjy with his sole possible entry into the public domain by allowing him to attend Easter service alongside others, no such sanctuary exists for Arthur "Boo" Radley in Lee's Maycomb, Alabama of the 1930s. Indeed, *Mockingbird* opens with a discussion of the limited institutions available to cognitively disabled individuals in Depression-era America: the state mental asylum, the jail, or the family cellar.

Boo's incarceration within the very center of the hamlet results in the communal mythologization of his mental impairment. The one thing that black and white can agree on in the segregated hamlet is that Boo's cognitive impairment poses a horrifying threat. In the end, the child narrator, Scout, learns that the real "horror" of small town life is the violence brought to bear on perceived – and ultimately specious - threats posed by African American and cognitively disabled men alike.[b]

Retelling the story of disability

While works such as *Winesburg, Ohio, The Sound and the Fury, Catcher in the Rye*, and *To Kill a Mockingbird* locate the source of disability as monstrosity in an uncomprehending social sphere, later twentieth-century American works spill over with disability experiences that inform perspectives claimed by authors as central to their worldview.

A host of disability references play a central role in late twentieth-century novels: Sylvia Plath's narration of her mental breakdown and the violence of her institutional experiences in *The Bell Jar* (1963); Oedipa Maas, the protagonist of Thomas Pynchon's *The Crying of Lot 49* (1967), recognizes the process of US historical "amnesia" by referencing the symptoms of an epileptic seizure; in *The Bluest Eye* (1970), Toni Morrison situates Polly Breedlove's limp and the mental illness of her daughter, Pecola, as traits that keep both women permanently disenfranchised from racialized mythologies of "physical beauty ... probably the most destructive idea in the history of human thought;" Wallace Stegner's Pulitzer Prize-winning novel, *Angle of Repose* (1971), tells the story of a wheelchair-user named Lyman Ward, who functions as the family archivist and escapes an uncomprehending, inaccessible contemporary world by imaginatively existing in the Victorian experiences of his grandparents during the settlement of the early West. This catalog of disability-based characterizations provides a glimpse into a voluminous closet of literary curiosities populating late twentieth-century American novels.

As the country responded to civil rights-based efforts to achieve equality for various minority groups, novels such as Katherine Dunn's *Geek Love* (1989) and Richard Powers's *Operation Wandering Soul* (1993) take inspiration from the efforts of the disability rights movement that culminated in the passage of the Americans with Disabilities Act in 1990. Both novelists emphasize the

b For more on Harper Lee's novel see Gregg Crane, "Law and the American novel," chapter 46 in this volume, 775–776.

experience of disability as an opportunity for creative subjectivity in an otherwise heteronormative, ableist world. Within these narrative traditions disabled people begin to find themselves identified as the bearers of a depth of experience akin to other marginalized communities. Representations of disability increasingly surface regarding the nature of social exclusion, the art of navigating intricately inaccessible environments, and the unique subjectivities forged in the crucible of a host of identity-based civil rights movements.

Geek Love brings to life a parade of what Sherwood Anderson refers to as "grotesques." Dunn's novel documents the exploits of an entire family of freak show actors in order to parody a quintessentially modernist mechanism of "high" literature – the epiphany – and links it to debased economic motivations: Aloysius Binewski's "brain child" is to actively manufacture children with severe disabilities for popular consumption. The novel satirizes the literary dependency upon "grotesque" bodies discussed throughout this chapter as a staple of American novelistic traditions. While Anderson's *Winesburg* narrator establishes a distance between his vision of grotesques and himself (despite his own disability status), Dunn self-consciously exploits the allure of the grotesque and, in doing so, indicts the prurient dream-work of art.

As the sole survivor of a family catastrophe, Dunn's narrator tells the story from the "knowing" perspective of a second-generation freak – the hunchback albino Olympia. The narrator dejectedly acknowledges her parents' secret disappointment in her relatively banal physical differences. In doing so, she introduces a division between her own "less interesting deformities" and the apocalyptic (and thus more "valuable") freakish qualities of her siblings: Arty, the quadruple congenital amputee named "Aqua Boy," conjoined sisters Elly and Iphy, and Chick, her clairvoyant brother. By linking disability representation with freak show-like hyperbole, *Geek Love* ironizes its own literary ancestry: Olympia and her freakish siblings embody the remnants of a past experiment gone awry.

In a direct revision of Simone de Beauvoir's argument in *The Second Sex*, Olympia states "that a true freak cannot be made. A true freak must be born."[10] The inversion expresses one of the crucial paradoxes of disability in the American novel: while the body hosts an array of parasitic social mythologies regarding abnormality and difference, it is also bound to a notion of biology as inborn essence. The Binewski children adeptly manipulate fantasies of bodily abjectness in order to carve out a niche in a fetishistic economy of affect-driven commodity capitalism. This overt manipulation of their bodies for profit leaves them ambivalently tethered to a physical fate from which they cannot escape.

Similar to Dunn's novel, Richard Powers's *Operation Wandering Soul* (1993) deviates uniquely from the portrayal of a single individual with disabilities.[c] The novel is set on a Los Angeles pediatric ward populated by children with disabilities, abandoned by their parents to the medical industry. Relegated to a hospital in the now dystopic center of Los Angeles, Powers's disabled children can play no role in supporting adult dreams of childhood transcendence. In this way, Powers dramatizes a definition of disability as that which inhibits children from imagining their own successful maturation through storytelling. There is, as theorist Robert McRuer argues, "no future for crips," in that few stories devote themselves to imagining productive life trajectories for people with disabilities and other marginalized identities such as queer, trans-, and intersexed bodies.[11]

The novel's title references disabled children set adrift to aimless wandering by adult communities rather than participating in any sort of purposeful journey. These children have to hunt out their own stories of purpose, for the adult stories surrounding them promise no viable path to maturation, given their "broken" bodies – and the novel thus imagines alternative trajectories on their behalf. In the pages of *Operation Wandering Soul*, the subjectivity of disability becomes mobile and multivoiced. In the pediatric unit, storytime kicks off with a reading of the Shinto folk tale, "The first child in the world was born deformed," a common origin myth for many cultures, including the Pima Indians, with whose myth this chapter began. The ward's adult volunteer story reader, Linda, realizes that the myth rationalizes the eradication of disabled children: the first man and the first woman make a reed boat for the "malformed" child (whom they bitterly name "The Leech") and abandon him to the whims of the ocean, allowing the couple to "begin again" with a more perfect offspring. As Linda searches for another story with a less distressing outcome, the disabled children intercede with questions about the fate of the "leech" child. This leads the storyteller to renarrate a life for the deformed child: Leech sails around the world (no need to walk if a boat provides your mobility), picks up bottled messages from other abandoned souls, and eventually runs into the famed historical traveler, Henry the Navigator, whose

c For a discussion of Richard Powers in the context of postmodernism, see Ursula Heise's essay in this volume ("Postmodern novels," chapter 58, 980). Bruce Robbins similarly cites Powers's experiments with narrative conventions ("The worlding of the American novel," chapter 66, note 3, 1105). For Powers's engagement with philosophy, see Robert Chodat ("Philosophy and the American novel," chapter 39, 666–667).

global exploits the disabled child's arrival precipitates. On the boat, the Leech dreams of other creatures like himself and avoids the "hard places" that will not accommodate his vessel.

Thus, Powers ironically inaugurates the arrival of the age of exploration by following the adventures of a disabled child tossed out to die in a reed boat on the sea. This imaginative act of narrating an alternative story for disabled children continues as the ward residents take up their own re-enactments of the latent disability subtext of fables such as Robert Browning's "The Pied Piper of Hamelin." Their performance emphasizes the exclusion of an all-gimp cast of disabled children ironically saved from the drowning fate of the other town residents because they cannot keep pace with the able-bodied dancers ahead of them.

Operation Wandering Soul merits attention for its complex rendition of multiple disabled points of view. For example, during the Pied Piper performance an excluded trio of disabled children form a union partially based on their awareness that each one fails to comprehend the different limitations of the others. Their mutual awareness of this exclusionary tendency in themselves constitutes an element of artistic realization that a more fully inclusive community of disabled people might demonstrate: every "outcast" holds interest among the others based on their unique experiences of otherness. The children fashion their connections on the pediatric ward into an alternative family circle that embraces its members and contests their devaluation beyond the hospital walls. While the non-disabled adults bequeath the children stories of the tragedy of impairment, the children, empowered by a group alliance based on disability, revise those narratives to interpret the nuances of disabled lives in a healthier manner.

The last frontier

In 1962, the literary critic Leslie Fiedler declared that disabled people represented a "last frontier" that American fiction was intent on conquering.[12] Why does disability erupt at so many turns of our national literature? This is a question with which we began and on which we will end. Disability represents a powerful yet largely un-interrogated conflict within the US national psyche. It is the site where the conflicted nature of American beliefs about "viable lives" gets acted out. Disability both reminds us of our vulnerability and at the same time asks us to recognize that bodily, cognitive, and sensory differences characterize a significant part of our shared experience as embodied beings.

In *A History of Disability* (1997), Henri-Jacques Stiker argues that disabled people's *integration* is not enough – we must press instead for the recognition of disability as *integral* to cultural understandings of difference.[13] While disability results in segregation within many cultures, it is integral to American literature. The works and writers discussed in this chapter invert popular media formulas by not professing to "solve" disability as a problem. Rather they portray the depths of doubt that reside in the recesses of shared beliefs about disabled bodies while also articulating new insights into the varied kinds of embodiment that attends experiences of disability.

We cannot truly know a culture until we ask its disabled citizens to describe, analyze, and interpret it.[14] Disabled peoples' once disregarded perspectives create a vantage point without which a country becomes less than its parts (to riff off John Winthrop's "perfect and best proportioned body" of Christ metaphor for utopian religious community in the early seventeenth century). Disabled perspectives provide readers with opportunities to reflect on an American cultural tendency that too easily assures itself of its own humanity. Rather, literary approaches to disability commonly demonstrate that the achievement of humanity must be actively re-evaluated in each social epoch and across generations.

Like other forms of equality, our relationship to disability is neither finished nor absolute. Some of our most enduring novels articulate the vantage point of socially disadvantaged peoples in a way that allows us to better understand the world as something unfinished, mutating, and, consequently, with the capacity to change. This is the politics of disability that literature unveils.

Notes

1. "The Story of the Flood," in *Aw-aw-tam, Indian Nights, Being the Myths and Legends of the Pimas of Arizona*, ed. J. William Lloyd (Westfield, NJ: The Lloyd Group, 1911), 47–49. http://sacred-texts.com/nam/sw/ain/index.htm.
2. Margarita Zamora, "Christopher Columbus's 'Letter to the Severeigns': Announcing the Discovery," in *New World Encounters*, ed. Stephen Greenblatt (Berkeley: University of California Press, 1993), 1–11.
3. A more extensive analysis of Winthrop's use of the extended metaphor of the perfect body of Christ can be found in chapter 1 of David Mitchell and Sharon Snyder, *Cultural Locations of Disability* (Chicago: University of Chicago Press, 2006), 52–55.
4. Leonard Cassuto, *The Inhuman Race: The Racial Grotesque in American Literature and Culture* (New York: Columbia University Press, 1997), xiv. For an in-depth discussion of Nietzsche's resignification of Emerson's concept of "inverse cripples" see David Mitchell and Sharon Snyder, "Montaigne's 'Infinities of

formes' and Nietzsche's 'Higher Men,' " in *Narrative Prosthesis: Disability and the Dependencies of Discourse* (Ann Arbor: University of Michigan Press, 2000), 82.

5. Rosemarie Garland Thomson. *Extraordinary Bodies: Figuring Disability in American Culture and Literature*. (New York: Columbia University Press, 1997), 95.
6. See Mitchell and Snyder, *Cultural Locations of Disability*, 45.
7. Henry Friedlander, *The Origins of Nazi Genocide: From Euthanasia to the Final Solution* (Durham: University of North Carolina Press, 1997), xii.
8. *A World Without Bodies*. DVD, 2002, directed by Sharon Snyder, Brace Yourselves Productions, twenty-eight minutes.
9. Flannery O'Connor, Introduction to *A Memoir of Mary Ann* (1961), in *Flannery O'Connor: Collected Works* (New York: Library of America, 2007), 831.
10. For explanation of this citation of Simone De Beauvoir's famous adage see Mitchell and Snyder. *Narrative Prosthesis*, 150, and Rachel Adams. *Sideshow U.S.A.: Freaks and the American Cultural Imagination* (Chicago: University of Chicago Press, 2001), 189.
11. Robert McRuer, "No Future for Crips: Queer Theory and the Limits of Tolerance," unpublished paper presented in "The Geo-Politics of Disability" lecture series at Temple University on September 23, 2008.
12. Leslie A. Fiedler, "The Higher Sentimentality," in Ken Kesey, *One Flew Over the Cuckoo's Nest: Text and Criticism*, (New York: Penguin Books, 1996), 386.
13. Henri-Jacques Stiker, *A History of Disability* (Ann Arbor: University of Michigan Press, 1997), 224.
14. David Mitchell and Sharon Snyder, eds. *The Body and Physical Difference: Discourses of Disability* (Ann Arbor: University of Michigan Press, 1997), back cover blurb by Louise deSalvo.

61

Model minorities and the minority model – the neoliberal novel

WALTER BENN MICHAELS

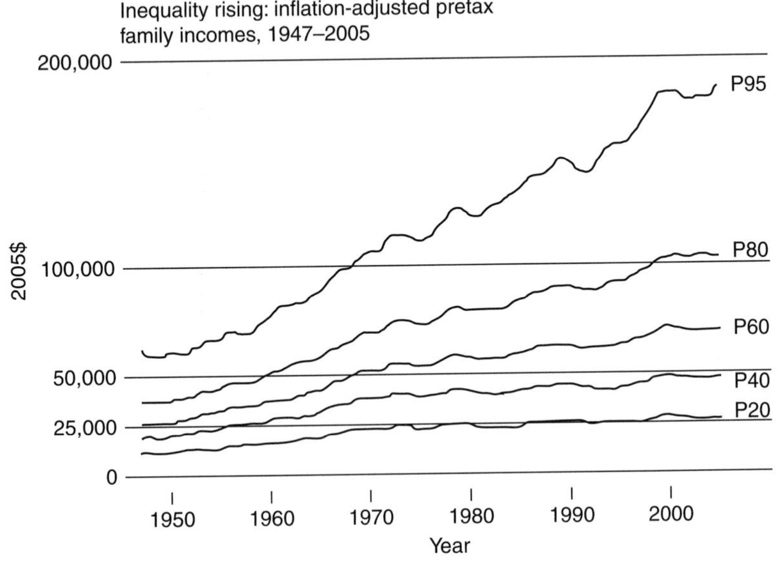

Table 3 Inequality rising: inflation-adjusted pretax family incomes, 1947–2005. Printed courtesy of Lane Kenworthy.

> Between the late 1940s and the mid-1970s incomes increased at roughly the same pace throughout the distribution; they doubled for each group. Since the 1970s the story has been quite different. At the 95th percentile, incomes have continued to rise. At the upper-middle levels (the 80th and 60th percentiles), they've increased at a moderate pace. In the bottom half of the distribution (the 40th and 20th percentiles), they've been fairly stagnant.
>
> Lane Kenworthy[1]

The first chapter of Chang-Rae Lee's 1995 novel *Native Speaker* contains a note given to the main character, a Korean-American named Henry Park, by his white wife when she leaves him. It's a list of epithets describing him as, among other things, an "illegal alien," an "emotional alien," a "stranger," "great in bed," a "follower," a "traitor," a "poppa's boy," "Yellow peril," "neo-American." And later in the novel – but earlier in his life – the novel applies another epithet to Henry. When the "poppa's boy" Henry is told by his father (in heavily accented English) that they are moving to a new house, a "very nice place" in a "nice neighborhood" near Fern Pond, Henry responds that he doesn't want to move, and that he especially doesn't want to move to Fern Pond because "all the rich kids live there." To which the father responds, "You rich kid now, Henry," and they move.

But if Henry's wealth is a relevant fact about him, it is not the fact that the novel itself is most interested in. What the novel cares about – as the wife's list suggests and its own title affirms – is what it calls Henry's "place in the culture," not his place in the economy. And this is true – indeed it is the defining characteristic – of what we might call the novel of identity more generally. Questions about what it means to be yellow or what it means to be American are questions about who we are rather than about how much (or little) we own, and while such questions have always played a significant role in American literature, they have, as the very structure of this volume suggests (how would it be organized if race, gender, disability, and sexuality were not available?), come to play an absolutely central role both in the literature and the literary criticism of the last thirty years. Furthermore, they have come to play this role at a time when anti-racism has replaced racism as the dominant mode of racialized discourse and, more striking still, at a time when the gap between the rich kids and the poor ones has been growing at an extraordinary rate. But the differences that matter in *Native Speaker* (or in, for example, Toni Morrison's *Beloved* [1987], Art Spiegelman's *Maus* [1986], Leslie Marmon Silko's *Almanac of the Dead* [1991], Demetria Martinez's *Mother Tongue* [1994], David Henry Hwang's *M. Butterfly* [1989], and Bharati Mukherjee's *The Middleman* [1988], most of which are discussed elsewhere in this volume) are not the ones between income quintiles. It's racial, cultural and sexual difference – the pathos of *Native Speaker*'s "yellow peril" and the complexities of its "neo-American" – that occupies center stage in these texts.

Both the problems and opportunities attending this choice are particularly striking for the Asian American novel, since Asian Americans today occupy, however unwillingly, not just the position of one among many minorities in

American life, but that of the "model minority." (Their predecessors were, of course, the Jews.) Indeed, it is precisely the rich-kid side of the dichotomy that has made them the model and it is the yellow peril side that has made so many want to resist it. When, in his recent book *Yellow* (2002), Frank Wu begins a chapter called "The Model Minority" with the declaration that you can't really "talk about Asian American experiences at all" unless you "kill off the model minority myth" along with the "stereotype" it represents, he is expressing in cruder terms *Native Speaker*'s skepticism about the seamlessness of assimilation. The emphasis on Asian American success, he says, "whitewashes racial discrimination."[2]

Nevertheless, the "myth" persists and, when you examine the most recent census data or the most recent figures on enrollment in elite universities, it's not hard to see why. Although Asian Americans make up only about 4 percent of the US population, they make up anywhere from 15 to 20 percent of the student body in, say, the Ivy League schools. One writer goes so far as to say, "the more selective the school, the higher the percentage of Asian students."[3] And they famously have the highest median income ($66,103) among racial groups recognized in the census. At the same time, however, it's not hard to see that the model minority myth does perpetuate racism and does have some victims. After all, the model part of model minority implies the existence of some other minorities who haven't followed it – and in the US we know very well who they are. African American students at those elite universities are under-, not over-represented. And the economic contrast is at least as striking as the educational one. Black households today have the "lowest median income ($33,916) among race groups."[4] In 2004, Asians represented 3.7 percent of households in the American population but 6.5 percent of those in the top 5 percent economically; African Americans were 12.2 percent of the population but they only represented 1 percent of the top 5 percent. So even though there are three times as many African Americans as Asian Americans, there are more rich Asians than rich black people. Indeed, it's this contrast between Asian and African Americans that generates the notion of the model minority – if Asians can overcome racism and succeed, why can't blacks? To which one answer – we might call it the Malcolm X answer – is that Asians can succeed precisely because they are not black and because in not being black they come to count in the US as white (i.e., not really as minorities at all). Alex Haley tells a famous story about Malcolm, watching immigrant kids newly arrived at what was then Idlewild airport, racing around and yelling at each other in whatever their native language was. By tomorrow, Malcolm said to Haley, "they'll know how to say their first English word – nigger."[5] The point of this story is only partly that in beginning to become American the children would begin to become racists; it is more importantly that they would themselves be racialized – they would become white. The American racial system – what is sometimes called the black/white binary – is, in this view, a machine that takes people (Slavs, Jews, Asians, whoever) and makes them white. And the most important part of this machine is black people – because it's by not being black that you get to be white.

Which obviously cannot be true if you think of Asian Americans, not to mention Jews, as minorities. When Henry Park remarks in *Native Speaker* that "It's still a black and white world," he is complaining about a perception that he believes has become outmoded. Asians, as Frank Wu says in *Yellow*, are "Neither Black Nor White." But, from Malcolm X's perspective, this isn't quite right and, indeed, *Native Speaker* itself dramatizes the way in which the black/white binary tends to be deployed rather than disrupted by the creation of the Asian American. John Kwang, the New York City politician for whom Henry finds himself working, begins the story of his own career in America by remarking that in the still segregated South he didn't count as "Colored" because, for instance, a "pretty white woman" in Fort Worth tells him he can use the restroom for whites. And, of course, in counting the Asian as white, the woman repeats the founding gesture of legalized segregation. The Supreme Court's decision in *Plessy v. Ferguson* – allowing passengers to be separated by race on public transportation – had distinguished only between black and white, a fact noted in his dissent by Justice Harlan. Our Constitution, Harlan famously proclaimed, is "color blind"; less famously, he also complained that the new racial laws would force American blacks into separate cars but would allow a "Chinaman" – a person belonging to "a race so different from our own that we do not permit those belonging to it to become citizens of the United States" – to "ride in the same passenger coach with white citizens."[6] In the segregated South, where the separate facilities are for "colored" and for "white," the "Chinaman" may not yet be eligible for citizenship but he is eligible to use the water fountains and to go to the bathrooms marked white.

Kwang, however, does not think of himself as white. He identifies with blacks, and he identifies the "black power" marches he sees up north – "*this* is America" – with America itself. Indeed, it's through this identification with blacks that Kwang becomes the particular kind of American he is – not just a successful politician but a successful "minority politician." That identification, however, is a fragile one. In the novel (as in the real world – think of the 1992 L.A. riots), there is tension between blacks and Koreans, in particular between upwardly mobile Korean shopkeepers and their not so upwardly mobile customers in black neighborhoods, and that tension comes to a head when one of the shopkeepers shoots and kills a customer he perceives as threatening. On the one hand, the Americanization of Koreans takes place through the identification of them as a minority, on the model of that original minority, black people. On the other hand, the conditions of American life – both legal and economic – distinguish them from the black model. They become the model minority because, following the Malcolm X view, they become white.

An early version of this trajectory is brilliantly described by Michael Rogin in his analysis of the first talking motion picture, *The Jazz Singer*, which starred Al Jolson, the great vaudeville star of the 1920s. In the movie, Jolson, the son of Jewish immigrants who became famous performing in blackface, plays a performer like himself, someone born Jakie Rabinowitz and now called Jack Robin. His ailing father, the cantor at a New York synagogue, wants Jakie to take his place for the service on Yom Kippur, the highest of Jewish holy days. But Jakie's first Broadway musical – in which he'll sing "Mammy" in blackface – is scheduled to open that same night. Choosing the musical over the synagogue, he not only becomes a star but also wins himself a cute gentile girlfriend. "Blackface," as Rogin puts it, "is the instrument that transfers identities from immigrant Jew to American." Putting on blackface, the Jew's identification with the African American helps establish his own Americanness. But blackface is also the instrument that separates the Jew from African Americans. Taking it off, his disidentification with the African American helps to establish his own whiteness. "The jazz singer rises by putting on the mask of a group that must remain immobile, unassimilable and fixed at the bottom."[7]

But if, for Rogin's Jews in the 1920s, blackface is a technology of assimilation and assimilation is the way to become both American and successful, for Asian Americans in the post-1965 period (and for middle- and upper-middle-class Americans more generally), a certain resistance to assimilation has performed the same functions. We can see part of the reason for this by comparing the racial context of immigration in the 1920s with immigration policy in the last quarter of the twentieth century. The Immigration Act of 1924 was passed during a period of intense nativism when it seemed to many that Jews and eastern Europeans could never be made white enough. For most of its history, the US had had no immigration laws – anyone who could get to the border could come in. But Californian hostility to Chinese immigration had produced one of the first immigration controls, the Chinese Exclusion Act (1882), and an increasing hostility to eastern European immigration eventually resulted in 1924 in what is often called the National Origins Act because it established national immigration quotas and thus sought to make racial identity the central consideration for determining eligibility for admission to the US. The point of the Act was to make sure that the US remained what the Act's sponsors said it had always been, a "Nordic" or "Anglo-Saxon" country. Acknowledging that other races had their virtues – "the Czech is a more sturdy laborer," as one Congressman put it, "the Jew is the best businessman in the world, and the Italian has a spiritual grasp and an artistic sense ... which the Nordic rarely attains" – the Congressman reminded his listeners that nevertheless, it was "the northern European, and particularly Anglo-Saxons[, who] made this country."

> Oh, yes; the others helped ... They added to it, they often enriched it, but they did not make it, and they have not yet greatly changed it. We are determined that they shall not. It is a good country. It suits us. And what we assert is that we are not going to surrender it to somebody else or allow other people, no matter what their merits, to make it something different ...[8]

In 1924, in the wake of World War I, this was a highly popular position. Only six votes were cast against the Act in the Senate, the House too voted overwhelmingly in its favor, and the result was a serious decrease in immigration, especially among the disfavored groups. But, by the 1950s, as the consequences of Nazi anti-Semitism became increasingly vivid and as the Civil Rights Movement became increasingly successful, race-based immigration policies began to look a lot less attractive. And in the wake of the Civil Rights Act of 1964, the Immigration Act of 1965 explicitly repudiated the racism of the National Origins Act, declaring that "No person shall receive any preference or priority or be discriminated against in the issuance of an immigrant visa because of his race, sex, nationality, place of birth or place of residence ..." This Act was passed almost as enthusiastically as its diametrically opposed predecessor had been (House 326–69, Senate 76–18), but where the 1924 Act had tamped immigration down, the 1965 Act opened it up. In 1960, the total American population was a little less than 180 million, about half a million of whom were Asian (about 18½ million were black). By 2005 the total population had swelled to a little under 300 million, 38 million of whom were black and 12½ million Asian.[9] So where the general population increased by a little less than 100 percent and the African American population increased by a little more than a 100 percent, the Asian American population increased by well over 2000 percent. Insofar, then, as the 1965 Act was designed to eliminate racial barriers to immigration, it succeeded beyond anyone's wildest dreams.

But the 1965 Act didn't simply repudiate racial criteria in the selection of appropriate immigrants; it replaced them with another and very different set of criteria. The National Origins Act gave preference to Nordics, the whitest of the white; the Act of 1965 offers preference to "qualified immigrants who are members of the professions or who because of their exceptional ability in the sciences or the arts will substantially benefit prospectively the national economy, cultural interests, or welfare of the United States" or who "are capable of performing specified skilled or unskilled labor . . . for which a shortage of employable and willing persons exists in the United States."[10] The 1965 Act, in other words, replaced national criteria with economic criteria; it replaced race with class.

Thus, for example, the post-1965 Korean immigrants were distinguished from their predecessors by the fact that (as the economist Marcus Noland puts it) "a significant number of them were educated members of the middle and upper-middle classes." And if the immigrants themselves, due to lack of language skills, etc. only rise to about the economic median of American life, their children (like *Native Speaker*'s author and like its main character) attain median incomes "nearly 40 percent higher than the national average" and go to college "at a rate that is twice the national average."[11]

This success story is sometimes understood as a consequence of the Asian commitment to Americanization and sometimes as a tribute to the supposedly distinctive attributes of Asian culture – the story of the model minority. But what it's really about is the successful importation of upper-middle-class status. In *Native Speaker*, Henry's mother tells him that his father went to "the best college in Korea." Her point is supposed to be that the father hates what he has ended up doing, owning a Madison Avenue grocery store. But what this really means is what Noland's statistics say it means – the educated members of the immigrant middle and upper-middle classes pass on their class status to their children. Henry goes to a good college too, and his creator, Chang-Rae Lee (whose own father immigrated to the US in 1968 and became a psychiatrist in New York) went first to prep school at Exeter and then to Yale. And the point is made even more explicitly in Bharati Mukherjee's acclaimed *The Middleman*, where, for example, one woman knows how to "behave well" in response to racism because she's been trained in "expensive girls' schools in Lausanne and Bombay," and where, in fact, most of the Asian characters know how to behave well since they are "Third World aristocrat[s]," or their fathers own a "steel company" and have (or had) "servants and two Mercedes Benzes." Sometimes, coming to America, they (like the father in *Native Speaker*) have lost some of the money and the class status. But then it's the responsibility of the children – "placed on earth to become accountants and engineers" – to get it back.

The point, then, is that what these characters have assimilated to (although assimilation is exactly the wrong word) is not so much America as it is the upper-middle class. And what has made it possible for them to do so is that they already were upper-middle class. They succeed not because of their Asian values (if Asian values make for success, how come there are so many poor people in Asia?) and not because of their eagerness to assimilate and adopt American values (there are lots of poor people in the US too) but because of their middle-class values. On the one hand, then, questions of cultural difference and cultural identity are profoundly irrelevant, as is the whole debate over assimilation or the refusal to assimilate; on the other hand, they are profoundly attractive, since they give us a picture not only of Asian Americans but of the social structure of the United States that, if it is deeply misleading, is also deeply gratifying. It's misleading because it represents an economic issue as a cultural one. Novels like *Native Speaker* make the central problems of American society a matter of identity instead of a matter of money. They encourage us to think that the important thing about Henry Park is the question of whether he's truly at home in American culture instead of the fact that, as his father says, he's a "rich kid." Thus, for example, the fact that he's married to a white woman presents us with the perennially attractive problem (think *Abie's Irish Rose*[12]) of the mixed marriage. In fact, however, intermarriage between Americans of Korean descent and white Americans is extremely common – more common, it seems, than intermarriage between rich and poor, which, according to the *New York Times*, "seems to be declining."[13] And insofar as people tend to marry within their class, Henry and his white wife are actually a very unmixed couple – they're both from wealthy families. But Americans like the difference between race and culture better than the difference between classes. We – especially the upper-middle-class writers and readers of books like *Native Speaker* and of essays like this one – prefer differences we're supposed to respect to differences which, at least from an egalitarian view, are not so respectable.

Another way to put this is to say that we like a vision of America organized around the concept of identity, especially (but not exclusively) racial or cultural identity, and we like thinking that the great problems that confront us are essentially problems of prejudice, both personal and structural. Which means that we like the difference between black people and white people or between whites and Asians much more than we like the difference between the rich kids and the poor ones. What poor people want is not respect but money, and a society that was committed to trying to give poor people what they want would be more committed to minimizing economic difference than to celebrating cultural difference. But over the last thirty years, as the gap between the rich and the poor has widened (in 1976, the top quintile of American wage-earners made 43.7 percent of all the money earned; the bottom quintile made 4.3 percent; in 2006, the top made 50.5 percent, the bottom 3.4 percent) and as class mobility in the US has declined (recent studies suggest it has fallen behind the supposedly lagging economies of western Europe; if you want to pursue the American Dream today, you need to learn German and move to Berlin), racism, sexism, and homophobia have proven to be much more attractive targets of disapproval than poverty and economic inequality.[14] Even – in fact, especially – our colleges (which have provided faculty positions for Lee and Mukherjee and many other writers and which provide readers for all of them) play a crucial, and crucially conservative, role in painting the picture of the US as a country composed of many different minorities rather than of a large majority falling further and further behind the one minority that matters most – the rich.

So for example, the outstanding fact about college students over the last thirty years is that they increasingly come from relatively wealthy families, families almost always in the top half of American wealth and overwhelmingly in the top quarter.[15] But when you look at the descriptions the colleges give of themselves, it's the ethnic diversity, not the wealth of their students, that they stress. And the intellectual activities of their faculty embody the same commitments. It's not just the number of identity-based courses, it's also the number of books and articles with identitarian topics. In their groundbreaking article, "Class, Multiculturalism and the *American Quarterly*," Larry Griffin and Maria Tempenis report that in 1965 (the year not only of the Immigration Act but also of the Presidential Executive Order on affirmative action) about 20 percent of the pages in the leading scholarly journal *American Quarterly* were devoted to what they call "multicultural themes" and the "diversity debate." By the mid-1970s that number had doubled and by 1996 it had doubled again – it was 80 percent.[16]

What scholars call the "surge in the growth of Asian American Studies Programs"[17] from the 1980s to the present is particularly revelatory here, since this surge is simultaneously a function of the extraordinary success of Asian Americans in American society – the model minority – and of ambivalence about that success, ambivalence about following in the footsteps of that earlier model minority and so becoming, like American Jews, white. This is what it means to expose the model minority as a myth, and to insist that race and racism are governing facts about contemporary American life. It's to choose the "illegal alien," "Yellow Peril" rather than the "rich kid" side of *Native Speaker*'s dichotomy. But, for reasons we have already begun to see, this answer – no matter how sincerely it's given – can't really be accepted at face value. For the experience of Asian Americans has in fact been much more like the experience of Jews than it has been like that of African Americans – a truth that *Native Speaker* itself dramatizes when it imagines a "rich old woman" in Henry's father's Madison Avenue store, describing him and his father as "Oriental Jews." The point is supposed to be about racism and anti-Semitism, but what it's really about is the irrelevance of anti-Semitism and even, in this case, of racism. Jews, essentially treated as white, were more the beneficiaries than the victims of racism in the officially racist America of the late nineteenth and early twentieth century. And Asians, since the passage of the explicitly anti-racist Immigration Act of 1965, have been the beneficiaries of the equally official anti-racism of the last half-century.[18] So what makes the Koreans like the Jews is not their shared victimization but their success, above all their economic success, a success in becoming like the "rich old woman" (which is to say, rich), which prejudice like her own has been unable to prevent. The moral of the story is the impotence of racism, not its power.

And this has been as true in reality as in fiction. *Native Speaker* doesn't say exactly where Chang-Rae Lee's Henry Park went to college but Daniel Golden's *The Price of Admission* (2006) tells what a real-life Henry Park's mother describes as the "devastating" story of the "discrimination" against Asians in college admissions. Even after the sacrifices she makes to get her son into the elite boarding school, Groton (she sells the family's "only investment property, an apartment building" in New Jersey), and even though Henry does very well at Groton and gets very high SAT scores, when it comes time to apply for college, he's turned down by several Ivy League schools and drops "like a falling leaf," his mother says, first to Johns Hopkins for his BA and then to medical school at the University of Kansas. Like the rich old lady in *Native Speaker* (but in a spirit of sympathy, of course, rather than distaste), Golden calls such Asians the "new Jews,"[19] the victims today of informal versions of the quotas that victimized Jews in the 1920s and 1930s. But, however real the injustice of the quota system (and, of course, you didn't then and don't now need quotas to keep African American students out of elite colleges), relegation to Johns Hopkins followed by a career as a doctor (the profession that in the US most brilliantly combines virtue and wealth) just isn't that tragic. The real point of the real-life Henry Park's story is that, just like the fictional Henry Park, he's a rich kid and that his parents' upper-middle-class status has been successfully passed on to him.

So what then does it mean to treat Asians as minorities on the model of African Americans? The answer here is more along the lines of the desire of the Korean politician in *Native Speaker* to hang on to his status as a "minority" politician. More generally, the rise of Asian American studies represents a desire, following the model of African American studies, to assert rather than efface minority status. Michael Rogin, as we have seen, described Jewish blackface as the effort to identify with African Americans and then, since the whole point of blackface is that you can take it off, to disidentify with them. We might see the rise of Asian American studies as following the same trajectory, but in a somewhat different context, a context in which anti-racism has replaced racism as the dominant mode of racialization and in which the point is therefore not the connection between racial status and economic success but the disconnect. The idea here is that resisting whiteness and insisting on your distinctive cultural identity – insisting on what Wu calls yellowness – makes your identity matter more than your wealth.

It's easy to see that this is a kind of blackface performance. The insistence on one's minority status counts as the insistence that one is crucially like blacks, which is to say, counts as putting the blackface on; the simultaneous economic achievement counts as the reminder that one is not after all black, that one can take the blackface off. But it would be a mistake to think of it as a performance that benefits simply or even mainly Asians – it works instead for the benefit of US society as a whole, which, as I have already suggested, loves the idea that your identity matters more than your wealth, loves the idea that being Asian or Jewish matters more than being rich, and especially loves the idea that being black or Latino matters more than being poor – unless, of course, you're poor *because* you're black or Latino, which is reassuring because it makes your poverty a function of racism rather than of capitalism.

Thus one of the central characters in Demetria Martinez's *Mother Tongue* is a Salvadoran refugee whose mother "washed clothes for the rich family" in their village and who fled the country sometime in the late 1970s because his association with a leftist priest has made him a target of the army. In the US, however, the problem of the oppression of "poor people" gets connected up with the problem of racism against "brown" people and, just as your identity matters more than your wealth in *Native Speaker*, it turns out to matter more than your poverty in *Mother Tongue*. Indeed, the happy ending of *Mother Tongue* involves the son of the long-since vanished refugee returning to El Salvador, learning to speak Spanish, and ceasing to feel his "heritage" as a "burden" when he learns to share it with people who "look like him."[20] Redescribing the political system that threatened the father as the cultural heritage that welcomes the son, the novel makes the social problem that begins it into a social solution that can conclude it.

Of course, part of what makes this possible is that El Salvador itself can be understood to have changed between the late 1970s and the mid-1990s. Its Civil War came to an end in 1992, and with it ended the wholesale human rights abuses and murders that produced refugees like *Mother Tongue*'s hero. But the poverty that caused the war in the first place did not end; on the contrary, the gap between the rich and the poor in 1994 (when the first elections were held there, and also when *Mother Tongue* was published in the US) was greater than it had been in the late 1970s. And it had become greater still by the end of the century. Why? Because, as the Congressional Research Service puts it, "In the 1990s, El Salvador adopted a 'neo-liberal' economic model, cutting government spending, privatizing state-owned enterprises, and adopting the dollar as its national currency."[21] So the rise of inequality in the US is matched by its rise in El Salvador, and, turning the battle against poverty into the search for identity, *Mother Tongue* simultaneously displaces and acknowledges them both.[22]

Novels like *Native Speaker* and *Mother Tongue* should thus be understood as elements in a larger discursive structure, one in which increasing appreciation of the values of identity is accompanied by increasing hostility to discrimination against identities, and in which the appreciation and the hostility are both accompanied by indifference to the increasing economic inequality that has been the hallmark of American society since the mid-1970s (the beginning, according to economists, of American neoliberalism). In the political theorist Nancy Fraser's terms, we might say that the novel of identity made questions of "recognition" more prominent than questions of "redistribution." More strongly, we might say that the focus on identity functions not just to distract people from the increase in inequality but to legitimate it.

This is what it means to say that the novel of identity shares the concerns of conservative institutions like law firms and brokerage houses as well as of liberal ones like universities. Markets are more efficient if race, gender, and sexuality are no obstacle to participating in them. And just as you don't want people's identity to stand in the way of their managing your workforce, you do want the workforce itself to feel their identity is being respected, even if (or especially when) their standard of living is not.

None of this implies, of course, that the people who so eagerly write and read about problems of identity may not also be concerned about the inequalities produced by neoliberalism; it just means that their interest in identity is not itself an expression of that concern. Nor does it mean that there are no differences between novels like *Native Speaker* and novels like *Mother Tongue*. *Native Speaker* is obviously a much more sophisticated and accomplished performance than *Mother Tongue*, a fact that is displayed in its more ironic relation to its title. But a certain self-criticism about the terms of identity has always been constitutive of the interest in it. Nothing is more common in the discourse of Asian America, for example, than the reminder that the very term both names and erases difference – what can it mean to lump people from India together with people from Korea? And nothing is more common in the discourse of identity more generally than the insistence that the very concept is problematic – because all identities are hybrid, or fictional or socially constructed. But the point of this insistence is not to change the subject; it is instead to make sure that it doesn't get changed, and that the relevant debates are about what it means to be a native speaker or about whether anyone really is a native speaker – that the debates are about the subject positions available within neoliberalism (within the political consensus that economic growth is the primary concern of the state and that competition in the marketplace is both the best technology of growth and the best guarantee of freedom) rather than about alternatives to it.

Francisco Goldman's *The Ordinary Seaman* (1997) elegantly suggests why. Its central character is a Sandinista fleeing the war for a job on a ship docked in Brooklyn, his adventures based on a true story of some sailors who found themselves "abandoned, unpaid and trapped" when the ship proved to be irreparably unseaworthy and its owners disappeared. But where the real-life event took place in 1982, the novel takes place in 1989 which means that when Esteban boards the *Urus* (in June), he's still thinking of himself as a "Communist," but by the time he escapes from it (in October), Honecker "has resigned in the German Democratic Republic" and "Los comunistas are going." "Are the Sandinistas still in power in Nicaragua?" he asks someone, and the answer, after the return of the American-financed Contras in August 1989 and the assassination of dozens of Sandinista candidates in the elections of 1990, will be no. Fortunately, he has prepared for this answer by getting himself a Nuyorquina girlfriend and spending "the night the Wall came down in Berlin" with her and "a bottle of red wine" while she helps "liberate" him from his "obsessive" loyalty to a past she "doesn't pretend to understand." This past is not about his heritage or his culture or his mother tongue – it's about his communism. But my point here is not that the prominence of identitarian concerns in these novels is a function of the fall of the Soviet Union. (Whatever the Sandinistas may have been hoping for, it's been a very long time since any US writers had high hopes for communism.) It is instead that that the prominence of identity naturalizes the unimaginability of any alternative to neoliberalism and so makes it easier for us to accept the inequality neoliberalism has produced.

At one point in *The Ordinary Seaman*, the crew are taunted by some kids they call "los blacks," or as the oldest of the crew-members calls them, "cruel delinquents." But Esteban, remembering some of the ideas the "political officer" attached to his army unit had taught him (about "proletarians," "democracy," the "Law of True Value," and the "*lumpen proletariat*"), says no. "Son lumpen," he tells the other sailors; "Lumpen jodido," he ads. "Fucked lumpen, just like us." Fucked lumpen are different from "los blacks" and "los gays," and the declaration that one should oneself be called a member of the fucked lumpen ("just like us") is different from, say, David Henry Hwang's declaration (in the Afterword to *M. Butterfly* [1989]) that "we prefer the term 'Asian' to 'Oriental,' in the same way 'Black' is preferable to 'Negro.'" Declaring yourself one of the "fucked lumpen" involves not only thinking that you're fucked because you belong to the lumpen but also thinking that the social system which creates the lumpen is fucked too. What you want, once you start thinking this way, is not for the lumpen to be respected, but for there to be no more lumpen. What you want, in other words, is not to value difference but to eliminate those differences that constitute inequality. But preferring black to Negro or Asian to Oriental – and preferring all of them both to "rich kid" and to "lumpen" – takes you in just the opposite direction. What you want is a world in which the fundamental conflicts have less to do with wealth than with race, space, gender, and sexuality, and in which the relevant projects center on maintaining identities by respecting differences (e.g. the national) or producing new identities by breaking down (which is to say, respecting other) differences (e.g. the transnational). This is the world of neoliberalism, the world in which identity and inequality have both flourished, and which the neoliberal novel simultaneously represents and enables.

Notes

1. Lane Kenworthy, "Consider the Evidence." http://lanekenworthy.net/2008/03/09/the-best-inequality-graph/.
2. Frank Wu, *Yellow* (New York: Basic Books 2002), 39, 69.
3. Tim Stafford, "The Tiger in the Academy," *Christianity Today* 50.4 (April 1, 2006).
4. US Census Bureau News (August 26, 2008).
5. Malcolm X, *The Autobiography of Malcolm X*, as told to Alex Haley (New York: Ballantine Books, 1973), 399.
6. *Plessy v. Ferguson*, 163 US 537 (1896), Justice Harlan dissenting.
7. Michael Rogin, *Blackface, White Noise* (Berkeley: University of California Press, 1998), 95, 92.
8. Representative William N. Vaile (Colorado), *Congressional Record* (April 8, 1924): 5922.

9. The 1990 figures are from US Census Bureau, *Race and Hispanic Origin of the Population by Nativity: 1850–1990*. www.census.gov/population/www/documentation/twps0029/tab08.html. The 2000 figures are from US Census Bureau, *Overview of Race and Hispanic Origin*, www.census.gov/prod/2001pubs/cenbr01-1.pdf
10. Immigration and Naturalization Act of 1965 in Randall Hansen, *Immigration and Asylum: From 1900 to the Present* (New York: ABC-CLIO, 2005), 1005–1006.
11. Marcus Noland, "The Impact of Korean Immigration on the US Economy," delivered at "Korean Diaspora in the World Economy" conference, Seoul, Korea, October 10, 2002. www.icasinc.org/lectures/noland2.html
12. *Abie's Irish Rose*, a comedy by Anne Nichols about Jewish–Catholic intermarriage, was a hit on the Broadway stage beginning in 1922 that was widely copied in film, radio, and television.
13. Tamar Lewin, *New York Times* (May 19, 2005). According to C. N. Le, the most recent data show that 60.8 percent of Korean women born in the US marry white men; 40 percent of the men marry white women. C. N. Le, "Interracial Dating and Marriage: U.S. Raised Asian-Americans," *Asian-Nation: The Landscape of Asian America*. www.asian-nation.org/interracial2.shtml (October 30, 2008). Of course, Lee's Henry is not American-born but he is American-raised.
14. The income inequality figures are from the US Census Bureau's Historical Income Tables – Households, www.census.gov/hhes/www/income/histinc/h02ar.html. The observation about lagging social mobility is from the Center for American Progress report, *From Poverty to Prosperity* (April 2007): "Studies show that the correlation between the earnings of sons and father (the standard measure of intergenerational mobility) is stronger in the U.S. than in many countries in Europe." www.americanprogress.org/issues/2007/04/pdf/poverty_report.pdf.
15. As Richard Kahlenberg puts it: "74 percent of students at the nation's top 146 colleges come from the richest socioeconomic quartile and just 3 percent come from the poorest quartile." *Left Behind: Unequal Opportunity in Higher Education*, www.tcf.org/Publications/Education/leftbehindrc.pdf.
16. Larry J. Griffin and Maria Tempenis, "Class, Multiculturalism and the *American Quarterly*," *American Quarterly* 54.1 (March 2002): 79.
17. Sharon Lee, Review of *In Defense of Asian American Studies*, *The Journal of Higher Education* 78.6 (November/December 2007): 721.
18. And the anti-racist novels of identity I am describing here thus differ crucially from the equally but differently (i.e. racist) identitarian novels of the 1920s (Fitzgerald, Cather, Hemingway *et al.*).
19. Daniel Golden, *The Price of Admission* (New York: Crown Publishing, 2006), 224.
20. Meanwhile, in case anyone has missed the identitarian point, the mother finally finds happiness with the son of Holocaust survivors.
21. Clare Ribando, *El Salvador: Political, Economic, and Social Conditions and Relations with the United States*, Congressional Research Service (2005), www.fas.org/sgp/crs/row/RS21655.pdf
22. Nancy Fraser, "From Redistribution to Recognition?" *New Left Review*, 212 (July–August 1995).

62

The American borderlands novel

RAMÓN SALDÍVAR

Novels written from and about the borderlands go against the grain of the normative binary narrative of American race relations. While "race" in the American social and cultural context has traditionally referred to the social and legal patterns of hierarchy and domination characterizing the relations between groups of blacks and whites, the borderlands novel posits a different racial narrative. The multiracial realities characteristic of the borderlands create social structures and discourses articulating a dialogical narrative of American social life based on multiplicity, heterogeneity, and difference. Individual and national identity is created, as Charles Taylor argues, dialogically, in response to and against others.[1] In a multiracial context the effects of this dialogical pattern are correspondingly complex, far-reaching, and unpredictable. The formal implications of this thematic and discursive difference are not self-evident, nor have they been a part of the traditional history of the American novel. Thus, even in eras when race in American discourse meant only "black" and "white," the presence in the borderlands of Native, Latino, and Asian people required the development of different discourses to articulate the heterogeneous complexities of individual and national identity. One consequence of the disruption of binary racial thinking in the borderlands novel is a need for different hermeneutical procedures in our understanding of its themes and forms.

Another salient characteristic of American borderlands novels that follows from their discursive heterogeneity concerns the racial pattern of hierarchy and domination – evident and explicit in some texts, dispersed and implicit in others. Structures of hierarchy and domination are never represented in the borderlands novel as simply the effects of singular social, legal, or economic conditions. Instead, borderlands novels figure structures of hierarchy and domination as arising from multiple historical factors that intersect with and underwrite each other in complex ways.

Given these patterns of heterogeneity and difference in racial discourse, how do borderlands novels describe the unity of American personal and national identity? What happens if, in the attempt to define a unifying national character, we find only difference at every turn? Within difference, how can we conceive of democratic communities and shared national identities? These questions strongly affect the formation of the American borderlands novel.

In positing the unity of national identity as a process articulated by the national motto on the Great Seal of the United States, *e pluribus unum*, Americans have often misprized the relative status of the *unum* in relation to the *pluram*.[2] That is, the politics of national identity require the citizen's allegiance to the *one* common good, where the common good reflects the shared identity of a *plurality* of all citizens.[3] Consistently, however, the unique differences of individuals, compounded by their social and racial otherness, are left out of the dialogue of national identity. The borderlands novel repeatedly reminds us of the erasure of some identities within the idea of multiplicity and the instability of the relationship between the one and the many in American history. This perspective extends to how borderlands novels understand social justice. Unlike writings that assume a racial binary, borderlands novels do not posit the absence, or elimination, of any *one* kind of domination and hierarchy as the key to the creating of a just, democratic society. They require, instead, that we imagine what kind of collective dialogue would follow from the recognition and removal of multiple layers of injustice, and, more importantly, what kind of national unity would be required to encompass multiple layers of difference.

Taking these thematic features into consideration, a case can be made for defining borderlands novels in formal terms. Noting the focus on stories of human emergence as a common generic move on the part of borderlands novels, their shared interest in how history functions in relation to fiction, and how realism as a mode is often redefined in fantastic terms, I discuss how form functions as a defining characteristic of borderlands narratives. I take here the instances of three novels to show that while borderlands novels remain firmly tied to the realist tradition, the thematic issues associated with the multiracial history of the American borderlands force specific adjustments in the way that realism functions in these texts. Accordingly, Américo Paredes's *George Washington Gómez* (1935–40; 1990), Cormac McCarthy's *Blood Meridian* (1985), and Leslie Marmon Silko's *Almanac of the Dead* (1991) illustrate how the modes of the *Bildungsroman*, the historical novel, and magical realism are revised in borderlands novels to represent the processes at work in the creation of unifying national visions within the context of differential trans-American New World cultures.

Borderlands novels depict the relationships between knowledge and power, between utopian progress and dystopian dehumanization, between history and myth, and most importantly, between physical violence and the violence of language, all as involved in the process of creating a singular national identity out of a region where identities remain multiple, complex, and often contradictory. Ultimately, the formal qualities of borderlands novels deeply affect how we understand the world, raising questions about what constitutes American or any other national identity.

The *Bildungsroman* in the borderlands: Américo Paredes, *George Washington Gómez* (1935–1940; 1990)

Américo Paredes's boy-hero, George Washington Gómez (dubbed "Guálinto" by his Spanish-speaking grandmother), represents the contradictions and limitations of the non-heroic historical position in his attempted construction of an authentic identity beyond ethnicity in the novel that bears his name.[4] Written between 1935 and 1940 but not published until 1990, *George Washington Gómez* addresses the central social issue of the modern era in the borderlands: the fate of the individual in relation to his communities in the process of modernization during the interwar years. The hero's story, however, emphasizes less the achievement of personal fulfillment than a representation of a nation's historical becoming. Concerned with the racialized subject's emergence into history (as the title suggests), *George Washington Gómez* is, therefore, what we might call a quintessential ethnic *Bildungsroman*, a category that Mikhail Bakhtin describes as "the novel of human emergence."[5]

One way in which a human being may emerge is in the complete integration of the social process with the development of the person.[6] In *George Washington Gómez*, Paredes gathers the historical raw material of popular memory concerning the integration of former Mexican territories into the United States after the Mexican–American War (1846–1848). This historical recollection lies at the core of Gúalinto's life, and his story of emergence. Like the traditional *Bildungsroman* hero, Guálinto undergoes an education in moral choice. The narrative shows him evolving from within as he negotiates those choices that simultaneously shape his destiny and control his fictional biography.

In Paredes's ethnic version of the *Bildungroman*, Guálinto's choice between existing norms and self-determined aesthetic ideals is ironized. Guálinto expresses his choice by embracing social practices that include the English language, his dress, speech, eating habits, religious and cultural practices as well as the intellectual protocols of the American middle class that he hopes will define him as an assimilated American. Operating in the context of early twentieth-century American racism, however, as a racialized subject he can do so only inconclusively.[7] Taken together, the social practices associated with an assimilated American identity constitute a set of powerful but highly unstable conditions that give meanings to the possibility of "moral choice" that are different from what they would be in times and places not shaped by conditions of race and ethnicity. In contrast to the traditional bourgeois novel of development, Guálinto's story of ethnic education and character formation is shaped not only by his premeditated acts of individual will but also by larger structures of race and geopolitical power. Composed earlier but published later than other borderlands novels that also focus on the hero's moral formation, such as José Antonio Villarreal's *Pocho* (1970), Tomás Rivera's . . . *And the Earth Did Not Part* (1971), and Rudolfo Anaya's *Bless Me, Última* (1972), Paredes's novel of emergence retrospectively sets the conditions for an understanding of ethnic and racial character formation in the borderlands novel as emergence into racial and social inequality.

In his daily interaction with Anglos, in blending into the world of American business, defense, and national security, and in his marriage with an Anglo woman, Guálinto makes what appears to be a set of reasonable moral choices in desiring to assimilate. Certainly, many middle-class Mexican Americans of the generation that came to personal and political maturity in the years of the Great Depression did choose to assimilate. Guálinto thus exemplifies how American society operates, allowing individuals to imagine broadly a spectrum of possibilities for subjective self-verification.

And yet, in narrating the parallel but ultimately different fates of Guálinto's sisters, Carmen and Maruca, who do not have even Guálinto's range of choices, Paredes also reflects on the limitations of self-determination for women of color in the borderlands. In the concluding sections of the novel, the sisters' Americanization as wives, mothers, and sisters occurs in both racial and gender-specific ways. Maruca marries "a middle-aged Anglo widower" and completely disappears from family history, while Carmen settles into the anonymity of Mexican American married life. These women's lack of alternatives render the category of "choice" problematic. May one choose to belong to a community? Who crosses its borders? In what directions may crossings proceed? Are there no mediators capable of moving across the symbolic and real borders of community, capable of creating a new hybrid, an assimilated nation of modern citizens in the transnational contact zone of the US–Mexico borderlands? What might a fully emancipated imagination unshackled from its binding limitations and capable of resolving these formidable questions look like?

Guálinto embraces the values of the American middle class, with insidious results. He does so at the cost of a cultural, political, and historical narrative that names him as a future "leader of his people" by putting into doubt who "his people" are. His birth name, "George Washington," becomes relevant here. How are we to imagine a new reality and articulate a new paradigm for conceiving of the multicultural politics that Guálinto intends to experience as he leaves behind his Mexican American upbringing and assimilates into white America? In what political language might our hero speak? What do the terms of political language mean in the context of subalternity and racial oppression within which his life must take shape? *George Washington Gómez* concludes with that additional set of open questions and a horizon of unresolved contradictions.

These are matters that novelists such as Helena María Viramontes in *Under the Feet of Jesus* (1996), Sandra Cisneros in *Caramelo* (2003), Karen Tei Yamashita in *Tropic of Orange* (1997), and Leslie Marmon Silko in *Almanac of the Dead* would later represent more sharply. At this early moment in the history of the borderlands novel, Paredes dramatizes these open-ended questions. In doing so he reveals the constructed quality of both universal and ethnocentric consciousnesses and shows, moreover, how personal identity can bolster repressive and limiting ideologies. In his fantasies and recurring dream, Guálinto imagines a history in which, under his leadership, "Texas and the Southwest . . . remain forever Mexican." For Guálinto in this instance, however, the possibilities of alternative histories remain only latent and repressed, situated within the anxiety resulting from the clash between history and the utopian imaginary.

Guálinto's dreams lead to the question in the novel whether in the aftermath of the American occupation of former Mexican territory post-1848, it was possible for Mexicans to claim membership in US society, claim political and social rights, and become recognized as active citizen-agents in the labor market and the public sphere while at the same time retaining the multiple differences of their original identity. Could one imagine a *trans*national state of mind and be both Mexican and American? And what would such a state of personal affairs implied by an achieved multicultural identity have to do with the creation of a just multiracial nation and polity? Writing during the crisis of national identity occasioned by the rise of the Cold War and its ruthless choices imposed in the name of national security, by the shattering conditions that have come to be known as postmodernity and at the time of the emergence of the late stages of post-industrial capital, Paredes looks back to mid nineteenth- and early twentieth-century history as he deliberates upon the features of the real and the imaginary in the borderlands, and leaves their resolution, signaled in the attenuated forms of daydream and fantasy, suspended in the narrative mode of contradictory emergence.

Unguessed kinships and optical democracy: Cormac McCarthy, *Blood Meridian, or The Evening Redness in the West* (1985)

Paredes's concerns with the critical possibilities of the ethnic *Bildungsroman* are paralleled by Cormac McCarthy's explorations of the formal possibilities of the historical novel in *Blood Meridian*. McCarthy's novel follows the story of "the kid," born in Tennessee in 1833, in his experiences with Captain John Joel Glanton's gang, a historical group of scalp hunters who massacred Indians and others in the US–Mexico borderlands in 1849–1850. Paired against him is Judge Holden, a massive, hairless, powerfully demonic man, apparently also drawn from the historical record. Much of the novel is based on Glanton gang member Samuel Chamberlain's late nineteenth-century memoir, *My Confession: The Recollections of a Rogue*, chronicling events of mayhem on the border.[8] Generally true to its sources, McCarthy's novel follows the kid across the nineteenth century, from his arrival in Nacogdoches, Texas to his participation in scalp-hunting expeditions in 1849 on the newly established US–Mexico border, culminating in his apparent brutal death at the hands of the Judge in an outhouse in Griffin, Texas in 1878.

McCarthy's novel acknowledges the conflict, discord, and violence that lie at the heart of American national identity. I focus on the force of violence and of the relationship between history and fiction in *Blood Meridian* to account for McCarthy's engagement with the American Southwest as a polyglot region where history and mythology merged symbolically to justify the interests of Manifest Destiny over the claims of indigenous peoples on both sides of the border. Reading *Blood Meridian*, with its uncompromising representations of brutality and carnage, is a difficult task. In numerous scenes of ruthless atrocity, McCarthy forces the reader away from human consciousness and toward the mindless materiality of violence. McCarthy makes us ponder whether in portraying the violence committed for the sake of nation-formation in the American borderlands, he is interested in debasing all human subjectivity or only particular forms of it. Ultimately, he would have us consider what kind of nation and democratic polity emerges from the brutal reduction of human consciousness to base materiality.

In its concern with the materiality of violence and its negation of human subjectivity, *Blood Meridian* also addresses questions of national identity. To be a citizen of a nation, an "American" or a "Mexican," for instance, is to know something about who you are and where you are but also about how, or if, you belong. National identity is thus knowledge about one's place in a community. National identity is more than just a social, legal, or psychological category, then; it is also a hermeneutic, an analytical category. As such it deeply affects how one understands the world. Life in the borderlands forces one to ask what kinds of knowledge qualify anyone as American, or any other nationality for that matter.

By working with such ideas, McCarthy forces us in *Blood Meridian* to examine the ideology of nation building. How are we to conceive democratic communities of shared provenance and common cause? What happens if, instead of a unified citizenry manifesting the destiny of a democratic organic nation we get only difference, or worse, *in*difference? What kind of democracy might the history that McCarthy displays as originary to the founding of a continental nation display? We get disquieting answers to these questions throughout *Blood Meridian* but perhaps nowhere more clearly than in this passage, concerning what the narrator refers to as the "optical democracy" of the landscape of the west:

> In the neuter austerity of that terrain all phenomena were bequeathed a strange equality and no one thing nor spider nor stone nor blade of grass could put forth claim to precedence. The very clarity of these articles belied their familiarity, for the eye predicates the whole on some feature or part and here was nothing more luminous than another and nothing more enshadowed and in the optical democracy of such landscapes all preference is made whimsical and a man and a rock become endowed with unguessed kinships.

How, when, and why is a man like a rock? If metaphorical identities emerge from a shared proper ground between the literal and figural aspects of the metaphor (the shared qualities that make Achilles into a lion in *The Iliad*, for example), in the case of *Blood Meridian*, what is the proper ground between the figural and literal aspects of the trope that allows men and rocks to occupy "with unguessed kinships" a shared identity? It turns out to be the act of violence itself, represented by the abstracting of forged similarities of "unguessed kinship" from out of the "neuter austerity" of the differential landscapes of the southwestern borderlands. Unlike other novels of the frontier, McCarthy's does not long for domesticity and repose.[a] Instead, it leaves us only with the dead weight of the past, and, in the Judge's words, the forlorn desire to build in stone "to alter the structure of the universe."

McCarthy's characters in *Blood Meridian*, in stark allusion to Psalm 91:6, rendered in the Authorized Version of the Bible (1611) as "the destruction that wasteth at noonday," wander the borderland satanically: "Spectre horsemen, pale with dust, anonymous in the crenellated heat." The borderlands they traverse divide the very structures of human order, "leaving what had been and what would never be alike extinguished on the ground behind them ... Above all else they appeared wholly at venture, primal, provisional, devoid of order. Like beings provoked out of the absolute rock ... of Gondwanaland in a time before nomenclature was and each was all." Following these characters through the day's meridian toward the red demise of the evening lands, we are no longer with the American Adam, setting out to create order in the garden, but in a more primal epoch, one without order and "in a time before nomenclature was." This linguistic homelessness signals the desolate nature of the "optical democracy" that McCarthy envisions as the substance of the borderlands and that hints at his novel's formal innovation in its revision of the historical novel. Not content with simply capturing the contradictions and fractures of its historical sources, in *Blood Meridian* McCarthy veers toward the neutered austerity of national narratives forged in sublime brutality and predicated as a whole from nothing more than the strange equality "of a man and a rock ... endowed with unguessed kinships." In doing so, McCarthy brings the historical novel to its limits as a form capable of capturing the economic and imaginary productive modes of its time.

Democratic landscapes: Leslie Marmon Silko, *Almanac of the Dead: A Novel* (1991)

Almanac of the Dead, like the other borderland novels discussed here, is also about the relation between history and fiction. But while those novels use the revised forms of the *Bildungsroman* and historical novel respectively to represent the borderlands, *Almanac of the Dead* does so in the different mode of magical realism in order to imagine a revolution of "the indigenous peoples of

a In her essay in this volume, chapter 31, "Imagining the frontier," Stephanie Le Menager notes that frontier novels increasingly situate violence away from the confrontation between "savagery and civilization" and "into the domestic space of the family," 525. Here and throughout her chapter, Le Menager emphasizes the violence of history-making and its role in the history-making of the American novel.

the Americas" against the European conquerors. "The Fifth World" imagined in *Almanac* is a reference to the pre-Columbian Indian belief that theirs, and ours, was a transitional time which had been preceded by four previous cosmic orders, "Suns," or world-creations. All had ended cataclysmically, as would one day the present Fifth, and last, world-creation as well.[9] However obscured from human perceptions the great patterns of history might be, for pre-contact Mesoamericans, "Within each Sun, time was understood as multi-dimensional and eternally recurrent," notes historian Inga Clendinnen.[10] Silko uses the metaphor of the "Fifth World" with its complex infolding of sequential and repeating temporalities to underscore the finite character of our own "Fifth World" and to structure the complex bundle of magical stories that will signal its demise. The utopian hope expressed in Silko's novel is that our "Fifth World" will be followed by the creation of another, "One World, Many Tribes," from the detritus of all previous universal calamities, even if the events of a new era remain problematic in their experiencing. If not entirely about the "end of history," *Almanac of the Dead* clearly contemplates the possible beginning of a new history. One of the novel's numerous characters, Angelita La Escapía, a Mexican Indian, is thus able at novel's end to muse that: "Poor Engels and Marx ... had waited and waited, year after year, for the successful revolution until their time ran out." "Now," she proclaims, "it was up to the poorest tribal people and survivors of European genocide to show the remaining humans how all could share and live together on earth, ravished as she was."

The revolutionary history envisioned in *Almanac of the Dead* is intimately connected to particular ideas of space and social relations. Figured by the "Five Hundred Year Map" in the front pages of the novel, the new history first admits the plurality of American social relations since before Columbus. Silko's map then offers this heterogeneity as an opportunity for the remaking of history. Utopian America will not be simply a pluralist society. Silko imagines instead a "Fifth World" founded on Native American forms and motivated by a return to pre-Columbian systems of community, polity, and justice: "Native Americans acknowledge no borders; they seek nothing less than the return of all tribal lands."

Moreover, Silko's "Five Hundred Year Map" is the space of Gloria Anzaldúa's borderlands, where "you are the battleground / where enemies are kin to each other; / you are at home, a stranger."[11] To negotiate this fabulous space will require what Walter Mignolo has called "border thinking," one of the consequences of European colonial expansion, bringing European languages, new ways of thinking about knowledge and power, into Asia,

Africa, and the Americas.[12] Silko's novel aspires to illustrate how the mapping of American space and the narrating of its vital social relations can generate an almanac of liberating political fantasy.

By beginning her novel with space and social relations and moving to border thinking, Silko considers the ways that material practices (of property distribution and ownership) and social relations (how ownership determines who you are and how you are regarded) are defined and limited by the very society they help create. Altering the social relations we create, Silko suggests, will also alter our relations to the physical surroundings within which we live, next to and amongst each other. In this way, the modern capitalist, liberal democratic nation-state – and its related vision of identity as autonomous, self-directed, and independent – is not the end of history but only one (deeply flawed) alternative. To undo the distortions of five hundred years of injustice and create a new conception of American identity will require an altogether different way of thinking and a wholly revised social geography.

The version of American identity that Silko imagines in *Almanac* is not, contrary to what Walter Benn Michaels suggests, simply an "ethnonationalism" founded on racial difference, which turns out to be "an ideology, not a source of identity at all."[13] In his chapter in this volume, Michaels characterizes the view of the American racial system as a binary mechanism "for taking people (Slavs, Jews, Asians, whoever) and mak[ing] them white" as obviously "not true if you think of Asian Americans, not to mention Jews, as minorities." Michaels dismisses identity factors as "neoliberal expressions" of "indifference to . . . economic inequality," in American society, arguing instead that "What you want . . . is not to value difference but to eliminate those differences that constitute inequality."[b] Who would disagree with that? But even while allowing for the post-racial framework he calls for, in which economic factors outweigh cultural ones in measuring assimilation to middle-class American life, Michaels's conception of race is too reductive to account for what happens in borderland fiction. Instead of indiscriminately and dismissively lumping all racial groups, "Slavs, Jews, Asians, whoever," together, Silko in *Almanac* attempts something far more difficult than simply pointing out racism in America. By concentrating precisely on the differences that constitute economic inequality, such as inequalities based on land ownership and wealth distribution, she shows how racial and cultural difference work inextricably

b See Walter Benn Michaels, "Model minorities and the minority model – the neoliberal novel," chapter 61, 1019, 1029. In the diagram that opens his chapter as elsewhere in his discussion, Michaels tends to blur the historical correlation between poverty, race, and ethnicity in American history.

with economic inequality to produce an unjust America. She thus assumes the task of imagining, in an American multiracial context, the possibility of creating equality within difference that goes beyond ethnonationalisms toward real justice and true democracy. In *Almanac* this utopian possibility is figured as a space of belonging and way of living together, that would serve as bases for the retaking of the land by the "ghost armies of the Americas leading armies of living warriors, armies of indigenous people."

The kind of democracy that Silko offers as an alternative to Michaels's ethnonationalism and McCarthy's optical democracy emerges most clearly in the chapter titled "Mistaken Identity." Explaining why the hunt for the fugitive Apache rebel Geronimo produced multiple Geronimos captured or killed, Old Mahawala claims that "the Apache warrior called Geronimo had been three, even four different men." "Of course the real man they called Geronimo, they never did catch. The real Geronimo got away." And the reason for this was that

> the tribal people here were all aware that the whites put great store in names. But once the whites had a name for a thing, they seemed unable to ever again recognize the thing itself . . . To them, a "rock" was just a "rock" wherever they found it, despite obvious differences in shape, density, color, or the position of the rock relative to all things around it.

Mahawala's concern with "the thing itself," before it has been adjusted to fit Euro-American requirements of reason and discourse, points to the particular kind of knowledge that operates in borderlands novels, forcing the issue of our basic understanding of the world and asking what kinds of knowledge qualify anyone as American or not.

McCarthy's "unguessed kinships" between a rock and a man had alluded to the violence of abstracted identities. Mahawala's concern with the relative self-identity of things (a rock is *not* just a rock but is also something uniquely situated relative to all things around it) leads in the opposite direction from McCarthy by drawing attention to the complexity that is suppressed when we look at things (and people) only in their general, abstractive qualities that can be appropriated and used. In contrast to the abstracting way of viewing the world, there is another, admittedly more difficult, way of seeing "the thing itself," as an independent existence, all the while maintaining its portion of shared identity with kindred things. Elsewhere, another character, old Calabazas, explains: "I get mad when I hear the word *identical* . . . There is no such thing. Nowhere. At no time. All you have to do is to stop and think." No standardization, no privileging of similarity over difference, no abstraction of metaphor over the thing itself. In imagining the possibility for a new era beyond the conditions of domination and injustice, Silko's characters begin by asking about the conditions necessary for the creation of identity within difference, equality within strangeness.

The complex plot movements in *Almanac of the Dead* ultimately converge in an uprising led by a coalition of native people, blacks, Mexicans and Mexican Americans, homeless men, Vietnam veterans, and a Korean hacker. In representing this group, Silko emphasizes their status as outsiders and refugees. But she also suggests how contemporary global capitalism misses the potentially significant differences that survive within (and at the margins of) the transformations created by 500 years of conquest in the Americas. *Almanac of the Dead* focuses on the shared fates of the subordinate subjects and disenfranchised social groups of American modernity. Linking multiple forms of homelessness, the novel represents this outsider status as a general attribution of subordination rather than as an identity politics. The point of identity politics in *Almanac* is not, as Michaels represents it, simply to glorify difference *as* difference. The point is precisely to understand and counter the ways that the ruling classes maintain material structures of inequality by manipulating relations of "race, space, gender and sexuality" to enforce the difference between subalterns and elites.[c] Here, the marvelous quality of an imagined new reality beyond inequality requires a magical form of realism as the novel muses about what differences in our conceptions of the world emerge if we see reality itself as a relational term. In this instance, then, as Fredric Jameson has argued, magical realism is not a literary trope, but a reality which is already fantastical and represents "the search of the libido or desiring self for a fulfillment that will deliver it from the anxieties of *reality but will still contain that reality.*"[14]

Constructing relational identity within difference leads Silko in *Almanac* to a payoff in the form of a state of affairs where multiple identities, national political cultures, and plural national collectivities may integrate into communities of shared fates without sacrificing their particularity. This way of thinking both counters the notion that "a 'rock' was just a 'rock' . . . despite obvious differences in shape, density, color, or the position of the rock relative to all things around it" and also allows for the abstraction of shared features among different things without ignoring their differences.

c Michaels, chapter 61, 1029. In the history of the novel, "magical realism" is the aesthetic innovation created precisely to represent and analyze the ideological confusions that structure the kinds of distortions in liberal and neoliberal narratives that Michaels here decries.

Angelita La Escapía can thus imagine at novel's end that "No human, individuals or corporations, no cartel of nations, could 'own' the earth; it was the earth who possessed the humans and it was the earth who disposed of them." In place of old local and national self-sufficiency and self-possession of the personal or corporate kind, we might have intercourse in every transpersonal and transnational direction with communities that do not "own" the earth but inhabit it as the provenance of their shared responsibilities to one another. *Almanac of the Dead* envisions oppositional practices and struggles that do not depend on simplistic identities, unities, or monologic representation. The novel asks us to consider instead whether it is possible to conceive of other models of identity and cultural struggle that are inclusive and expansive, and that allow for the accomplishment of a transnational "American" subject, *e pluribus unum*, without privileging the one over the many or resorting to the power of strange equalities. Such a model of relationality might hold us together in difference even as we share one another's fate in common. Silko's nonlinear, magical assembly of stories in *Almanac of the Dead* converges on forms that deliver her characters from the anxieties of 500 years of colonization while still containing that reality as a source of liberation. Only thus, she suggests, may we conceive of meaningful democratic participation in the determination of the political and cultural life of the nation and mutual deliberation about how to respond collectively to the challenges facing the communities of the Americas. By turning to a representation of the marvelous reality figured by a rejection of the unitary "identical" in favor of the "differences in shape, density, color, or the position" of a thing relative to all things around it, Silko brings the realistic mode of the borderlands novel to a climactic end.

In conclusion, what can we say are the features of the American borderlands novel? American borderlands novels are transnational; they respond to geopolitical influences outside the borders of the nation. They have as their central concern racial and economic structures of hierarchy and domination. These structures are multiple, contradictory, and cross-cutting. Borderlands novels are concerned with the place of the one (*unum*) in relation to the many (*pluram*) in multiple forms, with the individual in relation to the minority collective, or the minority person in relation to the hegemonic culture. They are not limited to one specific genre but can take shape as *Bildungsromane*, historical novels, and romances of different kinds, particularly as fantasy narratives in a modified form of magical realism.

Whatever shapes they do take, however, they respond to the tropes of difference seen in their thematics. Borderlands novels do not offer singular answers to the questions they pose, but they do propose alternative possibilities for social and personal life, in constructing visions of collectivity, beyond ideologies of race and nation. They are concerned with a sense of belonging, with the construction of individual, family, and domestic spaces that might constitute a national homeland, distinct from narrowly circumscribed nationalisms. They are concerned with the possibilities of a future emerging from the past that is nonetheless not determined by that past. Their heroes are non-heroic – they are the children, the homeless, the outsiders of the normative world who, in striving to belong to that world, confirm its impoverishment and stake out its alternatives. And lastly, perhaps most encompassingly, American borderlands novels are concerned with identity as a product of all of the multiple processes of relationality involved in the fashioning of identity. All of these factors necessarily alter the traditional conventions of the *Bildungsroman*, the historical novel, and magical realism. Ultimately, the formal qualities of borderlands novels affect deeply how we understand the world and, more importantly, how we can change it.

Notes

1. On Taylor's dialogic method, see Amy Guttman, "Introduction," in *Multiculturalism: Examining the Politics of Recognition* (Princeton: Princeton University Press, 1994), 7.
2. This misprision is the topic of David Foster Wallace's "E Unibus Pluram: Television and U.S. Fiction," *Review of Contemporary Fiction* 13 (1993): 151–194.
3. Guttman, "Introduction," 6.
4. On the non-heroic position, see Georg Lukács, The *Historical Novel*, trans. Hannah Mitchell and Stanley Mitchell (Lincoln: University of Nebraska Press), 37.
5. M. M. Bakhtin, "The *Bildungsroman* (1934–38)," in *Speech Genres and Other Essays*, ed. Caryl Emerson and Michael Holquist (Austin: University of Texas Press, 1981), 21.
6. This is the definition of the *Bildungsroman* that Walter Benjamin offers in the essay "The Storyteller: Observations on the Works of Nikolai Leskov," trans. Howard Eiland Edmund Jephcott, and others, in *Walter Benjamin: Selected Writings, Volume 3, 1935–1938*, ed. Howard Eiland and Michael W. Jennings (Cambridge: The Belknap Press of Harvard University Press, 2002), 146–147.
7. For a fuller discussion of the contradictions of assimilation, see Anthony Bogues, *Black Heretics, Black Prophets: Radical Political Intellectuals* (New York: Routledge, 2003), 11. Guálinto's is a classic instance of the experience of the assimilated middle classes under racist colonialism, as described by Frantz Fanon, *Black Skin, White Masks* (New York: Grove Weidenfeld, 1998).

8. See Samuel Chamberlain, *My Confession: The Recollections of a Rogue* (Austin: Texas State Historical Association, 1997).
9. Hugh Thomas, *Conquest: Montezuma, Cortés, and the Fall of Old Mexico* (New York: Simon & Schuster, 1993). Thomas notes that the pre-Columbian Mexica, following the calendar of the earlier Toltec civilization, had "constructed their history on a myth of eventual cataclysm": "This myth suggested that the world had already been through four eras, lit by four separate suns. The existing time, that of the Fifth Sun, would one day come to an end" (28).
10. Inga Clendinnen, *Aztecs: An Interpretation* (1993; Cambridge: Cambridge University Press, 1991), 36.
11. Gloria Anzaldúa, *Borderlands/La Frontera: The New Mestiza* (San Francisco: spinsters/aunt lute, 1987), 194.
12. Walter D. Mignolo, *The Idea of Latin America* (Oxford: Blackwell, 2005), 10–11.
13. See, Walter Benn Michaels, *The Shape of the Signifier: 1967 to the End of History* (Princeton: Princeton University Press, 2004), 24, 25.
14. Fredric Jameson, "Magical Narratives," in *The Political Unconscious: Narrative as a Socially Symbolic Act* (Ithaca, NY: Cornell University Press, 1981), 110. Jameson is here citing Northrop Frye, *Anatomy of Criticism* (Princeton: Princeton University Press, 1957), 193. The italics are Jameson's.

63
The rise of the Asian American novel

SUSAN KOSHY

Asian American literature falls outside the conventional criteria used to organize a literature, such as nationality, shared history, common culture, or racial identity. The term itself, Asian American, was an invention of the pan-Asian movement of the 1970s, and is used retroactively to organize and interpret a body of writing first produced when that category did not exist as a political or cultural identity. The works of the pre-1970s era were largely identified by the national origins of their writers or their subject matter as Japanese, Chinese, Korean, Indian, or Filipino American. The problem of referentiality also extends to contemporary or post-1970s literature by authors of Asian origin, fiction coeval with the category or produced in its aftermath. The civil rights struggles that birthed the term Asian American also led to the passage of the 1965 Immigration Act that profoundly changed the term's meanings. The 1965 Immigration Act reopened large-scale immigration from Asia after a hiatus of over forty years, and the influx of new immigrant and refugee populations transformed Asian Americans from a native-born to a largely foreign-born population and introduced new classes, religions, and nationalities – including Vietnamese, Hmong, Pakistanis, Sri Lankans, and Thais – to the constituency.[1] Nevertheless, while the communities, identities, subjectivities, and affiliations the term encompasses have continuously morphed, its efficacy as a rubric is based on its analytic rather than merely descriptive force. When the Asian American movement in the 1970s birthed the political fiction of pan-ethnic identity, it reconfigured the national origin-based affiliations of Asians into an aggregate identity that emphasized a shared political history of oppression and exclusion as Asians in the United States. The continuing relevance of the term is linked to its ability to offer critical readings of histories of racism and imperialism and alternative political visions of the future.

Thus, the project of naming Asian American literature manifestly resists closure. In contrast to a category such as African American literature that has gathered historical density and coherence over time and built a continuous tradition, Asian American literature is marked by historical ruptures and fractured by centrifugal forces. For that reason, most critics favor a broad definition of Asian American literature – as the works of Asian-origin writers living permanently in the United States, regardless of nativity. This flexibility, often perplexing to non-specialists, is an effort to account for the disjunctions in Asian American history, the discrepant integration of various Asian groups into the pan-ethnic collectivity, and the location of these texts at the intersection of overlapping traditions of postcolonial, world, and national literatures. The critical practice of inclusiveness in defining the field is a deliberate effort not to foreclose the contradictions produced by the category. It also foregrounds the historical and political dilemmas of identity and belonging that have shaped Asian American fiction.

We can identify three distinct periods in the development of the Asian American novel: novels mainly by immigrant Asian writers in the pre-World War II period (Etsu Sugimoto, Lin Yutang, H. T. Tsiang, and Onoto Watanna[2]); writings produced from the 1940s to 1970s by American-born and westernized Asian-born writers (including Louis Chu, John Okada, Diana Chang, Anor Lin, and Santha Rama Rao); and the works of a range of writers, immigrant and American-born, from the late 1970s to the present, books that have domestic, diasporic, and international audiences (such as those by Maxine Hong Kingston, Jessica Hagedorn, Bharati Mukherjee, David Wong Louie, Jhumpa Lahiri, Chang-rae Lee, Lê Thi Diem Thúy, and Sigrid Nunez).[3]

The periodization in this chapter, which uses the 1970s and 1980s as a marker for the transition from the modern to the postmodern, coincides with the chronology followed in most accounts of postmodernity, including Ursula Heise's in this volume.[a] However, in the Asian American novel, the "crisis in representation"[4] is embedded in the transformations of globalization and draws on three main sources: challenges to the material conditions of literary production, circulation, and consumption, or what Stuart Hall calls "relations of representation";[5] aesthetic and political responses to civil rights struggles in the USA and modernization and decolonization projects in Asia; and debates over the status and appropriate forms of fiction in "minor" literatures.

During the 1970s and 1980s, Asian American writers challenged prevailing norms through calls for access to publication, critiques of dominant

a Ursula Heise, "Postmodern novels," chapter 58.

representations of minority lives, and cultural recovery projects seeking to retrieve subjugated histories. The representational crisis was initially addressed as a matter of publishing a broader range of minority writers and encouraging narratives that countered stereotypical renderings of Asian and Asian American experiences. These calls for cultural inclusion fostered and drew strength from the growth of a domestic and international market for minority and Asian literature. The diversity and growing sophistication of reading publics inside and outside the USA also fueled formal and linguistic experimentation. In formal terms, the postmodern period represents for Asian American literature less a rupture with the realist modes of the modern period than an exponential expansion of styles and genres, in which realism retained an important but not dominant position. Realist techniques in the postmodern period were heightened through fertilization with reportage, diagrams, maps, and historical records, and supplemented with poetry, music, and visual media. In addition, new modes like magical realism, surrealism, collage, and parody emerged along with a proliferation of novelistic genres like spy novels, national allegories, epic novels, anti-*Bildungsromans*, and science fiction.

The crisis in representation that marked the transition to the postmodern period was also grounded in the political transformations of the civil rights era and anti-colonial and modernization struggles in the Third World. The pan-ethnic category Asian American produced new subjectivities and oppositional frames for generating historical and social knowledge. The movement's struggle for political representation was buttressed by the demand for cultural representation. Writers and activists associated with the movement were at the forefront of attempts to construct a canon of Asian American literature and promoted a definition of the literature that emphasized US-centricity, oral traditions, realism, anti-Orientalism, and anti-racism. Writers like Frank Chin, Jeffery Chan, Shawn Wong, and Lawson Inada advanced a model of Asian American identity that overturned stereotypes and constructed a literary tradition that defiantly asserted its Americanness.

The title of the anthology that launched the project of constructing an Asian American literature, *Aiiieeeee! An Anthology of Asian-American Writers* (1974), adopted the stereotypical representation of Asian American inarticulateness to reverse and recode its negative associations, turning it into a rallying cry. The *Aiiieeeee* project recovered, reprinted, and interpreted the work of neglected or forgotten Asian American novelists like Louis Chu and John Okada. However, the volume not only excluded the work of several less US-centric Asian American writers of the time, but also brought the *Aiiieeeee* writers and scholars into conflict with the stylistic and generic choices of others (Maxine

Hong Kingston, David Henry Hwang, and Amy Tan). The legacy of these initial attempts to formulate an Asian American literary tradition are mixed: on the one hand, the privileging of realist representation, political resistance, and materialist critique was a breakthrough that transformed the scope, power, and direction of Asian American writing; on the other hand, the masculinist strain, East Asian focus, and heteronormativity of the *Aiiieeeee* group generated constrictive models of artistic representation.[6]

But in relation to the development of the Asian American novel, perhaps the most salient aspect of the shift from the modern to the postmodern was the sudden and swift rise of the novel and its displacement of autobiography, till then the paramount Asian American long narrative genre. The dominance of autobiography and the secondary status of the novel for the first eighty years of Asian American literary production stemmed from an implicit ethnographic pact between Asian American writer and mainstream audience that placed a premium on cultural descriptions purveyed by insiders and discouraged formal experimentation. These constraints had three significant consequences: first, they positioned the author as a native informant; second, it privileged the genre of autobiography; and third, they constricted the development of the novel.

Although the dominance of autobiography and the ethnographic stance of the author have been noted by scholars, the relationship between these two aspects of Asian American literature and the belated development of the novel has not been examined.[7] I will argue that all three are linked to the slow emergence of the category of fiction in Asian American narrative. As Catherine Gallagher has pointed out, our affective investments in novels require a "cognitive provisionality" that depends upon the construction of conventions and protocols of plausibility. These fictional protocols enable the development of the novel because they allow novels to be read as "believable stories that did not solicit belief" rather than simply as facts or falsehoods.[8] However, the positioning of the Asian American author as native informant established rigid codes of facticity that worked against a readerly "disposition of ironic credulity" congenial to the production of novels.[9] The rapid growth of the Asian American novel in the 1980s was preceded by a burgeoning repertoire of fictional protocols in Asian American narratives, vividly illustrated by novels like Theresa Hak Kyung Cha's *Dictee* (1982) and Maxine Hong Kingston's *China Men* (1980).

The invention of fictional conventions took place not just in the texts themselves but was also catalyzed by fierce debates among Asian American writers and critics over the referential basis of literary forms in minority writing. Two watershed events in Asian American literary history were controversies over the incorporation of fictional material into autobiographies by Maxine Hong Kingston and Carlos Bulosan. As I discuss in greater detail later, the fallout from these debates fueled the growth of fiction and the novel, and created a more complex understanding of the vexed boundary between cultural and political representation in minority literature.

Arrested development: fictionality and the Asian American novel

The conditions that shaped early Asian American literature led to the arrested development of the novel and the hypertrophy of the autobiography. From the turn of the twentieth century till the 1970s, autobiography was the dominant genre for Asian American writers, leading to works like Lee Yan Phou's *When I Was a Boy in China* (1887), Lin Yutang's *My Country and My People* (1937), Younghill Kang's *East Goes West* (1937), Jade Snow Wong's *Fifth Chinese Daughter* (1945), Carlos Bulosan's *America Is in the Heart* (1946), Monica Sone's *Nisei Daughter* (1953), and Maxine Hong Kingston's *The Woman Warrior* (1976). However, while a few novels by Asians and Asian Americans began to appear by the early decades of the twentieth century, novels about Asia by white writers like Jack London, Pearl S. Buck, and James Michener dominated the mainstream market for Asian-themed fiction. Onoto Watanna, the first Asian American novelist, was also the only early Asian American novelist to enjoy a comparable level of popularity. Tellingly, her success stemmed in large part from her skillful mimicry of Orientalist imagery and plots, even as she subtly modified and reworked these formulae to explore sensitive subjects like interracial love, mixed-race identities, and racial nationalisms.[10]

Watanna's dexterous recoding of the staples of Orientalist narratives can be seen in her revision of the famous Madame Butterfly story. John Luther Long's popular short story "Madame Butterfly," the source for Giacomo Puccini's celebrated opera, appeared three years before Watanna's novel, *A Japanese Nightingale* (1902). Long's story focuses on a temporary marriage between a Japanese geisha and a callous American sailor who abandons her and then returns after marrying an American woman to reclaim his biracial child. Watanna reworks this narrative into a love story centered on a wealthy American, Jack Bigelow, and a part-Japanese, part-English geisha named Yuki.

While Long's story pivots on the Japanese woman's unrequited love for the American man, Watanna insists on the reciprocity and naturalness of their interracial desire.[11] Soon after his impulsive marriage to Yuki, Jack is beset by doubts about his enigmatic wife. His fearfulness and anxiety affect the reader, particularly because such behaviors have been projected in earlier versions of the Madame Butterfly story, such as Pierre Loti's *Madame Chrysanthemum* (1887), as signs of a Japanese geisha's greed, manipulativeness, and promiscuity. But the plot's ultimate revelation of Yuki's sincere devotion to her husband (at the end, Jack plans to sail with her toward America), sets this novel apart from most other interracial romances, where the incorporation of such desire within the American nation is unimaginable.[12] In winning the consent of her readers in this way, Watanna uses the Orientalist conventions of her fiction to rework their contents and expose American misconceptions of Asians.

Although the Asian American autobiography and novel were adjacent genres that emerged almost simultaneously, they performed different cultural work: autobiography came to be associated with the cultural-historical quotidian and the novel with the exotic-romantic. Most of the earlier novels by writers like Etsu Sugimoto and Onoto Watanna were set in China or Japan and featured romances, marriages, or intergenerational stories. However, during periods of political crisis, publication venues opened up for novels about war and occupation that are comparable to the current fascination with novels about Iraq and Afghanistan. The novels of Anor and Adet Lin (daughters of Lin Yutang), Han Suyin, and Mai-Mai Sze won a large readership at this time.[13] At these moments, the novel veered from its usual function of depicting exotic settings and "traditional" cultures and took on a testimonial role in which fiction approximated the functions of reportage. But these literary markets contracted as public interest waned or shifted. Before the 1950s, few Asian American novels were set in the United States or engaged the domestic context of settlement and immigration.

Autobiography, on the other hand, engaged everyday life and pivotal historical moments, but tethered these elements of plot and character to a conception of truth tied to factual accuracy and sanctioned political positions. Autobiographies that attested to the prospects for economic mobility or gender emancipation were particularly popular.

The clear demarcation in subject matter between the novel and autobiography, and the distinct kinds of referentiality they displayed, changed little until novelists turned to exploring the effects of racism on Asian American communities in the years following World War II. The attention to the harsher dimensions of displacement and marginalization led to the emergence of the realist novel and the covert novelization of the autobiography; it also produced a greater overlap between the two genres.

The realist fiction of H. T. Tsiang (*And China Has Hands* [1937]), John Okada (*No-No Boy* [1957]), and Louis Chu (*Eat a Bowl of Tea* [1961]) incorporated verisimilitude into the novel and instigated a discernible shift from the exotic-romantic to the familiar-quotidian. Verisimilitude proffered a language of the real to counter dominant myths about Asian American communities and further the creation of layered, lifelike social worlds in fiction. Chinese American writers like Tsiang and Chu were notably inspired by the leftist Chinatown literary movement, which emerged around Chinese-language journals and newspapers based in Chinatowns around the late 1930s and 1940s and drew on proletarian literature in the United States and China, experimenting to create a distinctively Chinese American idiom.[14]

These influences are noticeable in the focus on working-class life and immigrant struggles in Tsiang's *And China Has Hands*, which provides a satirical look at Wong Wan Lee's efforts to run a basement laundry business in New York's Chinatown. Lee uses his meager savings as a restaurant worker to buy the laundry, but his business collapses and he is eventually killed during a strike. The Chinatown presented in the novel is habituated by corrupt housing inspectors, prostitutes, thieves, Chinese students, waiters, and gamblers, and offers a striking contrast to the congenial, quaint, and exotic world depicted by Chinese-born contemporaries like Lin Yutang, *Chinatown Family* (1948), and Chin Yang Lee, *Flower Drum Song* (1957).[b]

Chu's *Eat a Bowl of Tea* extends the emergent social realist tradition of depicting the social decay of Chinatown in his wry novel about the Chinatown "bachelor society" in New York. The story centers on the marriage of Ben Loy, son of an aging Chinatown clubhouse proprietor, and Mei Oi, a young woman he returns to China to marry. The marriage is arranged by the fathers of the couple, old friends Wang Wah Gay and Lee Gong, but the happy arrangement goes awry when Ben Loy, a discreet frequenter of prostitutes, finds himself impotent with his new bride. Mei Oi is seduced by the notorious womanizer Ah Song and becomes pregnant. News of the scandal gets out and Wang Wah Gay cuts off Ah Song's ear in a fury. The two fathers leave Chinatown to escape public humiliation, and the young couple start a new life in San Francisco's Chinatown. In a neat comic turn captured in the title, Ben Loy's potency is restored when he drinks a brew of tea recommended by a Chinese herbalist. The novel, as Jeffery Chan notes, captures "the vision of a

b The emphasis on working-class struggles and socialist ideals links Tsiang's novel to other contemporary "immigrant tragedies," as Tim Prchal discusses in chapter 25, "New Americans and the immigrant novel," 428–431.

Chinatown community in transition from a bachelor to a family society . . . acknowledge[ing] the path of social and historical development that community traveled."[15] The depiction of the damaged gender relations of an aging male fraternity, tenuously linked to shadowy memories of wives and families left behind in China decades ago, and bound to each other by rituals of gossip, work, gambling, and paid sex, is unsparing and penetrating. Chu's realism and anti-exoticism are complemented by his efforts to create a distinctive Chinese American vernacular that incorporates Cantonese idioms and phrases.[16]

In realist novels like Chu's, fictionality provided cover for views outside the mainstream during the early Cold War era, when there was little public political expression of Asian American dissent. However, the unvarnished portrayals of Chinatown life in Chu's and Tsiang's fiction did not catch the attention of the mainstream public, which favored the quaint Chinatown novels of elite Chinese American writers or autobiographies set in this ethnic enclave. The new realist novels were dismissed by critics as crude or unfinished until the Asian American movement embraced them as precursors and models for a new generation of Asian American writers.

The other event of central importance to the emergence of the Asian American novel was the outing of fiction in autobiography. Debates surrounding two texts published as autobiographies, Carlos Bulosan's *America Is in the Heart* and Maxine Hong Kingston's *The Woman Warrior*, lay at the center of these controversies. They exposed the problems of enforcing a rigid distinction between fiction and nonfiction and led to a greater cross-fertilization between the novel and autobiography. In both cases, critics accused the authors of transgressing the boundaries between fiction and fact and of exaggerating and distorting the reality of Filipino American and Chinese American lives in the process. Kingston's critics – the most vocal of whom were Frank Chin and other writers associated with the *Aiiieeeee* project – accused her of selling out the Chinese American community in the name of feminism, of perpetuating stereotypes about Chinese Americans, and of purveying fake and inauthentic Chinese stories and legends for white consumption. In Bulosan's case, the charges of misrepresentation related to the details of the narrator Carlos's life and to several events included in the narrative.[17] Bulosan's narrator is described as an illiterate peasant who teaches himself to read and write in the United States; however, the author himself was a small-scale farmer's literate son who had nearly completed his high school education in the Philippines. Critics pointed out that some incidents (including a scene where the narrator is beaten, tarred, and feathered by white vigilantes) were not from the author's own experience. The exposure of these inconsistencies damaged the credibility of Bulosan's account, though revisionist readings of the text have argued that while these incidents may not have happened to Bulosan himself, they were drawn from events the author witnessed or heard about and, therefore, the autobiography should be read as a collective portrait of the community rather than a personal history.[18]

The incorporation of fictive elements in the autobiographies exposed the coerciveness of the implicit ethnographic contract in which the Asian American author served as the reader's native informant. On the surface, the idea of the autobiographical subject as native informant appears contradictory because in the Western tradition these two figures incarnate the poles of subjectivity and objectivity. That is, if the native informant is framed in the anthropological exchange as a non-subject and an objective source of cultural information, the conventional autobiographical storyteller embodies full, autonomous subjectivity. But in Asian American autobiography the two figures converge, transforming "I" into the sign and site of conflict. In a deft self-reflexive gesture, Kingston's narrator, Maxine, describes the paradox of pronouncing the American "I": "The Chinese 'I' has seven strokes, intricacies. How could the American 'I' assuredly wearing a hat like the Chinese, have only three strokes, the middle so straight . . . I stared at the middle line and waited so long for its black center to resolve into tight strokes and dots that I forgot to pronounce it." Here, the autobiographical I literally turns into cross-cultural uncertainty, interfering with Kingston's narrator's voice rather than enabling it.

The early debates about *The Woman Warrior* centered on its classification as an autobiography and its reliance on Orientalist stereotypes. Yet the text insistently foregrounds the position of an American-born Chinese in an assimilationist culture as structurally inauthentic. In the opening chapter, Maxine poses a conundrum for her co-ethnic readers: "Chinese Americans, when you try to understand what things in you are Chinese, how do you separate what is peculiar to childhood, to poverty, insanities, one family, your mother who marked your growing with stories, from what is Chinese? What is Chinese tradition and what is the movies?" This challenge, delivered in an abrupt shift from first to second person, points to the fictiveness of ethnic subjectivity and the unreliability of the narrator as a native informant. Yet these metafictional glosses interspersed in the text can hardly contain the charged scenes of racial and gender shame, rage, revenge, aversion, and sorrow that dominate *The Woman Warrior*, fueling radically different readings of its intentionality – Orientalist, anti-racist, sexist, and feminist.

The angry denunciations lobbed at Kingston by her critics and the "cultural mis-readings" of the novel by mainstream reviewers prompted a profound rethinking of the problems of voice, form, narrative authority, audience, and historical context in her writing.[19] The boundary between fantasy and fact, rendered indeterminate in *The Woman Warrior* to mirror the narrator's predicament as an American-born Chinese with tormented and tenuous links to her cultural identity, is luminously recast in the formal divisions of Kingston's next book, *China Men* (1980). Kingston wrote *China Men* to tell the story of four generations of male Chinese migration – the barely alluded to background to *The Woman Warrior*. *China Men* is composed, as Jinqi Ling points out, of six historical chapters (each centered on the immigration experience of a male ancestor of a different generation) sandwiched between mythical chapters dealing with ghost stories, legends, and folk tales that comment on the historical sections.[20] This dialectical structure intersperses "readerly text" (historical sections) with "writerly text" (mythical sections), highlighting the simultaneous inadequacy and necessity of representing minority histories in linear narrative form, while enlisting the reader to actively reconstruct the history, much as the narrator herself does.

The debates about *The Woman Warrior* and the changes in novelistic practice between *The Woman Warrior* and *China Men* fostered the rise of fictionality in Kingston's *oeuvre* and illustrate broader developments in Asian American literature. Kingston's book achieved a level of national recognition unprecedented for an Asian American writer, which, coupled with the runaway commercial success of Amy Tan's *The Joy Luck Club* (1989), established the growing appeal and broad reach of Asian American fiction. The earlier realist novels by Tsiang, Okada, and Chu had made major innovations to the novel, but they did not achieve the wide circulation or the cross-over appeal of Kingston's and Tan's works. The timing of Kingston's *The Woman Warrior*, converging as it did with the women's movement and the advent of multiculturalism, encountered a very different reception than the earlier realist novels. In the following decades, the changing literary market, the emergence of a new generation of Asian American writers, the establishment of creative writing programs that supported minority writers, and the invention of complex and variegated fictional protocols generated an outburst of literary activity that made the novel the pre-eminent genre in Asian American literature.

The contemporary Asian American novel

The controversy over Kingston's formal innovations in *The Woman Warrior* and her subsequent revision of genre, voice, and narrative technique in *China*

Men encapsulated many of the epistemological, aesthetic, and political shifts that marked the transition from modern to postmodern in Asian American literature. *The Woman Warrior* formulated identity as a problem rather than a solution (as the ensuing controversy powerfully demonstrated) and in doing so prefigured thematic and formal preoccupations that would be extended and reworked in the postmodern Asian American novel. The debates brought out the internal heterogeneity of Asian American identity and the growing strength of feminist and queer voices. In addition, Kingston's shift of scale from a spatial focus on Stockton's Chinese American community and a village in China (in *The Woman Warrior*) to a sweeping diasporic perspective spanning China, Hawaii, Alaska, the West Coast, New York, Florida, Cuba, Vietnam, and the Philippines (in *China Men*) anticipated the transnational and diasporic perspectives that became more prominent in the postmodern novel.

From the 1980s forward, the novel has been characterized by remarkable formal experimentation and a proliferation of new voices and themes. However, it is possible to distinguish two primary foci (with plenty of overlap): the local context of racialization under globalization and multiculturalism, and the transnational contexts of minority becoming shaped by migration, (neo)colonialism, and global capitalism. In novels with a US context, recurring themes of loss, unease, paranoia, and failure suggest that the cultural alienation of Asian Americans – a recurring theme in novels of the modern period (when Asian Americans were overtly excluded) – has not been resolved by their legal inclusion. Novels with a diasporic or international focus delineate the material and psychic costs of displacement linked to postcolonial crises of war and uneven development, the uncertainties of home in globality, the realities of racism in a geopolitical frame, and the ethical possibilities of cosmopolitanism. These two modes often merge, as in Bharati Mukherjee's *Jasmine* (1988) or Chang-rae Lee's *A Gesture Life* (1999), but whether fused or distinct, they are animated by a common set of concerns about the precariousness and elusiveness of belonging.

The formal innovations and thematic concerns of the postmodern Asian American novel set largely in the USA engage the complexities and contradictions of multiculturalism, at a time when overt legal barriers to equality fell at the same time as new identities proliferated as the site and source of conflicts and coalitions. These novels explore a world of what Richard Thompson Ford calls "racism without racists," in which racial conflicts and tensions emanate from "ambiguous facts and inscrutable motivations."[21] They highlight the fracture, paranoia, hysteria, and delirium that constitute the terrain of the post-civil rights era, extending in new forms the critique of the model minority position undertaken by Kingston and the earlier Asian American novelists.

Several postmodern novels, including Gish Jen's *Typical American* (1991), Bharati Mukherjee's *Jasmine*, Chang-rae Lee's *Native Speaker* (1995) and *A Gesture Life* (1999) turn obsessively to the idea of the model minority, exploring it as an uncanny figure for the limits and possibilities of what America is becoming and what becoming American means. Gish Jen's novel tells the story of the model minority as typical American through the tale of Ralph Chang's rise from foreign student to a home-owning, suburban-dwelling businessman and his subsequent free fall to economic disaster and personal tragedy. Ralph's Americanization is driven by his obsessive materialism and by his faith that money can alchemize race: "In this country, you have money, you can do anything. You have no money, you are nobody. You are Chinaman! Is that simple." Ralph's Americanization is powered by his Oedipal rebellion against the constraints of his father's world, his masculinist investment in the ideal of the self-made man, and his profane longing to become a "man-god." Following the loss of his business and home, Ralph recognizes the folly of his faith in the American dream of self-invention and upward mobility: "What escape was possible? . . . a man was as doomed here as he was in China . . . He was not what he made up his mind to be."

This insight is reinforced through the way that Jen formally revokes the *Bildungsroman*; until its very end, the book plots with satisfying symmetry the arc of Ralph's upward ascent and "Americanization," followed by his precipitous descent. A plot which had consecrated the attainment of every milestone of social mobility and Americanization (Part 1 ends with Ralph's marriage, Part 2 ends with Ralph moving into a new apartment and completing his PhD, Part 3 ends with his getting tenure, and so on) runs down, and temporal progress founders. An embryonic form, an anti-*Bildungsroman*, emerges in the penultimate chapter, appropriately titled "The Order, Lost." The novel concludes with Ralph reflecting on a moment from the past – when he had glimpsed his sister Theresa and colleague Old Chao floating in the swimming pool together – a moment that had been left out of the plot, but which is now retrieved. The inconsequentiality of the moment, its quotidian quality, irradiates it with meaning and sets it apart from the framework that had structured Ralph's story so far. Gish Jen's double gesture, taking up and abandoning the realist mode of the *Bildungsroman*, reveals the simultaneous appropriation and redeployment of realist modes, a move that characterizes many contemporary Asian American novels.

The concern with recovering ethical agency from a model minority identity ineluctably tied to the exigencies of social mobility and manifested in the destructive dynamics of family life, reappears in Chang-rae Lee's *Native Speaker* and *A Gesture Life*. Henry Park's camouflage as a spy in *Native Speaker* is a metaphor for his conditioning as a Korean American son and Asian American overachiever, but he divests his job of ethical content until he is forced to confront his role in an Asian American politician's downfall and the deportation of undocumented workers. Our last glimpse of Henry, after he stops working as a spy, is of him dressed in the playful costume of a "Speech Monster" helping his white American wife teach English to immigrant children. His retreat to the cramped space of public school classrooms, from where he exorcizes the fear of misspeaking English from the next generation of new Americans, reconstructs his racial identity as a lesson for how to transform immigrants into Americans. But the space afforded for such action is small and tenuous in comparison to the wide world of ambition and power in which he had earlier ranged. Similarly, *A Gesture Life* ends with a renunciation of the strategies of acquisition, possession, and acceptance that had passed for a successful life for the protagonist Doc Hata. Like *Native Speaker* and *Typical American*, *A Gesture Life* ends with the main character revoking his model minority identity. But all three novels merely hint at or leave unexplored the alternative trajectory of their protagonists' lives. They reside in the "not yet" of novelistic time.

On the surface, Bharati Mukherjee's *Jasmine* seems to offer a euphoric affirmation of the model minority that opposes the bleak readings of it by Gish Jen and Chang-rae Lee. *Jasmine* genders and sexualizes the stereotype, representing its heroine as a love goddess before whose irresistible beauty men succumb. And yet if we push away from an intentionalist reading of the novel (based on the author's statements about Jasmine's romance with America) to a feminist postcolonial reading, the contradictions in the representation of exuberant Americanization become apparent. Notwithstanding Jasmine's avowals of her love for the men who enable her mobility, their association with her leaves them dead or crippled, and the narration is rich with ambiguity about her power to elicit love and inflict death. Structurally, this contradiction can be traced to the effort to graft the plot of feminist maturation to a conventionally gendered love plot. The narrative energies of the feminist plot that cannot be channeled into the love plot erupt in the form of extreme violence that marks the heroine's progress across America. As Kristen Carter-Sanborn observes, the novel equivocates about Jasmine's agency in this violence – she has to assume the aspect of Kali to murder the sexual predator Half-Face, and Jasmine disavows the links between her identities: "Jyoti of Hasnapur was not Jasmine, Duff's day mummy and Taylor and Wylie's *au pair* in Manhattan; *that* Jasmine isn't *this* Jane Ripplemeyer having lunch with Mary Webb at the University Club today?"[22]

But if the love plot allegorizes Jasmine's Americanization and modernization and is accompanied by an undertow of death and violence, then how are we to read the terms of her consent to becoming American? On one level, Jasmine speaks of the desire to assimilate that drives her progress, "greedy with wants and reckless from hope." Yet Jasmine's repeated insistence that her various names signify roles she plays and not an identity she inhabits suggests that *Jasmine* may not be a novel of assimilation as much as a novel of passing. In this scheme, passing does not mean being taken for white, but remaining invisible by being taken for a stereotypical Asian. Viewing Jasmine this way aligns her more closely with Chang-rae Lee's Henry Park and Doc Hata, who pass as model Asian Americans in order that their purposes remain undetected. Yet while Henry Park and Doc Hata come to realize that the model minority is an abject identity, Mukherjee's *Jasmine* is more ambivalent, insisting that volition can turn abjection into empowerment: an illegal Punjabi woman can get out of Flushing with a fake green card; an au pair can become her employer's lover; an undocumented woman can become the banker's almost-wife.[c]

The tropes of spying, (tres)passing, disguise, and role-playing that suffuse Asian American novels of the 1980s and 1990s reveal the gaps between the ideals of emancipation and equality that drove civil rights struggles and their outcome in the liberal pluralism of a multicultural polity where recognition of diversity reifies and congeals identities. The passage from invisibility to recognition is a treacherous one, as these fictions remind us, because recognition may again endorse racial difference, however well intentioned.

While the center of gravity in these later novels lies in the post-civil rights tensions and identity politics of the United States, many contemporary Asian American novels broaden the frame to encompass alternative emphases on transnational ties or repressed histories of dispossession. The emergence of transnational audiences has led to new themes, storylines, and extensive formal experimentation in the contemporary novel. It has also broken down the compartmentalization of ethnic literature as a subnational canon, instead building intertextual linkages with Asian language and Asian Anglophone literatures.

c See Bruce Robbins, "The worlding of the American novel," chapter 66 in this volume, for a discussion of Mukherjee's representation of America in *Jasmine*, 1099.

Jessica Hagedorn's *Dogeaters* (1990) uses magical realism to excavate the layered histories of Spanish and US colonialism in the Philippines and to anatomize the insatiable consumption and brutal political repression of the country from the 1950s through the 1980s. The novel is set in Manila, where nominal independence belies the omnipresence of America through Hollywood movies, the visits of reporters, tourists, and GIs – and in the bloodlines and longings of the characters. Hagedorn imagines the postcolonial Filipino self as haunted by a transnational, ineluctable melancholy. The incoherence of the narrative, a dense concatenation of events, dialogue, and characters, suggests the failure of the postcolonial nation to plot its own destiny. The term "Asian American," when applied to this and many other Filipino American novels, refers to a neocolonial relation in which the native is already displaced, even in the homeland. As the characters in a disco joke to a German visitor, the Philippines has become a country of guests and ghosts. The cacophony of voices and media in the public sphere – radio, television, newspapers, films, gossip, love songs, prayers, advertisements – drown out the torture, sexual exploitation, poverty, and ecological catastrophe in the islands. Hagedorn's magical realism finds expression in labyrinthine anachronic plotlines, turgid dream sequences, copious religious, folkloric, and spiritual iconography that breaks down the boundary between reality and fantasy, exposing the gap between political realities and the mirage of development and sovereignty promoted by the elite.

Similarly, Lê Thi Diem Thúy's *The Gangster We Are All Looking For* (2003) reimagines the conventional realist immigrant plot of settlement and social mobility, instead mapping lines of flight and return between Vietnam and San Diego. Like *Dogeaters*, the novel is a disorienting collage of events, memories, images, and dreams. The story centers on a family of Vietnamese refugees broken by a war that follows them across the ocean; we might even consider *Gangster* to be a war novel of sorts, according to the more capacious framework laid out by John Carlos Rowe elsewhere in this volume.[d] Time and space in the novel reflect the unmooring of the protagonists. Time is fragmented and disjointed, while space is divided between land, sky, and water: to the narrator, the earth signifies entrapment, restriction, division; the sky opens up the horizon through the possibility of flight; but only the water represents death, rebirth, memory, and return. The book's epigraph translates the significance of water in the novel: "In Vietnamese, the word for *water* and the word for *a nation, a country*, and *a homeland* are one and the same: nu'ó'c."

d See John Carlos Rowe, "US novels and US wars," chapter 49.

Through the metaphor of water, the novel refigures the multiple meanings of belonging latent in the name of the original homeland to accommodate the condition of being between two places. This transpacific topography signifies a contemporary middle passage that rewrites traumatic loss as literally oceanic.

The "post" of Asian American postmodernity is ghost-ridden, an "after" of uneasy pasts, tenuous presents, and uncertain futures. Its nerve-center lies in disturbed belongings that result from wars, colonialism, and migration stretching over a century and a half and linking America and Asia. The Asian American category itself has been both a fiction and an incentive to fiction, a figure of and for transition. The history of Asian American novels highlights the need for constructing different frames (transoceanic, hemispheric, archipelagic, West Coast, diasporic) to situate Asian American writing. Finally, the development of the Asian American novel reveals that the formal changes in Asian American literature may not proceed in tandem with dominant literary movements, instead anticipating and following them in distinctive ways.

Notes

1. For a detailed analysis of the categorization of Asian American literature, see Susan Koshy, "The Fiction of Asian American Literature," *Yale Journal of Criticism* 9 (1996): 35–65.
2. Onoto Watanna is the pseudonym of Winnifred Eaton Babcock, who was part Chinese and part English.
3. It is important to note that the careers of some Asian American novelists cut across the historical divisions mentioned above and participate in and inflect literary movements in both periods.
4. Hans Bertens, *The Idea of the Postmodern: A History* (London: Routledge, 1995), 11.
5. Stuart Hall coins the term "relations of representation" to describe the struggle for access and control over the apparatus of cultural representation in black cultural politics. Stuart Hall, "New Ethnicities," in *Black British Cultural Studies: A Reader*, ed. Houston A. Baker Jr., Manthia Diawara, and Ruth H. Lindeborg (Chicago: University of Chicago Press, 1996), 164.
6. For a lucid and insightful defense of the project, see Jinqi Ling, *Narrating Nationalisms: Ideology and Form in Asian American Literature* (New York: Oxford University Press, 1998); for feminist, queer, and diasporic critiques, see King-Kok Cheung, "The Woman Warrior versus The Chinaman Pacific: Must a Chinese American Critic Choose between Feminism and Heroism?" in *Conflicts in Feminism*, ed. Marianne Hirsch and Evelyn Fox Keller (New York: Routledge, 1990), 234–251; David L. Eng, *Racial Castration: Managing Masculinity in Asian America* (Durham, NC: Duke University Press, 2001); Elaine H. Kim, "'Such

Opposite Creatures': Men and Women in Asian American Literature," *Michigan Quarterly Review* 29.1 (1990): 68–94; Koshy, "Fiction of Asian American Literature"; and Sau-ling Cynthia Wong, "Autobiography as Guided Chinatown Tour? Maxine Hong Kingston's *The Woman Warrior* and the Chinese-American Autobiographical Controversy," in *Multicultural Autobiography: American Lives*, ed. James Robert Payne (Knoxville: University of Tennessee Press, 1992), 249–279.

7. Elaine H. Kim, *Asian American Literature: An Introduction to the Writings and Their Social Context* (Philadelphia: Temple University Press, 1982); Viet Thanh Nguyen, *Race and Resistance: Literature and Politics in Asian America* (New York: Oxford University Press, 2002); Wong, "Autobiography as Guided Chinatown Tour?"
8. Catherine Gallagher, "The Rise of Fictionality," in *The Novel*, ed. Franco Moretti, 2 vols. (Princeton: Princeton University Press, 2006), 1:347, 340.
9. Felix Martinez-Bonati, "The Act of Writing Fiction," *New Literary History* 11 (1980): 35.
10. Notwithstanding her pioneering role as the first Asian American novelist, Onoto Watanna was until recently regarded as an ambivalent figure by Asian American critics. Her opportunistic act in passing as part-Japanese was seen in contrast to her sister Edith Eaton's open embrace of her Chinese ancestry. Edith Eaton took on the pen name Sui Sin Far and was a strong advocate of Chinese Americans in her journalistic and fictional work. Recent revisionist readings of the work of these two writers by Eve Oishi, Samina Najmi, Maureen Honey, Jean Lee Cole, Viet Thanh Nguyen, and Tomo Hattori have highlighted the complex gender and racial negotiations in their work.
11. Maureen Honey and Jean Lee Cole point to Watanna's use of Jack's perspective as the narrative point of view in the story as one of Watanna's key revisions to the Long story. "Introduction," in *Madame Butterfly/John Luther Long and A Japanese Nightingale/Onoto Watanna (Winnifred Eaton): Two Orientalist Texts*, ed. Maureen Honey and Jean Lee Cole (New Brunswick, NJ: Rutgers University Press, 2002), 7. For a detailed analysis of Long's story as an interracial romance, see Susan Koshy, *Sexual Naturalization: Asian Americans and Miscegenation* (Stanford, CA: Stanford University Press, 2004), chapter 1.
12. Koshy, *Sexual Naturalization*, chapter 1.
13. See Amy Ling, *Between Worlds: Women Writers of Chinese Ancestry* (New York: Pergamon Press, 1990).
14. According to Marlon H. Hom, the progressive Chinatown writers embraced social realism and regionalism as vehicles for representing the complex realities of Chinatown communities ("Chinatown Literature during the Last Ten Years [1939–1949] by Wenquan," *Amerasia Journal* 9.1 (1982): 75–100).
15. Jeffery Chan, "Introduction," in Louis Chu, *Eat a Bowl of Tea* (New York: Lyle Stuart, 1995), 4.
16. *Ibid.*, 2.

17. For a detailed account of these controversies, see Cheung, "Must a Chinese American Critic Choose," and Kim, *Asian American Literature*, 46–49.
18. The similarity between Richard Wright's *Black Boy* (1945) and Bulosan's autobiographical text are striking in this respect.
19. Maxine Hong Kingston, "Cultural Mis-readings by American Reviewers," in *Asian and Western Writers in Dialogue: New Cultural Identities*, ed. Guy Amirthanayagam (London: Macmillan, 1982), 55–65.
20. Ling, *Narrating Nationalisms*, 118–120.
21. Richard Thompson Ford, *The Race Card: How Bluffing about Bias Makes Race Relations Worse* (New York: Farrar, 2008), 32, 263.
22. Kristen Carter-Sanborn, " 'We Murder Who We Were': Jasmine and the Violence of Identity," *American Literature* 66.3 (1994): 573–593.

64

Toni Morrison and the post-civil rights African American novel

MICHAEL HILL

African American novelists of the 1950s cast long shadows.[a] In addition to Richard Wright, James Baldwin, and Ralph Ellison, worthy writers like Gwendolyn Brooks, Owen Dodson, Chester Himes, Mark Kennedy, Paule Marshall, Ann Petry, and J. Saunders Redding produced books that marked a Golden Age. This era was significant not only because nascent black luminaries received fellowships, access to eminent literary publications, and prestigious civic appointments,[1] but also because even among anonymous neophytes, there was an exponential increase in publication.[2] While this movement waxed through the 1950s, it was waning by the time the Civil Rights Act of 1964 passed. On one level, the African American novel's declining eminence can be attributed to the rise of the Black Arts Movement, a literary movement known for poetry and drama rather than extended fiction.[3] Yet a more accurate assessment detects an incubatory aspect of the 1960s. Not only were William Melvin Kelley, Frank London Brown, William Demby, and Margaret Walker crafting works that portended the future of black narrative, but also John A. Williams, Ernest Gaines, Clarence Major,[b] Ishmael Reed, and John Edgar Wideman commenced careers that would flower fully in the next three decades.[4] If a premonitory energy surrounded African American novel-writing in the 1960s, then 1970 signaled a shift. No figure exemplified this transition better than Toni Morrison.

a Lovalerie King summarizes the immediate post-World War II state of the African American novel in "Ellison and Baldwin: aesthetics, activism, and the social order," chapter 43, 719–721.

b Placing William Demby and Clarence Major in the context of "second-wave postmodernism," Ursula Heise suggests how their efforts in the 1960s and 1970s fit into and responded to a broader experimental mode in the American novel. See her essay in this volume, "Postmodern novels," chapter 58, 975.

Morrison stands as barely disputed champ of the African American novel. Although her celebrity status induces some observers to chide her for presumptive entitlement, a glance over her long professional life suggests that Morrison's current tendency to "strut" has an interesting history.[5] During the mid-1960s, she completed a draft of her first novel and began to circulate it. Initially, it aroused little interest, but Holt, Rinehart, and Winston eventually published the book, thereby beginning perhaps the most illustrious career in all of African American literary history. Morrison snipped in a 1994 afterword that upon its appearance, *The Bluest Eye* (1970) was "with very few exceptions ... dismissed, trivialized" and "misread," but A. Yemisi Jimoh notes more accurately that though the book "received faint praise from most, though not all, reviewers," high-profile reviews in the *New York Times Book Review* and *The New Yorker* gave Morrison "national recognition that was invaluable."[6]

If the reception of *The Bluest Eye* partook of some unevenness, the book itself displayed no such equivocation. Centered on Pecola Breedlove, an eleven-year-old black girl who lives in Lorain, Ohio, *The Bluest Eye* juxtaposes explicit portraits of self-loathing with implicit meditation on how to narrate such experiences. The result is a vexed testimony to the disintegration of a personality.[c] Defined by a middle class, a working class, and a set of pariahs, Lorain's black community notes Pecola's distress, yet it mangles the project of empathizing with her. When she seeks help in understanding her family's commitment to wearing the "cloak of ugliness," each class "clean[ed]" itself "on her" and felt "beautiful" as they stood "astride her" suffering. The lacerating climax of this novel is Cholly Breedlove's rape of Pecola, his daughter.[7] This act seems a perverse non sequitur, but Morrison, in what would become her patented complicating move, ties Cholly's transgression to a broader abdication of empathy. This abdication implicates not only Mr. Yacobowski, the white store owner who "need not waste the effort of a glance" on Pecola, but also Claudia and Frieda, Pecola's friends, who sense a quasi-predatory quality even in their pity for her.

The Bluest Eye scrutinizes how mainstream America's children's books and Hollywood-fueled cultural myths savage the black psyche,[d] yet it also attends

c In this volume, Maria Farland links Pecola's story to the "mental-breakdown narratives" that defined 1960s women's novels. In addition, she views Pecola's rape as an adjunct to later narratives that warn about men's inherent status as "sexual predators." See "Literary feminisms," chapter 56, 934, 938.

d Mark McGurl's focus on the ambivalent place of television and film in the American novel provides an excellent backdrop against which to contemplate Morrison's depictions of Pecola and her mother Pauline. See "The novel, mass culture, mass media" in this volume, chapter 41, esp. 696–697.

carefully to the way that the black community internalizes a debilitating penchant for white cultural emulation.[8] By 1973, when Morrison published her second novel, *Sula*, examining intraracial adjustments to broader socio-cultural realities had become an even more acute feature of her artistry. Highlighting the surprising truths of such explorations, the novelist made the pariah class a centerpiece of her narrative. In *Sula*, Morrison uses the small-town Ohio life that provided the context for *The Bluest Eye* to dramatize black female independence.

Sula Peace and Nel Wright possess contrasting personalities. Over two lives filled with deathly secrets, crushing betrayals, and belated revelations, they ultimately complement one another, reflecting Morrison's resuscitation of Zora Neale Hurston's pairing of Janie and Phoeby in *Their Eyes Were Watching God* (1937). The friendship also points to the resources that black women would have to marshal to "use each other to grow on."[e] Although this growth finally produces a convergence, the novel initially posits Sula and Nel as opposites. Sula matures in the Peace household, a space defined by needful promiscuity, murderous arson, and deceptively sacrificial maternity. Presided over by Eva Peace, Sula's grandmother, it is a domicile whose architectural idiosyncrasies match the whimsical nature of its proprietor. Where whimsy eventually becomes a governing spirit of Sula's character, Nel receives from her parents the full curriculum in propriety, complete with clothespins to narrow her Negro-inclining nose. If these disparate upbringings map to two destinies of black womanhood – bohemian free-spiritedness and bourgeois assimilation – then the fates of *Sula*'s principals illuminate other aspects of Morrison's artistic vision.

While the Bottom, the black neighborhood depicted in *Sula*, is the place that was razed "to make room for the . . . City Golf Course," Sula's insistent me-ness prevents her from being erased. Sula registers black feminist possibility. She eschews family life, declining to wed and sending her grandmother to a nursing home. She implodes conventional concepts of female ambition, attending college and traveling to whatever big city strikes her fancy. Finally, she revolutionizes fraternity. In the place of possessiveness and defensive affection, she presents a luxuriant narcissism that confounds and illumines the patterns of black community. Nel's final gesture in the novel provides

e Referencing *Their Eyes Were Watching God*, Elizabeth Freeman mentions the narrative importance of female friendship in "Reimagining genders and sexualities," chapter 57, 953–954.

evidence that she has learned Sula's lesson. After scorning Sula and the betrayal that had robbed her of so much, Nel visits Eva Peace at Sunnydale nursing home and listens to her suggest that there "never was no difference between" Nel and Sula. Baffled and offended by this equivalence, Nel leaves Eva, but the next day, after Sula's funeral, she confesses, "All that time, I thought I was missing [my husband] . . . [but] We was girls together." The girlhood that Nel and Sula share is not idyllic; it includes a joint participation in the drowning of a young boy and a confrontation with threatening whites that leads Sula to cut off the tip of one of her fingers. Nor is their succeeding womanhood any easier: their friendship is sundered for years when Sula sleeps with Nel's husband. Despite these difficulties, Nel and Sula discern "the slant of life that made it possible to stretch it to its limits"; thus, they grant one another an irrevocable permission to exult in being.

Sula was shortlisted for the 1975 National Book Award, and it suggested Morrison's continued ability to intrigue America's literary taste-makers. That near-miss, though, indicated the delicate choreography that "serious" African American novels required. Morrison reveals one aspect of this dancing in a discussion of *Sula*'s structure. She states that unlike any other of her works, this novel bridges the "threshold between the reader and the black-topic text" by constructing a "safe, welcoming lobby."[9] Put more crudely, she believes that *Sula* –albeit with aesthetic felicity – pays "deference . . . to the 'white' gaze."[10] That sensitivity to white spectatorship, a point of contention at least since Langston Hughes's "The Negro Artist and the Racial Mountain" (1926), had become combustible during the 1960s as the rhetoric of the Black Arts Movement (BAM) gained greater circulation. Where Amiri Baraka, a leading BAM spokesman, opined that "the Black artist's role in America . . . is to report and reflect so precisely the nature of the society" that "white men" will "tremble, curse, and go mad," Morrison admits that in her second novel, she also thought expansively about how a white readership could be eased into her fiction.[11]

In the early 1970s, Morrison was not the only African American novelist sorting through these issues. After the transformations prompted by the Civil Rights Movement, black literature emerged as a potentially fecund, yet increasingly indeterminate space. On one hand, writers embraced the expanded opportunities provided by political progress. At the same time, they sought a mode of expression that balanced individual prerogatives and social responsibility. During the 1950s, Ralph Ellison triumphed as an arbiter of novelistic excellence.[f] Stressing the formal challenges of extended fiction, he insisted that black writers suffered far more from technical deficiencies than from socio-political inhibitions.[12] His assessment made him a frequent official foil of the Black Arts Movement, but it also echoed resoundingly across the decades. Ellison's focus on craft became an abiding preoccupation of the post-civil rights African American novelist.

While Ellison's notion of craft blended black cultural references with frequently privileged white artistic models, the most adept practitioners of the Black Arts Movement advanced an artistry that extolled the utter sufficiency of blackness. Although African American novelists after the Civil Rights Movement would on the whole reject BAM's rhetoric as essentialist, they did admire the authority that the movement conferred on black culture. In fact, their confrontations with BAM yielded many of the recurrent themes that define the archive of contemporary African American expression, namely the cultural disorientation of the black middle class, the place of diaspora in the imagination of the black self, the possibilities for love in black existence, and the stakes of violence in black life. These themes, in combination with an insistence on formal innovation, afforded black novelists a highly productive opportunity to reconsider the imperatives both of their careers and their obligations (if any) to a broader racial fate. The results expose a literary tradition questing for and then repeatedly discovering its soul. The interplay between Toni Morrison and Ishmael Reed suggests the early stirrings of such discovery.

Ishmael Reed's *Mumbo Jumbo* (1972) offers "an extended commentary on the history of the black novel."[13] Where Morrison, in *The Bluest Eye* and *Sula*, engages the problems of African American storytelling via a midwestern narrative, Reed casts his madcap dash through history on an epic scale. He examines how Western civilization from the Crusades through the Jazz Age strove to stifle black creativity.[g] The spirit of this creativity, here figured as the "psychic endemic" Jes Grew, manifests a syncretist quality, but its chief antecedents are Egyptian cosmology, Haitian Vodun, and New Orleans-inspired jazz. Darryl Dickson-Carr observes that "one ironic trope in *Mumbo*

f Linking Ellison's "political detachment" to "a rigid dedication to form," Lovalerie King identifies the traits that aided his ascent within the American literati. See chapter 43, 718.

g Ursula Heise suggests that Reed's socio-political critique is "highly self-referential." Attending to his incorporation of "photos, handwritten letters and a bibliography," she concludes that *Mumbo Jumbo* is a part of a postmodernist moment that emphasizes the metafictional possibilities of the novel. See chapter 58, 970–971.

Jumbo concerns the practically inevitable ideological compromises that follow when African Americans . . . try to find their place by seeking white patronage."[14] Dickson-Carr's assessment illustrates how Reed, from a different slant than Morrison, also attends to the interrelationship between black expression and white onlooking. *Mumbo Jumbo* was the first book by an African American to be nominated for the National Book Award since 1957, when James Baldwin received that distinction for *Giovanni's Room* (1956). The fact that Morrison and Reed, two writers who employ radically divergent aesthetics, both garnered such recognition within a few years of each other suggests both an expanding mainstream capacity to detect black literary excellence and a growing consensus on the variety within black artistry. Thus, the 1970s African American novel sheds a frequently constricting feature, the belief in a uniform narrative practice. One more example affirms this contention and hints at why it is a key development.

Ernest Gaines published his first novel, *Catherine Carmier*, in 1964, and as he acknowledges in several interviews, he used Ivan Turgenev's *Fathers and Sons* (1862) as a guide.[15] Although Gaines's reputation grew with the appearance of his second book *Of Love and Dust* (1966), it was not until the 1971 publication of *The Autobiography of Miss Jane Pittman* that his critical and commercial stock afforded him celebrity status. A first-person narrative told by the text's 110-year-old eponymous protagonist, this work continued Gaines's chronicling of black life in the South. In addition, it marked the writer's firm entrenchment in narrative forms that owed less to European masters than to the folk rituals of segregated agrarian life. This is not to say that Gaines eschewed his earlier tutelage or renounced the influence of white writers like William Faulkner or Ernest Hemingway; rather, he folded the things that he learned from them into an overarching frame that more confidently incorporated the particulars of his Louisiana world. The results, while different from the products of Toni Morrison and Ishmael Reed, shared a similar fate with those two authors' early 1970s novels. Shortlisted for the 1972 Pulitzer, *The Autobiography of Miss Jane Pittman*, like *Sula* and *Mumbo Jumbo*, almost won a major literary prize. This additional close call with a pre-eminent marker of national literary value could be understood as an index of assimilation; however, the varied styles, politics, and temperaments of Gaines, Morrison, and Reed beg a more satisfying explanation. The "woodshedding" that black novelists completed in the 1960s prepared them technically while the cultural pride that the Black Arts Movement fostered alerted them to the rich and unique artistic possibilities of black life.[16] Thus, the 1970s, turning on the achievements of Morrison, Reed, and Gaines, instigated an inventiveness in the African American novel that continued unabated for at least fifteen years. A glance at three other novelists who began their careers in that milieu suggests the dynamism of that experimentation.

Gayl Jones's *Corregidora* (1975) impressed Toni Morrison as a paradigm-shifting performance. The elder writer confessed that "what was uppermost in my mind while I read her manuscript was that no novel about any black woman could be the same after this."[17] In one sense, Morrison's praise could be understood as self-interested. After all, as a Random House editor, she did tout Jones's work. Notwithstanding the cynical savvy of such an outlook, the raw sincerity of both *Corregidora* and Jones's second novel *Eva's Man* (1976) arrests simplistic cries of nepotism. By patiently and painfully recovering women's stories, both *Corregidora* and *Eva's Man* complicate earlier portraits of black heterosexual interaction and anticipate the darker side of the late twentieth-century fascination with eroticism. Where Jones delivers narratives of unremitting claustrophobia, Charles Johnson's first novel, *Faith and the Good Thing* (1974), engages interior consciousness via the narrative of relocation that also underlies Alice Walker's *The Third Life of Grange Copeland* (1970). In addition, Johnson's protagonist, Faith Cross, has been astutely compared to the central character in Ralph Ellison's *Invisible Man*.[18] Though their shared transition from the South to the North makes such comparisons inviting, the ideologies that animate Johnson's work place his character in an alternate philosophical universe. The extent of that alterity can best be understood in light of Johnson's second novel, *Oxherding Tale* (1982), which conveys its author's intent, *à la* Ellison, to place blackness in conversation with the broadest meditations on human existence. Where Ellison favored André Malraux, Johnson turns to Melville, Fielding, Sterne, and "most importantly" Hermann Hesse.[19] Johnson makes slavery the main subject of *Oxherding Tale*, but instead of returning to bondage as a site of physical domination and psychic disintegration, Johnson muses more broadly on the phenomenological meaning of enslavement. This brand of universalism not only makes Johnson a crucial forebear of younger black iconoclasts like Percival Everett and Jeffrey Renard Allen but also reveals how late twentieth-century black novels acknowledge their precursors even while insisting on fresh narrative approaches.

Gayl Jones and Charles Johnson provide two distinct solutions to the question of black art and white observation. Jones immerses her characters in an unrelieved probing of racial misery and thereby blunts the relevance of the white gaze. By contrast, Johnson places black experience squarely in the light of Asian and European philosophy. If these writers figuratively allude to their own artistry in their fiction, then John Edgar Wideman makes such thoughts explicit. After achieving acclaim as the first African American Rhodes Scholar since Alain Locke, Wideman wrote *A Glance Away* (1967), *Hurry Home* (1970), and *The Lynchers* (1973), three novels that were, according to Wilfred D. Samuels, more intent on establishing a "rudimentary hu(e)man and modernist experience" than on fully exploring "the unique qualities of African American existence."[20] Critics admired Wideman's works, lauding their universality, but eventually the writer found these estimates insufficient. In 1973, Wideman began an eight-year creative hibernation during which he embarked on a "discovery of and immersion in the work of black writers."[21] As a result, he started composing fiction that included intellectual characters who were more attuned to "the needs, concerns, and traditions of black people more generally."[22] Wideman's odyssey epitomizes both the insecurities of 1970s African American novelists and their resolve to dynamically search for solutions in a fusion of several priorities, a blend that is best understood as politicized virtuosity. One novel that reveals the textures of and the reactions to this combination is Toni Morrison's *Song of Solomon* (1977).

Macon Dead III, the protagonist of *Song of Solomon*, symbolizes a central dilemma of late twentieth-century blackness, the struggle to come to grips with upper-middle-class existence.[23] Poised between civil rights expectations and the more rancorous admonitions of black nationalism, Macon, nicknamed "Milkman" because of how long his mother nursed him, alternately manifests enervating entitlement and poignant ennui. These emotions occasionally erupt as full-blown controversies, but more often, they are vague contours only faintly glimpsed through the miasma of his family's history. That history becomes an enigmatic, yet telling riddle of modern black identity. Milkman's father, Macon Dead II, accrues his fortune via a real estate empire,[h] and harkening back to Tyree Tucker in Richard Wright's *The Long Dream* (1959) and Bill Hod in Ann Petry's *The Narrows* (1953), he represents entrepreneurship as a route to secure black masculinity.[i] While Macon achieves affluence, its soullessness mocks him. He turns to his son, hoping for redemption, but Milkman, scorning his father's fixation on commerce, eventually fights his

h Robert Levine suggests that Morrison's attention to real estate originates in the precarious nature of ownership in African American history. See "The early African American novel," chapter 16, 273–274.

i Describing the American "business" novel between 1865 and 1917, David Zimmerman observes that these books "aim to attach familiar meanings, emotional significance, and . . . philosophical and aesthetic import to the vertiginous economic changes transforming American culture." See his essay in this volume, "Novels of American business, industry, and consumerism," chapter 24, 409.

own self-indulgence and discovers the deep stakes of his kin and their legacy. This discovery entails not only repeating Grange Copeland's reverse Great Migration, this time from Michigan to Virginia, but also witnessing the suicide of his cousin, the violent radicalism of his best friend, and the lay-down-my-life-for-you generosity of his aunt.[24] Despite or perhaps because of these taxing tutelages, Milkman's journey metaphorically distills the way forward not just for African Americans in general but also for novelists particularly. To the latter group, Morrison suggests that there can be no seamless integration and no jettisoning of inconvenient truths. Just as Milkman must discover and accept the entire labyrinthine unruliness of his clan, the black artist must unflinchingly confront both a personal and a national past. Given the central role that this confrontation plays in the next decade of black novel-writing, perhaps it is fitting then that with *Song of Solomon*, Toni Morrison became the first African American since 1953 to win a major prize, The National Book Critics Circle Award, for a novel. Her efforts generated immense momentum.

By the early 1980s, African American novelists saw white readers' influence as less important. This change stemmed both from the emergence of a skilled, sizeable class of academic literary critics and the arrival of a raft of new talent.[25] While Ernest Gaines, Ishmael Reed, Paule Marshall, Toni Morrison, Charles Johnson, Alice Walker, and John Edgar Wideman took their place as seasoned artists who between them shared a double handful of mainstream fiction awards, increasingly and often through their own shepherding, they were forced to share the stage with up-and-comers like Percival Everett, David Bradley, and Jamaica Kincaid. Morrison, as an editor at Random House, directly promoted the careers of Leon Forrest, Gloria Naylor, Toni Cade Bambara, and Gayl Jones; Reed's work with the Before Columbus Foundation made him both a gadfly and a crucial facilitator.[26] The elder novelists' occupation of writer-in-residence positions made them more accessible. Consider for example that David Bradley, while a student at Penn, took creative writing courses from John Edgar Wideman.[27] Such contacts did not establish discipleship, but they did diminish the authority of Eurocentric and Anglo-American models of narration. The evidence can be seen in the diverse approaches that black novelists take to delivering their stories, and also in the prominence of themes like slavery, diasporic negotiations, middle-class angst, and black vernacular speech in their works. Published on the cusp of the new decade, novels by Bambara, Bradley, and Everett clarify these trends.

Bambara's *The Salt Eaters* (1980) presents Velma Henry, a veteran community organizer, whose experiences symbolize the challenges that attend the search for black unity. Disenchanted after a life spent agitating for social justice, Velma attempts suicide and subsequently consults a spiritual healer in hopes of re-balancing herself. Nelson George argues that Bambara's depiction "taps into the collective exhaustion of the generation that fought furiously for black advancement but" then found "itself confronting an unfinished agenda and middle age."[28] If Bambara casts this dilemma as a Southern and a midlife problem, then David Bradley and Percival Everett show that at the beginning of the 1980s, African Americans across wide geographic and age ranges were striving to re-anchor themselves in satisfying rituals of cultural definition. Bradley's second novel, *The Chaneysville Incident* (1981), chronicles its protagonist's return to his West Pennsylvania hometown after an absence of nearly a decade. The book's central character finds that his mentor's burial unexpectedly arouses unanswered questions about his father's death that he thought he had repressed, and he re-enters a world of hunting, pre-industrial existence, and racial intrigue that his life in Philadelphia had insulated him from. Craig Suder, the protagonist of Percival Everett's first novel, *Suder* (1983), is a third baseman for the Seattle Mariners. When he finds himself mired in the worst offensive drought of his career, Craig, at the behest of his manager, embarks on a wild journey that includes an interlude with an abused child and an elephant named Renoir. Unlike Bambara's and Bradley's protagonists, whose epiphanies require literal reconciliation within the context of black communities, Craig's situation involves squaring a Southern childhood with the almost absurd tableaux of his existence in the Pacific Northwest.[j] That negotiation becomes all the more fascinating when Everett suggests that on top of the traditional themes of male adolescence, Craig must sort through the possibility that he is pre-disposed toward the madness that so excruciatingly unraveled his mother's life.

That these portrayals should manifest such diverse locales even as they explore similar themes bespeaks two abiding truths of African American novels after the 1970s. First, the clustered production model that ruled from 1945 to 1960 had receded. It was no longer necessary to be in Chicago or New York in order to access cultural currents. In addition, despite dizzying aesthetic variegation, novelists were, by recourse and innovation, settling upon the master tropes of twentieth-century black representation. These tropes often carried prominent traces of what Claudia Tate has called "the manifest text" of blackness, [29] but just as frequently, in works from the early 1980s to the 1990s,

j Chester Himes predates Everett in exploring Westward migration as an adjunct to black masculinity. See Lovalerie King's discussion of Himes's *If He Hollers Let Him Go* in chapter 43, 720.

they reflected sensitivity to the contemplation of bourgeois ambivalence and diasporic complexity. Both are on display in the most highly decorated novel in the black literary tradition.

Alice Walker's *The Color Purple* (1982) still stands as the only African American novel to win both the Pulitzer Prize and the National Book Award.[30] Presented as a series of letters, this book tells the story of Celie, Nettie, Shug, Mister, and a whole host of others who move to and fro in a small Georgia town.

The Color Purple's climactic episode occurs when the songstress Shug and her erstwhile husband Grady prepare to leave Georgia after visiting with Celie and her husband Mister for several weeks. On the eve of their departure, Celie announces that she is leaving with them. Mister ridicules Celie's intention, and she replies with one of the most withering maledictions in all of African American literature: "Until you do right by me, everything you touch will crumble . . . everything you even dream about will fail . . . every lick you hit me you will suffer twice." This scene stokes immense rancor among commentators like Ishmael Reed because they feel that it is the culmination of Walker's demonization of black masculinity.[31] Such vitriol may be justified, but lost in debates about *The Color Purple* is the reconciliation between Celie and Mister that closes the book. On one level, this conclusion softens the novel's critique of sexism. By allowing Mister the luxury of genuine change, Walker could be seen as foisting responsibility for his repressive behavior onto another source. This analysis of Mister is undercut by the text's dim view of environmental determinism. Mister attributes his earlier disposition as much to cowardice as to the overbearing mandates of his father. While his prominence in *The Color Purple*'s latter pages could arouse intriguing speculation, the melodrama of Celie's reunion with her sister and children bespeaks an optimism that emphatically turns her misery into a prelude to epiphany. This portrayal suggests that while pain may be non-negotiable, the reaction to it matters infinitely more than the duress. Where Walker's embrace of such a possibility marks her distinctive position in the pantheon of late twentieth-century black novel-writing, it also suggests her distinction from other female novelists. A glimpse at two works by Gloria Naylor suggests why.

Contrasting the tendency to view Dixie as a space that foments sustenance and reconciliation, Naylor shows that the South can also contain despair-inducing repressions. For Willa Prescott and Ophelia "Cocoa" Day, two first cousins who feature prominently in *Linden Hills* (1985) and *Mama Day* (1988) respectively, the home place is Willow Springs, an island off the coast of Georgia and South Carolina that through a peculiarity of its history belongs to neither state. This amorphous quality becomes a metaphor of the anomalous position of the cousins as they leave the island and begin very different sorts of social ascents. Willa marries and moves to suburban Linden Hills, an exclusive subdivision that has been in her husband's family for several generations. Perverse mysteries lurk beneath the neighborhood's ordered exteriors,[k] and *Linden Hills* shows how wealth's destructive potential and social climbing's diabolical charades eventually lead to death. Cocoa goes to New York and marries in *Mama Day*, but the novel shows that joining the North and the South in the modern black psyche can be troublesome or even fatal. Naylor's novels capture the central conundrums of 1980s blackness, namely fears of racial betrayal, the perfidy of assimilation, and the search for cultural foundations. Shifting the ground of these considerations, several 1980s novels portray the African American contemplation of the black diaspora.

As early as *Brown Girl, Brownstones*, her 1959 debut novel, Paule Marshall offered a sustained consideration of the black immigrant experience in America. By the 1980s, she was still tilling this ground with works like *Praisesong for the Widow* (1983) and *Daughters* (1991). Joining her in these efforts were Jamaica Kincaid and Edwidge Danticat. Kincaid, through *Annie John* (1985) and *Lucy* (1990), extends Marshall's concentration on the young Caribbean female who must make sense of a world in physiological, geographic, and philosophical flux. For the black immigrant, the United States emerges as a space of surfeit. It is the nation where ostensibly the imagination can run free. But when the black immigrant confronts the reality of America in the works of Marshall and Kincaid, she quickly re-assesses all received myths and usually embraces a faith in her Carribbean heritage.[l] Edwidge Danticat is the youngest of this trio, and her explorations of Haiti bring a unique perspective to these matters. *Breath, Eyes, Memory* (1994) tells the story of a young black girl who has left Haiti to join her parents in New York City. This journey defines a chasm for the Haitian American. On one hand, life in New York means a sort of severance from the island past. Alternately, the enduring facts of ceremonies like testing, where a mother checks to make sure that her

k In her essay in this volume, Catherine Jurca analyzes *Linden Hills* in the broader context of American novels of suburban disaffection. See "The American novel and the rise of the suburbs," chapter 53, 888.

l Although he does not deal with black immigrants specifically, Tim Prchal's analysis of the differences between the melting pot and cultural pluralism suggest the stakes of their oscillation between an America of possibility and a homeland that never ceases to nurture. See "New Americans and the immigrant novel," chapter 25.

daughter is still a virgin, show that materially and metaphorically the hold of the island can never be escaped. If the protagonists of many of these books confront movement from an old homeland to a new one, then novels by Charles Johnson and Reginald McKnight, building on Alice Walker's enduring preoccupations, dramatize the African American return to Africa, a theme that literalizes the Afrocentricity debate in the 1990s between scholars like Henry Louis Gates, Jr. and Molefi K. Asante.[32]

Johnson, in the National Book Award-winning *Middle Passage* (1990) and McKnight in *I Get on the Bus* (1992) probe the implications of a sort of reverse Middle Passage. While scenes of African Americans looking at Africa have persisted in black literature, the cultural and academic conflicts of the Reagan–Bush era increased their significance. Foreign policies like Reagan's anti-embargo stance toward South Africa merged with domestic realities like the expansion of the prison-industrial complex to clarify certain contours of post-integration blackness. Facing these realities, novelists proffer clear-eyed portraits of African alternatives. Rutherford Calhoun, the nineteenth-century black protagonist of *Middle Passage*, tries to flee matrimony and his creditors by embarking upon a slave ship. When Rutherford confronts the cosmic repercussions of his collusion in the fate of the enslaved, he aids in a tribal mutiny and, once he makes his way back to the United States, decides that family life has its merits. Evan, the Peace Corps volunteer protagonist in McKnight's *I Get on the Bus*, is a distinctly late twentieth-century creation. Just as the romance of Africa fades in *The Color Purple*, the psychic pressure and the dizzying immensity of 1970s Senegal at first overwhelm him. Still, unlike Alice Walker, who in *Possessing the Secret of Joy* (1992) seemingly suggests the bankruptcy of African traditional culture, McKnight allows his protagonist to transform from a cynical American into a conscious, if still wary, appreciator of Senegalese complexity.

As a whole, post-civil rights African American novels bear markers of tremendous aesthetic and thematic refinement. During the 1980s, they moved from tentative explorations to commanding performances. In the 1990s, three commercial realities revealed intriguing dimensions of the black novel's development. First, the "Terry McMillan phenomenon" propelled black books into a perpetual place on bestseller lists. McMillan's career began with her self-published 1987 debut *Mama*, but her breakthrough work was *Waiting to Exhale* (1992), a book that sold over four million copies.[33] McMillan's success in relationship-themed black fiction promoted the careers of writers like J. California Cooper, Omar

Tyree, and Diane McKinney-Whetstone.[m] Beyond that category, two other commercially viable themes emerged in black fiction: crime and homosexuality.

Chester Himes's Coffin Ed and Gravedigger Jones detective novels of the 1950s and 1960s earned him international acclaim, and they also anticipated Walter Mosley's stories of the black private eye.[n] From the 1990 publication of *Devil in a Blue Dress*, Mosley has enjoyed perennial success. As with McMillan, his books have been transferred to the big screen and have cleared the way for African American crime novelists like Barbara Neely and Valerie Wilson Wesley.[34] Though detective fiction stands as a major achievement of late twentieth-century black writers, so is the expanded exploration of black masculinity. James Baldwin, in works like *Giovanni's Room*, *Another Country* (1962), and *Tell Me How Long the Train's Been Gone* (1969), claimed a mantle as one of the most forthright investigators of homosexuality in African American novels.[o] By the late 1980s, Baldwin's legacy was being furthered by Melvin Dixon's *Vanishing Rooms* (1990) and Randall Kenan's *A Visitation of Spirits*, two works that affirm homosexuality as a fact of black male experience.[35] Starting with his self-published debut *Invisible Life* (1991), E. Lynn Harris proved that black gay-themed fiction can control a substantial portion of the literary marketplace. Like Mosley, Harris has generated a string of bestselling books, and in the process, he has transformed the vocabulary of black sexuality.[36]

By the late 1980s, the African American novel had transformed from a brooding genre to a space of confident executions and unqualified critical and commercial successes. No events signal that truth more forcefully than the two novels that Toni Morrison wrote before she received the 1993 Nobel Prize. *Beloved* (1987) capitalizes on an interest in slave culture that had been mined in Margaret Walker's *Jubilee* (1966), Ernest Gaines's *The Autobiography of Miss Jane Pittman*, and Sherley Anne Williams's *Dessa Rose* (1986). Where those writers rode the immense wave of interest associated with Alex Haley's *Roots* (1976), Morrison approached the peculiar institution less as an epic, national drama than as a drama of interior consciousness. She began writing *Beloved* from a desire to chronicle "how [slaves] make a life," how they "relate[d] to

m Pamela Regis's account of how romance fiction achieved enormous popularity with women is clearly relevant to an understanding of Terry McMillan's career. See "Female genre fiction in the twentieth century," chapter 51 in this volume.

n For more on Himes's crime fiction, see Lovalerie King, chapter 43, 720–722.

o For an expanded discussion of Baldwin's importance to the tradition of gay-themed fiction, see Elizabeth Freeman's essay, chapter 57, 954–955.

one another."[37] In fulfilling this challenge, she produced one of the more arresting fictional accounts of the twentieth century.

The protagonist of *Beloved* is Sethe, a black single mother, who when confronted with the prospect of being returned to slavery in Kentucky, takes the life of one of her children and intends to kill the others. That act not only arouses the moral approbation of the broader black community but also occasions an intimate anguish within Sethe. She fiercely defends her actions, yet she knows that there is only one pardon that can truly take her off the cross. When Beloved, an enigmatic character who is alternately understood as the ghost of Sethe's murdered daughter and a distinct symbol of racial repression, shows up at Sethe's house, in Sethe's mind the opportunity to secure that pardon has arrived.[p] While *Beloved* examines a nineteenth-century reality, Morrison has said that she began the book by thinking about a "contemporary theme," the "complicated problems women have these days and have had for a long time in trying to juggle the requirements of nurturing, mothering, taking care of and becoming separate, complete individuals. And why is that a conflict."[38]

The capacity to address the historical residue that informs a contemporary reality becomes a hallmark not only of *Beloved* but also of the late twentieth-century African American novel more broadly. Hints of it can be detected in the heterosexual relationships in Morrison's *Tar Baby* (1981) and *Jazz* (1992) where the settings are the Caribbean and 1920s New York respectively, but the theme resonates most with the difficulties that black men and black women have establishing secure relationships. Perhaps, it is this dexterity that won for Morrison the crowning achievement of the Nobel Prize.

Morrison, along with Ishmael Reed, John Edgar Wideman, Alice Walker, and Ernest Gaines, bequeath a sense of authority to twenty-first-century African American novelists. Whether one needs models of irreverent satire or impassioned melodrama, the option exists for young black writers to consult a widely accomplished intraracial archive. One of the most celebrated black novels of the last decade of the twentieth century was Colson Whitehead's *The Intuitionist* (1999), and this book's explorations of ideological tension and urban technology certainly bespeak a familiarity with *Invisible Man*. But lurking in its sardonic understatement is also sensitivity to Reed's *Reckless Eyeballing* (1986) and *Yellow Back Radio Broke-Down* (1969). Likewise, Jeffrey Renard Allen's *Rails under My Back* (2001) not only hearkens to Leon

p For more on the haunted and haunting facets of *Beloved*, see Elizabeth Young, "Supernatural novels," chapter 13, 232–233.

Forrest's penchant for the big book but also Alice Walker's attentiveness to risky sites of cultural collision and John Edgar Wideman's insistent juxtaposition of wildly disparate intellectual influences. Mat Johnson's *Incognegro* (2008), Martha Southgate's *The Fall of Rome* (2002), Paul Beatty's *Slumberland* (2008), and Victor Lavalle's *Big Machine* (2009) all signal that the power of the pen cultivated by earlier black novelists will be wielded exuberantly by the next generation. Another development worth watching is short story master Edward P. Jones's entry into the pantheon of extended fiction. *The Known World* (2003), his highly honored first novel, aroused a fair amount of controversy since its central character is a slaveowning black man.[q]

The post-civil rights African American novel renovates black literary culture. Moribund ideas about aesthetic and commercial possibility get exploded, and a splendid array of laureled elders, seasoned hands, and young guns appears. Writers volley bitter recriminations across the gender line, and at the same moment, these women and men collaborate to carve out a technically accomplished, racially aware artistry. Consensus rarely forms, and with few exceptions, no predominant schools coalesce. Still, the observer can detect an archive.[39] This archive is labyrinthine, encompassing Trey Ellis's New Black Aesthetic, Toni Morrison's poetics of ineffability, and Ernest Gaines's "old fashioned modernism."[40] Despite the protean character of the African American novel after civil rights, its different strands converge in one insistence. While its grasp of craft involves a moving away from specific prescriptions of social responsibility, it never loses a sense of that obligation's efficacy.

Notes

1. Lawrence Jackson's *The Indignant Generation: A Narrative History of African American Writers and Critics, 1934–1960* (Princeton: Princeton University Press, 2010) offers the most meticulous account of African American literary culture during the 1950s. Robert Bone's *The Negro Novel in America* (New Haven: Yale University Press, 1965) provides a solid overview that is enhanced by Bernard Bell's *The Afro-American Novel and Its Tradition* (Amherst: University of Massachusetts Press, 1987) and *The Contemporary African American Novel: Its Folk Roots and Modern Literary Branches* (Amherst: University of Massachusetts Press, 2004).
2. During the 1950s, more than 125 novels by black writers were published. To put that number in context, only 180 novels by blacks were printed between 1853 (the year that the first African American novel appeared) and 1949. Thus, in a single

q Regarding the value system of Jones's novel, consult Amy Hungerford, "Religion and the twentieth-century American novel," chapter 44, 747.

decade, the total number of books by black novelists increased almost 70 percent. My statistics are based on Maryemma Graham's database of African American novels, "The Project on the History of Black Writing," www2.ku.edu/~phbw/, which is housed at Kansas University.

3. For revealing synopses of the Black Arts Movement, consult Gail Collins and Margo Crawford, eds., *New Thoughts on the Black Arts Movement* (New Brunswick, NJ: Rutgers University Press, 2006), and James E. Smethhurst's *The Black Arts Movement: Literary Nationalism in the 1960s and 1970s* (Chapel Hill: University of North Carolina Press, 2005).
4. Norman Harris's *Connecting Times: The Sixties in Afro-American Fiction* (Jackson: University Press of Mississippi, 1988) remains one of the few sustained analyses of the African American novel in the 1960s. While Harris offers greater coverage, James C. Hall, in *Mercy, Mercy Me: African American Culture and the American Sixties* (New York: Oxford University Press, 2001), presents a more textured account of how the decade influenced black cultural production.
5. In *The Economy of Prestige: Prizes, Awards, and the Circulation of Cultural Value* (Cambridge, MA: Harvard University Press, 2005), James English argues that because of her lobbying for the 1987 Pulitzer Prize, Toni Morrison "seems to have capitulated too fully to the awards mania" (237). The cue for labeling Morrison's present posture as a strut comes from a 1994 interview where she claimed that the Nobel Prize afforded her "license to strut." See Claudia Dreifus, "Chloe Wofford Talks about Toni Morrison", in *Toni Morrison: Conversations*, ed. Carolyn C. Denard and Toni Morrison (Jackson: University Press of Mississippi, 2008), 99.
6. Toni Morrison, "Afterword," in *The Bluest Eye* (New York: Plume, 1994), 216. For A. Yemisi Jimoh's opinions, see "The Bluest Eye," *The Literary Encyclopedia*, (September, 11 2003), www.litencyc.com/php/sworks.php?rec=true&UID=1425, accessed June 9, 2009.
7. Hortense Spillers has written insightfully on how *The Bluest Eye*'s incest scene revises the Trueblood episode in *Invisible Man*. See "The Permanent Obliquity of an In(pha)llibly Straight: In the Time of the Daughters and the Fathers," in *Black, White, and In Color: Essays on American Literature and Culture* (Chicago: University of Chicago Press, 2003), 230–250.
8. Directly engaging Kenneth Clark's sociological work, Morrison makes Claudia, her narrator, a compulsive destroyer of white baby dolls.
9. Toni Morrison, "Foreword," in *Sula* (New York: Plume, 2004), xv.
10. *Ibid.*, xvi.
11. Amiri Baraka, "State/meant," in *The Leroi Jones/Amiri Baraka Reader*, ed. William J. Harris (New York: Thunder's Mouth Press, 1991), 169.
12. For a sampling of Ralph Ellison's sentiments regarding black writers and their deficient technique, see "Brave Words for a Startling Occasion" and "The Art of Fiction," both of which are available in *The Collected Essays of Ralph Ellison*, ed. John Callahan (New York: Modern Library, 1995).

13. Henry Louis Gates, Jr., *The Signifying Monkey* (New York: Oxford University Press, 1989), 217.
14. Darryl Dickson-Carr, *African American Satire: The Sacredly Profane Novel* (Columbia: University of Missouri Press, 2001), 151.
15. For details about Gaines's indebtedness to Turgenev, see Ruth Laney's "A Conversation with Ernest Gaines," in *Conversations with Ernest Gaines*, ed. John Lowe and Ernest Gaines (Jackson: University Press of Mississippi, 1995), 60.
16. Taking a cue from musicians like Sonny Rollins, John Edgar Wideman uses the term "woodshedding" to describe an artist's private practice of his craft. See Wilfred Samuels, "Going Home: A Conversation with John Edgar Wideman," *Callaloo* 6.1 (1983): 45.
17. Toni Morrison, "Toni Morrison on a Book She Loves: Gayl Jones' *Corregidora*," in *What Moves at the Margin: Selected Nonfiction*, ed. Carolyn C. Denard and Toni Morrison (Jackson: University Press of Mississippi, 2008), 109.
18. Robert Butler links Faith to the protagonist of *Invisible Man*. See his essay, "The City as Psychological Frontier in Ralph Ellison's *Invisible Man* and Charles Johnson's *Faith and the Good Thing*," in *The City in African American Literature*, ed. Yoshinobu Hakutani and Robert Butler (Madison, NJ: Fairleigh Dickinson University Press, 1995), 123–137.
19. Rudolph Byrd, "*Oxherding Tale* and *Siddhartha*: Philosophy, Fiction, and the Emergence of a Hidden Tradition," *African American Review* 30.4 (Winter 1996): 550.
20. Wilfred D. Samuels, "John Edgar Wideman," in *The Oxford Companion to African American Literature*, ed. William L. Andrews, Frances Smith Foster, and Trudier Harris (New York: Oxford University Press, 1997), 775.
21. James Coleman, *Blackness and Modernism* (Jackson: University Press of Mississippi, 1989), 4.
22. *Ibid.*, 3.
23. Regarding the expansion of the black middle class, see Stephen and Abigail Thernstrom, *America in Black and White: One Nation, Indivisible* (New York: Simon & Schuster, 1997), and Philip A. Klinkner and Rodgers M. Smith, *The Unsteady March: The Rise and Decline of Racial Equality in America* (Chicago: University of Chicago Press, 2002).
24. Carol Stack engages the idea of the north to south reverse migration in *Call to Home: African Americans Reclaim the Rural South* (New York: Basic Books, 1996).
25. For reflections on this class of literary critics, see Houston A. Baker, "Generational Shifts and the Recent Criticism of Afro-American Literature," in *Within the Circle: An Anthology of African American Literary Criticism for the Harlem Renaissance to the Present*, ed. Angelyn Mitchell (Durham, NC: Duke University Press, 1994), 282–328, and J. Edgar Tidwell, "The Birth of a Black New Criticism," *Callaloo* 7 (October 1979): 109–112.
26. Cheryl A. Wall provides a thorough summary of Morrison's editorial activities. See her chapter "Toni Morrison, Editor and Teacher," in *The Cambridge Companion to Toni Morrison*, ed. Justine Tally (Cambridge: Cambridge

University Press, 2007), 139–148. For an overview of Reed's work with the Before Columbus Foundation, see Ishmael Reed, Kathryn Trueblood, and Shawn Wong, eds., *Before Columbus Foundation Fiction Anthology: Selections from the American Book Awards, 1980–1990* (New York: Norton, 1992).

27. Bradley talks about his time in Wideman's classes during a 1984 interview. See Susan Blake and James A. Miller, "The Business of Writing: An Interview with David Bradley," *Callaloo* 21 (Spring–Summer 1984): 36–37.
28. Nelson George, *Post-Soul Nation: The Explosive, Contradictory, Triumphant, and Tragic 1980s as Experienced by African Americans* (New York: Viking, 2004), 16.
29. Claudia Tate, *Psychoanalysis and Black Novels: Desire and the Protocols of Race* (New York: Oxford University Press, 1998), 4.
30. Although Walker receives what is understood as the "National Book Award," shifts in the name and the politics of that prize obscure her feat. For a discussion of the National Book Award, see English, *The Economy of Prestige*, 375n1. Also, see chapters 42–44 of Evelyn White, *Alice Walker: A Life* (New York: Norton, 2004) for commentary on Walker's awards and her reactions to them.
31. Calvin Hernton provides an account from the midst of this controversy in *The Sexual Mountain and Black Women Writers* (New York: Anchor, 1987).
32. Where Gates held that African culture, while a crucial touch-point in black life, could not be distilled to a singular set of beliefs, rituals, or practices, Asante argued that there were discernible values that coalesced in a coherent and an attainable worldview. See Dhyana Ziegler, ed., *Molefi Kete Asante: In Praise and in Criticism* (New York: Routledge, 1996), for a sampling of the salvos in this conflict.
33. For details on McMillan's career, especially the commercial viability of her novels, see Paulette Richards, *Terry McMillan: A Critical Companion* (Westport, CT: Greenwood, 1999), 1–20.
34. Charles E. Wilson's *Walter Mosley: A Critical Companion* (Westport, CT: Greenwood, 2004) contains specific information on Mosley. Regarding black detective fiction more broadly, consult Frankie Y. Bailey, *African American Mystery Writers: A Historical and Thematic Study* (Jefferson, NC: McFarland, 2008), and Stephen F. Soitos, *The Blues Detective: A Study of African American Detective Fiction* (Amherst: University of Massachusetts Press, 1996).
35. The development of black homosexual writing is treated in Charles I. Nero, "Toward a Black Gay Aesthetic: Signifying in Contemporary Black Gay Literature," in *Brother to Brother: New Writings by Black Gay Men*, ed. Essex Hemphill (Boston: Alyson, 1991), 229–252, and Kevin McGruder, "To Be Heard in Print: Black Gay Writers in 1980s New York," *Obsidian III* 6.1 (Spring 2005): 49–65.
36. For background on E. Lynn Harris, see Michael Hardin, "Ralph Ellison's *Invisible Man*: Invisibility, Race, and Homoeroticism from Frederick Douglass to E. Lynn Harris," *The Southern Literary Journal* 37.1 (2004): 96–120, and Kai Wright, "Documenting a Black Gay and Lesbian Literary Canon," *Black Issues Book Review* 6.4 (July / August 2004): 39.

37. Bonnie Angelo, "The Pain of Being Black: An Interview with Toni Morrison," *Time* (May 22, 1989): 120.
38. Toni Morrison, Interview with Don Swaim, *Wired for Books*. WOUB, Athens, OH. September 15 1987, wiredforbooks.org/tonimorrison/.
39. See Xiomara Santamarina, "'Are We There Yet?' Archives, History, and Specificity in African-American Literary Studies," *American Literary History* 20.1–2 (Spring/Summer 2008): 304–316, for more expansive thoughts on African American literature and archives.
40. Trey Ellis discusses his cultural theory in "The New Black Aesthetic," *Callaloo* 12.1 (Winter 1989): 233–243. The phrase describing Gaines is taken from Valerie Babb. See "Old-Fashioned Modernism: 'The Changing Same' in *A Lesson Before Dying*," in *Critical Reflections on the Fiction of Ernest J. Gaines*, ed. David C. Estes (Athens: University of Georgia Press, 1994), 250–264.

65

Hemispheric American novels

RODRIGO LAZO

> But the orgy of blood which followed, no man has written.
>
> William Carlos Williams[1]

In the acknowledgments to *The Ordinary Seaman* (1997), Francisco Goldman remembers coming across a 1982 newspaper article that inspired this novel about Central American laborers who are promised good wages to refurbish a ship, only to be abandoned aboard a "floating hellhole" on the Brooklyn waterfront. The ship owner's identity was unknown. "I was just back from a nearly two-year stay in Central America, balancing fiction writing with journalism and living in Manhattan," Goldman writes, "so it was the Central American connection that first drew my attention." The Central American connection is important not only to Goldman's personal history as a writer but also his novel and the history behind the exploitation recounted in the book. *The Ordinary Seaman* demarcates a relationship between New York as the economic capital of the United States and, on the other hand, a region that has been ravaged by the effects of US-funded wars. The setting highlights the economic power imbalance between two New Yorkers with $55,000 to invest in the purchase of a clunker ship and a crew that is duped into believing they have been hired legitimately to work in the maritime industry. With this picture of two guys operating an extra-national enterprise, the novel prompts readers to conceptualize a new space of economic interaction and abuse that brings together different parts of the hemisphere.

The context and setting of the novel are influenced by increasing economic globalization, military conflicts, and the migration of workers from one part of the Americas to another. Numerous events offer a historical backdrop. For one, the Sandinista Revolution of 1979 motivated years of US involvement in vicious Central American wars. These imperialist projects included the support for a counterrevolution that devastated the Nicaraguan countryside and hampered the economy so that thousands of Nicaraguans left their home country. In addition, the US supported a corrupt military regime in El Salvador during a civil war that sent hundreds of thousands of Salvadorans to Southern California, Washington, DC, and other destinations. As workers moved in a northern direction, their remittances moved south, and a process of greater economic interaction developed in the hemisphere. The signing in 1993 of the North American Free Trade Agreement (NAFTA), which includes Mexico, Canada, and the United States, represented renewed enthusiasm for trading blocs that would further integrate countries in the western hemisphere. Given these shifts in economic and geopolitical relationships, Goldman's book dramatizes the imbalance in economic relationships that crossed national borders in the 1980s and 1990s. Economic hierarchies in the Americas, the book shows, make it possible for a middle-class New Yorker to cash in on the poverty of Central America. The first mate of the *Urus*, Mark, draws an analogy between the workers on the ship and those who fill positions in various parts of the United States: "everywhere he goes he sees them: busboys, McDonald's, even working in pizza parlors now instead of Italians and Greeks."

There's no question that *The Ordinary Seaman* is a chronicle of international economic disparity, and Walter Benn Michaels is right to argue in this volume that the novel's critique of capitalist destruction transcends the politics of identity.[a] What *The Ordinary Seaman* does not do, however, is let the United States hide under a veneer of some amorphous postnational "empire" or neoliberal condition. When Mark reflects on what he and the ne'er-do-well "captain" Elias Tureen have done, he describes the men on the ship as "[o]ur little brown guys, property of Capitán Elias Cortés and First Mate Mark Pizarro." The third-person interior narration quickly emphasizes the limits of Mark's introspection: "When he says that, Your Honor, he's not being racist, naw, he's using self-mocking irony to serve honesty . . . Not all of them are little anyway, they're not *all* even brown." Mark is aware of the way labor is racialized in the United States, but he hides his culpability for abuse of the workers under ironic distance. Self-conscious about his racial assumption, Mark is less concerned about the more hyperbolic "irony" that situates him in a lineage with sixteenth-century Spanish conquistadors.[2] And yet that connection to Hernán Cortés and Francisco Pizarro is precisely why the main concern in *The Ordinary Seaman* is neocolonialism and the abuse perpetrated by an economic elite operating out of a liberal empire.

a Walter Benn Michaels, "Model minorities and the minority model – the neoliberal novel," chapter 61, 1028–1029.

Writers in the contemporary period sometimes conceptualize spaces of human interaction (e.g. the connection between New York and Central America) in relation to migration and its inequalities. These geographic and economic spaces, which do not adhere to national boundaries or regional designations, are an important characteristic of what I am here calling hemispheric American novels. The very term "hemispheric American" implies a spatial reconsideration. It must be taken as simultaneously repetitive and oxymoronic, and as a retort to the US appropriation of the word "America" in a national sense.[3] And yet it would be disingenuous to claim that noting this or even aspiring to move beyond it amounts to actual transcendence of the nation, especially not in a volume that focuses on the US novel. The argument here is more modest: certain novels call attention to complex settings that include people from various parts of the hemisphere who must negotiate power imbalances that have roots in the colonial history of the Americas. As a form, the novel offers a site where the types of interactions and spatial relationships that emerge in the hemisphere can be represented and conceptualized in language that sometimes breaks out of local and national limits. As Caroline Levander and Robert S. Levine have noted, the "analysis of the United States' engagements with a wide and surprising array of geographic entities helps to contextualize and clarify, rather than reproduce, the exceptionalism that has long been central to the nation's conception of its privileged place in the American hemisphere."[4] I take that point as a move toward a hemispheric approach rather than a presumptuous designation of a new field that would include all novels published in the Americas.

A hemispheric approach focuses on how the conception of an inter-American space is intertwined with the great violence that has been carried out in the name of colonial or imperialist triumph and economic success.[b] The "orgy of blood" in the epigraph from William Carlos Williams certainly should be a starting point for a consideration of hemispheric American interactions. But this is a starting point that recognizes the limits of representation; Williams implies that the "orgy of blood" has not been written because there is no way to gauge the devastation. "History begins for us with murder and enslavement, not with discovery," Williams writes, positing an "us" that is inclusive of multiple transatlantic influences and traditions in the Americas.[5] For Williams, the American grain includes the history of Spanish, French, and English

b While this approach shares Ramón Saldívar's conception of the multiple historical factors influencing structures of hierarchy, it de-emphasizes the question of race and national identity that Saldívar places at the center of his discussion of form in "borderlands" novels. See Saldívar, "The American borderlands novel," chapter 62, 1031–1032.

colonization of the hemisphere.[6] The first hemispheric American texts are written when Europeans begin to invent a "new world" populated by indigenous groups whose difference motivates violent conquest. Accordingly, one might say that one of the first hemispheric American "novels" is Bernal Díaz del Castillo's *Historia verdadera de la conquista de Nueva España* (True History of the Conquest of New Spain, 1632), an autobiographical account of Hernán Cortés's siege and capture of the Aztec capital.[7] Díaz's book contains a fantastic plot (a band of men take over an empire), memorable characters (Montezuma cowering), and a captivating narrative of a frightfully enchanting realm that has much in common with historical romance. Having participated in the historical events that motivate his hemispheric vision, he describes a new geographic area and portrays indigenous populations as evil and idolatrous in relation to the cultural and religious context of Spain. Díaz is but one example of the many accounts that led to an early modern discourse that invented the area known as the Americas. As Edmundo O'Gorman argued decades ago, America was invented in relation to European conceptions of the world. In other words, the notion of the hemisphere was produced as a process of interpretation that endowed the newly found lands with a meaning (and being) of their own; geographically, the Americas were conceived as the fourth part of the world, thus stretching the European sense of geography beyond Europe, Asia, and Africa.[8]

The novel as a popular form enters the ongoing re-invention of America in the late eighteenth and early nineteenth centuries as writers grapple with colonial legacies in light of new geopolitical arrangements. In this period, as in the present, the hemispheric American novel is a product of historical circumstances that call for an engagement with the past. As Gretchen Murphy shows elsewhere in this volume, novels published in the early nineteenth century often turned to colonial (Aztec) history to debate hemispheric political organizations and transatlantic opposition to Europe.[c] At the same time, they emphasized economic, racial, and national divisions that complicated the conception of hemispheric commonality. The types of divisions brought on by nation formation explain why even when novels focus on the indigenous past, they sometimes displace cultural difference in order to propose the type of unity demanded of the nation. Doris Sommer's 1991 *Foundational Fictions* showed how a variety of romance novels from various parts of the Americas – including James Fenimore Cooper's *The Last*

c Gretchen Murphy, "The hemispheric novel in the post-revolutionary era," chapter 33, 556–557.

of the Mohicans (1826), Juan Leon Mera's *Cumandá* (1879), and Gertrudis Gómez de Avellaneda's *Sab* (1841) – served as national allegories that combined the "desire for domestic happiness" with "dreams of national prosperity."[9] And while literary history can show influences that cross the hemisphere, for example in the way writers adapt Cooper's themes and concerns, literary influences do not necessarily mean a novel will present the type of conceptual space that I am associating with the hemispheric American novel.

Some of the most interesting examples of hemispheric American novels in the nineteenth century place slavery at the center of a violence that reaches across national lines, as evident in texts such as Martin Delany's *Blake; or The Huts of America* (1859–1862) and Herman Melville's *Benito Cereno* (1855). As Eric Sundquist and others have shown, *Benito Cereno* situates the frame of analysis of slavery in relation to the hemispheric effects of Spain's introduction of slavery to the Americas.[10] Like other hemispheric American novels, *Benito Cereno* offers a setting outside of the nation, opening with a ship anchored in the harbor of "a small, desert, uninhabited island toward the southern extremity of the long coast of Chile." The story is told largely through the limited and limiting perspective of Captain Amasa Delano, and one traditional allegorical interpretation posits that Delano is a New Englander who cannot envision the potential violence that slavery could unleash in the United States. But if we take the novel's setting off the west coast of South America seriously, then Delano's inability to comprehend the events points not only to slavery in the United States but also to "New World" slavery and, more generally, to Spanish America and "Spaniards" (Don Benito) more generally. Delano is suspicious of Spain but cannot see the hemispheric dimensions of a system that includes the participation of European planters in various Caribbean settings. The hemispheric setting of the novel is in 1799, early in the life of the US republic but prenational in a broader hemispheric sense because it precedes the wars of independence in the southern Americas. Not only does the ship's name, *San Dominick* (as well as the 1799 date for the action), point back to the black-led revolution in Haiti, but the many references to Spanish colonial history also remind readers that it was Spain's monarch Charles V who authorized the first official slave shipments from Africa into the hemisphere.[11] Instead of a radiant national pendant, the *San Dominick* shows "no colors." And it is within international waters that slaves aboard the *San Dominick* invert the hierarchy of the ship and of slavery itself. Like other hemispheric American novels, *Benito Cereno* looks back on the past, both the colonial period and the more recent history of revolution in the Americas, for an accounting of the American "orgy of blood." In the inability to propose a way out of the slavery's impasse (failure of the mutiny, subjection of the rebel slave Babo, death of Captain Benito Cereno, failure of vision), Melville's novella about a slave ship is an important literary historical antecedent to Goldman's *The Ordinary Seaman*.

The importance of slavery to hemispheric American novels in the nineteenth century allows us to begin seeing how a writer's context influences conceptions of contacts in the hemisphere. The two characteristics emphasized here for the hemispheric American novel, the introduction of a space outside the nation and the engagement with colonial history, emerge in different ways depending on the social, economic, and political context. Revolution in the Americas and slavery are important to the nineteenth century, and the question of racial hierarchies and the growing influence of the US empire continue to affect hemispheric conceptions into the early twentieth century. In the late twentieth century, as already noted, the rapid proliferation of technologies of globalization (transportation, media, communication), a growing economic disparity between the United States and countries of the southern Americas, and the increase in human migration from one part of the hemisphere to another become crucial elements to the development of a hemispheric American novel.

The "hemispheric American novel" should not be taken as a term that includes every novel written in and about the Americas, nor is it intended to cover every country. Rather than offer a field that brings together the US novel and the Latin American novel, a hemispheric American approach proposes a continual negotiation of spatial relationships and history. In other words, "hemispheric American" is not an *a priori* category. It is not an approach that calls for a bracketing of conceptual nations such as "United States" or "Mexico" and a bracketing of North/South oppositions. Instead, new spaces emerge in light of the past. We might start by asking, does a given novel complicate the way a reader views social, economic, and military relations in the hemisphere?

Consider Junot Díaz's Pulitzer Prize-winning *The Brief Wondrous Life of Oscar Wao* (2007), which suggests that late twentieth-century migration from the Dominican Republic to the United States is intertwined with a history of colonial exploitation. Díaz's testosterone-saturated narrator, Yunior, moves easily between New York street slang, anti-imperialist critique, and cultivated literary Anglophone culture. *Oscar Wao*, after all, is a riff on the name (and the cape) of England's best-known late Victorian queer aesthete. Yunior's own sense of lost love intertwines with the hilariously tragic destiny of the title character, a nerdy, corpulent boy in Paterson, New Jersey. Oscar Wao's unhealthy association with science fiction drives away women, and that causes him much suffering. He is only comfortable, it would appear, after a return to the country of his parents, except that the country turns out to be part of a tangle of violence and history. The narrative is hilarious because it constantly mixes up differences between countries (United States, Dominican Republic), languages (Spanish, English), and literary cultures (science fiction, the traditional canon).

The novel's panorama of violence links the rule of dictatorship to the legacy of conquest of America. The opening pages introduce the popular belief in *fukú*, a curse which "they say" (*dicen*) came first from Africa and led to the extermination of the indigenous Tainos. The narrator calls it "*fukú* – generally a curse or a doom of some kind; specifically the Curse and the Doom of the New World."

By situating the story of Oscar in the "New World," the opening of the novel shifts the frame of US-based literary culture toward a hemispheric perspective. With the novel constantly switching out of English and into Spanish, it invites both an Anglophone and Hispanophone pronunciation of *fukú*. Drawing a deliciously tenuous line between Columbus and Oscar, the novel reminds us how we have all been *fukú'd* in some way by the arrival of Spain's military, religious, and civil ambassadors in the regions that come to be known as America. *Fukú*, like history, has a way of repeating itself. In the twentieth century, says the narrator, some believe that *fukú* emerges with the rise of the Dominican Dictator Rafael Leonidas Trujillo and thus spreads from the Dominican Republic to Washington Heights in Manhattan.

The presentation of the curse allows the narrator to chart a path from the colonization of the Caribbean in the sixteenth century to the mid twentieth century and on to more contemporary forms of exploitation and violence. While *Oscar Wao* can be read as an immigrant narrative (and as a transnational novel with connections to two countries), it also offers another set of movements that go back to the transatlantic crossing to the so-called New World. In its first incarnation as a story in *The New Yorker*, "The Brief Wondrous Life of Oscar Wao" (2000) did not include details about the history of Oscar's family and its cursed past. In the novel version, that family history is added along with a variety of footnotes explaining references to the Dominican Republic and its culture as well as the experiences of "exiles" in the United States. Most prominent in the footnotes is the political history of the twentieth-century dictatorship in the country as well as the hemispheric past. These notes can be read as history-lite for readers who might not know that the USA invaded the Dominican Republic (and Haiti and Nicaragua and Cuba). As the novel weaves historical threads to nineteenth-century Cuba and twentieth-century Vietnam, it encourages a worldview that does not respect temporal borders or geographic regions. The hemispheric becomes a set of relationships that cross time and space in a variety of ways.

While Spanish colonization and the geopolitics of the southern Americas are important to *Oscar Wao* and other texts, some hemispheric American novels shift the space of analysis in other geographic and historical directions. In E. Annie Proulx's *The Shipping News* (1994), the northeast part of the hemisphere opens an alternate geographic conception. Quoyle, a down-on-his-luck newspaper reporter, seeks a way to escape the personal effects of an accident that killed his wife and left him a widower with two young daughters. The novel's most important setting emerges when Quoyle moves from bedraggled Mockinburg, a town in New York, to Newfoundland, returning to his ancestral homeland. Accompanied by his aunt, Agnis Hamm, Quoyle finds an area that is more ice than anything. Supposedly this place provides a clean slate for the two. "You've got a chance to start out all over again," Agnis tells him. "A new place, new people, new sights." But the irony is that the "new" place with new opportunities is also an old space tied to the Quoyle family's violent past.

Newfoundland appears unbearably cold and distant, yet seems to share in the economic desperation that affects points south, both in the United States and other countries. The "fishing's went down, down, down forty years sliding away into nothing," and efforts to bring industry to the area have failed. This hardship is connected to the novel's spatial configuration of hemispheric and transatlantic movement; the bounties of the sea attract people looking for riches and new beginnings. One character describes the Quoyles as pirates, "wrackers they say, come to Gaze Island centuries ago and made it their evil lair. Pirate men and women that lured ships onto the rocks." This history of violence, a piratical past that is familial, is what Quoyle must overcome as he establishes a new life for himself.

Some novels written originally in Spanish are exemplary hemispheric American novels although they have also been discussed in the context of national or Latin American literatures. Reinaldo Arenas's *El mundo alucinante* (1966), translated as *The Ill-Fated Peregrinations of Fray Servando* (1987), is a fantastic treatment in novel form of the wanderings of Fray Servando Teresa de Mier (1765–1827), a Dominican friar who spent much of his life on the run, leaping hemispherically and transatlantically from Mexico to England, Cuba, Spain, France, and the United States. In Arenas's novel, Servando reminds us of how the Americas emerged hemispherically in the late eighteenth and early nineteenth century, as wars of independence prompted widespread anti-European rhetoric and also motivated constitutional connections between the different countries of the hemisphere. At one point, we encounter Servando walking down the street in the United States, presumably in Philadelphia in 1821, carrying three great sacks of garbage which he had collected for subsistence. Suddenly, he hears "the news that in Mexico at last *independence had been declared.*" In the novel's first-person narration, Servando says, "And so with the Constitution in hand (for I had thrown down my sacks of garbage), I leaped for joy and landed (as a result of that same exceedingly joyous leap) on my own yearned-for soil." Constitutional debates in the early nineteenth century were hemispheric and transatlantic in scope both in terms of intellectual influences and print culture contexts. After leaping back to Mexico, Servando returns to the constitutional writing process. "There, with all the time in the world before me, I again read over the so-wished-for Constitution, and I began to emend it, marking it all over in its margins." This remarkable scene in which the sacks are quickly exchanged for a Constitution reminds us of the circulation of constitutional writings in English, Spanish, and in translation throughout the different countries of the hemisphere in the early nineteenth century.

But if Arenas's novel notes hemispheric interactions, it also warns how a hemispheric vision can sometimes be the result of a colonial effect. Servando turns to flight in order to define himself outside of the limits imposed by European conceptions and colonial subjection. "Until what distant day are we to remain in perpetual discovery by perpetually unseeing eyes?" That sense of being an effect of someone else's society and culture and struggling against it is a staple of writing on colonial conditions. *Fray Servando* situates this idea within the struggle for independence, but the novel also points to Arenas's concern – for he is a Cuban exile – about contemporary limits imposed by the nation-state and social constraints.

In the hemispheric American novel, the oppressive mechanisms of institutions and nation-states cross national borders, and some novels place the operations of empire at the center of their focus. *The Ordinary Seaman* offers a brutal set of questions about how US economic privilege can set off an exploitative relationship reminiscent of the other types of imperialist encounters. Esteban, the main character, contends with the death of his girlfriend, who has been killed in battle against the US-backed *contras*, leaving Esteban feeling dislocated in the world. The other workers in the story similarly flee the economic and political turmoil occasioned by conflicts that included wars in El Salvador, Guatemala, and Nicaragua, and the militarization of

Honduras, where it was possible in the 1980s to see the local military sporting US Army gear.[12] While these military conflicts drive the workers to New York, it is the inequality of economic resources that makes it possible for a couple of petty capitalist-wannabes, Elias and Mark, to send for the crew of the *Urus*. The book clearly delineates the difference between the privileged children of US middle-class wealth (along with their international friends) and, on the other hand, the workers aboard the ship, who are seeking hourly wages that are fairly low by US standards.

Captain Elias Tureen, by contrast, is almost forty and the child of a British journalist and Greek-American art gallery owner, schooled in Mexico City and at a private college in the United States. Using inheritance money from his father, Elias had joined his best friend Mark and paid $55,000 for the *Urus*. And the scheme: "Get one of those cheap flag of convenience registries and incorporations. Import the cheapest possible crew, even have them pay their own airfare. Work night and day, repair the ship fast, in a month to six weeks . . . should be able to get half a million dollars, *at least*, for a ship like this." In this novel's hemispheric economic configuration, nations no longer matter. The very notion of class would seem to be inadequate to describe the international economic hierarchies that facilitate the relations described in the book. Due to global inequity, the story suggests, two guys with a little money can hire workers illegally and keep them in conditions akin to slavery.

Understanding a neoliberal site of exploitation, whether global or hemispheric, does not necessarily remedy that situation. In this volume, Michaels argues that instead of valuing ethnic difference, *The Ordinary Seaman* rightly indicts a neoliberal system that creates conditions of oppression. Fair enough, but it is the Latino community in New York (Cuban, Mexican, and Central American together) that pulls Esteban out of the neoliberal "abyss" that "has been done to all of them." This is why Kirsten Silva Gruesz frames Esteban's connection to Latinos in relation to utopian possibilities.[13] I would argue that a US-based ethnic community is a solution only for some individual people who can get to one. Integration into a US group is no solution for the dead cook, Bernardo, nor for the workers who inhale themselves into a drugged oblivion and are unable to make their way back to land. Somewhere between Michaels and Gruesz, the novel fails to offer a solution to inequality or bring greater prosperity to all of the Americas. If anything, it asks, what happens to those who are *abyssed*? How many are out there dead without identification or even notification of their next of kin?

Questions about those who died on their way to work in the United States emerge as hemispheric references even in novels that are focused on local experiences. In Sandra Cisneros's *The House on Mango Street* (1984), for example, the character of Esperanza at one point writes about "Geraldo No Last Name," a worker killed in a hit-and-run. "No address. No name. Nothing in his pockets." While Cisneros's novel focuses on a local community and does not carve out a hemispheric historical space as such, the vignette about Geraldo offers a brief hemispheric turn that emphasizes the importance of migration.

Intricately connected to economic changes in multiple countries, migration might well be to the contemporary novel what slavery was to the hemispheric American novel of the nineteenth century. The passage in the United States of the Immigration Act of 1965 inspired large numbers of immigrants from Asia and Latin America to make their way to the United States, and along with them came seasonal workers and those who did not have papers to enter the country. This rise was connected to worldwide demographic shifts that included rapid population growth in the Middle East, Asia, and Latin America, as well as advances in technology that permitted rapid travel and communication. The abyss that yawns in *The Ordinary Seaman* is one of the possible inadvertent destinations. For Cisneros's Esperanza, the death of Geraldo speaks to a life without a past or future. He will never see or know the future, and neither will we see or know about his life. "And his home is in another country," Cisneros writes. "The ones he left behind are far away, will wonder, shrug, remember, Geraldo – he went north . . . we never heard from him again." The language she uses to describe Geraldo's journey mirrors Esperanza's own anxiety about leaving Mango Street and forgetting. "Friends and neighbors will say, What happened to that Esperanza?" Unlike Esperanza, Geraldo is unable to return to his town or anywhere else. Understanding what happened to him is impossible for his family. He is lost in a hemispheric space that does not provide liberation, part of a bloody history that has not been written.

In tracing out the spaces of hemispheric American novels, I have emphasized the link to historical events both past and present that prompt a consideration of hierarchies and relations of social and economic oppression that transcend national boundaries. While hemispheric conceptions make their way into novels in the nineteenth century as writers grapple with independence movements and slavery, in the contemporary hemispheric American novel immigration and the effects of globalization become part of the content of the novels and the historical panorama under which writers work.

Notes

1. William Carlos Williams, *In the American Grain* (New York: New Directions, 1956), 41.
2. The type of connection conceptualized by Mark resonates with the critique offered by Walter Mignolo and others working within a "coloniality of power" paradigm that proposes a continuum between Spain's conquest of the Americas and contemporary US economic and military operations, including the war in Iraq. Mark, however, cannot account for the effects of colonial violence on indigenous populations or take responsibility for his own participation. See Mignolo, *The Idea of Latin America* (Malden, MA: Blackwell, 2005), 11–44.
3. Ramón Saldívar and Paula Moya have taken up a similar turn toward the hemisphere, using the term "fictions of the trans-American imaginary." While I share their critical view of the national parameters of US literary history, I opt for a term that could be deployed outside of academia and engage directly in a broad array of discussions about the "American novel." See Saldívar and Moya, "Fictions of the Trans-American Imaginary," *Modern Fiction Studies* 49.1 (2003): 119.
4. Caroline F. Levander and Robert S. Levine, eds., *Hemispheric American Studies* (New Brunswick, NJ: Rutgers University Press, 2008), 3.
5. Williams, *American Grain*, 39.
6. For a study that analyzes Williams in relation to a literature of the Americas approach, see Vera Kutzinski, *Against the American Grain: William Carlos Williams, Jay Wright, and Nicolás Guillén* (Baltimore: Johns Hopkins University Press, 1987).
7. Bernal Díaz, *The Conquest of New Spain*, trans. J. M Cohen (New York: Penguin, 1963).
8. Edmundo O'Gorman, *The Invention of America* (Bloomington: Indiana University Press, 1961), 123.
9. Doris Sommer, *Foundational Fictions: The National Romances of Latin America* (Berkeley: University of California Press, 1991), 7.
10. Eric Sundquist, *To Wake the Nations* (Cambridge, MA: Harvard University Press, 1994), 140–154.
11. *Ibid.*, 136–140.
12. Visiting Tegucigalpa, Honduras with a group of students and professors in 1985, I found myself walking behind a group of Honduran soldiers whose gear was marked "US Army."
13. Gruesz argues that amidst the devastation *The Ordinary Seaman* produces moments of hope and utopian visions for future generations, but I would argue that the victories at the end of the novel are few and selective. In fact, the ending does not offer a way out of the hemispheric structures of oppression. Kirsten Silva Gruesz, "*The Ordinary Seaman* in Extraordinary Times," *Modern Fiction Studies* 49.1 (2003): 54–83.

66

The worlding of the American novel

BRUCE ROBBINS

It was not a street anymore but a world.

The first sentence of Don DeLillo's *Falling Man* (2007) describes lower Manhattan in the chaotic minutes after the attack on the World Trade Center on September 11, 2001. But it could also be read as a description of *Falling Man* itself, and perhaps also of the contemporary American novel in general. So read, the sentence would suggest that the American novel has recently become more worldly, whether because of 9/11 or in response to larger causes that 9/11 stands in for. This proposition is gently self-congratulatory, hence open to doubt. But there are also reasons for taking it seriously.

The street is what most novels take for their subject most of the time. It is by watching society at street level, so to speak, that the novel reader's sense of identity and relationship has mainly been formed. Most novels do not train our eyes to look very high or very low, or for that matter very far away; they do not encourage us to look at superstructures, or infrastructures, or the structuring force of the world capitalist system.[1] There are notable exceptions – some of them discussed in Cecelia Tichi's chapter in this volume[a] – but as a rule, worldliness is not natural to the novel.[2] This does not immediately change after 9/11. Like the protagonist in a suddenly darkened street that has been struck from above and from far away, the post-9/11 novel is first of all disoriented. If we can say that, like the street, the novel takes on the attributes of a world, the first meaning of this statement would have to be (this is how I understand Heidegger's sense of worlding) that the event has created its own unique local surround, a restricted time/space that replaces and cancels out any abstract planetary coordinates. In this sense the worlding of the novel would leave it less worldly rather than more.

a Cecelia Tichi, "Novels of civic protest," chapter 23.

If we want to argue nevertheless that the novel has indeed become more worldly, we need some clarity about those particular attributes of the world that we expect it to reproduce. Must it for example enter into the subjectivity of the hijackers and the logic of their attack, as *Falling Man* so boldly does? We are all connected, as the saying goes, but in different ways and at different scales: political, economic, ecological, and so on. What sort of interconnectedness are we asking the novel to apply its street smarts to? There are also questions of form. Street-level storytelling is associated with certain formal conventions of character, plot, point of view.[3] Which of these would have to be stretched or even replaced in order for the novel to embody a greater worldliness? And would such stretching and replacing necessarily be greeted as marks of literary success? Again, what exactly do we want? For some readers, true worldliness might require an honest confession of the novel's inability to tell meaningful stories of identity and relationship at the global scale; it might mean reflecting back to us the world's true meaninglessness. Others would ask for measurable achievement in reading the distant world with sympathy and accuracy, or at least a good-faith effort to make it as familiar as the streets where we work or live.

There is no doubt that, as the regions of the world that are obscurely tugging on each others' everyday life have increased, the demand has grown for better maps, more complex and reliable global positioning systems. But we cannot take for granted that the novel has managed to satisfy this demand. Does it indeed make the world more navigable? The plethora of questions above can be summed up in one large question. Has there in fact been a worlding of the novel?

A number of 9/11 novels suggest that the answer to this question may be no. In the face of large-scale impersonal violence, many of them retreat into domesticity – behind national borders, behind the door of the family home. In Claire Messud's *The Emperor's Children* (2006), for example, 9/11 interrupts like a moralizing *deus ex machina*, determined that the events should end in a return to order: an extramarital affair is broken up, an ambitious usurper has his projects foiled, a woman is reunited with her mother. Only one strand of the plot goes the other way: an uncomfortable young man, presumed killed in the towers, is enabled to disappear from his family without leaving a trace. In William Gibson's *Pattern Recognition* (2003), 9/11 provides the needed ethico-emotional excuse for the disappearance of a family member who was missing anyway. Because of the falling towers, both the absent father and the putatively villainous father-surrogate can finally be forgiven. In Joseph O'Neill's *Netherland* (2008), husband and wife split up over their reactions to 9/11, and to the American government's reactions to it. She says: "Our personal feelings don't come into the picture. There are forces out there." He says he is "a political-ethical idiot," and is clearly pleased to say so; he believes that only personal relations matter. The couple is reunited when his view more or less wins out.

DeLillo too takes 9/11 as an occasion to send his protagonist home to his estranged wife and child. When the word "world" comes up in *Falling Man*, it's often to indicate that ambitions are being scaled-back, life-complicating desires are being abandoned. "Keith used to want more of the world than there was time and means to acquire. He didn't want this anymore, whatever it was he'd wanted." "This was the world now," DeLillo writes. In "a time and space of falling ash and near night," the point seems to be that the novel's field of vision has contracted, not expanded. When the street becomes a world, perhaps we can see less rather than more of the world outside our borders. Seeing less may even be the goal we strive for. By this logic, worldliness is not an unambiguous ethical good. Perhaps the novel would be better off doing what the protagonist and his wife do late in *Falling Man*: "falling out of the world."[4]

Readers of American fiction should not be surprised by this anti-worldly moral. Rituals of retreat to a private or familial zone, whether fully comfortable or (more likely) not, make up an unbroken tradition in the novel before and since 9/11.[5] And often these celebrations of the private are tied to public events that, like 9/11, have some claim to the status of national trauma: the Vietnam War, the Soviet atom bomb test at the beginning of DeLillo's *Underworld* (1997), and the bursting of the dot-com bubble in the late 1990s, to which the title of Jonathan Franzen's *The Corrections* (2001) refers.[6] The sentiment that Franzen puts into the mind of his patriarch, another falling man, as he goes over the side of a cruise ship – "There was no solid thing to reach for but your children" – does something less than justice to the argument of Franzen's novel, as we will see, but it will certainly stand for many other withdrawals from worldliness.

One way to rationalize such withdrawals is to decide that the world outside the borders of the USA is incomprehensible, if entertainingly so. *Absurdistan*, the title of a novel by Gary Shteyngart (2006), is not a bad term for the generic place where, from the perspective of the American novel, the foreign *is* the absurd, or an inevitable object of satire – which is not to say that for Shteyngart the USA lacks its own targets of satire. Another possible term, from DeLillo's *Underworld* (1997), would be "The Museum of the Misshapens." It is there that US visitors can inspect the effects of radioactive testing and waste on two generations of Russian children. To a large extent, the novelistic treatment of historical suffering outside America's borders has resembled visits to such a museum – mercifully short visits. Between comic entertainment at the expense of foreign absurdities and the representation of foreign history as extreme suffering, the latter may sound as if it offers a more earnest educational payoff. But for the most part it too is subject to generic rules that severely limit the instruction it can deliver about the world and America's place in it.

One such rule is that history abroad will be never be less than atrocity, and atrocity abroad can then serve as the motivating event behind a "coming to America" story. In Bharati Mukherjee's *Jasmine* (1989), as in many other narratives of heroic American acculturation, the protagonist's country of origin – here, India – is vividly presented as a place of inscrutable and incurable ethnic violence.[7] Her fiancé is assassinated in a bombing, thus underlining the ineligibility of her homeland as a place to live and reproduce. The more painful the history, the more the protagonist is justified in leaving her home behind and coming to America. America, despite all the nasty obstacles it puts in the way of the would-be immigrant, cannot equal the nastiness of such a history.[8] Thus it can only figure as redemptive, a pattern that goes back at least as far as Abraham Cahan's *The Rise of David Levinsky* (1917). In Junot Díaz's *The Brief Wondrous Life of Oscar Wao* (2007), the abominations of the Trujillo dictatorship in effect take over large sections of a novel that initially seems to be about present-day Dominican Americans. The premise is that only this buried history, which explains the family's presence in America, can make sense of the twisted and passionate lives of the younger generation. But it is those American lives, not an ongoing life in the Dominican Republic, that must be made sense of. In Jeffrey Eugenides's *Middlesex* (2002), the so-called *Megali Katastrophe* of 1922, when Turkish troops slaughtered large numbers of Greek and Armenian Christians in Smyrna, is represented at some length (and in flagrant imitation of the Amritsar Massacre in Salman Rushdie's *Midnight's Children* [1981]).[9] But Eugenides (unlike Rushdie) allows the initial atrocity to dissipate gently into another coming-to-America narrative of perpetual self-fashioning. Unlike the trauma itself, the *scene* of the trauma disappears forever.

A similar structure shapes the treatment of the Holocaust in Michael Chabon's *The Amazing Adventures of Kavalier and Clay* (2000). The family left behind in Hitler's Europe motivates attempts at transnational rescue, but also attempts at upward mobility.[10] One might say that upward mobility in the USA is legitimated as a form of rescue directed at victims abroad.[11] But the same underlying schema, however inflected with irony, remains visible in Dave Eggers's *What is the What* (2006), the testimony of a boy who survives the ethnic cleansing in Sudan's Darfur region. Step one: atrocity in a foreign country. Step two: escape to the USA.

For all its limitations, the "coming-to-America" narrative must be counted as a valuable mode of novelistic worldliness. Even if it necessarily paints the world outside America's borders as a place of atrocity, subordinates that world to a more or less comforting storyline, and flatters the American destination, it also offers readers some chance – in the case of Díaz and Eggers, a considerable chance – to get inside foreign minds in the midst of foreign histories.

A different brand of worldliness results from the symmetrically opposite genre that sends characters not toward America but away from it, or what might be called the expatriate novel. In *The Sheltering Sky* (1949), Paul Bowles revises the tradition of Hawthorne, James, and Fitzgerald, which made Europe a dangerous playground for the rich and aimless, by moving beyond Europe and playing up both the danger and the aimlessness. According to Bowles's 1998 introduction, the novel was born from a dream he had in Fez.[12] The novel begins with an account of that dream: "He awoke, opened his eyes. The room meant very little to him; he was too deeply immersed in the non-being from which he had just come. If he had not the energy to ascertain his position in time and space, he also lacked the desire. He was somewhere; he had come back through vast regions of nowhere." "Non-being" and "vast regions of nowhere" are clearly what he is seeking outside the United States. Africa offers an opportunity to be unlocated; it is not in itself a location.

Like most novels, expatriate novels are often love stories of a sort, and what they do with this novelistic convention may be their best claim to a more strenuous worldliness. Non-locations like North Africa offer wealthy white people the opportunity for cheap, hassle-free sex, especially sex of kinds that are more likely to be exposed and punished at home. For this reason and others, these settings put interesting pressure on conventional relationships. The disintegration of the protagonists' marriage in Bowles (as in Fitzgerald's *Tender is the Night*) can be read as an effect of transnational space. But this space also permits new forms of bonding that in one way or other integrate the largeness of the world into the couple. *The Sheltering Sky*'s Kit, having run off into the desert and joined a caravan after Port's death, thinks at the moment of succumbing to a stranger's sexual advances: "She was alone in a vast and unrecognizable world, but alone only for a moment; then she understood that this friendly carnal presence was there with her." It's the vastness of the world that pushes them together, and the carnal-friendly bond thus produced may be appropriate to that vastness.

The first sentence of Norman Rush's novel *Mating* (1991) is "In Africa, you want more, I think." The "you" is specified as whites. What the white narrator wants is love. She and her white beloved both want equality, with the emphasis on gender equality; the beloved (an expatriate leftist intellectual) has set up a secret women-run utopian community in the Botswanan desert. But the privileges announced by the initial "you" are at odds with this egalitarian ideal, and the novel plays with the idea that love itself may also be at odds with it. As she begins to fall in love with the celebrity radical, who is a sort of ethical left-wing version of Joseph Conrad's Kurtz, the narrator comments: "[a]pparently my fate is to resonate against my will to representatives of certain elitisms I intellectually reject." She could be describing the fate of novel readers, especially in the presence of those oversize, seductive personalities capable of opening up for us a much wider world. By demanding unusual talents, worldliness seems to encourage the inequality of Pygmalion stories like Susan Sontag's *The Volcano Lover* (1992).

In *Mating*, where the reader's conventional investment in the love affair is cleverly channeled into a much less conventional investment in the success of the utopian community, the figure of the privileged expatriate shades imperceptibly into the figure of the do-gooder. The obvious difference between them – the latter seeks meaning, the former meaninglessness – might seem overshadowed by the privileges they clearly share. Still, the dominant tone is not always ironic, nor should it be. Despite the pervasive cynicism toward self-righteousness, innocence abroad, and the likelihood that the do-gooder will do unintended harm, this tradition has continued to suggest that justice may be more accessible or clearer in its outlines when viewed from abroad. Notable examples that refuse the temptations of easy irony and apolitical nihilism are Robert Stone's *A Flag for Sunrise* (1981), Robert Rosenberg's *This Is Not Civilization* (2004), and Benjamin Kunkel's *Indecision* (2005). The works of William Vollmann are interesting limit-cases where missionary zeal is combined with obtuseness about the world and proliferating ironies that may cancel themselves out, leaving the zealous obtuseness undefended.[13] Barbara Kingsolver's *The Poisonwood Bible* (1998) also falls into this category.

The geography of Jonathan Franzen's *The Corrections* seems very American: it sets the East Coast lives of the grown children against the midwestern values of their elderly parents. Yet the single largest cause of the family's miseries can only be mapped when the novel takes a comic detour through the poor nation of Lithuania. "Your country which saved us also ruined us," the Lithuanian Gitanas tells the expatriate Chip. Lithuania's port has been sold off to Orfic Midland, the same people who have bought and liquidated the railroad to which Chip's father devoted his life. The man who thinks as he falls that the only solid thing is his children has lost his foothold in the world as a result of the same theory – that "a railroad's first responsibility was to its stockholders" and not to provide service – and the same financial processes that turned Lithuania into "a zone of semi-anarchy, criminal warlords, and subsistence farming." This has much to do, though of course not everything, with how his children have turned out and why it's so hard to get them home for Christmas. To a remarkable extent, the key to the absurd and heart-wrenching unhappiness of this relatively prosperous midwestern family is to be found in another distant absurdistan.[14]

Appearances to the contrary, then, Franzen's middlebrow, family-chronicle form allows him to extend the avant-garde ambitions of Thomas Pynchon. Pynchon's *Gravity's Rainbow* (1973) begins with the inadequacy of the human sensorium to deal with global history. Like the V-2 missile, this history hits you before you can hear it coming.[15] If you want to understand why V-2s are falling on London, you can't just look at London. The rockets fall from high above; the launching sites are far away. In pursuit of their causes, you will have to spend some time as an expatriate. The secret you will find in the Zone will turn out to be bigger even than Nazi Germany; it will turn out to lie in a sort of conspiracy theory whose real agents are multinational corporations that work both sides of the World War II divide. This post-national answer need not be *the* answer. Blaming the United States is not, as it might seem, the only valuable content of worldliness. Neither Pynchon nor Franzen in fact identifies the US as the definitive origin or center of global capitalism, and in this I think they rightly avoid a (common) sort of negative exceptionalism. Yet when the novel manages not just to describe other places, but to describe the causal connections between those other places and ours, the prospect of blame will necessarily arise.

One brilliant response to the blame problem can be found in the work of Jamaica Kincaid. Kincaid's *Lucy* (1990) offers a series of strong causal linkages between American prosperity and Caribbean poverty. Yet at the same time the text allows readers to experience these linkages as evidence that Lucy's character is hate-filled, unforgiving, a pathologically compulsive blamer. The voice is a repository of historical injury, yet it is always qualified by a hint of possible unreliability. For example:

> Mariah decided to write and illustrate a book on these vanishing things [open land] and give any money made to an organization devoted to saving them. Like her, all the members of this organization were well off but they made no connection between their comforts and the decline of the world that lay before them. I could have told them a thing or two about it . . . I couldn't bring myself to point out to her that if all the things she wanted to save in the world were saved, she might find herself in reduced circumstances; I couldn't bring myself to ask her to examine Lewis's daily conversations with his stockbroker, to see if it bore any relation to the things she saw passing away forever before her eyes.

The finger points at a worldly causality that is not quite laid out even for us, but is still more forcefully blocked in its expression to characters like Mariah. Thus the emotional bond with Mariah takes on the depth and ambivalence of international causality itself, and so does the emotional bond with us. The American reader, who is told much that Lucy does not tell Mariah, can feel therefore like a privileged witness to the international causes of local emotion, but must also feel that, like Mariah, she or he may be a target of blame. The reader can also blame the narrator or the author in turn. We have little choice as readers but to pass through the question of blame, the question of responsibility for global injustice. It's the very substance of the narrative voice, which controls the entrance to the text.

Denis Johnson's *Tree of Smoke* (2007) suggests another way in which the structure of the world of nations can work its way into the novel's structure – in this case, its narrative perspective. Set in the Vietnam War, the novel plunges us into a confusion of plots and counter-plots, official and clandestine operations, and it does not even try to reduce this disorienting, topsy-turvy whirl to moral or even causal clarity. As if to underline the impossibility of locating oneself properly, scenes of murder are typically presented through the eyes of the victim. "He did not feel himself collapsing toward the water, and by the time he landed in it he was dead." This perspectival play is a kind of objective correlative for global incoherence. Here, it seems, an American agent is defending a Viet Cong agent by shooting a German assassin who was sent by his fellow Americans. Why? It is unclear, except that perhaps some sub-national, familial loyalty is involved. It's certainly not sympathy for the Viet Cong. No serious attempt is made to see the war from the Vietnamese side. It's as if such an effort would risk compromising the key premise of irreducible moral confusion. "With three beers in her head the ruckus seemed more uniformly unintelligible and pointless." The unintelligibility of the world might seem an argument for a retreat into privacy. Johnson seems to prefer the Graham Greene-like idea that only religion, which crosses national borders – Buddhism has been quietly built up as a counter-current to war on the Vietnamese side, paralleling Christianity on the American side – offers an alternative to murderous chaos.

It would be irresponsible to inquire into the worldliness of American fiction without making at least some passing reference to commercially successful genre fiction. A hypothesis worth exploring is that it is in genres like science fiction and the political thriller that the planet as a totality has become widely perceptible to readers and interestingly open to unfamiliar emotional identifications. But a first glimpse is not always decisive. Meaninglessness, which is the point for Johnson and Bowles, is sometimes also the main thing readers of American spy novels learn about the world outside their borders. Some, like the Jack Ryan novels of Tom Clancy, posit the essential goodness of the USA, though this one firm point contrasts with a slippery array of villains who are subject to change without notice, from Islamic terrorists to Colombia drug lords to neo-Nazis. In the Jason Bourne novels of Robert Ludlum, on the other hand, it would seem to be the American government that wants its agent dead. And this self-targeting pre-dates the end of the Cold War; *The Bourne Identity* was published in 1980. As in *Tree of Smoke*, the US government, all too easily represented by powerful rogue elements within it, is just another player in that shadowy arena of governments, movements, global corporations, and semi-autonomous agencies where no one occupies the high moral ground. This is a powerful alternative to belligerent patriotism, even if the moral is often, once again, the virtues of withdrawal from public action, especially in transnational territory.

In much science fiction, the modern nation-state is declared to be obsolete. Sometimes its much-anticipated disappearance makes way for a reassertion of older and equally questionable social forms, like the ethnic tribe. An example is Neal Stephenson's *The Diamond Age* (1995), where the Great Phyles, or tribes, that divide most of the world are Chinese and Japanese (each of them ethnically exclusive) and Anglo (which alone is open to other ethnicities). Civilizational self-flattery, which is likely to increase with the rise of East Asia, passes more easily in the guise of science fiction. The science fiction of William Gibson also turns to medieval romance for much of its plotting, which is set in a neo-feudal vision of geopolitics. But there are clear continuities with Gibson's non-sci fi novel *Pattern Recognition* (2003), which makes quite an extraordinary effort to suture personal experience and the impersonal realities of global capital.[16]

Pattern Recognition is another 9/11 novel, as I've said, but its worldliness has less to do with terrorism than with the global circulation of commodities. Its equivalent of the technologically augmented capacities that science fiction so often bestows on its characters is the protagonist's uncanny ability to predict the success or failure of corporate logos, an ability that is both a kind of critique of the global marketplace – logos pursue her from continent to continent, literally making her sick – and itself a marketable commodity. The plot will treat this ability as a disease, curing her of it after a climactic recognition and reconciliation scene with a figure who personally embodies the combined menace of international terror and of corporate capital. But the novel's central mystery features a kind of anti-logo circulating for free on the internet, and this mystery is solved when the placeless identities of the internet resolve into faces, recognized, in the streets of a city. Here the streets are worlds, and the world is in the street. The novel gives readers their accustomed pleasure and instruction, and it does so on a genuinely global scale.

Notes

1. A notable exception that does train us to see at a distance is Russell Banks's *Continental Drift* (1985). Banks couples a desperate coming-to-America story (a Haitian woman moving north into the USA) with the parallel narrative of a New England white man moving south, escaping from a quiet desperation of his own.
2. This is not to say that worldliness is a recent phenomenon. On the transnational dimension of the earliest American fiction, see Paul Giles, "Transatlantic currents and the invention of the American novel," chapter 1.
3. This would be a context in which to discuss experimental or avant-garde writing that tries to do without some or all of the conventions of reader identification, plot resolution, and so on. As a gesture toward this absent discussion, let me simply mention Richard Powers's interesting experiments in getting readers to identify with a specifically inhuman protagonist. These are most relevant to the global scale in *Gain* (1998), where the inhuman protagonist is a multinational corporation, a toxicity-producing artificial being whose life trajectory extends over many generations.
4. Here, as elsewhere in DeLillo, seeing "world domination" behind local people and objects is a special ability shared by terrorists and novelists. Like the novelist, the hijacker is ready to see the "entire life" he wants to destroy as both a consistent, coherent, judgeable "world" and as a sum of odd, random, and infinite particulars.
5. For a spirited defense of withdrawal in explicitly political terms, see John A. McClure, *Partial Faiths: Postsecular Fiction in the Age of Pynchon and Morrison* (Athens: University of Georgia Press, 2007).

6. On the rich connections between war, cosmopolitanism, and absurdity in American fiction, see John Carlos Rowe, "US novels and US wars," chapter 49.
7. Interesting comparisons, from the perspective of how extensively and fairly the society of origin is presented, include Carlos Bulosan's *America Is in the Heart* (1946) and Gish Jen's *The Love Wife* (2004). On Bulosan's treatment of history in the Philippines, see Rowe, chapter 49, 819, and Susan Koshy, "The rise of the Asian American novel," chapter 63, 1053–1054.
8. On the frustration of the "land of opportunity" ideal in narratives of immigration, see Tim Prchal, "New Americans and the immigrant novel," chapter 25.
9. Compare with the treatment in Hemingway's "On the Quai at Smyrna" from *In Our Time* (1925).
10. On the rescue motif in transnational fiction, see Russ Castronovo, "Imperialism, Orientalism, and empire," chapter 32, esp. 542–543.
11. For a qualification of this reading of the upward mobility story, see Bruce Robbins, *Upward Mobility and the Common Good* (Princeton: Princeton University Press, 2007).
12. For contrast see Barbara Kingsolver, *The Poisonwood Bible* (1998).
13. On Vollmann see Michele Hardesty, "Looking for the Good Fight: William T. Vollmann's *An Afghanistan Picture Show*," *boundary 2* (Summer 2009).
14. This doesn't mean the satire stops being funny: "Gitanas had created a satiric Web page offering DEMOCRACY FOR PROFIT: BUY A PIECE OF EUROPEAN HISTORY . . . Visitors to the site were invited to send cash to the erstwhile VIPPPAKJRIINPB17 – 'one of Lithuania's most venerable political parties' . . . and now a 'Western-leaning pro-business party' reorganized as the 'Free Market Party Company.' Gitanas's Web site promised that, as soon as the Free Market Party Company had bought enough votes to win a national election, its foreign investors would . . . become 'equity shareholders' in Lithuania Incorporated (a 'for-profit nation state')." Eventually the Web site will offer no-questions-asked access to wiretaps and the right to be called "Your Lordship" on Lithuanian soil (non-use punishable by flogging), among other perks.
15. On Pynchon as the highpoint of a certain worldly tradition, see John Carlos Rowe, "US novels and US wars," chapter 49, 828–829.
16. If any novel has managed to do the street as a world, it is perhaps DeLillo's *Cosmopolis*, whose protagonist is a financier and whose action is entirely taken up with a single cross-town ride, a ride that in very heavy traffic takes one full day.

67

The Native American Tradition

SEAN KICUMMAH TEUTON

In 1854 Cherokee outlaw John Rollin Ridge wrote *The Life and Adventures of Joaquin Murieta: The Celebrated California Bandit*, the first novel by a Native American. Years before, in 1839, Ridge's father John Ridge and others had gathered covertly to sign away Cherokee title to ancestral homelands in the east and to move the Cherokees west. For selling Cherokee land without consent of the nation, a band of traditionalists gathered one night at the Ridge house and brutally assassinated the father before the eyes of the son. John Rollin Ridge vowed revenge and one day killed a man he suspected to be one of his father's murderers. Fleeing to the California gold fields, John Rollin Ridge may have endured his banishment imagining himself the California bandit Joaquin Murieta, the Hispanic folk hero who robs the wealthy to support the weak throughout the land.[1]

Not all Native American novels bear such complex histories, but since *Joaquin Murieta* many Indigenous authors have sought in the novel a structure to develop characters as a means to raise social consciousness, and to resolve plots in which Natives depart and return to replenish community and land. Throughout this tradition, Native novelists transform the genre to meet intellectual and social needs facing Indigenous communities.[2] Whether masquerading or assimilating, resisting or recovering, the Native American novel persists, ironically, not only by preserving but in fact by rewriting narrative traditions. Yet from the arrival of the first American Indian novel, Native writers have been forced to meet the demands of a mainstream reading audience that often harbors inaccurate views of Native Americans.[3] Even though American Indians have been enrolled in American colleges since the seventeenth century, where they have learned to read and write in Latin and Greek as well as in English,[4] the concept of a Native American intellectual seems almost an oxymoron in the American mainstream.[5] Indeed, the North American savage was defined precisely by his lack of true language and, more specifically, writing.[6] Thus, in the sixteenth century and perhaps still today, to see an Indian writing is to see a figure neither savage nor civilized, but an aberration of each, and so no one at all. Today, that colonial desire for cultural authenticity or repulsion in the face of cultural corruption is triggered less by the image of the Native intellectual than by the Native literary work itself, particularly the novel.[7] As Native Americans were destroyed, the colonial and early republican imagination dealt with the guilt by dreaming up the image of the Vanishing American, who, though he must die, dies beautifully to yield to the flowering of Western civilization across America.[8] While that image has been exposed and decried in the American novel,[9] it seems allowed to remain in the Native American novel.

As recently as 1995, Native authors, perhaps in order to serve dominant reading markets, still seemed compelled to represent this vanishing. In *Reservation Blues* (1996), a novel about young Indian men starting a blues band, Spokane novelist Sherman Alexie claims merely to portray his community life as he well knows it, but Native critics contend Alexie is nonetheless accountable for representing Native worlds to a broader culture, which often expects American Indians to disappear.[10] *Reservation Blues* portrays multiple acts of self-destruction; many characters drink themselves toward early deaths. Alexie's explanation of Junior's suicide is most troubling. Because Alexie is not clear about the deeper, colonial roots of suicidal desire in Indian nations, many readers are led to believe that American Indians, as their own worst enemies, are just doomed. When Junior reappears to his friend Victor as a ghost, he offers no larger explanation for his own vanishing: "I wanted to be dead. Gone. No more." All Junior identifies as the source of his own despair is a lack of imagination. Since he could name the instances of racism and colonial oppression he relives shortly before pulling the trigger, it is puzzling that Junior finally sees "nothing." In the end, such nihilism evades contending with the federal sources of economic and cultural destruction on the Spokane Indian Reservation. Alexie portrays poverty and social dysfunction in the Spokane community in *Reservation Blues* as the unexamined and unlucky consequence of being American Indian in the world today.

Indians often must self-destruct in Native novels. In other Native novels, such as Blackfeet and Gros Ventre writer James Welch's *Death of Jim Loney* (1979), Chippewa writer Louise Erdrich's *Love Medicine* (1984), and Cherokee writer Thomas King's *Truth and Bright Water* (1994), Indians self-destruct in suicidal leaps, yet these novels seek to understand that destruction in its broader colonial context. Perhaps as mainstream American readerships confront our colonial history more squarely, Indian novelists will be able to put away the Vanishing American once and for all, to deal honestly with our history across colonial relations, and to redress crimes.

So, from its very beginning the Native American novel has negotiated – and even been complicit with – arduous psychological demands from readers moored to a colonial imagination. While accepting and marketing the image of the Vanishing American has always placed pressure on the Native American novel, there were and are alternatives in novelistic expression: assimilation to the dominant mainstream and, more subversively, masquerading or disguising an Indigenous narrative within a more acceptable allegory.[11] Our first novelist, John Rollin Ridge, thus set a bold standard in writing *Joaquin Murieta,* a work that carved out creative space for Ridge to declare his anger at numerous injustices: the ongoing theft of Cherokee lands in the southeast; the rape and murder of Cherokee citizens at the hands of the Georgia Guard; the betrayal of the federal government in upholding its 1832 Supreme Court decision and in allowing the ethnic cleansing of Cherokees from the southeast; and of course the assassination of his father. As a fugitive with light skin, a long beard (!), and a Western education, Ridge could easily have assimilated into the American mainstream as a journalist in northern California. Instead, he wrote behind his Indian name of Yellow Bird both to disguise his identity and, ironically, to declare his Indianness. Murieta briefly reveals his true self: "He dashed along that fearful trail as he had been mounted upon a spirit-steed, shouting as he passed: 'I am Joaquin! kill me if you can!'" Here only for a moment, the Cherokee rides a "spirit-steed" with "his long black hair streaming behind him." In that bold move to adapt what we might call a radical romance, Yellow Bird was indeed far ahead of his time.

As early as the late nineteenth century, in novels such as Creek writer Alice Callahan's *Wynema, A Child of the Forest* (1891) – the first Indian novel by a woman – the American Indian novel has also sought to express Indigenous realities not through disguise, but rather through assimilation. In *Wynema,* the white Methodist teacher Genevieve Weir, working in the Creek Nation, finds in the young traditional Creek woman Wynema all the promise of a wealthy Southern lady. Genevieve remains largely at the cultural center of this sentimental novel of women's rights,[12] and Wynema herself dreams of fulfilling Genevieve's suffragette virtues: "We are waiting for our more civilized white sisters to gain their liberty, and thus set us an example which we shall not be slow to follow."

The turn of the twentieth century is critically recognized as the nadir of Indian populations and cultural vitality in North America. After repeated federally sponsored removals and massacres, corrupt financial dealings with Indian subsistence on reservations, and the division of communal lands through the 1887 General Allotment Act, Native communities and their governments had been reduced to utter dependence on the federal government and its social planners, who saw the traditional ways of Indian people as impossible to maintain and even as the cause of their malaise.[13] By the early twentieth century, white and Native leaders promoting Indian "uplift," through organizations such as the Society of American Indians, sought to prepare Native Americans for citizenship by eradicating the last of their traditional cultures. Such an answer to the "Indian problem" was at that time viewed as progressive.[14] Indian novelists of the time often offered plots that placed white American culture at the center to which marginalized traditional American Indians aspired.

The novels by Cherokee writer John Milton Oskison perhaps best exemplify the Native novel of assimilation. Educated at Stanford and Harvard, editor and feature writer of *Collier's Magazine*, and an active member of the Society, Oskison wrote novels, such as *Wild Harvest* (1925) and *Black Jack Davy* (1926), set in Indian Territory – before Oklahoma statehood – that envision the arrival of white settlers as a pivotal moment to negotiate cultural changes. Perhaps most developed of these novels is *Brothers Three* (1935), which uses the struggle of three brothers to keep the family farm as an emblem of the cultural challenges facing Natives. Saving the farm has shaped many plots in the American novel, and here the central characters, though Indian by blood, promote the mainstream values of hard work and integrity in hard times. In order to engage American Indian cultural issues, Oskison allows traditional Native characters to make occasional entrances as minor players in the drama. To trace a similar assimilationist trend today, one might consider the recent novels of Louise Erdrich such as *The Last Report on the Miracles at Little No Horse* (2002).

By the 1930s, American lawmakers became aware of the disastrous consequences of allotment and reservation bureaucracy as exposed in the 1928 Meriam Report, a study sponsored by the Department of the Interior. Under the Roosevelt administration, Commissioner of Indian Affairs John Collier introduced the Indian New Deal, the 1934 Wheeler-Howard Indian Reorganization Act (IRA) to restore self-government on reservations. While assimilationist novels such as those by Oskison continued to present realist plots and characters, other Indian writers began to employ modernist techniques to question the necessity or even the possibility of Natives entering the mainstream. Osage writer John Joseph Mathews's *Sundown* (1934) is an interesting novel that straddles these two literary and cultural trends. The young protagonist, Challenge Windzer, lives in an Osage community that has recently experienced an oil boom, in which great new wealth offers to improve or destroy Osage life – depending on whether Chal is listening to his assimilationist father or his traditionalist mother.[15] Mathews employs both realist and modernist devices to tell the story of Chal, the author drawing on different conventions at key moments. When Chal is with his mother or gazing at Osage lands, all is presented with realistic clarity. However, when Chal must head to college, rush a fraternity, or confront the destructive power of alcohol, modernist fragmentation and internalized narrative memories gain full expression.

Cree anthropologist and writer D'Arcy McNickle, also writing during this time, completed two fine novels exploring the often hopeless predicament of American Indians, which McNickle himself describes as "wandering between two generations, two cultures." With *The Surrounded* (1936), McNickle set the prototype of the Native novel most recognized by contemporary audiences, complete with the serious treatment of colonialism and the power of oral traditions to resist it. Unlike earlier American Indian novels such as Okinagan writer Mourning Dove's *Cogewea, the Half-Blood* (1927), which offered protagonists of mixed Indian and white ancestry as "sad halfbreeds" both emotionally and psychologically ill-formed, McNickle's novels develop complex protagonists with mixed ancestry in order to ask difficult questions about Native American ancestral knowledge, cultural identity, and colonial change.[16] Ultimately, however, McNickle shows great doubts about whether American Indian people can successfully negotiate that change. Instead, McNickle suggests, Natives will either exist in flux, torn between the demands of both white and Indigenous cultures, or simply self-destruct. In *The Surrounded*, for example, when the wandering main character visits with his mother's family on the Flathead reservation and observes a traditional dance, he feels somehow embarrassed and out of place: "They were not real people." A trip to the mountains ends with him witnessing a murder committed by his mother and girlfriend, leaving him further disoriented and unmoored.

For decades McNickle worked on his most complex novel, *Wind from an Enemy Sky*, published posthumously in 1978,[17] about two elder Indian brothers, one a revered chief camped on traditional mountain lands, the other an assimilated farmer working in the nearby town, who have grown apart over the years but are now brought together by a terrible event. The government has suddenly dammed up the river that has sustained the Little Elk people for generations and, in reprisal, a young member of the tribe has shot dead a worker at the dam. Later, a well-meaning white anthropologist claims to have located in a museum the Little Elk people's invaluable beaver medicine, the power of which promises to save the people. The anthropologist, however, discovers it had been left to rot in a basement warehouse and so offers the Little Elks a Peruvian artifact instead. Such absurdly sad miscommunications between the Indians and the settlers continue a chain of tragic events in *Wind from an Enemy Sky*, through which McNickle reiterates his conclusions that Western and Indigenous worldviews are ultimately incommensurable.

One might also credit McNickle with developing the genre of the Native American historical novel. Reared on the early hope of John Collier to return tribal autonomy to Natives under the IRA, McNickle spent the years 1936–1952 working for the Bureau of Indian Affairs (BIA). On seeing the federal government begin to terminate tribes with the 1953 House Concurrent Resolution 108,[18] McNickle resigned. His sense of betrayal and pessimism is hardly masked in the above two novels, and perhaps explains his wish to write historical fiction. A year later, McNickle published *Runner in the Sun: A Story of Indian Maize* (1954), a delightful novel written for a young adult audience. The author takes us back to a pre-Columbian time in the cliff-dwelling southwest, when Indians faced a similar crisis threatening their environments and governments, cultures and societies. The novel's hero is a young man named Salt who is chastised by elders for seeking scientific explanations for their worsening drought and for suggesting their own beliefs on the subject to be superstitious. The banished Holy One sends Salt on a journey to Mesoamerica to discover a solution to the crisis, where Salt finds a new strain of corn and a new religious symbol to ensure their survival. In his final novel, the author offers here a positive vision of crisis, change, and renewal to Indian communities.[19] While one could argue that such a work of historical fiction is escapist, here McNickle leads Native youth to an earlier time when Western invasions were not the source of their crisis. Instead, readers are shown how an earlier Native community challenges those who abuse sacred knowledge with fear-mongering and intimidation, and how Natives use their scientific minds to identify and solve problems, seeking answers through hemispheric collaboration. Such historical fiction has gained Indigenous audiences, and perhaps for the same reasons then as today. Also writing during McNickle's time, Sioux author Ella Deloria's *Waterlily*, drafted in 1944 and published posthumously in 1988, returns to nineteenth-century Sioux life for a richly detailed account of camps, kinship, and religious and social customs. By the 1980s, American Indian writers shared their returns with a broad audience, in James Welch's *Fools Crow* (1986), in which the Blackfeet contend with the new moral crises of encroaching soldiers and disease, but also with generational differences and gender relations, or in Chickasaw writer Linda Hogan's novel about corruption during the Osage oil boom, *Mean Spirit* (1990).

Since as early as 1927, with the publication of Mourning Dove's *Cogewea, the Half-Blood*, Native American authors have harnessed the novel to engage the problem of maintaining an Indigenous identity in the face of European colonization. Born Christine Quintasket, Mourning Dove was a migrant farm worker in Washington state, where, after years of writing in her tent on evenings after laboring, she finally completed *Cogewea*. An Indian enthusiast named Lucullus McWhorter stepped in to edit her manuscript, eventually helping her publish the novel with his embellishments and in a very different form.[20] McWhorter probably had much to do with changing Mourning Dove's work into a popular Western romance, complete with villains and woeful pleas of halfbreeds in distress, with epigraphs to each chapter taken from "Hiawatha," among other works. The novel opens on a Montana cattle ranch on the Flathead reservation, where cowboys are Indians with mixed white and Native ancestry. The young woman Cogewea lives with her Indian family – her white father has left for good to the Alaska gold fields – and must decide between white and American Indian suitors: the dastardly scoundrel, Easterner Densmore, or the silent hero, "breed" James LaGrinder. While this rollicking novel bears all the inconsistencies of an invasive editor at odds with the author, *Cogewea, the Half-Blood* nonetheless displays well the challenges facing mixed-race Natives barred from either culture, when, for example, Cogewea enters a horse race dressed as a white woman and wins. On being discovered she loses her prize, the judge calling her a "squaw." And on entering a race for Native girls, she is told it's a race for Indians not "breeds."[a]

By the 1960s, Native American authors had begun to make the question – but also the recovery and the renewal – of Indigenous cultural identity the central theoretical and literary task in the Indian novel. While earlier writers such as Mourning Dove and McNickle saw the problem of mixed ancestry as central to understanding cultural erosion, the new writers saw Native identity – and even mixed ancestry – as the embodiment, the cause, and the solution to their colonial situation. Beginning around 1969 with the occupation of Alcatraz Island, a decade-long flurry of events came to define the era of Red Power and the Red Power novel: the 1972 march on Washington for the Trail of Broken Treaties; the 1973 takeover of Wounded Knee; the 1975

a For a different reading of *Cogowea*, see Tom Lutz, "Cather and the regional imagination," chapter 26, 447.

intervention of the American Indian Movement on the Pine Ridge reservation; the 1978 Longest Walk on Washington to re-enact the displacement of Indian peoples from their homelands. Between these touchstone events, elders, faith keepers, students, scholars, and activists organized dozens of occupations of stolen American Indian territories, staged takeovers of corrupt BIA offices, and filed multiple legal claims demanding the return of stolen lands and property, as well as compensation for centuries of cultural destruction. The movement drove the passing in 1968 of the Indian Civil Rights Act to recognize those rights in Indian country; in 1975 of the Indian Self-Determination Act to advance tribal self-governance; and in 1978 of the Indian Child Welfare Act and the American Indian Religious Freedom Act to protect Indigenous lives and customs.[21]

During this period, Native authors often placed individual and community cultural identity at the center of their novels: the protagonists cannot recover their lands, their pasts, and their lives until they reconnect with the elders, the healers, and other members of their communities. In so doing, they undergo a process of remembering and reinterpreting experiences of colonialism and related feelings of self-hatred. Upon achieving a more enabling picture of themselves in the Indian world, they are transformed. American Indians writing during the Indian Movement, and those influenced by it, respect the role of tribal knowledge, identity, and experience in explaining the rich realities of Native life – both the everyday stress of colonialist subjugation and the affirmation of Indian stories that engender cultural growth. Red Power writers thus situate American Indian identity as a concept central to forging knowledge of ancestral lifeways and homelands. Recognizing that the recovery of Native knowledge entails a complex process of interpretation, these authors elucidate just how American Indian people can awaken politically, reclaim a history, and build a community.[22]

While the American novel tends to celebrate leaving home to develop one's character, the Red Power novel often relies on the opposite movement. As Stephanie LeMenager argues in this volume, by the twentieth century, the frontier imagination had enabled the American novel to reinvent a world elsewhere, even at the evasion of troubling historical facts.[b] In the Red Power novel, however, American Indians have already left home, and their stories begin on their return, which marks the collective moment of cultural regeneration. [23] Most novels written during Red Power exude a yearning to return to the homeland from which protagonists have become estranged. In fact,

b Stephanie Le Menager, "Imagining the frontier," chapter 31.

the recovery and healing can take place only at home, through a process of self-reflection and reinterpretation of their past and present relationships, among trustworthy members of the tribal community. And when American Indians return with their discoveries, they must present this new knowledge to members of the tribal community. As Native storytelling is an intrinsically collective practice, so are the travels of the protagonists interpreted collectively, in the presence of elders, healers, and other listeners. These travelers are then cleansed and reintegrated. The community found in oral narrative, as Ursula Heise argues in this volume, appears frequently in the postmodern novel as a reaction to an often alienating modernity.[c] The Red Power novel thus explores how Native Americans might decolonize their nations by growing politically and culturally in a process that values the continuity of identity and experience in the production of knowledge.

The title of Kiowa writer N. Scott Momaday's first novel, *House Made of Dawn* (1968), refers to a Navajo healing ceremony meant to reintegrate tribal members as dwellers in the land. Momaday's protagonist, Abel, home from World War II and distanced from his land, cannot recover his tie to homeland until he comes to terms with his own bodily sense of self. In novels such as James Welch's *Winter in the Blood* (1974), the era's authors advanced their interests in American Indian cultural growth from the individual to the Native community, using characters' vexed relationship to the land as a vehicle to discuss tribal historical identifications with land. In *Winter in the Blood*, a young Blackfeet man experiences a political awakening, and, by recovering oral stories about the moral decisions of his ancestors, he recovers his masculinity and cultural identity.[24] Then, in novels such as Laguna author Leslie Marmon Silko's *Ceremony* (1977), the Red Power novel began to engage the political struggles that grow from and protect Native lands. In *Ceremony*, personal insight gained from religious experience provides knowledge that aids human consciousness,[25] as the protagonist Tayo recovers from a war that has damaged his ability to experience the world as a spiritually gifted Laguna man.

Half of all American Indians today reside in cities.[26] Some have argued that Indian people cannot live in metropolitan areas and maintain their cultural and spiritual lives and tribal communities, or that they must remain on reservations "given" to them by the United States, despite the reality that Native people have been migrating and resettling across the continent for thousands of years. Beneath this desire for cultural purity that these views

c Ursula Heise, "Postmodern novels," chapter 58, 974–977.

reflect lies the familiar binary of savagery and civilization, according to which European peoples bring cities and civilization to Native North America and diminish the savage world across the American frontier.[27] In this still under-examined view of American culture, Indian people must remain on the other side of a timeless "frontier" to be culturally pure, and, if they venture off to cities, they risk losing their culture and even plunging into the darkness of social degradation. On the other hand, if Native people succeed in the city, Americans may then consider the federal Relocation programs of the 1950s to be a success; Indians who carry briefcases are then thought to be absorbed, no longer a threat from the savage frontier – and no longer real Indians.

But Indigenous people in cities today might actually be drawing on a very old process of community-building and collective retribalizing to recall the aggregation of cities such as Cahokia (an ancient population center near what is now St. Louis, Missouri) or, more recently, the praying Indian towns of eighteenth-century New England, in which multiple tribes gathered to share culture and social relations, intermarry and create an entirely new tribal group.[28] In this exciting scenario, tribal members encounter members of multiple ethnic groups, contributing to the creative interaction and exchange of cultural values and practices. In fact, the intertribal activity of Red Power made possible a new political vision of Indian Country, and so Native writers today often represent the city as a setting of cultural exploration. Navajo writer Irvin Morris's *From the Glittering World* (2000) is a contemporary story of unceasing, restless movement away from and back to Navajo homelands, in a modern search for an explanation of colonialism and racism in the United States and Native America. Yet without an explanation of the central rootedness of the narrator, we would not appreciate his courage in leaving the safety of his lands and braving the city in his desire for knowledge. It is only through travel away from this secure relationship that the narrator gains a new perspective on his world, a vantage point above "my mother, the earth" through which better to understand the relations of power that have threatened to destroy both his people and the land.

The city's allure of new experiences, though, is not the only reason for the narrator's continual flight from home. At rock bottom in Gallup, he considers the source of his depression, addiction, and homelessness, and finds fear at the heart of his reluctance to go home: "I am afraid to face my own life. I am Indian. I am minority. I am dark and I am powerless." Significantly, the narrator suggests that his very experiences of the world beyond his nation have led him to "know too much," a condition that ironically also fuels his despair. In his unrelenting departures from home into the world of the city, the narrator of *From the Glittering World* leads his own discovery, however painful, of his own life, available to him only at a safe distance from home, in the city where "the sirens welcome me," and where he may also read "the tribal newspaper." Throughout *From the Glittering World*, the narrator learns to live with an ironic tension between reservation and city, between lived experience and read experience, where Indian life often makes more sense when read from a distance.

Because the Native American urban novel grows from a desire for cultural and social exchange in cosmopolitan spaces, it has become a vehicle for Indian writers who seek to address the lives of Indian women or queer Natives.[29] Laguna writer Paula Gunn Allen's *Woman Who Owned the Shadows* (1983) imagines lesbian life in San Francisco, while Janet Campbell Hale's *Jailing of Cecelia Capture* (1985) also takes her protagonist to the Bay Area to gain a law degree and disclose the legal control of the USA on Native women. As sexuality gains voice in *From the Glittering World*, so it does in Pomo author Greg Sarris's *Watermelon Nights* (1999), and especially in Creek writer Craig Womack's *Drowning in Fire* (2001), in which historical fiction concerning the pre-statehood Creek Nation intertwines with a richly woven gay coming-out narrative. Though perhaps occupying a genre all its own, Leslie Marmon Silko's *Almanac of the Dead* (1991) draws its force from Indigenous women in cities like Tucson and others over the hemispheric map.[30] The novel overturns our romantic assumptions that Native American women are bountiful, yielding care-givers by beginning with a scene of elder sisters Leche and Zeta cooking up drugs in their kitchen. Yet in its unprecedented hemispheric scope that combines actual historical events with Indigenous prophecy,[d] *Almanac of the Dead* is also a supreme Native novel of innovation.[31]

Indeed, from its inception and by very necessity, the Native American novel has been experimental, attracting and modifying subgenres to seek Indigenous cultural survival and development. At the vanguard of social and political movements during the last century, Indian writers have made the novel their place of both formal and social innovation. In formal terms, Native authors experiment with plot formulae, self-conscious narration, or simply the denial of novelistic expectations; in cultural terms, they place Indian people in unexpected conversations often halfway around the world,[32] where readers discover new possibilities for American Indian lives.

d Ramón Saldívar, in this volume, offers a fuller reading of *Almanac of the Dead*, which stresses how its formal innovations complicate themes of race and identity, especially along the US borderlands. See "The American borderlands novel," chapter 62, 1038–1043.

As early as the Red Power Indian movement of the 1970s, authors such as Anishinaabe writer Gerald Vizenor made the novel a place to imagine the relationship of intellectual health to tribal cultural health, in his words, "survivance."[33] In the sexually violent and controversial fantasy novel of apocalyptic pilgrimage, *Bearheart* (1978), Vizenor offers a message on dogmatic thinking, what he calls "terminal creeds." Belladonna Darwin-Winter Catcher, who is often confused about her Indianness, encounters "the hunter," who says: "Indians are an invention. . . . You tell me that the invention is different than the rest of the world when it was the rest of the world that invented the Indian . . . An Indian is an Indian because he speaks and thinks and believes he is an Indian, but an Indian is nothing more than an invention . . ." For her uncritical beliefs about Native culture, the hunters then execute Belladonna with a poison cookie, announcing that she "is a terminal believer and a victim of her own narcissism."

As Native American populations and economies continue to grow, and calls for greater autonomy from the federal government are increasingly answered, Indian authors will likely expand the artistic and cultural reach of the Indigenous novel beyond our present imaginations. James Welch, for example, imagined the moral consequences of Native Americans achieving advanced degrees and entering politics in *The Indian Lawyer* (1990), only further to test and to advance this cultural question beyond the continent and in the past century, in *The Heartsong of Charging Elk* (2000). Here, Oglala warrior Charging Elk sails to France to perform in a Wild West show, where he falls ill and is left behind, and decides to stay, forming a new family. In Meskwakie writer Ray Young Bear's *Remnants of the First Earth* (1996), poets are unleashed within novels to explore the creative power of poetic imagery in prose, where fantasy cannot be distinguished from reality, and whole passages appear in Mesquakie untranslated.[34]

Perhaps most excitingly, however, the Native American novel has become increasingly aware of itself as an art with real-world consequences for Indians' lives. Ojibwe writer David Treuer's *The Hiawatha* (2000), set in Minneapolis, is certainly an urban Indian novel, but as a novel of innovation, it draws its power from uncompromising plot devices and traumatized language. Complex phrases like "studied love" invite us to believe in characters that, via gratuitous murders, are abruptly taken from us. Thomas King also invites reflection on the Indian novel and its creation and purposes, with wonderful self-mocking humor. In *Green Grass, Running Water* (1994), white tourists visit the tribe's Dead Dog Café to see "real" Indians and to taste what they believe to be traditional dog meat hamburgers. Throughout, the narrator even reprimands the oral traditional Coyote figure (and presumably the rest of us) to "pay attention" and "forget about being helpful"; just "sit down and listen."

In writing the first Native American novel in the mid nineteenth century, John Rollin Ridge likely sought social refuge and intellectual health as much as artistic discovery or celebrity authorship. Like Ridge, Native authors over a century later sought in the novelistic form a subversive balm for colonial injustice. Yet leading up to that resistance, the American Indian novel at times has submitted to the desires of the American marketplace and readership. By the mid twentieth century, with the myths of the Vanishing American and the halfbreed caught between two worlds fully engrained, the novels of assimilation or its fateful impossibility might have seemed the only formal options available to the Native American novelist. But perhaps in the spirit of Yellow Bird, Indigenous writers in the late twentieth century and ever more today, have awakened, rekindled their fires, and breathed into the novel an Indian voice for tribal autonomy, cultural persistence, and social pluralism.

Notes

1. For more historical background, see James W. Parins, *John Rollin Ridge: His Life and Works* (Lincoln: University of Nebraska Press, 1991), esp. chapter 6.
2. Simon J. Ortiz, "Towards a National Indian Literature: Cultural Authenticity in Nationalism," *MELUS* 8.2 (1981): 7–13.
3. Louis Owens, *Mixedblood Messages: Literature, Film, Family, Place* (Norman: University of Oklahoma Press, 1998), 58–65.
4. Wolfgang Hochbruck and Beatrix Dudensing-Reichel, "'Honoratissimi Benefactores': Native American Students and Two Seventeenth-Century Texts in the University Tradition," in *Early Native American Writing: New Critical Essays*, ed. Helen Jaskoski (Cambridge: Cambridge University Press, 1996), 1–2; see Kristina Bross, *Dry Bones and Indian Sermons: Praying Indians in Colonial America* (Ithaca, NY: Cornell University Press, 2004), esp. 6–10.
5. Robert Warrior, "The Native American Scholar: Toward a New Intellectual Agenda," *Wicazo Sa Review* 14.2 (1999): 46–54; see Jace Weaver, *That the People Might Live: Native American Literatures and Native American Community* (Oxford: Oxford University Press, 1997), 16–23.
6. See, for example, Robert F. Berkhofer, *The White Man's Indian: Images of the American Indian from Columbus to the Present* (New York: Vintage, 1979); and Gordon M. Sayre, *Les Sauvages Américains: Representations of Native Americans in French and English Colonial Literature* (Chapel Hill: University of North Carolina Press, 1997), 179–217.
7. Hilary Wyss, *Writing Indians: Literacy, Christianity, and Native Community in Early America* (Amherst: University of Massachusetts Press, 2000), 3–6; on the novel, see

Bill Ashcroft, Gareth Griffiths, and Helen Tiffin, *The Empire Writes Back: Theory and Practice in Post-Colonial Literatures* (London: Routledge, 1995).

8. Richard Drinnon, *Facing West: The Metaphysics of Indian-Hating and Empire-Building* (Norman: University of Oklahoma Press, 1980). For a study of Christian conversion to solve the Indigenous presence, see Joshua David Bellin, *The Demons of the Continent: Indians and the Shaping of American Literature* (Philadelphia: University of Pennsylvania Press, 2001), ch. 1. For different aspects of the association of violence against Indians and "civilization," see Timothy Sweet, chapter 5, "American land, American landscapes, American novels"; Sandra Gustafson, chapter 6, "Cooper and the idea of the Indian"; Winfried Fluck, chapter 7, "The nineteenth-century historical novel"; and Stephanie Le Menager, chapter 31, "Imagining the frontier," in this volume.
9. James H. Cox, *Muting White Noise: Native American and European American Novel Traditions* (Norman: University of Oklahoma Press, 2006), chapter 5; and Elizabeth Cook-Lynn, *Why I Can't Read Wallace Stegner and Other Essays: A Tribal Voice* (Madison: University of Wisconsin Press, 1996).
10. Gloria Bird, "The Exaggeration of Despair in Sherman Alexie's *Reservation Blues*," *Wicazo Sa Review* 10.2 (1995): 47–52.
11. Louis Owens, *Other Destinies: Understanding the American Indian Novel* (Norman: University of Oklahoma Press, 1992), 32–40.
12. See Cari M. Carpenter, *Seeing Red: Anger, Sentimentality, and American Indians* (Columbus: Ohio State University Press, 2008), 29–53.
13. Frederick E. Hoxie, *A Final Promise: The Campaign to Assimilate the Indians, 1880–1920* (Lincoln: University of Nebraska Press, 1984).
14. Lucy Maddox, *Citizen Indians: Native American Intellectuals, Race, and Reform* (Ithaca, NY: Cornell University Press, 2005), 89–96.
15. For a reading of Chal's predicament in the context of community politics, see Robert Warrior, *Tribal Secrets: Recovering American Indian Intellectual Traditions* (Minneapolis: University of Minnesota Press, 1995), 46–57.
16. Robert Dale Parker, *The Invention of Native American Literature* (Ithaca, NY: Cornell University Press, 2003), chapter 3.
17. For publishing background, see John Purdy, *Word Ways: The Novels of D'Arcy McNickle* (Tucson: University of Arizona Press, 1990), 106–116.
18. On federal plans for the relocation of Native Americans, see Donald L. Fixico, *Termination and Relocation: Federal Indian Policy, 1945–1960* (Albuquerque: University of New Mexico Press, 1986).
19. Alfonso Ortiz, "Afterword," in *Runner in the Sun: A Story of Indian Maize*, by D'Arcy McNickle (Albuquerque: University of New Mexico Press, 1987), 245–254.
20. See Arnold Krupat, *Red Matters: Native American Studies* (Philadelphia: University of Pennsylvania Press, 2002), 76–97.
21. For a narrative history of the Indian movement, see Paul Chaat Smith and Robert Warrior, *Like a Hurricane: The Indian Movement from Alcatraz to Wounded Knee* (New York: New Press, 1996).

22. For a study of the Red Power novel and its legacy, see Sean Kicummah Teuton, *Red Land, Red Power: Grounding Knowledge in the American Indian Novel* (Durham, NC: Duke University Press, 2008).
23. William W. Bevis, "Native American Novels: Homing In," *Recovering the Word: Essays on Native American Literature*, ed. Brian Swann and Arnold Krupat (Berkeley: University of California Press, 1987), 580–620.
24. See the classic essays by Lawrence J. Evers, "Words and Place: A Reading of *House Made of Dawn*," in *Critical Essays on Native American Literature*, ed. Andrew Wiget (Boston: G. K. Hall, 1985), 211–230; and Kathleen Mullen Sands, "Alienation and Broken Narrative in *Winter in the Blood*," in Wiget, *Critical Essays*, 230–238.
25. See Ellen L. Arnold, "An Ear for Story, and Eye for the Pattern: Rereading *Ceremony*," *Modern Fiction Studies* 45.1 (1999): 69–92.
26. For a study of metropolitan Natives, see Susan Lobo and Kurt Peters, eds. *American Indians and the Urban Experience* (Walnut Creek, CA: Alta Mira, 2001).
27. Roy Harvey Pearce, *Savagism and Civilization: A Study of the Indian and the American Mind* (Berkeley: University of California Press, 1953; rev. edn., 1988).
28. Russell Thornton, "The Demography of Colonialism and 'Old' and 'New' Native Americans," in *Studying Native America: Problems and Prospects*, ed. Russell Thornton (Madison: University of Wisconsin Press, 1998), 33.
29. For a theory of Indigenous homosexuality, see Craig S. Womack, *Red on Red: Native American Literary Separatism* (Minneapolis: University of Minnesota Press, 1999), 275–279.
30. For comparative Indigenous hemispheric study, see Chadwick Allen, *Blood Narrative: Indigenous Identity in American Indian and Maori Literary and Activist Texts* (Durham, NC: Duke University Press, 2002).
31. For a reading of the "amplified witchery" in this novel, see David L. Moore, "Silko's Blood Sacrifice: The Circulating Witness in *Almanac of the Dead*," in *Leslie Marmon Silko: A Collection of Critical Essays*, ed. Louise K. Barnett and James L. Thorson (Albuquerque: University of New Mexico Press, 1999), 149–183.
32. See Philip J. Deloria, *Indians in Unexpected Places* (Lawrence: University of Kansas Press, 2004).
33. Kimberly M. Blaeser, *Gerald Vizenor: Writing in the Oral Tradition* (Norman: University of Oklahoma Press, 1996).
34. On Young Bear's ambiguity, see Michael D. Wilson, *Writing Home: Indigenous Narratives of Resistance* (East Lansing: Michigan State University Press, 2008), 134–146.

68

Contemporary ecofiction

JONATHAN LEVIN

Ecofiction is an elastic term, capacious enough to accommodate a variety of fictional works that address the relationship between natural settings and the human communities that dwell within them. The term emerged soon after ecology took hold as a popular scientific paradigm and a broad cultural attitude in the 1960s and 1970s.[1] Two key events helped spark this new environmental awareness: the controversy surrounding proposed dams on the Colorado River that led ultimately to the construction of the Glen Canyon Dam (begun in the mid-1950s and completed about ten years later), and the 1962 publication of *Silent Spring*, Rachel Carson's exposé of the environmental impact of toxic pesticides like DDT. Both generated widespread media coverage, bringing complex and urgent environmental issues and the ecological vocabularies that helped explain them into the American lexicon. Variations on these themes would thread their way through much writing about the environment for the next half-century. Before these controversies, few Americans thought about the unintended consequences of "progress" on the environment and its inhabitants. This innocence would be seriously challenged in the aftermath of Glen Canyon, *Silent Spring*, and the many environmental crises and controversies that followed.[2]

The 1960s and 1970s also saw a growing awareness and acceptance of the new tools being used by scientists, journalists, and others to understand the natural world. Ecology, which had first emerged among naturalists in the late nineteenth century, became the default framework through which many people would view the natural world. Grounded in evolutionary theory, ecology came to stand for the biological framework that foregrounds the interrelations among plants, animals, soil and other landforms, and climate that constitute and sustain any natural community.[3] This vision became linked to the growing concern for the fragility of particular ecologies. The "age of ecology" was also sometimes characterized by a utopian idealism, often associated with new forms of communal experience (especially during the counterculture movement of the 1960s and 1970s). Scientific ecologists often struggled against this association, mostly unsuccessfully because of the widespread sense that a better understanding of the interrelatedness of all life on the planet should be linked to a new consciousness about humans' place in the cosmic scheme of things. Several enduring ecological slogans entered the public consciousness around this time, such as "Think globally, act locally" and Barry Commoner's "Everything is connected to everything else."[4] With their emphasis on the powerful impact of even small or invisible actions as they are amplified along a chain of connections, these slogans helped make the ecological framework accessible and persuasive to many.

Variously influenced by these trends, contemporary ecofiction can be divided into three broad categories: wilderness narratives; stewardship narratives that weave together the linked fates of human communities and the land; and postnatural narratives that reject both wilderness and the land as dominant tropes or structural frameworks, turning instead to urban, suburban, and other postmodern landscapes to explore the complex and ambiguous ecological contexts of contemporary life. Wilderness narratives reflect popular mainstream environmental traditions, especially in their most classically preservationist mode. Stewardship narratives highlight the interaction of human communities and the land, reflecting environmentalist traditions that underscore the imperative of responsible stewardship. Postnatural narratives challenge most environmentalist frameworks. While authors in this group still highlight environmental destruction, they don't look to the "natural" setting – whether wilderness, agrarian landscape, or balanced ecological community – for relief from contemporary industrial or post-industrial trends. Nature, for many of these writers, has lost its status as pure and pristine. These late twentieth- and early twenty-first-century writers instead view "nature" as itself a kind of unnatural artifact, a hybrid of nature, engineering, and the media that invariably shape our perception of what passes as "natural."[5]

James Dickey's 1970 novel *Deliverance*, structured around the classic antagonism between urban and rural worlds, exemplifies the wilderness ethos. The narrative centers on a wild river that runs through a barely accessible stretch of Georgia wilderness now threatened with extinction by an impending dam project. Four mildly bored urbanites are looking to experience some of the last remaining wild land in the region, and the river and its surrounding woods are depicted as potentially redemptive for them. Lewis – an experienced outdoorsman and amateur survivalist – suggests that in the event of a total collapse of our human systems, he would move to the hills through which they are about to canoe: "You could make a kind of life that wasn't out of touch with everything . . . Where you could hunt as you needed to, and maybe do a little light farming, and get along. You'd die early, and you'd suffer, and your children would suffer, but you'd be in touch." Lewis's dream is a classic projection of the romantic imagination. He rejects the dehumanizing hollowness at the core of modern life in favor of experience in an uncorrupted and inaccessible natural setting, leading potentially to the kind of rebirth hinted at in the novel's title.

But if *Deliverance* is shaped by these urban/suburban male fantasies of an alternative social reality grounded in land depicted as "unvisited and free," it is also haunted by the truly alien otherness of the nature the trekkers encounter and the terrible human depredation Dickey associates with that nature. Dickey conveys this theme in many ways, including descriptive passages of animals (for example, an owl that perches on the narrator's tent as it hunts through the evening), the river (especially during several dangerous rapid runs), and, most dramatically, the assault by two local natives who brutally rape one of the narrator's group and threaten to rape and kill the narrator himself. On one level, this scene – probably best remembered for the raw, dehumanizing line from the film adaptation, "Squeal like a pig"[6] – suggests that beautiful, uncorrupted nature may harbor unimaginable horrors. On another level, these very horrors catalyze the narrator's own self-realization. One of the original group of four is killed during the journey, and the three survivors are pushed to their physical, mental, and moral limits. For Dickey's narrator, the intensity of the experience in nature actually leads to a paradoxical transcendence of that nature. By the novel's end, the dam has obliterated this natural setting, but it survives as a more intense reality in the narrator's imagination: "In me it still is, and will be until I die, green, rocky, deep, fast, slow, and beautiful beyond reality."

Deliverance is framed by an awareness that the wilderness is disappearing, and with it the only kind of space that could support such self-discovery. The novel does not offer much commentary on the natural or social costs of the rampant development exemplified by the dam. Lyrical as his descriptions of threatened nature are, Dickey focuses primarily on the narrator's inner journey. By contrast, Edward Abbey's classic 1975 wilderness novel, *The Monkey Wrench Gang*, offers sustained commentary on the shortsightedness and greed that drive humans' urge to develop the earth. *The Monkey Wrench Gang* is among the best-known and most beloved works of American environmental fiction, in part because the novel's environmental politics are so openly radical.[a] The novel follows four characters, all of them occupying different margins of society, as they set out to commit acts of eco-sabotage that will, they hope, reverse the trend of large-scale development in the region. They dream of destroying Glen Canyon Dam, which symbolizes for them the terrible destruction wrought throughout the American Southwest in the name of progress. The characters fix on Glen Canyon Dam because several of them fondly remember the canyons before they were submerged by the massive lake formed by the dam. Indeed, their evocations of this lost wilderness occasion some of the most lyrical writing in the novel.

Abbey's deep passion for the American Southwest wilderness suffuses *The Monkey Wrench Gang*. Almost everyone in the novel other than its four lead characters is depicted as insensitive to the extraordinary beauty and haunting mystery of the landscape. Some are driven by simple greed (the land is treated as a resource to be mined, harvested, or otherwise made profitable) and some by a shallow appreciation for nature shaped by what Abbey elsewhere calls "industrial tourism."[7] For the novel's ragtag band of eco-saboteurs, the remaining wilderness calls our entire industrial civilization into question. They adopt extreme measures because they despise the extreme measures that have transformed their beloved wilderness. Abbey's wilderness also becomes a proxy for the radical individualism that the novel presents as the only antidote to the bland uniformity rampant in contemporary American culture.

Abbey's radical environmental activism is best captured by the irreverent, often exaggerated style of the novel. The land itself is beautiful yet harsh and uninviting. The efforts of business and government to profit from its beauty by making it less demanding, more accessible, even more familiar for tourists strike the novel's principal characters as insulting and absurd, and inspire in them a series of exaggerated and comic anti-authoritarian gestures, from the burning down of billboards to the destruction of bulldozers, bridges, and (at least in their fantasies) dams. The novel's motto from Whitman, "Resist much. Obey little," encapsulates its spirit of anarchic resistance. By novel's end, the characters have not succeeded in much beyond delaying and making more expensive the various projects that they sabotage. But the spirit of resistance lives in them, and though all but one of them have been caught and chastened, the concluding scene makes clear that they have not lost their

a For a related reading of *The Monkey Wrench Gang*, see Cecelia Tichi's essay in this volume, "Novels of civic protest," chapter 23, 400, 403.

fight (a suspicion borne out by Abbey's posthumously published sequel, *Hayduke Lives!* [1990]).

Abbey's fiction offers an extended gloss on Thoreau's dictum from his essay "Walking" (1862), "In wildness is the preservation of the world." The allure of the wild, a direct legacy of the Romantic tradition, is a frequent theme in American environmental fiction. For Wallace Stegner, the wilderness narrative begins to shade into the stewardship narrative, especially as Stegner documents the taming of the West in his 1971 saga, *Angle of Repose*. Deeply committed to the preservation of wilderness, Stegner focuses on the essential connection between the great western wilderness and the people drawn to it. Unlike other wilderness writers, who value the immediacy and radical autonomy made possible by the setting, Stegner's narrator, like the author himself, values history, relationship, and connectedness, all of which he regards as crucial to the growth of the American West.[b] Telling the story of a family's experience of the West in the last half of the nineteenth century, the novel focuses on Susan Burling Ward, born into a genteel Hudson Valley family and married to an engineer who seeks his fortune primarily among the mines of the American West. The novel is narrated by Ward's grandson, Lyman Ward, a disabled historian who has retired to the family home in Grass Valley, California to write the story of his grandparents as they struggled to establish themselves in a variety of small mining towns and other potential "boom" towns in California, Colorado, Mexico, and Idaho.

Angle of Repose captures the paradox at the heart of Stegner's writing about wilderness and the West: "We were in subtle ways subdued by what we conquered." The novel's real focus is not the massive engineering project that the American West has become by the last half of the nineteenth century, but rather the process of character-building that takes place in this boom-and-bust setting. As Stegner comments in his 1960 "Wilderness Letter," "While we were demonstrating ourselves the most efficient and ruthless environment-busters in history, and slashing and burning and cutting our way through a wilderness continent, the wilderness was working on us."[8] The massive effort to conquer the wilderness ironically, and often tragically, taught many the values associated with the very wilderness that such efforts were designed to tame.

b For a comprehensive account of the idea of the frontier in American literature, including Stegner's novel, see Stephanie LeMenager's essay in this volume, "Imagining the frontier," chapter 31, esp. 515 for Stegner.

Susan Burling Ward, the narrator's grandmother in *Angle*, comes west loaded with the characteristic assumptions and preoccupations of a cultivated Easterner. Susan throws herself into her Western adventure, alternately encouraging and belittling her husband, pushing him toward his dream of making it big out west and condemning him for failing to secure for her the high-style Eastern comforts she dreamed of transplanting to the western territories. Like her husband, Susan learns humility through their failures – both as entrepreneurs and as companions – and like him, she learns to identify with the enduring values of the land, values that infuse spiritual depth into lives that might otherwise be stunted by their constant toil for material progress. This humility, framed by what Susan describes as "the West's bigness and impersonality," ultimately saves the couple and gets passed on to the narrator. Lyman's own humility is framed by his strong sense of how human conflict has shaped the history of his beloved West. By contrast, Lyman's young assistant Shelley Rasmussen toys with a more fashionable brand of utopian ecology, but Lyman will have none of such "soft-headedness" that "ignores both history and human nature." This leads him to the critical distinction between "civilization and the wild life": "I want a society that will protect the wild life without confusing itself with it." For Lyman Ward – and one suspects for Stegner himself – the ecological visionaries of the 1960s and early 1970s lack all depth of experience. They are right about nature, but wrong about the ways of the world.[9]

Although humankind may seek to mine wilderness for valuable minerals, harvest its trees for profit, or contain its waterways and their valleys for irrigation, energy, and recreation, wilderness remains completely indifferent to human aims and desires, and this indifference is at the heart of its appeal to so many writers in the wilderness tradition. Stegner belongs to this tradition, but his emphasis on the rise of a new Western culture deeply interconnected with the natural resources that supported the flourishing of that culture also points toward the stewardship tradition. For many, however, the idea of wilderness is antithetical to the notion of an appropriately balanced relationship between human communities and the land that supports the survival of those communities.[10] Native American writer Leslie Marmon Silko, for example, regards the land and all its diverse life forms as existing on a continuum with human communities and their history. For Silko, there is no genuinely individual encounter with the land, and the illusion of such an encounter is itself a sign of a diminished sense of history, community, and ecological relatedness. Humankind has forged its relationship to the land and its inhabitants over time, and that relationship is remembered and preserved through a series of rituals and stories that not only remind us of that relationship, but serve to restore us to it, both physically and spiritually.[c]

In Silko's 1977 novel *Ceremony*, the protagonist's early mental suffering is echoed by a drought in the land. Tayo has returned from the Second World War with a severe mental depression related to the Pacific island battle that led to the death of his beloved brother Rocky. Through Silko's technique of juxtaposing past and present, the novel's narrative suggests that, at least in Tayo's mind, the present-time drought in the American Southwest is related to Tayo's having prayed and chanted for the rain to stop years earlier, in the jungle during the war. Tayo has lost his sense of connectedness to the land and to the stories and rituals that bind the community to that land. He recalls a time when he and his brother climbed Bone Mesa and he "had felt that the sky was near and that he could have touched it." Stories mediated this belief: "Distances and days existed in themselves then; they all had a story. They were not barriers … [I]t depended on whether you knew the story of how others before you had gone." Tayo has lost faith in these stories and rituals, and the main action of the novel serves to remind him of their abiding power.[11]

For Silko, language and narrative traditions act as repositories of information and as instruments of ritual ceremony that form the basis of communal identity.[d] Silko never depicts the land Tayo traverses as an inaccessible wilderness but rather suggests that through words, stories, images, and rituals, Tayo and his community are intimately linked to this land. Tayo recovers the family cattle while rediscovering his physical and spiritual connection to a sacred mountain of his people. He then confronts his antagonists, members of the local Laguna community, at the symbolically weighty site of an abandoned Cebolleta land grant uranium mine, one of several in New Mexico that supported the development and deployment of the atomic bomb. By the end of the novel, Tayo confirms and completes his ritual healing by telling his story to the tribal elders, adding his to the collection of stories that together constitute the web of relations linking the human community with the land.

c In his discussion elsewhere in this volume of Silko's 1991 novel *Almanac of the Dead*, Ramón Saldívar similarly observes that for Silko, "altering the social relations we create … will also alter our relations to the physical surroundings within which we live" ("The American borderlands novel," chapter 62, 1040). Saldívar's discussion of the heterogeneity of the "borderlands novel" is helpful in understanding the contributions of Native American writers to contemporary traditions of literary ecology.

d For more on the social and political contexts that influenced *Ceremony*, see Sean Kicummah Teuton's essay in this volume, "The Native American tradition," chapter 67, 1115.

A similar pattern is evident in Chickasaw writer Linda Hogan's 1995 novel *Solar Storms*. Here again, a character loses all sense of connectedness to the land by spending time in the dominant culture. Set within the far northern waterways linking Minnesota and Canada, *Solar Storms* turns on the implied connection between the seventeen-year-old protagonist's personal trauma – her disfigurement and abandonment at a very young age by her mother – and the impending disaster to the waterfront community that is the anticipated result of dam projects further north in Canada. Having been raised in a series of foster homes outside her community, Angel initially feels no relationship to the land, its inhabitants, or even her own family. The journey north to fight the construction of the dam is also a journey back into Angel's family and tribal past that builds her confidence in her own identity and ambitions. Resistance to the dam construction is successful, but Angel and her companions learn upon their return home that other related dam projects threaten their village – and their traditional way of life – with flooding. Despite this threat, Angel has discovered her sense of self through her deep-rooted connection to the land, its waterways, and the community made possible by them: "we'd thrown an anchor into the future and followed the rope to the end of it, to where we would dream new dreams, new medicines, and one day, once again, remember the sacredness of every living thing." The means to imagine a better future is confirmed, thanks to the sense of restoration Angel has experienced through the course of the novel.

Native American writers are of course not alone in emphasizing the integration of community and shared traditions with effective and sustainable stewardship. Other ecologically minded novelists emphasize the interrelationship among people, their communities, and the traditions that link them to the land. Barbara Kingsolver's *Prodigal Summer* (2000) invokes both local, rural wisdom and principles of scientific ecology to frame broad ecological issues and underscore the often delicate interconnectedness of plant and animal species and the human communities that live alongside them. Kingsolver provides substantial discursive exposition of ecological principles, presented by characters who embody competing environmental perspectives. For example, in telling her curmudgeonly neighbor why she prefers organic methods of controlling insects to the pesticides he generously applies to his garden, Nannie Rawley offers a concise and informed critique of the use of pesticides like Sevin, which will, as she explains, ultimately serve to increase the population of the pests by killing their predators at the same time. Similar expositions accompany discussions of catastrophic tree infestations and the sexual lives of moths.

By putting characters with competing environmental agendas into conflict with each other, Kingsolver reflects on the challenges and opportunities faced by rural people addressing an array of pressing environmental problems. One character resists the conventional wisdom about best farming practices espoused by her deceased husband's relatives and devises a clever if much-ridiculed plan to raise goats for non-Christian religious holidays. This plan turns out to be both profitable and sustainable. Kingsolver also depicts an ongoing debate between a male hunter from out of state and a female forest ranger about the value of protecting predator species (in this case, coyotes). As the two become lovers, their debate becomes an extension of the novel's ongoing reflection on the relationship between individuals and the communities that sustain them – both animal and human. The novel closes by adopting the perspectives of the human hunter and the hunted coyote, suggesting that the supposed isolation of hunter and hunted is an illusion: "Solitude is a human presumption. Every quiet step is thunder to beetle life underfoot, a tug of impalpable thread on the web pulling mate to mate and predator to prey, a beginning or an end." For Kingsolver, this infinite web of relations is likewise the basis of community. Good stewardship of the land is based on a thorough understanding of the threads in that web, from the physiology of mating to the ecology of a garden, a family farm, or a national forest.

In contrast to Kingsolver's hopeful adaptations of rural traditions and ecological science, Don DeLillo's postnatural evocations of pervasive ecological anxiety suggest a community at severe risk. In *White Noise* (1985), which is structured around an environmental disaster ominously labeled by the media an "airborne toxic event," DeLillo is especially attentive to the ways in which language and visual media shape our awareness of environmental issues and crises. For most environmental writers, nature provides a foundation or refuge against which to measure the failures of our social institutions and new technologies. For DeLillo, that nature is no longer directly accessible. DeLillo's natural world is itself a product of these institutions and technologies, and our relationship to it is wholly shaped by our ways of talking about the world and representing it in visual and other media. Like the "most photographed barn in America" that the protagonist Jack Gladney and his colleague Murray visit early in the novel, nature is displaced by representations of nature.[e]

e For a discussion of *White Noise* in the context of postmodernism, see Ursula Heise's essay "Postmodern novels," chapter 58 in this volume, esp. 977–978. Heise usefully distinguishes DeLillo's postmodern juxtaposition of "satirical elements" with the largely "realist fashion" of DeLillo's literary style.

The "airborne toxic event" in the novel, though very real in the threat it poses, is ultimately just as elusive as the "most photographed barn in America." The event, caused by a train-car spill of Nyodene D., or Nyodene Derivative, forces a nine-day evacuation of many of the homes in the town of Blacksmith, including the Gladneys'. Information about Nyodene D. dribbles out, but that information is inconsistent and the reader is never entirely sure whether to trust it. At first the event is described as a "feathery plume," then as a "black billowing cloud," then an "airborne toxic event," and eventually a "cloud of deadly chemicals." Similarly, the symptoms associated with exposure change. The episode reveals a robust culture of expectation associated with environmental disaster. One family encountered during the evacuation is "wrapped completely in plastic, a single large sheet of transparent polyethylene." Jack eventually finds some official-looking tables and discovers that they are staffed by representatives from SIMUVAC, which he learns stands for "simulated evacuation." It turns out SIMUVAC has decided to use the real event "in order to rehearse the simulation." Later, Jack thinks to himself, "We'd become part of the public stuff of media disaster."

Like the most photographed barn in America, the toxic event itself becomes inseparable from its representation by radio and television reports, along with the people's desire to be reported on. Deprived of the opportunity to be intruded on, evacuees worry that their disaster doesn't stack up to those that do merit intrusive coverage. The conventions of environmental disaster have effectively displaced the disaster itself. DeLillo can take these conventions for granted in part because they had achieved such widespread recognition, primarily through the media DeLillo invokes, in the decades since the publication of Carson's *Silent Spring*. *White Noise* is less a call to environmental protection than a reflection on the ways in which our understanding of both the natural world and environmental disasters is now mediated by familiar narrative and visual conventions. The novel is not at odds with organized environmental action, but it does not offer any clear basis or framework for such action, either. Oddly, DeLillo's protagonist maintains a powerful feeling for the beauty of nature, even if the nature he describes is artificially enhanced by the same toxins that may be killing him.

Other postnatural writers maintain a sense of concern for the environment, but avoid the convention of lyrical description as a means of generating environmental sympathy. Carl Hiaasen's Florida-based crime novels provide a good example. In *Sick Puppy* (1999), Hiaasen addresses runaway development in Florida, a product of what he presents as the unholy alliance of corrupt business and government interests. Like most of Hiaasen's fiction, *Sick Puppy* is steeped in the political maneuverings of Florida's legislators, business people, and the lobbyists who join them together.[12] The novel is populated with characters whose insensitivity to the natural beauty of Florida underwrites the relentless development that has so transformed the Florida landscape. An investor is seeking to develop largely pristine Toad Island and is working to pass legislation that will support the construction of a new bridge, which in turn will constitute the first step towards the luxury golf community he hopes to build. Island residents who resist development present themselves as Thoreau-quoting environmentalists, but as Hiaasen's narrator notes, they do so only to raise the value of their property in hopes of making more money from the eventual development of the island. Even the well-meaning scientist hired to conduct an environmental survey of the island is forced to confess that the survey is not driven by high ideals but is rather designed to make "us appear responsible and concerned . . . to make sure the developers don't run into a snail-darter type of crisis."[13] As these examples suggest, Hiaasen finds corruption at every point along the political spectrum. Though the bridge to Toad Island is not built and the island remains undeveloped, Hiaasen includes neither extended lyrical descriptions of the place nor any impassioned arguments for its protection. The environmentalism that characterizes both the main character, Twilly Spree (who takes it upon himself to confront, sometimes violently, every litterer he encounters on the highway), and the former governor Clinton Tyree – a recurring character in Hiaasen's novels – resembles that of Abbey's Hayduke of *The Monkey Wrench Gang*: a series of exaggerated anti-authoritarian gestures aimed at the stupidity and greed that can think only of turning such unspoiled nature to profit. Spree and Tyree, however, have precious little left to protect: in Hiaasen's postnatural Florida landscape, the forces of development have proven hard to resist.

Moving far beyond Hiaasen's familiar atmosphere of big-time real-estate development, science fiction writer Kim Stanley Robinson projects a possible future in a world beset by climate change – induced by global warming – in his "Science in the Capitol" trilogy (2004–2007). Most of the series is set in Washington, DC, allowing Robinson to invoke familiar national landmarks to underscore the extraordinary nature of the flooding unleashed in the disaster. The series does include several interludes in classically "natural" settings: for example, an urban park, seemingly returning, after the flood, to its premodern condition; a Southeast Asian island-state that sinks due to the rising ocean levels; and the drought-damaged Sierra mountains where several characters go hiking. Even these scenes, however, underscore the extent to which nature as we currently know it no longer exists.[14]

Despite the devastation wrought by rising ocean levels and increased and intensified storm activity, Robinson remains surprisingly sanguine about the earth's future. Unlike radical environmentalists who suggest that technology and the worldview that supports it lie at the heart of our contemporary environmental crisis, Robinson is committed to the idea that scientifically informed ingenuity combined with a passion for the earth and its diverse inhabitants will generate new solutions to human-generated climate change. This faith in the human imagination hardly mitigates the destruction described throughout the series, but it does point the way toward a more sustainable future. In a surprising gesture toward the origins of a major line of thinking about nature in the United States, Emerson and Thoreau emerge in the final volume as visionary influences. The series ends with the suggestion that while scientific ingenuity cannot reverse the considerable damage already done, it can nevertheless propose new strategies of adaptation.

This promise of a better future is fairly constant in American ecofiction, though it is typically grounded in the return to relatively pristine places and the traditions that encouraged either the preservation of untamed wilderness or the stewardship of land respectfully adapted to human use. In Robinson's decidedly postnatural vision, the promise of a better future is less a function of a nature that exists apart from human ends than of a nature that includes the scientific and technological ingenuity that are sometimes regarded as the cause of our alienation from nature. This recognition is perhaps best exemplified by DeLillo's *Underworld* (1997), which highlights the link between the booming post-World War II American economy and the waste that economic engine generates. *Underworld* repeatedly invokes garbage, recycling, and the art of turning late twentieth-century American junk into quasi-sacred objects. Adopting an almost religious tone, DeLillo compares the massive Fresh Kills landfill on Staten Island to the Great Pyramids of Giza.[f] DeLillo would seem to be at once appalled by the extraordinary waste generated by contemporary American society while still moved by the combination of technical ingenuity and spiritual creativity applied to the problem. As the narrator observes late in the novel, "Maybe we feel a reverence for waste, for the redemptive qualities of the things we use and discard." The reverence for waste in DeLillo's novels turns on the recognition that our excessive consumption is fueled by a kind of quasi-spiritual seeking: a yearning for

f For a differently inflected reading of DeLillo's fiction in a religious context, focusing on DeLillo's use of ritual language, see Amy Hungerford's essay in this volume, "Religion and the twentieth-century American novel," chapter 44, 740–741.

connection with family, friends, community, and with whatever higher power is otherwise felt to be absent in our postmodern condition.

DeLillo and other postnatural writers significantly challenge the ecofiction that celebrates nature, wilderness, or the sacred bonds between humans and the land. The postnaturalists suggest that there is no such nature left to celebrate. But they are not for this reason without hope about the human future on the earth, since they recognize that without a model of pristine nature to preserve or protect, humans must exercise their technical ingenuity with even greater care and foresight. If this attitude leaves little basis for the traditional forms of environmental activism, which have typically relied on the idea of untainted nature to preserve, it nevertheless preserves the sense that humans must bear responsibility for the damage they inflict on the environment. And clearly, this responsibility still begins in the sense of reverence and wonder before the natural world, whether that world is regarded as a wilderness, a farm, or a more elaborately engineered hybrid, like the coastal cities that Robinson imagines will inevitably utilize all manner of ingenuity to stave off rising ocean levels or the ingenious mountains of garbage described with such awe by DeLillo.

Notes

1. For a concise overview of the history of the American environmental movement, see Kirkpatrick Sale, *The Green Revolution: The American Environmental Movement, 1962–1992* (New York: HarperCollins, 1993), and Philip Shabecoff, *A Fierce Green Fire: The American Environmental Movement* (1993; Washington, DC: Island Press, 2003). Also of particular interest for the advanced reader with an interest in the unfolding history of environmental science is Leslie A. Real and James H. Brown, eds., *Foundations of Ecology: Classic Papers with Commentary* (Chicago: University of Chicago Press, 1991).
2. On Carson's *Silent Spring*, see Roderick Frazier Nash, *The Rights of Nature: A History of Environmental Ethics* (Madison: University of Wisconsin Press, 1989), 79–82. On Glen Canyon and other related dam projects, see Donald Worster, *The Wealth of Nature: Environmental History and the Ecological Imagination* (New York and Oxford: Oxford University Press, 1993), 135–41, and Susan Zakin, *Coyotes and Town Dogs: Earth First! and the Environmental Movement* (1993; New York: Penguin, 1995), 135–185.
3. On the controversies surrounding scientific ecology, as well as on the critical disputes among ecologists, see Robert P. McIntosh, *The Background of Ecology: Concept and Theory* (Cambridge: Cambridge University Press, 1986).
4. "Think globally, act locally" is usually attributed to René Dubos, from a report prepared by Dubos and Barbara Ward for the 1972 United Nations Conference on

the Human Environment, "Only One Earth: The Care and Maintenance of a Small Planet." The phrase is also sometimes attributed to others, including David Brower, who has been credited with having used it in founding Friends of the Earth in 1969. Barry Commoner's slogan is from the first of his four laws of ecology, first presented in *The Closing Circle: Nature, Man, and Technology* (New York: Knopf, 1971).

5. Cynthia Deitering uses the term "postnatural" in her essay "The Postnatural Novel: Toxic Consciousness in Fiction of the 1980s," in *The Ecocriticism Reader: Landmarks in Literary Ecology*, ed. Cheryll Glotfelty and Harold Fromm (Athens: University of Georgia Press, 1996). In developing the link between toxic consciousness and the postnatural condition, Deitering cites Frederic Jameson's 1984 essay "Postmodernism, or the Cultural Logic of Late Capitalism" *New Left Review* 146 (July–August 1984): 59–92, and Bill McKibben's 1989 book *The End of Nature* (New York: Random House, 1989). Also influential in any formulation of postnatural hybrids like those described here is Donna Haraway,"A Cyborg Manifesto: Science, Technology, and Socialist-Feminism in the Late Twentieth Century," published in her 1991 volume *Simians, Cyborgs, and Women: The Reinvention of Nature* (New York: Routledge, 1991).
6. *Deliverance*, DVD, directed by John Boorman (1972; Burbank, CA: Warner Home Video, 2004).
7. See Edward Abbey, "Polemic: Industrial Tourism and the National Parks," in *Desert Solitaire: A Season in the Wilderness* (1968; New York: Touchstone, 1990), 39–59.
8. Wallace Stegner, "Coda: Wilderness Letter," in *The Norton Book of Nature Writing*, ed. Robert Finch and John Elder (1990; New York: Norton, 2002), 516, 515. The letter was written to David. E. Pesonen, who was working on the "wilderness portion" of the Outdoor Recreation Resources Review Commission report.
9. Stegner's emphatic insistence on the role of history in shaping nature anticipates the important work of environmental historian William Cronon, especially in *Nature's Metropolis: Chicago and the Great West* (New York: Norton, 1991). In his essay in this volume, Timothy Sweet offers a useful history of the ways in which depictions of the land in American fiction reflect the shifting social and cultural preoccupations and anxieties out of which that fiction was written. Sweet observes that in the novel's narrative structure "lay the capacity to understand any landscape as an embodiment of human history" ("American land, American landscape, American novels," chapter 5, 99).
10. There is a rich literature on wilderness and the idea of wilderness. See especially Roderick Frazier Nash, *Wilderness and the American Mind*, 4th edn. (1967; New Haven, Yale University Press, 2001); Max Oelschlaegger, *The Idea of Wilderness: From Prehistory to the Age of Ecology* (New Haven: Yale University Press, 1991); and William Cronon, "The Trouble with Wilderness," in *Uncommon Ground: Rethinking the Human Place in Nature*, ed. Cronon (New York: Norton, 1996). Also important to this history are Henry Nash Smith, *Virgin Land: The American*

West as Symbol and Myth (Cambridge, MA: Harvard University Press, 1950) and Leo Marx, *The Machine in the Garden: Technology and the Pastoral Ideal in America* (New York: Oxford University Press, 1964).

11. Silko elsewhere describes the role of storytelling and other forms of visual and oral culture in delineating "the complexities of the relationship which human beings must maintain with the surrounding natural world if they hope to survive in this place." See Leslie Marmon Silko, "Landscape, History, and the Pueblo Imagination," in Glotfelty and Fromm, *The Ecocriticism Reader*, 264–275.
12. Dana Phillips offers a suggestive reading of Hiaasen's 1987 novel set in the world of professional sport fishing, *Double Whammy*, in his essay "Is Nature Necessary?" in Glotfelty and Fromm, *The Ecocriticism Reader*, pp. 204–217. For a fascinating and challenging account of contemporary ecocritical practice, see also Phillips's *The Truth of Ecology: Nature, Culture, and Literature in America* (New York: Oxford University Press, 2003).
13. After the snail-darter, a tiny fish found only in Alabama and Tennessee, was listed as an endangered species, the Supreme Court ruled that construction on the Tellico Dam in Tennessee be halted. The dam was, however, eventually built, thanks to congressional legislation exempting the project from the Endangered Species Act and thereby allowing the dam's completion.
14. There is an extensive literature on greenhouse gas emissions, their relationship to climate change, and the current and potential impact of that climate change. Two influential accounts are McKibben, *The End of Nature* and Elizabeth Kolbert, *Field Notes from a Catastrophe: Man, Nature, and Climate Change* (New York: Bloomsbury, 2006).

69

Graphic novels

JAN BAETENS

"Comics are suddenly everywhere," claims Jared Gardner in one of the many scholarly essays that have been devoted to this cultural form in recent years.[1] And one of the places they are is certainly literature, more particularly the novel. It has now become perfectly thinkable that future editions of the Norton anthology or one of its many competitors will have a section on graphic novels. This situation is fairly new, for if comics have been knocking at literature's door for many decades now, where they occupy one of the niches of so-called paraliterature, the association with the novel is more topical. Of course, there has always been a flourishing branch of comics that specializes in the adaptation of literary material (*Moby-Dick* may be the best-represented example), but these productions were not considered literary works themselves –despite the undeniable quality of some of these adaptations. On the contrary, books like Will Eisner's *A Contract with God* (1978), Harvey Pekar's series *American Splendor* (seventeen issues, written between 1976 and 1993), Art Spiegelman's *Maus* (two volumes, 1986–1991), Daniel Clowes's *Ghost World* (1997), Chris Ware's *Jimmy Corrigan* (2000), Adrian Tomine's *Sleepwalk* (2002), Charles Burns's *Black Hole* (2005), to name just a few (though far from arbitrarily chosen), are nowadays often read as novelistic productions, albeit of a special kind.

How has this become possible, and what does it mean? Within the field of comics, it appears that a subgenre has emerged – the graphic novel – and its status has shifted from paraliterary to literary. Such an answer, which is not false *per se*, raises many other questions. The graphic novel, yes, fine, but do we only know what it is? What about comics that are not labeled graphic novels? For instance, do the "alternative comics," as Charles Hatfield[2] calls them, enter the category of the novel too? And why are there no "filmic novels"? (Well, there may be some, but they are considered films, not novels.) And what to think of graphic novels that have only pictures and no words, or only words that are placed outside the images, as captions rather than as speech balloons?

My main aim in this chapter will not only be to distinguish the subfield of the graphic novel from the broader field of comics (thereby transferring it to the world of the novel) but also to question all of these relationships – between comics and the graphic novel, between the graphic novel and literature – in the hope of better grasping the mutations of the novelistic domain itself. For part of what makes the graphic novel such an exciting object is what it does to the novel and how it is a (positive) response to what Mark McGurl calls in this volume the "preoccupation with mass visual culture in modern American fiction."[a] As I will argue, the graphic novel reveals deep transformations in the connections between novel and medium, the latter being no longer naturally seen as the word or the book, but hinting now toward the notion of what Marjorie Perloff calls the "differential text."[3] The new literary field as it was born in the early nineteenth century had already displayed a strong tension between the novel and the book-form. The emerging production of the graphic novel will further question the standard vision of the novel as a narrative work of verbal fiction between two covers.[b]

A short history of graphic storytelling

The graphic novel itself was not born within the novel, where the tradition of the illustrated novel has never been felt as a danger to the essentially verbal nature of the genre. Rather, it emerged from a very different field: that of visual print culture and visual storytelling by way of engraving. This tradition is much older than the comics, which started at the end of the nineteenth century when a new genre, later to be called the balloon strip, rapidly spread in the newspapers. R. F. Outcault's *The Yellow Kid* (1895) has long been considered the first example of this form of comics, although recent accounts are more nuanced.[4] Although narrative engravings, either individual images or sequences of images, have a very long history, the work by the Swiss author Rodolphe Töpffer (who published seven books between 1831 and 1846) is now generally acknowledged as one of the major starting points of graphic literature, by which I mean a new way of storytelling combining text and image in sequentially arranged frames. This new literature would claim many followers in Europe and the USA during the nineteenth century. Töpffer would have, for instance, a decisive influence on the genre of the woodcut

a Mark McGurl, "The novel, mass culture, mass media," chapter 41, 686.

b See Robert Coover, who argues that the history of the novel has always been determined by its changing relationships with the medium, "A history of the future of narrative," chapter 71.

novel, which used to have a real presence on both sides of the Atlantic Ocean until the 1920s.[5] His *histoires en estampes* ("engraved stories"), to follow the term he coined in his own writings on the genre, are clearly a forerunner of the contemporary graphic novel, so strong is their emphasis on storytelling, and therefore literature, as opposed to drawing (cartoon, caricature, etc.). Their basic mechanism is not the visualization of an existing script or scenario (for instance a gospel story) but the exploration of the narrative and expressive possibilities of the images (and words) in their sequential arrangements; finally, engraved stories are a practice whose cultural position is not easy to ascertain, but which offers innovative and original ways of combining texts and images in book form.

In the nineteenth century, graphic storytelling was not yet considered literature. Its culturally uncertain status prevented it from entering that world. The turn of the century appearance of the newspaper comics and their rapid orientation toward burlesque humor ultimately replaced Töpfferian graphic storytelling. (The latter's work would only be recovered many decades later, thanks to the pioneering work of scholars such as David Kunzle, made possible itself by the increasing institutionalization of the comics field and the effort of the genre to recover and reconstruct its own past.) Yet in spite of the breathtaking experiments of some early practitioners such as Winsor McCay (*Little Nemo*: 1905–1914) and George Herriman (*Krazy Kat*: 1913–1944), comics themselves are not, as were the Töpfferian engraved stories, a clear prototype of the contemporary graphic novel. First of all, they lack all cultural legitimacy: few other genres have been and remain so despised by high-cultural literati as American comics. Second, they focus less on storytelling than on comic effects, and this foregrounding of gag and slapstick reinforces their anti-literary character. Finally, the comics also witness the split between text and word: different people may be in charge of the drawings and the storyline. In this division of labor, the image is reduced to a merely illustrative role, which is in manifest contradiction with Töpffer's revolutionary intuitions.

The graphic novel as we know it today – exemplified by the works mentioned at the beginning of this chapter – is the result of the gradual transformation of these newspaper and magazine comic strips. The changes concern a variety of features – subject matter, style, internal and external constraints, etc. – whose shifts are far from linear and systematic. What is clear, however, is that the history in question is – at least in its beginning – extremely homebred. In more recent stages – roughly since the late 1970s – intercultural exchanges play a bigger role.

Between the newspaper and magazine funnies of the turn of the century and the graphic novel in its contemporary instantiation, three major evolutions deserve to be underlined.

The first transformation concerns the gradual opening of the comics to more elaborated forms of narrative and, relatedly, to a more serious or at least less childish tone. This is what happens with the creation of the adventure comics in the 1920s (travel stories, science fiction comics, detective comics, historical fiction, jungle stories, and so on). Technically, these comics take a serial form: instead of the daily or weekly gag, the comics try to tell stories, albeit always in their typical installment form. The mostly juvenile audience of these comics and their continuing link with the mass media (it is only today that they are republished in book form) still disqualify these adventure comics – despite their complex narratives – from the literary status of graphic novel.

A second transformation is the discovery of a totally new format, the comic book. The term "comic book" is somewhat misleading, since comic books more closely resemble cheap brochures, well known from the pulp publishing industry, than real books. Along with the comic book rapidly comes the exclusive link with a new type of character and story: the superheroes. It is not only for their "childish" and extremely repetitive content or formulaic style that comic books have such a bad reputation. On the one hand, the internal excesses of the genre – which unabashedly embraced gore and trash in the late 1940s – and, on the other, the external constraints of the comics industry, which imposed a crudely capitalistic, fully Taylorized production system, are both responsible for a lowbrow image that still prevails in many well-educated circles.

The comics industry has made various attempts to improve its image. Two examples of this (not very successful) policy were the adoption of the famous Comics Code (a system of self-censorhip established after the witch-hunt launched by psychiatrist Fredric Wertham's 1954 anti-comics pamphlet *The Seduction of the Innocent*, which linked the reading of comics with juvenile delinquency,[6]) and, in a different mode, the use of comics for didactic purposes (as in the *Classics Illustrated* series, a collection started in 1941 of readers' digests in comic form of the great classics of American literature).

The third transformation, the outburst of a new kind of comics during the countercultural 1960s, might be described as the return of the repressed. These were the years of the "underground" comics. These works, which did not respect the Comics Code's restrictions on the representation of sex and violence, were not allowed for sale in the official and monopolistic distribution venues of the industry and were therefore sold illegally either on the street or in "head shops" (which mostly specialized in the sale of drug paraphernalia). Technically speaking – and in matters of popular culture, issues of production technique are never a detail – it was the Xerox revolution that made the underground comics possible. Finally, just as important as the "illicit" subject matter – an illustration of the countercultural sex, drugs, and rock & roll credo – underground comics introduced two innovations which would prove crucial in the eventual appearance of the graphic novel. Underground comics innovated radically by bringing into play an unknown dimension of storytelling: autobiography, and, more generally, nonfiction. Several underground artists made use of the language of comics to question official history – for example Jaxon, author of various books that try to give voice to the Native American point of view (e.g. *Comanche Moon*, 1979). This was a truly groundbreaking shift, which would enable the comics to tap into new worlds of storytelling as well as to leave behind the constraint of humor that dramatically restricted the scope of the medium. Besides, the DIY (do-it-yourself) ideology of the underground comics also reactivated the merger of the verbal and the visual: story and drawings were no longer made by two different authors, as the very simplicity of making, distributing, and selling the comic strips made it possible once again for a single author to be in control of the process.

When in the late 1970s the label "graphic novel" appears – and it does so for the first time in connection with Will Eisner's collection of short stories, *A Contract with God* (1978) – it is almost by accident. Eisner was anything but a beginner. His *Spirit* character, one of the finest of the comic book era, had been appearing since 1940, and the author's work had always been characterized by the desire to do something more than the industry allowed him to do. The label itself had popped up by chance, during a discussion with the sales department of a bookshop. Its initial success was very modest. Despite Eisner's commitment to a revalorization of the comics genre, the importance of what happened in the late 1970s would only become visible after the publication of Art Spiegelman's *Maus*.

It was Art Spiegelman who would bring about the real change in the graphic storytelling field and whose significance for the institutionalization of the graphic novel would be vital. Spiegelman works at the crossroads of two traditions: the underground comic, of which he is a late but visually very creative representative; and the new tradition of European adult comics, which had been a mass phenomenon since the 1960s. Although often as irreverent as the former, the latter exploited very different styles and subject

6 Front cover illustration to Will Eiser's *A Contract with God*.

7 Scene from Art Spiegelman's *Maus I: A Survivor's Tale/My Father Bleeds History* (New York: Pantheon, 1986)

matter, especially in adult adventure fiction. (Perhaps the need to abandon fiction in favor of autobiography and documentary modes was less urgent in Europe given the absence of the superhero model; just as important a factor in this shift toward the documentary is the more general craving for the real as reflected in the nonfiction novel, as studied in this volume by David Schmid.[c])

In a sense, the graphic novel is the result of the encounter between these two worlds, which Spiegelman and his wife Françoise Mouly started to bring together in the seminal cross-cultural magazine *Raw* (1980–1991). All the major aspects of the contemporary graphic novel converged in *Raw*, and would become visible for the general public with the publication of *Maus* (started in 1972 as a three-page strip for *Funny Animals*, an underground journal, then serialized in *Raw* and eventually published in book form in 1986 and 1991). First, the use of autobiographical and documentary modes: in *Maus*, Spiegelman narrates the war memories of his father decades later. Second: the experimental use of new forms: Spiegelman uses an allegorical style of characterization (the historical figures are represented as animals, each nation being shown as a particular species), and his storytelling is metafictional (the narration of the events is not direct but mediated through a series of dialogues between son and father; the book also contains a detailed account of the way Spiegelman himself experiences both the situation of the oral storytelling and his own reworking of it in *Maus*). Third, Spiegelman's book bears various traces of its publication history: not only is the making of the book a key aspect of the story, but the whole economy and structure of the volume also bear traces of its genesis as an installment narrative and the specific rhythm that it entails.

Maus is not the only graphic novel of the 1980s, but it proved a watershed. In 1992, the Pulitzer Prize (a special award since there had been some trouble in classifying the book in the fiction or the nonfiction category) brought cultural legitimacy and literary recognition to *Maus*. Other books of the same period have been influential too: Moore's and Gibbons's *Watchmen* (1987) and Frank Miller's *Batman. The Dark Knight Returns* (1986), the two best-known representatives of the "adult turn" in the comic book industry, managed to seize with great acuity the postmodern *Zeitgeist* of the cyberpunk years. But although these creations helped to familiarize the public with the label of the graphic novel, they have never been embraced by a literary readership. Similarly, the work of Robert Crumb and his follower Harvey Pekar continues to be defined as (post-) underground comics rather than as graphic novels. It would take another

c David Schmid, "The nonfiction novel," chapter 59.

generation before authors like Charles Burns, Chris Ware, Daniel Clowes, or Adrian Tomine ceased to be evaluated not as "comics authors with a difference," but as graphic novelists. So after nearly two centuries, we seem to have returned to where we started with Töpffer: graphic storytelling. The cultural situation of the genre, however, has changed dramatically since the late 1990s, as demonstrated by steadily increasing attention from academic journals, specialized libraries, book series at university presses, scholarly conferences and exhibits, and so on. Scott McCloud's study, *Understanding Comics*,[7] would play the same role for the broader audience.

Toward an open definition of the genre

What exactly is a graphic novel? In the case of a genre whose boundaries are so blurred, it may not be appropriate to generate an essentialist, ontological definition. It is more useful to stick to a prototypical "family resemblance" approach and to bring to the fore a set of concrete rules that graphic novels more or less adhere to. Three extremely different elements appear paramount in this regard: the question of authorship; the issue of seriousness; and the material aspects of the host medium.

First of all, graphic novels have authors. More particularly, each has one single author who makes, signs, and owns the work. This may seem an absolute banality, but it hints at a major shift in comparison to the comic book industry, where authors are hired to do a job, where their work is supervised and controlled by an editor, and where ownership belongs to media corporations. The example of Jerry Siegel and Joe Schuster, the inventors of Superman who lost all control over and profit derived from their own character, is an infamous case in the history of the comics industry, where the author is undoubtedly the weakest link in the chain. Yet the difference between graphic novelist and comics author is not simply juridical. It also entails another, artistically more important dimension, the merger of the two authorial types that had been separated in the comic books industry: the scriptwriter and the visual artist. In the graphic novel, the author tends to be "complete," as he or is she is both author of the story and author of the drawings. This, too, marks a return to Töpffer, with great consequences for the literary appreciation of the genre. If the graphic novel becomes a "real" novel, it is not because of its novelistic pretext, as in the case of David Mazzucchelli's adaptation of Paul Auster's *City of Glass* (1994), or because of the presence of a "literary" scriptwriter (a situation that is quite familiar in Europe, but not in the USA), but because of the fact that there is now *one* author – and that it is the images themselves that can perform the telling of the story. The author, in other words, no longer needs to be in the first place a "writer"; what matters is that he or she is in charge of the whole process, even if the work is collaborative (as in the case of an adaptation, for instance, Mazzuchelli's graphic reinterpretation of *City of Glass*). There are also examples of multiple-author graphic novels, such as Alan Moore and Dave Gibbons's *Watchmen* (1986), but shared authorship is less the rule than the exception.

A second feature of the genre has to do with its subject matter, often described as "serious" or "adult" (the former term is more precise than the latter, which may connote pornography). Moreover, many graphic novels adopt an autobiographical stance, in the wake of the innovations of the underground generation. Both aspects are unquestionably linked. Autobiography, as opposed to the traditional escapist form of comics fiction, is interpreted as a warrant for the work's seriousness – as if it was easier to escape the paraliterary ghetto of the comics by rejecting fiction rather than by accepting it. In practice, however, autobiography is far from the only narrative mode of the genre. Think, for instance, of the morbid fantasies of Charles Burns, which have more to do, one hopes, with an imagination fueled by horror comics. More generally, the autobiographical tone of many graphic novels does not exclude fictional elements; even autobiographical graphic novels tend to be critical of the constraints of the "autobiographical contract." Already in the case of *Maus*, there were doubts about the fictional or nonfictional status of the work (*Maus* was initially placed on the fiction bestseller list of the *New York Times* but was shifted to the nonfiction list at the artist's request), and the same can be said of the family histories reworked by Chris Ware in his *Jimmy Corrigan* series. Autobiography in the graphic novel is never unproblematic, and in a typically postmodern move, its basic regime is that of metafictional autobiography, with a permanent reflection and feedback on the very traps of self-representation and authenticity.[d] (It should be stressed, however, that the graphic novel does not exhibit to the same extent as much postmodern fiction the material and stylistic heterogeneity of the successive types of metafiction: in the graphic novel, the "hand" of the artist remains mostly very recognizable, as the genre has strong auteur overtones which keep it close to certain aspects of high modernism.[8]) The link between autobiography and seriousness enables one to draw a line between the graphic

d On the metafictional tendencies within postmodernism, see Ursula Heise, "Postmodern novels," chapter 58, esp. 968–979.

novel and the comics industry, but does not rule out fantasy, humor, and phantasm.

Although this genre even allows a certain lack of realism, it produces a different reading and writing ethos, and it is precisely this ethical dimension that is needed to convert a work of graphic storytelling into a graphic novel. In the case of the American graphic novel, the extreme seriousness is reflected in the genre's fascination with themes like boredom, ennui, spleen, loss, suicide, trauma, etc., as exemplarily illustrated in the work by Chris Ware (or, to a lesser extent, Daniel Clowes), who pays a lot of attention to all the empty moments of waiting, losing time, dullness, in short uneventfulness, whereas the classic graphic literature is very much event- and even target-oriented. Lack of realism, however, is an idea that should be nuanced. Charles Burns's horrible science fiction nightmares disclose many of our contemporary anxieties, for instance about genetic manipulation. That Daniel Clowes's characters often behave as if they were living in a comics world, fits perfectly the mental universe of a certain type of youth. More generally, one might even argue that the graphic novel's seriousness has to do with its attempt to be socially relevant. The American graphic novel definitely wants to make statements about contemporary ordinary life –a dramatic difference from the European graphic novel, and a commitment to realism. (European works are much more experimental, graphically speaking, but have difficulties in leaving behind either pure fiction or the representation of the past.)

A third characteristic of the graphic novel encompasses a wide range of formal criteria concerning the host medium of the publication: the book. Here as well the situation seems very simple, but only at first sight. Unlike comics and comic books, graphic novels, even when they are prepublished in installment form, are from the very beginning conceived to appear in a book form resembling that of a novel – and, more important, to be sold alongside novels in bookshops. But the graphic novel craves a continuous modulation of its format, as opposed to the uniform appearance of both the comic books and traditional novels. The graphic novel rejects not only the exterior aspects of the comics industry's products, but above all their serialized logic. Graphic novels aim at being "one shot" publications, unadulterated by the necessity of continuing a character and a storyline as long as the market can absorb them. (The case is less clear, however, for graphic novels that emerge directly from the field of popular culture, such as Frank Miller's *Batman. The Dark Knight Returns*, or those by authors like Chris Ware and Daniel Clowes, who use recurring characters.) Unlike most novelists, graphic novelists pay great attention to design and layout issues, which they view as an integral part of their work. The most notable example here is Chris Ware's *Acme Novelty Library* (published since 1993), a brilliant illustration of Francis Ponge's aesthetic ideal: "each object its own rhetoric." On one point, however, the resistance to the novel format is absent: graphic novels are written as slowly as other novels, although this laboriousness may be hidden by the fact that many graphic novels continue to be published in installment form, for the graphic novel business is first of all not commercially viable if it bypasses the potentially lucrative prepublication stage in magazines and journals.[9] One might also argue that if the graphic novel completely abandons serialized comics, the genre condemns itself to losing the vitality of the popular culture that has always nourished it.[10]

The difficult balance between the one-shot policy of the graphic novel and the serialized forms common to mass media lays bare one of the fundamental problems of the genre, namely the uneasy relationship between a desire for novelistic forms and the persistent influence of nonnovelistic structures. Many so-called graphic novels are more collections of short stories (Burns, Tomine) or new versions of serialized works (Ware, Clowes) than actual graphic *novels*. Perhaps this is what makes graphic novels so excitingly new: they are neither novel nor nonnovel. At the same time, this new balance is what makes them such a fragile species of the novel. It is as if the genre functions best when it does not put between brackets its nonnovelistic aspects: narratologically speaking, the short story and the fragment; editorially speaking: the serialized installment; ideologically speaking, the ties with lowbrow culture.

The graphic novel as a literary genre

The graphic novel's multilayered nature also manifests itself in the new relationships between text and image that the genre has been elaborating from the very beginnings – a mission it shares with the work of the best representatives of the early comics age. George Herriman's *Krazy Kat*, for instance, is still an unchallenged example of the zigzag structure that defines the ideal of word and image in the graphic novel: neither illustration of the text by the image nor redundancy, but a back and forth between the two media, which can no longer be read separately. In the case of Herriman, this search for a new graphic storytelling language is echoed in the invention of a linguistically hybrid text – a dizzyingly sophisticated mix of phonic English and other languages – as well as in the attempt to create a permanent tension between the visual layout of the page as a unified whole and the sequential arrangement of the page units.

Such artistic ambitions of early comics and later graphic novels are shared by both the American and the European creators that inspire them. Yet the American graphic novel diverges from the European models in respect to some specific aspects of the word and image issue. One crucial difference is the greater importance given to the narrator's voice in American than in European graphic novels. Unlike their European counterparts, American graphic novelists like to foreground an explicitly "telling" presence, which the reader often sees also in the panels of the book. This presence is typically achieved through a "showing" modus: the visible presence of the narrator in the pages of the book is not subjective, as is its voice, but objective, for whereas the text is clearly uttered by the narrator, the drawings are not always made from the narrator's point of view. The overall effect of this massive presence of the verbal narrator is not quite the same as that of the cinematographic voiceover. In the graphic novel, the narrator's presence is being felt more as a "voice-with" that accompanies the images. Perhaps it is precisely this less overt impact of the "voice-with" that enables the tone of the narrative voice in the graphic novel to remain colloquial, an aspect which fits perfectly the genre's craving for realism. Graphic novels do not evince so much a craving for equilibrium between word and image as a privileging of the former at the expense of the latter.

For the literary appreciation and legitimization of the graphic novel, the treatment of the language issue is both vital and overrated. To start with this last point, there is now a general consensus that graphic novels are no longer supposed to have a literary subtext – either a pre-existing text or an original storyline. Nor must they have literary dialogue – however that may be construed – or indeed any dialogue at all. On the contrary, wordless graphic novels are highly appraised (although more in Europe than in the USA). It is accepted now that the literary aspect of a graphic novel is dependent on the storytelling capacities of the medium – which cannot be divided between verbal and visual components. This point is essential for comprehending the significance of the graphic novel to the larger field of the novel. For if on the one hand the graphic novel is more and more considered a part of the larger field of the novel, and if on the other hand the novelistic aspects of the graphic novel are determined less by its verbal, textual, and linguistic elements than by the narrative potential of a medium that combines words and images, this opposition raises a fundamental question about the relationship between novel and medium. If both the traditional literary novel and the newer graphic novel are now part of the same general novelistic field, one can only conclude that the novel itself – and not just the narrative behind it, as it has always been assumed – has become "differential" in the sense that Marjorie Perloff describes the migration of literary works in the multimedia environment of cyberculture: "[Differential texts are] texts that exist in different material forms, with no single version being the definitive one."[11] Novels, graphic novels, but also films, games, oral histories and so on, may merge increasingly in one global novelistic continuum –a subfield of the all-encompassing field of narrative.

But what about the despised superheroes comics? Here too, Art Spiegelman may have proven a prophetic voice. Not only has he reshaped underground comics (which he updated and upgraded in *Raw*); made possible, through *Maus*, the institutionalization of the American graphic novel; helped rediscover the lost heritage of the pre-superheroes comics in his serial book *In the Shadow of No Towers* – but he has also made a vibrant plea for one of the most typical, i.e. most extreme, practitioners of the superheroes comics at its most wild and crazy: Jack Cole, author of the 1950s character *Plastic Man*, a comic strip that transfers the extremities of the genre's narratives to the visual representation of the very "liquid" and systematically "morphed" protagonist. [12]

It will not come as a surprise that the reappropriation of the graphic novel by the literary novel owes more to the world of lowbrow comics than to the allegedly highbrow register of the graphic novel. Given the fact that the graphic novel itself is so deeply rooted in American popular culture – more specifically in superhero comics –one can understand why novelists eager to borrow from graphic storytelling do so not by turning to the graphic novel (which is in a certain sense too close in subject matter and general tone to be useful as a tool for innovation) but rather to comic books. Examples of this fascination can be found in recent books by Michael Chabon and Jonathan Lethem. In *The Amazing Adventures of Kavalier and Clay* (2000), Chabon retraces with great wit and imagination the well-researched history of the comic books' golden age, from the mid-thirties to the mid-fifties. Chabon's friend Lethem, who has the reputation of being a "genre-bender", is clearly influenced by comics. His 2003 novel *The Fortress of Solitude*, named for Superman's Arctic hideaway, deals with two young friends in Brooklyn who gain superpowers through a magic ring. This book also contains references to a famous series of the 1970s, "Omega the Unknown," published for ten issues by Marvel Comics, and now continued by Lethem – whose genre-bending has led him back from novel-writing to the universe of the comic books that inspired it.

The reappropriation of the graphic novel by the literary novel has been until now more myth than reality. What is actually happening is a reuse of the comic book intertext, in a typical move of the postmodern novel eager to plug into the world of popular culture. Even within the graphic novel itself, it is the beloved form of comics, the superheroes comics, that dominates most of the intertextual intercourse. Nevertheless, the return to these comic books is always very critical: Daniel Clowes denounces superheroes' daydreaming, and his often adolescent characters fall prey to the confusion between the real world and that of the comics; Charles Burns highlights the gloomy aspects of horror and science fiction, presenting physical decay and monstrosity in a deadpan way that increases the reader's uneasiness; Alan Moore and Dave Gibbons, as well as Frank Miller, portray the vigilante culture, one of the basic features of superheroes comics, as cryptofascist; Ware foregrounds the pathetic dimension of Batman-like figures (in his *Jimmy Corrigan*, a Batman-like figure appears as the superlative illustration of the loser); and Adrian Tomine's fictionalized comic book readers often behave like weirdos – or at least like the insecure and helpless people these books are supposed to be made for.

The most vibrant homage paid to comics culture is to be found in Art Spiegelman's *In The Shadow of No Towers*, yet this book, the author's very personal re-enactment of the 9/11 trauma, exemplifies in a splendid manner most of the paradoxes that characterize the graphic novel as an emerging field. The book is less a novel than a collection of serialized plates. Its authorship is multiple and shattered. If the first half of the book is close to the graphic novel universe imposed by former Spiegelman productions (albeit in a visually much more exuberant and expressionist way), its second half is, most strangely, an anthology of early twentieth-century comics. The book therefore refuses to continue the line opened by *Maus*.

In this regard, it is difficult to find a more "typical" example of graphic novel at the beginning of the twenty-first century. In more than one regard, *In The Shadow of No Towers* may initiate a move away from the more sanitized version of the graphic novel as it has been defined in this chapter, with its strong emphasis on the single-authored volume (as opposed to the multi-authored approach of many comic strip productions), the seriousness of its content (as opposed to the "bad taste" of much comic strip genre fiction), and its bookishness (as opposed to the capacity of the comic strip to appear in many less conventional formats). *In The Shadow of No Towers* not only rejects the newly dominating book form of the graphic novel, since it prefers an "unhandy" large format that sticks better to the dimensions of the early twentieth-century Sunday pages strips. It also stresses its roots in popular comics culture by its attempt to communicate with a broad and undifferentiated readership through (worldwide) publication in newspaper or magazine form. (In order to protest against the uncritical reporting on 9/11 in *The New Yorker*, Spiegelman offered the pages of his work in progress to other magazines, which ran it as ongoing commentary on the unfolding events.) By doing so, Spiegelman rediscovered a basic function of comics that the new structures of the graphic novel – with its strong orientation toward the book market – had been losing: the capacity of a permanent critical dialogue with the news of the day and therefore the possibility of playing a (healing) role in the daily life of its readers. Few other works are as marked by the vision of their author, by the gravity of their theme, and by the clever use of the book format as *In The Shadow of No Towers*, yet at the same time Spiegelman's work is also a profound reflection on the collective nature of the graphic novel, the vital necessity of humor and irony, and the relevance of serial publication. In this sense, one might say that if *Maus* has helped the graphic novel to gain its independence from the broader field of comics, *In The Shadow of No Towers* may prove a landmark in the renewed blurring of the graphic novel and the comic book, increasing rather than reducing the revolutionary force of the graphic novel as a challenging innovation within the genre of the novel itself.

Notes

1. Jared Gardner, "From the Editor's Chair," *American Periodicals* 17.2 (2007):139.
2. Charles Hatfield, *Alternative Comics. An Emerging Literature* (Jackson: University Press of Mississippi, 2005).
3. Marjorie Perloff, "Screening the Page/Paging the Screen: Digital Poetics and the Differential Text," in *Contemporary Poetics*, ed. Louis Armand (Evanston, IL: Northwestern Press, 2007), 379.
4. See David Kunzle, *The Early Comic Strip: Narrative Strips and Picture Stories in the European Broadsheet from c. 1450 to 1825* (Berkeley: University of California Press, 1973), and Charles Dierick and Pascal Lefèvre, eds., *Forging a New Medium. The Comic Strip in the Nineteenth Century* (Brussels: VUB University Press, 1998).
5. For a detailed survey of its most singular form, the wordless woodcut novels, see David Beronå, *Wordless Books. The Original Graphic Novels* (New York: Abrams, 2008).
6. See Fredric Wertham, *Seduction of the Innocent* (New York: Rinehart, 1954), and David Hajdu, *The Ten-Cent Plague: The Great Comic-Book Scare and How It Changed America* (New York: Farrar, Straus and Giroux, 2008).
7. Scott McCloud, *Understanding Comics: The Invisible Art* (New York: HarperCollins, 1994).

8. See also Hatfield, *Alternative Comics*.
9. *Ibid.*, 162.
10. See also Hillary Chute (2007), "Temporality and Seriality in Spiegelman's *In the Shadow of No Towers*," *American Periodicals* 17.2 (2007): 228–244.
11. Perloff, "Screening the Page," 379.
12. See Art Spiegelman, *Jack Cole and Plastic Man: Forms Stretched to Their Limits* (New York: Chronicle Books, 2001).

70

Twentieth- and twenty-first-century literary communities

DENEL REHBERG SEDO

The Great Books Foundation, The Big Read, Oprah, and online literary communities, such as those found on LibraryThing.com, are a few contemporary formations of literary communities – or sites of shared reading – that are the descendants of those identified by Barbara Hochman in chapter 36 in this collection. Twentieth- and twenty-first-century readers were and are still influenced by "cultural insiders (authors and literary commentators; educators and newly professionalized librarians),"[a] but social advances along with technological advances, such as radio, television, and the internet have had an impact on the practices and perceptions of shared reading, as well as the book choices readers make.

As Hochman argues, fiction-reading maintained its position as a contested social practice well into the twentieth century. She illustrates well fiction's contested terrain within late nineteenth-century social groups; this chapter picks up the story to identify some of the contemporary debates around reading literature, and in particular, what constitutes "good" literature. To do this, I focus on groups of readers, which are, of course, comprised of individual readers. Literary communities position reading not only as an individual activity but also as a social one, and they provide the analyst with opportunities to evaluate how literary taste and taste hierarchies are influenced by social structures.[b] By attending to the ideological and political basis of groups of readers, we may set the text aside as an object of analysis and instead emphasize the social structures that revolve around readers and their reading choices. In their interactions with contemporary formations such as the mass media, educational institutions, and government agencies,

a Barbara Hochman, "Readers and reading groups," chapter 36, 600.

b Nancy Glazener's "The novel in postbellum print culture" (chapter 20 in this volume) illustrates how publishers worked to create different reading publics as distinct commercial entities in the postbellum era. See esp. 345–348.

readers in groups demonstrate agency while also reflecting – and sometimes contesting – the hierarchical positions assigned to particular books and their readers.[1] The focus of this chapter, then, is on the complex social influences on book choice by groups.[2] First, I illustrate how mass media, and more recently, new media, along with other social changes such as those in formal education, have created an environment in which literary categories are expanded and become fodder for wide debate. The emergence of the "middlebrow" has become a symbol of the conflict between elite tastemakers and an expanding group of increasingly better-educated and independent-minded readers. While these forces have been brewing for a while, my discussion introduces the government as a relatively new significant influence in both individual and group reading choices. By promoting reading in general, the government perforce finds itself in a position where it is also recommending *what* people ought to be reading. The result, fueled by librarians who are happy to have the financial support no matter what strings may be attached, is that for the first time the national government has become a player in the canon-making enterprise. The final section of the chapter brings into view the rapidly evolving new media constellation that helps shape the relationship between an assertive middle-class readership and the intervention of the government, at a time of unprecedented complexity in the longstanding dialogue between elite and mass reading culture.[c]

The twentieth- and twenty-first centuries have seen major changes that have had great influence on the American reading public. The USA enjoys high literacy rates though women have higher prose and document literacy than men.[3] Technological changes have facilitated the increase in the production, distribution, consumption of, and responses to, novels. This increase in access to different kinds of literature, in part, has shifted elite cultural anxiety from the danger of novel-reading to concerns about particular novels as being dangerous at worst and trashy at best.[d] Throughout the past century, cultural commentators and scholars have debated the terms, value, and components of literary hierarchy. In short, the types of novels one owns or reads or admits to reading still act as cultural indicators.

Debates about the value of novels play out in educational settings, in libraries and other governmental agencies, and in various forms of media.

c In "A history of the future of narrative" (chapter 71 in this volume), Robert Coover considers the ways in which new media are reshaping narrative forms. It is beyond the scope of this chapter to suggest how government intervention might be doing the same, but this possibility may warrant the attention of literary critics.

d On the dangers of novel-reading in the nineteenth century, see Hochman, chapter 36.

Whatever the institution, broad social forces and power relations influence group reading choices and practices, most obviously through prescribed lists but also through the interpretive practices of those running the groups, published reviews, and broadcast book discussions. The new media culture of the past three decades – including radio, television, books, and the internet – not only facilitates the emergence of and access to nouveau literati such as Oprah Winfrey and other self-appointed literary tastemakers, but also provides vehicles for reader congregation and resistance.

Literary communities can be broadly categorized as formal (or institutional), semi-formal, and informal, according to their ideals, structures, and practices. Formal literary societies have been historically attached to educational, governmental, or religious institutions. Examples include the groups of pre-World War II African American belletristic literary societies identified by Elizabeth McHenry in her important reconfiguration of the idea of a homogeneous black community. McHenry brings to light the role of African American literary societies in the antebellum North and in post-Civil War literary culture, and argues that the groups provided some members of the black upper and middle classes with the education and self-confidence necessary for social action.[4] The literary circles of Chautauqua that began in 1874 and continue today are another example of formal literary communities. The ideological foundations of Chautauqua rest in liberal education for adults of all backgrounds, and were informed by an evangelical Protestant Christian philosophy of moral enlightenment.[5] (Even a group such as the Jewish Book Club that meets in the Temple Judea Mizpah at Northeastern Illinois University, shares this influence.[6]) These groups, however, illustrate well the messiness of an attempted taxonomy of literary societies using rigid descriptions. Contemporary groups might have their foundations in institutions, religious organizations, or ideologies, but members often break away to create their own rules, regulations, and practices. Elizabeth Long provides an example of this separation in her analysis of women's reading clubs in Houston, Texas.[7] One of the groups she studied had members who began their shared reading experiences in The Great Books program (described below), and brought their ideas of "good" literature and discussion practices to their new group.

Little evidence exists of literary societies that began in the nineteenth century and continued through to the late 1940s or even to the 1920s, presumably because most of the world was at war during much of that time. After World War II, formal adult education emerged to educate those sent to war and those who missed schooling to serve or work in the war effort. In 1947,

Maynard Hutchins and Mortimer Adler of the University of Chicago created The Great Books Foundation, which conceived of an ongoing liberal education as a way of bettering society. Spurred by the idea of war studies (later called general honors), a reading seminar designed by John Erskine for soldiers fighting in the trenches of the First World War,[8] the independent, non-profit educational organization's mission was – and is – to "provide people of all ages with the opportunity to read, discuss, and learn from outstanding works of literature ... [as] part of a grassroots movement to promote continuing education for the general public."[9] The Great Books Foundation claims it has "helped thousands of people through the United States begin their own discussion groups in libraries, schools, and community centers."[10]

The ideological beginnings of the Great Books Foundation were firmly ensconced in the educational philosophies of Hutchins and Adler, whose commitment to the Great Books lay in the belief that they were the foundation of progressive education. According to Daniel Born, Adler and Hutchins advocated a seminar-type book discussion of culturally sanctioned classics featuring close reading and dialogue between the discussion leader and the readers.[11]

Debate over what kinds of reading are appropriate continued into the twentieth century in both public venues and in private circles.[12] Born entertainingly retells the story of Adler and Hutchins meeting Gertrude Stein at a dinner party at which the question of which texts were "Great Books" came up in conversation, and an argument ensued over the value of teaching books in translation. The night ended with Stein slapping Adler across the head and leaving for a tour of Chicago with hired city police guides.[13] Adler later reminisced that while he was honored to be "bitch-slapped by the queen bee of American modernism," he had little respect for her argument. He writes: "The way I felt about her at that moment, I wished they had ... taken her for a ride Chicago-style."[14]

Used in elementary, high school, and university classrooms, the Great Books' trademarked method of discussion is called shared inquiry, in which the teacher or conversation leader poses questions about the text. Readers are encouraged to read closely, and to support their responses with specific references to selections from the text. Discussions focus on the selections, and readers are asked to fully explore the ideas within the selections before moving to ideas outside of them. Readers respond to one another instead of discussing the text with only the teacher or group leader.

The Great Books reading lists are not limited to traditional American classics. Rather, they range from Chekhov to Milton, and from Cather to

Hesse, with the Bible also appearing on the list. The chosen texts represent the enduring debates over what is appropriate reading material. Maintaining the liberal ideology of the program's co-founders, who believed in the direct link between literature and democracy and between democracy and freedom, Great Books staff and supporters assume that the classics allow readers to "meet and talk about enduring issues and ideas."[15]

Similarly, the ideological goal of co-authors Charles Van Doren and Adler was to make a university-sanctioned canon accessible to the general public, a mission they laid out in *How to Read a Book: A Classic Guide to Intelligent Reading* (1940). While they did not presume to offer "correct" readings, they recommended a list of 137 writers and books that would be "worth your while" to read. (Many of these books were [and remain] on the lists published by the Great Books program.) The authors also not so subtly imply that high-literary taste status, or cultural capital, can be gained by anyone who "learns to read" in the way that they teach, and by reading the books they recommend. Once a reader is "competent to judge" literary fiction, according to Adler and Van Doren, he or she "will probably find a large company of men and women of similar taste to share your critical judgments."[16]

Informal book clubs began appearing in the 1960s and the 1970s, coinciding with the rise of feminist consciousness-raising groups that were forming around North America at the time. A brief introduction to these groups may help to conceptualize the gender composition of – and hence reactions to – contemporary book clubs.

In reminiscing about feminism in the 1960s, Judith Harlan writes that the consciousness-raising gatherings were the backbone of an informal, unorganized network that promoted women-only meetings at which members "talked freely about the frustrations and restrictions they faced in their daily lives; they discussed society's underpinnings of sexism; and they experienced a 'click' as they suddenly understood the connection between society's sexism and the frustrations of their own individual lives."[17] In some contemporary American women's book clubs, membership and book discussion might not be as revolutionary as it was in these earlier groups, but many women still want their groups to be women-only spaces and will often work out social or personal conundrums through shared interpretations of the novel under discussion.[18] Later in the chapter I will discuss how these gendered spaces and practices influence literary debates.

First, however, it is important to contextualize contemporary communication systems. While present-day book clubs resemble the "grassroots" historical forms of literary communities in many ways, they are influenced by rapidly changing mediated forms of popular culture. Contemporary readers engage in social practices that are unique to the digitized spaces of twenty-first-century life. Online book groups, interactive fan-fiction sites where fans write their own fiction about favorite characters (such as Harry Potter) and share it with one another,[19] online retailers' and their customers' use of book reviews (as at Amazon.com), and book swapping and review websites mandate that we consider the changing authority of the reviewer. Literary blogs or LitBlogs, as they are often termed by their writers and readers, reconfigure traditional notions of cultural authority to allow almost anyone to become a writer, and anyone with interest and a computer connection can be a reviewer.[20] As Robert Coover illustrates in chapter 71 of this collection, the World Wide Web now provides a different means for production and distribution of texts.[e] The internet also provides reader access to other readers regardless of location, and thus provides access to yet another way to choose books. Online book clubs in their various iterations and formats are new forms of literary communities that work together with other forms of media, such as film and television, to create a cultural space in America that includes novels.

According to Cecilia Konchar Farr[21] and readers in more than thirty interviews and focus groups conducted in the United States,[22] "the general reader" or "real readers" (as opposed to professional readers who interpret literature for a living), are generally white, well educated, and mostly women.[23] Their selection process is not without conflict, especially in book clubs. On the one hand, readers want to demonstrate their cultural capital by choosing books that are viewed by cultural authorities as "worthy." On the other hand, readers need to actively consider the particular histories of pleasure reading and discussion, and also the taste hierarchies, within their book club.[24] Sometimes, the two hands cannot be joined together.

This author's research on the One Book, One Community phenomenon yielded a fine example of a semi-formal book club that serves specific readers' needs: the Huntsville (Alabama) Public Library African American Authors Book Club. Librarian Cleareaser Bone started and runs the club. Bone and other librarians responded to the lack of library-sponsored book clubs that choose African American novels or have African American storylines. The book club, called "Sister to Sister, Brother to Brother, African American Authors Book Club" has been reading together since March 2006. Although meetings are organized by librarians and held in the library,

e Coover, chapter 71, 1174–1179.

members bring reading suggestions to the meetings and vote on which novel or nonfiction books to read together. According to Bone,

> We try to cover different genres of literature, whether it was fiction, non-fiction. Whether it was anything from Tyler Perry's *Don't Make a Black Woman Take Off Her Earrings* (2007), or something, to non-fiction being, oh, what's the book . . . *Don't Play in The Sun* (2005). That was two non-fiction books, but two totally different, coming from two different points of view . . .[25]

This group's reading choices raise important points about processes of text selection. Non-professional readers look for books that they will enjoy reading, and also find intellectually stimulating and personally affecting. The diversity of US readers – with their different ethnic and cultural backgrounds, gender and sexual relations, social positions, religious affiliations – demands that novels reflect their own experiences, while teaching them how to operate in the world.[26] Similar to the women authors identified in this volume by Elizabeth Nolan, who work within and stretch the models and marketplace available to them to tell their stories, contemporary book club readers often look for an author whose experience will speak to their own.[f]

Ronald J. Zboray and Mary Saracino Zboray demonstrate earlier in this volume that – despite popular claims to the contrary – antebellum men purchased and read novels at least as frequently as women, and that both sexes often read them aloud in mixed-gender groups.[g] Their analysis demonstrates how little the cultural status of women's reading practices has changed over the past 300 years. Even today, mixed-gender or all-male literary communities are usually associated with "serious" literature and not often called book clubs but rather, "salons" or "reading groups." Contemporary women's book clubs, including the televised and online version of Oprah's Book Club, are associated with less serious fiction.[27] Cultural conflicts continue to revolve around "high" cultural and "low" or "popular" culture, with issues of gender thrown into the mix.

When the author Jonathan Franzen refused to appear on the popular television book club segment of *The Oprah Winfrey Show* to discuss his novel *The Corrections* (2002), he not so discreetly implied that viewers of the program could not also be readers of "serious" or "high" literature. To National Public Radio he said, "I feel like I'm solidly in the high-art literary tradition, but I like to read entertaining books and this maybe helps bridge that gap, but it also

f Elizabeth Nolan, "The woman's novel beyond sentimentalism," chapter 34.

g Ronald Zboray and Mary Saracino Zboray, "The novel in the antebellum book market," chapter 4, 80.

heightens these feelings of being misunderstood." Franzen accused Oprah's Book Club of being a "promotional vehicle for schmaltzy, one-dimensional novels."[28] Because Oprah's audience is predominantly female and the mass audience is often characterized as feminine, some critics believed that Franzen became the poster boy for the American white, male author under threat. His reactions, and Winfrey's subsequent decisions to un-invite him and then discontinue her hugely successful club, re-ignited debates about high and low literary and cultural classifications, with the arguments taking place in both popular and scholarly publications. Unlike the overtly gendered debates of previous eras, these contemporary conflicts also reflect anxiety about the state of the novel in an electronic era. Still, as Kathleen Fitzpatrick argues, the current debates stem from gendered anxiety in a society that associates mass culture with women "while real, authentic culture remains the prerogative of men."[29]

The first run of Oprah's Book Club lasted from 1996 to 2002. Most of the books picked were considered "middlebrow." While it was easy for some to classify all of the book choices made in that iteration of the club as "trash," some scholars and cultural workers were careful to differentiate among the texts. Shirley Kossick, for example, identified three distinct themes in Oprah's picks: (1) "triumph of the individual over apparently insurmountable odds"; (2) the challenges of women, and minorities, in general; and, (3) "the affirmation of the quality of life."[30] After a one-year hiatus, Winfrey reinvented the Book Club in 2003 to include four university-sanctioned "classics." And, in the fall of 2005, she opened her list to include memoirs and nonfiction. None of her current picks would be considered "middlebrow" fiction.

Celia Conchar Farr argues that cultural conflicts over the hierarchy of literary works arose in the early twentieth century as certain novels made their way into university English classes. Using textual analysis based in studying classical texts, poetry, and scripture, scholars critiqued the novels with the same vigor. American novels had to stand up to the same scrutiny. Some rose to the top of the lists and others were condemned to the proverbial trash pile. According to Farr, in the early 1900s, analytical standards were "increasingly hostile to the social aspects of novels. So novels became lowbrow or highbrow, bad or good by way of traditional standards of aesthetic merit that ... were aristocratic in origin and assumed the mediation of a discriminating few."[31]

The creation of "middlebrow" as a marketing category, according to Nicola Humble, was a gendered response to women writers and readers.[32] During the period from 1920 to 1950, according to Humble, critics who used the term "middlebrow" were reacting to the assumed audience of the book.

This claim is useful for contextualizing critical reactions to contemporary formations of literary communities. According to Humble, once a novel becomes popular – whether by bestseller status, Book-of-the-Month Club choice, or more recently, Oprah Winfrey's Book Club selection – it is excluded from serious attention. "A novel [is] therefore middlebrow not because of any intrinsic content, but because it [is] widely read by the middle-class public – and particularly the lower middle classes."[33] Issues of gender aside, the idea suggests that if many people are reading a book, it must possess limited cultural value. A bestseller cannot be literary. The more popular and economically successful a cultural artifact – such as a novel or book program like Oprah's Book Club – is, the more literary merit becomes suspect.[34]

Janice Radway argues that reviewers criticized members of the Book-of-the-Month club and its lists because of their power – both economic and cultural – to define good literature.[35] These reviewers' assumption was that good novels should stand out on their own; they should not be sanctioned by institutions. According to Radway, the perceived problem was not necessarily that so many people were participating in the Book-of-the-Month Club, but rather that the wrong cultural authorities were influencing people in their book selections.

Is this what bothers contemporary cultural critics about local, grassroots book clubs? Are the novels themselves under scrutiny, or are readers' responses and institutional programs suspect? Perhaps the concepts should not be considered separately. Book choice and discussion are intertwined in book club practices, and these functions can also create discontent among members of book clubs.[36] The friction arises from the interplay among literary analysis training, cultural distinction, group dynamics, and institutional agendas. Whether the reading lists are prescribed, created by the group themselves, or some combination, reading communities simultaneously work to inform readers' literary tastes, distinguish themselves from other readers (and citizens), and fulfill readers' self-perceived educational and social needs.

Enter the United States government. On December 20, 2005, the National Endowment for the Arts (NEA) released a press statement announcing its new nationwide reading program. The Big Read, as the program is called, is the NEA's response to a national study that found that reading in the USA was on a drastic decline. Chairman Dana Gioia says in the release that:

> If cities nationally unite to adopt The Big Read, our community-wide reading program, together we can restore reading to its essential place in American

> culture. Call me naïve, but I can actually envision an America in which average people talk about *To Kill a Mockingbird* and *The Great Gatsby* with the same enthusiasm as they bring to *Lost* or *Desperate Housewives*.[37]

According to that same release, literary reading in the USA is not only on the decline but reading for "pleasure and enlightenment" is *in crisis* (emphasis added). Modeled on successful "One Book, One City" programs in which citizens of a city or region are encouraged to all read the same book, The Big Read's aim is "to restore reading to the center of American culture," and, more implicitly, to educate and civilize American citizens through shared reading of "classic" books.

The Big Read is the NEA's response to their own research. The study, called *Reading at Risk (RaR)*, is drawn from data collected from the Survey of Public Participation in the Arts (SPPA), which was conducted by the Census Bureau in 2002. Only four of the questions were related to reading. Of the 17,000 American adults surveyed, 56.6 percent reported reading any book in the past twelve months, and 46.7 percent reported reading literature,[38] a category restricted to novels, short stories, plays, and poetry.

At the turn of the last century, cultural authorities lamented the *rise* of novel reading. The NEA has turned this around 180 degrees, while ignoring nonfiction reading in its description of the dire situation of the American reading public. The *Reading at Risk* study does not report participation by nonfiction readers or those who might read online. Instead, the main message of The Big Read is that reading a certain type of literary fiction will encourage civic engagement. Even if we consider the correlation between reading fiction and civic engagement, we must ask whether literature – much less a hierarchically determined literature – alone will create the informed citizenry that the NEA idealizes. To assign this duty to literature may ask too much. And, as Catherine Ross *et al.* have argued, to give such a task to reading can take away from the individual pleasures of books – in whatever form they might take and however they may be discussed.[39]

The Big Read program and its partners (ranging from the American Library Association to corporations like Boeing and Ford) fund more than 200 One Book, One Community-type programs across the USA. The participants in these programs are often provided with one of twenty-two books, many of which could be considered part of the traditional American canon, but some of which have also caused public conflict. For example, titles such as *Fahrenheit 451* (1953) and *The Great Gatsby* (1925) have as late as the 1980s been banned. Big Read participants also have access to a centrally produced reading guide and to book programs that sometimes, but not always, provide opportunities for alternate readings of the text.

There are currently three librarians who stage the Huntsville (Alabama) Big Read. For four years, the program was called Get into Reading, and was managed by the same small committee who chose the books, planned the program, wrote and distributed the promotional material and reader's guides, and facilitated the events, which included film screenings, art competitions, book group discussions, and historical re-enactments. Mary, one of the Huntsville Public Library's Branch Librarians who produces The Big Read, in addition to her regular responsibilities, reacted emotionally to news that they had received funding from the NEA program: "I cried a little bit and – it was like amazing because, you know, to go from a zero budget to $25,000 was pretty extraordinary." The NEA funding provided financial oomph that allowed Mary and her small group to continue with the programming that she herself calls "a unique way that people from different walks of life, different parts of the community, could connect."[40]

Such dedication speaks to the ideological, material, and emotional effort wrapped up in shared reading programming. Not unlike other event producers in the USA, Canada, and the UK, the Huntsville producers articulate ideals of community through shared reading and discussion. Those ideals, however, are not necessarily those promoted by the NEA. The national organization promises the public, funders, potential supporters, and politicians that a certain type of book acts as a conduit for discussion, for public engagement. Huntsville's Big Read 2007 book choice, Harper Lee's *To Kill a Mockingbird* (1960), seems particularly promising at a time when the American South struggled to make sense of the Jena 6, a case in which six black youths were arrested for the beating of a white youth. However, an analysis of the readers who attended and of the book discussion at the events suggests that neither were members of the African American community present nor were the readers willing to engage with the book's contemporary connection.

This onus on a novel and the discussions around it might be unfair. To create engaged citizens is important for a critically engaged, knowledgeable society, but to prioritize the cultural value of literary fiction assumes a form of elitism that endures from past centuries. The uniqueness of twentieth- and twenty-first-century print culture, however, lies in the social changes that have resulted largely because of increased literacy rates, levels of education, and changes in the way that mass media and the internet have created an environment in which literary categories are created, discussed, and contested by groups of assertive middle-class readers. Individual readers will bring to their literary communities – whether formal, semi-formal, or informal – their individual and collective histories and experiences informed by religion, education, media, and more recently, new media. Readers demonstrate agency within these confines by choosing their own, and perhaps multiple, groups – online, on television or radio, or face to face. And while the classification of "middlebrow" remains a symbol of the conflict between elite cultural authorities and this expanding group of increasingly independent-minded readers, the government is now an active player – through selective financial support – in the canon-making game.

Notes

1. See Dorothy Smith, *The Everyday World as Problematic: A Feminist Sociology* (Toronto: University of Toronto Press, 1987).
2. Contemporary American examples of comparative analysis of reading groups in and outside the academy include Jane Missner Barstow, "Reading in Groups: Women's Clubs and College Literature Classes," *Publishing Research Quarterly* 18 (2003): 3–17; and Temma Berg, "'What do you know?'; Or, The Question of Reading in Groups and Academic Authority", *Lit: Literature InterpretationTheory* 19.2 (2008): 123–154.
3. Mark Kutner, Elizabeth Greenberg, Ying Jin, Bridget Boyle, Yung-chen Hsu, Eric Dunleavy, and Sheida White, "Literacy in Everyday Life: Results from the 2003 National Assessment of Adult Literacy" (National Center for Education Statistics, Institute of Education Sciences, US Department of Education: Washington, DC, 2007). Accessed at http://nces.ed.gov/Pubs2007/2007480_1.pdf on October 4, 2008.
4. Elizabeth McHenry, *Forgotten Readers: Recovering the Lost History of African American Literary Societies* (Durham, NC: Duke University Press, 2002), 14. See also McHenry, "'Dreaded Eloquence': The Origins and Rise of African American Literary Societies and Libraries," *Harvard Library Review* 6.2 (1998): 32–56.
5. Barry D. Cytron, "The Chautauqua Literary and Scientific Circle in Iowa, 1880–1900," *Palimpsest* 59.6 (1978): 168–175; Andrew Chamberlin Rieser, *The Chautauqua Moment: Protestants, Progressives, and the Culture of Modern Liberalism* (Irvington, NY: Columbia University Press, 2003); John C. Scott, "The Chautauqua Vision of Liberal Education," *History of Education* 34.1 (January 2005): 41–59.
6. www.neiu.edu/~ncaftori/jbook.htm (Accessed September 6, 2008).
7. Elizabeth Long, *Book Clubs: Women and the Uses of Reading in Everyday Life* (Chicago: University of Chicago Press, 2003).
8. Gerald Graff, *Professing Literature: An Institutional History* (Chicago: University of Chicago Press, 1987), 135, cited in Daniel Born, "Utopian Civic-Mindedness: Robert Maynard Hutchins, Mortimer Adler, and the Great Books Enterprise," in *Reading Communities from Salons to Cyberspace*, ed. DeNel Rehberg Sedo (in progress).

9. www.greatbooks.org/ (accessed March 28, 2008).
10. www.greatbooks.org/about (accessed March 28, 2008).
11. Dan Born, "Utopian Civic-Mindedness."
12. Harold Bloom, *How to Read and Why* (New York: Scribner, 2000).
13. Born, "Utopian Civic-Mindedness."
14. Mortimer J. Adler, *Philosopher at Large: An Intellectual Biography* (New York: Macmillan, 1977), 139–140, cited *ibid.*
15. www.greatbooks.org/programs-for-all-ages/gb.html (accessed March 28, 2008).
16. Mortimer J. Adler and Charles Van Doren, *How to Read a Book: A Classic Guide to Intelligent Reading* (New York: Simon and Schuster, 1940; updated edition, 1972). Cited quotations are on pp. 350 and 214.
17. Judith Harlan, *Feminism: A Reference Handbook* (Santa Barbara, CA: ABC-CLIO 1998). "Click" was coined by Jane O'Reilly in the 1970s; it means "clicking-things-into-place-angry." See www.nymag.com/news/features/46167/ (accessed June 27, 2008).
18. Long, *Book Clubs*; DeNel Rehberg Sedo, "Badges of Wisdom, Spaces for Being: A Study of Contemporary Women's Book Clubs" (PhD diss., Simon Fraser University, Burnaby, British Columbia, 2004).
19. See, for example, Karen Hellenkson and Kristina Busse, eds., *Fan Fiction and Fan Communities in the Age of the Internet: New Essays* (Jefferson, NC: McFarland & Co., 2006).
20. See Sven Birkets's response to LitBlogs at: www.boston.com/news/globe/ideas/articles/2007/07/29/lost_in_the_blogosphere/?page=full (accessed July 31, 2007).
21. Cecilia Konchar Farr, *Reading Oprah: How Oprah's Book Club Changed the Way America Reads* (Albany: State University of New York Press, 2005).
22. The primary data described in this chapter is a result of a three-year, international project called "Beyond the Book: Mass Reading Event and Contemporary Cultures of Reading in the UK, USA and Canada" (www.beyondthebookproject.org). Qualitative and quantitative data was collected in Chicago, Huntsville (Alabama), and Seattle, in addition to six other sites in the UK and Canada.
23. The 2008 National Endowment for the Arts Survey (www.arts.gov/research/ReadingonRise.pdf) states that 31.9 percent of literary readers are Hispanic, 55.7 percent are white, 42.6 percent are African American, and 43.9 percent of other ethnicities report as readers. Of the men interviewed, 41.9 percent reported themselves as readers, while 58 percent of the women did. Sixty-one percent of the readers reported having a Bachelor's Degree or higher, and 55–64 was the highest age group to report having read a book not for work or school in the past year, with 58.4 percent. According to the 2008 Survey of Public Participation in the Arts on which this publication is based, nearly half (47.0 percent) of all adults read a novel or short story in 2008.
24. Rehberg Sedo, "Badges of Wisdom."
25. Personal communication with Cleareaser Bone, Huntsville, May 9, 2007.
26. Farr, *Reading Oprah*, 66.

27. Kathleen Rooney, *Reading with Oprah: The Book Club that Changed America* (Fayetteville: University of Arkansas Press, 2005).
28. David D. Kirkpatrick, "Winfrey Rescinds Offer to Author for Guest Appearance," *New York Times* (October 24, 2001). (Accessed at www.nytimes.com, April 20, 2008).
29. Kathleen Fitzpatrick, *The Anxiety of Obsolescence: the American Novel in the Age of Television* (Nashville, TN: Vanderbilt University Press, 2006), 205. The quote earlier in the paragraph is at 203.
30. Shirley Kossick, "Fiction and the Oprah Factor," *The Cape Librarian: Official Monthly Journal of the Cape Provincial Library Service* 46.6 (2002): 9.
31. Farr, *Reading Oprah*, 82.
32. Nicola Humble, *The Feminine Middlebrow Novel 1920s to 1950s: Class, Domesticity, Bohemianism* (Oxford: Oxford University Press, 2001).
33. *Ibid.*, 13.
34. Farr, *Reading Oprah*. In this volume, James L. W. West III argues that the cultural conflicts that resulted in the conglomeration of American publishing houses added fuel to the debate between aesthetic and commercial value. See chapter 47, "Twentieth-century publishing and the rise of the paperback," 794–795.
35. Janice Radway, *A Feeling for Books: The Book-of-the-Month Club, Literary Taste, and Middle-Class Desire* (Chapel Hill: University of North Carolina Press, 1997).
36. Berg "'What do you Know?'"; Rehberg Sedo, *Badges of Wisdom*.
37. www.nea.gov/news/news05/BigReadAnnounce.html (Accessed October 10, 2007).
38. National Endowment of Arts, *Reading at Risk: A Survey of Literary Reading in America, Research Division Report 46* (National Endowment of Arts, Washington DC, 2004), ix.
39. *Ibid.*, 5–7; Catherine Sheldrick Ross, Lynne (E. F.) McKechnie, and Paulette M. Rothbauer, *Reading Matters: What the Research Reveals about Reading, Libraries, and Community* (Westport, CT: Libraries Unlimited, 2005), 23.
40. Personal communication, May 23, 2006.

71

A history of the future of narrative

ROBERT COOVER

The future of the American novel begins in Sumer at the beginning of the Bronze Age something over 5,000 years ago with the development of a new technology called writing. Like all freshly invented technologies, the new writing system had to undergo a certain amount of experimental beta time (a millennium or so) before procedures became standardized and something like an accepted alphabet and grammar emerged, for one of the first things that was no doubt discovered was that writing was like speaking, but it was not speaking, and new protocols had to be formulated. Though it probably began as an accountancy mechanism for an agrarian society (some of the oldest written inscriptions concern grain harvests and the production of beer and its distribution), it eventually evolved into a more flexible and broadly applicable tool, opening up several new career opportunities – scribe, teacher, scholar, recorder, archivist, historian, preparer of tablets, mathematician, to name but a few – and making literacy a form of empowerment. Parents sent their children to writing schools to secure their futures. The cuneiform signs developed by the Sumerians were soon adopted by their neighbors and the technology spread throughout Mesopotamia, and eventually into South Asia, Africa, Europe, and on into the New World, a parallel but very different development getting off the ground in Asia two or three millennia after the Sumerians first pressed stylus to clay, promoted by Chinese priestly fortune-tellers. With a notable exception or two (e.g., the Mayans), all known writing systems of the world are believed to descend ultimately from either the early inventions of the Sumerians or those of the Chinese.

Though developed as a tool for commerce, Sumerian writing was inevitably taken up by storytellers, at that time also regarded as divinely inspired priests thanks to their magical writing skills, who committed to writing the oral tales of the tribe, mostly those about origins, laws, gods and mortals, cosmic and local warfare, and how things came to be as they are (the temple scribes having floated to the top, it was their intention of course to see that things stayed that way), and no doubt fashioned several new ones of their own. It was not an expensive technology: all it required was wet clay and a stylus for the composition and fire to bake it. There were surely everyday secular oral tales in circulation as well which did not get written down, perhaps because they were considered unworthy of an art and science deemed a gift of the gods, or simply because the taletellers were unschooled in the new technology. Probably also they did not toe the scribal line and, even if somehow published, would have been pulverized. The stories that were written down and preserved became common currency, making Sumerian language and culture a dominant scriptural force throughout the literate world, even after Sumerian civilization itself had decayed and collapsed, its language no longer spoken, somewhat in the way that Roman and Latin culture and language lingered authoritatively in the Christianized West.

Thus it was that, a millennium or so after the rise and fall of the Sumerians – it takes awhile for a new technology to settle in – an unknown Akkadian author or authors in the Old Babylonian period gathered together some loosely connected Sumerian myths and tales about a culture hero named Gilgamesh, and integrated them into a novel work of art for his or their own time and place: not a mere compilation of old tales from an ancient culture, but an innovative fictional rewrite, all the borrowed material at the service of a new theme, the contradictory elements of disparate fragments harmonized now into a single whole, and many elements, especially structural ones, probably completely original, especially those having to do with the friendship of Gilgamesh and Enkidu. The author or authors apparently converted Enkidu the servant, as he appears in all known Sumerian poems, into Enkidu the friend and rustic equal, thereby making more plausible the terrible shock Gilgamesh suffers at Enkidu's death, a shock powerful enough to send him off on his obsessive but futile quest for immortality or at least rejuvenation, which in turn gave the *Gilgamesh Epic* its coherent "plot" and its unity, becoming our oldest known sustained imaginative narrative and first generally acknowledged work of literature. There may have been others, of course, but this is what we have. Later revisions over the centuries padded the text out, framed the tale more clearly, threw in the popular flood story as entertainment, made some stylistic changes and greater use of recurrent motifs, and celebrated taletelling itself as the noblest of endeavors – inscribing his story, perhaps on the very walls of Uruk, was finally Gilgamesh's principal consolation and achievement after his unavailing visit to the Land of the Dead – but otherwise adhered to the original Old Babylonian adventure story, by then centuries old and part of the canon. With its lonely, larger-than-life hero and his trusted sidekick setting out to tame the hostile wilderness and the savage creature that inhabited it, with its awesome landscape, fierce male-bonding, suggestion of misogyny, and preoccupation with violent death, and with its muscularly written, but somewhat romantic style, the *Epic* might strike an American reader as a kind of proto-Western, not unlike the recent border novels of Cormac McCarthy, for example, though of course the pattern can be found throughout literary and folklore history.

The reason we know as much as we do about early Sumerian literature and that which followed in the early millennia of the age of writing is that it was recorded on clay tablets, among the most inexpensive and durable of all writing materials. Fired clay is susceptible to being broken and scattered and eroded by weather and water, but only stone is its match for longevity and stone is costly and difficult to work, suitable for monuments and tombstones maybe, but not for epics. Clay far outlasts papyrus, parchment, paper, and even leather, wood, and metal, and is more recognizable as a library artifact than, say, the bones and turtle shells used by the early Shang fortune-telling priests in China for their oracular inscriptions, few of which have been found. Clay tablets 5,000 years old have survived. Paper would have long since returned to nature.

The most complete extant version of the Gilgamesh Epic, discovered in bits and pieces in the ruins of Ashurbanipal's library a century and a half ago, was published in the Middle Babylonian period on twelve large clay tablets (eleven, to be precise, with a twelfth tablet appendix), rudely resembling in that manner the unbound pages of a codex, what we call a book, a technology that would not come into its own for another millennium and a half. In the intervening centuries, the preferred writing medium was the continuous papyrus scroll, developed in Egypt where the papyrus reeds grew. Its production became a significant contributor to Egypt's rising prosperity and power, though eventually, when papyrus became rare and failed to meet the demand of the increasingly literate world, it was augmented and somewhat superseded by parchment, made from prepared animal skins, which was more pliable for scrolling and less likely to come apart (stitched, not glued), provided a smoother writing surface, and was more readily available: a single handwritten Bible (the word derives from the Greek name for papyrus or scroll) required the slaughter of only about three hundred or so sheep, and sheep were everywhere. Papyrus and parchment were much better writing surfaces than wet clay, allowing for more fluid writing and works of greater length and subtlety, but their elaborate production – like that of the newly necessary pens and inks – was far more expensive, further separating the empowered literate from the illiterate mass, and they were much more susceptible to destruction, especially by fire. The legendary burning of the Great Library of Alexandria with its incomparable collection of irreplaceable handwritten scrolls lost forever remains one of literary history's most chilling horror stories.

Scrolls were divisible into chapters, or "books," were easily copied, boxed, and shelved, had developed sophisticated protocols over time such as spacing, paragraphing, and punctuation, were aesthetically appealing, and had been around for millennia, so even as the manuscript codex arrived – the page-turning "book," as we know it – scrolls were still widely seen as the true and permanent medium for extended writing such as literature and continued as such for some centuries, the codex format emerging from artless writing tablets made of strung-together sheets of wood with a renewable wax surface and not meant for posterity. Though scrolls worked well for sequential linear readings, however, they lacked pagination and a search mechanism, making spatial navigation through a long document (such as the Bible, for example) somewhat difficult. Various experiments were undertaken. Creating sideways columns instead of top-to-bottom run-on text led to folding the scrolls like an accordion (that great innovator Ovid may have been one of the first to try this, for the first-century Roman satirist Martial tells us: "This bulky mass of multiple folds / all fifteen poems of Ovid holds"), resulting in something like pages, and this in turn, over time, merged with the wax tablet technology to create the bound codex book with parchment and eventually paper pages. The codex was more transportable (you could take it to bed with you) and pagination eventually allowed for an index, writing's first sophisticated search mechanism, and one still much in use in print publishing. The classical world clung stubbornly to their tradition of writing on scrolls for awhile, but the Christian cult (seen by those being overtaken as barbarians) was spreading and its scholars and proselytizers overwhelmingly preferred the codex for Bible study and the exchange of theological tracts and notes, so eventually, as they conquered the Western world and erased much of the past, the codex form took hold and is still with us a millennium or two later. Most if not all the works mentioned in this volume were published using it.

Then in the middle of the fifteenth century came what was arguably the most revolutionary literary development since the Sumerian invention of writing itself: Johann Gutenberg's movable type. Gone suddenly was the scriptorium and the laborious copying by hand of manuscripts; in came the printing press and the mass-produced book, newspaper, magazine. The novel.

Much of the first half-century of this new technology was spent producing documents for the Church, making Bibles, plundering the Latin manuscript collections of the past, and adjusting to the changing protocols, for they soon found that printed books were like manuscript books, but they were not manuscript books. Print introduced new issues like font design (Gutenberg began with fonts that imitated scribal manuscripts as if trying to hide what he had done), ink production, binding and glues, formatting protocols, proofreading, footnoting as a kind of formalized marginalia, and so on. Out in the world, it created publishing houses, bookshops, public libraries. Their endeavors gave to all who could read the classic tongue access to texts once accessible only to the privileged few, denting the power structure and giving further impetus to the general awakening already taking place. The invention of the printing press in the age of Renaissance humanism would become the perfect Enlightenment tool. Meanwhile, in fourteen hundred ninety-two, while Columbus was sailing the ocean blue, Antonio de Nebrija published his groundbreaking *Gramática Castellana*, first of its kind in the European languages, stimulating the writing of original texts in the vernacular instead of in Latin, a practice pioneered a couple of centuries earlier by the likes of Chrétien de Troyes, Dante, Chaucer. Fewer than eight years after the *Gramática*, before the century turned, an anonymous author, but probably a young student classmate of Hernán Cortés named Fernando de Rojas from a *converso* family (*conversos* were Jews who converted to Christianity to avoid exile or being burned at the stake or otherwise humiliated, tortured, and killed by the Spanish Inquisition), published, in the Spanish language, the *Tragicomedia de Calisto y Melibea*, popularly known by way of its main character as the *Celestina* (in the earliest English translation: *The Spanish Bawd*), considered by some (I am one of those) as the second greatest literary work in the Spanish language. Multigeneric, it gave birth to both modern drama and to the novel, though as to the latter it took nearly another century of living with the book to get there. The full creative potential of a new technology is rarely understood at its inception. Much as in the *Gilgamesh Epic*, where we discover that the adventure tale we are reading has already been inscribed centuries before by the hero himself in a frame-tale celebration of the writing technology of the day, so in *Don Quijote*, widely held to be the first modern novel, the "ingenious hidalgo of La Mancha" is announced in Part Two as the now-famous hero of the already published Part One, thereby celebrating the writing technology and reading habits of the "new" print era, now a century and a half old. *Don Quijote* also features a lonely hero (one adjudged to have been driven mad by books) and his faithful rustic sidekick, challenging what the don perceives as a wilderness inhabited by the fantastic creatures of medieval romance, though now their story is richly inflected by irony, that irresistible characteristic peculiar to a majority of spine-bound, page-turning print novels, which perhaps has something to do with being able to flip back and reread what you've just read, the narrative existing in space as well as time.

The publishing industry also created a sudden surge in the demand for paper, especially with the rise of the literate bourgeoisie and their enthusiasm for books (new writing technologies create new audiences), stimulating a technological change in its production. In the pre-Gutenberg era the making of paper had relied primarily on recycled rags – thus, the famous ragmen – but now with rising costs and the linen and rag supply unable to meet the rising demand, various other fibers were tried, like cabbage and straw (Egyptian mummies were recycled to make wrapping paper, it is said, as one short-term solution to the paper shortage), the industry settling finally on pulped wood as its readily available basic ingredient; and then, as Europe moved into the Industrial Age, machines were invented capable of producing paper from wood in large continuous rolls. The mass production of cheap paper brought printing production costs down, making books and other reading materials available to everyone and, in that pre-film era, the novel became the entertainment medium of choice.

It was into the very heart of this booming democratizing print era, so receptive to the novel form, a form launched in part by New World travel narratives, that the United States of America was born. One could almost say: was written. The framers of the nation were all readers and writers, and no country before it had been so thoroughly founded upon literarily crafted documentation. Printing presses, public libraries, newspapers, paper mills were all in place nearly a century before the American Revolution, and played a significant role in fostering it and defining it. By the end of the war, there were newspapers in print throughout the former colonies, and the very first Constitutional amendment in the 1791 American Bill of Rights guaranteed freedom of the press and of expression. Less than a decade later, the Library of Congress was established, making the collecting of books a national hobby. Industrial paper mills and the abundance of wood, steam-powered printing presses, the opening up of the country by way of the railroads, nationwide public schooling focused on literacy, all contributed to the creation of a growing audience for American writing, including American novels, providing fulltime writing careers early on for the likes of Washington Irving and Fenimore Cooper, an opportunity that persists into this era of corporate publishing and the ubiquitous writing workshop. As might be anticipated, the new was largely imitative of the past, though that's a story told here in other chapters. One notable novelty in American fiction, however, was the fading away of the hieratic distinction between literary and everyday language, originally established by ancient Egyptian scribes and perpetuated in most modern cultures, thereby complicating to this day the translation of American fiction into other languages. Film, America's primary contribution to the universal history of imaginative narrative, being textually spare, moves about the world more easily, though dubbing and subtitles are of course dogged by the same difficulties, exacerbated by the increased emphasis on colloquial speech and the need for compression, but ameliorated by its general inconsequentiality.

Then in the middle of the twentieth century came what was arguably the most revolutionary writing development since Johann Gutenberg's movable type: the invention of the computer. The computer began as a kind of fancy calculator for science, applied mathematics, and commerce, much of the rest of the century being focused on tool design – transistors, semiconductors, and microprocessors, storage systems, browsers and modems, operating systems, and the like – and on such issues as networking, speed and portability, programming languages, computer-readable fonts, graphic user interfaces. But in 1991, roughly half a century after its invention (the full creative potential of a new technology is rarely understood at its inception), British high-energy physics researcher Tim Berners-Lee opened up the twenty-year-old internet to the general public by way of his creation of the nonproprietary World Wide Web, a global hypertext project intended as a computer-driven networked information management system for scholarly exchange, especially among physicists, but soon evolving into a flexible and broadly applicable tool, capable, as it turned out, of absorbing into its monadic 0/1 electronic universe almost all known forms of human expression. In anticipation of the future use of the web, Berners-Lee also introduced the HyperText Transfer Protocol (HTTP) that governs the World Wide Web and is traditionally – http://www – part of most web addresses; Uniform Resource Locators (URLs), our individual website addresses; and HyperText Markup Language (HTML), first of the standardized web language composition and text-formatting tools. The Mosaic web browser was launched in 1993 and transformed commercially into Netscape a year later, whereupon the historic worldwide rush to the internet was on.

Gone suddenly was the total reliance on printing presses and publishing houses with their cumbersome production, distribution, and warehousing practices, along with most other twentieth-century physical apparatuses of human communication, and in, to close out the millennium, swept the Digital

Age. The advent of the computer and World Wide Web opened up several new career opportunities – programmer (a kind of code scribe), computer technician, graphic designer, 3D modeler, sound engineer, software developer, hardware manufacturer, web designer, to name but a few, and not to neglect the rewriting of job descriptions in almost all existent disciplines and occupations – and made digital literacy in this globalizing era a form of empowerment. Parents now send their children to computer engineering and computer science schools to secure their futures. The platforms, languages, and procedures developed by the early designers of the new writing tools, primarily Americans or at American universities and entrepreneurial American companies, have become common currency throughout the globalized world, and the widespread adoption of American English as the shared tongue has made it the dominant scriptural force throughout the literate world, a dominance that will no doubt continue even should American civilization decline, somewhat in the way that Sumerian culture and language lingered authoritatively in the Mesopotamian region several millennia ago, far beyond the existence of Sumer itself.

As with all freshly minted technologies, this new writing system, using ACSII as its alphabet and hypertext as its grammar, has had to undergo a certain amount of experimental beta time (measured now in decades rather than millennia) as procedures gradually become standardized and something like a common coding language emerges, for one of the first things that was discovered is that electronic writing is like print writing, but it is not print writing, and new protocols have had to be formulated. Though much of these start-up decades has been devoted to composing and editing documents for conversion to print, emailing, and advertising, plundering the world's libraries for content and compiling textual data bases, engaging in scholarly, political, commercial, and amorous exchanges, and converting print media like newspapers and journals into print-imitative electronic formats, many writers, poets, game designers (sometimes seen as narrative artists of a sort), diarists, and filmmakers were drawn to the computer's word-processing and file management powers and to its conceptually original literary potential. Conjure up a new medium, and writers and artists will break in to play with it.

The earliest known "literary" experiment on the computer was Christopher Strachey's 1952 self-mocking love letter generator which created simple grammatical constructions with blanks to be filled in from appropriate implanted lists, using a random number generator as a recombinant text mechanism. It was written for an immediate successor to the first true stored-program computer – the "Manchester Baby" – built in 1948 at the University of

Manchester, England, and indeed, then only four years on, an invention still very much in its post-partum infancy. Poets drawn early to this new expressive domain over the decades that followed exploited its transformative, generative, and kinetic potential, while the first novelists to enter into it were fascinated primarily by the computer-specific novelty of hypertext with its linked networks of multidirectional text spaces and labyrinthine trails through mapped narratives. That most of these early experimental hypertext writers were Americans may have had something to do with the native affinity – in a nation that was itself an invention in a time of inventions, a cut-and-paste composite of clashing ethnicities accustomed to ceaseless change and an ever-expanding frontier – to spacious exploratory multivoiced narratives with arbitrary beginnings and no clear endings. These early experimental writers in the pre-World Wide Web era worked almost exclusively in text, partly because they were born and raised there and you start with what you know, but largely because the very limited capacities of computers and storage disks in those days dictated it, text being relatively memory-cheap. Their works, which examined the tantalizing new possibility of laying a story out spatially instead of linearly, inviting the reader to explore it as one might explore one's memory or wander a many-pathed geographical terrain, were published on low-density floppies (CD-ROMs not yet invented) and distributed by snail-mail, entering one's library as a book might. Reading them indeed was much like reading a book, except that they used links through unbound text spaces instead of turning pages, and they could only be read on a computer screen, and for some years only on Macintosh computers. Some electronic journals began to appear around 1990, but for the most part if these first hyperfictions (as they were sometimes called) were reviewed at all, they were reviewed in print, there perceived often as another experiment in the centuries-long history of vanguard fictions that have challenged the constraints and conventions of the book machine.

For a short time, it seemed that might be what digital narratives of the future would look like, but with the opening up of the internet in the mid-1990s via the World Wide Web and the invention of browsers, accompanied by expanding memory, improved interfaces, powerful search engines, the arrival of laptops and handheld devices with internet, television, image capturing, and telephony convergence, the massive shift of audience attention, and the explosive development of sophisticated networking, compositional, and hypermedia tools, it became clear that these early experiments have been to electronic literature what the early silents were to the movies: pioneer artworks making speculative use of a new technology still in transitional development.

That technology, though now globally dominant, has not yet settled – if we think of the computer's decadal growth in human terms, it's just past the toddler age, walking and talking but still struggling with its ABCs – but some indications of directions digital literature might take in the coming millennia are emerging. Importantly, new literary work will increasingly be published online, whether by authors or publishers, by direct website access, or by single-object downloads, simply because multimodal digital literature cannot step back into print, while all print literature can easily be moved into the computer. Indeed, it is there now, but for its final output and distribution stages, and has arguably become a mere subset of digitally produced literature. Authors may or may not choose to work exclusively in text, but the full range of audio, visual, and filmic media will be available to them and will often be integrated into their stories and poems. Codex-style bound books with paper pages will no doubt continue to be published for a time, centuries maybe, but even they will be produced on the computer, peddled online, and will frequently have ancillary websites enhanced by hypertextual and hypermedia elements, as well as reviews, interviews with the author, feedback zones, and other supplemental electronically accessed and interactive materials unavailable in the printed book. Because print novels now begin life as electronic texts, many will incorporate surface aspects of digital literature in their design and narrative strategies (in fact, many already do) and will be composed in environments impacted by the new media. Some electronic works will be released in their final authoritative version, others will appear serially in weblogs and online publications in the way that booklength print narratives have sometimes first appeared in newspapers and magazines, and some, though "finished," will mutate from week to week, by the whim of the author or by built-in text generation and morphing techniques or by reader interactions. If there are to be any library collectibles, they may have to be grabbed as secondary spinoffs in the manner of movie-lobby T-shirts, CDs and posters, and may represent only a passing phase of works perpetually in progress. The digital authors or their online publishers will have hands-on control over issues of color, font selection, and page design (as they do now), and the built-in linking mechanisms – whether triggered by mouse clicks, rollovers, keypad, voice commands, eye movements, screen touching, hand gestures, game joysticks or timers – can be used not only for hypertextual play, page-turning and the launching of hypermedia events, but also for accessing selected webwide data bases, whether of a general nature (e.g., language dictionaries, encyclopedias) or specific to the story or poem, a facility also available at any time of course to online readers who stumble into unknown territory, linguistic or otherwise, and need a little help.

Behind everything that appears on the computer screen lie layers of code and, as this is a kind of writing, too, authors will learn how to dip down and reshape it for their own unique purposes, as some are doing now, with the consequence, for some time to come at least, of continuous formal innovation, vanguard codework fostering vanguard literature. And vanguard everything-else: if the book is being affected by digitization, so are painting, sculpture, film, music, television, architecture, animation, photography, all the known arts of the past, as well as all forms of human discourse and cultural exchange, and under all of it lies mutable executable code. Nowhere is this designing and redesigning of the source code more actively a part of the creative writing process than in the development of computer and video games, which have had a trajectory parallel to that of digital poetry and fiction, though one that has been more robust (there was money to be made) and began earlier, their arcade boom predating kinetic poetry and hypertext fiction by a decade or two. Gaming is not the same thing as reading, but games – such genres as role-playing and adventure games, for example – have often striven for literary subtlety, style, complexity of plot and character, just as hypertext and network fictions have occasionally spiced their narratives with game elements and borrowed some of the innovative coding practices and sophisticated graphics. Advocates of the field see a continual blurring of the distinction between network fiction and games, or what they call interactive fiction (IF), with serious narrative art of the future partaking of both. These game elements may never satisfy the serious reader, whoever that may be, but new literary narratives may well employ navigational coding practices akin to those of computer games not transparent to the reader.

And where will that reader be? In bed perhaps with a bound book with paper pages, just as in the old days, the book downloaded to one's own computer or to that of one's local bookstore/printer; or with a handheld reading device or personal display glasses ("computer wearables," as such devices are called), and/or with earphones, being read to, maybe by the author herself, all devices usable as well on trains and planes and on the subway on the way to work and back, during lunch breaks, at the beach and on park benches. Most often, in the near future at least, the reader will be sitting in front of a computer screen, internet-linked and fully powered, but otherwise reading much as one has read for centuries at library desks or kitchen tables over an open book. Some large-scale narrative presentations now happen in museums and galleries as multiscreen and multimedia installations, and those will also continue to be reading spaces, especially for the avant-garde. Staged readings of electronic writing in which computer-projected wallsized screens of interactive text and images are accompanied by performance are already a popular commonplace, not unlike public poetry and fiction readings, and with the computerized convergence of sound, text, image, video, and animation, text-reading is increasingly a part of many art exhibits, video and film showings, and musical performances as well. Experiments over the past decade with immersive virtual reality facilities – typically, rooms made of movie screens with synchronized computer projection, the reader equipped with 3D glasses and often an interactive handheld device or glove, but also sometimes with body sensors – have included narrative, poetic, and theatrical artworks, and it is easy to imagine a future time, with the further development of something like the current plasma screens, when one's bedroom or living room could be turned into an immersive virtual reality chamber, story content supplied via internet downloads to rolldown screens in the manner of online movie rentals. Site-specific narrative projects have also been undertaken using 3D glasses and earphones in natural locations, the "real" world augmented by virtual persons, objects, texts, voices, actions, the reader a witness to the story taking place and sometimes one of its characters.

Of course there are many who object to any of this being called "literature." Certainly it does not look much like the traditional novel, that quintessential artifact of the age of print and the Industrial Revolution, and the ostensible topic, within American terms, of this volume. Even deep into this digital era, the page-turning book is still widely seen as the true and permanent medium for literature and other extended writing, electronic writing emerging from the artless chatter of the internet (the invasion of barbarians!) and, of no more substance than light, not meant for posterity. Powerful old technologies with their embedded infrastructures and all their investors and owners, employees, producers, sellers, collectors and users have a way of surviving tenaciously well beyond their dominant eras. It is a commonplace to say, using an argument once similarly made on behalf of papyrus and parchment scrolls in opposition to the codex, that the book will always be with us, that the computer may be an arena for literary writing of a sort, even eventually the primary one, but it cannot replace the deep reading experience – the power of the word alone to make a world – provided by the traditional novel. That may be so, but the trends in present-day reading habits, especially among the rising generations for whom the digital revolution is no novelty but simply the world into which they were born (new technologies create new audiences; they may even rewire the young brains that grow up on them), do not bode well for a long commercial life for novels or any other printed books: nearly three-quarters of all American adults are now on the internet, but a relatively minuscule number are still reading books. The digital revolution would seem to be irresistible and irreversible, the medium of choice (or perhaps choice is not even a factor) for the new generations, meaning that, if literature is to survive and continue to be a force in human lives, it will have to go there, speak to that audience.

The novel's future in this new expressive arena, impatient with extensive works in monomedia, would seem to be somewhat bleak, but if the notion of the "novel" be expanded to include all complex and lengthy narrative literature, there is no reason to suppose that storytelling, sometimes held to be that which, after language itself, most centrally defines humanity, will not eventually move as readily from page to computer screen, or its future equivalents, as it once moved from oral taletellers to clay to scroll to codex to printed book. Of course, changing technologies always reshape the very nature of the artistic enterprise, but there remains through all generations a desire for literary art that is intellectually and aesthetically written, organic, intentional, speculative, beautiful, entertaining, evocative, innovative if possible, a witness to the times. The authors of the Gilgamesh Epic and Book of Genesis were narrative artists, as were the poets "Homer," Virgil, and Ovid, not to mention the Hellenic romancers or prose fiction writers like Petronius. So, too, were Chrétien de Troyes, Dante, Boccaccio, Chaucer, Rojas, Cervantes, each using the technology of their era to reach their audiences and get their stories told. That no such widely acknowledged masters have as yet made their mark on the digital landscape is hardly surprising. All previous masters of a form were born into its technology and environed by it; so far, only for pre-teens is that really true today. It took millennia of cuneiform writing and the demise of the civilization that invented it before the first known extended narrative was composed using it, and then by a writer or writers working with ancient source materials in a language no longer spoken and requiring translation (the Akkadians also produced, on clay, the first known bilingual dictionaries). Don Quijote, obsessive reader of books, sallied forth from his library on his genre-establishing adventures a full century and a half after the invention of movable type, and after a massive amount of other published writing, once heralded, now largely forgotten, but probably necessary for Rocinante to get his footing. In America, book publishing had to wait nearly two centuries for the definitive American novel to appear, sending the nation out to sea on a doomed Nantucket whaling ship that it might find itself, and even then it took better than another half century, while Melville's reputation languished, before its value was finally understood. The new computer technology of our age is still developing and may well need another half-century to achieve some sort of maturity, assuming humanity's creative appetites outlast its destructive ones and we get that far, meaning that, even if digital novelistic masterpieces are improbably already being created, it will likely take at least that long for them to be recognized as such.

Meanwhile, as readers, we live in a rich and enviable time. We have at our fingertips, more accessible than ever, an unparalleled abundance of great writing, including great novels, with new works of print literature appearing by the shelfload every day – suddenly, as the book takes to its sickbed, everybody wants to write one – and at the same time we are also witnesses to the emergence of the exciting new writing medium of the future, able if we wish, thanks to the very technology making it happen, to write our way into the ongoing worldwide discourse (in the globalized digital era it will be increasingly difficult to speak of national literatures, or even to locate them) about that medium's development and its future impact on such treasured historic artforms as the traditional American novel.

A selected bibliography

(Note: Please see endnotes of essays for additional critical works.)

Aarseth,Espen. *Cybertext: Perspectives on Ergodic Literature*. Baltimore and London: Johns Hopkins University Press, 1997.

Adams, Rachel. *Continental Divides: Remapping the Cultures of North America*. Chicago: University of Chicago Press, 2009.

Allen, Chadwick. *Blood Narrative: Indigenous Identity in American Indian and Maori Literary and Activist Texts.*Durham, NC: Duke University Press, 2002.

Ammons, Elizabeth. *Conflicting Stories: American Women Writers at the Turn into the Twentieth Century*. Oxford: Oxford University Press, 1991.

Anderson, Benedict. *Imagined Communities: Reflections on the Origin and Spread of Nationalism*. London: Verso, 1983.

Anzaldúa,Gloria. *Borderlands/La Frontera: The New Mestiza*. San Francisco: Spinsters/Aunt Lute, 1987.

Arac, Jonathan. *The Emergence of American Literary Narrative, 1820–1860*. Cambridge, MA: Harvard University Press, 2005.

Huckleberry Finn as Idol and Target: The Functions of Criticism in Our Time. Madison: University of Wisconsin Press, 1997.

Armstrong, Nancy. *Desire and Domestic Fiction: A Political History of the Novel*. Oxford: Oxford University Press, 1990.

How Novels Think: The Limits of Individualism from 1719–1900. New York: Columbia University Press, 2006.

Armstrong, Nancy and Leonard Tennenhouse. *The Imaginary Puritan: Literature, Intellectual Labor, and the Origins of Personal Life*. Berkeley: University of California Press, 1992.

Awkward, Michael. *Inspiriting Influences: Tradition, Revision, and Afro-American Women's Novels*. New York: Columbia University Press, 1989.

Negotiating Difference: Race, Gender, and the Politics of Positionality. Chicago: University of Chicago Press, 1995.

Baetens, Jan. "Novelization, a Contaminated Genre?" *Critical Inquiry* 32.1 (Autumn 2005): 43–60.

Baetens, Jan, ed. *The Graphic Novel*. Leuven: Leuven University Press, 2001.

Babb, Valerie. *Whiteness Visible: The Meaning of Whiteness in American Literature and Culture*. New York: New York University Press, 1998.

Baker, Houston A., Jr. *Blues, Ideology, and Afro-American Literature: A Vernacular Theory*. Chicago: University of Chicago Press, 1984.

Modernism and the Harlem Renaissance. Chicago: University of Chicago Press, 1987.

Workings of the Spirit: The Poetics of Afro-American Women's Writing. Chicago: University of Chicago Press, 1991.

Bakhtin, M. M. *The Dialogic Imagination*. Translated by Caryl Emerson and Michael Holquist. Austin: University of Texas Press, 1981.

Banta, Martha. *Taylored Lives: Narrative Productions in the Age of Taylor, Veblen, and Ford*. Chicago: University of Chicago Press, 1993.

Barnes, Elizabeth. *States of Sympathy: Seduction and Democracy in the American Novel*. New York: Columbia University Press, 1997.

Baym, Nina. "Melodramas of Beset Manhood: How Theories of American Fiction Exclude Women Authors." In *The New Feminist Criticism: Essays on Women, Literature, and Theory*, ed. Elaine Showalter, 63–80. New York: Pantheon, 1985.

Novels, Readers, and Reviewers: Responses to Fiction in Antebellum America. Ithaca, NY: Cornell University Press, 1984.

Woman's Fiction: A Guide to Novels by and about Women in America, 1820–1870. Ithaca, NY: Cornell University Press, 1978

Bell, Bernard W. *The Afro-American Novel and Its Tradition*. Amherst: University of Massachusetts Press, 1987.

The Contemporary African American Novel: Its Folk Roots and Modern Literary Branches. Amherst: University of Massachusetts Press, 2004.

Bell, Michael Davitt. *The Development of American Romance: The Sacrifice of Relation*. Chicago: University of Chicago Press, 1980.

The Problem of American Realism. Chicago: University of Chicago Press, 1993.

Bellin, Joshua David. *The Demon of the Continent: Indians and the Shaping of American Literature*. Philadelphia: University of Pennsylvania Press, 2001.

Bender, John. *Imagining the Penitentiary: Fiction and the Architecture of Mind in Eighteenth-Century England*. Chicago: University of Chicago Press, 1987.

Bentley, Nancy. *The Ethnography of Manners: Hawthorne, James, and Wharton*. Cambridge: Cambridge University Press, 1995.

Frantic Panoramas: American Literature and Mass Culture, 1870–1920. Philadelphia: University of Pennsylvania Press, 2009.

Bercovitch, Sacvan, *American Jeremiad*. Madison: University of Wisconsin Press, 1978.

The Office of the Scarlet Letter. Baltimore: Johns Hopkins University Press, 1991.

The Rites of Assent: Transformations in the Symbolic Construction of America. New York: Routledge, 1983.

Bercovitch, Sacvan, ed. *The Cambridge History of American Literature*. 8 volumes. Cambridge: Cambridge University Press, 1994–2006.

Bercovitch, Sacvan and Myra Jehlen, eds. *Ideology and Classic American Literature*. Cambridge: Cambridge University Press, 1986.

Berlant, Lauren. *The Anatomy of National Fantasy: Hawthorne, Utopia, and Everyday Life*. Chicago: University of Chicago Press, 1991.

The Female Complaint: The Unfinished Business of Sentimentality in American Culture. Durham, NC: Duke University Press, 2008.

Berman, Carolyn Vellenga. *Creole Crossings: Domestic Fiction and the Reform of Colonial Slavery*. Ithaca, NY and London: Cornell University Press, 2006.

Beronä, David. *Wordless Books. The Original Graphic Novels*. New York: Abrams, 2008.

Best, Stephen Michael. *The Fugitive's Properties: Law and the Poetics of Possession*. Chicago: University of Chicago Press, 2004.

Birkerts, Sven. *The Gutenberg Elegies: The Fate of Reading in an Electronic Age*. New York: Faber and Faber, 1994; rept. 2006.

Blum, Hester. *The View from the Masthead: Maritime Imagination and Antebellum American Sea Narratives*. Chapel Hill:University of North Carolina Press, 2008.

Bolter, Jay David. *Writing Space: Computers, Hypertext, and the History of Writing*. Mahwah, NJ: Lawrence Erlbaum Associates, 1991.

Bone, Robert. *The Negro Novel in America*. New Haven: Yale University Press, 1965.

Boone, Joseph Allen. *Tradition Counter Tradition: Love and the Form of Fiction*. Chicago: University of Chicago Press, 1987.

Borus, Daniel H. *Writing Realism: Howells, James, and Norris in the Mass Market*. Chapel Hill: University of North Carolina Press, 1989.

Boyd, Anne E. *Writing for Immortality: Women and the Emergence of High Literary Culture in America*. Baltimore: Johns Hopkins University Press, 2004.

Bramen, Carrie Tirado. *The Uses of Variety: Modern Americanism and the Quest for National Distinctiveness*. Cambridge, MA: Harvard University Press, 2000.

Breitwieser, Mitchell. *National Melancholy: Mourning and Opportunity in Classic American Literature*. Stanford, CA: Stanford University Press, 2007.

Brickhouse, Anna. *Transamerican Literary Relations and the Nineteenth-Century Public Sphere*. Cambridge: Cambridge University Press, 2004.

Brodhead, Richard H. *Cultures of Letters: Scenes of Reading and Writing in Nineteenth-Century America*. Chicago: University of Chicago Press, 1993.

Melville, Hawthorne, and the Novel. Chicago: University of Chicago Press, 1976.

The School of Hawthorne. Oxford: Oxford University Press, 1987.

Brown, Bill. *The Material Unconscious: American Amusement, Stephen Crane, and the Economies of Play*. Cambridge, MA: Harvard University Press, 1996.

A Sense of Things: The Object Matter of American Literature. Chicago: University of Chicago Press 2003.

Brown, Gillian. *The Consent of the Governed: The Lockean Legacy in Early American Culture*. Cambridge, MA: Harvard University Press, 2001.

Domestic Individualism: Imagining Self in Nineteenth-Century America. Berkeley: University of California Press, 1990.

Buell, Lawrence. "American Literary Emergence as a Postcolonial Phenomenon," *American Literary History* 4 (October, 1992): 411–442.

New England Literary Culture: From Revolution through Renaissance. Cambridge: Cambridge University Press, 1986.

"The Unkillable Dream of the Great American Novel: *Moby-Dick* as a Test Case," *American Literary History* 20.1 (2008): 132–155.

Writing for an Endangered World: Literature, Culture, and Environment in the U.S. and Beyond. Cambridge, MA: Harvard University Press, 2001.

Burgett, Bruce. *Sentimental Bodies: Sex, Gender, and Citizenship in the Early Republic*. Princeton: Princeton University Press, 1998.

Butler, Judith. *Bodies That Matter: On the Discursive Limits of "Sex."* New York: Routledge, 1993.

Calderón, Héctor. *Narratives of Greater Mexico : Essays on Chicano Literary History, Genre, and Borders*. CMAS History, Culture, & Society Series. First edn. Austin: University of Texas Press, 2004.

Campbell, Donna M. *Resisting Regionalism: Gender and Naturalism in American Fiction, 1885–1915*. Athens: Ohio University Press, 1997.

Carby, Hazel V. *Reconstructing Womanhood: The Emergence of the Afro-American Woman Novelist*. Oxford: Oxford University Press, 1987.

Carpenter, Cari M. *Seeing Red: Anger, Sentimentality, and American Indians*. Columbus: Ohio State University Press, 2008.

Cassuto, Leonard. *Hard-Boiled Sentimentality: The Secret History of American Crime Stories*. New York: Columbia University Press, 2008.

The Inhuman Race: The Racial Grotesque in American Literature and Culture. New York: Columbia University Press, 1997.

Castiglia, Christopher. *Bound and Determined: Captivity, Culture-Crossing and White Womanhood from Mary Rowlandson to Patty Hearst*. Chicago: University of Chicago Press, 1996.

Interior States: Institutional Consciousness and the Inner Life of Democracy in the Antebellum United States. Durham, NC: Duke University Press, 2008.

Castronovo, Russ. *Beautiful Democracy: Aesthetics and Anarchy in a Global Era*. Chicago: University of Chicago Press, 2007.

Fathering the Nation: American Genealogies of Slavery and Freedom. Berkeley: University of California Press, 1995.

Necro Citizenship: Death, Eroticism, and the Public Sphere in the Nineteenth-Century United States. Durham, NC: Duke University Press, 2001.

Cawelti, John G. *Adventure, Mystery, and Romance: Formula Stories as Art and Popular Culture*. Chicago:University of Chicago Press, 1976

Chapman, Mary and Glenn Hendler, eds. *Sentimental Men: Masculinity and the Politics of Affect in American Culture*.Berkeley: University of California Press, 1999.

Charvat, William. *Literary Publishing in America, 1790–1850*. Amherst: University of Massachusetts Press, 1959; rpt. 1993.

"Melville's Income." In *The Profession of Authorship, 1800–1870*, ed. Matthew Bruccoli, Columbus: Ohio State University Press, 1968.

Chase, Richard. *The American Novel and Its Tradition*. Garden City, NY: Doubleday Anchor Books, 1957.

Cheng, Anne Anlin. *The Melancholy of Race: Psychoanalysis, Assimilation, and Hidden Grief*. Oxford: Oxford University Press, 2001.

Chodat, Robert.*Worldly Acts and Sentient Things: The Persistence of Agency from Stein to DeLillo*. Ithaca, NY: Cornell University Press, 2008.

Christian, Barbara. *Black Feminist Criticism: Perspectives on Black Women Writers*. New York: Pergamon Press, 1985.

Clark, Beverly Lyon. *Kiddie Lit: The Cultural Construction of Children's Literature in America*. Baltimore: Johns Hopkins University Press, 2003.

Clark, Suzanne. *Sentimental Modernism: Women Writers and the Revolution of the Word*. Bloomington: Indiana University Press, 1991.

Claybaugh, Amanda. *The Novel of Purpose: Literature and Social Reform in the Anglo-American World*. Ithaca, NY: Cornell University Press, 2007.

Clymer, Jeffory. *America's Culture of Terrorism: Violence, Capitalism, and the Written Word.* Chapel Hill: University of North Carolina Press, 2003.

Cohen, Daniel A. *Pillars of Salt, Monuments of Grace: New England Crime Literature and the Origins of American Popular Culture, 1674–1860*. New York: Oxford University Press, 1993.

Cott, Nancy. *The Bonds of Womanhood: "Woman's Sphere" in New England, 1780–1835*. New Haven, CT:Yale University Press, 1977.

Cowley, Malcolm. *After the Genteel Tradition; American Writers, 1910–1930*. Carbondale: Southern Illinois University Press, 1964.

Exile's Return: A Literary Odyssey of the 1920s. New York: Viking Press, 1951.

Cox, James. H. *Muting White Noise: Native American and European American Novel Traditions*. Norman: University of Oklahoma Press, 2006.

Crane, Gregg. *The Cambridge Introduction to the Nineteenth Century American Novel.* Cambridge: Cambridge University Press, 2007.

Race, Citizenship, and Law in American Literature. Cambridge, New York: Cambridge University Press, 2002.

Darnton, Robert. *The Case for Books: Past, Present, and Future*. New York: Public Affairs, 2009.

Davidson, Cathy N. *Revolution and the Word: The Rise of the Novel in America*. New York: Oxford University Press, 1986, rpt. 2004.

Davidson, Cathy N., ed. *Reading in America: Literary and Social History*. Baltimore: Johns Hopkins University Press, 1991.

Davidson, Cathy N., and Jessamyn Harcher, eds. *No More Separate Spheres! A Next Wave American Studies Reader*. Durham, NC: Duke University Press, 2002.

Davis, Lennard J. *Factual Fictions: The Origins of the English Novel*. New York: Columbia University Press, 1983.

Davis, Lennard J., ed. *The Disability Studies Reader*. New York: Routledge, 1997.

Dawes, James. *The Language of War: Literature and Culture in the U.S. from the Civil War through World War II*. Cambridge, MA: Harvard University Press, 2002.

Dekker, George. *The American Historical Romance*. Cambridge: Cambridge University Press, 1987.

Denning, Michael. *The Cultural Front: The Laboring of American Culture in the Twentieth Century*. London: Verso, 1997.

Culture in the Age of Three Worlds. London: Verso, 2004.

Mechanic Accents: Dime Novels and Working-Class Culture in America. London: Verso, 1987.

Dickson-Carr, Darryl. *African American Satire: The Sacredly Profane Novel*. Columbia: University of Missouri Press, 2001.

Dickstein, Morris. *Leopards in the Temple: The Transformation of American Fiction 1945–1970*. Cambridge, MA: Harvard University Press, 1999.

The Mirror in the Roadway: Literature and the Real World. Princeton: Princeton University Press, 2005.

Dillon, Elizabeth Maddock. *The Gender of Freedom: Fictions of Liberalism and the Literary Public Sphere*. Stanford, CA: Stanford University Press, 2004.

Dimock, Wai Chee. *Empire for Liberty: Melville and the Poetics of Individualism*. Princeton: Princeton University Press, 1989.

Residues of Justice: Literature, Law, Philosophy. Berkeley: University of California Press, 1996.

Through Other Continents: American Literature across Deep Time. Princeton: Princeton University Press, 2006.

Dimock, Wai Chee and Lawrence Buell, eds. *Shades of the Planet: American Literature as World Literature*. Princeton: Princeton University Press, 2007.

Dobson, Joanne. "Reclaiming Sentimental Literature." *American Literature* 69 (1997): 263–288.

Doody, Margaret Anne. *The True Story of the Novel*. New Brunswick, NJ: Rutgers University Press, 1996.

Dorman, Robert L. *Revolt of the Provinces: The Regionalist Movement in America, 1920–1945*. Chapel Hill: University of North Carolina Press, 1993.

Douglas, Ann. *The Feminization of American Culture*. New York: Avon Books, 1977.

Terrible Honesty: Mongrel Manhattan in the 1920s. New York: Farrar, Straus and Giroux, 1995.

Doyle, Laura. *Freedom's Empire: Race and the Rise of the Novel in Atlantic Modernity, 1640–1940*. Durham, NC: Duke University Press, 2008.

Drinnon, Richard. *Facing West: The Metaphysics of Indian-Hating and Empire-Building*. Norman: University of Oklahoma Press, 1980.

Duane, Anna Mae. *Suffering Childhood in Early America: Violence, Race, and the Making of the Child Victim*. Athens: University of Georgia Press, 2010.

Dubey, Madhu. *Signs and Cities: Black Literary Postmodernism*. Chicago: University of Chicago Press, 2003.

DuCille, Ann. *The Coupling Convention: Sex, Text, and Tradition in Black Women's Fiction*. New York: Oxford University Press, 1993.

DuPlessis, Rachel Blau. *Writing Beyond the Ending: Narrative Strategies of Twentieth-Century Women Writers*. Bloomington: Indiana University Press, 1985.

Edel, Leon. *Henry James*. Philadelphia: Lippincott, 1953–1972.

Edwards, Brent Hayes. *The Practice of Diaspora: Literature, Translation, and the Rise of Black Internationalism*. Cambridge, MA: Harvard University Press, 2003.

Elias, Amy J. *Sublime Desire: History and Post-1960s Fiction*. Baltimore: Johns Hopkins University Press, 2001.

Elliott, Emory. *Revolutionary Writers: Literature and Authority in the New Republic*. New York: Oxford University Press, 1982.

Elliott, Emory *et. al.* eds., *The Columbia History of the American Novel*. New York: Columbia University Press, 1991.

Elliott, Michael. *The Culture Concept: Writing and Difference in the Age of Realism*. Minneapolis: University of Minnesota Press, 2002.

Ellis, Markman. *The History of Gothic Fiction*. Edinburgh: Edinburgh University Press, 2000.

Ellison, Julie. *Cato's Tears and the Making of Anglo-American Emotion*. Chicago: University of Chicago Press, 1999.

Elmer, Jonathan. *On Lingering and Being Last: Race and Sovereignty in the New World*. New York: Fordham University Press, 2008.

Reading at the Social Limit: Affect, Mass Culture, and Edgar Allan Poe. Stanford, CA: Stanford University Press, 1995.

Eng, David. *Racial Castration: Managing Masculinity in Asian America*. Durham, NC: Duke University Press, 2001.

Ermarth, Elizabeth. *Sequel to History: Postmodernism and the Crises of Representational Time*. Princeton: Princeton University Press, 1991.

Ernest, John. *Liberation Historiography: African American Writers and the Challenge of History, 1794–1861*. Chapel Hill: University of North Carolina Press, 2004.

Resistance and Reformation in Nineteenth-Century African-American Literature. Jackson: University Press of Mississippi, 1995.

Evans, Brad. *Before Cultures: The Ethnographic Imagination in American Literature, 1865–1920*. Chicago: University of Chicago Press, 2005.

Ezell, Margaret J. *Social Authorship and the Advent of Print*. Baltimore: Johns Hopkins University Press, 1999.

Fabi, Guilia M. *Passing and the Rise of the African American Novel*. Urbana: University of Illinois Press, 2001.

Fabre, Geneviève and Michel Feith, eds. *Temples for Tomorrow: Looking Back at the Harlem Renaissance*. Bloomington: Indiana University Press, 2001.

Fahs, Alice. *The Imagined Civil War: Popular Literature of the North, and South, 1861–1865*. Chapel Hill and London: University of North Carolina Press, 2001.

Farr, Cecilia Konchar. *Reading Oprah: How Oprah's Book Club Changed the Way America Reads*. Albany: State University of New York Press, 2005.

Felski, Rita. *Literature after Feminism*. Chicago: University of Chicago Press, 2003.

Ferguson, Roderick A. *Aberrations in Black: Toward a Queer of Color Critique*. Minneapolis: University of Minnesota Press, 2004.

Ferraro, Thomas J. *Ethnic Passages: Literary Immigrants in Twentieth-Century America*. Chicago: University of Chicago Press, 1993.

Fetterley, Judith. *The Resisting Reader: A Feminist Approach to American Fiction*. Bloomington: Indiana University Press, 1978.

Fetterley, Judith and Marjorie Pryse. *Writing Out of Place*. Urbana: University of Illinois Press, 2003.

Fichtelberg, Joseph. *Critical Fictions: Sentiment and the American Market, 1780–1870*. Athens: University of Georgia Press, 2003.

Fiedler, Leslie A. *Love and Death in the American Novel*. New York: Criterion Books, 1960.

Fisher, Philip. *Hard Facts: Setting and Form in the American Novel*. New York: Oxford University Press, 1985.

Fishkin, Shelley Fisher. *From Fact to Fiction: Journalism and Imaginative Writing in America*. Baltimore: Johns Hopkins University Press, 1985.

Was Huck Black?: Mark Twain and African American Voices. New York: Oxford University Press, 1993.

Fitzpatrick, Kathleen. *The Anxiety of Obsolescence: The American Novel in the Age of Television*. Nashville, TN: Vanderbilt University Press, 2006.

Fleissner, Jennifer. *Women, Compulsion, Modernity: The Moment of American Naturalism*. Chicago: University of Chicago Press, 2004.

Fliegelman, Jay. *Declaring Independence: Jefferson, Natural Language, and the Culture of Performance*. Stanford, CA: Stanford University Press, 1993.

Prodigals and Pilgrims: The American Revolution against Patriarchal Authority, 1750–1800. Cambridge: Cambridge University Press, 1982.

Fluck, Winfried. "American Literary History and the Romance with America." *American Literary History* 21.1 (Spring 2009): 1–18.

" 'The American Romance' and the Changing Functions of the Imaginary." *New Literary History* 27 (1996): 415–457.

Foley, Barbara. *Radical Representations: Politics and Form in U.S. Proletarian Fiction, 1909–1941*. Durham, NC: Duke University Press, 1993.

Telling the Truth: The Theory and Practice of Documentary Fiction. Ithaca, NY and London: Cornell University Press, 1986.

Foote, Stephanie. *Regional Fictions: Culture and Identity in Nineteenth-Century American Literature*. Madison: University of Wisconsin Press, 2001.

Foreman, P. Gabrielle. *Activist Sentiments: Reading Black Women in the Nineteenth Century*. Urbana: University of Illinois Press, 2009.

Foster, Frances Smith. *Written by Herself: Literary Production by African American Women, 1746–1892*. Bloomington: Indiana University Press, 1993.

Francese, Joseph. *Narrating Postmodern Time and Space*. Albany: State University of New York Press, 1997.

Franchot, Jenny. *Roads to Rome: The Antebellum Protestant Encounter with Catholicism*. Berkeley: University of California Press, 1994.

Franklin, H. Bruce. *Future Perfect: American Science Fiction in the Nineteenth Century*. Oxford: Oxford University Press, 1966; revised and expanded edition, 1995.

Freeman, Elizabeth. *The Wedding Complex: Forms of Belonging in Modern American Culture*. Durham, NC: Duke University Press, 2002.

Freedman, Jonathan. *The Temple of Culture: Assimilation and Anti-Semitism in Literary Anglo-America*. New York: Oxford University Press, 2002.

Gardner, Eric. *Unexpected Places: Relocating Nineteenth-Century African American Literature*. Jackson: University Press of Mississippi, 2009.

Gardner, Jared. *Master Plots: Race and the Founding of an American Literature, 1787–1845*. Baltimore: Johns Hopkins University Press, 2000.

Gates, Henry Louis, Jr. *Figures in Black: Words, Signs, and the "Racial" Self*. New York: Oxford University Press, 1987.

The Signifying Monkey. New York: Oxford University Press, 1989.

Gates, Henry Louis, Jr., ed. *Reading Black, Reading Feminist: A Critical Anthology*. New York: Meridian Book, 1990.

Gates, Henry Louis, Jr. and Kwame Anthony Appiah, eds. *"Race," Writing, and Difference*. Chicago: University of Chicago Press, 1992.

Gilbert, Sandra M. and Susan Gubar. *The Madwoman in the Attic: The Woman Writer and the Nineteenth-Century Literary Imagination*, second edn. New Haven: Yale University Press, 2000.

No Man's Land: The Place of the Woman Writer in the Twentieth Century. New Haven: Yale University Press, 1988.

Giles, Paul *Transatlantic Insurrections: British Culture and the Formation of American Literature, 1730–1860* Philadelphia: University of Pennsylvania Press, 2001.

Virtual Americas: Transnational Fictions and the Transatlantic Imaginary. Durham, NC: Duke University Press, 2002.

Gillman, Susan. *Blood Talk: American Race Melodrama and the Culture of the Occult*. Chicago: University of Chicago Press, 2003.

Dark Twins: Imposture and Identity in Mark Twain's America. Chicago: University of Chicago Press, 1989.

Gilmore, Michael T. *American Romanticism and the Marketplace*. Chicago: University of Chicago Press, 1985.

Surface and Depth: The Quest for Legibility in American Culture. Oxford: Oxford University Press, 2003.

Gilmore, Paul. *The Genuine Article: Race, Mass Culture, and American Literary Manhood*. Durham, NC: Duke University Press, 2001.

Gilroy, Paul. *Black Atlantic: Modernity and Double Consciousness*. Cambridge, MA: Harvard University Press, 1993.

Glass, Loren. *Authors Inc.: Literary Celebrity in the Modern United States, 1880–1980*. New York: New York University Press, 2004.

Glazener, Nancy. *Reading for Realism: The History of a U.S. Literary Institution, 1850–1910*. Durham, NC: Duke University Press, 1997.

Goddu, Teresa A. *Gothic America: Narrative, History, and Nation*. New York: Columbia University Press, 1997.

Goldsby, Jacqueline. *A Spectacular Secret: Lynching in American Life and Literature*. Chicago: University of Chicago Press, 2006.

Gossett, Thomas F. *Uncle Tom's Cabin and American Culture*. Dallas, TX: Southern Methodist University Press, 1985.

Gould, Philip. *Covenant and Republic: Historical Romance and the Politics of Puritanism*. New York: Cambridge University Press, 1996.

Graff, Gerald. *Beyond the Culture Wars: How Teaching the Conflicts Can Revitalize American Education*. New York: Norton, 1992.

Greeson, Jennifer Rae. *Our South: Region, Nation, and World in U.S. Literature*. Cambridge, MA: Harvard University Press, 2010.

Gunning, Sandra. *Race, Rape, and Lynching: The Red Record of American Literature*. New York: Oxford University Press, 1996.

Habegger, Alfred. *Gender, Fantasy, and Realism in American Literature*. New York: Columbia University Press, 1982.

Halberstam, Judith. *Female Masculinity*. Durham, NC: Duke University Press, 1998.

Hale, Dorothy. *Social Formalism: The Novel in Theory from Henry James to the Present*. Stanford, CA: Stanford University Press, 1998.

Hall, David D. *Cultures of Print: Essays in the History of the Book*. Amherst: University of Massachusetts Press, 1996.

Hall, David D., ed. *A History of the Book in America*, vols. I–V. Chapel Hill: University of North Carolina Press, 2010.

Halttunen, Karen. *Murder Most Foul: The Killer and the American Gothic Imagination*. Cambridge, MA: Harvard University Press, 1998.

Handley, William R. *Marriage, Violence, and the Nation in the American Literary West*. Cambridge: Cambridge University Press, 2002.

Hapke, Laura. *Labor's Text: The Worker in American Fiction*. New Brunswick, NJ: Rutgers University Press, 2001.

Harper, Phillip Brian. *Framing the Margins: The Social Logic of Postmodern Culture*. New York: Oxford University Press, 1994.

Harris, Norman. *Connecting Times: The Sixties in Afro-American Fiction*. Jackson: University Press of Mississippi, 1988.

Harris, Sharon M. *Executing Race: Early American Women's Narratives of Race, Society, and the Law*. Columbus: Ohio State University Press, 2005.

Harris, Trudier. *From Mammies to Militants: Domestics in Black American Literature.* Philadelphia: Temple University Press, 1982.

Hart, James. *The Popular Book: A History of America's Literary Taste.* New York: Oxford University Press, 1950.

Hartman, Saidiya. *Scenes of Subjection: Terror, Slavery, and Self-Making in Nineteenth-Century America.* Oxford: Oxford University Press, 1997.

Hatfield, Charles. *Alternative Comics. An Emerging Literature.* Jackson: University of Mississippi Press, 2005.

Hayles, N. Katherine. *Electronic Literature: New Horizons for the Literary.* Notre Dame, IN: University of Notre Dame, 2008.

How We Became Posthuman: Virtual Bodies in Cybernetics, Literature, and Informatics. Chicago: University Chicago Press, 1999.

My Mother Was a Computer: Digital Subjects and Literary Texts. Chicago: University of Chicago Press, 2005.

Heise, Ursula K. *Chronoschisms: Time, Narrative, and Postmodernism.* Cambridge: Cambridge University Press, 1997.

Sense of Place and Sense of Planet: The Environmental Imagination of the Global. New York: Oxford University Press, 2008.

Hellekson, Karen and Kristina Busse, eds. *Fan Fiction and Fan Communities in the Age of the Internet: New Essays.* Jefferson, NC: McFarland & Co., 2006.

Hendler, Glenn. *Public Sentiments: Structures of Feeling in Nineteenth-Century American Literature.* Chapel Hill: University of North Carolina Press, 2001.

Hoberek, Andrew. *The Twilight of the Middle Class: Post-World War II American Fiction and White-Collar Work.* Princeton: Princeton University Press, 2005.

Hobson, Fred. *But Now I See: The White Southern Racial Conversion Narrative.* Baton Rouge: Louisiana State University Press, 1999.

Hochman, Barbara. *Getting at the Author: Reimagining Books and Reading in the Age of American Realism.* Amherst: University of Massachusetts Press, 2001.

Hogeland, Lisa Maria. *Feminism and Its Fictions: The Consciousness-Raising Novel and the Women's Liberation Movement.* Philadelphia: University of Pennsylvania Press, 1998.

Holland, Sharon. *Raising the Dead: Readings of Death and (Black) Subjectivity.* Durham, NC: Duke University Press, 2000.

Holloway, Karla F. C. *Bookmarks: Reading in Black and White.* New Brunswick, NJ: Rutgers University Press, 2006.

Moorings & Metaphors: Figures of Culture and Gender in Black Women's Literature. New Brunswick, NJ: Rutgers University Press, 1992.

Passed On: African American Mourning Stories: A Memorial. Durham, NC: Duke University Press, 2002.

Horwitz, Howard. *By the Law of Nature: Form and Value in Nineteenth-Century America.* New York and Oxford: Oxford University Press, 1991.

Howard, June. *Form and History in American Literary Naturalism.* Chapel Hill: University of North Carolina Press, 1985.

Publishing the Family. Durham, NC: Duke University Press, 2001

Hungerford, Amy. *The Holocaust of Texts: Genocide, Literature, and Personification.* Chicago: University of Chicago Press, 2003.

Postmodern Belief: American Literature and Religion since 1960. Princeton: Princeton University Press, 2010.

Hunter, J. Paul. *Before Novels*. New York: Norton, 1990.

Hutcheon, Linda. *A Poetics of Postmodernism. History, Theory, Fiction*. London: Routledge, 1988.

The Politics of Postmodernism. London, New York: Routledge, 1989.

Hutchinson, George. *Harlem Renaissance in Black and White*. Cambridge, MA: Harvard Univeristy Press, 1995.

Hutner, Gordon. *What America Read, 1920–1960*. Chapel Hill: University of North Carolina Press, 2009.

Irving, Katrina. *Immigrant Mothers: Narratives of Race and Maternity, 1890–1925*. Urbana: University of Illinois Press, 2000.

Irwin, John T. *American Hieroglyphics: The Symbol of the Egyptian Hieroglyphics in the American Renaissance*. Baltimore: Johns Hopkins University Press, 1980.

Doubling and Incest/Repetition and Revenge: A Speculative Reading of Faulkner. Baltimore: Johns Hopkins University Press, 1975.

Jackson, Blyden. *A History of Afro-American Literature*. Baton Rouge: Louisiana State University Press, 1989.

Jackson, Gregory S. *The Word and Its Witness: The Spiritualization of American Realism*. Chicago: University of Chicago Press, 2009.

Jackson, Leon. *The Business of Letters: Authorial Economies in Antebellum America*. Stanford, CA: Stanford University Press, 2008.

James, C. L. R. *Mariners, Renegades and Castaways: The Story of Herman Melville and the World We Live In*. Hanover, NH: University Press of New England, 1953; rpt. and revised edn., 2001.

James, Jennifer C. *A Freedom Bought with Blood: African American War Literature from the Civil War to World War II*. Chapel Hill: University of North Carolina Press, 2007.

Jameson, Fredric. *Archaeologies of the Future: The Desire Called Utopia and Other Science Fictions*. New York: Verso, 2005.

The Political Unconscious: Narrative as a Socially Symbolic Act. Ithaca, NY: Cornell University Press, 1981.

Postmodernism, Or, The Cultural Logic of Late Capitalism. Durham, NC: Duke University Press, 1991.

Jarrett, Gene Andrew. *Deans and Truants: Race and Realism in African American Literature*. Philadelphia: University of Pennsylvania Press, 2006.

Jehlen, Myra. *American Incarnation: The Individual, the Nation, and the Continent*. Cambridge, MA: Harvard University Press, 1986.

Five Fictions in Search of Truth. Princeton: Princeton University Press, 2008.

Johnston, John. *Information Multiplicity: American Fiction in the Age of Media Saturation*. Baltimore: Johns Hopkins University Press, 1998.

Jones, Gavin. *American Hungers: The Problem of Poverty in U.S. Literature, 1840–1945*. Princeton: Princeton University Press, 2008.

Strange Talk: The Politics of Dialect Literature in Gilded Age America. Berkeley: University of California Press, 1999.

Jordan, David M. *New World Regionalism: Literature in the Americas*. Toronto: University of Toronto Press, 1994.

Jurca, Catherine. *White Diaspora: The Suburb and the Twentieth-Century American Novel.* Princeton: Princeton University Press, 2001.

Kadlec, David. *Mosaic Modernism: Anarchy, Pragmatism, Culture.* Baltimore: Johns Hopkins University Press, 2000.

Kaestle, Carl F. *Literacy in the United States: Readers and Reading since 1880.* New Haven: Yale University Press, 1991.

Kaplan, Amy. *The Anarchy of Empire in the Making of U.S. Culture.* Cambridge, MA: Harvard University Press, 2002.

The Social Construction of American Realism. Chicago: University of Chicago Press, 1998.

Kaplan, Amy and Donald E. Pease, eds. *Cultures of United States Imperialism.* Durham, NC: Duke University Press, 1993.

Kaplan, Carla. *The Erotics of Talk: Women's Writing and Feminist Paradigms.* New York: Oxford University Press, 1996.

Kawash, Samira. *Dislocating the Color Line: Identity, Hybridity, and Singularity in African-American Narrative.* Stanford, CA: Stanford University Press, 1997.

Kazanjian, David. *The Colonizing Trick: National Culture and Imperial Citizenship in Early America.* Minneapolis: University of Minnesota Press, 2003.

Kazin, Alfred. *On Native Grounds.* New York: Harcourt, Brace & World, 1942.

Kelley, Mary. *Private Woman, Public Stage: Literary Domesticity in Nineteenth-Century America.* New York: Oxford University Press, 1984.

Kennedy, J. Gerald. *Imagining Paris: Exile, Writing, and American Identity.* New Haven: Yale University Press, 1993.

Kenner, Hugh. *A Homemade World: The American Modernist Writers.* New York: Knopf, 1975.

Kent, Kathryn. *Making Girls into Women: American Women's Writing and the Rise of Lesbian Identity.* Durham, NC: Duke University Press, 2003.

Kerber, Linda K. *Women of the Republic: Intellect and Ideology in Revolutionary America.* Chapel Hill: University of North Carolina Press, 1980.

Kim, Elaine H. *Asian American Literature: An Introduction to the Writings and Their Social Context.* Philadelphia, PA: Temple University Press, 1982.

King, Lovalerie. *Race, Theft, and Ethics: Property Matters in African American Literature.* Baton Rouge: Louisiana State University Press, 2007.

Knadler, Stephen. *Remapping Citizenship and the Nation in African American Literature.* New York: Routledge, 2009.

Kolodny, Annette. *The Land Before Her: Fantasy and Experience of the American Frontiers, 1630–1860.* Chapel Hill: University of North Carolina Press, 1984.

The Lay of the Land: Metaphor as Experience and History in American Life, and Letters. Chapel Hill: University of North Carolina Press, 1975.

Koshy, Susan. *Sexual Naturalization: Asian Americans and Miscegenation.* Stanford, CA: Stanford University Press, 2004.

Krupat, Arnold. *Red Matters: Native American Studies.* Philadelphia: University of Pennsylvania Press, 2002.

The Turn to the Native: Studies in Criticism and Culture. Lincoln: University of Nebraska Press, 1996.

The Voice in the Margin: Native American Literature and the Canon. Berkeley: University of California Press, 1989.

Krupat, Arnold and Michael A. Elliott. "Native American Fiction: 1945 to the Present." In *The Columbia Guide to Native American Literatures of the United States since 1945*, ed. Eric Cheyfitz, 127–182. New York: Columbia University Press, 2006.

Ladd, Barbara. *Resisting History: Gender, Modernity, and Authorship in William Faulkner, Zora Neale Hurston, and Eudora Welty*. Baton Rouge: Louisiana State University Press, 2007.

Landow, George P. *Hypertext 3.0: New Media and Critical Theory in an Era of Globalization*. Baltimore: Johns Hopkins University Press, 2006.

Lang, Amy Schrager. *The Syntax of Class: Writing Inequality in Nineteenth-Century America*. Princeton: Princeton University Press, 2003.

Lawrence, D. H. *Studies in Classic American Literature*. New York: Thomas Seltzer, 1923.

Lazo, Rodrigo. *Writing to Cuba: Filibustering and Cuban Exiles in the United States*. Chapel Hill: University of North Carolina Press, 2005.

Lears, Jackson. *No Place of Grace: Antimodernism and the Transformation of American Culture, 1880–1920*. New York: Pantheon Books, 1981.

Lehman, Daniel W. *Matters of Fact: Reading Nonfiction over the Edge*. Columbus: Ohio State University Press, 1997.

Le Menager, Stephanie. *Manifest and Other Destinies: Territorial Fictions of the Nineteenth-Century United States*. Lincoln: University of Nebraska Press, 2004.

Lentricchia, Frank and Jody McAuliffe. *Crimes of Art and Terror*. Chicago: University of Chicago Press, 2003.

Lerer, Seth. *Children's Literature: A Reader's History from Aesop to Harry Potter*. Chicago: University of Chicago Press, 2009.

Levander, Caroline F. *Cradle of Liberty: Race, the Child, and National Belonging from Thomas Jefferson to W. E. B. Du Bois*. Durham, NC: Duke University Press, 2006.

Levander, Caroline F., and Robert S. Levine, eds. *Hemispheric American Studies*. New Brunswick, NJ: Rutgers University Press, 2008.

Leverenz, David. *Manhood and the American Renaissance*. Ithaca, NY: Cornell University Press, 1990.

Levin, Harry. *The Power of Blackness: Hawthorne, Poe, Melville*. New York: Knopf, 1958.

Levin, Jonathan. *The Poetics of Transition: Emerson, Pragmatism, and American Literary Modernism*. Durham, NC: Duke University Press, 1999.

Levine, Lawrence. *Highbrow/Lowbrow: The Emergence of Cultural Hierarchy in America*. Cambridge, MA: Harvard University Press, 1988.

Levine, Robert S. *Conspiracy and Romance: Studies in Brockden Brown, Cooper, Hawthorne, and Melville*. Cambridge: Cambridge University Press, 1989.

Dislocating Race and Nation: Episodes in Nineteenth-Century American Literary Nationalism. Chapel Hill: University of North Carolina Press, 2008.

Martin Delany, Frederick Douglass, and the Politics of Representative Identity. Chapel Hill: University of North Carolina Press, 1997.

Lewis, R. W. B. *The American Adam: Innocence, Tragedy and Tradition in the Nineteenth Century*. Chicago: University of Chicago Press, 1955.

Limon, John. *The Place of Fiction in a Time of Science: A Disciplinary History of American Writing*. New York: Cambridge University Press, 1990.

Ling, Jinqi. *Narrating Nationalisms: Ideology and Form in Asian American Literature*. New York: Oxford University Press, 1998.

Lomas, Laura. *Translating Empire: Migrant Latino Subjectivity and American Modernities*. Durham, NC: Duke University Press, 2008.

Looby, Christopher. *Voicing America: Language, Literary Form, and the Origins of the United States*. Chicago: University of Chicago Press, 1996.

Lott, Eric. *Love & Theft: Blackface Minstrelsy and the American Working Class*. New York: Oxford University Press, 1993.

Loughran, Trish. *The Republic in Print: Print Culture in the Age of U.S. Nation Building, 1770–1870*. New York: Columbia University Press, 2007.

Lowe, Lisa. *Immigrant Acts: On Asian American Cultural Politics*. Durham, NC: Duke University Press, 1996.

Luciano, Dana. *Arranging Grief: Sacred Time and the Body in Nineteenth-Century America*. New York: New York University Press, 2007.

Lukács, Georg. *The Historical Novel*. Translated by Hannah and Stanley Mitchell. Boston: Beacon Press, 1963. Rpt. Lincoln: University of Nebraska Press, 1983.

The Theory of the Novel. Translated by Anna Bostock. Cambridge, MA: MIT University Press, 1971.

Lundin, Anne H. *Constructing the Canon of Children's Literature: Beyond Library Walls and Ivory Towers*. New York: Routledge, 2004.

Lutz, Tom. *American Nervousness, 1903: An Anecdotal History*. Ithaca, NY: Cornell University Press, 1991.

Cosmopolitan Vistas: American Regionalism and Literary Value. Ithaca, NY: Cornell University Press, 2004.

Lye, Colleen. *America's Asia: Racial Form and American Literature, 1893–1945*. Princeton: Princeton University Press, 2005.

Lynch, Deirdre Shauna and William B. Warner, eds. *Cultural Institutions of the Novel*. Durham, NC: Duke University Press, 1996.

Maddox, Lucy. *Removals: Nineteenth-Century American Literature and the Politics of Indian Affairs*. New York: Oxford University Press, 1991.

Mailloux, Steven. *Interpretive Conventions: The Reader in the Study of American Fiction*. Ithaca, NY: Cornell University Press, 1982.

Marcus, Greil and Werner K. Sollors, eds. *A New Literary History of America*. Cambridge, MA: Belknap Press of Harvard Univeresity Press, 2009.

Marr, Timothy. *The Cultural Roots of American Islamicism*. New York: Cambridge University Press, 2006.

Marx, Leo. *The Machine in the Garden: Technology and the Pastoral Ideal in America*. New York: Oxford University Press, 1964.

Maxwell, William J. *New Negro, Old Left: African-American Writing and Communism between the Wars*. New York: Columbia University Press, 1999.

McCann, Sean. *Gumshoe America: Hard-boiled Crime Fiction, and the Rise and Fall of New Deal Liberalism*. Durham, NC: Duke University Press, 2000.

A Pinnacle of Feeling: American Literature and Presidential Government. Princeton: Princeton University Press, 2008.

McCaskill, Barbara and Caroline Gebhard, eds. *Post-Bellum, Pre-Harlem: African American Literature and Culture, 1877–1919*. New York: New York University Press, 2006.

McClure, John A. *Partial Faiths: Postsecular Fiction in the Age of Pynchon and Morrison*. Athens: University of Georgia Press, 2007.

McDowell, Deborah E. *"The changing same": Studies in Fiction by African American Women*. Bloomington: Indiana University Press, 1995.

McDowell, Deborah E., and Arnold Rampersad, eds. *Slavery and the Literary Imaginatinon*. Baltimore: Johns Hopkins University Press, 1989.

McGann, Jerome. *Radiant Textuality: Literature after the World Wide Web*. New York: Palgrave, 2001.

McGill, Meredith L. *American Literature and the Culture of Reprinting, 1834–1853*. Philadelphia: University of Pennsylvania Press, 2003.

McGurl, Mark. *The Novel Art: Elevations of American Fiction after Henry James*. Princeton: Princeton University Press, 2001.

The Program Era: Postwar Fiction and the Rise of Creative Writing. Cambridge, MA: Harvard University Press, 2009.

McHale, Brian. *Postmodernist Fiction*. Second edn. London: Routledge, 1991.

McHenry, Elizabeth. *Forgotten Readers: Recovering the Lost History of African American Literary Societies*. Durham, NC: Duke University Press, 2002.

McKeon, Michael. *The Origins of the English Novel, 1600–1740*. Baltimore: Johns Hopkins University Press, 2002.

McKeon, Michael, ed. *Theory of the Novel: A Historical Approach*. Baltimore: Johns Hopkins University Press, 2000.

Meer, Sarah. *Uncle Tom Mania: Slavery and Transatlantic Culture in the 1850s*. Athens: University of Georgia Press, 2005.

Mendoza, Louis and S. Shankar, eds. *Crossing into America: The New Literature of Immigration*. New York: New Press, 2003.

Merish, Lori. *Sentimental Materialism: Gender, Commodity Culture, and Nineteenth-Century American Literature*. Durham, NC: Duke University Press, 2000.

Michaels, Walter Benn. *The Gold Standard and the Logic of Naturalism*. Berkeley and Los Angeles: University of California Press, 1987.

Our America: Nativism, Modernism, Pluralism. Durham, NC: Duke University Press, 1993.

The Shape of the Signifier: 1967 to the End of History. Princeton: Princeton University Press, 2004.

Michaels, Walter Benn and Donald E. Pease, eds. *The American Renaissance Reconsidered*. Baltimore: Johns Hopkins University Press, 1985.

Mickenberg, Julia. *Learning from the Left: Children's Literature, the Cold War, and Radical Politics in the United States*. New York, Oxford: Oxford University Press, 2006.

Miller, D. A. *The Novel and the Police*. Berkeley: University of California Press, 1988.

Miller, Perry. *Nature's Nation*. Cambridge, MA: Harvard University Press, 1967.

The Raven and the Whale. New York: Harcourt, Brace, 1956.

Minter, David. *A Cultural History of the American Novel: Henry James to William Faulkner*. Cambridge, New York: Cambridge University Press, 1994.

Mitchell, David T. and Sharon L. Snyder. *Cultural Locations of Disability*. Chicago: University of Chicago Press, 2006.

Narrative Prosthesis: Disability and Dependencies of Discourse. Ann Arbor: University of Michigan Press, 2000.

Mitchell, Lee Clark. *Determined Fictions*. New York: Columbia University Press, 1989.

Westerns: Making the Man in Fiction and Film. Chicago: University of Chicago Press, 1996

Mizruchi, Susan. *The Rise of Multicultural America: Economy and Print Culture, 1865–1915*. Durham, NC: University of North Carolina Press, 2008.

The Science of Sacrifice. Princeton: Princeton University Press, 1998.

Modeleski, Tania. *Loving with a Vengeance: Mass-Produced Fantasies for Women*. Hamden, CT: Archon, 1982.

Moon, Michael. *A Small Boy and Others: Imitation and Initiation in American Culture from Henry James to Andy Warhol*. Durham, NC: Duke University Press, 1998.

Moon, Michael and Cathy N. Davidson, eds. *Subjects and Citizens: Nation, Race, and Gender from Oroonoko to Anita Hill*. Durham, NC: Duke University Press, 1995.

Moretti, Franco. *Graphs, Maps, Trees: Abstract Models for a Literary History*. London: Verso, 2003.

Moretti, Franco, ed. *The Novel, Volume 1: History, Geography, Culture*. Princeton: Princeton University Press, 2007.

The Novel, Volume 2: Forms and Themes. Princeton: Princeton University Press, 2007.

Morrison, Toni. *Playing in the Dark: Whiteness and the Literary Imagination*. New York: Vintage, 1993.

Mott, Frank L. *Golden Multitudes: The Story of Best Sellers in the United States*. New York: Macmillan, 1947.

Moylan, Michelle and Lane Stiles, eds. *Reading Books: Essays on the Material Text and Literature in America*. Amherst: University of Massachusetts Press, 1996.

Murdy, Anne-Elizabeth. *Teach the Nation: Pedagogies of Racial Uplift in U.S. Women's Writings of the 1890s*. New York: Routledge, 2002.

Murphy, Gretchen. *Hemispheric Imaginings: The Monroe Doctrine and Narratives of U.S. Empire*. Durham, NC: Duke University Press, 2005.

Nealon, Christopher. *Foundlings: Lesbian and Gay Historical Emotion before Stonewall*. Durham, NC: Duke University Press, 2001.

Nelson, D. Dana. *National Manhood: Capitalist Citizenship and the Imagined Fraternity of White Men*. Durham, NC: Duke Univeristy Press, 1998.

The Word in Black and White: Reading "Race" in American Literature, 1638–1867. Oxford: Oxford University Press, 1992.

Nelson, Theodor Holm. *Literary Machines 93.1*. 1981. Sausalito, CA: Mindful Press, 1993.

Newbury, Michael. *Figuring Authorship in Antebellum America*. Stanford, CA: Stanford University Press, 1997.

Newman, Judie. *Fictions of America: Narratives of Global Empire*. New York: Routledge, 2007.

Newton, Adam Zachary. *Facing Black and Jew: Literature as Public Space in Twentieth-Century America*. Cambridge: Cambridge University Press, 1999.

Ngai, Sianne. *Ugly Feelings*. Cambridge, MA: Harvard University Press, 2005.

Nguyen, Viet Thanh. *Race and Resistance: Literature and Politics in Asian America*. New York: Oxford University Press, 2002.

Nicholls, Peter. *Modernisms: A Literary Guide*. Second edn. Houndmills, Basingstoke: Palgrave Macmillan, 2009.

Nickerson, Catherine Ross. *The Web of Iniquity: Early Detective Fiction by American Women*. Durham, NC: Duke University Press, 1998.

Noble, Marianne. *The Masochistic Pleasures of Sentimental Literature*. Princeton: Princeton University Press, 2000.

Nord, David Paul. *Faith in Reading: Religious Publishing, and the Birth of Mass Media in America*. New York: Oxford University Press, 2004.

North, Michael. *Camera Works: Photography and the Twentieth Century Word*. New York: Oxford University Press, 2007.

Okker, Patricia. *Social Stories: The Magazine Novel in Nineteenth-Century America*. Charlottesville: University of Virginia Press, 2003.

Orvell, Miles. *The Real Thing: Imitation and Authenticity in American Culture, 1880–1940*. Chapel Hill: University of North Carolina Press, 1989.

Otter, Samuel. *Melville's Anatomies*. Berkeley: University of California Press, 1999.

Owens, Louis. *Mixedblood Messages: Literature, Film, Family, Place*. Norman: University of Oklahoma Press, 1998.

Other Destinies: Understanding the American Indian Novel. Norman: University of Oklahoma Press, 1992.

Palumbo-Liu, David. *Asian/American: Historical Crossings of a Racial Frontier*. Stanford, CA: Stanford University Press, 1999.

Parker, Robert Dale. *The Invention of Native American Literature*. Ithaca, NY: Cornell University Press, 2003.

Patel, Cyrus. *Negative Liberties: Morrison, Pynchon, and the Problem of Liberal Ideology*. Durham, NC: Duke University Press, 2001.

Pearce, Roy Harvey. *Savagism and Civilization: A Study of the Indian and the American Mind*. 1953; rpt. and revised edn., Berkeley: University of California Press, 1988.

Pease, Donald E. ed. *National Identities and Post-Americanist Narratives*. Durham, NC: Duke University Press, 1994.

Petersen, Nancy J. *Against Amnesia: Contemporary Women Writers and the Crises of Historical Memory*. Philadelphia: University of Pennsylvania Press, 2001.

Peterson, Carla. *Doers of the Word: African-American Women Speakers and Writers in the North (1830–1880)*. New York: Oxford University Press, 1995.

Peyser, Thomas. *Utopia and Cosmopolis: Globalization in the Era of American Literary Realism*. Durham, NC: Duke University Press, 1998.

Phillips, Dana. *The Truth of Ecology: Nature, Culture, and Literature in America*. New York: Oxford University Press, 2003.

Pizer, Donald. *Realism and Naturalism in Nineteenth-Century American Literature*, rev. edn. Carbondale: Southern Illinois University Press, 1984.

Poirier, Richard. *A World Elsewhere: The Place of Style in American Literature*. New York, Oxford University Press, 1966.

Porter, Carolyn. *Seeing and Being: The Plight of the Participant Observer in Emerson, James, Adams, and Faulkner*. Middletown, CT: Wesleyan University Press, 1981.

Posnock, Ross. *Color and Culture: Black Writers and the Making of the Modern Intellectual*. Cambridge, MA: Harvard University Press, 2000.

The Trial of Curiosity: Henry James, William James, and the Challenge of Modernity. New York: Oxford University Press, 1991.

Powell, Timothy. *Ruthless Democracy: A Multicultural Interpretation of the American Renaissance*. Princeton: Princeton University Press, 2000.

Prchal, Tim and Tony Trigilio, eds. *Visions and Divisions: American Immigration Literature, 1870–1930*. New Brunswick, NJ: Rutgers University Press, 2008.

Pryse, Marjorie and Hortense J. Spillers, eds. *Conjuring: Black Women, Fiction, and Literary Tradition*. Bloomington: Indiana University Press, 1985.

Quayson, Ato. *Aesthetic Nervousness: Disability and the Crisis of Representation*. New York: Columbia University Press, 2007.

Rabinowitz, Paula. *Black & White & Noir: America's Pulp Modernism*. New York: Columbia University Press, 2002.

Labor and Desire: Women's Revolutionary Fiction in Depression America. Chapel Hill: University of North Carolina Press, 1991.

Radway, Janice. *A Feeling for Books: The Book-of-the-Month Club, Literary Taste, and Middle-Class Desire*. Chapel Hill and London: University of North Carolina Press, 1997.

Reading the Romance: Women, Patriarchy, and Popular Literature. Second edn. Chapel Hill: University of North Carolina Press, 1991.

Railton, Steven, director. Uncle Tom's Cabin and American Culture http://utc.iath.virginia.edu/

Regis, Pamela. *A Natural History of the Romance Novel*. Philadelphia: University of Pennsylvania Press, 2003.

Reid-Pharr, Robert. *Conjugal Union: The Body, the House, and the Black American*. New York: Oxford University Press, 2001.

Renker, Elizabeth. *The Origins of American Literature Studies: An Institutional History*. Cambridge: Cambridge University Press, 2007.

Reynolds, David S. *Beneath the American Renaissance: The Subversive Imagination in the Age of Emerson and Melville*. Cambridge, MA: Harvard University Press, 1988.

Faith in Fiction: The Emergence of Religious Literature in America. Cambridge, MA: Harvard University Press, 1981.

Reynolds, Larry J. *European Revolutions and the American Literary Renaissance*. New Haven: Yale University Press, 1991.

Richardson, Joan. *A Natural History of Pragmatism: The Fact of Feeling from Jonathan Edwards to Gertrude Stein*. New York: Cambridge University Press, 2007.

Rideout, Walter. *The Radical Novel in the United States, 1900–1954: Some Interrelations of Literature, and Society*. Cambridge, MA: Harvard University Press, 1956.

Rieder, John. *Colonialism and the Emergence of Science Fiction*. Middletown, CT: Wesleyan University Press, 2008.

Robbins, Bruce. *Upward Mobility and the Common Good*. Princeton: Princeton University Press, 2007.

Romero, Lora. *Home Fronts: Domesticity and its Critics in the Antebellum United States*. Durham, NC, Duke University Press, 1997.

Romines, Ann. *The Home Plot: Women, Writing and Domestic Ritual*. Amherst: University of Massachusetts Press, 1992.

Rosowski, Susan J. *Birthing a Nation: Gender, Creativity and the West in American Literature*. Lincoln: University of Nebraska Press, 1999.

Rowe, John Carlos. *At Emerson's Tomb: The Politics of Classic American Literature*. New York: Columbia University Press, 1997.

Literary Culture and U.S. Imperialism: From the Revolution to World War II. New York: Oxford University Press, 2000.

Rubin, Joan Shelley. *The Making of Middlebrow Culture*. Chapel Hill and London: University of North Carolina Press, 1992.

Rubin, Louis B. *The Curious Death of the Novel: Essays in American Literature*. Baton Rouge: Louisiana State University Press, 1967.

Rubin, Louis B. *et al.*, eds. *The History of Southern Literature*. Baton Rouge: Louisiana State University Press, 1985.

Ruttenberg, Nancy. *Democratic Personality: Popular Voice and the Trial of American Authorship*. Stanford, CA: Stanford University Press, 1998.

Ryan, Barbara and Amy Thomas, eds. *Reading Acts: U.S. Readers' Interactions with Literature: 1800–1950*. Knoxville: University of Tennessee Press, 2002.

Ryan, Mary P. *The Empire of the Mother: American Writing about Domesticity, 1830–1860*. New York: Haworth Press, 1982.

Ryan, Susan M. *The Grammar of Good Intentions: Race and the Antebellum Culture of Benevolence*. Ithaca, NY: Cornell University Press, 2003.

Said, Edward W. *Culture and Imperialism*. New York: Vintage, 1994.

Orientalism. New York: Vintage, 1978.

Saldívar, José David. *Border Matters: Remapping American Cultural Studies*. Berkeley: University of California Press, 1997.

The Dialectics of Our America: Genealogy, Cultural Critique, and Literary History. Durham, NC: Duke University Press, 1991.

Saldívar, Ramón. *The Borderlands of Culture: Américo Paredes and the Transnational Imaginary*. Durham, NC: Duke University Press, 2006.

Chicano Narrative: The Dialectics of Difference. Madison: University of Wisconsin Press, 1990.

Samuels, Shirley. *Romances of the Republic: Women, the Family, and Violence in the Literature of the Early American Nation*. New York: Oxford University Press, 1996.

Samuels, Shirley, ed. *The Culture of Sentiment: Race, Gender, and Sentimentality in Nineteenth-Century America*. Oxford: Oxford University Press, 1992.

Sanchez-Eppler, Karen. *Dependent States: The Child's Part in Nineteenth-Century American Culture*, University of Chicago Press, 2005.

Touching Liberty: Abolition, Feminism, and the Politics of the Body. Berkeley: University of California Press, 1993.

Schick, Frank L. *The Paperbound Book in America*. New York: Bowker, 1958.

Schueller, Malini Johar. *U.S. Orientalisms: Race, Nation, and Gender in Literature, 1790–1890*. Ann Arbor: University of Michigan Press, 1998.

Schweitzer, Ivy. *Perfecting Friendship: Politics and Affiliation in Early American Literature*. Chapel Hill: University of North Carolina Press, 2006.

Sedgwick, Eve Kosofsky. *Between Men: English Literature and Male Homosocial Desire*. New York: Columbia University Press, 1985.

Epistemology of the Closet. Berkeley: University of California Press, 1990.

Sedgwick, Eve Kosofsky, ed. *Novel Gazing: Queer Readings in Fiction*. Durham, NC: Duke University Press, 1993.

Seed, David. *American Science Fiction and the Cold War: Literature and Film*. Chicago: Fitzroy Dearborn, 1999.

Seltzer, Mark. *Bodies and Machines*. New York: Routledge, 1992.

Shamir, Milette. *Inexpressible Privacy: The Interior Life of Antebellum American Literature*. Philadelphia: University of Pennsylvania Press, 2006.

Shapiro, Stephen. *The Culture and Commerce of the Early American Novel: Reading the Atlantic World-System*. University Park: Pennsylvania State University Press, 2008.

Sherrill, Rowland A. *Road-Book America: Contemporary Culture and the New Picaresque*. Chicago and Urbana: University of Illinois Press, 2000.

Shi, David E. *Facing Facts: Realism in American Thought, and Culture, 1850–1920*. New York: Oxford University Press, 1995.

Shloss, Carol. *In Visible Light: Photography and the American Writer, 1810–1940*. New York: Oxford University Press, 1987.

Showalter, Elaine. *A Jury of Her Peers: American Women Writers from Anne Bradstreet to Annie Proulx*. New York: Alfred A. Knopf, 2009.

Sister's Choice: Tradition and Change in American Women's Writing. Oxford: Clarendon Press; New York: Oxford University Press, 1991.

Shukla, Sandhya and Heidi Tinsman, eds. *Imagining Our Americas: Towards a Transnational Frame*. Durham, NC: Duke University Press, 2007.

Shumway, David R. *Creating American Civilization: A Genealogy of American Literature as an Academic Discipline*. Minneapolis: University of Minnesota Press, 1994.

Silverman, Al. *The Time of Their Lives: The Golden Age of Great American Book Publishers, Their Editors and Authors*. New York: St. Martin's Press, 2008.

Slotkin, Richard. *The Fatal Environment: The Myth of the Frontier in the Age of Industrialization, 1800–1890*. Middletown, CT: Wesleyan University Press, 1985.

Gunfighter Nation: The Myth of the Frontier in Twentieth-Century America. New York: Harper Perennial, 1992.

Regeneration through Violence: The Mythology of the American Frontier, 1600–1860. Middletown, CT: Wesleyan University Press, 1973.

Smart, Robert Augustin. *The Nonfiction Novel*. Lanham, MD, and New York: University Press of America, 1985.

Smith, Henry Nash. *Democracy and the Novel: Popular Resistance to Classic American Writers*. New York: Oxford University Press, 1978.

Virgin Land: The American West as Symbol and Myth. Cambridge, MA: Harvard University Press, 1950.

Snyder, Katherine. *Bachelors, Manhood, and the Novel, 1850–1925*. Cambridge: Cambridge University Press, 1999.

Soitos, Stephen F. *The Blues Detective: A Study of African American Detective Fiction*. Amherst: University of Massachusetts Press, 1996.

Sollors, Werner. *Beyond Ethnicity: Consent and Descent in American Culture*. New York: Oxford University Press, 1986.

Interracialism: Black–White Intermarriage in American History, Literature and Law. New York: Oxford University Press, 2000.

Neither Black Nor White Yet Both: Thematic Explorations of Interracial Literature. Cambridge: Cambridge University Press, 1997.

Somerville, Siobhan. *Queering the Color Line: Race and the Invention of Homosexuality in American Literature*. Durham, NC: Duke University Press, 2000.

Sommer, Doris. *Foundational Fictions: The National Romances of Latin America*. Berkeley: University of California Press, 1991.

Spengemann, William C. *A Mirror for Americanists: Reflections on the Idea of American Literature*. Hanover, NH: University Press of New England, 1989.

Spiller, Robert E. *et al.*, eds. *The Literary History of the United States*. New York: Macmillan, 1948.

Spillers, Hortense J. *Black, White, and in Color: Essays on American Literature and Culture*. Chicago: University of Chicago Press, 2003.

Stecopoulos, Harilaos. *Reconstructing the World: Southern Fictions and U.S. Imperialisms, 1898–1976*. Ithaca, NY: Cornell University Press, 2008.

Stepto, Robert B. *From Behind the Veil: A Study of Afro-American Narrative*. Urbana: University of Illinois Press, 1979.

Stern, Julia A. *The Plight of Feeling: Sympathy and Dissent in the Early American Novel*. Chicago: University of Chicago Press, 1997.

Streeby, Shelley. *American Sensations: Class, Empire, and the Production of Popular Culture*. Berkeley: University of California Press, 2002.

Strychacz, Thomas. *Modernism, Mass Culture, and Professionalism*. Cambridge: Cambridge University Press, 1993.

Sundquist, Eric J. *Empire and Slavery in American Literature, 1820–1865*. Jackson: University Press of Mississippi, 2006.

The Hammers of Creation: Folk Culture in Modern African American Fiction. Athens: University of Georgia Press, 2006.

Strangers in the Land: Blacks, Jews, and Post-Holocaust America. Cambridge, MA: Harvard University Press, 2005.

To Wake the Nations: Race in the Making of American Literature. Cambridge, MA: Harvard University Press, 1993.

Sundquist, Eric, ed. *American Realism: New Essays*. Baltimore: Johns Hopkins University Press, 1981.

Suvin, Darko. *Metamorphoses of Science Fiction: On the Poetics and History of a Literary Genre*. New Haven: Yale University Press, 1979.

Sweet, Timothy. *American Georgics: Economy and Environment in Early American Literature*. Philadelphia: University of Pennsylvania Press, 2002.

Szalay, Michael. *New Deal Modernism: American Literature and the Invention of the Welfare State*. Durham, NC: Duke University Press, 2000.

Tabbi, Joseph. *Postmodern Sublime: Technology and American Writing from Mailer to Cyberpunk*. Ithaca, NY: Cornell University Press, 1995.

Tabbi, Joseph and Michael Wutz, eds. *Reading Matters: Narrative in the New Media Ecology*. Ithaca, NY: Cornell University Press, 1997.

Tamarkin, Elisa. *Anglophilia: Deference, Devotion, and Antebellum America*. Chicago: University of Chicago Press, 2008.

Tanner, Tony. *The American Mystery: American Literature from Emerson to DeLillo*. Cambridge and New York: Cambridge University Press, 2000.

City of Words: American Fiction 1950–1970. New York: Harper & Row, 1971.

Tate, Claudia. *Domestic Allegories of Political Desire: The Black Heroine's Text at the Turn of the Century*. New York: Oxford University Press, 1992.

Psychoanalysis and Black Novels: Desire and the Protocols of Race. New York: Oxford University Press, 1998.

Tawil, Ezra. *The Making of Racial Sentiment: Slavery and the Birth of the Frontier Romance*. Cambridge: Cambridge University Press, 2006.

Tennenhouse, Leonard. *The Importance of Feeling English: American Literature and the British Diaspora, 1750–1850*. Princeton: Princeton University Press, 2007.

Teuton, Sean Kicummah. *Red Land, Red Power: Grounding Knowledge in the American Indian Novel*. Durham, NC: Duke University Press, 2008.

Thiher, Allan. *Words in Reflection: Modern Language Theory, and Postmodern Fiction*. Chicago: University of Chicago Press, 1984.

Thomas, Brook. *American Literary Realism and the Failed Promise of Contract*. Berkeley and Los Angeles: University of California Press, 1997.

Civic Myths: A Law-and-Literature Approach to Citizenship. Chapel Hill: University of North Carolina Press, 2007.

Cross-examinations of Law and Literature: Cooper, Hawthorne, Stowe, and Melville. Cambridge: Cambridge University Press, 1987.

Thomson, Rosemarie Garland. *Extraordinary Bodies: Figuring Physical Disability in American Culture, and Literature*. New York: Columbia University Press, 1997.

Thrailkill, Jane F. *Affecting Fictions: Mind, Body, and Emotion in American Literary Realism*. Cambridge, MA: Harvard University Press, 2007.

Thurston, Carl. *The Romance Revolution: Erotic Novels for Women and the Quest for a New Sexual Identity*. Urbana: University of Illinois Press, 1987.

Tichi, Cecelia. *Exposés and Excess: Muckraking in America, 1900–2000*. Philadelphia: University of Pennsylvania Press, 2004.

Shifting Gears: Technology, Literature, Culture in Modernist America. Chapel Hill: University of North Carolina Press, 1987.

Todorov, Tzvetan. *The Fantastic: A Structural Approach to a Literary Genre*. Translated by Richard Howard. Ithaca, NY: Cornell University Press, 1975.

Tompkins, Jane P. *Sensational Designs: The Cultural Work of American Fiction, 1790–1860*. New York: Oxford University Press, 1986.

West of Everything: The Inner Life of Westerns. New York Oxford University Press, 1982.

Tracey, Karen. *Plots and Proposals: American Women's Fiction, 1850–90*. Chicago: University of Illinois Press, 2000.

Trachtenberg, Alan. *The Incorporation of America: Culture and Society in the Gilded Age*. New York: Hill and Wang, 1982.

Shades of Hiawatha: Staging Indians, Making Americans: 1880–1930. New York: Hill and Wang, 2004.

Trilling, Lionel. *The Liberal Imagination: Essays on Literature and Society*. New York: Viking Press, 1950.

Van Looy, Jan, and Jan Baetens, eds. *Close Reading New Media, Analyzing Electronic Literature*. Leuven: Leuven University Press, 2003.

Vizenor, Gerald. *Manifest Manners: Narratives on PostIndian Survivance*. Lincoln: University of Nebraska Press, 1999.

Vizenor, Gerald, ed. *Survivance: Narratives of Native Presence*. Lincoln: University of Nebraska Press, 2008.

Wadsworth, Sarah. *In the Company of Books: Literature and its "Classes" in Nineteenth-Century America*. Amherst: University of Massachusetts Press, 2006.

Waid, Candace. *Edith Wharton's Letters from the Underworld: Fictions of Women and Writing*. Chapel Hill: University of North Carolina Press, 1991.

Walcutt, Charles Child. *American Literary Naturalism, a Divided Stream*. 1956; Westport, CT: Greenwood Press, 1973.

Wald, Alan M. *Exiles from a Future Time: The Forging of the Mid-Twentieth Century Literary Left*. Chapel Hill: University of North Carolina Press, 2003.

Writing from the Left: New Essays on Radical Culture and Politics. New York and London: Verso, 1994.

Wald, Priscilla. *Constituting Americans: Cultural Anxiety and Narrative Form*. Durham, NC: Duke University Press, 1995.

Contagious: Cultures, Carriers, and the Outbreak Narrative. Durham, NC: Duke University Press, 2008.

Walker, Melissa. *Down from the Mountaintop: Black Women's Novels in the Wake of the Civil Rights Movement, 1966–1989*. New Haven: Yale University Press, 1991.

Wall, Cheryl. *Women of the Harlem Renaissance*. Bloomington: Indiana University Press, 1995.

Worrying the Line: Black Women Writers, Lineage, and Literary Tradition. University of North Carolina Press, 2005.

Ward, Gerald W. R., ed. *The American Illustrated Book in the Nineteenth Century*. Winterthur, DE: Winthherthur Museum; distributed by the University Press of Virginia, 1987.

Wardrip-Fruin, Noah and Nick Montfort, eds. *The New Media Reader*. Cambridge, MA: MIT Press, 2003.

Warner, Michael. *The Letters of the Republic: Publication and the Public Sphere in Eighteenth-Century America*. Cambridge, MA: Harvard University Press, 1990.

Publics and Counter Publics. New York: Zone Books, 2002.

The Trouble with Normal: Sex, Politics, and the Ethics of Queer Life. Cambridge, MA: Harvard University Press, 2000.

Warren, Kenneth W. *Black and White Strangers: Race and American Literary Realism*. Chicago: University of Chicago Press, 1993.

So Black and Blue: Ralph Ellison and the Occasion of Criticism. Chicago: University of Chicago Press, 2003.

Waterman, Bryan. *Republic of Intellect: The Friendly Club of New York City and the Making of American Literature*. Baltimore: Johns Hopkins University Press, 2007.

Watt, Ian. *The Rise of the Novel: Studies in Defoe, Richardson, and Fielding*. London: Chatto and Windus, 1957.

Weaver, Jace. *That the People Might Live: Native American Literatures and Native American Community*. New York: Oxford University Press, 1997.

Weinstein, Cindy. *Family, Kinship, and Sympathy in Nineteenth-Century American Literature*. Cambridge: Cambridge University Press, 2006.

The Literature of Labor and the Labors of Literature: Allegory in Nineteenth-Century American Fiction. Cambridge: Cambridge University Press, 1995.

Weinstein, Phillip. *What Else But Love?: The Ordeal of Race in Faulkner and Morrison*. New York: Columbia University Press, 1996.

Weisbuch, Robert. *Atlantic Double-Cross: American Literature and British Influence in the Age of Emerson*. Chicago: University of Chicago Press, 1986.

Wertheimer, Eric. *Imagined Empires: Incas, Aztecs, and the New World of American Literature*. Cambridge: Cambridge University Press, 1999.

West, James L. W., III. *American Authors and the Literary Marketplace since 1900*. Philadelphia: University of Pennsylvania Press, 1988.

Westfahl, Gary. *Mechanics of Wonder: The Creation of the Idea of Science Fiction*. Liverpool: Liverpool University Press, 1999.

Whiteside, Thomas. *The Blockbuster Complex: Conglomerates, Show Business, and Book Publishing*. Middletown, CT: Wesleyan University Press, 1981.

Wiegman, Robyn. *American Anatomies: Theorizing Race and Gender*. Durham, NC: Duke University Press, 1995.

Williams, Linda. *Playing the Race Card: Melodramas of Black and White from Uncle Tom to O. J. Simpson*. Princeton: Princeton Univeristy Press, 2002.

Williams Susan, S. *Reclaiming Authorship: Literary Women in America, 1850–1900*. Philadelphia: University of Pennsylvania Press, 2006.

Wilson, Christopher P. *Cop Knowledge: Police Power and Cultural Narrative in Twentieth-Century America*. Chicago: University of Chicago Press, 2000.

The Labor of Words: Literary Professionalism in the Progressive Era. Athens: University of Georgia Press, 1985.

Wilson, Edmund. *Axel's Castle: A Study in the Imaginative Literature of 1870–1930*. New York and London: C. Scribner's Sons, 1931.

Patriotic Gore: Studies in the Literature of the American Civil War. New York: Atheneum, 1962.

Wilson, Michael. *Writing Home: Indigenous Narratives of Resistance*. East Lansing: Michigan State University Press, 2008.

Wirth-Nesher, Hana. *Call it English: The Languages of Jewish American Literature*. Princeton: Princeton University Press, 2006.

City Codes: Reading the Modern Urban Novel. Cambridge: Cambridge University Press, 1996.

Wisse, Ruth R. *The Modern Jewish Canon: A Journey through Language and Culture*. New York: Free Press, 2000.

Womack, Craig S. *Red on Red: Native American Literary Separatism*. Minneapolis: University of Minnesota Press, 1999.

Wong, Sau-Ling Cynthia. *Reading Asian American Literature*. Princeton: Princeton University Press, 1993.

Wonham, Henry B. *Criticism and the Color Line: Desegregating American Literary Studies*. New Brunswick, NJ: Rutgers University Press, 1996.

Playing the Races: Ethnic Caricature and American Literary Realism. Oxford: Oxford University Press, 2004.

Yaeger, Patricia. *Dirt and Desire: Reconstructing Southern Women's Writing, 1930–1990*. Chicago: University of Chicago Press, 2000.

Young, Elizabeth. *Black Frankenstein: The Making of an American Metaphor*. New York: New York University Press, 2008.

Disarming the Nation: Women's Writing and the American Civil War. Chicago: University of Chicago Press, 1999.

Zafar, Rafia. *We Wear the Mask: African Americans Write American Literature, 1760–1870*. New York: Columbia University Press, 1997.

Zavarzadeh, Mas'ud. *The Mythopoeic Reality: The Postwar American Nonfiction Novel*. Urbana: University of Illinois Press, 1976.

Zboray, Ronald J. *A Fictive People: Antebellum Economic Development and the American Reading Public*. New York: Oxford University Press, 1993.

Zboray, Ronald J., and Mary Saracino Zboray. *Everyday Ideas: Socioliterary Experience among Antebellum New Englanders*. Knoxville: University of Tennessee Press, 2006.

Literary Dollars and Social Sense: A People's History of the Mass Market Book. New York: Routledge, 2005.

Zimmerman, David A. *Panic! Markets, Crises, and Crowds in American Fiction*. Chapel Hill: University of North Carolina Press, 2006.

Index